W9-CMS-031

FOR REFERENCE

Do Not Take From This Room

Encyclopedia of
AFRICAN HISTORY AND CULTURE

Encyclopedia of
AFRICAN HISTORY
AND CULTURE

VOLUME IV

THE COLONIAL ERA

(1850 TO 1960)

R. Hunt Davis, Jr., Editor

A Learning Source Book

☑®
Facts On File, Inc.

Encyclopedia of African History and Culture,
Volume 4: The Colonial Era (1850 to 1960)

Copyright © 2005 by The Learning Source, Ltd.

A Learning Source Book
Editorial: Brian Ableman, Christopher Roberts,
Bodine Schwerin, Ismail Soyugenc

Facts On File, Inc.
132 West 31st Street
New York NY 10001

Library of Congress Cataloging-in-Publication Data

Page, Willie F., 1929–
 Encyclopedia of African history and culture / edited by Willie F. Page; revised edition edited by R. Hunt
Davis, Jr.—Rev. ed.
  p. cm.
 "A Learning Source Book."
 Includes bibliographical references and index.
 ISBN 0-8160-5199-2 ((set ISBN) hardcover)
 ISBN 0-8160-5269-7 (vol. I)–ISBN 0-8160-5270-0 (vol. II)–
 ISBN 0-8160-5271-9 (vol. III)–ISBN 0-8160-5200-X (vol. IV)–
 ISBN 0-8160-5201-8 (vol. V)

 1. Africa—Encyclopedias. I. Davis, R. Hunt. II. Title.
DT3.P27 2005
960'.03-—dc22
                    2004022929

You can find Facts On File on the World Wide Web at
http://www.factsonfile.com
Design: Joan Toro, Joseph Mauro III
Maps: Sholto Ainslie, Dale Williams
Printed in the United States of America

VB PKG 10 9 8 7 6 5 4 3 2 1

This book is printed on acid-free paper.

For my students who have gone on to teach
about the African past and present

CONTRIBUTORS

General Editor

R. Hunt Davis, Jr., Ph.D., is professor emeritus of history and African studies at the University of Florida. He received a Ph.D. in African studies from the University of Wisconsin, Madison. Dr. Davis is an expert on the history of South Africa, African agricultural history, and the history of education in Africa. His published works include *Mandela, Tambo, and the African National Congress* (1991) and *Apartheid Unravels* (1991), along with numerous articles and book chapters. He served as director at the University of Florida Center for African Studies and is also a past editor of the *African Studies Review*.

Senior Authors

Agnes Ngoma Leslie, Ph.D., outreach director, Center for African Studies, University of Florida

Richard R. Marcus, Ph.D., assistant professor, Department of Political Science, University of Alabama, Huntsville

James Meier, Ph.D., adjunct assistant professor of history, University of Florida

Dianne White Oyler, Ph.D., associate professor of history, Fayetteville State University

Leah A. J. Cohen, M.A., graduate student in geography, University of Florida

Other contributors

Mohammad Alpha Bah, Ph.D., professor of history, College of Charleston; Brian Hollingsworth, doctoral student in African history, University of Florida; Bo Schwerin, M.A., creative writing, Johns Hopkins University

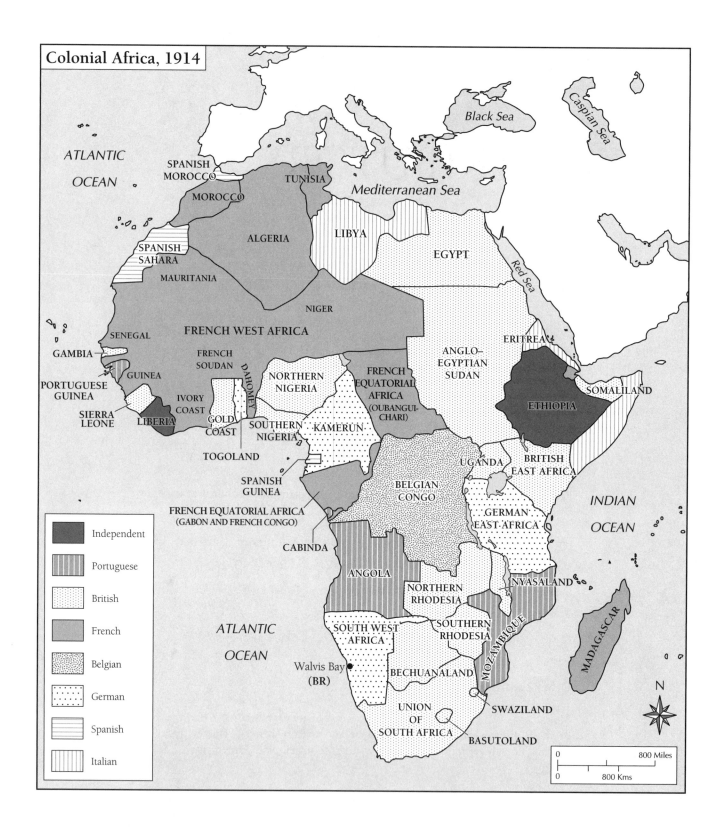

Colonial Africa, 1914

ATLANTIC OCEAN

SPANISH MOROCCO
MOROCCO
TUNISIA
Mediterranean Sea
Black Sea
Caspian Sea

ALGERIA
LIBYA
EGYPT

SPANISH SAHARA
MAURITANIA
NIGER
Red Sea

SENEGAL
FRENCH WEST AFRICA
ANGLO-EGYPTIAN SUDAN
ERITREA

GAMBIA
FRENCH SOUDAN
NORTHERN NIGERIA
FRENCH EQUATORIAL AFRICA (OUBANGUI-CHARI)
SOMALILAND

PORTUGUESE GUINEA
GUINEA
DAHOMEY
IVORY COAST
GOLD COAST
ETHIOPIA

SIERRA LEONE
LIBERIA
SOUTHERN NIGERIA
TOGOLAND
KAMERUN
BRITISH EAST AFRICA

SPANISH GUINEA
UGANDA

FRENCH EQUATORIAL AFRICA (GABON AND FRENCH CONGO)
BELGIAN CONGO
GERMAN EAST AFRICA
INDIAN OCEAN

CABINDA

ANGOLA
NORTHERN RHODESIA
NYASALAND

ATLANTIC OCEAN

SOUTH WEST AFRICA
SOUTHERN RHODESIA
MOZAMBIQUE
MADAGASCAR

Walvis Bay (BR)
BECHUANALAND

UNION OF SOUTH AFRICA
SWAZILAND

BASUTOLAND

N

Legend

- Independent
- Portuguese
- British
- French
- Belgian
- German
- Spanish
- Italian

0 ——— 800 Miles
0 ——— 800 Kms

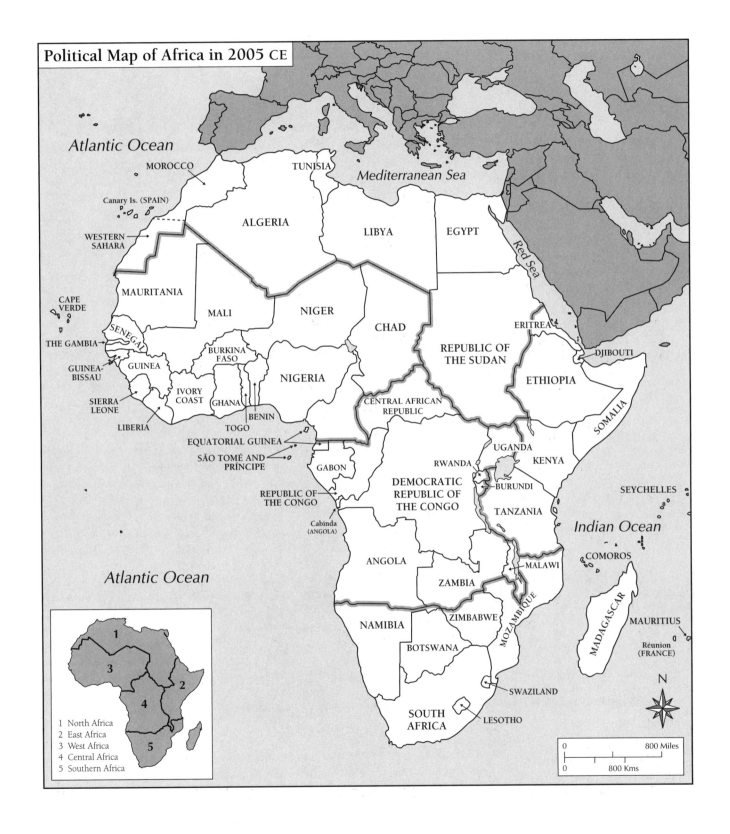

Political Map of Africa in 2005 CE

Atlantic Ocean

MOROCCO

TUNISIA

Mediterranean Sea

Canary Is. (SPAIN)

ALGERIA

LIBYA

EGYPT

WESTERN
SAHARA

Red Sea

MAURITANIA

CAPE
VERDE

MALI

NIGER

CHAD

ERITREA

SENEGAL

THE GAMBIA

DJIBOUTI

REPUBLIC OF
THE SUDAN

GUINEA-
BISSAU

GUINEA

BURKINA
FASO

ETHIOPIA

SIERRA
LEONE

IVORY
COAST

NIGERIA

CENTRAL AFRICAN
REPUBLIC

SOMALIA

GHANA

LIBERIA

TOGO

BENIN

UGANDA

EQUATORIAL GUINEA

KENYA

SÃO TOMÉ AND
PRÍNCIPE

GABON

RWANDA

SEYCHELLES

REPUBLIC OF
THE CONGO

DEMOCRATIC
REPUBLIC OF
THE CONGO

BURUNDI

Cabinda
(ANGOLA)

TANZANIA

Indian Ocean

Atlantic Ocean

COMOROS

ANGOLA

MALAWI

ZAMBIA

MOZAMBIQUE

MADAGASCAR

MAURITIUS

NAMIBIA

ZIMBABWE

Réunion
(FRANCE)

BOTSWANA

N

SWAZILAND

SOUTH
AFRICA

LESOTHO

0   800 Miles

0   800 Kms

1 North Africa
2 East Africa
3 West Africa
4 Central Africa
5 Southern Africa

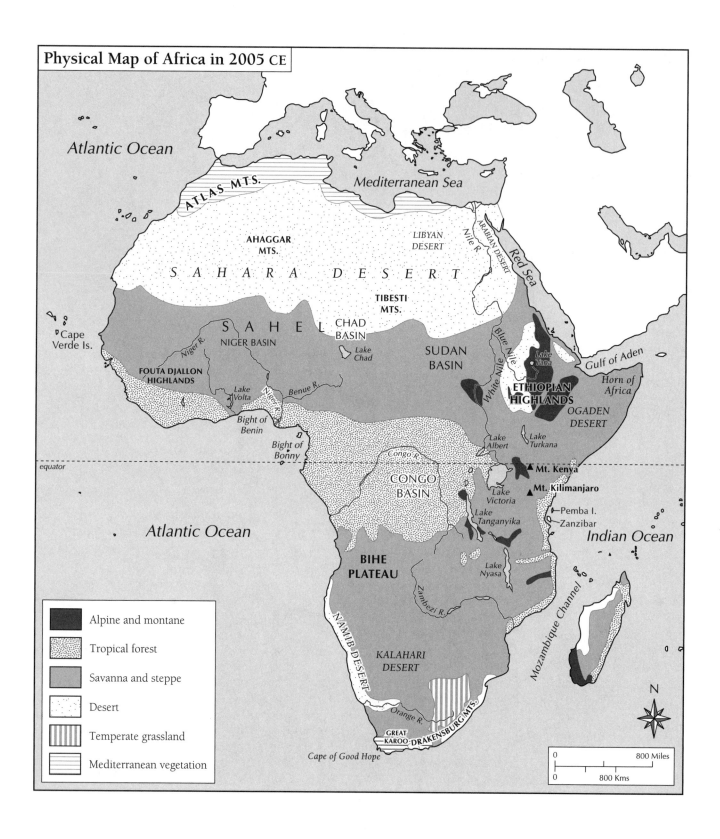

Physical Map of Africa in 2005 CE

Atlantic Ocean

ATLAS MTS.

Mediterranean Sea

AHAGGAR MTS.

LIBYAN DESERT

Nile R.

ARABIAN DESERT

Red Sea

S A H A R A   D E S E R T

TIBESTI MTS.

S A H E L

CHAD BASIN

Niger R.

NIGER BASIN

Cape Verde Is.

Lake Chad

SUDAN BASIN

Blue Nile

Lake Tana

Gulf of Aden

FOUTA DJALLON HIGHLANDS

White Nile

ETHIOPIAN HIGHLANDS

Horn of Africa

Lake Volta

Benue R.

Niger R.

OGADEN DESERT

Bight of Benin

Lake Albert

Lake Turkana

Bight of Bonny

Congo R.

▲ **Mt. Kenya**

equator

CONGO BASIN

Lake Victoria

▲ **Mt. Kilimanjaro**

Lake Tanganyika

Pemba I.

Zanzibar

Atlantic Ocean

Indian Ocean

BIHE PLATEAU

Lake Nyasa

Zambezi R.

NAMIB DESERT

Mozambique Channel

KALAHARI DESERT

Orange R.

GREAT KAROO

DRAKENSBURG MTS.

Cape of Good Hope

N

Legend

- Alpine and montane
- Tropical forest
- Savanna and steppe
- Desert
- Temperate grassland
- Mediterranean vegetation

0		800 Miles
0		800 Kms

CONTENTS

LIST OF ENTRIES

HOW TO USE THIS ENCYCLOPEDIA

This encyclopedia is organized chronologically, dividing the African past into five major eras. This division serves to make it easier to study the vastness and complexity of African history and culture. It also allows students and general readers to go directly to the volume or volumes they wish to consult.

Volume I, *Ancient Africa,* deals with Africa up to approximately 500 CE (roughly, in terms of classical European history, to the Fall of the Roman Empire and the dissolution of the Ancient World on the eve of the emergence of Islam). The volume also includes articles on the continent's key geographical features and major language families. In addition you will find articles that deal with certain basic aspects of African life that, in essential ways, remain relatively constant throughout time. For example, rites of passage, funeral customs, the payment of bride-wealth, and rituals related to spirit possession are features common to many African societies. Although these features can evolve in different cultures in radically different ways, their basic purpose remains constant. Accordingly, rather than try to cover the evolution of these cultural features in each volume, we offer a more general explanation in Volume I, with the understanding that the details of these cultural touchstones can vary widely from people to people and change over time.

On the other hand there are entries related to key cultural and social dimensions whose changes are easier to observe over time. Such entries appear in each of the volumes and include architecture, art, clothing and dress, economics, family, music, religion, warfare, and the role of women.

Volume II, *African Kingdoms,* focuses on what may be loosely termed "medieval Africa," from the sixth century to the beginning of the 16th century. This is the period that witnessed the rise and spread of Islam and, to a lesser degree, Arab expansion throughout much of the northern and eastern regions of the continent. It also saw the flowering of some of Africa's greatest indigenous kingdoms and empires. Other Africans, such as the Maasai and Kikuyu living in and around present-day Kenya, did

not live in powerful states during this time yet developed their own dynamic cultures.

Volume III, *From Conquest to Colonization,* continues Africa's story from roughly 1500 to 1850. During this era Africa became increasingly involved with the Atlantic world due to European maritime exploration and subsequent interaction through trade and cultural exchanges. This period also included the rise of the transatlantic slave trade, which in turn created the African Diaspora, and the beginnings of European colonization. As a result, it marks a period when the dynamics shaping African culture and society began to shift.

Volume IV, *The Colonial Era,* covers Africa during the years 1850–1960. This historical period begins with Europe's conquest of the continent, leading to the era of colonial rule. Political control enabled Europe to extend its economic control as well, turning Africa into a vast supply depot of raw materials. Volume IV also covers the rise of nationalist movements and the great struggle Africans undertook to regain their independence.

Volume V, *Independent Africa,* deals with the continent since 1960, when Africans began regaining their independence and started to once again live in sovereign states. (This process, of course, took longer in the southern portion of the continent than in other parts.) In common with the rest of the world's people, however, Africans have faced a host of new and challenging problems, some of which are specific to Africa, while others are of a more global nature.

In addition to the aforementioned cultural entries that appear in all five volumes, there are entries for each of the present-day countries of the continent as identified on the Political Map found at the front of each volume. Readers can thus learn about the key developments in a given country within a given time period or across the entire span of African history. There are also articles on individual ethnic groups of Africa in each of the volumes. Since there are more than a thousand identifiable groups, it has been necessary to limit coverage to the major or key groups within a given period. Thus, a group that might be historically important in one period may not be sufficiently important, or may not even have existed, in a period covered by one or more other volumes. Likewise, there are entries on the major cities of the continent for given time periods, including, in Volume V, all the present national capitals. Another key set of entries common to all volumes concerns historically important persons. In general, historians are more readily able to identify these individuals for recent periods than for earlier times. As a result the latter volumes contain more individual biographical entries. An exception here is the case of Ancient Egypt, where historical records have enabled us to learn about the roles of prominent individuals.

In preparing these volumes, every attempt has been made to make this encyclopedia as accessible and easy to use as possible. At the front of each volume, readers will find an introduction and a timeline specific to the historical era covered in the volume. There are also three full-page maps, two of which appear in all five volumes (the current political map and a physical map), and one that is specific to the volume's time period. In addition the front of each volume contains a volume-specific list of the photographs, illustrations, and maps found therein. The List of Entries at the front of each volume is the same in all volumes and enables the reader to quickly get an overview of the entries within the individual volumes, as well as for the five-volume set. Entries are arranged alphabetically, letter-by-letter within each volume.

Entry headwords use the most commonly found spelling or representation of that spelling, with other frequently used spellings in parentheses. The question of spelling, of course, is always a major issue when dealing with languages utilizing an alphabet or a script different than that used for English. Changes in orthography and the challenges of transliteration can produce several variants of a word. Where there are important variants in spelling, this encyclopedia presents as many as possible, but only within the entries themselves. For easy access to variant and alternate spelling, readers should consult the index at the end of each volume, which lists and cross-references the alternate spellings that appear in the text.

Each volume contains an index that has references to subjects in the specific volume, and the cumulative index at the end of Volume V provides easy access across the volumes. A cumulative glossary appears in each volume and provides additional assistance.

The entries serve to provide the reader with basic rather than exhaustive information regarding the subject at hand. To help those who wish to read further, each entry is linked with other entries in that volume via cross-references indicated by SMALL CAPITALS. In addition the majority of entries are followed by a **See also** section, which provides cross-references to relevant entries in the other four volumes. The reader may find it useful to begin with one of the general articles—such as the ones dealing with archaeology, dance, oral traditions, or women—or to start with an entry on a specific country or an historically important state and follow the cross-references to discover more detailed information. Readers should be aware that cross-references, both those embedded in the text and those in the **See also** section, use only entry headword spellings and not variant spellings. For those readers who wish to research a topic beyond the material provided in individual and cross-referenced entries, there is also a **Further reading** section at the end of many entries. Bibliographical references listed here guide readers to more in-depth resources in a particular area.

Finally, readers can consult the **Suggested Readings** in the back of each volume. These volume-specific bibliographies contain general studies—such as atlases, histories of the continent, and broad works on culture, society, and people—as well as specialized studies that typically cover specific topics or regions. For the most part, these two bibliographic aids contain those recently published works that are most likely to be available in libraries, especially well-stocked city and college libraries. Readers should also be aware that a growing number of sources are available online in the form of e-books and other formats. The World Wide Web is also a good place to look for current events and developments that have occurred since the publication of this encyclopedia.

LIST OF IMAGES AND MAPS IN THIS VOLUME

Photographs and Illustrations

Maps

INTRODUCTION TO THIS VOLUME

This volume covers a complex and event-filled period in African history. In 1850 most of the continent was under the rule of Africans, though there were portents of the colonial era to come. These included the French invasion and control over Algeria, beginning in the 1830s, various small colonial footholds on the West African coast, and the steadily expanding white settlement in South Africa. By 1960 Africa was again on its way to regaining its independence. Indeed, 1960 is sometimes called "the Year of Africa," since it marked the achievement of independence for so many African countries. The 110 intervening years saw the full-scale colonial conquest of Africa, the establishment of European colonial rule throughout the continent (except for nominally independent Liberia and for Ethiopia), the emergence of nationalist movements, and their gradual triumph throughout much of the continent in the 1950s. The end of the colonial era was not complete, however, until South Africa's democratic election, in 1994. These dramatic changes in the political scene found parallels in the economies, societies, and cultures of the continent.

During the last decades of precolonial independence, African leaders were busily engaged in state building. Egypt, under Khedive Ismail, extended its control over the Nilotic Sudan. To the southeast, a trio of strong emperors—culminating with Menelik—reestablished the political unity of Ethiopia. In the western Sudan, Islamic reformers such as al-Hajj Umar Tal continued establishing states based on Islamic principles, while the Sokoto Caliphate of northern Nigeria reached its zenith. The Ashanti Empire continued its expansion in the forest zone of West Africa, as did other states. Turmoil gripped Yorubaland, however, as various states struggled for supremacy in the aftermath of the Oyo Empire's collapse. In the East African interior, Kabaka Mutesa led Buganda to a position of regional dominance, while, further south, Mirambo built a powerful though short-lived state among the Nyamwezi. Zanzibar's ruling Busaidi dynasty of Arabs established control over much of the Swahili Coast and,

under Barghash, pushed inland along the trade routes from the coast. Further south, Lobengula consolidated Ndebele rule over much of present-day Zimbabwe, while in South Africa Cetshwayo was leading a resurgent Zulu kingdom.

Colonial rule brought a rapid end to the era of independent African states and powerful African rulers. The people of coastal cities and societies had for some time been in contact with Europeans and had been responding to or adapting elements of European culture to fit their own societies. These Westernized entities included the Fante Confederation and organizations such as the Aborigines' Rights Protection Society. Individuals who steered a middle course between their own African cultures and those of the European colonizers included Jamal al-Din al-Afghani, Edward Wilmot Blyden, Bishop Samuel Ajayi Crowther, James Africanus Beale Horton, and John Tengo Jabavu. Also, major European colonies had taken root in North Africa and South Africa well before the 1884–85 Berlin Conference that signaled the final European assault that ended in the continent's partition.

Colonialism became the dominant force in Africa after the 1880s, disrupting societies deeply rooted in their own histories and cultures. Africans often vigorously resisted, leading to extended conflicts such as the Cape Frontier Wars between the Xhosa and the Cape Colony, the Anglo-Ashanti Wars, and the Italo-Ethiopian Wars. Major battles included those at Omdurman, Isandlwana, and Adowa, the last two being rare African victories. Charismatic figures emerged to lead the African resistance, including Morocco's Abd el-Krim, Yaa Asantewa in the Ashanti Empire, Jaja and Nana Olomu in the Niger Delta, the Ndebele king Lobengula, and the Zulu king Cetshwayo. One of the more fervent forms of resistance emerged based on Islam. Leaders of Islamic anticolonial movements included Muhammad Ahmad al-Mahdi, the Khalifa Abdallahi ibn Muhammad, who led the Mahdiyya in the Sudan, and the Somali nationalist Muhammad Abdullah Hassan. After the colonial conquest, there were some initial armed revolts, such as the Chimurenga in Zimbabwe and the Maji-Maji Rebellion in Tanzania. On the whole, however, colonial military forces ruthlessly and effectively suppressed these uprisings. Large-scale revolutionary movements against colonial rule did not again resurface until after World War II had come to an end, in 1945.

Once colonial control was established, the European conquerors focused on how best to establish "colonial rule," which took a number of different forms following specific philosophies. Africans, in turn, had to come to terms with the colonial presence. Throughout the continent individuals such as Ferhat Abbas in Algeria, Egypt's Duse Mohammed Ali, Joseph Ephraim Casely-Hayford in the Gold Coast, Blaise Diagne in Senegal, Sir Apolo Kagwa in Uganda, Harry Thuku of Kenya, and South Africa's John L. Dube developed nascent political organizations and labor unions to assert African interests within the colonial framework. Many became involved with African-Americans in the context of Pan-Africanism, which helped promote the political demand of "Africa for the Africans" that helped spawn a more assertive African nationalism. A new generation of nationalists emerged that included Habib Bourguiba in Tunisia, Gamal Abdel Nasser of Egypt, Léopold Senghor of Senegal, Nnamdi Azikiwe of Nigeria, Ghana's Kwame Nkrumah, Jomo Kenyatta of Kenya, the Congo's Patrice Lumumba, and Zimbabwe's Ndabaningi Sithole. They founded political parties that promoted nationalism and independence. Ghana's independence, in 1957, marked the first major success. Usually independence came relatively peacefully, often facilitated by the United Nations. However, bitter and prolonged struggles took place in Algeria and in Kenya, and the reluctance of colonial powers to grant rights to Africans foreshadowed future conflict in the Portuguese colonies and southern Africa, more generally.

The influence of colonialism extended well beyond the political sphere. The colonial culture that evolved included a substantial religious dimension. Christianity played a significant social and political role throughout the continent, with a steady expansion under both European and African leadership that built on the missionary efforts of the previous century. This expansion, in turn, led to interaction with indigenous religions, regional variation, and the emergence of independent churches under individuals such as the Prophet William Wade Harris and Alice Lenshina. Parallel to the expansion of Christianity was a growth of Western-style education that included founding schools and universities such as Achimota College and Fort Hare College. This Western-style education increasingly took over from indigenous education and competed in the colonial era with Islamic education. A major development of education was the expansion of literacy in Arabic, European, and indigenous languages. Literacy, in turn, led to the emergence of popular newspapers and magazines. African published literature began to appear, with some authors, such as Tanzania's Shaaban Robert, utilizing indigenous languages. Others, such as Léopold Senghor and Chinua Achebe, wrote in the colonial languages. Significant cultural changes also took place in the spheres of architecture, art, and music. Many of these cultural changes were associated with the growth of cities and the evolving urban life and culture.

The colonial economy, too, underwent drastic changes and became increasingly geared to exports. Industrialization was limited outside of South Africa. Transportation and other aspects of the colonial infrastructure, including the further development of port cities and building of major dams, were primarily designed to facilitate the export economy. Agriculture was the economic mainstay. While subsistence agriculture continued to produce food crops, cash crops increasingly dominated the agricultural sector. African peasants grew many of the cash crops, especially in West Africa, but in the Belgian Congo and elsewhere, European concessionaire companies ran large plantations. White farmers predominated in southern Africa. Mineral exploitation was the other critical component of the colonial export economy, with large European-run firms such as Union Miniere controlling the mining industry.

By 1960, then, the political map of Africa had changed dramatically, as had African society and culture. As Africans entered a new era of independence, conditions of life would be vastly different from those of the years prior to 1850.

TIME LINE (1840–1964)

1840	Busaidi dynasty completes move of its capital from Oman to the island of Zanzibar
	As many as 100,000 Europeans are living in Algeria
1840s–1850s	Groundnuts (peanuts) become a valuable cash crop in the Senegambia region
1850–1860	Muslim Sokoto Caliphate reaches height of influence, encompassing more than 30 West African emirates
1853–1859	Muhammad Ali ibn al-Sanusi, a Sufi holy man, leads efforts to expel European colonialists from North Africa
1854–1873	Scottish missionary and explorer David Livingstone traverses southern and East Africa, adding much to Europeans' knowledge of the continent
1856–1857	Xhosa people kill their cattle in an ill-fated attempt to free themselves from British colonialism
1860–1884	Mirambo rules largest Nyamwezi state in present-day Tanzania
1864–1893	Ahmadu Séku leads West Africa's Tukulor Empire
1866	Discovery of the huge Eureka Diamond, near the Orange River, launches South Africa's Mineral Revolution

1868–1873	Non-Ashanti Akan states along the Gold Coast form the Fante Confederation
1869	Egypt's Suez Canal opens
1869–1887	Jaja rules over the merchant kingdom of Opobo, in Nigeria
1873–1874	Britain lays siege to Kumasi, the Ashanti capital, and declares the Gold Coast Colony, in present-day Ghana
1877–1893	Yoruba states engage in civil war in southwestern Nigeria
1879	Anglo-Zulu War in Natal, South Africa; Zulus win the Battle of Isandlwana only to later lose the war
1884–1885	European powers meet at the Berlin Conference to discuss the colonial partition of Africa, launching an intense period of colonial conquest
	Belgium's King Leopold gains international recognition of his personal rule over the Congo, leading to the Congo Free State
1885	The Mahdi, a warrior and holy man named Muhammad Ahmad, dies shortly after his victory over the Egyptian forces in the Sudan
1887	Ethiopian emperor Menelik II makes Addis Ababa his capital

Gold mining begins on South Africa's Witwatersrand

1888
De Beers Consolidated Mines founded, establishing diamond cartel in South Africa

King Lobengula signs a treaty with Cecil Rhodes, permitting Rhodes to search for minerals in Ndebele lands

1888–1892
Kingdom of Buganda is embroiled in religious civil war

1893
French defeat Tukulor Empire of Ahmadu Seku

1893–1914
Pacifist and human rights champion Mohandas Gandhi works among the Indian population in South Africa

1895
Failed Jameson Raid leads to the resignation of Cecil Rhodes as prime minister of Britain's Cape Colony

1896
Ethiopians defeat Italian forces at the Battle of Adowa

1896–1897
First Chimurenga rebellion in Southern Rhodesia (today's Zimbabwe)

1896–1901
Britain imports 30,000 indentured laborers from India to work on the railways in British East Africa

1897
British forces burn and loot Benin city in southern Nigeria

1898
Aborigines' Rights Protection Society founded in Gold Coast Colony (present-day Ghana)

France defeats Samori Touré's Mandinka empire in West Africa

1898–1899
Britain defeats Mahdist forces at Battle of Omdurman, establishing dominion over present-day Sudan

1899–1902
Anglo-Boer War in South Africa

1900
Muslim slave trader and empire builder Rabih bin Fadlallah is killed by French forces near Lake Chad

1903
Britain conquers Sokoto Caliphate in Northern Nigeria

1904–1908
Herero and Nama people are decimated during their rebellion against occupying German forces in South West Africa (today's Namibia)

1905–1906
Spirit medium Kinjikitile inspires unsuccessful Maji-Maji rebellion in southern German East Africa (present-day Tanzania)

1906
Bambatha, a Zondi chief, leads the last Zulu rebellion against British colonialists in Natal, South Africa

1908
Belgian government takes over the former Congo Free State of King Leopold II

1910
Formation of the Union of South Africa

1912
Moulay Hafid signs the Treaty of Fez, making Morocco a French protectorate

South African Native National Congress founded; it is later renamed the African National Congress

1914
Blaise Diagne of Senegal is first African elected as a deputy to the French National Assembly

1914–1918
World War I in Europe

1915
John Chilembwe leads failed "Rising" rebellion in Nyasaland (present-day Malawi)

1916	French forces put down final major Tuareg rebellion in Aïr
1917	Marcus Garvey moves his Universal Negro Improvement Association to New York, spreading message of racial pride and African unity
1919	League of Nations founded with Liberia and the Union of South Africa the only African states among its forty-two founding members
1920	English soap manufacturer William Lever acquires the Royal Niger Company to gain access to African palm oil
1921–1934	Thousands of African laborers die building the railway from Pointe-Noir to Brazzaville, in French Congo
1922	Doctrine of British colonial rule known as the "Dual Mandate" described in book published by colonial administrator F. J. Lugard
	The tomb of King Tutankhamun is discovered in Egypt
1924–1965	Humanitarian Albert Schweitzer directs his famed missionary hospital at Lambaréné, in present-day Gabon
1926	In Morocco, the Rif Republic of Abd el-Krim is dismantled by combined French and Spanish forces
1929–1930	Women of Aba, Nigeria, lead a successful revolt against British colonial taxation
1929–1939	Great Depression affects economic markets worldwide
1930	Ras (Prince) Tafari Makonnen from Harer becomes emperor of Ethiopia, taking the name Haile Selassie

1932	Antonio de Oliveira Salazar, the authoritarian prime minister, comes to power in Portugal
1935–1936	Italo-Ethiopian War in Ethiopia; Haile Selassie flees to England
1937	Gold Coast cocoa farmers strike to protest British agricultural policy in African colonies
	In Nigeria, Nnamdi Azikiwe founds *The West African Pilot*, an influential nationalist newspaper
1939–1945	World War II
1944	Heads of state of the Francophone African countries meet at Brazzaville to discuss post-war arrangements
1945	United Nations established, with Egypt, Ethiopia, Liberia, and South Africa among its founding states
1946	Felix Houphouët-Boigny and Ahmed Sekou found the African Democratic Assembly; effective African independence and nationalism movements spread throughout the continent
1946–1956	British colonial police, later joined by the British army, brutally repress anti-colonial Mau Mau insurrection, in Kenya
1947	Alioune Diop founds *Presence Africaine*, an influential journal for black intellectuals from around the world
1948	Afrikaner-led Nationalist Party wins South African elections and begins instituting racist apartheid laws
1949	With the slogan, "Self Government Now," Kwame Nkrumah founds the radical Convention Peoples Party in Gold Coast

1951	Libya's independence acknowledged by the United Nations
1952	*Palm Wine Drunkard*, by Amos Tutuola, is the first book written in English to be published by an African author
	Free Officers Committee, headed by Gamal Abdel Nasser, seizes power in Egypt
1953	Several hundred African workers killed by Portuguese colonial police in the Batepa Massacre, in São Tome and Príncipe
1953–1963	Nyasaland, Northern Rhodesia, and Southern Rhodesia united as the Central African Federation
1954–1962	*New Age,* a militant national newspaper opposing white rule, published in South Africa
	Algerian War coming to an end with France recognizing Algeria's independence
1955	Bandung Afro-Asian Conference, held in Indonesia, lays the groundwork for the Non-Aligned Movement
	Freedom Charter calling for a non-racial South Africa adopted by the multi-racial Congress of Democrats
1955–1959	Construction of the Kariba Dam, at the time, the largest dam project in the world
1956	Morocco, Tunisia, and Sudan achieve independence
1956	Egypt's Gamal Abdel Nasser nationalizes Suez Canal, leading to war with Britain, France, and Israel; UN peacekeeping forces intervene

1957	Ghana achieves independence
	Chinua Achebe's *Things Fall Apart* published
1958	Guinea declares independence
1958–1966	Hendrik Verwoerd, an ardent advocate of apartheid, serves as prime minister of South Africa
1959	The Pan-Africanist Congress, a black militant organization, founded in South Africa
1960	Benin, Cameroon, Central African Republic, Chad, Republic of Congo, Dahomey, Democratic Republic of Congo, Ivory Coast, Gabon, Madagascar, Mali, Mauritania, Niger, Nigeria, Senegal, Somalia, Togo, and Upper Volta all achieve independence
	Police kill 69 black protesters in Sharpeville, South Africa
	South Africa's Albert Lutuli awarded Nobel Peace Prize
1961	Tanganyika, Sierra Leone achieve independence
	Recently elected prime minister Patrice Lumumba assassinated, sparking political crisis in the Congo
1962	Algeria, Burundi, Rwanda, and Uganda achieve independence
1963	Kenya achieves independence
1964	Malawi and Zambia achieve independence

Aba Women's Revolt (1929–30) First major revolt by women in the West African region. Organized by rural women living in the Oweri and Calabar provinces of present-day NIGERIA, the revolt demonstrated the women's ability to organize powerful resistance to the British colonial administration in Eastern Nigeria. The Ogu Ndem, or Women's War, so surprised British administrators that, out of embarrassment, they preferred to call it a mere riot. There were many causes for the revolt, but the primary ones involved the economic policies implemented by the colonial administration in heavily populated Eastern Nigeria. The most onerous policy was the colonial TAXATION of Africans, which, during the Great Depression, brought tremendous hardship upon the people. As a result the simple attempt of a colonial census taker to question a woman in the village of Oloko sparked off the Aba Women's Revolt.

According to reports, a widow named Nawanyeruwa was asked by the census taker to state the number of people, goats, and sheep in her household. In the past the colonial census was taken for the purposes of increasing taxation. Convinced that this new census would again lead to a rise in taxes, the widow angrily asked the census taker, an IGBO man, whether his own mother was ever counted. (In traditional Igbo society, women did not pay taxes.) After the encounter Nawanyeruwa quickly rushed to the town square, where the women were meeting to discuss the present tax problem. Hearing the widow's story and believing that they would be the next to be counted, the women invited other women from the neighboring towns and villages to join them in protest.

In response to the call, within a few days more than 10,000 women gathered in the town. They pressured the warrant chief, an Igbo man named Okugo, to have the colonial government stop further taxation or resign his chieftancy. Women throughout Igboland took to the streets demanding not only that women be exempted from paying taxes, but that the unpopular warrant chiefs be removed from their positions immediately. Demonstrations and sit-down strikes took place in all major Igboland towns and cities. The outcry forced the British district officer to put Okugo on trial for assaulting two women during the revolt in Okolo, and the warrant chief was eventually found guilty and sentenced to two years imprisonment.

> The women who figured prominently in the Aba revolt are still admired in Igbo society. Nawanyeruwa is honored for sparking the revolt. The Oloko Trio—Ikonnia, Mwannedia, and Nwugo—became known as the "Emissaries of Peace, and Apostles on Non-Violence." Madam Mary Okezie (1906–1999) is remembered as the intellectual leader of the Nigerian women's movement, an elegant writer of petitions and letters.

Although the situation seemed improved, the women were outraged further when a reckless British driver accidentally hit and killed two of the protesters in Aba. In response, Aba women burned down government office buildings and European-owned businesses, causing the colonial administration to send the police and army to put down the revolt. Recognizing the power of the women's movement, the colonial administration struck a compromise with the women leaders from Oloko, asking them to end their revolt and go around the region to explain that women would never again be asked to pay taxes.

In 1930 the colonial administration set up a commission to study the causes of the revolt. The most important of the commission's many conclusions was that women should be given a greater role in the decisions affecting the way their society is run. In this way the women of the Aba revolt provided a precedent for the future role of women in Nigeria.

The Aba Women's Revolt was a harbinger of the influence that rural Igbo women would exert on future political activities. As a consequence of the revolt the system of warrant chieftancy was abolished, and women were appointed to the Native Court system, which was responsible for advising the colonial administration. These changes paved the way for the national political movements that led to Nigerian independence.

See also: COLONIALISM, INFLUENCE OF (Vol. IV); COLONIAL RULE (Vol. IV); RESISTANCE AND REBELLION (Vol. IV); WOMEN IN COLONIAL AFRICA (Vol. IV).

Further reading: Michael Crowther, *West Africa Under Colonial Rule* (London: Hutchinson & Co. Ltd, 1968).

Abbas, Ferhat (1899–1985) *Algerian nationalist*

The son of a middle-class family from Constantine, ALGERIA, Ferhat Abbas was a pharmacist by training. Until 1936 his political philosophy was that of a liberal reformer. He believed in assimilation with France and took part in a movement that demanded equal rights for Algerian Muslims under French rule. The objectives of Abbas and other *évolués,* as the more French-oriented Algerians were called, was to have Algeria become a full-fledged province of France with all its population being French citizens.

In 1938 Abbas reversed his thinking and became a nationalist. He founded a political party called the Algerian Popular Union, which advocated equal rights for French and Muslims and the preservation of Muslim culture. In 1943, during World War II (1939–45), Abbas helped to write the "Manifesto of the Algerian People," which called for an Algerian state but stopped short of demanding independence from France.

At the end of the war Abbas became a deputy to the Constituent Assembly, in Paris, where he spoke out in support of Algerian self-rule. French authorities arrested him in 1945 for participating in anticolonial demonstrations, not freeing him until the following year. Upon his release he founded a middle-class political party, the Democratic Union of the Algerian Manifesto, which in the 1946 legislative elections won 11 of the 13 seats allocated for Muslim Algerians in the Constituent Assembly.

The emergence of the rural, peasant-led NATIONAL LIBERATION FRONT (Front de Libération Nationale, FLN) at the forefront of the Algerian struggle against France caught Abbas by surprise. While increasingly supportive of the FLN cause, he did not become a member until April 1956, when he escaped from Algeria to CAIRO, EGYPT, to join the organization. In 1959 Ferhat Abbas became the first president of the Temporary Government of the Algerian Republic, in exile. His position as president was largely ceremonial, however, since the real power within the FLN lay with Ahmed BEN BELLA (1916–) and Houari Boumédienne (1927–1978).

After Algeria gained independence, in 1962, Abbas became president of the Algerian National Assembly, but President Ben Bella imprisoned him for opposing his attempt to reduce the National Assembly's role in government. When Boumédienne overthrew Ben Bella, in 1965, he released Abbas, who then focused on writing. Abbas provides an insider's view of the Algerian revolution through publications such as his 1980 book, *Autopsy of a War: The Dawn.* In 1992 the university in Sétif, which was founded in 1978, was renamed Ferhat Abbas University in his honor.

See also: BOUMÉDIENNE, HOUARI (Vol. V); COLONIAL RULE (Vol. IV); FRANCE AND AFRICA (Vols. IV, V); NATIONALISM AND INDEPENDENCE MOVEMENTS (Vol. IV).

Further reading: Abder-Rahmane Derradji, *A Concise History of Political Violence in Algeria, 1954–2000: Brothers in Faith, Enemies in Arms* (Lewiston, N.Y.: E. Mellen Press, 2002).

Abdallahi ibn Muhammad (Abdullahi ibn Muhammad; The Khalifa) (1846–1899) *Leader of the Mahdist movement in the Sudan*

A member of the nomadic Baggara ethnic group living in the DARFUR region of present-day Republic of the SUDAN, Abdallahi played an instrumental role in the creation of the Mahdist movement that transformed his native country in the late 19th century. Along with other Muslims of his time, he expected the coming of the *mahdi,* the long-awaited redeemer ordained by God to appear at "the end of time" to fill the world with his justice. In 1881, after a long search for this holy figure, he encountered Muhammad Ahmad (1844–1885) and proclaimed him to be the *mahdi.* In return, Muhammad Ahmad named Abdallahi as his *khalifa,* or successor, and gave him the title of "commander of the armies" with control over the administrations of the expanding Mahdist state. Muhammad Ahmad's aim was to overthrow the Egyptian colonial government of the Sudan. In the subsequent four years of fighting, Abdallahi commanded the Black Flag division of the Mahdist army, composed of Baggara warriors.

In 1885, less than six month after securing victory, Muhammad Ahmad, by then widely known as Muhammad Ahmad al-MAHDI, died. Abdallahi succeeded him as the leader of the MAHDIYYA, as al-Mahdi's movement had become known. Abdallahi chose Omdurman as his capital over the former capital of KHARTOUM, on the other side of the Nile River. Taking the title of *khalifa al-mahdi,* (the successor of the mahdi), Abdallahi consolidated his power over his rivals, ruling in an autocratic manner. A number of his policies caused discontent and rebellion, especially his abandonment of al-Mahdi's fiscal reforms and his return to the hated, Ottoman forms of taxation that al-Mahdi had condemned during Egyptian rule. Abdallahi also reinstituted a secular government managed by a bureaucracy made up of Sudanese civil servants who had worked for the previous Egyptian administration. Moreover, he continued to rule through a military rather than a civilian government.

For al-Mahdi, rule over the Sudan was to have been the first step toward a revived Islamic state; for Abdallahi, the goal was a strong Sudanese state. Accordingly, he struggled to formalize the Sudan's international boundaries by expanding east toward ETHIOPIA, north toward EGYPT, and west into the Sultanate of Darfur. Fighting erupted, with mixed results. In 1887 Mahdist troops made a successful large-scale raid deep into Ethiopia. In 1889, however, a combined British and Egyptian force soundly defeated the Abdallahi's army when it attempted to push into southern Egypt. Britain also was determined to avenge the death of British general Charles George GORDON (1833–1885), who had been killed at the siege of Khartoum in 1885. In a two-stage advance that began in 1896, British forces attacked and defeated the Mahdist state, with the final decisive confrontation at the Battle of OMDURMAN (1898). Khalifa Abdallahi escaped with some of his forces, only to be killed during his army's defeat at the Battle at Umm Diwaykarat, in 1899.

See also: COLONIAL CONQUEST (Vol. IV); ENGLAND AND AFRICA (Vol. IV).

Further reading: P. M. Holt, *The Mahdist State in the Sudan, 1881–1898,* 2nd ed. (Oxford: Oxford University Press, 1970); P. M. Holt and M. W. Daly, *A History of the Sudan: From the Coming of Islam to the Present Day* (London: Longman, 1988).

Abd el-Krim, Mohamed ben (Abdel Karim, Muhammad ben; Muhammad ibn Abd al-Karim al-Khattabi) (c. 1880–1963) *Moroccan political and military leader*

A member of a privileged Berber family, Abd el-Krim became a dedicated opponent of European rule in North Africa, organizing political and military resistance and founding a short-lived independent republic. Eventually, however, he was unable to resist the combined forces of Spain and France, which forced his surrender and sent him into exile.

Born in Adjir, MOROCCO, about 1880, Abd el-Krim was educated at both Spanish and traditional Muslim schools. This included two years at the renowned Qarawiyyin University, in Fez, where he studied Islam and was exposed to the Islamic reformist ideas of the Young Turks. Still quite young, he began a career in the colonial administration. After a brief period in the Bureau of Native Affairs, he became, in 1918, a judge in the Melilla district, along the northern Mediterranean coast of Morocco. His experiences there, transformed him, and he became convinced that North Africa should be free of COLONIAL RULE. While serving as a judge Abd el-Krim also edited the Arabic section of the local Spanish newspaper, *El Telegrama del Rif.*

Abd el-Krim's opposition to Spanish rule increased until it eventually landed him in prison. A series of adventures, including a prison escape, led him to Melilla once again, and then back to Adjir. There, in 1919, he began organizing more radical resistance to colonial rule. Within a short time he assembled an effective fighting force that, in July 1921, defeated a major element of the occupying Spanish army, capturing or killing thousands of soldiers; the Spanish commanding general was among the dead. Seizing on that victory, Abd el-Krim founded the Republic of the RIF, organized along modernist Islamic lines, with himself as its first president.

Abd el-Krim's republic proved to be short-lived. Although he was temporarily successful in defeating attempts at regaining control by both Spain and France, eventually those powers combined to send more than 250,000 troops against Abd el-Krim's independent republic. Outnumbered and possessing grossly inferior weapons, Abd el-Krim was forced to surrender on May 27, 1926. He was then exiled to RÉUNION ISLAND, where he spent the next 20 years of his life.

After World War II (1939–45) he was given permission to move to France. Still a committed anticolonialist, he switched destinations en route, and, in 1947, he accepted an offer of political asylum in CAIRO, EGYPT. There he remained active in anticolonialist affairs, heading the Liberation Committee of the Arab West. Abd el-Krim's staunch opposition to colonialism was not softened even by the arrival of Moroccan independence, in 1956. When King MUHAMMAD V (1910–1961) invited the aging rebel back to his homeland, Abd el-Krim refused, saying that he would not return until North Africa was free of all French troops. He died in Cairo on February 6, 1963.

See also: BERBERS (Vol. IV); FRANCE AND AFRICA (Vol. IV); RESISTANCE AND REBELLION (Vol. IV); SPAIN AND AFRICA (Vol. IV); SPANISH MOROCCO (Vol. IV).

Further reading: C. R. Pennell, *A Country with a Government and a Flag: the Rif War in Morocco, 1921–1926* (Boulder, Colo.: Lynne Rienner, 1986).

Abeokuta Capital of the Ogun State in present-day southwestern NIGERIA. Abeokuta was founded in 1830 by refugees from the Egba sub-group of the YORUBA that were seeking an escape from the civil wars that swept their country. Its name stems from this and means "refuge among rocks."

Within a decade of Abeokuta's founding, MISSIONARIES of the CHURCH MISSIONARY SOCIETY (CMS) arrived. Joining them were members of the KRIO group from SIERRA LEONE who had originated in the area but ended up as captives in the transatlantic slave trade. Abeokuta became a thriving commercial town as well as one of Yorubaland's centers of Christianity and Western-style EDUCATION. One of its most famous inhabitants was Samuel JOHNSON (1846–1901), an ordained Anglican minister and early historian of the Yoruba.

In the 1870s the more westernized elements in the Abeokuta citizenry established the Egba United Board of Management (EUBM) to share the governing of the town with the older elite. The EUBM sought to halt the expanding British colonial authority emanating from the LAGOS Colony. Ultimately, however, the EUBM proved to be a divisive force, and by 1872 it had lost most of its power.

As part of its attempt to arrest the rising tide of European influence, in 1867 the EUBM forced European CMS missionaries to leave Abeokuta. Later, even the Yoruba minister James "Holy" Johnson (c. 1836–1917) was expelled.

In 1893 the British forced Abeokuta to sign a treaty that limited its independence, and the community once again became a center of CMS activities. Still, it was not until 1914 that Abeokuta, by then a town of 60,000, came fully under British COLONIAL RULE. Even then, a spirit of independence remained. In 1918 anger at British colonial rule led local citizens to tear up the railroad tracks that ran through town on the way from the coast to the northern interior. There were a number of fatalities, which led to a dispatch of 1,000 British troops. The ensuing battle led to about 500 rebel deaths. This action restored British authority, which remained firmly established throughout the rest of the colonial period.

See also: ABEOKUTA (Vol. III); CIVIL WARS (Vol. V); COLONIAL CONQUEST (Vol. IV); COLONIAL RULE (Vol. IV); EGBA (Vol. III); ENGLAND AND AFRICA (Vol. IV); YORUBALAND (Vols. II, III).

Abidjan Former capital city of present-day IVORY COAST. The coastal city of Abidjan became part of FRENCH WEST AFRICA in 1893. Its location on the Ébrié Lagoon, an arm of the Gulf of Guinea, made Abidjan an ideal site for both a railroad and a port. Abidjan began to grow after it was made the terminus for a railroad from the interio, in 1904. Port facilities for ocean-going vessels were not built until after 1950, when the Vridi Canal was cut through the sandbar that protected the deep, sheltered lagoon from the Gulf of Guinea.

In 1934 the capital of the French colony of Ivory Coast was moved from Bingerville to Abidjan. At that time the inhabitants of Abidjan numbered only about 17,000. The city remained the administrative and commercial capital of the colony until 1960, when Ivory Coast declared its independence from France. Abidjan then became the capital of the new nation.

Abidjan's growth was a result of rapid colonial development. Large numbers of workers from Ivory Coast and other areas of French West Africa migrated to the city, drawn by the availability of jobs. The city also became the intellectual center of Ivory Coast when the National University of Ivory Coast was opened, in 1958. By the time of independence, in 1960, Abidjan's population had reached 180,000.

See also: ABIDJAN (Vol. V); FRANCE AND AFRICA (Vols. IV, V); HOUPHOUËT-BOIGNY, FÉLIX (Vols. IV, V); YAMOUSSOUKRO (Vol. V).

Aborigines' Rights Protection Society (ARPS) Early African-nationalist organization based in the GOLD COAST COLONY (today's GHANA). The late 19th and early 20th centuries saw an increase in African opposition to the expansion of European COLONIAL RULE. One expression of this opposition was the founding of the Fante National Political and Cultural Society. Organized in 1898 in the town of CAPE COAST, the organization assembled the educated Fante elite for the purpose of limiting the adverse impact of Western culture on traditional Fante culture. John Mensah SARBAH (1864–1910), a Western-educated lawyer, led the movement. While he and other society members approved of Western scientific knowledge, political ideas, and economic practices, they simultaneously opposed the excessive adoption of English ways and insisted that Africans should retain their names, their dress, and their languages. In short, they should not become "black Englishmen."

In 1897 the Fante National Political and Cultural Society transformed itself into the larger, multiethnic Aborigines' Rights Protection Society (ARPS). The first key issue for the ARPS was the Land Bill, which was legislation proposed by the British that would have given the colonial administration the power to take over all empty lands in the Gold Coast. The bill was strongly opposed by the people of the Gold Coast and of neighboring West African states as well. The ARPS was at the forefront of protests against the bill, reminding fellow West Africans about the detrimental results of the allocation of African land to white settlers in KENYA, SOUTHERN RHODESIA (today's ZIMBABWE), and SOUTH AFRICA. The ARPS used a formidable press campaign, particularly its own newly founded newspaper, the *Gold Coast Aborigines,* to criticize the Land Bill and British colonial policies in general. Members organized letter-writing campaigns to the British Parliament, and Sarbah, along with fellow lawyer and ARPS member Awoonor Renner, spoke out against the bill in the Gold Coast Legislative Council. In May 1898 the society sent a delegation to London to present its case to both the House of Commons and the British public. They were effective, for Parliament not only dropped the Land Bill, but also decided to abandon the equally unpopular Hut Tax legislation.

After the success of the anti–Land Bill campaign, the ARPS continued to pay attention to other bills before the British Parliament, requesting that the society be consulted before passing legislation affecting the Gold Coast. The ARPS opposed the imposition of direct taxes, called for better educational opportunities, and demanded constitutional reforms that would involve the Fante elite more broadly in government. By 1905 the demands had resulted in the construction of some elementary and secondary schools in Cape Coast.

The society also succeeded in bringing together Western-educated and traditional elites to oppose colonial policies and injustice. Above all else the question of land ownership was one on which both sides agreed. Within a few years, however, this solidarity faded when the British introduced indirect rule, a policy that gave the traditional rulers more power over their own people and greater influence with the colonial administration.

Other nationalist organizations emerged to challenge the primacy of the ARPS, and by 1927 the NATIONAL CONGRESS OF BRITISH WEST AFRICA had replaced it in importance. The legacy of the ARPS persisted, however, for it laid the groundwork for future West African NATIONALISM AND INDEPENDENCE MOVEMENTS.

See also: ENGLAND AND AFRICA (Vol. IV); COLONIAL RULE (Vol. IV); COLONIALISM, INFLUENCE OF (Vol. IV).

Further reading: A. Adu Boahen, *African Perspectives on Colonialism* (Baltimore: Johns Hopkins University Press, 1992); A. E. Afigbo, et al., *The Making of Modern Africa,* Vol. 2 (New York: Longman, 1990); Michael Crowther, *West Africa Under Colonial Rule* (London: Hutchinson & Co. Ltd, 1968).

Accra Capital of present-day GHANA, located on the Gulf of Guinea. Accra's origins lie in three principal coastal villages built by the Ga people, each of which played host to a European settlement: Nleshi, with a British fort; Kinka, with a Dutch fort; and, 2 miles away,

Osu, with a Danish fort. In 1850 the British purchased the Danish fort and consolidated their power by assuming control of the Dutch fort as well, in 1868. The villages and forts eventually merged to form Accra. Britain established the GOLD COAST COLONY in 1874, and in 1877 the colony's capital was moved from CAPE COAST to Accra.

Accra's development differed markedly from that of other colonial port cities in Africa. Its origins resulted in a dual African and colonial character, allowing the city to remain the center of Ga life while still serving as a colonial capital. This dual nature was perhaps reflected most clearly by Carl REINDORF (1834–1917), a Presbyterian minister of Danish and Ga heritage, who was an important figure in Accra and a chronicler of the history of the Gold Coast.

Although it had fewer than 20,000 inhabitants in 1891, by 1931 Accra had more than tripled in population. By the 1930s the city had developed much of what would be its present-day street plan, and growth proceeded at a rapid pace. In 1957 Accra became the capital of the newly independent nation of Ghana. On April 15, 1958, Accra hosted the initial Conference of Independent African States, the first pan-African conference held in an African city.

See also: ACCRA (Vol. II, III, V); ASHANTI (Vol. II); ASHANTI EMPIRE (Vol. III, IV); GA (Vols. II, III).

Achebe, Chinua (1930–) *Nigerian author*

Born Albert Chinualumogu Achebe in eastern NIGERIA, Achebe was raised as a Christian within IGBO cultural surroundings. He was educated in English and attended the Government College, in Umuahia, before going on to University College, IBADAN, where he was a member of its first graduating class, in 1953. While studying history and theology at the university he became interested in indigenous cultures and decided to use his Igbo name rather than his Christian one.

In the 1950s Achebe worked for the Nigerian Broadcasting Corporation. During this time he began to develop a distinctive literary voice that drew upon traditional culture. The negative portrayal of Africans in European novels prompted Achebe to launch his own literary career. The two books that influenced him the most in this regard were *Heart of Darkness* by Joseph Conrad (1857–1924), published in 1899, and *Mr. Johnson* by Joyce Cary (1888–1957), published in 1939. *Heart of Darkness* inspired Achebe to write, and *Mr. Johnson,* which was set in the familiar surroundings of his native Nigeria, gave Achebe a point of departure for refuting the negative stereotypes that Carey and other European authors presented when depicting Africans.

In 1958 Achebe published THINGS FALL APART, which earned him a global reputation as the foremost African novelist writing in English. He conceived of it as challenging the usual European portrayal of Africans. His method was to utilize the LANGUAGE and literature of the colonizer to challenge the very system of colonialism. This was the first of a number of both fiction and nonfiction books that were to make Achebe one of Africa's leading writers of the second half of the 20th century.

See also: ACHEBE, CHINUA (Vol. V); LITERATURE IN COLONIAL AFRICA (Vol. IV); LITERATURE IN MODERN AFRICA (Vol. V).

Further reading: Ezenwa-Ohaeto, *Chinua Achebe: A Biography* (Bloomington, Ind.: Indiana University Press, 1997).

Achimota College   Model, comprehensive secondary school located in ACCRA, GHANA. Originally Prince of Wales College, Achimota College was founded in 1927 by British governor Sir Gordon Guggisberg (1869–1930). The initial investment in the school, more than £600,000 sterling, was unusually large for launching an African school at that time. The student body was coeducational and consisted of both Africans and Europeans. The curriculum offered general secondary EDUCATION, post-secondary technical education, and teacher training. Within 10 years of its founding Achimota was also enrolling university students. Its student body was made up of 32 degree-track students in addition to 180 secondary students, and nearly 2,000 teacher-training students.

> The piano keyboard on the Achimota College seal symbolizes cooperation between blacks and whites. About 30 years earlier the African-American educator Booker T. WASHINGTON (1856–1915) may have been the first to utilize this symbol in this way.

Achimota's first principal was the Reverend. A. G. Fraser, a missionary from Britain. James E. K. AGGREY (1875–1927), a Ghanaian educated in North Carolina who had been strongly influenced by Booker T. Washington, was appointed assistant vice principal. The government absorbed the cost of tuition but required students to pay nominal school fees to enhance their respect for the education they received. Successful students competed for scholarships to study at British universities. Achimota College moved to a separate campus in 1948 and was called the University College of the Gold Coast. In 1957 the college's name was changed to the University of Ghana at Legon.

See also: EDUCATION (Vol. V).

Addis Ababa   Capital and largest city in ETHIOPIA, located on a plateau near the geographic center of the country. Ethiopia, its history dating as far back as the first century BCE, has had a number of capitals in the course of its rich history. Previous capitals fell into decline once the surrounding forests had been depleted for fuel and building supplies, and the kings and their courts moved on to more plentiful regions. Addis Ababa proved a more permanent seat of government than its predecessors.

In 1887 MENELIK II (1844–1913) founded Addis Ababa (meaning "new flower" in Amharic) in the SHOA province, where he was the ruler. In 1889, when Menelik became Ethiopia's emperor, he established Addis Ababa as the national capital. The city developed around the palace, Saint George's Cathedral, and the central market, known as the *Arada*.

Menelik's defeat of Italian forces in the Battle of ADOWA (1896) dispelled the threat of colonization and led to an influx to the city of European and Asian investors, merchants, and craftsmen, many of whom had a new respect for Menelik and Ethiopia. By 1900 the city's population had reached 40,000. The linking of Addis Ababa with the French-colonial port of DJIBOUTI via railway, in 1917, provided access to the sea and further solidified the city's status as Ethiopia's political and economic center.

> When Menelik, facing a wood shortage, planned to move the capital, the entrenched foreign population protested. As an alternative Menelik encouraged the planting of eucalyptus trees in a large-scale reforestation effort that eventually earned the city the nickname "Eucalyptopolis."

Ethiopia resisted colonization until 1936, when the government of Emperor HAILE SELASSIE (1892–1975) collapsed in the face of the invading Italian army. The resulting occupation, which lasted until 1941, had a tremendous impact on Addis Ababa. The Italians imposed a policy of neighborhood segregation, establishing Italian-only areas within the city. They changed the name of the Arada to the *Piazza* and converted it to a commercial district, moving the original market to Mercato. They also drove away many foreign proprietors, upsetting the local economy. Despite the social disruption caused by the Italian occupation the physical base of the city was much improved by the modern housing, roads, and other infrastructure constructed by Italian and Ethiopian workers during the occupation. By 1965 the city's population had surpassed 440,000.

See also: ADDIS ABABA (Vol. V); AMHARA (Vol. IV); AMHARIC (Vols. I, II); ITALY AND AFRICA (Vol. IV).

Adowa, Battle of (Battle of Adwa)

Decisive victory by Ethiopian forces, March 1, 1896, that led Italy to temporarily abandon its attempt to conquer ETHIOPIA. In 1889, the same year that he proclaimed himself *negus nagast* (king of kings) of Ethiopia, MENELIK II (1844–1913) entered into the Treaty of Wichele (Ucciali) with Italy. The Italians recently had occupied the Red Sea port of Assab, in ERITREA, where they established a colony. Menelik soon accused the Italians of misconstruing a clause in the treaty to claim a PROTECTORATE over Ethiopia, and in 1891 he denounced their claims. Confident that his forces, which he had been arming with modern weapons, were more than a match for any Italian invasion, Menelik then declared that he was ready to rid the region of the Italian presence.

Determined to put on a display of power, in 1895 the Italian government sent General Oreste Baratieri (1841–1901) to Ethiopia, where he met with some early success. Returning to Rome to a hero's reception, Baratieri vowed he would not only defeat the Ethiopian army, but would bring Menelik back to Rome in a cage. Menelik, however, had assembled a huge army of 196,000 soldiers, half of them with state-of-the-art weapons, near the Ethiopian town of Adowa. Baratieri was unaware of the size of the force opposing him until a column of 1,300 *askari* (Eritrean troops under Italian officers) was annihilated at Amba Alagi by a force of 30,000 Ethiopians. Baratieri then had his troops dig in at Adigrat, hoping to lure Menelik into attacking the relatively secure Italian positions. Menelik, however, could better afford to wait, for it was his home territory. Finally, after several long months and with his troops reduced to half their rations, Baratieri had no other choice but to attack.

The treacherous Ethiopian terrain, which had protected Ethiopians from their enemies for centuries, proved too much for the advancing Italian forces. Maneuvering in the dark and over a difficult and unfamiliar landscape, it was not long before they fell into complete disarray. Recognizing the plight of the opposing forces, the Ethiopians attacked. For a time the Italian force was able to hold them at bay. Eventually, though, the numbers and effective armaments of the Ethiopians proved insurmountable, and the Italians were completely defeated after having lost 289 of their officers, 2,918 European soldiers, and 2,000 *askari*. Others were missing or wounded, and several hundred were taken prisoner. Ethiopian casualties also were high, with 7,000 dead and 10,000 wounded.

News of the disastrous defeat caused an uproar in Italy, bringing down the government in power and leading to a change in policy toward Ethiopia. That October, with the Treaty of Addis Ababa, the Italian government made peace with Menelik, recognizing Ethiopia's independence. Around the world the people of the AFRICAN DIASPORA celebrated the news of the Ethiopian victory, seeing it as a sign of power and independence on the part of Africans and people of African descent.

A number of Europeans and *askari* were taken prisoner. Initially some 70 Italians and more than 200 *askari* were tortured to death before Menelik learned what was happening and put a stop to it. The prisoners were then marched to Menelik's capital, ADDIS ABABA, where they were held. Eventually the Italian government ransomed the European soldiers. The *askari*, however, met with a worse fate. As Tigrayans from Eritrea, they were considered to be traitors by Menelik, and they were given the traditional Ethiopian punishment for treason—the loss of the right hand and left foot.

See also: COLONIAL CONQUEST (Vol. IV); ITALY AND AFRICA (Vol. IV); PARTITION (Vol. IV); RESISTANCE AND REBELLION (Vol. IV).

Further readings: Haggai Ehrlich, et al., *Ras Aula and the Scramble for Africa* (New Jersey: Red Sea Press, 1996); Harold G. Marcus, *The Life and Times of Menelik II* (New Jersey: Red Sea Press, 1995).

Afghani, Jamal al-Din al- (Jamal al-Din Afghani)

(1838–1897) *Teacher, political agitator, and developer of a pan-Islamic philosophy*

Sayyid Jamal al-Din al-Afghani was an intellectual and activist who believed that Islam could find a middle position between a conservative rejection of everything Western and a liberal, blind acceptance of it. Politically he advocated pan-Islamism, a philosophy urging all Muslim nations to unite in combating European domination. He presented and defended his reformist and modernist view of Islam in newspaper articles, lectures, polemics, and other writings.

As a youth al-Afghani studied at various Quranic schools in Afghanistan, Iran, and India. He intentionally obscured whether he was born in Iran or Afghanistan and which of the two major sects of Islam—Shiite or Sunni—he belonged, believing that people in the Islamic world would accept or reject his ideas based on these factors.

In 1870 al-Afghani traveled to EGYPT and taught at al-Azhar University, in CAIRO. There he clashed with conservative Muslims over his reformist ideas. After leaving al-Azhar he opened an independent academy that attracted a number of young Egyptians who later became political leaders or Islamic reformers. These included Muhammad Abduh (1849–1905), one of the greatest

Muslim thinkers of the late 19th century, and Sad Zaghlul (1857–1927), the founder of the WAFD PARTY and leader of Egypt's independence struggle after World War I (1914–18).

Al-Afghani's opinions brought him into direct conflict with Khedive ISMAIL (1830–1895), viceroy of Egypt under the Ottoman Empire. Between 1870 and 1879 Khedive Ismail's thinking became more Eurocentric. In addition, Ismail's financial mismanagement had emptied the government treasury, and he was under great pressure from Egypt's European creditors. Al-Afghani chafed at the Egyptian government's commitment to secularization. He became politically active when Britain and France assumed control of Egypt's financial affairs. Seeking to implement a program of political and social reforms, al-Afghani branded Khedive Ismail's spending a mismanagement of public funds. He worked behind the scenes with Ismail's son, Muhammad Tawfiq Pasha (1852–1892), to depose Ismail. However, once Tawfiq became khedive, he ignored the reforms and in 1879 expelled al-Afghani from Egypt.

In 1881 al-Afghani published *The Refutation of the Materialists,* a book in which he asserted the superiority of Islam over other religions. Islam, he argued, was the religion best able to overcome materialism, which he viewed as the enemy of religion and culture. Al-Afghani's philosophy of Islamic renewal and resistance to Western domination continues to influence Egyptian thought today.

See also: ISLAM (Vol. II); ISLAM, INFLUENCE OF (Vol. IV); ISLAMIC CENTERS OF LEARNING (Vol. II); MALIKI SUNNI DOCTRINE (Vol. III); OTTOMAN EMPIRE (Vol. III); OTTOMAN EMPIRE AND AFRICA (Vol. IV); SHIISM (Vol. III).

African Democratic Assembly (Rassemblement Democratique Africain, RDA)

Multi-colony, multi-ethnic, political organization of FRENCH WEST AFRICA. In 1946, at the BAMAKO Conference, a group of African elites and politicians, led by Félix HOUPHOUËT-BOIGNY (1905–1993) and Ahmed Sékou TOURÉ (1922–1984), founded the RDA as the first inter-territorial political organization in Africa. The RDA called for full equality among all citizens and quickly became popular in IVORY COAST, Houphouët-Boigny's home. Eventually the RDA established a presence in all of French West Africa except MAURITANIA, and it also became active in other French African colonies such as CHAD and GABON.

Although Houphouët-Boigny claimed that the organization was not a political party, the RDA spawned associated, individual political parties in each of the constituent territories. In GUINEA, for example, the Democratic Party of Guinea, founded in 1947, evolved from the RDA. In addition, the RDA inspired opposition parties as the elites and politicians struggled with the concept of colonial federation. In SENEGAL, for example, Léopold SENGHOR (1906–2001) founded the Senegalese Democratic Bloc in 1948.

Those who followed Houphouët-Boigny supported the concept of territorialism, also endorsed by France, which envisioned each colony as an independent nation-state that would bargain on its own terms with France. In contrast, those who followed Senghor supported the concept of federation so that those colonies lacking resources (landlocked colonies like NIGER, UPPER VOLTA [now BURKINA FASO], and FRENCH SOUDAN [now the Republic of MALI]) would be more economically viable and thus able to negotiate with France from a position of strength.

Initially the RDA was radically anti-imperialistic and held strong ties with the French Communist Party. Although the French government was wary of this association, as well as the RDA's anti-imperialist ideology, France accepted and encouraged the growth of political parties as long as it felt that it could regulate them. France responded to the ideology and philosophy of the RDA by taking measures to diffuse its strength by running opposition candidates, removing supporters from government employment, and occasionally jailing its leaders. These moves weakened the RDA, and France eventually persuaded Houphouët-Boigny to split from the more radical RDA elements. He was also encouraged to sever the party's ties with the French Communists. As a result the RDA survived and soon resumed its prominent role in French West African politics. Houphouët-Boigny, for his part, became the most influential politician in French-speaking Africa.

See also: FRANCE AND AFRICA (Vols. III, IV, V); NATIONALISM AND INDEPENDENCE MOVEMENTS (Vol. IV).

African diaspora

The mass dispersion throughout the world of peoples of African culture or origin. The history of the African diaspora is tied, though not exclusively, to the SLAVE TRADE. The Indian Ocean and trans-Saharan slave trades, which existed centuries before their Atlantic counterpart developed, initiated the beginnings of African communities in the Middle East and Asia as early as the first century BCE. By the 18th century the practice of SLAVERY had resulted in groups of African captives on nearly every continent. To varying degrees of success, enslaved Africans struggled to maintain their cultural and ethnic identities under the immense hardships of slavery. Through their efforts the languages, values, and traditions of many African ethnic groups were spread throughout the world.

The African diaspora, however, was not a one-way phenomenon. In 1787, for example, former slaves from Britain, Canada, and the Caribbean founded the FREETOWN settlement in SIERRA LEONE, and in 1821 another group of freed captives from the United States established LIBERIA. These "repatriated" Africans, who themselves belonged to various ethnicities, developed new cultures that blended with Western influences. The results were the development of groups such as the KRIO in Sierra Leone and the Americo-Liberians in Liberia. These Africans were highly influential in bringing Western EDUCATION, culture, and ideas into Africa. These Western influences, however, were not always welcome.

Members of the African diaspora had an immense impact on African history during the colonial era. Many of the diaspora's leading figures of the time, such as Edward Wilmont BLYDEN (1832–1912), Marcus GARVEY (1887–1940), and W. E. B. DU BOIS (1868–1963) helped fuel African nationalism and develop PAN-AFRICANISM and NÉGRITUDE. They also created movements and organizations outside of Africa, such as the BACK-TO-AFRICA MOVEMENTS, the Harlem Renaissance, and the Nation of Islam.

See also: COLONIALISM, INFLUENCE OF (Vol. IV); ETHIOPIANISM (Vol. IV); RASTAFARIANISM (Vol. V); RECAPTIVES (Vol. IV); SLAVE TRADE, THE TRANSATLANTIC (Vol. III).

African National Congress (ANC) South African political organization that led the resistance movement against APARTHEID. Upon its inception, in 1910, the UNION OF SOUTH AFRICA made it clear that black Africans would not have an equal political voice. In response, Pixley ka Isaka Seme (1882–1951) invited all Africans to form a national organization to provide a platform for political action. As a result of Seme's call a broad spectrum of African leaders came together at Bloemfontein, in 1912, and founded the South African Native National Congress (SANNC), with John L. DUBE (1871–1946) as the organization's first president. Though it supported various strikes and protests during the early stages of its existence, the nascent SANNC took a decidedly conservative approach in its struggle against the racist South African government.

In 1914 the SANNC sent a delegation to Britain to convey African objections to the 1913 Natives' Land Act, which prevented Africans from buying land outside the "Native Reserves" and forced thousands of Africans from their homelands. The delegation included Dube and Sol T. PLAATJE (1876–1932), the SANNC's first secretary-general. Officials in Britain, however, responded to the group's concerns with determined apathy, and the delegation returned to South Africa having accomplished little.

Many of the SANNC's early leaders were educated in Britain and the United States, and they believed in the power of persuasion and the sanctity of the legislative process. As a result the SANNC was slow to gain a mass following. During much of the 1920s the Industrial and Commercial Workers Union, which fought against unfair working conditions through effective use of strikes and other militant actions, was more active and popular than the SANNC. In 1923 the SANNC changed its name to the African National Congress.

As the 1920s came to an end the ANC continued to founder in its fight against the South African government and in its efforts at gaining a larger base of support. As a result the organization experienced an internal rift between moderate and militant factions. The lack of results produced by the moderates allowed the ascension of a more radical leadership, with Josiah Gumede (1870–1947) assuming the ANC presidency, in 1927. Under Gumede's stewardship the organization began to work closely with the Communist Party of South Africa (CPSA). However, strong opposition to Gumede and his support for the CPSA perpetuated the ANC's infighting and led to Gumede's electoral defeat at the 1930 convention.

Gumede was succeeded by Seme, who attempted to return the ANC to a more moderate style. However, there was still a portion of the ANC's membership disillusioned with this approach, and the organization was effectively paralyzed by internal strife throughout the 1930s. In 1940 Alfred Xuma (1893–1962) became president of the ANC. Xuma was effective in making the ANC more efficient, but, like Seme, he was a moderate, and the call for a more aggressive form of resistance soon made Xuma's stance obsolete.

In 1944 a group of young ANC members, unhappy with the organization's moderate leadership, formed the African National Congress Youth League (ANCYL). The group was led by Anton Lembede (1914–1947) and also included Walter SISULU (1912–2003), Oliver TAMBO (1917–1993), and Nelson MANDELA (1918–). The ANCYL promoted African nationalism and believed that a militant resistance, including massive strikes and protests was the best way to achieve success in the fight against the South African government.

The ANCYL benefited from the increasing URBANIZATION that took place in South Africa during the 1940s, as the concentration of young African males in urban areas led to the formation of local activist organizations, whose members were mostly favorable toward the Youth League's call for militancy. At the same time the ANC, which had historically been composed of intellectuals and elites, evolved to include more working-class Africans in its membership. By 1947 the ANC Youth League had largely taken control of the ANC with Lembebe, Tambo, and Ashby Mda (1916–) sitting on the national executive committee.

During this time the ANCYL developed a model of activism called the Progamme of Action, which endorsed the active use of civil disobedience. In 1948 the South African National Party (NP), running on a pro-segregation platform, won the national elections, ushering in the era of apartheid. The NP's victory rallied support for the Program of Action. The following year James Moroko (1891–1985) of the Youth League was elected to succeed Xuma as ANC president, confirming the primacy of the Youth League faction within the organization. The ANC allowed women to join the organization beginning in 1943, and in 1948 the ANC Women's League was formed.

The rise of the ANCYL brought other changes to the ANC's philosophy on activism. The new leaders believed that the ANC could benefit by working with other activist organizations, and they soon created a joint planning council in collaboration with heads of the South African Indian Congress (SAIC). Emboldened by its alliances with other anti-apartheid groups, in 1952 the ANC launched a defiance campaign, calling on the population to defy apartheid laws with the hope that the resulting mass arrests would overwhelm the police and justice systems. The campaign garnered widespread support, and thousands were arrested. Though the effort failed to bring about any legislative changes, it strengthened the ANC's relationships with other activist groups and swelled the ANC's paid membership from under 10,000 to more than 100,000 in less than a year.

Seeking to coordinate South Africa's various anti-apartheid organizations, the ANC, SAIC, South African Coloured People's Organization, South African Congress of Democrats (a white anti-apartheid group), and the multiracial South African Congress of Trade Unions organized a mass meeting called the Congress of the People. At the congress, held in 1955, the groups introduced the FREEDOM CHARTER, an alternative to the apartheid system based on tenets of racial equality and the equal distribution of South Africa's land and resources. Near the end of the congress police surrounded the meeting, took the names of the attendees, and ordered them to leave.

The next year the government claimed that the Freedom Charter encouraged illegal, Communist activity. Using the 1950 Suppression of Communism Act, the government arrested 156 leaders of the ANC and other anti-apartheid organizations and charged them with high treason, a crime punishable by death. The trial lasted five years, but all of the defendants were eventually freed. During the trial the ANC was still active organizing strikes and campaigning against pass laws, which controlled the movement of black Africans throughout South Africa.

Though popular support for the ANC continued to increase, the organization experienced an internal rift toward the end of the 1950s. Some ANC members, calling themselves Africanists, were unhappy with the policy of cooperation with non-black organizations. Unable to reconcile their views with the non-racist policies of the ANC, the Africanists broke from the organization and founded the PAN-AFRICANIST CONGRESS (PAC), in 1959, with Robert SOBUKWE (1924–1978) as president.

Looking to upstage the ANC, the PAC organized an anti-pass-law campaign to begin 10 days before a similar ANC campaign was set to begin. In March 1960 the PAC urged people to gather at police stations without their passes and offer themselves for arrest. One of the larger demonstrations occurred in the city of Sharpeville, where more than 5,000 protesters gathered at the police station. Toward the end of the day, in a peaceful but increasingly tense atmosphere, police opened fire, killing at least 69 of the demonstrators.

The Sharpeville incident marked a turning point for the ANC, which soon was banned and had to move its operations underground. At the same time many within the ANC leadership came to believe that in order to achieve political change in South Africa they would have to accept the use of violence. This led to the formation of the ANC's military wing, Umkhonto we Sizwe. Mandela was named its commander in chief and began the ANC's armed resistance in 1961.

See also: AFRICAN NATIONAL CONGRESS (Vol. V); AFRIKANERS (Vols. IV, V); JABAVU, DAVIDSON DON TENGO (Vol. IV); POLITICAL PARTIES AND ORGANIZATIONS (Vols. IV, V); RESISTANCE AND REBELLION (Vol. IV); SHARPEVILLE (Vol. V); UMKHONTO WE SIZWE (Vol. V).

Further reading: Saul Dubow, *The African National Congress* (Stroud, U.K.: Sutton Publishing, 2000); Sheridan Johns and R. Hunt Davis, Jr., eds., *Mandela, Tambo, and the African National Congress: The Struggle Against Apartheid, 1948–1990: A Documentary Survey* (New York: Oxford University Press, 1991).

Afrikaans South African LANGUAGE of the AFRIKANERS, which was developed from a dialect of Netherlandic, or Dutch, spoken by European colonists in SOUTH AFRICA in the late 18th century. In the 19th century Christian MISSIONARIES began to codify the Afrikaans language to produce religious tracts. This effort ultimately led to the appearance, in 1859, of the Afrikaans language periodical *De Bode van Genadendal,* which published literature and accounts of church matters for black and white Christians. In 1876 a small group of white, Afrikaner nationalists established the first Afrikaans-only newspaper, *Di Patriot,* to promote the transformation of Afrikaans from a spoken to a written language. Codification of the language continued through 1915. Its standardization was completed under the auspices of the Afrikaner scholars of the Academy for Language, Literature, and Arts, which was established for that purpose in 1909.

The standardization of Afrikaans became the cultural core of the growing nationalist movement that arose after the ANGLO-BOER WAR (1899–1902). In 1925 Afrikaans replaced Dutch to become, with English, one of South Africa's two official languages. The political dominance of Afrikaans was institutionalized when the conservative,

Afrikaner-dominated Nationalist Party won a major electoral victory in 1948. Because it was the language of government, EDUCATION, and the political elite, Afrikaans came to represent white privilege and the statutory exclusion of other races through the ongoing implementation of APARTHEID.

See also: AFRIKAANS (Vols. III, V); LITERATURE IN COLONIAL AFRICA (Vol. IV); LITERATURE IN MODERN AFRICA (Vol. V).

Afrikaner Republics (Boer Republics)

Known individually as the TRANSVAAL and the ORANGE FREE STATE, states that emerged in the interior of SOUTH AFRICA during the latter half of the 19th century. Beginning in 1835 AFRIKANERS, who were settlers of Dutch and mixed European origins from the CAPE COLONY, began migrating north of the Orange River in search of arable land and hoping for greater independence from British COLONIAL RULE. Called the Great Boer Trek, the migration of Afrikaner *voortrekkers* (pioneers) led to conflict with several indigenous peoples, most notably the SOTHO, NDEBELE, TSWANA, and ZULU.

Formerly called *BOERS*, the Afrikaner settlers formed small states that were constituted as republics reminiscent of the Dutch Batavian Republic, which had briefly ruled the Cape Colony at the beginning of the 19th century. In 1845, however, Britain annexed NATAL, which lead to most of the trekkers retruning to the interior high veld. Then, in 1848, the British annexed the territory between the Orange and Vaal rivers, naming it the Orange River Sovereignty. In 1854, after Britain withdrew its claims to the area in the Convention of Bloemfontein, Afrikaner settlers declared the independence of the Orange Free State.

During the latter half of the 1850s the republics of the Transvaal united to form the South African Republic (SAR). But the discovery of precious minerals, first DIAMONDS, in 1867, and then GOLD, in 1886, sparked the interest of the British imperial officials. As a result of this so-called MINERAL REVOLUTION the British annexed the SAR in 1877. Three years later Afrikaners rose in rebellion and inflicted a significant defeat on the British at Majuba Hill, leading to British recognition of the SAR's independence, in 1881. Paul KRUGER (1825–1904) became the republic's new president. During this time tensions arose between Afrikaner farmers and the English-speaking miners and fortune seekers—perjoritavely called UITLANDERS.

In 1899 conflict erupted between Britain and the Afrikaner Republics. The subsequent hard-fought ANGLO-BOER WAR involved the large-scale use of guerrilla tactics by Afrikaner commandos. On the British side the war included the severe PACIFICATION of civilian populations, primarily through the use of concentration camps. Britain managed to finally stamp out Afrikaner resistance, and the Treaty of VEREENIGING, signed in May 1902, concluded the war. Both the SAR and the Orange Free State were granted self-government by 1907, and in 1910 they were incorporated into the UNION OF SOUTH AFRICA, along with Natal and the Cape Colony.

See also: ENGLAND AND AFRICA (Vols. III, IV, V); JAMESON RAID (Vol. IV).

Afrikaners

White South Africans, predominantly of Dutch or Huguenot Calvinist ancestry, who speak the LANGUAGE of AFRIKAANS and have historically held the belief of white and Christian supremacy. Used to refer to the Boer people, the term became more prevalent after the ANGLO-BOER WAR (1899–1902).

Between 1835 and the early 1840s many BOERS of the CAPE COLONY, though not the majority, moved farther inland to escape Britain's increasing influence on the political and social structure of the colony. Known as the "Great Boer Trek," the Boer migration met with determined resistance from various African tribes. Eventually, however, the Boers established secure settlements and founded the AFRIKANER REPUBLICS of the TRANSVAAL and ORANGE FREE STATE.

After the Anglo-Boer War the British quickly granted self-governing constitutions to the former Afrikaner states, now colonies of Britain. As Britain moved to incorporate the colonies into a union with the CAPE COLONY and NATAL, Afrikaners used their political position to ensure their continued dominance of the African population. Following the formation of the UNION OF SOUTH AFRICA the African population for the most part remained disenfranchised.

Unsatisfied with mere political domination, the Afrikaner-led union government pushed for further subjugation of the indigenous population. The Native's Land Acts of 1913 and 1936 confined African land ownership rights to less than 15 percent of the country's total land area. Further legislation reserved skilled employment for whites, limited African's from living permanently in the cities, and eventually ended the limited parliamentary representation for non-Europeans. These and other racist policies became the framework for the establishment of the APARTHEID system that was formally put into effect following the 1948 election.

Afrikaner Nationalism Afrikaners achieved their goals by dominating the political realm of the Union as well as that of the successor Republic of SOUTH AFRICA. From 1910 until 1994, when Nelson MANDELA (1918–) won election, every prime minister was an Afrikaner, including Louis BOTHA (1862–1919), Jan Christiaan SMUTS (1870–1950), J. B. M. HERTZOG (1866–1942), and D. F. MALAN (1874–1959). In addition, Afrikaners possessed cohesive political objectives and a sense of community that was lacking in their English-speaking counterparts. Together these characteristics of the Afrikaner population formed a strong foundation for Afrikaner nationalism.

Afrikaner nationalism was marked by its attempts to promote the use of the Afrikaans language over English, to gain full political autonomy from Britain, to alleviate the relative poverty of rural Afrikaners, and to further strengthen white supremacy. In 1914 the National Party (NP) was founded to advance these concerns, and the party grew quickly as Afrikaners became disillusioned by Prime Minister Botha's conciliatory relationship with Britain.

During the 1920s Afrikaner nationalists supported strikes by white LABOR UNIONS that were upset with a movement to relax the rules on labor preferences for whites working in the GOLD mines. In 1922 the strikers, having seized JOHANNESBURG, took up fortified positions and declared the establishment of the White Workers' Republic. Smuts, now prime minister, quickly crushed the rebel strikers. His victory was short-lived, however, for much of the white labor force began to support Hertzog, who subsequently won the 1924 election and became prime minister.

Hertzog immediately began implementing a legislative agenda that paralleled the ideology of Afrikaner nationalists. His efforts were soon stymied, as political and economic pressures related to the Great Depression (c. 1929–39) shifted Hertzog's focus from promoting Afrikaner nationalism to ensuring his reelection in 1934. To strengthen his position, Hertzog formed a partnership with the previously defeated Smuts. The Hertzog-Smuts partnership succeeded, and their newly formed United Party (UP) carried the elections; Hertzog remained prime minister and Smuts became his deputy prime minister. Many Afrikaners, however, were unhappy with the alliance. Some of those disillusioned with the UP helped form the Purified National Party, which was led by D. F. Malan.

In 1938 Malan helped organize a reenactment of the Great Boer Trek, which was to highlight the hardships of past Afrikaners. After the reenactment the Voortrekker Monument was constructed outside PRETORIA to commemorate and glorify the supposed heroic efforts of the Afrikaners and to depict the falsely alledged perfidy of Africans.

Despite Smuts's supposed moderate regard for Afrikaner nationalism, his partnership with Hertzog introduced a wave of legislation that decreased the rights of Africans. Still, the more ardent Afrikaner nationalists were

dissatisfied, and their discontent only swelled with the events of World War II (1939–45).

As war broke out, South Africa's leadership was split on what action the country should take. Hertzog preferred neutrality, while Smuts favored enlisting on the side of Britain, as South Africa had done in World War I (1914–18). Smuts prevailed in Parliament and once again became prime minister. Hertzog essentially was left out of South African political life until his death, in 1942.

Attracted by the tenets of Nazism, including its anti-semitic and "master race" ideologies, many Afrikaners supported alliance with Germany during World War II. Malan and the NP worked to suppress some of the more extreme pro-Nazi sentiment and organizations, especially as the tide of war shifted against Germany.

Afrikaner nationalists flocked to Malan and the NP, and after the war he was in a strong position to challenge Smuts and the UP in the 1948 elections. Running on a platform supporting total segregation, which they called *apartheid*, the NP, with the help of the unequal electoral weight given to Afrikaner-dominated rural areas, defeated Smuts. Malan became prime minister, and the NP took control of the government of South Africa. Afrikaner-nationalist ideology, even greater than that witnessed during the Hertzog era, infused the country's government.

See also: AFRIKANERS (Vol. V); GREAT BOER TREK (Vol. III); KRUGER, PAUL (Vol. IV); POLITICAL PARTIES AND ORGANIZATIONS (Vols. IV, V).

Further readings: Herman Giliomee, *The Afrikaners: Biography of a People* (Charlottesville, Va.: Univ. of Virginia Press, 2003).

Aggrey, James E. Kwegyir (1875–1927) *Prominent African educator during the colonial era*

James E. Kwegyir Aggrey was born in Anomabo in the Central Region of the British GOLD COAST COLONY (present-day GHANA). Educated in Wesleyan Methodist schools, he taught in Gold Coast mission schools before going to the United States to attend Livingstone College in Salisbury, North Carolina. He graduated with a bachelor's degree, in 1902. There he met Rose Douglas, whom he married, in 1905. In 1921 and 1924 Aggrey was the only African on the two Phelps-Stokes Commissions on EDUCATION in Africa. The commissions examined schools in colonial Africa and made policy recommendations. As a member of the two commissions, Aggrey served as an intermediary between blacks and whites. He also provided links between education in Africa and in the southern United States. In 1924 he was appointed assistant vice principal of the newly established ACHIMOTA COLLEGE in the Gold Coast. In 1927 Aggrey was in New York City writing his doctoral dissertation at Columbia University when he became ill and died suddenly. His wife returned to Salisbury, where she subsequently became a school principal.

agriculture At the middle of the 19th century the vast majority of Africans lived in rural areas and supported themselves through agriculture. Thus they were living as their ancestors had lived for many centuries or, in some parts of the continent, for millennia. Agricultural practices had not been unchanging in the past. Indeed, the "American food complex" of crops such as maize (corn), GROUNDNUTS (peanuts), and cassava had been spreading throughout large areas as major crops of the continent since about the beginning of the 16th century. Nor was

agriculture simply for subsistence purposes, for Africans had long been trading surpluses of what they raised for other foodstuffs or for items produced by craftspeople in another village. These trade items included iron axes and hoes, salt, baskets, and cloth, among other things. Even so, until the 19th century most agriculture involved producing long-familiar crops and raising familiar animal breeds for consumption at the local level.

By 1850 long-standing patterns of agriculture were already beginning to change in many parts of the continent. This change centered on the large-scale production of CASH CROPS for external markets. This was later to become a principal feature of African agriculture during the colonial period and afterward. European INDUSTRIALIZATION had created a market for agricultural commodities from the tropics, especially oil crops such as groundnuts and PALM OIL. African producers, mostly in West Africa, responded by producing crops designated for consumption outside the continent. For example, British imports of palm oil, which amounted to 1,000 tons in 1810, reached

Trying to fight off swarms of locusts, these South African agricultural laborers headed out to protect crops with insecticide. Photo taken c. 1935.
© *Wide World*

30,000 tons in 1953. The income generated from the sale of palm oil often went toward the purchase of imported European manufactured goods. In this way parts of Africa were beginning to become dependent upon world trade.

While West Africa was becoming increasingly engaged in producing cash crops prior to COLONIAL RULE, two areas of the continent were undergoing changes in agricultural practices due to the presence of European SETTLERS. These were SOUTH AFRICA, where Europeans had begun to settle and farm in the last half of the 17th century, and ALGERIA, where Europeans started settling by the 1820s. By the 1850s white farmers were becoming increasingly well established and were growing crops for European-style diets. The local population, with its land no longer used for traditional purposes, was reduced to working on white-owned farms for wages and had to fight for the right to work small garden areas and graze a few animals.

By the 1930s wine produced on white-owned farms in Algeria accounted for more than half of the colony's EXPORTS. Over the first half of the 20th century these farms were becoming increasingly mechanized. The result was a sharp decline in indigenous Algerian sharecroppers on whom the white landowners had at first depended for farm LABOR. By 1954 there were only 60,000 sharecroppers left from the 350,000 or so at the beginning of the century.

With the onset of colonial rule, cash-crop-commodity production for both export and settler farming expanded dramatically. Also, a new feature of the colonial ECONOMY emerged: the foreign-owned plantation. While groundnuts and palm oil produced by African farmers met local FOOD needs, RUBBER, sisal, and palm oil for export were increasingly grown on large, industrialized plantations. The huge Firestone rubber plantation in LIBERIA was a prime example.

African farmers also increasingly produced new crops strictly for export, including COCOA, COFFEE, and COTTON. Prior to World War II (1939–45), cash crops, whether grown by African peasant farmers, large-scale white commercial farmers, or European-owned plantations, constituted the core of African colonial economies.

Colonial governments therefore encouraged this production and engaged in agricultural research to improve the output of such crops. FOOD CROPS, on the other hand, were neglected. The agricultural labor force often was diverted to cash-crop production. In some areas, such as the

cocoa-producing regions of GHANA, this encouraged the cultivation of food crops in neighboring areas for sale to the workers on the cocoa farms. In many of the cotton-producing areas, however, the intensive labor demands of the crop led to a lack of sufficient labor for food crops. Severe food shortages often resulted. Nor did the economy promote the production of African food crops such as sorghum, yams, millet, and cassava for marketing to the growing urban areas. Colonial governments did support European farmers in producing crops for markets within Africa. An example is the South African government's support of the large-scale farming of maize for the South African cities. Conversely, there was a near total neglect of food crops grown by Africans for market. Instead the governments viewed African food-crop production as subsistence agriculture.

After World War II Africa underwent a dramatic population growth. Between 1900 and 1950 the population was growing at an already substantial annual rate of 1.2 percent. Then, in the 1950s alone, it grew by another 30 percent. The colonial emphasis on the production of export agricultural economies at the expense of food-crop production left Africa ill-prepared to increase or even sustain existing per-capita food production. This altered paradigm of African agriculture became another colonial legacy that burdened the newly independent African countries.

See also: AGRICULTURE (Vols. I, II, III, V); COLONIALISM, INFLUENCE OF (Vol. IV).

Ahmadu Séku (Ahmadu Sefu, Ahmadu ibn Umar Tal) (d. 1898) *Head of the Tukulor empire*

Ahmadu Séku was the son of a HAUSA-slave mother and the Islamic reformist UMAR TAL (1794–1864), who led the JIHAD that established the TUKULOR EMPIRE in the region of the Upper Senegal and Upper Niger Rivers in the 1850s. Umar Tal had resisted French colonial military expansion, but by the late 1850s the two sides established a cease-fire. Internal rebellions threatened Umar Tal's rule, and it was in an attempt to suppress one such rebellion, in Macina, that he was killed, in 1864.

His son, Ahmadu—one of 50 children that Umar Tal fathered—finally assumed his father's position after a bitter succession dispute. Ahmadu inherited two of the principal problems that had faced Umar as the leader of the Tukulor empire. First he had to struggle incessantly to suppress internal rebellions, and second, starting in the 1870s, he had to face a resurgence of French colonial ambition in the West African interior. Out of necessity, in 1887 Ahmadu's Tukulor empire and France formed a temporary alliance against common African opponents. Within two years, however, the French had resumed their COLONIAL CONQUEST of former Tukulor territories, folding them into the interior portions of FRENCH WEST AFRICA. Ahmadu resisted, but the French were too powerful, and by 1893 they had overwhelmed his forces. After staying on the move for a couple of years, Ahmadu settled in the SOKOTO CALIPHATE, his mother's homeland, where he died, in 1898.

See also: FRANCE AND AFRICA (Vols. III, IV, V); ISLAM, INFLUENCE OF (Vols. II, III, IV, V); MACINA (Vol. III).

Further reading: A. S. Kanya-Forstner, *The Conquest of the Western Sudan: a Study in French Military Imperialism* (London: Cambridge U.P., 1969); B. O. Oloruntimehin, *The Segu Tukulor Empire* (London: Longman, 1972).

Akan West African linguistic and ethnic group, located mostly in southern GHANA and IVORY COAST. Akan is part of the Kwa group of Niger-Congo languages. The Akan people are made up of several main dialect groups: the Ashanti, Fante, Akuapem, Akwamu, Akyem, Brong, and several others. In 1960 nearly 40 percent of the population of Ghana spoke a dialect of Akan, and it remains the most important LANGUAGE of the region. Akan is the language of the Ashanti religion, which is still actively practiced in Ghana.

Akan was the language of the Fante coastal peoples, who were among the first to experience direct COLONIAL RULE in West Africa. Akan was also the language of the ASHANTI EMPIRE, which flourished from the 17th century until the British, after a long and intense struggle, annexed it in 1895 as part of the GOLD COAST COLONY.

See also: AKAN (Vols. I, II, III); AKYEM (Vol. II, III); ASHANTI (Vol. II); FANTE (Vols. II, III); LANGUAGE FAMILIES (Vol. I).

Alexandria Port city on the Mediterranean Sea and second largest city in present-day EGYPT. The rich and diverse history of Alexandria extends back to the founding of the city by the Macedonian king, Alexander the Great (356–323 BCE), in 332 BCE. In addition to being a major port, the city became known as a cultural and EDUCATION center, and immigrants from many nations gave it an international feel. Symbols of culture and wealth were constructed, including the immense Alexandria library and the Pharos lighthouse, which by the second century CE was considered one of the Seven Wonders of the Ancient World.

After enjoying a reputation as one of Egypt's most important cities, Alexandria began a period of decline in 968, when conquering Arabs moved Egypt's capital to CAIRO. In 1517 Alexandria became part of the Ottoman Empire. By the time Napoleon Bonaparte (1769–1821) arrived to take the city in 1798, Alexandria had fallen from being the world's second-largest city to little more than a fishing village of approximately 5,000 inhabitants. The arrival of Napoleon's forces, however, marked a reintroduction of Egypt to the European world.

By 1805 Muhammad Ali (1769–1849) took control of Egypt as the Ottoman Empire's appointed pasha. Under this Albanian-born officer Alexandria's importance was revived. The opening of two waterways—the Mahmudiyya Canal, linking Alexandria to the Nile River, in 1820, and the SUEZ CANAL, in 1869—increased the port traffic. By 1881 there was a movement among citizens for Egyptian leadership of the city. Britain, which had been increasingly influential in Egypt, put down the movement and by the end of 1882 had assumed control of the country. At the beginning of the 20th century Alexandria's population stood at about 320,000, more than five times what it had been a half-century earlier. By this time the city had assumed strategic importance to Britain, as it served as the main naval base in the region during World War I (1914–18) and World War II (1939–45).

In 1957, after the Suez-Sinai War of 1956 (one of the ARAB-ISRAELI WARS), an anti-Western sentiment mounted and led to the forced exile of all French and British from Alexandria. By this time there were more than 1.5 million people living in Alexandria. Since then the city has embraced its Egyptian identity in place of its former international profile.

See also: ALEXANDER THE GREAT (Vol. I); ARABS (Vol. II); ARABS, INFLUENCE OF (Vols. II, III); ENGLAND AND AFRICA (Vols. III, IV, V); MACEDONIA (Vol. I); MEDITERRANEAN SEA (Vols. I, II); NILE RIVER (Vol. I); OTTOMAN EMPIRE AND AFRICA (Vol. IV); URBANIZATION (Vols. IV, V); URBAN LIFE AND CULTURE (Vols. IV, V); WORLD WAR I AND AFRICA (Vol. IV); WORLD WAR II AND AFRICA (Vol. IV).

Further reading: Michael J. Reimer, *Colonial Bridgehead: Government and Society in Alexandria, 1807–1882* (Boulder, Colo.: Westview Press, 1997).

Algeria North African country covering about 919,600 square miles (2,381,800 sq km) and bordered by the Mediterranean Sea and the present-day countries of MOROCCO, WESTERN SAHARA, MAURITANIA, MALI, NIGER, LIBYA, and TUNISIA.

Once part of the Berber Almoravid and Almohad empires in the 13th century and earlier, Algeria was the first country of the MAGHRIB to be ruled by the Ottoman Empire. In 1830 France conquered Algeria as part of its campaign to rid the Mediterranean of North African seaborne raiders known as *corsairs*. By 1837 the last provincial governor appointed by the Ottoman Empire had surrendered to the French. As soon as they were fully in control, France opened the country to European SETTLERS, and by 1840 there were approximately 100,000 Europeans living in Algeria.

In an effort to consolidate their control over the country, the French attacked the Berber-speaking peoples living in the mountainous region known as the Kabylia. The major resistance was led by Abd al-Qadir (1808–1883), who, after 15 years of opposing the French, finally surrendered, in 1847, and was exiled to Damascus, Syria. The majority of the indigenous people living in and farming the land taken over by the French were Muslim BERBERS and Arabs. Although they had not completely secured the southern boundaries of Algeria, the French stepped up their efforts to colonize the coastal region with its temperate climate, good rainfall, and rich soil. They gave grants of colonial land to French veterans as well as to Italians, Spaniards, Maltese, and Germans. Taxes paid by the indigenous Muslim population financed the colony of settlers, or colons, as they came to be known. By 1848 there were approximately 105,000 colons, whose primary occupation was farming COTTON, roses, tobacco, and grapes for wine.

Around 1850 the indigenous Muslim population suffered greatly from the loss of their fertile lands to colons and from plagues of locusts and disease that descended on the region. In 1852 Napoleon III (1808–1873) tried to reverse the colons' attempts to colonize the Berbers. For this he became in some ways the figure to whom the indigenous population looked for protection against colons' claims on their land.

During the Franco-Prussian War (1870–71) the Kabylia Berbers rebelled, led by the son of Abd al-Qadir. France brutally suppressed the revolt and gave the most fertile land in the Kabylia to new European settlers. When Napoleon III fell from power, in 1870, the European settlers exerted even greater influence in the region. Beginning in 1874 the French imposed the *indigénat*, a legal code for the indigenous Algerian population. The code allowed the government to accuse Muslims of a long list of illegal acts and then punish them with imprisonment or the confiscation of their property. In 1879 France administratively incorporated Algeria so that the Europeans living there could receive full French citizenship. Although administered by a governor-general, Algeria was reorganized into three French departments, or states, in which colons had the right to elect a municipal government and send deputies to the French National Assembly. While the Europeans were considered citizens, the Muslims were considered French subjects, thereby leaving them without the right to assemble, carry weapons, or move about within the country without permission. By 1880 the colons numbered about 375,000, but they successfully manipulated the local government and the French Assembly to maintain their advantage over local Muslims, who numbered about 3 million.

By the beginning of the 20th century European Algeria enjoyed the benefits of political and economic autonomy and had begun modernizing its infrastructure. Muslim Algerians, however, received little benefit from this modernization and continued to be burdened by poverty. The French National Assembly attempted to reward Algerian participation and support in World War I (1914–19) by offering French citizenship to Muslims if they would abandon Muslim law. The National Assembly hoped to increase Muslim representation in local government and give more property owners and veterans the right to vote. European Algerians, however, thwarted these efforts and retained political power.

The 1920s saw the rise of nationalism among Muslims who, because they had attended French-Arab schools in Algeria or had been educated in France, were more secular in their outlook and thinking. Seeking full citizenship rights as early as 1912, these nationalists had organized themselves under the name of the Party of Young Algeria. The "Young Algerians," as they were known, were led by Ferhat ABBAS (1899–1985), among others. They sought assimilation with France and equality of Europeans and Muslims.

In 1931 Ferhat Abbas published *De la colonie vers la province: le jeune Algérien* (From a colony toward a province: The young Algerian), a collection of articles by Algerian nationalists that made a case for citizenship in a province of France.

Another source of anticolonial resistance was Messali Hadj (1898–1974) and the French Communist party, which in 1926 founded L'Etoile Nord Africaine (The Star of North Africa) movement. It called for full independence from France and for a Muslim-controlled state.

A third reform movement, created after World War I in the rural areas of Algeria, was based on a common desire among many Muslims to resist further assimilation into French culture. This movement worked through Islamic NEWSPAPERS, publications, and EDUCATION to recreate an Arab cultural identity and to emphasize a return to the centrality of the Quran (the Muslim holy book) and the Hadith (the traditions of the Prophet Muhammad) . In 1931 one of the primary leaders of this movement, the religious scholar Abd al ben Badis (1889–1940), founded the Association of Muslims of Algeria. It sought to support his mission of combating assimilation and resisting French efforts to divide Arabs and Berbers. In response European Algerians banded together under a nationalist banner of being *pieds noirs* (descendants of the pioneer settlers) and dedicated themselves to the protection of white privilege.

Following the fall of France to Germany (1940) in World War II (1939–45), the pro-Nazi Vichy government controlled Algeria. Beginning in 1942, however, Algeria was the North African headquarters of the Allied forces. In 1944 General Charles DE GAULLE (1890–1970), the Free French leader, announced that French citizen-

1911, was considered a major statement of the Egyptian nationalist cause, and it led to Ali's participation in the First Universal Races Congress held in London that same year. The following year Ali founded *The African Times and Orient Review,* a journal that Ali declared to be dedicated to "the interests of the Coloured races of the World." *The Review,* which was published at various times as a monthly and a weekly, became a major platform for the ideas and ideology of pan-Africanism.

During this period Ali met the noted pan-Africanist Marcus GARVEY (1887–1940), who worked for *The Review* for a time. Ali, in turn, helped edit Garvey's newspaper, *Negro World,* while visiting New York.

During the early 1930s Ali moved to LAGOS, the capital of the British colony of NIGERIA, where he worked for the *Nigerian Daily Times* and the *Nigerian Daily Telegraph.* In 1932 he launched a weekly newspaper, the *Comet,* as a vehicle for promoting Nigerian nationalism. Shortly before his death, in 1944, Ali chaired the inaugural meeting of Nigeria's first nationalist political party, the National Council of Nigeria and the Cameroons.

See also: NATIONALISM AND INDEPENDENCE MOVEMENTS (Vol. IV); NEWSPAPERS (Vol. IV).

Alliance High School (1926–) Premier institution of secondary EDUCATION and the first secondary school in KENYA to provide a high-school curriculum to both male and female African students. In 1926 the European Alliance of Protestant Missions, in cooperation with the colonial government, founded Alliance High School in a town near the capital city of NAIROBI. Much of the money for building the initial facility came from funds that Africans had collected in memory of African soldiers who had died in World War I. The school opened with an all-male student body numbering 27. Women were admitted from 1938 until 1951, then, in 1948, a separate Alliance High School for Girls was opened nearby

Following a missionary heritage, Alliance High School provided an education in a Christian setting. Its students were the brightest and most promising young people from all over Kenya. They underwent a rigorous course of study that stressed service to the community and the nation, as stated in the school motto, "Strong to Serve." Graduates of Alliance High School became prominent in fields such as teaching, politics, law, architecture, engineering, and medicine.

From early on European missionaries dominated the school's teaching and administrative posts. The first African teacher was Eliud Mathu (d. 2002), who in 1944 became the first African member of Kenya's Legislative Council. In 1974 the school named its first African headmaster, Jackson M. Githaiga, and Africans have led the school ever since.

Amhara One of the major ethnic groups of modern-day ETHIOPIA that historically has exerted great influence over Ethiopian culture; also the name for the region covering approximately 171,000 square miles (442,890 sq km) in northwestern and north-central Ethiopia.

Under the restored Solomonic dynasty, which ruled Ethiopia from 1270 to 1974, all but one of Ethiopia's emperors came from among the Amhara. Historically Amharans also had made up the core membership of the ETHIOPIAN ORTHODX CHURCH. In 1889 MENELIK II (1844–1913), who was from the southern Amhara border kingdom of SHOA, became the Ethiopian emperor. Before becoming emperor, Menelik, as king of Shoa, expanded Amhara cultural and political dominance southward, establishing control over many OROMO areas.

As emperor, Menelik brought Amhara to even greater cultural prominence in an expanded Ethiopian empire. This dominance, however, stirred resentment among Tigrayans, especially since TIGRAY lay at the heart of the ancient city Aksum, out of which Ethiopia had emerged. Tigrayans also vividly remembered that the emperor preceding Menelik, YOHANNES IV (c. 1831–1889), was from Tigray.

Menelik's reign, which ended with his death, in 1913, was followed by a period when various princes from throughout Ethiopia fought to become the next emperor. Finally, in the mid-1920s, the Amharic-speaking Ras Tafari (1892–1975) consolidated his power and positioned himself to become Emperor HAILE SELASSIE. While under the brief Italian occupation prior to World War II (1939–45), the colonial administration tended to favor non-Amhara peoples of Ethiopia—Oromo, Tigrayans, and Somali Muslims—over the Amhara. With the restoration of Haile Selassie to the throne in 1941, however, the Amhara resumed their accustomed position of running the Ethiopian state. As the country modernized and the EDUCATION system expanded, LITERACY grew to unprecedented levels. Consequently, Amharic, as the official LANGUAGE of Ethiopian government, commerce, and education, grew in status vis-à-vis the country's other languages.

> The overthrow of Haile Selassie's government in 1974 and the subsequent Marxist regime ended the control of the Amhara nobility over national life. In 1989 Amharic lost its status as the official national language.

Amhara cultural dominance played an important part in the independence wars of neighboring ERITREA as well. In 1955 Amharic speaker Biteweded Asfaha Woldemikael (1914–) was made the chief executive of Eritrea, and his decision to change the official language of the Eritrean government from Italian to Amharic, replacing Tigrinya and Arabic, inflamed Eritrean ethnic rivalries that persisted through the rest of the century.

See also: AMHARA (Vols. I, III); AMHARIC (Vols. I, II); ITALO-ETHIOPIAN WAR (Vol. IV).

ANC See AFRICAN NATIONAL CONGRESS.

Anglo-American Corporation Giant MINING company that had an enormous impact on the economy of SOUTH AFRICA. In 1917 the Anglo-American Corporation of South Africa was established by Sir Ernest Oppenheimer (1880–1957). It was originally founded as a mining firm to exploit the rich GOLD deposits of the eastern WITWATERSRAND, a ridge to the east of JOHANNESBURG. The capital needed to start up the Anglo-American Corporation (AAC) was raised mainly in Britain and the United States, thus accounting for the company's name. In South Africa the AAC stood as the dominant player in the country's lucrative DIAMOND industry during the 1920s, becoming a major shareholder in DE BEERS CONSOLIDATED MINES, LTD., which remained a separate legal entity despite Oppenheimer's becoming its chairman in 1929. In time the AAC also became a force in the coal-mining, platinum-mining, and chemical industries and was also instrumental in developing the COPPER-mining industry in the COPPERBELT region of southern Central Africa. Upon Oppenheimer's death his son, Harry Oppenheimer (1908–2000), like his father a member of South Africa's Parliament, took control of the AAC.

In the context of South African politics the Oppenheimers were liberals and opposed the strict enforcement of APARTHEID. Opposition groups received funds from the Oppenheimers to challenge the ruling National Party, which was committed to a policy of white supremacy.

The AAC remains South Africa's largest company and one of the biggest mining and natural resource companies in the world. It is listed on both the Johannesburg and London stock exchanges.

See also: MINERALS AND METALS (Vols. IV, V); MULTINATIONAL CORPORATIONS (Vol. V).

Anglo-Ashanti Wars Series of armed conflicts between Britain and the ASHANTI EMPIRE that took place over most of the 19th century. Around the beginning of the 19th century the coastal trade of the Ashanti Empire,

in present-day GHANA, was threatened by the commercial activities of British merchants and expeditionary forces. Some Africans, however, especially those on the coast, saw the British as potential allies whose military backing would allow them to strike a significant blow against the powerful Ashanti. The local rivalries grew from the Ashanti practice of raiding neighboring kingdoms to take prisoners, which would later be traded for European goods or forced to work the Ashanti GOLD fields. By 1824 the Ashanti felt it necessary to expel their enemies from their territory, so they sent an army of an estimated 10,000 warriors to rout a smaller force made up of British, Fante, and Denkyira soldiers.

After the Ashanti victory over the British in 1824 the empire's leaders sent a message to any foreigners who might have designs on their territory, displaying the head of defeated British governor Charles MacCarthy (1769–1824) at the Ashanti capital of KUMASI.

In 1826 the British and their allies avenged their 1824 loss by defeating the Ashanti army at the Battle of Kantamanto, effectively putting an end to the first Anglo-Ashanti war. Following the war the Ashanti established peace with Britain and acknowledged the independence of other coastal peoples, including the Fante and Akyem. Because of their heavy losses the British reduced their military presence in the region and an extended period of relative peace followed.

In 1872 Britain bought the remaining Dutch forts along the Gold Coast, leaving it as the only European power in the region. Within a year violence erupted again. As the British moved inland toward Kumasi, Ashanti forces moved toward the coast to confront them. Although the skilled Ashanti bowmen, musketeers, and spearmen fought well, they could not repel the British forces, who were equipped with breech-loading rifles and artillery. In the end the British burned and looted Kumasi and forced the Ashanti to renounce their claims to all territories south of the Pra River. By 1874 Britain had formally declared the GOLD COAST COLONY over the entire coast, and Ashanti influence in the region declined over the next 15 years.

By the early 1890s the Ashanti were again building military strength and began efforts to end the British occupation of Kumasi. The British—who were now facing the additional threat of French colonial claims to the north and west of the Gold Coast—finally decided to secure its claim to the Gold Coast interior regions. In 1895–96 they assailed Kumasi with cannon fire, forcing the *asantehene* (king), Agyeman PREMPEH (1870–1931), to accept exile to avert a full-scale war and the total destruction of the Ashanti capital.

Following a short cease-fire, the Ashanti again restored their army, and by 1901 their leaders were no longer willing to abide the foreign occupation. Launching offensives under the direction of the bold military leader Yaa ASANTEWA (1850–1921), who was the mother of a prominent chief, the Ashanti began efforts to reclaim their city. Despite early victories, however, superior firepower—and the arrival of reinforcements from SIERRA LEONE and NIGERIA—helped the British to victory. Witnesses claimed that Yaa Asantewa was the last Ashanti person to lay down arms. The victory cemented the British claim to sovereignty over the Gold Coast, marking the end of the Anglo-Ashanti Wars and the beginning of the true colonial era in British West Africa.

See also: COLONIAL CONQUEST (Vol. IV); ENGLAND AND AFRICA (Vols. III, IV, V); PARTITION (Vol. IV).

Further reading: Robert B. Edgerton, *The Fall of the Ashante Empire: The Hundred-year War for Africa's Gold Coast* (New York: The Free Press, 1995).

Anglo-Boer War
Conflict within southern Africa lasting from 1899 to 1902. The war was the culmination of a series of disputes and conflicts between the AFRIKAANS-speaking BOERS of the TRANSVAAL and English MINING and imperial interests.

The Great Boer Trek of the mid-19th century had led to the creation of the AFRIKANER REPUBLICS of the Transvaal and the ORANGE FREE STATE. In 1877 the British peaceably annexed the Transvaal, but in 1880, unhappy with the timetable for the fulfillment of British promises of self-government, the Boers revolted. In 1881 an armistice was reached, but the status of Boer independence was still unclear.

This uncertainty within the Transvaal was further complicated, in 1886, by the discovery of GOLD. The find resulted in renewed British interest in the area as well as a mass influx of English mine capitalists, mine managers, and miners, who became perjoritavely known as UITLANDERS (outsiders) among the Boers they soon outnumbered. Despite their greater numbers the Uitlanders remained disenfranchised and exercised little political power. The unhappiness with the Boer government on the part of English colonial and imperial interests culminated, in 1895, with the ill-fated JAMESON RAID, which was designed to cause an uprising against Boer authority.

With the failure of the raid and Boer-English relations at an all-time low, both sides took measures to solidify their military positions in preparation for future conflicts. As British military reinforcement of the CAPE COLONY and NATAL grew, the Boer republics became convinced that Britain was preparing for war. In 1899 Paul KRUGER (1825–1904), president of the Transvaal, issued an ultimatum to Britain with a list of demands to be met within 48 hours. The demands went unfulfilled, and the Boers attacked the British on October 11, 1899.

Initially unprepared for war, the British met defeat in a number of early battles. An especially brutal period of British military failure, one in which they lost three major engagements, was named the "Black Week" (December 10–15, 1899). Despite their success the Boers were unable to administer a decisive blow to British forces, and eventually the arrival of British reinforcements rendered the Boer advantage fleeting.

At the beginning of 1900 Field Marshall Lord Frederick Sleigh Roberts (1832–1914) and his chief of staff, Lord Horatio Herbert KITCHENER (1850–1916), arrived in SOUTH AFRICA to take over command of the British forces. Their arrival marked a turning point in the war, as Roberts quickly went on the offensive. He lifted the Boer siege of cities such as KIMBERLEY and Mafeking, and in February his forces struck a devastating blow to the Boers with the defeat and surrender of General Piet Cronje (1835–1911). Roberts then began his march toward the Transvaal capital of PRETORIA. President Kruger fled to Europe, and Roberts entered the city unopposed in June. With the Boers on the defensive and spread thin, Roberts believed the war would soon be over. He thus relinquished command to Lord Kitchener.

The war was far from finished, however, as the Boers turned to guerrilla tactics with a focus on disrupting the British lines of communication and transportation. The Boer mounted riflemen, conditioned by years of living in the open environment of the vast southern African hinterland, made up a formidable and mobile fighting force that was difficult to capture. They lived off the land and restocked their ammunition and supplies with occasional raids on British outposts.

The Boers' elusiveness frustrated Lord Kitchener who, determined to end the war, abandoned conventional military tactics and began a "scorched-earth" offensive. Under this policy, Kitchener's troops sought to destroy anything that could sustain the Boer commandos. Thousands of Boer farms were razed, and the Boer women and children were interned in concentration camps, as were many African farm workers. Thousands died from malnutrition and disease in the camps, and the memory of their deaths helped fuel Afrikaner nationalism in the 20th century.

The Boers, on the run and desperate, made futile efforts at taking the offensive, but were consistently turned back by superior British forces. As Kitchener's tactics began to take their toll, the Boers eventually capitulated, signing the Treaty of VEREENIGING in 1902.

See also: BOTHA, LOUIS (Vol. IV); CAPE TOWN (Vols. III, V); ENGLAND AND AFRICA (Vols. III, IV, V); GREAT BOER TREK (Vol. III).

Further reading: Bill Nasson, *The South African War, 1899–1902* (London: Arnold, 1999).

Anglo-Egyptian Condominium

Anglo-Egyptian Condominium (1899–1955) Joint British and Egyptian government that ruled the territory that is present-day Republic of the SUDAN. The word *condominium*, from Latin, means "joint dominion," or "joint sovereignty."

Sudan had become part of an expanding EGYPT in 1821 when the forces of Muhammad Ali (1769–1849), the Ottoman viceroy of Egypt, invaded and annexed the Sudan. Subsequent Egyptian rulers repressed revolts and brought prosperity to the land. When Khedive ISMAIL (1830–1895), who governed Egypt from 1863 to 1879, came to power, his attempts to modernize and secularize Egypt caused deep resentment in the Sudan. In 1879, led by religious reformer Muhammad Ahmad al-MAHDI (1844–1885), the Sudanese began to resist Egyptian rule. By 1883 al-Mahdi's forces were in control of the Sudan. When al-Mahdi died in 1885 his *khalifa*, or successor, ABDALLAHI IBN MUHAMMAD (1846–1899), continued al-Mahdi's policies.

In 1898 a joint British and Egyptian military expedition reasserted Egyptian control over the Sudan, defeating the Mahdist forces at the Battle of OMDURMAN. Concerned about further Mahdist revolt, the British were unwilling to allow the Sudan to revert solely to Egyptian rule. Accordingly, on July 10, 1899, Britain established an agreement of joint authority called the Anglo-Egyptian Condominium, which remained in effect until 1955. By the terms of this agreement, the Sudanese state became a political entity separate from Egypt.

Dominated from the start by Britain, the condominium was not a relationship of equal partners. Though formally appointed by the khedive, the governor-general who administered the Sudan was actually named by the British. He officially reported to the British Foreign Office in CAIRO, but the governor-general administered the Sudan as if it were a British colony. Most of the administrative personnel were British army officers attached to the Egyptian army. Beginning in 1901 these administrators were gradually replaced by civilians from Britain. Egyptians filled the midlevel posts, and Sudanese held the lower-level positions. In 1910 the British-Egyptian alliance appointed a legislative council that retained power until 1948, when a partly elected legislative assembly superceded it.

With the overthrow of the government of King FARUK (1920–1965) in 1952, Britain and the new Egyptian government reached an agreement that called for Sudanese self-determination. Sudanese nationalists prevailed over those desiring continued union with Egypt, with the result that on January 1, 1956, the Sudan became an independent country.

See also: ENGLAND AND AFRICA (Vol. IV); GEZIRA SCHEME (Vol. IV); MAHDIYYA (Vol. IV).

Anglo-Zulu War (1879) Crucial conflict between the ZULU kingdom and Britain taking place in what is now the province of NATAL, in present-day SOUTH AFRICA. In 1872 the Zulu gained a capable, energetic, and ambitious new ruler, CETSHWAYO (c. 1826–1884), who ascended the throne after the death of Mpande (r. 1840–1872), his father. Cetshwayo was eager to maintain good relations with the neighboring British colony of Natal, but he was also intent on strengthening his own position within his kingdom. Thus he began to build up his army, a move that the British officials in Natal viewed with exaggerated alarm. British colonial power was expanding into the interior of South Africa at the time, in part because of the emergence of the DIAMOND MINING industry that was centered in KIMBERLEY. Britain had annexed the diamond fields in 1872, and in 1877 they seized control of the TRANSVAAL, one the two independent AFRIKANER REPUBLICS. Cetshwayo and the Zulus welcomed this move, since they had long been at odds with the BOERS, or AFRIKANERS, in the region. Their enthusiasm for Britain's presence in the interior of South Africa soon waned, however, as the British turned their focus on independent Zululand.

In 1878, on the basis of trumped-up charges stemming from a Zulu assault on opponents in Natal, the British high commissioner, Sir Henry Bartle Frere (1815–1884), issued an ultimatum to which he knew Cetshwayo would never agree. Essentially, he had demanded that the Zulu king forfeit his judicial authority, pay humiliating reparations, and disband the powerful Zulu army. When Cetshwayo's inevitable refusal came, the British invaded Zululand on January 11, 1879. This initiated the Anglo-Zulu War, a war fought between the armies of a modern, European industrial state and an African state that continued to rely, for the most part, on its traditional weaponry and methods of fighting.

The war was fought in two phases. Initially the British brimmed with confidence and believed that their 18,000 troops would readily defeat Cetshwayo. However, Lord Chelmsford (1868–1913), the British commander, was unprepared for the size, the discipline, and the courage of the Zulu army. The British invaded Zululand with Chelmsford in command of the central column. He divided his forces, and on January 22, at ISANDLWANA, the British suffered a crushing defeat. Using its traditional battle strategy and tactics, the Zulu killed more than 1,300 of the 1,700 troops, though they also suffered high casualties. Only the determined stand of a British garrison of 150 troops against 4,000 Zulu soldiers at Rorke's Drift managed to keep the British military disaster from becoming complete.

The second phase of the war began once the British regrouped, added reinforcements, and returned to the offensive. The Zulu managed to win some minor engagements, but they could not stave off a British military victory. In the end their tactics of seeking to engage their opponents in hand-to-hand fighting faltered in the face of breech-loading rifles. On July 4, 1879, Chelmsford reached the Zulu capital of Ulundi. After a fierce battle in which his 5,000 men defeated an army of 20,000 Zulu soldiers, the British commander burned Ulundi, which consisted largely of grass-woven, beehive-shaped dwellings, to the ground. The British also captured Cetshwayo and sent him into exile in CAPE TOWN. Britain had, with great difficulty, conquered the Zulu army, but it would not annex the Zulu kingdom until 1887.

See also: COLONIAL CONQUEST (Vol. IV); ENGLAND AND AFRICA (Vols. III, IV, V); WARFARE AND WEAPONS (Vol. IV).

Further reading: Jeff Guy, *The Destruction of the Zulu Kingdom* (London: Longman, 1979); Donald R. Morris, *The Washing of the Spears* (New York: Simon and Schuster, 1965).

Angola Southwest African country, about 476,200 square miles (1,233,400 sq km) in area, that is bordered by the Democratic Republic of the CONGO to the north and northeast, ZAMBIA to the east, NAMIBIA to the south, and the Atlantic Ocean to the west. Also part of Angola is the province of Cabinda, a coastal enclave separated from the main part of the country by the Congo River and a narrow coastal strip of the Democratic Republic of the Congo. Between 1850 and 1960 Angola evolved from being a major source for the Portuguese SLAVE TRADE to moving, albeit slowly, toward national independence.

By the turn of the 20th century Portugal was internationally recognized as sovereign in Angola. However, Angolans—among them, the KONGO, Mbundu, OVIMBUNDU, and Cuanhama peoples—began to stiffen their resistance to Portuguese rule in their homeland. As a result, Portugal's control became increasingly insecure in the decades leading up to World War I (1914–18).

By the 1930s, however, Portugal had reestablished its firm grip on the country. During that decade the conservative regime of Portuguese Prime Minister António Salazar (1889–1970) placed great emphasis on creating strong nationalist pride through maintaining Portugal's overseas possessions.

The marginalization of Angolans continued unabated through the World War II era (1939–45). Although SLAVERY was illegal, Angolan men were forced to work for the government without pay if they were unable to pay colonial taxes. As of 1950 a mere 30,000 of the estimated 4 million Africans in Angola enjoyed even minimal political or civil rights. The only African Angolans recognized by the state were the *assimilados,* so named for their having learned Portuguese and assimilated into Portuguese colonial society. The remaining millions of indigenous people were still considered "uncivilized" by the colonial authorities.

From 1950 to 1961 Salazar organized a wave of migration from Portugal to Angola, increasing the popula-

tion of whites from 80,000 to 200,000. However, this did not advance the official Portuguese aim of increasing assimilation within Angola. Instead the influx of immigrants further worsened the plight of Angola's African majority. The new arrivals, generally an uneducated lot, took jobs away from Africans in low-skill professions and reacted violently to liberal reforms favoring Africans.

African political consciousness developed rapidly after World War II. As colony after colony gained independence from European rule, Angolans, too, demanded liberation. Under the authoritarian rule of Salazar the colonial government had scoffed at Angolan liberation movements. However, the movements of the 1950s and 1960s—which often espoused liberal and Marxist ideologies—posed a much more serious threat to Portuguese rule. Early on the organization with the most influence was the Popular Movement for the Liberation of Angola (Movimento Popular de Libertação de Angola, MPLA), founded in 1956 and led by Agostinho Neto (1922–1979).

With the Angolan nationalist and liberation movements growing increasingly insistent, Portugal responded by sending in its secret police (PIDE). With tactics that included arbitrary arrest and imprisonment, PIDE became the most effective tool of the authorities for intimidating the populace and for quelling civil disturbances.

Portugal's policing action in Angola was part of a greater colonial scheme called *lusotropicology.* Under this largely fictional ideology, Portugal claimed to be creating a superior society that supported racial integration and Christian conversion. It also led Portugal to claim that it would never discuss self-determination for its overseas territories.

Despite Portugal's best efforts to continue its COLONIAL RULE, the tension in Angola eventually reached the boiling point, resulting in armed, rebel insurrection. In 1961 Holden Roberto (1923–), at the time a leader of the Union of Angolan Peoples, split from the group to form the more militant National Front for the Liberation of Angola (Frente Nacional de Libertação de Angola, FNLA). By the following year Roberto was organizing raids on Portuguese-owned businesses and farms as well as on government installations throughout Angola. The swiftness and lethality of the FNLA's early assaults shocked the Portuguese authorities and the international community alike and were met with a severe military response.

During the 1960s the fight for Angolan independence became more intense, resulting in other armed factions joining the fray. Ultimately this made Angola a key player during the Cold War between the forces of communism and the forces of democracy.

See also: ANGOLA (Vols. I, II, III, V); CHRISTIANITY, INFLUENCE OF (Vols. IV, V); COLD WAR AND AFRICA (Vols. IV, V); COLONIALISM, INFLUENCE OF (Vol. IV); INDEPENDENCE MOVEMENTS (Vol. V); NATIONAL FRONT FOR THE LIBERATION OF ANGOLA (Vol. V); NATIONALISM AND INDEPENDENCE MOVEMENTS (Vol. IV); NETO, AGOSTINHO (Vol. V); PORTUGAL AND AFRICA (Vols. III, V); RESISTANCE AND REBELLION (Vol. IV); ROBERTO, HOLDEN (Vol. V).

Further reading: Gerald J. Bender, *Angola Under the Portuguese: The Myth and the Reality* (Berkeley, Calif.: University of California Press, 1978); Linda Heywood, *Contested Power in Angola, 1840s to the Present* (Rochester, N.Y.: University of Rochester Press, 2000); John Marcum, *The Angolan Revolution, Vol. 1: The Anatomy of an Explosion (1950–1962)* (Cambridge, Mass.: M.I.T. Press, 1969).

anthropology and Africa Academic discipline concerned with the study of humans and their societies. Of particular concern to anthropology as a westernized social science has been an understanding of how human societies and their cultures have developed. In this regard, one of modern anthropology's defining works is *Primitive Culture*, published by Sir Edward Burnett Tylor (1832–1917), in 1871. This and similar works shifted the focus of early anthropology to the study of so-called primitive peoples, a focus that has remained to this day. This was particularly relevant to Africa during the time of European COLONIAL CONQUEST. In addition, with the establishment of COLONIAL RULE over most of Africa by 1900, European anthropologists began to utilize Africa to conduct studies of human society and culture. This enabled anthropologists to develop and test their theories while at the same time provide information to colonial administrators about the peoples they ruled.

The majority of the early anthropologists in Africa were scholarly amateurs who had developed a professional or personal interest in learning more about the people in whose midst they resided. Some were colonial administrators who had a goal of learning to govern more effectively. One of the most prominent and widely published of these amateur scholars was Robert Sutherland Rattray (1881–1938). A colonial official in the GOLD COAST COLONY (modern-day GHANA), he became the first government-appointed anthropologist in colonial Africa. Rattray's work, which primarily dealt with the Ashanti, was undertaken in the context of the system of "indirect rule," which allowed Britain to govern through local African rulers. Rattray's *Ashanti*, published in 1923, contained the type of detailed ethnographic information that helped facilitate British rule over the Gold Coast.

Over time anthropologist R. S. Rattray became acquainted with African societies and cultures firsthand rather than through formal academic study. As a youth he left school to join the sixth Imperial Yeomanry and fight in the ANGLO-BOER WAR in SOUTH AFRICA. At the end of the war he became an adventurer in southern Central and East Africa, where he began his study of African peoples. This led to the eventual publication of *Some Folk-lore Stories and Songs in Chinyanja*, with English Translation and Notes (1907), the first of his many books. In 1907 he joined the colonial administration of the Gold Coast Colony as a customs officer. There he studied the HAUSA language because the Hausa from northern NIGERIA made up much of the colonial police and army in British West Africa. After four years he went on leave to return to England to study anthropology at Oxford. He returned to the Gold Coast in time to join with the British assault on the German colony of TOGOLAND at the onset of World War I (1914–18), receiving a commission as captain, a title he used for the rest of his life. A few years after the war he received an appointment as the official government anthropologist of the colony, a position he held until his retirement at the end of 1929. In this position he conducted the research for several additional books, focusing on the Ashanti. In 1929 Oxford University recognized his work with the award of an honorary doctorate.

Christian MISSIONARIES made a significant addition to the ranks of early anthropologists in Africa. Their goal was the conversion of Africans to Christianity, and many missionaries believed that in-depth knowledge of African societies would facilitate this process. One such individual was the Swiss, Protestant missionary, Henri Alexandre Junod (1863–1934). Junod worked among the Tsonga people in the DELAGOA BAY region of MOZAMBIQUE for the better part of two decades before returning home in 1920. Early on he published a grammar of one of the Tsonga dialects. Then, in 1912 and 1913, he published his major work, a two-volume study entitled *The Life of a South African Tribe*. This classic study made the case for a scientific approach to ethnography based on the in-depth observation of one ethnic group over a long period of time. Junod published a revised, second edition of the work in 1927.

Another of these missionary-scholars, John Roscoe (1861–1932), was a contemporary of Junod. Affiliated with the CHURCH MISSIONARY SOCIETY in UGANDA from 1884 to 1909, Roscoe was closely associated with the BU-GANDA aristocrat, Sir Apolo KAGWA (1865–1927). As with Kagwa's

1905 study of his own people, Roscoe's *The Baganda: An Account of Their Native Customs and Beliefs* (1911) drew from numerous interviews that provided information gathered from those knowledgeable about Buganda's history. He returned to Uganda, in 1919, as the leader of the Mackie Ethnological Expedition, which was sponsored by the Royal Society to gather extensive information on the colony's peoples. In addition to publishing a general account of the expedition, Roscoe published detailed material on three of Uganda's ethnic groups.

Academic anthropologists did not begin working in Africa until the mid-1920s. One of these was the English social anthropologist Edward Evan Evans-Pritchard (1902–1973). Evans-Pritchard, who held a doctorate in anthropology from the London School of Economics, conducted field research among the Azande of the northern Congo and neighboring areas of what is today the Republic of the SUDAN. He later extended his studies to include the Nuer of southern Sudan.

Rather than producing descriptive studies of a single ethnic group, Evans-Pritchard constructed his studies around an issue in social theory. His first major work, *Witchcraft: Oracles and Magic among the Azande* (1937), dealt with the internal logic of a particular African belief system. His subsequent study, *The Nuer* (1940), examined the political organization of a people who lacked a formal system of government. These two works produced a fundamental shift in the direction of anthropological study of Africa and led to a host of both specialized and theoretically oriented studies.

By the 1930s the direction and emphasis of anthropology had changed, but it still continued to focus on what Europeans considered "primitive" or "traditional" societies. In some ways this represented a contrast with anthropology's initial period, during which amateur anthropology and colonial administration often went hand in hand. Instead academic anthropologists began to concentrate on a "traditional" Africa seemingly untouched by colonialism. It was not until after World War II (1939–45) that a few anthropologists began to study the effects of colonialism on Africans. These pioneers included J. Clyde Mitchell (1918–1995), who from 1946 until 1955 was a researcher at the Rhodes-Livingstone Institute in NORTHERN RHODESIA (today's ZAMBIA). In *The Kalela Dance* (1956), Mitchell wrote that he had "attempted an analysis of certain aspects of the system of social relationships among Africans in the towns of Northern Rhodesia." Such studies remained limited, however, as anthropologists mostly continued to pursue research on so-called traditional societies.

By 1960 anthropologists had produced substantial bodies of work on Africa's peoples. However, almost all of these studies were completed by outsiders, most of whom were British and based both in European universities and research institutes as well as the few universities on the continent. As such, anthropology remained very much a colonial discipline.

See also: ANTHROPOLOGY AND AFRICA (Vol. V).

Further reading: Jack Goody, *The Expansive Moment: The Rise of Social Anthropology in Britain and Africa, 1918–1970* (New York: Cambridge University Press, 1995); Sally Falk Moore, *Anthropology and Africa: Changing Perspectives on a Changing Scene* (Charlottesville Va.: University Press of Virginia, 1994).

apartheid AFRIKAANS word literally meaning "aparthood" or "separateness." Apartheid was the name given to the system of racial segregation and inequality that was incorporated into the laws of SOUTH AFRICA for much of the 20th century. It was grounded in the belief—held by most whites during the colonial era—that the people of Africa were inferior.

Though apartheid is largely based on the philosophy of white supremacy, also called *BAASSKAP*, many of the legislative acts that paved the way for a racially segregated South Africa were driven by economic considerations. Both the British administration and the subsequent Afrikaner leaders of South Africa were concerned with monopolizing the profits from the country's rich diamond and GOLD mines. As a result they continuously passed legislation that excluded black Africans from the economic benefits of the MINING industry. By 1893 Africans could not legally hold certain skilled positions in South Africa's mines. Black mineworkers also were forced to live in fenced, guarded compounds until they finished their work contracts.

In 1910, less than a decade after the British victory in the ANGLO-BOER WAR (1899–1902), Britain unified CAPE COLONY, NATAL, and the former AFRIKANER REPUBLICS of the TRANSVAAL and the ORANGE FREE STATE in the UNION OF SOUTH AFRICA. With no black parliamentary representation and an ineffective English-speaking electorate, the government of the union fell under control of the AFRIKANERS. Once in control of the union government, Afrikaners began passing legislation to give even greater preferential treatment to whites. Beginning in 1911 the all-white South African government systematically passed more than 300 laws to guarantee the separation and inferior social, political, and economic status of blacks and other non-whites in South Africa. The laws made it difficult, if not impossible, for blacks to secure jobs, to move freely about the country, to vote, and to mingle with whites.

One early law that established a foundation for later apartheid legislation was the Native's Land Act of 1913. This racist law designated less than 7 percent of the land in the union for blacks even though they made up more than two-thirds of the population. The remaining land was reserved for whites, who made up only one-fifth of the population.

Although protests went on for many years, in 1960 passbooks like this one were a fact of life for blacks under South Africa's apartheid policies. © *AP Wirephoto*

After the elections of 1948, during which the term *apartheid* entered the South African political vocabulary, the Afrikaner National Party (NP) assumed the reigns of power and quickly began passing wide-ranging, racist legislation. Laws passed in the 1950s divided cities into racially segregated areas and further restricted the freedoms of blacks and non-whites, including Indians, Asians, and CAPE COLOURED PEOPLE. The Bantu Education Act of 1953 established a separate system of EDUCATION for blacks, one in which they were taught only the skills necessary for them to partake in Bantu culture as defined by the government.

A leading proponent of apartheid was Hendrik VER-WOERD (1901–1966), who is frequently cited as the architect of the racist system. Verwoerd was minister of Native Affairs from 1950 to 1958 and was prime minister from 1958 until his death in 1966.

During the 1950s black political organizations such as the AFRICAN NATIONAL CONGRESS (ANC), the South African Indian Congress, and the more militant PAN-AFRICANIST CONGRESS organized rallies against apartheid. They especially targeted the pass laws, which made it mandatory for blacks to carry a passbook at all times.

A passbook contained a photo of its holder as well as other information such as address, employment record, and taxes paid. Not carrying a passbook was a crime, and during the 1950s an average of 500,000 people were arrested for this offense each year.

Despite the efforts of black activists, an increasingly oppressive police state backed the apartheid system, and the government became even harsher in suppressing opposition groups. Annoyed by international criticism of apartheid, the Union of South Africa became more defiant in its efforts to preserve the system. Apartheid continued unabated into the 1960s and became even more entrenched when, in 1961, South Africa broke all ties with the British Commonwealth and declared itself a republic.

See also: APARTHEID (Vol. V); BANTUSTANS (Vol. V); MANDELA, NELSON (Vols. IV, V); RACE AND RACISM (Vol. IV); RESISTANCE AND REBELLION (Vol. IV); UMKHONTO WE SIZWE (Vol. V).

Further reading: Saul Dubow, *Racial Segregation and the Origins of Apartheid in South Africa, 1919–36* (New York: St. Martin's Press, 1989); Leonard Thompson, *The Political Mythology of Apartheid* (New Haven, Conn.: Yale University Press, 1985); Nigel Worden, *The Making of Modern South Africa: Conquest, Segregation and Apartheid*, 3rd ed. (Malden, Mass.: Blackwell Publishers, 2000).

Arab-Israeli Wars   Series of conflicts in 1948–49, 1956, and later years between Arabs and Jewish settlers in Palestine. The Arab-Israeli Wars led to pan-Arab condemnation of Israel and roused most African countries to sever ties with what they viewed as a racist, Zionist regime.

The anti-Semitic feelings and acts that journalist Theodore Herzl (1860–1904) experienced in his native Vienna, Austria, led him to publish a book titled *Der Judenstaat* (The Jewish State, 1896). This book generated the political movement called *Zionism*, which had as its goal the establishment of a separate Jewish state in the region of Palestine.

The right of the Jewish people to a homeland in Palestine was acknowledged by the Balfour Declaration of 1917 and reaffirmed by the League of Nations in 1919. Small numbers of Jewish settlers had already begun to migrate to Palestine before World War I (1914–18). Immigration increased between World War I and World War II (1939–45) and after the wars. Thus by the late 1940s the population of Palestine was roughly one-third Jewish and two-thirds Arab. Conflict and tension marked the relationship between the two segments of people.

On October 6, 1946, the move to establish the modern state of Israel received strong support when United States president Harry S. Truman (1884–1972) released a statement indicating American support for a "viable Jewish state" in Palestine. Four months later Britain terminated its MANDATE over Palestine. On May 14, 1948, Israel became an independent nation. The first Arab-Israeli War broke out the same day.

This initial Arab-Israeli War is sometimes called the Palestine War of 1948 or Israel's War for Independence. A coalition of Arab forces from EGYPT, Transjordan (now Jordan), Iraq, Syria, and Lebanon occupied the Arab portion of Palestine and the Jewish section of Jerusalem. By early 1949 Israeli forces had driven back the Arab forces and occupied all of Palestine except for the Gaza Strip. Israel then signed armistice agreements with Egypt, Lebanon, Jordan, and Syria to establish Israel's new boundaries.

The second Arab-Israeli War, sometimes called the Suez War of 1956, broke out as a result of continued strain between the Arab world and Israel. Tensions had worsened when the Egyptian nationalist leader, Gamal Abdel NASSER (1918–1970), an outspoken advocate of pan-Arabism, became president of Egypt in 1954. The war had three chief causes. The Arab nations believed that Israel's continued presence in the Sinai Peninsula contradicted the 1947 United Nations PARTITION agreement, which mandated a Palestinian state as well as a Jewish state. Further upsetting the Arab states was Israel's unwillingness to repatriate the Palestinians who were displaced by the first Arab-Israeli War. The third and perhaps most important factor was that Nasser closed the SUEZ CANAL to Israeli ships. He also blockaded the Straits of Tiran at the entrance to the Gulf of Aqaba in order to gain control of shipping to the Israeli port of Eilat. Shortly thereafter Nasser caused an international crisis when he nationalized the canal.

France, Britain, and Israel secretly planned to regain control of the canal from Egypt, with Israel leading the operation. Israel invaded the Sinai Peninsula, which was Egyptian territory, overcame Egypt's defenses, and captured a majority of the peninsula. In 1957 a United Nations Emergency Force was stationed in the region, and peace was restored for the time. In March 1957, under pressure from the United States, Israel withdrew its forces from the territory it captured in Sinai. The canal was reopened under international control and Egyptian management. Israel won the war but did not gain any concessions from Egypt. Thus the stage was set for the Arab-Israeli war of 1967.

See also: ARAB-ISRAELI WARS (Vol. V); ARAB WORLD AND AFRICA (Vol. V); LEAGUE OF NATIONS AND AFRICA (Vol. IV); UNITED NATIONS AND AFRICA (Vol. IV).

Further reading: Samuel Decalo, *Israel and Africa: Forty Years, 1956–1996* (Gainesville, Fla.: Florida Academic Press, 1998); Chaim Herzog, *The Arab-Israeli Wars* (New York: Random House, 1982); Arye Oded, *Africa and the Middle East Conflict* (Boulder, Colo.: Lynne Rienner, 1987).

archaeology Archaeology involves the systematic recovery and study of material culture representing past human life and activities. It emerged as a modern academic discipline in the 19th century, and archaeologists began studying Africa from the discipline's inception. EGYPT and the ancient civilizations of the Nile were the focus of the earliest archaeological study in Africa. This study soon assumed its own particular set of concerns and developed into a discipline of its own called EGYPTOLOGY. It originated with the scholars who had accompanied Napoleon I (1769–1821) when he invaded Egypt in 1798. In 1858 the appointment of the French archaeologist Auguste Mariette (1821–1881) as conservator of monuments in Egypt and director of the Antiquities Service was an important milestone in the advancement of archaeology in Egypt. By 1900 the Egyptian Museum in CAIRO, which Mariette established, held a significant collection of artifacts.

Until the 1960s the work in Egypt was typical of the early practice of archaeology in Africa, which focused on literate civilizations of the Mediterranean areas and, to a lesser degree, the Horn of Africa. Archaeologists in this tradition focused on the monumental remains of past human culture and activities. The practice of archaeology gradually became much more scientific and careful in its approach. The English archaeologist William Flinders Petrie (1853–1942) pioneered this approach in Egypt.

Another important pioneer of scientific archaeology in Egypt was the American scholar George Andrew Reisner (1867–1942), who first started excavating in Upper Egypt in 1898. When work began on raising the height of the ASWAN DAM, in 1907, Reisner started an archaeological survey of the area between the First Cataract of the Nile and the border of the Republic of the SUDAN. From 1913 to 1916 he undertook extensive excavations at the site of Kerma located at the Third Cataract, at Gebel Barkal and related sites further to the south, and finally at the site of Meroë. His focus was on monumental remains of the Nubian kingdom of Kush, including its temples, pyramids, and cemeteries.

As archaeology developed in the 20th century, ancient Carthage and Roman North Africa, which took its place, were also subjects of interest. For example, in the 1920s archaeologists began to excavate the ancient Punic city of

Lepcis Magna, located in the TRIPOLITANIA region of present-day LIBYA. Founded in the 10th century BCE, Lepcis Magna grew as a Roman settlement until it was sacked in the year 523 CE. Many of its buildings have been amazingly preserved. Aksum, located in northeastern ETHIOPIA, was another literate civilization that attracted archaeological attention. In 1906 a German archaeological expedition undertook the first serious research, attracted by the distinctive towering carved granite stelae, one of which was 108 feet (33 m) tall. The founding of the Ethiopian Institute of Archaeology led to extensive research in the country in the 1950s and early 1960s.

In sub-Saharan Africa one of the few early monumental archaeological sites was Great Zimbabwe. Though not built by a literate culture, its massive stone walls and other impressive architecture attracted the attention of Europeans associated with prospector and MINING magnate Cecil RHODES (1853–1902). Unfortunately they looted the site in their search for GOLD and other valuable objects. By the time the first professional archaeologist, Gertrude Caton-Thompson (1888–1985), researched the sites in 1928, vandalism had sharply reduced the evidence available for recovery.

Gertrude Caton-Thompson first began working as an archaeologist in Egypt in 1921. She already had extensive research experience, including conducting an archaeological and geological survey in the Fayum region of Egypt and serving as the field director of the Royal Anthropological Institute before undertaking the archaeological survey of Great Zimbabwe. Her book, *The Zimbabwe Culture: Ruins and Reactions* (1931), was the first scholarly work on the topic and remains an important reference.

In sub-Saharan Africa the only other location where major archaeological research was conducted on literate societies with monumental remains was in the trading towns of the SWAHILI COAST. Significant research did not occur until the 1950s, with the work of James S. Kirkman (1906–1989). He focused on the external influence of ISLAM on the coast, as is evident from the title of his 1954 book, *Gedi the Great Mosque: Architecture and Finds*.

The second major trend in the practice of archaeology in Africa before 1960 was the interest in the prehistory of southern and eastern Africa. Here the focus was on both human origins and early human material culture. At the turn of the century SOUTH AFRICA, with its substantial European-settler population and research-oriented universities, initiated this concern with prehistory. Stone

implements such as axes and cutting tools that were found over several decades led to efforts to reconstruct the context in which they had been used. A key individual in this effort was Louis Albert Péringuey (1855–1924), who from 1906 until his death was the director of the South African Museum in CAPE TOWN. In the 1920s Professor A. J. H. Goodwin (1909–1959), who is viewed as South Africa's first professionally trained archaeologist, contributed valuable insights to African archaeology. In particular he came to understand that the Stone Age cultures of southern Africa needed to be understood on their own terms and not in terms of the nomenclature and classification of the Stone Age cultures of Europe. Others who built on this work included J. Desmond Clark (1916–2002), the long-time director of the Rhodes-Livingstone Museum in NORTHERN RHODESIA (now ZAMBIA).

Another dimension of prehistory had to do with hominid evolution. South Africa–based scholars took the lead here as well. In late 1924 Raymond A. Dart (1893–1988), the newly appointed chair of anatomy at the University of the WITWATERSRAND, in JOHANNESBURG, came into the possession of a child's skull which had been found at Taung in BOTSWANA (hence the popular name of the Taung Child). This was to be the first early hominid fossil known as *Australopithecus africanus* (southern ape of Africa). Dart's discovery launched the modern era of paleoanthropology. A subsequent find, in 1936, of the first adult *Australopithecine* in the Sterkfontein caves near Krugersdorp in the TRANSVAAL served to confirm the significance of Dart's assessment of the Taung skull.

Of great importance was the research conducted by the husband and wife team of Louis LEAKEY (1903–1972) and Mary LEAKEY (1913–1996). Their expeditions in various parts of East Africa in the 1920s and 1930s led to important discoveries of prehistoric tools in the Great Rift Valley. Their finds proved that hominids had inhabited this area far earlier than was commonly believed. In 1931 they began their work at Olduvai Gorge in present-day TANZANIA, and over the next three decades it became the world's most important site for research on the ancestors of modern humans. By 1961 the Leakeys had established that the ancestral human-like creatures in the region dated back more than 20 million years, far longer than anyone had anticipated.

By 1960 archaeologists had developed a detailed understanding of the material culture of the literate societies of North Africa and of past human life and activities in the region. Studies in the prehistory of eastern and southern Africa also pointed to Africa as the birthplace of human beings. However, little was known about the more recent past of the societies and cultures of sub-Saharan Africa. Moreover, archaeological scholarship was exclusively the domain of scholars of European origin and ancestry, although political independence was to lead to substantial new directions in the practice of archaeology on the African continent.

See also: ARCHAEOLOGY (Vols. I, II, III, V); CARTHAGE (Vol. I); GEBEL BARKAL (Vol. I); GREAT ZIMBABWE (Vol. II); HUMAN ORIGINS (Vol. I); KUSH (Vol. I); MEROË (Vol. I); OLDUVAI GORGE (Vol. I); STONE AGE (Vol. I); TAUNG CHILD (Vol. I).

Further reading: David W. Phillipson, *African Archaeology,* 2nd ed. (New York: Cambridge University Press, 1993).

architecture Indigenous architecture changed as Africans came more securely under European subjugation in the 19th century. Across the continent European-styled cities emerged, filled with indigenous African components. Ranging from wood structures in the tropical woodlands to sun-dried brick in the Sahara, indigenous African architecture depended upon the natural resources provided by the environment for construction materials. Found in many African villages, towns, and cities were round, thatch-roofed houses within walled enclosures that held extended families. Compounds included a central open courtyard, a communal meeting place, and perhaps a porch.

In Muslim areas the Arabian-style mosque combined with indigenous African mysticism and aesthetics to create unique local mosques. When Europeans or Americans settled in Africa they brought with them construction methods, materials, and ideas about architectural styles with which they were most familiar. European SETTLERS, traders, and MISSIONARIES constructed the buildings that they knew from their own cultures and used them as an expression of economic wealth and political authority. As these new urban planning and architectural styles were introduced, Africans contributed their own indigenous styles to create new African forms.

In the BACK-TO-AFRICA MOVEMENTS of the 1820s, African-Americans settled the colony of LIBERIA on the West Coast of Africa. Some brought with them architectural styles from North Carolina and Virginia. However, because they were not trained architects and because the construction materials available to them were different, Liberian houses resembled the settlers' former homes only in appearance. Other returnees who had been emancipated in Brazil found their way to LAGOS, in present-day NIGERIA, where a Brazilian quarter is identifiable by its architecture. Settlers also built a Brazilian-style cathedral in ABEOKUTA.

The European colonizers sought to change the face of urban Africa. Where urban areas already existed, Europeans often changed the city structure by adding a Europeanized city adjacent to the existing city. Where a specific architectural style existed, Europeans added or subtracted architectural elements to make a hybrid regional architecture called *arabisances*. Where no city existed, they executed urban planning. Until the 1950s European civil engineers built capital cities containing schools, hospitals, and government buildings. After the 1950s they increasingly used architects instead of engineers. In many cases Europeans adopted or adapted indigenous African design into their regional architecture. The porch is one such example. Europeans built two-story buildings that had a porch on both levels, windows parallel to each other, and louvered shutters that maintained privacy while allowing a breeze to pass through. Another indigenous element used by the Europeans was the central courtyard. In Saint-Louis, SENEGAL, the first colonial capital of FRENCH WEST AFRICA, houses were built around an interior courtyard and with a second-floor porch. Constructed in the 1950s and 1960s, buildings at the University of Ghana, in Lagos, are situated around an open courtyard.

In MOROCCO the French moved the capital from Fez to the existing city of Rabat to evade Moroccan resistance to their rule. As a consequence Rabat came to resemble a French city, with broad thoroughfares, streets intersecting at many different angles, and roundabouts. To the existing Arabian-styled Tetouan railway station the French added two towers reminiscent of medieval France. At the same time Muslim architects adapted to the changing urban environment by using Western building materials and techniques to build traditional-looking mosques.

The westernizing and modernizing of independent EGYPT was furthered by Khedive ISMAIL (1830–1895), who created a European-styled CAIRO adjacent to old Cairo in an effort to make his capital comparable to the grand capital cities of Europe.

The British brought with them English ideas of urban planning, artistic style, and housing construction. When they came to CAPE TOWN, SOUTH AFRICA, British planners used European architectural styles in construction. The Standard Bank building, for example, is in the Classical style, and St. George's Cathedral is in the Gothic style. Reflecting the segregation of South African society, British settlers built their houses with separate servants' quarters.

European architecture is evident in other British-ruled colonies as well. When the British planned ACCRA, in the GOLD COAST COLONY (present-day GHANA), they used Renaissance styles for construction of the customs house and post office. In Lagos they built Catholic and Anglican cathedrals in the Gothic style, but used the Italian Renaissance style for governmental buildings. Colonial architecture in NAIROBI, KENYA is characterized by Victorian-style buildings.

The French often created planned cities in the capitals of their colonies. In 1857 they built DAKAR (in present-day Senegal) with a plan based on the prevailing 19th-century, European Renaissance, urban design. Similarly, in 1893, the Europeans planning Conakry, in GUINEA, consciously designed buildings to resemble the neoclassical government buildings in Paris.

The Portuguese-designed city of Maputo, MOZAMBIQUE, has government office buildings in the colonial Renaissance style.

This photograph from around 1899 shows an example of the highly ornate Arab-style architecture of North Africa. © *Library of Congress*

Architectural changes appeared first in Africa's urban areas, but, in time, they also appeared in the rural hinterland. In some of these places, as Africans adopted and adapted new architectural styles, the traditional round, sun-dried brick houses with thatched roofs were replaced by European-styled, rectangular, multi-room houses made of concrete block with roofs of zinc or corrugated iron. Because of this shift in architectural styles, Africans traded the outdoor communal spaces and good ventilation of their traditional compounds for more modernized designs that often had stuffy interior spaces that overheated in the dry season.

Although many Africans adopted some European architectural styles, groups like the FULANI of Nigeria and the MAASAI of Kenya and TANZANIA continued their seminomadic lifestyle, even though the colonial administrations pressured them to become sedentary. As part of this lifestyle, they continued to live in portable, collapsible tents made of hides or found materials.

As urban areas grew rural peoples were attracted to their luxuries and the promise of jobs. Because they did not possess "proper" Western education, many of these people ended up working in an informal economy, providing needed goods or services. Unable to afford houses or apartments in town, these people often lived in "shantytowns" made from scrap lumber and metal. Those who could afford it rented one-room apartments, often sleeping indoors and using the city sidewalk for their living space. If these apartments were built around a courtyard, it was common for tenants to use that space like the communal areas in the rural village compound.

Until World War II (1939–45) the design of official buildings was reserved for European architects. In the 1940s and 1950s, however, Africans began going to professional schools to study architecture. Because, in general, they were trained in Europe or in the United States, many of these newly minted architects brought together Western rationalism and African mysticism to create a new, wholly African style.

See also: ARCHITECTURE (Vols. I, II, III); COLONIAL RULE (Vol. IV); COLONIALISM, INFLUENCE OF (Vol. IV); URBANIZATION (Vols. IV, V).

Further reading: Nnamdi Elleh, *African Architecture: Evolution and Transformation* (New York: McGraw-Hill, 1996); Nnamdi Elleh, *Architecture and Power in Africa* (Westport, Conn.: Praeger, 2002); Derek Japha, et al., *The Colonial City: Issues of Identity and Preservation* (Berkeley, Calif.: University of California Press: 1992).

armies, colonial European colonial powers deployed armed forces to their colonies to defend borders and also to suppress hostile indigenous populations (a process called PACIFICATION). Some European nations—France, Britain, Germany, Belgium, and Portugal—employed many black Africans in their colonial armies. Spain, on the other hand, recruited very few black-African soldiers but did have military units made up of African Berber mercenaries. These troops aided Francisco Franco (1892–1975) in his assaults on the Spanish mainland launched from North Africa during the Spanish Civil War (1936–39). Indigenous African troops were used as both soldiers and laborers, depending on the needs of the regular colonial armies.

In the 17th century the first colonial armies were sent by both France and Britain to the SENEGAMBIA REGION of West Africa. Soon both British and French military forces were recruiting local Africans to help them gain control of the coastal trading regions. These African units frequently proved effective in spite of the fact that basic training in the colonial armies included only instruction in the vernacular LANGUAGE of command, drill movements, handling a rifle, and marching. While peacetime recruitment often drew interest, during wartime, response was usually so low that colonial administrations had to force conscription on their African subjects in the 20th century. Both before and after World War I (1914–18) and World War II (1939–45), local chiefs were made to supply men from their populations. This practice was extremely unpopular and led to a number of protests. In addition, it was not uncommon for Africans recruited by forced conscription to desert.

French Colonial Armies The example of the French colonial armies illustrates the recruitment, uses, and changing roles of Africans in the military from 1850 to the era of African independence in the late 1950s and early 1960s.

In 1820 black Africans in France's Battalion d'Afrique (Africa Battalion), in SENEGAL, constituted only a small fraction of the soldiers in France's colonial army. By 1823, however, the French administration was able to field all-African units, and within a few years France employed African soldiers throughout its colonial empire. For example, WOLOF soldiers from Senegal were sent to MADAGASCAR in 1827 and a few years later they were even sent abroad to French Guyana, in South America.

Early on, Africans were used mainly as laborers to support French soldiers. However, the need for greater numbers of African soldiers increased as tropical diseases decimated the ranks of the white soldiers in sub-Saharan Africa. Although SLAVERY was formally abolished in France's colonies in 1848, in West Africa the French still increased their colonial ranks by purchasing slaves who they then indentured to military service for up to 14 years.

In Senegal the French military tried to rely on volunteer soldiers from the free population of Saint-Louis, but free African men usually rejected military service; the work was demeaning and men did not want to risk losing social status for associating and working with slaves.

In 1857 the governor of FRENCH WEST AFRICA, Louis FAIDHERBE (1818–1889), created the first permanent units of black soldiers for France, the TIRAILLEURS SÉNÉGALAIS. Unlike French commanders before him, Faidherbe believed that Africans could become effective combat soldiers, and he embarked on a campaign to change the status of Africans in the military. African troops had their own distinct uniforms and were segregated into their own companies with French officers. Trained to be infantry soldiers, the Tirailleurs received higher pay and incentive bonuses and shared in the spoils of war. The African troops were mainly drawn from savanna peoples, and the Bamana language became the secondary military vernacular after French patois. Since Africans could be promoted to the ranks of Native Officers, military service became the vehicle of advancement for Africans in French colonial society.

Following the French conquest of the empire of SAMORI TOURÉ (c. 1830–1900) in 1898, Touré's officers were incorporated into the Tirailleurs Sénégalais. Also, four of Touré's sons joined the cavalry units of the French Frontier Guard.

From 1890 until 1904 the demand for African soldiers outpaced the supply as France used the auxiliaries to subdue West African resistance to their occupation. French commanders paid enlistment bonuses to recruit soldiers and to encourage veterans to reenlist, and they also paid enlistment bonuses to troops who helped indenture more slaves.

In World War I Blaise DIAGNE (1872–1934), the French National Assembly delegate from Senegal, launched a recruitment campaign to increase the numbers of French troops fighting against the armies of the German colonies of KAMERUN (today's CAMEROON) and TOGOLAND. Armée d'Afrique units recruited by Diagne also were employed in Europe on the Western Front.

In 1919, after universal male conscription was systematically introduced in French West Africa, Muslim leaders who had witnessed the devastation of the European war wanted to protect their followers from unwanted foreign influence. They therefore discouraged them from joining the colonial army, risking French military reprisal.

During World War II FRENCH EQUATORIAL AFRICA provided the base of operations for the Free French resistance movement led by General Charles DE GAULLE (1890–1970). Tens of thousands of African troops helped de Gaulle and the allies to victory both at home in Africa and abroad.

Following the war, soldiers from the Armée d'Afrique provided internal security in French West Africa and French Equatorial Africa. Later, during the transition to independence between 1958 and 1960, French African colonial soldiers returned to their home territories to become the military and police forces for the newly independent nations. In many places French military officers continued to direct African enlisted personnel.

British Colonial Armies The experience of African troops in British colonies was similar to that of the troops in the French colonies. In the early 1800s the British Royal Africa Corps recruited local African troops for military service in both East and West Africa. British military policy in the 1860s revolved around the might of the British navy, since wherever Britain controlled the coast the interior fell under their control within 20 years. The ROYAL NIGER COMPANY used a navy on the Niger and Benue rivers for communication, to supply its outposts, and to protect its investment against smugglers.

In 1897 Colonel Frederick LUGARD (1858–1945) created the West Africa Frontier Force (WAFF) to be a federal, interterritorial army to combat French incursions into the region that was to become British-ruled NIGERIA. Commanded by British army officers with a small contingent of British non-commissioned officers (NCOs), the WAFF became the Royal West African Frontier Force (RWAFF), in 1928. In peacetime there was no shortage of men wanting to join the ranks of the military, and a clean bill of health was the determining factor for selection.

In the 1860s, Captain John Glover (1829–1885) formed a military force from HAUSA and YORUBA mercenaries. Known as "Glover's Hausas," they helped defend the colony of LAGOS and also fought in the ANGLO-ASHANTI WARS. Although English was the official language, Glover's troops spoke the Hausa language and it was used as the language of command. As late as 1950 British officers and non-commissioned officers appointed by the Colonial Office in West Africa were expected to learn Hausa.

In BRITISH EAST AFRICA the King's African Rifles (KAR) was formed in 1902. The KAR brought together soldiers from the former Central African Rifles Battalions of NYASALAND, the East African Rifles of the East Africa Protectorate, the KENYA Rifles, and the UGANDA Rifles. During World War I KAR units fought in the GERMAN EAST AFRICA campaigns.

In World War II the KAR expanded as Britain controlled more territories and participated in the 1942–43 Madagascar campaign. The first African officers were appointed about this time.

After the war the RWAFF increasingly played the role of safeguarding internal security. By 1956 each regiment was developed as a regional force, and served, in effect, as a nascent national army. For example, the Ghana Military Force became the Ghana Army at independence in 1957. Of Britain's former West African colonies, only The GAMBIA disbanded its army in favor of a civilian police force. The main task of the new armies was to maintain internal security, and the armies were supplemented with the addition of small navies and air forces. In East Africa the King's African Rifles trained as combat troops and were used to suppress the MAU MAU in Kenya.

German Colonial Armies In German protectorates (SOUTH WEST AFRICA, German South East Africa, Kamerun, and Togoland), the colonial forces were called the *Schutztruppe*. At the beginning of World War I German officers of the Schutztruppe commanded more than 1,500 African troops in Kamerun and more than 2,400 African troops in GERMAN EAST AFRICA. Although the Germans were known for their sometimes brutal racism in the administration of their African protectorates, it is thought that German officers treated African troops with a professional, if paternalistic, respect on the battlefield.

Belgian Colonial Armies By the end of the 1880s Belgium's King LEOPOLD II (1835–1909) had military personnel, the Force Publique, protecting his CONGO FREE STATE colony. Like other European colonial armies, the Force Publique recruited Africans into their ranks. Unlike other colonies, however, soldiers in the Belgian territory were inadequately supervised, and the armies often became nothing more than raiding parties for rogue administrators interested in personal gain.

During World War I, however, the Force Publique experienced some success in helping Britain contain the advancing German Schutztruppe in East Africa. Belgium also dispatched a Force Publique battalion to help France take parts of Kamerun from Germany. Similar to other European colonial armies, between the world wars, Belgian armies were used to preserve the peace and maintain internal security. During World War II African troops from the Congo aided the Allies in defeating German and Italian forces throughout the continent.

Unlike Britain and France, Belgium did not train African troops for officer positions. In 1961, when the Democratic Republic of the CONGO declared independence from Belgian rule, the lack of clear lines of command among African military personnel exacerbated the widespread instability of the country.

Portuguese Colonial Armies Around the time of World War I, in ANGOLA and northern South West Africa, Portuguese colonial armies recruited Africans, most notably Himba men, to help them pacify the region.

See also: COLONIAL CONQUEST (Vol. IV); COLONIALISM, INFLUENCE OF (Vol. IV); ENGLAND AND AFRICA (Vols. III, IV, V); FRANCE AND AFRICA (Vols. III, IV, V); PORTUGAL AND AFRICA (Vols. IV, V); WORLD WAR I AND AFRICA (Vol. IV); WORLD WAR II AND AFRICA (Vol. IV).

Further reading: Anthony Clayton, *France, Soldiers, and Africa* (London: Brassey's Defence Publishers, 1988); Anthony Clayton and David Killingray, *Khaki and Blue: Military and Police in British Colonial Africa* (Athens, Ohio: Ohio University Center for International Studies, 1989); James Lawrence, *The Savage Wars: British Campaigns in Africa, 1870–1920* (New York: St. Martin's Press, 1985); Paul Mmegha Mbaeyi, *British Military and Naval Forces in West Africa 1807–1874* (New York: Nok Publishers 1978); Timothy H. Parsons, *The African Rank-and-File: Social Implications of Colonial Military Service in the King's African Rifles, 1902–1964* (Portsmouth, N.H.: Heinemann, 1999).

art Dominated by indigenous works representing knowledge, power, and beauty in daily life, African art forms were influenced by European and American art in the 19th century and they, in turn, influenced the art of Europe and the Americas in the 20th century.

Because of the diversity of ethnic groups on the African continent, African art cannot be identified under the names of movements such as *impressionism* or *cubism* in Europe. Art among Africans has a function in society and is used for the beautification of daily life; it is a part of life rather than an imitation of it. Across the continent, style in African art is based on simplification and exaggeration for emphasis.

Much of African art is the symbolic representation of knowledge and power, both religious and political. A YORUBA divination tray is marked with important symbols known only to the *babalawo*, the diviner. Carved statues often represent ancestors who are well remembered and who work within the spirit world to help the family. An intricately carved staff can imbue its holder with power. The indigenous leader of KANKAN, GUINEA, for example, possesses a staff that has been passed from generation to generation. Among the Ashanti of present-day GHANA, a carved wooden stool represents the seat of power while the Golden Stool is the symbol for the collective soul of the Ashanti people.

Indigenous art for daily life is exhibited through carvings in wood, ivory, stone, and metals, cloth weaving, clay pottery, beadwork, and personal adornment such as scarification. A common purpose of indigenous artistic forms was, and still is, to generate beauty in daily life by decorating the practical and functional items in society.

The production of art is usually divided by gender in each society. For example, among the Senufo of present-day IVORY COAST, the men are the weavers and the women are the potters, while the converse may be true elsewhere. Whether male or female, however, the African artist must produce objects that are based on the aesthetically acceptable standards of the community.

Prior to the arrival of Europeans and later, Americans, the most obvious outside influence on African art came from Islam. In Islamic communities the symbols of religious power reflected Muslim aesthetic ideals, which prohibit statues or three dimensional representations but allow geometrical patterns and embellishments of scripture written in Arabic.

During the early 19th century some African descendants who had been removed to Europe and the Americas during the SLAVE TRADE, returned to Africa during the BACK-TO-AFRICA MOVEMENTS. These returnees brought with them the new art styles that they had learned, sharing them with indigenous Africans who then adopted and adapted these features into their own aesthetic sensibilities.

During the early 20th century African artifacts from Central and West Africa, especially masks, became fashionable items in curio shops and were displayed in the emerging ethnographic museums in Europe. At this juncture of European art history, artists were rebelling against the naturalist stereotypes and began incorporating African techniques of stylization to create a new artistic style. Although Europeans did not consider African artifacts to be on a par with European fine art, as European artists began referring to them more frequently, the artifacts became categorized as "tribal" or "primitive" art.

Credited with the "discovery" of tribal art in 1906, the French artist Henri Matisse (1869–1954) also introduced Spanish painter Pablo Picasso (1881–1973) to the simplified forms and earth tones produced by Africans. After visiting the Musée d'Ethnographie du Trocadéro in Paris, Picasso incorporated four different African masks in the creation of his renowned painting, *Les Demoiselles d'Avignon* (1907). This initiated the European art movement known as Primitivism, which in turn became the foundation for cubism, one of the most influential movements in the history of Western art.

See also: ART (Vols. I, II, III, V); DIVINATION (Vol. I); GOLDEN STOOL (Vol. III); MASKS (Vol. I).

Further reading: Jean-Baptiste Bacquart, *The Tribal Arts of Africa* (New York: Thames and Hudson, 1998); Suzanne Preston Blier, *The Royal Arts of Africa: The Majesty of Form* (New York: H. N. Abrams, 1998); Henry John Drewal and Margaret Thompson Drewal, *Gelede: Art and Female Power among the Yoruba* (Bloomington: Indiana University Press, 1990); Barbara E. Frank, *Mande Potters & Leatherworkers: Art and Heritage in West Africa*

(Washington, D.C.: Smithsonian Institution Press, 1998); Frank Herreman, *Facing the Mask* (New York: Museum for African Art, 2002); Hans Joachim Koloss, ed., *Africa: Art and Culture* (London: Prestel, 2002); Judith Perani and Norma H. Wolff, *Cloth, Dress, and Art Patronage in Africa* (New York: Berg, 1999).

Asantewa, Yaa (Queen Mother of Ejisu)
(1850–1921) *Leader of the Ashanti Empire*

Yaa Asantewa was born to the Ashanti royal family in the village of Ejisu, about 10 miles east of KUMASI, the Ashanti capital located in present-day south-central GHANA. Throughout her life her native region was the site of ongoing violence between the ASHANTI EMPIRE and the occupying British colonial forces. In 1874 Britain took control of Kumasi and declared the region part of its GOLD COAST COLONY. In 1888, following a bitter five-year civil war, the beleaguered Ashanti confederation chose Agyeman PREMPEH (1870–1931), a close ally of Yaa Asantewa's son, as the rightful *asantehene*, or king.

By 1896 the Ashanti were once again a powerful force in the region. In an attempt to reassert control over their colony the British advanced on Kumasi once more, capturing Prempeh in the process. In an attempt to bring the fighting to a quick end, the British demanded that the defeated *asantehene* be sent into exile. Capitulating to the demand, Prempeh, along with leading chiefs—including Yaa Asantewa's son—was eventually sent to the remote Indian Ocean island of SEYCHELLES. Without their king the Ashanti people rallied around Yaa Asantewa, who had assumed the powerful office of the Queen Mother in the absence of most of the Ashanti male leadership.

Early in 1900 the colonial governor of the Gold Coast, Sir Arnold Hodgson, made the mistake of demanding to sit on the Ashanti Golden Stool, a sacred object that represented the unity and independence of the Ashanti people. This unforgivable gaffe was met with the silent withdrawal of the Ashanti people, who immediately made plans for an attack on the British stronghold at Kumasi. Under Yaa Asantewa's active leadership, Ashanti warriors fought a fierce six-month battle for Kumasi. Eventually, in September 1900, British reinforcements with automatic weapons arrived to bring an end to the uprising, now remembered as the Yaa Asantewa War. According to some witnesses, Yaa Asantewa was the last Ashanti warrior captured. She, too, was sent to Seychelles.

In exile, Yaa Asantewa's encyclopedic knowledge of her own royal lineage was instrumental in helping Prempeh I compile *The History of Ashanti Kings and the Whole Country Itself,* begun in 1907. Proud and defiant to the end, she died in exile circa 1921.

See also: ASHANTI (Vol. II); COLONIAL CONQUEST (Vol. IV): GHANA (Vols. I, II, III, V): GOLDEN STOOL (Vol. III); WOMEN IN COLONIAL AFRICA (Vol. IV).

Ashanti Empire Territory ruled by the Ashanti, a West African AKAN group; at its height the Ashanti Empire covered most of present-day GHANA. In the 17th century the first Ashanti *asantehene,* or king, Osei Tutu (c. 1680–c. 1717), founded his capital of KUMASI, a market town along a trade route in the dense forests of the south-central region of present-day Ghana. With the sacred Golden Stool as a powerful symbol of unity, Osei Tutu and the succeeding *asantehenes* joined all of the local Ashanti chiefdoms into a formidable state.

Once it had centralized its power the Ashanti kingdom employed its massive and well-trained army to dominate other Akan kingdoms, including Denkyira and Akyem, as well as the MOSSI STATES to the north, such as Dagomba. Waging frequent wars, they captured thousands of prisoners, whom they used to increase their own ranks, to clear the forest for AGRICULTURE, and to work their lucrative GOLD fields. Prisoners were also traded on the coast for European goods. As a result of this military and commercial might the Ashanti kingdom evolved into an empire.

In 1807, however, Britain outlawed slave trading and began actively discouraging the trade in human captives on the southern coast of Ashanti territory (called the Gold Coast by Europeans for the massive amounts of the precious metal that were traded there). Over the next two decades British merchants and expeditionary forces continued to encroach on Ashanti territory, sparking the ANGLO-ASHANTI WARS, a series of battles that gradually weakened the Ashanti Empire during the 19th century.

In 1873 the British began an invasion of Kumasi, burning buildings and looting storehouses. The subsequent occupation of the city and the establishment of the British GOLD COAST COLONY to the south of Kumasi marked a shift in the region's power structure. Then, following the death of Asantehene Kwaku Dua II (d. 1884), a problem of succession embroiled the Ashanti in turmoil over who would be named the next *asantehene.* During this void in leadership, questions arose over the direction the empire should take. Some Ashanti chiefs and counselors recommended that the empire join with the Gold Coast Colony, while others vehemently disagreed. Since the Ashanti are a matrilineal society, royal women and queen mothers chose the *asantehene.* Queen Mother Yaa Akyaa (1845–1917) supported the accession of her son Agyeman PREMPEH (1870–1931), and after five years of civil war Agyeman Prempeh was finally appointed *asantehene.*

The internal warfare weakened the Ashanti Empire, but it did not fall easily. By 1896 its reorganized army attempted to expel the British from Kumasi. However, British forces overwhelmed the Ashanti army with superior firepower, seized Agyeman Prempeh, and eventually exiled him and his mother to the distant island of SEYCHELLES in the Indian Ocean.

Many Ashanti considered the exiling of Agyeman Prempeh to be a victory for their people. The primary objective was to preserve the sanctity of the Golden Stool, which, as the symbolic soul of their nation, was much more important than the destiny of any particular *asantehene.* The victorious British colonial governor demanded that the Ashanti royalty hand over the stool for him to sit on—an unpardonable offense that led to further conflict.

Because the rightful king and his mother had been exiled along with her own son, Yaa ASANTEWA (1850–1921), Queen Mother of a component state in the empire, assumed leadership. In 1901 she challenged the men by leading the last efforts to end the British occupation of Kumasi. Carrying a machete and a British-made 30.03 rifle, Yaa Asantewa led her army. Although eventually defeated, she escaped capture for three years. In the end, however, she, too, was exiled to the Seychelles.

After the Ashanti were defeated their gold fields were co-opted by British MINING interests, and the colonial administration set about building railroads from Kumasi to the coast. When Agyeman Prempeh was allowed to return to Kumasi, in 1924, he was celebrated once again as the mighty *asantehene,* but the former glory of the Ashanti Empire was a distant memory.

See also: ASHANTI (Vol. II); ASHANTI EMPIRE (Vol. III); COLONIAL CONQUEST (Vol. IV); ENGLAND AND AFRICA (Vols. III, IV, V); GOLDEN STOOL (Vol. III); OSEI TUTU (Vol. III).

Further reading: Ivor Wilks, *Asante in the Nineteenth Century: The Structure and Evolution of a Political Order* (New York: Cambridge University Press, 1975).

Asian communities During the colonial era large numbers of Asians were brought to Africa to supply British colonies with cheap LABOR. Some of these laborers were Chinese or Indonesian, but the majority were from India, which was part of the British Empire at the time. Significant Asian populations lived on the Indian Ocean islands of MADAGASCAR, MAURITIUS, and RÉUNION ISLAND, but the largest Asian communities lived, and still live, in SOUTH AFRICA and in BRITISH EAST AFRICA.

During the middle of the 19th century European-owned companies established South Africa's sugarcane industry along the Indian Ocean coast, in what was Britain's NATAL colony. Between the 1850s and 1910 the British administration recruited an estimated 150,000 Asians to work as indentured laborers for five-year terms. Most worked on the sugar plantations, but others were em-ployed as railway workers, miners, and domestic servants for British and Afrikaner households. At the end of their contracts many of the Indian laborers stayed in the area. By the end of the 19th century they had formed an educated middle class composed of merchants and small-business owners in addition to constituting a working class. As such, they were able to develop a measure of political influence that was unattainable to the country's black majority.

The most famous Indian to live in South Africa was a young, British-trained lawyer named Mohandas GANDHI (1869–1948). After arriving in DURBAN in 1893, Gandhi worked for more than 20 years as a social activist. His style of political leadership later had a profound impact on leaders of the AFRICAN NATIONAL CONGRESS.

In the 20th century the Afrikaner-dominated South African government tended to see the country's Indians as a homogenous community. Despite the government's tendency to lump the Indians together, however, there were religious, ethnic, and cultural differences among the various groups within the community. For example, some Indians were Hindi, some were Sikhs, and others were Muslims. In many ways immigrants from India's northern Punjabi district were as culturally distinct from the southern Goan Indians as they were from their Afrikaner neighbors.

Between 1896 and 1901 the British colonial government brought more than 30,000 indentured Indian workers to supply labor on the railway between the cities of KAMPALA, in present-day UGANDA, and MOMBASA, on the coast of KENYA. The workers who survived the difficult project settled throughout British East Africa, establishing Asian communities all down the SWAHILI COAST from Mombasa to DAR ES SALAAM, located on the coast of TANGANYIKA (present-day mainland TANZANIA).

Britain's East African railroads were notoriously difficult to build, and many workers died from disease brought on by poor living conditions and a harsh working environment. In addition, man-eating lions and other large predators terrorized the worker camps. In all an estimated 2,500 workers died during the construction of the Mombasa-Kampala railway.

Indian merchants along the Indian Ocean coast developed commercial ties to Asia and the Middle East, as well as throughout Africa. Similar to the Asian immigrants in South Africa, in the 20th century Asian settlers in East Africa made up an educated middle class that had some political power.

See also: ASIAN COMMUNITIES (Vol. V); ENGLAND AND AFRICA (Vols. III, IV, V); INDIAN OCEAN TRADE (Vol. II).

Further reading: Bill Freund, *Insiders and Outsiders: The Indian Working Class of Durban, 1910–1990* (Portsmouth, N.H.: Heinemann, 1995).

Asmara (Asmera) Capital and largest city of ERITREA, located near the Red Sea in the Eritrean highlands. Situated at an elevation of 7,700 feet (2,347 m), Asmara was originally a minor TIGRAY village before becoming the military headquarters of Emperor YOHANNES IV (1831–1889) of ETHIOPIA. His successor, Emperor MENELIK II (1844–1913), ceded Asmara and the surrounding region to Italy under the terms of the Treaty of Wichale (1889). Italy later used Asmara as a base from which to invade Ethiopia in 1895.

The following year, however, Ethiopia thoroughly routed the Italian invaders at the Battle of ADOWA, and the subsequent Treaty of Addis Ababa recognized Ethiopia's sovereignty and Italy's claim only to Eritrea. The Italian governor at the time selected Asmara over the port city of Massawa, some 40 miles (65 km) away, as the colony's capital because of its cooler highland climate.

Asmara came to assume the character of an Italian colonial city, and by 1925 had 10,000 inhabitants. A focal point of the city was the Piazza Roma Asmara, with the Bank of Italy, built in 1926, as one of its principal landmarks. Another important colonial building was the Catholic cathedral, erected in 1922. Yet in terms of its overall population, Asmara remained a Tigrayan city, with its indigenous population made up of equal numbers of Muslims and Ethiopian Orthodox Christians. In 1935, in an event that was a precursor to World War II (1939–45), Italy again utilized Asmara as its base for an invasion of Ethiopia. Although the Italian forces succeeded this time, British forces later defeated the Italians in 1941, restoring independence to Ethiopia and taking over Eritrea. The city continued as the British administrative capital until 1952, when a United Nations resolution made Eritrea a federated province of Ethiopia, with Asmara as its provincial capital. In 1993, when Eritrea became an independent nation, Asmara became the national capital.

See also: ASMARA (Vols. II, V); ITALY AND AFRICA (Vol. IV); UNITED NATIONS AND AFRICA (Vols. IV, V).

Aswan Dam Either of two Egyptian dams across the Nile River. The Aswan "Low" Dam was completed in 1902. It was supplanted in the 1960s by the much larger Aswan "High" Dam. Because EGYPT is relatively rainless, the annual flood of the Nile River is what makes the land suitable for farming. However, the volume of floodwater can change significantly from year to year—from 12 bil-

lion cubic meters in a lean year to 155 billion cubic meters in a heavy year. Egypt needed to control these floodwaters in order to guarantee a stable amount of water to grow crops for the country's expanding population. In addition, developing industries needed a new source of electricity to fuel their growth. A dam at Aswan, 590 miles (949 km) south of CAIRO, provided clear answers to both of these needs.

In 1898 Egypt employed British engineers to begin construction of what would be the first, or Low, Aswan Dam. A number of Britain's foremost engineers participated in the project, including Sir Benjamin Baker (1840–1907) and Sir John Aird. The dam was completed in 1902. Measuring over 100 feet (30 m) in height and nearly 1.5 miles (2.4 km) in length, the dam was an extraordinary engineering feat for its time.

It soon became apparent, however, that this was not sufficient. The primary problem was that the dam's reservoir area could not accommodate an extreme Nile flood. This produced dangerously high levels of water pressure against the dam's concrete and granite structure. Efforts to increase the height and width of the dam, first from 1907 to 1912 and then again from 1929 to 1934, failed to produce a significant solution.

Planning for a second Aswan Dam, located 4 miles (6.4 km) upstream from the first dam, began in the early 1950s. In November 1959 the Nile Water Agreement between Egypt and present-day Republic of the SUDAN paved the way for construction to begin on the Aswan High Dam. This new dam, which would not be completed until 1970, involved Cold War politics in its construction and produced sweeping changes not only in Egypt's topology, but in its native ecology and culture as well. The dam also affected the archaeological study of the remnants of the ancient civilizations of Egyptian Nubia and Sudanese Nubia.

See also: ASWAN (Vol. I); ASWAN DAM (Vol. V); COLD WAR AND AFRICA (Vol. IV) KUSH (Vol. I); MEDITERRANEAN SEA (Vols. I, II); NILE RIVER (Vol. I); NILE VALLEY (Vol. I); SUDAN, THE (Vol. II).

Atlantic Charter Declaration issued by the United States and Britain that seemed to promise a shift toward the end of colonialism. During World War II (1939–45) United States president Franklin D. Roosevelt (1882–1945) and British prime minister Winston Churchill (1874–1965) met aboard a warship in the Atlantic Ocean off the coast of Newfoundland. At the conclusion of this meeting, in August 1941, Roosevelt and Churchill issued a joint declaration that became known as the Atlantic Charter. It outlined their principles, intent, and vision for the postwar world that would follow upon the defeat of Germany and Japan. The third article of the declaration stated that the United States and Britain would "respect the right of all peoples to choose the form of government under which they will live," and that they sought to have "sovereign rights and self government restored to those [peoples] who have been forcibly deprived of them."

In the context of the NATIONALISM AND INDEPENDENCE MOVEMENTS occurring in most parts of Africa at the time—political efforts that sought a greater measure of power sharing, self rule, or outright independence—the Atlantic Charter appeared to signal a profound shift in Western policy toward the African colonies. African intellectuals widely quoted the third article, for it raised hopes for a drastically changed postwar political landscape, one in which Africans would exercise greater autonomy and work toward independence. When none of these expectations were realized after the war, the perceived duplicity of the declaration tended to embitter political moderates and give momentum to anticolonial nationalist movements.

See also: ENGLAND AND AFRICA (Vols. III, IV, V); INDEPENDENCE MOVEMENTS (Vol. V); UNITED NATIONS AND AFRICA (Vols. IV, V); UNITED STATES AND AFRICA (Vols. IV, V).

Awolowo, Obafemi (1909–1987) *Nigerian statesman and Yoruba national leader*

Popularly known as "Awo," Obafemi Awolowo was born to Christian parents in the YORUBA town of Ikene, in what was then the British PROTECTORATE of Southern NIGERIA. Because of his father's early death, Awolowo had a very difficult childhood. As a youth he attended various schools in towns in Western Nigeria before gaining admission, in 1927, to Wesley College, in IBADAN.

Forced to drop out of the college in 1928, he pursued various means of earning a living. In 1934 he moved to LAGOS and at various times engaged in money lending, public letter writing (most colonial Nigerians could neither read nor write), public transport, and produce trading. He did all of these with some success but also incurred huge debts and losses. In 1937 he married a businesswoman, Hannah Idowu Dideolu Adelana. During this period he also became active in the labor union movement, and in 1943 he was one of the founders of the Nigerian Trade Union Congress.

In 1944 he went to London to study law, and in 1946 he was admitted to the bar. After returning home the following year he established a law practice in Ibadan and also became active in the nationalist politics of the era. While in England he had founded a Yoruba cultural society among his countrymen there that became the nucleus of a new nationalist political party. This party, named the Action Group, was officially formed in 1950, with Awolowo as its first president.

From 1951 to 1959 Awolowo held posts of increasing responsibility in the government of the Yoruba-dominated Western Region, which began to demand self-rule within a federal Nigeria. In 1959 he was elected to the Federal House of Representatives in which, as head of the Action Group, he was leader of the opposition. In 1960, when Nigeria achieved independence, Abubakar Tafawa BALEWA (1912–1966), from the HAUSA-dominated Northern Region, became prime minister.

In 1963, as a result of an aborted coup attempt by the Action Group against Balewa's government, Awolowo was sentenced to 10 years in prison. He was released in 1966, however, following the military coup that put Yakubu Gowon (1934–), an officer from the Northern Region, into power. For the remainder of his political career, which ended in 1983, Awolowo was active in national politics. In 1987 the University of Ifé in Ilé-Ifé, Nigeria, was renamed Obafemi Awolowo University in his honor.

See also: AWOLOWO, OBAFEMI (Vol. V); GOWON, YAKUBU (Vol. V); NATIONALISM AND INDEPENDENCE MOVEMENTS (Vol. IV).

Azikiwe, Nnamdi (Benjamin Nnamdi Azikiwe) (1904–1996) *First president of independent Nigeria*

Azikiwe, an IGBO, was born in the town of Zungeru, in Northern NIGERIA. His father worked as a clerk for the British colonial army. Azikiwe received his early education in Calabar and later in LAGOS, where he was exposed to the philosophy of the pan-Africanist Marcus GARVEY (1887–1940) and met American-trained Ghanaian educator and minister James E. Kwegyir AGGREY (1875–1927). These events had a profound impact on the young Azikiwe.

In 1924 Azikiwe's father retired from his position after receiving humiliating treatment from a European coworker. Though the incident troubled Azikiwe, his father was able to use his retirement money to send Azikiwe to the United States to continue his education. He ultimately ended up at Lincoln University, in Pennsylvania, where one of his fellow students was Thurgood Marshall (1908–1993), who later became a U.S. Supreme Court justice. Although he was faced with persistent financial difficulties and discrimination, Azikiwe still managed to complete his studies and earn a master's degree in political science. His experience at Lincoln University was so positive that he strongly encouraged Kwame NKRUMAH (1902–1972), the first president of independent GHANA, to attend the school as well.

Azikiwe returned to Nigeria in 1934 and then moved to ACCRA, the capital of GOLD COAST COLONY (now Ghana), where he founded and edited a newspaper. He used the paper to criticize colonialism in West Africa, drawing the ire of colonial authorities, who charged him with sedition. Azikiwe was convicted of the charge, but the conviction was later overturned. The case was well publicized, and in 1937 Azikiwe returned to Nigeria as a nationalist hero.

In 1944 Azikiwe established the National Council for Nigeria and the Cameroons, as well as six NEWSPAPERS, including the *WEST AFRICAN PILOT*, through which he launched a massive anticolonial campaign. He branched out into economics as well, founding the African Continental Bank that same year. The colonial government reacted against Azikiwe's efforts, banning two of his papers, and rumors abounded of assassination plots against him. Azikiwe's popularity in Nigeria and beyond grew immensely, and in 1946 anticolonial radicals in Nigeria formed the Zikist movement, naming themselves after Azikiwe's nickname, Zik. In 1949 a European-police massacre of 18 African mine workers incited a Zikist riot, an event which led Azikiwe to distance himself from the movement.

In 1948 Azikiwe was elected president of the Igbo Union. Though still popular, he faced competition and criticism from organizations in Nigeria's other cultures, including the HAUSA and the YORUBA. The Hausa established the Northern People's Congress, in 1949, and the Yoruba, led by Obafemi AWOLOWO (1909–1987) formed the Action Group, in 1951. This heightened political activism and rivalry helped lead Nigeria to independence, in 1960, but it also increased the political and ethnic tensions that led to the outbreak of civil war within the first decade of Nigeria's independence.

Azikiwe continued to rise through the ranks of Nigerian politics until, in 1963, he assumed the role of independent Nigeria's first president.

See also: AZIKIWE, NNAMDI (Vol. V); NATIONALISM AND INDEPENDENCE MOVEMENTS (Vol. IV).

B

Ba, Amadou Hampate (1901–1991) *Malian historian and Muslim scholar*

Amadou Hampate Ba was born in Bandiagara, MALI, to a prominent Pular-speaking, Muslim family. As was common in his community, he received a Quranic education. He then became a follower of a prominent Sufi mystic and teacher. He also received a primary education in French, after which he became a junior clerk for the colonial government in UPPER VOLTA (today's BURKINA FASO). He worked as a research assistant, collecting historical and ethnographic texts for the Fundamental Institute of Black Africa (IFAN), a colonial research institute based in DAKAR, SENEGAL, with branches in other colonies of FRENCH WEST AFRICA. Ba's work with IFAN helped establish him as a historian and ethnographer. In the 1960s he directed the new Malian Institute for Research in Human Sciences and was Mali's ambassador to UNESCO (United Nations Educational, Scientific, and Cultural Organization). He retired to the city of ABIDJAN in IVORY COAST, where he concentrated on teaching, writing, and preaching.

The Pular (Peul) LANGUAGE enjoys widespread use in West Africa. In its various dialects, it is spoken by roughly 14 million people of FULANI background, from Fouta Jallon (modern GUINEA) through NIGER, MALI, NIGERIA, and CAMEROON. Fulani traders and merchants can be found in almost every major city in West Africa.

Amadou Ba wrote many works of nonfiction but only one novel, *L'Etrange destin de Wangrin* (The fortunes of Wangrin), published in 1973. His writings are notable for the extent to which they incorporate his detailed knowledge of his region's customs and ORAL TRADITIONS. Summarizing the importance of recording the past, he said "the death of an old man is like the burning of a library."

See also: LITERATURE IN MODERN AFRICA (Vol. V).

---

baasskap Term from AFRIKAANS literally meaning "master condition." In SOUTH AFRICA, it is applied to the concept of the white-minority domination over the majority, which was made up of Africans, CAPE COLOURED PEOPLE, and Asians. The origins of *baasskap* lay with SLAVERY during the Dutch East India Company and early British eras in the CAPE COLONY. As they migrated out of the Cape Colony into the interior, BOERS (later called AFRIKANERS) embraced this approach in dealing with the indigenous African people they encountered and eventually subordinated.

While *baasskap* became entrenched in social and economic relations between blacks and whites, it also had a legislative dimension. One of the earliest laws was the 1841 Masters and Servants Ordinance of the Cape Colony. Pass laws regulating the free movement of Africans were another example of legislated *baasskap*. With the National Party's electoral victory in 1948 and the emergence of APARTHEID in South Africa, *baasskap* reached its high point. The objective of the South African government was to consolidate and perpetuate political control by whites and thus ensure their social, economic, and cultural domination.

See also: ASIAN COMMUNITIES (Vols. IV, V); RACE AND RACISM (Vol. IV).

Baba, Shaikh Sidiyya (1862–1926) *Leading Muslim scholar and reformer in Mauritania*

The grandson of a highly revered and respected marabout, or Islamic holy man, Baba learned much from his grandfather about political leadership and political mediation. He also received a strong Islamic education from leading scholars of the southern Sahara region. Growing up in an era of European COLONIAL CONQUEST and expansion, Baba was interested in understanding the effects of European imperialism on Muslim countries. For example, he studied leaders such as Muhammad Ali (1769–1849), a Muslim who modernized EGYPT with the help of Europeans. With his broad knowledge of North African history, Baba turned his attention to reforming his own Moorish society in MAURITANIA.

Bands of warriors dominated precolonial Mauritania, and the marabouts were limited in their political authority. Baba sought to apply what he had learned about European power first to cooperate with the French in their colonial conquest, and then to utilize the French administrative presence to restructure the lines of political authority among Mauritanians. At the same time he worked to keep Mauritania autonomous during the colonial era. Baba also set up a French-Arabic school—the first in the country—at his camp at Boutilimit, located southwest of the capital in Nouakchott. The school trained what would become the country's first generation of leaders—these included some of Baba's own children—after Mauritania achieved independence, in 1960. In part, Baba's legacy was the creation of schooling that combined the best Islamic educational traditions with those of the French colonialists to meet the needs of Mauritania in the modern world.

See also: COLONIAL RULE (Vol. IV); COLONIALISM, INFLUENCE OF (Vol. IV); FRENCH WEST AFRICA (Vol. IV); ISLAM, INFLUENCE OF (Vol. IV).

Back-to-Africa movements

Various initiatives undertaken to return people of African descent in the Americas to Africa. Back-to-Africa movements were underway as early as the late 18th century, with efforts by British abolitionists and the Sierra Leone Company eventually leading to the establishment of SIERRA LEONE, a colony for repatriated Africans from Britain and the Americas. Similarly, by the 1820s the American Colonization Society had established the independent settlement of LIBERIA for repatriated African-Americans.

During the late 19th and into the 20th century one of the staunchest supporters of the Back-to-Africa movement was Bishop Henry McNeal Turner (1834–1915), whose disillusionment with the plight of American blacks made him call for emigration to Africa. Edward Wilmot BLYDEN (1832–1912), a West Indian who moved to Liberia, also encouraged American blacks to return to Africa.

One African-American abolitionist, Martin Robinson Delany (1812–1885), is characterized as an early black nationalist. After a varied career in MEDICINE, the military, politics, and publishing, Delany promoted repatriation of African-Americans to Africa. His efforts included an expedition to the NIGER DELTA (in present day NIGERIA), where he signed a treaty to settle African-Americans there in order to develop a COTTON industry. Although the outbreak of the U.S. Civil War (1860–65) diverted his attention to issues in America, individual families resettled in the delta region as a result of this effort.

In the early decades of the 20th century a second Back-to-Africa movement gained momentum under the direction of Jamaican-born Marcus GARVEY (1887–1940). Through his black nationalist organization, the UNIVERSAL NEGRO IMPROVEMENT ASSOCIATION, Garvey called for African-Americans and other members of the AFRICAN DIASPORA to return to the motherland, reclaim it, and establish a great African nation free from the control of whites. Garvey's impassioned speeches garnered enthusiastic support, but his mission was ultimately derailed by financial difficulties.

See also: PAN-AFRICANISM (Vols. IV, V).

Further reading: Stephen J. Braidwood, *Black Poor and White Philanthropists: London's Blacks and the Foundation of the Sierra Leone Settlement, 1786–1791* (Liverpool, U.K.: Liverpool University Press, 1994); Nemata Amelia Blyden, *West Indians in West Africa, 1808–1880: The African Diaspora in Reverse* (Rochester, N.Y.: University of Rochester Press, 2000); Tom W. Shick, *Behold the Promised Land: A History of Afro-American Settler Society in Nineteenth-century Liberia* (Baltimore: Johns Hopkins University Press, 1980).

Bagamoyo

Small Indian Ocean port city on northern coast of TANZANIA dating from the 18th century. Bagamoyo was a depot for the SLAVE TRADE and IVORY TRADE and gained importance as the first colonial capital of GERMAN EAST AFRICA.

Present-day Bagamoyo is a quiet place with a developing tourist trade that is very much at odds with the violence of its past history. Due to its location across a narrow strait from ZANZIBAR, the Omani Arab state that controlled the 19th-century East African slave and ivory trade, Bagamoyo became a principal port for the trade in human captives. In 1872 Roman Catholic MISSIONARIES seeking to suppress the slave trade founded a mission station outside the town that has remained an important church to the present day. Shortly after, in 1889, Bagamoyo figured in the German conquest of the area, and it became Germany's colonial capital. The city remained a German administrative center until Germany lost all its African colonies as a result of World War I (1914–18).

With the onset of British rule after World War I, Bagamoyo's administrative importance was eclipsed by the new colonial capital of DAR ES SALAAM. Bagamoyo's commercial power eroded as well, due to the rise of the port city of Tanga to the north. The Catholic mission, the old German governor's residence, and the fine coastal buildings remind present-day visitors and local residents alike of the town's former importance.

See also: SLAVERY (Vols. I, II, III, IV); SLAVE TRADE ON THE SWAHILI COAST (Vol. III).

Baker, Samuel (Sir Samuel White Baker) (1821–1893) *British explorer, adventurer, and administrator of the Sudan*

Baker had already led a full life of adventure in various parts of the world when, in 1861, he and his wife, Florence Von Sass, came to Africa in search of the source of the Nile River. Although he traveled both the Blue Nile and the White, he was unsuccessful in his attempt. Other explorers had preceded him. In 1863 Baker met the two men who had located the headwaters of that great river at Lake Victoria, the largest lake in Africa, in present-day TANZANIA and UGANDA. The explorers, John Hanning SPEKE (1827–1864) and James Augustus Grant (1827–1892), told Baker of rumors they had heard about another large body of water in the region. Using this information, in 1864 Baker came upon the large lake that he named Lake Albert Nyanza after Britain's Prince Albert (1819–1861), the consort of Queen Victoria (1819–1901).

Baker also was the first European to see Uganda's Murchison Falls (now Kabarega Falls), which he named for Roderick Murchison (1792–1871), president of the Royal Geographical Society.

Baker was knighted in 1866. Three years later he accepted an offer from Khedive ISMAIL (1830–1895) of EGYPT to lead a military expedition to the Upper Nile. His purpose was to suppress the SLAVE TRADE in what is now the Republic of the SUDAN and to promote commerce. Baker commanded the expedition under the titles of pasha and major-general of the Ottoman army. From 1869 to 1873 he administered the Equatoria Province of southern Sudan as governor general. Returning to Britain in 1874, he proved a passionate advocate for the abolition of the slave trade.

Baker wrote many popular books on hunting, nature, and, especially, his travels in Africa. After 1873 he pursued his life-long passions for big-game hunting and traveling.

See also: EXPLORATION (Vol. III); NILE RIVER (Vol. I); SLAVERY (Vols. I, II, III, IV).

Further reading: Michael Brander, *The Perfect Victorian Hero* (Edinburgh, U.K.: Mainstream, 1982); Richard Seymour Hall, *Lovers on the Nile* (London: Collins, 1980).

Balewa, Abubakar Tafawa (Alhaji; Sir) (1912–1966) *First prime minister of independent Nigeria*

Balewa was born to a Muslim family of humble background in what is now northern NIGERIA. He was educated at Katsina, where he obtained a teacher's certificate. After teaching from 1933 to 1945, he attended the Institute of Education at the University of London on a scholarship. Returning home in 1947, he was appointed a government education officer, but that same year he quit EDUCATION to begin a career in politics in the colonial Northern Region House of Assembly. Balewa continued to represent the Northern Region when the British replaced the House of Assembly with a federal House of Representatives, in 1951. Surprising for a representative from the Muslim-dominated north, Balewa held strong pro-West views and supported Western-style capitalism, which, in the strongly anticolonial and African-nationalist environment of the 1960s, contributed to his 1966 assassination.

In addition to being one of Nigeria's most prominent politicians, Balewa also became a best-selling novelist in 1934. His short work *Shaihu Umar,* written in HAUSA, relates the trials of a young Muslim man and his mother around the turn of the century, when SLAVERY and kidnapping were still very real threats in the Hausa-dominated region of Northern Nigeria. Through the story Balewa promotes the values and philosophy of Islam. It was translated and published in English in 1989.

The Nigerian federation became self-governing in 1954, and, along with Ahmadu BELLO (1909–1966), Balewa founded the conservative Northern Peoples Congress (NPC), one of the key political parties that formed the new coalition government. Other parties included the National Council for Nigeria and Cameroons, led by Eastern Nigerians Nnamdi AZIKIWE (1904–1996) and Herbert Macaulay (1864–1946), and the Action Group opposition party, representing the Western Region and led by YORUBA chief Obafemi AWOLOWO (1909–1987).

In 1957 the coalition government elected Balewa the first prime minister of the Federation of Nigeria, giving him executive and legislative powers. He retained the post when Nigeria achieved independence, in 1960, and continued to hold the position when Nigeria became a republic, in 1963. In 1960 Balewa was knighted by Britain's Queen Elizabeth II (1926–).

By the mid-1960s, however, Balewa's northern-oriented government had become corrupt, with many politicians reaping monetary benefits from their positions while much of the country suffered from poverty and starvation. In 1966, following several years of ineffective and divided national leadership, Balewa was assassinated in a military coup d'état led by junior officers of IGBO descent from southeastern Nigeria.

See also: COUP D'ÉTAT (Vol. V); NATIONALISM AND INDEPENDENCE MOVEMENTS (Vol. IV); POLITICAL PARTIES AND ORGANIZATIONS (Vol. IV).

Further reading: Trevor Clark, *A Right Honourable Gentleman: Abubakar from the Black Rock: A Narrative Chronicle of the Life and Times of Nigeria's Alhaji Sir Abubakar Tafawa Balewa* (London: Edward Arnold, 1991).

Bamako Current capital city of the Republic of MALI, located in the southwestern part of the country, on the Niger River. During the time of the Mali Empire (c. 11th through 15th centuries) the Bamako area was considered a center for Islamic learning. In 1883 the French officer Joseph GALLIENI (1849–1916) took control of Bamako, which at the time was populated by just a few hundred people. The French used the town as a military garrison during the French colonial wars, and in 1908 Bamako became the administrative capital of the former colony of FRENCH SOUDAN, which was administrated as part of FRENCH WEST AFRICA. At that time the Dakar-Niger Railway established a segment from Kayes, near SENEGAL, to Bamako, and the navigable portion of the Senegal River was linked with navigation on the Niger River, to facilitate the movement of bulk cargoes.

In 1946 a meeting of African political leaders in Bamako led to the founding of the AFRICAN DEMOCRATIC ASSEMBLY (Rassemblement Democratique Africaine, RDA), chaired by Félix HOUPHOUËT-BOIGNY (1905–1993) of IVORY COAST. The RDA was dedicated to greater African political rights and representation within the French colonial empire. In 1957 a subsequent meeting of the RDA in Bamako continued to argue for free association with France, but by then some of the key leaders were set on full independence. When Mali gained independence, in 1960, Bamako remained the capital.

See also: BAMAKO (Vols. II, III, V); FRANCE AND AFRICA (Vols. III, IV, V); NIGER RIVER (Vols. I, III); SENEGAL RIVER (Vols. I, II); TRANSPORTATION (Vol. IV).

Bambatha's Rebellion (Bambata's Rebellion)
ZULU uprising against white, colonial power in 1906. Bambatha (1865–1906) was the chief of the Zondi, a small branch (numbering only 5,500) of the Zulu people in the British colony of NATAL (now KwaZulu-Natal, in present-day SOUTH AFRICA). In 1905 he led opposition to a government poll tax that was to go into effect in January 1906.

This opposition grew, and in February 1906 African protestors killed two white policemen engaged in enforcing the tax. In response British troops, South African police, and volunteers from among the region's European SETTLERS launched a campaign of retribution against rebel suspects by destroying crops, confiscating cattle, and deposing chiefs.

White policemen were not the only targets of the rebels' ire. Many young Zulu men saw the capitulation of their elders to colonial demands as a betrayal and attacked their own leaders, too. In the trials that followed the rebellion it was not uncommon for fathers to testify against their sons.

Bambatha was deposed and fled into Zululand. He gathered support among opponents of the hated poll tax, though the rebellion never touched off a mass uprising. Natal imposed martial law in May, seeking to suppress the rebel forces intent on waging a guerrilla war. Bambatha promised his followers that a charm he possessed would deflect British bullets, an assertion that was later proved fanciful. The rebellion was easily put down, and Bambatha was killed and beheaded, in June 1906. By July the government was again in control, but unrest continued in the region for years.

Approximately 4,000 Zulu lost their lives in the armed rebellion, while only 24 whites were killed. The government charged the paramount Zulu king, DINIZULU (1868–1913), with 23 counts of treason, although the extent of his complicity was never clear. He was found guilty of harboring rebels, sentenced to four years in prison, and later exiled to the TRANSVAAL.

Bambatha's Rebellion clearly revealed to Africans the futility of mounting a military assault on the increasingly repressive white authorities. Instead Africans began to explore other forms of protest, which led to the establishment of the South African Native National Congress, in 1912, which later became the AFRICAN NATIONAL CONGRESS, in 1921. For whites in South Africa, Babatha's Rebellion highlighted their need for a centralized government that could suppress such large-scale uprisings among the African populations. Whites, for their part, responded with the creation of the UNION OF SOUTH AFRICA, in 1910.

See also: COLONIAL RULE (Vol. IV); RESISTANCE AND REBELLION (Vol. IV); POLITICAL PARTIES AND ORGANIZATIONS (Vol. IV).

Further reading: Benedict Carton, *Blood From Your Children: The Colonial Origins of Generational Conflict in South Africa* (Richmond, Va.: University of Virginia Press, 2000).

Banda, Hastings Kamuzu (Ngwazi Hastings Kamuzu Banda) (c. 1898–1997) *First president of independent Malawi*

Banda was born to CHEWA-speaking parents in what was then the British PROTECTORATE of NYASALAND (present-day MALAWI). He received his early education from MISSIONARIES and became a Christian. In 1914 Banda traveled to SOUTHERN RHODESIA (present-day ZIMBABWE), where he worked in a hospital and determined he would pursue a medical career. In 1916 he moved on to JOHANNESBURG, SOUTH AFRICA, finding work at a GOLD mine on the WITWATERSRAND. It was while working there that he received his first exposure to African nationalism. Banda also joined the African Methodist Episcopal Church (AME), in 1922, and through church funding was able to attend the AME Wilberforce Institute, in Ohio. From there he went on to earn his bachelor's degree from the University of Chicago. Then, in 1932, he attended Meharry Medical College, a leading center for training African-American doctors, which was located in Nashville, Tennessee. He received his doctor's degree in 1937.

Unable to set up a medical practice in Nyasaland due to the refusal of white nurses to work for a black doctor, Banda set up a practice in Liverpool, England. After World War II (1939–45), his practice became highly successful and brought him into contact with a number of African nationalist leaders, including Kwame NKRUMAH (1909–1972) of GHANA and Jomo KENYATTA (c. 1891–1978) of KENYA. Banda used his money and influence to help support local nationalist groups, particularly the Nyasaland African Congress.

In 1953 the British linked Nyasaland, NORTHERN RHODESIA (present-day ZAMBIA), and Southern Rhodesia into the CENTRAL AFRICAN FEDERATION. The African populations of Northern Rhodesia and Nyasaland, in particular, viewed the federation as an effort to extend the white electoral dominance of Southern Rhodesia to their countries and strongly opposed it. In 1957, at the request of the Nyasaland Congress, Banda returned home to lead the organization in protest against British plans to merge the federated territories into a single state. The Congress believed this plan would undermine the possibility of independence even more so than the federation and could even lead to South African-style APARTHEID in Central Africa. In 1959, after demonstrations turned violent, the British imprisoned Banda and disbanded the Congress. Working from prison, Banda formed the Malawi Congress Party, which quickly garnered members. Upon his release, in 1961, Banda was made the party's president for life. That same year the organization swept the elections to become the dominant opposition party.

As Nyasaland progressed toward independence, Banda served as the African leader in a short-term joint government made up of both blacks and whites. He then became prime minister, in 1963, which positioned him to assume the presidency of the independent Republic of Malawi, in 1966, a position he held until 1994.

See also: BANDA, HASTINGS KAMUZU (Vol. V); ENGLAND AND AFRICA (Vols. III, V); NATIONALISM AND INDEPENDENCE MOVEMENTS (Vol. IV).

Further reading: Colin Baker, *State of Emergency: Crisis in Central Africa, Nyasaland 1959–1960* (New York: Tauris Academic Studies, 1997). Philip Short, *Banda* (Boston: Routledge & Kegan Paul, 1974).

Bandung Afro-Asian Conference (1955) Widely viewed as the founding meeting of the Nonaligned Movement. On April 18, 1955, at the invitation of the prime ministers of Burma, Ceylon, India, Indonesia, and Pakistan, one of the more important international meetings of the post–World War II period took place in Bandung, Indonesia. Representatives of 29 Asian and African countries, mostly former colonies, met for six days to discuss mutual concerns and to develop a common foreign policy to deal with the pressures faced from the major powers. Heading the conference was senior statesman Jawaharlal Nehru (1889–1964) of India, assisted by Prime Ministers Sukarno (1901–1970) of Indonesia and Gamal Abdel NASSER (1918–1970) of EGYPT. The Bandung Conference laid the groundwork for the first summit conference of the global Nonalignment Movement, which was held in CAIRO, in June 1961. The purpose of the Nonalignment Movement was to allow smaller nations to follow their own political paths and avoid being dominated by the Cold War (1960–91) rivalry between the United States and the Soviet Union.

See also: COLD WAR AND AFRICA (Vol. V); NONALIGNED MOVEMENT AND AFRICA (Vol. V).

Bangui Capital city of the CENTRAL AFRICAN REPUBLIC, located just west of the Ubangi River. Inhabited by Niger-Congo farming peoples for thousands of years, the area around Bangui was a source of captives for both the transatlantic and Arab slave trades throughout the 18th and 19th centuries. In 1875 the military warlord RABIH BIN FADLALLAH (c. 1835–1900) incorporated the area into the Egyptian Sudan, but an 1887 agreement with the CONGO FREE STATE (today's Democratic Republic of the CONGO) granted the region to France. In 1889 France established a colonial military outpost at Bangui, and within five years the region had developed into the OUBANGUI-CHARI colony. The colony became a French overseas territory in 1946. The population of Bangui increased along with its role as an administrative center and trading port, and when the Central African Republic achieved its independence, in 1960, Bangui was named the capital.

See also: BANGUI (Vol. V); FRANCE AND AFRICA (Vols. IV, V); SLAVE TRADE, THE TRANSATLANTIC (Vol. III).

Banjul (formerly Bathurst) Current capital city of The GAMBIA, located at the mouth of the Gambia River. In 1816 a British naval captain acquired the sandy peninsula of Banjul Island through a treaty made with the local ruler. He renamed it St. Mary's Island and established a British military post, calling it Bathurst after the British Colonial Secretary. The British navy used Bathurst as a base to patrol the waters of the Gambia River in an attempt to control the SLAVE TRADE, which Britain had outlawed in 1807. As of 1818 the Banjul community had a civilian population of 700 made up of foreign merchants, freed slaves (known as Aku), and WOLOF-speakers and others from the SENEGAMBIA REGION.

Over the years commercial activities became increasingly important, especially with the dramatic growth in the export of GROUNDNUTS (peanuts) that began in the 1840s. Since it was navigable from the sea to more than 200 miles (322 km) inland, the Gambia River made an excellent route deep into the groundnut-producing regions of the interior. Although the city was once governed as part of the British colony of SIERRA LEONE, located to the south, in 1889 it became the capital of the British colony and PROTECTORATE of The Gambia. In 1965 when The Gambia gained independence, Bathurst maintained its status as the capital. The name was not changed to Banjul until 1973.

See also: BANJUL (Vols. II, III, V); ENGLAND AND AFRICA (Vols. III, IV); GAMBIA RIVER (Vol. II).

Bankole-Bright, H. C. (Herbert Christian) (1883–1958) *Sierra Leone medical doctor and a leading nationalist*

Herbert Christian Bankole-Bright was born on August 23 in the NIGER DELTA of present-day NIGERIA, where his father worked for the ROYAL NIGER COMPANY. Herbert Christian's grandfather, John Bright was a rich recaptive Aku-YORUBA merchant who in 1866 sent his son, Jacob Galba, to England to study MEDICINE. Jacob Galba had to cut his studies short, however, and he returned to FREETOWN, SIERRA LEONE to see his dying father and then take over his business.

Disappointed by his inability to continue his own medical studies, Jacob Galba Bright was determined that Herbert Christian, his son, would become a medical doctor. In 1904 Bankole-Bright left Freetown for Edinburgh, Scotland, where, in 1910, he completed his medical studies. He then entered the London School of Tropical Medicine to undertake advanced studies. In 1911 he married Addah Bishop, under whose father he had worked earlier as an apprentice.

Bankole-Bright returned to Sierra Leone in 1915 and opened a private practice in Freetown. Within a few years, however, he abandoned his practice for politics. Banky, as he was popularly known, criticized the British colonial ad-

ministration for its policies related to racial inequalities in salaries and employment opportunities, as well as for its restrictions on African participation in the government. To register his protests and criticisms of COLONIAL RULE, he utilized NEWSPAPERS, especially the *Aurora,* which he founded.

In 1920 Bankole-Bright participated in the conference of West African nationalists in ACCRA, GOLD COAST COLONY, that led to the founding of the NATIONAL CONGRESS OF BRITISH WEST AFRICA (NCBWA). Elected secretary-general, he participated in its delegation to London in an unsuccessful effort to meet with the top colonial officials.

It is thought that Bankole-Bright played a major role in the founding of the West African Student Union (WASU) during his 1920 visit to London. The WASU later played a significant part in the convening of the pivotal 1945 Manchester Conference, a meeting of future leaders of the Pan-African Movement.

Bankole-Bright and the other Sierra Leone delegates to the Accra Conference returned to Sierra Leone to found a local NCBWA branch, the National Council of Sierra Leone (NCSL), which became the country's first official political party. As the NCSL leader, Bankole-Bright intensified his criticism of the colonial administration and demanded African participation in the Legislative and Executive councils, which had always been dominated by Europeans. By 1924 his activism had succeeded in getting Bankole-Bright and a few other Western-educated Africans elected to the Legislative Council. They then began to clamor for representation in the Executive Council.

Bankole-Bright was also a champion of colony-PROTECTORATE separation in Sierra Leone's national politics. Accordingly, when the British colonial governor brought some traditional rulers from the protectorate region into the Legislative Council, Bankole-Bright and the KRIO council members objected. This rejection of people from the interior sowed the seeds of a bitter conflict between the Krios of the colony proper and indigenous Africans from the interior, which still had protectorate status. Traditional leaders and some Western-educated elites from the protectorate formed their own organizations to counter the Krio-dominated NCSL. The rift between the two segments of Sierra Leone society led to the founding of Sierra Leone's second political party, the Sierra Leone Peoples Party (SLPP), in 1951. Rivalry between the NCSL and SLPP continued until the late 1950s, when Bankole-Bright died and the NCSL went into decline.

See also: COLONIALISM, INFLUENCE OF (Vol. IV); CUMMINGS-JOHN, CONSTANCE (Vols. IV, V); ENGLAND AND

AFRICA (Vols. III, IV, V); NATIONALISM AND INDEPENDENCE MOVEMENTS (Vol. IV); PAN-AFRICANISM (Vols. IV, V); POLITICAL PARTIES AND ORGANIZATIONS (Vols. IV, V).

Barghash, ibn Said (c. 1833–1888) *Third sultan of Zanzibar*

Barghash was a son of Sayyid Said (1791–1856), the BUSAIDI sultan of Oman who, by 1840, had transferred his government to the island of ZANZIBAR. Upon Said's death one of his sons became the ruler of Oman, and another son, Majid bin Said (c. 1835–1870), became the *sayyid,* or sultan, of Zanzibar. Barghash disputed Majid's succession, but Majid had the support of the British consul. As a result, in 1859 Barghash was exiled to Bombay, India.

Barghash's two-year residence in the principal commercial center of British-ruled India enabled him to establish important contacts with Indian commercial and financial interests. He later used these contacts to his benefit in expanding Zanzibar.

Upon Majid's death, in 1870, Barghash became the third Busaidi sultan of Zanzibar. He extended the commercial empire in East Africa that his two predecessors had established. Its economic foundations were the booming SLAVE TRADE, which the British government opposed, and the IVORY TRADE. Among its holdings were the Arab plantations of the SWAHILI COAST that depended on enslaved labor to produce CASH CROPS such as cloves.

The obstacles that Barghash's territorial ambitions faced, however, were too great to overcome. First of all, although Arab traders, such TIPPU TIP (c. 1830–1905), were based in Zanzibar, they did not wish to be under the political control of its sultan. Second, strong African rulers, such as MIRAMBO (c. 1840–1884), also had no wish to submit to Busaidi rule. The third and greatest source of obstacles, however, came from the colonizing efforts of Britain and Germany.

Starting from the time they ruled Oman, the Busaidi sultans had close diplomatic relations with the British Empire. By the 1870s, however, the British consul to Zanzibar, Sir John KIRK (1832–1922), was increasing pressure on Barghash to adhere to the anti-slave-trade treaties that Barghash had signed. Because the slave trade was crucial to the Zanzibari economy, tensions mounted.

The German government asserted sovereignty over the region that was to become its colony of GERMAN EAST AFRICA, basing its claims on the treaties with mainland rulers that German explorer Karl PETERS (1856–1918) had collected in 1884. Barghash succumbed to the mounting pressure, and in 1885 he abandoned his territorial claims on the mainland, concentrating instead on governing Zanzibar. In 1890, two years after Barghash's death, Britain declared Zanzibar a PROTECTORATE.

See also: BRITAIN AND AFRICA (Vol. IV); COLONIAL CONQUEST (Vol. IV); GERMANY AND AFRICA (Vol. IV).

Barotseland

Province of western NORTHERN RHODESIA (present-day ZAMBIA). The region runs about 120 miles (193 km) along the Zambezi River, within its great flood plain. It was inhabited by the LOZI people, as they are currently known, one of the major ethnic groups in Zambia. (Lozi was the name given to the Luyi people by Kololo invaders, who came from the south in the first half of the 19th century.) The Lozi occupied Barotseland as far back as the 1600s.

The Kololo ruled from about 1838 until 1864, when the Lozi reestablished their control of the region. The Barotse kingdom had at least two centuries of established governmental and political organization as well as courts that had the power to enforce the laws. At its highest state of expansion in the 1800s, Barotseland extended into SOUTHERN RHODESIA (present-day ZIMBABWE). In 1890 Lubosi LEWANIKA (1845–1916), the king of the Lozi, negotiated a treaty with Cecil RHODES (1853–1902) of the BRITISH SOUTH AFRICA COMPANY that later brought the Lozi territory under the control of the British colonial administration. Barotseland was governed as part of Northern Rhodesia from 1924 to 1964, at which time it became a province of Zambia when that country gained its independence from Britain.

See also: COLONIAL RULE (Vol. IV); ENGLAND AND AFRICA (Vols. IV, V); PARTITION (Vol. IV).

Barth, Heinrich (1821–1865) *German explorer*

Born in Hamburg, Germany, Barth graduated from the University of Berlin, where he studied law, history, geography, and archaeology. He also studied Arabic in London. His initial experiences as an explorer came while traveling in Spain, EGYPT, and Palestine.

In 1850 Barth was invited by British missionary James Richardson (1806–1851) to join the expedition that ultimately made him one of the greatest explorers of Africa. Along with Adolf Overweg (1822–1852), a German geologist, Richardson and Barth set out to explore the area between Lake Chad and the Niger River in West Africa, in what is today the countries of CHAD and NIGER. The expedition was intended to establish a stronger connection with the Sefuwa kings of KANEM-BORNU, which had well-established trade and diplomatic relations with the Ottoman Empire. They also were hoping to conduct scientific studies and to help end the Saharan SLAVE TRADE.

The explorers began their journey in TRIPOLI, in present-day LIBYA, which was the northern terminus of the major trade route across the central Sahara desert. During the arduous Sahara crossing, Richardson died, leaving Barth to head the expedition. In 1851 Barth and Overweg reached KANO, one of the principal HAUSA city-states of northern NIGERIA. At this time it was one of the emirates of the SOKOTO CALIPHATE. They then proceeded to explore Kanem-Bornu territory around Lake Chad. In 1852 Overweg died, leaving Barth to journey on alone. He pressed on through the Sahel—the border of the Sahara—to the city of TIMBUKTU in present-day Republic of MALI. Weak and in failing health, Barth returned to Tripoli, in 1855, along the same route. He was only the second European since the Frenchman René Caillie (1799–1838) to have survived the trek to Timbuktu and back.

Through the course of his travels, Barth, who already spoke French, English, Arabic, and his native German, became familiar with several African languages, including West African Hausa, Songhai, Fulfulde (the FULANI language), and Kanuri (the Nilo Saharan language of Kanem-Bornu), as well as a number of TUAREG dialects. His linguistic studies established Barth as a pioneer in the scientific study of African languages.

In 1857–58 Barth published his experiences and findings in a massive, five-volume compendium entitled *Travels and Discoveries in North and Central Africa*, now considered a landmark work of geographic and anthropologic research. After his epic journey Barth never returned to Africa, dying in Berlin in 1865.

See also: HAUSA STATES (Vol. II, III); SAHARA (Vols. I, II); SAHEL (Vol. I); TUAREGS (Vol. I, II, III).

Basutoland Independent African kingdom surrounded by SOUTH AFRICA. Basutoland was the home of the SOTHO-speaking people known as the Sotho (-*suto* and -*sotho* are pronounced the same way). During the colonial era the country was the British PROTECTORATE that became independent LESOTHO (the country of the Sotho), in 1966.

Basutoland was forged largely through the efforts of Mshweshwe (1786–1870), the chief of the Sotho Kwena clan who ruled as king from 1823 to 1870. From Thaba Bosiu, his virtually impregnable mountain stronghold, Mshweshwe welcomed to his kingdom the many refugees displaced by the ZULU Mfecane (The Crushing) in return for their allegiance. He negotiated shrewdly with the British government and Boer settlers anxious to dispossess him and his people of their lands. During his long reign, which lasted from 1823 to 1870, he managed to hold his kingdom together despite intense pressure from encroaching BOERS. Even so, his kingdom lost much of its land, and it became incorporated into the ORANGE FREE STATE when that Boer republic was created, in 1854.

Because the Sotho were constantly embroiled in border skirmishes with their Boer neighbors, Mshweshwe appealed to British Queen Victoria (1819–1901) for protection. In

1868 Basutoland finally became a British protectorate. One year after Mshweshwe's death, however, it was annexed by the CAPE COLONY. Resistance toward Cape Colony rule erupted in the Gun War of 1880–81, which resulted from the attempt by Cape authorities to confiscate the guns of the Sotho and sell off their lands to white farmers. In 1884 Basutoland reverted to direct British control, this time with the status of a British High Commission Territory, an arrangement under which the Sotho people exercised considerable political autonomy over internal affairs.

During the latter half of the 19th century, the so-called MINERAL REVOLUTION of South Africa, which involved the discovery of unprecedented deposits of GOLD and DIAMONDS, transformed the economy of Basutoland. The MINING communities that sprang up in South Africa provided ready markets for Basutoland's agricultural produce as well as its renowned ponies. Also, it was common for Sotho men to labor in the mines or on white farms and send portions of their wages back to their families in Basutoland.

Throughout the 20th century Basutoland's economy continued to be intricately tied to South Africa's. In 1910 Basutoland narrowly averted being annexed to South Africa when the provinces of that country united as the UNION OF SOUTH AFRICA. Along with the other two High Commission Territories, BECHUANALAND and SWAZILAND, Basutoland remained under direct British rule. In 1959 a new constitution for Basutoland was approved, providing for an elected legislature and extending the country a greater measure of political autonomy. Basutoland returned to full independence as the Kingdom of Lesotho in 1966, led by King Mshweshwe II (1938–1996) and the prime minister, Chief Leabua JONATHAN (1914–   ).

See also: AFRIKANER REPUBLICS (Vol. IV); ENGLAND AND AFRICA (Vols. III, V); MFECANE (Vol. III); MINERALS AND METALS (Vols. IV, V); MSHWESHWE (Vol. III); THABA BOSIU (Vol. III).

Baya (Gbaya) Ethnic and LANGUAGE group of the present-day countries of NIGERIA, CAMEROON, the CENTRAL AFRICAN REPUBLIC, and the Republic of the CONGO. The Baya language is spoken by nearly 300,000 people, mostly in Cameroon. The Baya people are mostly subsistence farmers. While their primary farming areas are arable, the agricultural demands placed on the land are high, and when land becomes unproductive the Baya quickly migrate from place to place as a coping strategy. The fluid social divisions among the Baya, which cut across clan identities, contribute to their migratory patterns.

The Baya were highly influential in shaping the state of Cameroon, in both the colonial and independent eras. In 1928 brutal French rule in the Upper-Sangha region led to a massive three-year insurrection known as the Kongo Wara (the War of the Hoe Handle). The decentralized social structure of the Baya made them difficult for the French to contain. The result was a stronger French presence that remained in the region until 1981, well after Cameroon gained its independence, in 1960. Kongo Wara played an important role in bringing together support for NATIONALISM AND INDEPENDENCE MOVEMENTS in Cameroon and neighboring countries.

See also: ETHNIC GROUP (Vol. I).

Further reading: Philip Burnham, *Opportunity and Constraint in a Savanna Society: the Gbaya of Meiganga, Cameroon* (London: Academic Press, 1980).

Bechuanaland The British colonial entity that upon independence, in 1966, became the country of BOTSWANA. The landlocked territory of Bechuanaland was a vast, semiarid expanse measuring approximately 231,800 square miles (600,400 sq km). When the British declared the area a PROTECTORATE, in 1885, it was home to several TSWANA chiefdoms.

The "chuana" part of the word Bechuanaland is an alternative spelling based on the pronunciation of Tswana. Botswana, in the Tswana language, means "land of the Tswana people." Batswana refers to the Tswana people collectively.

In the early 1880s two small AFRIKANER REPUBLICS, Stellaland and Goshen, were pushing north into the southern Tswana area. British colonial interests, concerned with the German colonial presence in SOUTH WEST AFRICA (present-day NAMIBIA), sought to prevent the BOERS (later called AFRIKANERS) from blocking what they saw as their road from the southern coast into the interior. Thus in, 1885, Britain annexed the Tswana chiefdoms, with the Tswana area south of the Molopo River becoming the colony of British Bechuanaland. Ten years later this southern portion was incorporated directly into the CAPE COLONY, and the area north of the Molopo River became the Bechuanaland Protectorate.

About the same time, the *kgosi*, or king, KHAMA III (1835–1923) and two other principal Tswana kings traveled to England and successfully lobbied to prevent the colonialist Cecil RHODES (1853–1902) and his BRITISH SOUTH AFRICA COMPANY from annexing the protectorate to the new colony of SOUTHERN RHODESIA (modern-day ZIMBABWE).

Once the UNION OF SOUTH AFRICA was established, in 1910, Bechuanaland became, along with BASUTOLAND and SWAZILAND, a High Commission Territory under the direct administration of Britain's High Commissioner to SOUTH AFRICA. The British colonial administration basi-

cally neglected Bechuanaland, and, indeed, the administrative capital, Mafeking, actually was located south of the Molopo River in South Africa.

At independence Bechuanaland became Botswana, and was one of the continent's poorest countries. Unlike the African population of neighboring South Africa, however, Botswana's inhabitants had largely retained possession of their land and other resources. In the long run this, along with the discovery of DIAMONDS, enabled Botswana to become one of the most prosperous and stable countries on the continent.

See also: COLONIAL CONQUEST (Vol. IV); COLONIAL RULE (Vol. IV); COLONIALISM, INFLUENCE OF (Vol. IV); ENGLAND AND AFRICA (Vols. IV, V).

Further reading: Neil Parsons, *King Khama, Emperor Joe, and the Great White Queen: Victorian Britain through African Eyes* (Chicago: University of Chicago Press, 1998); Richard P. Stevens, *Lesotho, Botswana, & Swaziland: the Former High Commission Territories in Southern Africa* (London: Pall Mall Press, 1967).

Belgian Congo From 1908 to 1960, colonial name of today's Democratic Republic of the CONGO. From 1885 to 1908 Belgian Congo was known as the CONGO FREE STATE and was under the personal control of LEOPOLD II (1835–1909), the Belgian king. Measuring nearly a million square miles (2.6 million sq km) and covering the heart of the African continent, the Congo Free State was basically ruled as Leopold's private fiefdom. After the turn of the century reports of the abuse of Africans by both Leopold's agents and those of private CONCESSIONAIRE COMPANIES in the colony caused an international scandal. In 1908, one year before he died, Leopold was forced to turn over the colony to a reluctant Belgian government. It administered the colony until independence was finally granted, in 1960.

See also: BELGIUM AND AFRICA (Vol. IV); CONGO CRISIS (Vol. V); LEOPOLDVILLE (Vol. IV).

Belgium and Africa In the first half of the 19th century the government of Belgium was reluctant to engage in exploration or colonial activity in Africa. A small country sandwiched between France, Germany, the Netherlands, and the North Sea, Belgium was more concerned with defending its own borders in Europe.

However, Belgium's King LEOPOLD II (1835–1909), who succeeded his father to the throne, in 1865, saw in Africa an opportunity to increase his personal fortune. At the BERLIN CONFERENCE (1884–85), Leopold used clever diplomacy and deception to convince the European powers to accept his claim to nearly a million square miles (2.6 million sq km) of densely forested territory in the central African interior.

This photo, taken about 1940, shows an African village in the Belgian Congo. © *Wide World/Library of Congress*

Claiming a humanitarian, "civilizing" agenda, Leopold established the CONGO FREE STATE (today's Democratic Republic of the CONGO). In direct contradiction to his stated aims, however, Leopold instead ran his colony like a private concessionaire company. Although he never set foot in Africa, Leopold encouraged his agents to perpetrate unspeakable atrocities to force the indigenous populations to collect ivory and RUBBER. These products were then exported to Europe for his personal gain. By 1908 reports of the treatment of Africans in the Free State had caused an international scandal, and Leopold was forced to transfer the administration of the Free State to the Belgian government.

From 1908 to 1960 the Belgian government in Brussels ran the BELGIAN CONGO with heavy-handed tactics meant to ensure a profitable export economy. For the most part the Belgian administration succeeded, although other than administration officials and company owners few Belgians settled in the colony.

Despite Belgium's initial reluctance to administer African colonies, after World War I (1914–18), the country lobbied for a League of Nations MANDATE to administer the former German colony of RUANDA-URUNDI. There, the Belgian administration attempted to divide the population along ethnic lines in order to make it easier to govern. As a result, a minority ethnic group, the TUTSI, was promoted into a leadership role over the majority HUTU group. The Tutsi, who are generally lighter-skinned and taller than the Hutu, were given social and economic privileges not offered to the Hutu. Ethnic tensions between the two groups still rage today.

In an attempt to prepare the people in their African colonies for westernized, industrial development, the Belgian administration began to establish elementary schools and medical facilities. This development indicated not a new European altruism but a desire by the Belgian government to develop a minimally educated, relatively healthy work force that could be used to more efficiently extract and export the Congo's NATURAL RESOURCES. Little effort was made to establish secondary schools to improve EDUCATION among the African population.

In the interwar years the Belgian administration continued exporting rubber and also promoted plantation AGRICULTURE for PALM OIL and COFFEE. Nearly all exports passed though the colonial capital and river port city of LEOPOLDVILLE (today's Kinshasa), located on the Congo River. MINING, however, proved to be a more lucrative economic activity. Following discoveries of industrial-quality

DIAMONDS and vast COPPER deposits, Belgian-owned corporations, such as UNION MINIÈRE, quickly developed the mining industry in the Katanga region. Africans provided the labor for the industry, while the profits flowed back to Belgium.

During World War II (1939–45), German forces invaded and occupied Belgium, similar to the situation in France. The Belgian population, which was never fully convinced of the value of its African colonies, now saw that the resources supplied by its colonies would be all that Belgium could contribute to the war effort against Germany.

By the early 1950s Belgium embarked on a gradual 30-year plan to turn over the government of the colony to indigenous leadership. By the end of the decade, however, Congolese nationalists from various ethnic groups were clamoring for self-rule, and the pace of the independence process quickened. Congolese and Belgian leaders convened in Brussels, and in 1960 a new coalition government took control under the leadership of former rivals Joseph Kasavubu (1915–1969) and Patrice LUMUMBA (1925–1961). Despite nationwide independence celebrations, it soon became clear that the Belgian administration had not taken the proper steps to adequately prepare the country for a transfer of leadership. Within months the fledgling nation was plunged into crisis. The threat of civil war forced the evacuation of most of the remaining Belgian nationals.

See also: COLONIAL RULE (Vol. IV); CONCESSIONAIRE COMPANIES (Vol. IV); CONGO CRISIS (Vol. V); WORLD WAR II AND AFRICA (Vol. IV).

Further reading: Marie-Bénédict Dembour, *Recalling the Belgian Congo: Conversations and Introspection* (New York: Berghahn Books, 2000).

Bello, Ahmadu (Alhaji; Sir) (1909–1966) *Political leader and premier of Northern Nigeria*

A great grandson of Usman dan Fodio (1754–1817), founder of the Islamic SOKOTO CALIPHATE, Bello was born in Rabah, in northern NIGERIA. After working as a teacher Bello became the district head of Rabah, in 1934. In 1938, after a failed claim to the office of sultan, Bello instead took the honorary title of Sardauna of Sokoto. He also took the position of secretary of the Sokoto Native Authority within the British colonial administration.

In 1949 Bello helped found the Northern People's Congress (NPC) and later became its president. The NPC eventually became the foremost political organization in the predominantly Hausa-Fulani region of Northern Nigeria and a major factor in the movement for Nigerian independence from Britain. Bello went on to become Northern Nigeria's first premier, in 1954, and was one of Nigeria's triad of political leaders, the others being Obafemi AWOLOWO (1909–1987) in YORUBA-dominated Western Nigeria and Nnamdi AZIKIWE (1904–1996) in the largely IGBO region of Eastern Nigeria.

Bello was an active Muslim, as indicated by the honorific title Alhaji (the Pilgrim), meaning he completed the pilgrimage to the Muslim holy city of Mecca. However, Bello was also pro-West, as reflected in the honorific "Sir," which he received when knighted by the British queen. When Bello attempted to establish full Islamic law, or *sharia,* in Northern Nigeria, he was forced to back down after British objections. Bello's personal stance, however, allowed him to install elements of Islamic law without alienating the region's non-Muslim population or antagonizing the British.

In 1957, when the time came to appoint Nigeria's first federal prime minister, Bello preferred to remain premier of the Northern Region. Instead, Bello's NPC deputy, Abubakar Tafawa BALEWA (1912–1966) became the federal prime minister. Upon Nigeria's full independence in 1960, Bello continued his role as Northern premier, focusing on the North's growth and security.

See also: BELLO, AHMADU (Vol. V); ISLAM, INFLUENCE OF (Vols. II, III, IV); NATIONALISM AND INDEPENDENCE MOVEMENTS (Vol. IV); NORTHERN PEOPLE'S CONGRESS (Vol. V); USMAN DAN FODIO (Vol. III).

Further reading: John N. Paden, *Ahmadu Bello Sardauna of Sokoto: Values and Leadership in Nigeria* (London: Hodder and Stoughton, 1986).

Ben Bella, Ahmed (1916–) *First president of Algeria*

Born in Marnia, ALGERIA, into a poor peasant family, Ahmed Ben Bella served in the French army during World War II (1939–45) and reached the rank of master sergeant. He received both the Croix de Guerre and the Medaille Militaire for his valor and exemplary service. Upon returning to Algeria, in 1945, he learned of the harsh treatment that the French meted out at the so-called Sétif Massacre, which resulted in the deaths of thousands of anticolonial demonstrators. Ben Bella thereupon resigned from the French army and joined the Algerian Popular Party. He went on to lead the party's military wing, the Secret Organization (Organisation Secrète, OS), a group of revolutionary fighters who plotted the violent overthrow of COLONIAL RULE.

While many of the founders of the nationalist movement had come from the urban working class and from the peasantry, others, like Ben Bella, came from the ranks of the French military. They sympathized with the nationalists because they had been stationed in rural areas or in working-class districts. In 1948 Ben Bella robbed the Bank at Oran of 3 million francs to finance the OS.

Ben Bella was imprisoned in 1950 following an attack on a post office, but he escaped after two years. In 1953, while living underground in both North Africa and Europe, he was one of the key organizers of the Revolutionary Committee for Unity and Action (CRUA). In 1954 the CRUA evolved into the NATIONAL LIBERATION FRONT (Front de Libération Nationale, FLN), which later led the armed revolt against French rule. Ben Bella solicited and received funds and materials for his independence fighters from President Gamal Abdel NASSER (1918–1970) of EGYPT and President Habib BOURGUIBA (1903–2000) of TUNISIA. The French arrested Ben Bella again in 1956 and imprisoned him for six years. He was released after the signing of the Evian Accords (1962), under which Algeria received its independence. Ben Bella became the new nation's first prime minister.

See also: BEN BELLA, AHMED (Vol. V); FRANCE AND AFRICA (Vols. IV, V); NATIONALISM AND INDEPENDENCE MOVEMENTS (Vol. IV).

Further reading: Robert Merle, *Ahmed Ben Bella* (New York: Walker, 1967).

Benin City City in southern NIGERIA, located on the Benin River; capital of the Edo kingdom of BENIN. Benin City was the principal city within the ancient kingdom of Benin of the Edo people (also known as the Bini) from approximately the 15th through the late 19th centuries. The Edo kingdom, ruled by the *oba*, or king, exerted influence over the YORUBA, IGBO, Ijo, and Itsekiri peoples. The power of the *oba* and his state was symbolized by the massive moat and earth walls of the city, at places 57 feet (17.4 m) high and extending in a seven-mile (11.3 km) perimeter. These main city walls were at the heart of a system of protective walls that covered nearly 90 miles (145 km) of the kingdom.

The kingdom of Benin, which experienced a revival in the early 19th century, had a flourishing trade in PALM OIL, palm kernels, and other agricultural commodities. By the late 19th century, however, British merchants, in league with colonial authorities, were beginning to make deep inroads into kingdom of Benin's commerce. In 1897 Britain sent a diplomatic delegation to pressure Oba OVONRAMWEN (r. 1888–1914) to submit to their authority, but the delegation was ambushed and massacred. A British military force invaded the city in retaliation, setting fire to its buildings and homes. As the city burned many of its famed bronze castings and other works of ART were hauled away as war booty. Much of the art, some of it dating back to the 13th century, was sold to international traders, ending up in museums in England and elsewhere.

During the colonial era Benin City remained a center of Nigeria's palm oil and palm kernels industry, and in 1939 the colonial government set up the Nigerian Institute for Oil Palm Research there. A lumber industry also began to emerge in the 1930s.

Benin's *obas* depicted their history in bronze castings (actually made from brass) in the form of wall plaques. Some of the plaques dated back to the 15th and 16th centuries. The plaques were made using the cire perdu, or "lost-wax," method. The sculptor created a mold from plaster or clay and coated the mold with wax. Then, another coat of plaster or clay, this one perforated, was formed over the wax layer. The mold was then heated, causing the wax to melt and pour out through the perforations. The space that was once filled with wax was then filled with molten metal. Once the metal cooled, the clay or plaster mold was broken off and the metal casting was removed and polished. The technique is still common today.

See also: BRONZE (Vol. II); COLONIAL CONQUEST (Vol. IV); EDO (Vols. I, II); ENGLAND AND AFRICA (Vols. III, IV, V); IJO (Vols. II, III); ITSEKIRI (Vols. II, III); LOST-WAX PROCESS (Vol. II); OBA (Vol. II).

Further reading: A. F. C. Ryder, *Benin and the Europeans, 1485–1897* (New York: Humanities Press, 1969).

Benin, kingdom of Edo-speaking state located to the west of the Niger River in what is now southern NIGERIA; known for its complex ART pieces and success in trade. The origins of the kingdom date back to the 10th century and are intricately intertwined with those of its YORUBA-speaking neighbors. The Yoruba reportedly referred to the Edo-speakers as Ubinu, the name that Portuguese explorers referred to when they named the Bight of Benin. Benin's Oba Ewuare, who ruled from 1440 to 1473, is reported to have changed the name of the country to Edo. Edo-speakers referred to themselves as *Ovbiedo* (children of Edo) rather than the European name *Bini*.

The kingdom of Benin flourished between the 15th and 17th centuries, encompassing southeastern Yorubaland and some IBO territory on the east bank of the Niger River. Although it declined after that, the kingdom retained some of its power in the 18th and early 19th centuries through its involvement with European legitimate trade as well as the SLAVE TRADE. By 1807, however, the British abolition of the slave trade—combined with internal power struggles for the title of *oba*, or king—contributed to Benin's eventual decline. The kingdom remained a trading force throughout most of the 19th century, however, with the focus of commercial activity switching from human captives to goods such as PALM OIL and ivory.

During the latter half of the 19th century the British increased their demand for West Africa's natural resources, including palm oil, which was used as an industrial lubricant, and RUBBER, which became an important commodity after the development of the inflatable inner tube. Rich in both of these commodities, Benin became the target of British efforts to seize territory for its colonial empire.

In January 1897, followers of the reigning *oba,* OVONRAMWEN (r. 1888–1914), ambushed a British force that was sent to establish official colonial sovereignty over Benin. The attack shocked the British, who by mid-February had assembled upwards of 1,500 soldiers for a raid on the kingdom's capital, BENIN CITY. Despite fierce opposition, the British force eventually overwhelmed the kingdom's defenses, and the city fell on February 18, 1897. Initially Oba Ovonramwen escaped, but he was later captured and exiled to Calabar in southeastern Nigeria. Thereafter the kingdom of Benin was considered part of British colonial Nigeria.

During the siege on Benin City British soldiers set fire to the royal palaces and looted the city's many impressive sculptures and carvings made from bronze, ivory, and iron. The most prized of these were the brass busts that were constructed in tribute to each *oba.* Other artisan works stolen included intricate tapestries, bas-reliefs, and masks made of wood. The fire also destroyed a great deal of the intricate wood carvings in the royal palace. Much of the plundered art was then sold at auction by the British to offset the expenses of the war with Benin.

The kingdom of DAHOMEY, to the west of the kingdom of Benin, also flourished in the 17th through the 19th centuries. However, by 1904 Dahomey had become a colony of French West Africa. In 1960 Dahomey gained its independence from France and in 1975 changed its name from Dahomey to the People's Republic of Benin. So, although they are essentially unrelated, the modern-day country of Benin honors the former kingdom of the same name.

See also: BENIN, KINGDOM OF (Vols. II, III); COLONIAL CONQUEST (Vol. IV); ENGLAND AND AFRICA (Vol. IV).

Benin (Republic of) Country located on the Gulf of Guinea, bordered by BURKINA FASO and NIGER to the north, NIGERIA to the east, and TOGO to the west. The Republic of Benin covers approximately 43,500 square miles (112,700 sq km) and has a coastline about 75 miles (121 km) long.

The region of present-day Benin and Togo was long dominated by groups descended from the Aja kingdom. The large kingdom of DAHOMEY, in Benin, came about from the consolidation of the related Aja kingdoms of Abomey, Allada, and Ardra. Dahomey became wealthy from the SLAVE TRADE by acting as intermediary in the trading of captives to Europeans on the Guinea Coast throughout the 17th and 18th centuries. However, as that trade declined in the 19th century, Dahomey became increasingly dependent on trading PALM OIL, corn, and other agricultural commodities with Europeans.

About 1863 King Toffa (d. 1908) of Ardra, a kingdom known to Europeans as Porto Novo, signed a protection treaty with France, and his territory became an administrative center for spreading French colonial influence. By 1883 the French occupied much of the Dahomey kingdom. At the BERLIN CONFERENCE (1884–85), the other European powers recognized France's claims to the Dahomey region.

Benin during the Colonial Era: Dahomey Led by King Behanzin (d. 1906), Dahomey went to war with France in 1889–90 and again in 1892, both times seeking to limit France's influence in its territory. Despite a large army—which included upwards of 4,000 well-trained women warriors—Dahomey was unable to resist superior French firepower, and in 1892 France declared the PROTECTORATE of Dahomey. To quell possible uprisings, the French exiled Behanzin to the island of Martinique in the West Indies. With the opposition effectively removed, in 1894 the protectorate was declared a colony. Porto Novo became the colonial capital in part because of the support King Toffa had provided the French in the war against Dahomey.

One of the more prominent leaders of PAN-AFRICANISM in Paris after World War I was Prince Kojo Tovalou-Houénou (d. 1938), a nephew of the exiled Dahomean king Behanzin. A respected author and scholar, Tovalou-Houénou founded a pro-African organization he called the Universal League for the Defense of the Black Race.

In 1899 France incorporated Dahomey into the colonial confederation called FRENCH WEST AFRICA (Afrique Occidentale Française, AOF). As it did in its other West African colonies, France developed Dahomey's ports and railroads in order to facilitate the extraction of the region's valuable agricultural products. In the case of Dahomey, the crucial commodity was PALM OIL, which was used as an industrial lubricant in Europe. French companies built a port at Cotonou and constructed railroads to connect towns in the central and northern hinterlands with Porto Novo and Cotonou on the coast; the main line was completed by 1911.

The cost of development in the colony was paid by the taxes that the administration collected from Dahomean laborers who were forced to work on French projects. Although social development was not a priority of the French colonial administration, French Roman Catholic MISSIONARIES did establish elementary schools for the purpose of teaching French customs and LANGUAGE to select Dahomean students.

France's efforts to recruit Africans for military service in its colonial West African army, the TIRAILLEURS SÉNÉGALAIS, led to a popular revolt during World War I (1914–18) in northern Dahomey. The revolt was brutally suppressed, and Dahomean soldiers ultimately participated in the conquest of TOGOLAND (present-day Togo), the German colony to the west.

Joining Africans from other colonies in French West Africa, Dahomean soldiers fought on the side of the Free French during World War II (1939–45). Following the victory of France and the Allies, Dahomey became a member state of the FRENCH UNION, in 1946. This new arrangement allowed the country to elect its own representatives to the French Parliament.

When African independence movements forced the French Union to disband in 1958, Dahomey chose to become a self-governing polity within the French Community. For two years Dahomean political leaders struggled to achieve complete independence from France, finally accomplishing their goal, in 1960. The former colony officially became the independent Republic of Dahomey, with Hubert MAGA (1916–2000), a northerner representing the Dahomean Democratic Movement, elected as its first president. Maga's election did little to unite the disparate elements of Dahomey's population, however, and the nation was soon racked with political instability that continued into the 1970s.

In 1975 the Republic of Dahomey was renamed the People's Republic of Benin. The new appellation recalled the glory of the once-powerful Edo kingdom of BENIN, which was located in present-day Nigeria.

See also: ABOMEY (Vol. III); AJA (Vols. II, III); ALLADA (Vols. II, III); BENIN, REPUBLIC OF (Vols. I, II, III, V); COLONIAL RULE (Vol. IV); COLONIALISM, INFLUENCE OF (Vol. IV); FRANCE AND AFRICA (Vols. III, IV, V); PORTO NOVO (Vol. III).

Further reading: Patrick Manning, Slavery, Colonialism, and Economic Growth in Dahomey, 1640–1960 (New York: Cambridge University Press, 1982).

Berbers   Descendants of the peoples who inhabited North Africa before the Arab conquest in the seventh century. Berbers have long had a strong presence in MOROCCO and the central Sahara. Today numbering approximately 12 million, Berbers can essentially be divided into two groups: those living near the coast, who consider themselves Arabs and speak Arabic, and those living in the interior, who preserve their traditional languages and culture. From 1850 to 1960 Berbers living in the inaccessible and mountainous Kabylia region of ALGERIA and the RIF region of Morocco were among those who fiercely resisted European COLONIAL CONQUEST and imperialism.

See also: BERBERS (Vols. I, II, III); MAGHRIB (Vol. IV); TUAREGS (Vol. IV).

Further reading: Michael Brett, The Berbers (Oxford, U.K.: Blackwell, 1996).

Berlin Conference   International meeting, held from November 15, 1884 to February 26, 1885, that effectively divided vast amounts of African territory among major European powers. For centuries Europeans had dealt with Africa, engaging in everything from exploration to the trade in captives to religious conversion. For the most part, however, those activities had been confined to a limited area, typically along Africa's coastlines. As of 1875 merely one-tenth of Africa, mostly in the northern and southern extremities of the continent, had been claimed by European nations as colonies or PROTECTORATES.

The last quarter of the 19th century, however, saw an almost unchallenged rise in colonialist spirit among the European powers. Fueled in some cases by conservative governments seeking the status of empires and, in others, by a desire for wealth and commerce, European countries began to press for territorial expansion into the interior of Africa. As a result, by the 1870s, European governments had begun to fear that competition—or even more intense rivalries—in Africa might lead to unwanted conflicts in Europe itself. These governments, led by Otto von BISMARCK (1815–1898), the chancellor of the newly united Germany, met in Berlin to find a peaceful blueprint for colonial occupation of Africa.

The immediate cause of the conference came from Belgian activity in the Congo and Niger river basins. On behalf of his International African Association, Belgian king LEOPOLD II (1835–1909) sent Henry Morton STANLEY (1841–1904) on several expeditions into the Congo. By 1884 Portugal was worried that this Belgian expansion would threaten its long-standing position in ANGOLA, south of the mouth of the Congo River. With the help of Britain, a Portuguese-British commission was established to supervise activity along the Congo River. Fearing that his efforts in the Congo would be blocked by these old-line colonial powers, Leopold II appealed to Bismarck for help. The Berlin Conference, to which all major European powers and the United States sent representatives, was the response. Tellingly, no African state was represented.

Ostensibly the conference was to be concerned with humanitarian issues such as limiting the trade in human captives. In truth, however, the primary motive was carving up the vast amount of African territory that remained in the hands of African peoples. Over the course of many months the delegates forged an agreement that, in effect, created rules for colonial expansion. In doing so they divided Africa into a hodgepodge of zones of influence and even "nations"—regardless of original boundaries or of ethnic makeup—that lasted for decades and enabled European exploitation to continue without the threat of conflict closer to home.

The primary rules for colonial expansion created at the conference concerned "spheres of influence" and "effective occupation." A sphere of influence was simply an area along the coast that one of the conference members told the other conference members it had taken under its control. And under the agreements of the conference, taking control of a coastal area gave that particular European government power of virtually all the land directly linked to that area. This created corridors of territory, all of which would have access to the sea. The doctrine of effective occupation meant that in order to claim a particular territory a member of the conference had to have enough control of a region to insure trade and freedom of movement. This, the members believed, would eliminate conflicts between the conference members over particular territories.

The dash to accumulate colonies began with the signing of the Treaty of Berlin at the end of the conference. In addition to giving Leopold II full power over the Congo, the treaty clearly signaled the European powers that they could begin to take over the remainder of the continent. Virtually all of the conference members ultimately joined in the land grab. By 1900, for example, Britain had added of 4.25 million square miles (11 million sq km) to its empire, France had taken 3.5 million square miles (9.1 million sq km), Germany had gained one million square miles (2.6 million sq km), and even Italy had added 185,000 square miles (480,000 sq km). Indeed, by 1898 the only independent states south of the Sahara were LIBERIA, ETHIOPIA, and the two AFRIKANER REPUBLICS of the ORANGE FREE STATE and the TRANSVAAL.

Although all of this was accomplished, from the Europeans' perspective, with a minimum of conflict, it left a bitter legacy that marked Africa well into the 21st century.

See also: COLONIAL CONQUEST (Vol. IV); COLONIAL RULE (Vol. IV); ENGLAND AND AFRICA (Vols. III, IV); FRANCE AND AFRICA (Vols. III, IV); GERMANY AND AFRICA (Vol. IV); ITALY AND AFRICA (Vol. IV); PARTITION (Vol. IV); PORTUGAL AND AFRICA (Vols. III, IV); SPAIN AND AFRICA (Vol. V); UNITED STATES AND AFRICA (Vol. IV).

Further reading: S. E. Crowe, *The Berlin West African Conference* (Westport, Conn.: Greenwood, 1981).

Beta Israel Jewish people of ETHIOPIA. Isolated from the rest of the world's Jewish population, the Beta Israel (House of Israel) and their plight in largely Christian Ethiopia were finally acknowledged by the international Jewish community in the mid-1800s.

Though their origins are uncertain, the Beta Israel are known to be an ancient people whose history began well before Semitic farmers arrived in the region around 600 BCE. Religious warfare between the Beta Israel and the Christian Ethiopian monarchy spanned centuries until the 1700s, when the Beta Israel were fully defeated and forced to settle in the Lake Tana region in northwestern Ethiopia. Their situation within Ethiopia began to improve in the late 19th century.

Ethiopian Christians traditionally believed the Beta Israel to be possessors of evil magic, particularly the ability to transform into hyenas for the purposes of devouring Christian children. The status of the Beta Israel as a persecuted religious minority led them to be called *Falasha*, meaning "exiles" or "outsiders," a name now considered to be pejorative.

In 1769 the Scottish explorer James Bruce (1730–1794) documented the Beta Israel, estimating their population to be around 100,000. In spite of this the Beta Israel were virtually unknown to much of the world until the Jewish scholar Joseph Halevy became the first European Jew to visit the Beta Israel, in 1867. His pupil Jacques Faitlovitch (1881–1955) took up the Beta Israel cause in 1904, establishing Beta Israel committees in a number of countries and taking a number of the Beta Israel to Europe for education. In 1908 the rabbis of 44 countries acknowledged the Beta Israel as authentic Jews.

Between 1935 and 1941 the Beta Israel joined other Ethiopians in resisting the Italian invasion and occupation of Ethiopia. By 1955 the new nation of Israel had become involved with the Ethiopian Jews, helping to build schools and a seminary.

See also: BETA ISRAEL (Vols. I, II, III, V); JUDAISM (Vol. I); RELIGION (Vols. III, IV, V).

Bismarck, Otto von (1815–1898) *First chancellor of the united German Reich*

Son of a member of the landowning Junker aristocracy, by 1862 Otto von Bismarck had risen to become the prime minister of his native Prussia. Germany at the time was not a single country but rather a group of independent kingdoms, and Prussia was the most powerful of them. In 1871 German unity became a reality when the German princes, at Bismarck's instigation, proclaimed William I (1797–1888) the German emperor and established the German Reich. The archconservative Bismarck was the first chancellor, holding that post from 1871 to 1890. By 1884, the first year of the BERLIN CONFERENCE, at which the nations of Europe met to discuss the PARTITION of Africa, Germany had established itself as the major power of continental Europe.

Bismarck was under pressure from German merchants to find new markets for German goods and secure cheap sources of raw materials. As France and Britain extended their colonial empires into Africa and Asia, Bismarck feared that German traders would be denied access to those areas and the country would face the loss of money and prestige.

Bismarck sought to solidify Germany's position in Europe, and this became one of his primary goals at the Berlin Conference. Fourteen years earlier Prussia had vanquished France in the short Franco-Prussian War of 1870–71, and France's national pride remained wounded. Bismarck moved to soothe the French by encouraging France's colonial expansion and by obstructing her main colonial rival, Britain. Consequently, Bismarck claimed areas adjacent to territories where British influence and presence was growing. This move had the double effect of hindering British expansion and placating German mercantile interests. In 1884 and 1885, for example, he announced the establishment of German protectorates in GERMAN EAST AFRICA (present-day mainland TANZANIA, BURUNDI, and RWANDA), CAMEROON, and TOGOLAND (today's TOGO), as well as in the South Pacific. These colonies became important sources of raw materials for the German economy, especially PALM OIL, COTTON, COFFEE, COCOA, and RUBBER.

See also: COLONIAL CONQUEST (Vol. IV) GERMANY AND AFRICA (Vol. IV).

Further reading: Edgar Feuchtwanger, *Bismarck* (New York: Routledge, 2002).

Blaize, Richard Beale (1845–1904) *Prominent West African businessman*

Blaize was born in SIERRA LEONE to YORUBA-speaking, Christian parents who were RECAPTIVES. Like thousands of other recaptive Africans, they settled in FREETOWN after their slave ship had been intercepted by the British Anti-Slave Squadron, based in Freetown. Blaize attended a school operated by the CHURCH MISSIONARY SOCIETY and then began working as a printer. At age 17 he moved to his parents' Yoruba homeland, in NIGERIA, though his parents remained in Freetown for the remainder of their lives. Many other recaptives, or the children of recaptives, such as Samuel JOHNSON (1846–1901), did likewise. Blaize settled in LAGOS, which had come under British control in 1851, and continued working as a printer. He soon became the head printer for the printing press of the colonial government.

In 1875 Blaize left government employment to set up his own business. He had already engaged in small-scale trading, but he now became a full-time retailer and a wholesaler of imported goods from England. He also became involved in the export of such commodities as COTTON, PALM OIL, and palm kernels. Blaize married Emily Cole (d. 1895), whose father, T. F. Cole (1812–1890), was a recaptive who had settled in Lagos and was a leading merchant. His marriage to Cole facilitated his entry into the world of Nigerian commerce, and by the 1890s Blaize was the wealthiest African merchant in Lagos, heading a commercial printing press and becoming involved in the production of several Lagos NEWSPAPERS. Additionally, he was an important figure in local politics, mediating disputes between the British colonial government and the local Egba leadership in ABEOKUTA during the early 20th century.

In part Blaize's success came because, like many of his generation, he was raised and educated in Sierra Leone Colony. This helped him take advantage of the commercial opportunities linked with the rapid expansion of the production of CASH CROPS in West Africa.

By the end of the century, however, the situation was changing. British commercial interests, represented by individuals such as Sir George GOLDIE (1846–1925) and firms such as the ROYAL NIGER COMPANY, were able to squeeze the African merchants out of business. In the first half of the 20th century African participation in commerce came to be characterized by market-level traders, such as Madam Alimotu PELEWURA (1865–1951), rather than businessmen, such as Blaize, who headed large commercial firms.

See also: COLONIALISM, INFLUENCE OF (Vol. IV); ENGLAND AND AFRICA (Vols. III, IV).

Blyden, Edward Wilmot (1832–1912) *Liberian educator, statesman, and author*

Born of free parents in St. Thomas, the Virgin Islands, Blyden claimed IGBO ancestry. When he was 10 he moved to Venezuela. At age 18 he went to the United States to study at Rutgers Theological College in New Jersey, but was denied admission because of his race. In 1851, sponsored by the New York Colonization Society, which promoted the emigration of free Africans and former slaves to Africa, Blyden immigrated to LIBERIA to study at Alexander High School in MONROVIA, the capital.

Among his careers as an adult, Blyden was a minister, a teacher, and an educator. Ordained a Presbyterian minister, in 1858, he became principal of Alexander High School that year. Although self-taught after high school,

Blyden became a scholar. From 1862 to 1871 he was professor of classics at Liberia College. From 1875 to 1877 he served again as principal of Alexander High School. From 1880 to 1884 he returned to Liberia College as president. He resigned from the ministry in 1886.

A champion of African culture and nationalism, Blyden wrote regularly for NEWSPAPERS. From 1855 to 1858 he edited the *Liberia Herald.* In 1872 he founded and edited the *Negro,* published in FREETOWN, SIERRA LEONE, until its demise, in 1873. He cofounded the *West African Reporter* the following year.

Blyden was also called on to serve as a diplomat and politician. In 1861 he was the Liberian educational commissioner to Britain and the United States, and in 1862 he was named Liberia's commissioner to the United States, with the task of encouraging African-American emigration to Liberia. Blyden also served as Liberia's secretary of state and secretary of the interior.

After his presidential aspirations were frustrated in 1885, Blyden went to Syria to learn Arabic, which he later taught at Liberia College. He later divided his time between the colonies of Sierra Leone and NIGERIA. In 1906 he retired to Sierra Leone, where he continued publishing until his death, in 1912.

While Blyden served in many positions and capacities, he also made an important intellectual contribution by writing nonfiction books and pamphlets on Africa and Africans and their history and culture. He rejected the prevalent pseudo-scientific, racial thinking that asserted African inferiority, arguing instead that each race makes its own unique contribution to the world.

Beginning in the 1870s Blyden worked to unify English-speaking West Africans, particularly those living in Liberia and neighboring Sierra Leone. He hoped to establish a union of these two states, which in turn would serve as the nucleus of a larger English-speaking West African state that would promote and protect peoples of African descent everywhere. The ideas he presented in his books made him a precursor of the pan-African movement. These works include *A Voice from Bleeding Africa* (1856); *The Negro in Ancient History* (1869); *Christianity, Islam, and the Negro Race* (1887), considered his major work; *West Africa before Europe* (1905); and *Africa Life and Customs* (1908).

See also: LITERATURE IN COLONIAL AFRICA (Vols. IV, V), NÉGRITUDE, (Vol. IV), PAN-AFRICANISM (Vols. IV, V); UNITED STATES AND AFRICA (Vol. IV).

Further reading: Hollis Ralph Lynch, *Edward Wilmot Blyden* (New York: Oxford University Press, 1967); Hollis R. Lynch, ed., *Selected Letters of Edward Wilmot Blyden* (Millwood, N.Y.: KTO Press, 1978).

Boers Descendants of early European SETTLERS who established communities in portions of SOUTH AFRICA. Boers are descended from the Dutch, French Huguenot, and German settlers who arrived in the CAPE TOWN area of present-day South Africa as early as 1652. After Britain's annexation of the CAPE COLONY, in 1806, many Boers were vexed by British rule. Eventually, during the 1830s and 1840s, thousands of Boers began emigrating east in what came to be called the Great Boer Trek. As a result of their migration, the Boers established communities in what became the Republic of NATAL, the ORANGE FREE STATE, and the TRANSVAAL (also known as the South African Republic).

Though the indigenous populations of these regions fought the foreign encroachment, these *voortrekkers* (pioneers) eventually succeeded in displacing the indigenous African peoples already residing in the interior of southern Africa. Led by Andries Pretorius (1799–1853), the Boers combined military successes with a Calvinistic belief that they were God's chosen people, giving rise to a unique form of Boer, or Afrikaner, nationalism. Continued tensions between Boer settlers and the British colonial administration in southern Africa led to armed conflicts, first in 1880–81, and again in the ANGLO-BOER WAR of 1899– 1902, a brutal conflict won by the British.

The term *Boer* literally means "farmer," when translated from Dutch or AFRIKAANS. Because the word took on pejorative connotations during the decades of Anglo-Boer conflict, Boers came to identify themselves as AFRIKANERS by the end of the 19th century.

Following their defeat, the AFRIKANER REPUBLICS were incorporated into the UNION OF SOUTH AFRICA, which was formed in 1910. Despite losing the war, Boer leaders—including former Generals Louis BOTHA (1862–1919), J. B. M. HERTZOG, (1866–1942), and Jan Christiaan SMUTS (1870–1950)—held prominent positions in South Africa's early government. Continuing their legacy, Boer politicians dominated in South Africa until 1994, when the nation's black majority was first allowed to vote.

See also: BOERS (Vol. III); ENGLAND AND AFRICA (Vols. III, IV, V); GREAT BOER TREK (Vol. III).

Bondelswarts A NAMA community inhabiting southern NAMIBIA. The Bondelswarts suffered brutal repression by the German and South African governments when Namibia was colonial SOUTH WEST AFRICA. The German name *Bondelswarts* derived from the black band that adorned the heads of men entering battle. They had a reputation as a proud and independent nomadic people, grazing cattle and goats. The Bondelswarts actively resisted German colonial control, rebelling in 1896, and again from 1903 to 1906. SOUTH AFRICA took control of South West Africa as part of a League of Nations MANDATE after Germany lost its African colonies following World War I (1914–1918).

In 1922 the Bondelswarts initiated a rebellion against South African rule, prompted by a combination of incursions by white farmers, harsh police treatment, the incarceration of a popular leader, and most importantly, the imposition of a higher tax on hunting dogs. The exorbitant tax threatened their livelihood as hunters and was meant to intentionally pressure them into accepting wage LABOR work on white-owned farms. The South African government recruited about 400 whites near Windhoek to provide support for the police.

On May 26, 1922 the Bondelswarts were attacked at Guruchas by a force equipped with machine guns and two airplanes, which were used to bomb the Bondelswart forces. More than 100 Bondelswarts were killed, although approximately 200 men escaped. The following day the South African forces captured Bondelswarts women, children, and livestock. On June 8, 1922, at Berg Kramer, another attack resulted in an additional 53 Bondelswart deaths, putting an end to the rebellion.

The overwhelming force that the South Africans brought to bear against the Bondelswarts is revealed in the number of white casualties resulting from the conflict. Although more than 150 Bondelswarts were killed, not including women and children, and hundreds of others wounded, only two South Africans died in combat. The South African treatment of the Bondelswarts attracted international attention and resulted in the League of Nations appointing a commission of inquiry to investigate.

See also: GERMANY AND AFRICA (Vol. IV); LEAGUE OF NATIONS AND AFRICA (Vol. IV); RESISTANCE AND REBELLION (Vol. IV).

Covered wagons, like the one seen in an undated photo, were a part of Boer life on the South African frontier. © A. J. Bowland/New York Times

Botha, Louis (1862–1919) *Afrikaner general and the first prime minister of the Union of South Africa (1910–19)*

Louis Botha was born in Greytown, NATAL, on September 27, to a farming family that had participated in the Great Boer Trek into the South African interior. Beginning in 1886 he served as native commissioner in SWAZILAND and then entered the TRANSVAAL Parliament in 1897. Rising to the rank of general during the ANGLO-BOER WAR (1899–1902), Botha effectively employed guerrilla tactics against the British. He was instrumental in bringing the war to an end, accomplished through the Treaty of VEREENIGING.

In the war's aftermath Botha emerged as an able politician renowned for his conciliatory approach to controversial issues. In 1904 he became chairman of the Afrikaner political party Het Volk (the People), and three years later he became the first prime minister of the Transvaal colony. Upon the formation of the UNION OF SOUTH AFRICA, in 1910, he became its first prime minister.

Although he was an Afrikaner himself, Botha ultimately lost political ground to more adamant Afrikaner nationalists. This was caused by attempts to retain strong ties with the British Empire and to reconcile AFRIKANERS and English-speaking whites. In 1913–14 Botha further alienated Afrikaners through his strong-armed suppression of a white-mine-workers strike and a rebellion among Afrikaners opposed to South Africa's involvement in World War I (1914–18).

In 1915 Botha led the British and South African forces that conquered German SOUTH WEST AFRICA (today's NAMIBIA). He later represented South Africa at the Paris Peace Conference (1919) in Versailles, France. Botha died later that year while still serving as prime minister.

See also: GREAT BOER TREK (Vol. III).

Botswana Present-day country in southern Africa, bordered by ZIMBABWE to the northeast, SOUTH AFRICA to the southeast and south, NAMIBIA to the west and north, and ZAMBIA to the northeast. Botswana is a landlocked country with a total area of 231,800 square miles (600, 400 sq km). The western portions of Botswana are arid and contain the Kalahari Desert, which forces most of the region's inhabitants to live in the semi-arid east. The country's capital and largest city is Gaborone.

The TSWANA (pronounced "chuana") people, from whom the country got its name, were historically agro-pastoralists, meaning that they were both farmers and cattle herders. Their forebears migrated to the region before the middle of the second millennium, displacing the indigenous SAN hunter-gatherers. European Christian MISSIONARIES arrived in the country in the first half of the 19th century.

Botswana during the Colonial Era: Bechuanaland

In 1885 the British government declared a PROTECTORATE over the Tswana chiefdoms of the region. It was at this time that the area became known as BECHUANALAND. Five years later Britain imposed full COLONIAL RULE over the territory. From 1908 to 1910 the Tswana campaigned against inclusion in a proposed UNION OF SOUTH AFRICA, arguing that they should remain in a protectorate status. In 1910 the independent Union of South Africa was established, but Bechuanaland, along with SWAZILAND and BASUTOLAND (now LESOTHO), became High Commission Territories, administered by Britain's High Commissioner to South Africa. Due largely to its harsh landscape and perceived lack of mineral wealth, Bechuanaland was neglected by the colonial administration. As a reult, it remained a poor country until after its independence a half-century later.

Two years after the Union of South Africa was formed, a regional all-African organization was formed to promote African politics. However, because most political activists preferred British occupation to being incorporated into the Union of South Africa, the establishment of nationalist political parties in Bechuanaland started only in the 1950s. The argument for independence strengthened when South Africa's National Party, promoting the racist system of APARTHEID, won the South African elections in 1948 and 1953.

By 1960 many of Bechuanaland's local chiefs had been deposed by the colonial administration, leading to organized movements among a new generation of Africans poised to take over the country's leadership. Bechuanaland became independent Botswana, in 1966, with Sir Seretse KHAMA (1921–1980) becoming its first president. One year later DIAMONDS were discovered, and the country rapidly became one of the most prosperous in Africa.

See also: BOTSWANA (Vols. I, II, III, V); COLONIAL CONQUEST (Vol. IV); ENGLAND AND AFRICA (Vols. IV, V); GABORONE (Vol. V).

Further reading: Neil Parsons, *King Khama, Emperor Joe, and the Great White Queen: Victorian Britain through African Eyes* (Chicago: University of Chicago Press, 1998).

Bourguiba, Habib (1903–2000) *Tunisian nationalist and first president of independent Tunisia*

Born in Munastir, TUNISIA, during the period of French COLONIAL RULE, Bourguiba attended school in Tunisia before going to France to study law and become a lawyer. Returning home, he founded a nationalist newspaper, *L'Action Tunisienne* (Tunisian Action), and began a series of campaigns aimed at modernizing Tunisian society and defending Islamic cultural values.

Bourguiba joined the DESTOUR (Constitution) PARTY in 1920 but split from it in 1934. With Mahmoud Materi (1909–1972) and other young intellectuals, he formed a more radical version of the party called the Neo-Destour Party, which received the support of the General Confederation of Tunisian Workers. The party and the LABOR union worked together to establish underground cells throughout the country. In 1938 the two groups organized a demonstration over the dismissal of a worker, and a Neo-Destour leader was arrested. A further series of organized street demonstrations led to confrontations in which the police fired on the demonstrators, killing 112 and wounding 62. Bourguiba and other leaders were arrested, and later that year they were taken to France. Bourguiba remained under house arrest in Marseilles until 1943, when he returned to Tunisia.

A loyal supporter of the Free French government of General Charles DE GAULLE (1890–1970) throughout World War II (1939–45), Bourguiba refused to authorize political agitation against the French until the war had been won. His position changed, however, when Tunisians received no tangible reward for supporting France during the war. Consequently, Bourguiba left Tunisia in 1945 to seek international support for his country's independence. At home Tunisian nationalists engaged in targeted violence against the French. In 1950 France finally opened formal negotiations with Bourguiba, but in 1952 arrested him and other Neo-Destour leaders.

In 1955, however, weakened by its losses in the French–Indochina War (1945–54), the escalating Algerian war (1954–62), and the ongoing conflict with the Neo-Destour Party, France offered Bourguiba and Tunisia internal autonomy. Tunisia was to be governed by a bey, or ruler, who would be essentially a figurehead for the French. In keeping with his pragmatic tenet of "Take what you are offered and fight for better," Bourguiba accepted this arrangement.

Bourguiba's decision, however, split the Neo-Destour Party because an opposing faction was willing to settle for nothing less than total independence from France. In 1956 the Bourguiba faction gained an advantage and expelled the opposition leader, Salah ben Youssef (1908–1961), from the party. Bourguiba then purged ben Youssef's supporters, who were mostly young Islamic students or from the urban lower classes and from rural communities. The purge was not well received, and reaction forced Bourguiba to seek French assistance to quell the ensuing insurrection. Working gradually but persistently toward independence, Bourguiba continued negotiations with the French government, and in 1956 he concluded a treaty with France that gave Tunisia its full independence. In July 1957 Bourguiba was elected president.

Later that year Bourguiba inaugurated a Constituent Assembly to draft the country's new constitution. He created a modern, secular state, making Neo-Destour the only recognized political party. By 1959 he was in complete command of the state, exercising broad executive powers. Bourguiba assumed the role of master statesman

Habib Bourguiba, shown here in 1950, was the first president of independent Tunisia. © *New York Times*

and ruled through the cult of personality, with his ever-present photograph a constant reminder of his power.

See also: BOURGUIBA, HABIB (Vol. V); FRANCE AND AFRICA (Vol. IV); NATIONALISM AND INDEPENDENCE MOVEMENTS (Vol. IV).

Further reading: Derek Hopwood, *Habib Bourguiba of Tunisia: The Tragedy of Longevity* (New York: St. Martin's Press, 1992); Norma Salem, *Habib Bourguiba: Islam and the creation of Tunisia* (London: Croom Helm, 1984).

Brazzaville Major river port and capital city of the Republic of the CONGO, located in the southeastern part of the country. In 1883 the small village of Ntamo (also called *Ncuna*) became Brazzaville, three years after after French explorer Pierre Savorgnan DE BRAZZA (1852–1905) signed a treaty with Makoko, the local Teke king,

Strategically located on the north bank of the Congo River, near Malebo Pool, the city was designated the administrative headquarters of the French interests in western Central Africa, in 1903. It then served as the capital of French Equatorial Africa from 1910 to 1958. LEOPOLDVILLE (present-day Kinshasa), which served as the administrative center of the CONGO FREE STATE and, later, the BELGIAN CONGO, was located on the south bank of the pool.

The Malebo Pool marked the beginning of the navigable part of the Upper Congo River and, beyond it, the Congo-Ubangi waterway, which served much of FRENCH EQUATORIAL AFRICA. With the completion of the Congo-Ocean Railway, built between 1921 and 1934, this river shipping route connected the interior to the port at Pointe-Noire, located just north of the Angolan border on the Atlantic coast.

Built using African LABOR, the Congo-Ocean Railway was one of the most costly French colonial projects in terms of human lives lost. Exceptionally dangerous working conditions resulted in an estimated 15,000 to 20,000 deaths among the workers.

Once Brazzaville was established many Europeans moved into the city center, while Africans occupied sections in the northeast and the southwest of the city. During World War II (1939–45), after Germany invaded France, Brazzaville became the African center for the Free France. The French colonial governor, Adolphe-Félix Sylvestie ÉBOUÉ (1884–1944), opposed the Nazis and the puppet Vichy government of France and welcomed the escaped French general Charles DE GAULLE (1890–1970). During the first years of the war de Gaulle made Brazzaville the base for his Free French administration. It could serve this role because it was already the site of a major French military garrison.

In 1944 the heads of state of Africa's Francophone nations met in Brazzaville to call for reforms in the French colonial administration. The Brazzaville Conference, as the meeting became known, served as a starting point for the movement towards the French Congo's independence, which was attained in 1960. Independence did not come, however, without cost. Nationalist political parties were divided along regional lines, and in February 1959 deadly riots between rival parties broke out and continued until the French army intervened.

See also: BRAZZAVILLE (Vol. V); COLONIAL RULE (Vol. IV); CONGO (Vol. III); CONGO RIVER (Vol. I); FRANCE AND AFRICA (Vols. III, IV, V); URBANIZATION (Vols. IV, V); URBAN LIFE AND CULTURE (Vols. IV, V).

Further reading: Phyllis Martin, *Leisure and Society in Colonial Brazzaville* (New York: Cambridge University Press, 2002).

British East Africa Collectively, the British colonies of KENYA, TANGANYIKA, UGANDA, and ZANZIBAR. The origins of British East Africa lay in the imperial rivalries of the 1880s that led to the European PARTITION of Africa and the associated COLONIAL CONQUEST. In 1887 British private citizens formed an association that, the following year, was chartered by the British government as the Imperial British East Africa Company. Its purpose was to limit the expansion of GERMAN EAST AFRICA and to establish British claims to part of the region. An 1890 British-German treaty established both a British PROTECTORATE over Zanzibar and the British East Africa Company's claims to Kenya. In 1894 a British treaty with the kingdom of BUGANDA established the Uganda Protectorate.

In 1895 the British East Africa Company relinquished its territories to Britain, which then established the East African Protectorate. In June 1919, British East Africa became complete, when, under the terms of the Treaty of Versailles, which ended World War I (1914–18), the League of Nations made German East Africa into the British MANDATE of Tanganyika. The following year the East African Protectorate became Kenya Colony.

After World War II (1939–45) Britain coordinated the administration of its East African colonies more fully than it had during the interwar years. It established the East African High Commission, in 1948, which took over control of railways and harbors, posts and telecommunications, customs, research, and the income tax for all but Zanzibar. Upon gaining independence, between 1962 and 1963, the countries of East Africa continued this coordination under the East African Commons Services Organization.

See also: COLONIAL RULE (Vol. IV); COLONIALISM, INFLUENCE OF (Vol. IV); BERLIN CONFERENCE (Vol. IV); ENGLAND AND AFRICA (Vol. IV); LEAGUE OF NATIONS AND AFRICA (Vol. IV); WORLD WAR I AND AFRICA (Vol. IV); WORLD WAR II AND AFRICA (Vol. IV).

British Somaliland Northern region in the Horn of Africa that after 1887 was under British COLONIAL RULE. In 1960 British Somaliland was united with ITALIAN SOMALILAND to form the independent country of SOMALIA.

Britain's principal interest in Somaliland was to protect the sea routes to India. Britain had occupied Aden, across the Gulf of Aden from Somalia, as early as 1839. The region assumed new importance with the opening of the SUEZ CANAL in 1869. Eventually, to strengthen its position on the southern entrance to the Red Sea, Britain occupied the Somali area bordering the Gulf of Aden, establishing a PROTECTORATE over the region in 1887. The administrative center of the protectorate was the port of Berbera. By the time Britain established British Somaliland, its principal colonial rival, France, had already established the small colony of FRENCH SOMALILAND, centered on the port of DJIBOUTI, north of Berbera.

The British colonial presence was limited, but it was enough to provoke the ire of strict Muslims who viewed it as corrupting their Islamic society. By 1899 a local religious leader, MUHAMMAD ABDULLAH HASSAN (1864–1920), launched his first attack on the British. For the next 20 years British military forces, as well as those from ETHIOPIA and Italian Somaliland, which Hassan also attacked, were continuously engaged in battle with him. Only with his death, in 1920, did Somali resistance to British colonial rule end.

Unlike Italy, Britain did not place European SETTLERS in their region of Somaliland, since its interest in the region was strictly strategic. With the outbreak of World War II (1939–45), Italy briefly added British Somaliland to its East African empire, but combined British, South African, and Ethiopian forces quickly defeated the Italians. Britain governed all of Somaliland until 1950, when the Italians again ruled the southern area as a TRUST TERRITORY under the auspices of the United Nations.

In 1960 the British- and Italian-controlled areas of Somalia were united to become the independent United Republic of Somalia. The northern inhabitants of former British Somaliland, however, were left at a disadvantage, since MOGADISHU, on Somalia's southern coast, became the capital and focal point of development.

See also: ENGLAND AND AFRICA (Vols. III, IV, V); ITALY AND AFRICA (Vols. IV, V); UNITED NATIONS AND AFRICA (Vol. IV).

Further reading: I. M. Lewis, *A Modern History of the Somali: Nation and State in the Horn of Africa,* 4th ed. (Oxford, U.K.: James Currey, 2002).

British South Africa Company (BSAC) Commer-
cial company chartered by the British government and established by British entrepreneur Cecil RHODES (1853–1902) in 1889. The primary purpose of the British South Africa Company (BSAC) was to colonize southern Central Africa—including areas that are now ZAMBIA and ZIMBABWE—and then to capitalize on the extensive opportunities for MINING and land development. The 25-year charter the company received from Queen Victoria (1819–1901) also allowed the company to form banks, sign treaties with local rulers, and create its own police force.

The origins of the BSAC lie with the treaty that Rhodes and his colleagues persuaded the NDEBELE ruler LOBENGULA (1836–1894) to sign in 1888, granting the company the rights to his kingdom's potentially rich mineral resources. Two years later one of Rhodes's trusted deputies, Leander Starr Jameson (1853–1917), led a group of adventurers and fortune-seekers into present-day Zimbabwe. Skirting Ndebele territory, they set up fortified bases, including one that evolved into SALISBURY (present-day Harare). This intrusion led to conflict with the Ndebele that ended with their defeat and Lobengula's

death in 1893. The BSAC renamed the region SOUTHERN RHODESIA in 1895 in honor of Rhodes. Ndebele and SHONA rebellions known as the CHIMURENGA followed in 1896 but were quickly put down.

To the north, in present-day Zambia, the situation was much the same. In the 1890s the LOZI ruler, Lubosi LEWANIKA (1845–1916), made agreements with the BSAC that, under the British interpretation, gave them extensive rights to Lozi territories. While the Lozi kingdom retained some of its sovereignty, its lands effectively came under the Company's administration. In 1911 the initially separate Northeastern and Northwestern Rhodesia were combined into NORTHERN RHODESIA.

In 1895 the British South Africa Company supported a coup d'état attempt by British settlers living in the Boer-held TRANSVAAL region of SOUTH AFRICA. Under the leadership of Jameson, a force of 500 BSAC police and volunteers invaded the Transvaal in an attempt to wrest control from the BOERS. The coup failed, and Jameson was taken prisoner. For his complicity in the failed JAMESON RAID, Rhodes was forced to step down as prime minister of CAPE COLONY.

When the company's 25-year charter ended, in 1914, the British government granted it a 10-year extension, thereby employing BSAC officials as colonial administrators, of sorts, until 1923, at which time the white inhabitants of Southern Rhodesia were allowed self-rule. Northern Rhodesia went from company administration directly to the governance of the British Empire. The company, however, continued to hold mining and land development rights, reaping great financial rewards with the increased demand for Northern Rhodesia's vast resources of metals, especially COPPER.

The reign of the British South Africa Company came to an end in 1963, when Northern Rhodesia formed a new government, renamed itself Zambia, and took possession of its own land and mineral rights. Two years later, the company merged with two other corporations to create Charter Consolidated, Ltd., a name that recalls the original charter granted to Rhodes, in 1889.

See also: COPPERBELT (Vol. IV); ENGLAND AND AFRICA (Vols. III, IV, V); MINERALS AND METALS (Vol. IV).

Further reading: John S. Galbraith, *Crown and Charter: The Early Years of the British South Africa Company* (Berkeley, Calif.: University of California Press, 1974); Lewis H. Gann, *Birth of a Plural Society: The Development of Northern Rhodesia Under the British South Africa Company, 1894–1914* (Westport, Conn.: Greenwood, 1982).

Broederbond Secret society formed to further Afrikaner nationalism in SOUTH AFRICA. The term *broederbond* is AFRIKAANS and means "brotherhood." In the wake of the British victory in the ANGLO-BOER WAR (1899–1901), many young AFRIKANERS felt alienated from the dominant British. Impoverished and reduced both socially and culturally to second-class status, they sought ways to regain their lost authority. In 1918 several such Afrikaners formed Young South Africa, soon renamed the Afrikaner Broederbond. Their goal was to foster Afrikaner nationalism by providing cultural and educational opportunities for their fellow Afrikaners. In 1921 the group decided to make itself a secret rather than public organization.

Initially seeking to foster an Afrikaner lifestyle, including music and literature, it was not long before the Afrikaner Broederbond, or the AB as it was often called, became active politically. As a secret society, however, its work was known only through the activities of various "fronts," or public groups, such as the Federation of Afrikaans Cultural Societies, whose activities could withstand closer public scrutiny. The Broederbond's political activities increased quite rapidly during the 1920s and 1930s. One of the prime reasons for this was the merger, in 1934, of the South African Party, led by Jan Christaan SMUTS (1870–1950), and the Nationalist Party of J. B. M. HERTZOG (1866–1942) to form the United Party (UP). The more radical pro-Afrikaner elements of the Nationalists broke away and formed the "purified" National Party (NP) under D. F. MALAN (1874–1959), with the Afrikaner Broederbond as one of its leading support groups.

Broederbond popularity received another boost, in 1938, the year that marked the 100th anniversary of the Great Boer Trek and the subsequent wave of nationalist feeling among Afrikaners. Riding this sentiment, the Broederbond formed several new front organizations, including the Reddingdaadbond, which sought to improve the lot of poor Afrikaners, and the Ossewabrandwag, which was quickly transformed from a cultural organization into a paramilitary group.

As World War II (1939–45) approached the Broederbond actively opposed any South African involvement in a possible Anglo-German conflict. Indeed, many Broederbonders were decidedly pro-Nazi. When Smuts led South Africa into the war on the side of Britain, Broederbond members became vocal critics of the government's policy. With the victory of the NP over Smuts and the UP in the election of 1948, the views and policies of the Broederbond became the predominant ones of the government. At this point, so many of the nation's leaders were Broederbond members that the Broederbond and government often seemed one and the same. It is believed that every president and every prime minister of South Africa from 1948 until the downfall of the APARTHEID system, in 1994, was a member of the Broederbond.

Throughout this period the group's basic profile and its membership remained constant. All members were white, Afrikaans-speaking males who were rigorously screened and then approved by the existing membership. They pledged to maintain the secrecy of the organization and to further its goals as expressed in the organization's constitution. Although it presented itself as a fraternal or social organization, the Broederbond was organized along the lines of a paramilitary group. Its basic units were the branches, which, like revolutionary cells, were kept small, with no more than 20 members. Several branches were, in turn, under the jurisdiction of the central committees, which were located in towns and cities. Policy was decided not on the local levels but by the National Congress, which met every two years and to which the branches sent representatives. All this guaranteed secrecy for the organization and obedience to the commands of the National Congress and its administrative body, the Executive Council.

The Broederbond reached the peak of its power in the 1950s and early 1960s. Although the rise of anti-apartheid sentiment and the exposure of its activities by journalists caused it to lose some support during the 1960s and 1970s, the Broederbond still remained one of the dominant forces in South African politics.

See also: GREAT BOER TREK (Vol. III); POLITICAL PARTIES AND ORGANIZATIONS (Vol. IV).

Further reading: C. Bloomberg, *Christian-Nationalism and the Rise of the Afrikaner Broederbond in South Africa, 1918–1948* (London: Macmillan, 1990); Anthony Butler, *Democracy and Apartheid* (London: Macmillan, 1998); D. Harrison, *The White Tribe of Africa* (Berkeley: University of California Press, 1981).

Buganda Largest of the four kingdoms that make up present-day UGANDA; located on the northern shore of Lake Victoria. In 1856 a new Bugandan *kabaka,* or king, MUTESA I (c. late 1830s–1884), ascended the throne, and by the mid-1800s the Buganda kingdom was exerting political and military control over the other states in the region. Building further on the military strength of his predecessors, Mutesa equipped his army with firearms acquired from Arab traders from the SWAHILI COAST and ZANZIBAR in exchange for slaves and ivory. This was the state of affairs encountered by the first European visitors to the region, John Hanning SPEKE (1827–1864), in 1862, and Henry Morton STANLEY (1841–1904), in 1875. Both explorers met with Mutesa and were greatly impressed by him and by the kingdom's organization and military strength.

Mutesa was a shrewd and outward-looking ruler and recognized that the Europeans represented a new source of trade, useful goods, and ideas. He was thus open to Stanley's suggestion that MISSIONARIES come to Buganda. At

Stanley's request, in 1877 the Protestant CHURCH MISSIONARY SOCIETY established a mission, and shortly thereafter the Catholic Society of Missionaries of Africa, known as the White Fathers, also arrived. These groups, along with the coastal Muslim traders, successfully converted large numbers of Ganda (as Buganda's people are called) and struggled with each other to become the dominant RELIGION. Mutesa avoided conversion, electing instead to play the three sides against one another in order to obtain guns and other resources he needed to expand Buganda's borders. Upon Mutesa's death, in 1884, his son Mwanga II (c. 1866–1903) ascended the throne. Mwanga unsuccessfully attempted to ban all foreign religions and was subsequently deposed and exiled in 1888. The civil war that followed saw the brief victory of Muslim forces, which then were defeated by the Christians, who restored Mwanga. In his attempts to suppress foreign religion, Mwanga executed a number of his own court pages who were converted Catholics. (In 1964 the Catholic Church canonized these victims as saints, partly due to the efforts of Ugandan archbishop Joseph KIWANUKA [1899–1966].)

While in Buganda, Stanley witnessed the kingdom's military might. He observed 125,000 troops depart for the purposes of a single mission. The troops were to rendezvous with a fleet of 230 war canoes, just one part of Buganda's royal navy.

Continuing religious tensions between Catholics and Protestants, which reflected much deeper tensions within Bugandan society, erupted when British and German imperialists, led by Captain Frederick LUGARD (1858–1945) and Dr. Karl PETERS (1856–1918) respectively, came to Buganda, further polarizing the kingdom. British Protestant missionaries and their converts naturally supported British control, while the Catholic missionaries, who were French, supported the Germans (possibly in order to oppose the British) or continued independence. Ganda converts from both sides fought viciously until Lugard ended the conflict through the use of new military technology: the machine gun.

Britain's victory in Buganda led to an expansion of British territorial control and the eventual formation of the Uganda Protectorate, in 1894. Britain initially ruled the area through Buganda and Kabaka Mwanga II (c. 1866–1903), who had been restored to the throne, though Apolo KAGWA (1868–1927), the *katikiro* (prime minister), was the real power. When Mwanga began to oppose Britain he was replaced by his own infant son Daudi Chwa II (1897–1939). In 1900 the Buganda Agreement, willingly accepted by Buganda, established a fa-

vorable relationship between the African kingdom and the British colonial government. The agreement doubled Buganda's size and allowed it to remain largely autonomous. Buganda also secured private land tenure that kept the kingdom free of European SETTLERS and contributed to its autonomy. In 1952 the British governor of Uganda, Andrew Cohen (1909–1968), instituted reforms that gave Buganda's people majority control of their legislature, as well as control over EDUCATION, AGRICULTURE, and health services.

A crisis emerged in 1953 over British plans to incorporate Uganda into an East African Federation, along with KENYA and TANGANYIKA. Fearing a loss of their relative independence, Buganda strongly objected. The British responded by deporting the *kabaka* at the time, Mutesa II (1939–1969), and holding him in Britain. Negotiations in 1955, however, resulted in Mutesa's return to the throne, and plans for the East African Federation were scrapped. Uganda became independent in 1962, and Buganda remained a kingdom within the new country. Kabaka Mutesa II assumed the ceremonial office of president of the country, while a northerner, Milton OBOTE (1924–), became the prime minister.

See also: BUGANDA (Vols. II, III, V); CHRISTIANITY, INFLUENCE OF (Vols. II, III, IV, V); COLONIAL CONQUEST (Vol. IV); COLONIAL RULE (Vol. IV); COLONIALISM, INFLUENCE OF (Vol. IV); ENGLAND AND AFRICA (Vols. III, V); ISLAM, INFLUENCE OF (Vols. II, III, IV, V); PARTITION (Vol. IV).

Bunche, Ralph (Ralph Johnson Bunch)
(1904–1971) *Noted scholar and Africa adviser to the government of the United States*

Born into a humble family in Detroit, Michigan, Bunche moved to the warmer climate of Albuquerque, New Mexico at age 10 because of his parents' ill health. After their deaths two years later he was raised by his grandmother, "Nana" Johnson. Born into SLAVERY, she was a fervent supporter of African-American rights. In high school Bunche distinguished himself in history and English, becoming his class valedictorian. He attended the University of California at Los Angeles on an athletic scholarship, graduating summa cum laude in 1927 with a degree in international relations. He then received a scholarship to Harvard, where in 1934 he earned a PhD with an award-winning dissertation comparing French COLONIAL RULE in TOGOLAND (now TOGO) and DAHOMEY (present-day Republic of BENIN).

During his academic career Bunche taught at Howard University, from 1928 to 1950, and then at Harvard University, from 1950 to 1952. He also served on the boards of directors of various organizations and institutions, including Harvard's Board of Overseers, and was active in the civil-rights movement. He published two books, *A World View of Race* (1936) and *An American Dilemma* (1944). His view was that segregation was inherently incompatible with democracy and that racial prejudice lacked a scientific basis in biology or anthropology.

During World War II (1939–45) Bunche held important positions in the Office of Strategic Services and in the State Department, where he helped shape policy on Africa. In 1946 the United Nations (UN) secretary-general Trygve Lie (1896–1968) put Bunche in charge of the organization's Department of Trusteeship, which oversaw people living in countries without self-government. This led to his winning the Nobel Peace Prize, in 1950, for his efforts in mediating the conflict between Arabs and Jews in Palestine.

Bunche remained with the United Nations for the rest of his life, serving as undersecretary for special political affairs, UN special representative to the Democratic Republic of the CONGO, and undersecretary-general.

See also: UNITED NATIONS AND AFRICA (Vols. IV, V).

Further reading: Ben Keppel, *The Work of Democracy: Ralph Bunche, Kenneth B. Clark, Lorraine Hansberry, and the Cultural Politics of Race* (Cambridge, Mass: Harvard University Press, 1995); Brian Urquhart, *Ralph Bunche: An American Life* (New York: Norton, 1993).

Bunyoro Kingdom of precolonial UGANDA located in the Great Lakes region of eastern Central Africa, northwest of the kingdom of BUGANDA. Bunyoro was at its apex in the 18th century. By the mid-19th century, however, the kingdom was challenged by Buganda to the south and by Egyptian and Sudanese invaders to the north. As a result Bunyoro lost control over many of its outlying possessions. In 1872 Samuel BAKER (1821–1893), governor-general of Equatoria Province in the Egyptian-ruled Sudan, annexed Bunyoro territory as part of Egypt's push southward up the Nile. Led by Mukama KABAREGA (c. 1853–1923), the Banyoro, as the people of Bunyoro are sometimes called, resisted Egypt's authority, forcing the Egyptians, in 1888, to withdraw from the area.

During the early 1890s Buganda was in the midst of an exhausting religious civil war. Taking advantage of its neighbor's turmoil, Kabarega led Bunyoro to strengthen its military and centralize its power structure. This revival of Bunyoro eminence was soon challenged, however, as the British, led by Captain Frederick LUGARD (1858–1945), invaded from the south with the help of Protestants from Buganda. The reconstructed Bunyoro army held off the British for years, but in 1899 Kabarega was captured and exiled to the SEYCHELLES, in the Indian Ocean.

Kabarega's defeat marked the end of an independent Bunyoro. Britain then incorporated the kingdom into the Uganda PROTECTORATE and awarded half of Bunyoro's territory to Buganda for its help in the war. The Banyoro vigorously contested this division of land, and the issue remained a source of conflict in Uganda well into the 20th century.

See also: BUNYORO (Vols. II, III); COLONIAL CONQUEST (Vol. IV); ENGLAND AND AFRICA (Vols. III, IV, V); GREAT LAKES REGION (Vol. III); KITARA COMPLEX (Vol. II); RESISTANCE AND REBELLION (Vol. IV).

Further reading: Edward I. Steinhart, *Conflict and Collaboration: The Kingdoms of Western Uganda, 1890–1907* (Princeton, N.J.: Princeton University Press, 1977).

Burkina Faso Present-day country covering about 105,900 square miles (274,300 sq km), located in western Africa. Burkina Faso is bordered by The Republic of MALI to the west and north, by NIGER to the east, and by BENIN, TOGO, GHANA, and IVORY COAST to the south. Burkina Faso was named UPPER VOLTA under French COLONIAL RULE and for the first 23 years of independence.

The area of present-day Burkina Faso was originally inhabited by the Gurunsi, Bobo, and Lobi peoples. By the 15th century the powerful Gurma and MOSSI STATES had established hegemony over the region.

The Mossi States were organized strongly enough to resist attempts by neighboring Muslim empires to conquer their lands. Because of this, present-day Burkina Faso is one of the few countries of West Africa that does not have a Muslim majority.

These states (which included Yatenga, Fada-n-Gurma, Tenkodogo, and the dominant kingdom of Ougadougou), controlled the region until the late 1800s, when the French campaign of COLONIAL CONQUEST led to the establishment of a PROTECTORATE over Yatenga, in 1895. The fall of Ouagadougou to the French a year later effectively ended Mossi resistance. By 1897 the Gurma, Gurunsi, and Bobo had all succumbed to French colonial rule. An agreement with the British in 1898 established the borders between the new French territory and the British GOLD COAST COLONY (present-day Ghana). Despite the continued resistance of the Lobi, who made good use of poisoned arrows to fend off the French aggressors, by 1904 the region was added to the French colonial agglomerate of Haut-Sénégal-Niger (Upper Senegal-Niger).

Burkina Faso during the Colonial Era: Upper Volta In 1919 France split off Haute-Volta (Upper Volta) from Upper Senegal-Niger, which itself was later divided into FRENCH SOUDAN (present-day Mali) and Niger. All three colonies became part of FRENCH WEST AFRICA. For economic and administrative purposes, in 1932 the Upper Volta region was divided and distributed among Ivory Coast, French Soudan, and Niger. During the colonial period the economy increasingly relied upon money from laborers who migrated to neighboring Gold Coast Colony and Ivory Coast. Repatriated earnings from the migrants helped their families purchase consumer goods and pay their taxes to the colonial government. The French also promoted the agricultural production of CASH CROPS, especially COTTON and GROUNDNUTS (peanuts), for export.

Under pressure from the Mossi peoples, who wanted a separate territorial identity, the French reestablished Upper Volta, in 1947, as part of the FRENCH UNION. Following the French revision of colonial policies embodied in the *Loi Cadre* (Enabling Act) of 1956, Upper Volta became an autonomous country within the French Community. In 1960 the fully independent Republic of Upper Volta was established, with Maurice Yameogo (1921–1993), the head of the Voltaic Democratic Union, as its first president.

In 1984 Upper Volta was officially renamed Burkina Faso (meaning "the Land of Incorruptible Men") by president Thomas Sankara (1949–1987).

See also: BOBO (Vol. II); BURKINA FASO (Vols. I, II, III, V); COLONIALISM, INFLUENCE OF (Vol. IV); FADA-N-GURMA (Vol. III); FRANCE AND AFRICA (Vols. IV); LOBI (Vol. III); YATENGA (Vols. II, III).

Burton, Richard (Sir Richard Francis Burton) (1821–1890) *British explorer and writer*

Burton was the son of an army colonel and traveled extensively in Europe with his parents. He attended Oxford University—which he found boring—until he joined the East India Company's military and was deployed to Karachi and later Sindh, in India. There Burton displayed a remarkable proficiency for languages, learning Arabic, Persian, Hindustani, as well as a number of other dialects. Later in his life he would come to master 40 languages and dialects.

Working as an undercover intelligence officer, Burton developed techniques of assimilation and disguise that were essential on his later journeys. In 1853, disguised as a Muslim *hajji,* or pilgrim, Burton made a daring trip to the cities of Mecca and Medina, where non-Muslims were forbidden under penalty of death. He wrote about the experience in the landmark three-volume ethnological work, *Pilgrimage to El Medinah and Mecca* (1855–1856).

In 1854 Burton went on the first of his African expeditions with John Hanning SPEKE (1827–1864) in search of the source of the Nile River. Burton's extensive knowledge of Arabic and Islam proved useful in facilitating these expeditions, as the pair traveled along caravan routes fre-

quented by Zanzibari-based Arab merchants. Burton had to return to England to recover from an injury suffered when his caravan was attacked in Somaliland. Burton and Speke returned to Africa in 1857, and the following year they were the first Europeans to see Lake Tanganyika, which Burton mistakenly believed to be to be the source of the Nile. Burton fell ill and was unable to continue the expedition. Speke carried on, however, and came across and christened Lake Victoria, correctly declaring it the Nile's source. Speke returned to England before Burton and claimed much of the publicity for the expedition. Because of this and the dispute over the Nile's true source, Burton and Speke ended their friendship.

In the following years Burton visited and wrote about such disparate places as Utah, in the United States, and Iceland. In 1861 Burton married Isabel Arundell and became British consul to the Spanish island of Fernando Po. He would go on to be consul to Santos, Brazil, in 1864, to Damascus, Syria, in 1869, and finally to Trieste, Austria, in 1872. He died in Trieste in 1890.

Burton's literary efforts are as well known as his explorations. His English translations of the Indian erotica *The Kama Sutra of Vatsayana* (1883) and the mythic masterpiece *The Arabian Nights* (1885) became classics. His wife, under mysterious circumstances, burned many of his papers after his death.

See also: ARABIC (Vols. I, II); MECCA (Vol. II); MEDINA (Vol. III); NILE RIVER (Vol. I); SOMALI (Vol. II); TANGANYIKA, LAKE (Vols. I, II); VICTORIA, LAKE (Vols. I, V).

Burundi
Central African kingdom that regained independence from COLONIAL RULE in 1961. A very small, mountainous country of only 10,700 square miles (27,700 sq km), modern Burundi is bordered by RWANDA, TANZANIA, and the Democratic Republic of the CONGO. Lake TANGANYIKA lies along the southwestern border.

For centuries Burundi was an independent kingdom inhabited mostly by HUTU and TUTSI peoples. By the 1850s, when the first European explorers reached the area, the Tutsi had established themselves as an aristocratic ruling class. European colonization began in 1884, when German representatives of a forerunner of the German East Africa Company (GEAC) arrived in the region and began to sign treaties with local rulers granting Germany territorial control.

Burundi during the Colonial Era: Ruanda-Urundi In 1885 Burundi and the neighboring kingdom of Rwanda came under GEAC management in an administrative division called RUANDA-URUNDI. By 1891, however, the German imperial government had taken over its direct administrative control, and within a decade the territory was completely incorporated into GERMAN EAST AFRICA. In 1903 Burundi's Mwami (King) Gisabo (c. 1845–1908) signed the Treaty of Kiganda, which ceded the last remnants of sovereignty to Germany. The Germans set up their colonial administration at Usumbura, formerly a small village located on Lake Tanganyika.

German administration ended during World War I (1914–18), and in 1919 Ruanda-Urundi became a MANDATE of Belgium under the League of Nations. From the beginning Belgian rule favored the Tutsi aristocracy over the Hutu majority, and the Tutsi were given a great deal of say in a governmental system of indirect rule that Belgium continued until after World War II (1939–45). After the war the United Nations began to advocate democratic rule for Ruanda-Urundi, and in preparation for elections, two political parties developed. The Union for National Progress (Union Pour le Progrès National, UPRONA), spearheaded by the Tutsi prince, Louis Rwagasore (1932–1961), sought to serve both Tutsi and Hutu interests. On the other hand, the Christian Democratic Party (Parti Democrate Chretien, PDC) was supported by the Belgian government. In September 1961, UPRONA won the majority of seats in elections for the National Assembly, thereby making Prince Rwagasore the new prime minister. He was not to lead his government for long, however, as members of the PDC assassinated him the following month.

In 1962 the United Nations granted the division of Ruanda-Urundi into the independent nations of Rwanda and Burundi, with July 1 marking the official date of independence. Burundi opted to become once again a sovereign kingdom, with the long-reigning Mwami Mwambutsa (r. 1915–1966) assuming the office of head of state, a position that exercised real power. It also proceeded to change the name of the colonial capital from Usumbura to Bujumbura. However, the violent start to independent government and the Rwandan revolution (1959–1962) brought Hutu-Tutsi antagonisms to a boil. Continuous ethnic rivalries disrupted the country in the years that followed.

See also: BELGIUM AND AFRICA (Vol. IV); BUJUMBURA (Vol. V); BURUNDI (Vols. I, II, III, V); COLONIALISM, INFLUENCE OF (Vol. IV); ETHNIC CONFLICT IN AFRICA (Vol. V); ETHNIC GROUP (Vol. I); ETHNICITY AND IDENTITY (Vol. I).

Busaidi   The ruling dynasty of ZANZIBAR from 1840 to 1964. In 1741 the Busaidi dynasty founded by Said al-Busaidi (d. 1806) displaced the existing rulers of the southern Arabian kingdom of Oman. The center of their attention soon moved to the SWAHILI COAST of East Africa, where Omani Arab merchants had long been active.

In 1806 Sayyid Said (1791–1856) became sultan after murdering his brother, Said al-Busaidi. Sayyid Said sought to control the commerce of the coast first by consolidating his control over Zanzibar and then by commandeering more and more of the coast and offshore islands. In 1837 his dominance was complete when he defeated the Mazrui rulers of MOMBASA, the major port city on the coast of KENYA.

In 1840 Sayyid Said transferred the capital of his state from Muscat, in Oman, to ZANZIBAR CITY. This move put Said in a better position to exercise control over and profit from the booming SLAVE TRADE and IVORY TRADE.

Upon Said's death, in 1856, the kingdom was split between two of his sons, and the Zanzibar sultanate and the Omani sultanate became separate entities. Said's second son, ibn Said BARGHASH (c. 1833–1888), who ruled from 1870 to 1888, actively tried to establish a Zanzibari territorial empire in East Africa. Despite his efforts, Busaidi rule never extended much beyond the coast.

In the late 1880s European imperial ambitions ended the sultanate's territorial claims on the mainland. GERMAN EAST AFRICA took control of TANGANYIKA, and Kenya, to the north, became a British colony. Then, in 1890, a treaty between the German and the British colonies made Zanzibar a British PROTECTORATE. Under the protectorate the sultans remained the nominal rulers, but the real power rested with the British.

When Zanzibar became independent, in December 1963, the sultan and his circle of influential Arabs thought they would rule the country. However, a bloody revolt, in January 1964, drove the sultan from power, ending the Busaidi era of Zanzibar's history. Later that year Zanzibar joined Tanganyika to create TANZANIA.

See also: COLONIAL CONQUEST (Vol. IV); COLONIAL RULE (Vol. IV); TRADE AND COMMERCE (Vol. IV).

Further reading: Abdul Sheriff, *Slaves, Spices, and Ivory in Zanzibar* (Athens: Ohio University Press, 1987).

Busia, Kofi Abrefa (1913–1974) *Scholar and political leader from Ghana*

Born into a royal family within the Ashanti confederacy, in what was then the British GOLD COAST COLONY (now GHANA), Busia received his early education in church-run schools. He taught at ACHIMOTA COLLEGE, in ACCRA, before earning a scholarship, in 1939, to Oxford University, in England. Upon his return to the Gold Coast in 1941, Busia became one of the first Africans to serve as an officer in the colonial administration. Disappointed by the experience, he returned to Oxford for his doctorate degree in Social Anthropology. His doctoral thesis was published in London in 1951 under the title *The Position of the Chief in the Modern Political System of Ashanti*. In 1954 his academic pedigree allowed him to become the first African professor at the University of Gold Coast.

In 1951 Busia was elected by the Ashanti to the Gold Coast's Legislative Council, and the following year he became the head of the Ghana Congress Party (GCP), which stood in opposition to Kwame NKRUMAH (1909–1972) and his CONVENTION PEOPLE'S PARTY (CPP). The GCP represented the COCOA growers and the chiefs, while the CPP had a more populist appeal. Nkrumah, whom the British had jailed for his political activities, won a stunning victory. The British then invited him to form the colony's government as prime minister. Nkrumah won two more elections in 1954 and 1956. Busia was his party's only successful candidate in 1954. The GCP then joined the opposition National Liberation Movement (NLM) to try and defeat Nkrumah in 1956, with Busia becoming the NLM leader. Nkrumah's electoral appeal was simply too great to overcome, however.

Following Ghana gaining independence, in 1957, Nkrumah became prime minister and then, when Ghana became a republic in 1960, the president. Upon assuming power as the head of a sovereign Ghana, Nkrumah immediately acted to suppress his opposition. In 1958 he passed a Preventive Detention Act and used it to imprison more than a thousand of his opponents. One of the more prominent detainees, J. B. DANQUAH (1895– 1965), eventually died in prison for lack of medical care. Fearing such retribution himself, Busia went into exile, in 1959, teaching at the University of Leiden, in the Netherlands, and at Oxford. In 1966 Busia returned to Ghana after a coup overthrew Nkrumah, setting the stage for his rise to the office of prime minister.

See also: ASHANTI (Vol. II); ASHANTI EMPIRE (Vols. III, IV); BUSIA, KOFI (Vol. V); ENGLAND AND AFRICA (Vols. III, IV, V); NATIONALISM AND INDEPENDENCE MOVEMENTS (Vol. IV).

Cabral, Amílcar (Amílcar Lopes Cabral)
(1924–1973) *Writer and independence-movement leader in Guinea-Bissau and the Cape Verde Islands*

Cabral was born in Bafatá, in the mainland colony GUINEA-BISSAU, to parents from the CAPE VERDE ISLANDS. At the time Guinea-Bissau and the Cape Verde Islands, both located on the West African coast, were colonies of Portugal. Cabral received his early education in Cape Verde, where he excelled as a student. During the 1940s a severe drought hit the islands and this, exacerbated by harsh economic conditions brought on by World War II (1939–45) and Portuguese colonial policies, resulted in the death of nearly one-third of Cape Verde's population. Cabral was deeply affected by the disaster and Portugal's role in it, and he began to write poetry and short stories that demonstrated an anticolonial sentiment.

In 1945 Cabral traveled to Lisbon, Portugal, to study agricultural engineering. While there he helped found the Center for African Studies, in Lisbon. In 1952 he returned to Guinea-Bissau to work for the Department of Agriculture and Forestry Services. There he worked to complete an agricultural survey, traveling extensively in Guinea-Bissau and gathering information from the peasant population.

In 1956 Cabral became one of the founding members of the African Independence Party of Guinea and Cape Verde (Partido Africano da Indepêndencia da Guiné e Cabo Verde, PAIGC). One of West Africa's more active nationalist movements, the PAIGC aimed at liberating Guinea-Bissau and Cape Verde from Portugal to establish the two as a unified, independent country. Faced with oppressive Portuguese tactics similar to those employed in the colonies of ANGOLA and MOZAMBIQUE, the PAIGC abandoned their campaign of nonviolent protest. In its place they began to build a rebel military force in the neighboring Republic of GUINEA, which had become independent in 1958.

In 1962 Cabral and the PAIGC began a prolonged guerrilla war against the colonial government that eventually led to independence in 1974. Cabral, however, did not live to see it, as he was assassinated by the Portuguese secret police, in 1973.

See also: AFRICAN INDEPENDENCE PARTY OF GUINEA AND CAPE VERDE (Vol. V); CAPE VERDE, REPUBLIC OF (Vol. V); COLONIALISM, INFLUENCE OF (Vol. IV); NATIONALISM AND INDEPENDENCE MOVEMENTS (Vol. IV); PORTUGAL AND AFRICA (Vols. III, IV, V).

Further reading: Patrick Chabal, *Amílcar Cabral: Revolutionary Leadership and People's War* (New York: Cambridge University Press, 1983).

Cairo
Capital of EGYPT and largest city in Africa. Located along the Nile River, Cairo has long been the economic, political, and cultural center of Egypt. From the time of the Fatimid, Abbasid, and Ayyubid dynasties to the restoration of native Egyptian rulership in the 1950s, Cairo has endured as a symbol of Egypt's greatness and its challenges.

Modernization of Cairo By 1850 Cairo showcased many of the benefits of the reforms instituted by Muhammad Ali (1769–1849). While still resembling a medieval town, Cairo had undergone subtle changes, with its inhabitants becoming more educated and cosmopolitan than before. As a result Cairo developed an influential elite of teachers, bureaucrats, and engineers, all with an appetite for European comforts. The city's infrastructure at that time included the telegraph, and by 1854 railroad networks and regular train service to the Mediterranean coast was established. Also, by this time Cairo's population had increased, requiring an expansion of the physical city limits. Khedive ISMAIL (1830–1895), Egypt's ruler from 1863 to 1879— and grandson of Muhammad Ali—expanded the city from the Ezbekiyya Lake to the banks of the Nile, which more than doubled its area. Under Ismail the city's population grew from about 300,000 to 375,000.

After a trip to the Paris Exposition (1867), Ismail began guiding the transformation of Cairo into a city that would rival European capitals. He entrusted the modernization project to Ali Pasha Mubarak (1823–1893), an engineer known as Egypt's pioneer in EDUCATION.

Khedive Ismail planned to finance Cairo's modernization with the profits from the COTTON boom occasioned by the Civil War in the United States (1861–65). Unfortunately, this boom proved to be temporary, and the khedive's massive spending programs ultimately led to Egypt's financial collapse.

Between 1864 and 1865 the capital became a metropolis, with a Ministry of Public Works to coordinate urban planners and public utilities. Concessions were given to foreign companies to provide utilities to the area. One of the notable concessions granted to European companies was the one to the French Lebon Company, which supplied Cairo and some of its suburbs with gas for gas lighting. In 1865 Cordier, another French company, was given the concession to supply Cairo with municipal water. In anticipation of the opening of the SUEZ CANAL in 1869, a European-style quarter was built onto the western edge of the old city to impress visiting European dignitaries.

As a result of all this activity and the emphasis on a new, Europeanized environment, Cairo actually developed as two cities: a European-style city and an old, Muslim city. The transformation continued in 1868, when the municipal government was reorganized and Cairo was divided into new administrative units. Old suburbs were united and new suburbs were developed, all paving the way for northward expansion of the city.

The Department of Urban Planning began mapping the city and started to plan huge road construction projects. These included straightening and widening existing streets, connecting streets to open squares with roundabouts, and creating new streets that would extend into the desert. With all this development, Cairo began to attract large numbers of foreigners, some as tourists and others who took up residence and engaged in business and trade. The foreign population reached a total of 19,000 by 1882.

British Occupation In the late 19th century hostilities erupted between Britain and Egypt over the repayment of Egypt's foreign loans, many of which were made by British interests. The British occupation of Egypt in 1882 brought new challenges to Cairo. The British undersecretary of state, Sir Scott Moncrieff (1836–1916), managed the affairs of the city, and the Ministry of Public Works continued to grant concessions to foreign providers of public utilities, a practice that continued until 1937. During this period one of the major challenges facing the city was the growth of its population, which increased between 1882 and 1937 by 250 percent. Urban planners focused on land reclamation for the purpose of adding more capacity to the city for building construction.

Another achievement of this period was the development of a new suburb, Heliopolis, by the Heliopolis Oasis Company. Founded in 1906 by Belgium's Baron Edouard Empain (1852–1929) and Boghos Nubar Pasha (1825–1899), an Armenian national living in Egypt, the company constructed villas, apartment buildings, and hotels in a new suburb north of the city. Built on an old town but designed for Europeans, the community became the prototype of a satellite city in the desert.

Between 1894 and 1917 the same Baron Empain who built Heliopolis also gained the concession to provide Cairo with a tramway system. This network overlaid Ismail's planned city, but with the exception of Muhammed Ali Boulevard, the old city remained outside the network.

In 1902, after the British built the first ASWAN DAM, both banks of the Nile and those of the islands of Jazira and Rawdah had been stabilized, creating more land for construction. Large suburbs subsequently were laid out along the Nile, as were additional Western-style hotels. Bridge construction, which went on between 1902 and 1907, allowed Cairo to expand further westward; the arrival of automobiles, in 1903, accelerated the transformation of the city's street system. In 1915 British sanitary engineer James Carkett inaugurated the first sewer system, which serviced Cairo until the population density of the 1960s overburdened it.

Cairenes, as Cairo's residents are known, enjoyed improved public utilities, but there was a noticeable discrepancy in services provided for European Cairo and the homes of the indigenous people. As a result modern business activities moved to the north and west, where two landmarks became symbols of British occupation—the British army barracks and the British Residence.

In spite of its divided and colonial nature, by the 1930s Cairo had emerged as a modern capital and a center of learning and cultural activity. In 1922 Howard Carter (1874–1939) rekindled interest in Egypt by locating the tomb of Pharaoh Tutankhamun (r. 1361–1352 BCE), the artifacts of which are now displayed in the Cairo

Museum. In the area of popular culture, Cairo even developed a CINEMA industry, producing its first film with sound in 1932.

Growing Crises In spite of its geographical spread, and notwithstanding its cultural achievements, the main problem of the city remained population. The population of Cairo had doubled from 1882 to 1914, doubled again by 1942, and more than doubled again by 1966. This population explosion occurred through both natural increase and the migration of people from rural to urban areas.

The population problem, however, was not the only one facing Cairo in the years following World War II (1939–45). Tensions between Egyptians and the British colonial administration worsened considerably in the postwar era. These boiled over several times into the large-scale demonstrations and riots that marked the early 1950s. This culminated in the events that came to be known as Black Saturday (January 26, 1952), when mobs set the city ablaze and ravaged businesses that were owned or frequented by foreigners.

Soon afterward, when a coup d'état led to the ouster of King FARUK (1920–1965) and the installation of a military regime, Gamal Abdel NASSER (1918–1970) became the first native-born Egyptian to rule Egypt and Cairo since the age of the pharaohs. Unfortunately these events—coupled with the drawn-out battles between Egypt and the recently installed nation of Israel, to the east—did little to help the people of Cairo, who continued to suffer from unemployment, lack of housing, and a dearth of modern facilities for those living outside the Europeanized quarter. These problems, which continued to plague the city throughout the rest of the 1950s, emerged as crises in the 1960s.

See also: CAIRO (Vols. I, II, III, V); COLONIAL RULE (Vol. IV); CONCESSIONAIRE COMPANIES (Vol. IV); ENGLAND AND AFRICA (Vol. IV); OTTOMAN EMPIRE AND AFRICA (Vol. IV); URBANIZATION (Vols. IV, V); URBAN LIFE AND CULTURE (Vols. IV, V).

Further reading: André Raymond, *Cairo* (Cambridge, Mass.: Harvard University Press, 2000); Max Rodenbeck, *Cairo: The City Victorious* (New York: Vintage Departures, 1998).

Camara Laye (1928–1980) *Guinean author*

A speaker of the Maninka LANGUAGE, Camara Laye was born in Kouroussa, Upper Guinea, which is part of the present-day country of GUINEA. He was born into a respected Muslim family, and he studied in a Quranic school before attending Kouroussa's public elementary schools. He then went to the College George Poiret in the Guin-ean capital, Conakry, to study engineering. In 1947 he won a scholarship to study automotive mechanics at the Central School of Automobile Engineering in Argenteuil, France. After graduation he remained in France to work and to pursue further technical education at the College for Aeronautics and Automobile Construction.

While in France Camara Laye also began to pursue a literary career and studied at the National Conservatory of Arts and Crafts. His autobiographical novel, *L'Enfant noir* (Dark child), which is recognized as an early landmark in contemporary African writing, appeared in 1953. A highly idealized reminiscence of the writer's childhood in Kour-oussa, the book received the prestigious Prix Charles Veillon, in 1954. Critics of the novel, however, accused Laye of ignoring the political plight of Africans under COLONIAL RULE.

In 1956 Laye returned to Africa, spending time in DAHOMEY (present-day Republic of BENIN) and GHANA before returning to a newly independent GUINEA, in 1958. Despite the fact that he held a series of governmental posts, he became an outspoken critic of the government, eventually breaking with President Ahmed Sékou TOURÉ (1922–1984). In 1965 Laye left Guinea for exile in DAKAR. The following year he published *Dramouss* (translated, in 1991, as *A Dream of Africa*), a novel that depicted an African country ruled by a tyrannical dictator. Laye was also an essayist and writer of short stories. He died in Dakar, in 1980.

See also: FRANCE AND AFRICA (Vol. IV); LITERATURE IN COLONIAL AFRICA (Vol. IV); LITERATURE IN MODERN AFRICA (Vol. V).

Cameroon

Present-day country, 183,600 square miles (475,500 sq km) in area, in southern West Africa. Cameroon is bordered along its western coast by the Gulf of Guinea, to the north by NIGERIA and CHAD, and to the east and south by the CENTRAL AFRICAN REPUBLIC, the Republic of the CONGO, and GABON.

In the early 19th century a combination of ethnic and European influences marked the landscape of Cameroon. The northern regions came under the political control of the FULANI, a militant and militaristic Muslim people who had waged a JIHAD in neighboring Northern Nigeria and had established the SOKOTO CALIPHATE. Inspired by the successful Sokoto jihad, a northern-Cameroonian Fulani leader and scholar, Adama (1771–1848), launched a successful jihad in his home area. Between 1808 and 1820 Adama established an emirate that covered most of the region that makes up present-day northern Cameroon.

As the Fulani moved southward, however, they were finally repelled by the Mum kingdom, located in the central and western grassfields of Cameroon. During this time European and African slave traders dominated the regions to the south of Mum as well as along the territory's coast.

In the mid-1800s the SLAVE TRADE in Cameroon began to wane, as it did elsewhere in the Atlantic world. TRADE AND COMMERCE shifted to focus on NATURAL RESOURCES, particularly PALM OIL and ivory. As the dynamic of trade in Cameroon changed, Europeans began to expand their influence farther inland, diminishing the prominence of the coastal-based African merchants such as those from DOUALA.

In 1858 Alfred Saker (1814–1880), a British missionary, founded the city of Victoria. Saker believed the area held promising economic potential, and attempted to persuade Britain to make the area a PROTECTORATE. Britain wavered on the decision for nearly 30 years, and Germany took advantage of the lack of action. In 1884, after signing a treaty with Douala in the presence of a German gunboat, Germany declared the area a protectorate and named it Kamerun.

Cameroon during the Colonial Era: Kamerun

German COLONIAL RULE over the protectorate led to improvements in the territory's infrastructure and the introduction of large-scale plantation-based AGRICULTURE. Exports to Europe included plantation CASH CROPS, such as COCOA, COFFEE, and tea, as well as commodities harvested in the wild, such as RUBBER and ivory. However, the extent of German endeavors necessitated the widespread use of forced LABOR, the cruelty of which cost the lives of thousands of Africans.

After its defeat in World War I (1914–18) Germany ceded control of Kamerun to France and Britain. The two colonial powers split the colony, and the territories became League of Nations MANDATES, with France gaining the larger amount of area and incorporating it into FRENCH EQUATORIAL AFRICA.

British Cameroon Britain gained much less territory in Cameroon than France, and the land they acquired was divided into a southern and northern segment, separated by a portion of French Cameroon. The British, guided by the disjointed geography of their holdings, split the territory into two parts—Northern and Southern Cameroons—and placed each territory under a different administrative body within neighboring Nigeria.

In the early 1920s Britain sold some of Cameroon back to German plantation farmers. Their ownership did not last long, however, as Britain seized the land at the beginning of World War II (1939–45).

Northern Cameroons was administered by the Northern Region of Nigeria, while Southern Cameroons fell under control of Nigeria's Eastern Region. Dividing control over British Cameroon showed the lack of importance Britain placed on the governance of the territory.

The British, happy to use existing social controls, supported the local chiefs and expected them to provide administrative and economic guidance for the Cameroonian people. At the same time, however, the British imposed heavy taxes and monopolized the natural and commercial resources of the country.

French Cameroon (Cameroun) France took a more active role than Britain in its governance of Cameroon. The French instilled a French identity within the territory, instituting an intensive French-language program and destroying vestiges of the former German rule. France also developed the territory's economic potential, building railroads and increasing the land's agricultural output.

The French governance of Cameroon, however, was far from altruistic. Much of the development that took place in the territory was accomplished using forced labor. Although this practice was forbidden under the terms of the League of Nations mandate, it did not end until the BRAZZAVILLE Conference, in 1944.

Toward Independence During the 1950s Cameroon, much like the rest of colonial Africa, moved toward independence. Cameroon's independence, however, was complicated by the division of control over the territory between France and Britain. The process in French Cameroon was fairly straightforward. In the early 1950s France granted the colony a Legislative Assembly, and political parties became active. In 1957 the colony gained self-government within the French Community, and in 1960 French Cameroon gained independence and was renamed the Republic of Cameroon.

The situation in British Cameroon was more complex. Some political leaders favored reunification with French Cameroon. Some wanted integration into Nigeria. Still others preferred complete independence for British Cameroon. To settle the arguments surrounding unification and to complete Cameroon's path toward independence, in 1961 the British held a referendum asking British Cameroonians to decide their fate. The results were divided between the two parts of the colony, as the Northern Cameroons chose to become part of Nigeria, while the Southern Cameroons voted to reunite with French Cameroon. Later that year British Cameroon received its independence, and the results of the election were honored as the two divisions of the colony united with the territories they had voted to join.

See also: CAMEROON GRASSFIELDS (Vol. I); FRANCE AND AFRICA (Vols. IV, V); LEAGUE OF NATIONS AND AFRICA (Vol. IV).

Further reading: Emmanuel Chiabi, *The Making of Modern Cameroon* (Lanham, Md.: University Press of America, 1997).

Cape Coast Coastal West African city in southern GHANA. Cape Coast is one of the oldest towns in Ghana. It was originally a Fante fishing village, where in 1610 Portuguese tradesmen began their quest for the precious metal that gave this stretch of the West African coast the moniker Gold Coast. In 1653 Swedes built the Cape Coast Castle, which was used to hold and transfer African captives to the New World and Europe. The area was a important because of its strategic location for the transatlantic SLAVE TRADE, and many European countries fought for control of this and other sites in the area. The Cape Coast Castle also served as a fort to defend the area from armed incursions by trading parties from other European countries.

Cape Coast was the administrative capital of Britain's GOLD COAST COLONY until the capital was moved to ACCRA, the present-day capital of Ghana, in 1874. Prompted by the construction of early schools by European MISSIONARIES, Cape Coast earned a reputation as a center for EDUCATION. Today it is the site of a university and several well-known secondary boarding schools. It also still serves as a commercial port for the trafficking of fish, COCOA, coconuts, fruits, corn, and cassava. The city's castle is one of the Smithsonian Institute's World Historical Monuments, and tourism is an increasingly important activity.

See also: CAPE COAST (Vol. III); ENGLAND AND AFRICA (Vols. III, IV, V); FANTE (Vols. II, III); GOLD COAST (Vol. III); PORTUGAL AND AFRICA (Vols. III, IV, V); SLAVE TRADE, EXPANSION OF EUROPEAN INVOLVEMENT IN (Vol. III); SLAVERY (Vols. I, II, III, V).

Cape Colony First and largest of Britain's colonies in southern Africa. The Cape Colony underwent significant transformation in the decades preceding 1910, when the Cape Colony and three other self-governing British colonies came together to form the UNION OF SOUTH AFRICA. Except for a brief interlude of Dutch rule from 1803 to 1806, the Cape Colony had been under British rule since 1795. SLAVERY constituted a principal feature of life in the Cape Colony, but in 1834 the practice of selling human beings was abolished there and throughout the British Empire. Because it had a substantial settler population of BOERS (soon to be called AFRIKANERS) and more recent English immigrants, in 1853 Britain granted the colony limited self-government. Its constitution based the right to vote on wealth, not race. By 1872 the Cape Colony had become fully self-governing as far as its internal affairs were concerned.

In the latter half of the 19th century the eastern boundaries of the Cape Colony expanded dramatically beyond the Fish River, the original border between Xhosaland and the colony. Despite spirited resistance by the XHOSA people, the British prevailed, and the colony steadily expanded during the course of nine Cape Frontier Wars, which lasted for total of nearly 100 years. The CATTLE KILLING of 1856–57 significantly weakened the Xhosa, greatly facilitating a more rapid colonial expansion. Ultimately the colony grew to include the Transkei, as the territories to the east were known. The colony also expanded northward, and in 1895 Britain annexed the area known as BECHUANALAND (present-day BOTSWANA). The geographic area of the colony nearly doubled, and its population dramatically grew.

In the last quarter of the 19th century the economic importance of the Cape Colony decreased because of the discovery of vast deposits of GOLD and DIAMONDS in the interior of southern Africa. At the same time, however, the colony benefited from supplying agricultural commodities to the emerging MINING centers in the JOHANNESBURG and KIMBERLEY areas. CAPE TOWN, the colony's capital and the main gateway to the rest of the country, prospered following the construction of railroads to the mining centers.

During the ANGLO-BOER WAR (1899–1902) the colony was for a time the principal base for British operations. Significant fighting also occurred within its borders, at Kimberley and Makefing. When the Union of South Africa was formed, in 1910, the Cape Colony became the Cape Province, one of four provinces in the country. Prior to unification much greater economic and political freedoms were extended to black Africans in the Cape Colony than in other parts of the country, especially in the Boer-dominated provinces of the TRANSVAAL and ORANGE FREE STATE. As a result considerable controversy arose concerning what form racial relations in the Union of South Africa would assume. Ultimately a compromise was reached whereby the Cape Province retained its political institutions and traditions, but in the interior voting was restricted along racial lines.

See also: CAPE COLONY (Vol. III); CAPE FRONTIER WARS (Vol. III); MINERAL REVOLUTION (Vol. IV).

Further reading: Colin Bundy, *The Rise and Fall of the South African Peasantry* (London: James Currey, 1988); Noël Mostert, *Frontiers: The Epic of South Africa's Creation and the Tragedy of the Xhosa People* (New York: Alfred A. Knopf, 1992).

Cape Coloured People Term used in SOUTH AFRICA to describe people with a mixed racial heritage. Cape Coloured People constitute the largest population group in CAPE TOWN and the neighboring areas of the Western Cape Province, and over the first half of the 20th century they represented about 9 percent of the total population of South Africa.

With their origins dating back to the Dutch settlement of South Africa in the 1600s, the Cape Coloured People originally were the descendants of white settlers and indigenous Khoikhoi and SAN peoples. The Dutch settlers also imported slaves and political prisoners from Southeast Asia, known as Malays, to be workers on their farms. The Malays, too, were incorporated into the Coloured population, as were slaves from West Africa and MADAGASCAR. Along with the Dutch settlers of the CAPE COLONY, the Cape Coloured People began to speak AFRIKAANS, which is a LANGUAGE derived from Dutch but also incorporating many words and syntax from indigenous languages. Afrikaans, then, is as much the language of the Cape Coloured People as it is of the AFRIKANERS. In the 19th century, after the Cape Colony had passed into British hands, the term "Cape Coloured" came into common usage to describe this population of mixed-ethnic background.

Under the rule of both Britain and the UNION OF SOUTH AFRICA, the Cape Coloured People held an intermediary social position between the privileged whites and the disenfranchised Africans of the country. During the 1800s, for example, many of the Cape Coloured became skilled artisans and professionals. At the same time, however, because of the views held by many white South Africans regarding race, Cape Coloured People faced widespread discrimination, which restricted their educational and job opportunities and relegated them to a generally subordinate position within South African society.

Because of their social position the Cape Coloured People themselves were often divided in their attitudes toward the white-dominated government. Sometimes they supported the government in order to protect their limited privileges and sometimes they pushed for relief from the racial segregation prevalent in the 19th and 20th centuries in South Africa. This sense of being "in-between" led to a growing political consciousness. At the head of this movement was Dr. Abdullah Abdurahman (1872–1940), a Glasgow University graduate and medical doctor from Cape Town who, in 1903, joined the nascent African People's Organization (APO). Becoming president of the APO in 1905, Abdurahman shaped it into the leading organization promoting coloured political interests (for, despite its name it was principally a coloured organization). Abdurahman served for a quarter century on both the Cape Town City Council and the Cape Provincial Council.

As the 20th century progressed political involvement among the Cape Coloured People intensified. By the mid-1930s many young Cape Coloured were abandoning the moderate positions of their parents and joining the National Liberation League of South Africa, which was formed in 1935 and which called for a political alliance of all of South Africa's oppressed people against the white power structure. Among its leaders was Abdurahman's daughter, Zainunnissa "Cissie" Gool (1900–1963). The events occurring soon after the end of World War II (1939–45) reinforced this trend. The postwar political dominance by South Africa's conservative National party

allowed APARTHEID to systematically become the law of the land, and the government began codifying both the definition of the Cape Coloured population and the parameters of the group's rights and privileges. After 1948, for example, the Population Registration Act officially classified all South Africans as white, coloured, Bantu (Bantu being the apartheid-era term for individuals of African descent), or Indian.

Given the strictures of the apartheid regulations, classification within the government's divisions was critical for people's well being. Indeed, it could determine everything from the kind of job a person could have to where he or she might live to what sort of EDUCATION he might be entitled to. In spite of the government's protests that the racial classifications were objective in nature, the system frequently led, not simply to inequities, but to situations in which one sibling in a family would be classified as white while another might be classified as Cape Coloured.

Ethnic tests were a basic part of life for the Cape Coloured and other individuals during the apartheid era. Although officials often spoke of the objective or even scientific basis of their system, things were rarely that. Indeed, one of the government's more notorious "tests" for racial classification involved placing a pencil in a person's hair. If the hair sprang back when the pencil was twirled, the individual was regarded as Cape Coloured; if it did not spring back, the person was classified as "white." Using standards like this, the government created eight categories of Coloured people in South Africa: Cape Coloured, Malay, Griqua, Chinese, Indian, Other Indian, Other Asiatic, and Other Coloured. According to the government's system, people of Japanese origin were considered "honorary whites."

As reaction against apartheid widened and deepened during the late 1950s and 1960s, an increasing number of Cape Coloured People became more vocal in their opposition to the apartheid regime. Particularly disruptive during this period were two pieces of legislation. One, passed in 1950, forced people to relocate outside of "whites only" areas, and the other, passed in 1956, removed Coloured People from the common voting roll. By the end of the apartheid era, in 1994, the Cape Coloured population had for the most part joined those South Africans calling for an end to the country's race-based social stratification.

See also: AFRICAN NATIONAL CONGRESS (Vol. IV); KHOIKHOI (Vols. II, III); RACE AND RACISM (Vol. IV).

Cape Town Port city that was the first European settlement in present-day SOUTH AFRICA. Cape Town functioned as the administrative and military headquarters of the British CAPE COLONY, which was established in 1806, when Britain took control of the colony from the Dutch. The dual British and Dutch influence imprinted on Cape Town is still evident today in terms of its ARCHITECTURE, languages, peoples, and culture. During the 19th century Cape Town's primary role was the provisioning of ships passing by the Cape of Good Hope, approximately 30 miles (48 km) south of the city. However, the opening of the Egyptian SUEZ CANAL, in 1869, reduced the volume of maritime traffic because it was no longer necessary for ships to sail around the tip of Africa to travel between Europe and Asia. With the discovery of huge deposits of GOLD in the TRANSVAAL in the mid-1880s, JOHANNESBURG soon overshadowed Cape Town as South Africa's most important city.

Cape Town continued to grow and remain an important city, however. In 1867 the largest reservoir of DIAMONDS in the world was uncovered in KIMBERLEY. The city served as the main gateway into the interior and benefited greatly through increased trade and immigration. As a result, the population of greater Cape Town grew from 45,000 in 1875 to 171,000 in 1904. Reflecting this growth, villages on the periphery of the city's center developed into populous suburbs, such as Woodstock, Salt River, and Mowbray.

The racial composition of the city's population also began to change. Since its founding, in 1652, its main inhabitants had been Cape Town Europeans and CAPE COLOURED PEOPLE. The economic boom and the immigration of the late 19th century brought a sizeable number of Indian and Eastern European immigrants to the city. Even more significantly, large numbers of Africans, mainly XHOSA speakers from the eastern Cape Colony, filtered into Cape Town for the first time. By 1899 they numbered as many as 10,000. With the upsurge of Cape Town's economy and the pressing need for unskilled LABOR resulting from the ANGLO-BOER WAR (1899–1902), World War I (1914–19), and World War II (1939–45), this influx of Africans dramatically increased during the following 50 years.

Upon the creation of the UNION OF SOUTH AFRICA in 1910, Cape Town became the legislative capital. During the course of the 20th century Cape Town's importance remained tied to its role as a port. But the city also evolved into a manufacturing center, with TEXTILES its most important product. Owing to its beauty, pleasant summer weather, and excellent beaches, Cape Town became a major tourist destination for foreigners and South Africans alike. Part of Cape Town's attraction comes from its reputation for more liberal and relaxed relations between its different racial groups.

See also: CAPE OF GOOD HOPE (Vol. III); CAPE TOWN (Vols. III, V); DUTCH EAST INDIA COMPANY (Vol. III).

Further reading: Vivian Bickford-Smith, Elizabeth van Heyningen, and Nigel Worden, *Cape Town in the Twentieth Century: An Illustrated Social History* (Claremont, South Africa: David Philip Publishers, 1999); John Western, *Outcast Cape Town* (Minneapolis: University of Minnesota Press, 1981).

Cape Verde Islands Group of volcanic islands in the Atlantic Ocean off the coast of West Africa. Cape Verde is an archipelago of islands and islets located 360 miles (579 km) west of SENEGAL. They form the modern nation-state of the Republic of Cape Verde. Cape Verde (or Cabo Verde, in Portuguese) means "Green Cape," but despite the name, the climate is dry and the mountainous landscape is arid. Due to chronically low and irregular rainfall, drought has repeatedly afflicted the islands' human and animal populations.

Cape Verde is divided into the windward (northern) islands (Boa Vista, Sal, Santo Antao, São Nicolau, São Vicente), and the leeward (southern) islands (Brava, Fogo, Maio, and Santiago). They were a Portuguese possession from 1462 until 1975. Originally Cape Verde functioned as a Portuguese base for the SLAVE TRADE and other commercial activities along the West African coast.

The abolition of the slave trade in the 1870s damaged the islands' ECONOMY since it was not a productive area for the CASH CROPS that, on the mainland, had replaced the slave trade over the course of the 19th century. The islands had to rely instead on the servicing and repair of ships putting in at its harbors in the cities of Mindelo and Praia. The Cape Verde Islands remain inextricably linked to maritime commerce, as they are situated at a virtual ocean crossroads between Africa, Europe, and the Americas. Many of the islanders themselves work on ships or have emigrated to Portugal, New England, and elsewhere in the Atlantic region. The interaction of peoples from all over the world has resulted in an ethnically and culturally diverse population, part African and part European.

Responding to the oppression of Portuguese rule, Cape Verdean resistance coalesced into the African Party for the Independence of Guinea and Cape Verde, a nationalist liberation movement founded in 1956 and led by Amílcar CABRAL (1924–1973).

See also: CAPE VERDE, REPUBLIC OF (Vols. I, II, III, V); AFRICAN PARTY FOR THE INDEPENDENCE OF GUINEA AND CAPE VERDE (Vol. V); PORTUGAL AND AFRICA (Vols. III, IV, V).

Casely-Hayford, J. E. (Joseph Ephraim Casely Hayford) (1866–1930) *Ghanaian nationalist leader*

Known as a boy by his Fante name, Ekra Agyiman, J. E. Casely-Hayford was born in the coastal trading town of CAPE COAST in the British GOLD COAST COLONY (present-day GHANA). He was the son of an ordained minister and, through his mother, part of a prominent commercial family. He studied first at schools in his hometown and then went to SIERRA LEONE to attend FOURAH BAY COLLEGE. After returning to the Gold Coast Colony he worked as both a school principal and journalist before going to England to study law. In 1896 he returned home with a law degree.

In 1898 the first edition of his book, *The Truth about the West African Land Question,* was issued by the London publisher C. M. Phillips. Written on behalf of the ABORIGINES' RIGHTS PROTECTION SOCIETY, the book protested British policy regarding land ownership. Casely-Hayford was a legal colleague of John Mensah SARBAH (1864–1910), who organized the protection society. In legal briefs that he and Sarbah co-wrote, as well as in his own book, Casely-Hayford stressed the fact that, according to African customary law, all land is under ownership even if it appears abandoned or not under cultivation. Thus, he argued, the British government had no legal right to appropriate land for its own use. His defense forced the Gold Coast government to protect African land titles.

Casely-Hayford's writings also tried to explain to British authorities the value of local institutions. In 1903 the London publisher Sweet and Maxwell published his second book, *Gold Coast Native Institutions: With Some Thoughts Upon a Healthy Imperial Policy for the Gold Coast and Ashanti.* In it he argued that British administration, despite its professed policies to the contrary, inhibited the growth of nationalism and did not foster the emergence of self-government among Africans.

In 1911 Casely-Hayford published his third book, *Ethiopia Unbound.* In this book, the first novel written in English by an African, he is critical of uneducated traditional rulers, whom British administrators supported. The natural rulers of modern African societies, he argued, should be educated, westernized Africans.

After World War I (1914–18) Casely-Hayford began to adopt a broader, pan-Africanist outlook that stressed the achievement of self-determination through international cooperation among West Africans. He actively promoted his beliefs in his newspaper, the *Gold Coast Leader.* In 1920, with Dr. Akiwande Savage of NIGERIA, Casely-Hayford organized the NATIONAL CONGRESS OF BRITISH WEST AFRICA, which convened on three other occasions, 1923, 1925–26, and 1929–30. The conference was unable to gather broad support among Africans, however, and when Casely-Hayford died, in 1930, the National Congress died with him.

While he never saw the completion of many of his political objectives, Casely-Hayford made an important intellectual and political contribution to early PAN-AFRICANISM. His work is now seen as a precursor to the NATIONALISM AND INDEPENDENCE MOVEMENTS that were to sweep away COLONIAL RULE after World War II (1939–45).

See also: COLONIALISM, INFLUENCE OF (Vol. IV); DU BOIS, W. E. B. (Vol. IV); ENGLAND AND AFRICA (Vols. III, IV, V).

Further reading: Magnus J. Sampson, *West African leadership: Public Speeches Delivered by J. E. Casely Hayford* (London: F. Cass, 1969).

cash crops Agricultural products grown specifically for sale on the market rather than for personal consumption. From the earliest days farmers have traded or sold some of their surplus FOOD CROPS in order to obtain tools and utensils or other foods. Cash crops, on the other hand, are crops grown specifically for sale on the open market. Farmers use the income they receive from these crops to purchase goods and services, pay taxes and fees, and meet other needs. The market is thus a necessary mechanism. Without a market there would be no reason to grow cash crops.

Sugar Sugar was the first major cash crop in world history. Sugarcane, from which processed sugar is made, was first cultivated in Southeast Asia and Persia. In the 12th century Arab conquerors began to plant sugarcane in the eastern Mediterranean, where it soon was grown on large, plantation-like estates. In the 14th century, Europe, especially Venice and Spain, became involved in the sugar trade. Production spread to the Mediterranean islands of Cyprus and Sicily, where forced LABOR was often used to plant, harvest, and process the sugar. The locus of sugar production for the European market kept shifting steadily westward until the 16th century, when Portugal established sugar plantations in its Brazilian colonies. The sugar industry depended on the forced labor of captive Africans who were brought against their wills to work on these plantations.

The 17th century saw sugar production spread into the Caribbean, with continued expansion throughout the 18th and into the 19th centuries. Meanwhile, European planters also established sugar plantations on the Indian Ocean islands of MAURITIUS and RÉUNION as well as in NATAL Colony, in SOUTH AFRICA.

In the production and sale of sugar, one sees features that were typical of most later cash crops. It was grown for distant markets, the producers were not the principal consumers, the labor force was coerced, TRANSPORTATION systems emerged to move bulk commodities, political control over the areas of production lay elsewhere, and the principal beneficiaries were those who financed the system. In short, sugar was the ideal colonial export crop.

Palm Oil and Other Products Cash crops as a feature of colonial African economies predate the colonial period itself. The first major cash crop in West Africa was PALM OIL, which was also an important forest-zone food crop. In the early 19th century the Industrial Revolution began to spread through Europe, and machinery replaced hand labor in many industries. At a time before petroleum

The need for cash crops intensified Africa's perennial lack of water for agriculture. This undated photo shows a brick irrigation furrow that was designed to carry water to a citrus farm in South Africa. © *Smith's Photo Service/New York Times*

products were available as lubricants, factory owners needed a consistent supply of vegetable oils such as palm oil to keep machinery running smoothly.

> As part of the early 19th-century effort to suppress the SLAVE TRADE, European abolitionists promoted "legitimate commerce." They wanted the export of agricultural products to replace the trade in human beings.

Peanuts, called GROUNDNUTS throughout Africa, were another important "oil crop" that also was a food crop. In the 1840s farmers in the SENEGAMBIA REGION of West Africa started to export significant quantities of groundnuts, mainly to France. By the mid-1880s exports averaged nearly 30,000 tons (27,000 metric tons).

Much of the production of both palm oil and groundnuts was in the hands of peasant farmers, though some captive labor was also utilized. The full transformation of those crops into marketable commodities, however, was not done in Africa. Europe imported unprocessed palm oil and groundnuts for processing and distribution in various forms.

Cloves became another important export crop. In the 1830s Arab planters along the coastal zone of East Africa, which was under the control of the sultan of ZANZIBAR, established plantations that eventually produced 90 percent of the world's supply of cloves. Farmed by enslaved workers, the crops were grown specifically for export to the United States and elsewhere.

The Emergence of Single-Crop Economies Once the era of COLONIAL CONQUEST was complete, Africa's European rulers had to find a way to make their new possession profitable. Because the local African economies were primarily agricultural, one obvious answer was to promote cash crops for export. The income generated by agricultural EXPORTS could be used to purchase manufactured imports from Europe. Also, colonial governments could tax these imports and exports to obtain revenue for the administration of the colonies.

The export ECONOMY of many colonies came to rest on a single cash crop. Established peasant-produced cash crops such as groundnuts and palm oil continued to be important, and new crops, especially COCOA, emerged. In the 1890s, for example, farmers in Britain's GOLD COAST COLONY (modern-day GHANA) began to export cocoa. By

1911 the colony was exporting 40,000 tons (36,000 metric tons) annually to chocolate manufacturers such as the Hershey Chocolate Company, in the United States, and Cadbury Limited, in Britain.

The premier cash crop during the colonial era, however, was COTTON. Throughout the continent, colonial administrators promoted the production of cotton because the European powers wanted a cheap and controlled source of raw cotton for their textile mills back home. Cotton was grown mostly by peasant farmers. However, unlike cocoa, the price that farmers would get for their cotton was too low to stimulate production voluntarily. Thus, farmers were often coerced into planting this crop.

Westerners also established large plantations to produce export crops. In 1911 Lever Brothers, a British soap-making company, gained a concession of 1.9 million acres (768,888 hectares) in the BELGIAN CONGO (today's Democratic Republic of the CONGO) to produce palm oil for soap and other products. Also notable was the million-acre (404,678 hectare) plantation that the Firestone Tire and Rubber Company of the United States established in LIBERIA, in 1926. That plantation provided RUBBER for tire-manufacturing plants in the United States and also supplied the Allies with rubber during World War II (1939–45).

Sisal, used for making rope and twine, was another major plantation-produced crop. During the colonial era, it became the principal export crop of TANGANYIKA (part of present-day TANZANIA). Working conditions on the sisal plantations were for the most part very bad, and the plantation managers often resorted to coercion to maintain the needed number of workers.

Farming by Europeans In those parts of Africa with significant numbers of European SETTLERS, white farmers also produced cash crops for market. For example, the COLONS of ALGERIA grew wheat and tended vineyards. British farmers in KENYA planted COFFEE and raised dairy cattle; in SOUTHERN RHODESIA (today's ZIMBABWE), they planted tobacco. South Africa's white and mostly Afrikaner farmers grew maize (corn) as a cash crop to feed the country's numerous city dwellers. White South African farmers also exported citrus and other fruit to Europe and developed an extensive wine industry.

Working conditions for African laborers on many of the white-owned farms were often extremely harsh, especially in South Africa and in Algeria. However, black Africans had few options because they had lost so much of their productive lands to white farmers.

Conditions at Independence In the late 1950s and early 1960s the colonial era came to an end, and most African nations gained their independence from European rule. Because of practices inherited from their colonial past, however, the economies of the new African nations still depended significantly on income received from agricultural exports and from the MINERALS AND METALS industries, which were dominated by Europeans. In short, political independence did not translate into economic independence.

See also: AGRICULTURE (Vol. IV); CASH CROPS (Vol. V); COLONIAL RULE (Vol. IV); COLONIALISM, INFLUENCE OF (Vol. IV); PEASANTRY (Vol. IV); SLAVERY (Vols. I, II, III, IV); TRANSATLANTIC SLAVE TRADE (Vol. III).

Further reading: Ralph Austen, *African Economic History* (Portsmouth, N.H.: Heinemann, 1987).

Cattle Killing, The (1856–1857) Ill-fated "golden age," or millenarian, movement among the XHOSA that led to their final military and political demise as well as their dislocation. The teenaged prophetess NONGQAWUSE (c. 1840–1900) preached that if the Xhosa of the eastern CAPE COLONY would destroy their grain and kill their cattle, then their dead chiefs and heroes would rise from the dead and liberate the people from British colonial oppression. She promised that the Xhosa would be rewarded with new, strong cattle and abundant FOOD and that the European SETTLERS would be driven into the sea.

During this time many of the Xhosa's cattle had contracted lung sickness (bovine pleuropneumonia), a fatal disease that quickly spread to Xhosa herds after whites brought infected European cattle into the country in 1853. All told, it is estimated that at least 400,000 cattle were slaughtered by the Xhosa, either in conformity with Nongqawuse's prophecy or because they had become infected with lung sickness. As a result an estimated 35,000 to 50,000 Xhosa perished of starvation during 1856–57. Another 150,000 were forced to leave Xhosaland in search of food and employment on European-owned farms or in towns and cities of the colony.

The Xhosa fiercely resisted European military and cultural encroachment during the first half of the 19th century, but the devastation wrought by the cattle-killing movement dramatically weakened Xhosa unity and military strength. The Cape Colony's governor, George Grey (1812–1898), exploited the calamitous events following the cattle killing to strip powerful Xhosa chiefs of their political authority, military power, and economic independence. White settlers subsequently filtered into Xhosaland and acquired large tracts of land.

See also: CAPE FRONTIER WARS (Vol. III).

Further reading: J. B. Peires, *The Dead Will Arise: Nongqawuse and the Great Xhosa Cattle-Killing Movement of 1856–7* (Bloomington: Indiana University Press, 1989).

Central African Federation (Federation of Rho-desia and Nyasaland) (1953–1963) Short-lived alliance of British colonies made up of NORTHERN RHODESIA (present-day ZAMBIA), SOUTHERN RHODESIA (today's ZIMBABWE) and the PROTECTORATE of NYASALAND (now

MALAWI). Britain initiated the idea of the federation, arguing that it would benefit the three colonies economically. White settlers also hoped that the alliance would counteract the economic influence of SOUTH AFRICA. Because the capital of the federation was SALISBURY (present-day Harare), in Southern Rhodesia, the significant positions in the federation were held by white settlers living in that country. Industries and company headquarters were concentrated in Southern Rhodesia, while Northern Rhodesia and Nyasaland, which produced many of the commodities, were neglected. Black Africans pro-tested against the federation, which they felt was designed to impoverish Africans and benefit the white settlers. However, both white and black people in Northern Rhodesia and Nyasaland felt that Southern Rhodesia benefited most from the alliance. Roy WELENSKY (1907–1991), the second and last prime minister of the federation, opposed any changes to the power-sharing structure that would include black people or African-majority rule. Britain began plans to unify the federated territories into a single state, but demonstrations and strong nationalistic sentiment undercut the plan and led to the dissolution of the federation in 1963. In 1964, with the federation ended, Nyasaland and Northern Rhodesia became the independent countries of Malawi and Zambia, respectively. Due to the strength of white influence, however, Southern Rhodesia did not become independent Zimbabwe until 1980.

See also: COLONIAL RULE (Vol. IV); HARARE (Vol. V).

Central African Republic (CAR)

Landlocked country in the heart of Central Africa approximately 240,300 square miles (622,400 sq km) in size that is bordered to the north by CHAD, to the east by the Republic of the SUDAN, to the south by the Democratic Republic of the CONGO and the Republic of the CONGO, and to the west by CAMEROON. During the 17th and 18th centuries the small states of Central Africa were greatly disrupted by the SLAVE TRADE. Instability in the region continued in the 19th century, with militaristic traders such as RABIH BIN FADLAL-LAH (c. 1835–1900) raiding the region for captives and ivory. By the mid-19th century the Bobangi, a people living near the Oubangui (Ubangi) River, also were involved in the slave trade and seized captives from the neighboring Baya and Mandjia. This African-organized slave trade hindered the formation of relations between the different groups of people in the area, weakening the social structure of the region.

Central African Republic during Colonial Era: Oubangui-Chari

By the 1880s French explorers had entered the area. The settlement of BANGUI, the future colonial capital, was founded on the upper Oubangui River, extending the reach of the FRENCH CONGO. In 1894 the French declared the OUBANGUI-CHARI colony over the territory between the Oubangui and Chari rivers.

In order to minimize financial risk, France divided the territory among a number of private CONCESSIONAIRE COMPANIES, which administered their claims at their own cost. In their efforts to harvest the region's NATURAL RESOURCES and CASH CROPS, such as RUBBER, COFFEE and COTTON, these companies imposed forced LABOR on local Africans.

African resistance to French COLONIAL RULE resulted in a number of rebellions in Oubangui-Chari. All of these were eventually put down by the French, including the last and most significant revolt, the Kongo Wara Rebellion of 1928–31. After that uprising many Africans in the colony were forced to relocate to French-supervised villages.

In 1905 a governor-general in BRAZZAVILLE was placed in charge of Oubangui-Chari, as well as the colonies of CHAD, GABON, and French Congo. A year later Oubangui-Chari and Chad were administratively linked as Oubangui-Chari-Chad, though the two colonies would be separated again when they joined Gabon and the French Congo as parts of FRENCH EQUATORIAL AFRICA (Afrique Équatoriale Française, AEF), in 1910.

In 1940 Oubangui-Chari joined the rest of AEF in supporting the Free French forces of Charles DE GAULLE (1890–1970) during World War II (1939–45). All told, the colony sent about 3,000 troops to support the Allied efforts in North Africa and Syria. Upon the conclusion of the war, de Gaulle rewarded Oubangui-Chari and the other French African colonies with general French citizenship, the abolition of forced labor, and the right to send deputies to the National Assembly in France.

One such deputy was Barthélemy Boganda (1910–1959), the territory's first Catholic priest and a nationalist leader. Boganda formed the Movement for Social Development in Black Africa (Mouvement pour l'Evolution Sociale de l'Afrique Noire, MESAN) in 1949. When territorial assemblies were allowed, in 1956, MESAN dominated the elections.

As president of the Grand Council of French Equatorial Africa, Boganda proposed the independence of all of French Equatorial Africa as a single entity, with the intention of avoiding the political and economic problems that might arise from the independence of the individual territories. In the face of both French and local African objections to his plan, Boganda instead said "yes" to de Gaulle's oui-ou-non (yes-or-no) offer to the French African colonies, accepting autonomy for Oubangui-Chari as part of the FRENCH UNION. Oubangui-Chari became the autonomous Central African Republic in 1958, with Boganda as prime minister. In 1959 a constitution was established and Boganda became president, though he died later that year. In 1960 CAR became fully independent, led by President David Dacko (1930–   ).

See also: CENTRAL AFRICAN REPUBLIC (Vols. I, II, III, V); COLONIAL CONQUEST (Vol. IV); COLONIALISM, INFLUENCE OF (Vol. IV); FRANCE AND AFRICA (Vols. III, IV, V).

Further reading: Patrick Manning, *Francophone sub-Saharan Africa, 1880–1995,* 2nd ed. (New York: Cambridge University Press, 1998).

Césaire, Aimé (1913–   ) *West Indian and initiator of the Négritude cultural movement*

Aimé Césaire was born in Basse Point, Martinique, which was then still a French colony in the Caribbean. He received his primary education in Fort-de-France, the capital of Martinique. Then in the 1930s he went to Paris to study literature. While living in Paris he met Léopold SENGHOR (1906–2001) from SENEGAL and Leon-Gontran Damas (1912–1978) from Guyana. Together, in 1934, they founded the student publication *L'Etudiant noir* (African student) in which Césaire first gave expression to the ideas that were to crystalize into the NÉGRITUDE movement. He coined the term *négritude* in his 1939 poem, *Cahier d'un retour au pays natal* (Notebook of a return to my native land), which was originally published in the magazine *Volontes* and reprinted in other publications in 1944 and 1956. In the 1940s the term came to be applied to the nationalist pan-African literary and cultural movement that emerged among French-speaking intellectuals from Africa and the AFRICAN DIASPORA.

In 1939 Césaire and his family left France and returned to Martinique after the outbreak of World War II (1939–45). He and his wife taught school in Fort-de-France, and Césaire himself became active in politics and in the Communist party. He was elected mayor of Fort-de-France and deputy for Martinique to the French National Assembly in 1945. Although he renounced his Communist affiliation, in 1956, he continued to be politically active in Martinique until retiring from politics in 1993.

During the war's latter years Césaire also maintained an active literary career. In 1941 he founded a literary journal called *Tropiques,* which championed black culture. For a while he wrote mostly poetry; after 1955, however, he turned increasingly to drama as a vehicle for his ideas. Among his plays from this period are *Et les chiens se taisaient* (And the dogs kept quiet), from 1956; *La tragédie du roi Christophe* (The tragedy of King Christophe), written in 1963; *Une saison au Congo* (A season in the Congo), written in 1966; and *Une Tempete* (A Tempest), written in 1968. Both Césaire's poetic and dramatic themes include pride in his African heritage and culture and in African accomplishments. He also deals with the effects of DECOLONIZATION, cultural alienation, and a reconciliation of the past and present. His writing style often described as sur-

real, Aimé Césaire is firmly established among the most important black writers of the 20th century.

See also: FRANCE AND AFRICA (Vols. IV, V); LITERATURE IN COLONIAL AFRICA (Vol. IV); LITERATURE IN MODERN AFRICA (Vol. V).

Further reading: Gregson Davis, *Aimé Césaire* (New York: Cambridge University Press, 1997).

Cetshwayo (Cetewayo, Cetchwayo, Ketchwayo) (c. 1826–1884) *Last independent king of Zululand*

A wily political force as well as an able military leader, Cetshwayo overcame many opponents on his way to power. His father, Mpande (r. 1840–1872), had seized the ZULU throne from Cetshwayo's uncle, Dingane (r. 1828–1840). The elder of two sons, Cetshwayo had been declared Mpande's heir at an early age. His father, however, underwent a change of heart, and during the 1850s began showing favor to his younger son, Mbulazi (1827–1856). Eventually, this led to a civil war in which the forces of the two brothers battled for supremacy. Although Mbulazi was supported by the British from their neighboring colony of NATAL, in 1856 he was defeated and killed, leaving Cetshwayo the heir to the throne.

From 1857 until 1872, when Mpande died, Cetshwayo was effectively the king of Zululand, with his father holding the throne in name only. During this period Cetshwayo faced frequent incursions by the BOERS, who were intent upon pushing into Zululand from the TRANSVAAL. Cetshwayo responded by attempting to establish a diplomatic link with the British, who, interested in dominating southern Africa themselves, were intent on reducing Boer power. Thus Cetshwayo had reason to be optimistic when the British annexed the Boer South African Republic in April 1877.

Cetshwayo's optimism was short-lived, however, for Britain clearly saw a strong, independent Zululand as a threat to its rule in the region. Soon the British began a campaign to discredit Cetshwayo and justify intervention on their part. In 1878 Cetshwayo provided them with their excuse when his warriors raided Zulu opponents in Natal. In response the British authorities issued Cetshwayo an ultimatum that they knew he would reject: hand over the raiders, pay substantial reparations, and disband the powerful Zulu army.

When Cetshwayo's inevitable refusal came, the British invaded on January 11, 1879, thus initiating the ANGLOZULU WAR. Confident that their 18,000 troops would be more than enough for the situation, the British, under the leadership of Lord Chelmsford (1868–1913), were unprepared for both the number of warriors in Cetshwayo's army and the intensity of their efforts. At the Battle of ISANDLWANA, on January 22, the British suffered a crushing defeat, one of the worst ever for their overseas military forces. Ultimately, however, the sophisticated British weaponry proved to be more than a match for Zulu spears and shields. Following their defense of the hospital station at Rorke's Drift, the British went on to defeat Cetshwayo at Ulundi, on July 4. After the British victory Cetshwayo was sent to CAPE TOWN, where he was held prisoner for two years before being exiled to the neighboring area of the Cape Flats.

Cetshwayo, however, refused to give up the thought of returning to power, and he eventually went to London to plead his case to Queen Victoria (1819–1901). There he created a popular sensation while also impressing British leaders, who began to see Cetshwayo as an alternative to the chaotic squabbling among the various independent chieftains who had been left to govern Zululand after his defeat. Cetshwayo returned to Zululand from England early in 1883, and he soon was back on the throne. This time, however, the British took care to make sure that he had no army to support him.

Cetshwayo's return to power was not unopposed, and he immediately found himself in a civil war against the forces of Zibhebhu (1841–1904), who previously had been placed in charge of northern Zululand by Britain. The war went on from March to October, with Cetshwayo finally being defeated and forced from power. He died on February 8, 1884, possibly a victim of poison. He was succeeded by his son, DINIZULU (1868–1913), but the power of the throne was by that point much diminished.

See also: COLONIAL CONQUEST (Vol. IV); ENGLAND AND AFRICA (Vols. III, IV, V).

Further reading: John Laband, *Rope of Sand* (South Africa: Jonathan Ball, 1995); Donald R. Morris, *The Washing of the Spears* (South Africa: Jonathan Cape, 1965).

Chad

Landlocked country with an area of about 496,000 square miles (1,284,600 sq km), located in the central-Sudanic belt to the east of Lake Chad. This large nation is bordered by LIBYA to the north, the Republic of the SUDAN to the east, CAMEROON and the CENTRAL AFRICAN REPUBLIC to the south, and NIGER and NIGERIA to the west. Northern Chad stretches into the Sahara, but the country's southern region lies within the tropics.

In the middle of the 19th century the kingdoms of Bagirmi, KANEM-BORNU, and Wadai occupied the majority of the area making up present-day Chad. By the end of the 1890s, however, these once powerful Islamic states were overrun by the Sudanese warlord and slave-trader, RABIH BIN FADLALLAH (c. 1835–1900).

The French entered the region in 1890, but they were slow to establish a firm presence. They battled Rabih for years, finally killing him during the decisive Battle of Kousséri, in 1900. The death of Rabih opened the door to further French expansion, and by 1913 the conquest of Chad was complete.

French occupation of Chad was characterized by apathy in governance and an overall lack of infrastructural improvement and modernization. In 1905 the French organized Chad as a territory, which in 1906 was linked with OUBANGUI-CHARI. In 1910 Chad was placed under the umbrella of FRENCH EQUATORIAL AFRICA (Afrique Équatoriale Française, AEF). Under the AEF Chad was overseen by a French-appointed lieutenant governor, who took his orders from the AEF governor general in BRAZZAVILLE. The French did not give Chad the status of a separate colony until 1920.

Within Chad the French asserted control over only the southern regions, granting the rest of the colony a form of self-governance in return for local leaders ensuring security of the caravan trails and maintaining a semblance of law and order. This hands-off approach to governing was likely a result of a lack of resources and interest in the area, rather than any sense of propriety. As a result banditry and slave raids continued in central and northern Chad into the 1920s, and economic development in these regions was stagnant.

In the south the inhabitants initially welcomed the French. The colonial power had put an end to the SLAVE TRADE, introduced COTTON farming, initiated development projects, and built a few schools. But this goodwill toward the French was short-lived, as a head tax, cotton quotas, and the use of forced PORTERAGE and LABOR angered the populace. Relations with France improved, however, as a result of events of World War II (1939–45).

In 1939 France capitulated to Germany. A year later, Charles DE GAULLE (1890–1970) proclaimed a Free French government in BRAZZAVILLE, and Chad's lieutenant governor, Adolphe-Félix-Sylvestre ÉBOUÉ (1884–1944), was the first to recognize the exiled administration. During the war French interest and financial support in Chad grew, and the colony became the base from which Free France launched its attacks against Italian-occupied Libya.

After the war, in 1946, France allowed Chad to form a territorial legislature, which elected representatives to the French General Council of the AEF. The people of Chad were made French citizens and were allowed to elect representatives to the French legislative bodies. The real governing power, however, remained in France, and local politics were dominated by the Chadian Democratic Union (Union Démocratique Tchadienne, UDT), which represented the interests of French businesses and the traditional, noble leaders from the northern region of Chad.

During the 1950s, however, Chad, like many other French colonies, began the slow journey towards independence. The Chadian Progressive Party (Parti Progressiste Tchadien, PPT), comprised mostly of southern-Chadian intellectuals, represented Chadian interests and became the main opposition to UDT control of the government.

In 1956 the French enacted the *loi cadre* (Overseas Reform Act), which granted further autonomy to Chad and France's other African colonies. In 1957 the PPT dominated local elections, allowing the party's leader, Gabriel Lisette (1919–2001), to form the first African government of Chad.

In 1958 Chadians participated in the referendum on France's new constitution. Chad's representatives largely supported it, at the same time unanimously voting for a resolution making Chad an autonomous republic within the FRENCH UNION. Later that year, the AEF was terminated.

In March of 1959 Lissette's coalition government collapsed in the face of opposition from the Muslim north, but the PPT quickly regained control under the leadership of Francois-Ngarta Tombalbaye (1918–1975). Tombalbaye consolidated support to strengthen the PPT, and in 1960 was elected the first president of independent Chad. The country, however, was divided along a "fault line" shared with Nigeria and the Sudan, that of a Muslim north and a significantly Christian south. As with the other two countries, Chad also experienced civil war soon after independence.

See also: CHAD (Vols. I, II, III, V); COLONIAL CONQUEST (Vol. IV); COLONIAL RULE (Vol. IV); COLONIALISM, INFLUENCE OF (Vol. IV); FRANCE AND AFRICA (Vols. IV, V); TOMBALBAYE, FRANCOIS-NGARTA (Vol. V).

Further reading: Patrick Manning, *Francophone Sub-Saharan Africa, 1880–1995*, 2nd ed. (New York: Cambridge University Press, 1998).

Champion, A. W. G. (Allison Wessels George Champion) (1893–1975) *South African nationalist and trade union leader*

In 1893 Allison Wessels George Champion was born in NATAL to a ZULU family that had been educated by MISSIONARIES. As a young man he received what was at the time a considerable education for an African in southern Africa. In 1913 he left school to become a policeman in JOHANNESBURG and then worked as a clerk for a GOLD mine. He became involved in LABOR UNIONS as president of a mine clerks' association, which was formed in 1920. At the time many of the Africans who had lost their lands to white farmers moved to the cities in search of a livelihood. The rights of these urbanized Africans were promoted by the AFRICAN NATIONAL CONGRESS (ANC), founded in 1912, but many felt that the organization's tactics were too moderate. Accordingly, in 1918, Clements

KADALIE (1896–1951) founded the Industrial and Commercial Workers' Union (ICU) on the docks of CAPE TOWN. Open to everyone from sharecroppers to dock workers, the union opposed the increasing number of restrictions that the South African government imposed on the rights of Africans.

In 1925 Champion met Kadalie and joined the ICU as a union organizer. By the time he arrived in the port city of DURBAN in Natal, Kadalie's ICU was as well known as the ANC. By 1927 Champion had increased its numbers to include 70 percent of the Zulu urban workforce, many of whom worked in the city's bustling dockyards. He instituted successful court challenges of identification requirements, living restrictions, and local curfews imposed on Africans.

After a falling out with Kadalie, Champion founded a separate branch of the ICU in Natal, splintering the union, which by that time had about 100,000 members. In 1928, however, after a period of urban rioting caused by an ICU-led boycott of white businesses, Champion was banished from Durban for violating the Riotous Assemblies Act. The weakened ICU was itself in danger. By 1930, accused of Communist leanings and affected by the lack of skilled organizers, both branches of the ICU were foundering. Moreover, that year Champion was exiled from Natal.

Champion, however, continued to work for the betterment of the Zulu people. During the 1940s, after his return from exile, he was the founder and provincial president of the Natal branch of the ANC. In 1947 Champion helped to quell a period of violence and unrest in Durban between Africans and Indians.

In his later years Champion was a member of the central committee of the Zulu-based Inkatha Freedom Party. In 1975 he died in his home in Durban's Chesterville township.

See also: INKATHA FREEDOM PARTY (Vol. V).

Further reading: Shula Marks, *The Ambiguities of Dependence in South Africa: Class, Nationalism, and the State in Twentieth-Century Natal* (Baltimore: Johns Hopkins University Press, 1986).

Chewa Dominant ethnic group of MALAWI who also inhabit parts of ZAMBIA and ZIMBABWE. ChiChewa, the Chewa LANGUAGE, is part of the Bantu grouping of languages.

The Chewa, who trace their ancestry to the Luba region of present-day Republic of the CONGO, faced great difficulties and changes in the 19th century. From the south came the Ngoni, a ZULU offshoot, who used their military might to establish several conquest states that incorporated some of the Chewa people. From the east came militant YAO merchants engaged in the ivory and slave trades that extended from the SWAHILI COAST into the interior.

In the middle of the 19th century Christian MISSIONARIES began to establish a presence among the Chewa. Led by the example of Dr. David LIVINGSTONE (1813–1873), the missionaries sought to end the SLAVE TRADE. They also had established mission stations and schools by the 1870s, but these were located mostly to the north of the Chewa-populated areas. In 1889 the BRITISH SOUTH AFRICA COMPANY began to take control of the Chewa homeland, and by 1904 the British government had taken over, establishing the PROTECTORATE of NYASALAND.

African nationalist sentiments developed in earnest when Nyasaland was incorporated into the CENTRAL AFRICAN FEDERATION, in 1953. Fearing that the federation would institute the racist APARTHEID policies that were prevalent in SOUTH AFRICA, the Chewa people rallied behind the leadership of ChiChewa-speaker Hastings Kamuzu BANDA (c. 1898–1997) in the drive to end British COLONIAL RULE. Their support helped insure that Banda became prime minister when Nyasaland won its independence, in 1964. Two years later, when the country became the Republic of Malawi, Banda became its first president. As president he promoted the interests of the Chewa, including the use of Chichewa as an official language of Malawi.

While Christianity became a prominent RELIGION among the Chewa, they also continued to engage in older cultural practices that were linked to pre-Christian religious beliefs. These were most notably expressed through elaborate DANCE rituals involving the wearing of symbolic masks. These rituals and other important ceremonies, such as initiations and funerals, were conducted by members of secret dance societies known as Nyau. In this manner, deeply rooted Chewa cultural practices and beliefs persisted throughout the colonial era.

See also: BANTU LANGUAGES (Vols. I, II); CHEWA (Vol. III); CHRISTIANITY, INFLUENCE OF (Vols. IV, V).

Chilembwe, John (c. 1872–1915) *African Christian leader in Nyasaland (present-day Malawi)*

Born into a YAO family in the southern part of NYASALAND, Chilembwe was educated at the Scottish missionary school in Blantyre. About 1892 he was hired as an assistant by an unconventional British missionary named Joseph Booth (1851–1932). Booth differed from the local Scottish Free Church MISSIONARIES in that he treated Africans as equals, paying them fair wages and taking them on as partners in his mission projects.

In 1897 Booth took Chilembwe to America, helping him enroll at Virginia Theological Seminary and College. In America Chilembwe was exposed to the ideas of empowerment-minded black intellectuals such as Booker T. WASHINGTON (1856–1915) and W. E. B. DU BOIS (1868–1963). Within a few years, however, Chilembwe began to suffer from asthma, and in 1900 he returned to Nyasaland. He married and began serving as a foreign missionary for

the National Baptist Convention, a black-run American Christian organization. Upon his return, the people of Nyasaland showed great respect for his intelligence and abilities and flocked to his mission, the Providence Industrial Mission, which he developed into seven schools. Throughout the next decade Chilembwe built up the mission, spreading the message of Christianity and encouraging his nearly 2,000 students to empower themselves through EDUCATION and hard work.

Chilembwe's missionary teachings developed a proto-nationalism among Nyasa people. Nyasaland had become a British PROTECTORATE in 1891, and in 1912 the British administration imposed a hut tax to raise the money needed to run the territory. The tax was a great burden on the Nyasa people, many of whom were forced to work without wages for white settlers to pay their debt. Chilembwe resented this unfair taxation and quietly urged the people of his mission to refuse payment. His attitude turned even more anti-authoritarian at the onset of World War I (1914–18), when fighting between Germany and Britain over control of GERMAN EAST AFRICA spread to northern Nyasaland. Chilembwe could not understand why Nyasa's men were being made to fight for the whites who had taken their land, taxed them unfairly, and reduced them to colonial subjects in their own country. British authorities censored a bitter editorial that he wrote for the *Nyasaland Times*, and Chilembwe and his mission began to be viewed by the British as serious threats to the fragile stability of their protectorate.

Meanwhile Chilembwe began planning a rebellion. It is likely that he knew that his rebellion would not bring down the British administration, but he felt that a symbolic act of resistance was necessary at that time. In January 1915, The Rising, as Chilembwe's rebellion was called, began badly and only got worse. Although they did manage to kill three particularly harsh plantation managers, the rebels failed to secure the arms that they needed; they were easily subdued by British soldiers, who acted quickly and decisively. Not long after the short-lived rebellion Chilembwe was shot and killed by African police as he tried to cross the border into the Portuguese colony of MOZAMBIQUE.

See also: ENGLAND AND AFRICA (Vols. III, IV, V); RESISTANCE AND REBELLION (Vol. IV).

Chimurenga SHONA word meaning "fight" or "struggle," it came to signify a struggle for political and social rights and was applied by Africans fighting to liberate themselves from British COLONIAL RULE in SOUTHERN RHODESIA (today's ZIMBABWE). The word *chimurenga* is believed to originate from stories of the legendary Shona warrior, Sororenzou Murenga. Fighters who demonstrated great abilities were said to fight *chimurenga*, that is, as Murenga fought.

The BRITISH SOUTH AFRICAN COMPANY (BSAC), headed by Cecil RHODES (1853–1902), invaded NDEBELE and Shona lands in 1890, establishing the colony of Southern Rhodesia. The Rozwi state and other Shona kingdoms were in decline, but the Ndebele state of Chief LOBEN-GULA (1836–1894) remained militarily strong. In 1893 the BSAC provoked the Ndebele into a war that ended in their defeat and in Lobengula's death. Within a few years both the Ndebele and the Shona rose in rebellion against the company, which was weakened by the capture of many of its paramilitary police in the JAMESON RAID. The rising, known as the Chimurenga, was led not by the chiefs but by religious leaders. Although it had little chance for success, the Chimurenga was one of the most significant acts of RESISTANCE AND REBELLION against early colonial rule anywhere on the continent. The war ended a year later with a crushing British victory. Rhodes negotiated a settlement with the Ndebele leaders, but he engaged in a ruthless suppression of the Shona.

Mbuya Nehanda was the sister of Chaminuka, a Shona prophet. Nehanda herself prophesied a second Chimurenga, declaring that her "bones would rise again." Her prophecy came to pass nearly one hundred years later, with a second war for liberation, known as the second Chimurenga, breaking out in 1966.

See also: INDEPENDENCE MOVEMENTS (Vol. V); MWARI (Vol. III); SHONA KINGDOMS (Vol. III).

China and Africa China and Africa have a long history of trade. However, during the colonial period European interests dominated both China and Africa. China's relationship with Africa is thought to have begun in 100 BCE, with solid evidence of trade in the seventh century CE. Between 960 and 1270 trade relations grew between merchants in the Horn of Africa and China. In the 14th century, this culminated with the arrivval of 62 Chinese galleons and 100 auxiliary vessels in MOGADISHU and two other ports. This flotilla of Admiral Zheng He (1371–1433) marked a high point in early Sino-African TRADE AND COMMERCE. However, once the ships returned to China, conservative forces at the emperor's court gained control. These elements saw no need to continue such voyages, and China turned increasingly inward, shutting out the rest of the world.

The 19th century was a period of decline in China. The Industrial Revolution and the Western nations' pursuit of COLONIAL CONQUEST and foreign trade changed China's place in the world. Foreign governments—especially those of the United Kingdom, Russia, Germany, France, and the United States—expanded their influence in China and negotiated favorable treaties.

During this time, thinking that Chinese workers were more productive and trustworthy than Africans, the colonial powers began to use Chinese people as *coolies,* or unskilled laborers, for their expanding empires. As a result, in the late 19th century France and Britain brought Chinese workers to the plantations on the islands of MADAGASCAR, MAURITIUS, and RÉUNION, off Africa's eastern coast, in order to build the colonial ECONOMY. Within a decade of the end of the ANGLO-BOER WAR (1899–1902) between 70,000 and 100,000 Chinese laborers were brought to work in the British-owned GOLD mines in SOUTH AFRICA. During this time Germany, too, brought Chinese laborers to its colony in TANGANYIKA to build the central railway.

China continued to suffer from internal unrest and upheaval well into the 20th century. Between 1925 and 1949 the government of nationalist leader Chiang Kai-Shek (1887–1975) made little effort to develop an Africa policy. However, after the Chinese Revolution (1949) and the establishment of the People's Republic of China on the mainland, China's new Communist government sought to make allies in Africa. This change in policy was largely motivated by the opposition of Communist party chairman Mao Zedong (1893–1976) to European colonialism and the growing global influence of the United States. Most importantly, it was a period of Sino-Soviet détente, or relaxation of tensions, in which China hoped to thwart relations between the SOVIET UNION AND AFRICA.

The problem was that in 1949 the only independent African states were EGYPT, ETHIOPIA, LIBERIA, and SOUTH AFRICA. The close Western ties of the first three nations and the racist position of the APARTHEID government in South Africa made such relations impossible. The BANDUNG AFRO-ASIAN CONFERENCE (1956) served as a turning point. Chinese premier Chou Enlai (1898–1976) used this conference to establish China's first, new diplomatic relationship in Africa, with Egypt. The Marxist charge of NATIONALISM AND INDEPENDENCE MOVEMENTS across the African continent also served to invigorate African interest in ties with China. When independence came, many new African countries were poised to accept Chinese foreign aid and establish strong diplomatic relations. In all, 45 new African states established relations with China, with only IVORY COAST, MALAWI, ANGOLA, and LESOTHO choosing not to engage the Asian country.

See also: CHINA AND AFRICA (Vol. V); COMMUNISM AND SOCIALISM (Vol. V); MAO ZEDONG (Vol. V); TRADE AND COMMERCE (Vol. V).

Further reading: Alan Hutchinson, *China's African Revolution* (London: Hutchinson, 1975); Philip Snow,

The Star Raft: China's Encounter with Africa (Ithaca, N.Y.: Cornell University Press, 1989).

Chokwe Ethnic and LANGUAGE group of southern Central Africa. The Chokwe were originally seminomadic hunters along the upper Kwango and Kasai rivers. In the 17th and 18th centuries they came to be dominated by the Lunda states of ANGOLA. At the end of the 19th century the Chokwe established a powerful trade network that spanned land from the Congo basin to the Angolan coast. The Chokwe kingdom continued to grow, ultimately coming to dominate the Lunda in a brutal fashion. During this period Chokwe cultural practices expanded, evidenced today by the widespread style of their distinctive ritual masks.

The Chokwe kingdom collapsed under COLONIAL RULE in the early 1900s. Their disenfranchisement during the colonial era left them at the political margins. Today there are more than a million Chokwe speakers. Most are farmers living in either the Congo region or Angola, with about 45,000 in neighboring ZAMBIA.

The Chokwe played an important role in supporting the National Union for the Total Independence of Angola, a movement led by Jonas Savimbi (1934–2002) to establish an independent Angola.

See also: CHOKWE (Vols. I, II, III); LUNDA EMPIRE (Vol. III); NATIONAL UNION FOR THE TOTAL INDEPENDENCE OF ANGOLA (Vol. V); SAVIMBI, JONAS (Vol. V).

Further reading: Manuel Jordan, *Chokwe!: Art and Initiation Among the Chokwe and Related Peoples* (New York: Prestel, 1998); Manuel Jordan, *Chokwe* (New York: Rosen Publishing, 1997).

Christianity, influence of When Europeans arrived, African societies had their own individual, indigenous religions, many of which were characterized by belief in a single Creator and a pantheon of lesser gods and ancestors. With the arrival of European explorers, traders, and MISSIONARIES, however, Africans were increasingly exposed to Christian religious denominations, both Roman Catholic and Protestant. Although Catholics had been a presence on the continent for more than 300 years, dating back to Portuguese activities in West Africa, they did not send more missionaries until the latter half of the 19th century. At that time Charles Lavigerie (1825–1892) of France founded the Society of African Missions. Started in ALGERIA, these missions were also known as the White Fathers (1868) and White Sisters (1869).

While earlier Protestant groups had arrived along with explorers and traders in the 19th century, it was the abolition movement in Europe and America that inspired missionaries to return to work in Africa. Toward the end of the century, as the European colonial powers swarmed the continent, increasing numbers of Christian mission stations were established.

Indigenous African religions—as well as Islam—coexisted with the new proselytizing Christian RELIGION. However, Christianity made inroads only in areas where the influence of Islam was not strong. Individuals often became interested in Christianity because their own religions appeared to have failed them, as evidenced by the disruption of their indigenous lifestyles under the impact of the COLONIAL CONQUEST and subsequent COLONIAL RULE. The power of the written word, such as the Scriptures in the Bible, also made a great impression on traditionally non-literate societies.

THINGS FALL APART, a novel by Nigerian author Chinua ACHEBE (1930–), describes in detail the arrival and impact of Christianity in Eastern NIGERIA. In the book, indigenous religious beliefs and practices appear increasingly powerless in the face of Christianity, which steadily gains new converts.

While the missionaries attempted to recruit the sons of chiefs and other legitimate community leaders, most of those who flocked to the new religion were among those who never could have achieved high social positions locally. Unbeknownst to them, the first converts were setting themselves up to become the next generation of African leaders under colonial direction. The new Christians learned to speak, read, and write the European LANGUAGE of the colonial power and were educated to take support roles in the colonial administration. The most successful evangelization, however, was accomplished less formally, as individual converts took the new religion with them into the hinterlands, beyond the mission stations, and demonstrated the new religion by example.

Africans did not accept and practice all the precepts of Christianity presented to them. Instead they evaluated Christianity on the basis of their preexisting worldviews, which generally included local variations of indigenous religions. This, in some instances, led to an African form of syncretistic religion that blended European Christianity with indigenous religion or with indigenous customs.

The need for Africans to control religious knowledge, along with the suspicion that Europeans were not completely sharing that knowledge, led to the establishment of independent churches. The leaders of these churches often focused on healing and schooling and came to be seen as prophets by their congregations. The first major African Christian prophet of modern times, a XHOSA speaker named Ntsikana (c. 1760–1820), baptized himself before coming into direct contact with South African missionaries.

Later African prophets who founded Christian-based churches included William Wade HARRIS (c. 1850–1929), in LIBERIA; Simon KIMBANGU (c. 1887–1951), in the present-day Democratic Republic of the CONGO; Alice LENSHINA (1924–1978), in present-day ZAMBIA; Isaiah SHEMBE (c. 1870–1935), in SOUTH AFRICA; and John MARANKE (1912–1963), in present-day ZIMBABWE.

The Spread of Christianity Although Christians lived in North Africa during the early Christian period, Islam remained the stronger influence in that region. The settlers, or COLONS, who came to Muslim North Africa reintroduced Catholicism and began a new missionary movement. However, they found few converts among the Muslim population.

The center for the first African-born Protestants in West Africa was FREETOWN, SIERRA LEONE. There the CHURCH MISSIONARY SOCIETY (CMS) established a college for training missionaries at FOURAH BAY COLLEGE. This in turn helped the colony become a dissemination point for Protestants like Samuel Ajayi CROWTHER (1808–1891) to establish mission stations in LAGOS, ABEOKUTA, and Onitsha, in present-day Nigeria.

John Chilembwe, seen here performing a baptism ceremony about 1910, led one of many Christian movements that arose in Africa during the colonial period. © *Library of Congress*

In the 1870s New Livingstonia missionaries in East Africa revitalized the church at Lake Nyasa, and by 1900 BUGANDA had become Christian to a significant extent, with both the Roman Catholic and the Anglican Churches gaining converts. Many Ganda (as the people from Buganda call themselves in their Bantu language) then became active in spreading Christianity to neighboring societies.

In South Africa mission-school catechists became political and religious spokespersons for the community as early as 1820. Scots Presbyterians ordained the country's first African minister, Tiyo SOGA (1829–1871), in 1856. By the end of the century there were a number of ordained African ministers in the mission churches. However, African clergy became prevalent only after World War II (1939–45).

The most important indigenous actor in the early spread of Christianity was the catechist. In spite of the fact that catechists typically had minimal literacy, these people of African descent were the unpaid leaders of the congregation. Usually men, the catechists led prayers and hymns, preached the sermon, and were responsible for the upkeep of the church and school buildings. With close ties to the Europeans within the colonial structure, several catechists bore offspring who became leaders of the independent countries of Africa.

The 19th century witnessed a sustained missionary drive, with Bibles, prayer books, hymnbooks, and catechisms being translated into indigenous languages and printed and distributed to local congregations. After focusing exclusively on primary EDUCATION in the 19th century, the missionaries broadened the scope of their work in the 20th century to include secondary education, local hospitals, and clinics.

Christianity in Ethiopia During the 19th century European Christianity also had an influence in independent ETHIOPIA, one of the world's oldest Christian states. In 1830 the Church Missionary Society arrived in TIGRAY and established itself as co-religionists of the ETHIOPIAN ORTHODOX CHURCH. Although they were not allowed to penetrate the Ethiopian interior, the CMS missionaries built a rapport with Ethiopian Christians. Ethiopian leaders focused on creating a united front to challenge Islam on the coast. However, the real agenda of the Ethiopian princes was gaining access to Western technology and goods, especially firearms. This came about mainly because Ethiopia's AMHARA-speaking leaders were interested in consolidating their power in the region and were con-

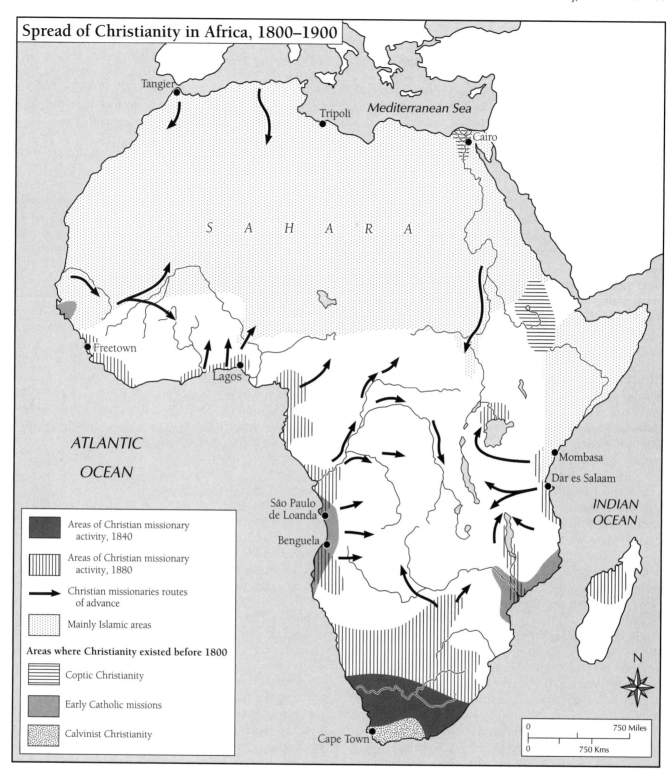

Spread of Christianity in Africa, 1800–1900

Tangier

Tripoli

Mediterranean Sea

Cairo

S A H A R A

Freetown

Lagos

ATLANTIC

OCEAN

Mombasa

Dar es Salaam

INDIAN
OCEAN

São Paulo
de Loanda

Benguela

Cape Town

N

	Areas of Christian missionary activity, 1840
	Areas of Christian missionary activity, 1880
→	Christian missionaries routes of advance
	Mainly Islamic areas

Areas where Christianity existed before 1800

	Coptic Christianity
	Early Catholic missions
	Calvinist Christianity

0   750 Miles

0   750 Kms

cerned about the threat posed by a modernized and militarized EGYPT.

Catholic missionaries who came to Ethiopia in the 17th century wanted to eliminate Ethiopian Orthodox Christianity, but Protestant missionaries tried to reform it. In 1860 the circulation of bibles by the British and Foreign Bible Society led to a religious movement in ER-ITREA that was reminiscent of the Reformation in Europe.

Emperor TÉWODROS II (1820–1868), who came to the throne as a reformer, allowed missionaries to distribute the Amharic Bible to replace the ones written in Ge'ez. When he imprisoned some British missionaries, however, a British military expedition defeated Téwodros's troops, leading to his eventual suicide. The Ethiopian Orthodox Church did not develop a specific missionary organization of its own until 1963. Although its missions were not sent to distant lands, it did use the Amharic language to spread Christianity in present-day Ethiopia as a part of Amharic imperialism.

See also: CHRISTIANITY, INFLUENCE OF (Vols. II, III, V); COLONIALISM, INFLUENCE OF (Vol. IV); ISLAM, INFLUENCE OF (Vols. II, III, V); KONGO KINGDOM (Vols. II, III).

Further reading: James L. Cox and Gerrie ter Haar, eds., *Uniquely African?: African Christian Identity from Cultural and Historical Perspectives* (Trenton, N.J.: Africa World Press, 2003); Elizabeth Isichei, *A History of Christianity in Africa: From Antiquity to the Present* (Grand Rapids, Mich.: W. B. Eerdmans Pub. Co., 1995); J. N. K. Mugambi, *Christianity and African Culture* (Nairobi, Kenya: Acton Publishers, 2002); Christopher Steed and Bengt Sundkler, *A History of the Church in Africa* (New York: Cambridge University Press, 2000).

Church Missionary Society (CMS) Organization established in 1799 with the goal of spreading Christianity worldwide. Formally known after 1812 as the Church Missionary Society for Africa and the East, the society was founded in Aldersgate, London, following the mid-18th-century revival of the Church of England (Anglican Church). Other groups interested in missionary work that were formed about the same time included the Baptist Missionary Society (1792) and the LONDON MISSIONARY SOCIETY (1795). In 1804 the Church Missionary Society (CMS) chose as its original mission field the British colony of SIERRA LEONE. There, following the British abolition of slavery in 1807, the CMS worked extensively among the RECAPTIVES, Africans whom the British Anti-Slavery Squadron freed from slave ships and brought to FREETOWN.

In its first decade the CMS sent only five MISSIONARIES abroad. However, because of the high death toll among its members in Sierra Leone, due mainly to malaria, the CMS considered training Africans for the ministry. To that end, in 1827 it founded a training institution that later became FOURAH BAY COLLEGE. The focus of CMS evangelism was EDUCATION, and each of its mission stations had a primary school attached to it. In 1845 the CMS opened a secondary school for boys (and in 1849, a separate school for girls), catering to Africans hailing from the West African coast. These mission schools were to provide the educational base for the growing number of Sierra Leonean Africans, who, as clergy, served to spread Christianity in Sierra Leone and other British-influenced areas.

Having Africans serving as the principal missionaries was in line with the philosophy of Henry Venn (1796–1873), the CMS general secretary who believed in an in-digenous, self-propagating, self-supporting church. Venn's approach resulted in the creation of the Niger Mission, launched in 1841, staffed mainly by African clergy. Beginning in 1864 the Niger Mission was led by an African bishop, Samuel Ajayi CROWTHER (1808–1891). With 10 priests and 14 catechists working under Crowther, the CMS soon was ministering to more than 600 Christians in the YORUBA-speaking areas of NIGERIA. One of their better-known priests was the Yoruba historian and peace-maker, Samuel JOHNSON (1846–1901).

After Venn's death, in 1873, however, the idea of an indigenous church increasingly gave way to a church controlled by Europeans, reflecting the increasingly colonial nature of the relationships between Europeans and Africans. Thus the CMS BUGANDA mission established by Alexander Mackay (1849–1890), in 1876, was largely run by Europeans.

Despite the volatile political situation in Buganda, especially following the death of Kabaka MUTESA I (c. 1830s–1884), the mission succeeded in converting many to Christianity. It did not, however, actively promote an African clergy. Thus, of the priests serving approximately 100,000 African Anglican Church members, merely 33 of them were Africans. It was only in the DECOLONIZATION era after World War II (1939–45) that the CMS and other missionary societies began to once again embrace Venn's vision of an indigenous African church.

See also: CHRISTIANITY, INFLUENCE OF (Vol. IV).

cinema An African film industry with African producers, directors, actors, and film editors did not exist in Africa before 1960. Because film is a powerful medium of communication, European colonial authorities tended to regulate access to film in their efforts to control information disseminated to their African subjects.

In SOUTH AFRICA, on the other hand, there is a rich history of filmmaking. As early as 1895 South African companies were using the early projection techniques to entertain and inform Boer and British miners in JOHANNESBURG. The first South African narrative film, *The Kimberley Diamond Robbery,* was produced in 1910.

Cinema in British Colonies The Colonial Office of the British Film Institute created the Bantu Educational Cinema Experiment in 1935. Through this experiment the British used film to help adult Africans understand and adopt British culture and values. It also was used to disseminate British propaganda during World War II (1939–45).

In 1939 the British established the Colonial Film Unit with branches in different parts of Africa for the purpose of scientific and medical education, war propaganda, and product marketing. Within 10 years the Colonial Film Unit had founded a film school at ACCRA, the capital of the GOLD COAST COLONY. At the school African students were trained to become assistants to the European production teams working in Africa. The Colonial Film Unit changed its name to Overseas Film and Television Center, in 1955, and began coordinating production units in Africa and providing funds for African filmmakers to purchase film equipment.

Although Britain institutionalized film production in its African colonies, it did not provide adequate cultural education for Africans to become overly interested in film in the postindependence era. Africans rarely got the opportunity to see themselves in the British-produced educational and documentary films, and Britain did not provide feature films through their embassies.

In 1950 the Gold Coast Film Unit produced a film based on a screenplay by John Hearsey entitled *The Boy Kumasenu* (60 minutes, black and white). Directed by Sean Graham, the film took the form of a documentary, using African actors to dramatize the inherently colonial theme of the transition between the traditionalism of so-called tribal Africa and the modern, implicitly European world of the 20th century.

The Gold Coast Film Unit became independent in 1950, but it continued to rely on British companies for postproduction. Moreover, African students received something less than a complete education in filmmaking: Rather than becoming independent directors or producers, students trained at this facility became assistants to Sean Graham, the Film Unit's director. However, at independence Kwame NKRUMAH (1909–1972) nationalized the country's film industry and his new Ghanaian government designed a sophisticated program for national film production.

Cinema in French-speaking Africa Colonies ruled by France and Belgium took separate paths to establishing their film industries. In 1928 the French Assembly passed a law to control film production in the colonies to prevent anticolonial themes. In 1934 the minister for the colonies, Pierre Laval (1883–1945), began enforcing the law and even extended it so that Africans were excluded from participating in film production both in front of and behind the camera. The first French-speaking-African film students were trained at the Institut des Hautes Études Cinématographiques (National Film School) in Paris. When Paulin S. Vieyra (1925–1987), the first African graduate of the school, was denied filming in Africa, he and his friends formed Le Groupe African du Cinéma and made films about Africans in Paris.

In the late 1950s and early 1960s French ethnographer-turned-filmmaker Jean Rouch (1917–) and writer and critic Georges Sadoul (1904–1967) influenced France to change its policy toward African involvement in film production. In part because of their efforts, the French administration created a demand for movies by providing feature films at the embassy movie theater (*cinématique*), where Africans could view contemporary European and American films and participate in a post-viewing discussion group with a French discussion leader.

The Belgians, for their part, used the British Colonial Film Unit as a model. In 1936 the Belgian government forbade unauthorized, foreign filmmakers from filming in the BELGIAN CONGO, so that Belgium alone could profit financially from film production in its colony. Belgium's tight control was also related to its desire to be able to determine the content of the ethnographic films being made about the region.

While the Belgian government had established a Board of Censors to approve indigenous participation in film production, in 1945, it prohibited Africans from attending either private or public movie theaters. The following year Catholic MISSIONARIES formed the Congolese Center for Catholic Action Cinema in an attempt to use film to convert Africans to Christianity. A few years later, however, the Film and Photo Bureau division of the Belgian Ministry of Information established a policy for producing films specifically for an indigenous audience. By 1952 a Congolese ciné-club in LEOPOLDVILLE (now Kinshasa) was teaching Africans how to make films.

See also: BELGIUM AND AFRICA (Vol. IV); CINEMA (Vol. V); COLONIAL RULE (Vol. IV); COLONIALISM, INFLUENCE OF (Vol. IV); ENGLAND AND AFRICA (Vols. III, IV, V); FRANCE AND AFRICA (Vols. III, IV, V).

Further reading: Imruh Bakari and Mbye B. Cham, eds., *African Experiences of Cinema* (London: British Film Institute, 1996); Manthia Diawara, *African Cinema: Politics & Culture* (Bloomington: Indiana University Press, 1992); John Gray, *Blacks in Film and Television: A Pan-African Bibliography of Films, Filmmakers, and Performers* (New York: Greenwood Press, 1990).

cloth and textiles In colonial Africa, as was the case for thousands of years, cloth woven from plant fibers, such as COTTON, or animal hairs, such as wool, was used for garments, blankets, burial shrouds, tents, and the like. Woven cloth could be made even more valuable by adding decorations, such as embroidery. During the 20th century embroidery was increasingly done on sewing machines. In areas where electricity was not available or prohibitively expensive, textile makers used older-style treadle sewing machines.

As trade with Europeans brought manufactured textiles into African markets, cloth increasingly became a prestige item. Although Africans continued to produce cloth locally, they also bought fabrics produced in European textile mills. The primary reason for buying European textiles was that it was cheaper to buy the fabric than to expend the required amount of time and effort to produce cloth for personal use. In addition, much of the European fabric was made using a batik, or wax-print, process that produced a more durable cloth. After conducting research in Africa, European manufacturers were able to replicate the colors and patterns preferred by specific ethnic groups. The leading producer of fabrics for African consumers was Vlisco Company, a Dutch concern founded in 1846. Vlisco was run by the van Vlissingens, a noted Dutch merchant family, whose producers learned the batik method for dyeing cloth from trading in the Dutch colony of Indonesia. By adopting the batik technique into its manufacturing process, Vlisco was able to dominate the African print-fabric market by the end of the 19th century. In the 20th century Africans incorporated the European batik methods into their own manufacturing process.

For a long time Africa's indigenous cloth has attracted travelers. An example of a textile popular with foreign visitors to Africa is the mud cloth produced in the Republic of MALI. The cloth is woven in strips and sewn together by men. Women then complete the cloth by using organic stains that produce a specific chemical reaction. Generally the mud cloth process uses a leaf solution and a mud dye that has fermented for about a year. The dyeing chemicals come from the iron tannate in the tannic acid from the leaves.

See also: CLOTH AND TEXTILES (Vols. I, II, III, V).

Further reading: John Picton, et. al., *The Art of African Textiles: Technology, Tradition, and Lurex* (London: Lund Humphries Publishers, 1995); Claire Polakoff, *Into Indigo: African Textiles and Dyeing Techniques* (Garden City, N.Y.: Anchor Press/Doubleday, 1980); Christopher Spring, *African Textiles* (Wakefield, R.I.: Moyer Bell, 1997).

clothing and dress The colonial era marked the second major revolution in African clothing and dress—the first being the changes that came with the arrival of Islam in the seventh century. Prior to the beginning of the colonial era in the late 19th century, European-style clothing was worn in only a few places in Africa. The BOERS, farmers of Dutch descent who had moved into SOUTH AFRICA beginning in the mid-17th century, retained their European styles. Also, people in the cosmopolitan Mediterranean ports of ALEXANDRIA, ALGIERS, TUNIS, and TRIPOLI regularly wore European clothing, especially on the occasions when they engaged in commerce with European merchants and traders. By the beginning of the 20th century, however, European styles were increasingly seen throughout the continent.

Following the long process of PACIFICATION and COLONIAL CONQUEST, European colonial administrators began developing a cadre of African professional bureaucrats. Most of these individuals, almost all males, worked in the national or district capital cities and occupied junior-level positions. They were required—sometimes by official rules and sometimes simply by social pressure—to adopt the attire of their white leaders. As a result, African men who hoped to advance within the colonial system abandoned their traditional dress and wore khaki shorts and short-sleeved shirts, similar to those worn by Europeans. In cooler climates, some even wore long pants, long-sleeved shirts, and neckties.

Women, on the other hand, were largely excluded from the urban centers during the colonial era. However, some women did succeed in migrating to the cities, even though it often was illegal and they rarely were able to find work once there. Because they were outside the employment mainstream, these women tended to maintain their customary habits of dress, wearing either Islamic attire or indigenous African clothing. Similarly, women living in rural areas tended to continue wearing whatever had been their traditional clothing before the onslaught of colonialism.

One of the more interesting developments related to African clothing lore concerns *kanga*, a cloth that originally appeared in the 19th century along the Swahili Coast. Since then, *kanga* has evolved into one of the continent's most popular and widely used garments. *Kanga* probably began when Zanzibari women took European kerchiefs and sewed them together into large rectangles. The resulting multicolored cloth quickly became very popular and was named *kanga*, the term for a noisy fowl known for its fancy feathers. During the early 20th century the fabric makers began printing words on the cloth, usually in Kiswahili. These words typically spelled out proverbs or amusing sayings. Today *kanga* is used for everything from headwraps to bodywraps. Babies are swaddled and carried in *kanga*. A woman might even split a piece of *kanga* in two so that she and a best friend can have matching outfits.

Also during the 20th century, European dress became more widespread due to the influence of Christian MISSIONARIES. Europeans tended to impose what amounted to a dress code on those Africans who attended their missions, issuing strictures against traditional garb, which, if it showed certain parts of the body, was considered immoral. A de facto European dress code was also in place at colonial schools in Africa. Furthermore, many African elites attended colleges and universities in Europe or the United States and adopted European dress as part of their attempt to find meaningful employment suitable to their level of education. In this way European dress became a sign of membership in a kind of quasi-elite, a bureaucratic or technocratic class suited for better jobs, housing, and overall living standards.

These same social pressures led many male government officers to go so far as to wear three-piece suits and other garments associated with the rich and powerful of Europe and the United States. This habit grew even more pronounced during the 1950s, when Africans began agitating for independence. By that time many Africans and Europeans alike saw the choice of European-style clothing as a sign of Africans' willingness and ability to take over the jobs of the colonial rulers.

See also: CLOTH AND TEXTILES (Vol. IV); CLOTHING AND DRESS (Vols. I, II, III, V); URBAN LIFE AND CULTURE (Vol. IV).

Further reading: Hildi Hendrickson, *Clothing and Difference: Embodied Identities in Colonial and Post-Colonial Africa* (Durham: Duke University Press, 1996).

cocoa (cacao) Major cash crop of the West African forest zone during the colonial period. The cocoa bean is the seed of the cacao tree (*Theobroma cacao*), which is indigenous to the Americas. The explorer Christopher Columbus (1451–1506) introduced cocoa beans to Europe, carrying them with him when he returned to Spain after his last voyage to the West Indies in 1502–04.

Seen here in 1958 on a plantation near Accra, Ghana, workers split cocoa pods and remove the seeds. © *Ghana Information Service/Library of Congress*

The growth of cocoa as a cash crop was directly linked to the development of candy manufacturing in the 1820s in Europe and the United States. By 1879 smooth chocolate became the standard, and manufacturers such as the Hershey Company of Pennsylvania developed a highly profitable candy business by combining locally produced milk with sugar from Cuba and cocoa that increasingly came from West Africa.

In the late 19th century the center of cocoa production shifted from Latin America to the Portuguese plantations on the islands of SÃO TOMÉ AND PRÍNCIPE, off the West African coast. By 1905 these islands had become the world's principal producers of cocoa. However, individual African farmers in the GOLD COAST COLONY (present-day GHANA) had begun to experiment with planting cocoa in 1879, and in 1891 they started to export it. By the 1920s the Gold Coast led the world in cocoa production.

Cocoa was a highly profitable enterprise. Between 1900 and 1939, production in the Gold Coast increased eightfold from 100,000 to nearly 800,000 tons (91,000 to 726,000 metric tons). Cocoa production spread to NIGERIA and IVORY COAST, which also became major producers. Félix HOUPHOUËT-BOIGNY (1905–1993), who served as president of Ivory Coast from 1960 to 1993, started his climb to political power in the 1940s by organizing his fellow cocoa planters.

By 1960 Africa produced three-fourths of the world's cocoa. Over the rest of the century, however, its share fell as other regions began to export cocoa in significant amounts. By the end of the 20th century Africa's world market share fell to about half of the 2.5 million tons (2.3 million metric tons) exported annually. By that time Ivory Coast had also surpassed Ghana as Africa's leading exporter of cocoa.

See also: AGRICULTURE (Vols. I, III, IV, V); CASH CROPS (Vol. IV); COLONIALISM, INFLUENCE OF (Vol. IV).

Further reading: Sara S. Berry, *Cocoa, Custom, and Socio-Economic Change in Rural Western Nigeria* (Oxford, U.K.: Clarendon Press, 1975).

coffee   An important cash crop in Africa beginning in the colonial era. Coffee is indigenous to Africa. It gets is name from the Kaffa region of ETHIOPIA, where one variety, *coffea arabica,* was first domesticated. By the mid-19th century coffee had become a popular beverage in both Europe and the United States, with steadily increasing consumer demand. However, despite its African origins and its continued popularity as a drink in Ethiopia, Latin American producers supplied as much as 95 percent of the world's coffee at that time.

Coffee production on a commercial scale in Africa did not take root until the late 19th century, when the continent fell under COLONIAL RULE. At that time coffee became one of the many CASH CROPS that European colonial governments promoted in an effort to develop export-generated income for their colonies. While African farmers in the GOLD COAST COLONY rejected coffee in favor of COCOA as a cash crop, coffee became the leading export of IVORY COAST. Early in the 20th century European SETTLERS in KENYA also raised coffee and prevented Africans from growing it.

Coffee production expanded rapidly in Africa after World War II (1939–45). By the 1960s the crop accounted for half or more of the total EXPORTS of ANGOLA, BURUNDI, Ethiopia, RWANDA, and UGANDA. By 2000 Africa produced nearly 20 percent of the world's coffee.

Coffee spread from Ethiopia to Yemen, where more systematic cultivation began. From the Arabian Peninsula it spread to Turkey, where a crude form of coffee as it is drunk today was first brewed from beans roasted over open fires. In the 1700s a French military officer took a single coffee plant to the Caribbean island of Martinique, and within 50 years coffee became a major cash crop there. From Martinique, the industry spread throughout Latin America.

See also: AGRICULTURE (Vols. I, III, IV, V); COFFEE (Vol. II); COLONIALISM, INFLUENCE OF (Vol. V); MONOCROP ECONOMIES (Vol. IV).

Cold War and Africa   The Cold War was a period of international tension and superpower rivalry between the United States and the Soviet Union (United Soviet Socialist Republic, USSR). It lasted approximately from the end of World War II (1939–45) through the early 1990s. The Cold War influenced the international political scene in Africa and across the globe.

The United States and the USSR, allies during World War II, emerged in the postwar era as the two great superpowers but with differing ideological aims. These differences affected all aspects of world politics, including Africa.

Within a few years of the end of the Second World War, several conflicts erupted as a direct result of the rising tensions between the United States and the USSR. One such conflict was the building of the Egyptian ASWAN DAM and its aftermath. Egypt's president, Gamal Abdel NASSER (1918–1970), viewed the dam project as essential for his country's economic development and modernization. He believed that the dam would generate electricity, improve river TRANSPORTATION, and expand the land area under cultivation through a major irrigation project. The United States, Britain, and the World Bank offered roughly $255 million in loans for the project. However, the United States withdrew its aid when EGYPT recognized the Communist government of China and reportedly received a zero-interest-loan offer from the USSR.

In retaliation for the withdrawal of Western aid, in July 1956 Egypt seized the SUEZ CANAL. Although the canal belonged to Egypt, it was operated by the Suez Canal Company, which was controlled by British and French interests. Both Britain and France believed that Egypt could not effectively run the canal and were keen on the use of force in order to guarantee its return. While the United States opted to remain out of the conflict, Israel became involved on the British and French side.

Israel began an attack on Egypt in October. When British and French paratroopers landed soon after, Egyptian forces retreated from the canal zone to protect their cities. Under pressure from the United States, and concerned that Egypt would move further into the Soviet camp, Britain called for a cease-fire early in November. As a result Egypt maintained control of the Suez Canal and began exacting tolls from passing ships.

Another important development during the early years of the Cold War that directly affected Africa was the emergence of the Nonaligned Movement (NAM). Founded in 1955 as an outgrowth of the BANDUNG AFRO-ASIAN CONFERENCE held in Indonesia, it came to involve most African states as they gained independence from COLONIAL RULE. Nasser, Kwame NKRUMAH (1909–1972), Patrice LUMUMBA (1925–1961), and other key leaders in the African independence movements were active in the NAM.

As a byproduct of the Cold War environment the NAM offered several attractive options for its members. First, it was a disinterested or "neutral" liaison for solving conflicts between the two superpowers. Second, the NAM assisted members in developing both non-capitalist and non-communist approaches to domestic policies. And, further, the NAM permitted member countries to receive developmental aid from both superpower blocs.

In the 1960s, when African nations across the continent moved out from under colonial domination, conflicts that divided people along ideological lines would become even more acute. As a result the Cold War came to have a much greater impact on Africa in the following years.

See also: COLD WAR AND AFRICA (Vol. V); COLONIALISM, INFLUENCE OF (Vol. IV); NONALIGNED MOVEMENT AND AFRICA (Vol. V); POLITICAL SYSTEMS (Vol. V); SOCIALISM AND COMMUNISM (Vol. V); SOVIET UNION AND AFRICA (Vol. V); UNITED STATES AND AFRICA (Vol. IV); WORLD WAR II AND AFRICA (Vol. IV).

colon Term adopted from the French word meaning "settler." *Colon* originally referred to a person, usually a farmer, who went to live in an area that his or her government wanted to control or to dominate. Later the word

became the root of the word *colonizer* and was also applied to an administrator of a colony.

In terms of policy, the colons found themselves caught between their home governments and the indigenous people in the regions where they settled. The treatment of the colons by their governments was arbitrary: Sometimes it benefited the government to protect the colons, and at other times it benefited the government to oppress them, just as the colons oppressed the indigenous people. In some cases children of colons were not considered first-class citizens of their home countries even though their parents were citizens in good standing.

ALGERIA and TUNISIA had the largest concentration of colons in French colonial Africa. Their English counterparts were concentrated in SOUTH AFRICA, SOUTHERN RHODESIA (present-day ZIMBABWE), and, to a lesser extent, KENYA. Portuguese settlers were primarily in colonial ANGOLA and MOZAMBIQUE, while Italians were settlers in LIBYA and ERITREA and Belgians in the BELGIAN CONGO. Most of colonial Africa, however, lacked significant settler populations.

See also: COLONIAL RULE (Vol. IV); SETTLERS, EUROPEAN (Vol. IV).

colonial conquest Process by which the European nations invaded and conquered the peoples of the African continent for the purpose of national aggrandizement and economic domination. For the most part the race to acquire colonies took place between 1880 and the outbreak of World War I (1914–18).

During the 19th century Europeans sought out raw materials and mineral wealth from Africa to fuel their INDUSTRIALIZATION. They also looked for markets in which they could create a demand for their manufactured goods. The competition was the greatest between Britain and France, which in the 18th century had fought each other over colonial empires in North America and India. By the 1850s Britain was already said to have "an empire on which the sun never set," and France was striving to match it.

The competition among European industrial nations for raw materials and markets led to the PARTITION of the African continent at the BERLIN CONFERENCE (1884–85). By this agreement the European colonizers claimed exclusive control over the coastal areas with which they had trade treaties, but they had to bring the interior regions under their control before they could declare possession.

In addition to commercial motivations, Europeans also developed social and cultural agendas for partitioning the African continent. To analyze social relationships, they began framing human interactions using the biological theories found in *Origin of the Species*, a landmark scientific study by Charles Darwin (1809–1882). Thus, they developed a pseudo-scientific racism that placed the white, industrialized nations at the top of civilization and

Local police officers, like those in this unit undergoing a military-style inspection in Nigeria, were an important feature of the European colonial system. Undated photo. © *Wide World/New York Times*

the dark-skinned, non-industrialized Africans at the bottom. This promoted the idea that Europeans had the responsibility of transmitting what they considered to be their "superior" culture to those whom they deemed as having no culture. This notion, known as the WHITE MAN'S BURDEN, was embodied in a poem of that name written by Rudyard Kipling (1865–1936) in 1899. Many negative stereotypes were thus created at this time as a rationale for Europeans' conquest of Africa.

The combination of commerce, Christianity, and cultural domination began with European traders and was followed by the Christian MISSIONARIES. Many Christian missions became centers of trade, like the Niger Mission of the CHURCH MISSIONARY SOCIETY at Onitsha, in present-day NIGERIA. Traders and MISSIONARIES called increasingly upon their home governments for support as they angered the indigenous people. Hence, these governments got into the business of the so-called civilizing mission. Believing that colonial control would facilitate Christian

conversion on the continent, missionaries acted politically in terms of their own best interest and that of their home countries. Reverend C. D. Helm of the LONDON MISSIONARY SOCIETY, for example, was the advisor to Chief LOBENGULA (1836–1894) of the NDEBELE in present-day ZIMBABWE. In 1888, when Cecil RHODES (1853–1902) sent a treaty for the chief to sign, Helm advised the chief to sign away his land and the mineral rights, thereby benefiting the Europeans. Ultimately, though, the BRITISH SOUTH AFRICA COMPANY had to resort to armed force in 1893 to defeat Lobengula and his armies. This defeat spelled the end of the Ndebele kingdom.

Throughout the continent European nations made treaties and resorted to military force in order to weave a tapestry of European domination over the continent. African resistance was often fierce, and at times African armies could defeat Europeans armies, as at the Battle of ISANDLWANA (1879). In almost every instance, however, European military power and resources proved to be too great, and they ultimately prevailed. As the saying at the time went, "Whatever happens, we have got the Gatling gun and they have not." It was only ETHIOPIA, which inflicted a decisive defeat on an Italian army at the Battle of ADOWA (1896), that managed to escape the process of colonial conquest.

See also: ANGLO-ASHANTI WARS (Vol. IV); ANGLO-ZULU WAR (Vol. IV); BELGIUM AND AFRICA (Vol. IV); COLONIAL RULE (Vol. IV); COLONIALISM, INFLUENCE OF (Vol. IV); ENGLAND AND AFRICA (Vols. III, IV, V); FRANCE AND AFRICA (Vols. III, IV, V); GERMANY AND AFRICA (Vol. IV); ITALY AND AFRICA (Vol. IV); OMDURMAN, BATTLE OF (Vol. IV); PORTUGAL AND AFRICA (Vol. IV); RESISTANCE AND REBELLION (Vol. IV).

Further reading: Bruce Vandervort, *Wars of Imperial Conquest in Africa, 1830–1914* (Bloomington: Indiana University Press, 1998).

colonialism, influence of Seventy years of COLONIAL RULE had a negative effect on Africans and their ability to manage the countries they inherited at independence. Beyond the fact that their countries were arbitrarily carved out of the continent, Africans have wrestled with the impact of the colonial legacy in many areas. The influence of colonialism can be seen in particular in the areas of administration, the ECONOMY, infrastructure, and society and culture in general.

Administration of the Colonies At independence Europeans expected the emerging African states to practice democracy. However, these same Europeans who practiced democracy at home acted in a highly authoritarian and sometime dictatorial manner in administering their African colonial possessions. Those Africans who pursued a colonial EDUCATION to work in the government did not learn about democracy in their textbooks nor did they learn about it in actual practice. Only Africans who were fortunate enough to study outside of the continent were able to gain a true understanding of the democratic process.

Africans who worked in the colonial bureaucracy were always assistants to the decision makers and did not experience the actual decision-making process until independence. At independence those within the European-trained African elite moved into governmental positions without the proper training for running government business. As a result they generally defaulted to governing their new countries in the same way they had learned under colonial rule.

Although political activity was a hallmark of European culture, the colonial governments did not promote political representation in Africa until after World War II (1939–45). Even at this late date the Europeans hoped to thwart independence by continuing a "divide and conquer" practice by promoting political parties on the basis of individual ethnic groups. Consequently, broad-based political parties were not widespread on the continent. Democracy was not common in most African societies, and a lack of exposure to democratic concepts and practical training resulted in bad decisions of governance. This in turn has been a major cause of Africans remaining economically dependent on the Western world. Because they are not natural to African systems of governance, POLITICAL PARTIES AND ORGANIZATIONS were largely ineffective. This has resulted in parties that either find it impossible to compromise or that produce one-party states. The idea that an authoritarian figure knows how to run the government effectively and efficiently has been expressed in the many military coups that have occurred since independence.

Colonial Culture When Europeans arrived on the continent they encountered many diverse African cultures. However, the Europeans did not appreciate African culture, largely because it was not Christian. Because of their racial and religious views, the European colonialists regarded African culture as inferior in the same way as they regarded Africans themselves to be biologically, morally, and intellectually inferior.

European assertions of the inferiority of Africans often took the form of claims that Africans were childlike. This was a frequent feature of colonial-era literature about Africa, as in the unenlightened writing of England's George A. Henty (1832–1902). As a newspaper reporter, he covered African events such as the ANGLO-ASHANTI WARS of 1873–74 before he turned to writing adventure stories for boys. A character in one of his books states that Africans "are just like children . . . always laughing or quarrelling . . . The intelligence of an average Negro is about equal to that of a European child of 10 years old."

Europeans imposed their own cultural norms in Africa. The French attempted to remove the cultural identity of the indigenous population through a policy of *assimilation*, which intended to change Africans into French people. The British, on the other hand, insisted on African acceptance of English LANGUAGE and EDUCATION in order to work for the colonial government. Because of policies such as these, Africans lost sight of much of their own cultures as they were co-opted into a colonial culture through European education.

The particular European languages of the colonizers became the official languages of their colonies. Thus, to land high-paying jobs in either the private or public sectors, Africans needed to learn European languages. The official language was taught in either mission or secular schools. In either case students learned the skills and knowledge, albeit a second-class knowledge, necessary to perform the tasks required of them in the government bureaucracy and in business. Education in many colonies was limited to males, often the sons of chiefs, selected by the Europeans for future subordinate positions within the colonial administration. Later, the number of both males and females attending elementary school increased. Some proceeded on to secondary school, and a very few went further on to university in the mother country. This last group became the elites of the country because they had assimilated into European culture. Learning the right European language and receiving a western-style education bestowed status.

The European missionaries brought Christianity with them. Students who attended mission schools were indoctrinated into the Christian denomination and were taught the "necessary skills" for life under a colonial regime. Missionary education generated the cadre of African clerics who would continue to spread the gospel and their understanding of the European culture in the rural areas. At independence most African nations retained the European language and educational system, and today nations in West, Central, and southern Africa are predominantly Christian.

Colonial Economy Through long-distance trade, precolonial Africa provided labor, raw materials, and mineral wealth that enriched the economies of Europe. After the general abolition of slavery in the 19th century the development of the so-called legitimate trade provided raw materials such as GROUNDNUTS (peanuts) and PALM OIL for European industry. In turn, Europe produced manufactured goods that were sold in African markets. During the colonial period the export orientation of the economy intensified, but Africans now had to trade with only one specific colonial power. Although the Europeans promised to "civilize" Africans, they did not promise to promote INDUSTRIALIZATION. As a rule the European governments intended to keep the populations in their African colonies economically underdeveloped and dependent.

In addition to mineral wealth the Europeans encouraged production of CASH CROPS such as RUBBER for industrial uses and COTTON for cloth. In colonies where there were not enough resources to grow the cash crop, workers were forced to migrate to urban areas and other colonies to earn wages to pay taxes in the newly contrived cash economy. Although slavery had been abolished, other forms of service substituted for it. Forced labor became a part of the structures of taxation. At independence African economies still depended on the industrialized nations and were unable to industrialize themselves.

Colonial Infrastructure Europeans contributed the expertise to the construction of infrastructure, but Afri-

cans paid for these technological improvements with their taxes. In many cases, because of harsh working conditions and tyrannical management, Africans also paid for the improvements with their lives. Colonial infrastructure centered on the ability to simplify and speed up the extraction of raw materials and minerals from the interior. TRANSPORTATION was the focus with the building of port facilities for coastal cities and roads and railroads that ran from the interior collection points to the coast. Consequently roads and railroads were specifically for economic and not social use. Communication, electricity, and the water supply were important to the capital cities, where Europeans dominated the upper levels of society. At independence colonial infrastructure remained poor, and few states had the ability to maintain it or expand it to meet the needs of the people.

Colonial Society The European-dominated relationship between the colonizers and the colonized strongly impacted precolonial social structures and relationships. European policies brought about the relocation of African males to the urban areas. However, the families of the men had to remain on their homesteads, which in many cases were a great distance away; the jobs were for men only. Consequently, at independence, office secretaries and clerks, hotel housekeeping staff, personal servants, waiters, and shopkeepers all were men. As an illustration of the disproportionate percentages of African men and women in urban areas, between 1934 and 1956 the percentage of males in the urban African population of SALISBURY (today's Harare) hovered between 85 and 91 percent. Many women remaining in the rural areas became female heads of household without the benefit of their husband's labor and sometimes without benefit of his wages.

Dress styles were another area where European culture had a major impact on Africans. Photographs from the early 20th century often showed members of the African elite dressed in the fashions of the Victorian era.

Europeans stressed EDUCATION as a way to have a job in the colonial private and public sectors, and Africans who aspired to a better standard of living above that of peasant farmer or unskilled laborer became very focused on obtaining an adequate education. Those people who were hired to work in the formal economy had to finish secondary school. However, many rural males who did not complete secondary education also came to the cities in search of jobs. Many of these people were self-employed in the informal economy. Without prospects, they lived in shantytowns adjacent to the city. As more men brought families to the city, more girls attended school, adding to the educated job pool, except that women were not allowed to have jobs in the formal economy. Women were relegated to the informal economy as self-employed in the service industries such as market traders, cooks, hairdressers, or in the illegal trades such as prostitution.

At independence the structure of colonial society remained very much in place, with the exception of more women being used in the workforce. Those who were educated were paid less than their male counterparts, those with minimal education performed low-paying jobs as secretaries, and those who were not educated remained in the informal economy.

See also: COLONIAL CONQUEST (Vol. IV); BRITAIN AND AFRICA (Vol. IV) FRANCE AND AFRICA (Vol. IV); GENDER IN COLONIAL AFRICA (Vol. IV); URBANIZATION (Vol. IV); URBAN LIFE AND CULTURE (Vol. IV); WOMEN IN COLONIAL AFRICA (Vol. IV).

Further reading: E. A. Brett, *Colonialism and Underdevelopment in East Africa: The Politics of Economic Change, 1919–1939* (New York: NOK Publishers, 1973); John Kent, *The Internationalization of Colonialism: Britain, France, and Black Africa, 1939–1956* (New York: Oxford University Press, 1992); Paul E. Lovejoy and Toyin Falola, eds., *Pawnship, Slavery, and Colonialism in Africa* (Trenton, N.J.: Africa World Press, 2003); Mahmood Mamdani, *Citizen and Subject: Contemporary Africa and the Legacy of Late Colonialism* (Princeton, N.J.: Princeton University Press, 1996).

colonial rule Prior to the second half of the 19th century Africans ruled themselves. There were exceptions to be sure—in ALGERIA, parts of SOUTH AFRICA, and small pockets of European control such as FREETOWN, SIERRA LEONE and LUANDA, ANGOLA. In addition, there were many cases in which Africans had participated with Europeans as equals in long-distance trade networks.

This changed with the onset of the Industrial Revolution, as the nations of Europe sought greater control over Africa and its NATURAL RESOURCES. This desire for greater control of the continent initially resulted in a rash of haphazard land grabbing and a burgeoning amount of conflict among the colonial powers. Needing to provide a structure to their efforts, the colonial powers decided to meet in what was called the BERLIN CONFERENCE (1884–85). There they formally divided Africa among themselves with little regard for the needs or desires of the indigenous population of the continent. Europeans then spent the next 20 years engaged in COLONIAL CONQUEST. In an effort to control the people of the lands they conquered, colonial administrators implemented various forms of colonial rule.

French Rule and Assimilation France initially pursued colonization with the idea that it would "civi-

lize" the people of the lands it conquered. The plan was to gradually introduce Africans to French culture with the goal that they would eventually become French citizens and an integral part of the "mother country." This concept of *assimilation* required Africans to abandon their own culture and adopt that of the French. French missionary and secular EDUCATION, in which an African child might stand and recite, in French, a history lesson that began "My ancestors, the Gauls..." provided the avenue toward citizenship.

The policy of assimilation largely failed. Prior to World War II (1939–45) only a few Africans from Algeria and the QUATRE COMMUNES of present-day SENEGAL succeeded in becoming citizens with voting rights in France. This was largely because these two colonial possessions were considered an extension of mainland France. Africans residing in French-controlled land outside these two areas were considered French subjects and had no rights as citizens.

French Rule and Association As French colonial interests increased and the process of assimilation stagnated, France abandoned the idea of assimilation and replaced it with a similar concept called *association*. This theory of governance allowed Africans to keep their indigenous culture but encouraged them to have a sense of pride and love for France as a mother country. The concept of association had less lofty goals for the relationship between France and its African colonies. As a result, France ceased providing Africans an opportunity to gain French citizenship.

Direct Rule Direct rule was another model for colonial governance in Africa. France, for example, established centralized administrations in urban centers that later became colonial capital cities. From these central points they would disseminate French culture, impose a foreign form of governance, and apply policies that would divide the indigenous peoples to lessen the possibility of organized RESISTANCE AND REBELLION.

Direct rule allowed the governments in Europe to enforce policies within their colonial possessions at a local level. In FRENCH WEST AFRICA, for example, the governor-general based in DAKAR took his orders directly from the minister of colonies in Paris. The governor-general would then pass these orders to a lieutenant-governor in each of the colonies in French West Africa. Colonies were further subdivided into *cercles* (districts) governed by a *commandant de cercle* (district commissioner). After receiving his orders, the *commandant de cercle* would then communicate directives to local chiefs, who in turn enforced the rules, initially made in France, on the local population.

The French desired their colonies to be self-sufficient and eventually return a profit to France and its people. In an effort to achieve this economic benefit, the French instituted colonial TAXATION. This forced Africans to acquire currency. To do this, some produced CASH CROPS or other resources valued by France. Others engaged in wage LABOR. Although SLAVERY had been abolished in Europe, the French required individuals to provide a certain amount of labor as part of their tax burden, forcing Africans to work for public projects such as building roads and railroads.

Company Rule The colonial powers of Europe did not always take a full interest in the governance of their possessions. Some governments granted vast tracts of land to European CONCESSIONAIRE COMPANIES, which used the land to harvest natural resources such as RUBBER and PALM OIL. Other companies received MINING concessions or were contracted to improve colonial infrastructure by constructing harbor facilities and railways. In order to conduct their business, the concessionaire companies, at their own expense, established and administered a system of government over the regions they controlled. They also set up a system of taxation and labor recruitment, which resulted in numerous abuses of the indigenous populations.

Indirect Rule Britain, meanwhile, largely practiced a form of governance known as indirect rule. Under this system the British integrated indigenous African rulers into the structure of the colonial administration, making them intermediaries between the British district commissioners and the colonial subjects. Although the British taught Africans the ways of British governance, they did not believe that Africans would assimilate British culture. The benefit of this method of colonial rule was that Britain did not require as many colonial officers to oversee the work of the colony. However, there were many cases in which the indigenous people, such as the IGBO, did not have one single leader but relied instead on a system similar to a direct democracy. To make this group fit into their colonial model, the British appointed chiefs to act as intermediaries for the people. Africans frequently viewed these appointees as illegitimate rulers who merely did the bidding of the colonial powers.

In his 1922 book, *The Dual Mandate in British Tropical Africa*, Frederick LUGARD (1858–1945) stated that the mission of the British Empire was "for liberty and self-development on no standardized lines . . . Such liberty and self-development can be best secured to the native population by leaving them free to manage their own affairs through their own rulers, proportionately to their degree of advancement, under the guidance of the British [administrative] staff, and subject to the laws and policy of the [British] administration."

British colonial governors frequently empowered local chiefs or appointees to collect taxes for the colony's coffers. Sometimes indigenous rulers misappropriated revenues. The British introduced a Native Court system to which people could bring their disputes and the Native Authority system to police the indigenous population. The Native Authority and Native Court systems, however, did not reflect indigenous law and custom, but rather the laws and customs imposed by the British.

Settler Rule While there were plenty of Europeans who traveled to Africa with the intent of someday returning to Europe, many European SETTLERS left their homes with the intent to remain in Africa permanently. Settler colonies were found in KENYA, NORTHERN RHODESIA and SOUTHERN RHODESIA (present-day ZAMBIA and ZIMBABWE, respectively), South Africa, Algeria, Angola, MOZAMBIQUE, ERITREA, and SOUTH WEST AFRICA (today's NAMIBIA). Settlers frequently alienated the indigenous people from their lands and forced them to work as wage laborers to pay taxes. There were also many instances of forced labor. These European immigrants demanded that special rights and protection be provided by colonial governments. The government applied harsh and racist policies toward the indigenous Africans to protect the interests of the outnumbered settlers. Later events in South Africa's history, most notably the institution of the APARTHEID system, illustrate this phenomenon quite clearly.

See also: BELGIUM AND AFRICA (Vol. IV); ENGLAND AND AFRICA (Vol. IV); FRANCE AND AFRICA (Vol. IV); GERMANY AND AFRICA (Vol. IV); ITALY AND AFRICA (Vol. IV); PARTITION (Vol. IV); PORTUGAL AND AFRICA (Vol. IV); SPAIN AND AFRICA (Vol. V).

Further reading: Michael Crowder and Obaro Ikime, eds., *West African Chiefs: Their Changing Status under Colonial Rule and Independence* (New York: Africana Publishing Corp., 1970); Bruce Fetter, ed., *Colonial Rule in Africa: Readings from Primary Sources* (Madison, Wisc.: University of Wisconsin Press, 1979); Prosser Gifford and William Roger Louis, eds., *France and Britain in Africa: Imperial Rivalry and Colonial Rule* (New Haven, Conn.: Yale University Press, 1971); Martin A. Klein, *Slavery and Colonial Rule in French West Africa* (New York: Cambridge University Press, 1998).

Comoros (Comoro Islands) Archipelago of four islands and several islets in the western Indian Ocean, 180 miles (290 km) off the coast of East Africa. Reflecting the unique position of the islands at the crossroads of Indian Ocean trade routes—which link Africa, Asia, and Arabia— Comorans are of diverse origins. Over the last 14 centuries, settlers from Indonesia, MADAGASCAR, the SWAHILI COAST of East Africa, Arabia, and Europe have left an imprint on the Comoro Islands, as have the many enslaved workers who either worked on the islands' plantations or passed through Comoros en route to another destination. Portugal was the first European nation to establish contact with the islands, in 1505.

In 1841 France established a formal presence on the island of Maore (called Mayotte by the French). By 1886 the other islands of Mwali (Mohéli), Njazidja (Grande Comore), and Nzwani (Anjouan) had become French protectorates.

In 1908 the administration of the Comoro Islands became the responsibility of the governor general of Madagascar, a neighboring Indian Ocean island nation to the south, which was also under French colonial control. Although most of the islands' lands are poorly suited to anything but subsistence AGRICULTURE, French and Shirazi Arab settlers managed large plantations. During the colonial period the Comoro Islands exported commodities such as ylang-ylang essence (used in the manufacture of perfume), vanilla, cloves, and COCOA. Comoros became a French overseas territory in 1947, giving it the right to representation in the French National Assembly, and the following year it shed its administrative ties to Madagascar. Local autonomy was granted in 1957, but the following year Comorans voted resoundingly to remain a French territory.

See also: COMOROS (Vols. I, II, III, V); FRANCE AND AFRICA (Vols. III, IV, V); INDIAN OCEAN TRADE (Vol. II); SHIRAZI ARABS (Vol. II).

concessionaire companies Privately owned European companies given authority by their native governments to establish control over and manage African colonial territories. European colonial powers made wide use of concessionaire companies, especially in the early stages of their efforts to carve out spheres of influence on the continent. These private companies, such as the ROYAL NIGER COMPANY, the BRITISH SOUTH AFRICA COMPANY, and the German East Africa Company, were granted the right to establish control over large tracts of land in regions with valuable agricultural or mineral resources. These companies in turn profited from their investments by securing raw materials for industrial production in Europe. They gathered the available raw materials, created markets for European manufactured goods, and introduced the use of currency. They also established military and political control and administered their territories at their own expense. However, because the companies were interested in short-term profits, they generally did not invest in infrastructure necessary to generate long-term returns.

Once the era of COLONIAL RULE was fully underway, European governments preferred to rule directly and revoked the rights of companies to administer and police territory. However, the companies often continued to operate, owning mineral rights or controlling vast tracts of land on which they grew CASH CROPS for export. The emphasis thus

shifted from establishing territorial claims during the era of PARTITION to developing the colonial economies.

See also: COLONIAL CONQUEST (Vol. IV); COLONIALISM, INFLUENCE OF (Vol. IV).

Congo, Democratic Republic of the (Congo-Kinshasa) Present-day country located in Central Africa measuring approximately 905,400 square miles (2,345,000 sq km). Located south of the Congo River, the Democratic Republic of the Congo has a short Atlantic Ocean coastline just south of the Angolan enclave of Cabinda. The country borders the CENTRAL AFRICAN REPUBLIC, the Republic of the SUDAN, UGANDA, RWANDA, BURUNDI, TANZANIA, and ZAMBIA, as well as ANGOLA and the Republic of the CONGO. Among the peoples who inhabited the region prior to the colonial era were the Luba, Lunda-Chokwe, Mongo, Yaka, Pende, and Azande.

Colonial Era: The Congo Free State and Belgian Congo By the middle of the 19th century the Congo River had become an important commercial waterway, and control of it therefore became increasingly important to the colonial interests of both Britain and France. In 1885 Belgian king LEOPOLD II (1835–1909) proclaimed his own African colony, naming it the CONGO FREE STATE. In 1908, the public exposure of human-rights abuses forced Leopold to turn the colony over to the Belgian government. It was then known as the BELGIAN CONGO until it became independent, in 1960.

Leopold's acquisition of the Congo was formalized by the BERLIN CONFERENCE of 1884–85. At that time the major European powers granted Leopold's International Congo Association sovereign power over the region. The writer and explorer Henry Morton STANLEY (1841–1904) played a key role in gaining international recognition of Leopold's claims on the basis of his 1879–84 expedition in the Congo basin, which Leopold sponsored. Leopold later convinced the Belgian government to make him the sole recognized authority over the vast area.

An early-20th-century description of LEOPOLDVILLE, the major commercial center of the Congo Free State, noted: "Trade is the life of Leopoldville. In the warehouses we see along the beach are stored rubber, ivory, palm oil, COFFEE, COCOA, lumber." This trade, however, benefited Europeans considerably and the African population very little, if at all. The colonial authorities often resorted to violence to obtain these commodities in the form of colonial TAXATION or compulsory labor for the state.

In 1960, as Congolese independence approached, people took to the streets of Leopoldville in celebration. © UPI/New York World-Telegram & Sun Collection/Library of Congress

With his territorial claims and personal authority solidified, Leopold then faced the tasks of gaining actual control of the land and making the colony profitable. Taking physical command brought Leopold and his agents into direct conflict with African rulers. The eastern third of Leopold's realm, for example, was controlled by the states in the trading federation controlled by Arab-Swahili trader, TIPPU TIP (c. 1830–1905). Realizing that he would need a large, armed force to take effective control of regions like these, Leopold established a colonial army, known as the Force Publique, composed of conscripted African soldiers and European officers. This armed force became a key element in Leopold's colonial rule.

By about 1887 Tippu Tip's influence in the region had declined, and he was forced to acknowledge Leopold's sovereignty. Leopold also came into conflict with other African rulers. One of the most notable of these was M'SIRI (c. 1830–1891), a NYAMWEZI trader who had established a kingdom through conquest over the people in the mineral-rich Katanga province in the southern Congo. Leopold's troops moved against his state and, in the course of negotiations between the two groups, M'siri was murdered. This opened the entire southern part of the Congo to mineral exploitation.

As in Katanga, Leopold's conquest of the Congo was a brutal process—and an expensive one. To recoup the tremendous outlay of personal funds he made, Leopold imposed heavy taxes and labor demands on the local population. As another means of raising money, he proclaimed that all lands not directly occupied by Africans belonged to the state. He then granted huge tracts of land for development by CONCESSIONAIRE COMPANIES. These companies used coerced labor to produce CASH

CROPS, which generated income for the state. COTTON and PALM OIL were the most immediate sources of wealth. But they were quickly replaced in importance by RUBBER, which grew wild. Of crucial importance to automobile production and other modern industries, RUBBER quickly became a vital product for the Congo, with EXPORTS growing from 110 tons (100 m tons) in 1890 to 6,614 tons (6,000 m tons) in 1901.

Leopold claimed to rule the Congo in a beneficent manner, promoting Christianity and EDUCATION. However, the truth was quite different. While both Protestant and Catholic MISSIONARIES were active, their work was a veneer that, for a short time, covered up the harsh realities of life for ordinary Congolese. Seeing the situation firsthand during his own experiences in Africa, the novelist Joseph Conrad (1857–1924) described the horrors of the Congo in his novel, *Heart of Darkness* (1902). Conrad's descriptions of what was happening in the Congo were so shocking that they have struck many readers—then and now—as being allegorical or symbolic rather than realistic. As a result, it was several more years before the true state of affairs in the Congo became widely known. It was then that E. D. Morel (1873–1924) and his Congo Reform Association, among other individuals and organizations, provided irrefutable information and generated sufficient international pressure to force King Leopold to turn over the Congo to Belgium, in 1908, which then ruled it as the BELGIAN CONGO until 1960.

In 1906 E. D. Morel published *Red Rubber: The Story of the Rubber Slave Trade Flourishing on the Congo,* which exposed and condemned the brutality of the Free State's rubber-collection regime. He specifically coined the term "red rubber" to connote the bloodshed involved.

Once in control, Belgium consolidated the colony into four semi-autonomous administrative provinces. Like Britain, Belgium tried to incorporate local African leaders to help administer its colony. However, the Belgian style of indirect rule did not make provisions for Congolese leaders to become more involved in the colonial government. As a result Belgium sent thousands of officials to settle in the Congo's administrative centers, including Leopoldville (now Kinshasa), STANLEYVILLE (now Kisangani), and ELIZABETHVILLE.

The resources that were major export items during Leopold's rule—especially rubber, ivory, and palm products—remained important trade items under Belgian administration as well. When world rubber prices dropped, however, the Congo's rubber industry trailed off. This de-

velopment also scaled back the widespread abuse that both corporations and the state employed to coerce Africans to perform the backbreaking work to harvest rubber for export.

After World War I (1914–18) the administration required Africans to produce agricultural products. Some, such as cotton, were grown for export. Others, such as rice, were grown to feed the settlers in the colony. In order to make its agricultural programs more efficient, the administration relocated thousands of Africans to indigenous farming settlements and imposed high production quotas. MINING, however, was the core of Congo's economy by the 1920s, with DIAMONDS and COPPER becoming the primary products. By the 1930s UNION MINIÈRE du Haut-Katanga, founded in 1906, was the world's largest copper-producing company. As in other parts of the continent, Africans were encouraged—or even coerced directly or indirectly by taxation—to leave their homes and take jobs in the mines. As a result Africans became the primary workforce in the income-producing mines, with Europeans providing supervision.

Although administration by the Belgian government put an end to the worst of the abuses seen during the rule of Leopold II, the Congo remained a relatively harsh and brutal colony. Education was limited, with little available to Africans beyond the most basic elementary level. Indeed it was not until the 1950s that the first universities were founded in the colony. The Belgian administration retained an equally firm control in the political arena, preventing even its own white colonial residents from taking part in elections until the late 1950s.

In spite of the repressive atmosphere, nationalism remained alive in the Congo. During the 1920s the religious movement of Simon KIMBANGU (c. 1887–1951) gained particular strength among the people of the colony. Proclaiming himself a prophet, Kimbangu assailed European cultural and religious institutions. Believing Kimbangu and his growing number of followers to represent a significant threat, the colonial authorities had him arrested in 1921. In spite of the Belgian actions, Kimbanguism survived, feeding increasing anti-Belgian and anti-European feelings among the people.

While nationalist feelings slowly continued to grow, during World War II (1939–45) the Congo remained loyal to the free Belgian government, even after it was defeated by Germany and was forced into exile. Pro-independence activists reemerged, however, in the postwar years. In response, Belgium launched what it called a Thirty-Year Plan for the gradual institution of Congolese self-government. Although the plan had widespread support within Belgium itself, it had little backing among Congolese nationalists, especially Joseph Kasavubu (1913–1969), leader of the ABAKO party, and the more leftist-oriented Patrice LUMUMBA (1925–1961). As other neighboring former colonies gained their independence, the calls for Congolese liberation grew louder and more insistent. By January 1959 rioting broke out, and very quickly the Belgian authorities became unable to control the situation. Within a year a conference in Brussels announced that Congo would become independent on June 30, 1960. Within two weeks of independence, however, a mutiny among officers in the police and armed forces plunged the new nation into what became known as the Congo Crisis, a period of instability and civil discord that was ended only by the intervention of the United Nations.

In 1971 Congolese dictator Joseph Mobutu Sese Seko (1930–1997) "re-Africanized" the geographical names of the Belgian Congo. For example, he renamed his country *Zaire;* Leopoldville became *Kinshasa;* Stanleyville became *Kisingani;* and Elizabethville became *Lubumbashi.*

See also: CONGO CRISIS (Vol. V); CONGO, DEMOCRATIC REPUBLIC OF (Vol. V); KASAVUBU, JOSEPH (Vol. V); KATANGA (Vol. V); MOBUTU SESE SEKO (Vol. V); NATIONALISM AND INDEPENDENCE MOVEMENTS (Vol. IV).

Further reading: Ch. Didier Gondola, *The History of Congo* (Westport, Conn.: Greenwood Press, 2002); Osumaka Likaka, *Rural Society and Cotton in Colonial Zaire* (Madison: University of Wisconsin Press, 1997); Georges Nzongola-Ntalaja, *The Congo from Leopold to Kabila: A People's History* (New York: Manchester University Press, 2002).

Congo Free State (1885–1908) Colonial state established in the Congo Basin by King LEOPOLD II (1835–1909) of Belgium. Today, the territory is the Democratic Republic of the CONGO. The ambitious ruler of a European country only 12,000 square miles (30,510 sq km) in area, Leopold used clever and able diplomacy to gain personal control of an African region of 905,063 square miles (2,300,000 sq km). His acquisition of the Congo began with the BERLIN CONFERENCE of 1884–85, at which Leopold's International Congo Association was recognized as the sovereign power over the vast Congo Basin. Leopold then persuaded the Belgian Parliament to authorize him to personally rule the area. It was then given the name Congo Free State, indicating that it was an area free from European COLONIAL RULE. Leopold's rule led to a system of abuses that eventually were exposed by various writers and organizations. The resulting international scandal forced him to turn control of the area over to the Belgian government, under which it became the colony known as the BELGIAN CONGO.

See also: BELGIUM AND AFRICA (Vol. IV).

Further reading: Adam Hochschild, *King Leopold's Ghost* (New York: Houghton Mifflin, 1998).

Congo, Republic of the (Congo-Brazzaville)
Present-day country located in western Central Africa measuring approximately 131,900 square miles (341,600 sq km). Located to the north of the Congo River, the Republic of the Congo has a short Atlantic Ocean coastline and borders GABON, CAMEROON, the CENTRAL AFRICAN REPUBLIC, the Democratic Republic of the CONGO, and the Angolan enclave of Cabinda.

Bantu-speaking peoples, including the Kongo, Vili (a Loango subgroup), Teke, and Sanga, inhabited the region prior to the colonial era. By the middle of the 19th century the Congo River had become an important commercial waterway and, therefore, control of it became increasingly important to the colonial interests of both Britain and France. In 1880 the Italian-born French explorer Pierre Savorgnan DE BRAZZA (1852–1905) negotiated a treaty with the Teke people that resulted in the establishment of a French PROTECTORATE on the northern bank of the Congo River.

Republic of Congo during the Colonial Era: French Congo In 1891 the FRENCH CONGO was officially declared a colony. At the time it included the territory to the west that is now Gabon. The colonial development of French Congo was similar to that of neighboring BELGIAN CONGO, with European CONCESSIONAIRE COMPANIES buying rights to the region's NATURAL RESOURCES, especially minerals, RUBBER, and ivory. The colonial ECONOMY in the French Congo was not immediately successful, and both the French administration and the European concessionaires recruited workers using forced LABOR schemes in order to maximize profits. Untold thousands of Africans from throughout the colony died from the brutal mistreatment and harsh conditions related to this labor system.

In 1905 de Brazza returned to French Congo to investigate the mistreatment of the indigenous people. His reports highlighted the abuses of the concessionaire companies and helped persuade the French government to diminish the administrative power of commercial concerns in the region. Even so, the practice of forced labor continued until the 1940s.

In 1903 France separated Gabon from French Congo, and the remaining portion was renamed Middle Congo. By 1910 France had taken control of Middle Congo from the concessionaire companies, uniting the colony with

OUBANGUI-CHARI (now the CENTRAL AFRICAN REPUBLIC) and CHAD to form FRENCH EQUATORIAL AFRICA (Afrique Équatoriale Française, AEF). Because of its strategic location on the Congo River, BRAZZAVILLE , in Middle Congo, was made the administrative capital of AEF.

After World War I (1914–18) France undertook the building of the Congo-Ocean Railway, which extended from the coastal city of Point-Noir to Brazzaville. Construction of the railway cost the lives of more than 10,000 African laborers, who died of physical abuse and horrendous living conditions. In 1928 this mistreatment sparked an African uprising, which the French quickly quelled.

During World War II (1939–45) relations between France and Middle Congo changed drastically. After France's surrender to Germany, Charles DE GAULLE (1890–1970) founded Free France in AEF, naming Brazzaville its capital. At the end of hostilities in Europe in 1944, France held the Brazzaville Conference, at which de Gaulle unveiled a reformed colonial policy. As part of the reforms France finally put an end to forced labor and guaranteed citizenship to all people within its colonies.

In 1946 France granted Middle Congo a Territorial Assembly and representation in the French Parliament, necessary steps on the way to self-government. In 1958 AEF was dissolved and Middle Congo, renamed the Republic of the Congo, moved toward independence. In August 1960 the country gained full autonomy, with Fulbert Youlou (1917–1972) becoming the first president. The period following independence was characterized by violence between the country's various political groups, which were divided along ethnic lines.

See also: COLONIALISM, INFLUENCE OF (Vol. IV); CONGO, REPUBLIC OF THE (Vols. I, II, III, V); FRANCE AND AFRICA (Vol. III, IV, V).

Convention Peoples Party (CPP)

Political party founded by Kwame NKRUMAH (1909–1972) that advocated immediate independence for the GOLD COAST COLONY from British COLONIAL RULE. The party's political activism led to the founding of the independent country of GHANA. Nkrumah established the Convention Peoples Party in 1949 after breaking away from the elite-oriented UNITED GOLD COAST CONVENTION (UGCC), for which he had served as general secretary. Feeling that the UGCC's focus on the interests of the middle class led it to ignore ordinary workers, Nkrumah and his new party advocated policies of positive action and immediate independence with the slogan of "Independence Now." The party was considered more radical than the UGCC in terms of fomenting public demonstrations against British rule, including illegal strikes.

The British colonial government imprisoned Nkrumah in 1950 for inciting riots with his Declaration of Positive Action, which demanded Gold Coast independence. While Nkrumah was in prison the CPP won the 1951 general election, thereby ushering Nkrumah, as the leader of the party, from the jailhouse to the state house. In 1952, still head of the CPP, Nkrumah became the Gold Coast's prime minister. The CPP dominated the Gold Coast elections, plebiscites, and referendums that led the colony to independence, in 1957, as the new nation state of Ghana.

As the 1960s began Nkrumah ruled in an increasingly arbitrary manner, and the CPP began functioning less as a true political party and more as a tool for individuals to further their own personal interests.

See also: ENGLAND AND AFRICA (Vols. III, IV, V); COLONIALISM, INFLUENCE OF (Vol. IV); COLONIAL RULE (Vol. IV); NATIONALISM AND INDEPENDENCE MOVEMENTS (Vol. IV); POLITICAL PARTIES AND ORGANIZATIONS (Vols. IV, V).

copper Malleable and ductile metal that became widely used in the early 20th century because of its excellent ability to conduct electricity. The use of copper has a long history in Africa, with both utilitarian and decorative applications. Beginning in the late 19th century the development of electricity as a commercially viable form of energy created a huge demand for copper, which was found to be the best material for electrical wiring and connectors. The widespread technological application of electricity coincided with the era of European colonization in Africa, and it was the colonized territories that turned out to hold some of the world's greatest copper reserves.

Large-scale commercial MINING of Africa's copper was concentrated in the COPPERBELT, a region that stretches across southern Central Africa. In 1906 a Belgian company, UNION MINIÉRE, began mining operations in the province of Katanga, in the BELGIAN CONGO (today's Democratic Republic of the CONGO). A few years later the South Africa-based ANGLO-AMERICAN CORPORATION began operations in NORTHERN RHODESIA (present-day ZAMBIA).

Today Zambia and the Democratic Republic of the Congo are two of seven countries (the others being Chile, Mexico, Peru, Russia, and the United States) that account for nearly 70 percent of the world's total copper reserves.

African miners—who were well paid compared to other laborers in the colonial era—provided the bulk of the workforce. However, due to the nature of the mining operations and mine ownership, the profits flowed abroad to the European colonial powers, with little benefit accruing to the producing countries. With the larger mining companies needing thousands of men to work the mines, major cities, such as ELIZABETHVILLE (present-day Lubumbashi) in the Congo, emerged in connection with mining operations. Railroads passing through these cities were built to haul the mined copper to ocean ports for shipment abroad, since the processing of copper into manufactured products occurred outside the continent.

After independence African countries took ownership of the mineral rights and of the mines themselves, but multinational corporations continued to operate the mines under very profitable contracts. Although new technological developments in the late 20th century have reduced the demand for copper somewhat, Africa continues to be a major producer of the metal.

See also: COLONIALISM, INFLUENCE OF (Vol. IV); COPPER (Vols. I, II); KATANGA (Vol. V); MINERALS AND METALS (Vols. IV, V).

Copperbelt Region stretching from the northern part of present-day ZAMBIA to Katanga province in the Democratic Republic of the CONGO that is believed to have the largest concentration of COPPER deposits in the world. The history of copper MINING in this area goes back many centuries, but between 1850 and 1960 the region's rich deposits caused unprecedented urban and industrial development as well as political upheaval.

Africans mined copper and used the metal for centuries before 1867, when the missionary and explorer David LIVINGSTONE (1813–1873) explored the Congo area and noted how the people of Katanga smelted copper ore into bars of 50 to 100 pounds (22.7 to 45.4 kg). Large-scale mining, however, started during the colonial era.

Reserves in the Copperbelt are now estimated at 100 million metric tons, representing about 30 percent of the world's total. Copper has provided Zambia and the Democratic Republic of the Congo with their major export incomes, with volumes amounting to a combined one million tons of copper metal per year. The Copperbelt region is the largest concentration of industry in sub-Saharan Africa outside SOUTH AFRICA.

In the BELGIAN CONGO a Belgian company, UNION MINIÈRE du Haut-Katanga, one of the world's largest copper-producing companies, started exploiting the region's resources in 1906. The city of ELIZABETHVILLE (present-day Lubumbashi) subsequently became the center of Belgian mining operations in Katanga.

In Zambia (then NORTHERN RHODESIA) commercial copper mining started in 1909 with the completion of major railway lines. The industry exploded in the 1920s when the BRITISH SOUTH AFRICAN COMPANY, founded by Cecil RHODES (1853–1902), granted trade and mining rights to other European-owned companies. The Selection Trust, a British company, developed Northern Rhodesia's first modern mine at the Roan Antelope deposit near Luanshya and started production in 1929. A second mine opened later in the year, followed by the opening of additional major mines between 1933 and 1965.

Commercial copper mining relies on ore mined both at the surface and underground, and the production and export of the metal is highly technical, requiring extensive LABOR and energy. As a result the mines in the Copperbelt could be developed only by big, multinational companies, whose economic strength later played a part in shaping the colonial policies of the short-lived CENTRAL AFRICAN FEDERATION (1953–63).

Especially after the 1920s, mining in the Copperbelt attracted workers of various ethnic groups from all over Africa, and the subsequent development of LABOR UNIONS and political parties related to the industry foreshadowed the nationalist movements that would sweep the continent in the years after World War II (1939–45).

Like DIAMOND MINING and GOLD mining, copper mining was a source of political conflict. Because of its mineral wealth, the province of Katanga resisted becoming a part of the Democratic Republic of the Congo when the former Belgian Congo was granted independence, in 1960. Supported by Union Minière, Moise Tshombe (1917– 1969), the provincial president of Katanga, tried to secede from the new, unstable republic. In response the republic sent government troops to subdue Tshombe, whose forces were assisted by Belgian troops. In the end the United Nations sent peacekeeping forces to restore order, but it was not until 1963 that Tshombe ended his plans for secession and accepted a UN-brokered National Conciliation Plan.

See also: ANGLO-AMERICAN CORPORATION (Vol. IV); COPPER (Vols. I, II); COPPER MINING (Vol. II); KATANGA (Vol. V); LUBUMBASHI (Vol. V); MINERALS AND METALS (Vol. V); MULTINATIONAL CORPORATIONS (Vol. V); TSHOMBE, MOISE (Vol. V).

Further reading: Jane L. Parpart, *Labor and Capital on the African Copperbelt* (Philadelphia: Temple University Press, 1983).

cotton The premier commercial crop of colonial Africa. Using various types of elaborate looms, African craftspeople have long woven cotton into cloth for trade as well as for their own use. In the medieval period the city of TIMBUKTU, in what is now MALI, was an important center for cotton, textile production, while in later times KANO and other northern Nigerian cities developed a significant non-mechanized, textile-manufacturing industry.

West Africa in particular has long been noted for its cotton cloth, although there also is evidence of cotton production along the SWAHILI COAST as far back as the 13th century and in other areas of the continent dating to the 11th century. In much of West Africa, as well as in other parts of the continent, the handicraft-based production of cotton TEXTILES has remained important into the 21st century and has held its own in competition with imported textiles.

Emergence of a European Textile Industry In the late 1700s and early 1800s the Industrial Revolution in Europe and North America brought about significant changes in the position and role of cotton production in Africa. The climate of Europe was not conducive to growing cotton, so in earlier days European merchants had purchased finished cotton goods from India and from West Africa. However, once the mechanized textile industry in Europe emerged, the demand shifted to raw cotton to supply Europe's own textile mills.

The first major sources of raw cotton for the European textile mills were the plantations of the southern United States, which were totally dependent upon an enslaved LABOR force. Cotton continued to be a major export crop from the southern states after the U.S. Civil War (1861–65), although much of the crop went to American textile mills in New England.

Cotton began to emerge as a commercial crop in ALGERIA, where in the mid-19th century European SETTLERS experimented with growing it for profit. During the U.S. Civil War, cotton growers in Algeria and other parts of Africa engaged in a brief boom period, as European textile mills were cut off from their usual suppliers in the southern United States. However, with the end of the war the cotton boom collapsed. In EGYPT, the loss of revenue was so severe that it contributed to the downfall of the government of Khedive ISMAIL (1830–1895) and started the country on the road to British domination. The cotton industry in Algeria also declined after the U.S. Civil War.

Effects of Colonial Conquest The late 19th and early 20th centuries was the period of COLONIAL CONQUEST and the establishment of COLONIAL RULE throughout the African continent. During this period cotton emerged as a major cash crop, that is, a crop grown for the export market rather than for domestic consumption. And in this case, it was an export market focused on Europe. Having conquered the African continent, the European colonial powers needed to find ways to profit from their colonies. One way was for the colonies to grow crops specifically for export to Europe. Cotton became an especially important export crop for two reasons. First, it could be grown by individual African farmers on a small scale without significant colonial investment in the factors of production. Second, the colonial powers could benefit their own national textile industries through a controlled source of raw material grown in their colonies.

On the African side of the equation, however, cotton was not generally a viable crop. Many parts of the continent lacked suitable climate and soils for cotton. In addition, the labor and land requirements for cotton production often interfered with FOOD production for domestic consumption. Nevertheless, European colonial authorities insisted that African farmers grow cotton, often using force to compel its production even though the market price was frequently very low. The BELGIAN CONGO and the Portuguese colony of MOZAMBIQUE were particularly notorious in this respect. Indeed, in Mozam-bique cotton gained a reputation among the local population as "the mother of poverty." In other parts of the continent, such as Northern NIGERIA, however, the long-standing domestic market for cotton textiles meant that the British were never successful in their attempts to promote cotton as an export crop.

After the Colonial Era Beginning about 1960, with the end of the colonial period and the arrival of independence, European countries were no longer able to compel individual African farmers to grow cotton. Nonetheless, cotton had become such an important part of the export-oriented economies of Africa that it continued to be a vital crop for such countries as CHAD, Egypt, Mali, Mozambique, and the present-day Republic of the SUDAN. Today Africa produces about 7 percent of the world's cotton and is responsible for about 12 percent of world cotton EXPORTS. Important, too, is cotton's continued significance for the local handicraft industries. Later in the 20th century locally produced cotton textiles, such as the famous Kente cloth of GHANA, came to be an important commodity for tourism and for export to Europe and the United States.

See also: CLOTH AND TEXTILES (Vol. IV); COTTON (Vols. I, II, III); TRADE AND COMMERCE (Vol. IV).

Further reading: Allen Isaacman and Richard Roberts, eds., *Cotton, Colonialism, and Social History in Sub-Saharan Africa* (Portsmouth, N.H.: Heinemann, 1995).

Crowther, Samuel Ajayi (Bishop) (1808–1891)
First African Anglican Bishop

Known at birth as Ajayi, Crowther was raised in the town of Osogun in the YORUBA-speaking region of present-day NIGERIA. The early 1800s were a chaotic time in Yorubaland because of the breakup of the old Oyo empire. When he was about 13 years old Ajayi was taken captive and sold into the transatlantic SLAVE TRADE. However, a naval vessel from the British antislavery squadron patrolling the coast intercepted his ship and released its human cargo in the colony of SIERRA LEONE, which had been founded in 1786 for the repatriation of freed slaves.

At the time, the Anglican CHURCH MISSIONARY SOCIETY (CMS) was actively engaged in Christianizing and educating Sierra Leoneans. One of its converts was Ajayi, who when baptized took the name Samuel Crowther, after an official of the CMS. Young Samuel enrolled in a school offering an industrial education, but in 1827 he was selected to attend FOURAH BAY COLLEGE, the new boys' secondary school in FREETOWN, Sierra Leone.

Meanwhile, the CMS was embroiled in a conflict over languages and Bible translation. Many clergymen did not wish to learn African languages, but the prevailing missionary practice was to spread the Gospel to people by means of their own tongues. This led the CMS to employ the Yoruba-speaking Crowther as an evangelist and also brought about his participation in the unsuccessful Niger Expedition (1841), which had the dual goal of Christianizing Africans and ending their enslavement. In 1842 Crowther went to London, where he attended the CMS Training College, and in 1843 he received ordination as an Anglican priest.

At about the same time, Yoruba-speaking Sierra Leoneans opened trade relations with the Yoruba in Nigeria. Many returned and settled in ABEOKUTA, bringing their Anglican version of Christianity with them. The CMS used their presence as an opportunity to establish a mission in Nigeria, with Crowther as an active participant. In 1857 the CMS appointed him as the leader of its Niger Mission; the same year he participated in the Second Niger Expedition. In 1864 Crowther traveled to England to be consecrated "Bishop of Western Equatorial Africa beyond the Queen's Dominions." By 1879 Nigeria supported 16 Anglican dioceses.

The very success of Crowther and his fellow African MISSIONARIES led to conflict with a new generation of European missionaries imbued with the pseudo-scientific racism of the late 19th century. They attacked his administration of the Niger Mission and in 1890 forced him to resign. Crowther's success as a missionary rested in his education, his commitment to his work, and in his knowledge of and sympathy with African culture. He was particularly adept at languages and wrote LANGUAGE texts to enable missionaries to communicate with his fellow Africans and to make the bible more easily accessible to Africans. A hallmark of his approach to missionary work was his patience and readiness to listen.

Beyond his translations and linguistic work, Crowther also spread knowledge about Africa through his written works. These included *Journal of an Expedition up the Niger in 1841* (with J. F. Schön; 1843), *Journal of an Expedition up the Niger and Tshadda Rivers* (1855), and *Gospel on the Banks of the Niger* (with J. C. Taylor; 1859).

See also: CHRISTIANITY, INFLUENCE OF (Vols. II, III, IV, V); OYO EMPIRE (Vols. II, III).

Further reading: Jesse Page, *The Black Bishop, Samuel Adjai Crowther* (Westport, Conn.: Greenwood Press, 1979).

Crummell, Alexander (1819–1898) *African-American missionary and educator*

Born in 1819 to an enslaved family in New York City, Alexander Crummell encountered many obstacles before he could achieve his goal of becoming an Episcopal priest. He was ordained in the Diocese of Massachusetts, in 1844, and in 1847 left for England. He entered Queen's College in Cambridge University and received a bachelor's degree in 1853. That same year he went to LIBERIA, where he spent 20 years as an Episcopal missionary. Working with Edward Wilmot BLYDEN (1832–1912), he hoped to establish Liberia as a black, Christian republic. After serving as principal of Mt. Vaughn High School in Maryland County, Liberia, Crummell became a professor at Liberia College in 1865. He returned to the United States in 1873 and became a church leader within the black community of Washington, D.C. In 1897 he founded the American Negro Academy, which promoted the publication of scholarly works about African-American history.

See also: CHRISTIANITY, INFLUENCE OF (Vols. II, III, IV, V); EDUCATION (Vol. IV); MISSIONARIES (Vols. III, IV, V).

Further reading: J. R. Oldfield, *Alexander Crummell (1819–1898) and the Creation of an African-American Church in Liberia* (Lewiston, N.Y.: E. Mellen Press, 1990).

Cummings-John, Constance (1918–2000) *Sierra Leonean educator and political figure*

Cummings-John was born into the KRIO (Creole) elite of FREETOWN, SIERRA LEONE. Her father had been city treasurer, and her future husband was a lawyer. She received an extensive education in Sierra Leone before going to London for teacher training. In 1936 she attended Cornell University in the United States for six months.

She did not, however, follow the normal path of an upper-class Freetown woman. While in London she became involved with PAN-AFRICANISM, in particular with the West African Youth League (WAYL), an organization founded by a fellow Krio, I. T. A. WALLACE-JOHNSON (1895–1965). Returning home in 1937, Cummings-John became a school principal but soon was helping Wallace-Johnson launch a local WAYL branch.

In 1938 Cummings-John campaigned for the Freetown city council as part of the WAYL challenge to the established political leadership of Dr. H. C. BANKOLE-BRIGHT (1883–1958). Winning the election handily, she served on the council from 1938 to 1942 and again from 1952 to 1966. As a city councilor she promoted expanded city services and was a staunch advocate of the market women who, as in other West African cities, were an important social and economic force. In 1952 she opened her own school for girls.

Also in 1952, Cummings-John founded the Sierra Leone Women's Movement to mobilize women throughout

Sierra Leone for the struggle for independence from Britain. She showed her own political independence by joining the Sierra Leone Peoples Party (SLPP) rather than a strictly Krio-based party. In 1957 she won election to the legislative council as an SLPP candidate. She resigned her seat shortly after, however, in the face of legal charges brought by Krio politicians in retaliation for her alliance with the SLPP. In 1966 Cummings-John returned to local politics. Elected Freetown's mayor, she became the first African woman to head a major African city.

See also: CUMMINGS-JOHN, CONSTANCE (Vol. V); NATIONALISM AND INDEPENDENCE MOVEMENTS (Vol. IV); PELEWURA, MADAM ALIMOTU (Vol. IV).

Further reading: *Constance Agatha Cummings-John: Memoirs of a Krio Leader,* LaRay Denzer, ed. (Ibadan, Nigeria: Sam Bookman, 1995).

D

Dadié, Bernard (1916–   ) *Statesman and author from the Ivory Coast*

Famous for his collections of African fables, folktales, and proverbs, Bernard Binlin Dadié believed that Africa's ORAL TRADITIONS were the moral center of African society. He also believed that these traditions could be the source of modern Africa's inner strength as Africans searched for freedom and equality in the 20th century.

Born in Assinie, near ABIDJAN in IVORY COAST, Dadié lived with his uncle and attended Catholic school in Grand Bassam. He then went to DAKAR, SENEGAL for further education. In Dakar he attended the prestigious ÉCOLE WILLIAM PONTY, where he took part in a movement that collected folklore and wrote dramas with African themes. In 1939 he became a civil servant and Director of Dakar's Institut Français d'Afrique Noire (IFAN).

In 1947 Dadié returned to Abidjan and became involved in Ivory Coast's independence movement. He worked on the newspaper published by the nationalist Democratic Party of Ivory Coast and subsequently spent 16 months in prison for participating in a nationalist demonstration. In 1981 Dadié published an account of his imprisonment titled *Carnet de prison* (Notebook from prison).

His work as a teacher, writer, and director of IFAN prepared him for the higher level offices he held in Ivory Coast's government. After 1957 Dadié served variously as first secretary of the ministry of education, director of information service, director of cultural affairs, inspector-general of arts and letters, director of fine arts and research, and minister of culture and information.

Besides compiling several collections of folktales, Dadié has also written six volumes of poetry, several plays, including *Monsieur Thogo-gnini* (1970), and a variety of novels, including the autobiographical *Climbié* (1956) and *Un Nègre à Paris* (*An African in Paris*; 1959).

See also: LITERATURE IN COLONIAL AFRICA (Vol. IV).

Dahomey FON-speaking kingdom located on the Gulf of Guinea, in West Africa; also the name of the PROTECTORATE and colony established by France in the same area. The economic basis of the kingdom evolved over the course of the 19th century from a dependence on the SLAVE TRADE to the production and trade of PALM OIL. France asserted its claim to the region in the era of PARTITION. In 1894 France deposed and exiled the reigning Dahomean king, Behanzin (d. 1906). In 1900 the French removed his successor and abolished the monarchy, thus ending the kingdom. In 1960 the colony of Dahomey became the Republic of Dahomey, with Hubert MAGA (1916–2000) becoming the country's first president.

See also: BENIN, REPUBLIC OF (Vol. IV); DAHOMEY (Vols. II, III); EDO (Vols. I, II).

Further reading: Patrick Manning, *Slavery, Colonialism, and Economic Growth in Dahomey, 1640–1960* (New York: Cambridge University Press, 1982).

Dakar Port city and capital of present-day SENEGAL located on the Cap-Vert Peninsula, the westernmost point of the African continent. Strategically located between Europe and southern Africa—and also a logical launching point for ships sailing from Africa to the Americas—Dakar has a long history as an important commercial port.

When the SLAVE TRADE was abolished, early in the 19th century, the cultivation and exportation of GROUND-

NUTS (peanuts) became the main economic activity of the Dakar region. After a period of struggle between the Dutch, British, and French, France took control of the area and built a fort in 1857. (The modern Place de l'Indépendence now stands on that site.) By 1884 the French had built a large military hospital, and by 1889 Dakar had working sewage and oil-streetlight systems.

In 1902 Dakar became the capital and administrative center for FRENCH WEST AFRICA when the center of government was moved there from Saint-Louis, about 125 miles (201 km) to the north. Beginning about 1907 the city experienced rapid growth following the completion of rail service to Bamako, a principal Niger River port located about 600 miles (966 km) to the east.

When the French colonized the Dakar area, most of its inhabitants were WOLOF. Consequently, Wolof speakers have predominated in the ethnic make-up of the city ever since, and an "urban Wolof" dialect has emerged that is the LANGUAGE of the streets.

In addition to being a bustling port, beginning in the 1920s Dakar also gained a reputation as a center of learning and research. The Pasteur Institute, a medical research facility, was founded in 1923, and in 1938 French environmentalist Théodore Monod (1902–2000) came to

Dakar to set up the French Institute of Black Africa, a noted center for historical and scientific research for French West Africans. The University of Dakar was founded in 1949.

As one of the more important ports on Africa's west coast, Dakar was constantly undergoing improvements to its infrastructure. As a result, by the time of Senegal's independence, in 1960, the city was connected by rail, air, and road to most major cities in West Africa.

See also: DAKAR (Vol. V); FRANCE AND AFRICA (Vols. III, IV, V); GORÉE ISLAND (Vol. III); QUATRE COMMUNES (Vol. IV).

dance Over many centuries a wealth of dance forms have emerged in Africa that incorporate the history, RELIGION, and traditional values of countless societies. For indigenous African societies, dance serves many purposes as a part of daily life. While movement patterns may vary greatly among ethnic groups, the indigenous form generally includes musicians and dancers who hold a rhythmic dialogue. Musicians speak by striking rhythm instruments, and the dancers answer by striking the ground with their feet. The rhythmic thumping of the dancers is often enhanced by ankle rattles.

Individuals or groups perform dances as part of ceremonies celebrating milestones in the life cycle. These events include initiation into adulthood or a particular age group, marriage, and death. Individuals also may perform dances that demonstrate social organization or religious ceremonies, including spirit-possession rituals.

Shown in 1950, colonial Dakar's Avenue William Ponty was a broad thoroughfare dotted with European-style shops. Note the clothing store at the left advertising "Haute Couture Dames." © *New York Times*

In this photo, taken in 1959, stilts are used to perform a traditional Guinean dance. © *Library of Congress*

Dance binds the people of the community together because it forces them to act as a team. At the same time dance dissipates physical and psychological tension through exercise. Although it is clear that dance plays various important social roles, it must be remembered that dance can also be done simply for recreation.

As greater numbers of Africans converted to Islam or Christianity, changes occurred in the traditional use of dance as ritual. For many of the individuals who chose to accept the practice of a new religion, dance for initiation ceremonies and in religious practices was curtailed. However, many of the same ceremonies were incorporated into other customs and traditions. For example, among rural Muslim societies, the performance of masquerade ceremonies, which had been a religious rite of passage, shed some of its strictly religious significance. Instead it became a more secular, cultural right of passage. As Africans created their own syncretistic religious movements based on Christianity or Islam, it was not uncommon for them to add dance back into their ceremonies.

In the rural areas members of dance clubs performed for recreation. For example, in KANKAN, a principle city of GUINEA, Mamaya dance clubs developed in the late colonial period from 1940 to 1960. Dressed in their best attire, men and women performed majestic dance steps while waving handkerchiefs. In urban areas, where people often were separated from their families and kin, dance groups based on ethnicity could be found performing ceremonies like those at home. During both the colonial and independence periods, Africa's urbanized elites learned ballroom dancing and used this European form to represent the competitive social dialogue between the musician and the dancer that existed in the past.

Both urban and rural bars and nightclubs also provided venues for dancing. In the cities the influence of Africans returning to Africa from Europe and the Americas brought a change in dance music as foreign rhythms were incorporated into African popular MUSIC. For example, in parts of West Africa in the 1950s, HIGHLIFE music generated a new form of recreational dance that improvised on old African patterns.

Since independence, African dance troupes frequently have visited the United States to demonstrate indigenous and popular dance culture of their region. Les Ballets Africains, the National Dance Company of the Republic of Guinea, is one such troupe.

See also: CHRISTIANITY, INFLUENCE OF (Vol. IV); DANCE (Vol. I); ISLAM, INFLUENCE OF (Vol. IV); MASKS (Vol. I); RELIGION, TRADITIONAL (Vol. I); URBAN LIFE AND CULTURE (Vols. IV, V).

Further reading: Wyoma and the dancers of Damballa, *African Healing Dance* [videorecording] (Boulder, Colo.: Sounds True, 1997); David Locke, *Drum Gahu: An Introduction to African Rhythm* (Tempe, Ariz.: White Cliffs Media, 1998); Kariamu Welsh-Asante, ed., *African Dance: An Artistic, Historical, and Philosophical Inquiry* (Trenton, N.J.: Africa World Press, 1996).

Danquah, J. B. (Dr. Joseph Kwame Kyeretwi Boakye Danquah) (1895–1965) *Scholar, lawyer, and political leader in Gold Coast Colony (today's Ghana)*

Born into a prominent AKAN family in what was the GOLD COAST COLONY (today's GHANA), Joseph B. Danquah was a respected scholar and moral philosopher before becoming a lawyer in order to fight against injustice. Beginning at age 20 he served as secretary to his brother, a paramount chief of Gold Coast's Akim Abuakwa state.

Then in, 1921, he traveled to London to study philosophy and law and to earn his doctorate.

Upon successfully completing his studies, in 1927, Danquah traveled extensively throughout Europe. Back in Gold Coast he founded the country's first daily newspaper in ACCRA, a small publication that he named the *Times of West Africa*. Using the newspaper to air his views to the public, Danquah regularly wrote editorial pieces—sometimes under the pseudonym Zadig—in which he criticized political hypocrisy and advocated human rights. In 1934 he was asked to serve as secretary of a Gold Coast delegation to the British Colonial Office, and in the 1940s he helped write legislation for constitutional reforms. He became a member of the Gold Coast Legislative Council in 1946.

Danquah wrote a play, *The Third Woman*, in 1943, and the following year he published *The Akan Doctrine of God*, a study in which he attempted to reconcile certain aspects of Christianity with traditional West African beliefs.

After World War II (1939–45) Danquah found inspiration in the NATIONALISM AND INDEPENDENCE MOVEMENTS that were spreading across much of Africa. In 1947 he was a member of "The Big Six," a group of educated lawyers and businessmen who founded the UNITED GOLD COAST CONVENTION (UGCC), a political party that called for independence from Britain with the slogan "Self-Government in the Shortest Time Possible." In 1949 Ghana's future first president, Kwame NKRUMAH (1909–1972), broke from the UGCC to form the more radical and nationalist CONVENTION PEOPLES PARTY (CPP). The CPP won the 1951 legislative assembly elections with the slogan "Self-Government *Now*," and in 1952 Nkrumah became the Gold Coast prime minister.

Danquah and the UGCC tried unsuccessfully to unseat Nkrumah in Gold Coast's legislative elections of 1954 and again in 1956, continuing the political rivalry that would eventually end in Danquah's death. Gold Coast declared its independence from COLONIAL RULE in 1957, and three years later the country became a republic. With Danquah's support, the new republic was renamed Ghana, recalling the glorious empire that dominated much of interior West Africa between the ninth and 13th centuries.

As soon as he was elected to head Ghana, Nkrumah rapidly began centralizing his power. He declared himself supreme commander of Ghana's armed forces and suppressed political rivals, including Danquah, whom he imprisoned, in 1961, on dubious charges. Danquah was

released in 1962, but as Nkrumah became increasingly autocratic Danquah criticized the morality and legality of Nkrumah's actions. Danquah was imprisoned again, in 1964, and put on a near-starvation diet, which weakened him physically but did not dampen the ardor of his criticism. In 1965, with his popularity flagging, Nkrumah planned to release Danquah to garner support, but Danquah died of heart failure before it could happen. The events that led to Danquah's death did much to increase opposition to Nkrumah's rule, and a year later he was deposed by a military coup d'état.

See also: BUSIA, KOFI (Vols. IV, V); COUP D'ÉTAT (Vol. V); ENGLAND AND AFRICA (Vol. IV).

Dar es Salaam (Dar al-Salam)

Indian Ocean port town and capital of present-day TANZANIA. One of the original villages of Dar es Salaam was named Mzizima, which translates to "healthy town" in KISWAHILI. Dar es Salaam literally means "haven of peace."

The area of Dar es Salaam was originally a group of Kiswahili-speaking FISHING villages founded in the 17th century on the Indian Ocean coast. As such, it was not a major port during the commercial heyday of the SWAHILI COAST, which spanned the 13th to the 15th centuries. However, the town of about 1,000 inhabitants began to grow after Sultan Majid bin Said (c. 1835–1870), the BUSAIDI ruler of ZANZIBAR, built his summer palace there in 1862.

The city expanded further after the German East Africa Company set up a trading center there in 1888. Then from 1891 to 1916 Dar es Salaam served as the capital of GERMAN EAST AFRICA, which included not only the mainland of present-day Tanzania but also present-day RWANDA and BURUNDI, to the northwest.

In the 1940s 78 rpm recordings of Cuban music made a big impact on the clubs in Dar es Salaam, as well as elsewhere in East and Central Africa. Local groups such as La Paloma, which was formed in 1948, began performing rumbas and other Cuban music, which remained popular into the 1960s.

In 1916 Britain took control of Dar es Salaam during the course of World War I (1914–18), making it the capital of TANGANYIKA, which after 1918 was held as a mandated territory under the provisions of the League of Nations. Britain gradually improved the city's infrastructure, constructing, for example, the Selander Bridge in 1930 to connect Dar es Salaam to its northern suburbs. In addition, after World War II (1939–45), the expanded production of sisal—a natural fiber used for cordage and twine—promoted economic growth and the further development of the city's port.

By 1957 the population had reached approximately 130,000, most of whom were Africans but with a strong Indian minority that controlled much of the city's commercial life. Dar es Salaam remained the capital when Tanganyika became independent, in 1961. It maintained its capital status when Zanzibar and Tanganyika united to form the nation of Tanzania, in 1964.

See also: DAR ES SALAAM (Vols. III, V); ENGLAND AND AFRICA (Vols. III, IV, V); GERMANY AND AFRICA (Vol. IV); RUANDA-URUNDI (Vol. IV); URBANIZATION (Vols. IV, V); URBAN LIFE AND CULTURE (Vols. IV, V).

Darfur Region in the western part of present-day Republic of the SUDAN, inhabited primarily by the Fur and Baggara peoples. A mountainous area dominated by dry plateaus, Darfur has long been inhabited by herders and subsistence agriculturalists. In the 17th century Fur sultans took control of the region from the Muslim dynasty of Kanem (located to the west, near Lake Chad), which had ruled the area since the 1200s. In 1874 British-backed forces from EGYPT invaded from the east, displacing the Fur rulers and adding the area to the region of the Sudan already under the rule of Khedive IS-MAIL (1830–1895).

For a brief time (1883–98), the region was ruled by the MAHDIYYA, an Islamic brotherhood. The Khalifa AB-DALLAHI IBN MUHAMMAD (1846–1899), who succeeded Muhammad Ahmad al-MAHDI (1844–1885) as the leader of the Mahdiyya, was a Baggara from Darfur. However, in 1899 the Mahdiyya, who had wrested control away from the "infidel" Egyptians in 1885, fell to combined British-Egyptian forces. The region was subsequently administered as part of Anglo-Egyptian Sudan by the ANGLO-EGYPTIAN CONDOMINIUM, a joint government.

Even under this condominium Darfur remained relatively independent. The British administration tended to allow local rulers to retain their positions of authority in order to keep the peace. At the outbreak of World War I (1914–18), however, Islamic leaders rose up against Anglo-Egyptian rule and declared their allegiance to the Muslim Ottoman Empire. In the fighting that followed, Darfur's Sultan Ali Dinar (r. 1898–1916) was killed, and his independent sultanate terminated, in 1916.

Generally, for the next 40 years Anglo-Egyptian rule in Darfur did not bring major changes to the day-to-day lives of the local peoples, especially those practicing a nomadic way of life. Some secular schools were established, but few attempts were made to promote Anglo culture, and Darfurians were left to dictate the direction of their region. Hence, beginning in the mid-19th century, Darfur's majority Islamic population—along with the rest of the Sudan—came increasingly under the influence of the Arab culture from which Islam sprang.

By 1953 Britain and Egypt had concluded an agreement by which all of the Sudan would be granted self-government, and, ultimately, independence was granted, in 1956.

See also: BAGGARA (Vol. II); COLONIAL CONQUEST (Vol. IV); DARFUR (Vols. II, III, IV); ENGLAND AND AFRICA (Vol. IV); FUR (Vols. I, II, III); ISLAM, INFLUENCE OF (Vols. II, IV, V).

De Beers Consolidated Mines, Ltd. South African DIAMOND-MINING cartel established by Cecil RHODES (1853–1902) in 1888. In the early 1870s, when diamond claims were being staked throughout the border areas of the CAPE COLONY, SOUTH AFRICA, two brothers, Johannes Nicolaas (1830–1894) and Diederik Arnoldus de Beer, purchased farmland at Zandfontein, near KIMBERLEY, for £50. Unhappy with the great numbers of miners who were flocking to the area, the brothers didn't hesitate to sell their otherwise not very profitable farm for £6,300. Despite the fact that they no longer owned the land, their former farm would provide the name for De Beers Consolidated Mines, Ltd.

Prior to the 1870s only India and Brazil were considered diamond-producing countries. But the fields around the De Beers farm proved exceptionally rich, and by 1880 South Africa was the world leader in diamond production, with export values exceeding $15 million annually. In 10 years the Kimberley mine alone produced more DIAMONDS than India had produced in more than 2,000 years as the leading production center of the precious gems.

Diamond mining in the Kimberley region began with many individual miners holding small claims. However, such an organizational structure became increasingly impractical as MINING moved from surface claims to deep holes. A process of amalgamation began about 1880, leading to a protracted battle for the overall control of the southern-African diamond fields. Rhodes and fellow Englishman Charles Rudd (1844–1916) formed a company to combine their holdings in the De Beers mine, thereby strengthening their position against another English mining company, Barnato Diamond Mining, owned by Rhodes's nemesis, Barney Barnato (1852–1897).

Rhodes and Rudd understood the dynamics of their market and knew that the flood of diamonds from Brazil greatly depressed the world diamond market in the 18th century. To avoid the same situation in Kimberley, their company attempted to control production in order to perpetuate the illusion of the scarcity of diamonds. By 1887 the deep pockets and ruthless business tactics of Rhodes and his financial backers forced Barnato into a merger with De Beers. When Barnato was finally bought out for £5,338,650 (about $25 million in 1887), Rhodes paid him with the biggest check ever issued up to that time.

De Beers Consolidated Mines Limited was established in March 1888, with Rhodes as its founding chairman. The company's holdings included the entire De Beers Mine, 75 percent of the claims in the Kimberley Mine, and a controlling interest in two other productive mines, Bultfontein and Dutoitspan. The four major De Beers shareholders—Cecil Rhodes, Barney Barnato, F. S. Philipson-Stow, and Alfred Beit—were appointed governors of the company. In 1890 De Beers forged an agreement with the newly formed London Diamond Syndicate, which agreed to purchase all of the diamonds they produced. For the next 30 years De Beers and the London Diamond Syndicate controlled the world diamond industry.

De Beers operations expanded to include open-pit, underground, alluvial (silt- or sediment-based), and marine diamond mines that attracted thousands of diggers, most of whom were young men. Although both black and white diggers provided LABOR in the mines, the operations were sharply segregated.

The De Beers diamond monopoly was broken for a time when new diamond fields were discovered near PRE-TORIA and in SOUTH WEST AFRICA (present-day NAMIBIA). Ernest Oppenheimer (1880–1957), an immigrant from Germany who founded Consolidated Diamond Mines in 1919, became a new leader in the field. In 1929 Oppenheimer was chosen president of the De Beers group and eventually united both companies in a cartel.

During the Great Depression of the early 1930s the demand for diamonds declined, and De Beers was forced to cease operations at all of its Kimberley mines. To ensure the industry's survival, De Beers concentrated instead on buying up all of the diamonds of "outside" (non-De Beers) producers. De Beers' mines recommenced limited production in the mid-1930s, but the markets remained depressed and the onset of World War II (1939–45) caused all of De Beers' mining activities to close down for the next four years. Since then De Beers has proved to be one of the most successful cartels in the annals of modern commerce. While the markets for other precious NAT-URAL RESOURCES, such as GOLD and silver, have fluctuated wildly in response to economic conditions, diamond values have advanced upward every year, with few exceptions, since the early 1930s.

See also: MINERAL REVOLUTION (Vol. IV); MINERALS AND METALS (Vol. V).

Further reading: Stefan Kanfer, *The Last Empire: De Beers, Diamonds, and the World* (New York: Noonday Press, 1993).

de Brazza, Pierre Savorgnan (1852–1905) *French explorer*

Italian by birth, Pietro di Brazza Savorgnani was the son of aristocratic parents. Desiring a naval career but faced with an unappealing opportunity with the Italian fleet, he enrolled in the French naval academy in 1870. By age 21 de Brazza had become a French citizen and changed his name.

After serving in the Franco-Prussian War (1870–71) de Brazza took part in a French antislavery mission to the west coast of Central Africa, landing in what is now the country of GABON. There de Brazza developed a strong interest in exploring the central African interior, which until that point was largely unknown to Europeans. In 1875 he returned to western Central Africa and made the first of his forays into the interior. His explorations earned him an offer of employment from the Belgian king LEOPOLD II (1835–1909), who was rushing to secure the lands of the Congo River Basin, mostly through the efforts of Henry Morton STANLEY (1841–1904). De Brazza instead launched a second mission for the French government, and began racing Stanley to establish control over the Congo region.

In 1880 de Brazza reached the Congo River and negotiated a treaty with the leader of the Teke people, King Makoko, establishing the foundation for the later PRO-TECTORATE of FRENCH CONGO. That same year de Brazza founded a French settlement on the north shore of the Malebo Pool, a town that later became BRAZZAVILLE.

After the BERLIN CONFERENCE (1884–85), which established the PARTITION of Africa among the European colonial powers, de Brazza was named commissioner general of the French Congo. He continued to expand French interests in the Congo, eventually securing an area three times the size of France itself. De Brazza supported fair wages for African workers and founded schools as well as employment and medical programs in the Congo. Despite becoming something of a celebrity in France, the antagonism of Leopold II and de Brazza's opposition to granting land to private interests eventually led to efforts to smear his image, and he was dismissed by the French government in 1898.

By 1905 conditions in the French Congo had begun to mirror those in the BELGIAN CONGO across the river, where SLAVERY and the excessively brutal treatment of the colony's African population had become commonplace. A reluctant de Brazza was commissioned to investigate the circumstances in the French Congo, where he uncovered extensive corruption and horrific treatment of Africans. In 1905, devastated and in failing health, de Brazza began the trip back to France but died while ashore in DAKAR, SENEGAL.

See also: COLONIAL CONQUEST (Vol. IV); COLONIAL-ISM, INFLUENCE OF (Vol. IV); COLONIAL RULE (Vol. IV); CONGO BASIN (Vols. I, II) CONGO RIVER (Vol. I); FRANCE AND AFRICA (Vols. III, IV, V).

decolonization
Gradual removal of colonial status. The process of decolonization in Africa began after World War II (1939–45), though the beginnings of nationalism

in the African colonies had long since taken shape. LIBYA (1951) and EGYPT (1952) were the first two colonies to emerge from European COLONIAL RULE, but the British GOLD COAST COLONY was the first to achieve independence through a successful nationalist movement, becoming independent GHANA in 1957.

The European colonial powers remaining after World War II differed widely in how much or how well they did (or did not) prepare their colonies for independence. Britain, suffering financially after the war and having already allowed for the independence of its colonial holdings in India, began to develop constitutional, African-led governments for its colonies in anticipation of full autonomy. This approach went rather smoothly in those colonies without European SETTLERS, but in colonies such as KENYA and SOUTHERN RHODESIA it meant strong resistance from local white interests. France attempted to maintain most of its colonies as part of the FRENCH UNION, but the war for independence in ALGERIA and similar struggles in Indo-China weakened France's imperialistic resolve. This eventually led to independence for all of France's African colonies by 1960. Drawn-out and excessively violent nationalist uprisings led both Belgium and Portugal to abandon their colonies, although in some cases the African independence movements had an opportunity to develop some of the organs and institutional capacity to govern their countries at the time of independence.

A common factor among all of the former colonies, however, was their struggle to develop as nations as well as to overcome the lingering effects of European domination. Even in countries that had established constitutions and governments before independence, such as Ghana, economic, political, and ethnic turmoil has often prevailed. To the present day the influence of COLONIALISM is still very much felt throughout Africa.

See also: BELGIUM AND AFRICA (Vol. IV); DEVELOPMENT (Vol. V); ENGLAND AND AFRICA (Vols. III, IV, V); FRANCE AND AFRICA (Vols. III, IV, V); INDEPENDENCE MOVEMENTS (Vol. V); NATIONALISM AND INDEPENDENCE MOVEMENTS (Vol. IV); NEO-COLONIALISM (Vol. V); PORTUGAL AND AFRICA (Vols. III, IV, V); POST-COLONIAL STATE (Vol. V); RESISTANCE AND REBELLION (Vol. IV); SPAIN AND AFRICA (Vol. IV); NEOCOLONIALISM AND UNDERDEVELOPMENT (Vol. V).

Further reading: Frederick Cooper, *Decolonization and African Society: The Labor Question in French and British Africa* (New York: Cambridge University Press, 1996).

de Gaulle, Charles (1890–1970) *French general and president*

De Gaulle took an interest in the military at an early age, studying at the Saint-Cyr Military Academy before joining the French infantry and seeing extensive action during World War I (1914–18). He also fought during the opening of World War II (1939–45) and served as undersecretary of state for defense and war. When de Gaulle's superior, Field Marshal Henri-Phillipe Pétain (1856–1951), assumed power in France and set about signing an armistice with the invading Germans, de Gaulle moved to England, where he continued to call for resistance against the German occupiers. He was sentenced to death in absentia by Pétain's Vichy government.

De Gaulle's call for support was immediately answered by Adolphe-Félix-Sylvestre ÉBOUÉ (1884–1944), governor of the French colony of CHAD. Following Éboué's lead, other sub-Saharan French colonies also sided with de Gaulle, and BRAZZAVILLE, in the FRENCH CONGO, became the capital of Free France. French colonies in North Africa and FRENCH WEST AFRICA, however, remained loyal to the Vichy government.

In 1940 the Free French failed in their attempt to capture the strategic port of DAKAR, SENEGAL. A year later, however, de Gaulle's Free French forces successfully collaborated with the British against the Italians in LIBYA and EGYPT. In 1943 de Gaulle moved the Free French headquarters to ALGIERS, ALGERIA, where he established the French National Committee, which was recognized by the Allied forces as Free France's official government-in-exile. As an Allied victory became imminent, the rest of France's African colonies sided with de Gaulle. In 1944, after a number of campaigns, de Gaulle led the Free French into liberated Paris. More than half of de Gaulle's troops who landed in France were TIRAILLEURS SÉNÉGALAIS, African-born soldiers.

In 1944, as head of France's provisional government, de Gaulle convened a conference at Brazzaville, where he acknowledged French colonial Africa's role in supporting his Free French movement. As a reward de Gaulle established a new relationship of assimilation between France and its African territories, halting the practice of forced LABOR, improving EDUCATION, and offering special citizenship to all Africans in the French colonies (this privilege was previously only for those living in the QUATRE COMMUNES). Political power in the colonies was decentralized, allowing territorial assemblies to form, and African deputies could now represent the colonies in the French Parliament. France still maintained a large measure of control over the colonies, however.

In 1946 de Gaulle resigned from the government over conflicts with various political parties. In 1958, however, he returned to the political scene, and he was elected president in December of that year. He immediately faced two issues in relation to Africa: the debacle of the war for independence in Algeria and the overall status of the African colonies. By this time the Algerian war of independence (1954–62) had become an exceptionally brutal conflict between the French and Algerian freedom fighters headed by the NATIONAL LIBERATION FRONT. De

Gaulle's decision to begin peace negotiations was highly controversial in France. Despite the threat of a breakaway faction of French military leaders known as the Secret Army Organization, de Gaulle won popular support and eventually secured Algeria's independence, in 1962.

De Gaulle addressed the status of France's African colonies, in 1958, with his famous *oui-ou-non* (yes-or-no) offer. The offer gave the African colonies two choices: become autonomous states in the FRENCH UNION, or become immediately and fully independent. De Gaulle actively campaigned for the colonies to join the Union, and only GUINEA chose immediate independence. However, by 1960 the French Union had failed and the other French colonies soon gained their independence as well. De Gaulle resigned from the presidency in 1969. He died a year later.

See also: FRANCE AND AFRICA (Vols. III, IV, V).

Delagoa Bay (Maputo Bay) Arm of the Indian Ocean located on the southeastern coast of MOZAMBIQUE, near the border with SOUTH AFRICA. Approximately 55 miles (88.5 km) long and 20 miles (32.2 km) wide, Delagoa Bay was known to Portuguese sailors as early as the 16th century. It was not until 1787, however, that they built a fort to protect the sailors and merchants who traded there. As commercial activity increased, the small town of LOURENÇO MARQUES grew around the fort.

In the 19th century trade in ivory and human captives flourished throughout Mozambique, and Lourenço Marques continued to grow. Although it was officially abolished, the SLAVE TRADE continued until the early 1860s, and the bay was coveted by the British, the Dutch, and South African BOERS looking to receive slave laborers. In 1875 France, acting as arbiter, awarded the disputed bay to Portugal, which had claimed possession all along. The bay gained further strategic importance with the development of GOLD mining along the WITWATERSRAND in the TRANSVAAL in the late 1880s.

In recent decades silt from the numerous rivers that discharge into Delagoa Bay, now called Maputo Bay, has decreased its depth, hindering access by larger ships. Plans are in place to dredge the bottom to restore its depth.

Transvaal president Paul KRUGER (1825–1904) directed the construction of a railway, completed in 1894, to connect JOHANNESBURG to Portuguese-controlled Delagoa Bay and thus lessen his state's dependence on the British-controlled areas of South Africa. By 1907 Lourenço Marques had grown so important that the Portuguese named it their colonial administrative capital, replacing the city of Mozambique, to the northeast. The bay, with its major port facilities, continued to serve the MINING and later manufacturing interests of the Johannesburg region.

See also: GAMA, VASCO DA (Vol. II); DELAGOA BAY (Vol. III); IVORY TRADE (Vols. III, IV); MAPUTO (Vols. III, V); PORTUGAL AND AFRICA (Vols. III, IV, V).

Destour Party Tunisian political party, later supplanted by the more militant Neo-Destour Party that led the way to independence for TUNISIA in 1956. Founded in 1920 by Sheikh Abdelaziz Thaalbi (1876–1944), the political party known as the Free Tunisian Destourian (Constitutional) Party never went beyond being a group of upper-class Tunisians. Its name reflects the fact that in 1861 Tunisia became the first Arabic-speaking country to adopt a constitution (in Arabic, *dustur*). The Ottoman Empire enacted a constitution later, in 1876, followed by Persia (modern Iran) in 1907.

Written constitutions that establish the fundamental principles by which the state is governed are of modern, European origin and are based on the rights of the individual. In contrast, according to traditional Muslim law, called *sharia*, all laws are considered to be revelations from God and are expressions of divine will.

In 1934 the radical wing of the Destour Party broke away to form the more militant Neo-Destour Party. The new party established underground cells throughout the nation, especially in the southern provincial cities. In the late 1930s the party agitated for independence through a series of organized street demonstrations. Police repression of this unrest resulted in hundreds of deaths, thousands of arrests, and the imprisonment of the party leadership. But this response only further served to establish the Neo-Destour Party and its leader, Habib BOURGUIBA (1903–2000), as the country's political vanguard.

When France granted political autonomy to Tunisia, in 1955, the Neo-Destour Party split because prominent left-wing politicians among its leadership were unwilling to accept anything less than complete independence. In 1956 the party expelled Salah ben Youssef (1908–1961), the leader of the party's left, and purged his supporters. These purges caused a major upheaval within the party and the government. Bourguiba, who was by then the prime minister, had to turn to the French for help in suppressing the resulting public disorder.

When France granted full independence to Tunisia, in 1956, Bourguiba instituted a one-party state and convened a Constituent Assembly to draft a new constitution. In 1963 a plot to assassinate Bourguiba heightened tensions within the party. At the same time diplomatic relations with France were souring because the French had refused to remove their forces from a military base in the Tunisian city of Bizerte. To consolidate his power Bourguiba reorganized the Neo-Destour Party and changed its name to the Socialist Destourian Party. In 1988 Zine El-Abidine Ben Ali (1936–   ) deposed Bourguiba and assumed the presidency. Ben Ali changed the name of the party to the Constitutional Democratic Rally and allowed a number of emerging political parties to compete for political office.

See also: NATIONALISM AND INDEPENDENCE MOVEMENTS (Vol. IV); SHARIA (Vol. II).

Diagne, Blaise (1872–1934) *Senegalese politician*

Born to a well-established WOLOF family on the island of Gorée, part of the French colony of SENEGAL, Diagne displayed an early talent for languages and learned to speak fluent French. He found employment as an interpreter in the colonial customs service and later became a customs official, working both in Africa and France. He became controller of customs in French Guiana, South America, in 1914.

At the beginning of the 20th century the Senegalese QUATRE COMMUNES (DAKAR, Saint-Louis, Gorée, and Rufisque) were considered to be full extensions of France and were allowed local self-government and the right to representation in the French National Assembly. *Assimilés,* or elites of European or mixed descent, had typically held the representative, or deputy, position. Diagne, in contrast, was part of the *évolués,* a group of mostly Muslim Africans whose influence was growing. In 1914 Diagne was elected deputy to the National Assembly, overcoming six European candidates and overall white opposition to become the first African to hold the position.

Diagne's personality and French patriotism helped him gain respect within the Assembly and, in 1916, win the passage of a law that boosted Franco-African rights. In 1917, with France facing a dire need for troops to fight in World War I (1914–18), French prime minister Georges Clemenceau (1841–1929) made Diagne a commissioner of the republic and assigned him the task of overseeing conscription in FRENCH WEST AFRICA. Diagne hoped that full African support of the French war effort would produce the reward of full citizenship for Africans in the French colonies, and he pursued the task wholeheartedly. All told he enlisted more than 180,000 African men. While Diagne was awarded the Légion d'honneur for his efforts, the rewards he had envisioned for Africans never materialized, and he ultimately declined the honor.

In 1919 Diagne was president of the first Pan-African Congress, which took place in Paris at the same time as the Versailles Peace Conference, which ended World War I. At the Congress he conferred with prominent pan-Africanists W. E. B. DU BOIS (1868–1963) and Marcus GARVEY (1887–1940), though the three leaders often did not agree.

In 1920 and again in 1924 Diagne was reelected to his post as deputy. He continued to be a firm supporter of African assimilation into French culture, establishing himself as a prime example of successful assimilation. While he vehemently opposed prejudice, he also defended colonialism and rejected independence and self-governance as viable options for the French African colonies. In 1931 Diagne became the undersecretary of state for the colonies, a French cabinet position. He was the first African to hold such a position and was at the time the foremost African in the French political realm.

Diagne's success was unprecedented and opened many doors for Africans in French West Africa. After Diagne, only Africans were elected to the deputy position from Senegal, including the poet and future Senegal president, Léopold SENGHOR (1906–2001). Despite this, Africans such as Senghor continued to oppose French COLONIAL RULE and the assertion of French cultural supremacy.

See also: (Vol. IV); FRANCE AND AFRICA (Vols. III, IV, V); GORÈE ISLAND (Vol. III).

diamond mining Africa's diamond-mining industry began soon after the 1866 discovery of the Eureka Diamond, a 21.25-carat specimen found in the alluvial sediment along the banks of the Orange River in the region of SOUTH AFRICA known at the time as Griqualand West. Until then India or Brazil produced most of the world's DIAMONDS.

In the early 1870s diamond-mining operations were carried out near the town of KIMBERLEY on 30-foot-square plots of land called *claims*. Prospectors usually bought individual claims from the Boer trekkers who had cleared and occupied the land, mostly for farming. Many miners worked alone, removing earth from open pits, one shovelfull at a time, and sifting through it in search of precious gems. Others pooled their resources to buy multiple claims and then hired large teams of workers who could dig, crush, and sift through tons of earth each day. Tens of thousands of prospectors and workers rushed into the area, and makeshift towns emerged practically overnight. Although both black and white diggers worked in the mines, all of the mine owners were white Europeans.

One of the consequences of the diamond revolution in Africa was the very real possibility that incredible wealth could be attained simply by owning the right piece of land. In light of this fact, land speculation, almost all of it done by European SETTLERS, led to aggressive colonizing efforts. The "annexing" of South African territories displaced the native peoples who were living there. Heavily armed, British MINING interests in South Africa eventually tried to forcibly remove the most determined groups, which included the ZULU, the XHOSA, and the PEDI. Ironically, however, the diamond mines could also work against colonization, as thousands of black workers spent their mine earnings on firearms, which they then used to prevent the further encroachment of both British and Boer farmers into their lands.

The most successful mining operations in South Africa vied for control of the industry, but no clear leader emerged until 1888, when an Englishman named Cecil RHODES (1853–1902) bought out the area's most productive mines and created DE BEERS CONSOLIDATED MINES, LTD. Rhodes's corporation continued to buy out competitors, eventually establishing a cartel that controlled production, limited supply, set prices, and generally held a monopoly on the industry. Despite Rhodes's death, in 1902, De Beers continued to dominate the industry.

By studying the dispersal of diamond deposits De Beers engineers figured that hundreds of thousands of years of water erosion had dislodged millions of carats of diamonds from the Orange and Vaal riverbanks, setting them tumbling toward the sea. In an attempt to locate these diamonds De Beers developed alluvial and marine mines in addition to the gigantic open pit mines found in Kimberley. Alluvial miners, those who worked river sediment and gravel, typically used the old but trustworthy washing pan technique. They placed sediment in a pan and swirled it, and as the lighter sediment poured over the sides, the denser minerals, including diamonds, sank to the bottom where they were easily spotted.

About 14.5 million carats of diamonds were recovered from Kimberley's largest diamond mine, nicknamed the Big Hole. When it closed, in 1914, the mining shaft of the Big Hole measured nearly 3,500 feet (1,097 m), the deepest hand-dug excavation in the world.

In 1908 a railroad worker found diamonds in the sand dunes near Kolmanskop, in German SOUTH WEST AFRICA (present-day NAMIBIA). Within a year Ernest Oppenheimer's Consolidated Diamond Mines recovered nearly 500,000 high-quality carats and seemed to be in position to rival De Beers for supremacy in the diamond industry. In 1929, however, Oppenheimer negotiated to become president of the De Beers group, and he eventually united both companies in a gigantic cartel.

In 1918 diamonds were first discovered in the Bakwanga Hills of the BELGIAN CONGO (present-day Demo-

cratic Republic of the CONGO), where the earth contained diamond-bearing pipes much richer than the ones in South Africa. Most of the diamonds from this region were of low quality, but technological advances made during World War II (1939–45) created many new uses for industrial diamonds. De Beers commenced large-scale mining, and by the mid-1950s the Congo was producing the majority of the world's diamonds. Unfortunately, the leaders of the Congo diverted the riches created by the country's mines to their own personal bank accounts, and the colony's people never reaped any benefits from their country's mineral wealth. Diamonds were discovered in other countries in West Africa, including LIBERIA, ANGOLA, and SIERRA LEONE, where De Beers had secured exclusive mining rights in 1935.

The South African diamond-mining industry reduced production during World War I (1914–18) and stopped all production for a few years during World War II. Since then, the industry has continued to be manipulated by the De Beers cartel and other industry leaders, guaranteeing the steady upward advance of diamond prices throughout the world.

See also: MINERAL REVOLUTION (Vol. IV).

diamonds For a thousand years Africa was known as a source of GOLD, but the majority of the world's DIAMOND MINING was done in either India or Brazil. That situation changed rapidly, however, in the years following the discovery of the 21.25-carat Eureka Diamond in 1866. Erasmus Jacobs (1851–1933), the son of a local farmer, picked up a "pretty pebble" along the banks of the Orange River in CAPE COLONY, SOUTH AFRICA and showed it to his neighbor, Schalk van Niekerk. Van Niekirk, who collected unusual stones, sent it to a mineralogist friend who positively identified it as a yellowish-brown diamond. Over the next few years diamonds were discovered in the area with increasing frequency, launching Africa's MINERAL REVOLUTION.

Before the end of the 19th century the South African town of KIMBERLEY, located between the Orange and Vaal rivers, had become the center of the world diamond trade. In 15 years the mines in and around Kimberley produced more of the precious gems by weight than had been produced in India, the former leading producer, in the previous 2,000 years.

For thousands of years diamonds have been valued around the world for their durability and beauty, and more recently for their industrial applications in boring and cutting other hard substances. In its rough form, a diamond resembles a piece of dull broken glass. In order to be transformed into a valuable gem, the rough diamond must be cut, shaped, and polished. In Europe the process was done for hundreds of years by master stonecutters, who had only chisels and crude hand tools at their disposal. Since the process of purchasing, cutting, polishing, and setting diamonds is long and costly, the gems have long been considered luxury items reserved for the elite.

In 1869 a Griqua shepherd boy discovered an 83-carat diamond that would eventually be cut into the 47.69-carat Star of South Africa. According to lore, when the rough diamond was displayed at a British Parliament session, one colonial secretary declared, "This diamond, gentlemen, is the rock upon which the future prosperity of South Africa will be built."

A diamond, the hardest naturally occurring substance known, is a crystal that is created when carbon is subjected to tremendous pressure and heat inside the earth. Because of the way they are formed, diamonds are often found in "pipes," or rock formations that form in the throats of extinct volcanoes. They are also located on riverbanks and distributed along coastal shelves. The world's largest gem diamond, the Cullinan, was discovered in 1905 in the Premier Mine of South Africa. In its natural state the Cullinan weighed 3,106 carats—substantially more than a pound!

See also: DE BEERS CONSOLIDATED MINES, LTD. (Vol. IV) MINERALS AND METALS (Vol. V).

Dinizulu (Dinizulu kaCetshwayo) (1868–1913) Zulu king

In 1884 the ZULU king CETSHWAYO (c. 1826–1884) died, and his son, Dinizulu, succeeded him. At the time Zululand was divided into 13 chiefdoms as a result of the British victory in the ANGLO-ZULU WAR (1879), and the territory was in the midst of a civil war. Wanting to ensure his safety, Dinizulu sought and received help from the BOERS of the TRANSVAAL, who declared him King of the Zulu and of Zululand. The Boers, however, were more interested in acquiring the territory of the Zulu than preserving Dinizulu's reign, and made vast territorial claims as a reward for their assistance.

Worried by the Boer demands, Dinizulu requested British intervention. In 1887 Britain annexed all of Zululand, sparking a rebellion by Dinizulu's followers. The rebellion was eventually put down, and in 1889 Dinizulu surrendered to the British and was charged with treason. He was convicted and exiled to St. Helena, though he was allowed to return in 1897 in the role of a British-paid paramount chief. In 1908 Dinizulu was again brought to trial by the authorities in NATAL because of suspected involvement in BAMBATHA'S REBELLION of 1906.

Dinizulu was sentenced to four years in prison but was released a year later when he was pardoned by his former ally, Louis BOTHA (1862–1919), who had become the first prime minister of the newly formed UNION OF SOUTH AFRICA. He was not, however, allowed to return to Zululand and was instead banished to a farm in the Transvaal, where he died. His standing among the country's African population was such that in 1912, the year before his death, he was one of eight paramount chiefs who were named honorary presidents of the newly formed AFRICAN NATIONAL CONGRESS.

See also: ENGLAND AND AFRICA (Vol. IV); SHAKA (Vol. III).

Diop, Alioune (1910–1980) Senegalese intellectual and founder of the journal Présence Africaine

Born into a French-speaking, Muslim family in Saint-Louis, SENEGAL, Alioune Diop received his bachelor's degree in 1931. He then studied philosophy at the University of Algiers, where he met French author and philosopher Albert Camus (1913–1960), and later traveled to Paris. He converted to Catholicism and briefly worked in the French colonial service.

In 1947 Diop founded the journal PRÉSENCE AFRICAINE, which quickly became the leading French-language journal focusing on Africa and the AFRICAN DIASPORA. Publishing works by black intellectuals, it became the focal point for NÉGRITUDE, a movement that gave expression to African cultural and literary values.

In 1949 Diop began the Présence Africaine publishing house. It published such important works as Nation negre et culture (Black nation and culture; 1955) by Cheikh Anta DIOP (1923–1986) and Discours sur le colonialisme (Discourse on colonialism; 1956) by Aimé CÉSAIRE (1913–). In all of his publishing endeavors Alioune Diop sought to promote the independence of black intellectuals from the influence of politics.

In 1956, with support from UNESCO, Diop convened the First International Congress of Black Writers and Artists in Paris, and in 1959 he convened a second such congress in Rome. He later brought together peoples of African descent at DAKAR, Senegal, in 1966 (the First World Festival of Negro Arts), at ALGIERS in 1969, and at LAGOS, NIGERIA, in 1977 (the Festival of Black and African Art and Culture).

See also: LITERATURE IN COLONIAL AFRICA (Vol. IV); PAN-AFRICANISM (Vols. IV, V).

Diop, Cheikh Anta (1923–1986) Senegalese historian, scientist, and writer

Born to a prominent family in Diourbel, SENEGAL, Diop was an outstanding student as a youngster. In 1945 he earned bachelor's degrees in mathematics and philosophy from schools in Senegal, and the following year he traveled to Paris to continue his studies at the University of Paris and at the Sorbonne University. In 1948 Diop wrote a linguistic study of the WOLOF, which was published in PRÉSENCE AFRICAINE, a leading African intellectual review.

While he studied for his doctorate in Paris, Diop was an ardent political activist, From 1950 to 1953 he served as the secretary-general of the AFRICAN DEMOCRATIC ASSEMBLY and helped establish the first Pan-African Student Congress, in 1951. Two years later he married Frenchwoman Louise Marie Maes, with whom he would have four children.

In the latter half of the 1950s Diop's reputation as a formidable Africanist intellectual continued to grow. In 1956, he participated in the first Congress of Black Writers and Artists, in Paris. Soon after, he presented his doctoral dissertation in which he argued against the prevailing view that ancient Egyptian civilization was Caucasoid and that instead it was black African at its core. This thesis was considered too radical at the time and was rejected by the academic board more than once. However, in the end Diop presented such a preponderance of scientific, linguistic, and anthropological evidence to back his theory that his dissertation was finally accepted in 1960. By this time it had already been published in Paris under the title of *Nations nègres et culture* (Black nations and culture, 1955).

Diop returned to Senegal to direct Africa's first radiocarbon laboratory, at the Fundamental Institute of Black Africa from 1963 to 1966. The lab was used to date various archaeological artifacts from throughout the continent and did much to reinforce the work that he had done in Paris in the 1950s. Throughout the late 1960s and into the 1970s he continued his work both as an activist and an intellectual, forming political parties and writing extensively on African culture and history.

See also: ANTHROPOLOGY AND AFRICA (Vols. IV, V); DIOP, CHEIKH ANTA (Vol. V); HISTORICAL SCHOLARSHIP ON AFRICA (Vols. IV, V).

Further reading: Cheikh Anta Diop, *African Origins of Civilization: Myth or Reality* (Chicago: Lawrence Hill and Co., 1983).

Diop, David (1927–1960) *Senegalese poet*

David Diop was born in Bordeaux, France, of a Senegalese father and a mother from CAMEROON. Raised by his mother after his father's death, he received his primary education in SENEGAL. Planning to study MEDICINE, he attended Lycée Marcelin Berthelot, in Paris, during World War II (1939–45). Poor health, however, made him a semi-invalid for most of his life and made him change his university studies from medicine to literature. He began to write poetry while still in school.

During the 1950s Diop returned to Africa and worked as a teacher in DAKAR. In 1958, because France had withdrawn its force of civil servants after GUINEA became independent, he volunteered to work in Guinea's educational system. David Diop and his family perished in 1960 in a plane crash returning to France from Dakar.

Although Diop lived most of his life in France, he expressed his emotional connection to his home in Senegal in his poetry. In 1948 his poems were published by Léopold SENGHOR (1906–2001) in *Anthologie de la nouvelle poésie nègre et malgache* (Anthology of the new black and Malagasy poetry). In the 1950s several of his poems were printed in PRÉSENCE AFRICAINE, the literary journal published by Alioune DIOP (1910–1980), to whom David was not related. David Diop's themes are anticolonial and pan-Africanist. His first book of poems, *Coups de pillon* (Hammer blows), published in 1956, called for Africans to retake control of the cultural aspects of their lives.

See also: FRANCE AND AFRICA (Vols. III, IV, V); LITERATURE IN COLONIAL AFRICA (Vol. IV).

disease in colonial Africa

When Europeans first arrived in Africa they encountered many Africa-specific diseases with which they were unfamiliar. As the continent came under COLONIAL RULE, Western scientists and medical providers slowly gained experience with these newly discovered diseases. Their work expanded Western medical scholarship into new realms, but these nascent encounters hardly encompassed the affect western Europeans' had on disease in Africa.

The actions of the colonial governments significantly changed the paradigm of disease in Africa. The Europeans, for example, brought with them diseases and strains of diseases that were virtually unknown in Africa before colonialism. And although the immediate impact of the diseases introduced by Europeans was not as devastating as that which occurred during the colonization of the Americas, the effects of these diseases on the indigenous population were long lasting and continued through the 20th century.

In southern Africa, for instance, tuberculosis was relatively rare, if present at all, in the early 1800s; in Europe, however, it was a major public health problem. As more Europeans arrived in southern Africa, the disease, fueled by poor working and living conditions, spread among the indigenous African populations and reached epidemic proportions by the 1920s. Remarkably, despite the availability of effective treatment, tuberculosis is still a major public-health problem in southern Africa, with infection rates at the end of the 20th century at least three times that of the rest of the world.

The increased presence of tuberculosis and other afflictions, however, depended upon more than their mere introduction into Africa by Europeans. Changes in social organization, employment strategies, and settlement patterns all contributed to the spread of these new diseases. Yet, though not fully culpable, the onset of colonialism combined with misguided policies and poor health care greatly affected these other contributors to the spread of disease.

For instance, forced employment by colonial interests in large-scale AGRICULTURE and MINING operations resulted in increased mass migration. In addition, as European SETTLERS took over the most fertile lands in areas such as ALGERIA, KENYA, and southern Africa, African populations were pushed onto lands of marginal value. This led to changes in settlement patterns and population densities, resulting in a dramatic increase in human contact, which assisted the spread of communicable diseases. Furthermore, the areas to which Africans relocated were sometimes not previously inhabited precisely because they were prime habitats for disease vectors. As a result, when Africans were forced onto these lands, their exposure to certain disease vectors increased.

On the economic front colonial influence on long-distance trade also aided the spread of disease. Although long-distance trade was well established in much of Africa for centuries prior to the colonial era, colonialism increased the number and diversity of trade interactions. As a consequence social interactions increased as people underwent regular trips to urban centers to buy and sell goods. This enabled disease to spread easily and quickly from one community to another, where the often unhygienic conditions of these communities did little to help control outbreaks.

As economic activities expanded, local ecology often changed, creating new habitats for disease vectors. Large-scale agriculture, especially irrigated fields, created ideal habitats for mosquitoes, which carry malaria. In addition, climatic changes, unrelated to colonialism, also affected the habitat for disease vectors. When droughts occurred, people suffered from malnutrition and raiding increased, again expanding human contact between communities as well as the chance to spread disease.

Colonialism, through land annexation and increased taxation, often resulted in widespread poverty for African populations. As poverty increased, so did malnutrition, which diminished the strength of individuals' immune systems. Unsanitary water, overcrowding, and a lack of FOOD were common in urban areas, which grew quickly as a result of URBANIZATION. These deficiencies, left unchecked in the indigenous population, allowed diseases to persist, and these difficulties began to hinder the interests of the colonial powers.

It became clear that in order to protect their LABOR force and their colonists, colonial governments had to address the problems of disease. As a result, Western health care facilities began to coexist with the already extensive systems of health and healing indigenous to Africa. The relationship between the two systems, however, was far from mutually beneficial, with health care providers from the West denouncing traditional healing as "pagan" and "unscientific." Despite this affront to traditional MEDICINE Western medical facilities made substantial gains in reducing the burden of some diseases, especially smallpox and sleeping sickness (trypanosomiasis). Additionally several schools of tropical medicine were established to study tropical illnesses.

In the early 1800s sleeping sickness, an often fatal disease transmitted by the tsetse fly, severely limited the expansion of colonial settlements in Africa, and in the 1850s numerous public-health programs were implemented with the objective of controlling the disease. Despite major epidemics from 1896 to 1906 and again in 1920, sleeping sickness was well under control by the 1960s. However, it sprang up again in many African nations after independence, and still affects an estimated half-million people in sub-Saharan Africa each year.

The scientific community was not the only group involved in combating disease in colonial Africa, as MISSIONARIES played an increasing role in administering medical care to the indigenous population. Missions in southeastern TANZANIA, for instance, had great success in treating yaws, a bacterial infection prevalent in conditions of overcrowding and poor sanitation. But though missionaries became a vital source of medical care, they frequently used health care as an access point to African communities, making sure not to neglect their goals of proselytizing and converting Africans to Christianity.

Indeed, during the colonial period, self-interest was the driving force behind many of the positive developments in the fight against disease. Still, some of the diseases present in Africa before Europeans arrived were successfully treated, and access to Western health care, though often times unequal, improved the overall quality of medical services available.

See also: CHRISTIANITY, INFLUENCE OF (Vol. IV); COLONIAL CONQUEST (Vol. IV); COLONIALISM, INFLUENCE OF (Vol. IV); DISEASE IN ANCIENT AFRICA (Vol. I); DISEASE

IN MEDIEVAL AFRICA (Vol. II); DISEASE IN MODERN AFRICA (Vol. V); DISEASE IN PRECOLONIAL AFRICA (Vol. III); HEALTH AND HEALING IN COLONIAL AFRICA (Vol. IV); TSETSE FLIES (Vol. II).

Further readings: Mario Joaquim Azevedo, Gerald W. Hartwig, and K. David Patterson, eds., *Disease in African History: An Introductory Survey and Case Studies* (Durham, N.C.: Duke University Press, 1978); K. David Patterson, *Infectious Diseases in Twentieth Century Africa: A Bibliography of Their Distribution and Consequences* (Waltham, Mass.: Crossroads Press, 1979); Oliver Ransford, *"Bid the Sickness Cease": Disease in the History of Black Africa* (London: J. Murray, 1983).

Djibouti, Republic of

Modern name of the small, northeast African country bordered by ERITREA, ETHIOPIA, SOMALIA, and the Gulf of Aden. Djibouti's NATURAL RESOURCES are meager, and much of its approximately 9,000 square miles (23,300 sq km) is desert or semi-desert terrain. Geographically, the country is extremely varied. In the north it is covered by rugged mountains, while the south and west are desert plains. Its highest point, Mount Mousa, at 6,768 feet (2,063 m), contrasts sharply with Lake Assal, at 515 feet (157 m) below sea level, the lowest point in Africa.

Djibouti is home to two main ethnic groups, the Afars (or Danakil), of Ethiopian origin, and the Issas, of Somali origin. Both share a nomadic past, speak related eastern Cushitic languages, and are predominantly Muslim.

Afar and Issa peoples of the Red Sea coast had established ties with French explorers beginning in the late 1830s. In 1862 France acquired the port of Obock from local sultans and, in anticipation of the completion of the SUEZ CANAL, sought to spread French influence in the Horn of Africa. Britain's presence at Aden, across the Bab al-Mandab Strait, further spurred France to action in the spirit of imperial rivalry. In 1888 France annexed the territory as a colony under the name of FRENCH SOMALILAND, and four years later it transferred the administrative capital from Obock to the city of Djibouti.

In the early 1890s the French commenced construction of a railroad to ADDIS ABABA, the capital of Ethiopia, hoping it would serve as Ethiopia's principal rail link to the rest of the world and establish Djibouti as an important trading point between Ethiopia and the sea. In 1946 French Somaliland became an overseas territory of France, and in 1958 the former colony became a member of the French Community, with representation in the French Parliament. Colonial policies tended to favor the Afar population, causing resentment among the region's Issas. In large part because of the discord between the Afars and Issas, full independence was slow in coming to French Somaliland. Following negotiations toward independence, in 1967 the nation was renamed the French Territory of the Afars and Issas. Later, in 1977, the country finally was granted full autonomy as Djibouti. Hassan Gouled Aptidon (1916–) was the country's first president.

See also: ADEN, GULF OF (Vol. II); AFAR (Vols. I, II, III); GOULED APTIDON, HASSAN (Vol. V); DJIBOUTI, REPUBLIC OF (Vols. I, II, III, V); DJIBOUTI, CITY OF (Vols. I, V); HORN OF AFRICA (Vol. I).

Douala

Principal port of the nation of CAMEROON located at the mouth of the Wouri River in the Gulf of Guinea. The city was originally the site of three villages in muggy swampland 15 miles (24 km) from the sea. It became a center for the SLAVE TRADE after the Portuguese arrived in the late 15th century.

> **In 1845, Alfred Saker (1814–1880), an English missionary who first translated the Bible into the Douala LANGUAGE, arrived in the region and soon signed an agreement with the local chiefs to abolish SLAVERY.**

By 1884 the region had fallen under the control of Germany as part of the colony of Kamerun. The port, which officially adopted the name Douala in 1907, served as the colonial capital from 1901 until 1916. The Germans filled in parts of the swamp in 1911 and constructed the first railroad, which ran a relatively short distance into the southeastern region of Kamerun, where most of the colony's CASH CROPS were grown. In 1919, after World War I (1914–18), the French assumed control of the city and continued to invest in the region by developing the port facilities and completing a rail link to Yaoundé. Beginning in 1940 the city served as the capital of the French Cameroons until Yaoundé became the capital, in 1946.

After World War II (1939–45) the city grew rapidly and had reached a total population of about 108,000 by 1954. The Wouri Bridge was completed in 1955. Stretching 5,900 feet (1,798 m) across the Wouri River, the bridge connected Douala by road with Bonabéri, which was a banana port at the time. With rail links to other African cities and a deepwater port, Douala was already a busy trading center. It later became an important industrial center for the independent nation of Cameroon.

See also: DOUALA (Vol. V); FRANCE AND AFRICA (Vols. IV); GERMANY AND AFRICA (Vol. IV); SLAVE TRADE, THE TRANSATLANTIC (Vol. III); URBANIZATION (Vols. IV, V); YAOUNDÉ (Vol. V).

Drum Monthly periodical published in JOHANNESBURG, SOUTH AFRICA, that featured articles, fiction, commentary, and photos focusing on the lives of black South Africans.

Robert Crisp, an Afrikaner, initially founded *Drum* as *The African Drum* in 1951. Under Crisp's guidance the magazine pandered to a condescending view of black Africans. The content made the magazine unpopular among the black population, not to mention unprofitable. Before the year was out Jim Bailey (1919–2000) took over the failing magazine and renamed it *Drum*, changing its focus to one centered on the social and political consciousness of black South Africans and the culture of Sophiatown, the vibrant epicenter of South African MUSIC during the 1950s. This shift in focus, along with juicy coverage of local crime and interracial relationships, increased *Drum's* popularity with black Africans, allowing the magazine to expand its circulation into other parts of the continent.

At a time when educational opportunities for Africans were limited, *Drum* offered an environment to learn journalism and PHOTOGRAPHY while on the job, and many noted writers and photographers worked for the magazine. *Drum's* first writer, Henry Nxumalo (d. 1957), also known as "Mr. Drum," was renowned for investigative works that unveiled the injustices of the racist South African regime. Nat Nakasa (1937–1965), another *Drum* writer, founded the literary magazine *The Classic* and was awarded a scholarship to study journalism at Harvard University in the United States. *Drum* photographer and later photoeditor, Jurgen Schadeberg (1931–1994), an Afrikaner, was a mentor to many aspiring African photographers including Peter Magubane (1932–), famed for documenting the injustices of APARTHEID.

Work such as Magubane's annoyed the South African government, and in 1965 the magazine was banned as an independent publication. *Drum* continued to come out, however, as a biweekly supplement to *The Golden City Post*, both of which were eventually sold to National Pers, a government-supported media conglomerate, in 1984.

See also: NEWSPAPERS (Vol. IV); NEWSPAPERS AND PRINT MEDIA (Vol. V); PRÉSENCE AFRICAINE (Vol. IV); URBAN LIFE AND CULTURE (Vols. IV, V).

Further reading: Anthony Sampson, *Drum: An African Adventure and Afterwards* (London: Hodder and Stoughton, 1983).

Dual Mandate Administrative doctrine put forth by British colonial governor Frederick LUGARD (1858–1945). In the first two decades of the 20th century the European colonial powers began to come under increased scrutiny and criticism for their COLONIAL RULE over Africa. Lugard—a veteran colonial governor with experience in both East and West Africa—wrote *The Dual Mandate* to defend the British approach to colonial government. He asserted that colonial governance should be based on a two-part approach that, first, promoted the best interests of indigenous peoples, and second, efficiently developed the NATURAL RESOURCES of a colony for economic profit.

Lugard's patrician attitude—and a certain amount of naïvete—regarding Britain's African colonies is evident throughout *The Dual Mandate*. Regarding "progress" in Africa, he writes, "in Africa to-day we are...bringing to the dark places of earth, the abode of barbarism and cruelty, the torch of culture and progress, while ministering to the material needs of our own civilisation. In this task the nations of Europe have pledged themselves to co-operation by a solemn covenant. Towards the common goal each will advance by the methods most consonant with its national genius. British methods have not perhaps in all cases produced ideal results, but I am profoundly convinced that there can be no question but that British rule has promoted the happiness and welfare of the primitive races."

The dual mandate theory also prescribed "indirect rule," an administrative system thought by the British to be the best way to help African people develop socially, politically, and economically while Britain profited from Africa's LABOR forces and natural resources. Under indirect rule colonial administrators levied taxes and advised local rulers, who continued to exercise authority over their territories. The system produced mixed results, however, as its quality and effectiveness tended to vary widely. In general, Britain's West African colonies met with better results than the East African colonies because, in Lugard's view, governors there tended not to get as involved in the local ways of conducting business and governmental functions. Despite continued criticism of the harshness and cruelty that seemed to be built-in features of indirect rule, the policy continued to be a mainstay in British-controlled colonies until 1947.

See also: ENGLAND AND AFRICA (Vol. IV).

Dube, John L. (John Langalibalele Dube)
(1871–1946) *African educator, newspaper editor, and minister*

John Dube was born to ZULU-speaking parents in the colony of NATAL in present-day SOUTH AFRICA. His family were members of the *amakholwa* (believers), Africans who, under the influence of MISSIONARIES, had converted to Christianity and adopted many other aspects of Western culture. In fact, Dube's father was one of the first ordained African ministers of the American Zulu Mission, which New England missionaries had established in Natal. In 1887 a young John Dube accompanied one of the missionaries to the United States and enrolled in Oberlin College, in Ohio. He studied in the college preparatory department until his return to South Africa in 1892. After marrying, in 1894, he became a teacher in the American Zulu Mission schools. Desiring to further his education but having no opportunity to do so in South Africa, Dube returned to the United States from 1896 to 1899 to attend the Union Missionary Seminary in Brooklyn, New York. He completed his studies and was ordained a minister in the Congregational Church.

Dube's two prolonged periods as a student in the United States had considerable significance for his later career. First, he was able to solidify his connections with American Congregationalists, who were to provide him with financial assistance and support for his work in Natal. But perhaps more importantly he became directly acquainted with African-Americans and their schools. In 1897 he presented talks at both Hampton Institute in Virginia and Tuskegee Institute in Alabama. He also met Booker T. WASHINGTON (1856–1915), who was a major influence on his subsequent career as an educator. Upon his return home Dube began planning a school modeled after Tuskegee, and in 1901 he opened Ohlange Institute. Dube was its principal, and the teaching faculty included his wife, his brother, and others educated in the United States. Ohlange was the first school for Africans in Natal that was run by Africans rather than white missionaries. Ohlange Institute's choir popularized the church hymn, "Nkosi Sikelel' iAfrika" (God Bless Africa), that became the anthem of the AFRICAN NATIONAL CONGRESS (ANC) and is today South Africa's national anthem.

In 1903 Dube founded and edited a newspaper, *Ilanga laseNatal* (the Natal Sun), which was published in both Zulu and English. As with Ohlange, Dube's purpose was to educate his fellow Africans and thus improve their lives. As he wrote in the first issue, the newspaper "should keep the people informed about events and show them ways of improving themselves." His activities as an educator and an editor led Dube and other educated Africans into increasing involvement in the struggle for African rights in the then highly segregated colonial society. In 1912, seeing the need for a strong political organization, they established the ANC. Dube was its first president, and his acceptance speech captured his own views and the spirit of the other founders of the ANC. "Upward!" he stated. "Into the higher places of civilization and Christianity—not backward into the slump of darkness." He served as ANC president until 1917, when he resigned over a major disagreement about what strategy to use to secure more land for Africans. Dube remained active in politics, however, often seeking ways to accommodate competing white and African in-

terests in South Africa. He also was proud of his Zulu heritage and increasingly promoted Zulu cultural and political interests.

Further reading: R. Hunt Davis, Jr., "John L. Dube: A South African Exponent of Booker T. Washington," *Journal of African Studies*, 2/4 (1975/76), 497–529; Shula Marks, *The Ambiguities of Dependence in South Africa* (Baltimore: The Johns Hopkins University Press, 1986).

Du Bois, W. E. B. (William Edward Burghart Du Bois) (1868–1963) *Scholar, sociologist, and black leader of the 20th century*

Du Bois was born in Great Barrington, Massachusetts, a town with an extremely small black population and a subtle racist undercurrent that influenced him in his youth. Du Bois excelled at his studies, earning two bachelor's degrees and a master's degree before becoming the first African-American to earn a doctorate from Harvard University, in 1895. His doctoral thesis, *The Suppression of the African Slave Trade in America*, continues to be an important source on the subject.

Du Bois taught in Ohio before moving on to university positions in Philadelphia, in 1896, and later in Atlanta. His scientific approach to social issues and his numerous groundbreaking studies of African-American life and race relations earned Du Bois the title of Father of Social Science.

Du Bois's ideological clashes with fellow African-American leader Booker T. WASHINGTON (1856–1915) resulted in his best-known book, *The Souls of Black Folk* (1903). In it, Du Bois challenged Washington's more accommodating, conservative views and espoused energetic protest as the only way of overcoming racism and affecting social change. That same year he put forth the famous concept of the "Talented Tenth," the small percentage of African-American society that could, with the benefits of higher EDUCATION, be the vanguard for an elevation of all African-Americans. To further his opposition to Washington, Du Bois founded the Niagara Movement, in 1906, which evolved into the National Association for the Advancement of Colored People (NAACP), in 1909.

By 1900 Du Bois had established himself as a leader in the Pan-African movement, which aimed to unite all people of African descent in a common fight for freedom and equality. Between 1900 and 1927 he organized or headed four Pan-African Congresses. His efforts met with varying success, a low point being the third congress, in 1923, which suffered from Du Bois's well-publicized feud with Marcus GARVEY (1887–1940).

Trips to Africa in 1923 and Russia in 1927 strengthened Du Bois's sense of black nationalism and made him sympathetic to Marxist ideals. In 1934 Du Bois resigned from the NAACP after vehemently criticizing the organization's direction.

At the Fifth Pan-African Congress, in 1945, Du Bois was lauded as a father of PAN-AFRICANISM. He was awarded the World Peace Council Prize in 1952 and the Soviet Lenin Peace Prize in 1959. Alienated by an American government suspicious of his communist leanings and disillusioned with the United States on the whole, Du Bois accepted an offer by Ghanian president Kwame NKRUMAH (1909–1972) to head the creation of an Encyclopedia Africana. In 1961 he became both a Ghanian citizen and a member of the Communist Party. Du Bois died in ACCRA, GHANA, in 1963.

See also: COMMUNISM AND SOCIALISM (Vol. V); UNITED STATES AND AFRICA (Vols. IV, V).

Durban Major port city on the Indian Ocean, located in eastern SOUTH AFRICA, in what was the colony of NATAL (today's KwaZulu-Natal province). The area of present-day Durban was home to African agro-pastoralists until 1824, when Shaka (1787–1828), the reigning ZULU king, gave British traders permission to settle on the coastal stretch of land. They founded Port Natal, renaming it Durban, in 1835, after Sir Benjamin D'Urban, the governor of the CAPE COLONY. Three years later the BOERS—who defeated Shaka's successor Dingane (1795–1840)—arrived in the area, establishing the Republic of Natalia. By 1845, however, clashes with the British led the Boers to abandon the area, and the British colony of Natal then emerged, with Durban as its main port and urban center.

In the mid-1800s Durban grew rapidly as British settlers immigrated to Natal, setting up businesses and developing a sugar industry. Workers imported from the Indian subcontinent supplied much of the LABOR needed for the rapidly growing sugar industry. Although they originally lived and worked on the sugar plantations, the Indian immigrants began to migrate into Durban proper in the early 20th century, eventually becoming a prominent part of the city's population. Also, black Afri-cans—mostly males—moved into the city to work on the docks and in other areas where manual labor was required.

In the mid-1880s the discovery of GOLD on the WITWATERSRAND in the TRANSVAAL led to the development of Durban's port. When the railway connection to the urban center of JOHANNESBURG was finally completed, in 1895, Durban soon became South Africa's leading port and a major trading center for the region's resources.

By 1900 the population of the city was approximately 55,700, and 20 years later it had risen to 90,500, one-third of whom were Africans. At that time many of the African residents were single male workers living in barracks. As the British authorities attempted to exercise more control over the growing numbers of laborers, African workers started to organize LABOR UNIONS and engage in strikes. One of Durban's early union leaders, A. W. G. CHAMPION (1893–1975), led union members in pitched battles against oppressive police restrictions in the 1920s and 1930s, getting banned from the city in the process.

In the 1930s the city's industrial sector began to boom, and over the next two decades the city, its industries, and its port all continued to grow. More African women and children also migrated to Durban, generally to the outskirts of the city, thereby dramatically increasing the population while simultaneously decreasing its male-to-female ratio.

See also: ASIAN COMMUNITIES (Vols. IV, V); DURBAN (Vol. V); ENGLAND AND AFRICA (Vols. III, IV, V); INDUSTRIALIZATION (Vols. IV, V); SHAKA (Vol. III); URBAN LIFE AND CULTURE (Vols. IV, V); URBANIZATION (Vols. IV, V).

Further readings: Bill Freund, *Insiders and Outsiders: The Indian Working Class of Durban, 1910–1990* (Portsmouth, N.H.: Heinemann, 1995); Paul Maylam and Iain Edwards, eds., *The People's City: African Life in Twentieth-Century Durban* (Portsmouth, N.H.: Heinemann, 1996).

Dyula Largely Muslim people who were influential traders in precolonial Africa. Speaking a LANGUAGE belonging to the widespread MANDE family of languages, the Dyula established extensive networks of TRADE AND COMMERCE linking West Africa's coastal and forest zones to the western region of present-day Republic of the SUDAN. The Sudan, in turn, was connected via trans-Saharan trade to markets in North Africa.

A new source of external trade opened for the Dyula in the 1400s, when they first encountered Portuguese merchants, who were the vanguard of Europeans arriving on the West African coast.

In the 19th century the forces led by the Dyula merchant and warrior SAMORI TOURÉ (c. 1830–1900) presented one of the primary challenges to French COLONIAL CONQUEST in West Africa. After using his trade connections to import weaponry and develop an army, Samori then conquered Dyula states south of the Niger River in the region of present-day IVORY COAST and LIBERIA. By the early 1880s Touré had established a West African empire surpassed in size only by the SOKOTO CALIPHATE and the TUKULOR EMPIRE. Relying on his military might and using Islam as a unifying force, Touré managed to hold onto his empire until clashes with French and British colonialists, begun in 1882, led to the empire's initial decline. Touré suffered his final defeat in 1898 at the hands of the French.

Today the Dyula compose an ethnic minority in BURKINA FASO, the Republic of MALI, Ivory Coast, GHANA, CAMEROON, The GAMBIA, GUINEA-BISSAU, and SENEGAL.

Most Dyula are Muslims, though some hold animist beliefs. Still known as merchants and businessmen, they also produce superb TEXTILES and pottery.

See also: DYULA (Vols. I, II, III); ISLAM, INFLUENCE OF (Vols. II, III, IV, V).

E

Éboué, Félix (Adolphe-Félix-Sylvestre Éboué)
(1884–1944) *French colonial governor*

Félix Éboué was born to a modest family in Cayenne, on the coast of French Guiana, in South America. At age 15 he was awarded a scholarship that brought him to Bordeaux, France. Between 1904 and 1908 he studied at the Paris Law School and the École Coloniale, a training school for colonial administrators. Upon completing his training Éboué was sent to FRENCH CONGO (today's Republic of the CONGO), where he was assigned to the OUBANGUI-CHARI region (in present-day CENTRAL AFRICAN REPUBLIC).

While he was in French Congo Éboué studied the people of the region, eventually authoring two anthropological monographs, *The People of Ubangi-Shari* and *The Musical Key to Drum and Whistle Languages.*

In 1932 Éboué was sent to Martinique, not far from his birthplace, but he was recalled to Africa two years later to serve as secretary general of FRENCH SOUDAN (present-day MALI). Soon Éboué was sent back to the French West Indies to serve as the first black governor of Guadaloupe. Then in 1938 he crossed the Atlantic yet again, when the French administration assigned him the governorship of CHAD, in northern Central Africa.

From Chad, Éboué watched the rise of Italian and German fascism, and quietly prepared his country for the coming conflict. When France fell to Germany in 1940 the Vichy government demanded that France's African colonies end relations with Britain. Éboué refused, believing that acceding to such a demand could undermine the best interests of Africans. Further establishing his antifascist position, he became the first French colonial governor to ally his forces with French general Charles DE GAULLE (1890–1970). Late in 1940 Éboué was appointed governor of all FRENCH EQUATORIAL AFRICA, which bordered Chad, a key territory to the later movement of Free French troops against the Italians in LIBYA.

Although Éboué was preoccupied with duties relating to World War II (1939–45), he still managed to direct the modernization of the schools and hospitals in territories under his stewardship. He was not sympathetic to the nascent African nationalist movements that were emerging at the time, but he believed strongly in the inherent equality of Africans and Europeans. He thus pushed for two-way cultural assimilation and consistently proposed policies that elevated Africans' status in the French colonies.

Éboué was a leading figure in the 1944 conferences in BRAZZAVILLE that defined postwar French colonial policy. After supporting Free France during the war Éboué felt justified in insisting that a victorious France give equal treatment to its African citizens. Unfortunately, he didn't live to see any of his proposed reforms implemented: Later that year, while in CAIRO, EGYPT, he died of a heart attack after suffering a bout with pneumonia. Described as "a soul free of all baseness," Éboué is now recognized as one of Africa's greatest and most compassionate colonial administrators and reformers.

See also: COLONIAL RULE (Vol. IV); FRANCE AND AFRICA (Vols. IV, V); NATIONALISM AND INDEPENDENCE MOVEMENTS (Vol. IV).

Further reading: Brian Weinstein, *Éboué* (New York: Oxford University Press, 1972).

École William Ponty (William Ponty School)
Training college for Africans, many of whom became the leaders of French-speaking countries after independence.

Founded in 1903 as the École Normale de Saint-Louis, the school was renamed École Normale William Ponty after the French colonial administrator and governor-general of FRENCH WEST AFRICA. It was moved from Saint-Louis to Gorée Island from 1913 to 1937, and then back to the mainland at DAKAR and Thiès. Originally established as a school for sons of chiefs and interpreters from throughout French West Africa, it also took the best pupils from academic departments of higher primary schools in French-speaking Africa. École William Ponty was comparable to its British counterparts, ACHIMOTA COLLEGE, in the GOLD COAST COLONY (present-day GHANA), and Makerere University, in colonial UGANDA.

One of the more prominent graduates of École William Ponty was Félix HOUPHOUËT-BOIGNY (1905–1993), who in 1960 became the first president of the independent IVORY COAST.

The school housed 50–80 male students aged 18–25. Their admission was largely based on local politics, and tuition was supported by scholarships. Although there was no entrance exam, there was an exit exam. The faculty was entirely European, and they offered a liberal arts curriculum similar to that of secondary schools in France. In addition to the basics, the curriculum included the arts—such as theater, poetry, MUSIC, and ART—along with history and sociology. The curriculum was intended to teach francophone Africans French knowledge and values—in essence to make them into black Frenchmen.

There were two educational tracks: teacher training and junior administrator training. The students who entered the teaching profession had an opportunity to complete on-the-job training at the facility. Those who left the school to enter government service did so as low-level administrators.

See also: EDUCATION (Vols. IV, V); FRANCE AND AFRICA (Vols. III, IV, V); GORÉE ISLAND (Vol. III).

economy The imposition of COLONIAL RULE furthered the transformation of the African economy that had begun with the era of the SLAVE TRADE. More and more, the LABOR and NATURAL RESOURCES of the continent were diverted to external use. For example, African workers labored in the MINING industry, which was developed by large European companies such as UNION MINIÈRE in the BELGIAN CONGO and the ANGLO-AMERICAN CORPORATION in SOUTH AFRICA. These produced the GOLD, COPPER, and other MINERALS AND METALS that were in demand in the Western world. African laborers also worked on Euro-

pean-owned plantations to produce COTTON, COFFEE, GROUNDNUTS (peanuts) and other CASH CROPS that Europeans needed for their own consumption. European firms such as the UNITED AFRICA COMPANY carried out the TRADE AND COMMERCE that resulted, with the profits flowing out of Africa and into the pockets of European investors.

It would be a mistake, however, to assume that older economic patterns completely disappeared in the face of the economic changes that occurred as a result of the influence of COLONIALISM. For example, AGRICULTURE continued to be the base of subsistence for the great majority of Africans. They continued to meet their own FOOD needs by growing FOOD CROPS, and local artisans such as blacksmiths and potters continued to produce many of the utensils and tools that these people needed. The increasing use of MONEY AND CURRENCY and the desire to buy consumer luxuries such as sugar or clothing, however, led to the increasing growth of the market economy in rural areas. Some farmers, such as those who grew COCOA in colonial GHANA, produced cash crops to generate income to meet the demands of colonial TAXATION. Others, especially in southern and Central Africa, engaged in migrant labor. Also, local smiths began to use imported scrap metal or materials brought by European colonialists to make tools and other items rather than smelting their own iron. Imported CLOTH AND TEXTILES provided the material for making clothes, thus undercutting local weavers.

Another area of dramatic economic change was in the area of TRANSPORTATION. Until the mid-19th century the continent's transportation needs were met by human porters, pack animals in certain regions such as the camels in the Sahara, and boats on rivers, lakes, and the coastal lagoons. In the colonial era Europe applied steam and then, when it was invented, the internal combustion engine to develop new modes of transportation in Africa. The result was the development of railroads, steam navigation, and road transport in the form of trucks and cars. Africans as well as colonial administrators and officials and European merchants and settlers benefited, though unequally, from the improved transportation system. The colonial era also witnessed the beginning of the decisive shift in the continent's economy from the rural to the urban areas, though this process would not be completed until after Africa achieved its independence from Europe.

The cumulative result of colonial rule was to lock Africa into a state of economic underdevelopment and dependency in place of the economic autonomy that had existed prior to the 16th century. As many observers have noted, the colonial African economy produced much that it did not consume, relying on imports to fulfill many of its needs.

See also: ASIAN COMMUNITIES (Vol. IV); COLONIALISM, INFLUENCE OF (Vol. IV); CONCESSIONAIRE COMPANIES (Vol. IV); ECONOMY (Vols. I, II, III, V); INDUSTRIALIZATION (Vol. IV).

Striving to educate as many people as possible, teachers worked with groups of students that included all ages, both adults and children, as shown here in this 1958 photo, in Ghana. © *Ghana Embassy/ Library of Congress*

education Africans established their own forms of education before the arrival of foreign traders, immigrants, and invaders. Each ethnic group had its own method of educating its young to become successful adults in society. With the changes in Africa in the 19th century, however, many young students were educated through less traditional methods in order to be prepared for their changing world.

For example, the traditional education of the Mende, a MANDE people in present-day SIERRA LEONE, GUINEA, and LIBERIA, involved an age-grade system by which children of a certain age were separated by gender and taught by their elders. The relationships forged with age mates during the three or four years of seclusion continued in the Poro Society, a secret society of initiated adult men, and the Sande Society, a secret society of initiated adult women. Mende knowledge typically was passed on orally, through ritual, and by example, and a successful "schooling" meant that young people were prepared to take their place among the adults in a community.

Later, with the introduction of indigenous LITERACY, a new form of African education emerged. For the first time students learned the written forms of their languages and began receiving their educations through script. In some cases, written codes had to be invented because foreign alphabets—Arabic or Roman, for example—could not accurately represent the indigenous language. Examples include the Vai syllabary and the N'ko alphabet. The Vai syllabary, invented by Duala Bukere in 1820, was used for interpersonal communication and for record keeping. In

the 20th century, Guinean scholar Souleymane KANTÉ (1922–1987) invented the N'ko alphabet and used it to transcribe into the Maninka LANGUAGE works of literature, history, SCIENCE, MEDICINE, and technology.

When Islam made inroads into an area, educational opportunities expanded to incorporate the religious education offered by Quranic schools. Children whose parents had converted to Islam would begin Muslim training at age five, studying with an imam or other teacher to memorize the Quran, the Muslim holy book. Teachers accomplished the Quranic education by writing one scripture at a time on a wooden board or slate and then helping the student memorize it phonetically. For those students whose first language was not Arabic, the teacher would also translate the text. In general, this process continued until the student had memorized all of the lessons.

Among some Muslim ethnic groups that also practiced the age-grade systems of education, children could be secluded for training to become an adult in society between the ages of nine and 12. After becoming adults those students who wanted to pursue Islamic learning even further could continue studying with the local imam or teacher or be recommended to an Islamic university, such as Al-Azhar in CAIRO, EGYPT.

When Europeans arrived they brought with them two forms of education, missionary and secular public. The intent of the MISSIONARIES was to spread Christianity and introduce European culture to Africans, whom they usually considered "uncivilized." For this purpose missionaries founded mission stations with churches and schools and recruited students from the surrounding indigenous population. Mission station schools were often boarding institutions so that students lived immersed in the European language and the religious principles of each school's particular Christian denomination. This type of education prepared Africans for work as assistants to the missionaries and as recruiters in their own communities. African Christians became lay leaders, such as music directors and Sunday school teachers. Some mission students, including Samuel Ajayi CROWTHER (1808–1891), Samuel JOHNSON (1846–1901), and Tiyo SOGA (1829– 1871), became fully ordained ministers in their own right.

As European governments became more involved on the continent, missionary schools expanded their curricula to include school subjects that would help enterprising members of the congregation to land jobs in the colonial ECONOMY. The evolution of FOURAH BAY COLLEGE, in Sierra Leone, was an example of such growth and development. While awaiting the development of a cadre of literate Africans during the early colonial period, the colonial officers used the European language as the official language of spoken communication. However, in many French colonies they adopted Arabic as the official language of correspondence because an existing cadre of literate Muslims already existed. Europeans then installed a colonial educational system to train their own cadre of literate workers who assumed positions in the public and private sectors of the economy serving as intermediaries between the Europeans and the general population. Many Muslims who helped pave the road to colonialism lost their jobs when the new Christian cadres were formed.

In response to the expanded role of these mission schools, Muslims offered a different kind of schooling that blended the Quranic and secular educations in the *madrasa,* a school that offered Islamic religious training and Arabic, as well as colonial languages and courses in grammar, math, science, and technology. This allowed the Muslim community to retain control over the religious instruction and moral values of their children while at the same time preparing them to take leadership positions as members of the cadre of indigenous intellectuals cultivated by most colonial administrations.

Under colonial education systems most local schools were elementary schools that provided up to six years of instruction, teaching students to read, write, and calculate. Some schools provided vocational courses that taught skills needed to participate in colonial construction projects or in the export AGRICULTURE industry. More advanced studies at the secondary level were available at boarding schools such as the ÉCOLE WILLIAM PONTY, in SENEGAL, and ACHIMOTA COLLEGE, in Britain's GOLD COAST COLONY (today's GHANA). Most such schools were located in the capital of the colony. Some, however, such as FORT HARE COLLEGE, in CAPE COLONY, SOUTH AFRICA, were located in rural areas. To enter a secondary school, students had to pass two exams, a comprehensive exit exam from the elementary school and an entrance exam for the secondary school. Students who completed the secondary program could become civil servants, teachers, or commercial agents for European companies.

Colonial education promoted the diffusion of spoken and written European languages. However, African graduates of this educational system lived in a cultural "no man's land," no longer a part of indigenous society but never able to meet European standards.

Although Muslim universities like Al-Azhar in Egypt and Sankoré in TIMBUKTU had long histories prior to European colonialism, the foundation of the present-day university systems in Africa is the outgrowth of European elementary and secondary education. Some schools that once focused on higher secondary education and technical education were adapted to become universities. École William Ponty, for example, began as the secondary École Normale in Saint-Louis. In 1827 Fourah Bay College, founded in FREETOWN, Sierra Leone, by the CHURCH MISSIONARY SOCIETY, became the first college in West Africa. In 1876 it became affiliated with Durham University, in England, and thus was able to offer university degrees. Although it was an independent institution the Liberia College, founded in MONROVIA in 1862, relied on funds from missionary and philanthropic groups in the United States. Achimota College developed into the University College of the Gold Coast in 1948. The South African College, founded in 1829, became the University of CAPE TOWN in 1918. And in UGANDA, Makerere College, founded in 1922, became an institution of higher education in 1937.

See also: CHRISTIANITY, INFLUENCE OF (Vols. II, III, IV, V); COLONIAL RULE (Vol. IV); COLONIALISM, INFLUENCE OF (Vol. IV); EDUCATION (Vol. V); ISLAM, INFLUENCE OF (Vols. II, III, IV, V).

Further reading: James P. Hubbard, *Education under Colonial Rule: A History of Katsina College, 1921–1942* (Lanham, Md.: University Press of America, 2000).

Egypt Country covering approximately 386,700 square miles (1,001,600 sq km) in the northeastern part of the African continent. It shares borders with the present-day states of LIBYA and the Republic of the SUDAN.

Ottoman Province Egypt's modern history as an independent nation begins in 1805, the year Muhammad Ali (1769–1849) secured recognition as governor of Egypt from its ruler, the Ottoman Sultan. By 1841 Egypt had become an autonomous province in the Ottoman Empire, as it would remain until the onset of World War I (1914–18), when Ottoman authority lapsed.

In 1863 Muhammad Ali's grandson, Khedive ISMAIL (1830–1895), became Egypt's ruler, and he remained in power until 1879. Remembered primarily for his role in promoting the modernization of Egypt, Ismail secured the title of Khedive (viceroy) from the sultan, which allowed Egypt even more independence within the empire.

During the 1860s the Egyptian economy benefited from the U.S. Civil War (1861–65), as the shortage of COTTON from the American South created a greater British demand for Egyptian cotton. With the windfall profits from cotton and loans from European bankers, Ismail fashioned parts of his capital city of CAIRO into a European-style city that attracted European expatriates and investors. In 1869, at the opening of the SUEZ CANAL, Ismail entertained European dignitaries at Egyptian expense in order to show off Egypt's urban and technological advances. The canal made Egypt a major world center of TRANSPORTATION and communication. In addition, succumbing to colonial ambitions, Ismail expanded Egypt southward along the Nile and took control of the Sudan.

Pasha was the highest official title of honor in the Ottoman Empire and always appeared after the person's name. Pasha was typically not a hereditary title, but it was used as one in 19th-century Egypt.

Khedive Ismail's initiatives modernized Egypt and helped to create a sense of national identity. Gradually, however, he lost control of his government through deficit spending and borrowing from European banks. The United States' reentry into the cotton export market after the Civil War did not help Egypt's finances, as it cut into the country's cotton sales. Egypt's problems forced Ismail to raise revenue to meet government expenses and pay back his loans. This led him to increase land taxes, sell Egypt's shares in the Suez Canal Company, and even dispose of personal assets like the royal silver. Even those actions failed to raise enough money, however, and he was forced to accept European oversight of his government until Egypt's loans could be repaid.

At the same time, Ismail came under pressure from political agitators, who opposed his westernized orientation, and from religious reformers like Jamal al-Din al-AFGHANI (1838–1897), who wanted to reduce European and secular influence in their country. Expressing a loss of confidence in the khedive, the British pressured the Ottoman sultan into dismissing Ismail in June 1879. Ismail's son, Mohammed Tawfiq Pasha (1852–1892), became khedive.

British Occupation As a result of Britain's behind-the-scenes maneuvering, important decisions about Egypt's governance were being made by Britons in London rather than by the khedive in Cairo or by the sultan in Istanbul. Egypt had become a British colony in all but name. The key institution promoting resistance to British rule and encouraging nationalism now became the army. Army officers, plotting against the government, thus became the nucleus of the first national party. Khedive Tawfiq, however, thought it more prudent to back Egypt's European creditors over the Egyptian nationalists.

In 1881 Egyptian officers led by Colonel Ahmad URABI (1841–1911) mutinied and forced Tawfiq to adopt a new constitution and hold elections. On the pretext of protecting their vital interest in the Suez Canal, the British and French intervened in 1882 in support of Tawfiq. The confrontation that ensued ended in the defeat of Urabi's nationalist forces and the British occupation of Egypt.

The British appointed Sir Evelyn Baring (1841–1917), later known as Lord Cromer, as consul general in Cairo. A brilliant financial administrator, he held the post from 1883 to 1907. Baring successfully rebuilt the Egyptian economy by increasing agricultural production and reducing the debt. Although the economy seemed to stabilize, Egyptians themselves were discontented because they felt the British blocked their advancement in government and in the professions. This was compounded by the fact that the public institutions created by Khedive Ismail, including public EDUCATION, health, and housing, were systematically neglected. Instead, investment was channeled into European-owned projects. Egyptians also resented the loss of their colony in the Sudan to the MAHDIYYA in 1885, blaming that loss on the British who now headed the Egyptian army.

Renewed strife emerged, in 1892, when Abbas Hilmi Pasha (1874–1944) succeeded his father, Tawfiq, as khedive. Abbas II fought with the British consul general over the right to appoint and dismiss his ministers and control the Egyptian army. Seeking to undermine British authority, Abbas built up a secret society of European and local supporters, including Mustafa Kamil (1874–1908), who emerged in 1895 as a palace propagandist. Kamil gradually turned Abbas's secret society into a revived National Party and founded a daily newspaper that promoted nationalist ideals. The National Party's main goal was the removal of British troops from Egypt. In 1906 Consul General Baring's mishandling of an incident involving British soldiers and local peasants enabled Kamil and the new nationalists to force Baring's retirement. Although

Kamil established the National party in 1907, succeeding consul generals were able to neutralize the nationalist threat. The new vehicle for this was a revamping of state agrarian policies, which placated Khedive Abbas and the more conservative landowners and won peasant support. By 1914 the National Party's leaders were in exile.

A British Protectorate The Ottoman Empire's long rule over Egypt gave way completely to a British PROTEC-TORATE in 1914 as a result of World War I (1914–18). The British desperately needed to hold on to Egypt because Britain depended on the Suez Canal to speed up communication and transportation between distant parts of its empire. The British deposed Abbas II and appointed Abbas's uncle, Husayn Kamil (1853–1917), whom they could control. Believing that Egypt would achieve independence after the war, Prime Minister Husayn Rushdi Pasha (1863–1928) stayed in office. With British attention directed toward the war, the quality of the British administration declined, and Egyptians suffered from overpopulation, food shortages, and the confiscation of goods and property.

Egyptian nationalism revived, in 1919, when Sad Zaghlul (1857–1927), a follower of Jamal al-Din al-Afghani, was elected vice president of the legislative assembly. Emerging as a prominent nationalist critic of the government and its British advisers, Sad Zaghlul notified the British High Commissioner, Sir Reginald Wingate (1861–1953), of his intention to form a delegation, termed *wafd* in Arabic, that would go to London to argue for Egypt's independence. Britain's Foreign Office refused to receive the delegation, however. Consequently, Sad Zaghlul organized a six-man delegation to present Egypt's case for independence at the Paris Peace Conference (1919) convened at the end of World War I. The delegation demonstrated its mandate by collecting signatures in support of independence.

In March 1919 the Rushdi cabinet resigned and the British exiled Sad Zaghul. Egypt erupted into a popular revolution—a general strike. Every social class demonstrated against the British protectorate. This outbreak forced the appointment of a new high commissioner, Lord Edmund Allenby (1861–1936), who had distinguished himself as a commander of British troops in Egypt and Palestine during World War I. Sad Zaghlul was allowed to go to Paris, and Egyptians went back to work with high hopes that the *wafd* would present its case and secure independence. The European powers, however, ignored the *wafd* and the issue of independence, never inviting the delegation to address the conference. From this delegation, however, Zaghul formed the Wafd Party, in 1919.

Continued unrest in Egypt forced the British to send a commission led by Sir Alfred MILNER (1854–1925) to investigate. Furious at their mistreatment, Egyptians organized a general boycott of the Milner commission. Al-

though Sad Zaghlul did speak with Milner, the two did not come to an agreement. Because an agreement could not be reached with the Egyptians, Britain decided to give up the protectorate and in 1922 unilaterally declared Egypt independent. This status was limited only by four conditions called "reserved points." These gave Britain the power to (1) protect British imperial communications in Egypt, (2) oversee Egypt's defense against foreign aggression, (3) protect foreign interests and minorities in Egypt, and (4) control the Sudan.

Independent Egypt Britain installed a new, independent Egyptian government led by King Fuad I (1868–1936), the 12th son of Khedive Ismail. A new constitution, modeled on Belgium's, also was put in place. Following the elections of 1923 King Fuad called on Sad Zaghlul to appoint a cabinet made up of Wafd ministers. The death of King Fuad in 1936 brought to power his teenage son, Faruk (1920–1965), under a regent. New elections held in 1936 were won by the WAFD PARTY. Mustafa al-Nahas (1879–1965) formed a Wafdist cabinet and successfully negotiated the Anglo-Egyptian Treaty (1936). This agreement guaranteed the British bases in Cairo and ALEXAN-DRIA. It also gave the British a 20-year lease on a large military base for defense of the Suez Canal. The Sudan question was left for later discussion.

For Egypt independence meant entering the world arena as a nation with a constitutional monarchy, cabinet ministers responsible to parliament, ambassadors, and membership in the League of Nations. However, under King FARUK, Nahas and his Wafdist cabinet lasted only 18 months. Faruk systematically found ways to exclude the Wafd Party from power by forming coalition governments of independent parties. Meanwhile the government did nothing to solve Egypt's pressing economic and social problems.

Since the politicians proved their incompetence, Egyptians looked for other solutions. Among those was the Society of Muslim Brothers (al-Ikhwan al-Muslimun), who wanted Egypt to abandon its secular government and return to traditional Islamic customs and institutions. Reacting against a century of westernizing reforms that had brought little or no benefit to the average Egyptian, the Muslim Brothers lashed out against Jews, Christians, and Western innovations.

In 1939 the onset of World War II (1939–45) transformed Egypt once again into a British army camp. Concerned that the existing government wanted Egypt to remain neutral, the British ambassador, Sir Miles Lampson (1880–1964), forced King Faruk to accept the British choice for prime minister. The new anti-German government was formed by Mustafa al-Nahas and his Wafd Party, which remained in power from 1942 to 1944.

Although few Egyptians had previously viewed themselves as Arabs, both King Faruk and the Wafd Party began to identify Egypt more closely with the Arab world.

In 1945 Egypt became a founding member of the Arab League. While preserving the sovereignty of each Arab country, the Arab League coordinated their efforts on key Arab issues. The most significant issue of the day was the possible creation of a Jewish state in Palestine. The formation in 1948 of the state of Israel prompted immediate Arab retaliation, and war between Israel and its Arab neighbors broke out on the same day that Israeli independence was announced. However, Egyptian forces were defeated in the Arab-Israeli war of 1948, and Egypt's old regime was discredited. New elections in 1950 brought back al-Nahas and the Wafd, who proposed an ambitious reform program beginning with the abrogation of the 1936 Anglo-Egyptian Treaty.

On January 26, 1952, the people of Cairo rebelled in what has become known as "Black Saturday." This revolt was as much a protest against al-Nahas's government as an expression of anger against foreigners, many of whose buildings were burned. Egyptian army officers seized power in a coup d'état. King Faruk was sent into exile. The leader of the revolutionary officers, Colonel Gamal Abdel NASSER (1918–1970), took power and was confirmed as president, in 1956.

President Nasser persuaded Britain to withdraw its troops from the Suez Canal, which had been Britain's principal interest in Egypt since the canal's opening, in 1869. He then nationalized the canal. This action resulted in a combined British-French paratroop invasion in October 1956. In a rare display of agreement during the Cold War era, however, the United States and the former Soviet Union pressured the British and French to withdraw, which they did.

Egypt's transition from Ottoman province to British protectorate and then from quasi-independence to full independence was then complete.

See also: ANGLO-EGYPTIAN CONDOMINIUM (Vol. IV); ARAB-ISRAELI WARS (Vol. V); COLONIAL RULE (Vol. IV); EGYPT (Vols. I, II, III, V); MUHAMMAD ALI (Vol. III); OTTOMAN EMPIRE AND AFRICA (Vol. IV).

Further reading: M. W. Daly, ed., *The Cambridge History of Egypt, Vol. 2: Modern Egypt, from 1517 to the End of the Twentieth Century* (New York: Cambridge University Press 1998); Arthur Goldschmidt, *Modern Egypt: the Formation of a Nation-State* (Boulder, Colo.: Westview Press, 2002); James Jankowski, *Egypt: A Short History* (Oxford, U.K.: Oneworld, 2000).

Egyptology Study of ancient EGYPT of the Pharaonic era (3000 BCE–30 CE), utilizing disciplines such as ART history, archaeology, and history. Egyptology as a field of study began after French forces, under Napoleon I (1769–1821), invaded Egypt in 1798. The scholars who accompanied Napoleon's forces sent home detailed descriptions of the antiquities they saw and unearthed, heightening European interest in ancient Egypt. Among the early, influential publications on Egypt was *Travels in Lower and Upper Egypt* (1802) by the artist Vivant Denon (1747–1825), who created a visual record of the ancient monuments and whom Napoleon later made director-general of museums.

Although Napoleon amassed a treasure of Pharaonic-era antiquities, he was forced to surrender them to the British, who had defeated him in Egypt in 1801 at the Battle of Alexandria. These spoils of war became the basis of the Egyptian collection at the British Museum in London. Until 1822, however, little was known about their purpose or significance. The details of ancient Egyptian life and culture were locked behind hieroglyphics, which to Europeans seemed an undecipherable writing system. That year, the scholar Jean-François Champollion (1980–1832) unlocked the meaning of the Rosetta Stone, a stone slab inscribed with three versions of the same text: one in hieroglyphics, one in Demotic (a common, simplified Egyptian script), and one in Greek. By comparing the hieroglyphics to the Greek and Demotic, Champollion was able to decipher them, giving the modern world access to knowledge of the ancient world. Because vast numbers of ancient Egyptian inscriptions could then be translated, Egypt's history and culture became better known than that of any other ancient civilization.

Further advances in Egyptology came in 1858 with the appointment of the French archaeologist Auguste Mariette (1821–1881) as conservator of monuments in Egypt and director of the Antiquities Service. The Egyptian government had established this bureau in 1835 to gain control over the country's ancient cultural heritage. Working without supervision and without any formal system for gathering and cataloging his findings, Mariette collected antiquities at a furious pace. Mariette subsequently established the Egyptian Museum in CAIRO to house what he and fellow archeologists unearthed. In 1900 the museum moved to its present building, which today houses more than 120,000 objects.

From 1881 until 1914 French archaeologist Gaston Maspero (1846–1916) served as director general of the Antiquities Service. He began to control the allocation of excavation permits in order to limit illegal excavations. During this period archaeologists were able to keep whatever artifacts the Egyptian Museum decided not to acquire for its collection. Consequently, many archaeologists, art collectors, explorers, and travelers came to Egypt, lured by the possibility of fame and wealth. In the process they made many amazing discoveries, including the tombs and mummies of many pharaohs and other notables in the Valley of the Kings in Upper Egypt.

Another major advance came with British archaeologist William Flinders Petrie (1853–1942), who, by applying scientific techniques to the study of Egypt's ancient past, established Egyptology as a scholarly endeavor. He is regarded as the first scientific excavator in the history of Egyptian archaeology. Until Petrie's time excavations of the ancient sites had lacked any methodical planning and produced a mixture of artifacts whose relationship to each other—and therefore full significance—was often unclear. Petrie demonstrated that through systematic excavation, an accurate chronological record of sites could be established.

Another well-known scientific Egyptologist of this period was Howard Carter (1874–1939), the British-born inspector general of monuments for Upper Egypt. With funds provided by his wealthy British patron, Lord Carnarvon (1866–1923), he supervised the excavations at Thebes and in the Valley of the Kings. These culminated in 1922 with the unearthing of the largely intact tomb of King Tutankhamun (r. c. 1361–1352 BCE) in 1922. Lord Carnarvon's death shortly after the discovery of King Tutankhamun's tomb gave rise to stories about a Mummy's Curse that haunted the tomb, causing the premature death of those who disturbed it. There is no evidence to support the existence of such a curse.

After World War II (1939–45) a renewed focus on ancient Egypt led a consortium of educational and cultural institutions to set up the American Research Center in Egypt (ARCE) as a private, not-for-profit organization committed to the conservation of Egyptian artifacts. ARCE supports researchers from across the globe to study all phases of Egyptian civilization.

See also: ARCHAEOLOGY IN AFRICA (Vols. IV, V); EGYPTOLOGY (Vol. V).

Further reading: Angela McDonald and Christina Riggs, eds., *Current Research in Egyptology 2000* (Oxford, U.K.: Archaeopress, 2000).

Ekwensi, Cyprian (Cyprian Odiatu Duaka Ekwensi) (1921–) *Nigerian writer*

Born to IGBO parents in Minna, Northern NIGERIA, Ekwensi excelled in his studies, particularly English, SCIENCE, and math. He attended the University of Ibadan, the Chelsea School of Pharmacy in London, and the School of Forestry in Western Nigeria. In 1944 Ekwensi gained employment as a forestry officer, and, ironically, considering his later urban focus, he drew inspiration for his writing from his job's bucolic milieu. In 1947 he published a collection of original short stories and Igbo folktales entitled *Ikolo the Wrestler and Other Igbo Tales*. Alongside his early writing career, Ekwensi also worked as a professor and a pharmacist.

A resident of large cities for much of his life, Ekwensi soon turned to URBAN LIFE AND CULTURE, particularly that of LAGOS, as his literary muse. Two novellas, *When Love Whispers* (1947) and *The Leopard's Claw* (1950), were Ekwensi's early efforts on urban themes, but *People of the City* (1954) truly established Ekwensi's subject and style.

Written in a journalistic tone, the novel follows jazz musician and reporter Amusa Sango through a series of interwoven plots taking place in Ekwensi's focal city of Lagos. The novel incorporates various aspects of city life, from crime and political corruption to MUSIC, NEWPAPERS, and business. *People of the City* became the precursor of Ekwensi's urban fiction, a genre he would develop further in the following decades. His accessible writing style and his choice of themes made him a popular author for a largely urban-based Nigerian readership that was already familiar with the journalism of Nigeria's lively press.

See also: IBADAN, UNIVERSITY OF (Vol. V); EKWENSI, CYPRIAN (Vol. V); LANGUAGE USAGE IN MODERN AFRICA (Vol. V); LITERATURE IN COLONIAL AFRICA (Vol. IV); LITERATURE IN MODERN AFRICA (Vol. V); NEWSPAPERS AND PRINT MEDIA (Vol. V); URBANIZATION (Vols. IV, V).

Elizabethville (Lubumbashi)

Second largest city and the principal industrial center of the Democratic Republic of the CONGO. Located in the COPPERBELT region of the Katanga province, the city of Elizabethville had a far different origin from the two other major colonial cities of the BELGIAN CONGO, LEOPOLDVILLE (present-day Kinshasa) and STANLEYVILLE (Kisangani). Those cities were founded because they were both strategically located at opposite ends of a 745-mile (1,240-km) navigable stretch of the Congo River, at a time when river steamers offered the most viable means of long-distance TRANSPORTATION. Elizabethville was situated far from any navigable river, but it lay above rich COPPER deposits.

> An early colonial-era source describes Elizabethville as "the boom town of the Congo. It has a white population of 3,000 and possesses every modern convenience. Its homes are supplied with electric current and running water, and its [white] inhabitants know the comforts of ice and of bathtubs."

In contrast to Leopoldville, however, a permanent African presence on the urban scene was readily accepted because a settled labor force, rather than a migrant one, was needed for the grueling task of extracting copper from the bowels of the earth. Rail links served to transport the copper to Benguela, ANGOLA, to the Kasai tributary of the Congo River, and to Northern Rhodesia.

While copper served as the basis of the ECONOMY, other industries for tobacco products, TEXTILES, food processing, brewing, and, of course, metalworking emerged. The city retained its stultifying colonial character until the mid-1950s, when the colonial government began to expand African EDUCATION, including establishing a university in 1955. Elizabethville became the capital of the breakaway Katanga state of Moïse Tshombe (1919–1969) from 1960 to 1963 and was the scene of fierce fighting between United Nations forces and Katanga's army. During that time many Belgians abandoned their homes and made a hasty departure from the country.

In 1966, along with other Congolese cities carrying colonial names, Elizabethville was renamed. Its new name, Lubumbashi, harked back to the African heritage of the Luba kingdom that dominated the region into the 19th century.

See also: BELGIUM AND AFRICA (Vol. IV); COLONIAL RULE (Vol. IV); COLONIALISM, INFLUENCE OF (Vol. IV); CONGO CRISIS (Vol. V); COPPER MINES (Vol. II); LUBA (Vol. II); LUBA EMPIRE (Vol. III); LUBUMBASHI (Vol. V); MINERALS AND METALS (Vol. V); TSHOMBE, MOÏSE (Vol. V); UNITED NATIONS AND AFRICA (Vol. IV, V); URBAN LIFE AND CULTURE (Vols. IV, V); URBANIZATION (Vols. IV, V).

Further reading: Bruce Fetter, *The Creation of Elizabethville, 1910–1940* (Stanford, Calif.: Hoover Institution Press, 1976).

England and Africa

England expanded its role and influence in Africa during the colonial era to become, along with France, a leading colonial power. During the second half of the 19th century Britain dramatically increased its presence on the African continent.

Up until 1707 England was its own kingdom. That year, it formed a union with Scotland under the name Kingdom of Great Britain. In 1801 the Kingdom of Great Britain, along with a conquered Ireland, became the United Kingdom. Throughout this time, the seat of British government was centered in London, England. For purposes of consistency, in volumes III through V of this encyclopedia, the articles specifically dealing with the relationship of Africa with the British are titled "England and Africa."

The opening up of Africa to European explorers, traders, and MISSIONARIES was made possible in part as a result of steam-powered boats and improved knowledge of waterways in the continent's interior. The availability of quinine as a prophylactic against malaria and the completion of the SUEZ CANAL in 1859 were also factors in this. In large part, Britain's efforts at COLONIAL CONQUEST were intended to replace the SLAVE TRADE with "legitimate trade." Also, British church leaders hoped that colonial expansion would facilitate the efforts of missionary societies to spread Christianity. However, Britain's imperialist aspirations were also driven to a large extent by the desire to gain greater access to Africa's potential markets and raw materials, as well as to outmaneuver their European colonial competitors.

During the PARTITION of Africa among Europe's leading powers in the 1880s, Britain established formal control over some of the continent's most strategically and economically vital regions. Britain's major colonial holdings ultimately included EGYPT and present-day Republic of the SUDAN in North Africa; GOLD COAST COLONY (now GHANA), NIGERIA, and SIERRA LEONE in West Africa; UGANDA and NORTHERN RHODESIA (now ZAMBIA) in Central Africa; BRITISH EAST AFRICA (now KENYA) in East Africa; and the UNION OF SOUTH AFRICA, SOUTHERN RHODESIA (now ZIMBABWE), and NYASALAND (now MALAWI) in southern Africa. After the end of World War I (1914–18), Britain also came to control some of Germany's previous colonies, including TANGANYIKA (now part of TANZANIA) and British TOGOLAND.

In administering its African colonial empire, Britain drew upon the philosophy devised by Frederick LUGARD (1858–1945) that was put forth as the DUAL MANDATE. Formulated while Lugard was serving as a colonial administrator, first in BUGANDA and then in the SOKOTO CALIPHATE in the Northern Region of Nigeria, this approach of indirect rule involved recognition of existing African kings, chiefs, and figures of authority. These indigenous leaders were permitted to rule as long as they recognized British supremacy and maintained certain colonial policies such as tax collection, recruitment into the military, and forced LABOR details.

The imposition of COLONIAL RULE, however, often met with militant resistance by Africans. In the Gold Coast Colony, the ASHANTI EMPIRE nearly managed to expel British colonial forces during the ANGLO-ASHANTI WARS. In southern Africa ZULU soldiers destroyed a British regiment at the Battle of ISANDLWANA, in 1879, though the resisting Africans eventually lost the ANGLO-ZULU WAR. The Zulus once again challenged British colonial control during the ill-fated BAMBATHA'S REBELLION of 1906–08. The AFRIKANER REPUBLICS also contested British encroachment, a conflict that culminated in the ANGLO-BOER WAR of 1899–1902. In all of these instances primary resistance met with failure and highlighted Britain's ability to quell rebellions through its command of advanced weaponry.

Militarily superior, Britain progressively tightened its grip over its African colonies and even established significant British settlements in certain desirable locales, such as Southern Rhodesia and Kenya. However, World War I and World War II (1939–45) had unfavorable impacts on Britain's economy and military capacity. These conflicts also contributed to the momentum of African nationalist

In spite of mass arrests and other repressive policies, by 1953 Britain was struggling to maintain control of its Kenyan colony during the Mau Mau insurrection. Here English policemen search a Kikiyu village for Mau Mau suspects. © *NEA photo*

organizations that were agitating for greater political power, and, ultimately, independence from colonial rule. The MAU MAU movement in Kenya, which developed during the late 1940s and 1950s, demonstrated the limitations of British colonial power. It also showed the high cost Britain would have to bear if it wanted to maintain its colonial holdings in the face of popular insurrections among its African colonial subjects. This cost increased as Africans educated in Europe and American universities formed a new and increasingly militant group that was unwilling to settle for anything short of complete political autonomy.

Recognizing the inevitability of the loss of its African colonies, by the 1950s Britain took steps to gradually transfer power to the African elites. In 1957 the Gold Coast Colony became the first sub-Saharan colony to attain full independence from Britain. Under the dynamic leadership of Kwame NKRUMAH (1909–1972), the country,

renamed Ghana, served as an inspiration for the many other African states that achieved independence from Britain in quick succession during the following six years.

See also: ENGLAND AND AFRICA (Vols. III, V); NATIONALISM AND INDEPENDENCE MOVEMENTS (Vol. IV); TRADE AND COMMERCE (Vols. IV, V).

Further reading: Barbara Bush, *Imperialism, Race, and Resistance: Africa and Britain, 1919–1945* (New York: Routledge, 1999); Trevor Royle, *Winds of Change: The End of Empire in Africa* (London: J. Murray, 1996).

Equatorial Guinea Present-day country in western Central Africa measuring some 10,800 square miles (28,000 sq km). Equatorial Guinea is made up of a continental region, bordered by CAMEROON and GABON, as well as five islands, the largest of which is Bioko (formerly Fernando Po). Malabo is the present-day capital.

In 1906 UNION MINIERE, a MINING corporation, was formed to begin exploiting the copper deposits on the Belgian side of the colonial border. Elizabethville, named in honor of Belgium's Queen Elizabeth, emerged in 1910. It had more in common with similar mining towns in SOUTH AFRICA, NORTHERN RHODESIA (today's ZAMBIA) and SOUTHERN RHODESIA (today's ZIMBABWE) than it did with the other commercial and administrative centers of the Congo. Whites occupied the more pleasant areas of the town, away from the noxious fumes of the refineries and smelters, while the African LABOR force occupied drab areas close to the mines, known at the time as the "native townships."

In 1858 Spain took control of Fernando Po from the British, and by the late 1870s the island was being used as a base for Spanish exploration of the African continent. In addition, they set up a penal colony to hold prisoners from Cuba, Spain's Caribbean colony. Spain also began developing COCOA and timber as the island's main exports. Typical of colonial-era labor, no Spaniards actually worked on the plantations. Instead, the authorities coerced Africans to do their work for them. Some of these laborers were of the local Bubi ethnic group, and others came from the Fang group, from the mainland.

It was not until 1900 that the Treaty of Paris formalized Spain's claims to Fernando Po and the neighboring continental territory, after which the region was known collectively as SPANISH GUINEA. The colony was divided into three administrative units: the island of Fernando Po, the islands of Annobón, Elobey, and Carrisco, and the continental Río Muni. Although the colonial economy on the islands was established, it wasn't until after the Spanish Civil War (1936–39) and World War II (1939–45) that development began on the continental lands. By the time the colony achieved its independence, in 1968, it had a strong export economy based on timber, cocoa, COFFEE, and PALM OIL.

In 1959 Spanish Guinea was made an overseas territory of Spain, meaning that all of its inhabitants, Africans included, were granted the rights and privileges of Spanish citizens. At the same time, however, NATIONALISM AND INDEPENDENCE MOVEMENTS were sweeping the continent, and Spain eventually extended self-rule to the territory, the name of which was changed to Equatorial Guinea in

1963. Equatorial Guinea became fully independent in 1968 with Francisco Macías Nguema (1922– 1979) as its first president.

See also: EQUATORIAL GUINEA (Vols. I, II, III, V); FANG (Vols. I, II); FERNANDO PO (Vol. III); MALABO (Vol. V); SPAIN AND AFRICA (Vol. IV).

Eritrea Present-day country located on the Red Sea in northeastern Africa that was a one-time Italian colony and Ethiopian PROTECTORATE. Bordered by DJIBOUTI to the southeast, the Republic of the SUDAN to the west, and ETHIOPIA to the south, Eritrea covers some 46,800 square miles (121,200 sq km).

Controlled at various times over the centuries by Aksum, EGYPT, Portugal, and the Ottoman Empire, Eritrea was originally settled by Sabeans from the Arabian Peninsula. Intermingling with peoples moving into the area from the northern Sudan, they survived primarily as pastoral nomads.

Eritrea during the Colonial Era Beginning with its purchase of the Red Sea port of Aseb in the late 1880s, Italy began a colonizing program that culminated, in 1890, with the formal declaration that Eritrea was an Italian colony. Large-scale immigration followed, and by the late 1930s more than 70,000 Italians had settled in the region. ASMARA, which soon took on the appearance of a colonial Italian city, became the colony's capital, primarily because of its location in the cooler and better-watered highlands. From 1936 to 1942, along with Ethiopia and ITALIAN SOMALILAND, Eritrea was administered as part of a colonial federation called ITALIAN EAST AFRICA.

To fulfill its dreams of empire Italy developed Eritrea's infrastructure, built roads and railways, and created an industrial zone. Although infamous for its harsh treatment of the Eritrean population as little more than cheap LABOR, the Italian colonial administration nevertheless helped contribute to Eritrean nationalism, as well as to the development of both a sizable working class and an educated urban population.

Following Italy's defeat in World War II (1939–45) Eritrea temporarily came under the control of Britain, which administered it as occupied enemy territory under the British Military Authority. After the formal end of the war the United Nations was entrusted with the region's future, ultimately choosing to unite Eritrea with Ethiopia. This decision, which was put into effect in the fall of 1952, was unpopular in Eritrea, where the population saw itself as different—economically, politically, and socially—from Ethiopia's. By 1961 armed resistance to Ethiopian rule had begun, continuing in various guises until 1993, when Eritrea's independence was finally formally recognized.

See also: AKSUM (Vols. I, II); COLONIAL RULE (Vol. IV); COLONIALISM, INFLUENCE OF (Vol. IV); ERITREA (Vols.

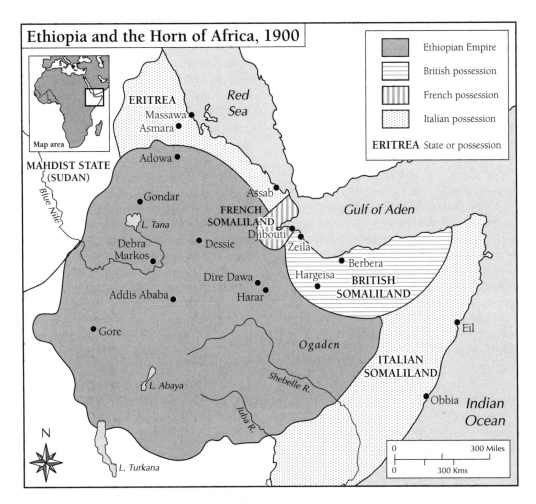

Ethiopia and the Horn of Africa, 1900

I, II, III, V); ITALY AND AFRICA (Vol. IV); OTTOMAN EMPIRE (Vols. II, III); PORTUGAL AND AFRICA (Vols. III, IV); SETTLERS, EUROPEAN (Vol. IV).

Further reading: Lionel Cliffe and Basil Davidson, *The Long Struggle of Eritrea for Independence and Constructive Peace* (New Jersey: Red Sea Press, 1988); Tekeste Negash, *Italian Colonialism in Eritrea: 1882–1941* (New York: Coronet, 1987).

Ethiopia Northeast African country covering approximately 435,100 square miles (1,126,900 sq km) that long resisted European colonial designs. Ethiopia, officially known today as the Federal Democratic Republic of Ethiopia, is a landlocked republic in the interior of the Horn of Africa. It borders the present-day states of DJIBOUTI, ERITREA, KENYA, SOMALIA, and the Republic of the SUDAN. In addition to the politically and culturally dominant AMHARA, Ethiopia hosts several other major ethnic groups, including the OROMO, TIGRAY, and Somali. Regarding RELIGION, approximately half the country's inhabitants are Muslims, while Christians make up 35–40 percent of the population. About 12 percent of the population is considered animist. Ethiopia claims one of the

world's earliest civilizations, as well as the Solomonic Dynasty, Africa's oldest monarchy.

By the mid-19th century Ethiopia finally emerged from the Zemene Mesafint, or Age of Princes, a protracted period of political anarchy (1768–1855). Stability and political reunification were achieved in part through the efforts of Lij Kassa (1820–1868), who extended the boundaries of the Ethiopian kingdom. Once he had consolidated power, in 1855, Kassa was crowned emperor, taking the name TÉWODROS II. Téwodros II sought to centralize and modernize Ethiopia, which involved importing Western technical advisors, reducing the power of feudal warlords, creating a national army, and taxing the holdings of the ETHIOPIAN ORTHODOX CHURCH. Amid diplomatic tensions with Britain, in 1867 Téwodros seized the British consul and other diplomats and retreated to the mountain fortress of Magdala. The British captured Magdala in 1868, but rather than allowing himself to be captured, Téwodros II committed suicide.

A four-year interregnum followed until Kassa Mercha, the governor of Tigray, assumed the throne in 1872, taking the name YOHANNES IV (1831–1889). During his reign, Yohannes was forced to focus his attention on quelling internal revolts and repulsing external threats.

Within Ethiopia the king of SHOA, the future Emperor MENELIK II (1844–1913), proved a powerful rival.

After the opening of the SUEZ CANAL in 1869, Italy sought to gain influence in the Horn of Africa. It captured the Red Sea ports of Aseb and Mitsiwa in present-day Eritrea and made inroads into Tigray before suffering a defeat at Dogali. In 1875 EGYPT invaded Ethiopia, also in pursuit of imperialist goals, but its forces were driven out the following year. Additionally, Yohannes IV had to contend with raids launched by Sudanese Mahdists, who were followers of the Islamic leader Muhammad Ahmad al-MAHDI (1844–1885). In March 1889, while fighting the Mahdists in the Sudan, Yohannes was killed. Menelik II declared himself emperor the same month, even though Yohannes IV had named his son as heir to the throne.

Despite having entered into a treaty of friendship with Menelik in 1889, Italy sought to establish a PROTECTORATE over Ethiopia in the early 1890s. Menelik resisted Italian attempts to gain influence, and the tensions culminated in the Battle of ADOWA, on March 1, 1896. A resounding loss for the Italians, the battle is still celebrated by Ethiopians as the most notable victory of any African army against a European power. Although Italy recognized Ethiopian independence in the Treaty of Addis Ababa, signed in October 1896, it retained control over Eritrea. Menelik expanded the boundaries of the Ethiopian state, mostly southward, between 1896 and 1906 to resemble the present-day borders. He also established a new capital at ADDIS ABABA. In addition, he began construction on a railway linking Addis Ababa to the port of Djibouti (completed in 1917).

Lij Iyasu (1896–1935), Menelik's grandson and designated heir came to power upon Menelik's death in 1913. He was deposed three years later by the country's Amhara nobility, which resented his attempts to integrate Muslims into the administration. Iyasu's support of the Central Powers during World War I (1914–18) also alienated Britain and France. Menelik's daughter, Zawditu (1876–1930), assumed the throne as empress, with Ras Tafari Makonnen (1892–1975), a cousin of Menelik, serving as prince-regent and the heir apparent. In 1928 Zawditu proclaimed Ras Tafari as king, and upon her death, two years later, Tafari had himself crowned Emperor HAILE SELASSIE.

Selassie undertook an ambitious program of modernization, which included drafting the country's first constitution, establishing a bicameral parliament, laying an extensive network of roads and communications, and abolishing SLAVERY. The success of Ethiopia's modernizing efforts, fueled by booming sales of COFFEE (the country's principal export), excited the envy of Italy's dictator, Benito Mussolini (1883–1945). He was intent on avenging Italy's defeat at Adowa and staking Italy's claim as a great imperial power. Italy invaded Ethiopia on October 2, 1935, and over the following seven months deployed poison gas and aerial bombardments to overcome the Ethiopian army. Despite Ethiopia's membership in the League of Nations since 1923 and that organization's commitment to collective security, its member states did not directly oppose Italy's flagrant violation of the league's core principles. Selassie fled into exile on May 2, 1936. Italy consolidated its control over Ethiopia, combining its administration with Eritrea and ITALIAN SOMALILAND to create ITALIAN EAST AFRICA. Prior to its occupation by Italy (1936–41), Ethiopia had been one of only two African countries to escape the imposition of COLONIAL RULE (LIBERIA was the other). Selassie returned to Ethiopia during World War II (1939–45), and liberated his country from Italian rule with the support of British and South African forces.

Ethiopia joined the United Nations as a charter member in 1945, and in 1963 Addis Ababa became home to the headquarters of the Organization of African Unity. With the backing of the United Nations, Eritrea was federated with Ethiopia in 1952, in the process securing Ethiopia's access to the Red Sea. Ethiopia enjoyed a relatively buoyant economy during the 1950s and 1960s as a result of profitable coffee EXPORTS. Internal dissent grew among those seeking significant land reform, however, especially those in opposition to the laws that gave large landowners and the ETHIOPIAN ORTHODOX CHURCH decided advantages. Despite concessions, which included a new constitution, the unequal distribution of land did not change. Selassie survived a coup d'état attempt by members of the imperial guard in December 1960, but ongoing conflict with Somalia and Republic of the Sudan over the next few years further eroded the emperor's popular appeal. After ruling Ethiopia for more than four decades, in 1974 Selassie was overthrown by the Dergue, a military junta.

See also: ETHIOPIA (Vols. I, II, III, IV); HORN OF AFRICA (Vols. I, V); ITALO-ETHIOPIAN WARS (Vol. IV); ITALY AND AFRICA (Vol. IV); LEAGUE OF NATIONS AND AFRICA (Vol. IV); OGADEN (Vol. IV); SOLOMONIC DYNASTY (Vol. II).

Further reading: Haile M. Larebo, *The Building of an Empire: Italian Land Policy and Practice in Ethiopia, 1935–1941* (Oxford, U.K.: Clarendon Press, 1994); Harold G. Marcus, *A History of Ethiopia* (Berkeley, Calif.: University of California Press, 1994).

Ethiopian Orthodox Church Long-time state church of imperial ETHIOPIA, theologically and organizationally distinct from Western Christian churches. The Ethiopian Orthodox Church dates back to the fourth century CE, when two evangelists, Frumentius and Aedesius, gained permission from Ezana, the king of Aksum, to spread the Christian RELIGION within the kingdom. Theologically close to the Coptic Church and other Eastern forms of Christianity, the Ethiopian church over the centuries also assimilated a number of beliefs and practices from traditional African religions. As a result it not only held fast to theological beliefs that had been deemed heretical in the West as early as the fifth century CE, but it also incorporated beliefs in various local spirits and devils. In addition, because of the emphasis the Ethiopian royal house placed on its supposed links to Israel's King Solomon and Queen Makeda (queen of Sheba), the church also incorporated traditional Jewish practices. These include circumcision, reverence for the Ark of the Covenant, and the observance of a Saturday (as well as a Sunday) Sabbath.

Although it technically remained independent, for centuries the Ethiopian church was headed by an archbishop appointed by the patriarch of the Coptic Church in ALEXANDRIA, EGYPT. Frequent tensions resulted from this arrangement as both the clergy and Ethiopian rulers strained against such foreign intervention. It was not until the 1920s, however, that an agreement was worked out allowing four Ethiopian archbishops to serve as auxiliaries to the Egyptian-appointed archbishop. This arrangement was, in turn, renegotiated in the wake of World War II (1939–45), at which time the head of the church was chosen from among the Ethiopian clergy.

Quite early in its history the Orthodox Church became the official religion of imperial Ethiopia, and it remained so in spite of large numbers of Ethiopian practitioners of both Islam and traditional religion. The institutions of the church and of the imperial throne were intertwined in complex ways. The church often seemed to exert influence in the selection of emperors in the same way that the emperors often had ways of exerting power over the church and its leaders. In the early 20th century, for example, the church played a key role in the overthrow of Lij Iyasu (r. 1913–1916), the grandson of the famous MENELIK II (1844–1913). Although he had been Menelik's personal choice as the next emperor, Iyasu had longtime links to Ethiopia's Muslim community, a situation that angered both the clerics of the church and the country's traditional-minded nobility. When Iyasu undertook policies that in their eyes undermined the supremacy of the church, both elements took action, first denying Iyasu a formal coronation for three years and ultimately overthrowing him and installing one of Menelik's daughters on the throne.

The interplay of the church and the imperial throne took another strange turn during the time of the ITALO-ETHIOPIAN WAR of 1935–36. Following Ethiopia's military defeat and the flight of Emperor HAILE SELASSIE (1892–1975), the Egyptian Coptic head of the church, Kerlos (d. c. 1942), collaborated fully with the Italian conquerors. The four main Ethiopian archbishops, however, did not collaborate, leading to widespread unpopularity for the church's head. Kerlos finally denounced the Italian invaders and was replaced by Ethiopia's fascist administrators. They installed an Ethiopian-born cleric who collaborated with them until his death, in

1939. When Haile Selassie was restored to his throne in 1941, he was confronted with two "heads" of the Ethiopian church, Kerlos—who had initially collaborated but who had ultimately rebelled and been deposed—and another who had been a willing tool of the Italian conquerors. Not liking either of the possibilities, the emperor played a waiting game. Within a year both archbishops died, and the emperor maneuvered to install a cleric more to his liking.

See also: AKSUM (Vols. I, II); ARK OF THE COVENANT (Vol. I); CHRISTIANITY, INFLUENCE OF (Vol. IV); COPTIC CHRISTIANITY (Vol. II); MAKEDA, QUEEN (Vol. I); TRADITIONAL RELIGION (Vol. I).

Ethiopianism Religious movement, begun in SOUTH AFRICA, that encouraged the development of African-led Christian churches independent of European influence. Ethiopianism and its message of African empowerment foreshadowed the NATIONALISM AND INDEPENDENCE MOVEMENTS that pushed for African equality in the political realm.

Some of the leaders of African churches worked in conjunction with independent black churches in the United States to develop a Christian theology more culturally appropriate to Africans. In 1915 one such leader, John CHILEMBWE (c. 1872–1915) of the Providence Industrial Mission, led an uprising against unfair British taxation in NYASALAND (present-day MALAWI). The rebellion failed, but it helped make conscientious Christians around the world more aware of the oppression faced by African Christians under COLONIAL RULE.

In the 1880s black missionary workers in southern and Central Africa were not allowed to move up in the hierarchy of paternalistic, European-run missionary churches. As a result black religious leaders began establishing their own independent churches with messages that better reflected the African perspective. In 1892 a former Protestant minister in South Africa, Mangena Mokone (1851–1931), founded such a church and used the term *Ethiopianism* to describe its Africa-centric beliefs.

Mentioned often in the Bible, where it is called Kush, Ethiopia not only held positive connotations for black Christians in Africa, but also served as a symbolic ancestral homeland for many people of African descent in North and South America. The historical glory of Kush and Ethiopia was a touchstone for many of the Africanist

During the colonial era, British East Africa became the world's largest exporter of sisal. In this undated photo, African women laborers dry the sisal before it is made into rope and twine. © *ECA Photo*

movements that became increasingly influential in the 20th century. Ethiopia's cultural independence, maintained even during the height of colonialism, made the kingdom an even more powerful symbol. The influence of Ethiopianism can be seen in the Africa-for-the-Africans movement, PAN-AFRICANISM, the BACK-TO-AFRICA MOVEMENT, African Zionism, and Rastafarianism. By the beginning of the 20th century independent African churches and numerous sub-sects were established in NIGERIA, CAMEROON, and GOLD COAST COLONY (now GHANA). By the 1950s churches with Ethiopianist views existed throughout West Africa and were present in KENYA, SOUTHERN RHODESIA (now ZIMBABWE), and NORTHERN RHODESIA (now ZAMBIA).

See also: BLYDEN, EDWARD WILMOT (Vol. IV); CASELY-HAYFORD, J. E. (Vol. IV); CHRISTIANITY, INFLUENCE OF (Vol. IV, V); GARVEY, MARCUS (Vol. IV); KUSH (Vol. I); RASTAFARIANISM (Vol. V); RELIGION (Vol. IV, V); RESISTANCE AND REBELLION (Vol. IV).

Further reading: Bengt Sundkler and Christopher Steed, *A History of the Church in Africa* (New York: Cambridge University Press, 2000).

Europe and Africa *See* BELGIUM AND AFRICA (Vol. IV); BERLIN CONFERENCE (Vol. IV); COLONIAL CONQUEST (Vol. IV); COLONIALISM, INFLUENCE OF (Vol. IV); COLONIAL RULE (Vol. IV); CONCESSIONAIRE COMPANIES (Vol. IV); DECOLONIZATION (Vol. IV); ENGLAND AND AFRICA (Vols. III, IV, IV, V); EUROPE AND AFRICA (Vol. V); EXPORTS (Vol. IV); FRANCE AND AFRICA (Vols. III, IV, V); GERMANY AND AFRICA (Vol. IV); ITALY AND AFRICA (Vol. IV); LEAGUE OF NATIONS AND AFRICA (Vol. IV); MISSIONARIES (Vol. IV); PARTITION (Vol. IV); PORTUGAL AND AFRICA (Vols. III, IV, V); SETTLERS, EUROPEAN (Vol. IV); SLAVE TRADE (Vol. IV); SPAIN AND AFRICA (Vols. IV, V); TRADE AND COMMERCE (Vol. IV); UNITED NATIONS AND AFRICA (Vols. IV, V); WORLD WAR I AND AFRICA (Vol. IV); WORLD WAR II AND AFRICA (Vol. IV).

exploration *See* BAKER, SIR SAMUEL (Vol. IV); BARTH, HEINRICH (Vol. IV); BURTON, SIR RICHARD (Vol. IV); EXPLORATION (Vol. III); KIRK, SIR JOHN (Vol. IV); NIGER EXPEDITION (Vol. III); SPEKE, JOHN HANNING (Vol. IV).

exports During the colonial era African economies shifted to single-commodity export systems in order to provide European markets with raw goods. The negative effects of these policies are still felt today. Prior to colonization there was vibrant trade between different parts of Africa—West Africa, the SWAHILI COAST, the Nile River Valley—and other parts of the world. Goods exported to the benefit of traders and coastal African states included grains, crops, wood products, oils, minerals, cloth, leather, and iron products. The arrival of colonial interests, however, changed the terms of trade.

Colonial states were required to seek economic self-sufficiency while providing cheap sources of raw goods to drive European markets. This led to one of the fundamental shifts in Africa during the colonial era—the focus on an export-driven ECONOMY. Economies that once were diversified were transformed into mono-mineral or MONOCROP ECONOMIES producing in large quantity that which they could best export to Europe. This process resulted in high economic volatility and an increased dependency of African economies on European markets.

For example, COTTON was grown in NIGERIA as early as the 15th century by farmers on small, mixed plots. In 1902 the British government began encouraging greater cotton production in Nigeria in an effort to reduce British reliance on cotton sources in the United States. By 1905 Nigeria was producing large amounts of cotton for the British market, and demand only increased with the onset of World War I (1914–18). By the 1920s cotton was the dominant Nigerian export, with 70 percent of all Nigerian cotton going to the United Kingdom. In spite of Nigeria's production, with the onset of World War II (1939–45) British-American ties were strengthened, and the need for Nigerian cotton was significantly reduced. As a result the price of Nigerian cotton collapsed, and the Nigerian export economy, so dependent on cotton, was severely damaged.

In the postwar period Britain made significant attempts to increase Nigerian cotton production—and, therefore, prices—but these efforts failed. The export promotion was driven by the United Kingdom's postwar crisis, not Nigerian economic need. In the end the United Kingdom was unable to revive the Nigerian cotton industry that it had created and then allowed to collapse.

Similar export schemes, such as Portuguese cultivation of cotton in ANGOLA and MOZAMBIQUE, French promotion of GROUNDNUTS (peanuts) in SENEGAL and rice in MADAGASCAR, and British promotion of COFFEE and tea in KENYA and UGANDA all led to similar economic dependencies and volatilities. Perhaps the greatest long-term impact of these export economies was the introduction of MINING in southern Central Africa. The development of the COPPERBELT, which extended from Katanga, in what was the BELGIAN CONGO, into the British colony of NORTHERN RHODESIA (present-day ZAMBIA), was especially important.

Some scholars argue that by extracting surplus goods, rather than investing them in development, European powers propelled their own economies forward while stifling African countries and reducing their potential for growth. Other scholars argue that this process linked hitherto independent African economies to the great potential of the global economy. Regardless, the impact of single-commodity export systems created during the colonial era is still felt today as countries struggle to retool their economies.

See also: CLOTH AND TEXTILES (Vol. IV); EXPORTS (Vol. V); TRADE AND COMMERCE (Vols. I, II, III, IV, V).

Further reading: Peter Duignana and L. H. Gann, *Colonialism in Africa 1870–1960: Vol. 4, The Economics of Colonialism* (London: Cambridge University Press, 1975); John R. Hanson, *Trade in Transition: Exports from the Third World, 1840–1900* (New York: Academic Press, 1980).

F

Faidherbe, Louis (1818–1889) *French general and scholar*

Born in Lille, France, Faidherbe studied at the École Polytechnique to become a military engineer. Beginning in 1844 he served abroad in ALGERIA and the West Indies. In 1852 he relocated to SENEGAL, a French colony on the coast of West Africa, serving as sub-director of engineers. Two years later he became governor of Senegal.

At the time, French Senegal was composed only of a coastal strip and the island settlement of Saint-Louis. As governor, Faidherbe began planning ambitious expansion, envisioning a French colonial empire extending to the Red Sea. In 1857 he founded the French fort that became the city of DAKAR, a major port and eventual capital of FRENCH WEST AFRICA and present-day Senegal. In 1858 he annexed territories inhabited by the WOLOF people.

The main opposition Faidherbe faced was from al-Hajj UMAR TAL (1794–1864), the head of the Tijaniyya Islamic brotherhood. In 1852 Umar declared a JIHAD that led to the founding of the TUKULOR EMPIRE, which eventually encompassed much of the land east of the Senegal River and along the middle Niger River. Faidherbe pushed the advancing Tukulors back, setting up French outposts along the Upper Senegal River. In 1860 he signed a treaty with Umar that restricted the Tukulor empire to the northern side of the Senegal River. With the annexation of Cayor and the other Wolof states in 1865, Faidherbe secured the land between the Senegal and Gambia rivers and created the foundation of what would become, in 1895, French West Africa.

Having extended France's colonial reach and having developed the economy of Senegal based on the peasant production of GROUNDNUTS (peanuts) as an export crop, Faidherbe resigned from his post as governor in 1861.

See also: COLONIAL CONQUEST (Vol. IV); FRANCE AND AFRICA (Vols. III, V).

family

In important ways, during the colonial era African family life and family structures remained rooted in traditions and values of the precolonial past. Among the most important of these was the notion that "a person is a person because of people," and that it is the people of one's family who are paramount in this sense. Individuals remained rooted in a network of social and economic family relationships that enabled them to meet the challenges of life. These included obtaining the necessary resources, such as bride-wealth to enter into marriage, assistance with work, support in old age, and so forth.

Despite the many continuities, however, African families began to undergo major changes. One of the most important of these was in the sphere of LABOR. Whereas earlier, most people worked within the context of the family enterprise, whether it be farming, trade, or some other activity, under COLONIAL RULE individuals increasingly worked outside and away from the family. These newly emerging patterns of labor took two forms. One was that of wage labor, which provided families with the resources for purchasing FOOD and other necessities rather than producing their own food and making or trading for other goods such as pottery or tools. This process was also closely linked to the growth of TRADE AND COMMERCE in the colonial ECONOMY, which also provided luxury goods for sale. The rapid rate of URBANIZATION was another factor that promoted wage labor.

Urbanization also was a factor in the other emerging labor pattern: labor migration. The development of the

MINING industry depended on a large pool of labor. The GOLD mines in SOUTH AFRICA drew migrant workers from hundreds of miles away, with that country's laws forcing men to leave their families in the rural areas. The COCOA farms of West Africa similarly depended on seasonal migrant laborers, who came mostly from the interior.

Not all families were affected by the shifts in labor, but the changes were drastic for those families that were affected. For example, wage labor meant working outside the family and therefore outside the family-based ECONOMY that had been typical of rural Africa for many centuries. Families thus lost some of their economic autonomy by becoming dependent on economic forces outside their control. This was the case even more so if workers migrated to the urban areas and lost access to land for farming. To some degree the extended family structure helped mitigate these changes, since some family members continued to reside in the rural areas and engage in AGRICULTURE.

With colonialism, the role of children also diminished, since their economic importance to the family was diminished. Sending a child to school only compounded the economic challenges because children then became an economic liability due to school fees and the need to buy books and clothing.

Finally, migrant labor was disruptive to the institution of marriage, as many male migrants never returned home to their wives and families. Sometimes this was because they had died while working their difficult jobs, but more often it was because they remained in the cities where they often started new families. Changes like these continued into the era of African independence.

See also: BRIDE-WEALTH (Vol. I); FAMILY (Vols. I, II, III, V).

Further reading: Mario Azevedo, "The African Family," in *Africana Studies: A Survey of Africa and the African Diaspora,* 3rd ed. (Durham, N.C.: Carolina Academic Press, 2004).

Fanon, Frantz (1925–1961) *French psychiatrist and philosopher*

Born in the French colony of Martinique in the Caribbean, Fanon had a middle-class upbringing. In high school he was taught by the poet Aimé CÉSAIRE (1913–   ), who exposed Fanon to the literary and cultural movement known as NÉGRITUDE. Fanon was especially attracted to the belief that there was a pan-African consciousness that, once developed, could help the people of the AFRICAN DIASPORA overcome political and social repression.

In 1943 Fanon left Martinique to fight alongside the Free French in World War II (1939–45). After the war he stayed in Lyon, France, where he studied MEDICINE and psychiatry. In 1952 he left France to serve as a psychiatrist for the colonial administration in ALGERIA. That same year Fanon published *Peau noire, masques blancs* (Black skin, white masks), in which he examined issues of colonization and racism. Turning away from the peaceful tenets of Négritude, he instead advocated violent rebellion as the only legitimate means of empowerment for the people of the colonized Third World. The work became a major influence for minority and opposition movements not only in Africa but also in America, Europe, Canada, and Northern Ireland.

Fanon resigned from his position and became an outspoken proponent of the Algerian nationalist cause. He even participated in the war, staying in rebel guerrilla camps, harboring Algerian fighters, and providing medical instruction to nurses. After being severely wounded in 1959, Fanon briefly served as the ambassador to GHANA for the provisional Algerian government. At this time he also established the first psychiatric clinic in Africa.

Fanon died in 1961 of leukemia while in Washington, D.C., one year before Algeria won its independence. That same year his book, *The Wretched of the Earth,* was published. Developed out of his experiences in war-torn Algeria, it became a virtual handbook of the black liberation movement.

See also: FRANCE AND AFRICA (Vol. IV); NATIONALISM AND INDEPENDENCE MOVEMENTS (Vol. IV).

Further reading: William W. Hansen, *A Frantz Fanon Study Guide* (New York: Grove Press, 1996); David Macey, *Frantz Fanon: a Life* (London: Granta Books, 2000).

Fante Confederation (Fanti Confederation) Alliance of kingdoms inhabited by the Fante people of the coastal region of present-day GHANA. Until it was dissolved in the 1870s this coalition of AKAN states, unofficially begun during the late 17th century, vied for political and commercial control of the region with the powerful ASHANTI EMPIRE, which also was made up of Akan groups.

During the era of the transatlantic SLAVE TRADE, a loose alliance of Fante kingdoms had established trading partnerships with Britain—ties that remained strong even after the British officially outlawed slave trading, in 1807. On the other hand the Ashanti, a group living to the north of the coastal Fante kingdoms, had allied themselves with the Dutch, who maintained trade in Fante territory.

In the 19th century a series of ANGLO-ASHANTI WARS—initiated, in part, by the encroachment of the Ashanti on Fante kingdoms—greatly weakened the Ashanti Empire. As a result, by the 1830s the Fante leaders had agreements with the Ashanti that secured their use of the coastal trading routes. Simultaneous agreements with Britain essentially made the collective Fante states a PROTECTORATE of the British Empire.

Eventually, in 1867, Fante opposition to foreign European trading activity came to a head when the British bought the remaining Dutch trading forts on the coast without seeking either the opinion or the approval of the Fante leaders, as had been the accepted custom. Further, the Ashanti were once again threatening Fante territory from the north, and the British were doing little to stop them. In 1868 Fante leaders proposed a more formal Fante Confederation, which assembled in 1871 at Mankessim, the center of Fante culture.

Although the British had encouraged the organization of the Fante Confederation, they also recognized that this newly constituted alliance could threaten their own hegemony on the coast. In an attempt to protect their interests the British arrested the Fante leaders and charged them with treason. The prisoners were soon released, but the British actions had successfully broken apart the confederation, which by 1873 was dissolved, leaving the British the sole authority in the region. In spite of these developments, however, the British and Fante remained allies, and the following year they combined to defeat the Ashanti at KUMASI, the Ashanti capital. After the victory Britain formally declared the GOLD COAST COLONY, and as part of the colony former Fante territory came under British protection and administration.

In the 17th century the Fante alliance was governed by a _brafo_, or high king, with the assistance of a high priest. In the 19th century, however, the Fante Confederation wrote a constitution that provided their state with a governing body, a judicial system, taxation, and an army.

See also: ASHANTI (Vol. II); FANTE (Vol. II); NETHERLANDS AND AFRICA (Vol. III); DENKYIRA (Vol. IV); ELMINA (Vol. III); ENGLAND AND AFRICA (Vols. IV).

Further reading: Mary McCarthy, _Social Change and the Growth of British Power in the Gold Coast: The Fante States, 1807–1874_ (Lanham, Md.: University Press of America, 1983).

Faruk, King (Farouk, Faruq, Farrukh)
(1920–1965) _King of Egypt (r. 1936–1952)_

King Faruk succeeded his father, King Fuad I (1869–1936), to the throne in 1936. Too young to rule in his own right, however, he ruled through a regent, Prince Mehmet Ali, until he was 18. Educated in EGYPT and Britain, Faruk was at first embraced by Egyptians because he was young, handsome, and wealthy, and because he represented the Arabic-speaking Muslim elite.

In the year that Faruk came to the throne, the nationalist WAFD PARTY won a majority of seats in the parliamentary elections. The new Wafd prime minister, Mustafa al-Nahas Pasha (1879–1965), and his cabinet negotiated the Anglo-Egyptian Treaty of 1936. Among its important provisions, the new treaty signed by King Faruk granted Britain a 20-year lease on a large military base for the defense of the SUEZ CANAL and additional military bases in ALEXANDRIA and CAIRO. In spite of the ANGLO-EGYPTIAN CONDOMINIUM of 1899, which placed the Sudan under joint British and Egyptian rule, the new treaty left Britain in almost total control of the Sudan. Although the Wafd Party continued to press for full Egyptian control over the Sudan, many Egyptians thought that the party had betrayed Egypt's best interests, bringing about a decline in its influence.

While Faruk appeared to have nationalist sympathies, Prime Minister al-Nahas Pasha's government lasted only 18 months. Thereafter Faruk, who like his father, King Fuad, saw the Wafd Party as a bitter rival, systematically found ways to exclude the party from power.

At the outset of World War II (1939–45) British military units were stationed in Egypt. Few Egyptians were pro-British, and Faruk tried to maintain the nation's neutrality despite the presence of foreign troops. The political conflict reached a peak when Faruk rigged the election of 1939 and installed a prime minister who favored neutrality. The British ambassador and high commissioner, Sir Miles Lampson (1880–1964), forced the king at gunpoint to call new elections and accept a pro-British government.

The return to power in 1942 of former Wafd prime minister Mustafa al-Nahas Pasha was taken as a public humiliation both of the king and of the Egyptian people, who nurtured their resentment of the British. After 10 years of Faruk's rule Egypt had lost its sovereignty, and Egypt's subjects had lost respect for their king.

In an effort to restore his popularity with the people, King Faruk attempted to assert himself as the leader of the Arab world. In 1945 Egypt became a founding member of the Arab League, allying Egypt with Syria, Lebanon, Iraq, Transjordan (now Jordan), Saudi Arabia, and Yemen, and became committed to the Arab cause in Palestine. However, the Arab-Israeli War of 1948 failed to halt the establishment of the state of Israel, and Egypt's defeat in this war further discredited Faruk's regime. The 1952 "Black Saturday" uprising in Cairo, led to a coup d'état by Egyptian army officers led by Colonel Gamal Abdel NASSER (1918–1970). Forced to abdicate, King Faruk was sent into permanent exile.

Faruk owned palaces, houses, a private train, and two yachts, but he especially favored cars. He collected 200 of them, including a Mercedes-Benz given to him by Adolph Hitler (1889–1945), the Nazi dictator of Germany. Because of his expensive lifestyle, Faruk became known as the Playboy King. Photographs from this time show a bloated, decadent figure who is unlike the young, handsome Faruk who first came to power.

See also: ARAB-ISRAELI WARS (Vol. IV); COUP D'ÉTAT (Vol. V); ENGLAND AND AFRICA (Vol. IV).

Further reading: William Stadiem, *Too Rich: The High Life and Tragic Death of King Farouk* (New York: Carroll & Graf, 1991); Adel M. Sabit, *A King Betrayed: The Ill-fated Reign of Farouk of Egypt* (London: Quartet, 1989).

Fashoda Village in southeastern Republic of the SUDAN that in 1898 was the site of an diplomatic standoff between Britain and France. Located on the western bank of the White Nile River in southern Sudan, the small town of Fashoda brought two of Europe's great powers to the brink of war. The BERLIN CONFERENCE (1884–85) had divided up the African continent and assigned portions of it to the various European colonial powers as "spheres of influence." This system encouraged France to try to secure a colonial domain running across the continent from FRENCH WEST AFRICA to FRENCH SOMALILAND, on the far eastern point of the Horn of Africa. For its part, Britain was most concerned with control of the entire Nile River Valley because of its imagined strategic importance to EGYPT, which it had occupied beginning in 1882.

In 1897 the French determined to occupy the sparsely populated territory of southern Sudan to support their east-west expansion. Under the command of Jean-Baptiste Marchand (1863–1934), French forces marched north from the administrative center at BRAZZAVILLE in Central Africa, reaching the outpost at Fashoda by the middle of 1898. There they beat back an attack by Islamic MAHDIYYA forces and awaited French reinforcements, who were to come from ETHIOPIA, to the east.

Britain, fresh off its victory over the Mahdiyya at the Battle of OMDURMAN, learned of the French activity and sent soldiers, led by Horatio Herbert KITCHENER (1850–1916), to assert its claim to the area. The larger British forces dared the bedraggled French to oppose them, and for a while the French government considered taking action. Eventually, however, French officials deemed it unnecessary to go to war over a remote outpost in the Sudanese desert. The crisis, now known as the Fashoda Incident or the Fashoda Affair, was solved through diplomatic negotiations back on the European continent. In the end Britain agreed to recognize French control of southern MOROCCO in the western Sahara, and France agreed to recognize English sovereignty in Egypt and Sudan.

See also: ENGLAND AND AFRICA (Vol. IV); FRANCE AND AFRICA (Vol. IV); PARTITION (Vol. IV).

Further reading: Hillas Smith, *The Unknown Frenchman: The Story of Marchand and Fashoda* (Sussex, U.K.: Book Guild, Ltd.: 2001).

FLN See NATIONAL LIBERATION FRONT.

Fon People of West Africa. The powerful Fon kingdom was part of DAHOMEY, which was centered in the southern portion of the present-day Republic of BENIN. The Fon, originally part of the Oyo empire in NIGERIA, reached the apex of their power in the middle of the 19th century, building their kingdom's wealth on the trade in enemy captives. Their culture was marked by an intricate political structure, with the king ruling over a hierarchy of government officials who oversaw the daily activities of the kingdom. The Fon were also noted for their annual festivals that included an airing of grievances, a review of policy decisions, and ritual sacrifices.

> **Fon religious practices centered around the *vodun*, or sacred spirits. Fon captives, transported to Cuba, brought with them their vodun beliefs, which would form the basis for the practice of the Voodoo RELIGION.**

During the early 1890s France invaded Dahomey in an effort to strengthen its position along the West African coast. The Fon king, Behazin (d. 1906), did not readily capitulate and battled the French until his defeat in 1892. He did not sign a treaty with France, however, and was exiled first to Martinique and then to ALGERIA. The French appointed a distant relative of Behazin as king, who did sign a treaty with France. The treaty established a French PROTECTORATE in the area and ended the independence of Dahomey, making it one of the last of the historical African kingdoms to succumb to European colonization.

> **During the war with the French, the exploits of Dahomey's women warriors came to light. Referred to as *Amazons* by Europeans, the 4,000 women soldiers were fiercely loyal to the king and were considered more skilled than their male counterparts.**

See also: COLONIAL CONQUEST (Vol. IV); FON (Vol. III); FRANCE AND AFRICA (Vols. III, IV, V).

Further reading: Stanley P. Alpern, *Amazons of Black Sparta: The Women Warriors of Dahomey* (New York: New York University Press, 1998); Edna G. Bay, *Wives of the Leopard: Gender, Politics, and Culture in the Kingdom of Dahomey* (Charlottesville, Va.: University of Virginia Press, 1998).

food As of the mid-19th century the food that Africans consumed came almost exclusively from the FOOD CROPS they grew or the livestock they raised. The principal foods people ate varied according to region and growing conditions, including climate and soils. For example, sorghum, which originated in Africa and was one the world's earliest crops, and pearl millet, another very early African crop, were ideally suited to the rainfall-based AGRICULTURE common to the drier savanna regions. Women used a mortar and pestle to ground these grains into flour that was then boiled with water to make porridges. In many countries porridges formed the food staple, and whenever possible people served them with soup made from various combinations of vegetables, fish, and meat.

People in UGANDA used ungerminated millet flour to prepare a sour porridge called *bushera*. Into this they then mixed freshly germinated millet to sweeten the porridge and give it a thinner consistency. The mix began to ferment in a few days to become an alcoholic drink.

Farmers in the highlands of ETHIOPIA grew *enset* (sometimes called the "false banana"), which looks like a large, thick, single-stemmed banana plant. Enset was the base for a fermented starch that was used to prepare a pancake-like bread known as *kocho*, which could also be served with raw ground beef mixed with butter and spices. Finger millet and teff, also among the earliest human crops, were important grains in Ethiopia. Basic to the diet of North Africans were barley and coarse bulgur wheat. Bananas, which first entered Africa from Southeast Asia 2,000 years ago, were a staple food in much of tropical Africa. In Uganda the central component of the diet was a dish known as *matoke* made from mashed unripe bananas steamed in banana leaves and often served with some meat stew.

After about 1500, crops originating in the Americas spread throughout much of Africa. The most important of these was maize (corn), which by the 1800s had become the most widely cultivated food plant in Africa. Other important American food crops were manioc (cassava), the sweet potato, and GROUNDNUTS (peanuts). By the late 19th century farmers in SENEGAL used their earnings from groundnut sales to buy rice exported to them by French planters in colonial Indochina. Increasingly, imports of non-traditional crops, such as white wheat, also supplied the sub-Saharan urban markets. This wheat was used for baking the bread that became "bachelors' food" in cities such as Yaoundé, where African males came to work, leaving their families behind.

Baked bread is an example of the western foods that accompanied COLONIAL RULE in Africa. Europeans wanted to consume food and beverages with which they were familiar, so they introduced their foreign diets along with other aspects of their culture to Africa. The English, for example, were a country of tea drinkers. In addition to establishing tea plantations in NYASALAND (today's MALAWI) and elsewhere, they established the custom of drinking tea, consumed with sugar and milk in their colonies. Shops in both rural and urban areas soon stocked tea, along with sugar and tinned milk, for their African customers. The German population of SOUTH WEST AFRICA (today's NAMIBIA), too, brought with them their taste for European-style drink. From the turn of the century until the end of WORLD WAR I (1914–1918), four large German-owned breweries—and a number of smaller ones—thrived.

By 1960 the patterns of African food consumption had changed considerably from a century earlier. Although for most people the food that made up their diet remained similar to earlier times, even for them items such as tea had become important for consumption. In the cities, these patterns had undergone even more significant change in the context of URBAN LIFE AND CULTURE.

See also: FOOD (Vols. I, II, III, V).

food crops Crops grown principally for consumption by the producers rather than as CASH CROPS, which are grown principally for the market. Food crop AGRICULTURE is often called *subsistence agriculture*. Until recent decades Africa has been overwhelmingly a continent of farmers who grew crops and raised livestock mainly to meet their own FOOD needs. Although African farmers may have sold or bartered some of their surplus production or given it up to meet the demands of colonial TAXATION, they did not grow food and other crops primarily for the market.

In the mid-19th century African farmers raised various types of crops for their own food. Some crops, such as sorghum and yams, were indigenous to the continent. Some, such as wheat and barley, were external to Africa but had been grown, particularly in North Africa, for thousands of years. Other crops were introduced within the past 1500 or so years. The first of these newer crops was the banana, which came into Africa from Southeast Asia in the second half of the first millennium. After 1500, crops originating in the Americas spread throughout much of Africa. The most important of these was maize (corn), which had become the most widely cultivated food plant in Africa by the 1800s. Other important American food crops were manioc (cassava), the sweet potato, and GROUNDNUTS (peanuts).

The early 19th century witnessed the emergence of cash crop production in Africa. Among the first cash crops were food crops such as groundnuts, first cultivated in the SENEGAMBIA REGION of West Africa, and PALM OIL, which originated in NIGERIA and DAHOMEY (today's Republic of BENIN). These crops also continued to make important contributions to the African diet.

With the onset of COLONIAL RULE, the production of cash crops accelerated at the expense of traditional food crops. This was especially true after the end of World War I (1914–18). The colonial agricultural research services concentrated on improving crops for export, neglecting the ones that Africans grew for their own food. Indeed, in SENEGAL rural Africans used their earnings from groundnut sales to buy rice exported by French planters in colonial Indochina. Market opportunities for locally produced food crops also developed within Africa at this time. For example, West African market women such as Madam Alimotu PELEWURA (c. 1865–1951) became an economic force by selling food grown in the rural areas to the urban LABOR force.

In southern Africa, agriculture was increasingly in the hands of European SETTLERS, who produced food for the rapidly expanding cities of JOHANNESBURG and CAPE TOWN. Government policy in SOUTH AFRICA and SOUTH-ERN RHODESIA had squeezed Africans off the land and forced them into wage labor. These displaced people then had to purchase their food instead of growing it as their ancestors had done.

By 1960 Africa's agricultural structure and food production capabilities were substantially different from what they had been a century earlier. The colonial emphasis on producing cash crops for export had diverted both land and labor from the production of food crops. Moreover, beginning about 1950 Africa's rate of population growth also accelerated, reaching 3 percent per year by 1960. This combination of stagnating, if not declining, food crop production and booming population had dire implications for the rest of the century. In essence, by the time that Africa was achieving its independence from colonial rule the food crisis of the late 20th century was already in the making.

See also: BANANA (Vol. II); CASSAVA (Vol. II); COLONIALISM, INFLUENCE OF (Vol. IV); EXPORTS (Vol. IV); FOOD CROPS (Vol. V); MILLET (Vol. I); PALM OIL (Vols. III, IV); SORGHUM (Vol. I); YAMS (Vol. I).

Further reading: R. Hunt Davis, Jr., "Agriculture, Food, and the Colonial Period," in Art Hansen and Della E. McMillan, eds., *Food in Sub-Saharan Africa* (Boulder, Colo.: Lynne Rienner Publishers, Inc., 1986); Jane I. Guyer, ed., *Feeding African Cities* (Bloomington, Ind.: Indiana University Press, 1987).

Fort Hare College First college for black students in SOUTH AFRICA. Fort Hare College was created in response to reports by a government commission that discovered that many African students were traveling overseas to pursue further EDUCATION. Concerned that the students might be exposed to "radical" ideas that would lead to involvement in politics upon their return home, the commission recommended establishing an institute of higher learning for Africans within South Africa. There were also strong advocates in the African community of such a higher education institution. Especially prominent in this respect were the newspaper editor John Tengo JABAVU (1859–1921) and the educator and political leader John L. DUBE (1871–1946).

Originally called the South African Native College, the school finally opened in 1916. At its opening the prime minister of the UNION OF SOUTH AFRICA, General Louis BOTHA (1862–1919), was the featured speaker and guest. Located in the town of Alice, in the Eastern Cape Province, the college was established on lands once occupied by the colonial military post of Fort Hare. Alice was also the site of the country's leading secondary school for Africans, Lovedale, which was operated by the Church of Scotland. In 1949 the college became affiliated with Rhodes University, located in nearby Grahamstown, and, the following year, the name of the institution was changed to the University College of Fort Hare.

Although it was segregated according to race, in many ways Fort Hare enjoyed a more relaxed racial climate than the country at large. Its student body included Africans, Coloureds, and Indians, and was made up of both men and women, who came from throughout southern and eastern Africa. Influential alumni of the college include Seretse KHAMA (1921–1980), who was president of BOTSWANA from 1966 to 1980, Robert Mugabe (1924–   ), the future president of ZIMBABWE, and Yusufu Lule (1911–1985), who briefly served as the interim president of UGANDA in 1979. Although the faculty was mainly white, two of its most respected professors, D. D. T JABAVU (1885–1959) and Zachariah Keodirelang Matthews (1901–1968) were black Africans. Matthews received the first bachelor's degree the college awarded in 1923 and later earned a master's degree in anthropology from Yale University.

Fort Hare offered its students a lively intellectual and political environment. Many of South Africa's most illustrious and influential African political figures attended Fort Hare in the late 1930s and early 1940s. Among these figures were the key AFRICAN NATIONAL CONGRESS leaders Nelson MANDELA (1918–   ), Govan MBEKI (1910–2001), and Oliver TAMBO (1917–1993); the founder of the PAN-AFRICANIST CONGRESS, Robert SOBUKWE (1924–1978); and Mangosuthu Buthelezi (1928–   ), founder and head of the Inkatha Freedom Party.

Following the imposition of APARTHEID policy in 1948, Fort Hare students staged frequent protests, which were often dealt with severely. In 1959 the South African government took control of Fort Hare and placed the school under the strictures of Bantu Education. Thereafter, Fort Hare College was transformed into an institution exclusively for XHOSA students.

See also: BANTU EDUCATION (Vol. V); FORT HARE COLLEGE (Vol. V).

Fourah Bay College First college in Africa offering a Western-style EDUCATION, located in FREETOWN, SIERRA LEONE. The CHURCH MISSIONARY SOCIETY (CMS) founded Fourah Bay College in 1827. Its primary goal was to train freed Africans and RECAPTIVES to become pastors who could help white MISSIONARIES spread the Christian gospel to the interior of West Africa. The origins of the college lay with the Christian Institution, which the CMS established in 1814 as a school and boarding home for liberated boys and girls. In 1827 CMS revitalized the Christian Institution with the formal establishment of Fourah Bay College. The early curriculum included an English course, Arabic, local languages, Latin, Greek, and Bible studies. The early phase of Fourah Bay College concentrated on Christian teachings and the creation of "Black English gentlemen." Classes taught mostly Western and English civilization to young Africans, who then became more assimilated into English culture.

Fourah Bay's first graduates included Samuel Ajayi CROWTHER (1808–1891), the first African Anglican bishop of West Africa and the future head of the CMS Niger Mission, and James Africanus Beale HORTON (1835–1883), who was sent to England after his studies at Fourah Bay to become a medical doctor. Horton later joined the British Navy, worked in the GOLD COAST COLONY, and became deeply involved with the FANTE CONFEDERATION and the rise of African nationalism in general. An important member of the faculty at this time was Edward Wilmot BLYDEN (1832–1912), also a strong proponent of black nationalism.

Among the many leaders of Fourah Bay College was an African-American, Edward A. Jones, who served as principal in the 1860s. Hailing from Charleston, South Carolina, Jones was an influential figure in the emergence of public displays of black nationalism.

In 1876 Fourah Bay College ceased being a strictly missionary institution and became associated with Durham University, in England. This affiliation led to a radical change of curriculum, with the college adding courses in secular subjects such as history, natural science, French, and German.

On the eve of World War II (1939–45) the colonial government took over the financial responsibility of Fourah Bay College, thereby giving it a solid public-funding base. It was also during this period that Britain established a review commission to make recommendations regarding the future of higher education in its West African colonies. As Sierra Leone moved toward DECOLONIZATION, the college soon entered a new phase of development, with additional degree and diploma courses. It also continued its history of offering theological training. New faculty and administrative personnel, some from overseas, were part of the expansion and renewal of the college, which continued into the 1950s and beyond.

In 1967 the University of Sierra Leone Act placed Fourah Bay under the umbrella of the new University of Sierra Leone, ending its affiliation with the University of Durham. Today, Fourah Bay College is run by Sierra Leoneans, most of whom are graduates of the college.

See also: CHRISTIANITY, INFLUENCE OF (Vols. III, IV, V).

France and Africa Using the principles of association and assimilation, France carved out a colonial empire in sub-Saharan Africa, dominating it economically, politically, and culturally from 1880 to 1960.

Establishing French Colonialism During the 19th century, already in possession of Mediterranean North African enclaves, France began establishing its tropical African empire in 1854, when Louis FAIDHERBE (1818–1889) was appointed governor of SENEGAL. Faidherbe used France's claim to its original enclave—the QUATRE COMMUNES of St-Louis, Gorée, DAKAR, and Rufisque—to reinforce the French position and spread French control throughout the Senegal River valley. Further south, in equatorial Africa, France signed treaties with local Mpongwe chiefs in GABON, which became the administrative center for the colonies to follow.

After the Franco-Prussian War (1870) Europe expanded its control in Africa in an effort to satisfy the demands of industrial capitalism. In this sense Africa represented little more than a source of cheap raw materials and new markets for finished products. In 1884–85, the European powers (and the United States) convened for the BERLIN CONFERENCE, which formalized the European PARTITION of the continent and largely established the political boundaries that would define Africa in the era of COLONIAL CONQUEST.

Also in the 1880s France renewed its efforts to expand in Africa. From his base in Senegal Joseph GALLIENI (1849–1916) employed the TIRAILLEURS SÉNÉGALAIS, African soldiers, to help his colonial troops gain control of the rest of France's claim in West Africa. About 1875 France moved into the interior of equatorial Africa, with Pierre Savorgnan DE BRAZZA (1852–1905) exploring territories drained by the Congo River, which emptied into the Atlantic Ocean just south of Gabon. Competing for control with the Belgians, de Brazza lay claim to the upper reaches of the Congo River by making treaties with local inhabitants, including the Teke. In an attempt to connect equatorial regions with French claims in West and North Africa, France also competed with other European powers for land in central and eastern Africa.

Because direct French rule depended on educated Africans to play key governmental roles, the colonial administration offered Africans some educational opportunities. However, because the French simultaneously relied on uneducated Africans for their commercial LABOR force, these opportunities were deliberately limited.

France was convinced of its cultural superiority and took seriously its responsibility to spread that culture to its colonies in Overseas France. The French administration encouraged West Africans to absorb and adopt French culture so that they could become French citizens (the process of *assimilation*). Acquiring French citizenship gave Africans the right to form political parties and voluntary associations and to vote for a representative to the French Assembly in Paris. Throughout its colonial territories France signed treaties of "protection" with indigenous rulers, guaranteeing French sovereignty but allowing for local indigenous rule to be loosely supervised by French officials (the process that became known as *association*). Faidherbe's model of indirect rule was the most practical option in terms of France's financial commitment to governing its new African empire. However, later governors adopted a policy of direct rule, by which France imposed a hierarchy of French administrators on African subjects without interest in developing a citizenry.

Development of French Colonial Federations
In 1895 France established a federation of colonies known as FRENCH WEST AFRICA (Afrique Occidentale Française, AOF). Colonies in AOF included Senegal, GUINEA, FRENCH SOUDAN (now MALI), UPPER VOLTA (now BURKINA FASO), IVORY COAST, DAHOMEY (now the Republic of BENIN), MAURITANIA, and NIGER. In 1910, based on the AOF model, France established FRENCH EQUATORIAL AFRICA (Afrique Equatoriale Française, AEF). Colonies in that federation included CHAD, FRENCH CONGO (now the Republic of the CONGO), OUBANGUI-CHARI (now the CENTRAL AFRICAN REPUBLIC), and GABON.

The Ministry of the Colonies in Paris administered the two federations, appointing a governor-general for each federation and lieutenant governors for individual colonies. The duties of the governor-generals included advising the French Assembly on legislation, submitting a budget to the Ministry of the Colonies, and implementing French law and policy within the federation. Except for African individuals in the Quatre Communes (in today's Senegal), who were French citizens, colonial inhabitants were extended few of the rights and privileges enjoyed by the European inhabitants of the colonies.

While metropolitan France (the *metropole*) administered defense and foreign policy, the colonies were required by law to be self-supporting through a system of forced labor and taxation, which included some form of personal tax (head tax or poll tax) to be paid in currency. Because the wealth of the federation of AOF was unevenly distributed, the colonies with more resources subsidized those that lacked them. As a consequence some colonies were able to pay for their own administration but unable to pay for important social programs, such as universal EDUCATION. Many West Africans went from being economically self-sufficient to needing to import FOOD because they devoted too much of their land and their time to producing CASH CROPS. The people of AEF, on the other hand, had even fewer resources and educational facilities than those of AOF. To encourage development, the Ministry of Colonies granted operating rights and large tracts of land to 40 CONCESSIONAIRE COMPANIES.

Prior to World War I (1914–18), France used African taxes to develop and exploit the colonies' economic resources. In addition to paying for the colonial administration, taxes were used to build infrastructure such as railroads and ports in order to export products needed for French industrial development. These export products were agricultural goods, such as COTTON, peanuts, COFFEE, and RUBBER, and also included mineral resources, such as iron ore, bauxite, GOLD, and DIAMONDS.

Colonies in AOF financed their projects through two major French concessionaires, the Société Commerciale de l'Ouest Africain and the Compagnie Française de l'Afrique Occidentale, both of which were monopolies. In a process typical of European concessionaire companies throughout the African continent, these companies received subsidies from France to trade with the colonies. They also engaged in price fixing for purchasing cheap raw materials from the colonies, sold finished products back to the colonies at inflated prices, and invested their profits at home in Europe. In AEF concessionaire companies used local labor to produce huge amounts of ivory and rubber, paying a fixed-rate annual payment of 15 percent of profits to the *metropole* but making no investment in local infrastructure.

French Colonialism during Wartime French colonialism was in full effect at the outset of World War I. Elected to the French Assembly from the Quatre Communes, Blaise DIAGNE (1872–1934) recruited soldiers from French-speaking Africa to fight in the war. In addition, the colonies provided supplies to maintain France's soldiers during wartime. Despite African loyalty, at the end of the war Africans found that the rhetoric of colonial leaders who spoke of "self-determination" referred only to Europeans. Hopes for African independence would have to be deferred.

Following the Paris peace talks, in 1919 the League of Nations gave France the former equatorial German colonies of Kamerun (now CAMEROON) and TOGOLAND (now TOGO) as mandates to administer until those colonies were ready to achieve independence.

During the inter-war years France changed its economic philosophy to actively invest *metropole* money into the development of the overseas territories so that they could more efficiently produce raw materials for the European industrial complex. However, French social investment in health and education had to be cut back when world economies collapsed during the Great Depression (c. 1929–39). As a result of economic hardship African farmers increased production, but the strategy failed when their increased production further lowered prices.

World War II (1939–45) marked a turning point in the relationship between France and Africa. Germany overran France in 1940 and formed the Vichy government (1940–44), which was made up of French administrators who collaborated with the Germans. When the Vichy government moved into AOF, West Africans were incensed that France would capitulate to German demands regarding its African colonies. Compounding their anger was the fact that West African soldiers had readily supported France's efforts in World War I. Eventually Africans in AOF became so dissatisfied with the racist policies instituted by the Vichy administration that they provided men and materials to support the Free French resistance. On the other hand, Adolphe-Félix-Sylvestre ÉBOUÉ (1884–1944), the African governor of Chad, remained loyal to Free France from the outset. He offered AEF and Cameroon as the home base for Free French troops and actively rallied African soldiers to the Free French cause. (By one count, more than half of the Free French troops were Africans.) As a reward for Éboué's initiative, Free French leader Charles DE GAULLE (1890–1970) confirmed Éboué as the governor-general over AEF.

Near the end of the war de Gaulle called the Brazzaville Conference (1944) and announced his prescription for a reformed relationship between the colonies and the *metropole*, one in which France and its colonies would constitute a federation.

In 1944 Félix Éboué created a category called *notables évolués*. This new term elevated the status of those African elite who had become well educated in French culture but who had not opted for French citizenship.

With the formation of France's Fourth Republic in 1946, de Gaulle's promises of a changed relationship were kept, in theory if not in practice. The French Assembly es-

tablished the FRENCH UNION (1946–58), a federation that allowed France, as the dominant partner, to continue its control of the colonies. The Union encouraged political activity among African parties such as the AFRICAN DEMOCRATIC ASSEMBLY (Rassemblement Democratique Africain, RDA), led by Félix HOUPHOUËT-BOIGNY (1905–1993). The RDA grew into a multiethnic party with branches in the colonies of both federations. A host of the political parties that came together to form the RDA evolved into nationalist movements when individual countries began achieving independence from France.

The End of French Colonialism The year 1954 witnessed major challenges to French COLONIAL RULE. First, in Indochina, Ho Chi Minh (1890–1969) defeated the French at the battle of Dien Bien Phu (in what is now Vietnam). Then in ALGERIA the NATIONAL LIBERATION FRONT stepped up its activities, launching a war of independence against French settlers that would drag on for eight bloody years. In 1956 TUNISIA and MOROCCO were granted independence, and the French government underwent constitutional reforms, culminating in the passing of the *Loi Cadre* (Overseas Reform Act), in 1956. The changes provided by this law altered the structure of relations between France and its colonies, breaking apart the existing federations in a process now referred to as *balkanization*. The new laws conferred specific powers over local affairs to a popularly elected territorial government, while France retained its role in decision-making in issues involving defense and foreign policy. This balkanization divided the colonies into two camps: the federalists and the anti-federalists. Federalism had its staunchest supporters in Senegal's Léopold SENGHOR (1906–2001), and Guinea's Ahmed Sékou TOURÉ (1922–1984); the anti-federalist movement was supported mainly by France, Houphouët-Boigny in Ivory Coast, and Léon M'Ba (1902–1967) in Gabon.

In 1958 de Gaulle and the Fifth Republic created the French Community, modeled after the British Commonwealth. But unlike the Commonwealth, France continued to control the foreign policy of its member states. De Gaulle toured the former African colonies (now territories) to encourage them to join the French Community, emphasizing the economic and social advantages in store for its members. In a referendum held in France and throughout francophone Africa on September 28, 1958, the only colony to vote "no" to the French Community was Sékou Touré's Guinea. Trying to avert other defections from the Community, de Gaulle took punitive measures against Guinea, recalling French officials from the country and instructing Guinea's French expatriates to return all French equipment to France. Ultimately France removed everything from telephones to the city plans for Conakry, the Guinean capital. However, the French Community lasted only until 1960, when member states were granted independence without the threat of punishment.

See also: COLONIALISM, INFLUENCE OF (Vol. IV); FRANCE AND AFRICA (Vols. III, V).

Further reading: Anton Andereggen, *France's Relationship with Subsaharan Africa* (Westport, Conn.: Praeger, 1994); Edward L. Bimberg, *Tricolor over the Sahara: The Desert Battles of the Free French, 1940–1942* (Westport, Conn.: Greenwood Press, 2002); Christopher Harrison, *France and Islam in West Africa, 1860–1960* (New York: Cambridge University Press, 1988); Francis Terry McNamara, *France in Black Africa* (Washington, DC: National Defense University, 1989); Gloria D. Westfall, *French Colonial Africa: A Guide to Official Sources* (New York: Hans Zell Publishers, 1992); Dorothy Shipley White, *Black Africa and De Gaulle: From the French Empire to Independence* (University Park, Pa.: Pennsylvania State University Press, 1979).

Freedom Charter Document adopted at the Congress of the People on June 26, 1955, establishing a vision for an alternative to the APARTHEID-based society that predominated in SOUTH AFRICA. Originally suggested at the Congress of the AFRICAN NATIONAL CONGRESS (ANC) in 1953, the idea of creating a statement of fundamental principles for a new South Africa was quickly accepted by the ANC's key allies, the South African Indian Congress, the South African Coloured People's Organization, and the South African Congress of Democrats. Over the next several years key principles and statements were worked out. Then on June 25 and 26, 1955, the Congress of the People met in Kliptown, near JOHANNESBURG. There the points of the charter were read aloud and approved by acclamation. As a sign of the difficulties ahead, at the end of the meeting heavily armed police officers arrived on the scene, and, alleging that treason was probably being undertaken, they took the names of the almost 3,000 delegates and ordered them to leave. In this way, at the same time that the announcement of the charter ushered in a vision of a new future for South Africa, the police response indicated the obstacles and tactics that would have to be overcome in order to achieve that future.

Among its other points the charter contained clauses dealing with right of the South African people as a whole—not just whites—to govern, equal rights for all national groups, sharing the land among those who work on it, equality of all South Africans before the law, equal human rights for all, the right of people to work and be secure, equal access to educational and cultural institutions for all South Africans, decent housing for all, and peaceful relations with other countries.

Not surprisingly the white, Afrikaner government of South Africa rejected the entire philosophy and the political sentiments underlying the Freedom Charter. It soon began a far-reaching crackdown on political opponents, arresting and jailing many and driving others into exile.

There were also African opponents of the Freedom Charter. For example, the "Africanist" bloc of the ANC seceded in 1959 to form the PAN-AFRICANIST CONGRESS, which maintained that Africans were the only rightful inhabitants of South Africa.

The Preamble of the Freedom Charter stated: "We, the people of South Africa, declare for all our country and the world to know: That South Africa belongs to all who live in it, black and white, and that no government can justly claim authority unless it is based on the will of the people; That our people have been robbed of their birthright to land, liberty and peace by a form of government founded on injustice and inequality; That our country will never be prosperous or free until all our people live in brotherhood, enjoying equal rights and opportunities; That only a democratic state, based on the will of the people can secure to all their birthright without distinction of colour, race, sex or belief; And therefore, we, the people of South Africa, black and white, together—equals, countrymen and brothers—adopt this FREEDOM CHARTER. And we pledge ourselves to strive together, sparing nothing of our strength and courage, until the democratic changes here set out have been won."

In the struggle to overthrow apartheid throughout the decades that followed, the ANC and its allies adhered to the philosophy of the Freedom Charter. When the country's first democratic elections were held in 1994, the ANC won an overwhelming electoral victory against both the representatives of the old political order and those who took the Africanist approach.

See also: LUTULI, CHIEF ALBERT JOHN (Vol. IV); MANDELA, NELSON (Vols. IV, V); SOBUKWE, ROBERT (Vols. IV, V).

Further reading: Suttner and Cronin, *Thirty Years of the Freedom Charter* (Athens, Ohio: Ohio University Press, 1987).

Freetown Capital and largest city of SIERRA LEONE, serving as the principal national port at the mouth of the Sierra Leone River. In 1787 the Sierra Leone Company led by Granville Sharp (1735–1813) founded what eventually became Freetown as a settlement for formerly enslaved Africans. The first group of settlers found unpleasant conditions. They lacked supplies and found the local people hostile to their enterprises. In 1788 a shantytown named Granville Town was erected, but a year later an attack by a local group completely destroyed the community. Undaunted, the Sierra Leone Company was able to find a new group of settlers—former slaves who were living in Nova Scotia—who in 1792 founded Freetown near the former site of Granville Town.

Because of its excellent harbor Freetown became a base for the British Anti-Slavery Squadron and was the site where the navy landed with RECAPTIVES seized from slave ships. The liberated slaves, many of whom came from the YORUBA area of present-day NIGERIA, established a society and ethnicity that was distinct from the indigenous population of Sierra Leone. They evolved into the Krios, with their own LANGUAGE, KRIO, which was a blend of various West African languages and English.

English MISSIONARIES with the CHURCH MISSIONARY SOCIETY (CMS) provided EDUCATION for the recaptives, and Freetown soon emerged as a center for erudition. In 1876 FOURAH BAY COLLEGE, which the CMS had established as a missionary and teacher training institution in 1827, began to offer academic degrees through an affiliation with the University of Durham, in England. Over the next several decades it became an important higher-education center for Britain's West African colonies.

In 1808 Freetown became an official British colony, and from 1821 to 1874 it served as the administrative center for all of Britain's West African holdings. As Britain established COLONIAL RULE over the Sierra Leone hinterland, Freetown became the colony's capital. The Krios dominated the cultural and commercial life of Freetown and also played an important political role.

The growth of formal colonial empires in West Africa in the late 19th century undercut much of the economic vitality of Freetown. The city slowly did grow, however, and a railway, built between 1896 and 1908, stretched 227 miles (463 km) into the interior and served to expedite the export of commodities such as PALM OIL.

The discovery of DIAMONDS in the 1930s contributed to an economic resurgence within the city. During World War II (1939–45), Freetown's port was a major Allied naval base for the South Atlantic. At Sierra Leone's independence in 1961, Freetown, with a population of about 130,000 and still very much a Krio city, became the national capital.

See also: COLONIALISM, INFLUENCE OF (Vol. IV); ENGLAND AND AFRICA (Vols. III, IV, V); FREETOWN (Vols. III, V); SLAVE TRADE (Vols. III, IV); URBAN LIFE AND CULTURE (Vols. IV, V); URBANIZATION (Vols. IV, V).

Further reading: Leo Spitzer, *The Creoles of Sierra Leone: Responses to Colonialism, 1870–1945* (Madison: University of Wisconsin Press, 1974).

French Congo (Middle Congo) Colonial name of what is now the Republic of the CONGO. By the middle of the 19th century the Congo River had become an important commercial waterway, piquing the colonial interests of both Britain and France. In 1880 the French explorer Pierre Savorgnan DE BRAZZA (1852–1905) negotiated a treaty with the Teke people, resulting in the establishment of a French PROTECTORATE on the northern bank of the Congo River.

In 1891 the French Congo was officially declared a colony, which at the time included the territory of GABON to the west. Just as in the neighboring BELGIAN CONGO, European CONCESSIONAIRE COMPANIES in French Congo bought the rights to the region's minerals and NATURAL RESOURCES and began developing a colonial export ECONOMY. Because of the tropical climate and difficult physical conditions in the colony, few of the companies succeeded right away. However, they did lay the groundwork for future exploitation, and their officers dominated the colony's early administration.

In 1903 Gabon became a separate colony and the remaining part of French Congo was renamed Middle Congo. By 1910 France had taken control of Middle Congo from the concessionaire companies and united the colony with OUBANGUI-CHARI (now CENTRAL AFRICAN REPUBLIC) and CHAD to form FRENCH EQUATORIAL AFRICA (Afrique Équatoriale Française, AEF). BRAZZAVILLE, in Middle Congo, was the administrative capital.

After World War I (1914–18) France developed the colony's infrastructure, including a major rail line from the coast to the interior, utilizing forced LABOR schemes to recruit African workers. During World War II (1939–45) relations between France and Middle Congo changed drastically. After France's surrender to Germany, Charles DE GAULLE (1890–1970) founded Free France in AEF, and named Brazzaville its capital. After the war, in 1944, France held the Brazzaville Conference, where de Gaulle unveiled a reformed French colonial policy. As part of the reforms France finally put an end to forced labor and granted citizenship to all people within its colonies.

In 1946 France granted Middle Congo a territorial assembly and representation in the French parliament. By 1958 AEF was dissolved and Middle Congo, renamed the Republic of the Congo, moved toward independence. In 1960 the country gained full autonomy, with Fulbert Youlou (1917–1972) becoming the first president.

See also: FRANCE AND AFRICA (Vol. III, IV, V).

Further reading: Patrick Manning, *Francophone Sub-Saharan Africa, 1880–1995* (New York: Cambridge University Press, 1998).

French Equatorial Africa (Afrique Équatoriale Française, AEF) (1910–59) Federation of four colonies in west-central and Central Africa including CHAD, Congo, OUBANGUI-CHARI (now the CENTRAL AFRICAN REPUBLIC), and GABON. Oubangui-Chari and Chad formed a single territory until 1920. The federal capital of French Équatoriale Africa (AEF) was BRAZZAVILLE (the capital of today's Republic of the CONGO),

Originally called the FRENCH CONGO, AEF was smaller in territory and population than FRENCH WEST AFRICA (Afrique Occidentale Française, AOF), France's other African colonial federation, which was established five years prior to the founding of AEF.

Generally the histories of AEF and AOF run along parallel lines. As with AOF, AEF was first defined by the borders drawn by European colonial powers at the BERLIN CONFERENCE (1884–85). The administrative structure of both AEF and AOF included a governor-general for the overall federation, with governors for the separate colonies reporting to him. Below the governors were the administrators of the *cercles,* or smaller administrative divisions. As with AOF, civilian administrators gradually took over from the military officers who had served as the first administrators during the period of COLONIAL CONQUEST. Administrative responsibilities included overseeing African civil servants and appointing African chiefs in the cantons, the districts into which *cercles* were divided. There was also, as in AOF, a necessity for interpreters, since French colonial officials usually lacked a familiarity with the local languages and customs of the people they governed.

France levied taxes on the African population and on commerce to help defray the costs of administering its equatorial African colonies. In contrast to AOF, however, AEF did not have a sufficient level of EXPORTS (mostly CASH CROPS) and imports (mostly manufactured goods from France) to provide a sufficient level of customs revenues to finance the colonial administration. France thus often had to provide subsidies out of its national treasury to meet expenses.

In addition to providing its own subsidies, the French government also relied on investments by huge private companies, large banks, and CONCESSIONAIRE COMPANIES to promote economic growth in French West Africa.

Although SLAVERY had been abolished in 1848, France imposed a policy of forced LABOR on its African territories in order to augment taxation. This labor disrupted the local social structure in myriad ways, since few Africans had other means to produce the French colonial currency that was used to pay the taxes. Using this labor AEF officials directed the construction of roads, railroads, and ports. The most dramatic use—and abuse—of such labor occurred between 1921 and 1934, with the construction of a 240-mile-long (386-km) railroad between the coastal port of Pointe Noire and inland Brazzaville. The brainchild of the minister of colonies,

Albert Sarraut (1872–1962), the project claimed the lives of some 10,000 African workers.

French Equatorial Africa played a significant role in World War II (1939–45). Because Governor-General Adolphe-Félix-Sylvestre ÉBOUÉ (1884–1944) was a strong supporter of Charles DE GAULLE (1890–1970), who presided over the Free French government, AEF served as the seat of government for the Free French. Also it was in AEF, in 1944, that de Gaulle held the Brazzaville Conference at which he promised a change in France's colonial policy after the war.

The AEF colonial structure remained largely unchanged until France instituted reforms in the 1940s and 1950s. By 1946 the creation of the FRENCH UNION gave each territory a legislative assembly, and territories of AEF, now considered overseas territories of France, elected their own representatives in the French National Assembly. Not long after, massive development projects improved the local infrastructures of each territory, leaving most of the region with serviceable railroads, ports, airports, roads, bridges, RADIO transmitters, and communication centers. There was also new French investment in health care and EDUCATION programs that produced a stronger and better-trained work force.

In 1958 de Gaulle came to power in France and offered the territories of AEF the choice of becoming autonomous states within a French Community or taking immediate and total independence. Led by Barthélémy Boganda (d. 1959) of Oubangui-Chari, AEF chose to join the Community, thereby ending the colonial administration of the federation.

See also: COLONIAL RULE (Vol. IV), COLONIALISM, INFLUENCE OF (Vol. IV), FRANCE AND AFRICA (Vols. III, IV, V).

Further reading: Patrick Manning, *Francophone sub-Saharan Africa, 1880–1995* (New York: Cambridge University Press, 1998).

French Morocco PROTECTORATE established by France in 1912 over most of the present-day country of MOROCCO. In 1904 France and Spain signed treaties to divide Morocco between them. French Morocco, by far the bigger portion, was administered from the colonial capital at Rabat, on the Atlantic coast. In response to rising Moroccan nationalism, in 1956 France restored Moroccan sovereignty and withdrew its administration.

See also: FRANCE AND AFRICA (Vol. IV); SPANISH MOROCCO (Vol. IV).

French Somaliland (1888–1967) Colonial name of the French-held territory in the Horn of Africa that is now called DJIBOUTI. The colony of French Somaliland, declared in 1888, served primarily as a port for trade goods

In parts of French Somaliland, long-distance communication was a challenge because of the lack of roads. In the 1930s, the French administration used young men like these Somalis to deliver messages, which they stuck through the tips of their spears. © *Wide World*

from the interior highlands of ETHIOPIA. In 1946 the colony became an overseas territory of France and a member of the FRENCH UNION. Then, following a 1958 referendum, the population of French Somaliland voted to join the French Community and was granted representation in the French Parliament.

In 1967 the country was renamed the French Territory of the Afars and Issas, and 10 years later the territory formally became independent Djibouti.

See also: ADEN, GULF OF (Vol. II); GOULED APTIDON, HASSAN (Vol. V); DJIBOUTI, CITY OF (Vol. V); FRANCE AND AFRICA (Vol. IV); HORN OF AFRICA (Vols. I, III); RED SEA TRADE (Vol. II).

French Soudan French colonial territory that in 1960 became the independent Republic of MALI. In 1890 the territory formerly called Upper Senegal was renamed French Soudan. Within five years the ruling TUKULOR EM-

PIRE of UMAR TAL (1794–1864) had fallen to French forces and French Soudan was made part of the newly formed colonial federation of FRENCH WEST AFRICA. The final major resistance to French control, the MANDINKA empire, collapsed in 1898, and by 1899 French PACIFICATION of the region was considered complete.

French Soudan became part of Haut-Sénégal-Niger (Upper Senegal and Niger) in 1904 but then reverted to French Soudan in 1919. France administered the territory through direct rule, governing through local chiefs who were appointed without regard to tradition or regional history and who reported to French officials at the *cercle* (district) level. Colonial authorities supported the cultivation of COTTON as the main export for the colony.

Following World War II (1939–45), in 1946 French Soudan's political leaders established the Sudanese Union, which had ties to the inter-territorial AFRICAN DEMO- CRATIC ASSEMBLY. With the reorientation of France's for- mer colonies in the French Community in 1958, French

Soudan became the internally autonomous Sudanese Republic. In 1960 the Sudanese Republic became the fully independent Republic of Mali, under the leadership of Modibo Keita (1915–1977), the Marxist head of the Sudanese Union-African Democratic Rally political party.

See also: COLONIALISM, INFLUENCE OF (Vol. IV); FRANCE AND AFRICA (Vols. III, IV, V).

French Union Federal association created by France in 1946 as part of its Fourth Republic Constitution. Disbanded in 1958, the French Union established a new political relationship between metropolitan France and its dependencies around the globe. After World War II (1939–45) the new constituents of the Fourth Republic reorganized France's relationship to its colonies by creating the French Union. In this configuration France continued its influence in Africa by remaining the dominant partner in a union with subordinate partners. These lesser members included the overseas department of ALGERIA, the newly formed overseas departments of RÉUNION IS-LAND, Guadeloupe, Martinique, and Guyana, and the French Overseas Territories, which included the African colonies. The Associated States—Indochina, MOROCCO, and TUNISIA—were given internal autonomy, although France controlled foreign policy.

The new constitution granted citizenship to all inhabitants of the colonies, put an end to the common colonial practice of forced LABOR, and established the organization known as FIDES, which was meant to help the colonies with economic and social development. As members of the French Union the African territories had the right to representation in three metropolitan bodies: the National Assembly (lower house), the Council of the Republic (upper house), and the Assembly of the French Union. The two African federations, FRENCH EQUATORIAL AFRICA and FRENCH WEST AFRICA, each maintained a legislative body called the Grand Conseil (Federal Council), which was made up of deputies sent by the member states. Most deputies were chosen by direct election from the territorial assemblies, which were elected by two colleges: College One comprised French residents and Western-educated Africans who had become French citizens; College Two comprised newly enfranchised Africans voting for the first time.

The French Union established a relationship between France and its African colonies that allowed the European country to maintain influence even after the colonies were granted independence. Direct popular elections, a legacy from the French Union, began the political process that led to independence. The union began to unravel in 1954 when the member states of Indochina withdrew. Two years later Morocco and Tunisia became independent, and in 1958 the constitution of the Fifth French Republic replaced the French Union with the French Community.

See also: COLONIALISM, INFLUENCE OF (Vol. IV); DE-COLONIZATION (Vol. V); FRANCE AND AFRICA (Vols. III, IV, V).

French West Africa (Afrique Occidentale Française, AOF) (1899–1959) A federation of eight colonies in West Africa including SENEGAL, GUINEA, FRENCH SOUDAN (now MALI), UPPER VOLTA (now BURKINA FASO), IVORY COAST, DAHOMEY (now the Republic of BENIN), MAURITANIA, and NIGER. French West Africa (AOF) was the larger of France's two colonial African federations—the other being FRENCH EQUATORIAL AFRICA. The AOF federal capital was DAKAR, Senegal.

At its inception the Federation of French West Africa was defined by boundaries drawn on the map at the BERLIN CONFERENCE (1884–85). By 1900 France had pacified the territory, and between 1904 and 1914 it consolidated its COLONIAL RULE in the region using a hierarchical form of administration. The French minister of the colonies appointed a governor-general, who oversaw the whole of AOF. Under him there was a governor, sometimes called a lieutenant-governor, for each individual colony, which was autonomous in terms of local budget, colonial TAXATION, and internal administration. Below the governor, each colony was divided into cercles (circles, or rings), each with its own administrator. At first these administrators were military officers, but as the period of COLONIAL CONQUEST unfolded, the post increasingly called for civilian administrators. Administrative responsibilities included appointing African chiefs and overseeing African civil servants.

Changes in administrative postings were so frequent, and the languages of AOF were so diverse, that French officials rarely stayed long enough at any one post to learn the LANGUAGE or customs of the people for whom they were responsible. Thus they had to rely on interpreters for communication. A typical cercle administrative structure included the European administrator, a principal assistant, one or two commissioners of indigenous affairs, a military detachment composed of a unit of the TIRAILLEURS SÉNÉGALAIS, an interpreter, a communications agent, and various other employees.

Each cercle was further sub-divided into cantons, each of which had a local, indigenous head. These local community administrators were the liaison between the colonial administrator and the African people. Besides serving to legitimize French rule, the major responsibility of local chiefs was to collect taxes and recruit LABOR, a role that made them very unpopular within their communities.

The French levied taxes to pay the costs of their colonial administration, and by doing so they disrupted the local social structure. These taxes had to be paid in French currency rather than in goods, and the need for the African population to earn hard currency led to the dissolving of certain local ties and the establishment of broader regional connections. By forcing normally sedentary farmers into a regional labor pool, the French created a more mobile population that foiled attempts to confine it within artificially drawn borders. And as they moved about, workers joined a large number of West Africans who traveled extensively in pursuit of Quranic EDUCATION.

The canton was an alien political form for many of the communities within AOF. Governor-General William Ponty (1866–1915) adopted the canton strategy from SAMORI TOURÉ (c. 1830–1900), who had drawn upon the social constructs of his empire's MANDE speakers. Believing that Samori's structure was the norm for the region, Ponty continued his policy with one important change: The French appointed the *chefs de canton* (canton chiefs). The French then made their selection on the basis of a willingness to collaborate with the colonial government rather than the legitimacy of their status within the chiefs' own communities.

In the first decade of the 20th century the tax burden on AOF subjects tripled. The French encouraged Africans to raise tax money by converting their arable land from the production of FOOD CROPS to the production of CASH CROPS for export. The French also directed Africans to join the labor forces on plantations that produced cash crops, and to transport and traffic in the preferred cash crop, GROUNDNUTS (peanuts). In general, however, the French never managed complete control of their colonial trade, and about 1910 barely half of the total of AOF exports were bound for France.

The colonial structure of French West Africa remained unchanged until massive reforms were instituted in the 1940s and 1950s. By that time the number of Europeans living in the colonies had increased, but, more importantly, Africans had become more acculturated to European ways. France invested heavily in postwar economic and social programs, allowing each AOF territory to develop its local infrastructure, including railroads, ports, airports, RADIO transmitters, communication centers, roads, and bridges. These improvements were the first steps toward INDUSTRIALIZATION, but they also improved the standard of living and allowed more people access to the ECONOMY. France's investment in the social programs in health and education produced a work force that was stronger, psychologically as well as physically.

Although SLAVERY was abolished in the colonies in 1848, France imposed a policy of forced labor on the AOF territories in order to augment taxes. The labor would be applied to public works projects, such as the building of roads, railroads, or ports.

With the creation of the FRENCH UNION in 1959, French West Africa ceased to exist as an administrative entity. All of its component territories became independent countries in 1960 (except for Guinea, which had become independent two years earlier).

See also: COLONIALISM, INFLUENCE OF (Vol. IV), FRANCE AND AFRICA (Vols. III, IV, V); PACIFICATION (Vol. IV).

Further reading: Patrick Manning, *Francophone sub-Saharan Africa, 1880–1995* (New York: Cambridge University Press, 1998).

Fulani (Fulbe, Peul) Mostly Muslim ethnic group, originally of West Africa, that continued to play an important role during the entire period of COLONIAL RULE. In their movements to support their pastoralist way of life, the Fulani conquered and absorbed various other peoples from present-day MALI and BURKINO FASO to NIGERIA and southern NIGER. Because of this they came to be identified not only with the TUKULOR EMPIRE but also with the powerful SOKOTO CALIPHATE, founded by Fulani reformer Usman dan Fodio (1754–1817) and subsequently ruled by his son, Muhammad Bello (1781–1837). The Sokoto Caliphate, with KANO at its center, was undoubtedly the largest centralized state in precolonial Africa.

British forces led by Frederick LUGARD (1858–1945) conquered and subdued the Fulani Sultanate and established colonial rule in Northern Nigeria between 1890 and 1903. However, the Fulani people continued to migrate throughout the region, and by the later colonial period they also had settled in parts of present-day CAMEROON and Republic of the SUDAN.

See also: COLONIAL CONQUEST (Vol. IV); ENGLAND AND AFRICA (Vols. III, IV, V); FULANI (Vols. I, II, III); FULBE (Vol. I); TUKULOR (Vols. II, III).

G

Gabon Country covering about 103,300 square miles (267,500 sq km) along the western coast of Central Africa. By the late 1800s the region that would become the modern nation of Gabon had fallen under French COLONIAL RULE. Today, Gabon is bordered by EQUATORIAL GUINEA, CAMEROON, the Democratic Republic of the CONGO, and ANGOLA.

Portuguese explorers were the first to arrive in the Gabon estuary in 1472. Other Europeans began to frequent the area shortly thereafter, trading with the local Mpongwe and Vili people. The Europeans exchanged weapons, alcohol, and cloth for wood, ivory, and human captives. The region's SLAVE TRADE was very lucrative until the 1840s, when the French signed treaties with Mpongwe chiefs ending the regional trade in humans and establishing French sovereignty over the coastal Mpongwe lands. In 1844 Roman Catholic MISSIONARIES arrived to further French influence, and in 1849 LIBREVILLE, the future colonial and national capital, was founded as a settlement for freed captives.

By the 1880s French explorers, most notably Pierre Savorgnan DE BRAZZA (1852–1905), had extended France's COLONIAL CONQUEST into the interior, establishing Franceville in 1880 on the upper Ogooué River. In 1885 the BERLIN CONFERENCE gave France rights to the region that included Gabon, and the following year Gabon became a part of the FRENCH CONGO. Libreville was then made the capital of the French Congo, with de Brazza as governor. In 1904 the capital was moved to BRAZZAVILLE, and Gabon became a separate colony until 1910, when it was brought under the umbrella of FRENCH EQUATORIAL AFRICA (Afrique Équatoriale Française, AEF).

As part of AEF, Gabon was subject to a number of unpopular colonial policies, including a head tax and a LABOR tax, as well as an economic development policy that allowed for CONCESSIONAIRE COMPANIES to exploit the local workforce to their own ends. Small-scale revolts occurred but were quickly put down by colonial authorities.

By the outbreak of World War II (1939–45) Gabon had developed a strong anticolonial yet paradoxically pro-French sentiment. Like the other colonies of AEF, Gabon supported the Free French movement led by General Charles DE GAULLE (1890–1970) during the war. After securing victory de Gaulle rewarded the African colonies with French citizenship, representation in the French National Assembly, and improved EDUCATION and health care, among other reforms. In 1958, in response to de Gaulle's *oui-ou-non* (yes-or-no) offer regarding total independence, Gabon chose to become an autonomous country under the FRENCH UNION. Two years later Gabon became fully independent, with Leon M'ba (1902–1967) as the country's first president.

See also: COLONIALISM, INFLUENCE OF (Vol. IV); FRANCE AND AFRICA (Vols. III, IV, V); GABON (Vols. I, II, III, V).

Further reading: Christopher Gray, *Colonial Rule and Crisis in Equatorial Africa: Southern Gabon, ca. 1850–1940* (Rochester, N.Y.: University of Rochester, 2002).

Gallieni, Joseph (General Joseph Simon Gallieni) (1849–1916) *French governor-general of Madagascar*

Born in France to Italian-immigrant parents, Gallieni was a good student, working his way out of poverty by enrolling in the military academy of Saint-Cyr. He entered the infantry as a second lieutenant, fighting in the Franco-Prussian War (1870–71). He then served in Africa, in the FRENCH SOUDAN, and later in Asia, in Tonkin, before being appointed governor of Upper SENEGAL, in 1886. After France exiled Queen Ranavalona III (1861–1917) of MADAGASCAR, in 1897, Gallieni became governor-general of Madagascar.

His strong-handed administration was marked by efforts to solidify French authority and power in the area. By recognizing differences among the region's various ETHNIC GROUPS—a policy known as a *politique des races* (politics of race)—he helped subvert Malagasy nationalism. Gallieni also made efforts to suppress Madagascar's monarchy and reduce British influence in the area. Equally important, he transformed the justice system by setting the French penal code alongside the existing Malagasy system.

One of the hallmarks of his administration was the use of taxation as an instrument of social and political policy. Customs duties, for example, were used to finance schools and hospitals. Taxation was also used as a means of persuading traditional subsistence farmers to turn to the growth of CASH CROPS for their income. Gallieni left Madagascar in 1905 and during World War I (1914–18) played a pivotal role in defending Paris at the First Battle of the Marne. He died of illness, in 1916.

See also: COLONIAL CONQUEST (Vol. IV); COLONIAL RULE (Vol. IV); FRANCE AND AFRICA (Vol. IV).

Gambia, The Long, narrow West African country of some 4,360 square miles (11,290 sq km) in size that is entirely surrounded by SENEGAL, save for its Atlantic coastline. Originally colonized in 1765, The Gambia was Britain's first African colony as well as the last British West African colony to gain independence, in 1965.

The Gambia was initially a region of interest for Portuguese traders. By the 1700s, however, the territory was contested by both Britain and France. The two colonial powers vied for control of the Gambia River's mouth, with outposts on the river's islands becoming a source of conflict. In 1765 the British established these island settlements as the colony of Senegambia. However, they eventually lost much of the colony to France.

In 1816 Britain purchased Banjul Island at the mouth of the Gambia River from the local African chief and established the fort and town of Bathurst with the intent of suppressing the SLAVE TRADE on the Gambia River. The British developed the policy of promoting so-called legitimate trade in CASH CROPS and natural products as an economic alternative to the trade in human captives. By the 1850s the production of GROUNDNUTS (peanuts) for export was booming, and would continue to develop extensively through the 1950s. Even today groundnuts are

virtually the Gambia's only significant export, making the country one of Africa's MONO-CROP ECONOMIES.

The British administered their settlement as part of their colony of SIERRA LEONE until 1843 when it became a crown colony in its own right. During this period British COLONIAL RULE was confined to the coastal zone. Between 1850 and 1866, however, Muslim and non-Muslim groups in the interior fought over religious differences and for control of the lucrative groundnut trade. British merchants profited from the sale of guns and powder to both sides. The British colonial officials were mainly concerned that the Marabout Wars—as the disputes among the local populations were called—did not disrupt trade.

The Gambia became part of Sierra Leone once again from 1866 to 1888. In 1889 negotiations with France, which had established COLONIAL RULE in Senegal, set The Gambia's present-day boundaries. The British colony ran the length of the Gambia River to the upper limits of navigation, some 200 miles (322 km) into the interior. The area of British rule extended 6.2 miles (10 km) from the center of the river on either bank, except for the seaboard and lower reaches of the river, where the colony was 30 miles wide. It was not until 1896, however, that the boundaries were fully marked.

On two separate occasions Britain attempted to cede The Gambia to France in exchange for other territories. Both attempts failed due to insufficient compensation, as well as to opposition in the colony and in Britain.

With the boundaries with French-ruled Senegal in place, the British turned to administering the PROTECTORATE they had established in the interior. Their policy was one of indirect rule in which local chiefs, both hereditary and appointed, ruled at the local level, reporting to British district commissioners. During World War II (1939–45), Gambian soldiers fought for the Allied cause, but by war's end the independence movement had gained considerable momentum in the country. The British responded in 1950 by replacing the system of indirect rule with elected local authorities. By 1960 The Gambia featured a number of political parties. Their efforts prompted Britain to grant independence to the small nation, in 1965.

See also: COLONIAL CONQUEST (Vol. IV); COLONIALISM, INFLUENCE OF (Vol. IV); ENGLAND AND AFRICA (Vols. III, IV, V); GAMBIA, THE (Vols. I, II, III, V); ISLAM, INFLUENCE OF (Vols. II, III, IV, V); SENEGAMBIA (Vol. III); SENEGAMBIA REGION (Vol. IV).

Further reading: Donald R. Wright, *The World and a Very Small Place in Africa: A History of Globalization in Niumi, the Gambia* (Armonk, N.Y.: M. E. Sharpe, 1997).

Gandhi, Mohandas (Mohandas Karamchand Gandhi; Mahatma Kandhi) (1869–1948) *Indian lawyer and political activist*

Although Mohandas Gandhi is best known for the part he played in the struggle for independence in India, he also played a pivotal role in the history of SOUTH AFRICA. To a large extent the techniques of passive resistance that he later employed to overthrow British rule in India were developed and honed in South Africa.

Born in India, Gandhi studied in London and then returned home to practice law. He came to DURBAN, South Africa, in 1893 to settle a legal case, but ended up staying in South Africa for the next two decades. In part his decision to remain was a response to the overtly racist treatment and gross social inequities directed against Indians living in South Africa. He resolved to fight the legislation, then under consideration, to deny Indians the right to vote, to impose a head tax on them, and to extend the period of indentured servitude for Indian laborers.

The British imported Indians from Madras and other regions of India to work as indentured servants in the sugar cane plantations in NATAL. In 1865 about 4,700 Indians were in Natal. In 1911 the number rose to 150,000. In 2000 the Indian population of South Africa, still centered in Natal, reached 1 million.

In 1894 Ghandi helped found the Natal Indian Congress to mobilize Indians against these measures. A pacificist, he helped organize an ambulance corps among Indians to tend to the wounded during the ANGLO-BOER WAR (1899–1902) and the 1906 BAMBATHA'S REBELLION. In 1903 he started the weekly newspaper *Indian Opinion* and founded two communal societies: the Phoenix Farm, close to Durban, in 1904, and the Tolstoy Farm, outside JOHANNESBURG, in 1910.

From 1906 onward he shifted his activism toward the TRANSVAAL, where he established a successful legal practice in Johannesburg, its largest city. He successfully opposed a humiliating Asiatic Law Amendment Ordinance, which sought to force all Indians to register with the authorities and be fingerprinted.

During this campaign Gandhi was imprisoned, as he was on several occasions in the following years. Courting arrest through passive resistance served as an effective means to protest against the powerful, white-dominated South African state. This strategy became known as SATYAGRAHA, combining the Indian words for "truth" and "hold firm." Gandhi organized the Satyagraha Association, which participated in high-profile efforts to combat the South African Supreme Court's decision that rendered all non-Christian marriages legally void. The association also organized strikes at coal mines and sugar plantations in Natal.

To resolve these conflicts with the Indian community, Jan Christiaan SMUTS (1870–1950), the future prime minister, met with Gandhi in June 1914. As a result of this meeting, Indian marriages were recognized, the head tax was abolished, and Indian indentured service was timed to end in 1920. In July 1914 Gandhi left South Africa for India. There, working to end British COLONIAL RULE, he became one of the world's most noteworthy individuals.

See also: ASIAN COMMUNITIES (Vol. V); RESISTANCE AND REBELLION (Vol. IV).

Garvey, Marcus (Marcus Mosiah Garvey) (1887–1940) *Jamaican-born social reformer and activist*

Born into poverty in Jamaica, British West Indies, Marcus Garvey rose to become one of the most influential black leader in the 1920s. His advocacy of economic and political activism stirred thousands of people, particularly in the United States, and his various reformist organizations and publications gave him an international forum.

One of 11 children, Garvey left his hometown of St. Ann's Bay at age 14, moving to Kingston, where he found work as a printer's apprentice. From the beginning he was a social activist, participating in Jamaica's first Printer's Union strike, in 1907. Travel in Latin America reinforced his sense of the injustices being done to black people, who, he came to believe, were victims of discrimination virtually everywhere.

In 1912 Garvey moved to London, where he found work at the *African Times and Orient Review*, published by the Sudanese-Egyptian journalist Duse Muhammad ALI (1867–1944). In London Garvey began to grow seriously interested in history, delving into both the history of Africa itself and the works of writers like Booker T. WASHINGTON (1856–1915).

Garvey's ideas found expression in 1914 in the formation of the UNIVERSAL NEGRO IMPROVEMENT ASSOCIATION (UNIA), which advocated not only an end to colonialism but also a raising of black consciousness throughout the world. Garvey moved to the United States in 1916, finding a receptive audience to his doctrine of activism and self-help. Using as his principle forum the newspaper that he founded, *Negro World*, he spread his ideas across the United States and virtually everywhere else inhabited by people of African descent.

In 1920 UNIA held its first international convention in New York City, where Garvey's speeches and public ap-

By 1920, when this photo was taken, Marcus Garvey had become known to many as the "Provisional President of Africa." © Keystone View Co. Inc./Library of Congress

pearances regularly drew crowds numbering in the thousands. Following a march down Harlem's Lenox Avenue, Garvey outlined his daring plan for the creation of an African nation-state to which people of African descent could emigrate. Convinced that blacks would never receive their full rights in any society in which they were a minority, Garvey called for the peoples of the AFRICAN DIASPORA to return to Africa. There, he maintained, Africans would enjoy political supremacy and, more than that, they, rather than white colonialists, would have control of the rich NATURAL RESOURCES available.

This idea, too, struck a chord, and it was not long before Garvey's UNIA had 1,100 branches operating in 40 countries. With membership soaring, Garvey established other activist groups as well as several business ventures. His Black Star Line, for example, purchased three ocean-going steamships, making it a pioneering black-owned business enterprise. Other groups, such as Negro Factories Corporation, founded a wide range of businesses in various locations. Garvey's power and influence at this time had become so great that he was even able to send a delegation to the League of Nations, appealing to that body to pass the former German colonies in Africa—lost

by Germany in the wake of World War I (1914–18)—over to UNIA for the founding of his proposed African nation-state.

By the late 1920s, however, Garvey and his movement began to encounter serious problems. Financial difficulties struck several of his business ventures, and membership began to decline. Beyond this, in a particularly conservative era, the radical nature of his ideas and the size of his following disturbed many individuals in power, and government agencies, both in the United States and abroad, began focusing on him. Eventually he was charged with mail fraud, the U.S. government maintaining that he and his associates had knowingly sent out materials urging investment in the Black Star Line even though they knew the venture was bankrupt.

Jailed in 1925, Garvey served his sentence in the Atlanta Federal Penitentiary. In 1927 President Calvin Coolidge (1872–1933) commuted his sentence, and Garvey was deported to Jamaica. Back in the land of his birth Garvey focused on politics, even running unsuccessfully for office. In 1935 he went to England, where he remained until dying, in relative obscurity, in 1940.

See also: BACK TO AFRICA MOVEMENT (Vol. IV); W. E. B. DU BOIS (Vol. IV); LIBERIA (Vol. IV); PAN-AFRICANISM (Vol. IV).

Further reading: Edmund David Cronin and John Hope Franklin, *Black Moses: The Story of Marcus Garvey and the Universal Negro Improvement Association* (Madison: University of Wisconsin Press, 1969); Marcus Garvey, et. al., *The Philosophy and Opinions of Marcus Garvey, or, Africa for the Africans* (Dover, Mass.: Majority Press, 1986).

gender in colonial Africa Aspects of gender relationships changed with the arrival of European colonists, who came with their own gender ideologies and began to manipulate human and NATURAL RESOURCES to benefit the export ECONOMY. Prior to the colonial era African men and women had well-defined realms of influence in their households and communities. Both men and women occupied leadership roles in their societies, although one rarely impinged upon the established role of the other. Custom defined the interactions and relationships of men and women before and after marriage and dictated the terms of marriage. In the household setting men and women observed specific divisions of the workload, although they often cooperated.

Even after the arrival of colonial governments, in many parts of Africa women continued in their role as subsistence farmers, providing FOOD for the family. However, men were recruited to work in the mines and cities as cheap wage LABOR, and it became increasingly difficult for women to rely on men to clear the fields for cultivation. Men, who previously had also been responsible for grazing the animals and constructing homes and other structures, had to leave their homes. Once in the cities men were forced to live in cramped quarters with other male migrants and were made to work long hours in difficult conditions. When men did not migrate they were encouraged to cultivate CASH CROPS for sale to European SETTLERS or for export. Although wives might weed or plant, men maintained control over all the profits from cultivation of cash crops, a practice that continues today.

In some parts of Africa, men, but not women, had access to agricultural extension services, EDUCATION, credit, and the most fertile land. However, despite the fact that the colonial authorities generally discouraged women from being active in the public sphere, women continued their long-standing practice of selling excess FOOD CROPS and crafts in local markets. In addition, women increasingly became the primary decision makers in their households when their husbands moved away. Women often sent food to their husbands in the cities, and men often sent money in the form of remittances to their wives in the countryside.

In the cities men lived without the support network that they had at home, since colonial policies discouraged the migration of women and children to towns. The demand for cooked food, bathing, laundry, and sex, combined with an increase in poverty among African women, resulted in an expanding market for prostitution. In fact, some prostitutes during the colonial era made more money than unskilled laborers by providing all or one of the "domestic services" mentioned.

Both men and women participated in ART and craft production long before colonial times. However, different sexes attended to different crafts. For instance, men tended to do ironworking, blacksmithing, and woodcarving, while women did pottery, basket making, weaving, and painting. These divisions continue today. If men in a particular region engage in weaving or basket making, women in that same area either do not do it, or, if they do, they use different tools from the men. There are often taboos, which vary with location or culture, that prevent women and men from engaging in the same particular activities or eating specific foods.

The arrival of Christian MISSIONARIES reinforced colonial gender ideologies. Whereas in some traditional religions it was the women who occupied positions of leadership, in European churches, the leaders were mostly men. Some forms of African Islam, with practices of purdah (seclusion of women from public) and veiling,

brought with them their own unique ideas about the female role. Islam, however, also brought basic, although not necessarily equal, rights to women in marriage and allowed females to seek divorce if these rights were not fulfilled.

See also: CHRISTIANITY, INFLUENCE OF (Vol. IV); COLONIALISM, INFLUENCE OF (Vol. IV); ISLAM, INFLUENCE OF (Vol. IV); URBAN LIFE AND CULTURE (Vol. IV); URBANIZATION (Vol. IV); WOMEN IN COLONIAL AFRICA (Vol. IV).

German East Africa Large German colony made up of territories that later became RWANDA, BURUNDI, and TANGANYIKA, the last of which made up the mainland portion of present-day TANZANIA. Its origins lay with the imperial rivalries of the 1880s and the aggressive German search for colonial possession during the era of the PARTITION of Africa and the associated COLONIAL CONQUEST.

In 1884 Karl PETERS (1856–1918), a private German adventurer, signed treaties with local rulers on the eastern coast of Africa, legitimizing Germany's presence in the region. Then Germany began its colonial conquest of the region that became known as Tanganyika. The German East Africa Company, organized in 1885, administered the colony.

German presence in the region disturbed Sultan ibn Said BARGHASH (c. 1833–1888), the BUSAIDI ruler of nearby ZANZIBAR, who claimed sovereignty over the Tanzanian coast. The ensuing tensions between Germany and Britain, which backed Zanzibar, ended in 1890 with a treaty between the two European powers. This treaty established a British PROTECTORATE over Zanzibar and halted German territorial expansion into what is today KENYA, to the north of Tanzania. The following year, the German government took over control of the colony from the German East Africa Company.

Much of what was produced by colonial plantations on the mainland, which before the German takeover had been delivered to Zanzibar for export, was now shipped directly by German merchants and shipping firms. These items included sisal (a natural fiber used to make twine), RUBBER, copra (dried coconut meat), COFFEE, GROUNDNUTS (peanuts), and COTTON. Other trade and export items included ivory, wax, and animal hides.

The use of military power characterized the colonial administration in East Africa. In its efforts to maintain tight control over the region, the German government used its colonial army to suppress indigenous revolts, such as the MAJI-MAJI REBELLION of 1905–07. Germany also used military might to defend its colonial possession against the British during World War I (1914–18).

When Germany lost the war, under the provisions of the Treaty of Versailles (1919), it also lost its colonial empire. Divided into mandates, or regions of direct control, by the League of Nations, German East Africa ceased to exist. The newly named Tanganyika became a British MANDATE, and the territory known as RUANDA-URUNDI, today the separate countries of Rwanda and Burundi, became a Belgian mandate. In addition, a small parcel of land along the Tanganyika-Mozambique border known as the Kionga Triangle fell under Portuguese control.

See also: GERMANY AND AFRICA (Vol. IV); LEAGUE OF NATIONS AND AFRICA (Vol. IV).

Germany and Africa During the 1880s, in an effort to keep up with the growing colonial empire of Britain, Germany rushed to gain territorial possessions in Africa. In 1884 Germany went from having no colonial possessions in Africa to declaring protectorates over Kamerun (now CAMEROON), TOGOLAND (now TOGO), and SOUTH WEST AFRICA (now NAMIBIA). The sudden German territorial claims, announced by the German chancellor Otto von BISMARCK (1815–1898), surprised the other European colonial powers and contributed to the meeting of the European powers at the BERLIN CONFERENCE later in the year.

Early German Encounters in Africa Though Germany did not officially claim territory in Africa until 1884, larger numbers of Germans began coming to the continent by the middle of the 19th century. During the 1850s German explorers, MISSIONARIES, and traders made inroads into Togoland, on the Guinea Coast of West Africa. One such explorer was Gustav Nachtigal (1834– 1885), who was instrumental in securing treaties from chiefs along the West African coast. Earlier he had traveled extensively through northern Africa, crossing the Sahara in 1869, to reach KHARTOUM.

Another early German explorer in Africa, Karl PETERS (1856–1918), founded the Society for German Colonization, which later funded his exploration. Working without the official sanction of the German government, Peters secured numerous treaties with chiefs in central East Africa. His zealous acquisition of territory greatly angered the sultan of ZANZIBAR, ibn Said BARGHASH (c. 1833–1888), who claimed to rule much of the affected area. Despite Barghash's hostility, in 1885 Germany declared the society's lands a PROTECTORATE, eventually transforming them into GERMAN EAST AFRICA.

German Colonialism Germany largely viewed its African possessions as a stimulus for its expanding economy, so obtaining NATURAL RESOURCES for export to Germany was a paramount concern. In particular, Germany sought to purchase ivory and PALM OIL and encouraged the cultivation of COFFEE, COCOA, and COTTON.

Germany's attempts to benefit from these new holdings were complicated by the fact that, compared to other European powers in Africa, Germany was unfamiliar in the intricacies of colonialism. As a result of this unfamiliarity, disorganization marked the initial governance of German territory in Africa. To compensate for their deficiencies, the Germans frequently used heavy-handed tactics in dealing with the indigenous populations within their possessions, resulting in numerous African uprisings.

In 1885 the HERERO of German South West Africa successfully resisted German intrusion until British forces from CAPE COLONY assisted in quelling them. About 20 years later, the Herero once more revolted against German occupation, and again met with initial success. The arrival of more German soldiers, however, turned the tide in favor of the Germans, and the Herero and their allies, the NAMA, were crushed.

> The German soldiers were led by the notorious Lothar von Trotha (1848–1920), who positioned his forces so that the Herero were compelled to escape into the unforgiving Kalahari Desert. He then ordered all Herero, armed and unarmed, within German Southwest Africa to be shot on sight. As a result, the Herero population nearly disappeared, as many of those who survived the initial military massacre were sent to concentration camps and died from overwork or disease.

In East Africa the German government took control of the colony from the German East Africa Company in 1891. Germany improved the infrastructure of the region, building railroads and ports to support an expanding trade economy. However, Germany instituted plantation AGRICULTURE that utilized forced LABOR and at the same time levied oppressive taxes upon the laborers. The despotic nature of German administration led to the MAJI MAJI REBELLION (1905–1906), in which thousands of Africans were killed and the Ngoni army was effectively destroyed.

German occupation in West Africa was similar to that of their other territories. Though Togoland was viewed as the *Musterkolonie* (model colony), and the administrative center of Lomé was developed extensively, forced labor and heavy taxation unfairly burdened the African population. The same could be said for the situation in Kamerun, where oppressive German rule resulted in the deaths of thousands.

However, German policy toward its African colonies did change after 1907 as the authoritarianism associated with Prussian rule began to wane. Germany invested capital for research in the fields of tropical MEDICINE and agriculture while augmenting the previous infrastructure improvements. As a result the African view of German occupation became one of measured respect. This era of improved relations was short-lived, however, as Germany, at the end of World War I (1914–18), ceded all of its colonial possessions under the terms of the Treaty of

Versailles. Britain, France, and Belgium then took over ruling the various former German colonies as mandates under the League of Nations.

German involvement in Africa was thus limited until the onset of World War II (1939–45). In 1940 France capitulated to Germany, and FRENCH WEST AFRICA fell to the control of the puppet Vichy government, which was loyal to Germany. In 1941 German forces under the leadership of General Irwin Rommel (1891–1944) landed in LIBYA. Making a push towards the SUEZ CANAL, Rommel gained initial success and proceeded as far as El Alamein in EGYPT. The British, however, led by General Bernard Montgomery (1887–1976), halted his advance and drove Rommel back into TUNISIA. American and British troops landed in MOROCCO and ALGERIA in 1942, creating a two-front war. The forces of Vichy France put up limited resistance before joining the Allies, and in 1943 Germany was forced from North Africa.

See also: COLONIAL CONQUEST (Vol. IV); COLONIALISM, INFLUENCE OF (Vol. IV); COLONIAL RULE (Vol. IV); WORLD WAR I AND AFRICA (Vol. IV); WORLD WAR II AND AFRICA (Vol. IV).

Gezira Scheme Agricultural project begun in 1911 in Gezira, the second-largest province in present-day Republic of the SUDAN. Starting as a small, private farm, the Gezira Scheme has since grown into a massive endeavor that today produces 60 percent of Sudan's total agricultural production. The project's first period of growth took place after 1925, following the construction of the Sennar Dam by the British colonial government in the Sudan. For the first time, large-scale irrigation was possible in the area along the west bank of the Blue Nile, south of KHARTOUM. Eager to develop the region's export commodities, Britain used the scheme to begin producing raw COTTON for shipment to its domestic textile factories.

The common practice of exporting agricultural commodities from colonial territories was usually detrimental to the local African economies. As the European powers grew cotton and other CASH CROPS to benefit their homelands, African economies got locked into a cycle of importing manufactured goods from abroad while producing commodities only for export.

Following Sudan's gaining independence, in 1956, the project underwent another period of rapid growth. Between 1957 and 1962 it increased in size by almost 1,000 percent. During that period, too, its products were

diversified, so that in addition to cotton, large quantities of wheat, GROUNDNUTS (peanuts), sorghum, vegetables, and fodder were grown. Animals that were raised included cattle, sheep, and goats. Today, the Gezira Scheme covers an area of more than 2.2 million *feddans* and involves more than 100,000 families living in more than a thousand villages. (A *feddan*, which is the unit of measurement used in Sudan, is a little larger than a customary acre.)

The project is now managed by a board of directors, half of whom are tenants. The tenant farmers pay approximately 4 percent of their proceeds from cotton back to the management. This allows them to use the land and water as well as various supplies, including fertilizers, insecticides and herbicides, and spare parts for their vehicles. Tenants also are entitled to use the light-rail system that operates within the project's area. Tenant fees are also used to pay for the project's government and its social development projects.

See also: AGRICULTURE (Vol. IV); COLONIAL RULE (Vol. IV); COLONIALISM, INFLUENCE OF (Vol. IV); ENGLAND AND AFRICA (Vol. IV); EXPORTS (Vol. IV).

Ghana Country with an area of 92,100 square miles (238,500 sq km) located on the coast of West Africa and bounded by the present-day countries of IVORY COAST, BURKINA FASO, and TOGO. During the colonial era Ghana was known as GOLD COAST COLONY.

Ghana in the 19th Century Britain became influential in the Gold Coast region through trading and missionary work. Coastal peoples, many from the Fante ethnic group, received MISSIONARIES in the 1820s and, consequently, the future colony began with a cadre of locally educated Fante elite. At the same time the ASHANTI EMPIRE controlled much of the region further inland, and they were strong enough to attack British invaders and Britain's Fante allies when they ventured too close to the Ashanti capital at KUMASI. These early battles were the start of nearly 70 years of sporadic warfare known as the ANGLO-ASHANTI WARS. Beginning in 1831, however, British and Fante relations with the Ashanti stabilized and remained that way for the next three decades. Captain George Maclean (1801–1847), the leader of the coastal merchants in the British colony, established order on the Gold Coast and was considered the real founder of British government there.

In 1844 Britain established direct control over the colony when Captain H. W. Hill and eight Fante chiefs made a unilateral declaration acknowledging British jurisdiction. It was during this period of stability, in about 1858, that British Basel missionaries introduced COCOA to the colony.

In 1863 the Ashanti became concerned about the British influence on the Fante and again began challenging

British authority in the region. By 1865 Britain, for its part, began to have second thoughts about its colonial commitment on the Gold Coast and even considered withdrawing. Concerned about the possible abandonment by the British, Fante leaders stepped up efforts to organize themselves to defend against an Ashanti invasion. By 1871, with British encouragement, the Fante chiefs agreed to a written constitution, thereby establishing the FANTE CONFEDERATION.

Having decided against withdrawal Britain redoubled its colonizing efforts in Gold Coast. Beginning in 1872 British forces took over the remaining Dutch trading forts on the Gold Coast. The withdrawal of the Dutch, who were former Ashanti trading partners and allies, rankled the Ashanti *asantehene*, or king. In protest, he sent soldiers to the coast. These forces were met by British soldiers who beat back the Ashanti and began a vicious campaign to quell further Ashanti resistance to British COLONIAL RULE. Flexing its imperial muscle, Britain invaded Kumasi, from 1873 to 1874, killing indiscriminately and burning homes and storehouses. With the Ashanti conquered, Britain established the Gold Coast Colony. Its administrative capital, originally at CAPE COAST, was moved to ACCRA in 1877.

Ghana during the Colonial Era: Gold Coast Colony In 1883 the Ashanti invited the British to mediate a succession dispute within the empire. This helped the British to put in place the next *asantehene*, Agyeman PREMPEH (1870–1931). The following year the European powers began partitioning the African continent at the BERLIN CONFERENCE, and Britain set about protecting the Gold Coast Colony interior from French and German expansion. Britain annexed kingdoms along the Volta River and made PROTECTORATE treaties with individual Ashanti states. Agyeman Prempeh refused to sign a treaty, however, instead attempting to reconquer those Ashanti states that signed with the British.

Kwame Nkrumah proclaimed Ghana's independence, March 6, 1957. *© Library of Congress*

Prempeh sent a delegation to London to assert Ashanti independence. Britain's government, however, had already made the decision to conquer the Ashanti, and in 1896 the British invaded Kumasi once again. Wanting to avert the devastation that accompanied the defeat of 1874, Prempeh agreed to be exiled to the SEYCHELLES, an island archipelago in the Indian Ocean, along with other Ashanti royalty.

In 1898 anti-British sentiment among the Ashanti erupted again. The rebellion was led by Yaa ASANTEWA (1850–1921), known as the Queen Mother of Ejisu, a fierce military leader whose son had been sent into exile with Prempeh. By the end of 1900, however, British reinforcements helped put down the rebellion and the PACIFICATION of the Gold Coast Colony was complete.

Trade in the Gold Coast had grown without major British investment in the late 19th century. However, because the world demand for cocoa was increasing, Britain and its missionaries distributed cocoa seedlings in the 1880s. Many of those Africans tha became engaged in growing cocoa were small farmers, who increased their earnings and participated in the colony's money economy. In order to increase the efficiency of cocoa exportation, by 1903 Britain moved the center of distribution from Kumasi to Accra, on the coast.

Gold Coast cocoa farmers had to sell their produce to a consortium of nine British companies that engaged in price fixing to keep their costs low and profits high. In 1937 the farmers protested by striking. Known as the GOLD COAST COCOA HOLDUP, the strike forced the British government to establish tighter controls over the colony's cash-crop economy.

By the end of the 19th century the British administration had built a network of rail lines from the interior to the coast. The infrastructure improvements encouraged economic growth and attracted European CONCESSIONAIRE COMPANIES to seek rights to exploit the region's MINING and timber resources. Along with CASH CROPS, GOLD, too, was moved by rail from Kumasi to the port at Sekondi.

In the 1890s the British administration and the colony's inhabitants came into conflict over land ownership. Traditionally Africans had not viewed land as being owned by a group or an individual; instead land was cared for by KINSHIP groups. Britain, on the other hand, tried to pass legislation to take ownership of all of the Gold Coast Colony territory that they designated "unoccupied" or "public" lands. This unpopular legislation prompted the politically conscious people of the Gold Coast to develop

organizations to retake control over the administration of their country.

A group of Western-educated African attorneys and businesspeople established the ABORIGINES' RIGHTS PROTECTION SOCIETY to try to gain more African input into the running of the colony. As early as 1850 Africans were nominated as unofficial participants in the Legislative Council that provided local opinion on colonial laws and the budget. However, following World War I (1914–18), the colony's elite wanted to change the composition of the Legislative Council so that Africans would be elected and would constitute a majority. In response British governor Sir Gordon Guggisberg (1869–1930) created provincial councils to advise the six African "unofficial" members of the Legislative Council.

From 1919 to 1927 Governor Guggisberg continued developing the Gold Coast's colonial economy and improving the infrastructure by using the financial resources from the boom years. Under his direction, British authorities built ACHIMOTA COLLEGE, Kolebu Hospital, and Takoradi Harbor, the Gold Coast's first deepwater port.

Despite these and other improvements made by Guggisberg's administration—and in contrast to the local African chiefs who participated in what they considered a colonial scheme—the colony's educated elite rejected the British overtures. Led by J. E. CASELY-HAYFORD (1866–1930), the Aborigines' Rights Protection Society founded the NATIONAL CONGRESS OF BRITISH WEST AFRICA to petition the British government in London for representative government.

The Road to Ghanaian Independence After World War II (1939–45) Gold Coast Colony was given a new constitution. However, the new middle class of clerks, merchants, mechanics, cocoa farmers, teachers, soldiers, and even unemployed school graduates was disillusioned by the failed promises of economic development, social improvement, and political self-determination. In 1947 the widespread discontent of the people ultimately led Dr. J. B. DANQUAH (1895–1965) and an association of educated elites to found the UNITED GOLD COAST CONVENTION (UGCC), which became the Gold Coast's first political party. Danquah is credited with coming up with the idea of changing the name of the independent Gold Coast to *Ghana*.

Believing the party needed the energy of more youthful members, Danquah invited Dr. Kwame NKRUMAH (1909–1972) to be the organizing secretary of the UGCC. Political riots in Accra in 1948 led to the detainment and deportation of a number of UGCC officials, including Nkrumah, but their nationalistic fervor was not to be denied. After his release Nkrumah moved to a more radical position of "Self Government *Now*," while Danquah worked with the British Coussey Committee to draw up a new Gold Coast constitution that would provide for local self-government.

Departing from the more gradualist program set forth by Danquah and the UGCC, in 1949 Nkrumah split to found the CONVENTION PEOPLE'S PARTY (CPP). As the leader of the CPP, Nkrumah was jailed for organizing a nonviolent, national strike that called for immediate independence. However, while Nkrumah was in prison, the CPP won the majority of seats in the first general elections held for the Legislative Assembly under the Coussey constitution. As a result Nkrumah was freed to serve as the leader of government business. In 1952 he became prime minister, sharing governmental power with the appointed British governor, Sir Charles Arden-Clarke. Five years later Nkrumah became the prime minister of the newly independent Gold Coast. Nkrumah renamed the nation *Ghana,* in honor of the glorious ancient African empire of the same name. In 1960 Ghana became a republic, with Nkrumah as its first president.

See also: COLONIALISM, INFLUENCE OF (Vol. IV); ENGLAND AND AFRICA (Vol. IV); GHANA (Vols. I, II, III, V).

Further reading: Kofi Nyidevu Awoonor, *Ghana: A Political History from Pre-European to Modern Times* (Accra, Ghana: Sedco Publishing, 1990); F. K. Buah, *A History of Ghana* (London: MacMillan Education, Ltd., 1980); Raymond E. Dumett, *El Dorado in West Africa: The Gold Mining Frontier, African Labor, and Colonial Capitalism in the Gold Coast, 1875–1900* (Athens, Ohio: Ohio University Press, 1998); Robert B. Edgerton, *The Fall of the Asante Empire: The Hundred-year War for Africa's Gold Coast* (New York: The Free Press, 1995).

gold   Prior to the arrival of Europeans on the African continent, gold and other NATURAL RESOURCES were under the control of Africans. In the 16th century Portuguese explorers began working with AKAN traders on the coast, exchanging European commodities, such as manufactured metal and CLOTH AND TEXTILES, for African gold. This area of West Africa subsequently became known to Europeans as the Gold Coast (present-day GHANA). Soon afterward a pattern of European interference and attempts to control the region's gold resources began to take hold, as more and more African gold was exported to Europe.

By the 19th century the West African goldfields had essentially been tapped, so the European powers looked elsewhere in Africa for other natural resources to exploit. However, when commercially viable gold deposits were discovered in the WITWATERSRAND, about 1886, the colonial MINING industry rapidly shifted to focus on gold in southern Africa. Ultimately the gold mines in southern African produced some of the greatest gold wealth in the world.

At first the capital needed for prospective mining and the heavy machinery needed for extraction came primarily from local sources. For example, mine owners often paid for gold mining with profits from the diamond industry, which was also booming. It was soon discovered, however, that mining southern Africa's deep, narrow gold veins needed more intensive investment than what could be offered by capitalists such as Cecil RHODES (1853–1902), who formed the Gold Fields of South Africa, Ltd., in 1887. As a result, Rhodes solicited investment from capital markets in London and New York, and the African gold industry became an international phenomenon. Most of the external investment in Africa before World War II (1939–45) went into the gold mines of SOUTH AFRICA.

In 1917 Sir Ernest Oppenheimer (1988–1957) used capital raised abroad to found the South Africa-based ANGLO-AMERICAN CORPORATION, which went on to become one of the world's largest mining and natural resource companies.

In general, investment in gold mines in southern Africa brought returns of between 5 and 9 percent, which was better than most other investment opportunities at the time. However, there was considerable variation in profitability, with 40 percent of the mines earning nothing and 35 percent earning considerably higher than average returns.

The extraction of gold and its shipment to Europe meant heavy investment in southern Africa's infrastructure, including roads, railways, and port facilities, as well. In addition, demand for miners was so great that much of the LABOR force migrated from all over southern Africa. This accelerated South Africa's development beyond that of other territories. It also led to URBANIZATION and the emergence of major cities such as JOHANNESBURG, DURBAN, and PRETORIA.

Although southern Africa was indisputably the prime location for gold extraction during the colonial period, deposits were found in the BELGIAN CONGO (today's Democratic Republic of the CONGO), TANGANYIKA (the mainland portion of present-day TANZANIA), and western Africa. The first European-run gold-mining activities in West Africa began in the 1880s, but gold mining there proved to have less impact on the ECONOMY than it did in South Africa. In West Africa small-scale, independent diggers were crucial to gold mining, while large private companies were the norm in southern Africa.

By 1961 Africa was producing about half of the world's gold supply. Even today the continent is one of the more profitable regions for the gold industry.

See also: ENGLAND AND AFRICA (Vol. IV); GOLD (Vols. I, II, III, V); MINERALS AND METALS (Vols. IV, V).

Gold Coast Cocoa Holdup (1937) Strike by COCOA planters in the GOLD COAST COLONY. The strike was in protest against the monopolistic practices of British cocoa buyers, who fixed cocoa prices at an artificially low price. By the 1930s the Gold Coast produced approximately 43 percent of the world's cocoa, the dry powder made from roasted cacao beans that is used to make chocolate. However, the producers were not able to get fair prices for their products because the system of colonial mercantilism designated the buyers to whom Africans could sell their CASH CROPS. A worldwide economic depression in the 1930s depressed agricultural commodity prices and intensified the economic plight of the producers.

In 1937 the nine British companies that were the designated cocoa purchasers fixed the prices they paid in an attempt to generate profits at the expense of producers. A typical response to such a practice in an open market might be to boycott imports from the unfair trading partner. In the Gold Coast, however, colonial policy prevented the colonies from manufacturing their own goods and, for this reason, there was no way to substitute for British manufactured imports. Moreover, since the colonial producers weren't allowed to seek alternative buyers for their crops, the only protest open to them was to withhold their cocoa from market and thus try to force a price increase.

This "cocoa holdup," as it became known, was disastrous for the farmers because perishable agricultural products, such as cocoa, could not be sold once they spoiled. It was also bad for the Gold Coast colonial economy since, at the time, cocoa EXPORTS made up 63 percent of the colony's total exports. The strike did, however, lead the British to establish government-run marketing boards to provide the producers of cocoa and other crops with a larger share of the price they received on the world market. The marketing boards also served to level out price fluctuations by paying lower prices to producers in profitable years and higher prices in lean years.

See also: AGRICULTURE (Vol. IV); COLONIAL RULE (Vol. IV); COLONIALISM, INFLUENCE OF (Vol. IV).

Gold Coast Colony West African British colony extending from present-day IVORY COAST to TOGO. Established in 1874, the colony became the independent country of GHANA in 1957.

Following its victory over the Ashanti in 1874, Britain established the Gold Coast Colony with its administrative capital at CAPE COAST (later moved to ACCRA). Over the next three decades Britain expanded its coast-based colony ,through the exercise of military incursions, to include the Ashanti state and the Northern Territories.

In the 20th century Britain built ports and an extensive railroad system using African LABOR. The railway system covered the Gold Coast forest area more effectively than any other transportation system in tropical Africa, allowing British and other European companies to extract the region's agricultural riches, including COCOA, which became the mainstay of the colonial ECONOMY.

Germany's loss of its African colonies in the aftermath of World War I (1914–18) led to British control of the western half of what was then TOGOLAND and its incorporation into the Gold Coast. The territory later was made part of independent Ghana in 1957, following a plebiscite, or vote of the people.

From 1919 to 1927, under the direction of Governor Sir Gordon Guggisberg (1869–1930), the Gold Coast Colony prospered in a boom economy. The economy faltered, however, first during the worldwide Great Depression of the 1930s and then again during World War II (1939–45).

Although they received a new constitution after the war, the people of the Gold Coast were unhappy with the postwar economy and their low level of participation in the government. There had always been a significant level of political consciousness among the colony's sizeable Western-educated elite, who organized both the ABORIGINES' RIGHTS PROTECTION SOCIETY in the late 19th century and the NATIONAL CONGRESS OF BRITISH WEST AFRICA in the interwar period.

In 1947 J. B. DANQUAH (1895–1965) founded the UNITED GOLD COAST CONVENTION (UGCC), which was the Gold Coast's first full-fledged political party. Two years later Kwame NKRUMAH (1902–1972) split from the UGCC to found the CONVENTION PEOPLE'S PARTY, a more radical organization that intensified the political opposition to continuing British rule with its demand of "Self Government Now." By 1957 the Gold Coast Colony achieved its independence, choosing the historically and culturally significant name, Ghana.

See also: COLONIALISM, INFLUENCE OF (Vol. IV); ENGLAND AND AFRICA (Vols. III, IV, V); GOLD COAST (Vol. III); NATIONALISM AND INDEPENDENCE MOVEMENTS (Vol. IV).

Further reading: F. K. Buah, A History of Ghana (London: MacMillan Education, Ltd., 1980).

Goldie, George (Sir) (1846–1925) *Trader and administrator who founded the Royal Niger Company*

Born George Dashwood Goldie Taubman, George Goldie was an influential British empire builder in NIGERIA during the 19th century. During the late 1860s he spent time in EGYPT and present-day Republic of the SUDAN and studied West African societies. Within two years of his arrival in Nigeria in 1877, he succeeded in carving out a monopolistic concern, the UNITED AFRICA COMPANY, from the many British trading companies operating in the region. By 1884, at his pleading, the British government established a PROTECTORATE over the Oil Rivers District of the NIGER DELTA. Two years later the government granted the United Africa Company a royal charter, and it became the ROYAL NIGER COMPANY, empowered with the administrative right to enter into treaties with African states. By the early 1890s it had established a monopoly over trade in the lower Niger Delta, displacing French and African traders.

In 1887 Goldie was awarded a knighthood in recognition of his assistance to Britain in securing its claims to southern Nigeria at the BERLIN CONFERENCE (1884–85). However, by the mid 1890s it became increasingly clear that Britain's interest in Nigeria would be better served by establishing a formal protectorate. A Goldie-led military expedition to northern Nigeria, in 1897, had been successful in crushing recalcitrant Muslim states in the region, but it touched off a conflict with France. The Royal Niger Company's charter was revoked, and in January 1900 Britain declared separate protectorates in southern and northern Nigeria. Goldie left Nigeria and, after spending time in China, SOUTH AFRICA, and SOUTHERN RHODESIA (today's ZIMBABWE), he returned to England, where he became the president of the Royal Geographical Society, in 1905. He declined several offers of positions in the colonies, including the opportunity to succeed Cecil RHODES (1853–1902) at the helm of the BRITISH SOUTH AFRICA COMPANY.

See also: COLONIAL CONQUEST (Vol. IV); ENGLAND AND AFRICA (Vol. IV); ROYAL AFRICAN COMPANY (Vol. III).

Gordimer, Nadine (1923–) *South African novelist and anti-apartheid activist*

Born to affluent, white, Jewish parents in the South African MINING town of Springs, near JOHANNESBURG in the TRANSVAAL, Gordimer's early education was interrupted by health concerns. Her mother, convinced her daughter had a weak heart, kept Gordimer at home for a good portion of her teenage years. As an alternative to loneliness, Gordimer became an avid reader and writer. She began to write fiction at age nine, and she was only 15 when she published her first story, "Come Again Tomorrow," in a South African magazine.

In her childhood Gordimer also began to develop the sensibilities that led her to rebel against the racist structure of South African society. Among the first experiences to alert the young Gordimer to the wrongs the white minority perpetrated against the oppressed African majority was the offensive treatment of African miners by white shopkeepers that she often witnessed. Such experiences became central to her writing.

After attending the University of Witwatersrand for one year, in 1944, Gordimer regularly published many stories in South African magazines throughout her twenties. Her collection of short stories, entitled *Face to Face,* which addressed the psychology of a society racially at odds with itself, appeared in 1949, one year after the formal institution of APARTHEID. Then, through the sponsorship of Afrikaner poet Uys Krige (1910–1987), Gordimer had a story published in 1951 in *The New Yorker,* an American magazine that would give her work its first international exposure and serve as a forum for her stories in future years. Two years later her first novel, *The Lying Days,* was published, followed by *A World of Strangers* (1958). Gordimer thus launched a career that ultimately placed her at the forefront of the literary anti-apartheid movement both in SOUTH AFRICA and throughout the world.

See also: GORDIMER, NADINE (Vol. V); LITERATURE IN COLONIAL AFRICA (Vol. IV); LITERATURE IN MODERN AFRICA (Vol. V).

Gordon, Charles George ("Chinese" Gordon) (1833–1885) *English soldier and governor general of the Sudan*

Following in his father's footsteps, Gordon chose a military career, entering the Royal Military Academy in his hometown of Woolwich, England, in 1848. Thereafter, he served in the Crimean War (1853–56) and was wounded in 1855. He also served in China during the Second Opium War (1856–60) and was instrumental in the suppression of the Taiping Rebellion (1851–64). His successes in China earned him the nickname "Chinese" Gordon.

In 1873 Gordon accepted an offer from Khedive ISMAIL (1830–1895) of EGYPT to become governor of Equatoria, a province in the southern part of present-day Republic of the SUDAN, taking the place of Sir Samuel BAKER (1821–1893). In 1877 Gordon was appointed governor general of the Sudan, DARFUR, and Equatoria. He actively worked to eliminate the region's SLAVE TRADE and put down a number of rebellions. Gordon resigned as governor general in 1879, following the dismissal of Khedive Ismail by the ruling Ottoman Empire, which was heavily influenced by Britain.

From 1880 to 1882 Gordon spent time in various capacities in India, China, the British CAPE COLONY in southern Africa, and Palestine. In 1883 King LEOPOLD II (1835–1909) of Belgium offered Gordon the opportunity to help establish the CONGO FREE STATE. Gordon accepted but the British government denied him permission, and the position instead went to Henry Morton STANLEY (1841–1904).

In 1884 Gordon was sent to the Sudan for his ill-fated final mission to organize the evacuation of Egyptian troops from KHARTOUM. There the troops were facing the advancing rebel forces of Muhammad Ahmad al-MAHDI (1844–1885), the messianic leader of the MAHDIYYA movement, who was attempting to free the Sudan from Egyptian rule. Instead of carrying out the planned evacuation, Gordon attempted to rally the defenders and hold Khartoum against the Mahdists. The British government of William Gladstone (1809–1898), however, was reluctant to support Gordon, and relief troops were not dispatched until late 1884. Khartoum fell in early 1885, two days before the troops came within sight of the city. Gordon was killed in the conflict, and the rebels displayed his head on a pike.

Gordon's gruesome death caused a great public outcry that eventually played a part in the downfall of Gladstone's administration. The British avenged Gordon's death, in 1898, at the Battle of OMDURMAN, where they defeated the Mahdi's successor, Khalifa ABDALLAHI IBN MUHAMMAD (1846–1899), and retook control of the Sudan.

See also: COLONIAL RULE (Vol. IV); ENGLAND AND AFRICA (Vol. IV).

government, systems of The late 19th century witnessed the most dramatic and far-reaching change in how authority was exercised in the history of Africa. While a European colonial presence had gradually taken hold on the continent, it was the PARTITION and subsequent COLONIAL CONQUEST taking place during the late 1800s that established COLONIAL RULE throughout virtually the whole continent. In general, colonial ministers and administrators within the governments of the European countries handed down directives for the colonial administrators in Africa, who were expected to carry out these directives by whatever means necessary.

The British, using a system of *indirect rule* that was refined by colonial administrators such as Frederick LUGARD (1858–1945), used local rulers and institutions to govern many of their African colonies. This style of governance worked best in regions where a strong local government already existed. Such colonies included NIGERIA, BUGANDA, and The GAMBIA. Belgium employed a similar system in RUANDA-URUNDI, a former German colony that became a Belgian MANDATE in the wake of Germany's defeat in WORLD WAR I (1914–1918).

Indirect rule was viable because it allowed the colonial powers to maintain control without having to commit an inordinate amount of resources or manpower. Instead, they were able to cajole the local governing elites into complying with the demands of the administration. In return, the local African leaders, their families, and sometimes their entire ethnic group received preferential treatment from the colonialists. Early on in the British PROTECTORATE of UGANDA, for example, the Buganda Agreement of 1900 gave vast landholdings and a measure of autonomy to Mwanga (c. 1866–1903), the *kabaka,* or king, of Buganda. In exchange, Mwanga aided the British by staffing the colonial police with Ganda (people from Buganda), who also administered the law and collected taxes for the British administration.

Unlike the British and the Belgians, the French employed a system called *direct rule.* Both direct and indirect rule used Africans to do the work of the colonial administrations. However, direct rule led the French to divide formerly unified territories and peoples in order to diminish the strength of local rulers and suppress any nationalistic tendencies among their colonial subjects. In addition, unlike the British administrators, direct rule meant that the French administrators hand-picked Afri-can officials to fill positions of power within the colonial governing structure. These French-assigned administrators often lacked the respect and legitimacy enjoyed by the Africans within the structure of indirect colonial rule.

Regardless of the kind of rule, the installation of colonial governments meant that long-standing African systems of government were dismantled or subordinated to what was essentially rule along Western lines. Within these structures, the ability to govern effectively depended greatly on the willingness of the authoritarian administrations to employ harsh controls—and even violence—to maintain their upper hand over the widespread and disparate colonial populations.

See also: DUAL MANDATE (Vol. IV); MANDATE (Vol. IV); GOVERNMENT, SYSTEMS OF (Vols. I, II, III, V); TRUST TERRITORY (Vol. IV).

groundnuts (peanuts) Agricultural commodity important for its nutritional value as well as for its oil, which has many uses. In the 16th century Portuguese traders brought the first groundnuts to Africa from South America. Groundnuts grow best in sandy soil and are very drought resistant, which made them an ideal crop to cultivate in Africa's sub-Saharan Sahel region.

Groundnuts—which are called peanuts in the United States—were successfully cultivated in large quantities in West Africa as early as the 1830s. By the end of the 19th century groundnuts were one of the region's most valuable CASH CROPS, especially in the SENEGAMBIA REGION, CAMEROON, GUINEA-BISSAU, and northern SIERRA LEONE. West African groundnut exportation was, and still is, centered on the coastal region from DAKAR, in SENEGAL, to the port city of BANJUL, in The GAMBIA.

The busy port of Dakar, seen in 1950, was a major link in the extensive groundnut (peanut) trade. © *New York Times*

The colonial development of AGRICULTURE in West Africa led to a sub-class of laborers known as "strange," or nonresident, farmers. These workers, almost always males, migrated to wherever there was a need for LABOR in order to make money to pay colonial taxes. In the Senegambia region farmers migrated twice annually from the hinterlands, first to plant the new groundnut crop, and then to harvest and transport the crop to the ports.

Groundnut cultivation also succeeded in parts of GOLD COAST COLONY (present-day GHANA), Northern NIGERIA, CHAD, and southern Sudan. Eventually, small farmers cultivated plots of groundnuts in parts of East Africa, as well. However, settlers in BRITISH EAST AFRICA failed in their attempts to establish large-scale groundnut cultivation in TANGANYIKA and UGANDA, where the soil proved to be too dry and hard.

Even now groundnuts and groundnut oil are among West Africa's most important EXPORTS. For example, today nearly 60 percent of the arable land in The Gambia is dedicated to groundnut cultivation.

See also: CASH CROPS (Vol. V); TRADE AND COMMERCE (Vols. IV, V).

Gueye, Lamine (1891–1968) *Senegalese lawyer and politician*

Although born in the FRENCH SOUDAN (now MALI), Gueye came from a family that originally was from SENEGAL. He studied law in France during World War I (1914–18) and then returned to West Africa, settling in Senegal, where he was the first black attorney in the French African colonies. Drawn to politics, he initially was a supporter of Blaise DIAGNE (1872–1934), the Senegalese deputy to the French National Assembly, although, in the course of time, the two became frequent political opponents.

After serving as mayor of DAKAR from 1925 to 1926, Gueye made several unsuccessful runs in legislative elections during the 1920s and 1930s. In 1935 he reorganized the Socialist Party, but was unable to win widespread support among the young members of Senegal's elite whom he had hoped would rally to his cause.

After World War II (1939–45) Gueye and Léopold SENGHOR (1906–2001) won the support of the French Section of the Worker's International, a socialist political party. This provided a base of political power that allowed Gueye to become mayor of Dakar once again, in 1946. Along with Senghor he was elected to the French National Assembly, but he lost the seat, in 1951, when he broke with Senghor. In 1958, after a 10-year split, Gueye and Senghor reunited to oppose the creation of autonomous African nations, advocating instead a federal system that would unite the newly independent African states.

Gueye's party remained in power in Senegal for the remainder of his life, and he was serving as president of Senegal's National Assembly when he died, in 1968.

See also: COLONIAL RULE (Vol. IV); FRANCE AND AFRICA (Vols. III, IV, V); NATIONALISM AND INDEPENDENCE MOVEMENTS (Vol. IV).

Guinea West African country on the Atlantic Ocean coast, some 95,000 square miles (246,100 sq km) in size, that takes its name from the term used to describe the coast of West Africa south of the western Sahara. Guinea is bordered by GUINEA-BISSAU, SENEGAL, the Republic of MALI, IVORY COAST, LIBERIA, and SIERRA LEONE. In 1849 the coastal region that included Guinea became a French PROTECTORATE. Later it was annexed with the name *Rivières du Sud*. Guinea, which had been a part of Senegal, became a separate French colony in 1891.

Guinea during the Colonial Era: French West Africa In 1895 Guinea became a component of FRENCH WEST AFRICA and Noël Ballay (1847–1902), the colony's first governor, named Conakry its capital. French control of the colony, however, was not solidified until 1898 with the capture of SAMORI TOURÉ (c. 1830–1900), the Muslim warlord who had led a vigorous resistance against French COLONIAL RULE.

France divided Guinea into 20 administrative *cercles* (districts), each headed by a French officer. The *cercles* were further divided into cantons headed by indigenous chiefs. Under French supervision, the chiefs collected a head tax from all persons over the age of eight, thereby generating sufficient revenue to meet most of the territory's administrative budget.

Unlike Senegal and FRENCH SOUDAN (present-day Mali), Guinea was slow to develop a significant cash-crop economy. After unsuccessful efforts to promote peanut production for export, colonial efforts switched to a focus of collecting wild RUBBER, which made up 73 percent of the value of all exports between 1892 and 1913. In 1914, however, the rubber market collapsed and never recovered. It was not until the development of banana plantations in the 1930s that Guinea had another significantly profitable export. After World War II (1939–45), MINING began to develop, first with iron ore between 1953 and 1966, and later with bauxite (aluminum ore), which became Guinea's major export after independence.

Conakry became an urban center and the administrative hub for the territory. It also was where students were recruited to become civil servants or junior commercial administrators. In addition to elementary and secondary schools, there were vocational schools with professional sections that offered special training for students who wished to be apprenticed in a skilled trade. AGRICULTURE was also taught, and students learned how to harvest GROUNDNUTS (peanuts) and collect rubber. These educational opportunities, however, were limited to a small segment of the population.

Although France had abolished SLAVERY in its colonies in 1848, most of the manual LABOR done in the territory, including farming, was carried out by laborers who were no better off than slaves. The French freed former slaves and captives in French Soudan and Upper Guinea, only to house them in "freedom villages," which became known as "villages of the commandant's captives" because the tenants were used as slave labor for French public works projects.

After World War II Guinea was the site of increased political unrest at all levels of government. As a result, the French encouraged Guinean Africans to identify with individual ethnic groups in an effort to dilute the potential power of nationalism. At the same time the indigenous, labor-based political party, Democratic Party of Guinea (Parti Démocratique de Guinée, PDG), sought a national Guinean consciousness.

The PDG began to organize support from disparate segments of the community, such as peasants, women, and the youth. Guinea was slow to experience political reforms, however, because its people had neither EDUCATION nor democratic experience, and the French colonizers dominated the electoral process until 1954.

Finally, under the leadership of the LABOR UNION organizer Ahmed Sékou TOURÉ (1922–1984), the PDG was able to challenge French control. Appealing to the groups targeted by the PDG, Touré used Islam to present a united front at the polls, and in 1956 he was elected to serve as the mayor of Conakry and as Guinea's deputy to the French National Assembly.

The Road to Guinean Independence In 1958 Sékou Touré resisted further French imperialism when French president Charles DE GAULLE (1890–1970) tried to recruit the territories to become members of the FRENCH UNION (similar to the British Commonwealth of Nations). Each of the French colonies was allowed to vote "yes" or "no" to this union, and de Gaulle campaigned in each colony trying to secure a "yes" vote.

When de Gaulle visited Guinea, Sékou Touré told de Gaulle that, in Guinea, "we prefer poverty in liberty to riches in chains." With a 95 percent negative vote, Guinea was the only colony to vote "no." In an effort to punish Guinea for snubbing de Gaulle and the French Union, France withdrew completely from Guinea, taking away financial support for development and favored-nations status for Guinea's EXPORTS. In addition, France encouraged its allies among the industrialized nations not to trade with its former colony. Guinea's neighbors, however, admired Guinea for having the power to resist the French, and they quietly continued their political and economic relations as before.

Guinea proclaimed its independence on October 2, 1958, and in November 1958 Sékou Touré joined Kwame NKRUMAH (1909–1972) in declaring a Union of West African States with a goal of implementing a United States of Africa, as idealized by PAN-AFRICANISM.

Guinea joined the United Nations in December 1958. Both the United States and the former Soviet Union quickly made overtures of alliance, but Guinea was determined to remain neutral in the Cold War. Thus Guinea began its existence as an independent nation both economically and politically isolated from the international community.

See also: COLD WAR AND AFRICA (Vols. IV, V); COLONIAL RULE (Vol. IV); COLONIALISM, INFLUENCE OF (Vol. IV); FRANCE AND AFRICA (Vols. III, IV, V); GUINEA (Vols. I, II, III, V).

Further reading: Martin A. Klein, *Slavery and Colonial Rule in French West Africa* (New York: Cambridge University Press, 1998); Patrick Manning, *Francophone sub-Saharan Africa, 1880–1995* (New York: Cambridge University Press, 1998); Jean Suret-Canale, *French Colonialism in Tropical Africa, 1900–1945* (New York: Pica Press, 1971).

Guinea-Bissau Country in coastal West Africa bordered by SENEGAL to the north and GUINEA to both the south and east and having an area of 14,100 square miles (36,500 sq km). The population of Guinea-Bissau is dominated by the Balanta and Fula peoples, with large Manjaca, MANDINKA, and Pepel minorities.

By the beginning of the 19th century the inhabitants of the Guinea-Bissau region already had a long history of relations with Portuguese merchants that was reflected in their LANGUAGE, culture, and trading practices. Portuguese traders had long relied on Guinea's population to supply their SLAVE TRADE, but when Portugal outlawed the trade in 1869, regional trade focused instead on GROUNDNUTS (peanuts), RUBBER, and ivory. Despite its long-standing activity in the region, however, Portugal did not begin its COLONIAL CONQUEST of the region in earnest until the latter half of the 19th century.

Guinea-Bissau during the Colonial Era: Portuguese Guinea By 1879 Portugal had succeeded in defining the boundaries of its territory on mainland West Africa, and the region then became known to Europeans as the colony of PORTUGUESE GUINEA. The European colonial powers later formalized their territorial claims with the PARTITION of the continent at the BERLIN CONFERENCE of 1884–85.

Because of its merchant activities Portugal had developed the coastal settlements of Portuguese Guinea by the 1890s. In the interior regions of the colony, however, there was less Portuguese influence. That began to change between the end of the 19th century and World War I (1914–18). This was when Portuguese forces engaged in military struggles with Africans in attempts to consolidate power in the region and maintain the borders of its colony, which were often in dispute.

> As they took control of the Guinea-Bissau region, the Portuguese benefited from discord between the region's Muslim and non-Muslim populations. West Africa's ongoing JIHADS, or holy wars, served to pit Muslims against those peoples who continued to follow traditional RELIGION, thereby making it more difficult to mount organized resistance to Portugal's efforts.

It took another 30 years of intermittent fighting before the interior of the territory was fully under Portuguese administration. The Bijagos archipelago, a group of islands off the Portuguese Guinea coast, came fully under colonial control only in 1936.

In 1941 Portugal moved the colonial capital from the island of Bolama to Bissau, a major commercial center and port town on the mainland. Later in the 1940s, in a northern border dispute, Portugal lost the Casamance River region, formerly a busy commercial center, to the French.

After World War II (1939–45) Africans began demanding the overthrow of European COLONIAL RULE throughout the continent. In 1952 Portugal compromised with the demands of nationalists in its African colonies and made the colonies—Portuguese Guinea, ANGOLA, and MOZAMBIQUE—overseas provinces. Despite the concession, Portugal still remained stubbornly determined to retain its colonial possessions and continued to use any means it could to deny its territories total independence. Indeed, the colonial credo declared that Portuguese unity would not allow for "transfers, cession, or abandonment."

In 1956 Amílcar CABRAL (1924–1973), along with Raphael Barbosa, secretly formed the African Party for the Independence of Guinea and Cape Verde (Partido Africano de Indepencia de Guine e Capo Verde, PAIGC). The clandestine group soon found many willing recruits and began agitating for improved social, political, and economic conditions for Africans in both Portuguese Guinea and the CAPE VERDE ISLANDS.

The situation in Portuguese Guinea was inflamed by the brutal treatment of Africans at the hands of the Portuguese police. One of the worst incidents occurred in Bissau at the port of Pidjiguiti, in August 1959. Police shot and killed 50 striking dockworkers, injuring as many as 100 others.

In 1960 the PAIGC moved its headquarters to Conakry, in neighboring Guinea, which had recently achieved independence from France. The following year it began its armed rebellion against the Portuguese government, which brought in more than 35,000 troops to maintain order. The protracted war for independence would conclude only in 1973, with Portugal finally recognizing an independent Guinea-Bissau in September of the following year.

See also: COLD WAR AND AFRICA (Vols. IV, V); GUINEA-BISSAU (Vols. I, II, III, V); INDEPENDENCE MOVEMENTS (Vol. V); NATIONALISM AND INDEPENDENCE MOVEMENTS (Vol. IV); PORTUGAL AND AFRICA (Vols. III, IV, V); SOVIET UNION AND AFRICA (Vols. IV, V).

Further reading: Malyn Newitt, *Portugal in Africa: The Last Hundred Years* (Harlow, U.K.: Longman, 1981).

Gungunyana (Gungunyane, Ngungunyana) (c. 1850–1906) *Ngoni king in Gazaland, in southern Mozambique*

Upon the death of his father, Mzila (c. 1810–1884), Gungunyana seized power to become king of the Ngoni living in south-central MOZAMBIQUE. Since Portugal was intent on claiming his multiethnic kingdom as part of its colonial territory, Gungunyana negotiated the Gazaland Concession with Britain in order to retain his sovereignty. The concession called for the BRITISH SOUTH AFRICA COMPANY (BSAC) to assist him in fending off Portuguese incursions in exchange for the kingdom's trading and mineral rights. The BSAC later recognized the Portuguese claim to the region, however, and Portugal responded with a military campaign to solidify control over Gunguyana's territory. The king resisted but was eventually defeated, in 1895. and exiled to the Azores Islands, where he died, in 1906. With Gunguyana's defeat the Gaza state, which had originated after his grandfather Soshangane (c. 1790s–c. 1859) was forced out of Zululand in the 1830s, came to an end.

See also: COLONIAL CONQUEST (Vol. IV); PARTITION (Vol. IV); PORTUGAL AND AFRICA (Vol. IV).

H

Haile Selassie I (Tafari Makonnen) (1892–1975)
Ethiopian emperor

Born into one of Ethiopia's leading families, Tafari Makonnen, as Selassie was named at birth, was the son of Makonnen Walka Mikael (1852–1908). The elder Makonnen was one of Ethiopia's most powerful military and political leaders. Until his death, he was considered by many to be the logical choice to succeed Emperor MENELIK II (1845–1913). Groomed from the start for a central role in a modernized ETHIOPIA, Tafari learned both French and Amharic from his French missionary schoolmaster. He also developed a respect for modern, European ways, which he believed were essential to the continued survival and independence of his country.

After the death of his father, Tafari went to the emperor's court, in ADDIS ABABA, where he continued his education and training. He remained there after Menelik II was succeeded by his grandson, Lij Iyasu (1896–1935). A weak ruler whose lack of seriousness and pro-Islamic leaning increasingly angered the traditionalists among Ethiopia's elite, Lij Iyasu was deposed in 1916. Seeking a compromise between various factions, the leaders of the coup replaced him with Menelik's daughter, Zawditu (1876–1930), who was made empress. As the respected son of an even more respected father, Tafari was appointed prince-regent and heir to the throne.

Tafari quickly began solidifying his position and taking control of the nation. Opponents were removed from positions of power or jailed. By the early 1920s he was firmly in charge of Ethiopia. When Zawditu died, in 1930, there was no one to oppose his final ascension to power, and he declared himself emperor on November 2, 1930, taking the name Haile Selassie I, meaning "Might of the Trinity."

As he had before becoming emperor, Haile Selassie endeavored to modernize the nation, encouraging education and the development of a more European-style government. One of his major accomplishments was the abolition of SLAVERY, long a part of Ethiopian traditions but which, until it was abolished, had prevented the nation's membership in the League of Nations.

As the 1930s continued, however, Ethiopia became the target of aggression on the part of the Fascist government of Benito Mussolini (1883–1945). In spite of numerous attempts at diplomatic solutions, Haile Selassie found his country invaded by Italian forces in 1935. Unable to mount much of a defense against the superior armaments and numbers of the Italian invaders, Haile Selassie could only appeal to the League of Nations for help. The league, afraid to anger the belligerent Italian dictator, failed to act, and by March 1936 Mussolini's troops were advancing on Addis Ababa, and Haile Selassie fled into exile.

As the voice of independent Ethiopia, Haile Selassie spent the early days of World War II (1939–45) in London. Then, backed by Allied forces, he was part of a force that eventually drove out the Italians and liberated Ethiopia, in 1941. After the end of the war he devoted much of his energy to his modernizing efforts, founding a university and even establishing what was then Africa's first airline.

Beneath these efforts, however, lay another aspect of both Haile Selassie and his regime. A firm believer in an autocratic system, as time went on he became even more rigid and more authoritarian. No longer content with simply governing his country, he engaged in shows of power, sweeping through the city of Addis Ababa in his limousines

Ethiopia's new emperor, Haile Selassie I (wearing crown), leaves his coronation ceremony, in 1930. © *Agencia Gráfica/New York Times*

or forcing court officials to prostrate themselves before him. Such actions were not unnoticed by elements that were growing increasingly disenchanted with the aging emperor.

Haile Selassie's flight from Mussolini's forces left him free to plead his nation's case. On June 30, 1936, he delivered a memorable address to the League of Nations, in Geneva, calling on the league and the stronger nations of the world to protect the weaker ones from aggression. The speech made him a major figure on the world stage and an important symbol of the victims of fascist aggression. In Ethiopia, however, Haile Selassie's flight was seen as a disgraceful break with a militaristic tradition in which leaders were expected to fight to the death rather than flee.

Meanwhile, external difficulties began to manifest, fueled to a large extent by the tensions of the Cold War. Neighboring SOMALIA was beginning to make claims on the OGADEN region, which Hailie Selassie believed to be part of Ethiopia. Meanwhile, ERITREA, which had been an Italian colony until the end of World War II, was demanding freedom from Ethiopia. By 1963 armed rebellion began in Eritrea, and the rebels received increasing amounts of aid from not only Islamic countries, which supported Eritrean Muslims, but also from China and the former Soviet Union. All of this initiated the downfall of Haile Selassie, who had held power in Ethiopia since the days of World War I (1914–18).

See also: ENGLAND AND AFRICA (Vol. IV); HAILE SELASSIE (Vol. V); ITALIAN SOMALILAND (Vol. IV); ITALY AND AFRICA (Vol. IV); RASTAFARIANISM (Vol. V).

Further readings: Harold G. Marcus, *Haile Selassie I: The Formative Years* (New Jersey: Red Sea Press, 1987); Anthony Mockler, *Haile Selassie's War: The Ethiopian–Italian Campaign, 1935–1940* (New York: Random House, 1985); Peter Schwab, ed., *Ethiopia and Haile Selassie* (New York: Facts On File, 1972).

Harris, William Wade (c. 1850–1929) *Liberian-born evangelist*

Born in LIBERIA into a Grebo family, Harris was raised in the Methodist Church, but then became affiliated with the Protestant Episcopal Church. He was intensely political at first, opposing the Americo-Liberian elite who controlled Liberia. Eventually he was imprisoned for participating in a pro-British rebellion to place Liberia under British rule.

In prison Harris claimed to have had a vision of the archangel Gabriel, and he declared that he was now a prophet, preparing the way for the returning Jesus Christ. Shedding European clothes and donning plain white robes, he began preaching a simple Christian faith, one free of almost all doctrinal complexity.

From 1913 to 1915 Harris, accompanied by two or three women, including Maame Harris "Grace" TANI (c. 1880–1958), walked from Liberia through IVORY COAST and into the GOLD COAST COLONY (today's GHANA), preaching and baptizing his new converts. While the women sang and danced he outlined his basic theology, proclaiming that God and Christ had come to defeat the spirits of traditional African religions and that his converts merely had to accept the Bible, follow the Ten Commandments, and destroy any traditionalist fetishes they encountered. After baptizing those individuals who accepted his message, Harris moved on, telling the new converts to join whatever Protestant church they might find nearby. Harris also appointed 12 "apostles," whom the converts were urged to follow if there was no church at hand.

Transforming conversion into an uncomplicated process—and not tampering with any new convert's individual practice of polygamy—Harris attracted thousands of adherents, including 120,000 in Ivory Coast alone. The strength of his following alarmed many officials, including the government of Ivory Coast, which deported him to Liberia.

It is believed that one of the reasons for the popularity of Harris's preaching was that he was willing to convert and baptize women, who had been neglected in the conversion attempts of other evangelists. Since many of the people to whom he preached came from matrilineal societies, this inclusion of women clearly must have had a powerful effect.

Harris died in Liberia, in 1929, but his churches continued after his death. Indeed, by the 1980s "Harrism" had become the largest single Protestant denomination in Ivory Coast.

See also: CHRISTIANITY, INFLUENCE OF (Vol. IV); MISSIONARIES (Vols. IV, V); POLYGAMY (Vol. I); PROPHETS AND PROPHETIC MOVEMENTS (Vols. IV, V).

Further reading: Gordon McKay Haliburton, *The Prophet Harris* (London: Longman, 1971).

Hasan, Mawlai al- (Moulay Hasan, Mulay Hasan)
(d. 1894) *Moroccan monarch*

Mawlai Hasan I, a member of the Alaoui dynasty, ruled MOROCCO from 1873 to 1894. Hasan tried to prevent the disintegration of his kingdom by utilizing his understanding of indigenous culture to control the different ethnic groups within his domain. He made annual tours of his state to personally collect taxes, administer justice, and display his military power to the various nomadic groups in the interior. Hasan also engaged in various forms of diplomacy with the encroaching European imperial powers in an effort to avoid any confrontation that they could use to justify usurping his authority. He resisted European attempts to lure Morocco into any situation in which it would lose its sovereignty.

The title *mawlai (moulay, mawlay, mulay)* is a term used to address a sultan, unless that sultan's name is Mohammed, in which case the term *sidi* is used.

As a monarch, Hasan made limited reforms in an effort to adapt his state to the new world order of the time. Because Europeans were competing to establish an exclusive political relationship with Morocco, Hasan divided up his various involvements with them so that no one European power could claim control over the whole coountry. In modernizing the army, for example, he sent some students to the British Royal Military Academy and others to Gibraltar. In 1876 he hired Sir Harry MacLean (1848–1920), an Arabic speaker who preferred dressing in Moroccan style, to be the chief instructor of the infantry school. The French then insisted that they train the artillery, sending their own instructor, Jules Erckman. In addition, Hasan employed a British chief of staff, Spanish cartographers, and Italian and German firms to build weapons. Efforts like these helped Hasan maintain Moroccan sovereignty during his rule, but European encroachment continued after his death, and independence was eventually lost under his son Mawlai Abdelaziz (r. 1894–1908).

See also: COLONIAL CONQUEST (Vol. IV); PARTITION (Vol. IV).

Hausa Dominant ethnic group in the region known as Hausaland, located in present-day northern NIGERIA. When Hausa people first came into contact with colonizing Europeans, the Hausa States existed as a part of the SOKOTO CALIPHATE, a FULANI-led Muslim empire.

Britain claimed Sokoto as part of its PROTECTORATE of Northern Nigeria, and, in 1900, the British launched an invasion on the pretext that the caliphate was violating

British laws banning the SLAVE TRADE. Led by High Commissioner Frederick LUGARD (1858–1945), the West Africa Frontier Force conquered Sokoto, emirate by emirate. While Hausa-Fulani soldiers fought valiantly, they could not survive the British Maxim machine gun, and the caliphate fell in 1903.

Lugard's task then became turning the Northern Territories into an administrative unit, which he accomplished by imposing indirect rule. By this policy the region's legitimate rulers, the emirs, were employed by the British administration to act as intermediaries between the new colonial government and the Hausa-Fulani people. Those emirs who supported Lugard retained their positions and those who didn't were replaced. As dependent rulers the emirs answered to British officials and acted as British agents in terms of tax collection and peacekeeping.

Despite the antislavery pretext for the British invasion of Sokoto, Lugard did not try to reform the existing Fulani-Hausa practice of keeping slaves. The primary reason for this was that agricultural production in the region, which was dependent on slave LABOR, was crucial to colonial TAXATION schemes.

While the system of indirect rule worked acceptably well for the British, it also worked to the benefit of the Hausa-Fulani emirs, who were able to exert their authority farther south into the Nigerian Middle Belt. Although they were sometimes forced to acquiesce to British law, the emirs continued to use Islamic law, or *sharia,* for judging local cases involving land disputes, divorce, debt, and slave emancipation. Such practices, along with the continual rejection of the imposition of British culture, kept the Northern Region relatively isolated from the other British colonial outposts in West Africa.

In 1914 Britain unified all of its regional protectorates into the colony of Nigeria, and by 1922 the administration had established a Nigerian Legislative Council for the largely non-Muslim southern provinces. It did keep its non-interference pact with the North, however, continuing to vest the emir-governors with legislative power.

It was only after World War II (1939–45) that Hausa-Fulani northerners looked toward the future of an integrated Nigeria, founding the Northern Peoples Congress (NPC) political party in 1949. In 1953, with nationalist sentiments rapidly growing, political riots erupted in the heavily populated, Hausa-dominated city of KANO. In LAGOS, the colonial capital, the House of Representatives voted for self-government in Nigeria by 1956. Soon, Hausa-speaking Abubakar Tafawa BALEWA

(1912–1966) formed the first All-Party Government and, as prime minister, helped lead Nigeria to complete independence in 1960.

See also: ENGLAND AND AFRICA (Vols. III, IV, V); HAUSA (Vol. I); HAUSA STATES (Vol. II, III).

Further reading: Philip Koslow, *Hausaland: The Fortress Kingdoms* (New York: Chelsea House Publishers, 1995); Paul Staudinger, *In the Heart of the Hausa States* (Athens, Ohio: Ohio University Center for International Studies, 1990).

health and healing in colonial Africa The spread of colonialism in the 19th and early 20th centuries introduced Western MEDICINE and health philosophies that transformed the landscape of health care in Africa. Two factors motivated colonial actions regarding health care—the desire to protect European officials and settlers, and the need to ensure the health of an indigenous LABOR force. The approaches used by Europeans to tackle these concerns varied in their efficacy. Moreover, these methods were at times heavy-handed and frequently in opposition to the traditional healing practices of the indigenous people.

Western Medicine Colonial administrators needed to protect European officials and SETTLERS from illness to ensure stability of the colonies. DISEASE IN COLONIAL AFRICA was widespread, and, understandably, the ideologies of Western medicine were the main influences on how colonial administrators reacted to the problem. At the time, Western medicine supported two theories of disease. The first theory, known as *contagion,* stated that certain diseases, such as smallpox and plague, were transferred from one person to another. The second theory, *infection,* stated that some diseases, such as malaria, were endemic to particular areas and not necessarily transferred from one person to another. These two theories greatly influenced the strategies used to improve and protect the health of Europeans in Africa.

The *infection* theory of disease was used in dealing with malaria, an inland disease to which Europeans had no immunity. Malaria, and the fear of contracting it, prevented Europeans from traveling into the interior of Africa except in more temperate regions, and curtailed the development of inland outposts. This constriction of travel may have aided Europeans in dealing with malaria, but other diseases found in Africa were not bound by geography.

In several cities colonial administrators, under the guide of the *contagion* theory, implemented a policy of segregation. They established separate sections for Europeans in order to minimize contact with Africans and, theoretically, limit disease transmission. For example, in FREETOWN, SIERRA LEONE, the suburb of Hill Station was created as a residential section exclusively for Europeans. Africans were allowed to work there during the day, but not allowed to stay overnight. African children were excluded entirely from Hill Station due to their strong association with disease. However, this approach often had limited success and was met by strong opposition in places where Africans held any political power.

In addition to protecting the health of its colonists, European administrators needed to protect the indigenous LABOR force that fed their countries' coffers. There were several ways in which health care was provided to Africans during the colonial period. Some health care was financed and administered by the colonial governments. In most locations, however, the quality of the health care provided by the government to Africans was far inferior to that provided to Europeans. In addition, Western-style medical facilities were only constructed in areas firmly under COLONIAL RULE, which were typically urban areas. Rural populations, therefore, did not have access to these facilities, and traditional healing continued to be the principal system of health care outside the cities.

Christian MISSIONARIES also provided Western health care to the indigenous population of Africa. However, their intentions in providing this care were at times far from selfless. Missionaries frequently used health care as an access point to African communities, reasoning that if they were able to provide assistance in curing disease, then the African people would be more willing to accept Christianity. Missionaries labeled traditional healing as pagan, which was likely a response to the traditional healer's role as both doctor and spiritual guide of a community. Despite the missionaries' efforts, some African populations, such as the MAASAI of southeastern TANZANIA, did not associate the arrival of missionaries with improved health. Rather, they equated missionaries with increased illness from exposure to new diseases and increased poverty from the oppression of colonial rule.

Western business interests that employed African workers also administered health care. Treatment, however, was usually limited to only the employee, and did not provide for the health of his or her family. This structure of health care resulted in limited success in reducing the prevalence of some of the more widespread illnesses, as treated employees returned to habitats still ripe with disease.

Some colonial administrators supported improving the health of all indigenous people as a tactic for stemming the spread of disease among the colonist population. Western health care systems were established across Africa, marked by the construction of hospitals and the initiation of vaccination programs. Despite the preventative nature of vaccination programs, the newly built hospitals and clinics frequently focused on the treatment of illnesses and their symptoms, rather than addressing their causes.

Traditional Healing The indigenous health and healing systems found within Africa during the 19th and early 20th centuries viewed illness and its causes differently than Western biomedicine. While Western medicine focused on ridding a patient's body of disease to ease physical suffering, traditional healing used a holistic approach under the theory that illness was frequently a manifestation of psychological, spiritual, or environmental problems. Traditional healers differ from their Western counterparts in that they are likely to play roles beyond that of doctor. African healers frequently take on the capacity of psychologist and spiritual leader, and people come to them for advice in areas beyond physical well-being.

The specifics of traditional healing in Africa vary from region to region. However, most traditional healing practices follow the basic theory of a need for equilibrium in every part of life. The individual, the community, the relationship between two or more individuals, or even the relationship between the human and spirit worlds—all are considered healthy when there is a state of balance. The moment that any of these become imbalanced, a patient can fall into a state of illness.

Traditional healers use divining bones to diagnose the problems of a patient. Divining bones are a collection of objects that represent different aspects of life, such as death, happiness, or luck, and are rolled like dice to make them "talk" to the healer. A healer's divining bones can consist of a variety of objects, including shells, rocks, and yes, actual bones.

When an illness is diagnosed, treatments are administered that reestablish balance, often using a healing method that increases the deficient element. For instance, if a patient is viewed as being "hot," cooling agents, such as water or sea plants, are applied to the patient. If an illness is associated with an environmental problem, then the treatment may include "healing" the environment in order to treat the patient.

See also: CHRISTIANITY, INFLUENCE OF (Vols. II, IV, V); COLONIAL CONQUEST (Vol. IV); COLONIALISM, INFLUENCE OF (Vol. IV); DISEASE IN MODERN AFRICA (Vol. V); HEALTH AND HEALING IN MODERN AFRICA (Vol. V); ISLAM, INFLUENCE OF (Vols. II, III, IV, V); MEDICINE MEN (Vol. I).

Further reading: Steve Feierman and John M. Janzen, *The Social Basis of Health and Healing in Africa,* (Berkeley, Calif.: University of California Press, 1992); Gloria Marth Waite, *A History of Traditional Medicine and Health Care in Pre-Colonial East-Central Africa* (Lewiston, N.Y.: E. Mellen Press, 1992).

Herero Bantu-speaking ethnic group living primarily in present-day NAMIBIA. Fierce conflicts between the Herero and German colonial forces resulted in the decimation of the Herero population. The greater Herero group is made up of various, largely pastoralist ethnic sub-groups, including the Herero, Himba, and Mbanderu. The Herero migrated to southwestern Africa from Central Africa during the 16th century. There they settled primarily in the central highlands north of present-day Windhoek, clashing periodically with the northward-encroaching NAMA people.

By the mid-1800s European explorers and MISSIONARIES had come to the area. Britain nearly annexed the region in the 1870s, but the BERLIN CONFERENCE of 1884–85 ultimately awarded it to Germany. As increasing numbers of German traders and missionaries settled in Hereroland, Herero chiefs, led by Chief Maherero (d. 1890), began forging treaties with the Germans, thinking the newcomers could be valuable allies in their ongoing territorial conflicts with the Nama. However, the Germans themselves became a more pressing problem than the Nama had ever been. The new settlers took Herero lands, stole their herds, and with the backing of German colonial police forces, drove the Herero to resettle in arid "native reserves," which barely supported grazing or subsistence farming.

When Chief Maherero died in 1890 he was succeeded by his son, Samuel MAHERERO (c. 1854–1923). Maherero agreed to "protection" treaties with the German settlers that alienated many of his fellow Herero chiefs and created a rift in the group. Coupled with an outbreak of disease among the cattle herds, these treaties weakened the Herero and allowed the Germans to further entrench themselves. By 1901 Hereroland had become part of the German colony of SOUTH WEST AFRICA.

Facing increasing oppression from the Germans, in 1904 Maherero rallied his people and launched a rebellion. Though initially successful, the tide quickly turned against the Herero. A planned coalition with the Nama fell through, and the Germans, under the command of Lieutenant General Lothar von Trotha (1848–1920), then brought their superior weapons and an army of 10,000 troops to bear. Using ruthless tactics, von Trotha won the decisive Battle of Waterburg (1904) and drove the Herero into the Kalihari Desert, poisoning the available water supplies and issuing an order calling for any Herero caught within the German-occupied territory to be killed. By 1907 the resistance had crumbled. Between German bullets, starvation, and the merciless elements of the Kalihari Desert, the Herero suffered near annihilation—75–85 percent of their people perished, while another 5–10 percent were driven into exile, mainly in BECHUANALAND (present-day BOTSWANA), to the east.

Following World War I (1914–18) South West Africa came under the control of SOUTH AFRICA, which forced the Herero into a segregated "homeland." South West Africa became independent Namibia in 1990. Today about 100,000 Herero (roughly 7 percent of Namibia's present population) live in the mostly arid region of northern Namibia, with smaller populations in Botswana and southern ANGOLA.

Herero women today often wear long dresses with multiple underlying petticoats, in imitation of the 19th-century Victorian style favored by the wives of German missionaries during the colonial era.

See also: COLONIAL CONQUEST (Vol. IV); COLONIALISM, INFLUENCE OF (Vol. IV); COLONIAL RULE (Vol. IV); GERMANY AND AFRICA (Vol. IV); HERERO (Vols. II, III); RESISTANCE AND REBELLION (Vol. IV).

Hertzog, J. B. M. (James Barry Munnik Hertzog)
(1866–1942) *Prime minister of the Union of South Africa from 1924 to 1939*

A fifth-generation South African, James Barry Munnik Hertzog was the seventh of 13 children born to Johannes Albertus Munnik Hertzog (1826–1895) and Susanna Maria Jacoba Hamman Hertzog (1831–1921). His father was originally a farmer, but he also became for a time one of the diggers on the diamond fields of KIMBERLEY. As a boy Hertzog attended school in Kimberley, where he came to dislike the non-AFRIKAANS-speaking outsiders who had flocked there to seek their fortunes. He attended college in Stellenbosch, CAPE COLONY, graduating with a bachelor's degree, in 1889, and then studied law in Holland, where he earned a doctorate. Within a few years of his return to SOUTH AFRICA in 1892, he was appointed as a judge.

From his days as a judge in the ORANGE FREE STATE, to his service as a division commander in the ANGLO-BOER WAR (1899–1902), to his administration as prime minister, J. B. M. Hertzog consistently served as a voice of the Boer, or Afrikaner, population of SOUTH AFRICA. Even before war broke out between the BOERS and Britain, Hertzog was a vocal nationalist, demanding that the Dutch LANGUAGE be taught on an equal footing with English in the schools of the Orange Free State. Then during the Anglo-Boer War he was an active military leader, fighting against the British until the very end of hostilities.

After the war Hertzog joined the government of the newly formed UNION OF SOUTH AFRICA, serving as minister of justice from 1910 to 1912. However, while leaders such as Jan Chritaan SMUTS (1870–1950) and Louis BOTHA (1862–1919) were seeking ways to reconcile the

Afrikaner and British elements within South Africa, Hertzog grew increasingly hostile to the British cause. He was especially scornful of any attempt to grant rights of virtually any kind to South Africa's majority African population. As a result, it was not long before he was dropped from the cabinet. This led Hertzog in 1912 to form the Afrikaner-oriented Nationalist Party, which stood for not only white supremacy but also Afrikaner dominance in South Africa.

After World War I (1914–18) Hertzog continued to build his Nationalist Party while opposing Smuts's ruling party. In 1921–22 Smuts's use of force to end a white-mine-workers' strike on the WITWATERSRAND led to a sharp rise in popularity for Hertzog's Nationalists. They won the election of 1924, and Hertzog became South Africa's prime minister. The economic crisis caused by the world-wide Great Depression of the early 1930s led him in, 1934, to join political forces with Smuts to form a coalition government under the new United Party. Hertzog remained prime minister until 1939, when he resigned after losing a parliamentary vote to have South Africa remain neutral rather than enter World War II (1939–45) on the side of the United Kingdom.

Hertzog's administration was marked by attempts to maintain Afrikaner predominance in South Africa's cultural, economic, and political life. A key factor in this was his success in keeping South Africa off the gold standard, which would have linked South Africa's currency to the price of GOLD. The effect was to keep the price of gold high, thereby supporting the South African gold industry and providing a much-needed boost to the economy during the 1920s and 1930s. Equally important to Hertzog's overall policies was his ability to prevent Africans from gaining political power. As part of this strategy, his administration pushed legislation to abolish the limited enfranchisement of Africans in the Cape Province, further limit African rights to reside in urban areas, and set up a limited form of self-government in the so-called Native Reserves, which were areas set aside for African occupation.

Despite strong African opposition organized by individuals such as D. D. T. JABAVU (1885–1959), in 1936 the parliament passed legislation that ended African voting rights. Africans were not re-enfranchised until 1994, when they helped elect Nelson MANDELA (1918–) the country's first African president. In effect, Hertzog strengthened existing white supremacy and set in motion those political forces that led to APARTHEID after 1948.

See also: AFRIKANERS (Vols. IV, V).

highlife The leading popular MUSIC form of the early post–World War II (1939–45) decades in GHANA and NIGERIA. Highlife reflects a blend of musical styles that gained widespread popularity starting in the late 1940s. It represented a fusion of indigenous musical forms and rhythms with the Big Band sound that was popular in the 1930s and early 1940s. Other influences that figure prominently in the highlife sound include West Indian calypso, military brass band music (usually associated with Africa's colonial era), and Cuban music. The pioneer highlife musicians were E. T. MENSAH (1919–1996) and his band, the Tempos, which he formed in ACCRA in 1948.

The rise of highlife coincided with several important political and social developments of the era. It was a period of growing nationalist sentiment, and many highlife songs had as their theme the injustices and indignities of COLONIAL RULE. Indeed, the authorities sometimes banned songs and arrested musicians. It was also an era of growing URBANIZATION, and the nightclubs and bars of Accra, LAGOS, and other major cities provided the venue for the highlife bands. Highlife also became popular with West Africans living abroad, especially in the cities of England. Many highlife songs, even love songs, dealt with the problems of everyday life that were associated with city living. While highlife remains popular in Ghana, with the rise of Congolese music in the 1960s, it ceased to be in the forefront of popular music styles.

See also: NATIONALISM AND INDEPENDENCE MOVEMENTS (Vol. IV); URBANIZATION (Vol. V); URBAN LIFE AND CULTURE (Vols. IV, V).

historical scholarship on Africa Scholarly writing about African history prior to 1960 was limited and largely superficial. In the 21st century students and others wishing to learn about African history can turn to encyclopedias, such as this one, for accurate information. These encyclopedias, in turn, rest upon a firm foundation of extensive and growing historical scholarship on the African past. This was not the case, however, a half century ago. Africa was still under COLONIAL RULE, few Africans had yet to receive a university EDUCATION, and fewer still were trained as historians. One of the earliest Africans who received formal training as a historian was the Nigerian scholar, Kenneth Onwuka Dike (1917–1983), who earned his PhD in history from London University in the mid-1950s. Prior to Dike, Africans writing about the past were non-professional historians documenting their own peoples. These included Reverend Carl REINDORF (1834–1917) from the GOLD COAST COLONY (today's GHANA), Reverend Samuel JOHNSON (1846–1901) of NIGERIA, Sir Apolo KAGWA (1865–1927) of UGANDA, and Silas Modiri Molema (c. 1891–1965) from SOUTH AFRICA. Otherwise, historical writing, as well as other kinds of scholarship about Africa, was basically the preserve of Europeans.

Europeans such as Heinrich BARTH (1821–1865) and David LIVINGSTONE (1818–1873) had written travel narratives about Africa from the early days of European contact with the continent. The tenor of this writing about

Africa changed as colonial rule became firmly established on the continent in the late 19th century. Europeans needed to justify their conquest and rule over the continent, and they did so by increasingly depicting Africa as "the dark continent," an image that still lingers. The tone was set early on for depicting Africans as backward, as in the title of former colonial administrator Sir Harry Hamilton Johnston's (1858–1927) 1913 book, *A History of the Colonization of Africa by Alien Races*. As suggested by the title, outsiders brought history to Africa, for according to Johnson, until they were "civilized" by outsiders, Africans were the "natural servant[s] of other races." If Africans were naturally servants, as Johnstone argued, or immature and underdeveloped children, as other propagandists for colonial empire wrote, then colonialism was justified. They believed, as did Oxford University professor Hugh Trevor-Roper (1914–) as late as 1966, that "There is only the history of Europeans in Africa. The rest is darkness—and darkness is not the subject of history." One of the few exceptions to such scholarship at this time was the work of W. E. B. DU BOIS (1868–1963), the foremost African-American educator. His scholarly work, *The Negro* (1915), constitutes one of the earliest efforts to claim for Africa its rightful place in world history.

After World War II (1939–45) it became clear that colonial rule in Africa was waning, and such assertions of a dark African past lost their utility. As African universities with their own departments of history emerged in the late 1940s and 1950s, historians of Africa began to write about the history of Africans rather than the history of Europeans in Africa.

See also: DIOP, CHEIK ANTA (Vols. IV, V); HISTORICAL SCHOLARSHIP ON AFRICA (Vol. V).

Horton, James Beale (Africanus Horton)
(1835–1883) *Medical doctor and pioneer in the African independence movement*

The son of an IGBO captive, James Beale Horton grew up in FREETOWN and Gloucester Village, in what is now SIERRA LEONE, where his father worked as a carpenter. After completing his initial education there, he won a scholarship and attended King's College and later Edinburgh University, in Britain, where he studied MEDICINE. He received his doctor of medicine degree in 1859. That same year he joined the British Army Medical Service as an assistant staff surgeon.

Horton served in the army for more than 20 years, rising to the rank of lieutenant colonel. During this time he published books on everything from tropical diseases to economics and politics. In spite of his achievements, British authorities, skeptical of having Africans in positions of authority, found various ways to slow his advancement. Despite being frequently shifted from assignment to as-

signment and denied the opportunity to serve as governor of Sierra Leone, Horton still maintained a positive outlook on African-British relations.

This outlook, though, did not prevent Horton from becoming a strong advocate of independence for African nations. While still a student he had adopted the name Africanus as a sign of pride in his heritage, and he consistently argued in favor of African rights and independence. His *Political Economy of British Western Africa*, published in 1865, for example, suggested that there be a West African University, modeled on universities in Britain, for the education of Africans. Three years later, in *West African Countries and Peoples*, Horton called for British authorities to adopt a gradual program of economic and educational development that would eventually lead to the establishment of independent, African-run states in the region. He became one of the initiators of a new state on the Gold Coast, known as the FANTE CONFEDERATION (or, sometimes, the Mankessim Confederation), which was established in 1868. Such political initiative, however, was not well received by the British authorities, and in 1874 Britain annexed the coastal states, establishing its new GOLD COAST COLONY, which covered modern-day GHANA. Indeed, in a period that was seeing an increase in colonialist and imperialist sentiment, his ideas soon became anathema to official British policy.

In 1880, at the age of 45, Horton retired from the army. Returning to Freetown, he established a bank through which he hoped to finance a growing network of African-owned-and-operated businesses. He did not live to see many results from his efforts, however, as he died of blood poisoning, only three years after his retirement.

See also: ENGLAND AND AFRICA (Vol. IV), NATIONALISM AND INDEPENDENCE MOVEMENTS (Vol. IV).

Further reading: Christopher Fyfe, *Africanus Horton* (Oxford, U.K.: Oxford University Press, 1972).

Houphouët-Boigny, Félix (1905–1993) *First president of the independent Ivory Coast*

Born into a family with extensive landholdings, Houphouët-Boigny was a member of the elite class in IVORY COAST. He attended medical school in DAKAR, SENEGAL, and worked as a doctor for Ivory Coast's Medical Assistance Service, where he gained a reputation as an effective healer. He also owned a plantation and had much success in AGRICULTURE.

Lacking in mineral resources, Ivory Coast, then a French colony, was mainly an agricultural producer. Its primary products were COCOA and COFFEE. In 1945 Ivorian farmers banded together as the African Agricultural Union, an organization of some 20,000 members that sought to change policies favoring Ivory Coast's white farmers. These policies were installed by France's Vichy government during World War II (1939–45). Houphouët-Boigny, who had first organized his fellow African planters in 1933, led the union. It would eventually form the base of his presidential ruling party, the Democratic Party of Ivory Coast (Parti Démocratique de la Côte d'Ivoire, PDCI).

In 1944 all of France's African territories were given the right to send representatives to the French National Assembly, a result of reforms granted by French general Charles DE GAULLE (1890–1970) as a reward for African aid to the French resistance during World War II (1939–45). This allowed for Houphouët-Boigny's election to the Assembly in 1946. That same year he helped found the AFRICAN DEMOCRATIC ASSEMBLY (Rassemblement Démocratique Africaine, RDA), a political party for the entirety of FRENCH WEST AFRICA, and at the BAMAKO Conference, also in 1946, he was elected the party's chairman.

The French Communist faction of the RDA began taking part in a series of demonstrations, strikes, and boycotts against the colonial government. Their efforts drew retribution throughout the territories, culminating in 1950 with the massacre of 13 African demonstrators by colonial police in Ivory Coast. Afterward, the RDA split from its Communist members, and Houphouët-Boigny redirected the party to form closer ties to France.

In 1958 France began the process of gradually granting independence to its African territories. Houphouët-Boigny and Senegal's Léopold SENGHOR (1906–2001), who was also a member of the National Assembly, participated in the creation of a law giving the territories near autonomy. Under the new system the African territories no longer sent deputies to the National Assembly, so Houphouët-Boigny focused his energies on building the PDCI. In 1960 Ivory Coast became fully independent, and in August of that year, Houphouët-Boigny was elected the country's first president.

See also: COLONIALISM, INFLUENCE OF (Vol. IV); COLONIAL RULE (Vol. IV); FRANCE AND AFRICA (Vols. III, V); HOUPHOUËT-BOIGNY, FÉLIX (Vol. V); NATIONALISM AND INDEPENDENCE MOVEMENTS (Vol. IV).

Hutu (Bahutu) Ethnic group found predominantly in the present-day countries of RWANDA and BURUNDI. There are two primary ethnic groups in Rwanda and Burundi, Hutu and TUTSI. Hutu make up nearly 85 percent of the population in each country. Historically the Hutu and Tutsi are very closely associated, with Hutu agriculturalists serving Tutsi clients. In the 18th and 19th centuries Hutus formed the lower social castes within Tutsi monarchies. During the colonial period the Belgian administrators of RUANDA-URUNDI observed the politically dominant Tutsi position, noted their markedly leaner and lighter-skinned appearance, and favored them within the colonial apparatus. Confronted with this type of institutional favoritism, in 1959 the Hutu rose up and launched a violent anti-Tutsi campaign.

As a result of their complementary, if sometimes violent history, Hutu and Tutsi share the same language in each country: Kinyarwanda, in Rwanda and the closely related Kirundi, in Burundi. The linguistic overlap and geographic proximity of Hutu and Tutsi make it more difficult to draw clear distinctions between the two groups than has been historically acknowledged.

See also: BELGIUM AND AFRICA (Vol. IV); HUTU (Vols. I, II, III, V).

I

Ibadan Second-largest city in southwestern NIGERIA and capital of the state of Oyo. Ibadan began as a small settlement that eventually grew into an influential YORUBA city-state. During the Yoruba Civil War (1817–35) the village's population expanded as people displaced by the war immigrated to Ibadan. In 1829 an army of soldiers from the Ife, Ijebu, and Oyo kingdoms set up a military camp in the village. The city steadily grew in military might, and in 1840 the warriors of Ibadan defeated the FULANI at the Battle of Oshogbo, putting a halt to the southward expansion of the SOKOTO CALIPHATE. Emboldened by its victory, Ibadan attempted to assert its authority over other Yoruba states, which led to an anti-Ibadan alliance and further war. Britain imposed a peace in 1886 and then in 1893 took over the town as part of its expanding colonial holdings in Nigeria.

In the early 20th century a railway was constructed, connecting LAGOS with KANO. The railway passed through Ibadan and provided a means to easily transport the city's agricultural goods. AGRICULTURE was the principal occupation for Ibadan's inhabitants, and as late as 1950 many men from Ibadan spent part of the year living and working on their land outside the city proper. Consequently Ibadan's residential pattern resembled that of a village rather than a city, with people residing in compounds that often had a hundred or more residents.

In 1962 Ibadan became the hub of Nigerian higher EDUCATION with the founding of the University of Ibadan. The city was not an important administrative center during most of the colonial era (1893–1960), but with a population of approximately one million in 1960, Ibadan remained a considerable city rife with commercial activity.

See also: ENGLAND AND AFRICA (Vols. III, IV, V); IBADAN (Vol. IV); IBADAN, UNIVERSITY OF (Vol. V); IJEBU (Vols. II, III); PALM OIL (Vol. III); URBAN LIFE AND CULTURE (Vols. IV, V); URBANIZATION (Vols. IV, V).

Further readings: Stephen Adebanji Akintoye, *Revolution and Power Politics in Yorubaland, 1840–1893: Ibadan Expansion and the Rise of Ekitiparapo* (New York: Humanities Press, 1971); P. C. Lloyd, A. L. Mabogunje, and B. Awe, eds., *The City of Ibadan* (Cambridge, Mass.: University Press, 1967); Ruth Watson, *Civil Disorder is the Disease of Ibadan: Chieftancy and Civic Culture in a Colonial City* (Athens, Ohio: Ohio Univ. Press, 2003).

Igbo (Ibo) People living chiefly in southeastern NIGERIA. The Igbo occupy the interior and hinterland regions of the NIGER DELTA. Living in city-states, they do not have one specific leader and instead practice a form of direct democracy by which an elder from each family represents that family in decision making for the community.

In the 18th century the Igbo came under attack from some of their Niger Delta neighbors, who conducted slave raids into their territory and subsequently incorporated many Igbo-speaking people into their own societies

In the 19th century the peoples of the Niger Delta acted as trading intermediaries between the Europeans on the coast and the merchants of the interior. In 1854, however, the presence of the British CHURCH MISSIONARY SOCIETY (CMS) began changing the situation. Led by African missionaries Samuel Ajayi CROWTHER (1808–1891) and the Reverend J. C. Taylor (freed YORUBA and Igbo, respectively), the CMS established its only successful Nigerian mission at Onitsha. Soon, at the request of fellow Igbos,

Taylor's missions expanded into Igbo villages along the Niger River into the delta. By 1859, feeling that the missions were too closely connected to the increasingly influential European traders, African traders began attacking the mission station.

In 1906, in spite of ongoing local resistance, the British colonial office took over the Niger Delta region as the PROTECTORATE of Southern Nigeria. By 1914, when it incorporated all of its regional protectorates into the colony of Nigeria, Britain imposed indirect rule, under which legitimate African rulers would govern under the watchful eye of the new colonial government. Indirect rule, however, could not work among the Igbo because they were not a state society, and there was no legitimate single ruler. Therefore, in 1919 the British Governor, Sir Hugh Clifford (1866–1941), appointed warrant chiefs to force the Igbo to fit the state society model.

In addition to the fact that the new British governor was illegitimate in the eyes of Igbo society, the warrant chiefs he appointed were unpopular because they were viewed as corrupt. Moreover, the "native courts" that the British established further alienated the Igbo when the courts' agents regularly abused their powers. As a result the Igbo resisted British occupation until as late as 1918.

British COLONIAL RULE provoked violent resistance among the region's women, as well. In 1929, for example, an Igbo warrant chief in the area of Aba began to revise the system of colonial TAXATION imposed on the area's residents. Fearing that they would be taxed and angry over the low prices they received for their agricultural goods, the women of Aba and Owerri began attacking the symbols of colonial rule, including the "native courts" and warrant officers. The ABA WOMEN'S REVOLT, as it became known, spread and forced British authorities to call in the police. On December 17, 1929, the police fired on a crowd of protesters, killing 32 and wounding 31 others.

In the 1940s significant numbers of Igbo began to migrate to the colonial capital of LAGOS, where they had moderate success in becoming middle-class workers such as clerks, railway workers, and storekeepers. They also increased their nationalistic political activity, with Igbo speaker Nnamdi AZIKIWE (1904–1996) and Herbert MACAULAY (1864–1946) forming the National Council of Nigeria and the Cameroons. Azikiwe, who became known as the father of modern Nigerian nationalism, led a general strike against the colonial government in 1945. As a chief architect of the country's independence, Azikiwe

was elected president of Nigeria when the country became a republic in 1963.

In May 1967 discontent and fear over the direction the Nigerian republic was taking led the Igbo-dominated Eastern Region to secede and form the Republic of Biafra. In turn this rebellion provoked a lengthy Nigerian civil war.

See also: BIAFRA (Vol. V); IGBO (Vols. I, II, III, V); JAJA (Vol. IV).

Ilorin Largely YORUBA city in western NIGERIA and capital of the Kwara State. Ilorin was the capital of a Yoruba kingdom within the Oyo empire until 1817, when the kingdom revolted and the empire collapsed. Ilorin eventually came under Muslim FULANI control under Abd as-Salam (d. 1842), who became emir of Ilorin and brought the city into the SOKOTO CALIPHATE. In the late 1830s as-Salam waged a JIHAD, spreading the Muslim empire eastward until he was defeated by the Yoruba warriors of IBADAN in 1840.

Located on the Awun River, Ilorin became a center of trade between Yoruba states and HAUSA territories. As British colonial influence expanded over the rest of Yorubaland, Ilorin persisted in keeping its autonomy. By 1897, however, the city had been conquered by Sir George GOLDIE (1846–1925) and the ROYAL NIGER COMPANY. In 1900, after sparking a conflict with the French, the Royal Niger Company had its charter revoked, and Ilorin fell under British COLONIAL RULE. It became the only Yoruba city in the British PROTECTORATE of Northern Nigeria. As a result it remained under the administration of the largely Hausa-Fulani northern region throughout Nigeria's turbulent colonial and early postcolonial history. In 1967 it became the capital of the newly created Kwara State.

Today Ilorin is an important market and manufacturing center. Manufacturing industries include FOOD processing, sugar refining, and iron working. The city also is a large nexus of local agricultural trade in yams, cassava, corn, GROUNDNUTS (peanuts), and COTTON, as well as handicrafts such as pottery and baskets. As the host city for the University College of Ilorin and the Kwara State College of Technology, Ilorin has become a center for EDUCATION, as well. Ilorin's population is primarily Muslim Yoruba.

See also: COLONIAL CONQUEST (Vol. IV); COLONIALISM, INFLUENCE OF (Vol. IV); ISLAM, INFLUENCE OF (Vols. II, III, IV, V); ILORIN (Vol. III).

Imvo ZabaNtsundu (African Opinion) Pioneering dual XHOSA- and English-language newspaper published in King William's Town, in the Eastern CAPE COLONY of SOUTH AFRICA. In November 1884, John Tengo JABAVU (1859–1921) initiated a new era of journalism in South Africa when he launched his weekly newspaper, *Imvo ZabaNtsundu*. NEWSPAPERS, such as *IsiGidimi SamaXhosa* (The Xhosa Messenger), founded in 1873, had been published in African languages by MISSIONARIES and aimed at African readerships. Indeed, Jabavu started his journalism career as an editor for *IsiGidimi,* but he and other such editors had to adhere to the editorial policy of the missionary publishers. *Imvo,* however, provided literate Africans with an independent voice. However, it was not a completely independent voice, because white commercial interests provided the capital to Jabavu and paid for advertisements carried in the paper.

Imvo published news items on a wide variety of subjects, including education, social news, and sports, but its editorials nearly always addressed the politics of the day. Their consistent focus was on establishing African civil and political rights in a country governed by whites, where the government treated Africans as colonial subjects and not as citizens. Africans, however, were not united politically, and in 1897 Walter Benson Rubusana (1858–1936) and other political opponents of Jabavu launched the rival *Izwi LaBantu* (Voice of the People). The early 20th century saw other African newspapers launched in South Africa, including the *Ilanga LaseNatal* (Natal Sun), edited by John L. DUBE (1871–1946), and the *Koranta ea Becona* (Bechuana Gazette), headed by Sol T. PLAATJE (1876–1932). Like Jabavu and Rubusana, Dube and Plaatje were very active in politics and played key leadership roles in founding the AFRICAN NATIONAL CONGRESS.

When Jabavu died, his son, Alexander Macaulay "Mac" Jabavu (d. 1946), took over the editorship of *Imvo.* By this time it had lost much of its earlier influence and readership, with its paid circulation having declined from a high of perhaps 4,000 to about 2,000 in the 1920s. The Argus Company, which owned major city newspapers such as the *Cape Argus,* took over *Imvo* in 1934. Mac Jabavu continued to edit the paper until his death. *Imvo* ceased publication in 1998.

industrialization Development of manufacturing capacity and infrastructure on a large scale. The onset of African industrialization can be traced back to the MINING industry in southern Africa. In the late 1800s, the discovery of DIAMONDS and GOLD in SOUTH AFRICA drew significant numbers of migrants from Europe as well as from the surrounding rural areas. The raw resources produced during this MINERAL REVOLUTION were exported to fuel the Industrial Revolution, which was well underway in Europe. As towns grew around the mines in Africa, other related industries developed in large-scale markets. Food processing, for example, became an important industry related to the agricultural production that was required to feed exploding urban populations.

Industrialization spread first through the mining territories in the BELGIAN CONGO (today's Democratic Republic of the CONGO) and NORTHERN RHODESIA (today's ZAMBIA). It also went on in areas in West Africa that had large amounts of NATURAL RESOURCES, such as SENEGAL and NIGERIA. Colonial authorities were more interested in exporting raw materials for their industries at home than in developing industries in Africa. Because of this, development in most colonies was generally limited to light industry.

> As late as the 1940s only South Africa and SOUTHERN RHODESIA (today's ZIMBABWE) had major steel and iron industries.

African colonies without major natural resources and minerals and metals, such as BECHUANALAND (today's BOTSWANA) and CHAD, were largely unaffected by foreign investment and the growth of urban markets.

During and after World War I (1914–18), progress in industrialization was relatively slow. However, the increase in demand for consumer goods and construction materials after World War II (1939–45) accelerated African industrialization, especially in the southern regions. While industrialization went hand in hand with URBANIZATION, African men in urban areas often maintained ties to rural areas because women and children usually remained on the farms cultivating FOOD CROPS for local consumption as well as CASH CROPS for trade or export. Indeed, AGRICULTURE—not industry—dominated the economies of most countries at independence.

See also: COLONIALISM, INFLUENCE OF (Vol. IV); EXPORTS (Vol. IV); INDUSTRIALIZATION (Vol. V).

Further reading: Lawrence J. Butler, *Industrialisation and the British Colonial State: West Africa 1939–1951* (Portland, Ore.: Frank Cass, 1997).

Isandlwana, Battle of (1879) ZULU victory over the British army. Military historians have called the Battle of Isandlwana the most dramatic military defeat suffered by British regular forces in all of colonial Africa. On January 11, 1879, the British launched an invasion of Zululand from their colony of NATAL, in SOUTH AFRICA. Their pretext was to halt alleged Zulu attacks on Boer settlers and neighboring African peoples by opposing supposed Zulu aggression and removing CETSHWAYO (c. 1826–1884), their king. The attack touched off the seven-month ANGLO-ZULU WAR.

Less than two weeks after the British marched into Zululand, an army (impi) of more than 20,000 Zulu soldiers, armed with traditional weapons, encircled a British force of approximately 1,700 camped at the mountain pass of Isandlwana. In the ensuing battle all but a handful of the invading force was lost—858 British soldiers and 471 of their African allies. Although between 3,000 and 4,000 Zulus died in the engagement, Isandlwana represented such a clear Zulu victory that it effectively undermined the widely held belief in British military invincibility.

Predictably the British launched a punitive campaign, which ended in the capture of the Zulu capital of Ulundi and a crushing Zulu defeat later that year.

Following the Battle of Isandlwana, a Zulu army proceeded to the British base at Rorke's Drift, approximately six miles (10 km) from Isandlwana. Against incredible odds, the base's garrison of 120 repelled the repeated assaults of waves of Zulu soldiers. The number of British soldiers cited for bravery during the engagement was such that, to this day, the Defense of Rorke's Drift saw the largest number of Victoria Crosses—Great Britain's highest military decoration—ever awarded to a regiment for a single action. Two feature-length films have been produced chronicling the events surrounding the battles of Isandlwana and Rorke's Drift: *Zulu* (1964) and *Zulu Dawn* (1979).

See also: COLONIAL CONQUEST (Vol. IV); ENGLAND AND AFRICA (Vols. III, IV, V).

Further reading: Adrian Greaves, *Isandlwana* (London: Cassell & Co., 2001); Ian Knight, *Great Zulu Battles, 1838–1906* (London: Arms and Armour, 1998); Rupert Furneaux, *The Zulu War: Isandhlwana and Rorke's Drift* (Philadelphia: J. B. Lippincott, 1963).

Islam, influence of Islam had had a major impact on Africa from its earliest days, spreading rapidly across North Africa and eventually becoming a religious, military, and social force in many areas south of the Sahara. As European colonization proceeded, beginning in the mid-19th century, the interaction between Europeans and Muslims went through various stages, from conflict to coexistence to cooperation. As a result Islam's influence during the colonial period became increasingly complex.

Islam in North Africa Foremost among the Islam-influenced areas was North Africa, where the religion had spread as early as the seventh century. Through the days of the Ottoman Empire, Islam had dominated the region. By the 1830s Muslim rulers in MOROCCO, ALGERIA, TUNISIA, and LIBYA, however, were battling Europeans intent on colonial domination. Although many of these regions in time fell under French, Italian, or even Spanish rule, Islamic resistance remained strong, and by the 1950s Muslim-led NATIONALISM AND INDEPENDENCE MOVEMENTS ultimately gained control.

Islam in West Africa Within present-day NIGERIA the FULANI jihads of the early 19th century eventually led to the formal establishment of Islamic states. The founding of these states, most notably the SOKOTO CALIPHATE, roughly coincided with the arrival of Europeans and the gradual imposition of COLONIAL RULE. During this period, Islamic institutions vehemently opposed European conquest. For example, the Sokoto consistently struggled against the attempts at COLONIAL CONQUEST of both Britain and France. Indeed, the Fulani aristocracy of the caliphate was able to hold off colonial conquest by both European powers for some time before finally being overwhelmed by the formidable British forces led by Frederick LUGARD (1858–1945) in the early 20th century.

Although the caliphate's resistance ultimately was defeated, the struggle was not entirely futile. Indeed, it was in part because of this determined resistance that Lugard eventually came forth with the governing policy known as indirect rule. This policy, which Lugard first instituted in this region, meant that the British colonial administration would have less governing to do, while the Muslim rulers would govern their own people directly.

In practice, the British colonial administration passed on its rules, requests, or even demands to the African Muslim rulers. They, in turn, had the responsibility of instituting such rules within the caliphate. Similarly, African objections, desires, and requests were transmitted for action by the British colonial administration. This policy proved quite successful from the British standpoint, especially in light of Britain's desire to use as few resources as possible in administering its overseas colonies. At the same time, from the point of view of the Muslim leadership, while it certainly was not a desirable alternative to independence, it did manage to leave them with some degree of control of their own people.

The effects of this linger even to the present day. Aided by their chief ministers or heads of administration—known as Waziris—as well as the emirs or state governors, the caliphs were able to organize the caliphates and the emirates as they saw fit. They established both national and state bureaucracies, political succession, and Islamic courts. In fact, in some areas British presence amounted to a single resident advisor, who dealt with the caliph or emirs only on matters of grave importance. As a result, British influence was far

Like all devout Muslims, these desert travelers faced Mecca, the birthplace of Muhammad, during prayer. The prayer ritual is repeated five times each day. This photo was taken in 1943. © *Underwood Stratton*

weaker in the heavily Islamic northern regions than it was in the rest of the colony. With indirect rule Fulani leadership managed to limit the advance of Western culture into their area. There were also negative effects to this, however. The preservation of Muslim culture came at the cost of some potentially advantageous features of Western life, including industrial technology and a more flexible, albeit more complex, capitalist economic system. Even to this day Nigeria's Northern Region maintains most of its Islamic institutions, while the southern regions are more Westernized.

In the SENEGAMBIA REGION of West Africa the competition between France and Great Britain often allowed Islamic leaders to maintain their independence. For example, under UMAR TAL (1794–1864), the TUKULOR EMPIRE remained independent. However, under Umar Tal's son and successor, AHMADU SÉKU (d. 1898), it could not. After resisting the French for some time, he ultimately was forced to sign an accommodation with them. Similarly, in neighboring GUINEA, the Muslim political and military leader SAMORI TOURÉ (c. 1830–1900) challenged the French coastal advance for many years. In his efforts Samori depended upon his fellow MANDINKA and other MANDE-speaking Muslims. He developed a highly trained fighting cadre of Muslims known as *Sofas*. An inspired leader, Samori successfully played the French

against the British for a long period of time until the two colonial giants finally realized that Samori had no intention of relinquishing control of his country. Ultimately, by 1898 he was subdued and banished to an island off the coast of GABON, where he died in 1900.

Islam in the Sudan and East Africa   Islam had taken deep root in the SWAHILI COAST many years before the arrival of Europeans. But, especially in the eastern Sudan, the concept of the *Mahdi* brought about a resurgence of Islam that had marked effects on European colonialism. In 1881 Muhammad Ahmad (1844–1885) proclaimed himself al-MAHDI, the long-awaited Muslim "redeemer" who, according to some Islamic traditions, would emerge to establish God's justice. Organizing a diverse group of followers called the MAHDIYYA, which also included non-Muslims, he sowed the seeds of Sudanese nationalism by uniting all peoples of the region to resist outside interference. Military successes enjoyed by the Mahdiyya, including the famous battle at KHARTOUM, inspired even greater revolts against colonialism.

Islam and European Colonial Rule   Elsewhere, in Central and southern Africa, the presence of Islam was initially limited. In Central Africa, however, large numbers of primarily Muslim immigrants began to arrive in the early 20th century, mostly in search of trade and work. This eventually led to a large Muslim presence that has continued to this day. In areas such as CAMEROON, CHAD, and Gabon, Muslim immigrants had arrived even earlier, allowing Islam to develop stronger roots. In SOUTH AFRICA, in contrast, it was Asian rather than African immigration that brought Islam, via the large number of migrant workers brought into the area from the Indian subcontinent.

In most parts of Africa Islam generally prospered under European colonial rule. The colonial effort to maintain law and order was highly favorable for the spread of the RELIGION. Moreover, the making of roads and railways made it possible for Islamic clerics to spread their religion toward the coast of West Africa as well as to the interior of Central and East Africa. The colonial administrators' use of Muslim leaders as agents of indirect rule further increased the power and respect of Muslim authorities throughout the continent. As a result, Muslim rulers maintained much of their power under colonial rule. Literate Muslims also were able to gain positions of authority within local and colonial bureaucracies, acting as court recorders and tax collectors, for example. This influence contributed to spreading Islam's influence in governmental as well as social and religious circles.

See also: ENGLAND AND AFRICA (Vol. IV); FRANCE AND AFRICA (Vol. IV); ISLAM (Vol. II); ISLAM, INFLUENCE OF (Vols. II, III, V); MAHDI, AL- (Vol. II); OTTOMAN EMPIRE AND AFRICA (Vol. IV).

Further reading: Nehemia Levtzion and Randall L. Pouwels, eds., *The History of Islam in Africa* (Athens, Ohio: Ohio University Press, 2000).

Ismail, Khedive (1830–1895) *Egyptian ruler*

Ismail, who came to power in 1863, was the grandson of Muhammad Ali (1769–1849), the ruler who established Egypt's de facto autonomy within the Ottoman Empire. Muhammad Ali's successors, Abbas (r. 1848–1854) and Said (r. 1854–1863), had allowed his modernizing reforms to languish, but the ascension of Ismail reinvigorated his grandfather's prior efforts to modernize EGYPT and recover an Egyptian national identity.

Ismail transformed Egypt's infrastructure, developing law courts, railroads, and telegraph lines, as well as creating new urban schools for both boys and girls. This drew Egyptians closer together and helped to foster a national identity. Ismail also patronized NEWSPAPERS in order to build up favorable public opinion. At the same time, he instituted the Egyptian Museum, the National Library, an opera house, a geographical society, and professional schools. As the SUEZ CANAL and other projects brought Europeans and European investment to Egypt, he entered the colonial competition for Africa by paying explorers and financing military expeditions into the Sudan and East Africa. Ismail rebuilt CAIRO, turning Egypt's capital into a modernized city to rival the capitals of Europe.

In 1859, four years before Ismail's ascension to power, construction began on the Suez Canal. In the wake of LABOR troubles the Suez Canal Company refused to pay the peasants who had been hired to dig, and this left the responsibility of paying the workers' wages to Ismail. Although foreign debt depleted the Egyptian treasury, the effect was at first barely noticeable, as Egypt was experiencing an economic boom due to the U.S. Civil War (1860–65). Since the war was preventing British textile mills from receiving their regular supply of American COTTON, the British were willing to pay any price for Egyptian cotton. Increased demand stimulated production, to the delight of both the Egyptian growers and the government.

Khedive Ismail spent lavishly for the opening of the Suez Canal in 1869. At his country's expense he invited many heads of state to stay at luxurious hotels in his newly renovated CAIRO, and to participate in all types of celebration activities. He even commissioned Giuseppe Verdi (1813–1901), the Italian composer, to write the opera *Aida* for the inauguration of Cairo's grand opera house.

After the U.S. Civil War the reentry of American cotton into the international market hurt the Egyptian economy, but Ismail did not reduce his spending. Still in need of money, he became dependent on loans, which he could secure only at high interest rates. By 1866 the crisis had become so severe that Ismail had to coerce Egyptian landowners to pay three years' taxes in advance in exchange for a promise of tax reductions in the future.

When Ismail had come to power in 1863 his title was pasha, or governor. In 1867, however, he paid an enormous fee to the Ottoman Empire to obtain the title of Khedive, which gave him a status closer to sovereign ruler of Egypt. His new rank allowed him to pass down his position to his son in Cairo rather than to a brother living in the Ottoman capital of Istanbul, in present-day Turkey. He also earned the right to take out foreign loans without Ottoman permission—a privilege that ultimately proved disastrous.

In 1875 Ismail sold Egypt's shares in the Suez Canal Company, 44 percent of the total stock, to the British government. Then, when Egypt could not repay its loans, European banks forced the country into bankruptcy. No longer confident in Ismail, the British asked the Ottoman rulers to dismiss him, and in 1879 Ismail had to turn over the khedivate to his son Tawfiq Pasha (1852–1892).

See also: MUHAMMAD ALI (Vol. III); OTTOMAN EMPIRE AND AFRICA (Vol. IV).

Italian East Africa (1936–42) Short-lived colonial administrative federation made up of the colonies of ITAL- IAN SOMALILAND, ERITREA, and ETHIOPIA.

See also: COLONIAL CONQUEST (Vol. IV); ITALY AND AFRICA (Vol. IV).

Italian Somaliland Colonial territory that included the eastern and southern portions of the Horn of Africa. The governmental seat of the colony was the port city of MOGADISHU. Italy began its colonial activity in the region in 1889, when it forged treaties with local sultans to establish a PROTECTORATE over what is today central SOMA- LIA. The territory grew to include regions to the north and south along the Benadir Coast, and by 1908 the borders of Italian Somaliland had been established through negotiations with both ETHIOPIA and Britain. The colonial territory grew again in 1925 with the annexation of a southern region known as Jubaland, which lay east of the

Juba (or Jubba) River in what was then the British colony of KENYA. The colony's economy rested on agricultural production of various CASH CROPS, involving both local LABOR and Italian settlers. The government actively promoted AGRICULTURE through research institutes, irrigation projects, and the like.

During the first decade of the 20th century the westward expansion of Italian Somaliland into the Somali hinterland had been contained by the presence of Ethiopian forces in the eastern province of OGADEN. By 1936, however, Italy had conquered much of Ethiopia, which was then united with Italian Somaliland to form Italian East Africa.

Control of the region shifted again during World War II (1939–45), when an army made up of combined British and Ethiopian soldiers conquered Italian Somaliland, in February 1941. The region remained under British rule until 1950, when it was made a TRUST TERRITORY of the United Nations. At that time—despite the fact

In 1935, while Italian troops moved into Ethiopia, men from Italian Somaliland were pressed into service to build modern canals to irrigate Italian-owned farmland. © *Library of Congress*

that Italy had lost its East African colonies in the postwar treaty of 1947—the United Nations decided that Italy should once again administer Italian Somaliland, for a definite 10-year period, while the region began the process of changing over to autonomous rule. Finally, on July 1, 1960, Italian Somaliland and its neighbor to the west, BRITISH SOMALILAND, were unified as the United Republic of Somalia.

See also: BENADIR COAST (Vol. III); ENGLAND AND AFRICA (Vol. IV); HORN OF AFRICA (Vols. I, V); ITALO-ETHIOPIAN WARS (Vol. IV); ITALY AND AFRICA (Vol. IV); SETTLERS, EUROPEAN (Vol. IV); UNITED NATIONS AND AFRICA (Vols. IV, V).

Italo-Ethiopian War   (1935–36) Conflict stemming from long-standing tensions between Italy and ETHIOPIA that culminated in a decisive Italian victory. The Italo-Ethiopian war is now seen as one of the precursors to World War II (1939–45) in that it forced Western democratic nations to take a stand against those nations, such as Italy, that were led by fascist regimes.

Italy's desire to rule Ethiopia dated to the late 19th century, but Ethiopia's Emperor MENELIK II (1844–1913) ended these early colonial aspirations through his victory at the Battle of ADOWA, in 1896. For nearly three decades afterward, the two nations maintained an uneasy peace, with Italy going so far as to back Ethiopia's bid for membership in the League of Nations, in 1923.

One ongoing point of contention, however, was the boundary between OGADEN, Ethiopia's southeastern province, and ITALIAN SOMALILAND. Tensions finally came to a head on December 5, 1934, with a pitched battle between opposing armies at an Ogaden watering stop named Welwel. Following the battle, Ethiopia, unable to oust the Italians from the border region, implored the League of Nations to investigate the matter while Italy, for its part, demanded both a formal apology and compensation from Ethiopia.

Italy's dictator, Benito Mussolini (1883–1945), used the incident at Welwel as an excuse to attack Ethiopia and add it to Italy's empire in the Horn of Africa. On October 3, 1935, the technologically superior Italian army began its attack on Ethiopia from bases in ERITREA and Italian Somaliland. Using poison gas and aerial bombing, the Italian forces soon held the advantage. Despite fierce Ethiopian opposition, within seven months the Ethiopian capital of ADDIS ABABA had fallen. Declaring victory, Mussolini designated his commanding general as viceroy of Ethiopia and Italy's king, Victor Emmanuel III (1869–1947) added Emperor of Ethiopia to his list of figurehead titles.

Prior to the fall of Addis Ababa, Emperor HAILE SELASSIE (1892–1975) had fled Ethiopia for Europe, where he went before the League of Nations to request assistance in deterring Mussolini. Although members of the League voiced their strong objections and issued sanctions on Italy, it was to little avail, as no other government was willing to challenge Italy's powerful dictator. Despite the inability of the League of Nations to defend Ethiopia, the Italo-Ethiopian War brought the emerging power of fascist regimes, especially those of Mussolini and Germany's Adolf Hitler (1889–1945), to the forefront of international concern. Fallout from the war, including the often brutal treatment of Ethiopians by the occupying Italian forces, would become motivating factors in the later independence struggles of African nations.

See also: COLONIAL CONQUEST (Vol. IV); ITALY AND AFRICA (Vol. IV); LEAGUE OF NATIONS AND AFRICA (Vol. IV).

Italy and Africa   Although Italy joined the scramble for African colonies relatively late, it made consistent moves during the 19th and 20th centuries to establish itself as a colonial power. Ultimately, however, Italian imperial ambitions were smashed in the wake of World War II (1939–45). Like Germany, Italy did not achieve national unity until well into the 19th century, giving Britain and France a head start in the race to PARTITION Africa. Still, Italy moved to take control over areas that it hoped would prove to be valuable, both as a matter of national pride and as a means of solving its chronic overpopulation problem.

The Horn of Africa The opening of the SUEZ CANAL in 1869 made the Horn of Africa of great strategic importance. Italy viewed this region as a place to relocate its un- and underemployed masses. So in 1882 Italy acquired Aseb Bay, on the Red Sea, later using it as a base of operations in 1885 to occupy Ethiopian-controlled Massawa, also on the Red Sea. Italy began encroaching on Ethiopian territory further inland until it was halted in 1887 by a military defeat. Rather than risking further possible defeat, the Italian government consolidated its coastal holdings by proclaiming the colony of ERITREA in 1890.

Meanwhile, in 1889 Italy had thrown its support behind the future Emperor MENELIK II (1844–1913) in the struggle for succession to the Ethiopian throne. After assuming power, Menelik signed the Treaty of Wichale, which Italy claimed made ETHIOPIA an Italian PROTECTORATE. Protesting that he had been duped, Menelik abrogated the treaty, but Italy continued its aggressive policies in regard to Ethiopia. In 1895 Italy launched a full invasion, only to suffer an embarrassing and crushing defeat at the Battle of ADOWA, in March 1896. Humiliated, Italy was forced to sign the Treaty of Addis Ababa (1896), recognizing Ethiopian sovereignty and putting a temporary end to its dreams of Ethiopian conquest. About the same time, Italy claimed a small protectorate over a region of Somaliland (now SOMALIA) not yet claimed by either Britain or France. The addition of further territory to the south became the basis for ITALIAN SOMALILAND, which, along with Eritrea, represented Italy's holdings in the Horn of Africa.

North Africa North Africa, closer than the Horn, also became an object of Italian colonial aspirations. Concerned over the French acquisition of MOROCCO and TUNISIA, Italy set about establishing itself as a colonial power in northern Africa. Using disputes with Turkey as a pretense, Italy embarked on the Turko-Italian War of 1911–12, seizing a substantial amount of territory of TRIPOLITANIA and Cyrenaica, in what is now LIBYA. By 1914 Italy had managed to occupy much of Libya, although it battled serious insurgency up through the 1920s. By the 1930s more than 40,000 Italian colonists had been sent to the territory. In 1934 the Italian government combined Tripolitania and Cyrenaica into the single colony of Libya, and then in 1939 the government made it a part of Italy itself. The Allied victory in North Africa during World War II, however, put an end to Italy's rule

there. Libya subsequently was placed under joint British and French military rule for the duration of the war.

Defeat in the Horn of Africa Throughout the 1930s and 1940s Italy expanded its holdings in Somaliland. During this same period the Italian dictator, Benito Mussolini (1883–1945), determined to avenge Italy's defeat at Adowa, moved aggressively on Ethiopia. Using border clashes as an excuse, Mussolini launched an all-out invasion in October 1935. Failing to secure much support from either individual countries or the League of Nations—which imposed only minor economic sanctions on Italy for its actions—Ethiopia fell, in May 1936. On June 1, 1936, Victor Emmanuel III, the figurehead king of Italy, was proclaimed the emperor of Ethiopia. Italy then proceeded to combine its holdings in Eritrea, Somaliland, and Somali-speaking Ethiopia to create what it called ITALIAN EAST AFRICA.

Italy's holdings in the Horn of Africa proved to be short-lived, however. With the outbreak of World War II, Italy invaded BRITISH SOMALILAND, only to be driven out

Like this officer, many Ethiopian soldiers set out from Harer in 1935 to defend their nation against Mussolini's invading armies. © Acme/Washington Star/Library of Congress

by combined British and South African forces, in 1941. The Allies quickly went on to conquer all of Italy's holdings in the region, including Ethiopia. In the wake of World War II the United Nations briefly returned the former Italian Somaliland to Italian control as a UN TRUST TERRITORY. The region was granted internal autonomy in 1956 and then full independence in 1960, putting to a final end Italy's dreams of empire in Africa.

See also: BERLIN CONFERENCE (Vol. IV); COLONIAL CONQUEST (Vol. IV); COLONIAL RULE (Vol. IV); ENGLAND AND AFRICA (Vols. III, IV, V); FRANCE AND AFRICA (Vols. III, IV, V); GERMANY AND AFRICA (Vol. IV); HAILE SELASSIE (Vol. IV); LEAGUE OF NATIONS AND AFRICA (Vol. IV); OTTOMAN EMPIRE AND AFRICA (Vol. IV); UNITED NATIONS AND AFRICA (Vol. IV).

Further reading: Patrizia Palumbo, ed., *A Place in the Sun: Africa in Italian Colonial Culture, from Post-Unification to the Present* (Berkeley, Calif.: University of Calif. Press, 2003).

Ivory Coast (Côte d'Ivoire)   West African country approximately 124,500 square miles (322,465 sq km) in size that is bordered to the east by GHANA, to the west by LIBERIA and GUINEA, to the north by MALI and BURKINA FASO, and to the south by the Gulf of Guinea. In the 18th and 19th centuries two groups of AKAN people, the Baule and the Agnis, migrated to the area now known as the Ivory Coast in an effort to escape the influence of the ASHANTI EMPIRE. The Agnis occupied the southeastern region of the Ivory Coast and founded the kingdoms of Sanwi and Indenie. Meanwhile, the Baoule moved into the central part of the country and established the kingdom of Sakasso in Senufo territory. To the north of the Akan kingdoms was the MANDE-speaking DYULA kingdom of Kong, which was founded in the early 18th century and served as a vital trade center to the region, prospering well into the 19th century.

Kong's rise as a center of commerce was not surprising, as the Ivory Coast region was a thriving trading community as early as the eighth century. Fittingly, ivory was long the chief export from the area, but over-hunting of elephants depleted their population to near extinction, and trade in ivory ended by the 18th century. The SLAVE TRADE also existed in the region, fostered by Muslim traders in the interior and Europeans along the coast.

Despite the relatively early presence of Europeans along the shore, beginning with the Portuguese in the 15th century, the hinterland remained unexplored by colonial powers through much of the 19th century. Then, from 1842 to 1843, the chiefs of the Grand Bassam and Assinie regions signed a series of treaties with the French naval officer Bouet-Williaumez (1808–1871) establishing a French PROTECTORATE over the territories. The French erected trading posts along the coast, but, still, they showed little interest in establishing a permanent presence in the hinterlands. This all changed, however, after the BERLIN CONFERENCE (1884–85), where the colonial powers agreed that annexation of the African coastline must be supported by "effective occupation."

In 1886 France assumed administrative authority over the region and began a program of exploration of the inland. The indigenous peoples of the area were not overly concerned by the initial influx of a few white explorers and their traveling parties. Between 1887 and 1889 local chiefs signed protectorate-forming treaties with various Frenchmen including Louis Binger (1856–1926), who was one of the first Europeans to traverse the interior of the Ivory Coast. The motivations of the African chiefs for signing over their lands with these treaties varied. Some believed the French would provide military help against their rivals, while others were probably deceived regarding the consequences of the agreements. In any case, by 1893 France had combined its various coastal protectorates to form the colony of Côte d'Ivoire.

Around the turn of the 20th century Ivory Coast was grouped with other French possessions in FRENCH WEST AFRICA, an administrative bloc commonly known by its French acronym, AOF, standing for Afrique Occidentale Française.

Ivory Coast During the Colonial Period: Côte d'Ivoire   When they realized France's expansionist intentions, Africans in Côte d'Ivoire began offering resolute resistance. Especially determined were the forces of SAMORI TOURÉ (c. 1830–1900), who used guerrilla tactics to fight the French for most of the 1890s. The French captured Samori Touré in 1898, allowing them to expand their influence inland and quell remaining resistance to complete the PACIFICATION process.

During the early part of the 20th century the French imposed taxes on the African population and instituted forced LABOR. The French also began a program of assimilation, extolling the supposed superiority of French culture and training an African elite in the ways of French bureaucracy. The introduction of civil service dismayed the traditional African leadership, as the French appointed rulers with no previous rights to power, reducing most of the legitimate leaders to insignificant figureheads.

At the onset of World War II (1939–45), France capitulated to Nazi Germany. At first all of FRENCH WEST AFRICA (Afrique Occidentale Française, AOF) offered support to the German-allied Vichy government, though many Ivorians supported the Free France government of Charles DE GAULLE (1890–1970). During the war the

Vichy government abused the African population of the colony by imposing quotas on already strained AGRICULTURE production and by increasing the use of forced labor.

After the war African political activity began to find a footing. In 1944 African farmers led by Félix HOUPHOUËT-BOIGNY (1905–1993) responded to the Vichy directives on agriculture by organizing the African Agricultural Union. This was eventually transformed into the Democratic Party of Ivory Coast (Parti Démocratique de la Côte d'Ivoire, PDCI), which was a base of support for Houphouët- Boigny.

In 1945 Côte d'Ivoire held its first election to determine the colony's two representatives to the French Assembly. The ballots were divided between French citizens and a limited African electorate, which chose Houphouët-Boigny as their delegate. He, along with the African delegates from other French possessions, pressed for reforms of colonial policy, and the French eventually acquiesced to some of the African delegates' demands.

In 1946 Côte d'Ivoire, along with the rest of France's African possessions, was designated an overseas territory. New rights for Africans, such as free speech and the right to assembly, accompanied this change and resulted in the rise of political activity. The PDCI, headed by the nearly autocratic leadership of Houphouët-Boigny, quickly gained popular support.

Empowered by his success at home, Houphouët-Boigny joined with other AOF leaders to form the AFRICAN DEMOCRATIC ASSEMBLY (Rassemblement Démocratique Africaine, RDA), which became a dominant force in AOF politics. The RDA was especially popular in Côte d'Ivoire, where the longstanding conflict between African and white farmers created an environment ripe for political activism. Soon, however, Houphouët-Boigny encountered French opposition to his party's activities. The PDCI, because of its association with the communist-influenced RDA, came under frequent attack from the colonial administration. In 1951, with the PDCI foundering, Houphouët-Boigny distanced himself from the more radical elements of the RDA. The tactic worked, placating the French, and reestablishing the influence of the PDCI and RDA.

In 1958 France called for a referendum to decide the fate of its possessions, allowing French territories to either to join the French Community as a self-governing republic or opt for complete independence and sever all ties with France. Côte d'Ivoire, along with every other African French territory except for GUINEA, chose to join the community. One year later elections for the legislature of the republic were held, with the PDCI winning all of the seats. The legislature elected Houphouët-Boigny prime minister, and in 1960 he became the country's first president.

See also: BAULE (Vol. III); FRANCE AND AFRICA (Vols. III, IV, V); IVORY COAST (Vols. I, II, III, V); NATIONALISM AND INDEPENDENCE MOVEMENTS (Vol. IV).

Further reading: Patrick Manning, *Francophone Sub-Saharan Africa, 1880–1995,* 2nd ed. (New York: Cambridge University Press, 1998).

ivory trade   Ivory became an important export in the 19th century in response to European demand. The time period witnessed the rise of the middle class in Europe, and in the days before RADIO and the phonograph, pianos were a fixture in most middle-class homes. This in turn led to an increasing demand for ivory for piano keys. The export of ivory from Africa dated back to ancient EGYPT, and it continued to be an important trade commodity for centuries. With the upsurge in European demand in the 19th century, the largest untapped source of ivory was the East African interior. The Arab merchant community of ZANZIBAR and the adjacent SWAHILI COAST were positioned to take advantage of this growing demand and aggressively pursued the ivory trade. By the late 1850s Zanzibar was exporting nearly 500,000 pounds (226,800 kg) of ivory annually. Ivory accounted for 40 percent of its EXPORTS.

Between 1880 and 1930, the trade in ivory led to the slaughter of thousands of elephants. *© Frank and Frances Carpenter Collection/Library of Congress*

The peoples of the interior, such as the NYAMWEZI and the YAO, undertook hunting elephants for their ivory. They also often worked as porters, transporting the ivory to the coast. As the century wore on, however, the coastal Arab and Swahili merchants pushed deeper into the interior and took over direct control of the trade routes. This expansion reached its zenith by the early 1880s with the move of TIPPU TIP (c. 1830–1905) into the eastern portion of present-day Democratic Republic of the CONGO.

In West Africa the 19th century saw the rise of so-called legitimate trade, primarily in CASH CROPS, in tandem with the efforts to abolish the SLAVE TRADE. While ivory was a commodity, as were cash crops, there were two principal differences with the commodity trade of West Africa. First, unlike commodities such as GROUND-NUTS (peanuts) and PALM OIL, ivory was not a readily renewable resource. Second, the export of ivory was inextricably linked to the export of slaves. Indeed, ivory and slaves dominated the export commodity trade of East Africa for most of the century. As with ivory, slaves were not an unlimited resource, and the collection of slaves was a highly destructive process. Human communities were being decimated along with the elephant herds in what was essentially a robber or predatory economic system. Such an economic system lacked any basis for productive and beneficial economic growth.

The ivory trade declined as the European PARTITION of East Africa undermined the Zanzibar-based trading system, as the ivory supply diminished with the killing off of the elephant herds, and as demand in Europe began to trail off. Despite the decline, the ivory trade never disappeared altogether, and the unsavory practice continues today.

See also: CONSERVATION (Vol. V); IVORY (Vol. II); IVORY TRADE (Vol. III); NATURAL RESOURCES (Vols. III, IV, V); TRADE AND COMMERCE (Vol. IV).

J

Jabavu, D. D. T. (Davidson Don Tengo) (1885–1959) South African professor and political leader

Jabavu was born in King William's Town, CAPE COLONY, the son of John Tengo JABAVU (1859–1921), the renowned editor of *IMVO ZABANTSUNDU*, a weekly newspaper for South Africans. Failing in the attempt to enroll his son in a white high school, John Tengo Jabavu instead sent him to Britain for his schooling. After attending a Society of Friends school in Wales, the younger Jabavu went on to obtain a bachelor's degree in English at the University of London, and a diploma in education from Birmingham University. After graduation Jabavu traveled to the United States. There he visited several historically black institutions, including the Tuskegee Institute, where he met its founder, the black intellectual, Booker T. WASHINGTON (1856–1915).

On his return to SOUTH AFRICA in 1915, Jabavu became the first African teacher at the new South African Native College, later known as FORT HARE COLLEGE. During his career there, which stretched to 1945, he taught a wide range of subjects, including social anthropology, Latin, history, and African languages. Even after other black faculty members were hired, he was far and away the most recognizable and popular African professor at Fort Hare, and he personally taught many of the most influential Africans who emerged as prominent nationalist leaders in southern Africa.

Not content with his role as an academic, Jabavu played active roles in extracurricular college activities and in the larger African community, championing causes of central importance to Africans. For example, he was tireless in promoting improved agricultural techniques among African farmers, writing instruc-

tional pamphlets and newspaper articles, lecturing widely in rural areas, organizing agricultural cooperatives, and in 1919 founding the Cape Farmers Association. Jabavu was also instrumental in organizing African teachers, assisting in the establishment of the Cape Native Teachers' Association (1920) and the nationwide South African Federation of Native Teachers (1921), both of which he led as president.

Jabavu assumed the role of spokesman for his people and engaged in many undertakings on the national political stage. He sought to realize the liberal ideal of a non-race-based Cape franchise, which involved a vaguely elitist notion of granting equal rights to all "civilized" men, regardless of race. He traveled widely, both abroad and in South Africa, to further the cause of Africans. Beginning in the mid-1920s he also was one of the leading figures in the Joint Council movement, which attempted to open lines of communication between leaders in the white and African communities. In 1929 Jabavu also helped found the South African Institute of Race Relations, which was dedicated to the same goal, serving as its vice president from 1932 to 1959. In the mid-1930s he assumed leadership of the movement to prevent the passage of the Native Bills, which aimed to abolish African franchise rights in the Cape Province. To this end, in 1935 he established, and assumed the presidency of, the All-African Convention. In 1943 Jabavu also cofounded the Non-European Unity Movement, which attempted to unite African, Cape Coloured, and Indian political constituencies across southern Africa.

Even as South Africa's black opposition became radicalized and more oriented to mass action in the late 1940s, Jabavu clung to his philosophy of elitist representation, racial reconciliation, gradual political reform, and moral uplift. By 1948, however, recognizing that he was out of step with political currents of his day, Jabavu retired from politics.

In addition to his public roles as an educator and politician, Jabavu was a passionate advocate for temperance, a prominent Methodist lay preacher, and a pianist of considerable talent. He also wrote poetry and many works of nonfiction in XHOSA and English, including a biography of his father, John Tengo Jabavu.

See also: CHRISTIANITY, INFLUENCE OF (Vols. IV, V).

Further reading: Catherine Higgs, *The Ghost of Equality: The Public Lives of D. D. T. Jabavu of South Africa, 1885–1959* (Athens, Ohio: Ohio University Press, 1997).

Jabavu, John Tengo (1859–1921) *South African newspaper editor and politician*

Raised in an African family of first-generation Christian converts, Jabavu attended Healdtown Missionary Institution, a Methodist school, and began his career as a mission schoolteacher at only 17 years of age. In 1881 he became editor of *Isigidimi sama Xhosa,* (The Messenger of the Xhosa), a newspaper published by Lovedale, a prominent missionary institution. After a falling-out with the newspaper's missionary publishers over his political views, Jabavu started his own newspaper, the weekly *IMVO ZABANTSUNDU* (African Opinion), in 1884. It was the first independent, African-language newspaper in SOUTH AFRICA. He used the influence he wielded through it to promote his politics among his African readership and to encourage eligible Africans to register as voters in the CAPE COLONY.

Championing many African causes, Jabavu emerged in the late 19th century as one of the continent's most influential African leaders. He initially threw his newspaper's support behind the Liberal Party, but when it increasingly adopted an anti-African position, he backed the Afrikaner Bond party instead. However, the white politicians of this party also betrayed his trust, and, in the process, Jabavu lost credibility for his ill-advised political alliances. During the ANGLO-BOER WAR (1899–1902) the government shut down his newspaper for more than a year because of his antiwar criticism. The closure seriously degraded the newspaper's financial situation in the years to follow.

In 1909 Jabavu joined an African delegation to London that protested the proposed constitution of the new UNION OF SOUTH AFRICA, believing that it threatened African franchise rights. Later, however, he made some serious political miscalculations, beginning with his decision to shun participation in the newly formed South African Native National Congress (later to become the AFRICAN NATIONAL CONGRESS), in favor of creating his own stillborn organization, the South African Races Congress.

Then, he supported the Natives Land Act (1913), a crucial legislative initiative designed to deny Africans the right to own or rent land in the vast majority of South Africa. His decision to back this bill was motivated by his friendship with J. W. Sauer (d. 1913), the white liberal politician who sponsored it. As a result, Jabavu suffered a resounding defeat in his 1914 bid for a seat on the Cape Provincial Council. In part, he had entered the election to spite Walter Benson Rubusana (1858–1936), who had started up a rival African-language newspaper. In challenging Rubusana, however, Jabavu drew away many of Rubusana's potential supporters, with the result that a white candidate won the seat. It was not until the election of 1994 that another African was elected on the basis of a common nonracial franchise to a legislative body in South Africa.

Forsaking politics, Jabavu campaigned for the establishment of an African college, and thanks in part to his protracted efforts, in 1916 the South African Native College (later renamed FORT HARE COLLEGE) came into being. He sat on its governing council, and his son, Davidson Don Tengo JABAVU (1885–1959), became the first African lecturer on its staff. Upon John Tengo Jabavu's death in 1921, his son Alexander Macauley "Mac" Jabavu (d. 1946) assumed the editorship of *Imvo ZabaNtsundu,* which continued publication until 1998.

See also: CHRISTIANITY, INFLUENCE OF (Vols. IV, V); MISSIONARIES (Vol. IV); NEWSPAPERS (Vol. IV).

Jaja (JaJa of Opobo, Jubu Jubogha) (1821–1891) *Influential merchant in the eastern Niger Delta*

Born a slave in Igboland, Jaja was named Jubo Jubogha by his first master, a trader from the small coastal trading state of Bonny. Intelligent and ambitious, Jaja quickly rose to lead one of the main merchant houses of the eastern part of the NIGER DELTA. As head of the trading group known as the Anna Pebble House, in Okoloma, Jaja engaged in an aggressive program designed to enlarge his house. He absorbed smaller houses, offered opportunities to younger traders, and encouraged initiative by offering to wipe out debts and granting trading concessions. As a result, within two years of his taking over the Anna Pebble House in 1862, Jaja had managed to add 15 houses to his group.

The rise of Jaja and his house was not well received by other groups, however, and by 1869 business competition had led to armed conflict. When a fire wiped out areas of Okoloma, including the armory of the Anna Pebble House, Jaja and his trade associates relocated to the island of Opobo. There they constructed an entirely new community, and Jaja declared himself king of Opobo.

Strategically located between Bonny and the source of goods in the interior, Jaja's kingdom of Opobo grew rapidly in power and importance. Indeed, because he had the might to deny others access to the best trade routes, he soon was able to charge hefty duties on goods passing through his region. In time Jaja's power and wealth grew so great that he started to eliminate the European coastal merchants altogether, shipping palm oil directly to Liverpool, England, himself.

As a ruler, Jaja steered an independent course, maintaining law and order with a traditional police force and conducting military exercises to keep his forces ready for conflict against any invader. Deeply mistrusting Christian MISSIONARIES, he did as much as he could to limit or even proscribe their evangelical activities. Instead he advanced the cause of traditional African religions, constructing shrines to important gods and ancestors. European-style EDUCATION, however, was encouraged, and beginning in 1873 he employed a succession of teachers to provide instruction to his and other children of Opobo. By the mid-1880s more than 60 boys and girls attended Opobo's school.

The extent of Jaja's power—as well as his willingness to use that power to dominate trade in the region—was not something the British interests in the area tolerated. Eventually they managed to get Jaja to sign a treaty by which his kingdom retained its independence but was put under British "protection." Since the treaty had little effect on Jaja's activities, the British soon took stronger action, luring Jaja to a meeting and arresting him. Taken to ACCRA in 1887, he was tried and convicted on charges of breaking treaties and restraining trade. Eventually he was exiled to St. Vincent's, in the West Indies, where he spent the next four years. In time he was allowed to return to Africa, but he died en route.

As the British had intended, Jaja's fate served as a warning to other leaders in the delta. Gradually they gave in to British demands, allowing Britain to take effective control of both the politics and economics of the region. Further, when it was discovered that quinine could be used to control malaria, the British soon took over the job of trading with the interior. This eventually put an end to the great African-run mercantile houses of the delta, and the city-states of the region, like Bonny, declined.

See also: BONNY (Vols. II, III); COLONIAL CONQUEST (Vol. IV); ENGLAND AND AFRICA (Vols. III, IV, V); IGBO (Vol. IV); NIGER DELTA (Vol. III); TRADE AND COMMERCE (Vol. IV).

Further reading: Ebiegberi Joe Alagoa, *Jaja of Opobo: The Slave Who Became a King* (London: Longman, 1970).

Jameson Raid Failed attempt in late 1895 to overthrow the Afrikaner government of the TRANSVAAL Republic and bring the Transvaal within the orbit of the British Empire. The Jameson Raid was engineered by Alfred Beit (1853–1906) and the prime minister of the British CAPE COLONY, Cecil RHODES (1853–1902). It was intended to further Rhodes's expansionist ambitions. Rhodes and Beit controlled the De Beers diamond mines. They also ran the BRITISH SOUTH AFRICA COMPANY, a commercial enterprise that all but governed the colony of Rhodesia, the ancestor of the present-day nation of ZIMBABWE. Dr. Leander Starr Jameson (1853–1917), administrator of Rhodesia for the British South Africa Company and a close friend of Rhodes, led the raid to bring down the government of Transvaal president Paul KRUGER (1825–1904). The raid was initiated to support a revolt among the mostly British UITLANDERS, or foreign settlers, as well as to serve Rhodes' designs for a united SOUTH AFRICA.

On December 29, 1895, with a force of roughly 500 mounted company police, Jameson set out from a base in British-held BECHUANALAND (today's BOTSWANA) and crossed the border into the Transvaal. The revolt among the Uitlanders in the Transvaal was prearranged to coincide with the Jameson invasion; however, it failed to materialize. On January 2, 1896, Transvaal soldiers surrounded and captured Jameson and his men, 16 of whom died in the skirmish. The Transvaal government turned Jameson over to the British to be tried in London. In addition many of the Uitlander conspirators in JOHANNESBURG were imprisoned.

The Jameson Raid led to Rhodes's resignation as prime minister of the Cape Colony. More importantly it heightened the distrust and tension between the British government and the AFRIKANER REPUBLICS (the Transvaal and the ORANGE FREE STATE) and between Uitlanders and AFRIKANERS. The raid underscored the republics' lack of military preparedness, which was redressed by better organization and improved armament. In general terms, the Jameson Raid and the controversy it engendered contributed significantly to the outbreak of the ANGLO-BOER WAR, in 1899. As for Jameson, he was able to rebound politically, wining election to the Cape Colony parliament in 1904. There he played an important role in events leading to the creation of the UNION OF SOUTH AFRICA in 1910.

Further reading: Elizabeth Longford, *Jameson's Raid: The Prelude to the Boer War* (London: Panther Books, 1984).

jihad (jehad) Meaning in Arabic, "fight" or "battle," *jihad* implies striving or struggling to achieve a higher moral standard following the path of God. Jihad is difficult to define because it cannot be precisely translated. In its most general sense it refers to the obligation of the individual Muslim and the Muslim community to make a sincere and noticeable effort to accomplish God's will, lead virtuous lives, and expand Islam. This may be done through preaching, education, and similar activities. It is Muslim belief that good deeds open the way to salvation and divine pardon.

Jihad also may refer to fighting to pursue justice and freedom and to oppose oppression. It is in this sense that jihad means war. Certain conditions, however, apply to determine what makes a just war. A jihad, for example, can be a defensive war or a war against an unjust regime, but it must be waged only against the government, not civilians. The concept of jihad cannot be used to justify a war that forces people to accept Islam. Jihad is often casually defined as "holy war," but in Islam, war is not considered holy. Muslim scholars explain that the notion of a holy war comes from Europe, where it was used to justify the Crusades (1096–1291) that Christians waged against Muslims.

Regarding jihad, the Quran (9:29) commands the faithful to "fight against those who do not believe in God or the Judgment Day, who permit what God and His messenger have forbidden, and who refuse allegiance to the true faith from those who have received scriptures, until they humbly pay tribute."

Two wars that meet these Islamic standards for a just war are the war that Muhammad Ahmad al-MAHDI (1844–1885) waged against the Egyptian colonial administration of the Sudan in the early 1880s and the war that MUHAMMAD ABDULLAH HASSAN (1864–1920) waged against the British and Italian colonial governments of SOMALIA in the early 20th century. Both were led by religious reformers and were fought to establish an Islamic state governed by Islamic law, or *sharia*.

See also: ISLAM (Vol. II); ISLAM, INFLUENCES OF (Vols. II, III, IV, V); JIHAD (Vol. II); QURAN (Vol. II); MAHDIYYA (Vol. IV); SHARIA (Vols. II, V).

Further reading: Rudolph Peters, *Jihad in Classical and Modern Islam,* (Princeton, N.J.: Markus Wiener Publishers, 1996).

Johannesburg South African city, 900 square miles (2,331 sq km) in size, that is both the major urban, financial, and commercial center of SOUTH AFRICA and the world's largest inland city. Once just an expanse of open savanna, Johannesburg was founded in 1886 after the discovery of GOLD in the nearby hill region known as the WITWATERSRAND. By 1899 it had become the world's most productive gold-mining region. The gold rush brought people from all over the world to South Africa. Initially the area was a jumble of miners' camps, but soon the government of the TRANSVAAL formally organized the area into the town of Johannesburg, which rapidly grew into a major city. By 1896 it had almost 100,000 people, making it the territory's largest city. By 1903 the city expanded to cover 82 square miles (212 sq km); the population reached 250,000 by 1914. Population growth slowed during the 1920s, reaching 400,000 by 1931, but then doubled to 800,000 by the end of World War II (1939–45).

Johannesburg's gold-mining industry and concomitant rapid growth were marked by political and social tensions. One source of these was the animosity between two groups of whites—AFRIKANERS (known prior to the 20th century as BOERS), who regarded the Transvaal as their homeland, and the UITLANDERS, European SETTLERS who possessed capitalistic and imperial interests in southern Africa. These divergent viewpoints came to a head with two armed conflicts—the Transvaal Revolt (1880–81) and the ANGLO-BOER WAR (1899–1902).

Another source of tension developed along social and class lines. Originally a rough-and-tumble mining camp, replete with alcohol and prostitution, the city later developed a middle class that began to impose its own Victorian social structures as their numbers and influence grew. Established residential areas emerged that reflected both class and racial divisions. The members of the white working class, increasingly AFRIKAANS-speaking, occupied their own areas, as did the largely English-speaking middle class. At the same time, indigenous Africans were segregated into largely impoverished and overcrowded areas located far from the main places of employment.

African mineworkers, forced to work the mines and live in single-sex compounds, were not only separated from whites, but also from their families, who usually remained in their rural homes. While these racial divisions never erupted into large-scale violence, class divisions within the white population did.

While the indigenous African residents of Johannesburg generally lived in poverty, their cultural life was vibrant. A lively MUSIC scene emerged in the Sophiatown and Alexandra townships after World War II, giving rise to such music greats as Hugh Masekela (1931–), Miriam Makeba (1932–), and Abdullah Ibrahim (1934–). DRUM, a periodical based in Johannesburg, covered the African music scene and also carried short stories and articles by African authors.

In 1922 white workers engaged in open revolt against the mine owners and the South African government, seizing control of the city. The army managed to suppress this "Rand Revolt," but only after 200 strikers had lost their lives. Despite its class struggles, Johannesburg quickly emerged as South Africa's preeminent city, as well as an international financial and commercial center. Johannesburg's vibrant economy has spanned more than a century, from the founding of its Stock Exchange in 1887 to the building of its modern skyline replete with metal and glass skyscrapers. Until recently, however, the highly visible, unsightly mine dumps served as a reminder that the city was built on the mining of gold.

In addition to mining, the policy of APARTHEID adopted in 1948 greatly influenced the layout of Johannesburg. Apartheid decreed that South Africans reside in areas established along racial lines. More specifically, the government sought to reduce the overall African population living within the municipal boundaries of its cities, and in 1955 it began to forcibly remove Africans from Johannesburg and resettle them in Soweto. This policy of rigid, legislated segregation characterized Johannesburg throughout the apartheid era (1948–94).

Since the end of apartheid many Africans have moved into areas of Johannesburg where they were previously not allowed to live. At the same time wealthy whites have begun moving from the downtown area, leaving behind an increasing crime rate and the reality of living among formerly disenfranchised neighbors.

See also: AFRIKANER REPUBLICS (Vol. IV); JOHANNESBURG (Vol. V); MAKEBA, MIRIAM (Vol. V); MASEKELA, HUGH (Vol. V); URBAN LIFE AND CULTURE (Vols. IV); URBANIZATION (Vol. IV).

Further reading: Peter Kallaway and Patrick Pearson, *Johannesburg: Images and Continuities: A History of Working Class Life Through Pictures, 1885–1935* (Braamfontein, South Africa: Ravan Press, 1986); Reuben Musiker, *Aspects of Johannesburg History* (Johannesburg: University of Witwatersrand Library, 1987).

Johnson, Samuel (1846–1901) *Yoruba educator, missionary, and historian*

Active both as a teacher and as a Christian missionary, Johnson played an important role in the recording of YORUBA history, a task that the Yoruba themselves had begun earlier in the 19th century. Johnson was born in FREETOWN, in what is now SIERRA LEONE. His father was one of Freetown's RECAPTIVES, the term used for people who had been liberated from slave ships by the British Navy. Johnson's father, who was originally from Oyo, in present-day NIGERIA, joined the CHURCH MISSIONARY SOCIETY (CMS) and eventually moved to Yorubaland.

After spending much of his youth among the Yoruba, Samuel Johnson was educated at the CMS Training Institution in ABEOKUTA, where many Christian Yoruba had settled upon their return to Nigeria from Sierra Leone. He completed his studies in 1865, becoming a schoolmaster and, in time, the administrator for several schools run by the Anglican Mission. He was ordained as a minister in 1888. The Anglican bishop for Nigeria at the time was the well-known Samuel Ajayi CROWTHER (1808–1891), who, like Johnson's father, was also a recaptive. During the 1870s and 1880s Johnson's work as a teacher and pastor led him to act as a peacemaker between various warring Yoruba states.

Samuel Johnson was not the only distinguished member of his generation in his family. His oldest brother, Henry, became an archdeacon with the Church Missionary Society. Another brother, Nathaniel, also worked as a teacher for the CMS. His younger brother Obadiah was one of the first Nigerians to become a medical doctor in the Western tradition.

During the 1880s Johnson began a serious study of the Yoruba peoples, writing a history and ethnographic text that he finally completed in the late 1890s. In 1897 he sent his finished manuscript to the main office of the CMS in London. There the manuscript languished and eventually was lost. Johnson's brother, Obadiah, reconstructed the manuscript from notes, and after Samuel's death he had it published as *A History of the Yorubas from the Earliest Times to the Beginning of the British Protectorate* (1921). Although present-day scholars have questioned some of Johnson's supposed discoveries and several of his underlying assumptions, Johnson's *History of the Yorubas* has long been considered a cornerstone of historical and ethnographic research.

See also: HISTORICAL SCHOLARSHIP ON AFRICA (Vol. IV); MISSIONARIES (Vol. IV); SLAVE TRADE (Vol. III); YORUBALAND (Vols. II, III).

Further reading: J. F. Ade Ajayi, *Christian Missions in Nigeria, 1841–1891; the Making of a New Elite* (London: Longmans, 1965).

Jonathan, Leabua (Chief) (1914–1987) *First prime minister of the independent Kingdom of Lesotho*

The great grandson of Mshweshwe (1786–1870), the founder of BASUTOLAND (present-day LESOTHO), Jonathan was heir to a minor chiefdom. He became a Catholic after receiving his education in a mission school. From 1934 to 1937 Jonathan labored in the South African GOLD mines, after which he became employed by the paramount chief regent and rose up through the administration to become the president of the Basuto courts.

Jonathan served in various high-level governmental positions, and in 1959 he founded the Basuto National Party (BNP). During this time Basutoland, a crown colony of Britain, was located wholly within the borders of SOUTH AFRICA, and was greatly affected by South Africa's APARTHEID policies. The BNP promoted improved relations with South Africa, in spite of the country's racist government. However, the party also rejected plans for Basutoland to join the UNION OF SOUTH AFRICA, favoring complete independence from Britain instead. Despite the party's relative lack of success, Jonathan managed to gain a seat in the Legislative Council. In 1962 he helped create a new constitution, which set the stage for Basutoland's independence from Britain and Jonathan's eventual rise to the position of prime minister.

See also: ENGLAND AND AFRICA (Vol. III, IV, V); MSH-WESHWE (Vol. III).

K

Kabarega, Mukama (c. 1853–1923) *Last independent king of Bunyoro*

In 1869 Kabarega became king of BUNYORO, a kingdom located in present-day western UGANDA. By the latter half of the 19th century it had ceded much of its territory and eminence to the kingdom of BUGANDA. Initially Kabarega met with resistance to his authority and was temporarily deposed before regaining power in 1872. After subduing his domestic foes Kabarega turned his attention to external opponents.

Early in Kabarega's reign, Egypt's Khedive ISMAIL (1830–1895) sent Samuel BAKER (1821–1893), the governor of Equatoria Province in Egyptian-ruled Sudan, to claim Bunyoro and the general Nile River headwaters region for EGYPT. Kabarega resisted, and his forces intermittently clashed with the Egyptian and Sudanese forces for years, finally forcing their withdrawal in 1888.

Between 1888 and 1892 Buganda, Bunyoro's longtime adversary, was engulfed in a religious civil war. Kabarega took advantage of the weakened state of his neighbor to centralize Bunyoro's power structure and expand the kingdom's territory, initiating a modest renaissance of Bunyoro power in the region.

Many African kingdoms of the time had no standing army, relying on a "call to arms" to attack or defend against enemies. Kabarega, however, transformed his personal guard into a standing army, equipping it with modern arms acquired from Arab traders.

By 1892 the civil war in Buganda had subsided as the kingdom fell to British control. Looking to expand their dominion, British forces, directed by Frederick LUGARD (1858–1945), invaded Bunyoro. Using guerrilla tactics, Kabarega led a five-year war of resistance, with his forces continuing the fight even after Kabarega fled to the Sudan, in 1894. Despite Kabarega's efforts, the British occupied Bunyoro in 1897. Kabarega, however, remained at large until 1899, when he was captured and exiled to the SEYCHELLES. He lived there for more than 20 years but was allowed to return to his homeland just before his death.

See also: COLONIAL CONQUEST (Vol. IV); ENGLAND AND AFRICA (Vols. III, IV, V); GREAT LAKES REGION (Vol. III); KITARA COMPLEX (Vol. II).

Kadalie, Clements (1896–1951) *South African trade union organizer*

Born Lameck Koniwaka Kadali Muwamba in NYASALAND (now known as MALAWI), Clements Kadalie briefly worked as a teacher in his homeland before going abroad in search of greater opportunity. After working in MOZAMBIQUE and ZIMBABWE, he settled in CAPE TOWN, SOUTH AFRICA, in 1918 and formed the Industrial and Commercial Workers' Union of Africa (ICU) the following year. With the ICU, Kadalie mobilized dockworkers and waged a surprisingly successful strike that resulted in higher wages at a time when black LABOR won few such victories. In the aftermath of the strike, membership in the ICU grew, spreading the general trade union organization throughout the country. In 1923 the ICU began publishing a newspaper, *Worker's Herald*, under Kadalie's editorship.

In response to labor unrest among black workers during the 1920s—in part, a product of the ICU's success—the government passed the Industrial Conciliation Act of 1924, which denied Africans the right of collective bargaining. By the mid-1920s the ICU claimed approximately 100,000 members, although its paid-up membership was considerably less. However gauged, the ICU was the largest union of black workers in South Africa and a powerful mass movement. Notably, it recruited from both urban and rural locales and across race lines, counting African, Coloured, and Indian workers among its ranks. The ICU was especially strong in NATAL, thanks to the efforts of the influential African nationalist leader, A. W. G. CHAMPION (1893–1975).

In an attempt to gain greater legitimacy within trade union circles, Kadalie went abroad in 1927 to seek support. As a result, the ICU became affiliated with the International Trade Union Congress, although its official application to the International Labor Organization was rejected. Over the next few years financial irregularities and personal differences among ICU leaders caused internal dissension. Repressive government measures further inhibited the organization's ability to function effectively. In 1929 Kedalie bowed to pressure from within the ICU and resigned as national secretary, establishing an independent ICU that operated out of East London. The influence of both branches of the ICU subsequently declined. However, Kadalie remained active locally in East London. He also participated in the African liberation struggle as a member of the AFRICAN NATIONAL CONGRESS until his death in 1951.

Further reading: Helen Bradford, *A Taste of Freedom: The ICU in Rural South Africa, 1924–1930* (New Haven, Conn.: Yale University Press, 1987); Clements Kadalie, *My Life and the ICU: The Autobiography of a Black Trade Unionist in South Africa* (New York: Humanities Press, 1970).

Kagwa, Apolo (Sir) (1865–1927) *Long-time* katikiro *(chief minister) of the Buganda kingdom*

As a young man Apolo Kagwa was one of the many pages at the court of the great *kabaka,* or king, MUTESA I (c. late 1830s–1884) during the time when Anglican MISSIONARIES of the CHURCH MISSIONARY SOCIETY (CMS) began their work in BUGANDA. Many of the young pages became converts of the CMS or their Catholic rivals. In 1886, two years after he had succeeded Mutesa I as *kabaka,* Mwanga II (c. 1866–1903) purged many of the converted Christian pages, executing 40 of them. Kagwa survived the political intrigues to become the leader of the Protestant faction during the civil wars among rival Protestants, Catholics, and Muslims that convulsed Buganda between 1888 and 1892. For his support in helping Mwanga remain *kabaka,* Kagwa became *katikiro,*

or chief minister, in 1890. Between then and 1897, when continuing religious warfare forced Mwanga into exile in the SEYCHELLES, Kagwa was a major force in the Protestant cause. He also was increasingly pro-British, since the British supported the Protestant cause.

Kagwa became the principal regent after Mwanga's exile—engineered largely by the British agent Frederick LUGARD (1858–1945)—and the signing of the Banda Agreement (1900). This agreement established British COLONIAL RULE over Buganda and the rest of UGANDA. As regent, Kagwa essentially ruled the country for the next decade and a half. He was also one of the kingdom's largest landholders. In 1902 Kagwa and his secretary, Ham Mukasa (1870–1956), traveled to Britain for the coronation of King Edward VII (1841–1910), and Kagwa received his knighthood in the process. Two years later Mukasa published an account of the journey, *Buganda's Katikiro in England.*

> As regent, Kagwa believed in the necessity to educate and train Buganda's youth and to promote academic excellence. He contributed directly to the EDUCATION of Buganda's youth by writing about Ganda history and culture. His history of Buganda's kings, written in the Ganda language, appeared in a translated and edited version as *The Kings of Buganda* (1971).

Crafty and autocratic, Kagwa was able to keep the friendship of the British while also maintaining a modicum of independence for his kingdom. Ultimately, however, conflicts with the young Kabaka Daudi Chwa II (1886–1942) and other younger politicians who had begun to chafe under his long-time leadership took their toll. In 1926 he was forced to resign after falling into a bureaucratic conflict with a British colonial administrator.

See also: COLONIAL CONQUEST (Vol. IV); ENGLAND AND AFRICA (Vol. IV); HISTORICAL SCHOLARSHIP ON AFRICA (Vols. IV, V).

Further reading: Ham Mukasa, *Buganda's Katikiro in England* (Manchester, U.K.: Manchester University Press, 1999).

Kampala City that became the capital of the British Uganda PROTECTORATE; located on the northern shore of Lake Victoria, near the site of the former BUGANDA capital of Mengo. The origins and development of the city of Kampala are closely related to the existence of the Buganda capital. In the 1840s Muslim traders reached Buganda and began exchanging firearms, cloth, and beads

for ivory and human captives. By the time the first European explorers reached the area in 1862, they found that trade routes were already well established, making the area of present-day Kampala strategically important to European nations with colonial designs. In the late 1870s the Anglican CHURCH MISSIONARY SOCIETY established itself in Kampala, soon followed by French Roman Catholic MISSIONARIES.

In 1881 a Buganda royal palace enclosure was built on Kasubi Hill, where royal tombs were located. By the end of the 1880s, however, a religious civil war had disrupted Buganda society, opening the way for European intervention. In 1890 Frederick LUGARD (1858–1945) declared the British Uganda Protectorate with Kampala the colonial capital. The growing city also became the headquarters for the British East Africa Company, one of many CONCESSIONAIRE COMPANIES that the European colonial powers used to assert territorial claims in Africa. (The colonial capital later was moved to Entebbe.)

In the early 1900s a railroad line was completed between MOMBASA, on the Indian Ocean coast, and Kisumu, on the northeastern shore of Lake Victoria, providing Kampala with greater access to Indian Ocean commerce. As a result, by the 1920s the area's COTTON, COFFEE, and sugar crops were important staples in the colonial ECONOMY.

As a result of the increased trade and commercial interests, the city attracted many Asian immigrants and became more racially diverse. There was a substantial amount of religious diversity as well, due to immigration and the continued arrival of Muslim traders and foreign missionaries.

In 1920 Makerere College was established—it became a university in 1949—and Kampala thus was established as a leading center for higher education in East Africa. In 1962 Kampala became the capital of the new independent nation of UGANDA. Two years later the city proper had an estimated population of 80,000, with about another 60,000 living in the surrounding area.

See also: ASIAN COMMUNITIES (Vols. IV, V); ENGLAND AND AFRICA (Vols. III, IV, V); IVORY TRADE (Vols. III, IV); KAMPALA (Vol. V); SLAVE TRADE (Vol. IV); SLAVE TRADE ON THE SWAHILI COAST (Vol. III); TRADE AND COMMERCE (Vol. IV); VICTORIA, LAKE (Vols. I, V).

Kanem-Bornu (Kanem-Borno) Historic trading empire made up of the separate kingdoms of Kanem and Bornu, located in west-central Africa, around Lake Chad. By the 19th century the former empire had been reduced to a collection of loosely affiliated smaller kingdoms located throughout the present-day countries of CAMEROON, CHAD, NIGER, and NIGERIA.

By 1808 parts of once wealthy and powerful Kanem-Bornu, including its western capital of Ngazargamu, had been incorporated through conquest into the SOKOTO

CALIPHATE. And in 1846 the death of the last Sefuwa *mai* (king) brought an end to the ruling dynasty that had lasted nearly 800 years. Taking over control of a much smaller Kanem-Bornu state was the al-Kanemi dynasty that the Sefuwa leadership had once asked for assistance against Sokoto. In the decades that followed, the al-Kanemi tried, with mixed success, to revive Kanem-Bornu's trans-Saharan trading operations.

Lake Chad was still in turmoil during the latter part of the 19th century. In the 1890s France, Germany, and Britain divided the region among themselves as part of the PARTITION process. About the same time, however, the Muslim slave trader and military commander, RABIH BIN FADLALLAH (c. 1835–1900), swept through Kanem-Bornu from the Sudan, to the east, with a large slave army, quickly controlling parts of the kingdom. During Rabih's short reign—he was killed in battle with French colonial forces in 1900—Kanem-Bornu was greatly weakened. By 1902 British forces also had moved into the region and eventually incorporated the western parts of the state into their Nigeria territory. Governing by means of indirect rule, Britain turned Kanem-Bornu over to the al-Kanemi *shehus* (chiefs), and the kingdom was subsequently divided into two separate emirates, Bornu and Dikwa.

During the course of World War I (1914–18) the victorious Allies stripped Germany of its claims to southern Kanem-Bornu territory. Later, in 1937, Dikwa eventually united with the neighboring state of Kukawa to form Nigeria's Borno State.

See also: ENGLAND AND AFRICA (Vol. III, IV); FRANCE AND AFRICA (Vol. IV); FULANI JIHADS (Vol. III); KANEM-BORNU (Vols. II, III); NGAZARGAMU (Vols. II, III); SEFUWA (Vols. II, III); TRANS-SAHARAN TRADE ROUTES (Vol. II); USMAN DAN FODIO (Vol. III).

Kankan MANDE town, located along the banks of the Milo River, a tributary of the Niger River, and the second leading city of present-day GUINEA. Kankan, an important Islamic center since the 18th century, maintained ties with the Islamic empire of al-Hajj UMAR TAL (1794–1864). Later, in the 19th century, Mande-speaking empire-builder SAMORI TOURÉ (c. 1830–1900) turned his war machine on Kankan when the city refused to aid him in his attack against other Muslims. After conquering the city and driving out the ruling Kaba family, Samori appointed a member of his own Muslim contingent to rule.

About 1890, as part of its efforts to diffuse regional solidarity, France occupied Kankan and reinstated the Kaba rulers. A large and varied number of products passed through the markets of colonial Kankan, ensuring a strong economy. By 1914 the city was serviced by a railroad, built by African forced LABOR, that enhanced the city's long-standing reputation as a major crossroads of trade routes from IVORY COAST, FRENCH SOUDAN (now the

Republic of MALI), and Guinea. By 1922 Kankan was recognized as the second-most important city in Guinea after the capital, Conakry.

Following World War II (1939–45) nationalist movements throughout Guinea looked to the Islamic leadership in Kankan as a model for regional organization.

Kankan native Souleymane KANTÉ (1922–1987) developed the N'ko alphabet, and by 1949 traders in the area were learning this writing system to use in their businesses.

See also: COLONIAL RULE (Vol. IV), COLONIALISM, INFLUENCE OF (Vol. IV); FRANCE AND AFRICA (Vols. III, IV, V); ISLAM, INFLUENCE OF (Vols. II, III, IV, V); KANKAN (Vol. V); URBANIZATION (Vols. IV, V).

Kano (Kano City)

One of the major HAUSA city-states in northwestern NIGERIA, located on the Jakara River. As a result of the far-ranging 19th-century JIHAD of Usman dan Fodio (1754–1817), Kano came under the rule of the SOKOTO CALIPHATE. The walled city continued to flourish as a major center for trans-Saharan trade and also as a center of textile manufacturing and cloth dyeing. It became the caliphate's principal commercial city. In 1851, European traveler and explorer Heinrich BARTH (1821–1865) estimated that its inhabitants numbered at least 30,000.

Heinrich Barth was eager to reach Kano, for, as he was to write in his *Travels and Discoveries in North and Central Africa (1857–1858)*, Kano "had been one of the great objects of our journey as the central point of commerce, as a great storehouse of information, and as the point whence more distant regions might be most successfully attempted."

In 1903 the British took control of Kano after they defeated Sokoto's military forces. However, the city continued to prosper, developing into a true urban center under British COLONIAL RULE. Britain built a railroad line to coastal LAGOS in 1912, which allowed for the shipment of CASH CROPS, particularly GROUNDNUTS (peanuts). Economic growth was particularly rapid in the aftermath of World War II (1939–45), and the population of Kano City had reached an estimated 130,000 by 1952.

See also: CLOTH AND TEXTILES (Vol. IV); ENGLAND AND AFRICA (Vols. III, IV, V); HAUSA STATES (Vols. II, III); ISLAM (Vol. II); ISLAM, INFLUENCE OF (Vols. II, III, IV, V); KANO (Vols. II, III, V); TRANS-SAHARAN TRADE ROUTES (Vol. II); USMAN DAN FODIO (Vol. III).

Kanté, Souleymane (1922–1987) *Guinean intellectual and creator of the indigenous N'ko alphabet*

Souleymane Kanté was born in Upper GUINEA near the city of KANKAN. His father, Amara Kanté, was one of many youths brought to the region by SAMORI TOURÉ (c. 1830–1900) to study at the region's superior Quranic schools. Amara Kanté then became a Quranic teacher, opening a school near Kankan. His reputation as a teacher attracted many students from across FRENCH WEST AFRICA to study under him alongside Souleymane and his four brothers and two sisters. After Amara Kanté's death in 1941, Souleymane's elder brothers continued the school. The following year Souleymane traveled to IVORY COAST, where he sold Arabic books, taught himself the colonial LANGUAGE of French, and read a wide range of literature.

While living in Bingerville, the capital of the colonial Ivory Coast, Kanté read a journal article written by a Lebanese journalist that stated Africans were inferior because they had no indigenous written form of communication. This was a position that reflected the prevailing racism of colonialism. African languages, the article alleged, were like those of birds, impossible to transcribe. Shocked and insulted, Kanté set out to prove the article's author wrong.

Working with his own Maninka language, from 1945 to 1947 Kanté tried to use Arabic script for writing Maninka, which belongs to the MANDE group of languages. As he worked he discovered that Arabic script could not accommodate the tonality of the Mande languages. He next attempted to use the Roman alphabet, and although its use of accents made it better suited for writing the language, it proved too imprecise for much of the Maninka vocabulary. Based on this trial-and-error approach, Kanté concluded that borrowed alphabets were unsuitable for writing African languages and that he would have to construct his own alphabet to reflect the tonality—an essential feature—of the Mande languages.

Kanté struggled for several years to create an indigenous alphabet before announcing his success on April 14, 1949. Kanté gave his invention a culturally significant name, *N'ko*. In all the Mande languages the pronoun *N* represents the pronoun "I," and the Mande verb *ko* represents the verb "say." By choosing the name *N'ko*, "I say," Kanté united all Mande speakers with just one phrase. This term also recalled the unifying epic of the Mande past, that of Sundiata, in which the history of Mande cultural dominance knew men of valor who said, "N'ko."

After reworking and refining his alphabet, Kanté spent the rest of his life using the N'ko alphabet to translate books into Maninka. Equally important, he used the alphabet to write down and record indigenous Mande knowledge. Believing that Africans needed to learn in their African languages and that learning an indigenous alphabet would eliminate illiteracy, Kanté encouraged everyone to learn the alphabet. This, he asserted, would allow them to write down knowledge and personal experiences to preserve indigenous knowledge.

Because many Mande-speakers were Muslims, Kanté, using N'ko, translated the Quran into Maninka. Before his translation could be published, 10 Islamic scholars from Guinea had to verify its accuracy, and a report had to be filed in Saudi Arabia. In addition Kanté transcribed works from the disciplines of literature and linguistics, as well as the social and physical sciences. He also wrote textbooks, a dictionary, and an encyclopedia. These works essentially standardized the Maninka language in its written form.

Souleymane Kanté formally presented his alphabet to newly independent Guinea's president, Ahmed Sékou TOURÉ (1922–1984) in 1959, who then rewarded Kanté with a substantial monetary prize. Touré also requested that Kanté and his family return to Guinea from Ivory Coast, where they had been living. When Kanté reached Kankan, he discovered that the N'ko alphabet had preceded him by 10 years, and it had already become an accepted tool for literacy.

See also: EDUCATION (Vols. IV, V); ISLAM, INFLUENCE OF (Vols. II, III, IV, V); KANTÉ, SOULEYMANE (Vol. V); LITERACY (Vols. IV, V); SUNDIATA (Vol. II).

Further reading: Dianne White Oyler, *The History of the N'ko Alphabet and its Role in Mande Transnational Identity: Words as Weapons,* (Cherry Hill, N.J.: Africana Homestead Legacy Press, 2003).

Kariba Dam Hydroelectric dam, spanning the Kariba Gorge of the Zambezi River on the border of ZAMBIA and ZIMBABWE. Construction on the Kariba Dam began in 1955 as a joint venture between British colonies of NORTHERN RHODESIA, SOUTHERN RHODESIA (present-day Zambia and Zimbabwe respectively) and NYASALAND (present-day MALAWI), which at that time made up the CENTRAL AFRICAN FEDERATION. The dam was intended to harness the waters of the Zambezi River, the fourth-largest in Africa, and to create hydroelectric power. It also had the political purpose of strengthening the federation. At its completion in 1959, the Kariba Dam was the largest in the world, with a reservoir, named Kariba Lake, approximately 175 miles long and up to 20 miles wide.

The construction of the dam resulted in massive changes to the area's population and ecology. The creation of Kariba Lake flooded the traditional lands of the Gwembe Tonga, displacing more than 50,000 people and forcing them to move to higher, less arable land. The reservoir also destroyed the habitats of numerous animals, and as the water level rose it left many creatures stranded on islands. In what came to be known as Operation Noah, nearly 7,000 animals, ranging from impala to rhinos, were rescued by boat. Many more, however, drowned.

The name *Kariba* is taken from a large rock that originally rose from the Zambezi River at the entrance to the Kariba Gorge. The local population believed that the rock was the home of the river god Nyaminyami. They predicted that the god's wrath would doom any attempt to dam the Zambezi. Remarkably in 1957 and 1958 the river flooded twice, causing much damage to the unfinished dam. The second flood was so large that it was predicted to happen only once every 10,000 years. In spite of this, the dam was completed, and the river god's home now lies beneath 100 feet of water.

After the Central African Federation broke up in 1963, there were considerable political tensions over the distribution of the dam's electricity between African-ruled Zambia and white-ruled Rhodesia (which had dropped the "Southern" from its name). After nearly 15 years of armed struggle, Rhodesia became independent Zimbabwe, and a more cooperative relationship developed with Zambia. This led to a new set of arrangements for supplying electricity to Zimbabwe's rapidly growing urban areas and to the mines and cities of Zambia's COPPERBELT, a region rich in COPPER and other ores. The reservoir became a healthy new habitat for fish populations and supports a thriving fishing industry. In 1997 the Gwembe Tonga Project was initiated to help stabilize the Gwembe Tonga community and address the social and environmental impact of the Kariba Dam.

See also: ZAMBEZI RIVER (Vols. I, III).

Kaunda, Kenneth (1924–) *First president of independent Zambia (1964–1991)*

Kenneth David Kaunda was born in 1924 to Christian MISSIONARIES at Lubwa Mission in the northern part of what was then the British colony of NORTHERN RHODESIA (present-day ZAMBIA). His father, David, was sent by the Presbyterian Livingstonia Mission in NYASALAND (present-day MALAWI), in 1904, to work as an evangelist in Zambia. His mother, Helen, was one of the first female school teachers in Northern Rhodesia. Because his parents were from Malawi, Kaunda was not aligned with any of Zambia's ethnic groups. This worked to his advantage later in his political career because he was seen as being less inclined to favor one ethnic group over another.

Kaunda went to school at Lubwa Mission School and trained as a teacher. In 1941 he went to Munali Secondary School in Lusaka, eventually returning to Lubwa Mission as a boarding master. He married Betty Banda (1928–) in 1946, and they had nine children.

Kaunda's first involvement in politics came in the early 1950s, when he joined the Northern Rhodesia African Congress, later called the AFRICAN NATIONAL CONGRESS (ANC), led by Harry Nkumbula (1916–1983). An efficient organizer, Kaunda quickly rose in the party's leadership ranks, becoming the secretary general in 1953. In 1958 he formed the Zambia African National Congress (ZANC). The colonial administrators, however, banned this party the following year, and Kaunda was sent to prison for nine months for holding an illegal meeting. He was one of many subsequent presidents of African countries sentenced to prison for opposing COLONIAL RULE. In 1960 Kaunda was released from prison and was soon elected president of a new party, the UNITED NATIONAL INDEPENDENCE PARTY (UNIP). Kaunda led UNIP to a sweeping electoral victory in 1964, thereby becoming the first president of independent Zambia.

See also: CENTRAL AFRICAN FEDERATION (Vol. IV); COLONIALISM, INFLUENCE OF (Vol. IV); ETHNICITY AND IDENTITY (Vol. I); KAUNDA, KENNETH (Vol. V); NATIONALISM AND INDEPENDENCE MOVEMENTS (Vol. IV).

Further reading: Richard S. Hall, *Kaunda, Founder of Zambia* (London: Longmans, 1965); Kenneth Kaunda, *Zambia Shall Be Free* (London: Heinemann, 1962).

Kenya Present-day country, some 224,900 square miles (582,500 sq km) in size, located in eastern equatorial Africa and sharing borders with ETHIOPIA, Republic of the SUDAN, UGANDA, TANZANIA, and SOMALIA; Kenya was under British COLONIAL RULE from 1895 to 1963.

Since the 16th century cities along the Kenyan coast, including MOMBASA and Malindi, were busy ports for the trading of African goods, including ivory, animal hides, and human captives. By the mid-1830s the Kenyan coast was controlled by the BUSAIDI sultan of ZANZIBAR, off the coast of present-day Tanzania. In contrast to central Tanzania, however, it wasn't until much later in the century that Zanzibari Arabs and coastal Swahili merchants were able to control trade routes into the interior from the Kenyan coastal ports they ruled. These routes remained in the hands of Kamba merchants until the 1880s, when Arab merchants were finally able to establish direct links with the kikuyu and other peoples residing beyond the Kamba lands. The MAASAI, who were particularly militant, provided another barrier to establishing trade routes.

The first Europeans to venture into the interior were the German MISSIONARIES Johan Ludwig Krapf (1810–1887) and Johannes Rebmann (1820–1876) from the CHURCH MISSIONARY SOCIETY. They traveled in the interior in the late 1840s seeking sites for mission stations, but they were unsuccessful. More than three decades passed before further exploration was conducted. By that time, the Maasai and other peoples of the interior had been greatly weakened due to warfare and rampant epidemics among both people and cattle.

The decline of the Maasai opened the way for European COLONIAL CONQUEST. In 1883 Joseph Thomson (1858–1895) became the first British explorer to successfully pass through Maasai lands. In 1887 the British East Africa Association, led by Sir William Mackinnon (1823–1893), claimed concessionary rights to the Kenyan coast from the sultan of Zanzibar, and in 1890 Britain and Germany divided the interior, with the British claiming the territory north of the mouth of the Umba River. The association was awarded a royal charter, and, as the Imperial British East African Company, it administered the territory from 1888 to 1895. By 1895 the company had exhausted its resources and was unable to extend its activities beyond the coast. At that time the British government stepped in, establishing the PROTECTORATE of BRITISH EAST AFRICA.

British East Africa Britain maintained its East Africa protectorate mainly as a corridor between the coast and the more lucrative, inland UGANDA protectorate. In 1895 construction began on a railroad from Mombasa to Lake Victoria, and by 1901 the railroad was complete, effectively bisecting Maasai lands. Although the protectorate administration was able to enter into diplomatic agreements with the Maasai, resistance to the British venture was fierce, especially among the Nandi, who resisted until 1905.

The construction of the British railway led to the development of NAIROBI, which began as a settlement for rail workers and eventually became the capital of the protectorate.

The completion of the railroad in 1901 coincided with the incursion of the first European SETTLERS into the region. By 1903 these settlers had begun to seize lands belonging to the Maasai and the agriculturalist Kikuyu groups who lived in the fertile highlands north of Nairobi. In 1904 British settlers established the first plantation, and by 1910 COFFEE was the region's major cash crop. Dispossessed Africans were relocated to crowded "native reserves" and were forced to LABOR on settler farms or to find work in Nairobi. The loss of their lands, along with the excessive colonial hut tax policy, forced labor practices, and the *kipande,* an identification card required of all Africans, formed a growing list of grievances that fueled the rise of Kenyan, and particularly Kikuyu, nationalism.

Because of violent African opposition to the railway, Britain brought in workers from India to help with the construction. Some of these workers stayed behind once the project was completed, and Indian traders who had previously operated on the coast also began to move to the interior, seeking land. This led them into direct conflict with the white settlers in the highlands region, who refused to treat Indians as equals, politically or economically. White and Indian settlers remained locked in dispute well into the 1920s. In 1927 the troubles ended when Indian settlers accepted a five-seat minority in the colony's Legislative Council.

Kenya during the Colonial Era: Kenya Colony

Following World War I (1914–18), Britain offered war veterans the opportunity to acquire cheap land in the British East Africa protectorate, resulting in a threefold increase in the European population. In 1920 the protectorate became the Kenya Colony, and the coastal region leased from the sultan of Zanzibar became the Protectorate of Kenya.

Conditions for Kenya's black population, however, continued to be miserable. In response, Africans developed organizations to bring their grievances to light. The Young Kikuyu Association (later, the Kikuyu Central Association), founded in 1921 by Harry THUKU (1895–1970), took the forefront in this effort, and was joined by other groups, such as the Young Kavirondo Association, which was formed a year later. Groups like the Young Kikuyu Association were the starting points for Kenya's eventual African leaders, including future president and nationalist icon Jomo KENYATTA (c. 1891–1978). Toward the end of World War II (1939–45), in which Kenyan troops fought on the side of the victorious Allies, the colonial government became the first in East Africa to allow an African representative to take part in the colony's Legislative Council. By 1951 the number of African representatives to the council had increased to eight.

Any political headway, however, was halted by the MAU MAU movement, a rural Kikuyu uprising that had begun in the 1940s and became increasingly violent in the early 1950s. Aimed at driving white settlers off of Kikuyu lands, in 1952 the Mau Mau movement led the colonial government to declare a state of emergency. Large numbers of Kikuyu were rounded up by British authorities and placed in concentration camps and "protected villages," and many Kikuyu leaders in Nairobi were imprisoned. These included Jomo Kenyatta, who was by then the head of the Kenya African Union. By the end of the 1950s Britain managed to suppress the Mau Mau uprising, but not until more than 150,000 Kikuyu lost their lives from fighting or deprivation.

Despite its lack of immediate results the Mau Mau movement did convince Britain that a state headed by the vocal white settler minority was unfeasible, and in 1960 Africans were given the majority in the Legislative Council. The new situation led to the formation of two major political parties, the Kenya African National Union (KANU), a largely Kikuyu and LUO party, and the Kenya African Democratic Union (KADU), made up of representatives from smaller ethnic groups. KANU leaders Tom MBOYA (1930–1969) and Oginga ODINGA (1912– 1994), both Luo, helped secure Jomo Kenyatta's release from prison, and the revered Kikuyu nationalist then led KANU to political dominance. Elections in 1963 installed Kenyatta as prime minister, and in December of that year Kenya Colony and the Kenya Protectorate

In 1954, during the infamous "Operation Anvil," thousands of people suspected of Mau Mau sympathies were herded through barbed-wire enclosures at the reception camp at Langata. © *Library of Congress*

merged to form independent Kenya. One year later the country became a republic with Kenyatta as president.

For the international community Kenya and British TANGANYIKA (present-day Tanzania) became, and to some extent still remain, the region most commonly associated with notions of Africa. This came about mainly due to works of a number of popular writers, most prominent among them being the Danish author Karen Blixen (1885–1962, better known by her pen name, Isak Dinesen) and the American writer and Nobel Prize winner Ernest Hemingway (1899–1961). Writing as Dinesen, Blixen used her experiences on a coffee plantation in colonial Kenya between 1914 and 1931 for her most famous work, the memoir *Out of Africa* (1938). Hemingway visited East Africa twice, in 1933 and 1954, and his experiences translated into works such as the short story "The Snows of Kilimanjaro" (1933) and *The Green Hills of Africa* (1935). For some time after their publications, the writings of Blixen and Hemingway came to define, for better or worse, the popular image of Africa.

See also: ASIAN COMMUNITIES (Vols. IV, V); COLONIALISM, INFLUENCE (Vol. IV); ETHNIC GROUP (Vol. I); KENYA (Vols. I, II, III, V); RESISTANCE AND REBELLION (Vol. IV).

Further reading: Bruce Berman, *Control & Crisis in Colonial Kenya: The Dialectic of Domination* (Athens, Ohio: Ohio University Press, 1990); Joanna Lewis, *Empire State-Building: War & Welfare in Kenya, 1925–52* (Athens, Ohio: Ohio University Press, 2000); B. A. Ogot and W. R. Ochieng', eds., *Decolonization and Independence in Kenya* (Athens, Ohio: Ohio University Press, 1995).

Kenyatta, Jomo (Johnstone Kamau, Kamau Ngengi, Kamau Wa Ngengi) (c. 1891–1978) *Kenya's first president*

Born in Kikuyuland, in BRITISH EAST AFRICA (present-day KENYA), Kenyatta was not sure of the year of his birth, since the KIKUYU traditionally keep track of people's ages by their initiation groups rather than their birth years. Named Kamau wa Ngengi at birth, he attended mission schools near NAIROBI and was baptized a Presbyterian, taking the name Johnstone.

Young Kenyatta worked at various jobs, including carpentry, before taking a position with the water company in Nairobi. By the early 1920s he was involved in the nationalistic Young Kikuyu Association, and he helped build several such organizations over the next few years.

He became the general secretary of the Kikuyu Central Association (KCA) in 1928, and also edited its newspaper, *Muigwithania*. In 1929 the KCA sent Kenyatta to London in an unsuccessful attempt to seek redress for what had become a massive white land grab.

The years immediately following World War I (1914–18) saw a surge in white immigration to Kenya, with more than 9,000 Europeans settling in the Nairobi area alone. Determined to turn Kenya into what they called a "white man's" country, officials of both the British government and the colonial administration encouraged white immigration by setting aside vast amounts of land that, traditionally, had belonged to Africans. This policy particularly affected—and angered—the Kikuyu and the MAASAI, who lost nearly 7 million acres (2,832,800 hectares) to white settlers during the post-World War I period.

Kenyatta returned to England in 1931. He remained in Europe for the next 15 years, traveling and studying in England, on the continent, and in the Soviet Union. His study at the London School of Economics with Bronislaw Malinowski (1884–1942), the famed anthropologist renowned anthropologist, resulted in the publication of *Facing Mount Kenya*, in 1938. A book about Kikuyu social and cultural life, it was one of the first books ever written by an African nationalist about his own society. During this period he also became acquainted with a number of other African nationalists, many of whom were even more revolutionary than he was.

After World War II (1939–45) Kenyatta returned to Africa, where, as president of the Kenya African Union, he set about drawing attention to the plight of the Kikuyu people and other Kenyans whose land had been usurped by whites. With speeches, street marches, and demonstrations, he did more than attract attention; he built an organization whose membership reached upwards of 100,000. Although Kenyatta's magnetic personality drew thousands to his cause, others, particularly among young Kikuyu, were not satisfied with his relatively moderate approach to both land reappropriation and the drive for independence. By the late 1940s the MAU MAU movement had begun its attempts to reclaim Kenya's land for Africans, destroying white-owned farms and murdering white settlers and African supporters of the government in the process.

The colonial authorities and the British government responded by instituting the kind of "state of emergency" measures that came to characterize antinationalist efforts in many other African countries. Finally the British sent in troops, arrested Kenyatta and other Kikuyu leaders, moved Kikuyu people onto guarded reserves, and suspended African political activity. In 1953 they charged and convicted Kenyatta of being a leader of Mau Mau in a highly political trial and sentenced him to seven years of hard labor. While the authorities endeavored to quell the Mau Mau, Tom MBOYA (1930–1969) and other nationalist leaders worked to free Kenyatta and gain independence. When Kenyatta's sentence was served, the colonial administration was unwilling to free him, despite the fact that it claimed to have put down the Mau Mau insurrection. Kenyatta was held until his case brought to light scandals involving the colonial administration, forcing Britain to reexamine its role in Kenya.

Despite his given and baptismal names, the man who eventually would lead Kenya chose for himself a name based upon the Kikuyu word for the simple beaded belt worn by African workers. Although there are different stories and varying details, according to the most prevalent telling of the tale, about 1909 Kenyatta appeared at a Scottish-run mission school with his only "clothing" consisting of a *mucibi wa kinyata,* as the workers' belts were called, and a few wire bracelets. When he became involved in nationalist politics, the young man used the word for that belt as his name, in tribute not only to the thousands of African workers who wore them but also as a reminder of the humble origins from which he came.

In 1960 Britain finally realized that it could no longer hold onto Kenya, and it began taking steps to move towards independence. For Kenyatta this meant release from prison. It also meant, not long after, the reestablishment of Africans' right to form political parties, which resulted in the Kenya African National Union (KANU), the party formed by Kenyatta and others to press for independence.

Free, Kenyatta became, even at the age of 70, a dominant figure on the Kenyan scene. As the president of KANU, he continued to push for Kenyan independence alongside Tom Mboya, Oginga ODINGA (1911–1994), and Daniel arap Moi (1924–   ). In 1963, when Kenya became an independent nation, Kenyatta was its first prime minister, urging the various elements of the new nation to draw together with the slogan, *Harambee!* (Pull together!).

See also: ENGLAND AND AFRICA (Vol. IV); HARAMBEE (Vol. V); KENYA AFRICAN NATIONAL UNION (Vol. V); KENYATTA, JOMO (Vol. V); LABOR UNIONS (Vol. IV); NATIONALISM AND INDEPENDENCE MOVEMENTS (Vol. IV).

Further reading: Robert B. Egerton, *Mau Mau: An African Crucible* (New York: Free Press, 1989); Jomo Kenyatta, *Facing Mount Kenya* (New York: Vintage Books, 1965).

Khama III (Kgama III) (1835–1923) *King of the Ngwato people in Bechuanaland (present-day Botswana)*

Khama III became king of the Ngwato in 1875. A staunch Christian convert, he quickly imposed his beliefs on his people, outlawing traditional religion and imposing other measures, such as prohibition of alcohol, that were unpopular with his subjects. To strengthen his position, Khama allied himself with Christian MISSIONARIES in the region, including John Mackenzie (1835–1899).

The Ngwato faced persistent threats from the neighboring NDEBELE people, as well as from encroaching BOERS, who were increasingly laying claim to lands in the interior. Under the influence of the missionaries, Khama decided the British were key to the preservation of his throne. Persuaded by Mackenzie's pleas, Britain declared the colony of BECHUANALAND in order to halt the advance of the Boers and block the interests of other European colonial powers, as well. By 1910 the southern part of the colony was annexed to the CAPE COLONY and became part of SOUTH AFRICA. Khama's kingdom, in the north, became part of the British PROTECTORATE of Bechuanaland.

In 1894 the BRITISH SOUTH AFRICA COMPANY, headed by Cecil RHODES (1853–1902), sought control of the Bechuanaland Protectorate, with the intention of incorporating it into SOUTHERN RHODESIA (present-day ZIMBABWE). Khama and two other prominent TSWANA kings, Bathoen (1845–1910) and Sebele (1842–1911), traveled to England to contest Rhode's claim. With the aid of the LONDON MISSIONARY SOCIETY and other humanitarian organizations, the Tswana men were able to convince the British government to allow the Tswana to maintain control over the protectorate rather than turning it over to Rhodes. A highllight of the visit was the meeting between the Tswana and Queen Victoria (1819–1901), whom King Khama greatly impressed.

In 1923 Khama died of pneumonia, but his legacy of a country free from South African rule was intact. His grandson, Seretse KHAMA (1921–1980), became the first president of independent Bechuanaland (renamed BOTSWANA) in 1966.

See also: COLONIAL CONQUEST (Vol. IV); ENGLAND AND AFRICA (Vols. III, IV, V).

Further reading: Neil Parsons, *King Khama, Emperor Joe, and the Great White Queen: Victorian Britain through African Eyes* (Chicago: University of Chicago Press, 1998).

Khama, Seretse (Sir) (1921–1980) *First president of independent Botswana (1966–1980)*

Seretse was the grandson of Kgosi KHAMA III (1835–1923), ruler of the Ngwato people of central BOTSWANA and a hero from the Boer Wars. When his father died in 1925, the four-year-old Seretse was proclaimed *kgosi*, or king, of the Ngwato, with his uncle Tshekedi Khama (1905–1959) his guardian and regent.

Although he was often sick as a child, Seretse Khama was a studious and active adolescent. He received a degree from FORT HARE COLLEGE, in neighboring SOUTH AFRICA, and was sent to England to study law. After finishing his studies in Britain, Seretse married a white Englishwoman named Ruth Williams. This caused great distress to his uncle Tshekedi, to say nothing of the British colonial administration, but it did not keep Seretse from being welcomed home as the rightful *kgosi* of the Ngwato, in 1948.

At the time of Seretse's return Botswana, located just north of South Africa, was still known as BECHUANALAND, a British PROTECTORATE. The British administration in Bechuanaland relied heavily on South Africa and its NATURAL RESOURCES, and therefore took an intense interest in the affairs of the neighboring country. The administration at that time hoped that a pro-British party would win the next all-white elections and assume control of the territory from the pro-Afrikaner Nationalist party, which had won the 1948 elections. British officials felt that Khama, a popular and capable traditional ruler, presented an obstacle to their political maneuvering in Bechuanaland, so the British Commonwealth relations minister declared him "unfit to govern" and exiled him and his wife to England in 1951. In 1956, after years of mounting pressure from international civil organizations, a new Commonwealth relations minister welcomed Khama, by then frail from diabetes, back to Bechuanaland.

In the early 1960s Khama would shine as a popular and effective leader in Bechuanaland's independence movement. In 1965 he became prime minister following the country's first universal franchise elections, and then in 1966 he was elected president of the newly declared Republic of Botswana.

See also: COLONIAL RULE (Vol. IV); ENGLAND AND AFRICA (Vol. IV); NATIONALISM AND INDEPENDENCE MOVEMENTS (Vol. IV).

Further reading: Willie Henderson, Neil Parsons, and Thomas Tlou, *Seretse Khama, 1921–1980* (Braamfontein, South Africa: Macmillan, 1995).

Khartoum

Capital city of present-day Republic of the SUDAN located near the confluence of the White and Blue Nile rivers in north-central Sudan. In 1821, on a site near the town of Halfaya, Khartoum began its modern existence as an Egyptian army camp. It received its name, which means "elephant's trunk" in Arabic, because of the long shape of the peninsula it occupies between the White and Blue Nile rivers. The main caravan route north to CAIRO passed through Khartoum, which caused the city to grow rapidly as a trading and administrative center. By 1850 a palace, which still stands today, was built for the Ottoman-Egyptian governor-general. In 1885 the forces of the MAHDIYYA captured and destroyed the city and killed the Egyptian governor-general, Charles George GORDON (1833–1885), ending Egyptian rule of the city. The Mahdiyya then built their capital at Omdurman, just across the river.

In 1898 the British recaptured Khartoum, and the city became the administrative seat of the ANGLO-EGYPTIAN CONDOMINIUM government of the Sudan, which it remained throughout the colonial period (1899–1955). During this time the British rebuilt the city. The rail line from Wadi Halfa, a city near the upper limits of navigation on the Egyptian Nile, reached Khartoum in 1899. Additional railway construction over the next couple of decades connected the city to the Red Sea and regions farther to the south. By the early 1900s the revived city had a population estimated at 14,000. Khartoum continued to grow as a commercial, TRANSPORTATION, and administrative center, so that in 1964 the city, by then the capital of a newly independent Sudan, had an estimated 135,000 inhabitants.

See also: BLUE NILE (Vol. I); COLONIAL RULE (Vol. IV); ENGLAND AND AFRICA (Vols. III, IV, V); KHARTOUM (Vols. I, III, V); AL-MAHDI, MUHAMMAD AHMAD (Vol. IV); OTTOMAN EMPIRE AND AFRICA (Vol. IV); URBANIZATION (Vols. IV, V); WHITE NILE (Vol. I).

Khayr al-Din (d. 1889) *Tunisia's leading 19th-century political figure*

Khayr al-Din, a popular Ottoman military officer who came to TUNISIA in 1839, eventually became prime minister and one of the great Muslim political reformers of the mid-19th century. He began his political career at a time when Tunisia was still under the rule of the Ottoman Empire. Khayr al-Din and other members of the ruling class and the middle class thought that the Tunisian state should become a constitutional monarchy and be more democratic. This philosophy of government embodied European political ideas as well as a return to the basic principles of Islam practiced in the early Muslim community.

In 1861 the bey, or governor, Muhammad al-Sadiq (r. 1859–1882), promulgated a constitution that provided for the separation of powers and limited the bey's authority over the other branches of government. Khayr al-Din became the first president of the new supreme council. He resigned in 1862, however, because Prime Minister Mustafa KHAZNADAR (1817–1878) blocked full implementation of the new constitution. Widespread protests against high taxation subsequently forced the government to suspend the constitution. Under pressure from France the bey dismissed Khaznadar in 1873 and replaced him with Khayr al-Din.

The Quran requires that the affairs of the Muslim community be run by mutual consultation, or shura. In the early days of Islam, the caliphs, or chief rulers, were elected by the councils of elders.

Khayr al-Din took office at an increasingly difficult time for Tunisia. The International Financial Commission (representing Italy, France, and Britain) had taken control of government revenues, expenditures, and debt repayments. Although limited to spending only one-third of Tunisia's revenue, Khayr al-Din immediately began modernizing Tunisian institutions and initiated a wide variety of reforms in the administration. His honesty and efficiency were well respected.

In addition to reforming government, Khayr al-Din also sought to reform the administration of religious affairs, especially by attempting to persuade the *ulama* (a community of learned Muslim men) to accept European methods of government. Furthering EDUCATION, he established Sadiqi College on estates confiscated from ex-prime minister Khaznadar. The college was a multilingual school for training civil servants along European educational lines but also within Muslim traditions. Khayr al-Din failed in his efforts to modernize Tunisia within the Islamic tradition, however, because European imperial ambitions were too great. The European powers forced the bey to dismiss Khayr al-Din from office in 1877. France increasingly assumed control over Tunisia, and by 1884 it had established a formal PROTECTORATE over the country.

See also: COLONIAL CONQUEST (Vol. IV); FRANCE AND AFRICA (Vol. IV); ISLAM (Vol. II); ISLAM, INFLUENCE OF (Vols. III, IV); OTTOMAN EMPIRE AND AFRICA (Vols.III, IV).

Khaznadar, Mustafa (Georgios Stravelakis)
(1817–1878) *Tunisian prime minister*

Born Georgios Stravelakis in Kardamila, Chios, Greece, which was then part of the Ottoman Empire, Mustafa arrived in TUNISIA as a young man in the service of the Ottoman Sultan. He became a companion of the future bey, or Ottoman governor, of Tunisia, Ahmad I bin Mustafa Bey (r. 1837–1855), and married his sister. When Ahmad became bey, he appointed Mustafa Khaznadar head of the treasury. (*Khaznadar* is actually the Turkish term for "treasurer.") Khaznadar eventually became prime minister, as well, a position he held until 1873.

Khaznadar used his position and connections to enrich himself to such an extent that his greed eventually undermined Tunisian autonomy. In return for money, he and the governmental officials loyal to him supported European commercial and banking interests in Tunisia. Khaznadar also systematically undermined governmental reforms intended to curb his power. The result was that the Tunisian government was forced to borrow money from European bankers to pay its debts. Khaznadar then skimmed off a portion of the loans in the form of large commissions, making himself extremely wealthy in the process.

In 1873 Tunisia's financial matters had become so tangled and the national debt so great that the government was forced to turn over control of its treasury to the International Financial Commission, which oversaw Tunisia's finances and managed the country's debt. That same year, under pressure from France, the bey dismissed Khaznadar from office and appointed his rival, KHAYR AL-DIN (d. 1889), prime minister.

For his part, Khaznadar was able to escape punishment. He had deposited large amounts of money abroad and had secretly received French citizenship in 1851. After his dismissal as prime minister, he went to Paris. His French connections protected him when the Tunisian government sought to prosecute him for embezzlement.

See also: COLONIAL CONQUEST (Vol. IV); FRANCE AND AFRICA (Vol. IV); OTTOMAN EMPIRE AND AFRICA (Vol. IV).

Further reading: L. Carl Brown, *The Tunisia of Ahmad Bey, 1837–1855* (Princeton, N.J.: Princeton University Press, 1974).

Kikuyu KENYA'S largest ethnic group, living primarily in the highland region around Mount Kenya, northeast of NAIROBI; the Kikuyu played a central role in the struggle for Kenyan independence. The Bantu-speaking Kikuyu migrated to their present-day homelands in the 16th century, establishing a presence in the region and trading extensively with the neighboring MAASAI and Okiek peoples. By the 1880s, however, the Kikuyu had come under British COLONIAL RULE, and by 1903 British settlers had begun to displace the Kikuyu from their highland territory. An almost exclusively agricultural people, the Kikuyu were tied closely to the land. Their culture, like that of the Maasai, was severely disrupted by the loss of approximately 27,000 square miles (69,930 sq km) to European SETTLERS in the years following World War I (1914–18).

Many Kikuyu were forced to become "squatters" on what was once their own land, only to be subsequently evicted by white settlers who did not want successful African farmers as competitors. The Kikuyu were often forced either to become fully dependent and work the white settlers' lands for low wages or to relocate to the city of Nairobi to find jobs.

The Kikuyu population in Nairobi became the central force behind Kenyan nationalism and the movement for independence from British rule. In 1921 Harry THUKU (1895–1970) founded the Young Kikuyu Association, which became a major outlet for Kikuyu grievances. Key issues were white rule, insufficient wages, the head tax, the *kipande* identification card all Africans were required to carry, and the appropriation of Kikuyu lands by the white settlers. Among the members of the Young Kikuyu Association was Jomo KENYATTA (c. 1891–1978), who became the inspirational leader of the Kenyan independence movement as well as the country's first president. In 1928 the Young Kikuyu Association became the Kikuyu Central Association, with Kenyatta as its general secretary.

Kikuyu frustration with the continued loss of land to white settlers came to a boil in the 1940s, with the Kikuyu launching a rural campaign of LABOR strikes and vandalism designed to frighten away the European encroachers. Returning African veterans who had served overseas during World War II (1939–45) were among many of those participating in the militant actions. By the 1950s the uprising, which became known as the MAU MAU movement after the name of a local mountain range, had become more organized and increasingly violent. In 1952, following the assassination of British loyalist Kikuyu Chief Warihiu, colonial authorities declared a state of emergency and arrested Kikuyu leaders in Nairobi, including Kenyatta. For the next three years the mostly Kikuyu Mau Mau fighters struggled against superior British forces. The British attempted to stamp out Kikuyu nationalism by rounding up thousands of Kikuyu and interning them in concentration camps and "protected" villages. It was estimated that by 1954, one-third of all Kikuyu men in KENYA had been imprisoned by colonial authorities. By 1955 the Mau Mau movement was defeated, but, despite massive casualties, it did achieve some positive results. The long struggle attracted international attention to the plight of the Kikuyu and Kenyans overall and convinced the British government that minority rule by the white settlers was an unfeasible situation. By 1960 African majority rule was established in Kenya, and, over the next three years leading up to independence, the Kikuyu assumed a major role in the developing political scene.

See also: COLONIALISM, INFLUENCE OF (Vol. IV); ENGLAND AND AFRICA (Vols. III, IV, V); KIKUYU (Vols. I, II, III, V); NATIONALISM AND INDEPENDENCE MOVEMENTS (Vol. IV); RESISTANCE AND REBELLION (Vol. IV).

Further reading: Jomo Kenyatta, *Facing Mount Kenya* (New York: Vintage Books, 1965); Robert L. Tignor, *The Colonial Transformation of Kenya: The Kamba, Kikuyu, and Maasai from 1900 to 1939* (Princeton, N.J.: Princeton University Press, 1976).

Kimbangu, Simon (c. 1887–1951) *Congolese religious leader*

Simon Kimbangu was born in the Central African town of Nkamba, in the Belgian-run colony then known as the CONGO FREE STATE (now the Democratic Republic of the CONGO). His father was a leader of traditional RELIGION, but in 1915 Simon was converted to Christianity by MISSIONARIES from the British Baptist Missionary Society. He soon became a catechist, with the task of instructing candidates for baptism. Intensely religious, he believed that he had a vision from God commanding him to preach and heal.

In 1921, while working as a migrant worker in LEOPOLDVILLE (today's Kinshasa), Kimbangu began a public ministry as a preacher. He was reputed to be a healer, and large crowds came to hear him speak. Kimbangu came to be called Ngunza, or "prophet," and his birth village of Nkamba was later renamed New Jerusalem. His sons and followers named the independent church he founded the Church of Jesus Christ on Earth by the Prophet Simon Kimbangu.

Kimbangu's church combined Baptist and traditional beliefs and opposed drinking, polygamy, dancing, and smoking, as well as sorcery and WITCHCRAFT of any kind. Kimbangu identified God with Nzambi Mpungu, the supreme god in some traditional African creation myths, and preached God's closeness to his people. Many Africans of the time believed that the Europeans held back the true secrets of Christianity in order to maintain a hold over the people. Consequently, as a prophet, one to whom people believed God spoke directly, Kimbangu had great moral authority among his followers.

In 1969 the Church of Jesus Christ on Earth became a member of the World Council of Churches. Widespread in Central Africa, it is the largest denomination in the African independent church movement.

Although Kimbangu avoided any kind of political message in his preaching, his movement fed on anti-European sentiment and soon took on political and nationalist overtones. Belgian authorities became concerned and feared a massive uprising. Kimbangu eluded the

Belgians' first attempt to capture him but later turned himself in. In 1921 he was sentenced to death, but King Albert I (1875–1934) of Belgium commuted his sentence to life imprisonment in ELIZABETHVILLE, in the Belgian Congo, where he died 30 years later.

Belgian authorities tried to suppress Kimbangu's church. However, led by his youngest son and successor, Joseph Diangienda (1918–1992), it went underground, spawning a variety of related sects. Kimbangu himself became a symbol of Congolese nationalism. In 1956 Diangienda formed a church council and began a move to legitimize the church. In 1959 colonial authorities officially recognized the church, but in 1960 after national independence, its rights were again restricted.

See also: BELGIUM AND AFRICA (Vol. IV); COLONIALISM, INFLUENCE OF (Vol. IV); PROPHETS AND PROPHETIC MOVEMENTS (Vol. IV).

Further reading: Martin Marie-Louise, *Kimbangu: An African Prophet and His Church* (Grand Rapids, Mich.: Wm.. B. Eerdmans, 1976).

Kimberley Capital city of the Northern Cape Province and historic center of the diamond trade in SOUTH AFRICA. Named in honor of Lord Kimberley, the British Secretary of State for the colonies, the city is located between the Orange and Vaal rivers, about halfway between CAPE TOWN and JOHANNESBURG.

Kimberley's first diamond, *The Eureka*, was found in 1866 by Erasmus Jacobs (1851–1933), the son of a farmer. A few years later diggers found hundreds of the valuable gems at Zandfontein, at a farm owned by two brothers, Johannes Nicolaas (1930–1894) and Diederik Arnoldus de Beer. By the mid-1870s more than 30,000 people had moved into the area, all hoping to make their fortunes in the diamond trade. The population continued to climb so that by the 1880s, it had reached 70,000.

Kimberley is so closely identified with DIAMOND MINING that the diamond-bearing earth that is crushed and sifted in the process is known as kimberlite. The kimberlite found at Colesberg Kopje held so many diamond deposits that the entire hill was gradually removed, leaving behind the world's deepest hand-dug excavation. The 700-foot-deep (215-m) excavation, which has a perimeter of nearly a mile (1.6 km) is no longer an operating mine. It is now popularly known as Kimberley's "Big Hole," and along with a recreated MINING town/museum, it is now a popular tourist attraction. *The Eureka* can be viewed in the museum at the site.

In short order the land around Kimberley was bought up and divided into small plots, or claims, that measured about 30 feet square. Barney Barnato (1852–1897), a young Englishman who came to CAPE COLONY in 1873, was one of many who made huge profits from the small plots in Kimberley. By 1883 he had merged his Barnato Diamond Mining Company with the Kimberley Central Mining Company.

Cecil RHODES (1853–1902), another young Englishman, was enjoying similar success in Kimberley. He joined forces with English entrepreneur Charles Rudd (1844–1916) to gain control of the major mining operations in the area, including Barnato's. By 1888 Kimberley's diamond mining industry, accounting for 90 percent of the world's supply, was a cartel controlled by Rhodes's company, DE BEERS CONSOLIDATED MINES, LTD.

The city of Kimberley was also the site of some important battles of the ANGLO-BOER WAR (1899–1902). During the siege of Kimberley (1899), thousands of women and children were lowered into the mine for protection from long gun attacks by the BOERS.

Kimberley is known as a "city of firsts." In 1896 South Africa's first School of Mines opened there, and the city was also the first in the Southern Hemisphere to install electric street lighting. In 1912–13 British officials established the continent's first flight school, which evolved into headquarters of the South African Air Force.

In 1912 Sir Ernest Oppenheimer (1880–1957), the diamond magnate who took control of the De Beers mines when Rhodes died in 1902, became the first elected mayor of the municipality of the city of Kimberley. In 1914 work on the big Kimberley mine was suspended, but by that time more than 20 million tons of earth had been excavated and almost 6,630 pounds (3,000 kg) of DIAMONDS found. Today Kimberley is an administrative, commercial, and TRANSPORTATION center with a population of about 210,000.

See also: MINERAL REVOLUTION (Vol. IV); MINERALS AND METALS (Vol. V).

Further reading: Robert Vicat Turrell, *Capital and Labour on the Kimberley Diamond Fields, 1871–1890* (New York: Cambridge University Press, 1987); William H. Worger, *South Africa's City of Diamonds: Mine Workers and Monopoly Capitalism in Kimberley, 1867–1895* (New Haven, Conn.: Yale University Press, 1987).

kingdoms and empires As of 1850 Africans still maintained major kingdoms and empires throughout the continent. In West Africa the ASHANTI EMPIRE was expanding from central GHANA southward toward the coast and northward toward the interior; the kingdom of BENIN continued to control the trade of southern NIGERIA. In the interior the Islamic TUKULOR EMPIRE established by UMAR TAL (1794–1864) was approaching its apex. The MANDINKA empire, led by SAMORI TOURÉ (c. 1830–1900), would come to control much of the same territory in the coming decades. The SOKOTO CALIPHATE exceeded both the Tukulor and Mandinka empires in size and strength.

Though not a kingdom, per se, EGYPT rose to international prominence during the short reign of Khedive IS-MAIL (1830–1895). South of Egypt, in ETHIOPIA, rulers in the kingdoms of AMHARA and SHOA had consolidated their power and created a practically impregnable empire in the Ethiopian highlands. To the south, on the East African coast, Arab sultans of the BUSAIDI dynasty, in ZANZIBAR, established a vast trading empire that stretched from the Benadir Coast of SOMALILAND in the north to MOZAMBIQUE in the south. The Busaidi sultanate depended on trade with kingdoms further inland, such as BUGANDA, BUNY-ORO, BURUNDI, and RWANDA, which thrived until the 1890s. These latter kingdoms did not even come into contact with Europeans until the 1860s.

Militaristic merchants like TIPPU TIP (c. 1830–1905), in East Africa, and RABIH BIN FADLALLAH (c. 1835–1900), near Lake Chad, organized slave armies to protect and extend networks that became influential trading empires.

On the west coast of southern Central Africa, the formerly glorious KONGO kingdom was greatly reduced by the transatlantic SLAVE TRADE. In present-day eastern SOUTH AFRICA, however, the collection of Nguni kingdoms making up the ZULU empire controlled the region. Zulu "offshoot" states also thrived, including the Gaza kingdom, in MOZAMBIQUE, and the NDEBELE kingdom, founded by Mzilikazi (1790–1868), a former Zulu general. The Ndebele conquered the SHONA kingdoms as they expanded northward. The expansion of the Zulu empire, affected through military domination, caused the displacement and relocation of a number of peoples in South Africa, thereby bringing about the establishment of SWAZILAND and the SOTHO kingdom, both of which flourished.

European Colonization Whereas the 17th- and 18th-century conflicts between Africans and Europeans were generally based on issues surrounding TRADE AND COMMERCE, by the early part of the 19th century, it was the actual territorial rights of sovereign African nations that were threatened by European encroachment. By the 1820s the Ashanti Empire and Britain had fought the first of the ANGLO-ASHANTI WARS. In ALGERIA France had colonized provinces by 1837, and by the 1850s and 1860s African kingdoms across the continent were under siege. In South Africa, the Sotho and XHOSA kingdoms fought

with the BOERS for territorial rights. In Egypt, Britain was well on its way to colonial occupation.

Ultimately, in 1884–85 the European powers convened at the BERLIN CONFERENCE to discuss the partitioning of the African continent in anticipation of COLONIAL CONQUEST. The meeting, which lasted several months, signaled the beginning of the end of most of Africa's independent states. In fact, by 1898 the only major African empire still truly autonomous was Ethiopia, thanks in large part to its victory over Italian forces at the Battle of ADOWA.

In spite of European colonization, in many of the kingdoms that had not been destroyed in war, the colonial administration was carried out through the same families that ruled the formerly independent states. In the Sokoto Caliphate, for example, British colonial administrator Frederick LUGARD (1858–1945) developed the DUAL MAN-DATE policy of COLONIAL RULE, whereby Africans were kept on to run the local government under the watchful eye of British governors. Nevertheless, this policy of "indirect rule," as it often was called, hardly offered the benefits of self-rule that the kingdoms enjoyed previously.

Largely because of the British policy of indirect rule in Sokoto, that region later produced Sirs Abubakar Tafawa BALEWA (1912–1966) and Ahmadu BELLO (1906–1966), the first leaders of independent Nigeria.

At independence in the 1950s and 1960s, it was not the precolonial kingdoms that became the new states (except for a few small states such as SWAZILAND and BASU-TOLAND [now LESOTHO], which had a constitutional monarchies). More typical was the situation in Buganda, where the royal heir, Kabaka Sir Edward Frederick Mutesa II (1939–1969), became the first president of independent UGANDA, in 1962. His election was based on the privileged position that the Buganda kingdom held within the larger Uganda colony when it was under the rule of Britain. As a result, in 1966 Milton OBOTE (1925–), the Ugandan prime minister, ousted and exiled Mutesa II. As a northerner, Obote came from outside of the Buganda power structure and demanded access for all ethnic groups to the benefits of state in the new republic.

See also: KINGDOMS AND EMPIRES (Vol. II); KINGDOMS AND EMPIRES OF EASTERN AFRICA AND THE INTERIOR (Vols. II, III); KINGDOMS AND EMPIRES OF THE HORN OF AFRICA (Vol. III); KINGDOMS AND EMPIRES OF THE LOWER GUINEA AND ATLANTIC COAST (Vol. II, III); KINGDOMS AND EMPIRES OF THE MAGHRIB (Vols. II, III); KINGDOMS AND EMPIRES OF SENEGAMBIA (Vol. II); KINGDOMS AND EMPIRES OF

WEST AFRICA (Vol. III); KINGDOMS AND EMPIRES OF THE WEST AFRICAN SAVANNA (Vol. II).

Kinjikitile (Kinjikitile Ngwale) (d. 1905) *Leader of the Maji-Maji Rebellion*

Very little is known about Kinjikitile Ngwale beyond his role in stoking the fires that eventually erupted in the MAJI-MAJI REBELLION, a mass uprising by the African peoples of GERMAN EAST AFRICA (in the region of present-day TANZANIA) against German colonizers. The Germans had imposed abusive LABOR practices on Africans in the region, forcing them to neglect their own farms in order to cultivate government lands for the production of CASH CROPS such as COTTON. The Africans labored in conditions similar to SLAVERY, facing the threat of whippings if they did not work hard enough. These circumstances, coupled with excessive taxation and insufficient wages, imparted a deep current of anger and resentment against the German oppressors. Kinjikitile proved to be the factor that tipped the scales in favor of rebellion.

Kinjikitile was a spirit medium, a person who claims the ability to converse with the supernatural world. Such mediums played major roles in African attempts at RESISTANCE AND REBELLION against COLONIAL RULE throughout Africa, most notably perhaps in SOUTHERN RHODESIA (present-day ZIMBABWE), where the SHONA prophet Mbuya Nehanda (d. 1898) and other spirit mediums led the first CHIMURENGA war (1896–97) against the British colonial government. Kinjikitile himself claimed to be possessed by a snake spirit named Hongo. Calling himself Bokero, Kinjikitile traveled throughout the region, calling for an uprising to drive out the Germans. The key to success, he believed, was the use of magic water (*maji maji*, in Swahili) which, when imbibed and sprinkled over the body, would render the African fighters impervious to German bullets.

The magical *maji maji* that Kinjikitile offered as protection against German bullets was made up of water, castor oil, and millet seeds.

Kinjikitile's anticolonial messages inspired Africans across tribal boundaries, and his "war medicine" offered them hope of defeating the superior arms of the German troops. By 1905 the Germans had become sufficiently concerned with Kinjikitile's activities that they had him arrested and hanged for treason. His death, however, only served to spark the movement he had been fomenting, and, in that same year, the Maji-Maji Rebellion broke out. Though it would not last much longer than a year, the rebellion would ultimately result in the deaths of more than 200,000 Africans from violence and famine.

See also: GERMANY AND AFRICA (Vol. IV); SPIRIT POSSESSION (Vol. I).

kinship Term that refers to the organization of family life and defines relationships through rights, duties, privileges, and responsibilities with regard to social life. Family members are kin because they are related either through descent (parentage) or through marriage (affinity). Each society constructs its concept of kinship. In most societies kinship is determined by either matrilineal (from the mother) or patrilineal (from the father) descent. Until the period of the SLAVE TRADE matrilineal and patrilineal descent patterns in Africa were more or less equally distributed across the continent. In the post–slave trade era of the 19th century, however, many matrilineal societies became patrilineal. The causes for the shift can be traced to the influence of COLONIAL RULE, especially in those areas where CASH CROPS formed a mainstay of the rural ECONOMY. Since men, as a rule, controlled the disposition of cash crops, they wanted control of the land on which the crops grew. Moreover, they wanted to be able to pass their land down to their sons. In a typical matrilineal society, the sons and daughters of mothers, rather than fathers, would inherit the valuable land.

Patrilineal families generally live in extended family communities. In many rural areas, an extended family includes grandparents, parents, and children. In this setting, the male elder of the family controls a communal tract of land, and it is his duty to apportion that land to the other male family members.

Under the patrilineal structure all the men in a family are related by descent through the male line, and they marry women from other families. The men's daughters marry away from their families but do not lose membership in their fathers' families. Within patrilineal societies, the men retain the privilege of directing social organization, and elder men direct younger men and women. Children, and hence their LABOR, belong to the father and his family. In cases of death or divorce, each society has constructed rules addressing the change of relationship of the widow or divorcee to the family. In most cases, however, if the woman has children, then she can stay within the husband's family to take care of and be with her children. If she chooses not to stay, then she can return home to her natal family but often has to leave her children behind.

At the outset of the colonial period in Africa the community of kin was more important than the individual. Land, property, and wealth belonged to the group and benefited the group as a whole. However, colonialism introduced to Africans a new concept of societal formation based on the primacy of the individual. Widespread migration of laborers to cities and farms only increased this sense individualism. Today, the concept of the individual who belongs to any number of groups has replaced the importance of kinship in many settings.

See also: COLONIALISM, INFLUENCE OF (Vol. IV); GENDER IN COLONIAL AFRICA (Vol. IV); POLYGAMY (Vol. I); URBANIZATION (Vols. IV, V).

Kirk, John (Sir) (1832–1922) *British physician, naturalist, and influential consul general to the sultan of Zanzibar*

Kirk received his medical education in Edinburgh, Scotland, and afterwards served in the Crimean War (1854–56). In 1858 he accompanied David LIVINGSTONE (1813–1873) on his second Central African expedition, serving as the group's physician and naturalist. In 1859 Kirk and the other members of the expedition became the first Europeans to see Lake Nyasa. His stint on the expedition ended in 1863 due to illness. Kirk's experience in Africa earned him a position as acting surgeon for the British political agency in the island of Zanzibar, the seat of the sultanate of ZANZIBAR, which ruled much of the SWAHILI COAST.

Kirk is also well known as a naturalist and botanist. During the expedition in Africa, he identified a number of species that now bear his name, from Kirk's Red Colobus (a kind of monkey) to Kirk's Dik-Dik (a tiny antelope). He also created a botanical garden in Zanzibar.

Kirk rose through the ranks in Zanzibar, becoming assistant political agent, in 1868, and consul-general, in 1873. During this time Kirk became a powerful influence on ibn Said BARGHASH (c. 1833–1888) and in many ways was a shadow ruler of the sultanate. In 1873 he persuaded Barghash to sign a treaty abolishing the SLAVE TRADE on the SWAHILI COAST, a practice that until that time was one of Zanzibar's economic mainstays. Following the PARTITION treaty between Britain and Germany in 1885, Kirk used his influence to gain territorial rights from the sultanate that would lead to the formation of BRITISH EAST AFRICA. Kirk retired from his consular position in 1887.

Kirk continued to serve the British government, journeying to the Niger River in 1895 and thereafter joining a committee to oversee the construction of the UGANDA railroad. He was knighted in 1900.

See also: ENGLAND AND AFRICA (Vols. III, V); SLAVE TRADE ON THE SWAHILI COAST (Vol. III).

Kiswahili (KiSwahili, Swahili) Bantu-based LANGUAGE spoken in eastern Africa, primarily in the present-day countries of TANZANIA, KENYA, and UGANDA. Africa's second-most widely spoken language behind Arabic, Kiswahili was influenced greatly by Persian and Arabic language and also assimilated many European words during the period of COLONIAL RULE in Africa.

Kiswahili is the maternal tongue of the Waswahili (Swahili people), a loose association of East African coastal ethnic groups, as well as of Swahilized Arabs who live on the coast from the Horn of Africa to MOZAMBIQUE. The origins of the Kiswahili language are unclear, but there is evidence that the language has existed on Africa's east coast for over a thousand years. Contact over the years with traders from Arab regions, Persia (present-day Iran), India, and China led to a great many borrowed words entering the language, though it remains to this day a distinctly Bantu tongue.

Other theories of the origins of Kiswahili hold that the language evolved from Arabic, and that it is a product of intermingling African and Arabic cultures rather than an authentic African tongue. However, archaeologists have found evidence of Kiswahili culture from long before Arab or Persian traders came to Africa's shores. The influence of COLONIALISM can be credited for these doubts about the long history and remarkable development of Kiswahili language and culture.

The spread of Kiswahili as an inter-ethnic lingua franca, or common language, from the coastal regions into the interior of East and Central Africa was largely due to the growth of TRADE AND COMMERCE in the mid- and late 19th century. It first spread along trade routes as merchants based in ZANZIBAR CITY and along the East African coast pushed into the interior. By the latter part of the century, traders such as TIPPU TIP (c. 1830–1905) had established a powerful presence as far inland as the eastern portions of the present-day Democratic Republic of the CONGO. The spread of the trade routes occurred in areas where people mostly spoke a Bantu language, which made Kiswahili a readily adopted language for trade.

Kiswahili and Colonialism As East Africa came under the colonial rule of Britain, Germany, and Portugal, Kiswahili came to play a major role in colonial administration. Those European officials in the region who bothered to learn an African language learned Kiswahili. It became the language of local administration and was spoken by members of the the police and the army. This was particularly true in GERMAN EAST AFRICA (present-day Tanzania), where German authorities used Kiswahili exclusively as the language of communication with the colonial subjects.

The British also used Kiswahili as a common means of communication for their African colonial force, the King's African Rifles, whose members spoke a wide range of maternal languages. British officers also used the language to communicate with their African troops. In the 1930s African scholars led a British attempt to standardize the language, basing their efforts on the Zanzibar City dialect known as Kiunjuga. As with many other aspects of East African life, Kiswahili was permanently marked by colonialism, with many English, Portuguese, and to a lesser extent, German words entering the language.

While a majority of Kiswahili words are of Bantu origin, many common words, including the name Swahili itself (from the Arabic *sawa hili,* meaning "of the coast"), come from languages not indigenous to sub-Saharan Africa. Words such as *chai* (tea) and *serikali* (government) come from the Persian Farsi language. Arabic words include the numbers *sita* (six), *saba* (seven), and *tisa* (nine). European words include the Portuguese-derived *kasha* (box) and *pesa* (money), the English-derived *baiskeli* (bicycle) and *basi* (bus), and the German-derived *shule* (school).

Written Kiswahili predates colonialism, with the earliest examples coming from the early 1700s. Because of its widespread usage and its long history as a written language, in Arabic script and later in Latin script introduced by the Portuguese, Kiswahili was convenient for educators in the colonial period to use in their primary schools. (European languages were used at the secondary and university levels.) The adoption of Kiswahili in schools had the negative effect, however, of limiting the development of literacy in other indigenous languages. Kiswahili also became the language of choice for NEWSPAPERS and RADIO in East Africa, and eventually for television as well.

Kiswahili was popular in colonial East Africa not only because it was already widespread but also because it was considered politically neutral. Outside of the countries sharing the SWAHILI COAST, it had no attachment to any specific ethnic group. After independence, English or French became the official language of most of the countries where Kiswahili was widely spoken, but Kiswahili became the second language of the people and the language of unity in the face of the region's multiplicity of languages. In West Africa, HAUSA, MANDE, and WOLOF served a similar purpose as linguae francae.

Kiswahili Literature Early examples of Kiswahili literature were mostly epic poetry, called *utendi,* which combines Arab verse and Bantu song. As the language evolved under the influence of colonialism, so did its literature. Particularly important in this regard was the Kiswahili poet and essayist Shaaban ROBERT (1909–1962), who utilized the *utendi* form in conjunction with new, experimental modes to help create a modern Kiswahili literary style. As colonialism gave way to independence, other East African writers, such as Muhammad Saleh Farsy, Muhammad Said Abdulla, and Faraji Katalambulla all contributed to the establishment of a significant body of Kiswahili literature ranging from poetry to essays to romance and detective fiction. Today, Kiswahili has perhaps the richest literary tradition of any African language.

Kiswahili Today At the present, there are as many as 50 million Kiswahili speakers, though only perhaps two million of these are native speakers (the rest use it as a secondary language). The language has 15 major dialects, all of which are mutually intelligible. It is an official language of several countries, including Kenya, Uganda, and Tanzania, where the efforts of President Julius NYERERE (1922–1999) made Kiswahili practically universal. The language is also used by significant numbers of people in RWANDA, BURUNDI, the Democratic Republic of the Congo, MALAWI, ZAMBIA, MOZAMBIQUE, and SOMALIA. Kiswahili is used less frequently in the southern part of the Republic of the SUDAN, the Republic of the CONGO, the COMOROS, and northern MADAGASCAR. Because of political and cultural connections between ZANZIBAR and Oman on the Arabian Peninsula, migrants of Arab descent from East Africa now living in Oman, about one-third of the population, also speak Kiswahili.

See also: BANTU LANGUAGES (Vol. I); KISWAHILI (Vols. II, III); LANGUAGE FAMILIES (Vol. I); LITERATURE IN COLONIAL AFRICA (Vol. IV); LITERATURE IN MODERN AFRICA (Vol. V).

Kitchener, Horatio Herbert (Lord) (1850–1916)
British soldier and administrator in the Sudan and South Africa

For many Victorian Britons, Kitchener personified the ideal imperial hero. After stints in Palestine and Cyprus, during the 1870s Kitchener went to EGYPT in 1882. He rose to the rank of adjutant-general and in 1892 assumed command of the Egyptian army. Four years into his command Kitchener led a savage campaign against the Islamic separatists known as the MAHDIYYA, or Mahdists, in present-day Republic of the SUDAN. The campaign culminated in 1898 with the defeat of the Mahdists at the battle of OMDURMAN. By then the Mahdists were under the command of the Khalifa ABDALLAHI IBN MUHAMMAD (1846–1899). In the process, Kitchener avenged the humiliating 1885 defeat of the British and Egyptian forces led by Charles George GORDON (1833–1885) at KHARTOUM. After his victory on the battlefield Kitchener ordered 20,000 of the enemy wounded to be massacred "as humanely as possible," and he was subsequently dubbed the "butcher of Omdurman." He also forced the withdrawal of French forces from FASHODA (present-day Kodok), on the Upper White Nile, thus frustrating French designs on the Egyptian Sudan.

During the ANGLO-BOER WAR (1899–1902) Kitchener assumed supreme command of the British forces in SOUTH AFRICA. Again Kitchener gained renown for the ruthless methods he employed to force the BOERS to capitulate. The creation of an extensive network of blockhouses linked by barbed wire, the pursuit of a scorched-earth policy, and the establishment of concentration camps for Afrikaner women and children were controversial but ultimately successful measures. Still, it took Kitchener nearly two years to stamp out Boer resistance, and at a high cost. Some 30,000 farmsteads were destroyed and an appallingly high number of civilian deaths in the unsanitary concentration camps left a legacy of inveterate hatred for the British among Boers (later known as AFRIKANERS).

In 1902 Kitchener became commander-in-chief of the Indian army, finally returning to Africa in 1911 to take the position of consul general of Egypt and the Sudan. In addition to the many exalted positions he held within the British Empire, Kitchener's efforts for the empire were rewarded with several titles, including earl, baron, and viscount. In 1914 he became secretary of state for war and proved instrumental in recruiting British troops for World War I (1914–18). He drowned in the North Sea in 1916 when the cruiser conveying him to Russia hit a mine.

See also: COLONIAL CONQUEST (Vol. IV).

Kiwanuka, Joseph (Joseph Nakabaale Kiwanuka) (1899–1966) *First African-born Catholic bishop of the modern era*

Kiwanuka was born to Catholic parents in Nakirebe, in the BUGANDA kingdom of UGANDA. In 1914 he entered seminary and, after studying philosophy and theology, became an ordained priest in 1929. He then traveled to Rome to continue his studies at the Angelicum University, where he excelled, earning a licentiate (the equivalent of a master's degree) in Church Law and then a doctorate. Kiwanuka's academic accomplishments were

unprecedented for an African and led to a more welcoming policy for Africans who sought to enroll in other Italian and European institutions.

In 1934 Kiwanuka became the first African member of the Society of Missionaries of Africa, also known as the "White Fathers" due to their white clothing. After five years of pastoral work and a teaching appointment at the seminary where he originally trained, Pope Pius XII (1876–1958) consecrated Kiwanuka as Bishop of Masaka in 1939. He became the first African bishop in the modern Church. In 1960 he became Archbishop of Rubaga.

As a leader of the church in Africa, Kiwanuka worked to integrate elements of African culture, including MUSIC, into Christian worship. He also was a proponent of diversifying the MISSIONARIES of Uganda, in opposition to the British colonial policy of allowing only British and English-speaking missionaries into the colony. Kiwanuka's rise to positions of influence in the Catholic Church paved the way for other Africans to follow the same path. In fact, one of Kiwanuka's African students at the Katigondo seminary, Laurean Rugambwa (1912–1997), was appointed bishop and later became the first African-born cardinal in 1960.

Kiwanuka died in February 1996, just as independent Uganda plunged into the political turmoil that led prime minister Milton OBOTE (1925–   ) to assume total control of the country.

See also: CHRISTIANITY (Vols. I, II); CHRISTIANITY, INFLUENCE OF (Vols. II, III, IV, V); RELIGION (Vols. III, IV, V).

Koko, King (Frederick William Koko) (c. 1835–1898) *King of the small Niger Delta state of Nembe*

Over the course of the 19th century the growing European demand for vegetable oils and other products from Africa led to increased production and trade in CASH CROPS such as PALM OIL. In the NIGER DELTA a number of small trading states, of which Nembe was one, had prospered on the basis of their share in this commerce. British merchant interests were also drawn to this profitable trade.

In 1879 George GOLDIE (1846–1925) brought together the separate private British firms trading in the Delta to form the ROYAL NIGER COMPANY (RNC). The British government was also expanding its political control of the Southern Region of NIGERIA, and in 1885 Britain declared a PROTECTORATE over much of the Nigerian coast. In turn Britain handed over the administration of the Niger Delta portion of the protectorate to the RNC. The trading company then used its position to try to monopolize the export and import trade.

In 1889 Koko (r. 1889–1896) became Amanyanabo (King) of Nembe in the midst of the struggle of the Niger Delta states to maintain their commercial role. Prior to becoming king Koko had been a Christian and a church leader. However, to strengthen public support for his kingship, he resumed the traditional religious practices and observances of his people.

Even before he became king Koko watched as the British moved against other states. Two years earlier, in 1887, the British had exiled JAJA (1821–1891) of Opobo, the most important power in the Niger Delta. In 1894 they ousted the Itsikeri chief, NANA OLUMU (c. 1852–1916), from the governorship of the Benin River. Consequently, Koko decided to make a preemptive strike.

Early in 1895 Koko dispatched a fleet of 20 war craft to attack the RNC depot at Akassa. In reprisal for the Akassa Raid, British forces launched a full-scale land and sea war that destroyed the city of Nembe and many nearby towns. Koko was forced to flee into the interior where he died three years later. The war, however, brought the RNC monopolistic practices under criticism and led to loss of the RNC's government charter. In 1899 the territories once managed by the RNC were reorganized into the Protectorate of Southern Nigeria.

See also: BRITAIN AND AFRICA (Vol. IV); COLONIAL CONQUEST (Vol. IV); TRADE AND COMMERCE (Vol. IV).

Kongo (Bakongo)

Large ethnic group of western Central Africa. Collectively the Kongo people are sometimes called *Bakongo*. The Kongo kingdom was a major state and European trading partner in the 17th century. By the latter half of the 19th century, however, economic and ethnic strife had dismantled the kingdom. During the 20th century Kongo leaders were prominent in the independence movements in ANGOLA and the BELGIAN CONGO (now the Democratic Republic of the CONGO).

Following the BERLIN CONFERENCE (1884–85) most of the area of the Kongo kingdom was incorporated into the Portuguese colony of Angola. The rest of the former kingdom became part of the Belgian colony of the CONGO FREE STATE, which in 1908 became the Belgian Congo.

Kongo in Angola A mostly agrarian people, the Kongo people had few opportunities to improve their economic and social standing under European COLONIAL RULE. During the first half of the 20th century Angolan Kongo men were forced to leave their villages to LABOR on Portuguese plantations in order to pay colonial hut taxes; political opposition was quickly and brutally repressed, and explicit political activity was banned.

After World War II (1939–45), African NATIONALISM AND INDEPENDENCE MOVEMENTS began to gain momentum throughout the continent. By 1954, Kongo leaders had established the Union of Peoples of North Angola (UPNA) to further their goals during the period of decolonization that was looming. At the time the political climate in Angola was more repressive than that in neighboring Belgian Congo. For this reason UPNA had its base of operations in the Kongo-dominated city of LEOPOLDVILLE (now Kinshasa) in the Belgian Congo.

In 1957 the UPNA petitioned for the United Nations to create an independent Kongo state. However, with its leadership coming exclusively from the Kongo ethnic group, the UPNA found it difficult to get widespread support for its goals in Angola. For this reason, in 1958 the name of the organization was changed to the Union of Angolan Peoples (Unão das Populações de Angola, UPA) in order to appeal to all Angolans.

As the UPA became more insistent in its demands for independence, the Portuguese regularly jailed groups of Kongo activists. A breaking point came in 1961 when attempts to free jailed Kongo freedom fighters turned violent. Frustrated UPA members raided Portuguese-owned farms throughout the northern Angolan countryside, killing hundreds in the process. The Portuguese police responded with extreme violence to crush the uprising, and, in the months following, hundreds of thousands of Kongo people fled Angola for refuge in the Congo.

In 1961 a Kongo group led by Holden Roberto (1923–) founded the National Front for the Liberation of Angola (Frente Nacionale de Libertação de Angola, FNLA). Growing out of the UPA, the FNLA began a long and bloody armed rebellion against Portuguese colonialism. Although European colonial powers had withdrawn from most of the African continent by the mid-1960s, the FNLA—along with other armed ethnic rebel groups—waged their independence battle until 1975.

Kongo People in Belgian Congo The rule of Belgian King LEOPOLD II (1835–1909) in the Congo was especially harsh. Similar to the situation for the Kongo people in Portuguese Angola, Kongo men in the Congo were forced to labor for large European companies in order to pay the exorbitant taxes charged by the colonial administration.

About the same time that Angola's Kongo leaders established the UPNA, leaders in the Congo founded the Bakongo Tribal Association (Alliance des Bakongo, ABAKO), also in Leopoldville. Led by Joseph Kasavubu (1913–1969), ABAKO became a political force as independence neared, and in 1957 the party won a great majority of the seats in pre-independence elections.

Despite the promise of national elections, though, the Belgians let the independence process lag, causing some Kongo leaders to begin agitating for immediate change. In January 1959 ABAKO scheduled a meeting to discuss the foundering independence process, but nervous Belgian authorities closed their meeting place and tried to disperse those who had assembled. This suppression sparked a violent reaction among ABAKO leaders that quickly spread throughout Leopoldville. Rioting in the city was suppressed with brutal force, and as many as 49 Congolese were killed and many more were injured. The violence sent a clear message to the Belgian authorities, who then accelerated the independence process. Within a year the Belgian Congo became the independent Republic of the

Congo, with Kasavubu the nation's first president. Unfortunately the hasty preparations for Congolese independence left the country vulnerable to ethnic and regional divisions that quickly left the country in crisis.

See also: KONGO (Vols. II, III); KONGO KINGDOM (Vol. II, III); PORTUGAL AND AFRICA (Vols. III, IV, V).

Krio Language spoken in SIERRA LEONE; also the people who speak the language. In the area around Sierra Leone Krio has been spoken, both as a primary language and as a lingua franca, for more than 200 years. For the most part, those for whom Krio is their first language are the descendants of RECAPTIVES, or slaves rescued at sea from North American-bound slave ships or returned to Africa from overseas locations. Based on English, Krio is in this way similar to the other Creole languages spoken in various parts of Africa. However, it has its own particular characteristics based on the languages spoken by the recaptives and returnees from North America who were settling in FREETOWN and the adjacent peninsula from the beginning of the 19th century.

Creole languages began as pidgin, or simplified, languages but later were adopted as primary languages as their use became more formalized and they developed characteristics of an established language.

By the mid-1800s Krio was widely used not just by the descendants of the recaptives but also as a means for people to communicate with those of different ethnic groups. Still in use today, it is one of the official languages of Sierra Leone and is widely used as a second language.

See also: ETHNIC GROUPS (Vol. IV); LANGUAGES (Vol. I).

Kruger, Paul (1825–1904) *Political figure in independent Transvaal, in present-day South Africa*

Known as "Oom Paul" and the "old lion of the TRANSVAAL," Stephanus Johannes Paulus Kruger was born October 10, 1825, on his family's farm in the CAPE COLONY. Kruger's family, originally from Prussia, had come to SOUTH AFRICA in the early 18th century. In 1835 the Krugers moved north to settle on the far side of the Orange River. There they met Hendrik Potgieter, one of the leaders of the Great Boer Trek. Joining Potgieter and his caravan of Dutch-speaking BOERS, the Krugers moved on, eventually settling in the Transvaal.

Determined and precocious even as a youngster, Kruger reportedly taught himself to read and write. By the time he was 16 he owned his own farm; at age 17 he

was a married man; at age 21 he was a widower, having lost both his wife and daughter. He married again shortly after, this time to his late wife's cousin, with whom he had 16 children.

As a member of one of the founding Boer families of the Transvaal, Kruger came to politics rather naturally. In the 1860s he served as Commandant General of the Transvaal army. When Britain annexed the Transvaal in 1877, Kruger became one of the leading opponents of the British action, even journeying to London to lobby against it. Unable to convince the British to relinquish control of the region, he returned to South Africa where he joined with Martinus Praetorius and Piet Joubert to fight for Transvaal independence. When the Boers won the first Boer War, in 1883 Kruger became the president of the independent Boer Republic of Transvaal.

With the discovery of GOLD in the region, the Transvaal was swept up in the economic transformation that became known as the MINERAL REVOLUTION, with population and commercial interests growing rapidly. As president, Kruger was as outspoken as ever, particularly in his attempt to maintain Boer dominance over the waves of new immigrants who flooded into the Transvaal region. Continued opposition to the British inroads into the Boer regions remained a hallmark of Kruger's administration.

Despite his fervent patriotism and the economic boom, Kruger did not prove a particularly popular leader. He came under frequent criticism for his policies, especially his tendency to award jobs and commercial situations on the basis of personal friendship. In spite of this, he managed to be reelected to office on four different occasions, the last time in 1898, when the second Boer War broke out.

Too old to fight, Kruger guided the Boer forces from the capital. As the British marched on PRETORIA, however, Kruger was forced to flee. There he sought vainly to enlist European support for his struggle against the British. Eventually he settled in Switzerland, where he died in 1904.

Further reading: Stephanus Johannes Paulus Kruger, *The Memoirs of Paul Kruger, Four Times President of the South African Republic* (Kennikat Press, 1970); Johannes Meintjes, *President Paul Kruger: a Biography* (London: Cassell, 1974).

Kumasi (Coomassie) Capital of the ASHANTI EMPIRE, located among the hills of a wet, dense forest in the south-central region of present-day GHANA. Kumasi was founded in the mid-17th century by the Ashanti (Asante) king, Osei Tutu (1680–1717). As the capital of the Ashanti Empire, it grew in importance along with the empire's expanding power and territory. By virtue of its location on a north-south trade route, Kumasi had one of the largest markets in the region.

The city suffered during the ANGLO-ASHANTI WARS of 1873–74, when a British invasion destroyed the palace of the *asantehene* (Ashanti king). In 1896, after a brief period of weakness, growing Ashanti strength caused the British to depose the Ashanti ruler, Agyeman PREMPEH (1870–1931), and establish a PROTECTORATE. In the early 1900s Kumasi became part of the British GOLD COAST COLONY. Although its importance as a trade town initially declined, Kumasi's status returned as it became the center of the region's COCOA production. By 1903 a railroad connected Kumasi to the port of Sekondi-Takoradi, to the southwest. Twenty years later, another line linked Kumasi to ACCRA, to the southeast. Following the establishment of the rail lines, the town grew rapidly and modernized its infrastructure with sewer and water systems. In the 1930s and 1940s, as the population climbed from about 36,000 to 78,500, Kumasi lost much of its Ashanti character; by 1948 less than half of the city's inhabitants were of Ashanti descent.

See also: ASHANTI (Vol. II); ENGLAND AND AFRICA (Vols. III, IV, V); KUMASI (Vols. III, V).

L

labor In general black Africans performed the work required to maintain Europe's colonial economies. In the middle of the 19th century, as the era of exploration came to a close and the colonial era opened up, Europeans tended to view Africa as a vast reservoir of raw materials to be extracted for the benefit of their increasingly industrialized countries. The African population, too, was seen as little more than a natural resource, a limitless manual labor pool to be used to develop the colonies' large-scale export economies. Outside of SOUTH AFRICA, which had a large working-class British immigrant and Afrikaner population, *labor* for Africa's whites meant skilled labor rather than manual labor, which was delegated to Africans.

Slave Labor and Forced Labor In principle Europeans wanted to abolish the practice of slave labor in their colonies. Although the SLAVE TRADE had been officially abolished by the middle of the 19th century, the practice of SLAVERY continued unchanged in many parts of Africa. In many traditional West African agrarian communities slaves were a much-needed segment of the agricultural labor force. Following abolition they were simply reclassified as tenant or hired labor. In some West African Muslim communities, where polygyny was accepted, female slaves were reclassified as wives. However, for the labor needs of the European colonialists, the practice of slavery was replaced by the equally nefarious practice of forced labor.

Forced labor was first instituted by the European CONCESSIONAIRE COMPANIES that claimed territorial, trade, and MINING rights throughout Africa in the 19th century. European governments gave these large, privately owned corporations the authority to do what they deemed necessary to maintain regional control in their efforts to ex-

ploit agricultural and mineral resources. As a consequence the companies created security forces that used threats of violence to "recruit" African laborers, who were then forced to work long days under brutal conditions for little or no pay. If workers failed to meet absurdly high production quotas, they were denied food and water. Repeat offenders were beaten, and it was not uncommon for an especially militant or disruptive laborer to disappear, never to be seen again.

In France's colonies the African population was subject to a system of regulations called the *indigénat*. Passed by the French government in 1881, this set of laws was specifically designed to limit the freedoms of Africans under French COLONIAL RULE. One of the provisions of the *indigénat* was the right of colonial administrators to inflict punishments on Africans without obtaining judgement from the court, and a frequent form of punishment was hard labor.

Taxation and Colonial Labor Recruiting Schemes Hiring schemes in the colonies were given a patina of legitimacy by being connected to colonial TAXATION. After the BERLIN CONFERENCE of 1884–85, many European governments declared protectorates over African territories. According to the agreements they drew up, the European colonial powers reserved the right to tax the African population in order to raise the income needed to pay the costs of running a PROTECTORATE. Head taxes, poll taxes, and so-called hut taxes levied on African villages had to be paid in the colonial currency, but most rural Africans had no opportunity to earn currency. As a result villages were forced to supply the government with laborers in exchange for paying taxes. These laborers, almost always young men, were forced to leave their villages to work wherever they were needed. Some were sent to mines, plantations, or processing plants; others were made to work on administration projects including the building of roads, railroads, bridges, and port facilities.

> The practice of forced labor disrupted African rural life in countless ways. To recruit workers the colonial authorities required village leaders, who were by rule older males, to hand over young, able-bodied males. The rifts between the generations often erupted in violence, with young males attacking or even killing village elders—sometimes their own fathers—rather than submitting to forced labor.

Despite widespread protests the colonial taxation system persisted, preserved by the threat, and often the implementation, of violence. It was not uncommon for colonial forces to burn homes and even murder the inhabitants of a village that refused either to pay the tax or supply the labor.

Colonial taxation was a less volatile issue in West Africa, where many Africans were able to pay taxes with profits from CASH CROPS, especially COCOA, GROUNDNUTS (peanuts) and palm products. However, in East Africa, where colonial governments forced farmers to grow less profitable, more labor-intensive crops such as COTTON and COFFEE, the tax burden was onerous.

Prior to World War I (1914–19) some of the worst atrocities related to forced labor were reported in the Portuguese colony of MOZAMBIQUE and in the CONGO FREE STATE, in southern Central Africa. Under the administration of Belgium's King LEOPOLD II (1835–1909) and his equally cruel administrators, millions of Congolese people lost their lives harvesting RUBBER and ivory for export to Europe. When a series of newspaper articles exposed the conditions in the Congo, international objections to Leopold's methods forced him to pass control of the colony to the Belgian government in 1908.

Tenant Labor Taxation was not the only means by which colonial administrations forced Africans to work. In colonies with large populations of European SETTLERS, for instance, the most fertile agricultural land was seized by whites and then leased back to the African farmers who formerly lived and worked on it. Like colonial taxes, the land leases had to paid in either currency or labor. Some pastoralist groups such as the KIKUYU of KENYA were forced to trade their labor for grazing rights to the lands that had belonged to their forbears for centuries. Land-

This undated photo shows a typical scene from a colonial-era tobacco farm in Rhodesia. Laborers were supplied with only the simplest tools to plant and harvest cash crops. © *Smith's Photo Services/New York Times*

lease schemes such as these were common in SOUTHERN RHODESIA, ALGERIA, and SOUTH AFRICA, as well.

In South Africa colonial policies created a huge itinerant work force. In some regions this work force was made up of nearly the entire young male segment of the population. Although these up-rooted workers had to move often to find new employment, they usually upheld their filial duties and sent part of their income back to their families, who remained in the rural areas. These young men congregated in increasingly urbanized areas and were among the first Africans integrated into the colonial cash economy. Many of them became relatively cosmopolitan, acquiring a taste for manufactured goods and Western-style urban living that was foreign in the villages they left behind.

Following World War I the face of African labor began to change as workers formed LABOR UNIONS. African workers found that widespread labor strikes could bring the colonial economy to a grinding halt and gave them the best opportunity to affect changes. Their demands usually included provisions for better working conditions, improved food and housing in the labor camps, better pay, and shorter workdays. By the end of World War II (1939–45), however, the labor union demands began to include calls for the end of colonialism. In this way, many of Africa's labor leaders evolved into the founders of African NATIONALISM AND INDEPENDENCE MOVEMENTS.

See also: LABOR (Vols. I, II, III, V).

Further reading: Frederick Cooper, *Decolonization and African Society: The Labor Question in French and British Africa* (New York: Cambridge University Press, 1996); Bill Freund, *The Making of Contemporary Africa: The Development of African Society since 1800*, 2nd ed. (Boulder, Colo.: Rienner, 1998).

labor unions (trade unions) Organizations that bring together workers in the interest of improving wages, working conditions, and benefits. Africans organized labor unions in response to the deplorable working conditions that prevailed in the colonies. The fundamental reason that European nations established African colonies was to gain access to vast mineral and agricultural wealth. At the time, MINING, farming, and transportation technology was crude and still required massive amounts of hard LABOR. However, outside of the few colonies that had large numbers of European SETTLERS, whites generally refused

to perform manual labor in Africa. As a result, beginning in the 19th century, the European colonial administrations began devising ways to recruit African labor on a huge scale.

The Origins of African Labor Organizations Although slavery had been outlawed throughout the colonies by the early 20th century, the colonial labor-recruiting schemes often amounted to legalized SLAVERY, with workers forced to toil in impossibly difficult conditions for little or no pay. The concept of African workers' rights did not exist, and, therefore, labor contracts emphasized only the workers' obligations, leaving no recourse for addressing the issues related to backbreaking work, long hours, inadequate housing, poor sanitation, poor food, and limited contact with families.

Even before the end of the 19th century railroad workers in the British colony of NIGERIA were trying to organize to demand better working schedules. The colonial authorities, however, responded by making it illegal for Africans to form their own organizations. In general both the European administrations and the owners of the European CONCESSIONAIRE COMPANIES that ran many of the colonial projects either ignored the demands of African workers or used armed guards who rapidly—and often brutally—repressed their activities.

The African labor union movement began in earnest as World War I (1914–18) approached, about the same time that the ideas of European socialism were becoming better known in Africa and elsewhere around the world. Socialism, as a system based on collective action of the working classes, became influential among African laborers and labor organizers.

In SOUTH AFRICA, as in Nigeria, African-led labor unions were difficult to establish because of legal obstacles. To circumvent this Africans instead joined "mutual aid societies," which served many of the same organizing purposes. By World War I, however, both unions and mutual aid societies were gaining influence throughout South Africa, especially in urban areas, where labor pools developed. In 1919 pioneering labor leader Clements KEDALIE (1896–1951) formed the Industrial and Commercial Workers' Union of Africa (ICU), whose original members were dockworkers in CAPE TOWN. Thanks to union leaders such as A. W. G. CHAMPION (1893–1975), the ICU soon had a membership of more than 150,000, with farm and industry laborers joining the dockworkers.

White Labor Unions White labor unions were common only in South Africa, where thousands of working-class British immigrants and AFRIKANERS labored in the mines and in industrial jobs. In the depressed economic environment that followed World War I, South Africa's major companies began hiring more black and Asian laborers, to whom they could pay less money to do the same job. As a result, Afrikaner workers organized unions to demand increased hiring of whites.

The antilabor government of Jan Christiaan SMUTS (1870–1950), tried to suppress South Africa's unions, both black and white. In 1922, at Benoni, Smuts even resorted to dropping bombs on the headquarters of striking, white mineworkers. It was estimated that more than 200 strikers were killed in the bombing. Rather than dissuade South Africa's labor leaders from further action, the government attack served only to galvanize and bring an element of militancy to the labor movement.

In southern Africa white laborers shunned alliances with African workers and formed their own unions. Roy WELENSKY (1907–1991), the white-supremacist who helped form the CENTRAL AFRICAN FEDERATION, led a white railroad-workers' union in NORTHERN RHODESIA (now ZAMBIA).

The Growth of African Labor Unions As the African labor movement gained momentum throughout the 1930s and 1940s, African-owned NEWSPAPERS served as labor's mouthpiece. Journalists such as Nnamdi AZIKIWE (1904–1996), who later became the first president of independent Nigeria, wrote daily editorials in his WEST AFRICAN PILOT to bring public attention to the abuses suffered by African workers under COLONIAL RULE.

In 1945 Michael "Pa" Imoudu (1902–) the prime figure of the Nigerian labor movement, led a railway workers' strike that finally forced Britain to negotiate with the African labor leaders. Nigeria's National Institute for Labour Studies was renamed in his honor in 1994.

African workers quickly came to see the power of acting en masse when strikes by farmers, miners, dockworkers, or railway workers brought the colonial ECONOMY to a grinding halt. In the 1940s both Britain and France granted their colonial subjects the right to organize labor unions but, in spite of these labor reforms, most major European-owned corporations still refused to engage in collective negotiations with African workers. Companies that needed unskilled labor simply hired "scabs," or replacement workers. For trades that required more specialized skills, such as railway workers, companies stubbornly chose decreased production and lower profits rather than share the wealth. As the influence of the African unions increased, however, union member-

ship also rose dramatically. Eventually corporations were left no option but to negotiate with African labor leaders.

In 1946 a strike in FRENCH WEST AFRICA involving more than 75,000 railway workers led France to abolish its policies of forced labor. Within months African workers also had organized successful strikes in the French colonies of TUNISIA, ALGERIA, and GUINEA. In the British colonies workers successfully mobilized against colonial oppression in NORTHERN RHODESIA (now ZAMBIA), KENYA, TANGANYIKA (now TANZANIA), and SIERRA LEONE.

In the 1950s, as NATIONALISM AND INDEPENDENCE MOVEMENTS emerged across the continent, the demands of African laborers came to include the withdrawal of the colonial oppressors and the right to self-rule. In this way labor leaders became political leaders, as well. These men included Tom MBOYA (1930–1969) in Kenya, Obafemi AWOLOWO (1909–1987) in Nigeria, I. T. A WALLACE-JOHNSON (1895–1965) in Sierra Leone, and Ahmed Sékou TOURÉ (1922–1984) in Guinea.

Touré, especially, based his political party, the Democratic Party of Guinea (Parti Democratique de Guinée, PDG), on worker and peasant interests. In 1958 the PDG led the movement toward DECOLONIZATION by voting "no" to continued membership in the FRENCH UNION, thereby becoming a symbol of the importance of African labor alliances for the new era of independence.

Senegalese writer and filmmaker Ousmane Sembene (1923–) relied on his experience as a dockworker to write *The Black Docker,* and he chronicled the four-month railroad workers strike on the Dakar-Niger railway (1947) in his novel, *God's Bits of Wood,* written in 1960.

See also: LABOR UNIONS (Vol. V).

Further reading: Frederick Cooper, *Decolonization and African Society: The Labor Question in French and British Africa* (New York: Cambridge University Press, 1996); Bill Freund, *The Making of Contemporary Africa: The Development of African Society since 1800,* 2nd ed. (Boulder, Colo.: Rienner, 1998).

Lagos Major West African port city and most populous urban center in NIGERIA, as well as its former capital. Lagos is located on a series of low-lying islands bordering lagoons on the Bight of Benin in the Atlantic Ocean, a location that encourages water-borne traffic. In the late 15th century the site that became Lagos—a YORUBA fishing village named Eko—was visited by Portuguese traders, who named it after a port in their own country. It soon became a major trading center for slaves, ivory, and peppers. After the abolition of the SLAVE TRADE, however, Lagos became a major port for exporting PALM OIL and palm kernels. Heavy commercial activity led to the installation of a British consul in the 1850s, and in 1861 the British took formal control.

For a while Lagos was ruled from the GOLD COAST COLONY (today's GHANA), to the west, but in 1886 it became a separate crown colony. As such, Lagos was the base for British colonial expansion in southern Nigeria. By 1914 it had become the capital of the Colony and PROTECTORATE of Nigeria (which included both Northern and Southern Nigeria). Under the British colonial administration, the region's ECONOMY was focused on the export of CASH CROPS, and its burgeoning markets attracted migrants from Europe, SIERRA LEONE, and other parts of Nigeria, expanding the city dramatically. The popularity of Lagos's NEWSPAPERS was a testament to the town's lively intellectual and political life.

Petroleum production began in the 1950s and soon became the major economic activity for both Lagos and Nigeria in general. When Nigeria gained its independence in 1960, Lagos became the capital. Following the Biafran War in the mid-1960s, the city began to flourish again, with Nigeria's oil production booming and international oil prices favorable to suppliers.

By 1971 the population of Lagos had grown to approximately 900,000. Because of overcrowding, Nigerian officials began plans to move the capital to the less populated town of Abuja, located about 311 miles (500 km) to the northeast.

See also: ABUJA (Vol. V); BIGHT OF BENIN (Vol. III); ENGLAND AND AFRICA (Vols. III, IV, V); LAGOS (Vols. III, V); OIL (Vol. V); PORTUGAL AND AFRICA (Vols. III, IV, V) SLAVERY (Vols. I, II, III, V); URBAN LIFE AND CULTURE (Vols. IV, V); URBANIZATION (Vols. IV, V).

Further reading: Takiu Folami, *A History of Lagos, Nigeria: The Shaping of an African City* (New York: Exposition Press, 1982).

language As a rule Africans are multilingual, speaking a "mother language" as a first language and one or more other languages for specific purposes in society. Language is a primary indicator of cultural identity. When describing an ethnic group, it is usually by the language the people speak. For example, people who speak the HAUSA language are generally referred to as "the Hausa." In this way language is a powerful psychological link among people of a specific ethnic group because it can shape how they see and think about themselves and their world.

When a language is spoken over an extended geographical area, it is likely that the groups that speak it do not use the same form of the language. Modern linguistic studies tend to value these language variations equally. Hence, the word *dialect*—which implies that there is a standard version of the language of which the dialect is a sub-standard version—is not an appropriate term for describing individual language variations in Africa.

Language in the Precolonial Era Prior to the PARTITION of the continent by European colonial powers (1884–85), Africans spoke a wide variety of vernacular languages that changed according to the influences of their social environment. In the 17th and 18th centuries, some languages on the continent disappeared as whole societies were decimated by the conflict produced by the SLAVE TRADE. At the same time, new languages continually emerged along with the changes brought about by the arrival and subsequent dispersal of groups of linguistic outsiders. In SOUTH AFRICA, for example, the Dutch-based language AFRIKAANS developed as European SETTLERS penetrated the region and had less and less contact with Dutch speakers from their European homeland.

Africans often adopted a lingua franca—or language used for inter-group communication—where they came into contact with other African languages through trade. While a specific ethnic group speaks its mother tongue as a *vehicular language* for everyday communication, many non-native speakers might use it as a second language to communicate specifically for trade. In West Africa, for instance, the MANDE languages are the linguae francae for traders who speak Bamana, DYULA, MANDINKA, and Maninka. These languages are used in the present-day countries of MALI, NIGER, GUINEA, The GAMBIA, and IVORY COAST. In East Africa the Bantu language KISWAHILI developed as a trade language along the East Africa coast and throughout the interior regions penetrated by the coastal trading networks. The use of Kiswahili expanded rapidly over the course of the 19th century.

Africans came into contact with non-African languages through trade and conquest. North African merchants along the Mediterranean coast spoke European languages, including Greek and Latin in the post-classical era, but the use of these languages did not spread outside the port cities. The earliest non-African language that penetrated the interior regions of the continent was Arabic, brought by conquest to North Africa and by trade to West and East Africa. In North Africa, well before the 19th century, Arabic became the first language of the majority of the population except for parts of ALGERIA and MOROCCO, where Berber languages remained entrenched. In sub-Saharan Africa, learning Arabic as a commercial language enabled Africans to obtain some of the riches generated by long-distance trade across the Sahara desert or across the Indian Ocean. In addition to being used for trade, Arabic was, and still is, the language of Islam. Depending upon the context Africans learning Arabic were either fluent in the language or learned just enough to function in the society where it was spoken.

Many Africans came into contact with European languages during the era of the slave trade or in the period of legitimate trade that followed. For this reason coastal ethnic groups were first to encounter these languages. In most cases Africans were the ones who learned the European languages. However, because they learned the languages informally, they often created "pidgin" or "creole" languages that blended the European language with local African tongues. If no lingua franca existed when the European language penetrated the coast, a pidgin language became the vernacular language used for trade. Portuguese-based creoles were the earliest such languages. The KRIO language spoken in SIERRA LEONE, which is a blend of English and the coastal indigenous languages (including Portuguese creole), is a later example.

European Christian MISSIONARIES followed the traders to the African coast. In their efforts to attract converts, they tried to learn the local African languages so that they could translate the Bible and make it accessible. Those African language variations that were reduced to written form tended to become the "standard" form of the language for the purposes of the colonial authorities and therefore superceded other, spoken variations. Mission schools generally used written indigenous languages at the elementary level and the European colonial language at the higher levels, a practice that was followed in the system of colonial EDUCATION that developed later.

Language during the Colonial Period In the latter half of the 19th century European colonial powers began imposing alien governmental and language systems on Africans. Believing that the colonial culture was superior to that of Africans, few Europeans bothered to learn African languages. This was especially true in those colonies with substantial numbers of European settlers.

The colonizers generally wanted the sons of chiefs to adopt the European language and culture so that these young men would eventually form a cadre of junior administrators for both government and business. In many cases, however, legitimate indigenous leaders resisted the Europeans and refused to send their sons to colonial schools. Consequently many of the first Africans who went to mission schools were children of families that were not a part of the traditionally recognized power structure. Because of this, by learning the language and accepting European Christianity, some sons of lesser leaders were able to bypass those who had been considered the rightful heirs of the legitimate leadership.

Throughout Africa colonial policy insisted on the primacy of the colonial language to the point that students and colonial-educated officials were punished if they were caught using indigenous languages. Within a few decades these mechanisms allowed the colonial language to supplant indigenous African languages as the official language of most African countries.

By the mid-20th century a group of European-educated elites had emerged. Since they found it easier to gain the favor of colonial authorities, this group produced many of the leaders of the newly independent nations of Africa.

Today most Africans speak an indigenous African language as a first language, perhaps a local lingua franca, and a colonial language. A fine example of this multilingualism is the African intellectual Souleymane KANTÉ (1922–1987), in Guinea, who spoke the Maninka language, Arabic (as a second language, a lingua franca for Muslims), and French (the colonial language). The Kenyan author Ngugi wa Thiong'o (1938–   ) speaks KIKUYU, Kiswahili as the lingua franca, and English (the colonial language). Language diversity continues to mark the continent, and today there are more than 2,000 African languages spoken in Africa.

See also: COLONIAL RULE (Vol. IV); COLONIALISM, INFLUENCE OF (Vol. IV); ETHNIC GROUP (Vol. I); ISLAM, INFLUENCE OF (Vol. IV); LANGUAGE FAMILIES (Vol. I); LANGUAGE USAGE IN MODERN AFRICA (Vol. V); LITERACY IN COLONIAL AFRICA (Vol. IV); NGUGI WA THIONG'O (Vol. V).

Further reading: Bernd Heine and Derek Nurse, eds., *African Languages: An Introduction* (New York: Cambridge Univ. Press, 2000); Ian Maddieson and Thomas J. Hinnebusch, *Language History and Linguistic Description in Africa* (Trenton, N.J.: Africa World Press, 1998); Vic Webb and Kembo-Sure, *African Voices: An Introduction to the Languages and Linguistics of Africa* (Cape Town; Oxford University Press, 2000).

law and justice The installation of COLONIAL RULE led to tremendous changes in the legal systems of Africa. In the mid-19th century there were two major types of legal systems in Africa, as well as other, minor ones. One was the system of *sharia,* a written law associated with Islam. This system had been in place in North Africa for centuries. However, with the establishment and expansion of theocratic Islamic states, it became more widespread in large areas of sub-Saharan Africa, most notably in the SOKOTO CALIPHATE. Elsewhere on the continent African societies had their own systems of governance and law. While these were very diverse, depending on the nature of social and political organization in any given society, they have been grouped under the rubric of "traditional law." A third type of legal system, that commonly seen in Europe, was also present, but to a much more limited degree.

The Dutch brought Roman-Dutch law to SOUTH AFRICA, and then in 1806 the British introduced English common law when they took control of the CAPE COLONY. In ALGERIA the French settlers, called COLONS, lived under French law. Also, by the 1850s Europeans had managed to impose their own commercial law in matters of TRADE AND COMMERCE between themselves and Africans.

The fundamental change that colonial rule brought to law in Africa was the disassociation between government and those who were under it. The new colonial rulers did not share the beliefs and values, including legal values, of those they ruled. Europeans brought with them their own legal systems that had evolved over the centuries in Europe. Where European SETTLERS were a significant component of a colony's population, as in South Africa and Algeria, European legal systems were put fully in place. Also, throughout colonial Africa, legal matters among Europeans or between Europeans and the local population fell under the jurisdiction of European colonial courts.

The principal issue that colonial administrations had to address, however, was what system of laws to utilize for legal relations between the rulers and the ruled and relations among the ruled. This led to a great deal of experimentation at first.

Secular Law vs. Religious Law

European colonial authorities had the fewest difficulties with Islamic law, for they readily saw that it was a well-developed system of jurisprudence. Basically, matters of civil law were left in the hands of the existing system of courts. Matters of criminal law, however, became a more mixed situation. Thus, in Northern Nigeria, for example, Britain utilized the system of jurisprudence already in place in the Sokoto Caliphate as part of their approach to governance based on the notion of *indirect rule*. Of course when there was a conflict between Islamic notions of criminal justice and those of Europeans, the latter prevailed. Thus the impact on Africans was minimal in civil matters, but when it came to criminal matters, the values and precedents of an alien legal system prevailed. Fundamentally, European legal systems were based on a secular approach to the law, while *sharia* was based on theology.

At independence the new governments inherited operating, secular legal systems at the national level, which they continued to utilize. This, however, created tensions with the more religious elements in their societies, who thought that the withdrawal of European rule meant that *sharia* should be restored as the rightful system of law. In short, colonial rule had introduced a secular-religious fault line.

Traditional Law

Colonial administrations faced much more complex issues when it came to traditional law, not the least of which was defining it. Islamic law was written law, so Europeans who read Arabic could understand it. Traditional law was oral. Second, while there were different schools of Islamic law, there was nonetheless a consistency in its basic principles. With traditional law there was a great diversity among African societies. Almost every colony yoked together disparate ethnic groups, each with its own legal system. Also, there was a matter of how law operated from society to society. To complicate matters, in some instances, colonial conquest had destroyed the political system and thus the basis of law within that society. As a result the European powers found themselves in the challenging situation of attempting to understand how the peoples they ruled had conducted their legal affairs. This was a pressing issue, because it greatly affected the effectiveness and stability of colonial administration.

Throughout colonial Africa, European administrators sought to understand traditional law so that they could refer to it for administrative purposes. The operating principle was to utilize what was often termed *customary law*. In the words of a Supreme Court ordinance from the GOLD COAST COLONY, customary law should be followed as long as it is not "repugnant to natural justice, equity, and good conscience."

Early on, colonial administrators such as Col. John Maclean (1810–1874), who in the 1850s was an official over the XHOSA in South Africa, gathered information with the assistance of a number of missionaries on the workings of Xhosa law. Similarly, the government of the Gold Coast Colony (today's GHANA) appointed R. S. Rattray (1881–1938) as government anthropologist for the purpose of generating information on the colony's population, including its laws. Gradually the colonial governments were able to codify traditional law into systems they could both understand and utilize for administrative purposes.

In 1858 Colonel John Maclean published a compilation of Xhosa law entitled *Compendium of Kafir Laws and Customs*. As a colonial official, he had found it difficult in legal matters to reconcile what he understood of indigenous laws and customs with the prevailing Roman-Dutch laws of the Cape Colony. His *Compendium* was an effort to provide a systematic study of Xhosa (Kafir) jurisprudence to facilitate the work of colonial officials with responsibilities for administering the Xhosa.

Colonial Law as a Means of Control Colonial authorities developed legal systems for purposes other than good administration. Among the most prominent of these reasons was to control the populace. Concern with generating sufficient LABOR supplies for the colonial economy was one particular area of concern. A common measure for this purpose was the pass laws. In southern Africa, officials used laws to regulate the flow of labor to the urban areas and for restricting agricultural workers to the white-owned farms on which they lived.

Colonial laws were also used to control the free expression of ideas. For instance, in 1921 officials in the BELGIAN CONGO imprisoned the religious leader Simon KIMBANGU (c. 1887–1951), fearing that the political and nationalist overtones of his preaching would cause a massive uprising. He spent the rest of his life in prison. Nnamdi AZIKIWE (1904–1996) raised the ire of the authorities for his stringent criticism of British colonial rule in the columns of the newspaper he edited in the Gold Coast in the mid-1930s. The British authorities charged and convicted him of sedition, but the conviction was later overturned. As the struggle for independence intensified after World War II (1939–45), the European authorities brought charges against many African political leaders. One of the most glaring examples was South Africa's so-called Treason Trial, which resulted when the government accused 156 prominent political opponents of treason, a charge punishable by death. The trial dragged on for five years before the government's case collapsed without any convictions, but it served the purpose of seriously hampering the anti-apartheid movement.

At independence African countries inherited legal systems that were radically different from those that had existed in the mid-19th century. All had national legal systems based in one degree or another on the secular legal tradition of the former colonial powers. For much of the citizenry of these countries, however, these were alien legal concepts, unanchored in their own cultural and social traditions.

See also: COLONIALISM, INFLUENCE OF (Vol. IV); GOVERNMENT, SYSTEMS OF (Vol. IV); LAW AND JUSTICE (Vols. I, II, III, V).

Further reading: Kristin Mann and Richard Roberts, eds., *Law in Colonial Africa* (Portsmouth, N.H.: Heinemann Educational Books, 1991).

League of Nations and Africa International organization that failed to protect African peoples from the predations of European colonial powers during the 20th century; a forerunner of the United Nations. The League of Nations was established on January 25, 1919, as part of the Paris Peace Conference following World War I (1914–18), with its first formal meeting being held in 1920. Aside from the white-ruled UNION OF SOUTH AFRICA, LIBERIA was the only other African country among its founding 42 members. (ETHIOPIA joined in 1923, and EGYPT became a member in 1937.) In an attempt to achieve collective security, the member states of the League of Nations pledged to preserve peace through disarmament and the diplomatic resolution of international disputes. Shortly after its creation it issued mandates that named the victors of the war (including Britain, France, Belgium, and SOUTH AFRICA) as trustees of the African territories previously held by the powers defeated in World War I (Germany and the Ottoman Empire).

The colonies of GERMAN EAST AFRICA (present-day TANZANIA, RWANDA, and BURUNDI) were divided among Britain and Belgium; the colony of German SOUTH WEST AFRICA (present-day NAMIBIA) was entrusted to South Africa; and parts of both Kamerun (present-day CAMEROON) and TOGOLAND (present-day TOGO) were entrusted to both France and Britain.

Despite their obligation to act as stewards, or trustees, safeguarding the welfare of the African populations of these mandated territories, the trustee powers effectively administered them as if they were their own colonies. The League of Nations' overall record for preserving peace and security proved dismal, though the refusal of the United States to join had seriously weakened it from the outset. The organization's failure to maintain peace in Ethiopia in 1935 was an especially inglorious episode in its history, as fascist Italy's modern military machine crushed the Ethiopian army and forced Emperor HAILE SELASSIE (1892–1975) to flee. This manifest violation of the core principles of the League of Nations' charter, and the ineffectual response of its member states, incited outrage throughout the African world and became a turning point in galvanizing anticolonial African nationalism. A series of other aggressive acts by militaristic states like Germany, Japan, and Italy exposed the ineptitude of the League of Nations and brought about its demise. In 1946 it formally dissolved itself and was superseded by the United Nations.

See also: BELGIUM AND AFRICA (Vol. IV); ENGLAND AND AFRICA (Vols. III, IV, V); FRANCE AND AFRICA (Vols. III, IV, V); GERMANY AND AFRICA (Vol. IV); ITALY AND AFRICA (Vol. IV); UNITED NATIONS AND AFRICA (Vols. IV, V); WORLD WAR I AND AFRICA (Vol. IV); WORLD WAR II AND AFRICA (Vol. IV).

Leakey, Louis (1903–1972) *Anthropologist and paleontologist*

Raised in KENYA by his missionary parents, Louis Leakey was, even as a child, fascinated by Africa and its past. He studied the ways of the KIKUYU people with whom he was raised, and in his teens he was already collecting arrowheads and other ancient artifacts. By the time he completed his studies in anthropology at Cambridge

University, in England, he believed the history of modern humans actually began in Africa, not in Europe or Asia.

Beginning in the 1920s and 1930s Leakey carried out expeditions in East Africa. In 1929, for example, he made an important discovery of prehistoric tools in the Great Rift Valley, a discovery that proved that hominids had inhabited this area far earlier than commonly believed. In 1931 he began his work at Olduvai Gorge, a region to which he returned many times in the next three decades, and which he believed held unparalleled secrets to the human past.

Over the years the work of Louis Leakey, along with that of his wife Mary and his son Richard, proved just this. Again and again Leakey's discoveries at Olduvai and at sites in Kanjera, near Lake Victoria, pushed back the boundaries of human history. By 1961 Leakey had established that the history of human-like creatures in the region went back more than 20 million years, far longer than anyone had anticipated. *Zinjanthropus boisei* (later known as *Australopithecus boisei*), *Homo erectus, Homo Habilis,* and *Kenapithecus wickeri* were all Leakey discoveries. Leakey was also the first to find fossilized evidence to show that, at times in the prehistoric past, different kinds of hominids probably inhabited the Olduvai area at the same time.

Leakey's career was not without controversy, however, as the scientific community often attacked his methods and findings. Nevertheless, by the time of his death in 1972, he was considered one of the preeminent anthropologists and paleontologists in the world, receiving numerous professional honors. His work also established a family tradition for scientific exploration that was carried on by his wife Mary and his son Richard (1944–   ) and daughter-in-law Meave (1942–   ).

See also: ARCHAEOLOGY IN AFRICA (Vols. IV, V); *HOMO ERECTUS* (Vol. I); *HOMO HABILIS* (Vol. I); *HOMO SAPIENS* (Vol. I); HUMAN ORIGINS (Vol. I); OLDUVAI GORGE (Vol. I); LEAKEY, MARY (Vol. IV, V); LEAKEY, RICHARD (Vol. V); LEAKEYS, THE (Vol. I); RIFT VALLEY (Vol. I).

Further reading: Sonia Cole, *Leakey's Luck: The Life of Louis Seymour Bazett Leakey, 1903–1972* (London: Collins, 1975); Louis Leakey, *Adam's Ancestors* (New York: Harper, 1953); Virginia Morell, *Ancestral Passions: The Leakey Family and the Quest for Humankind's Beginnings* (New York: Touchstone Books, 1996).

Leakey, Mary (1913–1996) *Archaeologist, anthropologist and paleontologist*

Born in 1913 to artistic parents, Mary Leakey was raised in Britain, Italy, and France. She was living with her family in the French region of the Dordogne when she became fascinated with the rock art and tools that were being discovered in the local caves. This sparked a life-long study of ancient creatures and artifacts.

Although she never completed her formal university education in either archaeology or paleontology, Leakey began fieldwork early in life. She also developed an ability to illustrate artifacts and specimens. It was this latter talent that led to her relationship with the well-known paleo-archaeologist Louis LEAKEY (1903–1972), whom she met in 1933 and whose book, *Adam's Ancestors,* she illustrated.

In 1934 she left for Africa with Louis Leakey, whom she married in 1936, embarking on a career that would bring her fame as well as the respect of the world's scientific community. She began her African work before World War II (1939–45) at digs near Lake Nakuru, in KENYA, and in Olorgesailie, south of NAIROBI. It was after the war, however, that she made her most noteworthy discoveries. The first of these came in 1948, during an expedition on Rusinga Island, near Lake Victoria. There she discovered fragments that she eventually reconstructed into the skull and jaws of a creature known as *Proconsul africanus,* a 20-million-year-old, common ancestor of humans, monkeys, and apes.

Beginning in the 1950s Leakey made similarly important discoveries at Olduvai Gorge, in northern TANZANIA. There she discovered the famous "Zinj," an example of *Australopithecus boisei* dating back some 1.75 million years. Not long after that, she discovered *Homo habilis,* perhaps the earliest tool-making hominid.

Even before her husband's death in 1972 Mary Leakey was doing significant research on her own. Her work continued during the 1970s and 1980s. By this time her son, Richard (1944–   ) and daughter-in-law Meave (1942–   ) had become prominent researchers in their own rights.

See also: ARCHAEOLOGY IN AFRICA (Vols. IV, V); *HOMO ERECTUS* (Vol. I); *HOMO HABILIS* (Vol. I); *HOMO SAPIENS* (Vol. I); HUMAN ORIGINS (Vol. I); OLDUVAI GORGE (Vol. I); LEAKEY, MARY (Vol. V); LEAKEY, RICHARD (Vol, V); LEAKEYS, THE (Vol. I); RIFT VALLEY (Vol. I).

Further reading: Mary Leakey, *Disclosing the Past* (Garden City, N.J.: Doubleday, 1984); Virginia Morell, *Ancestral Passions: The Leakey Family and the Quest for Humankind's Beginnings* (New York: Touchstone Books, 1996); Barbara Williams, *Breakthrough: Women in Archeology* (New York: Walker, 1981).

Lenshina, Alice (Mulenga Mubisha) (1924–1978) *Bemba prophetess in colonial Northern Rhodesia (present-day Zambia)*

Alice Lenshina was born Mulenga Mubisha in a small village near the Scottish Presbyterian Lubwa Mission at Kasomo, in the British colony of NORTHERN RHODESIA (present-day ZAMBIA). She came from the Bemba people, who, because they were organized along matrilineal KINSHIP lines, gave women a prominent role in society. Mubisha first began to attract attention in 1953 when she claimed to have had visions in which she died and went to heaven, where she received divine inspiration. She claimed that Jesus had given her a new Christian message that was specifically for Africans, and that upon returning to the world she was to spread it.

When Mubisha told her story to the head Lubwa missionary, he accepted it and encouraged her to testify to her experiences in area churches. In addition the MISSIONARIES also gave her religious instruction, helped her study the Bible, and then baptized her, giving her the Christian name, Alice. Once baptized she continued to preach and spread the word, attracting a large following. In 1955, however, following a quarrel with the Presbyterian missionaries, Alice and her husband were expelled from the church. She responded by starting a movement she called *Lumpa* (which, in the Bemba LANGUAGE, means "excelling all others"), and taking the name Lenshina, meaning "queen."

At the heart of Alice Lenshina's message was a personal interpretation of Christianity that held baptism—which only she could perform—as the central ceremony. Also key was her attack on WITCHCRAFT and sorcery, which proved immensely popular among a people who believed that human misfortune was due to the malevolence of others who were witches. (This religious syncretism, or blending of Christian with indigenous beliefs, was a fairly frequent phenomenon in various parts of the continent.) In addition she condemned a number of traditional African practices, including polygamy, and looked with disfavor at alcohol consumption.

Within a few years Alice Lenshina attracted a following of approximately 100,000 people, including many who had been members of established Christian churches. She built a huge cathedral in Kasomo, which she renamed Zion, where she expected Jesus to appear at his Second Coming. The members of her LUMPA CHURCH composed their own hymns, to which they could better relate than the essentially foreign Catholic and Presbyterian hymns. Because of its popularity the Lumpa Church presented a challenge to the colonial government, whose earthly authority it rejected. Lenshina refused to register her church with the government, and by 1958 she was urging church members to oppose colonial taxes and form their own villages in defiance of the authority of chiefs. With her encouragement, her followers also withdrew from membership in the African political parties—such as the UNITED NATIONAL INDEPENDENCE PARTY (UNIP)—that were mounting an increasingly strong challenge to COLONIAL RULE. Indeed, Lumpa Church members and UNIP members often clashed, setting the stage for the violence that would come to pass between the government of independent Zambia and Lenshina's church in 1964.

See also: BEMBA (Vol. III); CHRISTIANITY, INFLUENCE OF (Vols. IV, V); INDEPENDENCE MOVEMENTS (Vol. V); LENSHINA, ALICE (Vol. V); NATIONALISM AND INDEPENDENCE MOVEMENTS (Vol. IV); PROPHETS AND PROPHETIC MOVEMENTS (Vol. IV); RELIGION (Vols. IV, V); RESISTANCE AND REBELLION (Vol. IV); WITCHCRAFT (Vol. I).

Further reading: Andrew Roberts, "The Lumpa Church of Alice Lenshina" in *Protest and Power in Black Africa,* Robert Rotberg and Ali Mazrui, eds. (New York: Oxford University Press, 1970).

Leopold II, King (1835–1909) *Belgian king who ruled over the colonial Congo Free State (present-day Democratic Republic of the Congo)*

Born in 1835, Leopold II succeeded his father to the Belgian throne in 1865. Leopold's early years in power were noteworthy for both his personal interest in philanthropy and the rapid expansion of Belgium's commercial, industrial, and colonial interests. The latter part of his reign, at least in terms of his personal reputation, was vastly different.

In conjunction with the noted Anglo-American explorer Henry Morton STANLEY (1841–1904), Leopold organized the International Association for the Exploration and Civilization of the Congo in 1876. Less than a decade later, in 1884–85 an international conference meeting in Berlin, Germany, placed what became known as the CONGO FREE STATE under Leopold's personal rule.

What followed was a record of cruelty and exploitation that shocked even the normally callous colonialists of the day. By leasing concessions to various contractors and by the extensive use of forced LABOR, Leopold and his agents were able to extract vast amounts of wealth and raw materials from the region—at virtually no cost to themselves. The cost was borne by all of the Congolese people, with millions of them meeting unnatural deaths and millions of others having the normal rhythms of their lives totally disrupted.

The exposure of the scandalous nature of Leopold's administration of the Congo began with a simple discovery by a British shipping agent named Edmund Dene Morel (1873–1924). Leopold's ships, Morel observed, left for the Congo loaded not with trade goods but with soldiers and firearms. The ships returned, however, filled with valuable cargoes of raw materials. Sensing that no legitimate commerce could account for this, Morel began a personal investigation that led to a series of articles titled "The Congo Scandal," which appeared in the journal *The Speaker,* in 1900. As news of Morel's discoveries spread, Leopold became one of the era's most notorious figures.

By 1908 the public exposure of the details of Leopold's administration, including the use of forced and even slave labor, led him to turn the Congo region over to the Belgian government. Leopold died not long afterward in 1909 and was succeeded by a nephew, Albert I. Leopold left a legacy of oppressive rule that has haunted the Congo ever since and which reappeared in full force under the government of Joseph Sese Seko Mobutu (1930–1997) in the latter part of the 20th century.

See also: BELGIAN CONGO (Vol. IV); BELGIUM AND AFRICA (Vol. IV); COLONIAL CONQUEST (Vol. IV); COLONIAL RULE (Vol. IV); CONCESSIONAIRE COMPANIES (Vol. IV): CONGO, DEMOCRATIC REPUBLIC OF (Vols. I, II, III, V); MOBUTU SESE SEKO (Vol. V); SLAVE TRADE (Vol. IV).

Further reading: Adam Hochschild, *King Leopold's Ghost* (Boston: Houghton Mifflin, 1998).

Leopoldville Long-time capital of the BELGIAN CONGO, named for King LEOPOLD II (1835–1909). Located on the banks of the Congo River in the present-day Democratic Republic of the CONGO, about 320 miles (515 km) from the Atlantic Ocean, Leopoldville was built on the site of two villages, Nshasha and Ntamo. In 1881 the Anglo-American journalist and explorer Henry Morton STANLEY (1841–1904) acquired a trading post on the site, naming it in honor of his patron, Leopold II, King of the Belgians. He selected the site because it was at the head of Pool Malebo (formerly known as Stanley Pool), a lake-like area of the Congo River where navigation on the river's upper stretches ends. Below the Pool Malebo, the river cascades off the escarpment in a series of 32 rapids over some 240 miles (430 km), ending at Matadi. The river then is navigable for its final 83 miles (134 km) to the Atlantic Ocean.

Once the railroad from Matadi reached Leopoldville in 1898, its strategic geographical position as the terminus of navigation for the Congo River assumed great commercial importance. Virtually all of the imports and EXPORTS of the CONGO FREE STATE passed through its docks and warehouses. A fleet of 75 small, wood-burning steamers plied the nearly 6,000 miles (9,600 km) of navigable waterways of the Congo Basin. Travel on the river took considerable time, however. For example, the 1,000-mile trip from Leopoldville to STANLEYVILLE took up to 18 days.

With the building of the railway from Matadi in 1898, commercial development increased and the town began to grow. The Roman Catholic church erected a cathedral, in 1914, which was the same year that an oil pipeline reached the city. Air service began in 1920. By 1923 the colonial government of the then Belgian Congo formally accorded Leopoldville city status and transferred its capital there from Boma.

For many years Leopoldville remained largely a city for Europeans, with the authorities considering African workers as only temporary inhabitants who were to return to their rural villages at the end of their employment. Gradually, however, such racial residential restrictions were eased. The worldwide Great Depression of the early 1930s caused a slump in Leopoldville's commerce, but by the late 1930s and early 1940s the city resumed its growth in both population and area, primarily as new residential neighborhoods were added for the influx of industrial workers. By 1940 its 50,000 inhabitants made it the largest city in Central Africa. At independence in 1960 the population had climbed to 400,000, and the overall area of the city was more than twice what it had been only a decade earlier. The foundations of the megacity that it was to become had been laid. Leopoldville became the capital of the new republic. Its name was changed to Kinshasa in 1966, after Joseph Sese Seko Mobutu (1930–1997) came to power.

See also: BELGIUM AND AFRICA (Vol. IV); CONGO (Vol. III); CONGO RIVER (Vol. I); MOBUTU SESE SEKO (Vol. V).

Lesotho Small, mountainous country, 11,700 square miles (30,300 sq km) in area, that is wholly surrounded by SOUTH AFRICA. The origins of modern Lesotho (pronounced as "lesutu" and meaning "the country of the SOTHO people") lie with the founding of the Sotho kingdom of BASUTOLAND in the early 1830s, by King Mshweshwe (1786–1870). A shrewd negotiator, Mshweshwe led the Sotho people (also called the Basotho) from 1823 until his death in 1870. In the latter years of his reign, however, the Sotho people lost a war and much of their best farming lands to the BOERS of the neighboring ORANGE FREE STATE.

Lesotho during the Colonial Era: Basutoland To prevent the total loss of Sotho lands, Mshweshwe successfully persuaded the British to establish a PROTECTORATE over the remaining area of Basutoland in 1868. Beginning in 1871 Basutoland was under the rule of the British CAPE COLONY, but in 1884 it reverted to rule by Britain itself as a High Commission Territory. Along with the other two High Commission Territories of BECHAUNALAND (modern-day BOTSWANA) and SWAZILAND, Basutoland managed to remain autonomous from the UNION OF SOUTH AFRICA, which was formed in 1910. Basutoland became the independent nation of Lesotho in 1966.

Although Lesotho managed to remain politically separate from SOUTH AFRICA, it became fully dependent economically on the country that surrounded it. To a significant degree it became another of South Africa's so-called native reserves, where Africans resided but had to leave in order to find employment on farms and mines and in the industrial and TRANSPORTATION sectors; the loss of lands in the mid-19th century made this dependency inescapable. Since the wages of African workers in South Africa were very low, Lesotho became a very impoverished country during the period of COLONIAL RULE. Politically its people avoided the full impact of the racist APARTHEID laws of South Africa, but they were much affected by it economically.

See also: AFRIKANER REPUBLICS (Vol. IV); ENGLAND AND AFRICA (Vols. III, IV, V); LESOTHO (Vols. I, II, III, V); MFECANE (Vol. III); MINERALS AND METALS (Vols. IV, V); MINING (Vol. II, III, IV, V); MSHWESHWE (Vol. III); THABA BOSIU (Vol. III).

Further reading: Richard P. Stevens, *Lesotho, Botswana, and Swaziland: The Former High Commission Territories in Southern Africa* (New York: Praeger, 1967).

Lessing, Doris (1919–) *British novelist, feminist, and anticolonialist*

Born Doris May Tayler to British parents living in Iran, Lessing was six years old when her father moved the family to a farm in SOUTHERN RHODESIA (now ZIMBABWE). The farm failed, however, and Lessing's mother struggled valiantly to maintain a white-settler lifestyle for her children. Her mother would prove to be a major influence on Lessing's writing and the later development of her feminist ideals.

Lessing attended school in the capital city SALISBURY (present-day Harare), but she dropped out at age 13. No longer taking classes, she managed to transform herself into an intellectual through extensive reading on politics, literature, and sociology. In 1937 she married. After having two children, however, she divorced, finding the traditional domestic role of wife and mother too restrictive. She then became active with a Communist group called the Left Book Club. Through the club she met her next husband, Gottfried Lessing, with whom she had a son. After her second marriage also ended in divorce, she moved to London with her young son, in 1949. She returned to Rhodesia only once, in 1956, many years prior to the country's independence in 1980.

In 1950, Lessing published her first novel, *The Grass is Singing*. The story of a white farmer's wife who has an affair with a black servant who ultimately murders her, the novel brutally depicts the nature of both race and gender relations in colonial Southern Rhodesia. Two years later the novel *Martha Quest* began the largely autobiographical *Children of Violence* series (1951–59), books that explore the psychological and social concerns of a European woman growing up in southern Africa. Less-

ing's social criticism and outspoken opposition to colonialism and racism resulted in her being declared a "prohibited alien" by the Rhodesian government. However, by this time Lessing had established a reputation as an important writer whose anticolonial, feminist views were increasingly difficult to ignore.

Lessing's novels, novellas, stories, and poems written in the 1950s and 1960s are predominantly autobiographical, depicting the clash of cultures Lessing witnessed in colonial Africa. Her other books during this period include *The Habit of Loving* (1953), *Fourteen Poems* (1959), and *In Pursuit of the English* (1960), a nonfiction account of her experiences in working-class London.

See also: COLONIALISM, INFLUENCE OF (Vol. IV); COMMUNISM AND SOCIALISM (Vol. IV); LESSING, DORIS (Vol. V); LITERATURE IN COLONIAL AFRICA (Vol. IV); LITERATURE IN MODERN AFRICA (Vol. V); SETTLERS, EUROPEAN (Vol. IV); WOMEN IN COLONIAL AFRICA (Vol. IV).

Lewanika, Lubosi (1845–1916) *King of the Lozi people of western Zambia (r. 1878–1884, 1885–1916)*

The best known and most influential of all LOZI rulers, Lubosi Lewanika expanded the Lozi kingdom until it covered more territory than it ever had before. When he came to power, the kingdom was at a weak point, having endured a Makololo invasion as well as a period of disunity among the various Lozi factions. In 1884 an attempted coup forced Lewanika into exile for a year, but he later regained his throne after winning a costly war to safeguard his position. Apart from insecurity at home, Lewanika also faced the constant threat from the militaristic NDEBELE kingdom to the south, in present-day ZIMBABWE.

In order to secure his position, Lewanika turned to a French missionary, Francois Coillard, who advised him to ask for British protection. Lewanika's friend, the Ngwato king KHAMA III (1835–1923), who lived in present-day BOTSWANA, had already accepted British protection. Realizing that European control was inevitable, Lewanika asked for the British to extend a PROTECTORATE over his kingdom as well, which preserved the kingdom's quasi-autonomous status under British COLONIAL RULE.

In 1890 Lewanika and the BRITISH SOUTH AFRICA COMPANY (BSAC) agent, Frank Lochner, signed the first treaty giving the company MINING rights. Lewanika signed additional treaties with the BSAC, unwittingly reducing his sovereignty. During the first years of World War I (1914–18) Lewanika provided material support to the British, for which he got little recognition. Although during his reign he ceded much of his authority to the British, Lewanika also instituted policies that developed an educated Lozi elite, which maintained Lozi unity after his death in 1916.

See also: BAROTSELAND (Vol. IV); LOZI (Vol. III).

Lewis, Samuel (Sir) (1843–1903) *Mayor of Freetown, Sierra Leone*

Attorney, municipal official, and critic of the colonial government, Lewis was a lifelong advocate of African rights and peaceful relations among the different cultures and heritages within SIERRA LEONE. Born in 1843 to YORUBA parents who were RECAPTIVES (the term used for people liberated from slave ships by the British Navy) from NIGERIA, Lewis attended school in FREETOWN and then went to England to study law. He returned home as only the third person of African descent to qualify to practice law in Sierra Leone. Initially he chose to remain an independent attorney rather than a government official, deciding that this would allow him to maintain the freedom he needed to criticize the government and advocate the causes in which he believed.

Successful in defending many of his clients, Lewis built a reputation as a dedicated spokesperson for Africans and African causes. Eventually he gave in to requests that he serve in government and became a member of the Legislative Council and, in time, the mayor of Freetown. In 1896 he was the first West African to be knighted by the British crown.

Considered a progressive, he supported African rights and increased contact and understanding between peoples of the coast and those of the interior parts of the region. Such contact, he believed, would not only benefit the Creole, or KRIO, elite of the colony, of which he was a member, but also the peoples of the interior.

See also: ENGLAND AND AFRICA (Vol. IV).

Further reading: J. D. Hargreave, *A Life of Sir Samuel Lewis* (Oxford, U.K.: Oxford University Press, 1958).

Liberia

Independent republic on the Atlantic coast of West Africa measuring approximately 38,300 square miles (99,200 sq km) and bordered by SIERRA LEONE, GUINEA, and IVORY COAST. Although Liberia was the only black state in Africa to entirely avoid European colonial occupation in all of its forms, from an African perspective, the creation and development of Liberia followed a pattern similar to COLONIAL CONQUEST.

In 1807 Britain banned the transatlantic SLAVE TRADE, and opposition to SLAVERY in general became more vocal. Sierra Leone became a home to free blacks who had been living in London and Canada as well as RECAPTIVES freed by Britain from slave ships on the high seas. In the United States abolitionists saw the coastal region south of Sierra Leone as a prime location to establish a settlement for America's free blacks and emancipated slaves.

The American Colonization Society (ACS), founded in 1816, administered the colony until 1841, when the settlement received its own constitution and Joseph J. ROBERTS (1809–1876), became its first black governor. In 1847 Liberia became fully independent, with Roberts as

the first president. MONROVIA, named after American president and ACS member James Monroe (1758–1831), became the capital.

By 1860 Liberia had negotiated treaties with local African leaders to extend the new nation's coastline to about 600 miles (966 km) in length. By 1870 approximately 13,000 free blacks had immigrated to Liberia, though that number that did not increase significantly thereafter. This colonization by black Americans represents the largest migration ever to be made *out* of the United States.

Though Liberia was initially given formal recognition as a country by a number of European nations, it was not until 1862 that the United States also recognized the Liberian government, due to concerns that the slave-holding southern states would not allow for a black ambassador in Washington, D.C.

Border Disputes The Liberians had significant trouble in securing the territory of their country. Conflicts with Britain in Sierra Leone and France in Ivory Coast continued until treaties were signed in 1885 and 1892. Regardless, British and French encroachment continued in more subtle ways. Under the pretext of quelling indigenous African rebellions, the European powers used military alliances with Liberia to claim territory. After the colonial troops were no longer needed, they simply remained in Liberia and became "squatters" on Liberian land. By 1910 Liberia's original land claims were reduced by almost half.

After 1920 European encroachment trailed off, but the Liberian government was saddled with debt and was unable to establish its reach more that 20 miles (32 km) inland. Through loans from the United Kingdom and the United States, however, the Americo-Liberians, as the initial settlers and their descendants came to be known, gradually began to control larger portions of land in the face of resistance by indigenous Africans.

Financial Troubles During its early years the republic suffered growing pains, particularly in financial terms. In 1871 President Edward J. Roye (1815–1872) secured a large loan from Britain—for the purposes of funding new schools and roads—without consulting the Liberian Congress. The move was unpopular and ultimately led to Roye's removal from office. In 1912 another loan was taken from an international group of bankers. With this latest loan the country seemed headed for financial stability. However, the outbreak of World War I (1914–18) devastated the economy, reducing it to a quarter of its previous levels.

Following the war, in 1926 Liberia received much-needed foreign investment from the Firestone Tire and Rubber Company, which established a million-acre (4,047 sq km) RUBBER plantation there. Another large loan secured by Firestone finally allowed Liberia to consolidate its debts. However, by 1931 economic conditions brought on by the worldwide Great Depression once again undercut Liberia's prosperity, and the country was forced to place a moratorium on its loan payments. Assistance from the League of Nations proved to be more hassle than help.

World War II (1939–45) began Liberia's movement toward relative financial stability. The country was the main supplier of rubber for the Allied forces, and a defense contract signed with the United States in 1942 provided for the building of roads, an international airport, and a deepwater port for Monrovia. Following the war the country further developed its infrastructure. Extensive deposits of iron and other minerals were discovered and mined, and revenue collected from ships registered under the Liberian flag also contributed to a boom in the Liberian economy. By 1951 Liberia was financially solvent for the first time in its history. The economic success did not extend beyond the dominant Americo-Liberian upper class, however.

Ethnic and Class Tensions A major issue facing the Liberian government was how to incorporate the indigenous African peoples into the new nation. Tensions between the two groups were immediate. Indigenous Africans believed the settlers to be weak and unable to properly make use of the land to survive, while the settlers believed the Africans were uncivilized and in need of moral and intellectual guidance in the Western tradition. In 1929 President Charles D. B. King (1871–1961) modeled Liberia's new Booker Washington Institute on the Tuskegee Institute, a training school in Alabama exclusively for blacks.

When Liberia's constitution was established the settlers made up merely one percent of the new country's population. However, the constitution failed to address the rights of indigenous Africans. As a result, under the political domination of the True Whig Party, a virtual caste system developed with mulatto, or mixed race, Americo-Liberians in Monrovia at the top of a power pyramid. African-Americans and West Indians of African descent formed the second tier, while recaptives (called *Congos* in Liberia) were third. The indigenous Africans were the lowest caste, and were treated accordingly.

Tensions between the Liberian government and the Africans of the interior resulted in numerous battles, as the government attempted to extend its authority. In 1868 the Liberian Frontier Force (LFF) was created to patrol the African interior and collect taxes, which were levied even though Africans of the interior were without representation in the government and were restricted

from voting. A year later the Department of the Interior was formed, again without the participation of Africans from Liberia's interior.

In 1929 the League of Nations investigated claims that Liberian government officials were forcing indigenous Africans into LABOR as personal porters and as workers on government projects. The government also was accused of having a contract with the Spanish government to provide labor on the island of Fernando Po, capturing Africans for that purpose and taking a fee per worker. The scandal led to the resignation of president Charles D. B. King in 1930 and fully revealed the extent of discrimination by the Americo-Liberian elite against the African majority.

The election of William TUBMAN (1895–1971) to the presidency in 1944 led to improved ethnic relations for a time. Tubman made numerous efforts to balance the interests of the elite minority with the African majority, including giving indigenous Africans the right to vote and embracing traditional African customs and dress. In 1958 Liberia enacted its first laws against racial discrimination. However, despite Tubman's efforts and the new legislation, ethnic tensions in Liberia continued to be a major issue.

See also: ETHNIC CONFLICT IN AFRICA (Vol. V); LEAGUE OF NATIONS AND AFRICA (Vol. IV); LIBERIA (Vols. I, II, III, V); THE UNITED STATES AND AFRICA (Vols. IV, V).

Libya North African country measuring approximately 680,000 square miles (1,761,200 sq km) and situated on the central Mediterranean coast. Libya has a dry and often extreme desert interior and is bordered by TUNISIA, ALGERIA, NIGER, CHAD, the Republic of the SUDAN, and EGYPT.

Libya under Ottoman Rule Although Libya was semi-independent under the rule of the Ottoman Empire, in 1835 the Ottomans reestablished direct administration to protect its province from the increasing threats of European colonization. At the time, the country was divided into the coastal regions of TRIPOLITANIA and Cyrenaica, and the interior region of Fezzan.

In the 1840s the Muslim leader Muhammad Ali ibn al-SANUSI (1787–1859) established the headquarters of his Sanusiyya religious brotherhood in Cyrenaica, in eastern Libya. Recruiting followers from among the local population, the Sanusiyya eventually developed into a significant political force.

By the 1860s Europeans were showing interest in Libya, with investors from France, Italy, and Britain establishing businesses in coastal towns. In the early 1880s Europeans colonized Tunisia, Libya's neighbor to the west, forcing many Muslims to move to Tripolitania, in western Libya, for the religious freedom that the Ottomans afforded.

The Ottoman Empire allowed separate religious communities to govern themselves as long as internal laws did not conflict with Ottoman law. For example, in the 1880s a Jewish merchant community of approximately 15,000 lived with almost complete autonomy along the Libyan coast.

Libya under European Colonial Rule European colonization arrived later in Libya than most of the rest of the continent. After the 1878 Berlin Congress, Italy was allowed by the other European colonial powers to claim Libya as a territory in its Mediterranean sphere of influence. At first Italy lacked sufficient force for outright COLONIAL CONQUEST. Instead it began acquiring land and establishing medical missions, educational institutions, and businesses. Only in 1911 did Italy move to seize Libya as a colony. Until the end of World War I (1914–18), however, Ottoman and Sanusiyya forces were able to confine Italian forces to the Tripolitania coast. At the end of the war the defeated Ottoman Empire was stripped of its North African provinces and forced to cede control of Tripolitania to Italy.

Within five years of the end of the war Italy's leader, Benito Mussolini (1883–1945), set out to conquer all of Libya, claiming that it formerly had been part of the Roman Empire. With all of Tripolitania under firm control, by 1923 Mussolini launched an assault on the interior regions, starting a war that lasted nearly a decade. Italian forces moving east met with fierce Sanusiyya resistance in Cyrenaica, leading to a brutal war of attrition. In the course of the fighting the Italians put numerous Libyans into concentration camps, where many died of disease and malnutrition. The protracted war effort evolved into a campaign to eradicate much of Libya's indigenous population, with the Italian government confiscating vast expanses of fertile land and redistributing it among newly arriving Italian settlers. Those indigenous people who survived the concentration camps were left to settle in less fertile lands.

By 1940 110,000 Italians lived in Libya, and by 1960 they numbered 500,000. The Italian government began to develop Libya's infrastructure, including roads and railroads, sanitation, and medical care. While they suppressed the Sanusiyya and exiled its leaders, the Italians did abide the practice of Islam. The colonial administration helped maintain mosques and shrines, monitored Ramadan activities, organized pilgrimages to Mecca, and granted limited Italian citizenship to Muslims. It did not, however, provide Libyans with EDUCATION or technical training, and thus created a large, unskilled LABOR force.

The Path to Libyan Independence Libya was a major theater in World War II (1939–45). With Italy's defeat the victorious Allied powers presided over the peace conference that was called to decide what to do with Libya. Ultimately, the country was turned over to the United Nations, which in 1951 granted the country independence as the United Kingdom of Libya, a constitutional monarchy. The head of the Sanusiyya, Sayyid Idris (1889–1983), became King Idris I, with his heirs designated as his successors. The new king, however, had little support outside his home base in Cyrenaica.

Until 1958, when oil was discovered in Libya, the country was so poor that it could pay its debts only through loans it received from industrialized nations like the United States.

See also: CYRENE (Vol. I); FEZZAN (Vols. I, II, III); ITALY AND AFRICA (Vol. IV); LIBYA (Vols. I, II, III, V); OTTOMAN EMPIRE AND AFRICA (Vols. III, IV); SETTLERS, EUROPEAN (Vol. IV); UNITED NATIONS AND AFRICA (Vols. IV, V).

Further reading: Ali Abdullatif Ahmida, *The Making of Modern Libya: State Formation, Colonization, Resistance, 1830–1932,* (Albany, N.Y.: State University of New York Press, 1994); Claudio G. Segre, *Fourth Shore: The Italian Colonization of Libya,* (Chicago: University of Chicago Press, 1974).

literacy The ability to read written texts in Africa dates back to ancient times. The educated clerics and people of the upper classes read hieroglyphics, in present day EGYPT, Meroitic script, in present-day Republic of the SUDAN, and Ge'ez script, in present day ETHIOPIA. Historically, however, indigenous Africans have depended more on oral culture than written to transmit knowledge from one individual and generation to the next. Many ethnic groups had a social caste of historians who were the custodians of ORAL TRADITIONS, and elders passed family histories from one generation to the next through spoken word.

Written forms of foreign languages arrived on the continent at different times and spread by means of trade or conquest. Levels of reading proficiency varied from group to group, and an ability to read did not guarantee functional literacy in a foreign LANGUAGE.

Both conquest and trade brought literacy in the Arabic script to the West African and Central African interiors. Arabic is the language of Islam, and converts learned the language in the course of learning the Quran, the Muslim holy book. For many West Africans, conversion to Islam was spurred by an interest in the riches that could be gained through the long-distance trade that, in some places, was the exclusive arena of Muslims. Other West Africans were interested in the script for keeping track of their commercial activities. For example, the ruler of ancient Ghana, in the western Sudan, used Arabic script for recording the empire's tax records. It was also used for record keeping among the Indian Ocean traders who spoke KISWAHILI.

For most African Muslims at this time, Arabic literacy was demonstrated through the "reading" of texts they had memorized. Although many Africans did not speak Arabic as a first language, they still memorized the Quran in that language. The imam, or religious leader, supplied them with translations and interpretations. Africans who became functionally literate in Arabic tended to be those who chose to become Muslim scholars. Many went on to study Islamic theology at Muslim universities like al-Azhar in CAIRO, Egypt.

During the colonial period Europeans founded Christian missionary schools and public schools to train Africans to work in government and business. In an attempt to provide a similar EDUCATION to help ensure colonial employment, Muslims, too, began a new type of school, the *madrasa.* In the *madrasas,* Muslim instructors taught languages—both Arabic and the colonial language—as well as subjects including SCIENCE, math, history, and literature. Some Muslim Africans, the FULANI of GUINEA, for example, used Arabic script phonetically to write their indigenous languages.

Inspired by Arabic script, King Njoya of the Mum people (c.1873–1933) created the Mum script, which is used in present-day CAMEROON. As an act of national pride, Njoya wrote the history of his people and placed it in his local museum.

Widespread literacy in European languages came later, arriving first on the coasts, where European traders used the Roman alphabet to keep records in their own languages. Soon Christian MISSIONARIES followed the traders and explorers, converting many Africans and teaching literacy in their particular European language. At mission schools Africans learned European languages written in the Roman alphabet and were better able to work with the Europeans who were establishing themselves on the coast. Some missionaries translated the Bible into local indigenous languages that were written in the Roman alphabet. As colonial governments established themselves by the end of the 19th century, colonial schools were established to teach Africans the skills necessary to work for the Europeans in government and business.

Influenced by both Islam and Christianity, some indigenous Africans created their own "holy scripts." These included the Ibibio-Efik alphabet, which was created about 1930 along the present-day NIGERIA-Cameroon border. The YORUBA "holy alphabet" was devised in western Nigeria at about the same time.

Indigenous Africans who could not read came to recognize the potential advantages of literacy in a variety of ways. In the 1820s a man named Duala Bukere, who lived on the coast of present-day LIBERIA and spoke Vai (a MANDE language), was surprised to see that his employer, a Portuguese slave trader, was able to learn of Duala's misbehavior through a written letter. Inspired, Bukere created the Vai syllabary, which was used for keeping trade records and for interpersonal communication. Other indigenous groups in the region, including the Mende, Loma, Kpelle, and Bassa, base their scripts on the Vai syllabary.

In 1949 in response to hearing the denigrating remark that Africans had no culture because they did not have an indigenous writing system, Souleymane KANTÉ (1922–1987), a Muslim from Guinea, invented an alphabet called N'ko. Kanté first tried to write his Maninka language in the Arabic script and the Roman alphabet. However, when these writing systems proved unable to accurately reproduce the tones of spoken Maninka, he created his own symbols, eventually settling on an alphabet of 27 letters. Kanté encouraged people to use the N'ko alphabet to communicate in writing with family and friends and to record local and family histories. To further spread the Maninka N'ko alphabet, Kanté also produced a large compendium of translated and transcribed works of history, theology, science, and MEDICINE.

See also: AKSUM (Vols. I, II); CHRISTIANITY, INFLUENCE OF (Vols. II, III, IV, V); HIEROGLYPHICS (Vol. I); GE'EZ (Vol. I); ISLAM, INFLUENCE OF (Vols. II, III, IV, V); LITERATURE IN COLONIAL AFRICA (Vol. IV); NEWSPAPERS (Vol. IV).

Further reading: David Dalby, ed., *Language and History in Africa* (New York: Africana Publishing Corporation, 1970); Dianne White Oyler, "A Cultural Revolution in Africa: The Role of Literacy in the Republic of Guinea since Independence" in *International Journal of African Historical Studies* Vol. 34, No. 3 (2001).

literature in colonial Africa During the colonial era creative writing—including novels, poetry, prose, and plays—were written in European as well as indigenous languages.

Precolonial Literature In the precolonial period indigenous literature in non-Islamic areas primarily consisted of oral storytelling and poetry. Written drama and fiction, however, were produced in eastern Africa. In ETHIOPIA the Amharic LANGUAGE was written in the Ethiopic script known as Ge'ez. As a result, written literature was predominantly found in Islamic areas, where the main form of literature was nonfiction devoted to religious subjects. However, a substantial amount of poetry also was produced, primarily by upper-class religious leaders. One of the most notable of these poets was Usman dan Fodio (1754–1817) of the SOKOTO CALIPHATE, who composed 400 poems in Arabic as well as in the FULANI and HAUSA languages.

Colonial Literature   The long-standing patterns began to change during the colonial period with the introduction of the European Roman alphabet as well as European languages and literatures. Africans then began translating their oral literature using European languages and literary formats. This type of Europeanized literature developed in urban areas where the different literatures interacted with one another.

By custom African men became the colonial authors because, in many indigenous societies, women were prohibited from public speaking. This pattern did not truly end until the coming of independence, at which time women began entering the public forum. Once they did so women began writing, using their own authentic voices to describe life in male-dominated colonial societies.

As time went on the focus of much of this literature became the colonial experience itself, and by the 1950s many African writers used both fiction and nonfiction in this way. Primary concerns were a critique of colonialism and a simultaneous attempt to validate indigenous African traditions in the face of the imposition of European cultures. Ironically, many African authors had to acquire precisely the kind of European EDUCATION and "culture" they were rebelling against in order to gain access to the media through which they could work to overthrow colonial political and cultural domination.

By the 1950s the novel as a genre had become the main vehicle with which Africans could challenge both COLONIAL RULE and European perceptions of Africans and their culture. In French territories this tradition began as early as 1921, with *Batouala, véritable roman nègre* (Batouala, a true black novel). Written by René Maran (1887–1960), it is a tale of the harsh life endured by Africans during the colonial era. Although Maran actually was born on the Caribbean island of Martinique, he spent much of his youth in Africa. *Batouala* generally is considered the first African work to be published in French. Critically acclaimed for this and other works, Maran went on to become the first African to win the illustrious Prix Goncourt.

This tradition of challenging colonial rule and European perceptions of Africa took a step forward with the publication of *Palm-Wine Drunkard*, written by Amos TUTUOLA (1920–1997). Published in 1952, this was the first novel by an African to be published in English. A few years later, leading Nigerian author Chinua ACHEBE (1930–) published *Things Fall Apart* (1958). This well-known book represented a major attempt to counteract the misconceptions of African life and culture prevalent in European society and literature at the time.

Literature, like so many aspects of African life and culture, developed differently in different parts of the continent. In West Africa, for example, literature emerged later in the French colonies than in the British colonies. In part this was because the British system of indirect rule allowed more freedom of expression than the French policy of conformity through assimilation. In addition, unlike their counterparts in the French territories, Christian MISSIONARIES in British West Africa translated the Bible into indigenous languages. This led Africans to begin expressing their own ideas in writing, using the Roman alphabet to represent their own indigenous languages. The first literature in this region appeared as early as 1789, when Olaudah Equiano (c. 1745–1797) wrote a description of his life as a slave. Later J. E. CASELY-HAYFORD (1866–1930) wrote political essays as well as works justifying African culture.

In FRENCH WEST AFRICA the first major writings appeared in the journal PRÉSENCE AFRICAINE, which was founded by Alioune DIOP (1910–1980). Over the years the journal provided a forum for Africans writing in French, especially for those extolling African virtues via the NÉGRITUDE movement. In the same vein, CAMARA LAYE (1928–1980) wrote his autobiography, *L'Enfant noir* (Dark child). Appearing in 1953, the book juxtaposed the author's reminiscences of indigenous culture with the changes wrought by his European-style education. Similarly, the novel by Ousmane Sembéne, *Le Docker noir* (The black docker), which was published in 1956, agonizes over cultural syncretism.

Meanwhile, also in French West Africa but on another front, Souleymane KANTÉ (1922–1987) directly challenged the belief widely held among Europeans that Africans had no real "culture." After inventing the N'ko alphabet, Kanté devoted the remainder of his life to translating and transcribing works of Arabic and European nonfiction. He also wrote an exhaustive chronicle of the 4,000-year history of the MANDE people of West Africa.

On the other side of the continent, in East Africa, writers were also taking on the role of political activists, challenging and criticizing colonial administrations. In East Africa, however, English and KISWAHILI were the dominant literary languages. Some authors, such as Ngugi wa Thiong'o (1938–), wrote in both of these languages as well as an indigenous language. One of the most important works to appear in this region was *Facing Mount Kenya*. Published in 1938 and written by Jomo KENYATTA (c. 1891–1978), this ethnographic work brought the culture of the KIKUYU people to public attention in Britain and other European countries. At the same time it praised and defended indigenous culture and launched stinging criticisms of colonialism.

In contrast to West and East Africa, in SOUTH AFRICA missionaries played a major role in the transition from oral to written literature. For example, the XHOSA-speaking missionary Tiyo SOGA (1829–1871) translated the Christian classic, *Pilgrim's Progress* by John Bunyan (1628–1688), into Xhosa. Similarly, missionary newspapers, including *Isigidimi samaXhosa* (The Xhosa Messenger), published poetry and stories written by literate Africans. These early endeavors carved the way for a number of African writers who emerged during the 20th century. Sol T. PLAATJE (1876–1932), for example, was a newspaper writer and political leader who also translated several Shakespearean plays into his native TSWANA language. Another South African, S. E. K. MQHAYI (1875–1945), drew on the Xhosa oral tradition for his poetry. On the other hand, Archibald Campbell Jordan (1906–1968) drew not on Xhosa oral tradition but on stories from his childhood for his 1940 novel *Ingqumbo Yeminyanya* (The Wrath of the Ancestors). Another important South African literary figure, Peter Abrahams (1919–) grew up in the slums of JOHANNESBURG to become perhaps the first black South African to actually make a living as a writer. Abrahams' 1946 book *Mine Boy*, which describes the life of an African miner, established him as an important author while he was still in his twenties.

A unique phenomenon in South Africa was the development of a large number of white authors. Writing in English and in AFRIKAANS, these authors became noteworthy figures in Africa as well as on the international scene. One of the most important of these writers was Olive Schreiner (1855–1920). Her autobiographical novel, *The Story of an African Farm*, made her a major figure on the literary scene. Even more prominent, however, was Alan PATON (1903–1988), whose *Cry the Beloved Country* was published in 1948. Dealing, like so much of South African literature, with race and oppression, it was perhaps the most widely read and acclaimed novel to come out of Africa to date. Meanwhile, a group of Afrikaans-speaking poets, known as the Dertigers, had emerged during the 1930s. One of its most prominent members was N. P. van Wyk Louw (1906–1970). Interestingly not all of the writers working in Afrikaans were white, for it also was the language of most of South Africa's CAPE COLOURED PEOPLE. The widely admired poet Adam Small (1936–), for example, is just one of several non-white writers who worked primarily in Afrikaans.

At the other end of the continent, the European presence also made an impact in EGYPT. There two trends emerged from the impact of Europe on poetry, which was the dominant form of literature within the country. On the one hand, there was a continuation and a reinforcement of traditional literature, written in Arabic and dealing with Islamic themes. As part of this general movement, Sami Pasha al-Barudi (1834–1904), Ismail Sabri (1854–1923), and Hafix Ibrahim (1870–1932) initiated a revival of classical Arabic poetry. This was later taken to greater heights by Ahmad Shawqi (1869–1932).

On the other hand was the next generation of poets. Through their education they were even better acquainted with European culture, and they broke, though not completely, with the classical Arabic tradition. These writers also were more overtly political. One of the key figures of this group was Ahmad Zaki Abou Shadi (1892–1955). The group that he founded in 1932, known as the Apollo Group, stimulated a surge in anthologies and *diwan* (volumes of collected verse).

In Egypt prose also began to emerge as a form of literature, which in turn led to the development of the Egyptian novel during the 1940s. The 1952 military coup that ended the Egyptian monarchy transformed Egyptian literary as well as political life. One of its major effects was to usher in a Realist school of writing. Foremost among the writers of these novels was Abd al-Rahman al-Sharqawi (1920–1987), who wrote about the harshness of Egyptian peasant life.

Everywhere on the continent the colonial era brought great changes to the literary traditions of Africa. In much of the continent it meant moving from oral to written literature in both indigenous and Western languages. In the Islamic regions it brought a challenge to the older, long-established literary traditions. Regardless of region or religious background, however, as their literature developed, African writers came to address these and other transformations that were taking place during the colonial era and in its wake.

See also: BETI, MONGO (Vol. V); COLONIALISM, INFLUENCE OF (Vol. IV); FOLKLORE (Vol. I); GORDIMER, NADINE (Vols. IV, V); LESSING, DORIS (Vols. IV, V); LITERACY (Vol. IV); LITERATURE IN MODERN AFRICA (Vol. V); ORAL TRADITIONS (Vols. I, IV); SCHREINER, OLIVE (Vol. V); USMAN DAN FODIO (Vol. III).

Further reading: Douglas Killam and Ruth Rowe, eds., *The Companion to African Literatures* (Bloomington, Ind.: Indiana University Press, 2000); Yakubu A. Nasidi, *Beyond the Experience of Limits: Theory, Criticism and Power in African Literature* (Nigeria: Caltop Publications Limited, 2001); Jonathan P. Smithe, ed., *African Literature: Overview and Bibliography* (New York: Nova Science Publishers, Inc., 2002); Wole Soyinka, *Myth, Literature, and the African World* (New York: Cambridge University Press, 1990).

Livingstone, David (1813–1873) *Scottish missionary and explorer*

The most famous European explorer of Africa in the 19th century, Livingstone became a celebrity whose exploits aroused widespread popular interest in Europe. He spent two years acquiring a medical degree and then, in 1838, joined the LONDON MISSIONARY SOCIETY (LMS). He had hoped to be sent to China but was prevented by the ongoing Opium War (1839–42). Thus, in early 1841, just months after ordination, he arrived in Africa.

Livingstone first stayed at Kuruman, BECHUANALAND (modern-day BOTSWANA), with the Reverend Robert MOFFAT (1795–1883), the man who had motivated his interest in missionary work. Livingstone soon established his own mission station to the north of Kuruman, working among the TSWANA people. In 1845 he married Moffat's eldest daughter, Mary (1821–1862). By 1849 Livingstone had begun to explore widely throughout southern Africa, hoping to uncover territories that were unknown to Europeans.

After Livingstone's wife and children returned to England in 1852, his explorations became even more extensive. From 1854 to 1856 he made his way across Africa, first reaching ANGOLA and then traveling eastward until he reached the mouth of the Zambezi River on the Indian Ocean coast. On this journey he encountered a great waterfall on the upper Zambezi known to local inhabitants as "the smoke that thunders." Livingstone renamed it Victoria Falls in honor of Queen Victoria (1818–1901) of Britain.

After his return to England the proceeds of a lecture tour about his explorations left him financially secure. Wanting to explore more widely than the London Missionary Society could support, he resigned from the LMS and took a government post. From 1858 to 1863 he led the British-backed Zambezi Expedition to explore the interior of Africa. He believed that if MISSIONARIES and merchants could remain in the interior, the SLAVE TRADE could be replaced with so-called legitimate trade—commerce in commodities rather than human beings. However, various misfortunes, including his wife's death from malaria, turned the Zambezi expedition into a disaster. Returning to England with neither converts nor sources of agricultural products, he was considered a madman and a failure.

From 1865 to 1873 Livingstone explored East Africa, mainly in modern-day MALAWI and TANZANIA, seeking the source of the Nile River. In 1871 the American journalist Henry Morton STANLEY (1841–1904) followed in Livingstone's path to verify the reports of his death. Refusing to return to England with Stanley, but in failing health, Livingstone resumed his ultimately futile search for the source of the Nile. In 1873 he died near Chitambo, ZAMBIA. His body was buried in London's Westminster Abbey. His heart, however, was laid to rest under a tree in Chitambo.

During his travels Livingstone distinguished himself as a geographer, botanist, cartographer, and ethnographer, as well as a missionary and explorer. His literary legacy includes a large body of journals, notebooks, and letters and three published books. These writings gave an invaluable account of southern and Central Africa and its peoples in the mid-19th century. Their greatest contribution, however, was the attention they focused on the scope and horrific brutality of the slave trade in Africa.

See also: CHRISTIANITY, INFLUENCE OF (Vols. IV); EXPLORATION (Vol. III); MALARIA (Vol. V); NILE RIVER (Vol. I); SLAVERY (Vols. I, II, III); ZAMBEZI RIVER (Vol. III).

Lobengula (1836–1894) *Last king of Matabeleland, home of the Ndebele people, in present-day Zimbabwe*

Son of Mzilikazi (1790–1868), the first NDEBELE king, Lobengula was born in 1836 near present-day PRETORIA, SOUTH AFRICA. After Mzilikazi's death in 1868, two years of internal dissension passed before Lobengula ascended the throne. He then crushed a number of challenges to his power and established his capital at the location of one of his more brutal victories, naming it Bulawayo, which translates as "the place of killing." An imposing man and the ruler of every aspect of the Ndebele nation, Lobengula developed a military state with an army nearly 20,000 strong.

At the end of Mzilikazi's reign, minor GOLD deposits were found along the Umfuli River, a mere 70 miles (113 km) south of the Ndebele capital. Europeans flocked to the region, and though Lobengula disliked the white presence in his lands, he also made extensive use of their knowledge and resources. One European in particular, Dr. Leander Starr Jameson (1853–1917), became an influential presence in the king's court, acting as Lobengula's personal doctor and treating him for alcoholism and gout.

In 1886 a major gold deposit was discovered in the WITWATERSRAND, near JOHANNESBURG, SOUTH AFRICA. Prospectors anticipated finding even more gold further north, in Matebeleland and Mashonaland, home of the SHONA people. This issue arose at the BERLIN CONFERENCE (1884–85), where the European nations addressed the issue of colonial PARTITION. At the conference's conclusion Matabeleland and Mashonaland were established as British territories. Britain allowed foreign interests to operate in these territories with permission from the local kings, and Lobengula was courted by Germans, AFRIKANERS, and Portuguese, all seeking to negotiate claims to the region's mineral wealth. Ultimately, however, it was Charles Rudd (1844–1916), an associate of British diamond MINING magnate Cecil RHODES (1853–1902), who won Lobengula's permission in exchange for monthly payments, rifles, and a promise that no more than 10 whites would enter Matabeleland at any one time.

The ensuing relationship was an uneasy one, with Lobengula becoming increasingly suspicious of British aims. Jameson, who was one of Rhodes's most trusted associates, managed to placate the Ndebele ruler and negotiated permission for the Rhodes-led BRITISH SOUTH AFRICA COMPANY (BSAC) to construct a road through Matabeleland and into Mashonaland. This led in 1890 to the establishment of the settlement of SALISBURY (present-day Harare) and the British colony of SOUTHERN RHODESIA (present-day ZIMBABWE).

"Did you ever see a chameleon catch a fly?" Lobengula is reported to have asked the Reverend Charles Helm, a European missionary residing among the Ndebele. "The chameleon gets behind the fly and remains motionless for some time, then he advances very slowly and gently, first putting forward one leg and then another. At last, when well within reach, he darts his tongue and the fly disappears. England is the chameleon and I am that fly."

Ndebele raids on the Shona, over whom Lobengula claimed sovereignty but who now lived in the area claimed by the BSAC, prompted clashes with the British. In 1893, after a minor Ndebele raid, Jameson sent troops to Bulawayo. There the British soundly defeated a much larger Ndebele force, and Lobengula fled to the north. A British patrol sent to capture him was wiped out by Lobengula's vanguard. However, in 1894, weakened by illness and the defeat of his people, Lobengula died under mysterious circumstances. (It is thought that he may have poisoned himself, though he perhaps also died of smallpox.) He was survived by three sons, but they were prevented by the British from assuming the throne, and the Ndebele kingdom permanently collapsed.

See also: COLONIAL CONQUEST (Vol. IV); ENGLAND AND AFRICA (Vols. III, IV, V); SHONA KINGDOMS (Vol. III).

London Missionary Society (LMS)

Founded in 1795 as the Missionary Society and renamed the London Missionary Society (LMS) in 1818, the organization had as its goal to spread the knowledge of Christ "among heathen and other unenlightened nations." The LMS was one of several important missionary organizations founded at about the same time as an outgrowth of the evangelical movement in Britain and North America. It began as an interdenominational society of independent churches, the Church of England, and Presbyterian clergy and laymen but soon was run predominantly by Congregationalists.

The initial LMS mission in 1796 was to Tahiti, and the society also sent MISSIONARIES to eastern and south Europe. During the 19th century the LMS expanded its scope to include Asia, Australia, and Africa—specifically Central Africa, MADAGASCAR, and southern Africa.

The LMS was governed by a board of directors. Separate committees oversaw particular aspects of mission work. The examinations committee, for example, selected the individuals to be sent to specific lands. One of the pioneer LMS missionaries to Africa was the Reverend Robert MOFFAT (1795–1883). Another was his son-in-law, the well-known David LIVINGSTONE (1813–1873).

The rapid expansion of mission work in Africa caused financial strain. This led the LMS to encourage indigenous churches to become self-financing and self-governing. As a result the role of foreign missionaries declined, and local clergy and lay people became increasingly prominent in running their own churches.

In 1966 the LMS merged with the Commonwealth Missionary Society to form the Congregational Council for World Mission, which was further restructured in 1977 to become the Council for World Mission.

See also: CHRISTIANITY, INFLUENCE OF (Vol. II, III, IV, V); CHURCH MISSIONARY SOCIETY (Vol. IV).

Lourenço Marques (Maputo)

Major port and capital city of MOZAMBIQUE, located on DELAGOA BAY, an arm of the Indian Ocean in southern East Africa. In the late 19th century the discovery of GOLD in the TRANSVAAL, to the southwest of Lourenço Marques, created a windfall for the town. As thousands of miners rushed to the JOHANNESBURG area, Lourenço Marques, as the closest seaport, had to modernize its infrastructure and port facilities to handle the flow of immigrants and the trade that developed after their arrival. Between 1877 and 1892 Mozambique's foreign trade increased by approximately 300 percent, with much of the increase due to the traffic at Lourenço Marques.

Lourenço Marques was named after the Portuguese explorer and trader who first visited the area in 1544. In 1787 the Portuguese built a fortress called Nossa Senhora da Conceião (Our Lady of Conception), around which the town grew.

European SETTLERS and merchants, too, began to migrate to the town, creating new markets. Unfortunately these new arrivals, with their colonialist attitudes and practices, oppressed the local African people, who were displaced from their land. The town grew further with the completion of the railroad link with PRETORIA in 1894. At the same time, a substantial number of south Asian merchants—Indians and Pakistani among them—migrated to the town from across the Indian Ocean. By the early 1900s Lourenço Marques was a bustling town with a poor African majority, a smaller, wealthier European minority, and a large Asian population.

Upon Mozambique's independence in 1975 Lourenço Marques remained the capital. A year later the city was renamed Maputo, the name of the site prior to the arrival of Portuguese sailors.

In 1907 Lourenço Marques, with its population at 6,000 and rising, replaced Moçambique, a city located on a small island about 1,000 miles (1,609 km) to the northeast, as the capital of Portuguese East Africa. With its modern colonial facilities, the city had long ceased to resemble the malarial, depressed trading post of mid-century. Growth continued throughout the 20th century, with the population reaching about 65,000 by 1960.

Located on a picturesque stretch of East Africa's Indian Ocean shoreline, Lourenço Marques was a particularly comfortable city for its Portuguese inhabitants, but far less so for its African majority, whose living conditions and prospects for improvements were so poor that many left the area.

See also: ASIAN COMMUNITIES (Vols. IV, V); MAPUTO (Vols. III, V); PORTUGAL AND AFRICA (Vols. III, IV, V); URBAN LIFE AND CULTURE (Vols. IV, V); URBANIZATION (Vols. IV, V).

Further reading: Jeanne Marie Penvenne, *African Workers and Colonial Racism: Mozambican Strategies and Struggles in Lourenço Marques, 1877–1962* (Portsmouth, N.H.: Heinemann, 1995).

Lozi Major ethnic group found in the western part of present-day ZAMBIA. Smaller populations of the Lozi people are found in present-day ZIMBABWE, NAMIBIA and BOTSWANA. Lozi—who have also been called Luyi, Silozi, Rozi, Tozvi, Rutse, Kololo and Rotse, hence BAROTSELAND—includes several sub-groups with similar cultural and linguistic characteristics. *Lozi* is a more recent name, which replaced the name *Luyi*. The Lozi LANGUAGE is a Bantu language that belongs to the Niger-Congo family of African languages.

The Lozi region, called *Bulozi* (belonging to the Lozi) or *Barotseland*, is situated in the plain of the Zambezi River, where annual floods leave a bed of rich alluvial soils. Due to the heavy flooding in February or March, the Lozi shift their homes temporarily to higher ground in the forest region each year, returning to their normal residences after the rains. Led by their king they celebrate this event, called *Kuomboka*, which means "get out of water."

The Lozi, then known as the Luyi, occupied Barotseland in the 1600s, intermarrying with other groups, including the Kololo, who entered the kingdom later. A SOTHO-speaking group from SOUTH AFRICA, the Kololo invaded in 1838 and ruled the Luyi kingdom until 1864, when they were finally overthrown. In 1878 Lubosi LEWANIKA (1845–1916) took over as *litunga*, or king, and built a powerful state. However, European imperial interests were impinging on the area as elsewhere in Africa, and from the 1890s, Barotseland came increasingly under British COLONIAL RULE, ending up part of the colony of NORTHERN RHODESIA. Though their political independence had been lost, the Lozi were able to retain their cultural and ethnic identity.

See also: BANTU LANGUAGES (Vol. I); COLONIAL CONQUEST (Vol. IV); ENGLAND AND AFRICA (Vols. III, IV, V); KUOMBOKA CEREMONY (Vol. V); LOZI (Vol. III); NIGER CONGO (Vol. I); LEWANIKA, MBIKUSITA INONGE (Vol. V).

Luanda Capital city and major port of ANGOLA, located in the northern part of the country, on the Atlantic coast. The city's Portuguese name, Luanda, is taken from *loanda*, a Kimbundu word meaning "flat land." From the 17th through the 19th centuries Luanda developed into a center of the Portuguese SLAVE TRADE, predominantly sending African captives to Brazil. As the town grew the region's different ethnic groups melded into a distinctive Creole Afro-Portuguese culture. During the first half of the 19th century the slave trade diminished, and the export of CASH CROPS such as COTTON, PALM OIL, and COFFEE became more important. Trade in other local products, including copal (a tropical tree resin used in making varnish), leather, and cassava flour also flourished. This economic growth was accompanied by population growth.

After the BERLIN CONFERENCE (1884–85) the low-lying city center was taken over by immigrating Europeans and named the *Baixa* district. These new settlers displaced many urban Africans, who relocated to form communities, called the *musseques*, on the surrounding slopes and uplands. The population of the *musseques* grew with the migration of Africans from the interior. The mixture of peoples created a lively African community that fostered social cohesion and political consciousness. Later, as a result of the politicized atmosphere, the *musseques* became the birthplace of Angola's NATIONALIST AND INDEPENDENCE MOVEMENTS.

During the early 20th century Luanda's education system proved well-designed and encouraged cultural exchange and open-mindedness among the city's African, *mestiço* (mixed-race), and European population. This created a more diverse and equitable atmosphere than that found in most other colonial African cities, especially those developed by the Portuguese.

Following World War II (1939–45) a rise in global coffee prices helped to expand economic opportunities in Angola. The resulting employment boom attracted thousands of rural people to Luanda, and between 1940 and 1960 the population of the capital increased four-fold. Also, beginning in the 1950s the colonial government offered incentives to Portuguese nationals to emigrate to Luanda to aid in the development of industry.

In 1961 Angola's various nationalist movements began waging civil war against the Portuguese colonial forces and against one another. Before long the threat of violence in the rural areas became overwhelming, and throngs of rural Angolans fled to Luanda and other urban areas for refuge. The civil war dragged on until 1975, when Portugal finally abandoned its African colonies.

See also: COLONIAL RULE (Vol. IV); COLONIALISM, INFLUENCE OF (Vol. IV); LUANDA (Vols. III, V); PALM OIL (Vol. III); PORTUGAL AND AFRICA (Vols. III, IV, V); SLAVE TRADE, TRANSATLANTIC (Vol. III); URBAN LIFE AND CULTURE (Vols. IV, V); URBANIZATION (Vols. IV, V).

Lugard, Frederick (Sir, later Lord Frederick John Dealtry Lugard) (1858–1945) *British colonial administrator*

Born in India to missionary parents, Frederick Lugard began his career in the military, serving abroad in the Afghan wars, the Sudan, and Burma. He went to England after being severely wounded and eventually took a position with the British East Africa Company in UGANDA in 1890. There he spent two years helping to establish Britain as the primary European power in the region. A vehement advocate of British imperialism, Lugard refused to accept his employer's decision to withdraw from Uganda in light of spiraling costs and international criticism of Lugard's treatment of French MISSIONARIES. Returning to England, he lobbied for a continued British presence in the region, publishing a book, entitled *The Rise of Our East African Empire* (1893), which outlined his vision of British dominance of the region.

In 1894 Lugard went back to Africa, this time journeying to West Africa in the employ of the ROYAL NIGER COMPANY. He remained in the area that would eventually become NIGERIA for several years, first opposing French expansion into the region and then taking command of the West African Frontier Force, a military unit he organized to help the Royal Niger Company further its interests. In 1900 the British government revoked the company's charter and took direct control over the region,

placing Lugard in charge. As high commissioner Lugard first battled the resistant Islamic states of the SOKOTO CALIPHATE. After defeating them he set about organizing the region into an administrative whole. By supporting local rulers and their courts—while at the same time eliminating SLAVERY and instituting a more humane system of justice—Lugard was able to establish British authority effectively and efficiently.

Lugard's work and policies in Nigeria gave rise to a doctrine that became known as *indirect rule,* by which the British could control their African colonies through local rulers and institutions. Adopted in other regions, it proved beneficial to the British colonial government in many areas, particularly those in which people were not separated by sharp ethnic divisions. In 1922 Lugard outlined his ideas for colonial administration in *The Dual Mandate in British Tropical Africa,* a book in which he argued that indirect rule represented the best way for Britain to profit from its colonies while also helping them develop socially, politically, and economically. The book was essentially a defense of colonialism in the face of the criticism that arose after World War I (1914–18).

In 1902 Lugard accepted the position of governor of Hong Kong, serving from 1907 to 1912. He then returned to Nigeria, where, beginning in 1912, he set about combining Britain's separate Northern and Southern Nigeria protectorates. Lugard had to put down rebellions, develop the Nigerian administrative system, and deal with the threat of German military incursions from their colony of Kamerun (present-day CAMEROON). Finally, after two years of difficult work the task of unification was completed January 1, 1914.

Although officially retired after 1919, Lugard remained active in public affairs for the remainder of his life, serving first with the Privy Council and then, from 1922 to 1936, as a member of the League of Nations' Permanent Mandates Commission.

See also: BRITISH EAST AFRICA (Vol. IV); COLONIAL CONQUEST (Vol. IV); COLONIAL RULE (Vol. IV); ENGLAND AND AFRICA (Vol. IV); PARTITION (Vol. IV).

Lumpa Church
Large and influential African church movement established in 1955 by Alice LENSHINA (1924–1978). Alice Mulenga Mubisha Lenshina was a self-proclaimed prophetess among the Bemba peoples of present-day northern ZAMBIA. She claimed that she had

died four times and had gone to heaven, where she received divine instructions to spread God's word.

In 1953 Lenshina was baptized by Scottish Presbyterian MISSIONARIES (although she was later expelled from the Presbyterian church). Within a few years she established her own religious movement, which she called *Lumpa* (meaning "excelling all others" in the Bemba language). Eventually this church became one of the largest and most powerful religious movements in Zambian history, with approximately 150 congregations and as many as 100,000 members by 1956. Donations from members enabled the church to acquire property—including a chain of stores—and to build a large brick cathedral at its headquarters in Kasomo, Lenshina's birthplace. The church developed its own hymns based on indigenous songs and accompanied by MUSIC played with indigenous instruments. In this way members related to Lumpa services much more closely than they had when the missionary churches used traditional European hymns and instrumentation. The Lumpa Church attracted members in part because of its promise of salvation to believers and also because of its syncretistic blending of African and European belief systems. It also appealed to people because it denounced such social vices as divorce, drinking, and smoking. In addition the Lumpa Church prohibited polygamy.

As Lenshina's church expanded it began challenging not only the norms of established churches and the powers of traditional leaders, but also the colonial and national state. Rejecting taxation, the church even went about forming its own villages. As a result, violent clashes between the Lumpa Church and the government became common. After Zambia's independence in 1964, members of the new governing party, the UNITED NATIONAL INDEPENDENCE PARTY (UNI) destroyed Lumpa members' homes and their church buildings. Church members retaliated by murdering seven UNIP members and assaulting others. Zambian police and army units responded, resulting in the deaths of at least 700 church members. Following the incident the church was banned.

Following a government amnesty, in 1968 an estimated 20,000 Lumpa followers emigrated to the present-day Democratic Republic of the CONGO. Many other members joined or rejoined Christian churches that in turn sought to incorporate more Bemba features into the church liturgy.

See also: BEMBA (Vol. III); CHRISTIANITY, INFLUENCE OF (Vols. IV, V); INDEPENDENCE MOVEMENTS (Vol. V); LENSHINA, ALICE (Vol. V); NATIONALISM AND INDEPENDENCE MOVEMENTS (Vol. IV); PROPHETS AND PROPHETIC MOVEMENTS (Vols. IV, V); RELIGION (Vols. IV, V).

Further reading: Andrew Roberts, "The Lumpa Church of Alice Lenshina," in *Protest and Power in Black Africa*, Robert Rotberg and Ali Mazrui, eds. (New York: Oxford University Press, 1970).

Lumumba, Patrice (Patrice Emery Lumumba)
(1925–1961) *First prime minister of the independent Democratic Republic of the Congo*

Born to Catholic parents in the village of Onalua, in Kasai province of the BELGIAN CONGO (present-day Democratic Republic of the CONGO), Patrice Lumumba was educated at nearby mission schools. In 1944 he moved to STANLEYVILLE (today's Kisangani), a thriving port city on the Congo River, where he took a job as a postal clerk. In 1951 Lumumba wed 15-year-old Pauline Opangu in a marriage arranged by his father. Although initially resistant to the marriage, Lumumba eventually fathered at least eight children by Pauline, who became his trusted confidante.

Lumumba became involved in the political issues that were facing the Belgian Congo during his early adulthood. Hoping that he could unite the ethnically diverse Congolese, he took classes to improve his French, the lingua franca of Central Africa, and he also learned KISWAHILI and several Congolese dialects. Africans in the Congo had not yet organized political parties, but predecessor organizations, such as Stanleyville's African Government Employees Association, were in existence. Lumumba rose through its ranks, serving as secretary and eventually president. He also wrote editorials in local political NEWSPAPERS, establishing a reputation as a recognizable nationalist leader who was unafraid to speak out on the most important issues.

By 1954 Lumumba was a leading political figure in Stanleyville, meeting with King Baudouin (1930–1993) of Belgium, who was touring the country, and traveling to Belgium as a representative of the first Congolese delegation to discuss political reform. Lumumba's forceful style and outspokenness caught the attention of the white Belgian administrators in Stanleyville. They accused him of embezzling funds from the post office and sentenced him to two years in prison. Within a year, however, Lumumba's supporters in the community raised the money he was accused of taking, thereby buying his freedom. (After his release Lumumba challenged the verdict and cleared his name on appeal.)

Despite his support in the African community, Lumumba no longer felt welcome in Stanleyville. In 1957 he moved to LEOPOLDVILLE (present-day Kinshasa), where he continued his political activism. Belgian colonial authorities were now allowing African political parties to exist, and Lumumba took the lead in forming the Congolese National Movement (MNC), helping turn it into a broad coalition of groups lobbying for Congolese independence. Late in 1958 Lumumba represented the MNC at the All-African People's Conference held in ACCRA, GHANA, where he met with the head of this newly independent country, Kwame NKRUMAH (1909–1972). Nkrumah was a strong advocate of PAN-AFRICANISM and continental unity, which Lumumba also now embraced.

In October 1960 Patrice Lumumba attempted to rally his supporters in his efforts to regain office. © UPI/New York World-Telegram & Sun Collection/Library of Congress

In Leopoldville Lumumba took a job as sales representative for Polar Beer, a beverage company. Within a year the intelligent and cheerful Lumumba was sales manager for the whole company.

As the 1950s came to a close and independence became seemingly inevitable, new political parties sprang up. Many, however, disagreed with Lumumba's call for a unified country with a strong central government and instead called for a Congo federation, with individual regions or provinces retaining authority. The most vocal provinces were dominated by certain ethnic groups, such as the Lunda and KONGO, that had been removed from power during the colonial period.

As the different groups quarreled over the direction of the country, Lumumba gave an impassioned speech at a Stanleyville MNC conference that resulted in violent street rioting in which up to 30 people lost their lives. In response the colonial authorities arrested Lumumba for inciting the riots and sentenced him to six months in jail. The Stanleyville riots were just part of a larger wave of unrest that was sweeping through the Belgian Congo, so the colonial authorities called for the Congolese representatives to meet in Brussels, Belgium. Initially, the MNC was represented by Joseph-Désiré Mobutu (1930–1997), a little-known compatriot of Lumumba's. However, when the MNC delegates refused to continue the conference without Lumumba in attendance, Belgian authorities released him, for they had by then decided to grant independence to the Congo and thus wanted to facilitate the process.

Following the Brussels meeting, a national election was scheduled for June 1960, with independence coming soon after. Lumumba's MNC party, with its advocacy of national unity, and the ABAKO party, with its ethnic-based approach and led by Lumumba's long-time rival Joseph Kasavubu (c. 1910–1969), won the most votes in the election. Following negotiations a coalition government was declared, with Lumumba the prime minister and Kasavubu the president. Mobutu was made secretary of state for national defense.

During his Independence Day speech on June 30, 1960, Lumumba recalled the brutality of the former Belgian rule, again inciting widespread riots. On July 5 the army mutinied against its white Belgian officers. Many in the country's white population fled the country as it descended into chaos. The Congo Crisis had begun. Within 18 months Lumumba was murdered by his political rivals.

See also: BELGIUM AND AFRICA (Vol. IV); COLONIAL RULE (Vol. IV); COLONIALISM, INFLUENCE OF (Vol. IV); CONGO CRISIS (Vol. V); DECOLONIZATION (Vol. IV); INDEPENDENCE MOVEMENTS (Vol. V); LUMUMBA, PATRICE (Vol. V); MOBUTU SESE SEKO (Vol. V); NATIONALISM AND INDEPENDENCE MOVEMENTS (Vol. IV).

Further reading: Thomas Kanza, *Conflict in the Congo: The Rise and Fall of Lumumba* (Harmondsworth, U.K.: Penguin, 1972); Crawford Young, *Politics in the Congo: Decolonization and Independence* (Princeton, N.J.: Princeton University Press, 1965).

Luo (Lwo, Lwoo, Dholuo, Kavirondo)

Third-largest ethnic group in KENYA, after the KIKUYU and the Luhya; also the Nilotic language they speak. Luo speakers live primarily in UGANDA, western Kenya, and northern TANZANIA, in the Lake Victoria region. Like the Kikuyu the Luo became highly active in the evolving Kenyan political scene toward the close of the colonial era.

Originally from the upper Nile region, the Luo migrated south to their present-day homelands by the end of the 15th century. Largely pastoralists, they also turned to AGRICULTURE and fishing and intermingled extensively with local Bantu speakers. However, toward the latter half of the 19th century, the European presence in the region increased dramatically. By 1895 Britain had established the PROTECTORATE of BRITISH EAST AFRICA over Luo-occupied territories. Construction was begun on a railroad from MOMBASA, on the coast, to Kisumu, on Lake Victoria. Upon its completion in 1901, the railroad solidified the British presence in the interior. By the 1930s European SETTLERS, mostly British, had seized for their own cultivation millions of acres of lands previously held by Africans.

In response to the oppressive colonial regime, the Luo developed a political resistance closely tied to that of the Kikuyu. In 1922, one year after the formation of the Young Kikuyu Association, the Kikuyu James Beauttah established the Young Kavirondo Association, supported mainly by the Luo and Luhya. Like the Young Kikuyus, the Young Kavirondos protested white-settler rule, insufficient wages, the head tax, the *kipande*—an identification card all Africans were required to carry—and the theft of their land. Unlike the Young Kikuyu Association, however, by 1923 the Kavirondo organization fell under the influence of European MISSIONARIES, who gradually shifted the organization from a political focus to a humanitarian one. Also, dissension among the Luo tended to limit their political effectiveness.

A number of Luo became major players in the Kenyan struggle for independence. For example, Tom MBOYA (1930–1969) and Oginga ODINGA (1912–1994) were instrumental in founding nationalist organizations and supporting Jomo KENYATTA (c. 1891–1978), the Kikuyu and Kenyan nationalist leader who was imprisoned in 1952 as part of the British backlash against the MAU MAU movement. Both leaders helped found the Kenya African National Union, which became the leading political party in Kenya following the 1961 elections. When Kenya received full autonomy in 1963, with Kenyatta as president, both Mboya and Odinga assumed high-ranking roles in the government, assuring the Luo a prominent role in Kenyan politics in the early years of independence.

See also: COLONIALISM, INFLUENCE OF (Vol. IV); ENGLAND AND AFRICA (Vols. III, IV, V); NATIONALISM AND INDEPENDENCE MOVEMENTS (Vol. IV).

Further reading: B. A. Ogot, *History of the Southern Luo* (Nairobi, Kenya: East African Publishing Company, 1967).

Lusaka

Commercial center and colonial capital of NORTHERN RHODESIA (present-day ZAMBIA), located north of the Zambezi River on a plateau that rises 4,200 feet (1,280 m) above sea level. Named after a local African leader, Lusaka was founded in the 1890s when the BRITISH SOUTH AFRICA COMPANY established control over the region. Lusaka began as a station on a railway line and evolved into a commercial center for white farmers. By 1924 the British Colonial Office had taken over the administration of Lusaka, and in 1935 the town replaced Livingstone as the capital of Northern Rhodesia. Soon after that, the manufacturing of foodstuffs, beverages, clothing, and cement began.

Not long after World War II (1939–45) the Zambian independence movement gained momentum in Lusaka. In 1948, for example, the independence-minded Northern Rhodesia African Congress was founded there. By 1951, under the able leadership of Kenneth KAUNDA (1924–), the organization had become the Zambian African National Congress. During the 1950s and 1960s Lusaka was a hotbed of political activity, with opposition parties moving their operations there so that they could directly confront the colonial government. The population, which was estimated at 30,000 in 1950, increased to about 126,000 by 1964.

The original plan of Lusaka followed that of an "English garden city," with main roads leading to the town center. Impressive buildings were also planned and, by the time of independence, these included the State House, the High Court, the Secretariat, and the Anglican Cathedral.

When Northern Rhodesia became independent Zambia in 1964, Lusaka bore the signs of racial segregation in all spheres. Schools, hospitals, cinemas, residences, and even shopping centers were segregated according to white, black, Indian, and Coloured quarters. There were separate shopping centers for whites and blacks, with the shops for black people owned mostly by the Asian-settler community.

The town featured only a few major public buildings and roads, so the new government faced the huge task of building an infrastructure to accommodate the growing population. Within a few years of independence, the new administration had either finished or begun building Zambia's first university, an international airport, the impressive National Assembly building, a major network of roads, as well as administrative and commercial buildings. Lusaka was quickly transformed into a cosmopolitan city, hosting major national and continental events.

See also: ENGLAND AND AFRICA (Vols. III, IV, V); INDEPENDENCE MOVEMENTS (Vol. V); LUSAKA (Vol. V); NATIONALISM AND INDEPENDENCE MOVEMENTS (Vol. IV); URBAN LIFE AND CULTURE (Vols. IV, V); URBANIZATION (Vols. IV, V).

Lutuli, Albert (Chief Albert John Mvumbi Luthuli) (1898–1967) *President of the African National Congress and first African awarded the Nobel Peace Prize.*

Lutuli was born in SOUTHERN RHODESIA (now ZIMBABWE), where his father was an interpreter for Seventh Day Adventist MISSIONARIES. While still an infant Lutuli lost his father and was sent to his family's ancestral home of Groutville, in the colony of NATAL. In Groutville he lived with his uncle, the locally-elected chief, and attended the mission school. As he entered into adulthood Lutuli trained to become a teacher, attending Adam's College, near DURBAN, eventually joining the school's faculty.

In 1935, at the request of town elders, Lutuli returned to Groutville, where he became the elected chief. With the encouragement of his friend John L. DUBE (1871–1946), Lutuli joined the AFRICAN NATIONAL CONGRESS (ANC) in 1945. Dube died a year later, and Lutuli was elected to succeed him on the Native's Representative Council, initiating his career in national politics. In 1951 Lutuli won election as Natal provincial president of the ANC. The next year he provided strong leadership during the Defiance Campaign, a countrywide, nonviolent campaign against racist pass laws. As a result, the South African government ordered him to resign either his cheiftancy or his position in the ANC, which Lutuli refused to do. The government removed Lutuli from the position of chief in 1952, but his reputation as an uncompromising leader spread.

Later that year Lutuli was elected president general of the ANC. Despite governmental bans on his activities, Lutuli continued to write speeches and occasionally attend ANC conferences, providing respected leadership as the organization fought to gain support among the populace. Lutuli was arrested in 1956 along with 155 other African leaders and charged with high treason. Eventually released, Lutuli continued to lead the fight for African equality in SOUTH AFRICA, and in 1961 he received the Nobel Peace Prize. Confined to house arrest in his later years, Lutuli used his time to dictate his autobiography, *Let My People Go.*

See also: RESISTANCE AND REBELLION (Vol. IV).

Lyautey, Louis H. G. (Marshal Louis Hubert Gonzalve Lyautey) (1854–1934) *French colonial administrator in Morocco*

Born into a family with a long tradition of military service, Lyautey attended the renowned French military academy, Saint-Cyr, and, after serving as a cavalry officer, was stationed in Indochina under the well-known colonial administrator General Joseph GALLIENI (1849–1916). He then became Gallieni's chief of staff on MADAGASCAR, helping Gallieni solidify French control of that island.

In 1900 Lyautey assumed command of a territory in French colonial ALGERIA, and by 1903 he was promoted to general and given the plum assignment of the Algerian territory of Oran and its important port city. There he was responsible for restoring order and enforcing treaties, tasks at which he excelled. In 1912 he became high commissioner of MOROCCO, where he spent most of his remaining military career pacifying the populace. Unlike other colonial administrators, for whom military action was the primary instrument of COLONIAL RULE, Lyautey preferred to use a show of force and manipulate ethnic and other long-standing rivalries among the local population rather than engage in outright warfare. As a result he created what many viewed as a "model" example of the colonization process, bringing European MEDICINE, EDUCATION, and other benefits while still preserving many local customs and traditions. After serving as the French minister of war during World War I (1914–18), Lyautey returned to Morocco, where he was finally successful, after long years of fighting, in putting down the rebellion led by Mohamed ben ABD EL-KRIM (c. 1880–1963). France, however, did not completely establish its control over the whole of Morocco until 1934, nine years after Lyautey had retired.

See also: FRANCE AND AFRICA (Vol. IV); RIF (Vol. IV).

Further reading: William A. Hoisington, Jr., *Lyautey and the French Conquest of Morocco* (New York: St. Martin's, 1995).

Maasai (Masai) Pastoralist ethnic group of the Great Rift Valley region of southern KENYA and northern TANZANIA. Devastated by disease, the Maasai were not stong enough to resist the COLONIAL CONQUEST of their lands. The Maasai migrated to their current homelands in the 15th and 16th centuries. By the 1800s they had established an organized nation and had earned a reputation as fearsome warriors. Dependent exclusively on their cattle herds for nearly all of their needs, the Maasai continuously sought to expand their grazing territories and their herds. Some of the region's other ethnic groups, such as the Luhya, had to defend themselves against frequent Maasai raids. Others, such as the KIKUYU, lived on higher lands unsuitable for cattle and thus established peaceable trading relations. Ultimately Maasai dominance was so complete that even armed Arab slave traders traveling through Maasai lands had to pay tribute to gain safe passage.

Cattle are central to Maasai life. Social standing is based on the ownership of cattle. They also play a crucial role in daily life. Cowhide is used for bedding, shoes, and other items. Cow dung is mixed with mud to build houses. A staple of the Maasai diet is cow milk mixed with cow blood, which is tapped from the cow's jugular without actually killing the animal. Cattle, however, are rarely used for meat by the Maasai, who keep sheep and goats for that purpose.

By the 1830s the Maasai were falling victim to internal dissention, with clan warfare arising over cattle and grazing rights. These conflicts weakened the Maasai's powerful grip on the region, resulting in the loss of land and cattle and opening the Maasai to raids from other peoples. In the late 1800s European MISSIONARIES and explorers preceded the imposition of British COLONIAL RULE. During this same period the Maasai suffered a series of devastating epidemics. Their cattle were ravaged by pleuro-pneumonia and rinderpest, which reduced the Maasai herds to 20 percent of their original size. Famine and drought followed, as did smallpox and cholera, which were brought to the region by Europeans. By 1890 the Maasai population had diminished from around 500,000 to a mere 40,000.

Despite the prowess of their warriors, the Maasai were no longer able to field effective opposition to British encroachment. A final turning point came with the British-built railroad, which by 1899 reached Maasai lands on its way from MOMBASA, on the Kenyan coast, to Lake Victoria. Determined to complete the railroad and facilitate greater access to the interior, the British stamped out the already weakened Maasai resistance. In 1904 they forced the Maasai to sign an agreement that diminished their lands to a third of their original size. By 1910 the Maasai lands had been split in half by the railroad, and over the next three years the Maasai were relocated to reserves far from their homeland.

Beginning in 1914 the Maasai took their case to the colonial courts, but they gained back only minor tracts of land. In the 1930s the British encouraged other peoples to settle in Maasai lands to help reduce "congestion," and by World War II (1939–45), tax policies and the imposition of a cattle quota to provide food for soldiers resulted in the loss of another 70 percent of the Maasai herds. Unfortunately, independence for Kenya in 1963 did little to alleviate Maasai land troubles.

See also: COLONIALISM, INFLUENCE OF (Vol. IV); ENGLAND AND AFRICA (Vols. III, IV, V); MAASAI (Vols. I, II, III, V).

Further reading: Thomas Spear and Richard Waller, eds., *Being Maasai: Ethnicity & Identity in East Africa* (Athens, Ohio: Ohio University Press, 1993).

Maba Diakhou Ba (c. 1809–1867) *Islamic scholar and military leader in the Senegambia region of West Africa*

Maba Diakhou Ba was born into a devout Muslim family living in the kingdom of Baddibu, which straddled the Gambia River. His father provided him with his early education, and he then went on to study with other leading Islamic scholars in what is today SENEGAL. Maba returned to Baddibu and established himself as a popular Islamic teacher, with whom students from all over the SENEGAMBIA REGION came to study.

Throughout Maba's lifetime, Islamic clerics in the region fervently continued the jihads, or holy wars, that reformers had begun in the 18th century in an attempt to both ward off European "infidels" and convert the region to Islam. Maba himself was sympathetic to the project of the respected cleric, UMAR TAL (1794–1864), who was interested in establishing an Islamic TUKULOR EMPIRE in the region between the Senegal and Gambia rivers.

Political division in Baddibu pitted the Soninke on one side, and the Marabouts on the other. The difference was that the Marabouts, a term meaning "holy men," were religious and the Soninke were not. The symbol of this division became drinking: Marabouts abstained from consuming alcoholic beverages on religious grounds and castigated their opponents for imbibing.

In the 1850s Maba returned to Baddibu to teach and study. The more strict and observant Muslims, including Maba, became increasingly frustrated with the impiety they observed in Baddibu's rulers. Finally, in 1861, hostilities broke out between the parties, made more complex by a military intervention that Britain launched to protect its trade in Baddibu's GROUNDNUTS (peanuts), an important export commodity. Eventually Maba and the Marabouts triumphed, and Baddibu was subsequently ruled as a theocratic state according to Islamic law, or *sharia*. After the victory, nearby Muslim states turned to Maba for leadership, and he soon engaged in a series of wars to estab-

lish theocratic rule over the region. By 1865 he was able to field a well-disciplined army of 10,000 men.

From their colonies at the mouth of the Senegal River, both Britain and France worried about the growing power of Baddibu and were especially concerned by Maba's apparent ability to unite the area's Muslims across ethnic lines. In response Senegal's French colonial governor, Louis FAIDHERBE (1818–1889), sent two expeditions to attack Baddibu. Though the French forces could not defeat Maba at first, the ongoing local disputes in Baddibu eventually led to Maba's downfall. In an 1867 battle his army was defeated and Maba was killed. Baddibu, though still independent of COLONIAL RULE, never recovered from Maba's death and disintegrated into internal factions.

Although he had failed to establish a permanent theocratic state in Senegambia, Maba did much to spread Islam throughout the area. Prior to Maba, Muslims were a minority in Gambia's population, but a majority of the country's people now follow Islam.

See also: CASH CROPS (Vol. IV); ENGLAND AND AFRICA (Vols. III, IV); FRANCE AND AFRICA (Vols. III, IV); ISLAM, INFLUENCE OF (Vols. II, III, IV, V); JIHAD (Vol. II); MARABOUT WAR (Vol. III); SENEGAMBIA (Vol. III); SHARIA (Vols. II, V); TORODBE (Vol. III).

Macaulay, Herbert (Herbert Samuel Heelas Macaulay) (1864–1946) *Nigerian political leader*

An outspoken opponent of COLONIAL RULE as well as of the racial injustice that generally accompanied it, Herbert Macaulay was a leading force in the movement that eventually led to independence for NIGERIA. The son of a missionary and the grandson of the famous bishop Samuel Ajayi CROWTHER (1808–1891), Macaulay was educated in mission schools before becoming a clerk in the LAGOS public works department. After studying in England he returned to Lagos, where he became the chief surveyor for the colony.

While in the civil service Macaulay found that he could no longer tolerate the racial discrimination he witnessed in the course of his duties, and he resigned his post. He then went into private practice, becoming a leading critic of British rule, using articles in the *Lagos Daily Times* to develop and spread his ideas. Consistently opposing British efforts to expand or even maintain their administration in Lagos and Nigeria, he fought against everything from fees for a public water system to British efforts to redistribute land.

In 1922 Macaulay organized the Nigerian National Democratic Party, in Lagos. The goals of the party were the same as Macaulay's: self-government, nondiscrimination in both the public and private sectors, compulsory primary EDUCATION for children, and the establishment of higher education at the secondary and university levels.

Toward the end of his life Macaulay became active outside Lagos, too, presiding over the 1944 meeting of the Nigerian Union of Students that eventually gave rise to Nigeria's first national political party, the National Council of Nigeria and the Cameroons (NCNC). His close political ally at the time was Nnamdi AZIKIWE (1904–1996), who took over the full leadership after Macaulay died while touring on behalf of the NCNC.

See also: ENGLAND AND AFRICA (Vol. IV); NATIONAL-ISM AND INDEPENDENCE MOVEMENTS (Vol. IV); NEWSPA-PERS (Vol. IV).

Further reading: Tekena Tamimo, *Herbert Macaulay* (London: Heineman, 1976).

Madagascar

Island located in the Indian Ocean about 242 miles (390 km) off the coast of MOZAMBIQUE on the southern coast of East Africa. Mozambique measures approximately 226,700 square miles (587,200 sq km). In Madagascar there are 18 ethnic groups, the largest and most powerful of which are the MERINA, who make their home in the central highlands. In 1787 King Andrianampoinimerina (c. 1745–1810) came to power, reuniting a Merina kingdom that had been divided among four warring rulers. He built a sizable army, created a rigid class structure, installed seven royal agents to act as mediators between him and his people, and fashioned both a general council of advisers and an inner council of 12 chiefs.

On Andrianampoinimerina's death in 1810, his son, Radama I (r. 1810–1828), took power. With British assistance, Radama centralized Merina control over much of the island. In the 1850s and 1860s French influence grew in Madagascar's capital, Antananarivo. Radama I was succeeded by Queen Ranavalona (1828–1861), who developed local industries with the help of French entrepreneurs. Ranavalona and the royal court converted to Christianity and welcomed French MISSIONARIES.

In 1883, in the early days of the reign of Queen Ranavalona III (r. 1883–1897), the French started a campaign of conquest, taking control of the key port cities of Tamatave and Majunga. In December 1885 France and the Merina signed a treaty mandating that the government pay an indemnity of 10 million francs for the French to leave Tamatave. The queen sought British assistance, sparking French reprisals. In 1894 France insisted that the government agree that all foreign affairs would be handled through the French resident-general, and on October 1, 1895, France established a PROTEC-TORATE over Madagascar. Receiving little support from Queen Ranavalona to institute indirect rule, the French abolished the monarchy on February 28, 1897, installing General Joseph GALLIENI (1849–1916) as Madagascar's governor-general.

Gallieni established a unified rule over the entire island, transforming existing administrative and economic structures into those of a modern state. He implemented a notorious *politique des races* (politics of race) to perpetuate ethnic differences and deflect the growth of Malagasy nationalism. Within the system, the favored status of the Merina people galvanized an ethnic division that persists in Madagascar to this day. Yet by the 1920s it was clear that even a *politique des races* would not contain growing nationalism.

The nationalist movement was invigorated by World War II (1939–45), when, with the help of Prime Minister Winston Churchill (1874–1965) of Great Britain, General Charles DE GAULLE (1890–1970) won Madagascar for the Free French side. Several thousand Malagasy soldiers, conscripted into the French army, served in North Africa and other combat zones. After their return these veterans became nationalist leaders and agitated for independence. In 1946, when France made Madagascar an overseas territory of the French Republic, four Malagasy representatives were elected to serve in the Constituent Assembly in Paris. Political parties proliferated on the island. In March 1947 nationalists launched a rebellion against French rule. The uprising soon engulfed a third of the island. By the time the last of the rebels surrendered in 1949, an estimated 100,000 people had died. Yet the push for independence continued. In 1956 France granted self-government to its other overseas territories, including Madagascar. The country finally became independent on June 26, 1960.

See also: ANDRIANAMPOINIMERINA (Vol. III); COLONIAL CONQUEST (Vol. IV); COLONIAL RULE (Vol. IV); FRANCE AND AFRICA (Vol. IV); MADAGASCAR (Vols. I, II, III, V); RACE AND RACISM (Vol. IV).

Further reading: Mervyn Brown, *A History of Madagascar* (Princeton, N.J.: Markus Wiener Publishers, 2000); Jennifer Cole, *Forget Colonialism: Sacrifice and the Art of Memory in Madagascar* (Berkeley, Calif.: University of California Press, 2001); Pier M. Larson, *History and Memory in the Age of Enslavement: Becoming Merina in Highland Madagascar, 1770–1822* (Portsmouth, N.H.: Heinemann, 2000).

Maga, Hubert (1916–2000) *First president of the independent Republic of Dahomey (present-day Republic of Benin)*

Born in Parakou, in east-central DAHOMEY (now the Republic of BENIN), Hubert Maga was educated at the elite ÉCOLE WILLIAM PONTY in DAKAR, SENEGAL. He then worked as a teacher before becoming a territorial councilor for northern Dahomey, in 1947. Three years later he was elected to represent Dahomey in the French National Assembly, serving as a deputy until 1958.

In 1958, when the FRENCH UNION disbanded and Dahomey became an autonomous member of the French Community, Maga became the country's prime minister. He was charged with the difficult task of uniting Dahomey's disparate ethnic groups in the drive for independence. He succeeded, and in 1960, following a referendum for total independence from France, he was elected president of the new Republic of Dahomey.

In the 1950s Maga led the Dahomean Democratic Movement, a political party that he would later merge with the Dahomean Republican Party to form the Dahomean Progressive Party, which became the coalition government of Dahomey between 1958 and 1960.

The nation that Maga inherited was poor and divided along ethnic and regional lines. Maga, a northerner, was accused by southern Dahomeans of squandering huge amounts of French aid on such unpopular projects as the construction of a presidential palace. In 1963, amid increasing pressure from political opposition, Maga was ousted in a coup d'état by his friend Christophe Soglo (1909–1984), the commander of Dahomey's small army. Although deposed as president, Maga was kept on as Soglo's foreign minister. Maga returned to power and, from 1970 to 1972, was the de facto head of state as chairman of Dahomey's Presidential Council.

See also: COUP D'ÉTAT (Vol. V); ETHNICITY AND IDENTITY (Vol. I); FRANCE AND AFRICA (Vols. III, IV, V).

Maghrib (Maghreb) Region of Northwest Africa along the Mediterranean Sea; it extends from the Atlas Mountains to the coast and includes present-day MOROCCO, ALGERIA, TUNISIA, and part of LIBYA. Much of the coastal region of the Maghrib had been conquered by the Ottoman Empire, which ruled it through much of the 19th century. Under Ottoman rule, individual political entities, however, enjoyed considerable local autonomy, and Morocco never came under Ottoman control. The corsair fleets of coastal cities such as ALGIERS helped finance local governments through their raiding of Mediterranean shipping. As European navies grew in power in the Mediterranean and pushed the corsairs back, coastal-based governments, mostly Arab in make-up, were squeezed and resorted to taxing rural areas. In the process these governments sought to extend their control over the Berber-speaking interior, which in turn led to rebellion.

European governments took advantage of this turmoil and the weakening of the Ottoman Empire to carve out colonies from the Ottoman provinces of the Maghrib. European SETTLERS, who became known as COLONS, emigrated to North Africa, attracted by the temperate climate and fertile soils of the coastal regions. Algeria,

which the French first invaded in 1830, was the first to fall in this process of expansion. This was followed by the French conquest of Tunisia, in 1881, and the Italian conquest of Libya, in 1911. Only in Morocco did the earlier government survive, but it did so as a French PROTECTORATE, with its powers greatly diminished, between 1912 and 1956.

European invaders frequently encountered staunch resistance in the Maghrib. In Morocco, for instance, a former colonial administrator named Mohamed ben ABD EL-KRIM (c. 1880–1963) led an effective political and military resistance against French and Spanish encroachment. He even declared the short-lived independent Republic of the RIF. Eventually, however, the Europeans were able to establish control over the entire region. More settlers followed, especially in Algeria. But the spirit of independence did not die, and following World War II (1939–45), one after another of the countries of the Maghrib gained its independence. In Algeria, violence accompanied the struggle for independence. In Tunisia, however, it came fairly peacefully.

See also: COLONIAL CONQUEST (Vol. IV); FRANCE AND AFRICA (Vol. IV); ITALY AND AFRICA (Vol. IV); NATIONALISM AND INDEPENDENCE MOVEMENTS (Vol. IV); OTTOMAN EMPIRE AND AFRICA (Vol. IV).

Further reading: Ali Abdullatif Ahmida, ed., *Beyond Colonialism and Nationalism in the Maghrib: History, Culture, and Politics* (New York: Palgrave, 2000).

Mahdi, Muhammad Ahmad al- (Muhammad Ahmad ibn Abdallah) (1844–1885) *Sudanese religious leader*

Born in the town of Dongola, in the northern part of present-day Republic of the SUDAN, Muhammad Ahmad ibn Abdallah was a deeply religious person who ultimately led an Islamic renewal movement that was to change the course of Sudanese history. He never traveled outside the Sudan and thus received his education from Sudanese Muslim teachers. Initiated into the Sammaniyya, a reformist Sufi Muslim order, he gained a reputation for holiness and supernatural powers as a result of his teaching and preaching. He actively spoke out against non-Islamic practices such as the wearing of amulets, the consumption of tobacco and alcohol, the wailing of women at funerals, MUSIC in religious processions, and visiting saints' tombs.

To cure the social ills of the Sudan, Muhammad Ahmad ibn Abdallah called on Muslims to observe customary Sudanese religious practices and to conduct human affairs in accordance with the precepts of Islamic law, or *sharia*. Most significantly for the history of the Sudan and the wider region, he represented a direct challenge to Egyptian rule on the grounds that it was oppressive and unjust.

As was a frequent practice among Sufi orders, a band of devout followers gathered around Muhammad Ahmad. Committed to his vision of a more just Sudanese society, these loyal followers came from far away to meet with him at Aba, his island retreat located on the White Nile, some distance south of KHARTOUM.

In 1881 Muhammad Ahmad declared that he was the Mahdi, the long-awaited redeemer ordained by God to appear at the end of time to fill the world with divine justice. Instrumental in this declaration was ABDALLAHI IBN MUHAMMAD (1846–1899), a devout Muslim who became Ahmad's disciple and, later, his designated successor, or *khalifa.*

The concept of the Mahdi is an important element among the Sufi religious orders. The term itself occurs in neither the Quran nor in the traditions of the prophet Mohammed. Rather, it is a popular belief that held that a redeemer would emerge from the chaos and trouble associated with the end of the world and would establish God's justice. To many Sudanese people the social disorder and disruption of the Sudan in the 1870s and 1880s seemed just such a time.

The Mahdi's religiously based challenge to Egyptian authority so alarmed the governor-general that he dispatched a military force to seize Muhammad Ahmad and suppress his movement. The Mahdi and the Ansar, as his followers were known, drove off the Egyptian force, however, and then retreated to a more remote region. This "victory" lent credibility to Muhammad Ahmad's claim to be the Mahdi and inspired dissident elements from across the Sudan to join the Ansar. An ill-advised expedition by an Egyptian provincial governor against the Ansar ended in total disaster, making the Egyptian position increasingly tenuous.

Political events in EGYPT itself further weakened the response to the growing Mahdist challenge. In 1881 Ahmad URABI (1841–1911) led a successful revolt against the khedive's government. In 1882 the British invaded Egypt, restored the khedive, and occupied the country. In the Sudan further uprisings and major military defeats at El Obeid in early 1883 and at Shaykan toward the end of the year doomed Egyptian rule in the Sudan. As a last ditch effort, the Egyptian government sent the British hero, General Charles George GORDON (1833–1885), to Khartoum as governor-general. He arrived in early 1884, but Khartoum was soon besieged by the Mahdi's forces. The city fell to the Ansar in January 1885, with Gordon dying in the fighting, two days

before a relief expedition arrived. The Mahdi himself died six months later. Abdallahi, his *khalifa,* took over control of the MAHDIYYA, as the Mahdi's movement had become known.

Although joint British–Egyptian control over the Sudan was reestablished in 1899 by agreements called the ANGLO-EGYPTIAN CONDOMINIUM, Muhammad Ahmad is still considered the "Father of Independence" by many Sudanese.

See also: ENGLAND AND AFRICA (Vol. IV); ISLAM (Vol. II); ISLAM, INFLUENCE OF (Vols, II, III, IV); *SHARIA* (Vols. II, IV); SUFISM (Vols. II, III).

Further reading: P. M. Holt, *The Mahdist State in the Sudan, 1881–1898,* 2 ed. (Oxford, U.K.: Oxford University Press, 1970).

Mahdiyya (1885–98) Movement and government founded by Muhammad Ahmad (1844–1885), later called al-MAHDI. The Mahdiyya controlled the northern two-thirds of the Sudan from its capital at Omdurman.

Neighboring EGYPT had first established control over much of the Sudan in the 1820s, during the reign of the Ottoman pasha Muhammad Ali (1769–1849). His grandson, Khedive ISMAIL (1830–1895), further extended Egyptian control in the 1860s and 1870s to include an area on the upper Nile about half the size of the continental United States. Khedive Ismail's governor-general for the Sudan, now a province of Egypt, was the British general, Charles George GORDON (1833–1885).

Britain established a PROTECTORATE over Egypt in 1882, after first deposing Khedive Ismail, in 1879, and then defeating the nationalist forces of Ahmad URABI (1841–1911). Britain refused, however, to get involved with the growing challenges that Egypt faced from the south, in the Sudan. Gordon resigned, left the Sudan, and was replaced by an Egyptian, Muhammad Rauf (1832–1888). A crisis in governance was shaping up in the Egyptian Sudan, presenting an opportunity for revolution.

A religious mystic and teacher named Muhammad Ahmad ibn Abdallah took advantage of this opening to lead an Islam-inspired campaign to force the Egyptians, who were viewed as oppressors, out of the eastern Sudan. In 1881 he announced to his followers that he was the Mahdi, the long-awaited redeemer ordained by God to appear at the "end of time" to fill the world with divine justice. His declaration was supported by ABDALLAHI IBN MUHAMMAD, a devout Muslim in search of the Mahdi, who became Muhammad Ahmad's disciple. In return the Mahdi named Abdallahi his *khalifa* (lieutenant, successor).

At times of crisis in the Islamic world it was common for ordinary Muslims to look for the appearance of the Mahdi. Not surprisingly, therefore, as the situation in the Egyptian Sudan worsened, people began to follow Muhammad Ahmad and accept his declaration. Support came from three sources. The first two were genuinely pious Muslims and those with grievances against the Khedive's government. The third element was made up of Baggara cattle nomads who resented the taxes imposed by the Egyptians and who became the core of the Mahdist fighting forces.

Governor-General Muhammad Rauf did not take the emergence of the Mahdiyya seriously enough at first and failed to quash the incipient rebellion. A small force of his troops, using modern weapons, were defeated by the Mahdi's forces. The Sudanese saw this victory as a sign that Muhammad Ahmed was truly the Mahdi. As a result, the Mahdiyya grew in size and strength and soon were in open rebellion against their Egyptian rulers. As his forces recorded more victories, the Mahdi's reputation and stature in the Muslim community grew even greater. In 1883 he achieved a major victory over Egyptian forces by capturing El Obeid, southwest of the capital of KHARTOUM. The Egyptian government then sent General Gordon, charging him to make peace with the Mahdi or to evacuate Khartoum. Gordon failed in his mission and was defeated and killed in 1885 while trying to defend Khartoum. The Mahdi died shortly thereafter, as the British sent a force to defeat him.

After the Mahdi's death his followers organized an independent state under the *khalifa*, Abdullahi. Their capital was at Omdurman, across the river from Khartoum. With its army victorious, this Mahdist state dedicated itself to the expansion and purification of Islam in the Sudan. Internal problems, however, soon began to arise. Khalifa Abdullahi failed to replace the civil servants who had worked for the previous regime and were still loyal to it. He also made the mistake of reinstating the Egyptian system of taxation that had long caused Sudanese resentment.

The Mahdist Sudan fell into a period of conflict and tension. Some of this was caused by competition among the Mahdi's three core groups of supporters, and some was caused by its attempts to expand its borders. It also faced the very real threat that Egypt, now a British protectorate, would attempt a reconquest. That attack finally came in 1896, when a combined British and Egyptian military force invaded the Sudan. The campaign ended with an Anglo-Egyptian victory over the Mahdist state at the Battle of OMDURMAN, in 1898, and the Khalifa's death in battle, in 1899. Despite the collapse of the Mahdist state, however, the Mahdiyya survived as both a political and a religious movement, playing an active role in the affairs of the modern-day Sudan.

See also: ANGLO-EGYPTIAN CONDOMINIUM (Vol. IV); JIHAD (Vol. IV).

Further reading: P. M. Holt, *The Mahdist State in the Sudan, 1881–1898,* 2nd ed. (Oxford, U.K.: Oxford University Press, 1970).

Maherero, Samuel (c. 1854–1923) *Leader of the Herero people in South West Africa (present-day Namibia)*

Born about 1854, Samuel Maherero became the leader of the HERERO following the death of his father, Chief Maherero, in 1870. During the initial years of his reign, the younger Maherero focused on the long-standing war between the Herero and the neighboring NAMA people, with whom the Herero had engaged in raids and skirmishes for decades.

By the 1890s, however, Maherero faced a new challenge in the form of the rapidly developing German colonial empire in SOUTH WEST AFRICA. From a handful of MISSIONARIES, in the mid-1880s, the German presence had steadily grown until, by 1901, it had reached more than 3,000 farmers and other settlers. Beyond this, the number of well-armed and well-trained German troops in the area was steadily increasing. Although he was reluctant to relinquish either territory or control, Maherero initially sought ways to accommodate the German colonists and their armed forces. Risking the anger of many of his subchieftains, in 1894 he even signed a treaty that allowed Germany to place Hereroland under its PROTECTORATE.

That the treaty was a disastrous mistake became clear almost immediately. Not long after it was signed, a small subgroup of the Herero, the Herero Mbandjeru, rebelled against the German forces. Maherero, however, was bound by his treaty and denied them support. To make matters worse, disease wiped out vast numbers of Herero cattle in 1897, bringing Maherero's people to the brink of starvation and forcing them to accept menial jobs under the Germans on railways and in mines.

By the turn of the century the situation had reached a crisis, with the white population steadily increasing and the Herero being consistently cheated of land and cattle. Finally, in 1903, when the BONDELSWARTS, a neighboring Nama clan, rebelled against the German administration, Maherero saw his chance to expel the foreigners and launched his own revolt.

The Germans realized the seriousness of the threat posed by the Herero revolt and quickly made peace with the Bondelswarts before turning their attention to Maherero's rebels. Led by ruthless commander Lothar von Trotha, the well-equipped German army put in motion a battle plan that led to one of the most brutal chapters in the history of colonial Africa. Von Trotha forced Maherero's army toward Waterberg, northeast of Windhoek, and surrounded them, forcing the Herero to retreat toward the Omaheke Desert. Then Von Trotha issued what amounted to an extermination order, declaring that any Herero—man, woman, or child—found within the borders of German-claimed territory would be killed. By 1905 more than 65,000 Herero had died, trapped in the desert without food or water or hunted down and killed by von Trotha's troops. What had once been one of the region's major ethnic groups was virtually wiped out.

Maherero, however, survived, along with three of his sons. Making his way across the northern Kalahari Desert, he reached British territory and settled in BOTSWANA, where he lived until 1923. Eventually he was buried back in his homeland, where to this day people gather to commemorate him and the other Herero leaders.

See also: COLONIAL CONQUEST (Vol. IV); GERMANY AND AFRICA (Vol. IV); KALAHARI DESERT (Vols. I, II); RESISTANCE AND REBELLION (Vol. IV).

Further reading: Horst Drechsler, *Let Us Die Fighting* (Westport, Conn.: Lawrence Hill, 1981).

Maji-Maji Rebellion (1905–06) Uprising among Africans in the southern region of GERMAN EAST AFRICA (present-day TANZANIA) against the oppressive German colonial authorities; it led to the deaths of more than 200,000 Africans from combat and starvation. By the late 1890s Germany had fully established its COLONIAL RULE over German East Africa. The colony was utilized as a source of ivory, and the colonial administration levied heavy taxes on the African population to generate revenue to cover the costs of administration. The German authorities often collected taxes through violence and intimidation. They also installed a forced-LABOR program, requiring African farmers to neglect their own farms to work on government lands in order to produce CASH CROPS, such as COTTON. African laborers received negligible wages, and were often beaten if deemed not productive enough.

At the beginning of the 20th century the spirit medium KINJIKITILE (d. 1905), who claimed to be possessed by a snake spirit, began spreading anticolonial messages throughout the southern area of German East Africa. He asserted that the spirits were calling for the Germans to be driven out. He convinced Africans throughout the region that use of a magic water (*maji maji*, in Swahili) would protect them from German bullets and thus insure their military success. Kinjikitile gained a large following, enough that the Germans had him arrested and executed in 1895 on charges of treason.

With Kinjikitile's death African hatred and resentment boiled over. That same year, the revolt began in the Matumbi hills, where conscripted African workers refused to labor in the government cotton fields. The rebellion then spread, not necessarily in an organized fashion, but in spontaneous outbursts that involved several different ethnic groups. The Maji-Maji fighters targeted Europeans in general, including MISSIONARIES and administrators.

The colonial administration dismissed the early stages of the rebellion as merely a minor riot caused by "sorcery and copious beer drinking following a good harvest." Though initially caught off-guard by the rebellion's ferocity and rapid spread, the Germans recovered almost immediately. Maji-Maji assaults on German ma-

chine gun posts quickly proved the ineffectiveness of Kinjikitile's magic water.

The rebellion's turning point came at Mahenga, a town about 180 miles (290 km) west of DAR ES SALAAM. There German soldiers armed with two machine guns slaughtered thousands of comparatively lightly armed Maji-Maji fighters. The Ngoni, who contributed an army of 5,000, suffered the brunt of the losses. The Maji-Maji Rebellion ultimately marked the destruction of the Ngoni people.

By 1907, using superior armaments and a "scorched-earth" policy, the Germans had fully suppressed the revolt. The devastation of much of the region's land led to a massive famine that resulted in more deaths than the rebellion itself. In all, casualties from the rebellion and the subsequent famine numbered nearly 250,000.

The Maji-Maji Rebellion offers excellent examples of how the history of an event may be skewed or altered by varying perceptions. When Britain took over German East Africa as a League of Nations MANDATE (it became British TANGANYIKA), British historians made a point of highlighting German colonial atrocities. This may have been for the purposes of justifying Britain's own control of the region and portraying themselves in a better light through comparison. The British also suggested that the role of spirit guidance and magic in the rebellion demonstrated how the Africans were not advanced enough to govern themselves.

In addition, the general perception of African unity against the Germans may not be entirely true. Interviews with elder members of the Lurugu people suggest the Lurugu were relatively open to the German presence in the region, seeing the Germans as potential allies against the Mbunga people who had been raiding Lurugu villages.

The Maji-Maji Rebellion and revolts in German SOUTH WEST AFRICA (present-day NAMIBIA) at about the same time alerted Germany and the rest of Europe to the deep currents of RESISTANCE AND REBELLION that ran through the African populations they had colonized. Germany immediately altered its colonial policies in East Africa, easing the use of violence as a means of enforcement and encouraging higher levels of EDUCATION and health standards for Africans.

In a larger scope the rebellion demonstrated a level of anticolonial unity among African peoples that was not previously seen in the colonies. The Maji-Maji Rebellion also served as inspiration for those who, in the 1960s, led the struggle for an independent Tanzania.

See also: BONDELSWARTS (Vol. IV); CHIMURENGA (Vol. V); ENGLAND AND AFRICA (Vols. III, IV, V); GERMANY AND AFRICA (Vol. IV); NATIONALISM AND INDEPENDENCE MOVEMENTS (Vols. IV, V); NGONI (Vol. III); SPIRIT POSSESSION (Vol. I).

Malan, D. F. (Daniel Francois Malan) (1874–1959)
South African prime minister (1948–1954) and founder of the National (or Nationalist) Party

Born near Riebeek West, Cape Province, SOUTH AFRICA, Malan was a childhood friend of his future political rival, Jan Christiaan SMUTS (1870–1950). After earning a doctorate in divinity from the University of Utrecht in Holland, Malan returned home to take up duties as a minister of the Dutch Reformed church. An ardent Afrikaner nationalist and champion of the AFRIKAANS language, he left the ministry in 1915 to became editor of *Die Burger* (The Citizen) a pro-Afrikaner CAPE TOWN daily newspaper. He entered parliament in 1918, and in 1924 he became minister of the interior under J. B. M. HERTZOG (1866–1942), the Nationalist Party prime minister. In 1933, however, Malan broke with the Hertzog faction of the Nationalist Party over Hertzog's political alliance with Smuts against the extreme nationalists. Malan then formed the hardline Purified Nationalist Party.

Malan favored neutrality during World War II (1939–45) and reconciled with Herzog, who also favored neutrality. Together they formed the National Party, which maintained a minority vote in the House of Assembly during the war years. After the war, in 1948 Malan led the National Party to a surprising electoral victory over Smuts's United Party. Malan then became both prime minister and minister of external affairs.

Malan and the National Party were committed to the policy known as APARTHEID, or "separateness," that sanctioned white supremacy and the political, economic, and social subordination of black South Africans. Malan stepped down as prime minister in 1954 after winning further gains for the National Party in the national elections of 1953. He then retired from political life.

See also: AFRIKANERS (Vol. IV, V).

Malawi
Present-day southeastern African country measuring about 45,700 square miles (118,400 sq km) in size and surrounded by TANZANIA, MOZAMBIQUE, and ZAMBIA. From the late 1800s until 1964 Malawi languished under British COLONIAL RULE as the colony of NYASALAND.

By the 18th century the SLAVE TRADE, which had existed in the region since the ninth century, began to flourish as Portuguese contact created a new market for Arab and Swahili merchants. By the turn of the 19th century the lucrative trade in captives had brought the militaristic Ngoni people to the region. It also brought the YAO, who became dominant slave traders in the area east of Lake Malawi (Lake Nyasa). KISWAHILI-speaking traders from the coast spread Islam to the Lake Region and the Shire Highlands in the 1860s. Christianity was introduced through the efforts of the Scottish missionary and explorer David LIVINGSTONE (1813–1873), who alerted the European community to the horrors of SLAVERY in East Africa. By the early 1870s Christian MISSIONARIES had established a European presence, and by the 1890s British forces had eliminated the region's slave trade. The missionaries desired the protection afforded by a colonial government, and the people of Malawi also were wary of the influence of diamond mogul and imperialist Cecil RHODES (1853–1902) as well as the potential for a Portuguese annexation of the region. This led the British to establish the Shire Highlands Protectorate, in 1889. In 1891 the Shire Highlands Protectorate became the British Central African Protectorate, and in 1907 the territory was named Nyasaland.

Malawi during the Colonial Era: Nyasaland
The British set about building an infrastructure of roads and railways, and CASH CROPS such as tea and tobacco were grown on large European-owned plantations. The small community of European SETTLERS constituted the primary interest of the colonial government, and African needs were continuously neglected. To fund the administration of the colony, Britain implemented a "hut tax" and gradually suppressed traditional African farming methods, essentially forcing Africans to either work on plantations or find jobs outside of Nyasaland to support themselves. Large numbers migrated to SOUTH AFRICA to form part of the LABOR force in the GOLD mines and elsewhere.

One of the migrants from Malawi was Clements KADALIE (1896–1951), who founded an important labor union, the Industrial and Commercial Workers' Union, which became the first African mass movement in South Africa.

Though some African groups had initially welcomed colonial rule, many, such as the Yao and the CHEWA, put up firm resistance. In 1915 the Yao missionary John CHILEMBWE (c. 1872–1915) initiated a revolt called "The Rising" in response to British oppression. The rebellion was quickly put down, but Chilembwe's efforts inspired future nationalist movements.

In 1944 Nyasaland's first political party, the Nyasaland African Congress, came into being. Five years later

Africans were finally allowed seats on the protectorate's legislative council. The potential for increased participation in the colonial government by the African majority vanished, however, when the British, against vehement African protest, linked Nyasaland with NORTHERN RHODESIA (present-day Zambia) and SOUTHERN RHODESIA (now ZIMBABWE) to form the CENTRAL AFRICAN FEDERATION in 1953.

The federation was intended to give the colonies the economic stability needed to rival the influence of South Africa. Africans in Nyasaland, however, saw the move as a reassertion of colonial rule and a step toward an entrenched, white-dominated minority government like that of the virulently racist regime in South Africa. The federation's capital was established at SALISBURY, in Southern Rhodesia, and most of the industrial and financial strength of the federation was concentrated in that colony. Nyasaland received hardly any of the supposed benefits of federating, adding fuel to the burgeoning nationalist movement in the PROTECTORATE.

In 1957 the Nyasaland African Congress leader, Hastings Kamuzu BANDA (c. 1898–1997), led protests against British plans to merge the federated colonies into a single state. By 1959 anticolonial demonstrations were turning violent, leading the British authorities to declare a state of emergency, imprison Banda, and ban the congress. While in prison Banda founded the Malawi Congress Party, becoming the party's president-for-life after his release in 1961. The nationalist efforts led the British to abandon their plans for further consolidation of the colonies, and in 1963 the Central African Federation was dissolved. That year, Banda became prime minister, a position he retained until the following year, when Nyasaland became independent Malawi. In 1966 the country became a republic, with Banda as its president. Due to years of British colonial neglect, Banda inherited a country that was among the poorest on the continent.

See also: ENGLAND AND AFRICA (Vols. III, IV, V); MALAWI (Vols. I, II, III, V); NATIONALISM AND INDEPENDENCE MOVEMENTS (Vol. IV).

Further reading: Martin Chanock, *Law, Custom, and Social Order: The Colonial Experience in Malawi and Zambia* (Portsmouth, N.H.: Heinemann, 1998).

Mali   Present-day central West African nation, about 478,800 square miles (1,240,100 sq km) in size, stretching north into the Sahara desert, where it shares borders with ALGERIA and MAURITANIA. Other countries bordering Mali include (east to west) NIGER, BURKINA FASO, IVORY COAST, GUINEA, and SENEGAL. The population is concentrated in the southern half of the country in the watershed of the Niger River. Beginning in 1890, the region of modern Mali became part of France's colonial empire as the colony of FRENCH SOUDAN.

French Soudan was the site of parts of the empires of Ghana and Mali, two of Africa's most celebrated states. In the middle of the 19th century, two Islamic empires, the TUKULOR EMPIRE of UMAR TAL (1794–1864) and the smaller MANDINKA empire of the DYULA warlord SAMORI TOURÉ (c. 1830–1900), had come to dominate the region. France, however, indicated its colonial intentions in 1855, when it founded a fort at Médine, in the Niger River valley. By 1880 France had claimed the territory as French Upper Senegal but faced formidable resistance to further incursion from the Tukulor and Mandinka forces. In 1890 France renamed the territory French Soudan.

Mali during the Colonial Era: French Soudan Ultimately France defeated the Tukulors in 1893, and two years later French Soudan became part of FRENCH WEST AFRICA (Afrique Occidentale Française, AOF). Samori Touré's Mandinka Empire, the final major resistance to French control, collapsed in 1898.

A somewhat amorphous territory, in 1904 French Soudan was made part of the administrative federation of Haut-Sénégal-Niger (Upper Senegal–Niger) but then became French Soudan again, after the Upper Volta (present-day Burkina Faso) and Niger colonies were split off, in 1919 and 1922, respectively. France administered Soudan with its customary policy of indirect rule when and where it could, governing through appointed local chiefs. The colonial ECONOMY revolved around the cultivation of COTTON and GROUNDNUTS (peanuts) for export.

The Republic of Mali was named after the Mali Empire, recalling the region's past glory. Mali's first president, Modibo Keita, claimed the Mali emperors as his ancestors.

After World War II (1939–45) France allowed French Soudan to establish political parties as part of French colonial reforms. These parties eventually merged to form the Sudanese Union, which was tied to the interterritorial AFRICAN DEMOCRATIC ASSEMBLY. In 1958 French Soudan became the Sudanese Republic, an autonomous member of the French Community, with the Sudanese Union-African Democratic Rally as its dominant political party. The next year, the Sudanese Republic linked with Senegal to form the Mali Federation. The federation was short-lived, however, as political differences led Senegal to secede a year later. In 1960 the Sudanese Republic became the fully independent Republic of Mali, under the Marxist leadership of Modibo Keita (1915–   ).

See also: COLONIALISM, INFLUENCE OF (Vol. IV); FRANCE AND AFRICA (Vols. IV, V); GAO (Vol. II); MALI, REPUBLIC OF (Vols. I, II, III, V); MALI EMPIRE (Vol. II); KEITA,

In this photo, taken in 1937, Muslim worshippers in the city of Jenne, in French Soudan (today's Mali), gathered near the wall of the mosque. © *New York Times*

MODIBO (Vol. V); SONGHAI (Vols. II, III); SUNDIATA (Vol. II); TIMBUKTU (Vol. II).

Further reading: Patrick Manning, *Francophone Sub-Saharan Africa, 1880–1995*, 2nd ed. (New York: Cambridge University Press, 1998).

Mami Wata (Mammy Water) Water spirit revered primarily in the coastal regions of the West and Central Africa. In the 20th century a number of the spirit's attributes were controversially linked to the influence of COLONIALISM. Mami Wata is the pidgin English name for the powerful water spirit also known by the names Ezenwaanyi, Nnekwunwenyi, Ezebelamiri, and Nwaanyi mara mma. Belief in Mami Wata is found mainly in the regions of the present-day Republic of BENIN, TOGO, southwest GHANA, NIGERIA, as well as CAMEROON and the Democratic Republic of the CONGO. Its origins are somewhat unclear. The Mami Wata deity seems to have first appeared in southern Nigeria in the early 20th century. However, the Mami Wata priesthood, known as the Mamaissii, is also associated with Dahomean Vodoun, the

ancient RELIGION based on spirit worship and the precursor of the Vodou religion practiced in Haiti.

Flora Nwapa (1931–1993), one of the first Nigerian women writers to be published in English, used Mami Wata extensively in her writing, most notably in her children's book *Mammywater* (1979). Scholars have noted that Nwapa used the spirit as a symbol of feminist ideals, since Mami Wata embodies the sense of independence characteristic of urban women with their significant degree of economic autonomy.

Mami Wata is worshipped primarily in coastal or riverine areas, where drownings and other aquatic disasters are attributed to the spirit. However, Mami Wata is also a spirit of excess and overabundance and is believed to sometimes bestow great wealth on her favored followers. Devotees of Mami Wata wear the spirit's colors, red and white, with red representing the corporeal, such as blood, illness, and heat, and white representing the spiritual, such as clarity, transparency, and truth. Typically depicted as a fair-skinned mermaid with long black hair and large, piercing eyes, Mami Wata also is often shown with snakes wrapping her torso, representing the supernatural as well as the male aspect of the water spirit sometimes assumes.

Despite her ties to abundance and wealth, followers of Mami Wata believe the spirit is barren, or infertile. In Nigeria Mami Wata is often considered the cause of barrenness and venereal disease (which can be a cause of infertility), though she is also believed to grant fertility to barren women who devote themselves to the spirit. The spirit is also believed to have the ability to take the form of a promiscuous woman, and thus prostitutes are often referred to as *mami watas*. Mami Wata's association with the rampant problem of veneral disease in Africa demonstrates how attributes of the spirit have been influenced by the problems related to URBANIZATION.

Though there is a long tradition of belief in water spirits in Africa, Mami Wata displays unique, if controversial, ties to colonialism. Anthropologists have suggested Mami Wata's image, with light-colored skin and "European" features, symbolizes the power and wealth of the white woman during the period of COLONIAL RULE in Africa. On the other hand, many images of the deity come from the Indian Hindu tradition. Mami Wata's typical representation as foreign and as possessing, as well as desiring, wealth (in modern times, her shrines often feature consumer products such as designer perfumes and sunglasses) also seems to indicate that her image has been highly influenced by colonialism and urbanization.

Other anthropologists have pointed out that in Africa white has long signified the world of spirits. There are also known traditions involving the use of chalk to whiten the skin to symbolically counteract the "redness" of people in states of high emotion or sickness. Though the influence of colonialism on the cult of Mami Wata is debatable, the symbolic possibilities are difficult to ignore and may well be representative of African attempts to assimilate the disruptive effects of colonialism and accelerated urbanization into long-standing indigenous spiritual traditions.

See also: NWAPA, FLORA (Vol. V); RELIGION, TRADITIONAL (Vol. I).

mandate Order or commission from the League of Nations to establish a responsible government over a conquered territory in the aftermath of World War I (1914–18). In Africa the League of Nations authorized the victorious Allies, or mandatories, to administer the colonies that Germany forfeited as a result of their defeat. At the conclusion of the First World War, control over the former German colonies passed to France, Britain, and Belgium. The French received the larger parts of TOGO (formerly the German colony of TOGOLAND) and CAMEROON (formerly Kamerun), both located in western Africa. Britain received a smaller portion of Togoland, which it administered together with the neighboring GOLD COAST COLONY (known today as GHANA). Britain also received the western part of Cameroon, which it administered along with the colony of NIGERIA, Cameroon's neighbor to the west.

The colonies of the former GERMAN EAST AFRICA were mandated to Britain and Belgium, with Britain receiving TANGANYIKA (today's TANZANIA) and Belgium receiving RUANDA-URUNDI (the present-day countries of RWANDA and BURUNDI). German SOUTH WEST AFRICA (today's NAMIBIA) was handed over to SOUTH AFRICA, since the South African army had wrested the territory from Germany at the outset of the war.

This apportioning of African lands was not merely a repeat of the European PARTITION that came about from the BERLIN CONFERENCE of 1884–85. Instead the mandates were placed under the jurisdiction of the League of Nations, a body created to protect the people in European colonies from the predations of the colonizing powers following the war. The new organization assigned its mandates in the spirit of the "Fourteen Points" described by American president Woodrow Wilson (1856–1924) regarding the reestablishment of world peace. Among the points was a call for the impartial adjustment of all colonial claims based on the equality of the interests of the indigenous population. In other words, contrary to the prewar administration of the former German colonial territories, the mandatories were now supposed to run the colonies in a manner that provided equally for the advancement of Africans.

The mandated territories were to be held in trust until Africans were able to control their own affairs. Most Western observers believed that a century would be required to complete the transformation. However, the devastation resulting from World War II (1939–45) and the rapid emergence of AFRICAN NATIONALISM AND INDEPENDENCE MOVEMENTS that followed in its wake led the European countries to disengage quickly from the mandate system. With the collapse of the League of Nations in 1946, the mandates were reconstituted as TRUST TERRITORIES under the auspices of the United Nations. By 1962 all the trust territories except South West Africa had become independent nations.

The situation for the people of South West Africa was complicated by the fact that, unlike the other African mandates, their territory was administered as an integral part of South Africa, as if it were a northern province. Because of the nature of South Africa's administration and the intransigence of its APARTHEID government, it was not until 1990 that South West Africa became the independent country of Namibia.

See also: BELGIUM AND AFRICA (Vol. IV); COLONIAL RULE (Vol. IV); ENGLAND AND AFRICA (Vol. IV); FRANCE AND AFRICA (Vol. IV); GERMANY AND AFRICA (Vol. IV); INDEPENDENCE MOVEMENTS (Vol. V); LEAGUE OF NATIONS AND AFRICA (Vol. IV); UNITED NATIONS AND AFRICA (Vol. V).

Further reading: Michael D. Callahan, *Mandates and Empire: The League of Nations and Africa, 1914–1931* (Brighton, U.K.: Sussex Academic Press, 1999).

Mande (Manding, Mandingo, Mandingue) A diverse population of some 46 LANGUAGE communities dispersed throughout West Africa but predominantly in present-day GUINEA and the Republic of MALI. While the term Mande represents a group of many languages, four of them are mutually intelligible: MANDINKA, Maninka, Bamana (Bambara), and DYULA. The Mande languages appear to have originated in the region of the headwaters of the Senegal, Gambia, and Niger rivers.

Most Mande-speaking peoples trace their historical origin to the ancient West African Empire of Mali, which spoke Maninka. They base their heroic origins on the epic of Sundiata, the traditional founder of the Mali Empire. With their common language and shared historical past, the Mande, despite being spread across a large geographic area, retained a cultural identity.

Photographed in 1947, these Mande musicians from the French colony of Upper Niger are playing traditional flutes. © *New York Times*

A shared Mande cultural identity aided SAMORI TOURÉ (c. 1830–1900), a late-19th-century Dyula leader, in building a large state in the western savanna regions. Samori spoke Maninka and utilized Mande political institutions for anchoring his state at the local level. However, after the French defeated Samori in 1898, much of the Mande-speaking heartland became a part of France's colonial empire.

French authorities originally intended for the Mande-speaking territories to be part of the larger FRENCH WEST AFRICA. Because of cultural continuity and a history of strong governance, though, the French found it difficult to bring these territories into the fold. In an effort to diminish Mande strength, France tried to divide and conquer, creating individual colonial entities that broke apart the Mande-speaking population, grouping them instead with members of other language families. For example, Maninka speakers were split between the colony of FRENCH SOUDAN (present-day Mali) and Guinea, and those in Guinea were grouped with 19 other language groups living between them and the coast. Despite the efforts of the French, however, most Mande speakers were able to cross the artificially contrived borders, thereby allowing their commercial activities to continue to thrive.

See also: BAMANA (Vol. I); BAMBARA (Vols. II, III); FRANCE AND AFRICA (Vols. III, IV, V); MALI EMPIRE (Vol. II); MANDE (Vols. I, II); SUNDIATA (Vol. II).

Mandela, Nelson (Nelson Rolihlala Mandela; Madiba) (1918–) *South African lawyer and resistance leader*

Mandela was born in the village of Qunu, located in the XHOSA-speaking Transkei region of the eastern Cape Province of SOUTH AFRICA. His father, a high counselor to the paramount chief of Thembuland, died when Mandela was still a young boy. After his father's death Mandela was placed in the care of the paramount chief and was raised to become the principal counselor to the heir to the chieftaincy. Eschewing the local affairs and politics of the Transkei, Mandela instead studied to become a lawyer.

After being dismissed from FORT HARE COLLEGE for his part in a student demonstration, Mandela went to JOHANNESBURG and completed his degree via correspondence at the University of South Africa. While completing his degree Mandela joined the AFRICAN NATIONAL CONGRESS (ANC) in 1942, quickly joining a burgeoning youth movement within the organization led by Anton Lembede (1914–1947).

This group of young ANC members included Walter SISULU (1912–2003) and Oliver TAMBO (1917–1993), whom Mandela had befriended at Fort Hare. They thought that the gradualist tactics of the ANC leadership were ineffective and believed that a more prudent course

of action was to promote African nationalism with the goal of self-determination. In 1942 they formed the African National Congress Youth League, which quickly exerted influence within the ANC power structure.

In 1950 Mandela was elected to the ANC national executive committee, and in 1952 he was elected national volunteer-in-chief. The duties of this position included traveling the country to organize resistance related to the ANC's defiance campaign, which called for mass civil disobedience in response to South Africa's racist APARTHEID legislation. Mandela was arrested for his role in organizing the defiance campaign. Moreover he was banned from attending ANC gatherings and was prohibited from leaving Johannesburg.

In December 1952 Mandela and Oliver Tambo opened a legal partnership in Johannesburg. Their endeavor was the first black law office in the country.

Mandela was arrested again in 1956 along with 155 other political activists and charged with high treason, a crime punishable by death. Mandela and the codefendants were detained while the five-year trial progressed. A highly respected lawyer, Mandela acted as defense attorney for the accused, ultimately earning acquittals for the most serious charges. He was eventually released but the trial brought about a change in Mandela's ideology of resistance. In 1958 he married Nkosikazi Madikizela (1934–), who was known as Winnie and became a prominent freedom fighter in her own right.

In 1960 the South African government banned the ANC, and Mandela and his colleagues were forced to go underground to continue their resistance movement. By 1962 they had come to the conclusion that the use of violence was inevitable, leading to the formation of the ANC's military arm, Umkhonto we Sizwe (Spear of the Nation), with Mandela as commander-in-chief.

See also: AFRIKANERS (Vols. IV, V); MANDELA, NELSON (Vol. V); RESISTANCE AND REBELLION (Vol. IV); UMKHONTO WE SIZWE (Vol. V).

Further reading: Nelson Mandela, *Long Walk to Freedom* (New York: Little Brown & Company, 1995).

Mandinka
West African people who are part of the larger MANDE group; also the name of the LANGUAGE spoken by these people. Speakers of Mandinka and the closely related Maninka claim descent from groups that were once a part of the Mali Empire. Their languages are two of the four mutually intelligible forms of the larger Mande group, which consists of 46 separate languages in

all. Because they are understood by speakers of other Mande languages, Mandinka and Maninka have long been used as the lingua franca of trade and commerce across much of West Africa.

Many Mandinka speakers ultimately fell under British COLONIAL RULE in GAMBIA. However, those Mandinka speakers who were part of the TUKULOR EMPIRE of UMAR TAL (1794–1864) fell within the French colonial orbit following Umar's defeat, in 1863. After 1898 Maninka speakers, too, came under French control, as the French extended their influence eastward following the defeat of SAMORI TOURÉ (c. 1830–1900).

Today the Mandinka ethnic group can be found stretching from the mouth of the Gambia River inland across the West African savanna region. Mandinka speakers live mostly in The Gambia, GUINEA-BISSAU, and SENEGAL, and Maninka speakers are found throughout MALI, GUINEA, BURKINA FASO, SIERRA LEONE, and LIBERIA.

See also: MALI EMPIRE (Vol. II); MANDINKA (Vol. II).

Maranke, John (1912–1963) *Prophet and founder of an apostolic African church in Zimbabwe*

John Maranke was born Muchabaya Ngomberume, in northeastern SOUTHERN RHODESIA (present-day ZIMBABWE), to the daughter of a prominent SHONA chief. He took his mother's clan name of Maranke when, on July 17, 1932, he had a revelation inspiring him to preach Christianity.

After receiving an elementary education at a Methodist mission school, Maranke worked as a laborer in the town of Umtali. He then experienced a long period of illness during which he had dreams that culminated in his revelation. Afterward Maranke believed himself to be a new John the Baptist, and he set out to baptize and proselytize among his close circle of family and neighbors. Eventually he founded a church, Humbowo Hutswa we Vapostori (The New Revelation of the Apostles), claiming that his visions were providing further guidance on its structure and rituals. His church's practices drew heavily on the Christian Old Testament, the teachings of Christian MISSIONARIES, and older indigenous religious beliefs. Healing was also an important component of church ritual.

During the 1940s and 1950s Maranke continued to develop the Vapostori church, and upon his death in 1963, his two sons, Abel (d. c. 1988) and Makebo (d. 1992) took over the church leadership. In the decades since African independence, as with many other African Pentecostal churches, the Vapostori Church has continued to grow and attract large numbers of new adherents. Presently, more than 70 years after its founding, the Vapostori church, also known as the Apostolic church of John Maranke, has more than a half-million members.

> The latter years of the colonial era in Africa saw the rise of many PROPHETS AND PROPHETIC MOVEMENTS. Like Maranke, their founders often claimed to be guided by visions that followed a near-death experience.

See also: CHRISTIANITY, INFLUENCE OF (Vols. II, III, IV, V); HEALTH AND HEALING (Vols. IV, V); RELIGION (Vols. III, IV, V).
Further reading: Bennetta Jules-Rosette, *African Apostles: Ritual and Conversion in the Church of John Maranke* (Ithaca, N.Y.: Cornell University Press, 1975).

Margai, Milton (Sir Milton Augustus Striery Margai) (1895–1964) *First prime minister of independent Sierra Leone*

A mild-mannered conservative who remained pro-British throughout his life, Margai was the son of a wealthy merchant. Educated in the best schools in SIERRA LEONE, he graduated from FOURAH BAY COLLEGE, in FREETOWN. He then went to England to pursue his medical studies at the University of Durham and the Liverpool School of Tropical Medicine.

From the late 1920s until the 1950s Margai served in Sierra Leone as a medical officer in the government service, where he became known for his work in prenatal and postnatal care. He was also instrumental in training midwives and in improving conditions for children in the country.

Margai's mild manner did not preclude political activism. Although he was a life-long moderate, he was a prominent nationalist and one of the key figures in Sierra Leone's independence movement. Rising from the Bonthe District Council, to which he was first elected in 1930, he eventually served in the Protectorate Assembly. In 1946 he joined the Sierra Leone Organization Society, the ancestor of the Sierra Leone People's Party (SLPP), which was founded during the early 1950s by Margai and his brother Albert (1910–1980). Freetown politician Constance CUMMINGS-JOHN (1918–2000) helped organize women's support for the party. The SLPP was Sierra Leone's first nationalist party, and it consistently advocated a path of self-government for Sierra Leone within the British Commonwealth.

Through the early 1950s Margai assumed a number of increasingly important political roles, rising from the legislative council to the executive council, and by 1953 to the ministries of health, AGRICULTURE, and forestry. In 1954 he became chief minister when Sierra Leone was granted self-government, and he was reappointed chief minister in 1957. During the latter part of the 1950s

Margai's SLPP was split, as his brother Albert, who was more radical, led a splinter group to form a rival political party. Still, Milton Margai held on to power and was named premier, and later prime minister, as the country moved toward full independence. He died in office on April 28, 1964, after a short illness. Albert Margai succeeded Milton as prime minister but lacked his popularity, and in 1967 he lost the election to Siaka Stevens (1905–1988).

See also: ENGLAND AND AFRICA (Vol. IV); NATIONALISM AND INDEPENDENCE MOVEMENTS (Vol. IV).

Marrakech (Marrakesh) City in west-central MOROCCO, located at the foot of the Atlas Mountains. Founded in 1062 during the era of the Almoravid Empire (c. 1060–1146), Marrakech developed into a prosperous commercial center for trans-Saharan trade. After serving as the capital under the Sadis, in the 16th century the city became a military post for the successor Alawite rulers. In 1912 the Mauritanian leader, Ahmad al-Hibah, took control of the city in an effort to stave off French COLONIAL CONQUEST. The French defeated him that same year and captured Marrakech. During the subsequent period of French COLONIAL RULE, which lasted until Morocco gained its independence in 1956, the modern part of the city was built. It contrasts sharply with the ancient sector of the city, called the medina.

By 1920 a railroad connected Marrakech to the coastal ports of Casablanca and Safi, thus enhancing the city's role as a center of commerce. Since independence in 1956 the city has continued as an important commercial center and has become a significant tourist destination. The population was estimated at 243,000 in 1960.

See also: ALMORAVIDS (Vol. II); ATLAS MOUNTAINS (Vol. I); FRANCE AND AFRICA (Vols. III, IV, V); MARRAKECH (Vols. II, III, V); SADIAN DYNASTY (Vol. II); URBAN LIFE AND CULTURE (Vols. IV, V); URBANIZATION (Vols. IV, V).

Mau Mau Name, meaning "Burning Spear," given to KIKUYU guerilla fighters during a long period of violent insurrection in KENYA during the 1940s and 1950s. Although the roots of the Mau Mau rebellion lay in the whole history of British involvement in Kenya, the more immediate cause lay in the 20th-century land policy of the Kenyan colonial government.

In the years following World War I (1914–18) the colonial authorities encouraged emmigration from both Britain and continental Europe, appropriating thousands of square miles of land for the new settlers. As immigrants arrived, more and more land was taken, primarily from the Kikuyu ethnic group. By the 1940s just a few thousand Europeans owned nearly one-third of Kenya's land, mostly in the fertile highlands, while millions of Africans were forced to live on inferior land that they could never officially own.

Protests against the government's policies took place throughout the 1920s and 1930s, but despite the efforts of Jomo KENYATTA (c. 1891–1978) and other Kikuyu leaders, no lasting changes were affected. The situation finally came to a head as Africans who had served Britain during World War II (1939–45) returned home to find that Britain was not keeping either of its wartime promises to return land to Africans and rescind discriminatory social policies.

In 1946 security forces at a demonstration in NAIROBI killed several demonstrators, sparking violent acts of retribution throughout the Kenyan countryside. During this period of instability a revolutionary Kikuyu cadre emerged, eventually calling itself the Land Freedom Party (LFP). The main goal of the LFP was the end of minority white rule. Unlike the more conservative Kenya African Union, which had led antigovernment protests since the 1920s, the LFP rebels were willing to use violence to achieve their ends.

The LFP army was an assemblage of cells, or units, usually numbering no more than a hundred fighters per cell. Their weapons were simple, usually bows and arrows, spears, short machetes, or firearms that were either homemade or captured from settlers and British soldiers. In spite of their lack of supplies the LFP army soon built itself into a formidable force. In the months that followed the initial flurry of violence, activity by Mau Mau, as the rebel movement was by then called, was limited. However, as sympathy for their goals grew, and as fear of Mau Mau attacks increased, the rebels grew stronger.

A key element to the strength of the movement was the so-called Mau Mau oath. Drawing on Kikuyu traditions in which oaths are considered sacred bonds, Mau Mau members pledged never to inform on one another and to drive whites from power, killing them if necessary. The pattern of sporadic Mau Mau attacks with a limited government response continued for several years. In 1952, however, the Mau Mau assassinated a well-known supporter of the British, Chief Wariuhu, and the government clamped down immediately. Within two weeks Britain declared a state of emergency, and as thousands of British troops poured into the country, the colonial government began a massive roundup of Kenyan political leaders. In the initial sweep more than 4,000 Africans, among them Jomo Kenyatta, were detained.

When Mau Mau activity continued, the British government arrested and detained more Kikuyu and forcibly moved others to "protected" villages where they lived under the total control of the colonial authorities. In trying to suppress the Mau Mau uprising the British raided and destroyed entire communities, often torturing detainees and holding them without charges or trials.

In April 1954, as part of what was called Operation Anvil, colonial police rounded up the entire African population of the city of Nairobi, separating out approximately 70,000 Kikuyu from the 100,000 detainees. More than 30,000 of these Kikuyu were then taken to prison camps and their families sent to overcrowded "native reserves." Given such tactics, it is not surprising that by late 1954 almost one-third of all Kikuyu men had been put in prison.

Throughout Kenya the colonial authorities instituted a system of quick and immediate "justice." Taking the Mau Mau oath became a capital offense under the rules of the state of emergency, and public hangings—outlawed in Britain a century earlier—became commonplace in Kenya. More than 1,000 Africans were hanged between 1953 and 1956. Those oath takers who were spared the gallows were coerced under the threat of torture to take counteroaths, or "cleansing vows," by which they foreswore Mau Mau and pledged their loyalty to the colonial government.

Although Mau Mau activity had declined markedly by 1956, the authorities still refused to lift the state of emergency, and they continued to hold tens of thousands of Kikuyu in detention. Following an incident in which a group of Mau Mau prisoners were beaten—and 11 of them killed—a public outcry finally made the government release the remaining detainees and relax the state of emergency.

The Mau Mau uprising marked a military defeat for the Kikuyu, but it forced the Kenyan and British authorities to reevaluate East African colonial policy. Within months of lifting the state of emergency, talks were underway in London to effect a transitional government that would place Kenya on the road to independence and majority rule.

See also: ENGLAND AND AFRICA (Vol. IV); MBOYA, TOM (Vol. IV); NATIONALISM AND INDEPENDENCE (Vol. IV); RESISTANCE AND REBELLION (Vol. IV).

Further readings: Frank Furedi, *The Mau Mau War in Perspective* (Athens, Ohio: Ohio University Press, 1989); Wunyabari O. Maloba, *Mau Mau and Kenya* (Bloomington, Ind.: Indiana University Press, 1998); David Throup, *Economic & Social Origins of Mau Mau 1945–53* (Athens, Ohio: Ohio University Press, 1988).

Mauritania Present-day country of northwestern Africa, some 398,000 square miles (1,030,800 sq km) in size and bordered by ALGERIA, MALI, SENEGAL, and WESTERN SAHARA; during the 19th century the region of present-day Mauritania fell prey to the French campaign of COLONIAL CONQUEST in West Africa.

The Maures, who were the indigenous Arabic peoples controlling the region's trade, had established profitable coastal commercial ties with the Portuguese in the 15th century. Maure traders charged European traders a *coutume,* or annual fee, for trade rights. During the 19th century, however, attempts by the Maure to reestablish their own sovereignty in the region met with defeat at the hands of French colonial forces.

By 1840 France had laid claim to Senegal and was expanding its West African colonial empire, which led to their control over neighboring Mauritania. Under the French governor of Senegal, Louis FAIDHERBE (1818– 1889), French troops conquered the Maure Walo kingdom and launched assaults on the Brakna and Trarza emirates. Despite the Maure effort to capture Saint-Louis, in 1855 France was victorious, establishing a PROTECTORATE over the defeated Maure and ending the *coutume* payments. This success led Faidherbe to send expeditions to the interior in both 1859 and 1860 to extend French COLONIAL RULE beyond the coast. However, successive colonial administrators after Faidherbe failed to build on his initiative, and by the start of the 20th century, France had done little to strengthen its control over Mauritania. The *coutume* had by this time been reinstated, a telling sign of France's administrative weakness and the Maures' staunch independence.

Mauritania during the Colonial Era The situation changed under a new policy of "peaceful penetration" initiated by French administrator Xavier Coppolani (1866–1905). From 1901 to 1905 Coppolani, who came to be known as the "Pacific Conqueror" by the Maure, employed divide-and-conquer tactics along with efforts at protection and peace. At the time the Maure were involved in constant internal warfare and raiding and were enthusiastically supplied with firearms by French commercial interests in St-Louis who became rich through the weapons trade. Much to the dismay of these French companies, Coppolani negotiated with two of Mauritania's three most powerful marabouts, or Islamic leaders, Shaikh Sidiyya BABA (1862–1926) and Shaikh Saad Bu, winning their support for a French-imposed peace over the region. By 1904 Coppolani had established firm French control over the Senegal River valley, eventually extending French power into the south-central area of Mauritania. Also in 1904 France established Mauritania as a protectorate separate from Senegal, and later that year it became the Civil Territory of Mauritania.

Coppolani's campaign of PACIFICATION failed in the northern Adrar region, however, where the third influential marabout, Shaykh Ma al-Aynin, sided with MOROCCO in its claims to Mauritania. Coppolani was killed in 1905, and three years later France began to conquer the Adrar through force. Although occasional conflicts occurred as late as 1955, France had effectively subdued any resistance by 1912.

In 1920 Mauritania became part of FRENCH WEST AFRICA (Afrique Occidentale Française, AOF). The administration of Mauritania differed from that of the other AOF colonies, however, in that the marabouts were instrumental in the governance of the colony. Also, due to France's relatively late "pacification" of Mauritania, many of the *cercles,* or administrative subdivisions, of the colony were headed by military commanders. Maure warrior leaders were also enlisted in the colonial government, in keeping with Coppolani's original efforts at maintaining peace in the region.

During World War II (1939–45) the pro-German Vichy government of France assumed control of AOF, installing racist policies and practicing increasingly brutal forms of forced LABOR. Toward the end of the war Mauritania and AOF came to side with the Free French forces of Charles DE GAULLE (1890–1970). In 1944, as a reward for French African colonies' contribution to the war effort, colonial reforms were instated, including an abolition of forced labor and an expansion of EDUCATION and health care. In 1946 the new French constitution established Mauritania and the other French African colonies as overseas territories of the FRENCH UNION. French citizenship was granted to all, as was the right to vote, to form territorial assemblies, and to send representatives to the French National Assembly.

In 1946 suffrage was limited to only a few groups, such as government officials, property owners, and the members of trade and LABOR UNIONS. The right to vote was gradually extended to a wider range of people until 1956, when it became universal in the French African colonies.

In 1946 Mauritania's first political party, the socialist-minded Mauritanian Entente, was formed by the Senegalese leaders Léopold SENGHOR (1906–2001) and Lamine GUÈYE (1891–1968). Headed by Horma Ould Babana, the Mauritanian Entente handily won the 1946 territorial assembly elections but was defeated just as easily in 1951 by the Mauritanian Progressive Union (MPU). Babana fled to Morrocco, where he formed the National Council of Mauritanian Resistance.

In 1956 the Loi Cadre, or Overseas Reform Act, gave the French African colonies domestic autonomy, and Moktar Ould Daddah (1924–) became prime minister. Daddah was immediately faced with the problem of Mauritania's sharply divided populations. The northerners, who were mostly of Arab descent, supported union with Mo-

rocco. Mauritanians in the south, on the other hand, more closely identified with the populations of sub-Saharan Africa and preferred to join Mali and Senegal in the Mali Federation. The latter group formed parties such as the Gorgol Democratic Bloc and the Union of the Inhabitants of the River Valley to oppose the northern, pro-Morocco Maures. In response to the desires of both factions, Daddah called for unity, and in 1958 the MPU, the Mauritanian Entente, and the Gorgol Democratic Bloc merged to form the Mauritanian Regroupment Party. The new party supported total independence, rejecting union with Morocco or the Mali Federation. Unity did not last long, however. In 1958 the Mauritanian National Renaissance Party, or Nahda, was formed in opposition to the Regroupment Party's desire to keep close ties with France.

In 1958 Mauritania became an independent member of the French Community, and in that same year it became the Islamic Republic of Mauritania. In 1960 it declared full independence. Daddah once again brought together the various sides of Mauritania's political scene, becoming the country's first president, in 1961. The nation's various political parties, including Nahda and Daddah's Mauritanian National Union, merged to form the Mauritanian People's Party, which was declared the only legal party in Mauritania.

At independence the vast majority of the population lived in the rural areas in the southwestern part of the country, subsisting either on farming in the river regions or by means of nomadic PASTORALISM. The country had very few university graduates and less than a thousand high school students. Its TRANSPORTATION infrastructure was extremely rudimentary, with few paved roads and no port facilities. Nouakchott, Mauritania's national capital, had been only a small village as late as 1958, when a massive construction project was started to accommodate 15,000 residents.

See also: COLONIALISM, INFLUENCE OF (Vol. IV); FRANCE AND AFRICA (Vols. III, IV, V); MAURITANIA (Vols. I, II, III, V); NOUAKCHOTT (Vols. II, V).

Further reading: David Robinson, *Paths of Accommodation: Muslim Societies and French Colonial Authorities in Senegal and Mauritania, 1880–1920* (Athens, Ohio: Ohio University Press, 2000).

Mauritius   Island nation in the Indian Ocean, situated approximately 500 miles (805 km) east of MADAGASCAR. Although it measures only 720 square miles (1,870 sq km), by the 1850s Mauritius was the sugar capital of Britain's empire, producing than 100,000 tons (90,718 metric tons) each year. In the sugar fields, LABOR had been done by African slaves brought from the mainland, but in 1935 Britain, which acquired Mauritius from France in 1814, abolished SLAVERY throughout its empire. By the 1830s indentured laborers imported from British-ruled India were doing the bulk of the work in the sugar industry. It was not until the 1870s that the indenture system was officially terminated, but even after that, conditions for the workers remained horrible. By the early 20th century more than 450,000 Hindu and Muslim laborers had been brought to the island to work the plantations. The Mauritian sugar industry, however, had already begun to decline after the 1860s. Producers cut costs, centralized production, and encouraged individuals to pool their capital to establish small farms, thus worsening the conditions of the workers. These efforts proved incapable of stopping the slide, and the island never regained its former economic significance.

Despite being a British colony, the island continued to hold on to its French linguistic and social traditions. The Franco-Mauritian elite class—made up primarily of plantation owners, officials, and other people of wealth—retained its political power. It was not until the early 20th century that the Creole middle class, made up of both people with mixed-race ancestry and descendants of African slaves, achieved inroads into the political system. The Indo-Mauritians, traditionally forced to the bottom of the island's social ladder, did not make any significant progress in terms of political or social power until well into the 1920s and 1930s.

In the era of DECOLONIZATION following World War II (1939–45) Mauritius moved slowly toward nationhood. A new constitution in 1947 and another in 1958 gradually extended the franchise and broadened the political base of power. However, discord arising from the island's ethnic diversity—which was compounded by the entrenched political power of the elite—consistently led to conflict, including periods of rioting, in the years leading up to independence in 1968.

See also: CASH CROPS (Vols. IV, V); COLONIAL RULE (Vol. IV); COLONIALISM, INFLUENCE OF (Vol. IV); ENGLAND AND AFRICA (Vols. III, IV, V); ETHNIC CONFLICT IN AFRICA (Vol. V); FRANCE AND AFRICA (Vols. III, IV, V); MAURITIUS (Vols. I, II, III, V); MONO-CROP ECONOMIES (Vol. IV).

M'baye d'Erneville, Annette (1926–) *Senegalese poet best known for writings emphasizing a love of humanity and the empowerment of African women*

Born in Sokone, Western SENEGAL, M'baye was educated at the Saint-Joseph de Cluny à Saint-Louis and the École Normale d'Institutrices, a teacher's college for girls located near DAKAR. She ultimately became general superintendent of the École Normale before continuing her studies in Paris. In 1959 M'Baye returned to Senegal, where she became the commissary of Regional Information, in Diourbel. In 1963 she founded the magazine *Awa*, and shortly thereafter became Program Director for Radio Senegal. She published her first book of poetry, *Poèmes africains*, in 1965. This was followed by *Kaddu*

(1966), *Chanson pour Laïty* (1976), *Le Noël du vieux chasseur* (1983), and *La Bague de cuivre et d'argent* (1983). Her fine poetry and journalistic leadership have made M'Baye one of the influential African literary voices of her generation.

See also: LITERATURE IN COLONIAL AFRICA (Vol. IV); LITERATURE IN MODERN AFRICA (Vol. V).

Mbeki, Govan (1910–2001) *South African political activist, intellectual, and journalist*

Govan Mbeki was born into a staunch Wesleyan Methodist family in the Transkei, located in the Eastern Cape Province, SOUTH AFRICA. He remained closely connected to the region and its peasant population for the duration of his life. After graduating with a bachelor's degree in political studies and psychology from FORT HARE COLLEGE in 1937, he assumed a teaching position at Adams College in NATAL. This missionary-administered secondary school fired him, however, because of his political activism, most notably relating to the AFRICAN NATIONAL CONGRESS (ANC), which he joined in 1935. To make a living he managed a cooperative store, and from 1939 to 1943 he edited *Territorial Magazine* (later renamed *Ikundla yaBantu*). In the early 1940s Mbeki also served as a representative to the Transkeian Territories General Council, which was a regional legislative body with limited authority over local matters.

Mbeki's first loyalty was to the ANC, a political body that his able leadership helped to build into a strong and disciplined organization in the Eastern Cape. In 1943 his literary and intellectual talents were utilized in the drafting of "African Claims," a seminal ANC document that called for the principles of the ATLANTIC CHARTER to be applied to the treatment of blacks in South Africa. In 1954 he became editor of the Eastern Cape for *NEW AGE*, a political newspaper. Mbeki was instrumental in organizing the Congress of the People, held July 25–26, 1955, in Kliptown, outside JOHANNESBURG. This conference resulted in the formulation of the FREEDOM CHARTER, which subsequently served as the blueprint for the struggle of the ANC and other black opposition groups dedicated to overthrowing APARTHEID. Mbeki continued as an active member of the ANC for the remainder of his life and lived to see his son, Thabo Mbeki (1942–) elected president of South Africa in 1999.

See also: MBEKI, GOVAN (Vol. V); NATIONALISM AND INDEPENDENCE MOVEMENTS (Vol. IV).

Mboya, Tom (Thomas Joseph Odhiambo Mboya) (1930–1969) *Trade unionist and political activist in Kenya*

Born to LUO parents who were field workers on a sisal plantation, Mboya saw first-hand the hardships and poverty that were part of life for most Africans in colonial

KENYA. Receiving an elementary education, he was forced to drop out of secondary school in order to help send his siblings to school. He had two years further training as a sanitary inspector and after graduation found employment in NAIROBI, where he also became active in trade union affairs.

Mboya soon organized a national union of government workers, which in turn led to his developing a network of contacts with union leaders in both Britain and North America. By 1953, at the age of only 23, he became the general secretary of the new Kenyan Federation of Labor, which was, in the absence of African-dominated political parties, the only national organization speaking for Africans in Kenya.

After a period studying in India and at Oxford University, in England, Mboya visited the United States to establish study programs for Kenyan students. Returning to Kenya in 1956, he immediately put his organizational experience to work, using demonstrations and political pressure to force the British colonial authorities to provide Africans with civil liberties. As those rights began to be granted—including the right to establish political parties—Mboya began the People's Convention Party, which had as its slogan the words that became a catchphrase among the African nationalist and independence movements: *Uhuru Sasa*, or "Freedom Now." In 1957, in the first Kenyan election in which Africans were allowed to vote, Mboya was elected to the Legislative Council.

For the next half-dozen years Mboya was a leading figure in the drive for Kenyan independence. In 1958 he served as the chair of the All-African Peoples' Conference, where such future African leaders as Patrice LUMUMBA (1925–1961), Kwame NKRUMAH (1909–1972), and Robert Mugabe (1924–) met to formulate strategies for furthering the cause of African independence. He also was instrumental in obtaining the release from prison of the prime symbol of the Kenyan independence movement, Jomo KENYATTA (c. 1891–1978), and in setting up the multiracial government that guided Kenya in the transition to independence. A firm believer that newly independent nations like Kenya needed the stability of a single-party government, Mboya also was one of the initial organizers of the Kenya African National Union, the party that dominated the nation during the early days of independence.

See also: ENGLAND AND AFRICA (Vol. IV); LABOR UNIONS (Vol. IV); MBOYA, TOM (Vol. V); NATIONALISM AND INDEPENDENCE MOVEMENTS (Vol. IV).

Further reading: Tom Mboya, *Freedom and After* (Boston: Little Brown & Company, 1963).

medicine While traditional medicine has sustained the African population for thousands of years, Western biomedicine is relatively new to Africa. In the 19th century, a few Africans—James Africanus Beale HORTON (1835–1883) is an example—trained abroad as medical doctors and returned to Africa to practice. However, it was the institution of colonialism that was largely responsible for the introduction and spread of Western biomedicine across Africa.

At the time when colonial doctors and MISSIONARIES were establishing African biomedical clinics, a new way of understanding disease was gaining momentum in the West. The new, SCIENCE-based framework, called the *germ theory* of disease, upended African traditional medical systems that often attributed the source of disease to human or supernatural agents. In light of the germ theory, missionary healers chastised African patients for using traditional medicine, which the Europeans thought of as irrational WITCHCRAFT.

The colonial and missionary healers tended to lump all of the non-Western traditional medical practices into one category, thereby devaluing the different medical systems and treatments that were, and still are, available in Africa. Different traditional medical systems successfully used herbs, rituals, prayers, charms, minerals, animal products and byproducts, song, DANCE, offerings, and foods for treatment of many different biological and social conditions. As Western-style medicine became more common, however, traditional healers began to incorporate some of the Western medicines into their practice, as well.

Victoria Hospital at Lovedale Institute in the eastern Cape Province of SOUTH AFRICA is an example of the hospitals that medical missionaries established in many parts of the continent. Founded by Church of Scotland missionaries in 1898, it immediately established an experimental nursing school for Africans, which, by 1902, evolved into a three-year nursing course. In 1908 one of the early course graduates, Cecilia Makinwane (b. 1880), became the first registered African nurse in South Africa. To honor Makinwane's accomplishment, the South African government in Mdantsane named a 1,450-bed hospital for her.

The practice of Western biomedicine spread especially rapidly after World War II (1939–1945), when inexpensive drugs, many developed during the war, became more widely available. In general the first Africans to have access to Western medicine were the laborers and residents who lived near the urban areas, where the colonial doctors also lived. The more rural areas, however,

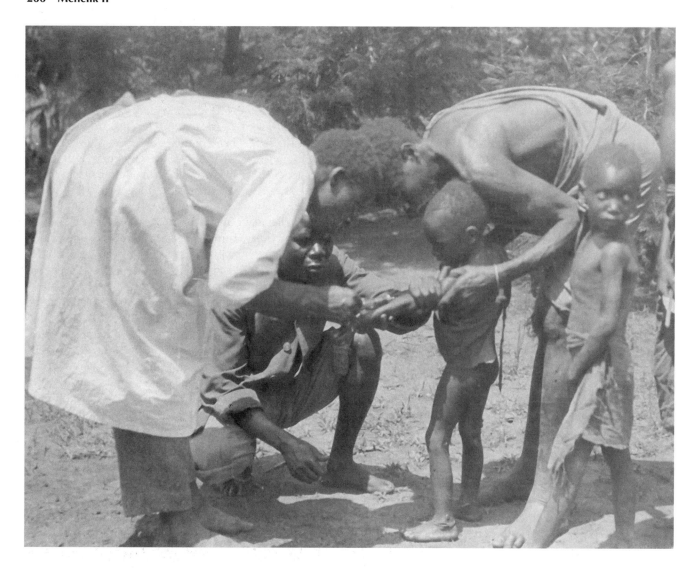

By the early 1940s, when this photo was taken, innoculations against sleeping sickness were an important step forward for Western-style medicine in tropical Africa. © *Actualit/New York Times*

were exposed to colonial medicine only through missions. While colonialism was responsible for forcing traditional healers to keep their practices secret from, it was also responsible for numerous positive changes in health conditions. For example, vaccination programs begun during the period eventually led to the elimination of diseases, such as smallpox, that had long plagued the continent.

See also: COLONIALISM, INFLUENCE OF (Vol. IV); DISEASE IN COLONIAL AFRICA (Vol. IV); HEALTH AND HEALING IN COLONIAL AFRICA (Vol. IV) MEDICINE (Vols. I, II, III, V).

Further reading: Philip D. Curtin, *Disease and Empire: The Health of European Troops in the Conquest of Africa* (New York: Cambridge University Press, 1998); Adell Patton, Jr., *Physicians, Colonial Racism, and Diaspora in West Africa* (Gainesville, Fla.: University Press of Florida, 1996).

Menelik II (Sahle Mariam) (1844–1913) *Ethiopian emperor*

One of Africa's greatest 19th-century rulers, Menelik II took his name from the reputed founder of ETHIOPIA, the legendary son of King Solomon and Queen Makeda (of Sheba). During his long, tumultuous reign, he transformed Ethiopia into a relatively modern state with a strong army. Born in 1844, Menelik was the grandson of Sahle Selassie (1795–1847), who set himself up as the ruler of the independent kingdom of SHOA. From an early age, Menelik—or Sahle Mariam, as he was named at birth—was raised at the royal court of the Ethiopian emperor TÉWODROS II (1820–1868), who conquered Shoa and took both Menelik and the youngster's mother to his capital. There Menelik learned the arts of war and politics, rising to be the governor of Shoa. Eventually Menelik fell out of royal favor when Téwodros suspected him of joining regional warlords in a planned rebellion. Menelik was imprisoned but fled to Shoa, where he crowned himself king.

Menelik's early reign in Shoa offered glimpses of policies he would follow later in life. For example, in a time of religious animosity and strife he exercised religious tolerance, allowing Islam and traditional African religions to be practiced along with the Coptic Christianity of his own ETHIOPIAN ORTHODOX CHURCH. He also played a wily political game, attempting to maintain a neutral path in the tangled web of Ethiopian, British, and Mahdist interests. Equally important, he recognized the need for Ethiopia to modernize and gain access to European technology, especially in weaponry. He felt this was crucial for countering the increasingly aggressive moves of the European powers. Toward that end he purchased state-of-the-art weapons from Italy and France and hired Europeans to instruct Ethiopians in everything from military science to ARCHITECTURE.

When Téwodros was succeeded on the Ethiopian throne by Kassa (1831–1889), who took the name of YOHANNES IV, Menelik initially made moves to try to take power from the new emperor. In the end, however, he negotiated a compromise in which he exchanged recognition of Yohannes's authority for guarantees that he would succeed Yohannes as emperor. In the meantime he continued to rule in Shoa, forging treaties with various European nations and expanding his borders southward into Harer.

Téwodros met his end in 1868, after becoming involved in a complex dispute with Great Britain. The British military force sent to Ethiopia easily defeated Téwodros, who committed suicide rather than surrender. The emperor's quick defeat further convinced Menelik of the need to develop a modern, well-equipped army.

Yohannes's rule came to an end in 1889. Facing encroachments from Italy in the east, and from the Sudanese Mahdists in the west, Yohannes attempted to defend his

As they prepare to receive U.S. president Theodore Roosevelt's Diplomatic Treaty Mission of 1903–04, Emperor Menelik II and members of his royal court entered the Aderach, or Audience Hall, in the palace at Addis Ababa, Ethiopia. © *Library of Congress*

kingdom from both enemies. Ultimately he was not successful, and he was defeated and killed by the Mahdists in March, 1889.

Realizing that Ethiopia might easily slip into feudalism or even anarchy, Menelik worked quickly to consolidate his power. Armed as they were with sophisticated weapons, his forces were able to put down opposition from the various princes and warlords who held local power in the country. However, the newly crowned emperor was less decisive in dealing with external threats. Not sure that his forces would be able to defeat an all-out Italian invasion, Menelik preferred to negotiate rather than directly confront Italy. He therefore held back, signing the Treaty of Wichale and allowing the Italians to set up their colony in neighboring ERITREA.

Ultimately, that treaty was to prove the undoing of Italy's further colonial aspirations in Africa. Apparently using the kind of subterfuge that had marked many Europeans' dealings with African leaders, the document was issued in two versions, one Italian and the other, Amharic. The two were apparently not the same, with the Amharic version guaranteeing Ethiopia's independence and the Italian version essentially reducing Menelik's kingdom to an Italian PROTECTORATE. When he discovered the deceptive strategy, Menelik took decisive action. Rejecting the treaty, he declared his full intention to oppose any Italian attempts at taking control, backing up his assertions with new arms purchased from France and Russia. Italy, on its part, dispatched an army under General Oreste Baratieri (1841–1901), the celebrated Italian hero who vowed to capture Menelik and bring him to Rome in a cage.

Despite a few initial successes, Baratieri proved no match for Menelik, who amassed a force of almost 200,000 soldiers, the majority of them equipped with modern rifles. Learning too late of the size of the force opposing him, Baratieri found himself not only isolated deep within Ethiopian territory but also pressed by his own government to achieve a quick victory.

Both sides dug in to relatively secure positions, where they remained until a lack of food and the urgings of the Italian government finally forced Baratieri to advance. At the Battle of ADOWA, on March 1, 1896, the Italians met with defeat unlike any other suffered by modern Europeans in Africa. Unable to hold off Menelik's troops, Baratieri's force 20,000 was routed, taking upwards of 10,000 casualties. To add to the humiliation, several hundred Italians and their Eritrean allies were taken prisoner and held in Menelik's capital of ADDIS ABABA until they were ransomed by the Italian government.

Menelik used his victory to secure a treaty guaranteeing Ethiopian independence. To the surprise—and disapproval—of many Ethiopians, however, he did not attempt to negotiate a complete Italian withdrawal. Instead, possibly in order to use the Italians in his international diplomatic game or possibly because he was not sure he could win a full-scale war with a major European power, he allowed Italy to keep its colony in Eritrea.

Hailed as a major military victor, Menelik was visited and courted by diplomats from virtually every European nation. Secure in his power, he continued the policies he had begun earlier, modernizing his nation and making sure that it would remain independent. He built roads, railroads, and bridges, encouraged the use of European MEDICINE and technology, and instituted monetary and postal systems for the nation. He also developed schools, hospitals, and even hotels. Above all, he increased the centralized authority of the emperor and the bureaucrats who carried out his commands.

Many of Menelik's achievements proved short-lived, however. Not long after the turn of the 20th century, he began suffering a series of seizures that left him increasingly incapacitated. He tried to set up a line of succession that would allow his grandson, Lij Iyasu (1896–1935), to take power. For a time Menelik's brilliant and powerful queen, the Empress Taitu (c. 1840–1918), was able to hold on to power, ruling in her husband's name. Upon his death, however, the weak and incompetent Iyasu came to the throne, which he held only a few years. With Iyasu's fall from power in a 1916 coup d'état, Ethiopia returned to a short period of the decentralization until, in the 1920s, HAILE SELASSIE (1892–1975) began to reconsolidate Ethiopia on his way to becoming emperor.

See also: COPTIC CHRISTIANITY (Vol. II); MAHDI, AL-MUHAMMAD AHMAD (Vol. IV); MAKEDA, QUEEN (QUEEN OF SHEBA) (Vol. I); MAHDIYYA (Vol. IV); ENGLAND AND AFRICA (Vol. IV); ITALY AND AFRICA (Vol. IV).

Further reading: R. H. Kofi Darkwah, *Shoa, Menelik and the Ethiopian Empire* (London: Holmes and Meier, 1976); Harold G. Marcus, *The Life and Times of Menelik II* (New Jersey: Red Sea Press, 1995); Chris Prouty, *Empress Taytu and Menelik II* (New Jersey: Red Sea Press, 1987).

Mensah, E. T. (Emmanuel Tettey) (1919–1996)
Ghanaian musician and band leader

In the aftermath of World War II (1939–45), a new MUSIC form, HIGHLIFE, emerged in West Africa. It was heard first in GOLD COAST COLONY (present-day GHANA) and then in NIGERIA. At the forefront of this musical genre was E. T. Mensah. Beginning in 1930, as a schoolboy in his hometown of ACCRA, Mensah played the piccolo in the student Accra Orchestra. Within a few years he and his brother started the Accra Rhythmic Orchestra. By this time he had also started playing the saxophone and trumpet. Indeed, it was as a trumpeter and singer that he was to gain fame. During the Second World War European musicians with a jazz background influenced the existing dance bands such as those of Mensah and his brother.

Mensah began to experiment with a blend of American swing, West Indian calypso, older indigenous music forms, and other musical genres, leading to his particular brand of highlife music. He also moved away from the big band format that had held sway on the popular music scene to play in smaller groups, such as his own Tempos, which he founded in 1948. This was also a period of increasing political activity due to heightened NATIONALISM AND INDEPENDENCE MOVEMENTS and also increasing URBANIZATION with a new and vibrant URBAN LIFE AND CULTURE. E. T. Mensah and the Tempos captured the spirit of the times, and his musical influence spread to Nigeria, where he was soon touring. It was not long before the music reached England, where several cities had significant West African and West Indian populations who picked up and spread highlife music. In 1953 Mensah and his band made a highly successful tour of England, where he recorded what were to be some of his biggest hits. By all accounts the high point in Mensah's career was performing with the great American jazz musician, Louis Armstrong (1900–1971), who came to Ghana in 1957 to help celebrate its independence.

The emergence of a new popular form of African music in the 1960s, known as Congolese, was to eclipse highlife in popularity. Mensah continued to perform and record highlife songs, as did others he influenced, but they were no longer in the forefront of popular music in West Africa. However, for his admirers, who were many, Mensah always will remain the "king of highlife."

Merina Largest ethnic group of the island nation of MADAGASCAR. The Malagasy-speaking Merina had near-complete control of the island before it became a French PROTECTORATE, in 1895. The early Merina evolved out of the mixing of the indigenous African Vazimba people and the Indonesian Hova. After nearly one hundred years of warfare, the two groups began assimilating into one another. By the 15th century the Merina had founded a small kingdom in the elevated central plateau of Madagascar. By the end of the 18th century, the Merina king Andrianampoinimerina (c. 1745–1810) had established his capital at Tananarive (which is now called Antananarivo). There he centralized his power and forged a powerful kingdom known as Imerina.

The Merina had gained much of their prosperity through the SLAVE TRADE, exchanging captives for European firearms. King Radama I (c. 1793–1828) ended the slave trade in return for British military supplies, which were used to further Merina dominance over the various coastal peoples. Radama also opened his kingdom to MISSIONARIES who, through their efforts to educate and win converts, helped spread Merina culture even further. Radama's successor, his wife Ranavalona I (r. 1828–1861), was strongly anti-foreign, first outlawing Christianity and then, in 1837, expelling all foreigners from Imerina. Ranavalona's son, Radama II (1829–1863) reestablished European ties during his two-year reign from but was assassinated for his pro-French position. By the 1880's, under Queen Ranavalona II (r. 1868–1883), who converted to Christianity, and Ranavalona III (1861–1917), the highly-centralized Merina state came to dominate all of Madagascar save for parts in the south and west.

In 1883 the French began their COLONIAL CONQUEST of Madagascar. By 1895 French troops occupied Tananarive, and the Merina soon came under French COLONIAL RULE. The Merina monarchy was abolished in 1897, and Queen Ranavalona III was deported to ALGERIA, where she remained for most of her life.

Under the Fench policy of *politique des races* (race politics), the Merina benefited more than the other Malagasy peoples on the island. Regardless, Merina nationalism grew during World War I (1914–18) and World War II (1939–45), in which Malagasy troops played a role. Madagascar was under the control of the French Vichy government until the British seized the island in 1942, turning it over the Free French the following year. In 1947 Merina and other Malagasy nationalists rebelled, but the French crushed the uprising.

At independence, in 1960, Philibert Tsiranana (1910–1978) of the Tsimihety people assumed the presidency of Madagascar and established policies that favored the coastal regions over the inland Merina. However, due to their long-time dominant position on the island and the favoritism they received during the colonial era, the Merina continue to be prominent within the civil service, business, and professional sectors of Madagascar.

See also: ANDRIANAMPOINIMERINA (Vol. III); FRANCE AND AFRICA (Vols. III, IV, V); INDONESIAN COLONISTS (Vol. II); MERINA (Vol. III); RACE AND RACISM (Vol. IV).

Milner, Alfred (Sir; Lord Alfred Milner) (1854–1925) *British administrator in South Africa*

Milner excelled as a student, attending Oxford before a brief stint as a journalist. He became the private secretary to Lord Goschen (1831–1907), who, in 1890, used his influence to appoint Milner as the undersecretary of finance for the British colonial administration in EGYPT. In 1892 Milner published *England in Egypt,* which documented British involvement in Egypt and argued for an even greater British presence in the country.

Milner's reputation earned him the positions of high commissioner of SOUTH AFRICA and governor-general of the CAPE COLONY. He faced problems caused by the failed JAMESON RAID (1895), an even that aggravated tensions between the governing BOERS and British UITLANDERS of the TRANSVAAL Republic. Milner became concerned that, without heightened involvement, Britain would lose its

South African interests, and he spoke out for the equal treatment of Uitlanders in the AFRIKANER REPUBLICS of the Transvaal and ORANGE FREE STATE. He also saw the GOLD mines of the WITWATERSRAND in the Transvaal as an essential economic resource for establishing British dominance in Africa. Various strategies for gaining an upper hand in the region, conducted by both Milner and Joseph Chamberlain (1836–1914), secretary of state for the colonies, led to the eventual outbreak of the ANGLO-BOER WAR (1899–1902).

Britain annexed the Transvaal and Orange Free State while the war was ongoing, and in 1901 Milner was called upon to administer the states. The following year Milner helped draft the Treaty of VEREENIGING, which ended the war.

As the Governor of Transvaal, Milner guided the reconstruction of the war-ravaged, economically depressed Boer territories. Facing a LABOR shortage in the gold mines, Milner made the highly controversial move of importing indentured Chinese workers. He continued his efforts in South Africa until 1905.

See also: ASIAN COMMUNITIES (Vol. IV); COLONIAL CONQUEST (Vol. IV); COLONIAL RULE (Vol. IV); ENGLAND AND AFRICA (Vol. IV).

Mineral Revolution Period at the end of the 19th century marked by the discovery of large mineral deposits in modern-day SOUTH AFRICA. Africans mined and traded GOLD long before the arrival of Europeans. In the late 1860s, however, the traditional role of minerals in African society changed. In 1866, alluvial DIAMONDS were discovered in the Vaal River. Soon after, dry deposits of diamonds were found at what would become the city of KIMBERLEY. The discovery initiated a massive migration to what was a sparsely populated region. In 1871, Britain annexed the diamond fields in the face of opposing Boer claims from the ORANGE FREE STATE (OFS) and the TRANSVAAL.

By the 1880s Kimberley had quickly expanded to become the largest city in the southern African interior. DIAMOND MINING at Kimberley became the underpinning of the region's economy. Imports to CAPE COLONY and NATAL increased dramatically, allowing their governments to make improvements to infrastructure. At the same time, diamonds soon eclipsed agricultural products as the colonies' primary EXPORTS, and a regional banking system began to take root to handle the changing financial environment. The capital-intensive nature of diamond mining led to a consolidation of the small-scale miners, and the industry ultimately fell under the control of Cecil RHODES (1853–1902) and the company he headed, DE BEERS CONSOLIDATED MINES, LTD.

In 1886 the discovery of gold in the WITWATERSRAND ushered in a new phase to the Mineral Revolution. After the find, thousands of miners, 10 times the number at Kimberley, descended upon the area. A MINING camp emerged, eventually becoming the city of JOHANNESBURG, which would quickly eclipse Kimberley in importance.

Unlike the earlier diamond discovery, the gold deposits were located in a gold-bearing reef that required deep mine shafts, extensive machinery, and a complex refining process. The deposits were also within the borders of the Transvaal Republic, which was under the Boer government of Paul KRUGER (1825–1904). Though vexed by the chaos brought by the influx of foreigners, whom they termed UITLANDERS, the BOERS realized that the tax income generated by the mines gave them the opportunity to establish their freedom from British influence.

Despite the Boers' goal of autonomy, by the 1890s the British colonies to the south moved closer to unification with the Boer republics of Transvaal and the OFS. The British victory in the ANGLO-BOER WAR (1899–1902) ultimately resulted in the unification of the defeated Boer republics with the Cape Colony and Natal to form the UNION OF SOUTH AFRICA in 1910.

The effects of the Mineral Revolution went far beyond the political reorganization of southern Africa. The LABOR required by the new industries resulted in massive African migration to the region, especially from ZIMBABWE (called SOUTHERN RHODESIA at the time) and MOZAMBIQUE. The free movement of laborers, however, forced the mining industry to offer incentives to attract the needed workforce. The resulting power of African laborers became a problem for the colonial administrators, who sought to maintain white supremacy in the region. As a result Africans were subjected to pass laws, which were used to monitor and restrict their movements and which compelled them to live in mineworker compounds that essentially functioned as forced-labor camps. The concentration of the laborers gave rise to new urban centers and the phenomena of URBANIZATION. Eventually the shift in settlement patterns destroyed African rural life and made the traditional homestead economy unsustainable.

The era of the Mineral Revolution also was marked by an improvement in communication capabilities and infrastructure, particularly in railroad and port construction. The new railroads granted unprecedented ease of access to the southern African interior and created opportunities for agricultural trade, though most of the larger farms capable of taking advantage of these opportunities were owned by white farmers employing cheap or forced African labor.

See also: MINERALS AND METALS (Vols. IV, V).

minerals and metals Valuable metals lying near the earth's surface—among them GOLD, iron ore, and COPPER—have been mined in Africa for thousands of years. However, the extraction of metals and equally valuable minerals changed dramatically when European colonialists realized the extent of Africa's natural resource wealth. The first major thrust to exploit mineral resources on a large scale came in the 1860s, after the discovery of DIAMONDS, in present-day SOUTH AFRICA. In the 1880s the discovery of nearby gold reserves prompted further exploration of resources in Africa and sparked what is now called the African MINERAL REVOLUTION.

In the late 1800s rich copper reserves were discovered in what became known as the COPPERBELT, in NORTHERN RHODESIA (present-day ZAMBIA) and in Katanga (present-day Democratic Republic of the CONGO).

Even prior to the era of full-fledged colonialism European CONCESSIONAIRE COMPANIES were developing large-scale, heavy MINING techniques to exploit difficult-to-extract minerals, such as gold, zinc, and cobalt. In South Africa major mining activities also focused on coal, which was plentiful and was used to provide power for both the mining industry and, in later years, the railway.

Mining developed in other parts of the continent, as well, in the 1900s. For example, tin and coal were being extracted from Nigerian soil as early as 1902. Large diamond deposits were discovered in SOUTH WEST AFRICA (present-day NAMIBIA), ANGOLA, and SIERRA LEONE by 1920. Industrial diamonds were mined for export in the BELGIAN CONGO as early as the 1920s. Britain's GOLD COAST COLONY (today's GHANA) supplied manganese; the country also exported bauxite (aluminum ore) on a small scale, and gold on a major scale, during this period.

Until the 1930s mining was developed mainly in southern Africa and along the West African coast. After World War II (1939–1945), however, mineral extraction developed rapidly in other parts of West Africa, as well. In the 1950s bauxite was discovered in GUINEA, and American and European mining concerns began exploiting iron reserves and diamonds in LIBERIA. Iron deposits were discovered in MAURITANIA in 1935, but large-scale extraction did not begin until 1960.

By 1960 African resources made up a large portion of the world's mineral and metal supply. African copper accounted for approximately 22 percent of the world's supply; African cobalt accounted for 77 percent of world supply; manganese accounted for 22 percent; diamonds, 95 percent; gold, 52 percent; and platinum accounted for 30 percent of the world's output. In addition Africa's non-metal mineral deposits, such as phosphates and asbestos, made up a large share of the world market.

Between 1950 and 1975 increasing development and industrialization led to worldwide demand for Africa's NATURAL RESOURCES. However, the minerals and metals themselves were not the only resources exported from the continent. The profits from the mining industry, too, flowed out of Africa and into the coffers of foreign mine owners and investors. Despite the fact that they made up the majority of the mining LABOR force,

Africans themselves received negligible benefits from the stripping of their lands.

See also: COLONIALISM, INFLUENCE OF (Vol. IV); MINERALS AND METALS (Vol. V).

mining Mining was a major activity in Africa long before European colonists arrived in great numbers in the 1800s. One of the world's oldest iron mines, believed to have been active more than 45,000 years ago, is located in SWAZILAND, in SOUTH AFRICA. Africa has a rich history of iron smelting for agricultural tools and weapons, and the precolonial kingdoms of western Africa also used locally mined GOLD dust for currency in trading.

Before the end of the 19th century European-owned mining operations in Africa were extracting large amounts of gold, COPPER, and DIAMONDS from mines in southern Africa. And by the end of the colonial era minerals and metals extracted from African mines also included tin, nickel, bauxite, uranium, zinc, coal, lead, and agricultural phosphates.

The mining economy began to change substantially with the discovery of copper in the 1850s and diamonds in the 1860s, in an area that is today part of South Africa. Initiating what became known as Africa's MINERAL REVOLUTION, the discovery of these deposits led to an influx of prospectors, smugglers, and adventurers. New companies formed quickly—including Rio Tinto-Zinc, DE BEERS CONSOLIDATED MINES, LTD., and Consolidated Gold Fields—and dominated the mining industry for the next century. The latter two were founded by the influential British colonialist Cecil RHODES (1853–1902), who went on to found the BRITISH SOUTH AFRICA COMPANY (BSAC). One of the principal objectives of the BSAC was to speculate on the exploration for, and exploitation of, gold deposits in ZIMBABWE (which was colonial SOUTHERN RHODESIA). Any profits from the mining industry were reinvested to extract additional NATURAL RESOURCES.

Once mineral resources were discovered in great quantities in Africa, the colonial powers focused their energies on extracting these resources as rapidly and inexpensively as possible. With this imperative, cheap LABOR became a priority. In 19th-century South Africa, European SETTLERS made up the majority of miners. During the late 1800s, however, greater numbers of black Africans were recruited and coerced into working in the mines. Between 1907 and 1922 major strikes by white miners caused mine owners to hire even more black African laborers, who could be coerced to do the same work as white miners but for less pay.

The conditions in and around mines were often unsafe and demeaning. Mining employers usually required miners to live near the mines in cramped, unsanitary housing. Laborers went long stretches without contact with their families, working long hours in dangerous conditions for very little pay. Private companies that bought concessions to the mineral rights through colonial agreements reaped the profits from the mining industry. African laborers, on the other hand, did not benefit very much from the lucrative mining industry. Investments that could have gone to better working conditions instead were used to facilitate the further extraction of raw resources for consumption by an increasingly industrialized Western Europe.

The pattern of mineworker repression held for many areas in present-day South Africa and, to some degree, in the COPPERBELT region of today's Democratic Republic of the CONGO (the former BELGIAN CONGO). There were, however, other mining operations in the Copperbelt that maintained much less control over the lives of the miners. Some even encouraged families to migrate together to the mining towns.

After World War II (1939–45) and into the 1970s the mining industry expanded along with the world demand for minerals and metals. Large-scale, industrial mining took place all over the African continent, including copper mining in ZAMBIA and present-day Democratic Republic of the Congo, iron ore mining in LIBERIA, bauxite mining in GUINEA, and uranium mining in NAMIBIA and NIGER. Diamond and gold mining continued in GHANA (the former GOLD COAST COLONY) and SIERRA LEONE. Spanish corporations mined phosphates in MOROCCO, and tin was mined in northern NIGERIA. The thoroughgoing European exploitation of Africa's mineral resources—and its labor force—left many nations dependent on the mining industry even after independence.

See also: COLONIALISM, INFLUENCE OF (Vol. IV); METALS (Vol. I); MINERALS AND METALS (Vols. IV, V); MINING (Vols. II, III, V).

Mirambo (c. 1840–1884) *Political leader of the Nyamwezi people of Tanzania*

In the 19th century the interior of East Africa was the site of a dramatic increase in both the SLAVE TRADE and IVORY trade. This was also a time of turmoil and upheaval that provided opportunities for ambitious individuals to carve out positions of authority and power for themselves. One such man was Mirambo, a leader of the NYAMWEZI people living in the west-central region of present-day TANZANIA.

The Nyamwezi were particularly well-situated to take advantage of the growing volume of trade, since the major trade routes from the coast to Lake Tanganyika ran through the heart of their country. Mirambo utilized this strategic position and his own leadership skills to build a large Nyamwezi state in the third quarter of the 19th century.

Sometime after 1850, upon the death of his father, Mirambo inherited the chieftainship of a small Nyamwezi state. He then set out to establish his control over neighboring Nyamwezi chiefdoms, utilizing the innovative ZULU-style military techniques and strategies introduced by Ngoni military bands that had pushed into the area from southern Africa.

By the late 1860s Mirambo had built the largest of the Nyamwezi states. Other Nyamwezi chiefs sought to ward off Mirambo's growing power by using their ties with Arab traders from the SWAHILI COAST, who had set up a trading center in Tabora. In the early 1870s, after several years of fighting that severely disrupted the trade routes, Mirambo and the sultan of ZANZIBAR, ibn Said BARGHASH (c. 1833–1888), reached an agreement. This pact recognized Mirambo's authority over the area in return for not interfering with the Arab trade network, allowing Mirambo to continue building his state.

Mirambo's state attracted the attention of a number of European visitors, such as the adventurer Henry Morton STANLEY (1841–1904), who called Mirambo "the Napoleon of Central Africa." In 1880, however, two Englishmen were killed in Mirambo's territory. This caused the British, whose influence in Zanzibar was growing, to view Mirambo in an increasingly negative light. British hostility in turn undercut Mirambo's alliance with the sultan's government, which then began to support Mirambo's Nyamwezi opponents.

In 1884 Mirambo's armies were already on the defensive when their leader died of throat cancer. His state did not long survive his death, as ambitious rival Nyamwezi leaders expanded their own territories. Eventually, however, German soldiers incorporated the Nyamwezi area into GERMAN EAST AFRICA.

See also: COLONIAL CONQUEST (Vol. IV); TRADE AND COMMERCE (Vol. IV).

Further reading: Norman R. Bennett, *Mirambo of Tanzania* (New York: Oxford University Press, 1971).

missionaries Individuals who worked to convert non-Christians to Christianity and who, for the most part, worked as members of organized missionary societies associated with major denominations. There were also individuals within Islam who engaged in missionary work, but in Africa, the term "missionary" has come to be associated with Christianity.

The late 18th century witnessed an upsurge of evangelism among European Christians. They often broke away from established churches, such as the Church of England, to found new denominations, such as the Methodists. They also founded missionary societies, including the LONDON MISSIONARY SOCIETY (LMS) in 1795 and the CHURCH MISSIONARY SOCIETY (CMS) in 1799, to promote their efforts both domestically and overseas.

The late 1700s also saw the rise of the movement to abolish the SLAVE TRADE and, later, the practice of SLAVERY itself. The British were the first to do this, abolishing the slave trade in 1807. Africa soon became a focal point of European missionary activity, with the earliest missions established in West Africa and SOUTH AFRICA. British abolitionists founded the Province of Freedom, which became SIERRA LEONE, in 1787, and CMS missionaries arrived in 1804. Much of their early focus was on EDUCATION for the purpose of acquiring LITERACY needed to read the Bible and other religious material. This led to more advanced schooling, including the founding in 1827 of FOURAH BAY COLLEGE.

In CAPE COLONY and neighboring areas of present-day South Africa, sustained missionary activity began in 1792 with the arrival of German Moravians to work among the Khoikhoi. The first group of LMS missionaries arrived three years later, and by 1816 the LMS was fielding 20 missionaries, making it the largest missionary body in the region. Two of its missionaries, Robert MOFFAT (1795–1883), who arrived in 1817, and Dr. David LIVINGSTONE (1813–1873), who arrived in 1841, came to epitomize 19th-century missionary activity in Africa.

Western-style EDUCATION formed a major component of mission work, with early missionaries contributing significantly to reproducing African languages in writing. Moffat, for example, worked exhaustively on Setswana, the LANGUAGE of the TSWANA people. Mission schools began to produce well educated Africans, some of whom became ordained ministers and missionaries among their own people. Indeed, under the leadership of Henry Venn (1796–1873), the CMS carried out its Niger Mission to the YORUBA-speaking area of modern-day NIGERIA through the agency of individuals educated first in Sierra Leone. These included Samuel Ajayi CROWTHER (1808–1891), who was ordained in 1843, and later consecrated as the first African Anglican bishop, in 1864. A counterpart of Crowther in South Africa was Tiyo SOGA (1829–1871), who was ordained as a Presbyterian minister, in 1856, and played a key role in translating the New Testament into the XHOSA language.

As the era of PARTITION of Africa among the European powers began later in the century, missionary societies became increasingly reluctant to work through Africans such as Crowther and Soga. Thus, the CMS mission to BUGANDA, which began in 1877, was entirely in European hands. Such exclusion from positions of authority and leadership in the mission churches sparked independent churches such as that led by Isaiah SHEMBE (c. 1870–1935), in South Africa, and the LUMPA CHURCH, founded by Alice LENSHINA (1924–1978), in colonial ZAMBIA. In IVORY COAST, Liberian-born William Wade HARRIS (c. 1850–1929) attracted thousands to his independent church with his charismatic preaching. Leaders such as these three were considered prophets, and their prophetic movements proved to be powerful organizing forces. For this reason, they often ran afoul

of colonial authorities, as did Simon KIMBANGU (c. 1887–1951), whom the colonial authorities in the BELGIAN CONGO arrested, in 1921, and held in prison until his death in 1951.

After World War II (1939–45), in keeping with the process of DECOLONIZATION, mission churches tried to broaden their appeal to Africans. This led them to ordain an increasing number of Africans as ministers. Their schools had already turned out many of the leaders of African NATIONALISM AND INDEPENDENCE MOVEMENTS. These missionaries encouraged, albeit inadvertently, the emergence of the independent churches that after 1960 increasingly contested the Western churches for adherents among the faithful.

See also: CHRISTIANITY, INFLUENCE OF (Vols. II, III, IV, V); KHOIKHOI (Vols. II, III); MISSIONARIES (Vols. III, V); PROPHETS AND PROPHETIC MOVEMENTS (Vol. IV); RELIGION (Vols. III, IV, V); SHEPPARD, WILLIAM (Vol. IV).

Further reading: Adrian Hastings, *The Church in Africa: 1450–1950* (New York: Oxford University Press, 1994); Andrew F. Walls, *The Missionary Movement in Christian History: Studies in the Transmission of Faith* (Maryknoll, N.Y.: Orbis Books, 1996).

Moffat, Robert (Reverend) (1795–1883) *Missionary and linguist in southern Africa*

Raised in a Presbyterian family in Scotland, Moffat went to England and apprenticed to become a gardener. There, influenced by Methodist preachers, he joined the LONDON MISSIONARY SOCIETY and committed himself to bringing Christianity to Africa. He arrived in CAPE TOWN in 1817, and a year later he was sent to a mission station in Namaqualand, a region in the northern CAPE COLONY (present-day southern NAMIBIA). In 1821 he was reassigned to BECHUANALAND (present-day BOTSWANA). There he worked first in the settlement of Dithakong and later in Kuruman, where he stayed for 50 years.

During a sabbatical in England (1839–43) Moffat met and recruited David LIVINGSTONE (1813–1873) for missionary work in Africa. In 1845 Moffat's eldest daughter, Mary, married Livingstone, who went on to achieve fame as an explorer as well as a missionary.

While in Kuruman, Moffat became proficient in the LANGUAGE of the TSWANA people, a Bantu tongue known as Setswana, and compiled a grammar of the language. He translated the New Testament into Setswana and had it published in London in 1840. Later he also translated the Old Testament as well as a hymnbook and the classic Christian morality tale *Pilgrim's Progress*, by John Bunyan (1628–1688).

Moffat won many converts and achieved great popularity. During the 1820s he established a close friendship with Mzilikazi (c. 1790–1868), the king of the NDEBELE, whose people were migrating through Bechuanaland at that time. In the late 1830s, however, the Ndebele were pressured by Afrikaner incursions and moved on. They ultimately settled in the southwestern part of modern-day ZIMBABWE, and Moffat lost contact with the king. The two met again in the 1850s after Moffat had journeyed across the Kalahari Desert. Although Moffat never succeeded in converting Mzilikazi to Christianity, in 1859 the Ndebele king allowed the first permanent mission station to be built in his kingdom. The station was run by Moffat's son, John Smith Moffat (1835–1918). The presence of this mission station in Zimbabwe helped pave the way for British MINING and colonizing expeditions in the 1880s and ultimately, in 1893, the conquest of the Ndebele by Cecil RHODES (1853–1902).

In 1870 the senior Moffat and his wife returned to Britain, where he continued his scholarly work in linguistics, wrote his memoirs, and sought to recruit others for missionary work.

See also: AFRIKANERS (Vol. IV); BANTU LANGUAGES (Vol. I); MISSIONARIES (Vols. III, IV); NAMA (Vols. III, IV); NAMALAND (Vol. III); RELIGION (Vols. III, IV).

Mogadishu Capital and principal port of SOMALIA, located in the southeastern part of the country, on the Indian Ocean. Mogadishu was a successful trading center as early as the 10th century, when Arab and Persian merchants came to the area. In 1892 the sultan of ZANZIBAR leased the port at Mogadishu to Italy, which was interested in colonizing the Horn of Africa. By 1905 the city had become the capital of ITALIAN SOMALILAND, taking on the characteristics of an Italian colonial city, with a Roman Catholic Cathedral and European-style colonial administrative buildings and housing. The Italians also developed a school system for the Somalis, with a government school to teach Italian.

The Sultan of Zanzibar took control of Mogadishu in 1871. He built the Garesa Palace, which today houses a museum and library.

By the outbreak of World War II (1939–45), some 8,000 Italians lived in the colony, most of whom were civil servants and their family members. British troops occupied the city early in the war and favored the forces of Somali nationalism against fascist Italian interests. This set the stage for a clash in Mogadishu between Italian settlers and Somali nationalists. The violence began in 1948 and left scores dead and injured on both sides. The King's African Rifles—the British colonial regiment in East Africa—restored order.

Although Italy was on the losing side in World War II, the Italian government once again administered Mogadishu from 1950 until 1960, when the United Nations declared the city part of a TRUST territory. In 1960, when Mogadishu became the capital of independent Somalia, the population of the city stood at approximately 86,000.

See also: ARAB COASTAL TRADE (Vols. I, II); BENADIR COAST (Vol. III); ENGLAND AND AFRICA (Vols. III, IV, V); ITALY AND AFRICA (Vol. IV); MOGADISHU (Vols. II, III, V); NATIONALISM AND INDEPENDENCE MOVEMENTS (Vol. IV); PERSIAN TRADERS (Vol. II); UNITED NATIONS AND AFRICA (Vols. IV, V); URBAN LIFE AND CULTURE (Vols. IV, V); URBANIZATION (Vols. IV, V).

Mombasa Major port city on the East African coast of present-day KENYA. Mombasa's history from the 16th century through the 19th century is marked by a number of shifts in power. The Portuguese maintained an unsteady dominance over Mombasa, which was the primary town on the SWAHILI COAST, from the early 16th century until 1698. After years of struggle, Omani Arabs finally drove the Portuguese out and the Omani Sultanate assumed control. Bitter feuding between the rival Masrui and BUSAIDI dynasties ended with Mombasa under the rulership of Busaidi Sultan Sayyid Said (1791–1856).

In 1841 Said moved the capital of Oman from Muscat to the island of ZANZIBAR, just to the south of Mombasa, establishing the sultanate of Zanzibar. The city of Zanzibar became a center for the Indian Ocean SLAVE TRADE as well as a major depot for the IVORY TRADE. Mombasa flourished economically, providing Zanzibar with a steady supply of captive humans and ivory. At mid-century the population stood at about 10,000.

In 1873 the British, who had long exerted influence within the sultanate, forced the sultan ibn Said BARGHASH (c. 1833–1888) to abolish the slave trade, though this did little to suppress trade activity. With colonial aspirations and the ostensible desire to permanently shut down the slave trade, Britain, in a PARTITION agreement with Germany, assumed control of Kenya and UGANDA, in 1886. In 1887 Britain secured concessions along the Kenyan coast from Sultan Barghash, and in 1888 the Imperial British East Africa Company made Mombasa its headquaters for the administration of Kenya. The company's financial difficulties led to intervention by the British government, which established the East African Protectorate, in 1895.

Mombasa was capital of the PROTECTORATE until 1906, when the capital was moved to the new colonial city of NAIROBI.

In 1901 a railroad linking Mombasa, with its population of about 25,000, to Kisumu, on Lake Victoria, ensured that Mombasa continued as a major port of entry to East Africa and facilitated trade to Uganda and the interior. Until the end of World War I the city had been confined to a 7.5 square-mile (16 sq km) island, but continued economic growth led to its expansion to the mainland by 1930. The African LABOR force on the railways and harbors also grew steadily and became increasingly well organized. Strikes in the aftermath of World War II (1939–45) heralded the beginning of the nationalist movement on the coast.

Another post–World War II development was the beginning of tourism. The early tourists were white SETTLERS from SOUTH AFRICA and SOUTHERN RHODESIA. At the time of Kenya's independence, in 1963, Mombasa was a vastly different city than it had been under the Busaidi sultans, but it still remained largely a Muslim, KISWAHILI-speaking town.

See also: BRITISH EAST AFRICA (Vol. III); ENGLAND AND AFRICA (Vols. III, IV, V); GERMAN EAST AFRICA (Vol. IV); GERMANY AND AFRICA (Vol. IV); MASRUI (Vol. III); MOMBASA (Vols. II, III, V); OMANI SULTANATE (Vol. III); PORTUGAL AND AFRICA (Vol. III); SAYYID SAID (Vol. III); SLAVE TRADE ON THE SWAHILI COAST (Vol. III); TOURISM (Vol. V).

Mondlane, Eduardo (Dr. Eduardo Chivambo Mondlane) (1920–1969) *Major figure in Mozambique's independence movement*

Born in Manjacaze, a town in southern MOZAMBIQUE, Mondlane was raised by his widowed mother, who instilled in him a desire for education. Against seemingly insurmountable odds, he attended, first, a local school, which he entered at the age of 11, and then a series of mission and religious schools. He completed his secondary education in SOUTH AFRICA, where he won a scholarship. From there Mondlane went on to the University of Witwatersrand, also in South Africa. In spite of the fact that he was one of only 300 blacks on a campus of 5,000 students, he became a campus leader. This visibility, however, brought Mondlane to the attention of the white South African authorities, the newly elected Nationalists, whose racist APARTHEID policies were hostile to any signs of black leadership. Refusing to renew his student residence permit, in 1949 they effectively banned him from completing his education in South Africa.

Back in Mozambique Mondlane organized a national student union known as UNEMO. This and other political activities led to his arrest by the Portuguese colonial government, in October 1949. Seeking a way to more closely monitor Mondlane's activities, the Mozambican authorities arranged for him to study at the University of Lisbon, in Portugal, where he was subject to constant surveillance. In Portugal, however, he also met other future leaders from elsewhere in Portuguese Africa, including Agostinho Neto (1922–1979) of ANGOLA and Amílcar CABRAL (1924–1973) of GUINEA-BISSAU. A scholarship gave Mondlane the opportunity to attend Oberlin College, and at the age of 32 he enrolled as an undergraduate student in the United States. At Oberlin he met his wife, Janet Rae Johnson (1920–), and completed his bachelor's degree. From there he continued on, earning a Ph.D. in anthropology from Northwestern University and doing postdoctoral study at Harvard University.

Mondlane accepted a job with the United Nations, in New York City, where he became a close friend of Tanzanian Julius NYERERE (1922–1999), who urged him to consider using TANZANIA as a base of operations in the drive for Mozambique's independence. After joining the faculty of Syracuse University, Mondlane went to DAR ES SALAAM, Tanzania, in the summer of 1962. There, along with representatives of several Mozambican groups, he formed the Front for the Liberation of Mozambique (FRELIMO). Elected president of FRELIMO, Mondlane left the classroom behind to devote himself full-time to the independence movement.

See also: COLONIAL RULE (Vol. IV); FRONT FOR THE LIBERATION OF MOZAMBIQUE (Vol. V); MONDLANE, EDUARDO (Vol. V); NATIONALISM AND INDEPENDENCE MOVEMENTS (Vol. IV); PORTUGAL AND AFRICA (Vols. III, IV, V).

money and currency Under COLONIAL RULE the various objects that had been used as money for the growing TRADE AND COMMERCE gave way to standardized coins and paper notes issued by governments. By the early 19th century Africans still exchanged what was, essentially, "commodity money," such as salt bars, cowrie shells, and the like. Silver coinage, however, was increasingly used for the external trade involving Europeans. The earlier forms of money survived well into the colonial period for purposes of exchanges among Africans at the local level. However, as part of developing both the colonial state and the colonial ECONOMY, European administrations issued coins and paper bank notes at rates that were tied to the value of money in the home countries. They also took the name of the home country currencies. Thus, in BRITISH EAST AFRICA there were shillings, in EGYPT, the Egyptian pound, and in FRENCH WEST AFRICA, the West African franc.

The transition from older currencies led to inconveniences and dislocations for Africans, but this was not a concern of the colonial authorities. Rather, they wanted to see the full monetization of the economy. In the first place, this facilitated colonial TAXATION by providing a standardized and readily transferable form of money. Africans were forced to either sell goods they produced, usually CASH CROPS, or work for wages to pay taxes. In turn the tax receipts could be used to pay the costs of administration, including the wages of Africans in the civil service or other parts of the government.

Monetization of markets also promoted the taxation of both imports and EXPORTS in terms of duties. After receiving colonial currencies for the commodities they sold in the market for export to Europe, African producers then had easily exchanged money to buy goods imported from Europe. This became increasingly important as Africa became more fully integrated into the world economy during the colonial period. On the other hand, this also exposed Africans more fully to global economic fluctuations. The Great Depression of the 1930s, for example, had a major impact on both African producers and consumers. The process of URBANIZATION and the development of extensive wage-labor forces would have been severely impeded without the availability of standardized currencies. In the rural areas, on the other hand, except for paying taxes, money tended to be hoarded and saved for "rainy day" contingencies.

Monetization also allowed governments to regulate commerce by imposing currency controls, which they began doing early in the colonial period. As European countries attempted to recover from the economic devastation of World War II (1939–45) they stopped permitting the free exchange of their currencies, including those of the colonies, into other currencies. In the British case, the currency reserves of the colonies were generated by trading surpluses. These, in turn, helped support the value of the British pound sterling. France used this system to retain tight control over monetary allocations within its colonies.

By 1960 the economies of most African countries were fully dependent on the use of standardized government-issued currencies for the purchase of goods and services in the formal sectors of the economy. Although barter continued to be important in the exchange of locally produced foodstuffs and services in the rural areas—and in some aspects of the informal urban economy, as well—the governments of newly independent countries were positioned to issue their own national currencies.

See also: COLONIALISM, INFLUENCE OF (Vol. IV); MONEY AND CURRENCY (Vols. I, II, III, V).

mono-crop economies Economic structure common in colonial Africa in which a colony was largely dependent on the export of a single cash crop. AGRICULTURE constituted the principal economic activity throughout Africa at the time of the COLONIAL CONQUEST and the PARTITION of the continent among the European colonial powers. Once they had taken control of the continent, these occupying powers sought ways to develop their colonies' economies. Historically, colonial occupiers ma-

nipulated their colonies to cover the costs of COLONIAL RULE and, if possible, to generate a profit, too. This was no different in Africa, and the taxation of agricultural commodities for export was an obvious solution.

Colonial authorities promoted the production of crops for export back to their own countries, where the crops would be consumed or processed for use in manufacturing. Generally, the focus was on a single cash crop. Thus, EGYPT and the the Sudan became heavily dependent on exporting COTTON to Britain for use in British textile mills, while MALI and CHAD were in a similar situation with France. GROUNDNUTS (peanuts) were another such cash crop, with the SENEGAMBIA REGION developing a mono-crop economy around that export. In the mid-1920s Firestone started its massive RUBBER plantations in LIBERIA, leaving the country's economy dependent on that one crop.

Mono-crop economies have a number of disadvantages in contrast to multi-crop economies. First, monoculture—the growing of a single crop over large areas—is highly susceptible to plant diseases and insects, as well as variability in the weather. For example, swollen shoot disease in COCOA trees led government agricultural agents in the British GOLD COAST COLONY to destroy diseased trees. In the second place, such economies are very vulnerable to market price fluctuations, over which they have little control. It was a combination of the destruction of diseased trees and low prices that led cocoa farmers to stage the GOLD COAST COCOA HOLD-UP, in the late 1930s.

Some colonial economies became as dependent on the export of a single mineral as others did on a single cash crop. For example, in the African COPPERBELT, a region that spanned NORTHERN RHODESIA (present-day ZAMBIA) and the Katanga province of the BELGIAN CONGO, colonial authorities focused economic development solely on the production of COPPER.

At the time of independence, most African countries were locked into a dependence on the export of one or two major commodities. Decades of colonial rule had produced a situation in which, in the words of a popular saying, "Africa produces what it does not consume and consumes what it does not produce."

See also: CASH CROPS (Vol. IV, V); COLONIALISM, INFLUENCE OF (Vol. IV); DEPENDENCY (Vol. V); EXPORTS (Vols. IV, V); NEO-COLONIALISM (Vol. V); UNDERDEVELOPMENT (Vol. V); DEVELOPMENT (Vol. V); TRADE AND COMMERCE (Vols. IV, V).

Seen here in 1942, the "The Waterside," Monrovia's business district, remained quiet even during the tumultuous days of World War II.
© Ziff-Davis photo

Monrovia Capital and principal port of LIBERIA, located at the mouth of the St. Paul (Mesurado) River, on the Atlantic Ocean. The American Colonization Society (ACS) founded Monrovia in 1822, when it sent the first shipload of former slaves there to establish what grew into Liberia. The ACS purchased land from a local chief and named the new settlement after James Monroe (1758–1831), the United States president. The town grew as more former slaves and freedmen arrived from the United States and the British West Indies and as people migrated from the countryside. The foreign immigrants, known as Americo-Liberians, adopted a colonialist attitude toward the indigenous Africans, which led to tensions and clashes.

In 1848 Liberia declared itself independent from the ACS and made Monrovia the national capital. (However, the United States did not officially recognize the country until 1862.) About the same time that Liberia declared independence, Liberia College (the future University of Liberia) was established, with Edward Wilmot BLYDEN (1832–1912) and Alexander CRUMMEL (1819–1898) becoming its first two professors. The new institution put Monrovia on its path to becoming the educational center of Liberia.

During World War II (1939–45) United States forces expanded the capacity of the port, and the economy sub-sequently grew based on the export of iron ore and RUBBER. In 1961 Monrovia, with a population of about 115,000, hosted the conference that initiated the anti-colonial Organization of African Unity.

See also: MONROVIA (Vol. V); MONROVIA GROUP (Vol. V); ORGANIZATION OF AFRICAN UNITY (Vol. V); UNITED STATES AND AFRICA (Vols. IV, V); URBAN LIFE AND CULTURE (Vols. IV, V); URBANIZATION (Vols. IV, V); WORLD WAR II AND AFRICA (Vol. IV).

Morocco Country in northwest Africa, 279,400 square miles (723,600 sq km) in size, bordering the Mediterranean Sea and the Atlantic Ocean. Neighboring countries of present-day Morocco include ALGERIA and WESTERN SAHARA. Because of Morocco's key position at the crossroads of Mediterranean and Saharan trade routes, European colonial powers occupied the region during the 19th and 20th centuries.

During the reign of Moulay Abderrahame (r. 1822–1859) Morocco resisted European imperialism. By supporting Algerian resistance against the French and by using diplomatic ties with Britain, Morocco managed to repel French incursions. This approach led to the Treaty of Tangier (1856), an agreement with Britain that made the port of Tangier, on the Strait of Gibraltar, a free-trade port. It also made Tangier's British citizens autonomous, freeing them from Moroccan taxes and allowing them to be subject to British, rather than Moroccan, law.

In 1859–60, following Morocco's defeat in the Tetuan War, Sultan Muhammad IV (r. 1859–1873) was forced to cede to Spain territories in the southern part of the country, along the Atlantic coast of the far western Sahara. The peace treaty at the conclusion of the war gave Spain control of Morocco's customs house in order to pay down the Moroccan war debts. Under this arrangement one-half of the proceeds went to pay the war indemnity to Spain, and one-half went to pay off British creditors. When the Europeans rejected an increase in tariffs for Moroccan imports, the sultan resorted to increased domestic taxation, creating discontent in a population already suffering from the effects of a series of poor harvests (1871–76).

Muhammad was succeeded by Mawlai al-HASAN (r. 1873–1894), who renewed efforts to keep Moroccan territory free of European control. To this end he sought to westernize the country and modernize the army. Al-Hasan's efforts, however, were neutralized during the reign of his immediate successor, Moulay Abdelaziz (r. 1894–1908). In 1904 Spain and France signed a secret treaty that divided Morocco into a northern Spanish zone and a southern French zone. This led in 1912 to the declaration of the protectorates of FRENCH MOROCCO and SPANISH MOROCCO.

Morocco during the Colonial Era: French Morocco and Spanish Morocco France appointed Marshal Louis H. G. LYAUTEY (1854–1934) as resident-general to share power with the Moroccan sultan. With Lyautey, France attempted to apply lessons learned from earlier colonial experiences to the occupation of Morocco. Although the French administration chose the government cabinet and controlled the army, it allowed for the continuation of the indigenous Moroccan social and political structure. Lyautey made Rabat, on the Atlantic coast, the new political capital and developed Casablanca as a seaport; instead of taking over existing towns, French settlers built new westernized towns.

Following the divide-and-rule approach that had proved successful elsewhere, the French colonizers used their economic influence to co-opt the Moroccan elite, which included provincial governors, religious leaders, urban merchants, and members of the ruling family. The colonizers also sought to pit Arabic-speaking urbanites against the Berber-speaking rural population.

By the 1930s more than 200,000 French citizens had settled in Morocco. During World War II (1939–45) Morocco was the site of Allied military bases for prosecuting the war.

Although French and Spanish COLONIAL RULE met with continual resistance, the official quest for Moroccan independence began only during the reign of MUHAMMAD

V (1909–1961), who came to power in 1927. In 1944, toward the end of the war, Muhammad issued the Independence Manifesto, calling for Moroccan independence and the reinstitution of the monarchy. Muhammad's historic speech, delivered in Tangier, rekindled national consciousness and resistance to foreign occupation.

The most significant resistance to European imperialism was put up by the BERBERS of the RIF Mountains, in northern Morocco. Beginning in 1893 the Riffi—people of the Rif—fought against Spanish encroachment from the Atlantic and Mediterranean coasts. Their armed rebellions took many Spanish lives and forced Spain to fortify its coastal garrison town of Melilla.

When the Treaty of Fez (1912) awarded Spain the mountains near the Riffi enclaves of Melilla and Ceuta, Moroccan military commander Mohamed ben ABD EL-KRIM (1882–1963) led a resurgence of the Riffi resistance. At first, Abd el-Krim succeeded largely because the Spanish forces lacked leadership and equipment. In 1925, however, French forces joined with the Spanish, and, with superior weaponry and organization, the French subdued the Riffi resistance. Ultimately they exiled Abd el-Krim to RÉUNION ISLAND in the Indian Ocean.

By 1952 there were mass demonstrations across North Africa against continued French COLONIAL RULE. In Morocco, France met this challenge by dethroning Muhammad and sending him to MADAGASCAR, in 1953. The French administration replaced the popular leader with an aged relative, Mohammed bin Arafa, causing widespread resentment among the country's nationalists, who rallied to support the exiled king. By 1955 the situation was so volatile that France allowed Muhammad V to return. Once he was restored to power, Muhammad V led negotiations to put an end to the Spanish and French protectorates, and in 1956 Morocco officially declared itself an independent constitutional monarchy.

The new government, dominated by the Istaqlal Party, set about founding schools and universities, establishing local elected assemblies, and improving the country's infrastructure. Muhammad also restored Islamic practices that had been suppressed under foreign rule and successfully fought to clean up government corruption. By 1960 Morocco had formally recovered most of the territory that had been stripped from it by Europeans, with the exception of the southwestern region that later became the country of Western Sahara.

See also: COLONIAL CONQUEST (Vol. IV); COLONIALISM, INFLUENCE OF (Vol. IV); ENGLAND AND AFRICA (Vols. III, IV, V); FRANCE AND AFRICA (Vols. III, IV, V); MOROCCO (Vols. I, II, III, V); MAGHRIB (Vols. I, II, III, IV, V); NATIONALISM AND INDEPENDENCE MOVEMENTS (Vol. IV); RESISTANCE AND REBELLION (Vol. IV); SETTLERS, EUROPEAN (Vol. IV); SPAIN AND AFRICA (Vols. III, IV);

Further reading: Moshe Gershovich, *French Military Rule in Morocco: Colonialism and its Consequences* (London: F. Cass, 2000); C. R. Pennell, *Morocco since 1830: A History* (New York: New York Univ. Press, 2000).

Mossi States (Moshe, Moose, Mohe, Mosi)

Confederation of states including Yatenga, Fada-n-Gurma, Nanumba, Ouagadougou, Mamprusi, Tenkadogo, and Dagomba located in northern present-day GHANA and in BURKINA FASO. Due to their interior location, the Mossi did not participate directly in the coastal trade. Only after the Europeans defeated the coastal and forest-zone kingdoms during the PARTITION of Africa did they seek to develop a trading relationship with the Mossi.

The French and the British competed with each another to establish a monopoly that would control trade in the interior region bordering the upper Niger River. After the British conquered the ASHANTI EMPIRE, they moved further into the interior and incorporated some Mossi peoples into their new colony of the Gold Coast. The French gained control of much of the region by defeating the TUKULOR EMPIRE under AHMADU SÉKU (d. 1898), in 1896, and the MANDINKA Empire under SAMORI TOURÉ (c. 1830–1900), in 1898. The Mossi leader, the *mogho naba*, rebuffed the French request to sign a trade treaty, however, and the French invaded Ouagadougou, in 1896. Because they met significant resistance from the Mossi people, they adopted a policy of indirect rule. They created the colony of the Upper Ivory Coast, which later became the UPPER VOLTA territory, in 1919. In 1947 the borders of Upper Volta were finalized. (In 1984 the name of the country was changed to Burkina Faso, meaning "Land of the People of Dignity.") The Mossi today make up more than half of Burkina Faso's population.

See also: COLONIAL CONQUEST (Vol. IV); ENGLAND AND AFRICA (Vols. III, IV, V); FRANCE AND AFRICA (Vols. III, IV, V); MOSSI STATES (Vols. II, III); NIGER RIVER (Vol. I).

Further reading: Elliot Skinner, *The Mossi of the Upper Volta* (Stanford, Calif.: Stanford University Press, 1964).

Mozambique

Country located in southeastern Africa bordered by SOUTH AFRICA and SWAZILAND to the south, ZIMBABWE and ZAMBIA to the west, and MALAWI and TANZANIA to the north. Mozambique covers 297,800 square miles (771,300 sq km) and has a 1,750-mile (2,816-km) coastline on the Indian Ocean. While the coastal regions are generally low-lying, the elevation in the central and northwestern areas of the interior rises to 5,000 feet (1,524 m), with several higher points.

Between 1850 and 1975 Mozambique was ruled by Portugal, although at the beginning of this period, Portuguese control was largely limited to the coastal fringe and the Zambezi River valley. As the Portuguese attempted to expand the area under their COLONIAL RULE, they encountered organized African resistance.

There were several major nodes of resistance in the 19th century, one of which was the Ngoni peoples. In the mid-19th century, under the leadership of Shoshangane (d. 1859), the Ngoni arrived in Mozambique from the NATAL region of SOUTH AFRICA. Fleeing the military campaigns of the ZULU leader, Shaka (1787–1828), the Ngoni invaded the Gaza state of south-central Mozambique. At first the Ngoni in the Gaza state were sufficiently strong to reduce the Portuguese trading posts in their area to tributary status. The Portuguese became involved in the succession disputes after Soshangane's death and in 1862 helped Mzila (c. 1810–1884) gain the throne, which initiated Portugal's claims of authority over the country.

Although Mzila and his successor, GUNGUNYANA (c. 1850–1906), sought diplomatic relations with the British, by 1891 Britain recognized the Portuguese claims to Mozambique. Portugal then mounted a determined military effort to establish authority over the rest of southern Mozambique. Wielding modern weaponry, including machine guns, Portuguese forces defeated Gungunyana by 1895 and exiled him to the Azores Islands.

In 1890 Gungunyana entered into a concession agreement with the BRITISH SOUTH AFRICA COMPANY of Cecil RHODES (1853–1902), believing that such ties would help him stave off the mounting Portuguese pressure. He did not realize, however, that he was negotiating with agents of a private individual and company and not official British diplomats. The assistance he sought in maintaining his sovereignty through this agreement thus never materialized.

A second pocket of active African resistance was led by Joaquim José da Cruz, also known as Nyaude. He established a base of operations that enabled him to levy tolls on traffic along the Zambezi River, which flows through central Mozambique on its course to the Indian Ocean. Portuguese attacks against Nyaude's position failed in both 1853 and 1869, but in 1888 the Portuguese finally were able to secure the area, which by then was ruled by Nyaude's son. The Portuguese then exiled those they captured.

Resistance efforts such as these left Portugal in a tenuous position in terms of its claims to control over Mozambique. Cecil Rhodes and his British South Africa Company took advantage of this situation and claimed jurisdiction over substantial areas of Mozambique. In 1891, however, Portugal reached an agreement with Britain that allowed it to reestablish some of its territorial claims in Mozambique. Portugal then continued to rule the area as a colony until independence in 1975.

The agreement struck between Portugal and Britain solidified Portugal's hold on territory in Mozambique. However, the agreement gave Britain territories in central southern African that effectively put an end to the previous Portuguese hopes of creating a region of control linking Portugal's African holdings from Mozambique, on the Indian Ocean, to ANGOLA, on the Atlantic Ocean.

Mozambique during the Colonial Era Portugal set about reorganizing its administration of Mozambique in the late 19th century. It had long used the *prazo* system to stake its claims to the Zambezi valley. (*Prazos da coroa,* loosely translated as "terms of the crown," were crown grants given to distinguished colonials of Portugal.) While grants such as the *prazos* had their legal limitations, in reality, the *prazeros* were basically independent. Living on a distant continent with little communication—or fear of punishment, for that matter—some *prazeros* exceeded their territorial claims; many others continued to enslave Africans, despite Portugal's official abolition of SLAVERY in Africa. The *prazero* system remained in effect up until the 1880s, but in the era of the colonial PARTITION of Africa it outlived its purpose. Most historians agree that the abandonment of the Portuguese *prazo* system was responsible for the much more destructive system of colonialism that followed.

By the end of the 19th century Portugal had secured its claims to Mozambique but had not yet effectively occupied much of the interior. To do so, it handed over the administration of large areas of the country to CONCESSIONAIRE COMPANIES. Three, all founded in the 1890s, were of particular importance: the Mozambique Company, the Niassa Company, and the Zambezia Company. Interestingly, these companies were controlled and financed by the British. The companies were responsible for planning and developing MINING ventures and plantations for producing CASH CROPS for export. Also, they

were responsible for constructing railroads between Mozambique and neighboring countries. These development projects relied primarily on forced African LABOR. In addition, Portugal relied heavily on the taxation of African workers for financing its colonial government. As a result, in order to pay the taxes, tens of thousand of Mozambican men entered into migratory labor to work on the GOLD mines located along South Africa's WITWATERSRAND.

In order to further solidify its control over Mozambique, Portugal undertook a series of military campaigns during the early 20th century, finally leading to the effective occupation of the Manica, Zambezia, and Niassa regions. These campaigns were necessary because the private companies were too weak to establish needed control on their own. Intensification of Portuguese control eventually reduced the need for the private companies, so Portugal ultimately revoked private charters. Even after the conclusion of major military operations, in 1917, sporadic revolts occurred, including one in the Zambezia region (1917–1921) and a tax revolt in Mossuril (1939).

Mozambique and the Salazar Regime A new phase in the colonial history of Mozambique began with a change of government in Portugal, in 1926. That year a coup d'état led to the creation of the Estado Novo (New State), which eventually brought to power the dictator Antonio Salazar (1889–1970), in 1932. From that time until the end of Salazar's dictatorship in 1968, the existing pattern of colonial exploitation intensified, with coerced labor, forced cultivation of COTTON and other cash crops for export, excessive taxation of Africans, and low wages. Thus the system of colonial rule was even further streamlined to benefit the Portuguese colonizers at the expense of the colonized. Until the end of the Second World War (1939–45), the number of European SETTLERS remained small, and most lived in the colonial capital of LOURENÇO MARQUES (today's Maputo) or the port city of Beira. After the war, however, the government promoted emigration from Portugal to the African colonies, so that independence in 1975 an estimated 250,000 Portuguese resided in Mozambique.

African resistance against Portuguese control and the abuses associated with it had never ceased. However, from the 1930s until independence, Mozambique witnessed ever-increasing levels of civil unrest. Several protests occurred in the port city of Lorenço Marques between the 1930s and the mid-1950s. The first significant action of this sort was carried out by dockworkers in late 1930. The second occurred in 1948, and it led to several hundred Africans being deported or imprisoned in São Tomé, an island off the coast of Angola. In 1956 yet another rebellion resulted in the death of 49 dockworkers. Portuguese efforts at suppressing the rebellions were often brutal.

Fearsome repression, often resulting in wholesale death, was also a continuing aspect of Portuguese control over the Mozambican countryside. For example, in 1960 members of the Makonde people in northern Mozambique were arrested after failing to secure a petition to create an African association. Those arrested were taken to an unknown location, but only after the murder of more than 600 Africans, including several important chiefs who protested their detention.

After World War II most colonial powers began the DECOLONIZATION process that would lead to independence for their former colonial charges. Portugal, on the other hand, was determined to maintain a strong hold over its African colonies, including Mozambique, Angola, and GUINEA. In this setting it was not surprising the African nationalism dating from earlier in the 20th century became even more acute during the 1950s and 1960s. The triumph of Mozambican independence, however, would not occur until 1975, following a prolonged and bitter 13-year war.

See also: COLONIAL CONQUEST (Vol. IV); COLONIALISM, INFLUENCE OF (Vol. IV); NATIONALISM AND INDEPENDENCE MOVEMENTS (Vol. IV); MOZAMBIQUE (Vols. I, II, III, V); PORTUGAL AND AFRICA (Vols. III, IV, V); RESISTANCE AND REBELLION (Vol. IV).

Further reading: Ronald Chilcote, *Portuguese Africa* (Englewood Cliffs, N.J.; Prentice-Hall Inc., 1967); Thomas H. Henriksen, *Mozambique: A History* (London: Collings, 1978); Malyn Newitt, *A History of Mozambique* (Bloomington, Ind.: Indiana University Press, 1995).

Mphahlele, Ezekiel (Es'kia Mphahlele, Bruno Eseki) (1919–) *Acclaimed South African writer, critic, and scholar of African literature*

Born in PRETORIA, SOUTH AFRICA, Mphahlele married Rebecca Mochadibane, in 1945, and began teaching high school while earning a bachelor's degree at the University of South Africa. After graduating in 1949 he taught for three years before being banned from the classroom for his anti-APARTHEID activism, which included protesting the Bantu Education Act, a segregationist law typical of South Africa in that era. Turning away from teaching, he worked for the influential black urban DRUM magazine, in JOHANNESBURG, writing essays and acting as the fiction editor from 1955 to 1957. At that time, Mphahlele left South Africa to lecture in English and literature, first at the University of Ibadan, in NIGERIA, and then at other universities in Africa, Europe, and the United States.

Mphahlele published his first collection of stories, *Man Must Live and Other Stories,* in 1947; his autobiography, *Down Second Avenue*—a vivid, politically aware account of growing up in segregated Pretoria township—came out in 1959. Mphahlele continued writing throughout the 1960s and beyond, turning out critical essays, novels, and poetry, and also editing collections of African literature and poetry for university presses. He is widely regarded as one of the foremost authorities on African literature in English.

See also: BANTU EDUCATION (Vol. V); IBADAN, UNIVERSTIY OF (Vol. V); LITERATURE IN COLONIAL AFRICA (Vol. IV); LITERATURE IN MODERN AFRICA (Vol. V); MPHAHLELE, EZEKIEL (Vol. V); URBAN LIFE AND CULTURE (Vols. IV, V).

Mqhayi, S. E. K. (Samuel Edward Krune Mqhayi) (1875–1945) *Xhosa writer and poet from South Africa*

S. E. K. Mqhayi was born among the rural XHOSA-speaking people of the eastern Cape Province of SOUTH AFRICA. As a boy he learned about Xhosa traditions, culture, and oral literature, and he came to appreciate praise poems, known as *izibongo,* and the vocabulary and literary skills they required. Mqhayi attended local church-affiliated schools, and in 1891 he went on to the highly esteemed Lovedale School, which was run by Scottish Presbyterian MISSIONARIES. There he trained as a teacher, a profession he practiced intermittently along with working on several African-run NEWSPAPERS. His journalistic career, which continued into the 1920s, included a stint, from 1920 to 1922, as editor of IMVO ZABANTSUNDU (African Opinion), which had been founded by the pioneer African journalist, John Tengo JABAVU (1859–1921). In 1925 Mqhayi settled near King William's Town in the eastern Cape Province and devoted the rest of his life to his writing and to visiting among his own Xhosa people.

As an author who drew on Xhosa oral literary forms to produce written works, Mqhayi played a role for Xhosa literature similar to what Tanzania's Shaaban ROBERT (1909–1962) did for KISWAHILI, especially in terms of his poetry. Some of his work drew on Christian themes, as in the case of his early novel *U-Samson* (1907), which utilized the biblical story of Samson to critique modern society. This was followed by *Ityala lamaWele* (The Legal Case of the Twins), which drew on both Genesis 38:27–29 and Mqhayi's memories of the indigenous court proceedings of his childhood, and which some critics consider to be his most important prose work. Mqhayi's later utopian novel *U-Don Jadu* (1929) dealt with the theme of an integrated Christian South Africa drawing on both its indigenous African and immigrant European heritages. Following up on his training as an educator, Mqhayi sought to inform his fellow Xhosa by writing about important African historical figures. In 1925, for example, he produced a biography (1925) of John Knox Bokwe (1855–1922), one of the leading Africans of his day. Mqhayi also translated into Xhosa an English-language biography of Ghanaian educator James E. Kwegyir AGGREY (1875–1927).

Praise poetry, or *izibongo,* traditionally was the highest form of literary art among the Xhosa. The poet, or *imbongi,* employed highly figurative speech to not only praise but also speak candidly about the qualities of his subject. When the United Kingdom's Prince of Wales visited South Africa in 1925, Mqhayi "praised" him with the following poem:

Ah Britain! Great Britain!
Great Britain of the endless sunshine!
She hath conquered the oceans and laid them low;
She hath drained the little rivers and lapped them dry;
She hath swept the little nations and wiped them away;
And now she is making for the open skies.
She sent us the preacher; she sent us the bottle,
She sent us the Bible, and barrels of brandy;
She sent us the breechloader, she sent us cannon;
O, Roaring Britain! Which must we embrace?
You sent us the truth, denied us the truth;
You sent us the life, deprived us of life;
You sent us the light, we sit in the dark,
Shivering, benighted in the bright noonday sun. *

In spite of his success as a writer of prose, Mqhayi was best known—in his own time and since—for his poetry, especially for his reworking of the oral heritage of *izibongo* into a written form. This was a form that resonated with the Xhosa audiences he addressed and that continues to shape the work of Xhosa poets in the early 21st century.

See also: COLONIAL RULE (Vol. IV); ENGLAND AND AFRICA (Vol. IV); LITERATURE IN COLONIAL AFRICA (Vol. IV).

Further reading: A. C. Jordan, *Towards an African Literature: The Emergence of Literary Form in Xhosa* (Berkeley, Calif.: University of California Press, 1973).

* Note: the translation of Mqhayi's poem is by Jordan in *Towards an African Literature,* p. 27.

Msiri (Msidi, M'siri, Mushidi) (c. 1830–1891)
Nyamwezi trader and self-proclaimed king in what is now the Congo province of Katanga.

Born in NYAMWEZI region of west-central TANZANIA in 1830, Msiri was the son of an influential figure in the East African long-distance caravan trade. Establishing close relationships with various chieftains along the trade routes, Msiri quickly expanded his father's commercial network. Key to this was his use of profits from the sale of COPPER, ivory, and human captives for the purchase of guns, powder, and ammunition. With these he was not only able to control his trade routes but soon was able to carry out his own slave raids.

By 1856 Msiri's influence in the region allowed him to turn his trading enterprise into a kingdom, known as Garenganze, which eventually grew to include all of Katanga east of the Lualaba River, in present-day Democratic Republic of the CONGO. From Msiri's capital of Bunkeya, his traders traveled east and west, ultimately stretching his direct trade links to places as far away as the SWAHILI COAST and the neighboring Indian Ocean island of ZANZIBAR, which was then the commercial hub of the East African trade. This was done in cooperation with powerful Swahili and Arab traders in the interior, such as TIPPU TIP (c. 1830–1905).

In the late 1880s and early 1890s, however, Msiri increasingly came into contact with Belgians in the CONGO FREE STATE, which was expanding rapidly as the forces of King LEOPOLD II (1835–1909) seized control of vast regions to the north of Katanga. This land-grab culminated in December 1891 with the arrival in Bunkeya of Captain William Stairs (1863–1892), a Canadian-born British officer in the service of King Leopold. Originally resistant to the idea of acknowledging Leopold's sovereignty, Msiri eventually acquiesced. Late in the negotiations, however, a Belgian officer found himself surrounded by Msiri's warriors and, in a panic, shot and killed Msiri, touching off what quickly became a massacre. Eventually Msiri's kingdom was replaced by the Bayeke kingdom, which had begun its ascendancy in the region during the mid-1800s. Soon, however, the Congo Free State and NORTHERN RHODESIA, which was administered by the BRITISH SOUTH AFRICA COMPANY, placed the entire area firmly under COLONIAL RULE, bringing to an end the era of powerful East African traders and state builders such as Msiri.

See also: BELGIUM AND AFRICA (Vol. IV); COLONIAL CONQUEST (Vol. IV); IVORY TRADE (Vol. IV); SLAVE TRADE (Vol. IV); TRADE AND COMMERCE (Vol. IV).

Muhammad V (Side Muhammad Ben Yusuf) (1910–1961) *King of Morocco*

Never noted as a firebrand, Muhammad was handpicked for the Moroccan sultanate by the French colonial authorities, who believed that he would be an acquiescent ruler. However, to their surprise, Muhammad became an effective nationalist leader, able to force the issue of Moroccan independence and ultimately, in the mid-1950s, to liberate his country.

Taking the throne in 1927 as Muhammad V, he at first followed a fairly moderate course. By the mid-1930's, however, he became increasingly nationalistic, urging the French, for example, to abandon their policy of having two different legal systems for Morocco's Arabs and BERBERS. He also created an annual Throne Day holiday on which his speeches would foster nationalist sentiments and activities.

Although loyal to the Allies during World War II (1939–45), Muhammad V grew even more nationalistic during the war years, encouraged, in part, by American president Franklin D. Roosevelt (1882–1945), who had advised him to press for independence from France.

By 1951 he was so openly identified with the independence movement that the French fomented rebellions against him. In 1953 he was deposed and exiled, sent first to the Mediterranean island of Corsica and then to the Indian Ocean island of MADAGASCAR. During his absence, however, civil disruptions and even terrorism increased so rapidly in Morocco that France, already facing rebellion in nearby ALGERIA, was forced in November 1955 to allow him to return and resume the throne. In March 1956 he succeeded in negotiating a treaty with France that gave Morocco full independence.

As the sultan of an independent nation, Muhammad V took a moderate stance in many areas, while taking firm control of the nation. Retaking the throne in 1957, he pursued a policy that asserted his own personal authority over the nation. As the decade went on, however, he gradually passed more and more of the daily control of the nation to his son Hassan, who favored a more active government. Finally, in 1960, he turned over the reigns of government to Hassan, who became King Hassan II (1929–1999), after his father's death. Muhammad remained king, in name only, until his death in 1961.

See also: COLONIAL RULE (Vol. IV); FRANCE AND AFRICA (Vol. IV); HASSAN II (Vol. V); NATIONALISM AND INDEPENDENCE MOVEMENTS (Vol. IV).

Further reading: C. R. Pennell, *Morocco Since 1830: A History* (New York: New York University Press, 2001).

Muhammad Abdullah Hassan (Sayyid Muhammad Abdille Hassan) (1864–1920) *Nationalist and resistance leader in Somalia*

Hassan was born in northern Somali territory in the Horn of Africa. As a boy he began his Islamic education and by age 10 he could read the Quran. While still a teenager he set up his own school to teach the Quran, and soon his reputation for learning and piety earned him the honorific title of *sheikh*. In his late teens he signed on as a crew member on a trading vessel that traveled the Somali coastal regions, and he also traveled overland to the Sudan. About that time, his homeland came under British COLONIAL RULE as the PROTECTORATE of BRITISH SOMALILAND.

After his travels Hassan returned home and married before setting out in 1894 on the pilgrimage to Mecca, the holy Islamic city in Saudi Arabia. It was in Mecca that he met Sayyid Muhammad Salih (d. 1919) and joined the religious brotherhood, the Salihiyya, that Salih had founded.

Upon returning to the Somali port city of Berbera, Hassan proselytized on behalf of the Salihiyya in opposition to the well-established Qadiriyya brotherhood. He

also became increasingly anti-British, believing that colonial rule was corrupting and destroying the Islamic way of life among his people. Calling for the expulsion of the British but unsuccessful at gaining many followers, he moved back to his home area, gradually amassing a large following of devout supporters. In 1899 he launched his first incursion against the colonial occupation.

Hassan was a poet as well as a skilled orator, both admired traits among the Somali people. His oratory was probably the main reason for his success in gaining a following.

For the next 20 years Hassan led a fierce resistance against the forces of ETHIOPIA in the contested area of the OGADEN, where his father's family originated, and British Somaliland. The British initially derided Hassan, dubbing him the "Mad Mullah" for his messianic teaching. They underestimated him, however, as he consistently eluded capture and commanded an army that at its height numbered 15,000.

In 1904, after a series of defeats, Hassan fled to ITALIAN SOMALILAND, where he stayed until 1907. He then returned to British Somaliland and continued his attempts to drive out the colonial powers. In 1920 the British Air Force delivered a crushing bombardment on Hassan's position. Killed in the raid, Hassan died as a martyr to his followers and as one of the forefathers of Somali nationalism.

See also: ENGLAND AND AFRICA (Vols. III, IV, V); COLONIAL CONQUEST (Vol. IV); ISLAM, INFLUENCE OF (Vols. II, III, IV); RESISTANCE AND REBELLION (Vol. IV); SUFISM (Vols. II, III, IV).

music A vital facet of life in Africa, music commemorates important occasions for both individuals and communities. It complements other mediums of expression such as DANCE, theater, and oral tradition. It accompanies and organizes the rhythms of work, and it provides entertainment and comfort. The many musical styles that have developed across Africa share certain common features that distinguish them as uniquely African. At the same time, however, the breadth of diversity makes it impossibly to treat "African music" as a unified entity.

Instruments The diversity of African music is evident in the vast number of distinctive African instruments that can be heard throughout the continent. Africans do not normally categorize instruments in a fashion comparable to that of Western musicologists, but their instruments can be roughly fitted into the same broad categories, which include drums (membranophones), wind instruments (aerophones), stringed instruments (chordophones), and self-sounding instruments (idiophones). In spite of this, it must be remembered that instruments often take on a highly personal role for African musicians, in large part because musicians typically craft their own instruments.

The nature and scale of African societies can influence the type of instruments utilized by members of a given community. Historically, Africans living in highly centralized and hierarchical states have tended to see the human voice as very important. At the same time, among these peoples musical instruments tend to be fewer in number. In contrast, in smaller, less tightly organized societies, man-made instruments occupy a more prominent place. Ecology and the particular materials available also determine what instruments appear in different settings. For example, not surprisingly drums are most commonly utilized in regions that are heavily wooded.

Throughout African societies, drums play a pivotal role, especially in West Africa. Drums come in many sizes and shapes and are constructed of varied materials. The bodies of drums are fashioned from wood, gourds, and clay, while the skins of cows, goats, and reptiles typically serve as drum membranes. Among the more recognizable African drums are the hourglass-shaped West African tension drums, widely known as *talking drums*. These can produce sounds that mimic human voices, and, for the initiated, convey messages. The goblet-shaped *djembe* drums of GUINEA and the bowl-shaped *ngoma* drums of southern Africa are also distinctive.

Wind instruments, which include the flute, trumpet, oboe, and whistle, are made of calabashes, wood, ivory, the horns of cattle, in addition to metal. Large horn bands often arose in powerful kingdoms, most notably in West Africa and the Great Lakes region. Brass bands sprang up in the latter half of the 19th century, directly influenced by military bands of the colonial powers. The impact of Cuban music on West African dance music has been especially influential in spreading brass wind instruments.

Although the lute, zither, musical bow, and lyre are widely employed stringed instruments, perhaps the most celebrated African stringed instrument is the 21-string kora, which is part lute and part harp. In West Africa, especially in the Sahel region among the MANDE, the kora is closely associated with the griot (also known as a *jeli* or *jali*). Griots, who function as oral historians, praise singers, counselors, and minstrels, recite epic poetry and perform praise singing, invariably accompanied by a kora. This underscores a general trend in African music, linking music with oral literature. During the course of the 20th century, particularly after World War II (1939–45), the guitar became an increasingly important instrument among African musicians.

There are two principal types of self-sounding instruments: the xylophone and the lamellophone. The defining characteristic of this class of instruments is that the body of the instrument vibrates to produce sound. The xylophone, usually referred to as a balafon or marimba, is constructed of wooden bars fastened to hollowed-out gourds that resonate with sound when struck with sticks.

The lamellophone is a kind of thumb piano, commonly known as the mbira, *kalimba,* or *sansa,* and is most prevalent in southern and Central Africa. It is normally constructed with 10 metal straps, which are attached to a resonator of wood. (See photo on p. 219 of Vol. II.)

The human voice, too, serves as an important musical instrument. Possibly the most distinctive African vocal style is call-and-response singing. This involves a soloist calling and the chorus responding collectively to the soloist's prompt. Although call-and-response is practiced throughout Africa, it is among the ZULU of SOUTH AFRICA that the traditional call-and-response a cappella, choral music known as *isicathamiya* has gained the greatest following.

Social Role Music is interwoven into the everyday fabric of African societies and cannot be understood properly outside the context of its cultural settings. It serves a wide range of functions and is at the heart of many social, cultural, religious, and commercial activities. Important life transitions, such as initiation cere-

In this photo taken in 1957, father and son both enjoy playing a marimba in Sanniquellie, Liberia. © *Library of Congress*

monies, weddings, and funerals require specific forms of music. Similarly, the veneration of ancestors, healing ceremonies, and spirit possession ceremonies all must be accompanied by the appropriate music. Music can also signal the presence of a deity, or it can be used to summon one. Specific instruments are associated with certain spiritual or curative properties. For instance flutes and horns are widely associated with spirits.

The making of music is normally not limited to a select cadre of professional musicians, even though the latter exist. More generally, African men and women are expected to acquire skill in singing and dancing as a step in becoming full members of a given society. In undergoing initiation to adulthood, they receive instruction in song and dance.

African Musical Styles One cannot speak of African music as if the incredibly diverse array of Africans universally embrace one monolithic form. Many different styles have evolved as part of a dynamic and ongoing process of blending between indigenous musical genres. The coming together of diverse musical styles has also resulted from the migrations of distinct African peoples throughout the continent. Wherever groups have migrated, they have introduced new musical forms that have influenced and become integrated with the music of the region, adding to the adaptability and sophistication of African music. Given the dynamic and fluid nature of African musical forms, the suggestion that African music was in some sense static and unchanging prior to COLONIAL CONQUEST would be historically incorrect. It would also be misleading to characterize African musical styles as traditional and Western or Arabic musical influences as modern or modernizing.

With increasing European penetration of Africa during the 19th century, and finally, the imposition of formal COLONIAL RULE, African music became increasingly influenced by Western music. Christian music, in the form of Protestant hymns and Catholic liturgical chants, had a significant impact in West and Central Africa. In North and East Africa, Middle Eastern and Arabic influences were more pronounced. Indian music, too, made inroads in eastern Africa, particularly with the establishment of significant Indian communities in UGANDA, KENYA, TANZANIA, and South Africa.

Interestingly some of the external musical styles that have exercised the greatest impact on African musicians were introduced by communities of the AFRICAN DIASPORA. *Goombay,* a music that developed among the Jamaican Maroons, is one such example. This style spread throughout West Africa in the early 19th century, after being introduced into SIERRA LEONE by freed Maroons. Jazz, ragtime, and reggae provide further instances of music created by persons of African descent, who have drawn on African musical traditions, and who have, in turn, influenced African music.

Each region of Africa boasts distinctive varieties of music, reflecting both indigenous musical styles and the musical traditions of different colonial powers. As a result, to a certain extent, there are broad similarities in the contemporary musical forms of English-speaking, French-speaking, and even Portuguese-speaking Africa. For example, in the former West African British colonies of NIGERIA, GHANA, and Sierra Leone, the guitar has left an indelible imprint on musical expression. The term *palm-wine music* refers in a broad way to the music of the African coast, which blended indigenous musical styles with those introduced by European sailors. As a result Western instruments such as accordions, harmonicas, and guitars were adapted by African musicians.

The original Jamaican Maroons were enslaved Africans who were freed as the Spanish fled Jamaica, then a possession of Spain, in front of a British invasion. Receiving their name from the Spanish word *cimarrón,* meaning wild or untamed, the Maroons settled in the island's tropical forests and proved very effective at resisting British control, fighting a series of wars with the colonial authorities over roughly 75 years. Groups of escaped slaves also joined the Maroons and swelled their numbers.

Guitar bands known as HIGHLIFE bands flourished in Ghana and Nigeria in the post World War II era, especially in the urban areas. Among the notable bandleaders were E. T. MENSAH (1919–1996) and Nana Ampadou (1945–   ). They also drew upon calypso, Cuban rhythms, and the big-band sound that was popular at the time in the United States and Europe. In Nigeria, *juju,* a guitar band style closely associated with the YORUBA, has become extremely popular, owing in part to the popularizing efforts of I. K. Dairo (1930–1996). In *juju* music, Western keyboards, accordions, and pedal steel guitars are mixed with Yoruba percussive rhythms. In Central Africa, *soukous,* which drew on Cuban rumba music, attained great popularity as early as the 1930s. In South Africa, the *marabi,* a keyboard style of music, evolved in the black townships in the early 20th century. By the 1920s, influenced by African American jazz bands, it had incorporated the big band sound and given birth to groups such as the Jazz Maniacs. It continued to evolve into a uniquely South African jive music known as *mbaqanga.* Perhaps the most famous South African musical group, the Jazz Epistles, emerged from the *mbaqanga* tradition. Formed in 1959, the Jazz Epistles featured Abdullah Ibrahim (1934–   ), who was then known as Dollar Brand, on the piano,

Hugh Masekela (1931–) on the trumpet, and Kippi Moeketsi on the alto sax. Their first recording, made in 1960, marked the beginning of modern South African jazz.

I. K. Dairo was not initially a professional musician, although he was only 12 when he joined his first band. As with so many of his contemporaries, he was a migrant worker, and he also was a small-scale trader. However, he continued to work as a musician until 1956, when he formed in his own band, which in 1959 became the Blue Spots. As part of his effort to take *juju* music to new levels, he researched Yoruba ORAL TRADITIONS. As a composer, instrumentalist, and vocalist, he drew on Yoruba call-and-response traditions, the Yoruba talking drums, the accordion, and rhythms from Latin America. His standing among his fellow musicians was such that when he died, in 1996, no Nigerian musicians performed for five days, and the RADIO carried only his music.

See also: COLONIALISM, INFLUENCE OF (Vol. IV); GRIOT (Vol. II); IBRAHIM, ABDULLAH (Vol. V); MASEKELA, HUGH (Vol. V); MUSIC (Vols. I, II, III, V); SITI BINTI SAAD (Vol. IV); THUMB PIANO (Vol. II); URBANIZATION (Vols. IV, V); URBAN LIFE AND CULTURE (Vols. IV, V).

Further reading: Samuel Ekpe Akpabot, *Form, Function, and Style in African Music* (Ibadan, Nigeria: Macmillan Nigeria, 1998); Alan P. Merriam, *African Music in Perspective* (New York: Garland, 1982).

Mutesa I, Kabaka (c. late 1830s–1884) *Ruler of the kingdom of Buganda, in present-day Uganda*

Mutesa I reigned as *kabaka*, or ruler, of the kingdom of BUGANDA from 1852 to 1884. During these years he increased the kingdom's commercial contacts with Arab traders from the SWAHILI COAST, who had first arrived at the royal court in 1844, eight years before Mutesa's reign began. Also during his reign, Europeans were admitted into the kingdom for the first time.

Mutesa I was an autocratic ruler, known for the great rewards and severe punishments he meted out to those he felt deserved them. However, upward mobility in his kingdom was based on achievement rather than social rank. As a result his capital became a magnet for ambitious and adventuresome subjects. The *kabaka* himself was head of a military and civil bureaucracy that served

solely at his pleasure. Buganda was prosperous and militarily superior to neighboring kingdoms, and eager to expend its influence over them.

Mutesa increased Buganda's wealth by raiding neighboring states to get slaves and ivory. These items were traded to Arab merchants in exchange for firearms and COTTON. For a time, because it supported his dealings with the Arabs, Mutesa observed the traditional Muslim practice of fasting during the month of Ramadan. However, in 1877, because he wanted European support against incursions from EGYPT, he also welcomed Christian MISSIONARIES into his kingdom.

Mutesa's court was first visited by Europeans in 1862, when an expedition led by John Hanning SPEKE (1827–1864) passed through Buganda in search of the source of the Nile River. Next to arrive, in 1872–73, were the British army officers Samuel BAKER (1821–1893) and Charles George GORDON (1833–1885), in command of Egyptian troops in the service of Khedive ISMAIL (1830–1895). The two men were probing southward in search of trade and territorial expansion, and Mutesa saw the visit as an opportunity to help mount an expedition against the neighboring kingdom of BUNYORO. The Anglo-Egyptian group, however, preferred to advance up the Nile and offered no assistance.

In 1875, when British journalist Henry Morton STANLEY (1841–1904), visited Buganda, he counted 125,000 troops and 230 war canoes in readiness for a single campaign against the kingdom of Busoga to the east.

Mutesa was never converted to Christianity, despite the presence of missionaries from the CHURCH MISSIONARY SOCIETY, whom he had allowed into the country after 1877. Catholic missionaries arrived in 1879. Eventually, rival Protestant, Catholic, and Islamic religious factions emerged, reflecting some of the deeper social and political tensions in the kingdom. In 1884 Mutesa I died in his capital at Lubaga Hill, a walled city with a population of 40,000. He was succeeded by his son, Mwanga II (c. 1866–1903), in an orderly transition of power. Unlike Mutesa, however, Mwanga was weak and vacillating, and Buganda soon entered a period of unrest.

See also: BUSOGA (Vol. III); RAMADAN (Vol. II); TRADE AND COMMERCE (Vol. IV).

Further reading: S. Kiwanuka, *A History of the Kingdom of Buganda* (London: Longman, 1971).

N

Nairobi Capital of BRITISH EAST AFRICA (also known as Kenya Colony), located in the fertile central highlands of present-day KENYA; the city retained its capital status after Kenyan independence, in 1963. Nairobi was founded, in 1899, as a camp for British colonists and Asian laborers working on the Mombasa-Uganda railroad. Due to its high elevation (5,500 feet; 1,676 m) and pleasant climate, the camp soon attracted Asian merchants, British settlers and officials, and Africans from throughout the region. By 1905 the British had moved their colonial capital to Nairobi from the coastal city of MOMBASA.

Nairobi took its name from the MAASAI term, Enkare Nairobi, meaning "place of cool waters."

During the early 20th century Nairobi's commercial and economic sectors continued to develop despite several regional outbreaks of bubonic plague. European SETTLERS, attracted by the agricultural potential of the fertile surrounding area, gave the town a British colonial character, in terms of both its ARCHITECTURE and its segregated residential areas. In order to accommodate European settlers, however, the British administration forced many black Kenyans from their land. The people most seriously affected by this land policy were the KIKUYU (Gikuyu), Kenya's largest indigenous ethnic group. In light of the British land grab, many Kikuyu migrated to Nairobi and began to form political organizations with the aim of getting their land back. The future president of independent Kenya, Jomo KENYATTA (c. 1891–1978), was one of the prominent leaders of this political process.

After World War II (1939–45), because of a substantial expansion in manufacturing, Nairobi added an industrial sector to its existing commercial and government sectors, bringing an influx of African migrants. Some of these new arrivals were able to find housing in legally recognized African residential areas, but many settled as illegal squatters. At the same time, the nationalist MAU MAU movement challenged the colonial order to face the reality of Kenyan independence, which was finally achieved, in 1963, after decades of Mau Mau violence and British reprisals. At independence, Nairobi, with an estimated population of 266,800, remained the capital.

See also: ASIAN COMMUNITIES (Vols. IV, V); COLONIAL RULE (Vol. IV); COLONIALISM, INFLUENCE OF (Vol. IV); ENGLAND AND AFRICA (Vols. III, IV, V); NAIROBI (Vol. V); URBAN LIFE AND CULTURE (Vols. IV, V); URBANIZATION (Vols. IV, V).

Further readings: W. T. W. Morgan, ed., *Nairobi: City and Region* (New York: Oxford University Press, 1967).

Nama Ethnic group of southern NAMIBIA that today makes up approximately 5 percent of the country's population. From 1904 to 1908, the Nama revolt against German colonial occupation nearly led to their annihilation. Known by the early European colonists as Khoikhoi, the Nama were first driven northward from their original home to an area near the Orange River, along Namibia's southern border with SOUTH AFRICA. During the mid 1800s the Nama moved again, this time to a region near Windhoek, the present-day Namibian capital, located in the central highlands. This semi-arid region of grasslands and shrubs has been their homeland ever since.

A pastoral people who have survived for centuries as subsistence farmers and herders, the Nama have a vital musical and poetic tradition. Storytelling, for which they are renowned, has been one of their primary ways of keeping their history and traditions alive in the present day. Their LANGUAGE uses various clicking sounds and is in the Khoisan language family that also includes the SAN languages.

During the first decade of the 20th century the Nama joined with the HERERO in a rebellion against German COLONIAL CONQUEST that lasted nearly four years. Following a period of German expansion in their territory, in January 1904, the Herero rose up against COLONIAL RULE, initially killing more than 100 settlers and troops. The German colonial authorities responded with particularly brutal force. Still, in October 1904, the Nama, in spite of long-standing differences that in the past had frequently led them into conflict with the neighboring Herero, joined the uprising.

Led for much of the time by their leader Hendrik WITBOOI (1830–1905), the Nama steadfastly refused to surrender even in the face of a particularly ferocious German PACIFICATION effort. German troops embarked on a campaign of torture, lynching, and mass murder after their commander, Lothar von Trotha (1848–1920), gave orders to kill any Nama or Herero who did not leave the territory. By the time the rebellious Herero and Nama put down their weapons, in 1908, thousands had been killed, and another 15,000 Herero and 2,000 Nama had been herded into concentration camps where they became subjects of medical experiments, sexual abuse, and forced LABOR. Ultimately, as many as 60,000 Herero— almost 80 percent of their population—and 50 percent of the Nama population of 20,000 people lost their lives.

It took decades for the Nama to recover from the disaster, but by the middle of the 20th century, although somewhat lessened in power and influence, they once again had become one of the main ethnic groups of the Namibian region.

See also: GERMANY AND AFRICA (Vol. IV); KHOIKHOI (Vols. II, III); KHOISAN (Vol. I); MAHERERO, SAMUEL (Vol. IV); SOUTH WEST AFRICA (Vol. IV).

Namibia Mineral-rich country located in southwest Africa on the Atlantic Ocean. A German colony called SOUTH WEST AFRICA from 1884 to 1915, Namibia measures 318,300 square miles (824,400 sq km) in area and has a mostly arid and semiarid climate. It is bordered by ANGOLA, BOTSWANA (called BECHUANALAND during the colonial era), and SOUTH AFRICA. The most influential groups in Namibia include the OVAMBO, who constitute about 50 percent of the population, the HERERO, NAMA, and Afrikaner and German minorities.

By 1860, SAN hunter-gatherers, Namibia's original inhabitants, had been pushed into the Kalahari desert by Bantu-speaking agro-pastoralists, such as the Ovambo and the Herero, who eventually came to dominate the north and central areas. In the meantime the Khoisan-speaking Nama peoples had established control over the southern portions of the territory. The Nama and the Herero clashed frequently over land, which both needed for grazing their herds, until increasing incursion by German explorers and traders gave the two peoples a common enemy.

By the 1870s the British had established the settlement of WALVIS BAY and seemed set to establish COLONIAL RULE over the entire area. However, the cost of such a venture proved prohibitive, and Germany, through a combination of dubious treaties, military force, and outright theft, began to annex territory. By the end of the 1880s, Germany had established the colony of South West Africa. As of the early 1900s the Germans had gained total control of the southern and central regions, using genocidal tactics to virtually annihilate the resisting Herero and Nama peoples.

After Germany's defeat in World War I (1914–18), South Africa governed South West Africa under a MANDATE from the League of Nations. After World War II (1939–45) South African prime minister Jan Christiaan SMUTS (1870–1950) sought to convince the newly formed United Nations (UN), which replaced the League of Nations, to permit South Africa to incorporate South West Africa as a fifth province. Opposition to South Africa's racial policies led the United Nations to reject the overture and to have South Africa administer the country as a UN TRUST TERRITORY instead. South Africa, however, refused to accept UN oversight and instead continued to administer South West Africa "in the spirit of the League (of Nations) mandate."

As a result of South Africa's administration, the South West African economy was closely tied to that of South Africa, with South African MINING companies realizing huge profits that would have been impossible without African LABOR. Likewise, the country's commercial fishing and farming industries were expanded using black laborers while profits went to white-owned South African companies and farms.

In line with NATIONALISM AND INDEPENDENCE MOVEMENTS elsewhere in postwar Africa, Namibian groups began efforts to rid themselves of South African rule. The Herero, who had suffered under brutal conditions during the earlier German colonial era, officially petitioned for British trusteeship. When that proved impossible, in 1946, the Herero leaders began asking the United Nations to support an independent Namibia. They received little help, however.

Because of the country's established system of racial inequality, progress toward independence was slow. Treating the territory as a fifth province of South Africa, the Afrikaner-led government gave parliamentary representation to its white residents. For the rest of the population, it implemented its APARTHEID policies and denied Africans and mixed-race people access to the political system. They also refused to issue passports to Namibian activists, thereby keeping them from garnering support from abroad. Moreover, following decades of colonial rule, Namibians lacked the economic means to pressure the South African government to change.

As the situation worsened, Namibians began organizing protests by any means possible, with African and mixed-race miners forming unions and holding strikes. Similarly, youth groups, sometimes aided by European missionary church organizations, made vocal demands for civil rights.

Finally, in 1956, the Herero paramount chief, Hosea Kutako (1870–1970), succeeded in getting a representative to petition the United Nations for help. Although progress was still slowed by the bureaucratic foot-dragging of the South African government, independence movements were emerging all over the African continent, and it seemed that Namibian independence was not far off.

In 1959 Namibians founded their own independence-minded political party, the South West Africa National Union (SWANU). It continued the UN petition process, called for better EDUCATION and health services for Africans, and demanded a more equitable distribution of the country's land and NATURAL RESOURCES. At the same time, SWANU began smuggling members across the border to British Bechuanaland (soon to be independent Botswana) to train as freedom fighters.

For some Namibians, however, SWANU was too accommodating to the South African government. Among them was Sam Nujoma (1929–   ) and members of his Ovamboland People's Organization, which broke from SWANU to create the South West Africa People's Organization (SWAPO), a more militant group that approached the independence movement with greater urgency. However, as they had done with SWANU, the South African government refused to recognize Nujoma's party and banned meetings; independence was still a long way off for Namibia's people in 1960.

See also: COLONIALISM, INFLUENCE OF (Vol. IV); GERMANY AND AFRICA (Vol. IV); NAMIBIA (Vols. I, II, III, V); NUJOMA, SAM (Vol. V); RESISTANCE AND REBELLION (Vol. IV); SKELETON COAST (Vol. III).

Nana Olomu (c. 1852–1916) *Prominent trader and political leader of the Itsekiri people of the Niger Delta*

The abolition of the SLAVE TRADE and the emergence of "legitimate trade" in products demanded by an indus-trializing Europe led to a growth in CASH CROPS for export. One of the most important of these was PALM OIL, with Southern NIGERIA emerging as the major producer. African traders acted as intermediaries in this commerce, buying palm oil in the interior, transporting it to the coast, and selling it to British merchants. The Itsekeri people on the northwestern edge of the NIGER DELTA were among those most deeply involved in this trade.

Nana Olomu's father was the leading Itsekiri trader of his time, and Nana in turn became the wealthiest trader of his day. His wealth meant power, and, in 1884, though he faced internal political opposition, he became governor of the Benin River. At the urging of the British consul, this office had been established by the Itsekiri traders more than 30 years earlier to control the region.

The profitable trade of the delta became increasingly attractive to British merchant interests. In 1879 George GOLDIE (1846–1925) brought together the separate private British firms trading in the delta to form the ROYAL NIGER COMPANY (RNC). The British government, which had been signing treaties with coastal rulers in preparation for the BERLIN CONFERENCE (1884–85), established a PROTECTORATE over the region. Britain then ceded administrative responsibility of the Niger Delta to the RNC.

A struggle to control trade ensued between the RNC and the Delta trading states. In the Itsekiri case, the commercial struggle ended in war, in 1894, with the British eventually the victors. Nana surrendered to the British authorities, who then tried him on various charges. Nana was found guilty and was sent into exile in ACCRA, the capital of the British GOLD COAST COLONY. He resided there until 1906, at which time he was allowed to return home. He died in 1916.

See also: ENGLAND AND AFRICA (Vol. IV); COLONIAL CONQUEST (Vol. IV); KOKO, FREDERICK WILLIAM (Vol. IV); TRADE AND COMMERCE (Vol. IV).

Further reading: Obaro Ikime, *Merchant Prince of the Niger Delta: the Rise & Fall of Nana Olomu, Last Governor of the Benin River* (London: Heinemann Educational, 1968).

Nasser, Gamal Abdel (Gamal Abdal, Gamal Abdul) (1918–1970) *Egyptian president and Arab leader*

Gamal Abdel Nasser was born in a poor suburb of ALEXANDRIA, a seaport city in northern EGYPT. The son of a postal worker with southern-Egyptian peasant roots, Nasser was educated at the Egyptian Military Academy when it was opened to non-aristocratic students. In 1938 he graduated from the academy and joined the officer corps. Together with fellow army officers, he helped to found a secret society, the Free Officers Movement, whose aim was to combat both governmental corruption and British imperialism. He fought in the 1948 Arab-Israeli War and was wounded in battle. In 1952 General

Muhammad Naguib (1901–1984), a hero of the Arab-Israeli War, led the Free Officers in a bloodless coup d'état that forced King FARUK (1920–1965) into exile.

In 1953 the Free Officers formed the Revolutionary Command Council (RCC), which Nasser secretly dominated. Empowered to govern the country for three years, the RCC banned all political parties but the Arab Socialist Union. It abolished the monarchy, named the popular General Naguib president, and declared the country a republic. Nasser's public role was minister of the interior. Policy differences between Nasser and Naguib, however, soon resulted in a power struggle between the two leaders.

In 1954 Nasser deposed Naguib, named himself president, and began a sweeping social and political revolution known as Arab Socialism, that also included a program of land reform. A decree limited the total acreage any Egyptian could own to slightly more than 200 acres (80 hectares). All lands above this amount were purchased from the owner by the government and distributed to landless peasants.

Under Nasser the government increased spending on free public EDUCATION, passed progressive LABOR laws, and improved public health and housing. He also enlarged the army and the police, turned Faruk's palaces into government offices, and allowed national monuments to decay. To build popular support for his reforms, Nasser rewrote schoolbooks, filling their pages with images of a prerevolution Egypt populated with oppressed peasants and imperialist masters. He also expanded Egypt's participation in the Arab League. In 1956 Nasser was officially elected president of Egypt under a new constitution that made Egypt an Arab, socialist state and gave Nasser broad executive powers.

Following a policy of nonalignment that Nasser called "positive neutralism," Egypt resisted taking sides with either the Western powers or the Soviet Union during the Cold War (1947–91). Instead Egypt willingly accepted monetary aid from both sides. As a reaction to this policy, the United States and Britain withdrew their financing from the ASWAN HIGH DAM, a massive flood-control project that Nasser supported. Nasser responded by nationalizing the Suez Canal Company, intending to use its profits to finance the dam. Judging Nasser's actions a threat to the canal, Britain, France, and Israel united to attack Egypt, strip away the Sinai Peninsula, and reoccupy the SUEZ CANAL zone. The United States and the Soviet Union intervened to stop the Suez War (or Suez-Sinai War, as it is sometimes called), and UN troops were stationed in Sinai as peacekeepers. In the end, Egypt kept the canal and received assistance from the Soviet Union to construct the Aswan Dam. Nasser's government then expelled thousands of British and French citizens and confiscated their property. This defiance of former colonial powers like Britain and France made Nasser a hero in the Arab world.

In 1958 Egypt and Syria formed the United Arab Republic, or UAR, as it was often called, with Nasser as head of state. Nasser hoped that the UAR would someday include every Arab land. The new state lasted only three years, until 1961, when Syria withdrew, but Nasser continued to call Egypt the United Arab Republic until his death.

Nasser's dream of Arab unity was an expression of his belief in pan-Arabism. His book, *The Philosophy of the Revolution* (1959), maintained that the European nations intentionally divided the Middle East into many different states in order to keep them politically and economically vulnerable. A unified Arab world, he contended, could stand up to the West. In defense of Arab Socialism, he noted how foreigners extracted wealth from Egypt but left it under-industrialized and dependent upon CASH CROPS such as COTTON. He further believed that oil profits should be divided equally among all the states in the region.

As Egypt entered the 1960s, the political situation in the region, worsened by Nasser's refusal to recognize the state of Israel, remained volatile. Egypt's defeat by Israel in the Suez War of 1956 caused him to divert money into building up Egypt's armed forces. Egypt also began to accept military aid from the Soviet Union, which sold weapons to the other Arab countries as well. Continued conflict with Israel marked the upcoming years of Nasser's life.

See also: NASSER, GAMAL ABDEL (Vol. V); SOVIET UNION AND AFRICA (Vols. IV, V).

Further reading: Dominique De Roux, *Gamal Abdel Nasser,* notes de Michel Marmin (Lausanne, Switzerland: Age d'homme, 2000); James Jankowski, *Nasser's Egypt, Arab Nationalism, and the United Arab Republic* (Boulder, Colo.: Lynne Rienner Publishers, 2002).

Natal Former British colony and now a province of present-day SOUTH AFRICA. During the first half of the 19th century the region that is now Natal was home to ZULU groups that were trying to repel an influx of Boer settlers, who were migrating to the area in large numbers. After years of warfare, in about 1840 the BOERS secured tracts of land through treaties with the Zulu leader, Mpande (1798–1872), and established the settler colony of Natalia. At the same time, however, Africans who had been forced from the region by the Zulu Mfecane (a military campaign of territorial expansion) began to return to Natal, eventually outnumbering the white settlers and destabilizing Boer control of the colony.

Britain took advantage of the instability in the region and claimed the area as a PROTECTORATE in 1843. As a result most of the AFRIKAANS-speaking Boers in Natal migrated to the two interior AFRIKANER REPUBLICS—the TRANSVAAL and the ORANGE FREE STATE (OFS). Natal was then governed as an extension of CAPE COLONY until 1856, when the British proclaimed the region a crown colony.

Under British rule white farmers began to experiment with growing a number of CASH CROPS for both local consumption and export. Sugar became increasingly important. Unable to recruit sufficient African LABOR, the colony decided, in 1858, to import indentured workers from India. Within a few years more than 6,000 Indians arrived in Natal, and they continued to do so until the end of the indenture system, in 1911. Joined by other Indian immigrants, they came to outnumber the white population by the end of the century. As they left the sugar estates at the end of their indenture, they became small-scale farmers or entered commerce.

The Indians' struggle against discriminatory legislation led to the arrival of the young lawyer Mohandas GANDHI (1869–1948) in Natal, in 1893. Over the next two decades he developed the nonviolent resistance practice of *SATYAGRAHA*, which he was then to implement in India in the ultimately successful effort to end British rule there.

In the latter half of the 19th century, Natal and the surrounding regions were marked by constant conflicts among Boer, Zulu, and British interests, the bloodiest of these conflicts being the ANGLO-ZULU WARS. By 1897, however, the Zulu were defeated, and their territory, Zululand, was officially made part of Natal. The Boers invaded the colony during the ANGLO-BOER WAR (1899–1902), but they were eventually repelled by British forces.

Despite Britain's military might, the Zulu continued to resist COLONIAL RULE into the 1900s. The Zulu king DINIZULU (1868–1913) was charged with treason for his role in leading rebellions against the British in 1889 and 1908. This resistance, however, was insufficient to oust the British from the region. In 1910 Natal joined Cape Colony, the Transvaal, and the OFS to form the UNION OF SOUTH AFRICA.

See also: CETSHWAYO (Vol. IV); ENGLAND AND AFRICA (Vol. IV).

National Congress of British West Africa
Inter-territorial political body founded by J. E. CASELY-HAYFORD (1866–1930), the Gold Coast intellectual. Casely-Hayford believed that the most effective path to West African independence involved cooperation among all Africans. In 1920, following the conclusion of World War I (1914–19), a new current of African nationalism offered Casely-Hayford and his Nigerian colleague, Dr.

Akiwande Savage, a chance to organize a conference in support of West African self-determination.

The conference, attended by West African leaders and held in ACCRA, passed resolutions calling for various reforms. These included an end to British-controlled judiciaries, economic and political equality for Africans, and African input on the political direction of the former German colonies. (Germany lost its colonies, including TOGOLAND [now TOGO] and Kamerun [part of today's CAMEROON] in West Africa, when it lost the war; Britain and France shared control of these two colonies under the MANDATE system of the League of Nations.) At the end of the conference the leaders made their gathering a permanent entity, naming it the National Congress of British West Africa (NCBWA).

The NCBWA met on three other occasions, in 1923 in FREETOWN, SIERRA LEONE; in 1925–26 in Bathurst, The GAMBIA; and in 1930 in LAGOS, NIGERIA. At the later meetings the congress had to repeat many of its original demands, exposing its inability to organize the masses and bringing to light the lack of engagement by the colonial governments. Despite its inability to gain the reforms in COLONIAL RULE that it sought, the NCBWA was a precursor of the more militant—and more successful—West African nationalist movements that formed after World War II (1939–45).

See also: NATIONALISM AND INDEPENDENCE MOVEMENTS (Vol. IV); POLITICAL PARTIES AND ORGANIZATIONS (Vol. IV).

Further reading: J. Ayodele Langley, *Pan-Africanism and Nationalism in West Africa, 1900–1945: A Study in Ideology and Social Classes* (Oxford, U.K.: Clarendon Press, 1973).

nationalism and independence movements
Anticolonial in its origins, nationalism constituted a set of political ideas that over time gave rise to independence movements seeking to end COLONIAL RULE in Africa. In the late 19th century, many African societies put up a spirited resistance to European COLONIAL CONQUEST. In the early decades of the colonial era, widespread RESISTANCE AND REBELLION gave testimony to continued African unwillingness to accept colonial rule. Gradually, however, African opposition shifted to a different political realm. Whereas initial resistance and subsequent rebellions were largely attempts to restore the old order, some Africans began to look forward to a new order. The impetus for rising nationalism was the deep dissatisfaction with being subjects of colonial empires rather than citizens of their own societies. However, the shape that nationalism took drew from the dominant currents of political thought in Europe at the time.

The patterns of political thinking that can be labeled nationalism first emerged among those who had received

African Independence

Map legend:

- Countries that have retained their independence
- Countries gaining independence by 1945
- Countries gaining independence 1945–54
- Countries gaining independence 1955–64
- Countries gaining independence since 1964
- Countries gaining independence from an African state

* Sovereignty is disputed as of 2004.

Map labels:

MOROCCO 1956 · TUNIS 1956 · Mediterranean Sea · WESTERN SAHARA* 1976 · ALGERIA 1962 · LIBYA 1951 · EGYPT 1922 · Red Sea · MAURITANIA 1960 · MALI 1960 · NIGER 1960 · CHAD 1960 · SUDAN 1956 · ERITREA 1993 · SOMALILAND REPUBLIC declared 1991 · SENEGAL 1960 · GAMBIA 1965 · GUINEA-BISSAU 1974 · BURKINA FASO 1960 · GUINEA 1958 · SIERRA LEONE 1961 · IVORY COAST 1960 · GHANA 1957 · BENIN 1960 · NIGERIA 1960 · CENTRAL AFRICAN REPUBLIC 1960 · DJIBOUTI 1977 · ETHIOPIA · SOMALI REPUBLIC 1960 · LIBERIA · TOGO 1960 · CAMEROON 1960 · EQUATORIAL GUINEA 1968 · SÃO TOMÉ & PRÍNCIPE 1975 · GABON 1960 · DEMOCRATIC REPUBLIC OF THE CONGO 1960 · UGANDA 1962 · KENYA 1963 · REPUBLIC OF THE CONGO 1960 · RWANDA 1962 · BURUNDI 1962 · TANZANIA 1961 · Cabinda (ANGOLA) · COMOROS 1975 · ATLANTIC OCEAN · ANGOLA 1975 · MALAWI 1963 · MOZAMBIQUE 1975 · ZAMBIA 1964 · MADAGASCAR 1960 · NAMIBIA 1990 · ZIMBABWE 1980 · BOTSWANA 1966 · SWAZILAND 1968 · LESOTHO 1966 · SOUTH AFRICA 1910 · INDIAN OCEAN

a Western-oriented EDUCATION. As the historian Robert W. July (1918–) observed, "The educated African was the parent of the independent African." Among the earliest people to argue for a new political direction for Africa was the Liberian educator and political thinker Edward Wilmot BLYDEN (1832–1912). Blyden made a significant contribution to West African intellectual history by articulating ideas about African nationalism and PAN-AFRICANISM. Similarly, in EGYPT, the 1881 mutiny of Egyptian army officers led by Colonel Ahmad URABI (1841–1911) was an attempt to force the khedive to adopt a more nationalist stance and a new constitution and elections.

With the defeat of independent African states in SOUTH AFRICA, African leaders such as the CAPE COLONY newspaper editor John Tengo JABAVU (1859–1921) began calling for African participation in the parliamentary government. His position also highlights the significant role that NEWSPAPERS played in spreading ideas of nationalism in an era before RADIO became widespread.

African nationalists began to form overtly political organizations, although for the most part they were not yet dedicated to political independence. In 1912, for example, young, French-educated Muslims in ALGERIA organized the Party of Young Algeria. These "Young Algerians," led by Ferhat ABBAS (1899–1985) were seeking full French citizenship rights. They also desired assimilation with France and civil and social equality between mostly Christian Europeans and Muslims. That same year witnessed the founding of the AFRICAN NATIONAL CONGRESS (ANC), in South Africa, as a challenge to European SETTLERS who dominated the country's political life. The first generation of ANC leaders was also seeking full citizenship rights.

There was an upsurge of African nationalism and associated political organizations in the aftermath of World War I (1914–18). Nationalists focused on the Fourteen Points of U.S. president Woodrow Wilson (1856–1924). In particular they looked to his fifth point, which called for an impartial adjustment of all colonial claims. The guiding principle for that adjustment was that the interests of the indigenous population must have equal weight with the claims of the government. At the Paris Peace Conference, in 1919, a group of young Egyptian nationalists arrived, organized into a delegation (*Wafd* in Arabic) to press the assembled Allied powers for Egyptian independence. Though they were unsuccessful, they then constituted the WAFD PARTY, which was the country's leading political party until 1952. Nationalists in the four British West African colonies formed the NATIONAL CONGRESS OF BRITISH WEST AFRICA, which existed throughout the 1920s. It called for an end to British-controlled judiciaries, economic and political equality for Africans, and African input on the political direction of the former German colonies. In KENYA, a young government clerk, Harry THUKU (1895–1970), in 1921 helped launch the East African Association and the Young Kikuyu Association, which were the first of several political organizations to form in that colony. The intellectual currents of NÉGRITUDE and PAN-AFRICANISM also helped stimulate African nationalism in the 1920s and the 1930s, since they also were addressing the colonial condition.

For many Africans, the Italian invasion of ETHIOPIA in 1935 marked the beginning of World War II (1939–45) instead of the more conventional European-centered date of 1939. This event heightened feelings about liberation for many nationalists. They were particularly incensed by the failure of the major colonial rulers in Africa to come to the assistance of one of the three African member states of the League of Nations. The fall of France to Germany in 1940 greatly weakened France's long-term hold on its colonial empire, as did the British defeats in Asia at the hands of the Japanese. As the Allied leaders attempted to rally their demoralized populations, the colonized peoples were listening. Thus, in 1943, the ANC published a document entitled "The Atlantic Charter from the Standpoint of Africans within the UNION OF SOUTH AFRICA," which called for full African participation in the country's educational, political, and economic activities.

In the aftermath of the war African nationalism became much more assertive and vigorous, and the earlier political organizations transformed into political parties calling for independence. In NIGERIA, for example, Nnamdi AZIKIWE (1904–1996) established, in 1944, the National Council for Nigeria and the Cameroons. He also founded six NEWSPAPERS, including the *WEST AFRICAN PILOT*, through which he launched a massive anticolonial campaign. Although the colonial government banned two of his papers, Azikiwe had helped unleash political forces that would lead Nigeria to independence and, in 1963, Azikiwe to the presidency. Likewise, in GHANA, Kwame NKRUMAH (1909–1972) returned from England in 1947 to work as a political organizer. In 1949 he formed his own political party, the CONVENTION PEOPLE'S PARTY (CPP), to press for immediate independence for the GOLD COAST COLONY, which became Ghana in 1957.

In the colonies that constituted FRENCH WEST AFRICA, African political leaders, led by Félix HOUPHOUËT-BOIGNY (1905–1993) and Ahmed Sékou TOURÉ (1922–1984) met in BAMAKO (in what was then FRENCH SOUDAN), in 1946. There they formed the multi-colony, multiethnic AFRICAN DEMOCRATIC ASSEMBLY (Rassemblement Democratique Africain, RDA). Although Houphouët-Boigney claimed that the organization was not a political party, the RDA quickly spawned associated, individual political parties in each of the constituent territories. Touré then used the GUINEA branch of the RDA, the Democratic Party of Guinea, to lead his country to independence in 1958. The other French West African colonies became independent countries in 1960.

Nationalism and the movement toward independence often evolved into a violent liberation struggle. This was particularly true in Algeria and Kenya, where both countries had white settler populations that were determined to hang onto their privileged way of life. By 1948, frustrated with the continuing determination of the COLONS to stymie any meaningful Muslim political advance, revolutionary

Algerian fighters founded the Organisation Sécrete (Secret Organization) and plotted the violent overthrow of colonial rule. Ahmed BEN BELLA (1916–   ), who was to become president of independent Algeria in 1963, was one of its key leaders. By 1954 it had evolved into the NATIONAL LIBERATION FRONT and led the prolonged and bloody war that brought independence in 1962.

The struggle in Kenya was neither as prolonged nor as destructive of human life, but it nonetheless was both costly and bloody. It took the form of the MAU MAU movement and lasted from the late 1940s until the mid-1950s. Though the British security forces managed to suppress it, the Mau Mau fighters succeeded in propelling the British government to grant independence to Kenya. The events in Algeria and Kenya were a forecast of later wars of liberation in the Portuguese colonies and in Rhodesia (today's ZIMBABWE).

By 1960 the forces of African nationalism had crafted independence movements throughout much of the continent that brought an end to decades of colonial rule. Elsewhere this independence did not truly arrive for years. The struggle for independence was to last the longest for the countries of southern Africa.

See also: DECOLONIZATION (Vol. IV); INDEPENDENCE MOVEMENTS (Vol. V); POLITICAL PARTIES AND ORGANIZATIONS (Vols. IV, V).

Further reading: Toyin Falola, ed. *Africa.* Vol. 4. *The End of Colonial Rule: Nationalism and Decolonization* (Durham, N.C.: Carolina Academic Press, 2000).

National Liberation Front (Front de Libération Nationale, FLN) Independence movement of ALGERIA that, from 1954 to 1962, led the armed resistance to French COLONIAL RULE. After World War II (1939–45), movements calling for Algerian independence emerged throughout the country. One such organization was the Movement for the Triumph of Democratic Liberties (Mouvement pour le Triomphe des Libertés Démocratiques, MTLD), founded by Messali Hadj (1898–1974). In 1947 the MTLD created the Special Organization (Organisation Spéciale, OS) as a secret military wing. The OS was founded to manage and carry out covert military operations against French occupation when political channels were unavailable. When the French police dissolved the OS, in 1950, its leader, Ahmed BEN BELLA (1916–   ), created the Revolutionary Committee of Unity and Action (Comité Révolutionnaire d'Unité et d'Action, CRUA) to replace it.

The leaders of CRUA, including Ben Bella, were located in CAIRO and known as the "externals," while CRUA members within Algeria were known as "internals." In early 1954 CRUA leaders began to organize an armed resistance against French occupation. Later that year, CRUA was renamed the National Liberation Front (FLN). The

FLN then separated itself from military action by creating the National Liberation Army (Armée de Libération Nationale, ALN) to fight Algeria's war of independence.

In November 1954 the FLN began its rebellion, with the ALN launching multiple attacks against government and commercial targets throughout Algeria. The initiation of armed resistance soon garnered the support of a host of other Algerian nationalists, including Ferhat ABBAS (1899–1985), who was considered the founder of Algerian nationalism.

One group that did not align itself with the FLN was the National Algerian Movement (Mouvement Nationale Algérien, MNA), which was founded by Messali Hadj after the failure of the MTLD. Concerned with opposition to its leadership position within the independence struggle, the FLN eventually destroyed the MNA in Algeria. However, the MNA still held strong support among Algerian nationals in France, so the FLN responded by building up its own support in France. Taking their fight to Europe, the two resistance groups engaged in bloody "café wars" that left almost 5,000 dead.

As the ALN fought military battles against French occupation, the FLN attempted to gain the political support of the Algerian population. At the same time, French settlers known as COLONS began to form vigilante units to hunt down suspected FLN members. Though the French government did not sanction the colon actions against the FLN, the colonial police tacitly approved of the anti-FLN campaign.

French animosity toward the FLN increased dramatically after an incident at Phillipville, in 1955, in which the FLN killed more than 100 civilians. French forces retaliated in kind, claiming to kill more than 1,000 ALN members (though the FLN put the number of Muslim deaths, including non-FLN members, at more than 10,000). In 1956 France arrested FLN externals who were in Algeria for a leadership meeting and interned them for the duration of the war.

The FLN battle to gain self-determination was put in jeopardy, in 1958, with the return to power of Charles DE GAULLE (1890–1970). De Gaulle quickly introduced a referendum to decide the status of Algeria, and exhorted rebel leaders to participate in elections. The FLN, fearful that the referendum could undermine popular support, refused de Gaulle's invitation and set up a government-in-exile led by Abbas. Called the Provisional Government of the Algerian Republic, it was located in TUNIS, the capital of neighboring TUNISIA. The FLN continued to use guerrilla tactics in an attempt to disrupt the referendum vote. Ultimately, however, the FLN was unsuccessful, and 96 percent of Muslim voters supported Algeria's continued relationship with France.

Originally a loosely disciplined group of less than 1,000 men, the ALN gradually evolved into a fighting force of more than 40,000. Over time the ALN came to occupy areas of the Algerian countryside, driving out French police forces and even collecting taxes in certain instances. All told the ALN's struggle against French occupation cost the lives of more than 1,000,000 Algerians.

By 1959, however, the international community was pressuring France to grant Algeria its independence, and domestic French opposition to the conflict with the FLN was running high. Finally, in 1961 France and the FLN sat down to talks that led to a cease-fire in March 1962. Later that year, Algeria was granted independence.

See also: FRANCE AND AFRICA (Vols. III, IV, V); INDEPENDENCE MOVEMENTS (Vol. V); NATIONAL LIBERATION FRONT (Vol. V); RESISTANCE AND REBELLION (Vol. IV).

Further reading: Benjamin Stora (translated by Jane Marie Todd), *Algeria, 1830–2000: A Short History* (Ithaca, N.Y.: Cornell University Press, 2001).

natural resources   Africa has benefited from its diverse natural resources for generations. Historically, Africans used natural resources in a more sustainable manner than in the recent past, partly due to much lower population densities. When Europeans arrived in Africa, however, they recognized the wealth of natural resources and designed colonial economies to exploit as many resources as possible. The subsequent extraction and export of resources helped fuel the Industrial Revolution in Europe, which, by that time, had greatly reduced its own natural resources.

The natural resources of principal importance during the colonial period were related to AGRICULTURE and MINING. Africa's volcanic areas, such as the Rift Valley of East Africa, contain very fertile soils, while other areas have very old soils that have leached their nutrients over thousands of years and are no longer productive. Under colonialism, African farmers in both types of environments were encouraged and coerced—through the imposition of taxes or the threat of violence—to cultivate CASH CROPS for export rather than traditional subsistence crops.

Cash crops grown during this period included COFFEE, tea, tobacco, sisal, GROUNDNUTS (peanuts), sugar cane, COCOA, palm products, and trees for lumber. Many of the agricultural economies of African countries today remain dependent on the production of cash crops.

Although GOLD, COPPER, and iron ore had been mined in Africa long before Europeans arrived, the colonial focus on extracting MINERALS AND METALS resulted in what came to be called the African MINERAL REVOLUTION. Beginning in the latter half of the 19th century, European mining companies began investing in heavy machinery to extract large quantities of mineral resources at depths previously impossible to mine. With prospectors digging mines wherever they could, southern, Central, and West Africa soon became the focus of extensive diamond, gold, iron, and copper mining.

The harvesting and extraction of all these natural resources required human capital resources, as well. Africans exclusively provided the needed LABOR. As colonial subjects, hundreds of thousands of Africans, usually men, were either coerced or forced to leave their villages to work in the mines or on plantations for little or no money.

After World War II (1939–45) Europeans finally came to realize that Africa's natural resources were, in fact, being overused. As a result concepts that had not previously been of concern, such as the depletion of forests and the preservation of Africa's natural and wildlife resources, became a priority. By end of the colonial period, governments were beginning to create nature reserves and national parks, although often without consultation of indigenous populations. In addition, concerns about agricultural productivity lead to the implementation of soil erosion management techniques.

See also: COLONIALISM, INFLUENCE OF (Vol. IV); CONSERVATION (Vol. V); NATIONAL PARKS (Vol. V); NATURAL RESOURCES (Vols. III, V); WILDLIFE (Vol. V).

Ndebele (Matabele)   Bantu-speaking people living primarily in present-day ZIMBABWE who trace their origins to the ZULU of SOUTH AFRICA. In 1823 the Ndebele leader Mzilikazi (1790–1868) broke away from the Zulu king Shaka (1785–1828) and, along with a number of followers, settled in the region of present-day PRETORIA, South Africa. There they assimilated or conquered surrounding peoples, adding to their numbers. The continued threat posed by the Zulu and by encroaching BOERS prompted Mzilikazi, in 1837, to migrate to what became Matabeleland, located in the southwest of present-day Zimbabwe. Founding their capital at Bulawayo, the Ndebele used their military might to conquer and incorporate many of the local SHONA people into their state, while raiding others living outside their borders.

The Ndebele kingdom was short-lived, however. LOBENGULA (1836–1894) became king in 1870, two years after Mzilikazi's death, and ruled with a strong hand. Even so, he and his people faced an influx of Europeans drawn by the discovery of GOLD deposits south of Bulawayo. In 1888 Lobengula granted mineral rights in Matabeleland to the BRITISH SOUTH AFRICA COMPANY (BSAC), headed by Cecil RHODES (1853–1902), in exchange for firearms and ammunition. Rhodes then used this concession to move white settlers into the region, thus circumscribing Ndebele authority and power.

After the Ndebele raided Shona villages in territory controlled by the BSAC in an attempt to reassert their authority, the British stormed Bulawayo in 1893. Lobengula went into exile, where he eventually died. His heirs were never allowed to claim the Ndebele throne, and the settlers claimed their lands as part of the new British colony of SOUTHERN RHODESIA (now Zimbabwe). In 1896, however, the Ndebele rose in a rebellion called the CHIMURENGA and regained some of their land and herds in the peace settlement that followed.

Though their kingdom passed out of existence, the Ndebele people and culture persisted and today are a major ethnic group in Zimbabwe. While many continue to live in rural areas, raising maize (corn) and herding cattle, others became urbanized or engaged in migrant LABOR. Many also became political activists, contributing to the nationalist struggle that resulted in Zimbabwe's independence in 1980.

See also: BANTU LANGUAGES (Vol. I); COLONIAL CONQUEST (Vol. IV); ENGLAND AND AFRICA (Vols. III, IV, V); NGUNI (Vol. III); SHAKA (Vol. III).

Négritude A nationalist, pan-African literary and cultural movement among French-speaking intellectuals from Africa and the AFRICAN DIASPORA. Négritude emerged from the political activities of people of African descent living in the French Caribbean possessions of Guadeloupe, Martinique, and French Guiana. As citizens of France, politicians from these islands had begun to articulate an identity that affirmed racial pride well before the emergence of the formal Négritude movement on the eve of World War II (1939–45).

The word *négritude* was first used by writer and politician Aimé CÉSAIRE (1913–) of Martinique in his 1939 poem "Cahier d'un retour au pays natal" (Notebook of a return to my native land). The central figure of the poem is a black West Indian who returns to his home island from France. He represents the legacy of French colonialism and the various threads of African cultural identity that, intertwined, produce a unique racial endowment called *négritude*.

Césaire and like-minded, French-speaking black intellectuals developed the concept to generate a movement representing a collective identity for people of Africa and the African Diaspora. These people, they argued, shared a common culture, history, and experience of cultural domination.

The Négritude movement, though, was not only concerned with issues of culture and history. One of its major contributions lay in the arts. By adapting the French LANGUAGE to African conditions, it helped create new poetic and literary forms.

Although the Négritude movement originated in the French Caribbean, intellectuals from these islands were not alone in expressing the positive values of racial pride. Césaire, in fact, gave American poet Claude McKay (1890–1948) of the United States credit for expressing the values of Négritude in his verse. McKay, Langston Hughes (1902–1967), and other writers of the Harlem Renaissance in the United States gave testimony to a rich black culture. *The Souls of Black Folk* (1903) by W. E. B. DU BOIS (1868–1963) was also a critical contribution to the formulation of Négritude thought.

Négritude became the literary and cultural arm of the Pan-African movement, which insisted on the need for black equality if people of African heritage were ever to participate fully in the global community. PAN-AFRICANISM helped bring an end to formal COLONIAL RULE in Africa and prompted greater black intellectual and cultural autonomy.

See also: FRANCE AND AFRICA (Vols. IV, V); LITERATURE IN COLONIAL AFRICA (Vol. IV); LITERATURE IN MODERN AFRICA (Vol. V); NEOCOLONIALISM (Vol. V); *PRÉSENCE AFRICAINE* (Vol. IV); SENGHOR, LÉOPOLD (Vols. IV, V).

Further reading: Abiola Irele, *The African Experience in Literature and Ideology* (Bloomington, Ind.: Indiana University Press, 1990); Colette V. Michael, *Negritude: An Annotated Bibliography* (West Cornwall, Conn.: Locust Hill Press, 1988).

New Age Militant national newspaper published in SOUTH AFRICA from 1954 to 1962. By the 1950s South African presses offered a broad range of NEWSPAPERS, published for a wide variety of readerships, black and white. Alongside the mainstream, big-city dailies such as the *Star,* published in JOHANNESBURG, and the *Cape Argus,* in CAPE TOWN, were those papers that served as voices of protest and resistance against the political system that supported white supremacy. The protest papers became increasingly militant after the Afrikaner National Party won the 1948 election and began institutionalizing racism under the guise of APARTHEID.

One of the papers that most vigorously opposed white supremacy was the *Guardian.* Founded in 1937 as a LABOR UNION newspaper for African, white, and Coloured unionists, intellectuals, and politicians in Cape Town, the *Guardian* quickly attracted a broad national readership. At the same time, however, it upset government authorities. In 1952 the police raided its offices and issued banning orders against its editor, Brian Bunting (1920–). As part of its survival strategy the *Guardian* underwent a series of name changes before becoming *New Age,* which it remained from 1954 to 1962.

In its incarnation as *New Age,* the paper reached the peak of its influence. By 1958 it had a paid national circulation of 30,000 and a readership of about 100,000. Its popularity among African, Cape Coloured, and liberal white readers was a testament to the quality of its writers and their fearlessness in attacking unjust government policies. Among the writers was noted political journalist Govan MBEKI (1910–2001), who was the editor and branch manager of the paper's Port Elizabeth office in the eastern Cape Province from 1955 to 1962. During that time the columns of the *New Age* covered race issues (including anti-pass-law demonstrations), LABOR abuses, and industrial disasters such as the Coalbrook Mine collapse that killed more than 400 miners in 1960. Chief Albert LUTULI (1898–1967), the president of the AFRICAN NATIONAL CONGRESS, rightly described the paper as "the fighting mouthpiece of African aspirations."

It was precisely because it was such a strong champion of African rights in the increasingly repressive and politically hostile environment of apartheid South Africa that *New Age* was forced to cease publishing. Following the police massacre of peaceful protesters at Sharpeville in March of 1960, the paper wrote in-depth stories under bold headlines that declared the event a "mass slaughter." In response to the subsequent nationwide disturbances, the government cracked down, declaring a state of emergency. It closed the doors of *New Age,* arresting Bunting and other staff members.

The paper reappeared later in 1960, boldly continuing its coverage of the South African political scene. However, the state was becoming even more repressive, and the publication of *New Age* was officially prohibited on December 1, 1962. The paper changed its name to *Spark,* but the following year the government closed it down for good. Bunting, who had been editor since 1948, was forced to leave the country, ending the 25-year history of the *Guardian* and its successor newspapers. Those tumultuous 25 years witnessed a steady decline in the freedom of the press in South Africa to the point that it virtually disappeared in the early 1960s.

See also: COMMUNISM AND SOCIALISM (Vol. V); NATIONALISM AND INDEPENDENCE MOVEMENTS (Vol. IV).

newspapers Print media first became widespread in Africa during the 19th century, as colonial governments sought to control the African population by communicating to them what the rulers wanted them to know. The first newspapers were hand produced and published under the direction of the British government. Some publications ran for only a few editions, but, by 1900, there were more than 70 newspapers printed in West Africa alone.

Colonial Newspapers Africa's first newspapers were gazettes, or small, official government publications. The first gazette, the *Cape Town Gazette and African Advertiser,* ran for only three months, in 1800. The following year, the *Royal Gazette and Sierra Leone Advertiser* began publication in FREETOWN. The *Royal Gold Coast Gazette,* published in present-day GHANA, was a handwritten newspaper that began publication in 1822. The gazettes were sold in the streets by hawkers who earned a small commission.

In East Africa, journalism was dominated by British settlers. The region's first newspaper was the *East Africa and Uganda Mail,* published in MOMBASA, KENYA in 1899. Other British-run newspapers included the *East African Standard,* in NAIROBI; the *Uganda Argus,* printed in KAMPALA; and the *Tanganyika Standard,* printed in DAR ES SALAAM. These publications presented conservative views in favor of white settlers and opposed black liberation.

Newspapers in West Africa were also greatly influenced by the British. Beginning in the 1940s, a newspaper conglomerate called the London Mirror Group published British-style newspapers including the *Daily Times* and *Sunday Times of Lagos,* in NIGERIA; the *Gold Coast Daily Graphic* and *Sunday Mirror,* in ACCRA; and the *Sierra Leone Daily Mail,* in Freetown. The Mirror Group newspapers trained journalists, including some Africans, and used modern printing presses and photo equipment. Features in these papers included news headlines, professional news reporting, editorials, sports news, and special-interest sections such as women's pages.

In southern Africa, print media were dominated by Argus South African Newspapers, which, starting in the 1950s, controlled the major news publications in SOUTHERN RHODESIA (now ZIMBABWE), NORTHERN RHODESIA (now ZAMBIA), and SOUTH AFRICA. Argus published the *Rhodesian Herald* and the *Sunday Mail* in SALISBURY (now Harare), the *Chronicle* and *Sunday News* in Bulawayo, and the *Umtali Post,* in Umtali (now Mutare). In Zambia, the Argus Group published the *Northern News* (later called the *Times of Zambia*) and the *Sunday Mail.* Reflecting the racist attitude of the white government in South Africa, the country's Argus newspapers tended to ignore the black majority. These newspapers included *The Star* of JOHANNESBURG, the *Sunday Times,* the *Cape Times,* and the *Cape Argus.*

Missionary Newspapers The important role that European MISSIONARIES played in the culture and politics of colonial Africa extended to the press, as well. They devoted space in their media to attacks on societal ills as well as to articles that attempted to persuade people to convert to Christianity. Because of their status of being related to, and yet outside, the colonial government, missionaries enjoyed the privilege of a greater freedom of expression. However, by criticizing the colonial government they were seen as being on the Africans' side, and they sometimes incurred the ire of colonial authorities.

Beginning in 1859, the first newspaper in Nigeria, *Iwe Irohin Fun Awon Ara Egba ati Yoruba* (Newspaper for the Egbas and the Yoruba), was written and typeset by hand in the YORUBA language and published by Henry Townsend of the Anglican Church Mission Society.

African Newspapers As might be expected, Africans saw newspapers as a means not of supporting the status quo, but of spreading anticolonial ideas and promoting nationalism. Since, in the 19th century, Africans generally lacked the financial and mechanical resources required to establish media operations, they had to import printing presses and machines from Europe or, more rarely, acquire them second-hand from failed colonial newspapers.

One serious early journalist was Charles Force. In 1826 Force, a freedman from the United States, brought a small, hand-operated printing press to MONROVIA, LIBERIA and set up the *Liberia Herald,* a four-page monthly. Although Force died not long after establishing the *Herald,* it continued publication for more than 30 years under different editors, including Edward Wilmot BLYDEN (1832–1912), an anticolonial activist from the West Indies.

In South Africa the first newspaper to cater to a black readership was IMVO ZABANTSUNDU (African Opinion), launched in 1884 by John Tengo JABAVU (1859–1921). The newspaper was published both in the XHOSA language and in English. Despite Jabavu's death, *Imvo ZabaNtsundu* continued publication until 1998.

Between 1836 and 1977 the non-white South African population—including black Africans, Cape Coloureds, and Indians—was served by more than 800 publications that varied in size and frequency of printing.

Newspapers were a particularly important tool for the Kenyan independence movement. The first African-owned newspaper in Kenya was *Mwigwithania* (meaning "work and pray" in Kikuyu). First published in 1928, *Mwigwithania* was edited by the future leader of the Kenyan independence movement, Jomo KENYATTA (c. 1891–1978). Newspapers like Kenyatta's became so effective that, by the time of the MAU MAU movement in the 1940s and 1950s, British authorities were suppressing the African press by denying publishers their licenses, blocking their newsprint supply, or by banning them outright.

In LAGOS, Nigeria, the publication of the WEST AFRICAN PILOT marked a major development in the history of black newspapers in Africa. Founded by Nnamdi AZIKIWE (1904–1996) and launched November 22, 1937, the *West African Pilot* became the medium for some of the strongest printed attacks on colonialism. Its initial circulation of 12,000 doubled by the 1940s, making the newspaper unparalleled in both the size of its readership and the extent of its influence.

At one point British authorities even arrested Azikiwe for pieces published in the newspaper, fearing that certain pieces printed in the *West African Pilot* might foment rebellion within the African population. In spite of this setback, however, Azikiwe went on to establish a chain of six newspapers throughout Nigeria.

Newspapers during Independence In the late 1950s and early 1960s the press in Africa reflected the mood of the political environment. In Rhodesia, Roy WELENSKY (1907–1991), who later became prime minister of the short-lived CENTRAL AFRICAN FEDERATION (1953–1963), ran the *Northern News* from 1944 until 1950, at which time he sold it to Argus. Welensky ensured that the paper conformed to his white-supremacist political views by appointing its editor and writing the editorials himself. At the same time, African nationalists were using newspapers to claim the right to be heard, the right to print people's views without government interference, and the right to self-government. In Northern Rhodesia, African-owned newspapers provided a voice to those who spoke out against both colonialism in general and Welensky's racist government. These papers included *African Times* (1957–58), published by Elias Mtepuka, and *African Life* (1958–61) published by Sikota Wina (d. 2002), who later became a prominent politician when Northern Rhodesia became independent Zambia.

At the end of the colonial period many of the continent's major newspapers were owned and run by foreign news groups. However, after independence, feeling that the foreign-owned print media did not serve the needs of their people, many African governments seized control of major newspapers.

The United Nations reported that, by 1964, there were 220 daily newspapers in Africa with a total circulation of 3 million.

See also: COLONIAL RULE (Vol. IV); INDEPENDENCE MOVEMENTS (Vol. V); NATIONALISM AND INDEPENDENCE MOVEMENTS (Vol. IV); WALLACE-JOHNSON, I. T. A. (Vol. IV).

Further reading: Frank Burton, *The Press of Africa: Persecution and Perseverance* (New York: African Publishing Co., 1979); William A. Hachten, *The Growth of Media in the Third World: African Failures, Asian Successes* (Ames, Iowa: Iowa State University Press, 1993); Helen Kitchen, ed., *The Press in Africa* (Washington D.C.: Ruth Sloan Associates, Inc., 1956).

Niger Landlocked modern-day country, approximately 458,100 square miles (1,186,500 sq km) in size, that is bordered to the north by ALGERIA and LIBYA, to the east by CHAD, to the south by NIGERIA and Republic of BENIN, and to the west by BURKINA FASO and the Republic of MALI. The northern region of Niger is dominated by the vast and arid Sahara desert, an area inhabited by TUAREGS since the 11th century. Heading south, the terrain becomes increasingly fertile and supports pastoral herding as well as AGRICULTURE.

In the 1840s the once-great KANEM-BORNU empire, which had ruled southeastern Niger, was near its end. At the same time the expansion of the FULANI-ruled SOKOTO CALIPHATE, centered within northern Nigeria, was also ending. The Kanem-Bornu and Fulani declines allowed for the expansion of the HAUSA kingdom of Damagaram throughout much of southern Niger, giving rise to a Hausa cultural renaissance.

In the latter half of the 19th century, the beginning of a prolonged drought in the region enabled the Tuaregs to extend their control further south. Despite this expansion of Tuareg influence, southern Niger remained an area of convergence for multiple kingdoms and people, many of them refugees from the warfare that pervaded the region.

Niger during the Colonial Period: Upper Senegal and Niger; French West Africa European colonialism reached Niger relatively late, with the southern states of Dosso and Gaya signing treaties with the French during the 1890s. Tuareg people were not as accommodating, and they zealously resisted France's efforts of COLONIAL CONQUEST. Tuareg resistance prevented the French from establishing a firm control of Niger for more than 20 years.

In 1900 Niger was established as a French military dominion and placed under a succession of administrative bodies. In 1903 it was grouped with other territories of the Sudan to form Senegambia and Niger. This area became Upper Senegal and Niger one year later and then was placed under the administration of FRENCH WEST AFRICA (Afrique Occidentale Francaise, AOF).

Another severe drought, this one lasting from 1913 to 1915, caused widespread famine in the region and motivated a migration of Niger's population to the south. This migration impaired Tuareg control of the northern areas of the country. Despite their weakened state the Tuaregs, angered by newly imposed taxes and the French recruitment effort for World War I (1914–19), engaged in a widespread rebellion from 1916 to 1917. The insurgence was brutally suppressed, and the French, satisfied the country was secure, transferred the governance of Niger to a civilian administration. In 1922 France declared Niger a colony, ushering in an era of relative peace.

In the period between the two world wars Niger underwent changes similar to those of other African colonies, marked by a rapid spread of Islam and the expansion of agriculture with the help of improved irriga-

tion. During this time the French practice of forced LABOR increased and was used to expand the country's infrastructure.

During World War II (1939–45) Niger followed the lead of the other AOF colonies and, in 1942, pledged its loyalty to the Vichy government within German-occupied France. After the war French constitutional reforms opened the door to self-government, as France granted Africans French citizenship and representation in the French National Assembly.

Within Niger, local advisory legislatures were organized as political participation among the population increased. The first political party of Niger was the Sawaba (Independence) Party, headed by Djibo Bakary (1922–1998). In the 1958 referendum on continued alliance with France, Bakary encouraged a vote of "no." Niger voted to join the French Community, however, and Bakary's attempt to defeat the referendum served only to anger France. With French support, Hamani Diori (1916–1989), leader of the Niger branch of the AFRICAN DEMOCRATIC ASSEMBLY (Rassemblement Démocratique Africaine, RDA), quickly rose to prominence. Diori led the RDA to a position of power in Niger and eventually exiled Bakary to GUINEA. In 1960, upon Niger's independence, Diori became the country's first president.

See also: BORNU (Vol. II); DIORI, HAMANI (Vol. V); FRANCE AND AFRICA (Vols. III, IV, V); KANEM (Vol. II); NIGER (Vols. I, II, III, V).

Further reading: Patrick Manning, *Francophone Sub-Saharan Africa, 1880–1995*, 2nd ed. (New York: Cambridge University Press, 1998).

Niger Delta Largest river delta in Africa, located in southern NIGERIA; also known to Europeans in the 19th century as the Oil Rivers because of the local PALM OIL trade. The environment of the Niger Delta caused the peoples there to develop differently from their IGBO and YORUBA neighbors. Delta ethnic groups—including the Itsekiri, Ijaw, Urhobo, and Ogoni—lived in mangrove swamps and sustained themselves through fishing and trade, purchasing staple crops from the interior, and selling sea salt, palm products, and other trade items that were convenient for long-distance commerce. Once they had thrown off the yoke of conquest by the kingdom of BENIN, these people established city-states that grew wealthy first from the SLAVE TRADE in the 18th century and then from other forms of commerce in the 19th century. Because they were adept at traveling by canoe, these delta traders became the intermediaries between interior markets and European merchants, whose ships could not navigate the shallows of the Niger Delta. Through their trading associations, delta peoples were able to purchase European weapons, which allowed them to procure goods from interior markets by force if necessary.

In a society based on patron-client relationships, delta peoples purchased Igbo slaves and incorporated them into their extended families, whose members—both slave and free—produced wealth for the house. Slaves of ability and intelligence could eventually buy their freedom because they were encouraged to generate house income from which they received a commission. Trade-driven, Niger Delta city-states such as Warri, Nembe (known to the British as Brass), Calabar, New Calabar, and Ubani (Bonny) were cosmopolitan, with multilingual inhabitants who spoke at least one indigenous LANGUAGE, Igbo, as well as a pidgin English in order to trade with the Europeans. Although each city-state was successful in conquering interior lands for trade, no one city-state succeeded in unifying the region under a single government.

Britain was interested in creating a palm-oil monopoly in the Oil Rivers, and in 1849 it appointed John Beecroft (1790–1854) as consul to the region. Beecroft established the Courts of Equity, through which conflicts among traders could be resolved. From 1850 to 1870, trade in the Delta increased, making the region a commercial hot spot as Europeans began staking territorial claims in Africa.

In 1869 JAJA (1821–1891), a former slave of Igbo descent, left Ubani. By the following year he established the independent trading kingdom of Opobo. Although Jaja sent soldiers to help the British in the Anglo-Ashanti War of 1873, he openly resisted their policy of free trade. Fearing his power, the British finally accused him of illegal trade and exiled him to the West Indies, in 1887.

Britain declared a PROTECTORATE over the Oil Rivers in 1887, and in 1914 it consolidated the administration of the Niger Delta together with other protectorates to create the colony of Nigeria. As early as 1921 Britain was offering oil exploration rights to private petroleum companies. However, oil was not discovered until 1956, which again made the Niger Delta a focal point of European interest. The development of its oil reserves brought incredible wealth to Nigeria but also sparked civil war, government corruption, dissent, and violence in the years following Nigerian independence, in 1960.

See also: NANA OLOMU (Vol. IV); NIGER DELTA (Vols. I, V); OIL (Vol. V); TRADE AND COMMERCE (Vol. IV).

Nigeria Large West African country, 356,700 square miles (923,900 sq km) in size, located on the Atlantic coast and bounded by the present-day nations of CHAD, CAMEROON, NIGER, and Republic of BENIN. The dominant ethnic groups in Nigeria are the HAUSA-speaking FULANI, in the north; the YORUBA, in the southwest; and the IGBO, in the southeast, near the NIGER DELTA.

Although Britain established a coastal PROTECTORATE as early as 1849, Africans in the interior continued to control their own governments. Their primary contact with Europeans was with traders, who wanted to monopolize their markets, and with MISSIONARIES, who wanted to convert them to Christianity. From 1850 until the BERLIN CONFERENCE (1884–85), British expansion in Nigeria was largely the result of the actions of these traders and missionaries. After 1885, however, the British government moved swiftly to annex all the territory that comprises modern-day Nigeria

In the middle of the 19th century, the majority of the region's trade was in PALM OIL, which moved primarily through the ports of the Niger Delta. Commercial activity in the delta boomed, with African traders acting as intermediaries between the interior producers and the European traders who remained on the coast because of the delta's shallow waters.

In 1849 Britain appointed adventurer and trader John Beecroft (1790–1854) the first British Consul for the Bights of Benin and Biafra, two areas along the Nigerian coast. In an effort to maintain British trade in the region, Beecroft and the coastal rulers established a court of equity to solve problems arising between African and European traders. Beecroft was officially there to promote trade, but he also took the opportunity to extend the British sphere of influence, using warships to force local indigenous leaders to sign British treaties.

As steamship TRANSPORTATION on the Niger River improved, the palm-oil trade spread to the interior. By 1860 British companies had established trade from Hausaland, in the north, all the way to LAGOS, on the coast; by 1865 direct trade with interior merchants was as important as that on the coast.

In the mid-19th century, wars were frequent among the Yoruba states of western Nigeria. In 1861 Britain annexed Lagos—a Yoruba-dominated town—in anticipation of a potential French annexation of warring Yoruba states. By 1863 regional trade had diminished to a trickle, and the new British lieutenant governor, John Hawley Glover (1829–1885), used military force to stop the Yoruba infighting and permit trade to resume. Glover's intervention did not put an end to Yoruba hostilities but it did serve to extend British authority further into the interior.

In 1865 the British Parliament came to the conclusion that the colonial government had assumed too much responsibility in West Africa, and it therefore advocated phasing out all activity on the Nigerian coast. However, traders and missionaries forced the government to reevaluate its decision. Ultimately Britain's reasons for maintaining its Nigerian holdings were economic as well as nationalistic. British industry could not afford to lose access to the region's valuable NATURAL RESOURCES, especially palm oil. This, combined with the threat of invasion by other European colonizers, in particular, France and Germany, led the British to declare the Nigerian protectorates.

Near the close of the 19th century, the kingdom of BENIN declined and began to withdraw from trade. This soon became the focus of British intervention. In 1897 a British agent named Phillips demanded an audience with the *oba* (king) of Benin during the Ague Festival, a most sacred festival during which the *oba* was forbidden to meet with anyone who was not an Edo. Phillips persisted, and when he and his contingent entered Benin, they were ambushed and killed. Responding quickly, Britain conquered Benin within six weeks, and British-dominated trade in the region resumed.

With British trade along the southern coast largely unchallenged, Britain looked to expand its colonial influence into the SOKOTO CALIPHATE, in northern Nigeria. Britain was competing with France for control of the interior Niger River basin. Ultimately, fringe areas of Sokoto became part of the French colonies that are today BURKINA FASO and Niger.

Between 1900 and 1906, British forces led by Sir Frederick LUGARD (1858–1945) gained control of Sokoto in a methodical, step-by-step process against a well-established Muslim state. With the capture of the city of Sokoto, and the subsequent defeat of the fleeing sultan in 1903, the conquest seemed complete. As High Commissioner for Northern Nigeria, Lugard successfully initiated a policy of indirect rule by which the legitimate emirs governed as intermediaries between their people and the new, British colonial government.

The policy of indirect rule did not fare so well in Southern Nigeria. Many African groups in the southern region did not have social structures built around a single leader, making the northern model of indirect rule impossible. As a result, in 1919 the British administration assigned warrant chiefs to help them govern the Niger Delta and Igbo peoples. The African warrant chiefs were unpopular because the position was illegitimate in the eyes of local people. Many of them also were perceived as being as corrupt as the British administrators they represented.

Nigeria during the Colonial Era On the eve of World War I (1914–19) the Britain unified its various Nigerian protectorates to form the single colony of Nigeria. However, it continued to administer the north separately from the south. After the war, victorious Britain encouraged the expansion of its trade and industry, and Africa emerged as a market for the consumer goods that were unavailable during the war. However,

from 1930 to 1938, the worldwide Great Depression sharply cut back production and profits. Nigerian small farmers suffered, too, since the prices of their goods fell.

By the end of the 1930s Nigerians were beginning to imagine an independent Nigeria. These early nationalist stirrings gained momentum when Britain and the United States signed the ATLANTIC CHARTER (1941), pledging to respect the rights of all peoples to choose the form of government under which they lived. After World War II (1939–45) Nigerians actively supported PAN-AFRICANISM by attending Pan-African Congresses; they further demonstrated nationalist fervor by participating in the first General Strike, which occurred in 1945 and paralyzed all essential services in the country.

In 1946 the drafting of the first Nigerian constitution, the Richard's Constitution, showed that the British government was willing to meet some of the nationalist demands for a greater degree of self-government. Further revisions were made to the constitution in 1951, 1953, 1954, and 1957, by which time Nigeria was nearly prepared for self-government.

In 1960 the country finally became independent as a federal republic composed of three states, each of which was dominated by a major ethnic group: the Hausa, in the Northern Region; the Yoruba, in the Western Region; and the Igbo, in the Eastern Region. Lagos was the federal capital. The political dialogue in the fledgling country divided people along regional lines, which were also ethnic lines. The Northern People's Congress (NPC) was the main party of the Northern Region, the most populous of Nigeria's three states. The NPC was led by Ahmadu BELLO (1909–1966) and Abubakar Tafawa BALEWA (1912–1966), who was prime minister at independence. The National Council of Nigeria and the Cameroons, led by Nnamdi AZIKIWE (1904–1996), was dominant among Igbo voters. The Action Group, headed by Obafemi AWOLOWO (1909–1987), enjoyed the support of most Yoruba speakers.

Political tensions and rivalries at the time of independence were heightened by the question of who were the principal beneficiaries of independence. Because a British-style EDUCATION opened the doors for governmental participation and economic advancement, the Yoruba were the first to benefit from British employment. This was because Lagos, a Yoruba town, was the capital. The country's first institute of higher learning, the University of IBADAN, was constructed in the heart of the Yoruba area.

The next groups to benefit from independence were the Igbo and Ibibio, who had been the beneficiaries for many years of widespread missionary schools. Educated Igbo and Ibibio became middle-class clerks, railway workers, and storekeepers, and many also migrated to Lagos to take up well-paid government positions.

Despite having one of their own as the prime minister, the northerners benefited the least from independence. This was due in large part to the fact that Christian missionaries and their schools did not enter the Northern Region. British colonial officials were careful not to offend the sensibilities of the region's Muslim leaders, upon whom they depended to keep the peace, and so they refused to give missionaries permission to work there. With a general absence of British schooling, few northerners had readied themselves to participate in the new government in Lagos.

The political, social, and economic tensions existing in Nigeria at independence soon erupted, and by the middle of the decade the country was embroiled in a lengthy and bitter civil war.

See also: BIAFRA (Vol. V); COLONIAL RULE (Vol. IV); COLONIALISM, INFLUENCE OF (Vol. IV); ENGLAND AND AFRICA (Vols. III, IV, V); HAUSA STATES (Vol. III); NATIONALISM AND INDEPENDENCE MOVEMENTS (Vol. IV); NIGERIA (Vols. I, II, III, V).

Further reading: Adeline Apena, *Colonization, Commerce, and Entrepreneurship in Nigeria: The Western Delta, 1914–1960* (New York: Peter Lang, 1997); Anthony Oyewole and John Lucas, *Historical Dictionary of Nigeria* (Lanham, Md.: Scarecrow Press, 2000); Jonathan T. Reynolds, *The Time of Politics: Islam and the Politics of Legitimacy in Northern Nigeria, 1950–1966* (San Francisco: International Scholars Publications, 1999).

Nkomo, Joshua (Joshua Mqabuko Nyongolo Nkomo) (1917–1999) *Nationalist leader in the struggle for Zimbabwe's independence*

Joshua Nkomo was born in the Matabeleland region of SOUTHERN RHODESIA (now ZIMBABWE) to a prosperous, cattle-raising family. After obtaining an elementary education at a Catholic mission school, Nkomo worked as a carpenter and truck driver to fund his education in SOUTH AFRICA. There he attended Adams College, in DURBAN, and the Jan Hofmeyr School of Social Work, in JOHANNESBURG. Upon his return to Zimbabwe, in 1947, Nkomo took up a position as a social worker with Rhodesian Railways and also served as a lay preacher. In 1951 he completed his bachelor's degree by correspondence through the University of South Africa. In 1952 he became general-secretary of the Rhodesian Railways Employees' Association, and, under his leadership, the labor union came to represent 3,000 members among its 22 branches.

About that time, Nkomo also became increasingly involved in politics, heading a branch of the Southern Rhodesian African National Congress (SRANC), in Bulawayo, the country's second largest city. Despite his vocal opposition to the CENTRAL AFRICAN FEDERATION—which brought together Southern Rhodesia, NORTHERN RHODESIA (now ZAMBIA) and NYASALAND (now MALAWI) into one federation—in 1953 Nkomo stood for office in elections for the country's newly formed parliament but was unsuccess-

ful. In 1957 the SRANC and another independence-minded political organization, the African National Youth League, merged, and Nkomo became the new president of the reconstituted organization. It became the leading opposition group to white COLONIAL RULE.

In February 1959, while Nkomo was attending an anticolonial conference in CAIRO, the SRANC was banned and 500 of its members detained. Rather than return home, Nkomo stayed in EGYPT for several months and then moved to London to organize opposition to Southern Rhodesia's white government. The following year, after former members of the banned AFRICAN NATIONAL CONGRESS formed a successor organization, the National Democratic Party, Nkomo was elected its president in absentia.

See also: LABOR UNIONS (Vol. V); NATIONALISM AND INDEPENDENCE MOVEMENTS (Vol. IV); NKOMO, JOSHUA (Vol. V).

Nkrumah, Kwame (Francis Nwia Kofi Nkrumah) (1909–1972) *First president of Ghana*

Kwame Nkrumah was born Francis Nwia-Kofi Ngonloma, in the British GOLD COAST COLONY (today's GHANA). He was educated at the Prince of Wales' College at Achimota (ACHIMOTA COLLEGE), with Dr. James E. Kwegyir AGGREY (1875–1927) as his mentor. Nkrumah became a teacher in the early 1930s and then left to pursue higher education in the United States. He attended Lincoln University, in Pennsylvania, where he earned two bachelor's degrees, the second in theology. Nkrumah then completed a master's degree in education at the University of Pennsylvania. While there, he helped to found the African Students Association of America and Canada.

The prominent Nigerian nationalist Benjamin Nnamdi AZIKIWE (1904–1996) also earned degrees from both Lincoln University and the University of Pennsylvania and encouraged Nkrumah to follow in his footsteps.

In 1945 Nkrumah went to London to study law and work on his doctoral dissertation. However, he became involved with the prominent West Indian pan-Africanist, George Padmore (1905–1959). Abandoning his studies, he helped organize the Fifth Pan-African Congress, at Manchester. Nkrumah served as the co-chair of the congress with W. E. B. DU BOIS (1868–1963). About the same time, Nkrumah also was made vice president of the West African Students Union. In line with his increasing nationalist thinking, he changed his name to Kwame Nkrumah, taking his last name from his school days when

In 1960 Dr. Kwame Nkrumah wore traditional clothing as he was sworn in as the first president of the Republic of Ghana. © *New York World-Telegram & Sun Collection/Library of Congress*

a teacher wrote down his name incorrectly and choosing the name Kwame (meaning "Saturday born").

In 1947 Nkrumah wrote his first book, *Towards Colonial Freedom.* The vision espoused in his book led to Nkrumah's selection by Dr. J. B. DANQUAH (1895–1965), a prominent Ghanaian political figure, to serve as the organizing secretary for the UNITED GOLD COAST CONVENTION (UGCC), a newly founded political organization. Nkrumah's work for the UGCC included organizing nonviolent demonstrations against British rule. In 1948 he founded the *Accra Evening News,* a newspaper that had the goal of educating the population of the Gold Coast on the pressing need to rid themselves of British colonialism. Also in 1948, Nkrumah was one of the UGCC executive members, known as the "Big Six," who the British detained in the colony's Northern Territories because of their militant activities.

Upon his return from detention Nkrumah was dismissed from his post as general secretary of the UGCC because of differences with Danquah and others. In the aftermath of his dismissal Nkrumah formed his own political party, the CONVENTION PEOPLE'S PARTY (CPP), in 1949. The CPP was more radical than the UGCC and appealed to the middle and lower economic classes rather than to the elites represented by the UGCC. Nkrumah's approach was one of positive action, and his

slogan was "Self-Government Now." In 1950 Nkrumah was arrested for encouraging demonstrations that turned into riots in ACCRA. The following year, while still in prison, he was voted into office as the CPP swept the elections by winning 34 out of 38 seats; he was then released from prison to participate in the new government. In 1952, in anticipation of Gold Coast independence, Governor Sir Charles Arden-Clarke (1898–1962) invited Nkrumah to begin forming a new government as the prime minister of the Gold Coast Colony. Maintaining the momentum begun in 1951, Nkrumah and the CPP continued winning widespread popular support. Finally, following elections in 1957, he became prime minister of the newly independent state of Ghana.

For his domestic policy, Nkrumah tried to reverse the poor planning and mismanagement of the colonial period. Diversifying the economy and attracting foreign investment, he embarked on a five-year plan that he hoped would strengthen Ghana's position in the world ECONOMY. In the country's AGRICULTURE sector, Nkrumah removed the monopoly enjoyed by foreign companies like the UNITED AFRICA COMPANY and introduced incentives to COCOA producers. By diversifying agriculture and introducing mechanized farming, Nkrumah tried to reduce Ghana's dependence on foreign foodstuffs. He further moved the country toward INDUSTRIALIZATION by encouraging manufacturing and by establishing lending institutions, including the central Bank of Ghana. Nkrumah's government set up a nationalized airline, Ghana Airways, and a shipping company, the Black Star Line, named after the failed shipping company of Marcus GARVEY (1887–1940), whom Nkrumah greatly admired. It also established a relatively modern RADIO and television station with an emphasis on education and entertainment. In order to promote education and welfare, Nkrumah's government promoted literacy and trained workers through vocational classes.

In foreign policy, Nkrumah's vision—not only for Ghana but also for the entire continent—revolved around PAN-AFRICANISM. For example, in April 1958 he invited representatives from the independent African countries (EGYPT, ETHIOPIA, Ghana, LIBERIA, LIBYA, MOROCCO, Republic of the SUDAN, and TUNISIA) to meet in Ghana. Then, in December, he convened an All-African Peoples Conference, in Accra, to discuss the end of COLONIAL RULE throughout the continent. It was the first such Pan-Africanist conference on African soil, and it attracted many African political leaders. Regarding Ghana's alignment in the Cold War, Nkrumah adopted African Socialism and remained neutral in a manner similar to presidents Gamal Abdel NASSER (1918–1970), of Egypt, and Sékou TOURÉ (1922–1984), of GUINEA.

In 1960 Nkrumah led Ghana in becoming a republic, with Nkrumah himself assuming the presidency. Ghana prospered during the first years of his tenure as president.

The country's stable economy led the masses to support his costly industrial programs, his expansion of infrastructure, and his far-reaching social programs. However, support for his programs plummeted as Ghana's economy declined along with the fall in the world price of cocoa in the mid-1960s.

See also: COLD WAR AND AFRICA (Vols. IV, V); COLONIALISM, INFLUENCE OF (Vol. IV); ENGLAND AND AFRICA (Vols. III, IV, V); NATIONALISM AND INDEPENDENCE MOVEMENTS (Vol. IV); NKRUMAH, KWAME (Vol. V).

Further reading: David Birmingham, *Kwame Nkrumah: The Father of African Nationalism* (Athens, Ohio: Ohio University Press, 1998); Richard Rathbone, *Nkrumah & the Chiefs: The Politics of Chieftaincy in Ghana, 1951–1960* (Athens, Ohio: Ohio University Press, 2000).

Nongqawuse (c. 1840–c. 1900) *Prophetess among the Xhosa people of South Africa*

Born about 1840, Nongqawuse was orphaned and raised by her uncle and her guardian, Mhlakaza, in the Transkei region of the eastern CAPE COLONY, SOUTH AFRICA. In her mid-teens she claimed that she was visited by "new people," or the spirits of her XHOSA ancestors. She related how they instructed her to convince the Xhosa to kill their cattle, destroy their stores of corn, and not sow the next harvest. If the Xhosa carried out these directions and refrained from practicing WITCHCRAFT, Nongqawuse's "new people" promised that, in return, the Xhosa would receive large numbers of healthy cattle and bountiful harvests, and that kinsmen killed in recent wars with the British would return from the dead. Nongqawuse's message found a receptive audience among the Xhosa: At the time lung sickness ravaged Xhosa cattle herds, and the Xhosa had already surrendered much of their land to the Cape Colony during the Cape Frontier Wars.

Nongqawuse's prophesies started to gain attention in April 1856, and during the next 15 months she was able to convince important Xhosa chiefs to place trust in her. The end result of her unfortunate prophesies exacted a steep price among her people. Some 400,000 cattle were destroyed, somewhere between 35,000 and 50,000 Xhosa died of starvation, and probably three times that number were forced to leave their lands in search of food and employment. Although the particulars of Nongqawuse's life after the anticipated "new people" failed to materialize are somewhat murky, it seems reasonably certain that she was handed over to the British colonial authorities, taken to CAPE TOWN in 1858, and confined there. After being released, she apparently returned to the eastern Cape Colony, married, had two daughters, and died about 1900 on a farm near Alexandria.

One of the most prolonged struggles between Africans and Europeans, the Xhosa Wars, also known as the Cape Frontier Wars and the Kaffir Wars, were fought intermittently for 100 years (1779–1879). The eighth and most costly of the Xhosa Wars ended in 1853, with much Xhosa territory opened to European settlement.

See also: CAPE FRONTIER WARS (Vol. III); CATTLE (Vol. I); PROPHETS AND PROPHETIC MOVEMENTS (Vol. IV).

Further reading: J. B. Peires, *The Dead Will Arise: Nongqawuse and the Great Xhosa Cattle-Killing Movement of 1856–7* (Bloomington, Ind.: Indiana University Press, 1989).

Northern Rhodesia Colonial territory that became the present-day country of ZAMBIA. In 1890 LOZI king Lubosi LEWANIKA (1845–1916) signed a treaty that gave the BRITISH SOUTH AFRICA COMPANY (BSAC) mineral prospecting rights in his kingdom. Taking advantage of the equivocal wording of the treaty, the BSAC soon came to control the whole territory and ruled it until 1923, when Britain took over direct administration.

For administrative purposes the BSAC initially divided the territory into Northwestern Rhodesia, with headquarters at Kalomo, and Northeastern Rhodesia, with headquarters at Fort Jameson (now Chipata). Later, in 1911, the two regions were merged and renamed Northern Rhodesia after BSAC founder Cecil RHODES (1853–1902). Its capital city initially was the southern town of Livingstone, overlooking the Victoria Falls, but, in 1935 the seat of government was moved to LUSAKA. From 1953 to 1964 Northern Rhodesia was aligned in the CENTRAL AFRICAN FEDERATION with the two neighboring British protectorates of SOUTHERN RHODESIA (now ZIMBABWE) and NYASALAND (now MALAWI). On October 24, 1964, Northern Rhodesia emerged from the colonial yoke as independent Zambia.

See also: COLONIAL CONQUEST (Vol. IV); COLONIAL RULE (Vol. IV); ENGLAND AND AFRICA (Vols. III, IV, V); PROTECTORATE (Vol. IV).

Nyamwezi Second-largest ethnic group of present-day TANZANIA. The Nyamwezi played a critical role as middlemen in the 19th-century trade between the SWAHILI COAST and the East African interior. The Nyamwezi, who speak a Bantu language, are an agricultural and cattle-raising people living in west-central Tanzania. Historically they had lived in small chiefdoms rather than a single, large state.

In the 19th century the Nyamwezi were strategically located to take advantage of the IVORY TRADE and SLAVE TRADE, both of which were expanding inland from the Indian Ocean coast. Early in the century young Nyamwezi men began working as porters. They carried heavy loads of ivory tusks and COPPER from the interior to coastal ports such as BAGAMOYO and returned home with trade goods. By mid-century, Arab and Swahili traders established trading centers in the interior. One of these was Tabora, founded in 1852 in the heart of the Nyamwezi region.

Trade and associated political turmoil led to rivalries among Nyamwezi chiefs. Many of these chiefs sought to create larger states that could control and profit from the expanding trade. The most notable was MIRAMBO (c. 1840–1884), who by the late 1860s had built the most powerful of the Nyamwezi states. His state did not long survive his death, however. It disintegrated in the face of opposition from rival Nyamwezi leaders.

Within a few years, while the colonial powers continued to amass territory in East Africa, German soldiers incorporated the Nyamwezi into the colony of GERMAN EAST AFRICA. The Nyamwezi today number about 1.8 million people. They continue to farm largely on a subsistence basis but also grow CASH CROPS such as COTTON and tobacco. Tabora is a major railroad, commercial, and administrative center.

See also: TABORA (Vol. III); TRADE AND COMMERCE (Vol. IV).

Nyasaland

Nyasaland (1889–1964) Colonial name of the British PROTECTORATE in southeastern Africa that became the independent country of MALAWI. The British claim to the region of Nyasaland was originally established, in 1889, as the Shire Highlands PROTECTORATE. As early as the 1850s, Scottish MISSIONARIES had visited the area, failing in their goal to convert large numbers of Africans but managing to disrupt the regional SLAVE TRADE, which gradually dwindled. When British colonial forces arrived, they faced great resistance from the region's YAO, CHEWA, and Ngoni peoples, but eventually they were able to establish COLONIAL RULE. Throughout the PACIFICATION process, the local IVORY TRADE remained strong. The protectorate was renamed Nyasaland in 1907.

In 1953 Nyasaland was joined with SOUTHERN RHODESIA (now ZIMBABWE) and NORTHERN RHODESIA (now ZAMBIA) to form the CENTRAL AFRICAN FEDERATION. The federation was unpopular with the African population of Nyasaland, and opposition to the federation and British oppression in general gave strength to a powerful nationalist movement, led by Hastings Kamuzu BANDA (c. 1898– 1997). After struggling with violent African demonstrations the British disbanded the federation in 1963, and in 1964 Nyasaland became independent Malawi.

Nyasa is the local word for "lake." Present-day Lake Malawi was formerly known, redundantly, as Lake Nyasa.

See also: NATIONALISM AND INDEPENDENCE MOVEMENTS (Vol. IV).

Nyerere, Julius

Nyerere, Julius (Julius Kambarage Nyerere) (1922–1999) First president of Tanzania

Nyerere was born in 1922 in Butiama, TANGANYIKA. His father was the chief of the Zanaki, one of the country's smaller ethnic groups. Young Nyerere attended a local primary school and then the government secondary school at Tabora, which at the time was the only secondary school for Africans. About this time he converted to Catholicism, taking the name Julius.

In 1945 Nyerere obtained a teaching certificate from Uganda's Makerere College (later to become Makerere University) and then returned to Tabora to teach at a Catholic mission school. He later went to study at the University of Edinburgh, where, in 1952, he received a master's degree in economics and history. He thus became Tanganyika's first university graduate. After graduation he again took up teaching, this time at a Catholic school near the colonial capital of DAR ES SALAAM. About that time, Nyerere also married Marie Gabriel Magige, with whom he eventually had eight children.

Having been involved in the anticolonial movement while a student in Edinburgh, Nyerere became active in politics upon his return to Tanganyika. He again participated in the Tanganyika African Association (TAA), which he had initially joined at Makerere. Founded by British colonial officials as a forum for soliciting African ideas, the TAA proved inadequate for furthering the cause of African nationalism and bringing an end to COLONIAL RULE. As a result, in 1954, Nyerere and others formed the country's first political party, the Tanganyika African National Union (TANU) out of the TAA. The party became a strong, nonviolent popular movement.

Because Britain ruled Tanganyika first as a League of Nations MANDATE and then as a TRUST TERRITORY under the auspices of the United Nations (UN), it had to report to the United Nations on its administration of the country. Nyerere made use of this situation to make the case for independence before the UN Trusteeship Council, first in 1956 and again in 1957.

In 1958, elections for the Legislative Council led to TANU winning 28 of 30 seats. Two years later Britain granted Tanganyika limited self-government, with Nyerere, the TANU leader, becoming chief minister. He became prime minister when Tanganyika attained independence, in 1961, and then he became president when the country became a republic, in 1962.

Nyerere became known by the honorific title *mwalimu,* the KISWAHILI word for teacher. In many respects he was a teacher for his entire adult life, first in schools and then as the leader of a newly independent nation.

In 1963, following a popular revolution on the island of ZANZIBAR, off the coast of mainland Tanganyika, Nyerere took the lead in merging the two separate states of mainland Tanganyika and Zanzibar to create the United Republic of TANZANIA. He remained president until voluntarily stepping down in 1985.

See also: EDUCATION (Vols. IV, V); ENGLAND AND AFRICA (Vols. III, IV, V); INDEPENDENCE MOVEMENTS (Vol. V); MISSIONARIES (Vols. III, IV, V); NATIONALISM AND INDEPENDENCE MOVEMENTS (Vol. IV); NYERERE, JULIUS (Vol. V); TANZANIA AFRICAN NATIONAL UNION (Vol. V); UNITED NATIONS AND AFRICA (Vol. IV).

Further reading: Cranford Pratt, *The Critical Phase in Tanzania, 1945–1968: Nyerere and the Emergence of a Socialist Strategy* (New York: Cambridge University Press, 1976); William Edgett Smith, *We Must Run While They Walk: A Portrait of Africa's Julius Nyerere* (New York: Random House, 1971).

Obote, Milton (Milton Apolo Obote) (1924–)
Ugandan independence and political leader

Obote was born in the northern part of UGANDA and educated at missionary schools. He then attended secondary school at Busoga before going to Makerere College (now Makerere University), in KAMPALA, the Ugandan capital. He left Makerere after two years without graduating and went to the neighboring British colony of KENYA during the 1950s to work. He first became involved in politics by working for a time with the dynamic Kenyan labor-union leader and political nationalist, Tom MBOYA (1930–1969). When he returned to Uganda in 1956, Obote continued his political activities, becoming a leader in the Uganda National Congress, one of several Ugandan nationalist parties spearheading the drive for independence from Britain.

After serving in various appointed and elected legislative posts, Obote became president of the Uganda National Congress party. In 1960 he merged his party with elements of the Uganda People's Union, a rival party, to form the more powerful Uganda People's Congress. A year later, still striving to unite the country's disparate forces, Obote joined with Kabaka (King) Yekka's Buganda Party, creating a political party large enough to compete with the dominant Democratic Party. Victorious in the elections preceding independence, Obote became prime minister as Britain withdrew from Uganda in 1962, and the country gained independence.

See also: BUGANDA (Vols. II, III, IV, V); ENGLAND AND AFRICA (Vol. IV); NATIONALISM AND INDEPENDENCE MOVEMENTS (Vol. IV); OBOTE, MILTON (Vol. V).

Further reading: Kenneth Ingham, *Milton Obote* (London: Routledge, 1994).

Odinga, Oginga (Jaramongi Oginga Odinga)
(1912–1994) *Luo political leader in Kenya*

Born in Bondo, in the Nyanza province of KENYA, Odinga was the only child in his LUO family to receive an education. He attended the ALLIANCE HIGH SCHOOL near NAIROBI and then completed his studies at Makerere College, graduating in 1939. He worked in EDUCATION until 1946, teaching at the Church Missionary School in Maseno and serving as headmaster at the Maseno Veterinary School. In 1947 he left teaching for business and opened the Luo Thrift and Trading Corporation. He also became politically active by reviving the Luo Union organization.

It was also in 1947 that Odinga became involved in politics as a member of the Kenyan Legislative Council. He became a fervent nationalist and supporter of the KIKUYU leader Jomo KENYATTA (c. 1891–1978), who headed the Kenya African Union. After the British colonial government imprisoned Kenyatta for his alleged leadership of the MAU MAU movement, Odinga ignored the opportunity to assume the forefront of the independence movement. Instead he dedicated himself to campaigning for Kenyatta's freedom. In 1960 he helped found the Kenya African National Union, and when the party had significant results in the 1961 elections, Odinga was able to secure Kenyatta's release. When Kenyatta became president of independent Kenya, in 1963, he rewarded Odinga with the vice presidency. They were soon to part ways, however, over their differing approaches to Kenya's path to development.

See also: DEVELOPMENT (Vol. V); NATIONALISM AND INDEPENDENCE MOVEMENTS (Vols. IV, V); ODINGA, OGINGA (Vol. V).

Ogaden Low plateau area of southeastern ETHIOPIA that was important seasonal pasture land for Somali nomads. Prior to becoming Ethiopia's emperor, the king of SHOA, MENELIK II (1844–1913), began expanding into this region and other southern areas outside the Amharic-speaking core of Ethiopia. The region, however, continued to be contested terrain between Ethiopia and ITALIAN SOMALILAND and thus essentially went unadministered in the early 20th century. Sayyid MUHAMMAD AB-DULLAH HASSAN (1864–1920) took advantage of the lack of either Ethiopian or Italian governmental control to use the region as a refuge for his anticolonial forces. Until his death in 1920, Hassan used Ogaden in his effort to rid SOMALIA of colonial rulers, launching attacks on the Ethiopian- and Italian-controlled areas as well as on BRITISH SOMALILAND.

As Somalia moved toward independence, in 1960 the British- and Italian-ruled areas were unified. Somali leaders then sought to regain control of the Ogaden in order to create a united "Greater Somalia" with the other traditional Somali territories of DJIBOUTI, which was still FRENCH SOMALILAND, and the Northern Frontier District of the then British colony of KENYA. The United Nations, however, recognized Ethiopia's control of the Ogaden.

Somalia's irredentism led at first to low-level conflict, and then major fighting, from 1964 on. It was only in the late 1970s that Cuban troops and Warsaw Pact support enabled the leftist government of Ethiopia to establish firm control over the region. The disintegration of Somalia's central government in the 1990s reduced the challenge to Ethiopia's control of the Ogaden.

Irredentism is a term that comes from the word *irredenta*, a territory historically or ethnically related to one political unit but under the political control of another.

See also: COLONIAL RULE (Vol. IV); ITALY AND AFRICA (Vol. IV).

Olympio, Sylvanus (Sylvanus Epiphanio Olympio) (1902–1963) *First president of the Republic of Togo*

Born to a powerful family in LOMÉ, the capital of what was then French TOGOLAND, Olympio was a member and later leader of the Committee of Togolese Unity (Comité de l'Unité Togolaise, CUT). The CUT supported reduced ties with France and the reunification of the Ewe, a large ethnic group in southern French TOGO. The colonial PARTITION of the Ewe homeland had left the Ewe

population split between colonies ruled by three separate European powers: the British GOLD COAST COLONY (present-day GHANA), German Togoland, and French DAHOMEY (present-day Republic of BENIN). When German Togoland was divided into British Togoland and French Togoland following World War I (1914–18), the Ewe were split further. Following World War II (1939–45), Olympio used his influence as president of the Togo Assembly and deputy to the French National Assembly to promote the Ewe cause. Ultimately, however, his efforts failed, as British Togoland voted to join with the Gold Coast in 1956. The Gold Coast and British Togoland became independent Ghana the following year.

Also in 1956, French Togoland became an internally autonomous republic in the FRENCH UNION. Elections that year brought Olympio's brother-in-law, Nicholas Grunitzky (1913–1969) of the Togolese Progress Party, to power as prime minister. Olympio and the CUT protested the results, and in 1958 the United Nations supervised a new election, which the CUT won handily. Olympio became prime minister and then president when Togo gained full independence in 1960. In 1961 he was officially elected president, and Togo became a one-party state, with the CUT dominating the legislature.

In 1960 Olympio turned down an offer by Kwame NKRUMAH (1909–1972), the Ghanian president, to join Togo with Ghana. Insulted, Nkrumah closed Ghana's border with Togo, causing Togo, the smaller country, significant economic difficulty.

Olympio quickly became unpopular among the Togolese. Despite having driven most of his opposition into exile, Olympio's strict economic policies and authoritarian tendencies caused dissatisfaction, especially among Juvento, the youth wing of the CUT. Also, his refusal to fund an increase in the army's personnel soon made him an enemy of Togo's small military establishment. In 1963 the military staged a coup d'état, overthrowing Olympio and assassinating him in the garden of the United States embassy, where he sought refuge. The coup was the first of many in sub-Saharan Africa in the postcolonial era.

See also: COLONIALISM, INFLUENCE OF (Vol. IV); ETHNICITY AND IDENTITY (Vol. V); FRANCE AND AFRICA (Vols. III, IV, V); NATIONALISM AND INDEPENDENCE MOVEMENTS (Vol. IV).

Omdurman, Battle of (1898) Conflict that marked the end of the Mahdist state in what is now the Republic of the SUDAN. In 1898 a combined British and Egyptian

military expedition under the command of Sir Horatio Herbert KITCHENER (1850–1916) launched a campaign to reassert control over Sudan, which was officially a province of EGYPT. Forces loyal to Mahdist leader, ABDALLAHI IBN MUHAMMAD (1846–1899), had driven the Egyptian government from the Sudan, culminating in the capture of KHARTOUM in 1885 and the death of British general Charles George GORDON (1833–1885).

The reconquest took place in two stages. First, Kitchener moved south from Egypt, systematically defeating Mahdist forces and capturing key towns. He simultaneously built a railroad to support his southward advance. In the second stage, Anglo-Egyptian forces pushed into the heart of Sudan. At this point they attacked Omdurman, the Mahdist capital, which was situated across the Nile River from the old capital of Khartoum. Supported by gunboats anchored in the Nile, Kitchener's army of 15,000 was able to defeat 43,000 Mahdist troops. Although Abdallahi ibn Muhammad escaped, he was pursued and later killed in battle, in 1899. Following those events, Britain and Egypt jointly ruled Sudan under the terms of an agreement known as the ANGLO-EGYPTIAN CONDOMINIUM (1899) until its Sudan's independence, in 1956.

See also: AL-MAHDI, MUHAMMAD AHMAD (Vol. IV); MAHDIYYA (Vol. IV).

Further reading: M. W. Daly and P. M. Holt, *A History of the Sudan: From the Comin g of Islam to the Present Day* (London: Longman, 1988); Peter Harrington and Frederic A. Sharf, eds., *Omdurman, 1898: The Eyewitnesses Speak. The British Conquest of the Sudan as Described by Participants in Letters, Diaries, Photos and Drawings* (London: Greenhill Books, 1998).

oral traditions The social values, guidelines, and histories that form the spoken record of societies. While African societies have maintained their oral traditions since the colonial period, literacy in foreign languages and the new writing technology imposed by the colonizers—and maintained after independence—brought about irreversible changes to oral tradition.

The necessity for writing down the oral genre comes from the desire to preserve it, on the one hand, and the need to legitimize precolonial history through a written text, on the other. Although Europeans were not generally interested in preserving and maintaining African oral traditions, Western anthropologists and historians have been interested in collecting the stories and, later, arguing their validity.

Changes in the maintenance and transmission of the oral tradition did not immediately change with the arrival of Christian MISSIONARIES and the colonial government. On the contrary, African oral traditions were so deeply entrenched in the medium of the spoken word that their conversion to writing evolved over time. By the 20th century, however, writing technology was changing both the composition and performance of indigenous African history.

During the colonial era a number of African literary figures wrote in the LANGUAGE of the colonists. But many also were inspired by the language and oral traditions of their own cultures. For example, S. E. K. MQHAYI (1875–1945) drew heavily on his knowledge of XHOSA oral literature. In GERMAN EAST AFRICA (present-day TANZANIA), poet Shaaban ROBERT (1909–1962) made use of his extensive knowledge of oral verse forms in writing his KISWAHILI poems.

In much of West Africa, for example, the knowledge of oral tradition was typically controlled by a cultural caste known as griots (from French), or *jeliw* (from MANDE). These storytellers are local cultural historians who have the responsibility of maintaining the accuracy of the tradition as it is passed down. The storyteller must excite the audience by his accurate yet creative and compelling understanding of the contribution to the events made by the audience's ancestors. This type of oral tradition is history, but it also is performance ART. The storyteller often relates the words in song, accompanied by performances on musical instruments such as the *balafon* (xylophone), *kora* (stringed harp), and drum. In this way, the oral nature of the literature is kept alive as it is passed from generation to generation.

However, once the free-flowing oral tradition is transcribed into the local language—or translated and transcribed into a foreign language—it exists in a fixed form. This means that anyone who is literate has access to knowledge that was previously the specialized knowledge of one group. It also means that if the story is now passed down in a written form, the storyteller or historian loses the ability to adapt the performance of the tradition according to the values of the audience.

As oral traditions are performed and transcribed by anthropologists and historians, the story that passes into the repository of Western knowledge focuses on only that one version, which becomes the "official" history. An example of an oral tradition that has been recorded and read in Western classrooms is the epic of the first Malian king, Sundiata. His oral tradition is presented in prose form, originally as a poem and song. At some point, a single indigenous historian wrote down a version of the poem. That one version was then translated and transcribed by one publisher. The publisher's translation, whether accurate or not, became the "official" version of the epic sold in Western markets, regardless of whether it was the version accepted by the indigenous culture.

***

Newly created oral traditions may or may not follow the established pattern of orality. The oral tradition that has been created around the Maninka-speaking intellectual Souleymane KANTÉ (1922–1987) differs from the Sundiata oral tradition because it was immediately recorded in the written form of the Maninka language and preserved in the indigenous N'ko alphabet.

***

See also: GRIOT (Vol. II); ORAL TRADITIONS (Vol. I); SUNDIATA (Vol. II).

Further reading: Stephen Belcher, *Epic Traditions of Africa* (Bloomington, Ind.: Indiana University Press, 1999); John William Johnson, Thomas A. Hale, and Stephen Belcher, eds., *Oral Epics from Africa: Vibrant Voices from a Vast Continent* (Bloomington, Ind.: Indiana University Press, 1997).

Orange Free State (OFS) Boer province (1854–1902) in the central highveld of SOUTH AFRICA, north of the Orange River. The region of the Orange Free State was inhabited by the Griqua and SOTHO peoples when, in the 1830s, Boer farmers from the CAPE COLONY began entering the area to establish their own independent republic.

The Boer migration, called the Great Boer Trek, was followed by an influx of British settlers. Over strong Boer objections, the British presence led, in 1848, to the region's annexation by Britain as the Orange River Sovereignty. By 1854, however, economic and military problems led Britain to cede sovereignty of the territory to the BOERS, under the provisions of the Bloemfontein Convention. The Boers established a republic with a parliamentary system, naming it the Oranje Vrystaat, or Orange Free State (OFS), and retaining Bloemfontein as the capital. Their government specifically served only white settlers.

Wars between the OFS and neighboring BASUTOLAND in 1858 and 1865 led to Boer expansion at Sotho expense. For its part, Britain, which wanted to check OFS expansion, annexed the remaining area of Basutoland in 1868. Then, in the late 1860s, Britain also annexed the western part of the OFS after great deposits of DIAMONDS were discovered near KIMBERLEY. It was, however, British conflict with the Boer government of the TRANSVAAL that led to war between Britain and the Boers.

The ANGLO-BOER WAR (also known as the South African War) finally broke out in 1899. The OFS sided with its fellow Boer republic of the Transvaal against Britain. Early on, the republican armies held sway against the British, but by May 1900, the tide had turned, and Bloemfontein fell to British forces. Boer guerrillas extended the fighting into 1902, when the Treaty of VEREENIGING ended the war. The Orange Free State became the British-ruled Orange River Colony, which was incorporated into the newly formed UNION OF SOUTH AFRICA as the Orange Free State Province in 1910.

See also: AFRIKANERS (Vol. IV); DIAMOND MINING (Vol. IV); ENGLAND AND AFRICA (Vols. III, IV); GREAT BOER TREK (Vol. III); NETHERLANDS AND AFRICA (Vol. III); ORANGE RIVER (Vols. I, III).

Oromo Large, mostly Muslim ethnic group living in the Horn of Africa; also the LANGUAGE they speak. The Oromo are mostly agriculturalists and constitute the majority population in ETHIOPIA, inhabiting the central region of Oromia (Oromiyya). Today they also reside in parts of SOMALIA, KENYA, Republic of the SUDAN, ERITREA, and DJIBOUTI.

***

Made the capital by Amharan Emperor MENELIK II (1844–1913), ADDIS ABABA was originally named Finfinnee, and served as the capital of Oromia. The Oromo still call the city Finfinnee and hope for its return to Oromo control.

***

In the latter half of the 19th century, when European colonization of Africa began in earnest, the Oromo had the dubious distinction of being one of the few African peoples to be colonized by other Africans—in this case, Amharic-speaking Ethiopians. Ethiopian emperors YOHANNES IV (r. 1844–1889), from Tigray, and Menelik II (r. 1889–1913), from SHOA, suppressed the Oromo people in a campaign that is now described plainly as genocide. With superior organization and European weaponry, Menelik stripped the Oromo of any power in Ethiopian society and brutally forced them into positions of servitude and even outright SLAVERY. It is estimated that during Menelik's reign, Ethiopia's Oromo population shrank from approximately 10 million to 5 million, with many people forced to take refuge in neighboring countries.

Menelik's grandson and designated heir, Lij Iyasu (r. 1913–1916), was the son of the Oromo governor of Wello, a region in northeastern Ethiopia. Although never formally crowned, Iyasu enjoyed the status of emperor during his short reign, which was characterized by national programs aimed at restoring Oromo independence. A Muslim, Iyasu was forced from power by Ethiopian princes and the leaders of the ETHIOPIAN ORTHODOX CHURCH. In 1926 Ras Tafari (1892–1975) claimed the Ethiopian crown. Iyasu died following a military campaign in Afar, and Ras Tafari went on to become Emperor HAILE SELASSIE.

The Amharic-speakers who ruled Ethiopia referred to the Oromo as the *Galla*, a derogatory term of uncertain origin. To the Amhara, the connotations of the term *Galla* included pagan, uncivilized, outsider, enemy, slave, and inferior. European historians and writers, who used the more widely translated Amharic literature on the subject of the Oromo, have perpetuated the use of the Galla label, even to the present day.

In the 1930s, under Haile Selassie (1892–1975), Ethiopia continued its political, economic, and social subjugation of the Oromo people. By 1935, however, the country was more concerned with defending itself from Italian invasion than with the Oromo. As Italy's forces launched offensives from the Red Sea, some Oromo soldiers defected to support them against the Amhara-dominated Ethiopian national forces. Despite Ethiopia's modernized army, by 1936 Italy claimed victory, forcing Haile Selassie into exile. For the Oromo, the Italian victory granted a short reprieve from the brutal treatment they received under Selassie's regime. In a situation that was rare in colonial Africa, the victory of the European forces actually improved the lot of an indigenous people. However, following Italy's defeat in World War II (1939–45), Haile Selassie returned to the throne, and Ethiopia's national policies once again marginalized the Oromo population.

See also: ETHNIC CONFLICT IN AFRICA (Vol. V); OROMO (Vols. I, II, III, V); OROMO PEOPLE'S DEMOCRATIC ORGANIZATION (Vol. V).

Further reading: P. T. W. Baxter, Jan Hultin, and Alessandro Triulzi, eds., *Being and Becoming Oromo: Historical and Anthropological Equiries* (Lawrenceville, N.J.: Red Sea Press, Inc., 1996); Mohammed Hassen, *The Oromo of Ethiopia: A History, 1570–1860* (New York: Cambridge University Press, 1990).

To call attention to what he believed to be unfairly high taxes, in 1930 an Oromo chieftain gathered together a number of his countrymen and provided each of them with a long piece of lumber. The group then waited near a palace window in hopes of gaining the attention of Ethiopia's emperor. © *New York Times*

Ottoman Empire and Africa Exercising sovereignty over the majority of North Africa as of the 16th century, the Ottoman Empire played an important role in Africa until it was dissolved in the wake of World War I (1914–18). Ottoman sovereignty over the countries of North Africa dated to the mid-16th century. During the 17th and 18th centuries, however, Ottoman control increasingly came to be exercised through local rulers who, while acknowledging the Ottoman sultan's ultimate authority, were granted power over virtually all local affairs.

As the 18th century came to an end, the Ottoman sultans began losing effective control of the region. In EGYPT, for example, by the middle of the 19th century, Egyptian nationalist Duse Muhammad ALI (1769–1849) and his successors had guided that country toward even greater autonomy than before. They governed their state with only the barest acknowledgement of the sovereignty of the sultan in Istanbul. Elsewhere, in 1830, the French forced the Ottoman bey, or governor, to flee ALGIERS, and France soon established its COLONIAL RULE over all ALGERIA. Within a few years France had extended its influence east to TUNISIA, which it eventually invaded and claimed by 1881.

Only in LIBYA was the Ottoman sultan able to retain a substantial degree of control. Following the BERLIN CONFERENCE (1884–85), however, as the European powers scrambled to divide up Africa among themselves, Britain and France encouraged Italy to extend its sphere of influence to include Libya. Although Italy made moves toward colonization, it was not until 1911 that it was able to engineer a crisis with the Ottoman government and invade TRIPOLI. The sultan's troops—led by the future leader of post-Ottoman Turkey, Mustafa Kemal Ataturk (1881–1938)—could only retreat inland, where they organized indigenous resistance to the Italian invasion. Facing further hostilities in his Balkan provinces, the Ottoman sultan ultimately sued for peace and, in 1912, relinquished control over Libya's two provinces, TRIPOLITANIA and Cyrenaica. Italy took control of the region's government, although the sultan was allowed to maintain a figurehead position as religious leader of Libya's Muslims. Later, following the Ottoman defeat in World War I (1914–18), even this arrangement was abandoned, and the long presence of the Ottoman Empire in North Africa came to an end.

See also: COLONIAL CONQUEST (Vol. IV); ENGLAND AND AFRICA (Vols. III, IV, V); FRANCE AND AFRICA (Vols. III, IV, V); ITALY AND AFRICA (Vol. IV); PARTITION (Vol. IV); OTTOMAN EMPIRE AND AFRICA (Vol. III).

Further reading: Asli Çirakman, *From the "Terror of the World" to the "Sick Man of Europe": European Images of the Ottoman Empire and Society from the Sixteenth Century to the Nineteenth* (New York: Peter Lang, 2002).

Oubangui-Chari French colony in Central Africa covering the area of present-day CENTRAL AFRICAN REPUBLIC.

Until the late 1800s, Central Africa was largely untouched by COLONIAL CONQUEST. By 1894, however, the French declared a colony in the territory between the Oubangui (Ubangi) and Chari rivers, in the heart of the African continent. In 1906 France linked the colony's administration to that of neighboring CHAD to form Oubangui-Chari-Chad. Four years later Oubangui-Chari-Chad was united with two other French colonies, GABON and FRENCH CONGO (now part of the Republic of the CONGO) in an administrative region called FRENCH EQUATORIAL AFRICA. After World War II (1939–45), Oubangui-Chari moved toward independence and in 1958 became autonomous as the Central African Republic. In 1960 the nation became fully independent, with David Dacko (1930–) as its first president.

See also: DACKO, DAVID (Vol. V); FRANCE AND AFRICA (Vols. IV, V).

Ovambo Largest ethnic group in NAMIBIA, they form roughly two-thirds of the country's population. The Bantu-speaking Ovambo were central to the country's independence movement. In the 14th century the Ovambo had migrated from the upper regions of the Zambezi River and settled in the area of present-day southern ANGOLA and north-central Namibia. By the late 19th century, however, Europeans had begun to establish a presence in southwestern Africa, and Germany was awarded a sphere of influence over the region during the BERLIN CONFERENCE (1884–85). Through the use of underhanded treaties, police force, and outright theft, Germany gradually imposed COLONIAL RULE over much of the area. In response to escalating oppression, the HERERO and the NAMA of central and southern Namibia launched rebellions that were brutally quashed by German troops. Though the Ovambo participated in one battle during the Herero rebellion (1904–07), the Germans did not resort to military force to establish their rule in Ovamboland. Rather, they entered into treaties with the individual chiefs to lay claims to sovereignty over the northern region, a process they completed in 1910.

After World War I (1914–18) Germany's colony of SOUTH WEST AFRICA became a League of Nations MANDATE under the supervision of SOUTH AFRICA. South Africa then used military force to consolidate its control of Ovamboland. It maintained its administration of the region after World War II (1939–45) and essentially considered it as a fifth province under APARTHEID rule. Under colonial rule Ovamboland became a colonial backwater, supplying migrant LABOR for the other parts of the colony. As a result its inhabitants lived in considerable poverty.

In 1959 Ovambo activists Samuel Nujoma (1929–) and Andimba (Herman) Toiva ja Toivo (1924–) formed the Ovamboland People's Organization (OPO). That same year, in conjunction with the Herero-led South West African National Union, the OPO began organizing resistance to apartheid relocation policies. The OPO's activities led to a South African backlash, and Nujoma was forced into exile.

While Nujoma was in exile Ovamboland continued to be a hotbed for the independence movement. The OPO evolved into the South West Africa People's Organization (SWAPO) and expanded beyond its Ovambo roots. In 1989, after South Africa finally surrendered its claim to the territory, Nujoma returned from exile and led SWAPO to victory in the national elections. Namibia became independent in 1990, and Nujoma assumed the presidency. As of 2004 Nujoma and the largely Ovambo SWAPO continued to dominate the Namibian political scene.

See also: COLONIAL CONQUEST (Vol. IV); COLONIALISM, INFLUENCE OF (Vol. IV); GERMANY AND AFRICA (Vol. IV); SOUTH WEST AFRICA PEOPLE'S ORGANIZATION (Vol. V).

Ovimbundu Ethnic group of the Benguela Plateau in present-day ANGOLA. By the 18th century the Bantu-speaking Ovimbundu had established 22 kingdoms in the Benguela highlands. The Ovimbundu underwent a series of economic changes during the colonial era. Trade with the Portuguese was established by the late 1700s, and by 1800 the Ovimbundu had come to dominate the regional trade of captives and ivory. Though the Portuguese campaign of colonial conquest had begun as early as 1575, with the establishment of the coastal stronghold of LUANDA, the Ovimbundu resisted colonial rule until 1902. The outlawing of the slave trade and the construction of the Benguela railway, in 1904, undermined the Ovimbundu's trade superiority, and the Ovimbundu became involved in the rubber trade until that, too, declined in the early 1900s. The Ovimbundu then turned to CASH CROPS, such as COFFEE, as the backbone of their ECONOMY. By the 1960s, soil conditions and encroaching Portuguese settlers forced a large percentage of Ovimbundu males to labor on Portuguese coffee plantations, in the cities of Luanda and Lobito, or in industrial plants.

Perhaps the most cohesive ethnic group in colonial Angola, the Ovimbundu benefited from the establishment by MISSIONARIES of a number of Christian villages, complete with schools and health clinics. The Ovimbundu's strong economic background and general solidarity made them a powerful popular base for anticolonialist efforts led by Jonas Savimbi (1934–2002) and his national Union for the Total Independence of Angola (União Nacional para a Independência Total de Angola, UNITA),

formed in 1966. After Angola achieved independence in 1975, UNITA continued to fight in a civil war with its rival, the Popular Movement for the Liberation of Angola. Largely because of Ovimbundu support, Savimbi and UNITA were able to continue the war until Savimbi's death in 2002.

See also: COLONIALISM, INFLUENCE OF (Vol. IV); NATIONALISM AND INDEPENDENCE MOVEMENTS (Vol. IV); OVIMBUNDU (Vols. II, III); PORTUGAL AND AFRICA (Vols. III, IV, V); SAVIMBI, JONAS (Vol. V).

Ovonramwen (r. 1888–1897; d. 1914) *The last* oba *(king) of the powerful Edo kingdom of Benin*

Ovonramwen came to power as the *oba* of the kingdom of BENIN in 1888, a time when British COLONIAL RULE was expanding throughout southern NIGERIA. When his father, Oba Adolo (r. 1848–1888), died, a struggle for the throne ensued. Eventually Ovonramwen gained power by killing his rivals. However, his kingdom was shrinking rapidly due to increasing British encroachment. In 1892 Britain and Benin negotiated a treaty that, from the British perspective, established Benin as a British PROTECTORATE. Ovonramwen, on the other hand, ignored the treaty.

Through various means Britain was bringing the other rulers of southern Nigeria within its colonial orbit, and, after 1895, Benin alone retained its independence. The people of Ovonramwen's kingdom practiced human sacrifice in their traditional rituals, which the British saw as a convenient excuse for intervening in Benin's internal affairs. In January 1897 the consul-general of Britain's Niger Coast Protectorate set off to BENIN CITY, the kingdom's capital. Under the threat of military action, Ovonramwen and his counselors were pointedly asked to submit to British colonial authority, which they refused. When a small British party was massacred—in an action instigated by some of Ovonramwen's African opponents—the British launched an invasion with an already assembled force of 1,500 soldiers. Ovonramwen failed to defend Benin City, but he retreated into the countryside, continuing to resist the British authorities before finally surrendering in August. With its COLONIAL CONQUEST of southern Nigeria complete, Britain then deported the *oba* to the city of Calabar, in southeastern Nigeria, where he died in 1914. After Ovonramwen's death, Britain restored the Benin kingship as a largely ceremonial office, installing his son, Aiguobasinmwin as *oba*.

See also: ENGLAND AND AFRICA (Vols. III, IV, V).

P

PAC See PAN-AFRICANIST CONGRESS.

pacification Term used by Europeans to describe the intimidation and violent suppression used to subdue resistance to COLONIAL CONQUEST in Africa. Pacification, or "making peace," was a process begun after the PARTITION of Africa by the European powers in 1884–85. It typically involved dispatching heavily armed COLONIAL ARMIES into territories occupied by indigenous African peoples. The armies met with fierce resistance throughout the continent. However, since European armaments were usually far more advanced and lethal than those used by Africans, European pacification campaigns were usually successful at achieving the goal of securing a territory for further colonial development.

Whenever possible, European armies employed African mercenaries to aid them in ridding an area of a common enemy. Typically these mercenaries were paid with a share of the plunder taken from a conquered village.

All of the European colonial powers—France, Britain, Belgium, Germany, Spain, Portugal, and Italy—embarked on pacification campaigns of some kind in Africa. Pacification was intended to establish an easy and effective occupation and to create an environment that would increase the potential for prosperity for future white settlers. Despite the patina of legitimacy that the colonial powers gave to their efforts, the process was often marked by contemptible actions on the part of the European soldiers, their leaders, and security officials. Crimes committed in the name of pacification included the arbitrary killing of people, including women and children; the enslavement of captives; the burning of villages and crops; and the stealing of cattle and other livestock. As a rule, any African resistance to European pacification efforts was crushed quickly and viciously.

Although most of the colonies were considered "pacified" by the onset of World War I (1914–18), some remote areas of Africa remained unsecured for European colonial administration as late as the 1930s.

See also: BELGIUM AND AFRICA (Vol. IV); BRITAIN AND AFRICA (Vol. IV); FRANCE AND AFRICA (Vol. IV); GERMANY AND AFRICA (Vol. IV); ITALY AND AFRICA (Vol. IV); PORTUGAL AND AFRICA (Vol. IV); RESISTANCE AND REBELLION (Vol. IV); SPAIN AND AFRICA (Vol. IV).

palm oil The liquid extracted from the fermented fruit of the oil palm. The oil palm was long one of the important West African FOOD CROPS, and in the 19th century it became one of the region's leading CASH CROPS. During the 19th century the increased use of machinery brought about a corresponding increase in the need for lubricating oils. In the same period, abolitionists who were vigorously engaged in attempts to suppress the SLAVE TRADE actively promoted "legitimate trade" in agricultural products and other goods to replace the infamous trade in human beings. Palm oil—and also palm kernels—readily fit both needs.

In parts of western Africa, palm oil was a key export for decades prior to European colonization. This palm plantation worker in Cameroon collected palm seeds, which were then processed for their versatile oil. © *National Archives*

By 1850 Britain alone was importing some 30,000 tons of West African palm oil annually. Over the second half of the century, palm-oil EXPORTS, mostly from NIGE-RIA, averaged about 50,000 tons annually. While some palm trees were planted, most of the production came from controlled groves of wild palms. Most of those engaged in the production were small-holder farmers.

Palm oil continued as a major cash crop for Nigeria and other parts of West Africa during the colonial period. Furthermore, European plantations also began to play a role. Chief among these were the plantations in the BEL-GIAN CONGO (today's Democratic Republic of the CONGO) owned by the British Lever Brothers Company. In 1911 William Lever won the right to use up to 1.9 million acres (750,000 hectares) of palm-bearing land to get palm oil for his company's soap business.

The market for palm oil expanded after World War II (1939–45), when further advances in refining the oil made it possible to use unhydrogenated palm oil in processed food products. This led to a rapid expansion of palm oil exports and the spread of palm oil production to other parts of the world. By 1982 Malaysia, in Southeast Asia, had become both the world's largest pro-

ducer and exporter of palm oil. Nigeria, with about half the total for Africa, remains the largest African producer of palm oil.

See also: AGRICULTURE (Vol. IV); COLONIALISM, IN-FLUENCE OF (Vol. IV); PALM OIL (Vol. III).

Further reading: D. K. Fieldhouse, *Unilever Overseas: the Anatomy of a Multinational, 1895–1965* (Stanford, Calif.: Hoover Institution Press, 1978); Susan M. Martin, *Palm Oil and Protest* (Cambridge, U.K.: Cambridge University Press, 1988).

Pan-Africanism Idea that all people of African descent share histories, interests, and concerns and should unite to develop their common culture. The founding of the Pan-Africanism movement is typically credited to Henry Sylvester Williams (1869–1911), a scholar from Trinidad, West Indies, who founded the African Association in 1897. A year later the African Association called for a meeting to consider the oppression of the AFRICAN DIASPORA in a world increasingly dominated by whites. Many black intellectuals from the Americas and the West Indies embraced the idea, and the African Association, which changed its name to the Pan-African Association (PAA), planned the first Pan-African Congress (not to be confused with the PAN-AFRICANIST CONGRESS of SOUTH AFRICA).

The tangible results of the First Congress, held in London in 1900, were minimal, and two years later, the PAA disbanded as a result of internal discord and financial difficulties. Other pan-African events not connected to the PAA included an International Conference held at the Tuskegee Institute by Booker T. WASHINGTON (1856–1915) that attracted both African and African-American attendees.

However, largely because of the efforts of African-American W. E. B. DU BOIS (1868–1963), the Pan-African Congress reconvened in 1919, 1921, 1923, and 1927. Marcus GARVEY (1887–1940), a black leader from Jamaica, also attended these early congresses.

The 1919 congress is known as the First Pan-African Congress (PAC), and it coincided with the Paris Peace Conference held at Versailles ending the World War I (1914–18). Attendee W. E. B. Du Bois wanted to address the Paris Peace Conference to suggest that the PAC have input into the disposition of the African colonies stripped from Germany and Italy. Although Du Bois was able to speak with conference officials, the delegation was not allowed to present its case at the conference.

As the 20th century progressed, Pan-Africanism stimulated African political activity, becoming a theme that bound Africa's various NATIONALISM AND INDEPENDENCE MOVEMENTS. The African colonies sided with their respective colonizers in World War II (1939–45), but African support for the Allied war effort did not prevent them from looking for ways to achieve independence. At the conclusion of World War II, the Fifth Pan-African Congress met in Manchester, England, to discuss the immediate future of Europe's African colonies. Although the meeting was relatively unheralded, it served to galvanize the world's black leaders. Attendees of the event included Kwame NKRUMAH (1909–1972), the future leader of GHANA; Jomo KENYATTA (c. 1891–1978), the future president of KENYA; Hastings Kamuzu BANDA (c. 1898–1997), the future president of MALAWI; and Obafemi AWOLOWO (1909–1987), a prominent Nigerian nationalist.

In 1947, Senegalese author Alioune DIOP (1910–1980) founded *PRÉSENCE AFRICAINE,* a literary journal devoted to furthering the intellectual Pan-Africanist movement known as NÉGRITUDE.

See also: INDEPENDENCE MOVEMENTS (Vol. V); PAN-AFRICANISM (Vol. V).

Pan-Africanist Congress (PAC)
Militant black opposition organization in SOUTH AFRICA that emerged from the AFRICAN NATIONAL CONGRESS (ANC). The Pan-Africanist Congress was founded on April 6, 1959, by disaffected members of the African National Congress. The ideological basis for the PAC can be traced back to the 1940s and the formation of the ANC Youth League, a branch of the ANC that called for mass demonstrations and a variant of African nationalism known as *Africanism.* Among its key members was Robert SOBUKWE (1924–1978), a staunch Africanist who cofounded the PAC and later became its first president. During the 1950s, Africanists within the ANC grew increasingly disenchanted with its policy of multiracialism and its willingness to admit whites, Indians, and Coloureds as members or as allies. Africanists were opposed to the Charterist movement, which stemmed from the FREEDOM CHARTER of 1955, and which embraced the principle that South Africa belonged to all its peoples, regardless of race. They also felt that this approach weakened the forces against APARTHEID and reinforced the patronizing colonialist image of Africans as incapable of providing their own leadership. The PAC was explicitly an African nationalist organization, and, impatient with the organization-building approach of the

ANC leadership, determined to win African rights through militant action supported by the masses.

The PAC identified with and sought to emulate the continent-wide struggle of African peoples against white COLONIAL RULE. In particular, it looked to Kwame NKRUMAH (1909–1972), who led GHANA to independence in 1957. The PAC believed it was necessary for Africans to forge their own future to boost self-confidence and adopted the slogan "Africa for the Africans." Sobukwe led the Africanists out of the ANC in late 1958, and in April 1959 he and other dissatisfied ANC members founded the PAC at Orlando, a suburb of JOHANNESBURG. Sobukwe was elected its first president.

The PAC also formed its own labor-union organization called the Federation of Free African Trade Unions of South Africa. In March 1960 the PAC organized a campaign of defiance, which led to the Sharpeville massacre, in which 69 African protesters where shot dead by South African police. The subsequent harsh government repression resulted in the imprisonment of Sobukwe and the banning of the PAC, the ANC, and other opposition organizations.

See also: NATIONALISM AND INDEPENDENCE MOVEMENTS (Vol. IV); PAN-AFRICANIST CONGRESS (Vol. V); SHARPEVILLE (Vol. V).

Further reading: Gail M. Gerhart, *Black Power in South Africa: The Evolution of an Ideology* (Berkeley, Calif.: University of California Press, 1978); Tom Lodge, *Black Politics in South Africa since 1945* (New York: Longman, 1983).

partition
While the origins of European colonies or "spheres of influence" can be traced back to the Portuguese maritime exploration of the 15th century, it was not until the late 1800s that full-scale colonialism took shape. In the early 19th century the prohibition of the SLAVE TRADE by Britain signified an international economic shift, with Africa being perceived not as a source of LABOR but as a source of raw materials for use by industrial Europe. Thus, access to African resources became an essential part of economic policy. As late as the 1870s, however, European states had not yet embarked a policy of COLONIAL CONQUEST, as they were largely able to obtain what they wanted through trade and commercial treaties. By 1875 only about one-tenth of the continent had been colonized, with the main areas being in the extreme northern and southern parts of the continent.

A number of developments changed the relationship between Europe and Africa. INDUSTRIALIZATION led to new European advances in communications (e.g., the telegraph), TRANSPORTATION (e.g., improved steam navigation and railroads), and military technology (e.g., the machine gun). Europe thus developed a huge technological advantage over African states and peoples. Further, advances in tropical MEDICINE (e.g., the use of quinine to control malaria) enabled Europeans to operate in the tropical zones with fewer setbacks from disease. These advancements gave Europeans the tools they needed to occupy the continent.

Though the slave trade persisted even into the 20th century, Europe's efforts to suppress it played a large role in shaping imperial aims in Africa during the late 19th century. Many MISSIONARIES and explorers engaged in activities with the stated goal of ending SLAVERY on the continent. Though they were not always successful in their endeavors, these missionaries and explorers did expand Europe's influence and provide the avenues through which the United Kingdom and other European countries established the foundations of their African colonial empires.

The motivation for colonial conquest stemmed largely from increased rivalry among the European countries on both economic and political grounds. Developments came to a head when King LEOPOLD II (1835–1909) of Belgium and his International African Association laid claim to large portions of the Congo River Basin. Increasing diplomatic tensions in Europe led German chancellor Otto von BISMARCK (1815–1898) to organize the BERLIN CONFERENCE, in 1884. This diplomatic gathering was ostensibly concerned with humanitarian issues, but it actually intended to establish guidelines for the amicable European partition of Africa. All of the major European powers were present, along with the United States, but there were no African representatives. The conference recognized Leopold II's claims in the Congo region and, more significantly, it concluded that any colonial power could claim a "sphere of influence" over an African territory if it first secured "effective occupation" of that territory.

Upon the conclusion of the conference in 1885, the partition of the continent commenced in earnest. Fueled by nationalistic pride, political rivalry, and the promise of economic gain (which was amplified by the discovery of DIAMONDS, GOLD, and other MINERALS AND METALS), European states rapidly laid claim, on paper at least, to broad swaths of African territory. Establishing control on the ground was frequently a much slower process, due in large part to African RESISTANCE AND REBELLION. In some instances, as when Ethiopian emperor MENELIK II (1844–1913) defeated an Italian army at the Battle of ADOWA in 1896, the resistance was successful. By that date, however, all of Africa, save ETHIOPIA, LIBERIA, MOROCCO, and the AFRIKANER REPUBLICS of the TRANSVAAL and the ORANGE FREE STATE, were at least nominally under European COLONIAL RULE.

Even the countries that maintained their sovereignty after 1896 fell in some way under the influence of colonialism. The Transvaal and the Orange Free State became British possessions after the ANGLO-BOER WAR (1899–1902). France and Spain had divided Morocco by 1912. Liberia, established as a colony for Africans freed from slavery in America, was essentially an economic colony of the United States. And from 1936 to 1941 Ethiopia was occupied by the forces of fascist Italy.

Though Africans would struggle against European colonizers for years to come, and though the balance of colonial power would shift as well, by the beginning of World War I (1914–18) the partition of Africa was complete. The results were a haphazard imposition of colonial borders, dividing territories with no concern for the traditional or ethnic boundaries of the Africans living there. Essentially a reorganization of hundreds of cultures and societies, the lines of partition shaped the formation of present-day African nations, and remained an influence even after the reestablishment of Africa's independence.

See also: BELGIUM AND AFRICA (Vol. IV); ENGLAND AND AFRICA (Vols. III, IV, V); EUROPE AND AFRICA (Vols. IV, V); FRANCE AND AFRICA (Vols. III, IV, V); GERMANY AND AFRICA (Vol. IV); ITALY AND AFRICA (Vol. IV); NATURAL RESOURCES (Vols. III, IV, V); PORTUGAL AND AFRICA (Vols. III, IV, V); PROTECTORATE (Vol. IV); UNITED STATES OF AMERICA AND AFRICA (Vols. IV, V).

Further reading: H. L. Wesseling, *Divide and Rule: the Partition of Africa, 1880–1914* (Westport, Conn.: Praeger, 1996).

pastoralism Lifestyle of people whose economic, cultural, and social institutions center on livestock such as cattle, sheep, camels, and goats. In many pastoralist societies, the number of animals owned by determines the prestige of the owner. Among some groups, the TSWANA of southern Africa, for instance, cattle also might serve as the foundation of the group's political structure. During the era of COLONIAL RULE, European colonial administrators often tried to force pastoralists, such as the MAASAI of East Africa, to settle and begin a sedentary existence. Pastoralism, however, has persisted into the 21st century.

See also: PASTORALISM (Vol. I).

Further reading: Dorothy L. Hodgson (ed.), *Rethinking Pastoralism in Africa: Gender, Culture & the Myth of the Patriarchal Pastoralist* (Athens, Ohio: Ohio University Press, 2000); M. A. Mohamed Salih, Ton Dietz, and Ghaffar Mohamed Ahmed Abdel, eds., *African Pastoralism: Conflict, Institutions, and Government* (London: Pluto Press in association with OSSREA, 2001).

Paton, Alan (1903–1988) *South African author and political activist*

Born in 1903 in Pietermaritzburg, in present-day KwaZulu-Natal, SOUTH AFRICA, Alan Paton became one of South Africa's most celebrated authors. His widely read novel, *Cry, the Beloved Country*, published in 1948, poignantly highlighted the racial tensions that divided his country's European and African populations. The novel has been the basis for the 1950 musical, *Lost in the Stars*, by Maxwell Anderson (1888–1959) and Kurt Weill (1900–1950), as well as two feature-length dramatic films, released in 1951 and 1995.

Paton is well known for his other novels, which include *Too Late the Phalarope* (1953) and *Ah, But Your Land is Beautiful* (1981). He also wrote biographies, most notably of the South African politician Jan Hofmeyr (1894–1948) and the Archbishop of CAPE TOWN, Geoffrey Clayton (1884–1957). Both of these works appeared in 1964. In addition, Paton wrote a play called *The Lost Journey* (1959) about the famous British missionary and explorer, David LIVINGSTONE, (1813–1873).

Paton first worked as a schoolteacher and then entered social work, eventually serving as the principal of the Diepkloof Reformatory in JOHANNESBURG. Paton's political activities grew out of deeply held principles. A public critic of APARTHEID and racial discrimination, he was a founder—and later president—of South Africa's Liberal Party, which challenged the country's racial policy. (The government banned the Liberal Party in 1968.) While his political activities did little to deter apartheid, as an author, Alan Paton contributed significantly to undermining the credibility of the South African apartheid state.

See also: LITERATURE IN COLONIAL AFRICA (Vol. IV); LITERATURE IN MODERN AFRICA (Vol. V).

Further reading: Peter F. Alexander, *Alan Paton: A Biography* (Oxford, U.K.: Oxford University Press, 1994).

Pedi Large ethnic group living in the Northern Province of SOUTH AFRICA. The Pedi, also known as the Northern SOTHO or Bapedi, first established a kingdom around the beginning of the 17th century, in the region between the Vaal and Limpopo rivers, in present-day South Africa. It was not until the late 1700s, however, that all of the Pedi were united under King Thulare (d. 1824), after which they came to dominate the TRANSVAAL. In the early 1800s the Pedi came under attack from the marauding NDEBELE, led by their chief Mzilikazi (1790–1868). The militaristic ZULU expansion, known as the Mfecane (The Crushing), further threatened the Pedi. In the aftermath of the Ndebele and Zulu attacks, Thulare's former kingdom was left in shambles. Led by Thulare's son, Sekwati (d. 1861), the Pedi relocated east of present-day PRETORIA, where they gradually recovered much of their lost power.

Under Sekwati, the Pedi made peace with the Zulu and also granted land to the east of the kingdom to the BOERS, who had arrived in the region during the Great Boer Trek. Conflicts between the Pedi and the Boers immediately erupted as the Boers encroached on Pedi land and accused the Pedi of stealing livestock. Violence broke out in 1838, 1847, and 1852, before Sekwati negotiated a peace that lasted until his death in 1861. During the ensuing power struggle, Sekwati's son Sekhukhune (d. 1882) defeated and exiled his brother Mampuru (d. 1883), assuming the Pedi throne.

After GOLD was discovered in the settlement of Pilgrim's Rest, in 1873, the Pedi began working the mines for far less compensation than their white counterparts. Conflict over pay and over Boer trespassing on Pedi land led to war in 1876. While the Pedi sent the Boers into retreat, Boer attacks on crops and livestock left the Pedi starving. One year later, however, the Boers themselves were weakened when the British annexed the Transvaal. Sekhukhune then launched a war against the British, winning a number of battles before being soundly defeated in 1879. In 1896 the British divided the Pedi kingdom in two, creating a rivalry that further weakened the group.

Following the British defeat of his brother's Pedi kingdom, Mampuru plotted to kill Sekhukhune, a plan he carried out in 1882. Mampuru was caught one year later by South African authorities and executed for Sekhukhune's murder.

Shortly after the formation of the UNION OF SOUTH AFRICA, in 1910, the Pedi were forced to live in cramped "native reserves." In 1959 the Pedi were confined to Lebowa, part of the APARTHEID homeland system designed to segregate and manage the African population in South Africa. Only the fall of apartheid toward the end of the 20th century allowed the Pedi to finally emerge from the shadow that fell over them during the era of COLONIAL RULE. By that time nearly four million Pedi were living in northern South Africa, and the Pedi LANGUAGE, today one of 11 official languages spoken in the country, was spoken by nearly 10 percent of the population.

> Mass graves discovered in Lebowa in 1986 suggest the "homeland" government responded brutally to any dissent within its jurisdiction, though no one has been held responsible for the deaths.

See also: COLONIAL CONQUEST (Vol. IV); COLONIAL-ISM, INFLUENCE OF (Vol. IV); ENGLAND AND AFRICA (Vols. III, IV, V); ETHNICITY AND IDENTITY (Vol. V); GREAT BOER TREK (Vol. III); MFECANE (Vol. III); MZILIKAZI (Vol. III).

Pelewura, Madam Alimotu (c. 1865–1951) *Political figure and leader of market women in Lagos, Nigeria*

Alimotu Pelewura, a YORUBA-speaking Muslim, came from a humble background. The daughter of a fish trader, she went to work alongside her mother at an early age, without a formal education. Her husband died young, and she never remarried. Madam Pelewura then focused her energies on organizing and leading her fellow market women, who mostly came from backgrounds similar to her own.

In LAGOS, NIGERIA, as in many other parts of West Africa, women were the principal distributors and retailers of food and many other goods. They thus played a critical economic and social role in the life of the region's cities and towns. Furthermore, as the market ECONOMY expanded during the colonial era, with increases in the production of CASH CROPS and a growing wage-LABOR force to sell to, the opportunities for market women correspondingly grew. For the most part they operated on a small scale, working out of stalls in the marketplace. Collectively, however, they exercised considerable power, and they were aware that by organizing they could promote their interests.

By 1910 Madam Pelewura had emerged as the leader of the market women of Lagos, a position formally acknowledged by the *eleko* of Lagos, who was the city's *oba* (ruler). By the 1920s, some 8,000 Lagos market women organized the Lagos Market Women's Association, with Pelewura as its president.

As president of the association, Madam Pelewura oversaw the administration of the Ereko Market, which was the central market in Lagos. The market women paid small weekly dues to the association, which in turn actively worked on their behalf. The association became so powerful that, by the early 1930s, the British colonial administration grew alarmed. They did not like seeing Africans, especially African women, exercising so much power. Indeed, in the 1930s, when the colonial government sought to move the Ereko Market to a less desirable location, Madam Pelewura organized large-scale protests that

blocked the move. Such successful obstruction of a colonial government's plans was highly unusual and a sign of the influence wielded by Madam Pelewura.

During World War II (1939–45) Pelewura and her association again clashed with the British authorities. This time Britain sought to impose price controls and take direct control over the distribution of *gari*, a flour made from cassava tubers and the basic foodstuff in most of the region. This led to continuous tension and strife between the Lagos Market Women's Association and colonial administrators throughout the war period.

Because of her leadership role, Madam Pelewura continued to be actively involved in politics. She was generally effective at ensuring the continued support of the *eleko* and his councillors for the market women's interests. She also became embroiled in the emerging nationalist politics that sought to challenge the political status quo of the colony. She became a political ally of Herbert MACAULAY (1864–1946), one of Nigeria's earliest nationalist politicians, and founder, in 1923, of the Nigerian National Democratic Party (NNDP). Macaulay recognized the benefits of having the market women and their leader backing NNDP activities.

After the war Pelewura, who was then over 80, continued to participate in both nationalist and local politics. The *eleko* conferred additional recognition on her as a representative of the common people before his court. She was also selected to take part in a political delegation to London to protest Britain's postwar plans for Nigeria, but she was too frail to make the trip. Indicative of the respect she had earned among the population of Lagos, when she died in 1951, more than 25,000 people joined the funeral procession to the cemetery.

See also: COLONIAL RULE (Vol. IV); NATIONALISM AND INDEPENDENCE MOVEMENTS (Vol. IV); WOMEN IN COLONIAL AFRICA (Vol. IV).

Peters, Karl (1856–1918) *German explorer*

Born September 27, 1856, in Neuhaus an der Elbe (in present-day Germany), Peters was the son of a clergyman who studied history and philosophy. During a stay in England he became convinced of the need for Germany to develop a colonial empire. To this end, in 1884 he founded the Society for German Colonization.

Operating without official sanction from the German government, Peters ventured into eastern Africa, meeting with numerous African leaders, signing treaties, and acquiring territory for his society. These were for the most part areas that ibn Said BARGHASH (c. 1833–1888), the sultan of ZANZIBAR, claimed to rule. In the wake of the BERLIN CONFERENCE of 1884–85, Otto von BISMARCK (1815–1898), the German chancellor, declared the society's lands to be a German PROTECTORATE, thus forming part of what came to be known as GERMAN EAST AFRICA.

Known for his harsh policies, as well as for his extreme nationalism, Peters served in the German colonial administration from the capital at BAGAMOYO, on the northern coast of TANGANYIKA (present-day mainland TANZANIA). In 1897, however, the imperial colonial commissioner in the German legislature called Peters to account for cruelties committed during his administration, effectively putting an end to his career in Africa. He died in September 1918, in Woltorf, Germany.

See also: GERMANY AND AFRICA (Vol. IV); PARTITION (Vol. IV).

photography Photography was invented in Europe around 1839, and photographic studios were set up in EGYPT and SOUTH AFRICA as early as the 1840s. Soon photographers were operating in LUANDA, ANGOLA and FREETOWN, SIERRA LEONE, as well. In East Africa, Indian photographers set up large, commercial studios in KENYA, TANZANIA, and ZANZIBAR. The clients at these studios were mostly Europeans who sat for portraits, but photographers also took pictures of cultural scenes and places of interest.

Anthropologists and ethnographers used photographic images in Africa extensively during the second half of the 19th century. However, many of the so-called anthropological portrayals of Africans were set up in ways that, ultimately, reinforced negative stereotypes of both Africa and its peoples.

Adventurous photographers were attracted to scenic Egypt and the Nile region. Among them was Austrian artist Richard Buchta, who photographed the upper Nile and northern UGANDA. Scientists and adventurers traveled to other remote regions of Africa, as well. Some explorers employed photographers for their expeditions. For example, British explorer and missionary David LIVINGSTONE (1813–1873) brought along John KIRK (1832–1922), a naturalist and physician, to take pictures of his Zambezi expedition of 1858–62.

Around 1870 improvements in photographic technology led to an increase in the number of studios in Africa's capital cities and major towns. Photographers of this era used heavy "box cameras," which did not have shutters. Instead, they exposed large negatives that they retouched and printed. (The later integration of a darkroom in the camera meant that a negative could be produced on printing paper and processed immediately.) Continued technological advances in photography resulted in simpler processing techniques and lower prices

for pictures. Colonial governments encouraged lowering the costs of photography, since they often compelled Africans in the colonies to carry identity pictures issued by colonial administrations.

The first locally manufactured cameras appeared in NIGERIA and GHANA in the 1920s. During this period new uses for photography came about, including photo reportage and news photography. Also, images of Africa were coveted by research institutions and magazines such as *Life* and *National Geographic*. DRUM magazine, which became Africa's most popular periodical in the 1950s, employed African photojournalists like Peter Magubane (1932–) of South Africa.

A number of professional African photographers began garnering fame in the early 20th century. One was Alex Agbaglo Acolatse (1880–1975) from the GOLD COAST COLONY (now Ghana). In TOGOLAND (now TOGO), which was then ruled by Germany, he became one of the first African professional photographers. His images can be seen in German archives.

In Sierra Leone two brothers, Arthur and Alphonso (1883–1969) Lisk-Carew, founded a studio in Freetown in 1905. Their business included selling postcards, stationery, and photographic equipment and supplies. The British colonial government recognized the brothers' professionalism and contracted them to record government events for propaganda purposes. The Lisk-Carews' work can be seen in British archives.

During the 20th century photography quickly grew into a profession, with talented and creative African photographers adapting their techniques to suit their environments. In the 1940s the number of African-operated photographic studios increased greatly, due in large part to the introduction of medium-sized cameras, low-priced enlargers, and electrification, which allowed for the use of artificial lights in studios.

By the 1950s photography was widespread, and the range of events that photographers were contracted to cover broadened to include formal government and political events, traditional ceremonies, religious events, weddings, funerals, and sports contests. However, as was the case around the world, African photographic studios began to decline after the 1960s. At this time new technologies allowed individuals to use less expensive cameras and film to process their own photographs.

See also: PHOTOGRAPHY (Vol. V).

Plaatje, Sol T. (Solomon Tshekisho Plaatje) (1876–1932) *Tswana journalist, novelist, and political activist in South Africa*

Born on a farm called Dornfontein, on October 9, 1876, Plaatje was educated at nearby Pniel mission station and, subsequently, at a mission school in Beaconsfield, CAPE COLONY. Quickly distinguishing himself as a student, he progressed rapidly, eventually earning an appointment as a pupil-teacher, a post that he kept from 1892 to 1894. In 1894 he moved to KIMBERLEY, in northern Cape Colony, where he took a job as a letter carrier, one of the few occupations that could provide advancement for Africans.

His job at the post office gave Plaatje an entrance to the more educated and cosmopolitan element of Kimberley's African population, people who worked as teachers, court interpreters, clerks, and members of the clergy. Plaatje soon was involved in a variety of community affairs, serving as the secretary for local cricket clubs, singing with the Philharmonic Society, and joining the South Africans' Improvement Society, whose meetings and discussions formed the beginnings of his political activity. By 1898, the year in which he also married Elizabeth M'belle, the sister of his life-long friend Isaiah Bud M'Belle, Plaatje's English had become proficient enough for him to take a job as a court interpreter, one of the most prestigious jobs available to Africans at the time.

A gifted linguist, Plaatje spoke several African languages, including his own TSWANA, plus SOTHO, XHOSA, ZULU, and Koranna as well as the European languages of English, Dutch, and German.

Taking up a position with the court in the town of Mafeking, Plaatje found himself in a smaller, less cosmopolitan community. But there, too, he managed to find companionship among educated and politically aware individuals, the most noteworthy of whom was Silas Telesho Molema, a member of one of the region's most influential families.

With the outbreak of the ANGLO-BOER WAR, in 1899, Mafeking was attacked by Boer forces from across the TRANSVAAL border. During the siege that followed Plaatje was asked to type a diary being kept by a white magistrate, Charles Bell. Responding to Bell's words, Plaatje eventually began recording his own thoughts and reactions to the siege in a work that many years later, in 1976, would be published as *Mafeking Diary: A Black Man's View of a White Man's War.*

In 1901 Silas Molema purchased a newspaper called *Koranta ea Becoana* (Tswana Gazette) and appointed Plaatje editor. With articles in both Tswana and English, the paper quickly became, under Plaatje's leadership, a weekly periodical that brought messages of progress and EDUCATION to the African population as well as advocacy of constitutional rights. Although, by 1902, Plaatje had left his job with the court and was devoting more time to the paper, the enterprise was never economically viable,

and by 1908 its financial ground was foundering. In 1910, however, Plaatje found support among several wealthy Africans for another newspaper, this one called *Tsala ea Becoana* (The friend of the Tswana). For a time this newspaper—the second of three Plaatje eventually would establish—provided him with both income and a forum for his ideas.

During this period, when the UNION OF SOUTH AFRICA was created and its white leadership became more conservative and more restrictive, Plaatje was increasingly drawn into the political arena. By 1909 he had become one of the leaders of the South African Native Convention and was instrumental in the transformation of this loosely knit organization into the South African Native Congress, the ancestor of the AFRICAN NATIONAL CONGRESS (ANC), in 1911. Serving as the ANC's first corresponding secretary, Plaatje put his experience as a journalist and newspaper editor to work.

In 1913 his concerns about the well-being of the African people coalesced into his opposition to the 1913 Native Land Act, which he believed would have disastrous effects on the African population. With Plaatje's encouragement, protests were held, representatives were sent to the capital in CAPE TOWN, and money was raised to send a delegation to London to voice Africans' opposition to the measure.

In 1914 Plaatje sailed for London as part of the ANC's delegation, an effort that, ultimately, was unable to affect either the rejection or even the modification of the measure. When the rest of the delegates returned to South Africa, Plaatje decided to remain in England where he worked on a manuscript about African life (*Native Life in South Africa*) and continued to press for African rights. While the bulk of his time in England was spent on his effort to galvanize opinion against the Land Act, Plaatje managed to find time to take on several other projects, including writing an essay on Shakespeare and several books on Tswana LANGUAGE and culture. These books, which included a volume of traditional Tswana proverbs, were part of Plaatje's growing fascination with finding ways to preserve Tswana culture in the face of the seemingly unstoppable advance of European influence. Asserting the innate value—rather than the "backwardness" observed by Europeans—of Tswana language and culture, Plaatje's writings represented an early and significant step in preserving Tswana identity.

In 1917 Plaatje returned to South Africa, where his activities soon brought him to the attention of the government. Breaking with the ANC's policy of refraining from overt criticism of the government, he spoke out against South African policies and was arrested on a number of charges.

Plaatje soon returned to London, in 1919, hoping to draw attention to injustices and discrimination in South Africa. These efforts soon carried him beyond England to Canada and the United States, where he held forth at a series of speaking engagements that kept him abroad until 1923. When he returned to South Africa he found conditions even worse for Africans. Making his living once again as a writer and journalist, he continued to serve as a leader and spokesperson of the African cause.

Plaatje's works of fiction drew him considerable attention and, in North America, sales. They included *The Mote and the Beam*, a tale of a sexual relationship between a black and a white in South Africa, and *Mhudi*, a historical novel about early South African life.

See also: BECHUANALAND (Vol. IV); LITERATURE IN COLONIAL AFRICA (Vol. IV); NATIONALISM AND INDEPENDENCE MOVEMENTS (Vol. IV).

Further reading: Solomon Plaatje, *Selected Writings* (Athens, Ohio: Ohio University Press, 1998); Brian Willan, *Sol Plaatje: African Nationalist, 1876–1932* (Berkeley, Calif.: University of California Press, 1984).

political parties and organizations African political organization was generally suppressed, and, in some places, declared illegal during the era of COLONIAL RULE.

However, even before the end of the 19th century, Africans were organizing to protest European colonialism. For example, in 1897 Western-educated African lawyers in the British GOLD COAST COLONY founded the ABORIGINES' RIGHTS PROTECTION SOCIETY to voice opposition to British claims on African territories.

In the first decades of the 20th century, Africans continued founding political organizations, including the AFRICAN NATIONAL CONGRESS (1912), in SOUTH AFRICA, and the NATIONAL CONGRESS OF BRITISH WEST AFRICA (1920), in Gold Coast Colony. Following World War II (1939–45), political organization revolved around the various African NATIONALISM AND INDEPENDENCE MOVEMENTS across the continent. Many of these movements evolved into recognized political parties that vied for seats in post-independence governments.

See AFRICAN DEMOCRATIC ASSEMBLY; CONVENTION PEOPLE'S PARTY; NATIONAL LIBERATION FRONT; PAN-AFRICANIST CONGRESS; UNITED GOLD COAST CONVENTION; UNITED NATIONAL INDEPENDENCE PARTY; WAFD PARTY.

See also: POLITICAL PARTIES AND ORGANIZATIONS (Vol. V).

Further reading: M. A. Mohamed Salih, ed., *African Political Parties: Evolution, Institutionalization and Governance* (London: Pluto Press, 2003).

porterage A form of transport used for TRADE AND COMMERCE when animal-drawn transport is impractical or unavailable or if river transport is impossible. Porter-

Shown "headloading," these women porters carry rice to the market in Dar Es Salaam, in c. 1900. © *Francis C. Fuerst/New York Times*

age, sometimes called headloading, was very common prior to widespread motor and rail transport and was frequently used to transport CASH CROPS and other trade items to market.

In the West African forests and rain forests TRANSPORTATION is difficult because tropical diseases such as sleeping sickness, which affects both animals and humans, restrict the use of draft animals. Consequently, humans must carry their own loads, and the most effective way to do this is through headloading. The practice is common in portions of East Africa, as well. In contrast, porterage did not play a role in trans-Saharan trade because of the availability of camels.

Children learn the skill of headloading at a very early age, using it while collecting firewood and bringing water from a well or stream. Through such repeated practice, they strengthen their neck muscles so that they can carry weights as heavy as 50 pounds while walking with their hands free.

In both East and West Africa, traders conducted long-distance overland trade through porterage. Both slave laborers and professional porters were used to transport heavy loads, including ivory. Some ethnic groups, such as the NYAMWEZI of TANZANIA, were particularly adept at porterage and plied their skills professionally. Porterage was one of the few ways in which African men could earn a cash wage to pay colonial taxes.

Today, however, porterage is no longer the factor in long-distance trade it was in the past. Still, it is regularly practiced throughout Africa in both rural and urban areas. Indeed, women carrying produce and other goods to market in this convenient and inexpensive fashion is a familiar sight.

See also: TRADE (Vols. I, II, III); TRADE AND COMMERCE (Vols. IV, V).

Portugal and Africa Portugal's colonial presence in Africa was the longest of the European powers. From the latter half of the 19th century onward, Portugal shored up its occasionally harsh COLONIAL RULE. By the beginning of the 1960s, however, African nationalist movements in Portugal's colonies had begun the inexorable movement toward independence.

For centuries Portugal's activity in Africa was limited primarily to the SLAVE TRADE on both the east and west coasts of Africa. However, in the 19th century, the slave trade was largely abolished, and Portugal gradually turned its attention to colonizing several territories where it already had a presence. In southwestern Africa, the Portuguese controlled ANGOLA; in the southeast, they were the main European power in the MOZAMBIQUE region; and in West Africa, where the Portuguese had traded with coastal peoples since the 15th century, they held the territory that would become GUINEA-BISSAU. Portugal's colonial

territorial expansion gained momentum in the middle of the 19th century and culminated in the Portuguese participation in European PARTITION of Africa at the BERLIN CONFERENCE in 1884–85.

About 60 years prior to the Berlin Conference, Portugal lost its colony of Brazil, in South America. Portugal saw in Africa a chance to revive its hopes for empire, and in the late 19th century, its interest in Africa evolved to take on nationalistic and imperial—rather than purely economic—characteristics.

At the beginning of the 20th century Portugal's territorial claims in Africa were much larger than the areas actually under its control. And as Portugal increased the vigor of its colonial efforts, it faced more instances of RESISTANCE AND REBELLION by indigenous Africans. These acts were often brutally repressed by the Portuguese authorities and frequently resulted in large-scale death and destruction.

As part of Portuguese attempts to settle and pacify African territories, the Portuguese government began officially sanctioning the emigration of its citizens from Portugal. These efforts, however, did not meet with much success, since the settlers took African land and jobs and caused social upheaval. Generally the Portuguese settlers took up residence in the colonies' major urban ports such as LUANDA, in Angola, and LOURENÇO MARQUES, in Mozambique. The majority of the settlers who didn't move to the ports tried to establish plantations, which typically were worked by underpaid African laborers in harsh conditions. Others worked with European CONCESSIONAIRE COMPANIES to exploit regional resources.

The Republic of Portugal faced a crisis in the early 1920s, resulting in a military coup d'état in 1926. By 1932 the country was under the leadership of Antonio de Oliveira Salazar (1889–1970), who abolished the old constitution and instituted an authoritarian state, which he led as prime minister, until 1968. As part of his sweeping economic reforms, Salazar quickly imposed direct rule over Portugal's African colonies. Even though the dream of a Portuguese-African empire was hardly becoming a reality, Salazar encouraged a steady flow of Portuguese settlers to Africa. Portuguese migration to the colonies even accelerated during the period following World War II (1939–45).

Portugal was officially neutral during World War II and, therefore, neither gained nor lost African territory as a result of the war. In the latter half of the 1940s, African NATIONALISM AND INDEPENDENCE MOVEMENTS began pressing for an end to colonial rule. As a concession to nationalist demands, Salazar revised the Portuguese constitution to change the status of Portugal's African territories from colonies to overseas territories. Change was slow in coming, however, and, by the 1950s, the independence movements were agitating for true independence. Salazar responded by allowing a secret colonial police force, known as PIDE, to use violence, intimidation, and even murder to subvert the efforts of the independence movements. In turn Africans in the Portuguese colonies turned to guerrilla warfare in order to pressure Portugal to withdraw.

Male Portuguese settlers in Africa had a long history of producing children with African women, and by the beginning of the 20th century, the Portuguese colonies—especially in western Africa—had sizeable mixed-race populations. A Portuguese doctrine, described by the term *lusotropicology,* proposed that part of Portugal's mission in Africa was to fuse the Caucasian and Negroid races to form a "superior" Portuguese-African race. Conversion to Catholicism also played an important role in the doctrine.

In Angola the most effective nationalist movement proved to be the Popular Movement for the Liberation of Angola (Movimento Popular da Libertação de Angola, MPLA), a Marxist-oriented organization led by Agostinho Neto (1922–1979). The National Front for the Liberation of Angola (Frente Nacional para a Libertação de Angola, FNLA), a pro-West liberation organization led by Holden Roberto (1923–   ), also joined in the fighting. Because of their opposing ideologies, the two major Angolan independence movements ended up warring with each other, as well as with the Portuguese colonial government. In addition, as the war dragged on, the former Soviet Union and the United States became involved, thereby making Angola a front of the Cold War between the superpowers.

In Mozambique the Portuguese government was opposed by the Liberation Front of Mozambique (Frente de Libertação de Moçambique, FRELIMO), and in West Africa the independence struggle was led by the African Party for the Independence of Guinea and Cape Verde (Partido Africano da Independência da Guiné e Cabo Verde, PAIGC). By the mid-1970s the sustained efforts of all of these organizations, along with a regime change in Portugal, were responsible for achieving African independence for Portugal's former colonies.

See also: COLD WAR AND AFRICA (Vols. IV, V); PORTUGAL AND AFRICA (Vols. III, IV).

Further reading: David Birmingham, *Portugal and Africa* (New York: St. Martin's Press, 1999); Malyn Newitt, *Portugal in Africa: The Last Hundred Years* (London: Longman, 1981).

Portuguese Guinea Low-lying West African coastal colony held by Portugal until independence, as GUINEA-BISSAU, in 1973. From the 15th century until 1879, Portuguese settlements and commercial activities on the West African mainland were administered from the CAPE VERDE ISLANDS, located about 500 miles (805 km) off the coast of Portuguese Guinea. In 1879, however, Portugal established a new administrative center on the island of Bolama, off the mainland coast, and began running colonial trading stations from there.

The territory of Portuguese Guinea was occupied by several African ethnic groups, including the Balanta, on the coast, and the Fula, MANDINKA, Manjaca, and Pepel in the interior. The Portuguese colony included the 30-plus islands of the Bijagos Archipelago but was surrounded on all sides by French-claimed territory. Following the Portuguese abolition of the SLAVE TRADE, in 1869, GROUNDNUTS (peanuts), RUBBER, wax, and ivory became the main colonial trade items.

From the time of its founding, Portuguese Guinea was the site of often brutal efforts by the Portuguese to establish colonial control in the interior regions. Decades of repression and mistreatment erupted in nationalist sentiments after World War II (1939–45), with Africans calling for an end to European COLONIAL RULE. The Portuguese were not compliant, however, and in the mid-1950s Amílcar CABRAL (1924–1973) formed the African Party for the Independence of Guinea and Cape Verde (Partido Africano de Independencia de Guine e Capo Verde, PAIGC) and began an armed insurgency against Portuguese government forces.

The regional war continued into the 1970s, with the PAIGC finally declaring independence in 1973. The declaration was ratified in 1974, and the former colony took the name Guinea-Bissau. Amílcar Cabral, the longtime PAIGC leader, had been assassinated early in 1973. As a result, prior to independence, Amílcar's half-brother, Luis Cabral (1931–   ), who was also the PAIGC deputy secretary, was elected Guinea-Bissau's first president.

See also: PORTUGAL AND AFRICA (Vols. III, IV, V).

Further reading: Malyn Newitt, *Portugal in Africa: The Last Hundred Years* (Harlow, U.K.: Longman, 1981).

Prempeh I, Agyeman (Nana Agyeman Prempeh I, Nana Kwaku Dua III) (1870–1931) *The 13th asantehene (king) of the Ashanti in Ghana*

Known for resisting British colonial overtures, Agyeman Prempeh I ruled the ASHANTI EMPIRE, in present-day

GHANA, from 1888 until his death in 1931. He assumed the throne after a bitter five-year civil war to crown the successor to Kwaku Dua II, who died, in 1884, after a 40-day reign. The war pitted Prempeh's supporters, who included Yaa ASANTEWA (1850–1921), a powerful queen mother of one of the states of the confederation, against a group of Ashanti king-makers supporting Prempeh's cousin, Yaw Atwereboana, who they thought would seek closer ties with the British colonial administration. This attitude alienated the majority of the Ashanti people, who had been waging war against Britain for decades, and Agyeman Prempeh I finally assumed power in 1888. The Ashanti struggled to maintain independence until, in 1896, a British expeditionary force attacked KUMASI, the Ashanti capital, arresting Prempeh in the process. A year later, the British claimed the territory as part of their Gold Coast PROTECTORATE.

Violence flared again in 1900, when British colonial governor Sir Arnold Hodgson demanded to sit on the Ashanti Golden Stool, the sacred symbol of Ashanti sovereignty. In light of this grave insult, Ashanti insurgents, led by Yaa Asantewa, who was acting as queen mother, attacked and destroyed the British fort in Kumasi. Britain, which had long struggled to subdue the proud and independent Ashanti people, responded to the attack with its full imperial force, crushing the uprising and declaring the Ashanti kingdom a British colony in 1901.

Prempeh, who remained in British custody, chose exile over subjecting his people to a protracted war against the heavily armed British forces. Originally he was imprisoned in Elmina Castle on the southern coast of Ghana, and then, in 1897, he was sent to SIERRA LEONE, where a continuous flow of Ashanti visitors caused the British to move him again, this time to the remote island of SEYCHELLES, in the Indian Ocean. There he began compiling *The History of Ashanti Kings*, an important English text for understanding the history of the Ashanti kingdom.

Yaa Asantewa was the most important source for *The History of Ashanti Kings*. A member of the Ashanti royal dynasty, she possessed extensive knowledge of the oral history of her lineage, which she shared with Prempeh when they were both in exile on Seychelles.

By the early 1920s various organizations had convinced the British that Prempeh no longer represented a serious threat to the administration of the GOLD COAST COLONY and that it would be in their best interest to release him. In November of 1924 Prempeh returned to Kumasi

from Seychelles to a hero's welcome. The British recognized him only as the chief of Kumasi, but the Ashanti people treated him as true royalty. Prempeh lived in circumstances befitting his royal stature until his death in 1931. He was succeeded by his nephew Osei Tutu Agyeman Prempeh II (r. 1931–1970).

See also: COLONIAL RULE (Vol. IV); ENGLAND AND AFRICA (Vols. IV, V); GOLDEN STOOL (Vol. III); HISTORICAL SCHOLARSHIP ON AFRICA (Vol. IV).

Further reading: Agyeman Prempeh, E. Akyeampong, A. Adu Boahen, N. Lawler, T. C. McCaskie, I. Wilks, eds., *The History of Ashanti Kings and the Whole Country Itself and Other Writings* (London: British Academy, 2003).

Présence Africaine Literary journal dedicated to fostering the writings of black Africans. Established in 1947 by Senegalese author Alioune DIOP (1910–1980), *Présence Africaine* has been committed to the publication of works by black African intellectuals and others within the AFRICAN DIASPORA, regardless of philosophy or politics. In the 1950s *Présence Africaine* became one of the chief voices for NÉGRITUDE, the pan-Africanist literary movement. Authors whose work appeared in the journal not only gave expression to the value of their African culture and heritage, but also revitalized pan-Africanist goals.

Présence Africaine advertises that "Since 1941, Africans, Madagascans, and West Indians in Paris have been preoccupied with affirming the 'presence' or ethos of the coloured communities of the world, defending the originality of their way of life and the dignity of the culture."

At first *Présence Africaine* received validation on the world stage by virtue of its editorial committee, which included the well-known European intellectuals Jean-Paul Sartre, Albert Camus, Emmanuel Mournier, and André Gide. In time, however, the white, European editors were discreetly dropped in favor of French- and English-speaking black Africans.

See also: LITERATURE IN COLONIAL AFRICA (Vol. IV); LITERATURE IN MODERN AFRICA (Vol. V); PAN-AFRICANISM (Vol. IV).

Pretoria Administrative capital of SOUTH AFRICA, located in the north-central part of the country in what is now Gauteng Province. By 1855 migrants of the Great Boer Trek had established themselves in the TRANSVAAL region and had begun to see the need for an established capital to function as a center of Boer influence. Marthinus W. Pretorius (1819–1910), who later served as the first president of the South African Republic (1857–77), founded the city of Pretoria in response. He named it after his father, Andries Pretorius (1798–1853), one of the prominent leaders of the Great Trek.

In 1938 Afrikaner nationalists commemorated the centenary of the Great Boer Trek with a reenactment involving columns of ox-drawn Boer wagons. Coming from across the country, the wagons converged on the newly erected Voortrekker Monument, which stood on a prominent hill on the southern edge of Pretoria. The famous Battle of Blood River, in which Andries Pretorius defeated a ZULU force 20 times the size of his own, is commemorated in bas-relief on the stone wall surrounding the monument. In the years following the centennial celebration, the monument became a significant physical reminder of Afrikaner nationalist history, playing a key role in preserving and promoting it.

In 1860 Pretoria became the capital of the South African Republic. However, it remained a small frontier town with residents numbering fewer than 5,000 until the discovery of GOLD on the WITWATERSRAND in the 1880s. Indeed, even in the aftermath of the MINERAL REVOLUTION—and despite rail lines that, by 1894, linked it directly to both CAPE TOWN and DELAGOA BAY—Pretoria continued to grow slowly. As a result, in contrast to the booming MINING center of JOHANNESBURG barely 31 miles (50 km) to the south, Pretoria remained an AFRIKAANS-speaking city rooted in its Boer past. Its role as the capital of an independent Afrikaner state ended in 1900, when British forces captured it in the course of the ANGLO-BOER WAR (1899–1902). The war ended with the signing of the Treaty of VEREENIGING at Melrose House, which still is one of Pretoria's important historic sites.

In 1910, Pretoria, with a population of about 55,000 people, became the administrative capital of the newly formed UNION OF SOUTH AFRICA. The impressive Union Buildings, designed by Sir Herbert Baker (1862–1946), one of the foremost architects of his day, were built to house the country's administrative office.

Pretoria grew much more rapidly once it became a national capital, with a city center devoted to government offices as well as numerous commercial and industrial enterprises. It was a highly segregated city, however, with separate residential areas for whites, Africans, and Asians. This segregation became even more pronounced in 1948, with the introduction of APARTHEID laws. By 1960 the population of the city proper was 303,700, with an additional 120,000 in the adjoining black, urban townships.

See also: AFRIKANER REPUBLICS (Vol. IV); AFRIKANERS (Vols. IV, V); ASIAN COMMUNITIES (Vols. IV, V); BOERS (Vols. III, IV); ENGLAND AND AFRICA (Vols. III, IV, V); GREAT BOER TREK (Vol. III); PRETORIA (Vol. V); URBAN LIFE AND CULTURE (Vols. IV, V); URBANIZATION (Vols. IV, V).

Further readings: Joy Collier, *The Purple and the Gold: The Story of Pretoria and Johannesburg* (Cape Town, South Africa: Longmans, 1965).

prophets and prophetic movements Beginning in the latter half of the 19th century, it became increasingly common for African individuals to emerge as prophets, beginning religious movements that continued after their death. These prophets, who claimed to have been directed by God to preach to their people, generally combined elements of indigenous RELIGION with Christianity, which had been introduced by European MISSIONARIES. Often the prophetic movements attracted large numbers of people who no longer found the answers they were seeking in older religious beliefs but also found that the Christian message as preached by the missionaries left something to be desired.

See CHIMURENGA; CHRISTIANITY, INFLUENCE OF; HARRIS, WILLIAM WADE; KIMBANGU, SIMON; KINJIKITILE; LENSHINA, ALICE; MARANKE, JOHN; NONGQAWUSE; SHEMBE, ISAIAH; TANI, MAAME HARRIS "GRACE."

See also: PROPHETS AND PROPHETIC MOVEMENTS (Vol. V).

protectorate Political relationship in which one state surrenders a portion of its sovereignty to another while usually retaining some control over internal governance. During the late 19th and early 20th centuries, many African lands were designated as protectorates by the European colonial powers. Typically the relationship resulted in the colonial power exerting its will over the protectorate in issues regarding foreign affairs and commercial enterprises. A protectorate differed from a colony in that it was technically separate from the protector and ostensibly retained some rights of self-government. Frequently, however, becoming a protectorate was only an intermediate stage on the road to annexation and complete loss of sovereignty.

See also: BERLIN CONFERENCE (Vol. IV); COLONIAL CONQUEST (Vol. IV); COLONIAL RULE (Vol. IV); PARTITION (Vol. IV); TRUST TERRITORY (Vol. IV).

Quatre Communes French term meaning "four communes" or "four townships," referring to the western SENEGAL ports of DAKAR and Rufisque, the island of Gorée, and the island city of St-Louis. In the 1870s the French began extending voting rights to all male inhabitants of their colonies, and by 1887 the Quatre Communes were incorporated as French territories, with representation in the French Chamber of Deputies.

Senegal's political situation was complex throughout the 19th and into the 20th century. In the first half of the 19th century, the ports of Saint-Louis and Gorée—essentially the extent of the French holdings in West Africa—were busy centers of the French trade in captives and gum-arabic. (Dakar and Rufisque went largely undeveloped until the late 19th century.) By 1848, however, the French had outlawed the trade in human captives and extended some rights of French citizenship to the inhabitants of their colonial territories in Senegal.

The French term *commune,* the second word of Quatre Communes, indicates a French political division known as a *commune de plein exercice.* This was a municipality that exercised full representation at the French Assembly in Paris.

In 1854 Louis FAIDHERBE (1818–1889) became governor of France's colonies in Senegal, and French colonial operations soon expanded. French incursions into the Muslim-dominated interior regions made the political situation even more complex, with some citizens given rights of French citizenship while others were ruled by whatever system of government was already in place. By the late 1850s the French had begun to develop Dakar in order to export GROUNDNUTS (peanuts) back to Europe. After the completion of the Dakar–to– Saint-Louis railroad, in the mid-1880s, Dakar's growth exploded, and in 1902 Dakar replaced Saint-Louis as the administrative capital of FRENCH WEST AFRICA. Rufisque, located a few miles down the coast from Dakar, prospered along with the new capital.

In the decade leading up to World War I (1914–18), the French maneuvered to revoke some of the civil rights of the Senegalese people, especially Muslims. However, in spite of this, Blaise DIAGNE (c. 1872–1934), the first black African to be elected to the French Assembly, led the nation's efforts to support France in the war, recruiting upwards of 180,000 African troops to fight on the European continent.

During World War II (1939–45), when France was occupied by German forces, the collaborationist Vichy government in France stripped the people of the Quatre Communes of most of their civil rights. After the Allied victory, however, the French restored civil and political rights to what they had been before the war. Postwar politics in the Quatre Communes was dominated by Lamine GUÈYE (1891–1968) and Léopold SENGHOR (1906–2001), who, in 1960, led the nation to independence.

See also: FRANCE AND AFRICA (Vols. III, IV, V).

R

Rabearivelo, Jean-Joseph (1901–1937) *Malagasy poet from Madagascar*

Rabearivelo was born into an aristocratic MERINA family in Antananarivo, MADAGASCAR. French COLONIAL RULE had impoverished Madagascar's elite, however, and Rabearivelo grew up relatively poor. From an early age, he was an avid reader of French literature, which gave him an intense desire to go to France. He never had the opportunity to leave Madagascar, however.

In 1923 he became a proofreader at a small publishing house in Imerina, in the central highlands of Madagascar. That same year, Rabearivelo's first publication appeared in the journal *Anthropos,* and in 1931 he started his own journal, *Capricorne.* He also became a member of the prestigious Malagasy Academy and completed several acclaimed plays and volumes of poetry. Unlike many other African-born writers of his generation, Rabearivelo refrained from outward political activism in his poetry, preferring instead to focus on his dark and fractured interior world.

Despite his literary accomplishments, any rise in Rabearivelo's position or income was blocked by the oppressive French colonial administration. The administration finally offered to send him to France, but it rescinded the offer shortly thereafter. It is thought that this final insult precipitated Rabearivelo's suicide by poisoning on June 22, 1937.

See also: LITERATURE IN COLONIAL AFRICA (Vol. IV).

Further reading: Moradewun Adejunmobi, *Jean-Joseph Rabearivelo, Literature, and Lingua Franca in Colonial Madagascar* (New York: Peter Lang, 1996); Simon Gkandi, *Encyclopedia of African Literature* (New York: Routledge, 2002).

Rabih bin Fadlallah (Rabeh Zubair) (c. 1835–1900) *Muslim reformer and military empire builder in the Lake Chad region*

Rabih's military career began when he was a lieutenant of Rahma Mansur al-ZUBAYR (1830–1913), who was engaged in trading for ivory and slaves in the Bahr-al-Ghazal region of present-day southern Republic of the SUDAN. When the the Sudan's British administrator, General Charles George GORDON (1833–1885), moved against al-Zubayr in the efforts to suppress the SLAVE TRADE, Rabih found himself on his own, but with an army under his command.

Though he claimed that he supported Muhammad Ahmad al-MAHDI (1844–1885) and his reform of Islam, Rabih was more of a military adventurer than a Muslim reformer. Setting out to build an empire for himself in the central sub-Saharan savanna, in 1892 he seized the capital of Bagirmi in present-day CHAD, and he then moved on to KANEM-BORNU. By 1896 he had completed its conquest and was in the process of building his own dynasty in Bornu when he in turn became ensnared in the European COLONIAL CONQUEST of this region. He had a strong and well-armed force of some 20,000 soldiers, and he was able to inflict a few defeats upon the French in early skirmishes with them. However, as was the case with other powerful contemporary leaders in the West African interior, such as SAMORI TOURÉ (c. 1830–1900) and AHMADU SÉKOU (d. 1898), the European colonial forces were simply too powerful. Rabih died fighting the French in 1900, and Britain, France, and Germany divided his domains among their West African colonies of NIGERIA (Britain), Chad (France), and Kamerun (Germany).

See also: CHAD, LAKE (Vols. I, III); ENGLAND AND AFRICA (Vols. III, IV, V); FRANCE AND AFRICA (Vols. III, IV, V); GERMANY AND AFRICA (Vol. IV); ISLAM, INFLUENCE OF (Vols. II, III, IV, V); PARTITION (Vol. IV); RESISTANCE AND REBELLION (Vol. IV).

race and racism Race as a means of division is a social construct rather than a biological fact, for in biological terms, all human beings belong to a single race. Racism consists of the social interaction among humans involving and deriving from behaviors and attitudes that differentiate humans on the basis of the assumed existence of races.

Human societies have long viewed each other in what could be termed racial stereotypes, but these views usually were in terms of social characteristics. Thus, during much of the era of the SLAVE TRADE, Europeans often spoke of African societies as "primitive" and "savage" in contrast to their own supposed state of being "civilized." These were not, however, considered innate or immutable characteristics. As a result some early MISSIONARIES were able to accept as counterparts—if not exactly equals—people such as the Nigerian Samuel Ajayi CROWTHER (1808–1891) and the South African Tiyo SOGA (1829–1871) based on their educational accomplishments and their commitment to the Christian faith.

In the mid-19th century, however, views and beliefs about race took on a biological dimension. Central to this was the work of Charles Darwin (1809–1882), in particular his seminal work *On the Origin of Species by Means of Natural Selection, or the Preservation of Favoured Races in the Struggle for Life,* which was published in 1859. While Darwin was referring to flora and fauna, not human beings, his explanation of the mechanism by which species evolved—natural selection—was embraced by those who wished to use race to explain the differences among human societies. The application of Darwin's ideas to human beings became known as Social Darwinism, with the social economist Herbert Spencer (1820–1903) and his notion of the "survival of the fittest" playing a particularly prominent role. Other writers of the time were also coming to similar conclusions, including Comte de Gobineau (1816–1882), who utilized a "scientific" concept of race to explain the rise and fall of civilizations. Dividing humanity into three races—black, yellow, and white—de Gobineau deemed whites the superior race and "pure," Aryan whites the most superior of all.

For Africa, the most significant aspect of these "modern" views of race was that they came to the fore during the late-19th-century surge of European imperialism that led to the PARTITION of Africa. For many Europeans the COLONIAL CONQUEST and COLONIAL RULE that followed needed an intellectual justification, something that Social Darwinism conveniently supplied. Simply put, whites alleged that blacks were biologically inferior and thus were incapable of ruling themselves. A corollary of that argument implied that whites had a moral responsibility to rule over Africans for their own good and welfare. This justification was expressed in Rudyard Kipling's pro-imperialist poem, The "White Man's Burden."

Africa's colonial rulers and the scholars who accompanied them cast everything about Africa in racial terms. For example, C. G. Seligman (1873–1940), an anthropologist writing in 1930, stated that the languages of West Africa consist of words that for the most part "are simply monosyllables . . . like the syllables in a child's first reading book." He also wrote that sub-Saharan history was "no more than the story of the permeation through the ages . . . of the Negro and Bushman aborigines by Hamitic blood and culture." He categorized these Hamites as Caucasians who were "the great civilizing force of black Africa" before the colonial period.

The racism that emerged from theses intellectualized views of human beings pervaded colonial rule. It could result in raw exploitation, as in the brutality associated with the Belgian interests in the CONGO FREE STATE or the harshness of APARTHEID in SOUTH AFRICA. It could also result in the type of indifference to human suffering that resulted in the tens of thousands of deaths from disease and neglect among African porters in the Carrier Corps in the East African theater of World War I (1914–18). A similar situation involved the thousands of Africans who died in building the railway from the coastal port of Pointe Noire to BRAZZAVILLE in the early 1930s. In its less harsh dimensions, racism guided the approach to administration in the colonies, in which Africans were treated as subjects and not citizens. In those colonies without significant numbers of European SETTLERS, this approach had a relatively benign side to it, expressed in notions of "trusteeship" and "association." However, in colonies with a large settler population, such views led to oppression of the indigenous black population. The unfair and demoralizing land alienation that characterized these colonies was but one example of this.

Africans responded vigorously to European views on race and the notions of racial superiority. African intellectuals such as Edward Wilmot BLYDEN (1832–1912) also used the idea of racial differences in arguments. However, they wrote about the past achievements of the "Negro race," its positive inherent attributes, and the values of its culture. At the same time, the Francophone intellectuals of the NÉGRITUDE movement followed much the same line of thought, asserting an African cultural identity intertwined with the legacy of French colonialism and embodied by a unique racial endowment. Taking the notion of black achievement still further, in the mid-20th century, the Senegalese historian and scientist Cheikh Anta DIOP (1923–1986) argued that ancient Egyptian civilization was not of Caucasian descent, as the prevailing view at the time would have it, but instead black African at its core.

In the political arena, Africans such as Sol T. PLAATJE (1876–1932), Kwame NKRUMAH (1909–1972), and Julius NYERERE (1922–1999) implicitly and explicitly rejected the racist assumptions that underlay colonial rule. They had little problem tapping into the anger Africans held over the humiliation they experienced at the hands of colonial administrators, businesspersons, missionaries, and settlers. Concurrently, LABOR leaders such as A. W. G. CHAMPION (1893–1975) and Clements KADALIE (1896–1951) were able to build LABOR UNIONS around African workers' demands for improved wages and working conditions as well as their resentment over racial slights and injustices.

Ideas of race—and the racism it engendered—were closely associated with the rise of colonialism, but they were also linked to its demise. Indeed the fatal weakness of colonialism was that defining the realities of the colonial situation in racial terms blinded those in positions of power. The colonialists' general failure to consider African views and desires led future African leaders such as Nigeria's Nnamdi AZIKIWE (1904–1996) to deny the legitimacy of colonial rule and demand political independence. This later led to the rise of African NATIONALISM AND INDEPENDENCE MOVEMENTS and eventually to the end of the colonial era.

See also: ANTHROPOLOGY AND AFRICA (Vols. IV, V); COLONIALISM, INFLUENCE OF (Vol. IV); HISTORICAL SCHOLARSHIP ON AFRICA (Vols. IV, V); WHITE MAN'S BURDEN (Vol. IV).

radio Radio was introduced to most African countries because, as in the case of Britain, the European powers wanted to extend domestic radio broadcast systems to other countries within their spheres of influence. Colonial governments originally saw the radio as a propaganda tool rather than a means of development, and early broadcasts were in the languages of the respective European colonial powers.

The first radio broadcast in Africa occurred as part of a British Empire broadcasting experiment on December 19, 1932, in NIGERIA. On that day the British Broadcasting Corporation (BBC) inaugurated the world's first regularly scheduled shortwave overseas service. Because the broadcasts were in English, they were accessible only by the educated and affluent members of the population. Almost 10 years later, in ZAMBIA, the British first broadcast news in indigenous languages. During World War II (1939–45) they used local languages to report on the progress of Allied forces, many of whom were African. Though electrical service was rare in rural Africa, some chiefs did have radio sets powered by large batteries.

In the British colonies, two patterns of establishing radio stations emerged. The first was that of retransmitting programs from British Empire Broadcasting Service, and the second was that of setting up a station with its own programs. The British, who tended to centralize their broadcasting, used unified controlled short wave transmissions covering a large territory. The Portuguese, on the other hand, favored a decentralized system to serve individual provinces. The French used a mixture of regional and national broadcasting systems called *radio diffusion nationale*. Policies established by the respective colonial powers often were carried over in the countries that gained independence. For instance, both the British and French exercised state radio monopolies that the African governments perpetuated after independence.

The first popular radio that was affordable to many Africans was manufactured by Ever Ready in 1949. Called the "Saucepan Special"—the prototype was built in the shell of a metal saucepan—it became popular in African townships and rural areas despite its rather steep price of about $14. A decade later, the "Saucepan Special" was replaced by the transistor radio, which became so popular that people carried them everywhere, even to the fields and on social outings. The radio had such a major impact on the lives of many Africans that, instead of singing songs and telling fireside stories, they listened to radio programs and music from other parts of the world.

By 1955 there were more than 1 million radios in sub-Saharan Africa, and 10 years later that number exceeded 7 million. By the end of the 20th century there were more than 100 million radios in Africa.

See also: COLONIAL RULE (Vol. IV); COLONIALISM, INFLUENCE OF (Vol. IV); NEWSPAPERS (Vol. IV); RADIO AND TELEVISION (Vol. V); TELECOMMUNICATIONS (Vol. V).

Further reading: Richard Fardon and Graham Furniss, eds., *African Broadcast Cultures: Radio in Transition* (Westport, Conn.: Praeger, 2000); Graham Mytton, *Mass Communication in Africa* (London: Edward Arnold, 1983).

recaptives Africans freed from slave ships intercepted by British navy patrols on the high seas off the coast of West Africa. Most recaptives were sent to FREETOWN, the capital of SIERRA LEONE, where they were considered free on arrival. A small number of recaptives also were delivered to LIBERIA, Sierra Leone's neighbor to the south. From 1807, when Britain outlawed its SLAVE TRADE, until 1870, more than 50,000 Africans were removed from slave ships and relocated to Sierra Leone.

Along with freed slaves from the United States; Nova Scotia, Canada; and islands in the West Indies, the recaptives formed a distinct class of society in Sierra Leone. Called *Krios*, members of this new group generally respected Western culture and took to the belief in EDUCATION and self-improvement. During the 20th century, the children of educated recaptives comprised a formidable group that lobbied for African control of both church and state.

Samuel Ajayi CROWTHER (1808–1891), the first African bishop of the Anglican church, was a recaptive originally from NIGERIA. Samuel JOHNSON (1853–1901), a noted YORUBA teacher, missionary, and historian, was the son of recaptive parents.

See also: CHRISTIANITY, INFLUENCE OF (Vol. IV); ENGLAND AND AFRICA (Vol. IV); KRIO (Vol. IV).

Further reading: Akintola Wyse, *The Krio of Sierra Leone: An Interpretive History* (London: Hurst, 1989).

Reindorf, Carl (Reverend Carl Christian Reindorf) (1834–1917) *Ghanaian minister and Gold Coast historian*

Carl Reindorf was the son of Christian Reindorf (1806–1865), a merchant of Danish and Ga-Dangme parentage, and Anoa Ama (a.k.a. Hannah, 1811–1902), a Ga-Dangme woman from ACCRA, GHANA. In many ways, Reindorf's social background was thus representative of Accra, a city that evolved from Ga-Dangme and European roots and the place where Reindorf spent much of his life. In 1842 Reindorf enrolled in a Danish school at Christianborg Castle in Accra. He was baptized in 1844 and continued his education at the Presbyterian Basel mission. In 1855 he became a missionary, teaching Bible interpretation and literacy in Ga. He took the position of assistant teacher at Akropong Seminary in 1860 and went on to head the Basel middle school at Christianborg Castle.

While Britain was still struggling to establish its rule over the GOLD COAST COLONY (present-day Ghana), Reindorf served as an assistant surgeon during the Ada-Awuna War (1866) and the Ga-Akwamu War (1869–70) and was commended by Britain for his efforts. He was ordained as a full minister of the Presbyterian church in 1872, and he was appointed minister for the village of Mayera near Accra, where he founded a school for boys.

It was after his retirement in 1893 that Reindorf produced his most lasting achievement, *A History of the Gold Coast and Asante*. This extensive work covers Ghana's history beginning in the precolonial era to 1860, giving histories of not only the Ga-Dangme but also the Akwamu, Akyem, Fante, and Ashanti as well. Much of its content reflected what he had first learned as a child about Ga-Dangme culture and society from his paternal grandmother.

See also: ASHANTI (Vol. II); ASHANTI EMPIRE (Vols. III, IV, V); AKWAMU (Vol. III); AKYEM (Vols. II, III); DENMARK AND AFRICA (Vol. III); ENGLAND AND AFRICA (Vols. III, IV); FANTE (Vols. II, III); GA-DANGME (Vols. II, III); GOLD COAST (Vol. III); MISSIONARIES (Vol. IV); TRADING STATIONS, EUROPEAN (Vol. III).

religion During the colonial era, religion played a crucial role in determining the conditions of African societies and economies and, hence, African history.

African Traditional Religions The number of practitioners of African traditional religions declined as Islam and Christianity continued to spread inland from the coastal regions. Even so, African traditional religions were, and still are, popular and widely distributed throughout the continent. African animistic or traditional belief systems are so diverse that it is impossible to define them. The practice of traditional religions remains exceptionally strong in parts of West Africa, in parts of present-day MOZAMBIQUE, and in the southern region of the present-day Republic of the SUDAN.

Islam and Africa Because Islam came to the continent so early, many Africans consider it an indigenous religion. In the 19th century a great number of Africans converted to Islam for various reasons, often financial. In some cases, Muslims conquered an area and the indigenous people wanted to avoid paying an exorbitant tax levied on non-Muslims. Others wanted to gain access to the wealth generated by the long-distance trade that tended to exclude non-Muslims. Still others appreciated LITERACY in Arabic script—a skill often acquired as a feature of Islamic conversion—because it allowed them to keep better business or governmental records.

Of course there were those who genuinely preferred the Islamic religion. Africans found it relatively easy to accept Islam because it allowed for the incorporation of some of their existing customs and traditions into Islamic practice. In marriage, for example, many Africans believed that you could have as many wives as you could support and treat equitably; in traditional Islam, a man may have as many as four wives if he can support and treat them equitably.

In West Africa, where Islam already had a long history, Islamic brotherhoods provided people with a tool of social organization. For example, the various Islamic states controlled by the SOKOTO CALIPHATE or the TUKULOR EMPIRE would have been impossible to unify without the influence of Islamic Sufi brotherhoods. In the Sudan, the MAHDIYYA brotherhood organized significant anticolonialist resistance, as did the Sanusiyya brotherhood in ALGERIA and modern-day LIBYA. The Salihiyya brotherhood, led by MUHAMMAD ABDULLAH HASSAN (1864–1920), fought to keep Somaliland (present-day SOMALIA) free of Christian and European influence.

Christianity in Africa Christian MISSIONARIES, both Catholic and Protestant, were very active in Africa during the 19th century, especially in Central and southern Africa and along the west coast. Where they could gain the trust of the local African population, Europeans set up missions and set about converting people and spreading Western-style EDUCATION.

Similar to conversion to Islam, a number of Africans converted to Christianity for reasons other than faith. Some wanted access to the wealth associated with the long-distance European trading network, run primarily by Christians. Others, who observed the shift of power to the Europeans with better technology, foresaw that conversion to the new religion might allow them to participate in the spoils of governance. Still others appreciated the record-keeping potential of literacy in European and African languages. And, as with Islam, some converts truly preferred the tenets of Christianity to their original religion.

Unlike Islam, however, Christianity was not as readily adaptable to the African cultural profile. In the case of marriage, for example, the African norm was polygyny (more than one wife) while the Christian missionaries promoted monogamy (one man, one wife).

By the latter half of the 19th century, African missionaries were becoming more common, and the Anglican Church had consecrated its first African bishop, Samuel Ajayi CROWTHER (1808–1891), from NIGERIA. With the growing number of Christian communities, prophetic movements, too, emerged with more regularity.

Syncretism In the cases of both Islam and Christianity, Africans generally did not accept the outside religion exactly as it was. Instead they evaluated the new religion in terms of the one that they already knew and selected the things they liked about the new religion without completely renouncing their original religion. An example of this combination of religions, called *syncretism*, would be the practice of Muslims "protecting" themselves by wearing amulets containing Quranic scripture instead of indigenous fetishes. Another example is the identification with and combination of indigenous gods and Catholic saints.

In some cases the reasons for choosing Islam or Christianity were based on the participation of the religion's adherents in the SLAVE TRADE. Many indigenous people of West Africa chose Islam over Christianity because, in their experience, the slave traders had been Christian. However, in East Africa, many indigenous people chose Christianity over Islam because, for them, the majority of slave traders had been Muslim.

In addition to African traditional religious beliefs, Islam, and Christianity, there were other religions that had a presence on the continent in the colonial era. In ETHIOPIA, where Coptic Christianity dominates, the African Jewish community known as the BETA ISRAEL were a persecuted minority for centuries. Also, in 1875, Africa's first Hindu temple was built in DURBAN, in SOUTH AFRICA, to serve the large number of Indian Hindi laborers there.

See also: RELIGION (Vols. I, II, III, V); CHRISTIANITY, INFLUENCE OF (Vol. IV); ISLAM, INFLUENCE OF (Vol. IV); PROPHETS AND PROPHETIC MOVEMENTS (Vol. IV); SUFISM (Vol. IV).

Further reading: Brenner, Louis, *Controlling Knowledge: Religion, Power, and Schooling in a West African Muslim Society* (Bloomington, Ind.: Indiana University Press, 2001); André Droogers and Sidney M. Greenfield, eds., *Reinventing Religions: Syncretism and Transformation in Africa and the Americas* (Lanham, Md.: Rowman & Littlefield, 2001); Charlotte A. and Frederick Quinn, *Pride, Faith, and Fear: Islam in Sub-Saharan Africa* (New York: Oxford University Press, 2003); Benjamin C. Ray, *African Religions: Symbol, Ritual, and Community* (Upper Saddle River, N.J.: Prentice Hall, 2000); Lamin Sanneh, *West African Christianity* (Ossining, N.Y.: Orbis Books, 1983).

resistance and rebellion Actions by Africans included both overt forms of resistance against the initial COLONIAL CONQUEST and more covert resistance against COLONIAL RULE carried on during the decades of colonial administration. Africans resisted European efforts at establishing territorial control over their lands long before the era of PARTITION that began in the 1880s. In SOUTH AFRICA, for example, the XHOSA fought a series of nine Frontier Wars (1779–1878), first against Boer settlers and subsequently against the British colonial government of the CAPE COLONY.

When France embarked upon its conquest of ALGERIA in 1830, it achieved fairly rapid initial success against the provincial governors who had reported to the Ottoman Empire. In the Kabylia, however, the French then ran up against the strong resistance of the BERBERS, who undertook a bitter and prolonged 16-year struggle before finally surrendering in 1847. In what is today GHANA, the ASHANTI EMPIRE fought several major wars with Britain between 1824 and 1896 before finally capitulating. EGYPT witnessed the emergence of Colonel Ahmad URABI (1841–1911), who incited a popular movement for the protection of Egypt and the defense of Islam against the growing foreign presence. This led to a British military invasion in 1882, the defeat of Urabi, and Britain's annexation of Egypt.

The BERLIN CONFERENCE (1884–85) marked a fuller phase of European colonial conquest and expansion. It also initiated greater African resistance, which ranged throughout the continent and varied in size and intensity. In the NIGER DELTA, for example, merchant princes such as JAJA (1821–1891) and NANA OLOMU (c. 1852–1916) fought and ultimately lost what amounted to trade wars against British merchants who were backed by the British Royal Navy and who wanted to break the African merchants' hold on trade with the Nigerian interior. France embarked on major military campaigns in the West African interior in hopes of adding vast tracts of territory to its empire. SAMORI TOURÉ (c. 1830–1910), who had begun building his own large, multiethnic, Muslim state in the 1860s, was one of those who, beginning in the late 1880s, fiercely resisted French expansion. He was finally captured in 1898.

Across the continent, African states large and small opposed the European colonial expansion. Sometimes they experienced temporary success on the battlefield, but only Emperor MENELIK II (1844–1913) of ETHIOPIA was fully successful in his resistance, defeating an Italian army at the Battle of ADOWA, in 1896. By the eve of World War I (1914–18), the overt stage of African resistance was basically concluded, although Berber resistance in MOROCCO effectively fought off both the French and the Spanish for much of the 1920s.

The establishment of colonial rule, however, did not end African opposition against the Europeans occupying their lands. One of the earliest rebellions, occurring in 1896, was mounted by the NDEBELE and the SHONA against the BRITISH SOUTH AFRICA COMPANY (BSAC). The BSAC, which only three years earlier had defeated the Ndebele kingdom, had great difficulty in suppressing this uprising, known as the CHIMURENGA. German colonial occupation faced major rebellions in both GERMAN EAST AFRICA (present-day TANZANIA) and SOUTH WEST AFRICA (today's NAMIBIA). The 1905–06 MAJI-MAJI REBELLION in

Police wielded clubs to disperse women during a demonstration in Durban, South Africa, in 1959. © AP

the former resulted in more than 200,000 African deaths from combat and famine. Meanwhile, in South West Africa, the HERERO revolt of 1904–07 forced Germany to call in 10,000 troops in order to quash it. There were many other such revolts of varying magnitude and success. Almost inevitably, however, the occupying colonial powers managed to suppress them. With the firm establishment of colonial administration, the rebellions seemed more and more hopeless and faded away.

The end of overt rebellions did not mark the end of resistance to the colonial takeover. Instead Africans adopted more covert forms of resistance that occasionally resulted in overt violence. Colonial TAXATION often provoked resistance. In southeastern NIGERIA, for example, in what has become knows as the ABA WOMEN'S REVOLT (1929–1930), local women mounted a strong protest against the threat of new taxes. Typical of the reaction of the colonial authorities, the police were called in force to suppress the Nigerian women. The compulsory growing of CASH CROPS led to more subtle forms of resistance. For example, MOZAMBIQUE peasants often would boil COTTON seeds before planting them, causing the crop to fail. This would enable them to spend their time growing FOOD CROPS for their own consumption instead of cotton, which was labor-intensive and produced very little profit.

The formation of LABOR UNIONS, through which Afri-can workers sought to improve their incomes and working conditions, constituted a form of resistance as well. For instance, by the early 1920s Egyptian workers had begun to agitate for eight-hour workdays and the right to organize and bargain collectively, as well as other rights enjoyed by workers in Europe. Some of the earliest strikes took place in 1924. As Egypt became increasingly industrialized, especially after 1930, worker militancy grew accordingly. Shortly after World War II (1939–45) a series of strikes gripped the country, with the colonial administration calling in both the police and the army to suppress them. Such LABOR militancy and unrest were part of the country's wider economic and social problems that led, in 1952, to the military overthrow of the Egyptian puppet monarchy and the establishment of Egypt as a republic.

Africans also expressed their discontent with colonial rule through RELIGION. While not necessarily overtly political in the way that tax protests could be, religion could lead to direct open resistance, as in the case of the LUMPA CHURCH. When the church's founder, Alice LENSHINA (1924–1978), first began to preach, she addressed social ills in a way that challenged white-missionary authority. By the late colonial period, however, her church was challenging the right of the NORTHERN RHODESIA colonial authorities to tax church members. Lenshina was never imprisoned, but in 1921 colonial authorities in the neighboring BELGIAN CONGO did arrest Simon KIMBANGU (c. 1887–1951), fearing that his preaching was generating opposition to their control. He remained in prison the rest of his life.

Neither resistance nor rebellion was able to halt or overthrow colonial rule, but such actions served to undermine and weaken it. In this way, at least, they helped pave the way for the emergence of the African NATIONALISM AND INDEPENDENCE MOVEMENTS that in many ways embodied the same spirit.

See also: CHRISTIANITY, INFLUENCE OF (Vols. II, III, IV, V); COLONIALISM, INFLUENCE OF (Vol. IV); ISLAM, INFLUENCE OF (Vols. II, III, IV, V).

Further reading: Clifton C. Crais, et al., eds., *White Supremacy and Black Resistance in Pre-industrial South Africa: The Making of the Colonial Order in the Eastern Cape, 1779–1865* (Cambridge, UK: Cambridge University Press, 1992).

Réunion Island French island located in the Indian Ocean and measuring about 970 square miles (2,512 sq km). Part of the Mascarene Archipelago, Réunion is located roughly 420 miles (680 km) east of MADAGASCAR and 110 miles (180 km) southwest of MAURITIUS.

Britain seized Réunion during the Napoleonic Wars (1805–15), along with Mauritius and the SEYCHELLES, but returned it to France as part of the 1815 Treaty of Paris. Under British rule, sugarcane was introduced to the island, and Réunion quickly became a mono-crop economy run by an elite class of sugar barons, with most of the arable land devoted to sugar production.

Britain led the campaign to abolish SLAVERY in Réunion and Mauritius in the 1830s, leading France to bring in indentured laborers from Asia to work the sugar plantations. The presence of Asians led to the emergence of a highly diversified, Creole-speaking population. However, French remained the official LANGUAGE, and the islanders tended to be Catholic in their religious persuasion due to the presence of French MISSIONARIES.

During the reign of French emperor Napoleon Bonaparte (1769–1821), Réunion was known as Bonaparte Island.

The 1869 opening of the SUEZ CANAL marked the end of Réunion's economic success, as the island gradually ceased to be an important shipping center. In 1946 the island became a French *département*, similar to a county or state, and Saint-Denis was named its capital. Though calls for independence have occasionally unsettled Réunion, the island remains, for the most part, content with its strong ties to France.

See also: FRANCE AND AFRICA (Vols. III, IV, V); MONO-CROP ECONOMIES (Vol. IV); RÉUNION ISLAND (Vols. III, V).

Rhodes, Cecil (Cecil John Rhodes) (1853–1902)
Financier and British empire builder

One of the more colorful—and controversial—figures of the colonial period in Africa, Cecil Rhodes was a prospector, financier, politician, and architect of imperialism, playing the game of statecraft with both astonishing success and failure. While his efforts resulted in the acquisition of enormous amounts of wealth and territory for Britain, they fell short of his goal of complete British domination of Africa "from Cape to Cairo."

Early Life Born July 5, 1853, Rhodes was the son of an Anglican clergyman. Suffering from poor health, he was sent to the warm climes of Africa, where he was to join his brother, Herbert (1845–1879), on a COTTON farm in NATAL. Arriving there at the age of 17, he found that Herbert had left for the newly discovered diamond fields near KIMBERLEY. In time, Herbert returned, and the two brothers attempted to make a viable venture out of the farm. It did not take long for it to become clear that the diamond fields held a better chance of success for the brothers. Indeed, his various business ventures relating to DIAMOND MINING proved so lucrative that, by the time he was 20, Cecil Rhodes had made himself a substantial fortune.

> Cecil Rhodes never abandoned his belief that a proper education was important, personally, professionally, and socially. In 1873 he returned to England and enrolled in Oxford University. He then divided his time between Kimberley and Oxford, completing his university studies while simultaneously amassing incredible wealth.

Rhodes as Financier The secret of Rhodes's diamond fortune lay not in multiple individual discoveries. Instead he did what so many 19th-century tycoons did, creating a monopoly that controlled virtually all aspects in the production of a given commodity. During the 1870s and 1880s, in the early stages of his career, Rhodes formed partnerships with others like himself—prospectors and owners of small mines. He eventually united these small holdings into DE BEERS CONSOLIDATED MINES, LTD., an organization that controlled a substantial amount of the MINING industry in southern Africa. Rhodes then acquired the only competing organization of size, the Kimberley Mine of Barney Barnato (1852–1897), taking control of it in 1888. This allowed Rhodes to dominate virtually all of Kimberley's diamond production. When GOLD was discovered in the TRANSVAAL, in the mid-1880s, he quickly acquired large stakes in those mines as well, although he never established the commanding position in gold mining that he did with DIAMONDS.

> So complete was Rhodes's monopoly, that by 1891 he controlled 90 percent of the world's known diamond production.

Politics and Statecraft Unlike some other tycoons who entered politics later in life and only after amassing their fortunes, Rhodes's financial and political careers moved in lockstep almost from the beginning. To Rhodes, politics was seen as a means of both building his own personal wealth and increasing the size of the British Empire. From his youth Rhodes was a committed imperialist who envisioned British domination reaching not only across Africa, but across the entire globe. The fact that the spread of British power could also increase his own wealth was to him simply a matter of good fortune.

Rhodes began his political career in 1881, when he was elected to the CAPE COLONY Parliament. As one of the richest individuals in southern Africa, he was then able to use his political position as a stepping stone to even more power. In 1882 he served on a commission whose task it was to bring peace to fractious BASUTOLAND. There he encountered the famous General Charles George GORDON (1833–1885), who impressed Rhodes with his ability to get his way, not necessarily by military force, but through meetings with African leaders. It was a lesson that Rhodes himself would try to apply, with mixed success, throughout his career.

Early on, Rhodes began to envision a "Cape-to-Cairo" corridor of British dominance, an area that would open vast areas of mineral and other wealth to British settlement, as well as help Britain control much of Africa. Standing in his way, however, were not only African governments and leaders, but also Belgians, Germans, and other Europeans who had joined the scramble for African colonies. Hoping to achieve his goal through negotiation, Rhodes helped forge several agreements between Africans, BOERS, and British interests in BECHUANALAND (today's BOTSWANA), from 1882 to 1885. Some agreements managed to solve crises of the moment; others left hanging issues that were not resolved until after the ANGLO-BOER WAR (1899–1902). In 1888, after several years of careful preparations, Rhodes persuaded King LOBENGULA (1836–1894) to concede exclusive mining rights in his Matebeleland kingdom to Rhodes. Rhodes then quickly secured a charter for a new business venture, the BRITISH SOUTH AFRICA COMPANY, to develop the territory. Now having what was, in effect, total control of this vast territory, in 1890 Rhodes sent pioneers into both Matebeleland and Mashonaland (the two major areas of what is now ZIMBABWE), which were soon renamed Rhodesia in his honor.

From 1890 to 1895 Rhodes served as prime minister of the CAPE COLONY. One of the most significant pieces of legislation he introduced prefigured the Bantustans of the later APARTHEID era. He also moved to limit the already restricted franchise rights of Africans. When it came to the Boers of the Cape Colony, he proved particularly adept at diplomatically bridging the gaping division between them and the English-speaking settlers of the Colony.

During this period Rhodes had frequent dealings with Paul KRUGER (1825–1904), at the time president of the TRANSVAAL, who was fiercely opposed to any political rights for either British settlers, who were dubbed UITLANDERS (foreigners), or black Africans. Kruger was intent on maintaining Boer control of his state's internal politics and its autonomy from any British imperial encroachment. Kruger had managed to close off most of the open routes through the Transvaal, extracting heavy customs duties on all goods entering or transiting the state. This policy outraged Rhodes, who was eager to gain access to the supposed gold fields that lay north of the Limpopo River in present-day Zimbabwe. He became increasingly eager to take action against Kruger and the Boers. This, combined with his desire to relieve what he alleged to be injustices perpetrated against the Uitlanders in Boer territory, led Rhodes to disaster.

The Jameson Raid On December 29, 1895, Rhodes's hand-picked administrator of the Matebele territories, Leander Starr Jameson (1853–1917), launched a military attack, appropriately called the JAMESON RAID, into the Transvaal. Although the action was ostensibly taken in order to protect the Uitlanders from persecution, in truth, it was a maneuver intended to force the Uitlanders to rise in rebellion against the Boers in order to establish British control over the Transvaal and its gold-mining region. The Uitlanders did not respond, however, and the invaders were quickly routed, with the entire band either killed or captured.

Ultimately Jameson and his cohorts were tried and sent to prison, the Boers strengthened their hold over the Transvaal, and Rhodes was forced to resign as prime minister of the Cape Colony.

Rhodes's Final Years The remainder of Rhodes's life was marked more by failure and bitterness than his earlier success. In 1896 he took part in the suppression of a revolt in Matebeleland by helping to negotiate a settlement with NDEBELE leaders. But after that, no longer holding any direct political power, he was forced

to concentrate his energies on developing the region that bore his name. On a personal level the situation was equally bleak. Although he never married, Rhodes became involved in scandals centering around a notorious Russian adventuress, Princess Catherine Radziwill (1858–1941), who was eventually sent to prison after forging documents in Rhodes's name. Afflicted with heart disease, Rhodes was physically unable to play much of a part in the Anglo-Boer War, though he was involved in the siege at Kimberley. Nor did he live to see the end of that conflict, which, ironically, brought Britain the full control of South Africa that Rhodes had desired for so long. He died at home in a seaside suburb of CAPE TOWN in 1902.

Rhodes's will left the bulk of his fortune for philanthropic uses, in particular for the famous Rhodes Scholarships that financed study at Oxford for students from the British Commonwealth, the United States, and Germany. For many years only white males were eligible to apply.

See also: AFRIKANER REPUBLICS (Vol. IV); AFRIKANERS (Vol. IV); COLONIAL CONQUEST (Vol. IV); COLONIAL RULE (Vol. IV); ENGLAND AND AFRICA (Vol. (IV) PARTITION (Vol. IV).

Further reading: Robert Rotberg, *The Founder: Cecil Rhodes and the Pursuit of Power* (New York: Oxford University Press, 1988); Antony Thomas, *Rhodes: Race for Africa* (New York: St. Martin's Press, 1997).

Rif (Riff) Rugged mountainous area in northern MOROCCO that became a stronghold of Berber resistance to Spanish and French colonial governments; also the name given to the Berber resistors. Bounded by the Mediterranean to the north and the Rif Mountains to the south, the Rif region covers a stretch of northern Morocco from Tangier, near the Strait of Gibraltar, to the western border with ALGERIA. Historically the region was the home of various independent Berber peoples, most of whom traded and practiced limited subsistence farming of figs and olives.

In 1893, fearing further encroachment by Spaniards into their territory, fierce Berber forces from throughout the Rif attacked the Spanish settlement at Melilla, on the Mediterranean coast. Spain responded by sending 25,000 troops to push the BERBERS back into the mountains. To keep peaceful relations with Spain, the Moroccan sultan agreed to make reparations and vowed to help suppress the Rif in the future.

Rif is an Arabic word meaning "edge of the cultivated area," which accurately describes the region's harsh environment.

The 1912 Treaty of Fez divided Morocco into a southern French Zone and a northern Spanish Zone. This demarcation did little to change the political situation in the region, however, and the pattern of Berber resistance in the Rif continued. The militant leader Ahmad al-Raisuli (d. 1925) began calling for the removal of Spanish troops. He had previously been a Spain-appointed governor in northern Morocco, but when Spain began expanding its territorial claims in the Rif, al-Raisuli led attacks against the Spanish forces in and around Melilla, beginning in 1919.

Al-Raisuli eventually surrendered to Spanish authorities in 1922, after which time he actually fought alongside the Spanish against the forces of his longtime rival, Mohamed ben ABD EL-KRIM (c. 1880–1963), a Berber military commander and respected scholar who was successfully organizing forces to impede the movement of Spanish troops throughout Rif. In 1921–22 Spain sent a battalion to subdue Abd el-Krim, but his forces destroyed the Spanish troops, numbering almost 20,000, igniting what would come to be known as the War of Melilla, or the Rif War. Following his victory, in 1923 Abd el-Krim declared an independent Islamic Rif Republic in the Spanish-occupied territory.

The army of the Republic of the Rif was highly organized and fought with state-of-the-art weapons, including machine guns and mountain howitzers, and by 1924 Abd el-Krim's military successes had caused Spain to withdraw its troops from the Moroccan interior to concentrate on defending its coastal enclaves.

In an attempt to solidify the legitimacy of his republic, Abd el-Krim assembled a legislature, tried to get diplomatic recognition from Britain and France, and even negotiated with European companies to offer them MINING rights in the Rif. The fledgling nation's hopes were dashed, however, as numerous international treaties had secured Spain's international claims to the territory.

Despite the early success of the Rifi—Berber inhabitants of the Rif—against the Spanish in the north, their short-lived republic began unraveling when they attempted to rid the southern region of French occupation. In short order, the French and Spanish combined their forces to secure the Melilla port and force Abd el-Krim to fight on both northern and southern fronts. As a testament to their organization and fierceness, the Berber forces managed to engage upwards of 300,000 combined Spanish and French troops in the Rif. In the end, however, Abd el-Krim surrendered to the French, in 1926, and was exiled to RÉUNION Island, a French territory in the Indian Ocean. After its defeat the Republic of the Rif disintegrated, and the Spanish resumed their relatively peaceful occupation of the region until the Spanish Civil War (1936–39), during which time Generalissimo Francisco Franco (1892–1975) used northern Morocco to launch attacks against the Spanish Republic.

See also: COLONIAL RULE (Vol. IV); FRANCE AND AFRICA (Vols. III, IV, V); RESISTANCE AND REBELLION (Vol. IV); SPAIN AND AFRICA (Vols. III, IV).

Further reading: Jose E. Alvarez, *The Betrothed of Death: The Spanish Foreign Legion During the Rif Rebellion, 1920–1927* (Westport, Conn.: Greenwood Publishing Group, 2001).

Río de Oro See WESTERN SAHARA.

See also: PORTUGAL AND AFRICA (Vol. III); RÍO DE ORO (Vol. II); SPAIN AND AFRICA (Vols. III, IV, V); DAKHLA (Vol. V).

Robert, Shaaban (1909–1962) *Tanzanian poet and essayist*

Robert was born near Tanga, in GERMAN EAST AFRICA (present-day TANZANIA). Although his father was Christian, Robert followed the Islamic faith. While Robert's life is not well documented, his work helped establish a modern literary style for the KISWAHILI language while also preserving traditional African verse forms. He mixed these traditional forms with experimental ones and often used the *utendi* verse form, which was reserved for narration and didactic themes. In this way he served to link classical and modern Swahili literature. Among Robert's works are *Kufikirika* (The conceivable world) (1946), *Maisha yangu* (My life) (1949), *Maisha ya Siti Binti Saad, mwimbaji wa Unguja* (Life of Siti Binti Saad, poetess of Zanzibar) (1958), and *Insha ya mashairi* (Essays and poems) (1959). While writing for much of his adult life, he supported himself by working as a civil servant for the British colonial government of TANGANYIKA. A government monthly published many of his poems. Robert died in DAR ES SALAAM, Tanzania, in 1962. A volume of his complete works, entitled *Diwani ya Shaaban*, was published posthumously in 1966.

See also: LITERATURE IN COLONIAL AFRICA (Vol. IV); SWAHILI COAST (Vols. II, III).

Roberts, Joseph J. (Joseph Jenkins Roberts)

(1809–1876) *American-born statesman and independent Liberia's first president*

Born a free black in Norfolk, Virginia, Joseph J. Roberts trained as a boatman, shuttling goods between Norfolk and Petersburg, Virginia. After his father died his mother and six siblings emigrated to LIBERIA, on the West African coast, in 1829. The family built a house on their allotted land and established a successful store in MONROVIA, supplying traders with PALM OIL, hides, wood, and ivory.

At the age of 24, Roberts was named high sheriff of the colony by the American Colonization Society, which oversaw the administration of Liberia. As sheriff he helped to collect taxes and keep the peace between colonists and the indigenous African peoples who lived near the Monrovia settlement. Following his success as sheriff, in 1839 Roberts was selected as the colony's lieutenant governor. A year later, following the death of Liberia's white governor, Thomas Buchanan (the brother of future U.S. president James Buchanan), Roberts became Liberia's first black governor.

Both Britain and France had colonial interests on the coast of West Africa (territories that would later become SIERRA LEONE and IVORY COAST, respectively), but neither country recognized Liberia as an independent nation. Seeing that this could lead to territorial disputes, Roberts and the American Colonization Society decided that the colony should become an independent republic. In 1846 the Liberian legislature voted in favor of independence, and Governor Roberts won the colony's first election to become the first president of the Republic of Liberia. Roberts sailed to Europe to get formal recognition of his new republic, and by 1849 Britain, Belgium, and France all recognized Liberia and established diplomatic ties. The United States officially recognized Liberia much later, in 1862.

After securing international recognition, Roberts's next order of business was to establish Liberia's borders, which he did through negotiations with indigenous rulers in the region. Roberts smartly gave some of these rulers positions in the republic's legislature, which gave him greater leverage in local disputes, including his attempts to curtail the illegal SLAVE TRADE that continued in the interior. After four terms as president, Roberts declined a fifth term, and Stephen Benson (1816–1865) assumed the presidency in 1855.

For the next 15 years Roberts served as a major general in the small Liberian army and as a respected foreign diplomat to France and Britain. He also helped establish Liberia College in 1856, serving as its first president and teaching classes in jurisprudence and international law. In 1871 Edward J. Roye (1815–1871), the incumbent president of Liberia, was removed following an embezzlement scandal, and Roberts was again asked to lead the country. He served out a sixth term as president before his death in 1876. Roberts's birthday, March 15, is celebrated as a national holiday in Liberia.

See also: UNITED STATES AND AFRICA (Vol. IV).

Royal Niger Company

One of a number of CONCESSIONAIRE COMPANIES that European powers utilized to establish colonial footholds in Africa. The Royal Niger Company (RNC) began operation in the NIGER DELTA in the 1870s, trading in commodities such as PALM OIL, palm kernels, and other CASH CROPS.

The origins of Royal Niger Company lay with George GOLDIE (1846–1925), one of a number of British merchants trading in the lower Niger region. In 1879 he organized the UNITED AFRICA COMPANY to further his trading operations, changing its name to the National Africa Company in 1882. It became the Royal Niger Company in 1886, when it received a British charter that provided British military protection and the rights to secure and administer any territories obtained through negotiations with local rulers. The company then took over the administration of Britain's Oil Rivers PROTECTORATE, with the exception of the Niger Delta, which was under the control of the Liverpool traders. The Company established its headquarters at Asaba, which was located inland on the lower Niger River.

Competing with French and German entrepreneurs, Goldie and his agents secured trading agreements with peoples located along the Niger and Benue rivers, in present-day NIGERIA. By establishing a network of trading stations along the navigable waterways in the interior, Goldie broke long-term trading agreements between European merchants and coastal African rulers that had restricted foreigners to trading at the region's ports. The company governed the territory that it controlled by administering a rudimentary justice system, which it supported with gunboats. Although Goldie's charter was based on free trade in the Niger Basin, he imposed tariffs on non-British goods and seized smuggled goods, punishing purchasers who lived in areas under RNC control. The RNC also supported MISSIONARIES and enforced the anti-slave-trade efforts of Britain. The company extended its area of operation into northern Nigeria when it secured agreements with the SOKOTO CALIPHATE in 1884 and with Borgu in 1894.

The growing rivalry between Britain and France during the process of PARTITION led British prime minister Lord SALISBURY (1830–1903) to conclude that the British government would have to directly take over colonial administration in Nigeria if Britain was to retain control of this important region. Thus in 1900 the RNC surrendered its administrative role to British colonial authorities. It received full compensation for its administrative infrastructure and half the royalties on all minerals produced in Nigeria for the following 99 years.

See also: BORGU (Vol. III); COLONIAL CONQUEST (Vol. IV); COLONIAL RULE (Vol. IV); ENGLAND AND AFRICA (Vols. III, IV, V); TRADE AND COMMERCE (Vol. IV).

Further reading: Geoffrey L. Baker, *Trade Winds on the Niger: The Saga of the Royal Niger Company 1830–1971* (London: Radcliffe Press, 1997).

Ruanda-Urundi Region wtihin GERMAN EAST AFRICA that came under Belgian administration as a League of Nations MANDATE following World War I (1914–18). In 1962 the territory was split to form the present-day nations of RWANDA and BURUNDI.

See also: BELGIUM AND AFRICA (Vol. IV); GERMANY AND AFRICA (Vol. IV).

rubber Elastic substance harvested from tropical trees. In colonial Africa, rubber collected in the wild was a highly valued commodity. Africans traded rubber with Europeans prior to the colonial era. In 1840, however, the process of vulcanization was discovered, allowing for many industrial uses that were previously impossible. By the 1890s both the demand and the uses for rubber were increasing rapidly, and European CONCESSIONAIRE COMPANIES rushed to the CONGO FREE STATE and FRENCH WEST AFRICA to stake claims on territories where wild rubber trees grew.

Using forced LABOR schemes, companies marched African laborers into the forest to collect the sap from wild rubber trees and vines. As the sap coagulated, or hardened, it was rolled into balls for easy TRANSPORTATION.

Rubber collectors are seen at work in French Equatorial Africa in 1943. © *Library of Congress*

Africans in the Congo Free State who failed or refused to meet unrealistically high production quotas were beaten, mutilated, and even murdered. The crimes perpetrated by Europeans in Congo Free State made that colony a symbol of colonial abuse.

In West Africa—especially in GUINEA, IVORY COAST, and SIERRA LEONE—wild rubber was typically harvested by local workers and sold to European export companies at prices that were kept artificially low by the British administration. By 1900 Britain was importing as much as 20,000 tons of wild African rubber.

Harvesting rubber can kill the tree. During the colonial period, European companies looking for cheap rubber and hardwoods contributed to the degradation of Africa's tropical forests that continues to this day.

The market for African rubber began to decline about 1910, when Asia began producing the commodity more cheaply. In Malaysia the collection of rubber sap on Britain's colonial plantations required far less labor and time than what was required for harvesting wild African rubber. Moreover, newspaper reports had sparked international condemnation of the scandalous worker abuse in the Congo Free State, forcing European concessionaires to run their operations on a smaller scale.

In the 1920s the African rubber industry shifted again. At the time, about two-thirds of the world's rubber production was supplying the automobile industry in the United States. Britain, however, controlled the world supply of rubber and therefore was able to control prices, as well. In light of this, in 1926 the American Firestone Company established a one-million-acre plantation in LIBERIA in order to control its own rubber supply. According to the concession agreement, the Firestone Company had to pay off a huge Liberian debt to Britain, but, in exchange, it gained unprecedented influence in Liberia's governmental affairs. By 1930 the company had colluded with the Liberian government to recruit up to 30,000 workers, perhaps a third of whom received no pay and were, in effect, slaves. In addition, the Liberian economy became so dependent on Firestone that the American dollar became the country's official currency in the 1940s.

During World War II (1939–45), when Japan took control of British rubber plantations in southeast Asia, the Firestone plantation in Liberia became a main supplier of rubber for the Allied forces. As late as the 1960s, there were still as many as 20,000 workers on Firestone's Liberian plantation.

See also: CASH CROPS (Vols. IV, V).

Rwabugiri, Kigeri IV (d. 1895) *Powerful Rwandan mwami (king) just prior to the era of German colonialism*

Before the ascension of Rwabugiri to the throne in 1865, RWANDA had gone through centuries of territorial consolidation that had expanded the core state of Nyignya. Once in power Rwabugiri took the name Kigeri IV and used a series of military campaigns to unite most of the remaining independent smaller states in the region. (Some northern kingdoms remained independent.)

With his power centralized, Rwabugiri was able to extend the reach of the royal political structures into the outskirts of the kingdom. At the same time, Rwabugiri took the opportunity to significantly increase the authority ascribed to the *mwami*. Using his new powers, he seized land and dismissed the claims of regional sovereignty made by the clan chieftains who had ruled under the traditional system.

Of TUTSI heritage, Kigeri IV appointed other Tutsi to positions of importance. This ethnic preference magnified the cultural differences between the Tutsi and HUTU. Though sometimes seen as comprising a different social class, the Hutu actually had long interacted with the Tutsi on relatively equal footing. As a result of Rwabugiri's policies, however, the Tutsi-Hutu dynamic shifted to one more clearly defined by roles of social superiority (Tutsi) and subjugation (Hutu). COLONIAL RULE, particularly during the period of the Belgian MANDATE, reinforced this stratification. This change was a precursor to the problems of 20th-century Rwanda, where a society divided between the politically dominant Tutsi and the numerically superior Hutu erupted into a devastating civil war.

After Rwabugiri's death, in November 1895, his son, Mibambwe Rutarindwa (d. 1896) succeeded him as *mwami*. The following year, political intrigue led to Mibambwe's assassination and his replacement by Yuhi IV Musinga (r. 1896–1931). The battle for succession greatly reduced the political power of the *mwami*, and within a few years, Rwanda had become a part of GERMAN EAST AFRICA.

See also: BELGIUM AND AFRICA (Vol. IV); GERMANY AND AFRICA (Vol. IV); MWAMI (Vol. III).

Rwanda
Mountainous eastern Central African kingdom that regained independence from COLONIAL RULE in 1962. Covering only 9,600 square miles (24,900 sq km), present-day Rwanda is bordered by BURUNDI to the south, TANZANIA and UGANDA to the east, and the Democratic Republic of the CONGO to the west. Lake Kivu lies along the western border.

At the BERLIN CONFERENCE (1884–85), Germany claimed the region occupied by two long-standing African states, Rwanda and Burundi. Both states were inhabited largely by the agriculturist HUTU ethnic group but were politically dominated by the pastoralist TUTSI group.

Rwanda during the Colonial Era: Ruanda-Urundi
By the early 1890s German explorers had arrived, and the process of German COLONIAL CONQUEST had begun. At the time, Kigeri IV RWABUGIRI (r. 1860–1895) was still the *mwami* (king) of a powerful and expanding kingdom. His death, in 1895, led to a succession dispute among his sons. Compounded by the rise of German colonialism, the conflict caused divided loyalties among Rwanda's lesser chiefs and weakened the centralized power of the *mwami*. Ultimately the victor in the struggle over the throne, Yuhi IV Musinga (r. 1896–1931), actively collaborated with the German authorities, who, by 1906, were fully in control of his kingdom. Rwanda became part of GERMAN EAST AFRICA and was administered, together with the neighboring kingdom of Burundi, as RUANDA-URUNDI.

Between 1910 and 1912 the Schutztruppe, the colonial force of imperial Germany, made several military expeditions to quell an ongoing popular uprising in northern Rwanda. The failed uprising was led by northern Hutu groups called Kiga, who had remained independent when Rwabugiri centralized his power in the late 19th century. Underscoring the regional differences that plagued Rwanda, Tutsi soldiers and some southern Hutu assisted the Germans in putting down the Kiga rebellion. Their collaboration elevated the Tutsi in the eyes of the German colonialists but embittered the northern Hutu.

German colonial rule in East Africa did not last long. After Germany was defeated in World War I (1914–18), Ruanda-Urundi came under Belgian control as a League of Nations MANDATE. In 1925 the mandate was joined administratively with the BELGIAN CONGO. Belgium managed Ruanda-Urundi through indirect rule, endowing the Tutsi with political dominance over the Hutu, who were largely reduced to indentured laborers. However, EDUCATION provided by Catholic MISSIONARIES led to a growing group of educated Hutu who chafed under the old feudal system that the Belgians had continued because it simplified their rule. The largely Hutu peasantry was also engaged in producing exportable CASH CROPS, especially COFFEE, on the country's rich soils. Population growth, however, was making adequate land for crops and herds increasingly scarce, which added to social unrest.

After World War II (1939–45), Belgium retained Ruanda-Urundi as a TRUST TERRITORY, this time mandated by the United Nations, the successor to the League of Nations. By the mid-1950s, the relationship between Rwanda's Tutsi and Hutu populations had become extremely volatile, with the Hutu majority calling for more autonomy from the Belgian administration as well as relief from Tutsi domination. Beginning in late 1959, armed rebels representing the Party for Hutu Emancipation began a "peasant revolution." Led by Gregoire Kayibanda (1924–1976), Rwanda's Hutu deposed the Tutsi monarch, Kigeri V Ndahindirwa, and launched a campaign of anti-Tutsi violence that led to the death of many thousands and drove thousands more into exile.

As the revolution continued through 1960–61, Hutu representatives replaced many Tutsis in government at the local level, and Kayibanda declared Rwanda a republic. In 1962 Belgium recognized the Kayibanda government, granted Rwanda independence, and began withdrawing from the country. Independence did not bring peace, however, and the ethnic hatred spawned in Rwanda during the colonial era persisted into the 21st century.

See also: BELGIUM AND AFRICA (Vol. IV); COLONIALISM, INFLUENCE OF (Vol. IV); ETHNIC CONFLICT IN AFRICA (Vol. V); GERMANY AND AFRICA (Vol. IV); KAYIBANDA, GREGOIRE (Vol. V); RWANDA (Vols. I, II, III. V).

S

Sadat, Anwar as- (1918–1981) *Anticolonialist who became president of Egypt*

Born in the town of Mit Abul Kom, near CAIRO, Anwar Sadat grew up during the period of British COLONIAL RULE in EGYPT. In 1938 he enrolled in the Egyptian Military Academy in Cairo and upon graduating was stationed at a remote outpost. There he met Gamal Abdel NASSER (1918–1970), and the two helped found the Free Officers Organization, a secret organization dedicated to overthrowing British rule in Egypt.

Sadat had 12 siblings and his upbringing was a humble one. Ordinarily, his background would not have merited entrance to the Egyptian Military Academy, which was attended by the upper class. His father, however, managed to persuade an Egyptian aristocrat to assist his son, and Sadat was eventually enrolled in the academy.

A staunch anticolonialist, Sadat supported Nazi Germany with the hope of driving the British from Egypt. He was arrested twice for collaborating with German forces during World War II (1939–45). After the war Sadat joined an underground movement opposed to the puppet Egyptian monarchy headed by King FARUK (1920–1965). Sadat was again arrested, in 1946, for antigovernment activities. He was released in 1948 and a year later rejoined the army and given the rank of captain.

Sadat, however, still desired an Egyptian government free from British influence. In 1952 the Free Officers Organization staged a coup d'état, overthrowing King Faruk and eventually installing Nasser as president. Sadat became Nasser's communications officer and ran a newspaper, *Al Gumhuriah* (The Republic), that was the voice of the Free Officers' movement. Under Nasser, Sadat later served in a number of high-level government positions, including the vice presidency, from 1964 to 1966 and again in 1969–70. In 1970, during Sadat's second term as vice president, Nasser died, leaving Sadat to assume the presidency.

See also: ARAB-ISRAELI WARS (Vols. IV, V); COUP D'É-TAT (Vol. V); ENGLAND AND AFRICA (Vols. III, IV, V); SADAT, ANWAR AS- (Vol. V).

Further reading: Kirk J. Beattie, *Egypt during the Sadat Years* (New York: Palgrave, 2000); Thomas W. Lippman, *Egypt after Nasser: Sadat, Peace, and the Mirage of Prosperity* (New York: Paragon House, 1989).

Salisbury (Harare)

Capital city of colonial SOUTHERN RHODESIA (now ZIMBABWE), located in the northeastern part of the country. Salisbury was founded in 1890 by the Pioneer Column, a police force of the BRITISH SOUTH AFRICA COMPANY (BSAC), which established colonial control over the region on behalf of Cecil RHODES (1853–1902). The settlement was named in honor of British prime minister Robert Lord SALISBURY (1830–1903).

The BSAC envisioned Salisbury as a center for the MINING of GOLD, similar to JOHANNESBURG, but the anticipated gold wealth never materialized. Instead the town developed as a commercial and government center serving the white settler population engaged in commercial AGRICULTURE. Industry was never the focal point of investment during the era of COLONIAL RULE, so most of Salisbury's African inhabitants were employed in the service sector; whites held managerial positions or were skilled workers.

In 1891 the city was redesigned following a grid pattern, with wide boulevards and avenues replacing the initial haphazard settlement pattern—a new layout that facilitated the racial segregation that was imposed by the BSAC.

Beginning in 1896 the system of taxation that British colonial authorities imposed on Southern Rhodesia's rural villages forced many African men to seek work in Salisbury, creating a housing shortage. This rural-to-urban migration increased further once the town's economy was strengthened by the completion of rail links to Beira, MOZAMBIQUE, in 1899, and to SOUTH AFRICA via Southern Rhodesia's TRANSPORTATION hub at Bulawayo, in 1902.

The area of Salisbury designated for white residents, known as "Avenues," expanded north and east of the central business district, while the African residential area was located to the south of the city, downwind from the emissions of the city center. In 1935 Salisbury became an official city, with a population of approximately 32,000, of whom about 30 percent were white. Growing rapidly after World War II (1939–45), the city became the capital of the CENTRAL AFRICAN FEDERATION, a political alliance that brought together Southern Rhodesia with two other British colonies, NORTHERN RHODESIA and NYASALAND. White immigration from Britain after the war helped fuel this growth further, as did continued African immigration, still mostly male, from the rural areas. Despite the government's attempt to maintain segregation, by 1941 three-quarters of the male African workers resided in shacks on their employers' property in the Avenues section.

By 1961 the city's population exceeded 300,000, with whites still constituting about 30 percent of the total. After independence Salisbury was renamed Harare after a hill located above the settlement of a local Shona chief.

See also: ENGLAND AND AFRICA (Vols. III, IV, V); HARARE (Vol. V); RACE AND RACISM (Vol. IV); SETTLERS, EUROPEAN (Vol. IV); URBAN LIFE AND CULTURE (Vols. IV, V); URBANIZATION (Vols. IV, V).

Further reading: Teresa A. Barnes, "We Women Worked so Hard": Gender, Urbanization, and Social Reproduction in Colonial Harare, Zimbabwe, 1930–1956 (Portsmouth, N.H.: Heinemann, 1999).

Salisbury, Robert Lord (1830–1903) British statesman in Africa

Born in 1830, Robert Arthur Talbot Gascoyne-Cecil was the son of the second Marquis of Salisbury. Educated at Eton and Oxford, Cecil was then sent by his father on a two-year voyage to various territories of the British Empire. The first-hand experience of Britain's widespread imperial interests helped him to get elected to Parliament in 1853, at the age of 23. In 1868 Cecil's father died, making him the third Marquis of Salisbury.

During his long career as a Tory member of Parliament, Salisbury was a staunch yet practical conservative. He gained a reputation as a skillful politician and capable foreign diplomat and, following the elections of 1885, Salisbury served simultaneously as prime minister and foreign secretary. He was briefly out of office but returned as prime minister in 1886, and it was during this second administration that Salisbury left his mark on British political history.

A reluctant imperialist, Salisbury presided over the acquisition and maintenance of British colonies in Africa, including KENYA, UGANDA, NIGERIA, SOUTHERN RHODESIA, and NORTHERN RHODESIA. He tended to be satisfied with coastal colonial enclaves, which could be more easily secured by Britain's naval supremacy. Though a devout Anglican, Salisbury nevertheless was not an active proponent of MISSIONARIES and instead tended to favor a more traditional lifestyle among the indigenous population of Britain's African colonies. Salisbury was consistently critical of the brutal actions of British expansionist Cecil RHODES (1853–1902), and reportedly was "unimpressed" by Rhodes's obvious kowtowing in naming the capital of SOUTHERN RHODESIA after him.

Under his leadership Britain showed a willingness to defend its colonial territories but tried whenever possible to avoid foreign wars. This policy became increasingly difficult toward the end of the 19th century as the PARTITION of the continent among the various European colonial powers intensified. In 1890, with Germany, and 1891, with Portugal, Salisbury's administration established treaties to define colonial boundaries in East Africa. Then, in 1898, Britain and France came to the brink of war over a territorial dispute in the region that is now southeastern Republic of the SUDAN. Known as the FASHODA Incident, the crisis was brought on by Britain's insistence on maintaining control over the upper Nile in the face of France's attempts to establish dominion across the entire African continent, from West Africa to the Nile. Eventually they agreed on the boundaries between their spheres of influence.

In 1899, however, hostilities did erupt with the onset of the ANGLO-BOER WAR, which continued until 1902. Salisbury's diplomatic approach proved to be ineffective in mediating the disputes between the imperialist British colonial administration of South Africa and the BOERS, or AFRIKANERS, of the TRANSVAAL, who sought to maintain their independence from Britain. Salisbury despised the fighting, calling it "Joe's War" in reference to Joseph Chamberlain, his appointed Colonial Secretary, who vigorously supported Britain's colonial expansion. Though the war did end with the Treaty of VEREENIGING (1902), it cast a pall on the closing years of Salisbury's political career. He resigned as prime minister in 1902 and died the following year.

See also: AFRIKANER REPUBLICS (Vol. IV); COLONIAL CONQUEST (Vol. IV); ENGLAND AND AFRICA (Vol. IV).

Further reading: David Steele, *Lord Salisbury: A Political Biography* (New York: Routledge, 2001).

Samkange, Stanlake (1922–1988) *Scholar, novelist, journalist, political activist, and publisher from Zimbabwe*

Stanlake John Thompson Samkange was born to a distinguished family in the Zvimba Communal Lands of ZIMBABWE (then known as SOUTHERN RHODESIA). His father, Thomas Samkange (1887–1956) was a prominent Methodist minister and political activist, while his mother, Grace Mano Samkange (c. 1895–1985) was a member of a church women's organization known as *manyo*. At the time that the young Samkange was a student, churches were responsible for administering Western-style schools for Africans. He attended the local Methodist school and then a Methodist boarding school, the Waddilove Institute, in ZIMBABWE. In keeping with their progressive attitudes, the Samkanges wanted their son to receive the best education possible, so they sent him to Adams College in NATAL and then to FORT HARE COLLEGE, in the eastern Cape Province of SOUTH AFRICA.

Upon graduating Samkange returned home, teaching at a government school and then working as a freelance journalist. Influenced by the example of Booker T. WASHINGTON (1856–1915), Samkange wanted to start a school, Nyatsime College, to be modeled after Washington's Tuskegee Institute, in Alabama. Work on organizing the college began in the early 1950s. Samkange then spent two years in the United States, 1957 to 1959, pursuing a master's degree from Syracuse University, in New York. His visit enabled him to generate African-American support for his school, which finally opened in 1962.

From 1951 to 1966, except for his two years at Syracuse, Samkange was extremely active in Zimbabwean national politics. He was committed to ending white political dominance of Southern Rhodesia, but he was not a revolutionary nationalist. His approach—and that of the organizations to which he belonged, such as the Bantu Congress, the All-African Convention, the United Rhodesian Party, and the Central African Party—was essentially one of working toward gradual reform from within the political system. Thus, when Rhodesia announced its unilateral declaration of independence from Britain in November 1965, Samkange was not in position to support the armed independence struggle movement that followed.

See also: CHRISTIANITY, INFLUENCE OF (Vols. IV, V); EDUCATION (Vols. IV, V); NATIONALISM AND INDEPENDENCE MOVEMENTS (Vol. IV); SAMKANGE, STANLAKE (Vol. V); SIT-HOLE, NDABANINGI (Vols. IV, V); UNILATERAL DECLARATION OF INDEPENDENCE (Vol. V).

Further reading: Terence Ranger, *Are We Not Also Men?: The Samkange Family and African Politics in Zimbabwe, 1920–64* (Portsmouth, N.H.: Heinemann, 1995).

Samori Touré (Samori, Samori Turé, Samory Touré) (c. 1830–1900) *Mande-speaking empire builder in West Africa*

Born into a DYULA family living in the interior GUINEA savanna town of Konyan, Samori Touré descended from Muslim merchants who had turned to farming. His family was closely allied with the Kamara clan, and adhered to the Kamara's traditional RELIGION. However, Samori Touré himself left farming to become a merchant, which helped him reconnect with his Islamic Dyula heritage.

During the first half of the 19th century Muslims contended with those who practiced indigenous African religions for control over the savanna peoples. Muslim Sisé warriors conquered Samori Touré's hometown and captured his mother, whereupon he joined the Sisé army. Quickly learning military skills, he soon distinguished himself as a soldier. By 1861 he struck out on his own and imposed his leadership on his mother's non-Muslim Kamara kinspeople. He then used his skills to help his family resist the spread of Sisé Islamic imperialism. Although his army was weak, he demonstrated extraordinary tactical ability, and through the 1860s he extended his authority over the Dyon and Milo river valleys.

By 1873 Samori Touré had disassociated himself from his non-Muslim elders and established Bisandugu, in present-day Guinea, as the capital of the centralized state he was constructing. He divided his empire into cantons, with a governmental head that was either his relative or friend, assisted by a war chief. The cantons served to unite ethnic groups and families who had been previously at war with one another.

> The army was the basis for Samori Touré's political authority. It consisted for the most part of captives trained from their youth to serve as professional soldiers. Known as *sofa,* they were infantrymen armed with rifles. At critical moments Samori Touré could field an army of 10,000 to 12,000 well-armed, highly trained, and effectively led *sofa.*

Between 1875 and 1879 Samori Touré went on to conquer the entire upper Niger valley from Siguiri to Kouroussa. The addition of this territory gave him a common border with the TUKULOR EMPIRE of al-Hajj UMAR TAL

(1794–1864), with whom Samori Touré negotiated a treaty. By the beginning of the 1880s Samori had seized the Muslim city of KANKAN and destroyed his previous oppressors, the Sisé empire. The Samori empire, also known as the MANDINKA empire, was by this time the third largest in West Africa, after the Tukulor empire and the SOKOTO CALIPHATE.

Unlike Usman dan Fodio (1754–1817) of the Sokoto Caliphate or al-Hajj Umar Tal of the Tukulor empire, Samori Touré did not establish his empire to fulfill a jihad designed to spread Islam. His empire was secular in nature, but Samori Touré chose Islam as the unifying force through which he could legitimatize his personal rule over his ethnically diverse subjects. Although he waged war against other states ruled by Muslim clerics, Samori Touré surrounded himself with Muslim advisers. He even took the title *almami,* the equivalent of imam, and in 1884 he began the process of converting all of his subjects to Islam.

Samori Touré tried to expand his empire along trade routes, but the West African Muslim empires had begun to suffer the encroachment of European colonial powers, and he came up against the French imperialist expansion at BAMAKO. He was able to maintain a semblance of his empire through minor fighting and treaties, and he also used his mercantile relations with the British in SIERRA LEONE to supply his armies with rifles from FREETOWN. However, in spite of Samori Touré's best efforts, beginning in 1882 the French began a systematic campaign of COLONIAL CONQUEST against his Mandinka empire.

Employing guerrilla warfare, Samori Touré held off French troops while also carving out a new state in the region of present-day GHANA and IVORY COAST. By 1894 Samori Touré had retreated to his new empire, using scorched-earth tactics to devastate the lands left to the French. However, he realized too late that he needed help from other African states against the French invasion. By 1898 the French had conquered the Mandinka empire and captured Samori Touré after he fled to what is now LIBERIA. After his capture the French deported Samori Touré to GABON, on the Central African Atlantic coast, where he died in exile.

See also: AHMADU SÉKU (Vol. IV); FRANCE AND AFRICA (Vols. III, IV, V); FRENCH WEST AFRICA (Vol. IV); ISLAM, INFLUENCE OF (Vols. II, III, IV, V); KINGDOMS AND EMPIRES (Vol. IV); RESISTANCE AND REBELLION (Vol. IV); SOKOTO CALIPHATE (Vol. III); TRADE AND COMMERCE (Vol. IV); USMAN DAN FODIO (Vol. III).

San Khoisan-speaking people of the Kalihari Desert region of southern Africa, living primarily in present-day BOTSWANA, NAMIBIA, ANGOLA, and northern SOUTH AFRICA. Among the most ancient of African peoples, the San have existed as semi-nomadic hunter-gatherers in southern Africa for anywhere from 20,000 to 30,000 years. By the third century BCE, however, Bantu-speaking peoples had migrated from the north and settled in San lands. This expansion of Bantu speakers eventually pushed the San into the inhospitable, semi-arid regions of the Kalahari Desert.

"San," derived from the NAMA word *saan,* meaning "bush-dwellers," is only one of many names applied to these people. They are also widely known by the pejorative term "Bushmen," as well as by the names Khwe and Basarwa. Anthropologists today consider the use of the term "San" as appropriate, despite the fact that the word had taken on derogatory connotations in the Nama LANGUAGE.

The arrival of Dutch settlers in the 1600s presented further problems for the San, who lived just beyond the borders of the CAPE COLONY. The BOERS, as the settlers were known, saw the San as dangerous and helplessly barbaric. This low opinion of the San, coupled with the raids the San conducted to capture Boer cattle, led to a drawn-out extermination campaign by the Boers. The sporadic Boer-San conflicts, lasting from 1676–1861, ultimately resulted in the destruction of much of the San population. The remaining San continued to be marginalized, oppressed, and even enslaved by both black and white farmers throughout the period of COLONIAL RULE in southern Africa. Their lands stripped from them and their hunting traditions drastically limited, the San were essentially confined to the Kalahari desert, where the adverse conditions served as their only protection.

The San are still very much marginalized, most notably in Botswana, where they have been repeatedly dispossessed of their lands and forbidden to carry out their usual hunting practices. As recently as 2002 the San, considered "Stone Age creatures" by Botswana's government, were forced off their lands in Botswana in what has been viewed as an attempt at ethnic cleansing. The government has compared the attempt to rid the country of the San to the culling of elephants.

By the 20th century, the San people numbered around 100,000, with the largest populations living in Botswana and Namibia. Continuing to live through foraging, along with some AGRICULTURE and animal husbandry, many San had also been forced to work as cheap farm LABOR.

See also: COLONIALISM, INFLUENCE OF (Vol. IV); ETHNIC CONFLICT IN AFRICA (Vol. V); ETHNICITY AND IDENTITY (Vol. V); SAN (Vols. I, III).

Further reading: Robert J. Gordon, Stuart Sholto Douglas, *The Bushman Myth: The Making of a Namibian Underclass* (Boulder, Colo.: Westview Press, 2000).

al-Sanusi, Muhammad Ali ibn (Sidi Muhammad b. Ali al-Sanusi) (1787–1859) *Sufi Muslim leader in Arabia and North Africa*

Born in the Algerian town of Mustaghanim, al-Sanusi was initially educated at small, local Quranic schools, or *zawiyas*. He then completed his formal studies in 1805 at the university mosque of the Qarawiyyin, in Fez, MOROCCO. He continued his studies at other Islamic universities, including the famed al-Azhar in CAIRO, EGYPT. After performing his hajj, or pilgrimage, to Mecca, al-Sanusi became a disciple of Ahmad bin Idris al-Fasi (1760–1837). Although he was trained as a teacher, al-Sanusi went on to write prolifically throughout his life, authoring more than 40 works.

In ALGERIA in 1837, al-Sanusi created the Sanusiyya brotherhood, a Sufi group that was criticized by some traditional Islamic scholars for al-Sanusi's overly original doctrinal interpretations. At the same time, French colonialists were taking control of much of the region, and al-Sanusi was drawn into conflicts with them. In an effort to avoid further problems with Europeans, in 1843 al-Sanusi moved his headquarters east to coastal Cyrenaica (in present-day LIBYA), a city that remained under Muslim Ottoman control. There he established a Supreme Council and a school at al-Bayda, attracting a number of followers, mostly from among the region's indigenous rural population.

In 1853 al-Sanusi's growing concern with further French encroachment in North Africa led him to direct his followers to take a more militant stance. At the same time, however, he retreated from the coast to the interior, settling at Jaghbub, a Saharan outpost on the route to Cairo. Finding refuge from the conflicts and modernization that accompanied French colonialism, al-Sanusi pursued a lifestyle reminiscent of that of the prophet Muhammad (c. 560–632). At his desert retreat he created a Quran-based social model that attracted rural people and nomads to his brotherhood. Because he advocated respect for, and duty to, the Ottoman Empire, the Ottoman administration exempted him from paying a property tax, instead allowing the Sanusiyya to collect tithes, or voluntary contributions, from its members.

Al-Sanusi died in 1859, respected as a scholar and remembered as one of the early advocates of North African independence from Europe. Following his death, the Sanusiyya Supreme Council ruled until al-Sanusi's sons were properly prepared to assume control. When the time was right the political leadership of the brotherhood was assumed by Muhammad Ahmad al-MAHDI (1844–1902), and the religious leadership was given to Muhammad al-Sharif (1846–1896), who directed the Sanusiyya university at Jaghbub.

See also: COLONIAL CONQUEST (Vol. IV); EDUCATION (Vol. IV); FRANCE AND AFRICA (Vols. III, IV, V); ISLAM, INFLUENCE OF (Vol. II, III, IV); ISLAMIC CENTERS OF LEARNING (Vol. II); QURAN (Vol. II); NATIONALISM AND INDEPENDENCE MOVEMENTS (Vol. IV); OTTOMAN EMPIRE AND AFRICA (Vol. IV); SUFISM (Vols. II, III, IV).

Further reading: Knut S. Vikør, *Sufi and Scholar on the Desert Edge: Muhammad b. Ali al-Sanusi and his Brotherhood* (Chicago: Northwestern University Press, 1995).

São Tomé and Príncipe
Small country, made up of two islands totaling 390 square miles (1,010 sq km), located off the Atlantic Ocean coast of GABON. The Portuguese first came to these two islands in the late 15th century. The Portuguese crown granted land for settlements on the island of São Tomé in 1493, and on neighboring Príncipe island by 1500. In the mid-1800s the economic focus of the islands' Portuguese-owned plantations turned from sugar to the production of COFFEE and COCOA, and cocoa production became increasingly important as the demand in Europe and the United States increased. By 1908 São Tomé and Príncipe had become a leading world cocoa producer.

The Portuguese-owned plantations, or *roças*, on São Tomé and Príncipe used African laborers, many of whom were brought from the Central African mainland. Although the Portuguese abolished SLAVERY in their African colonies in 1876, conditions on the "legitimate" *roças* remained harsh and abusive long after.

During the 1900s, poor pay and brutal working conditions created great dissatisfaction among the plantation workers in São Tomé and Príncipe. In 1953 riots finally erupted. In their attempts to quell the uprising, Portuguese security forces and police killed several hundred Africans. The killings came to be known as the "Batepa Massacre," and today the government observes the anniversary of this event as a national day of remembrance.

In the 1950s and 1960s resistance to colonial oppression grew, and an organized independence movement developed under the leadership of the Movement for the

Liberation of São Tomé and Príncipe, based in neighboring mainland Gabon. In 1975 the two islands gained independence as the nation of São Tomé and Príncipe.

See also: CASH CROPS (Vol. V); INDEPENDENCE MOVEMENTS (Vol. V); PORTUGAL AND AFRICA (Vols. III, IV, V); SÃO TOMÉ AND PRÍNCIPE (Vols. I, II, III, V).

Sarbah, John Mensah (1864–1910) *Barrister and statesman of the Gold Coast (present-day Ghana)*

John Mensah Sarbah was of Fante origin and came from CAPE COAST, a coastal commercial town in the British GOLD COAST COLONY (now GHANA). As a teenager he went to London to study law and in 1887 was called to the English bar, thus becoming the first African barrister from the Gold Coast. Sarbah's early legal writing posited the argument that British rule of African lands was illegitimate. At the same time, however, Sarbah realized that regardless of the lawfulness of Britain's COLONIAL RULE, British occupation of his native land was not likely to end soon. As a consequence Sarbah focused on increasing African participation in the colonial administration and called for an expansion of self-government as a British colony.

In 1894 the British set forth the Crown Lands Bill as a guideline to determine the ownership of land within the Gold Coast. African opposition to this legislation was strong, and in 1897 Sarbah helped found the ABORIGINES' RIGHTS PROTECTION SOCIETY as an opposition group to the British land policy. In addition, as a member of the Gold Coast legislative council, Sarbah used his position to promote the argument that land ownership should be based on African law. Sarbah's efforts paid off with the eventual failure of the proposed legislation and the maintaining of customary land ownership rights.

In addition to being an accomplished lawyer, Sarbah was also a respected author. He wrote numerous legal treatises including *Fanti Customary Laws,* in 1897, and *Fanti National Constitution,* published in 1906. These works examined ways in which the Fante, having been exposed through trade to Western ideas and institutions over 300 years, could draw on their own traditions as well to develop a distinctly Fanti approach to government within the framework of British colonial rule.

See also: ENGLAND AND AFRICA (Vols. III, IV, V); FANTE CONFEDERATION (Vol. IV); LAW IN COLONIAL AFRICA (Vol. IV).

Further reading: Bjorn Edsman, *Lawyers in Gold Coast Politics c. 1900–1945: From Mensah Sarbah to J. B. Danquah* (Stockholm: Almquist & Wiksell International, 1979).

satyagraha Political and spiritual principle of nonviolent protest against injustice developed by Mohandas GANDHI (1869–1948) during his stay in SOUTH AFRICA, from 1893 to 1914. Gandhi's principal concern was finding a way to overcome the superior might of the British colonial administration to win rights for the country's Indian community. *Satyagraha* comes from a Sanskrit word and translates roughly as "truth force" or "soul force."

In 1906 the British administration in the colony of NATAL proposed a set of laws that discriminated against Indians, many of whom were indentured workers in the colony's sugarcane fields. Seeking a way to force the government to withdraw the legislation, Gandhi developed *satyagraha* as a revolutionary form of political protest. Drawing on the lives and teachings of the Buddha (563–483 BCE), Socrates (470–399 BCE), Jesus Christ (4 BCE–29 CE), and Leo Tolstoy (1828–1910), Gandhi envisioned a means of defying the laws that he believed were unjust. It was hoped that those who imposed and upheld the unjust laws would reconsider them when faced with the calm resolution of activists inspired by the spirit of love and truth inherent in *satyagraha*. This novel form of political action empowered the oppressed masses and served as an important part of Gandhi's spiritual philosophy.

Upon his return to India, Gandhi successfully employed *satyagraha* to organize Indians into forcing the British to end COLONIAL RULE in that country. *Satyagraha* influenced the struggle for black rights waged by the AFRICAN NATIONAL CONGRESS in South Africa as well as the Civil Rights Movement in the United States during the 1950s and 1960s.

See also: ASIAN COMMUNITIES (Vols. IV, V); RESISTANCE AND REBELLION (Vol. IV).

Further reading: M. K. Gandhi, *Satyagraha in South Africa* (Baltimore: Greenleaf Books, 1980).

Schreiner, Olive (1855–1920) *Noted South African intellectual, pacifist, suffragette, and author*

Olive Schreiner was born at the Lutheran Mission Station at Wittebergen, in the eastern CAPE COLONY, SOUTH AFRICA. Raised in a Calvinist household by her German father and English mother, both MISSIONARIES, she read voraciously and began writing her own stories and essays at a young age. After working as a governess for wealthy AFRIKANER farmers for 11 years, in 1881 Schreiner traveled to England. There she abandoned her original plan to study medicine, and within two years she found a publisher for her autobiographical novel, *The Story of an African Farm*, which met with immediate success. The radical anti-imperial political views she expressed in her book gave Schreiner a reputation as a rising Victorian intellectual.

Schreiner returned to South Africa in 1889 and continued writing fiction and essays. Three years later she married Samuel Cronwright, an ostrich farmer. In 1895 her first child died shortly after birth; subsequently, she would suffer a series of miscarriages. Schreiner put her energies into writing. Over the next decades she attacked imperialism, especially the activities of mining magnate Cecil RHODES (1853–1902), and criticized Britain for its part in the ANGLO-BOER WAR (1899–1902). In fact, the British authorities interned her for a year for supporting the BOERS. After the turn of the century she wrote forcefully in support of women's suffrage and was an outspoken opponent of violence, particularly the brutality of World War I (1914–18). After a bout with depression Schreiber died of heart failure in 1920.

Throughout her life Schreiner immersed herself in philosophical texts and espoused what were considered radical ideas on pacifism, politics, and sexuality. In some recent scholarly criticism, Schreiner is called to task for her negative portrayal of native African people in her fiction, but her works are invaluable for understanding the effects of South Africa's history of war and oppression on its women.

See also: LITERATURE IN COLONIAL AFRICA (Vol. IV); WOMEN IN AFRICA (Vol. IV).

Further reading: Carolyn Burdett, *Olive Schreiner and the Progress of Feminism: Evolution, Gender, Empire.* (Hampshire, U.K.: Palgrave Macmillan, 2001).

Schweitzer, Albert (1875–1965) *German-born humanitarian, writer, theologian, and doctor*

Albert Schweitzer was born at Kaysersberg, near Strasbourg in the Alsace region of Germany (now France). Educated in both Germany and France, he studied science, music, and theology before devoting his life to serving humanity.

In 1902 Schweitzer became the principal at a theological seminary at the University of Strasbourg, where he was inspired to become a missionary. Between 1905 and 1913, he studied medicine at the university, raising money for a hospital that he planned to build in Africa. In March 1913 he and his wife left Europe for Lambaréné, in rural FRENCH EQUATORIAL AFRICA (present-day GABON). Upon his arrival Schweitzer converted an abandoned chicken coop into a crude hospital building, where he treated patients both young and old who suffered from ulcerated and infected sores and a variety of tropical diseases, including sleeping sickness and malaria. Many patients also suffered from leprosy.

About 1915 Schweitzer formulated the central thought that would come to symbolize his unique brand of humanitarianism: reverence for life. When he and his

wife, Helene (1879–1957), returned to Europe in 1917, he spent the next seven years writing, teaching, lecturing, and giving concerts to raise funds for his Lambaréné hospital, which was in dire financial trouble throughout the World War I years (1914–18). In 1923 he published the first two volumes of his epic work, *The Philosophy of Civilization,* in which he articulated his ideas on "reverence for life." In 1924 he returned to Africa, alone this time, to rebuild his hospital and continue his missionary work.

Back in Africa Schweitzer continued to write, publishing numerous memoirs and essays including *On the Edge of a Primeval Forest* and *From My African Notebook,* in which he recorded his experiences as a doctor and missionary. During World War II (1939–45) Schweitzer maintained the hospital at Lambaréné, relying on contributions from various support groups, including The Albert Schweitzer Fellowship, in the United States.

In recognition for his work as a dedicated humanitarian, Schweitzer was awarded the 1952 Nobel Peace Prize. He used his $33,000 prize to expand the hospital at Lambaréné and build a leper colony.

In the 1940s and 1950s Schweitzer continued his humanitarian work in Africa, occasionally going abroad to lecture or receive awards. In 1959 he returned for good to Lambaréné. He died in 1965 at the age of 90. A product of his era, Schweitzer is remembered for a somewhat contradictory legacy as a compassionate missionary, pacifist, and humanitarian of the first order, who at the same time exhibited an autocratic and paternalistic attitude toward Africans.

See also: DISEASE IN COLONIAL AFRICA (Vol. IV); HEALTH AND HEALING (Vols. IV, V); MISSIONARIES (Vol. IV).

Further reading: James Brabazon, *Albert Schweitzer: A Biography* (Syracuse, N.Y.: Syracuse University Press, 2000).

science Scientific discovery and advances are well documented in ancient African history. However, European colonization of the continent tended to undermine African scientific discovery, labeling African knowledge "inferior" to Western knowledge. In general, when anthropologists studied indigenous knowledge during the colonial period it was to maintain a record for museums or to understand the so-called native mind in order to control the continent more efficiently. Rarely were such investigations intended to learn anything substantive that might inform Western scientific methods.

The primary goal of Western science in colonial Africa was to aid in the extraction of resources to the European nations. Colonizers used scientific advances to improve MINING techniques, to improve the health of Europeans residing in Africa and of laborers working in their enterprises, and to create African markets for European goods.

Often, indigenous technologies and information systems were actively discouraged or even banned. For example, in some areas of Africa indigenous medical practitioners were jailed. The Nigerian iron-smelting industry of precolonial times was undermined by the importation into Africa of scrap iron that flooded the market and diminished the demand for local iron products. This and similar actions had the effect of stalling indigenous creativity and technological advances during this period.

Due to the enormous mineral wealth of some places in Africa, the earth sciences—which included geologic exploration—and the field of engineering were two major areas of focus during the colonial era. Western scientific exploration was also brought to Africa in order to export and exploit other areas of its natural environment. Botanists returned from Africa with hundreds of species of native plants to be examined and labeled in research centers in Europe, such as the Royal Botanical Gardens at Kew, in England. The European perspective was that new species were officially "discovered" only after they were incorporated in the Western taxonomic systems, despite the fact that Africans had known about and used these species for thousands of years. Europeans also set up colonial botanical gardens to experiment with the importation of economically useful plants.

During the colonial period little effort was made to educate the African population in the disciplines of Western science. This was partly due to the racist belief, intimately connected to so-called scientific discoveries made during the SLAVERY period, that viewed indigenous African populations as biologically inferior to Western races. The creation of scientific research centers in Africa did not begin until after World War II (1939–45). An example of the rare colonial institute that served African scientists was the Fundamental Institute of Black Africa (known by its French acronym, IFAN), in DAKAR, SENEGAL. At this center of scientific research, African scholars such as Cheikh Anta DIOP (1923–1986) were able to conduct scientific inquiry with assistance of respected French scholars.

See also: COLONIALISM, INFLUENCE OF (Vol. IV); MINERALS AND METALS (Vol. V); NATURAL RESOURCES (Vols. IV, V); SCIENCE (Vols. I, II, III, V).

Senegal Present-day country with an area of 76,000 square miles (196,800 sq km) that is defined to the north and northeast by the Senegal River, which generally follows the country's northern border with MAURITANIA. Senegal is bordered to the east by MALI, to the south by GUINEA and GUINEA-BISSAU, and to the west by the Atlantic Ocean. A unique geographic feature of Senegal is that it nearly surrounds the country of the GAMBIA.

By the mid-19th century, the indigenous people of Senegal were quite familiar with European influences. The region had long been a major center of TRADE AND COMMERCE, with the French building a factory in St-Louis as early as 1659. Much of the early economic activity in the area centered around the SLAVE TRADE, but when the trade was outlawed by the French in 1848, the region's indigenous people turned to the cultivation of GROUNDNUTS (peanuts) as their main source of income.

During this time the dynamic of everyday life was changing in Senegal. The Senegal River cities of St-Louis and Gorée were introduced to the French policy of *assimilation,* which was based on the belief that French culture was superior to that of the indigenous people. As a result, a divide developed between those who accepted assimilation—the mixed-raced *métis* and African river traders—and those who ignored or disdained the fledgling westernization of the region.

This latter group was composed mostly of Africans living beyond the coastal trading centers. The WOLOF to the east were one such group. Though the French-appointed governor Louis FAIDHERBE (1818–1889) annexed their territory in 1858, the Wolof, whose leaders were Islamic converts, fought a war of resistance against the French COLONIAL CONQUEST of the SENEGAMBIA REGION until 1886. Further opposition came in the form of the Tukolor leader UMAR TAL (1797–1864), who battled the French along the Senegal River Valley until a truce was declared in 1860.

As African resistance in Senegal eased, France embarked on expanding the infrastructure of its territory. The French founded the city of DAKAR in 1857, and in 1885 a railroad was constructed between it and St-Louis. This sparked the growth of Dakar to the point that, by the turn of the century, the city was the largest in Senegal and the seat of the colonial government.

While Senegal expanded in size and in EXPORTS, the policy of assimilation continued, and Africans gained rights that were unheard of in other parts of the continent. The cities of Saint-Louis, Dakar, Gorée, and Rufisque were governed by democratically elected municipal administrations and together formed the symbolic QUATRE COMMUNES (Four Townships) of Senegal. In 1879 the French granted full male suffrage to those who could prove that they had lived within the Quatre Communes for five years. As a result Africans could participate in electing Senegal's deputy to the French Parliament. Later in 1879, Senegal formed a legislative council that was vested with authority over local administrative and financial matters.

Despite their voting rights, Africans in Senegal were unable to exercise much influence over Senegalese politics. France exerted as much control as possible over the legislative council, while French merchants used operatives within the territory to protect their commercial interests. The local political environment was controlled by the *métis*, who through their wealth and education held sway over the African majority. Election fraud was pervasive during this time, and, if necessary, the *métis* could buy the support of the African electorate.

Senegal during the Colonial Era Near the end of the 19th century the number of French settlers arriving in Senegal began to increase, and in 1895 the territory was officially declared a French colony. Later that year Senegal was incorporated into FRENCH WEST AFRICA (Afrique Occidentale Française, AOF), and Dakar was named the capital of the new federation.

In the early 20th century the policy of assimilation was transformed into one of *association*, which accepted the legitimacy of African heritage, though only as subordinate to French culture. For Africans in French territories, this shift resulted in new difficulties, including capricious governance and increased use of forced LABOR. Africans within the Quatre Communes, however, viewed themselves as French citizens, and were troubled by France's attempts to deny their constitutional rights.

Between 1907 and 1914 France gradually revoked the citizenship of Africans within the Quatre Communes. In 1910, in an attempt to defend their political position, Africans formed a political party, the Young Senegalese, and were able to elect a small number of representatives to the legislative assembly. Despite the efforts of the Young Senegalese, Africans continued to lose their rights until the election of Blaise DIAGNE (1872–1934) in 1914 as deputy to the French Parliament. Diagne, the first African to hold the position, successfully fought for African rights, and in 1916 his efforts helped the people of the Quatre Communes to regain citizenship. Diagne's success in the battle for Senegalese citizenship was in large part a result of his accomplishment, during World War I (1914–18), of recruiting thousands of men from AOF for the French army. African conscripts contributed greatly to the western front, marked by the exploits of the TIRAILLEURS SÉNÉGALAIS.

After the war Diagne proposed an extension of citizenship to the rest of AOF but met with little success. Following his initial efforts at expanding the rights of Africans, Diagne, a staunch believer in *assimilation*, frequently supported French colonial policies. This fostered a constant but weak opposition, with the deputies who succeeded him emulating Diagne's politics. As a result, true empowerment of Senegal's African population did not occur until after World War II (1939–45).

In 1946 Léopold SENGHOR (1906–2001) and his political mentor, Lamine GUÈYE (1891–1968), were elected to represent Senegal in the French Constituent Assembly. Senghor, who was a poet and intellectual, focused his attention on organizing disparate groups of the African populace in a movement towards integration of French and African culture. In 1958 he supported Senegal joining the French Community but soon after realized the inevitability of political independence.

In 1959 Senegal joined with Mali to form the Mali Federation, which was granted independence in 1960. The federation was short-lived, however, as the countries separated two months later, with Senghor elected as Senegal's first president.

See also: COLONIALISM, INFLUENCE OF (Vol. IV); COLONIAL RULE (Vol. IV); FRANCE AND AFRICA (Vols. III, IV, V); GORÉE ISLAND (Vol. III); SENEGAL (Vols. I, II, III, V); SENEGAMBIA (Vol. III); SENEGAL RIVER (Vols. I, II).

Further reading: Michael Crowder, *Senegal: A Study of French Assimilation Policy*, rev. ed. (London: Methuen, 1967); William J. Foltz, *From French West Africa to the Mali Federation* (New Haven, Conn.: Yale University Press, 1965).

Senegambia region West African territory covering approximately 80,000 square miles (207,200 sq km) that includes the present-day states of SENEGAL and The GAMBIA. During the colonial era, the Senegambia region was the center of the production and trade of GROUNDNUTS (peanuts). Originally brought to the area from South America by Portuguese settlers in the 17th century, groundnuts thrived in the semi-arid savanna climate of the western part of the region.

Bounded by the Senegal River to the north, the Gambia River to the south, and the Atlantic Ocean to the west, the Senegambia region was home to diverse groups including the WOLOF, MANDINKA, FULANI, Jola, Serahuli, Tukulor, and Serer peoples. By the mid-19th century three significant developments that were to affect the region for the remainder of the century were apparent.

The first of these developments was the growing importance of groundnuts as an export cash crop. Increasing European demand for vegetable oils led to the heightened production and export of groundnuts via the highly navigable Gambia River. By 1851 Britain was exporting more than 11,000 tons of groundnuts, most of which were crushed for a versatile oil that could be used for cooking, for soap production, and for lubricating machinery. Senegal's groundnut production was even greater than the Gambia's, rising to average exports of 29,000 tons per year between 1886 and 1890. St-Louis, at the mouth of the Senegal River, was the center of the French groundnut trade.

The second development was the further spread of Islam in the region, sparked by the jihads that had begun earlier in the century. Of particular importance was the jihad of al-Hajj UMAR TAL (1794–1864). Stimulated by his example, Maba Diakhou Ba (1809–1867), a respected Mandinka Muslim teacher, or marabout, launched a war against the local chiefs to establish a state based on Islamic law. After the death of Ba, the Wolof leader Lat Dyor Diop (1842–1886) continued the effort. As a result of these "marabout wars," the centuries-old process of Islamization of the region was brought to a successful conclusion.

> **Today groundnuts are still a chief crop in both Senegal and The Gambia. A good groundnut harvest in Senegal produces more than 1 million tons of groundnuts.**

By 1864 Lat Dyor had already faced French colonial expansion and been defeated, forcing him to ask Ba for refuge. In 1882 he again confronted the French and fought against them until his death in battle in 1886. His story introduces the third theme, that of European COLONIAL CONQUEST and the imposition of COLONIAL RULE. The British and the French utilized their coastal strong points, such as Banjul Island, at the mouth of the Gambia River, and Gorée Island and St-Louis, in Senegal, as bases to expand their rule. Particularly important in this process was the French governor of Senegal, Louis FAIDHERBE (1818–1889), who in the 1850s began an aggressive policy of expansion. By 1889, in the aftermath of the BERLIN CONFERENCE (1884–85), which set the ground rules for the European PARTITION of the continent, Britain and France had divided the Senegambia region between them, with the much larger portion falling under French rule.

See also: CASH CROPS (Vol. IV); ENGLAND AND AFRICA (Vols. III, IV, V); FRANCE AND AFRICA (Vols. III, IV, V); ISLAM, INFLUENCE OF (Vols. III, IV, V); SENEGAMBIA (Vol. III); SENEGAMBIA CONFEDERATION (Vol. V).

Senghor, Léopold (1906–2001) *Author and first president of Senegal*

Léopold Sédar Senghor was born into a Serer-speaking family living in Joal, near DAKAR, SENEGAL. Although he grew up in predominantly Muslim surroundings, his mother raised him as a Roman Catholic. He attended mission schools and then entered the seminary in Dakar. When he protested the racism he encountered, however, the church rejected him as a candidate for the priesthood, and he left to attend the Dakar Lycée. Recognized as a brilliant student, Senghor graduated in 1928 and won a scholarship to study at the prestigious École Normal Supèrieure in Paris. As France's cultural and political capital, Paris drew students from across the French colonial empire, and while there Senghor met Aimé CÉSAIRE (1913–), from Martinique, and Léon Damas (1912–1978), from French Guyana, whom he joined in founding a literary review, *L'Etudiant noir* (The black student), in 1934.

Senghor's intellectual and social ventures and encounters took place not in Africa but in Europe, where he was introduced to the wider French-speaking black world, the world of the AFRICAN DIASPORA. However, he also established close ties with France, even becoming a good friend of Georges Pompidou (1911–1974), the future French president. In 1935 Senghor lived up to the academic reputation he established in Dakar by becoming the first of many prominent Africans to graduate from the prestigious Sorbonne with the Agrégation de l'Université, France's highest academic distinction.

> **Aimé Césaire and Léon Damas introduced Senghor to black American writers of the Harlem Renaissance. These figures included Claude McKay (1890–1948), Countee Cullen (1903–1946), and Langston Hughes (1902–1967).**

After finishing school Senghor taught in France until the outbreak of World War II (1939–45), when he joined the French army. Captured by the Germans, he was briefly a prisoner of war until being released. He then returned to teaching but also joined the French resistance. When the war ended he became involved in politics. In 1945 he was elected as a deputy from Senegal to the French parliament, focusing increasingly on the issue of self-government for France's colonies. In 1956, however, he suffered a major defeat at the hands of Félix HOUPHOUËT-BOIGNY (1905–1993), a political rival and later president of IVORY COAST. Houphouët-Boigny defeated Senghor's party in the 1956 French legislative elections in every French colony except Senegal. Senegal became a republic in 1959 and, in 1960, Senghor became president, a position he held until resigning in 1980.

Parallel to Senghor's emergence as a major political figure was his growing stature as a poet and cultural figure. His *Chants d'ombre* (Shadow songs, 1945) gained him a reputation as a spokesperson for the growing pan-African literary and cultural movement called NÉGRITUDE. Along with Alioune DIOP (1910–1980), in 1947 he cofounded the journal PRÉSENCE AFRICAINE as a platform for Négritude writers. Senghor's political and literary activities reinforced each other, for they both reflected his belief in the uniqueness of the African personality and its right to coexist in equality with the European personality.

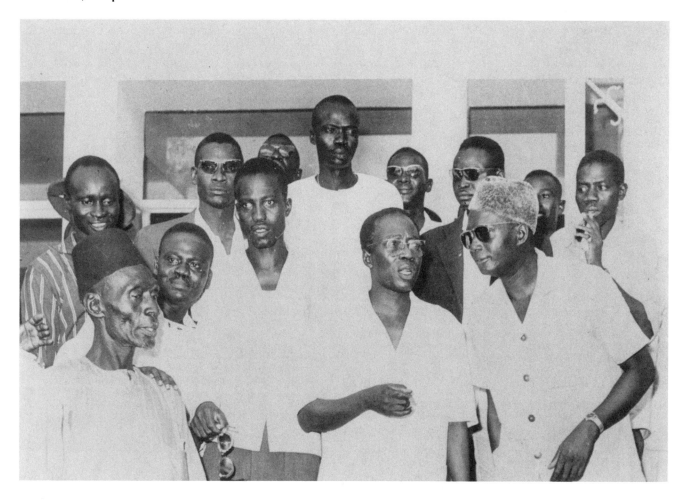

Léopold Senghor, center, wearing clear glasses, is seen with a group that proposed to secede from the Mali Federation in 1960. © *New York World-Telegram & Sun Collection/Library of Congress*

See also: FRANCE AND AFRICA (Vols. IV, V); FRENCH WEST AFRICA (Vol. IV); LITERATURE IN COLONIAL AFRICA (Vol. IV); LITERATURE IN MODERN AFRICA (Vol. V); NATIONALISM AND INDEPENDENCE MOVEMENTS (Vol. IV); PAN-AFRICANISM (Vols. IV, V); SENGHOR, LÉOPOLD (Vol. V).

Further reading: Janet G. Vaillant, *Black, French, and African: a Life of Léopold Sédar Senghor* (Cambridge, Mass.: Harvard University Press, 1990).

settlers, European Europeans who immigrated to colonies in Africa to make their permanent home on the continent, in contrast to those who came to work for a period of time as government officials, for commercial firms, or for other reasons. The earliest European settlement in Africa took place in the second half of the 17th century, when approximately 2,500 people settled in the then Dutch-ruled CAPE COLONY. By 1793 they numbered about 13,830. Subsequent immigration to SOUTH AFRICA brought the European settler total to 250,000 by 1870. About that time, the discovery of large deposits of DIA-

MONDS and GOLD led to significant immigration. As a result, by 1911, the total white population of the newly founded UNION OF SOUTH AFRICA was about 1.3 million people (out of a total population of 6 million). The settler population continued to expand so that it reached 3.1 million in 1960 and 6.1 million at present (out of a total 43.5 million).

The other area of significant early European settlement was in ALGERIA at the opposite end of the continent. France embarked upon its conquest of the country in 1830, and by the end of the decade there were already 100,000 Europeans, known as COLONS, living there. Their numbers continued to grow so that by 1880, 375,000 colons lived amidst Algeria's Muslim population of approximately 3 million. By 1954 there were almost one million colons in the country.

European settlers were also demographically significant in TUNISIA (250,000) and MOROCCO (363,000). The violent war for Algerian independence (1954–62) led, by its end, to a vast emigration of colons, so that today Europeans number less than 1 percent of the population. The same holds true for the populations of MOROCCO and TUNISIA today.

The northern and southern extremes of the continent drew large numbers of settlers early on. In part this was because these regions are in temperate zones outside the tropics and so were conducive to European settlement in terms of climate, AGRICULTURE, and a disease-free environment. Although significant settler populations developed in some tropical African colonies, none reached the numerical or percentage size of those in southern Africa and North Africa. Where Europeans did settle, it was largely in the highland areas where conditions more nearly approximated the temperate environments. These settlers also arrived much more recently, for they came only after COLONIAL RULE was firmly in place. Thus, most of the other settler colonies were in East and southern

Central Africa. The most prominent was SOUTHERN RHODESIA (today's ZIMBABWE), which had about 11,000 white settlers in 1900 and 136,000 at mid-century (out of a total population of 4 million). KENYA had approximately 39,000 in 1950, while there were 80,000 in ANGOLA and 52,000 in MOZAMBIQUE by that time. NAMIBIA, NORTHERN RHODESIA (today's ZAMBIA), LIBYA, and ERITREA also had substantial settler populations at mid-century.

Settler colonies exhibited many common features. Socially, the barriers between the indigenous population and the settlers were much stronger and more visible than elsewhere on the continent. Economically Africans were much more likely to have to work for whites in wage LABOR. This was due primarily to the large-scale European appropriation of African lands. South Africa exhibited the most extreme situation: By 1913 only 7 percent of the

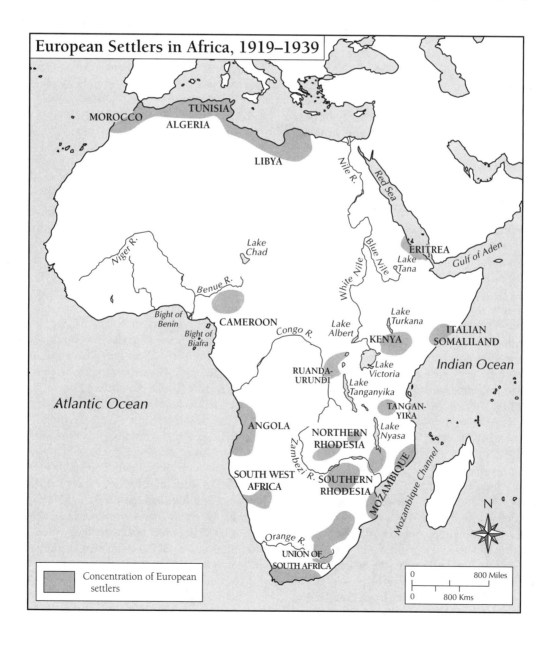

European Settlers in Africa, 1919–1939

country's land surface remained in African hands. In Algeria two-fifths of the farmland was in colon hands by mid-20th century. Southern Rhodesian settlers already owned more farmland than Africans did by 1930, and subsequently they obtained additional land at African expense.

Land distribution reflected the political facts of colonies with large settler populations. While elsewhere European colonial administrators at least argued that they were ruling on behalf of the indigenous population, in the settler colonies this was not even an issue. Again it was in South Africa and Algeria that the settlers achieved the greatest political power. The creation of the Union of South Africa in 1910 effectively made it a fully self-governing country under the control of the white electorate. Algeria's colons gained the political upper hand by 1870, electing representatives for both local and French governing bodies. They never gained the full autonomy of the white South Africans, however. Even where settlers did not gain such an extent of political power, they were the principal beneficiaries of colonial administration.

Because of the entrenched positions of the settler communities, the settler colonies faced the most violent struggles as their African majorities sought independence. The Algerian war was the bloodiest all, with perhaps 10 percent of the population killed in the struggle. In the early 1950s Kenya's British settlers faced violent outbreaks from members of the MAU MAU movement demanding the return of land to Africans. It took a 14-year struggle before Rhodesia became independent Zimbabwe in 1980. In the 1960s and early 1970s Portugal fought protracted and ultimately unsuccessful wars before its African colonies became independent. Only South Africa escaped an all-out war of liberation, due largely to the fact that its fully independent status led to a negotiated transfer of power from white to African hands in the early 1990s. As a result, that country retains a substantial white population. This was not the case for most other former settler colonies, where most settlers emigrated at the time of independence.

See also: AFRIKANERS (Vols. IV, V); BOERS (Vols. III, IV); COLONIALISM, INFLUENCE OF (Vol. IV); ENGLAND AND AFRICA (Vols. III, IV, V); FRANCE AND AFRICA (Vols. III, IV, V); INDEPENDENCE MOVEMENTS (Vol. V); NATIONALISM AND INDEPENDENCE MOVEMENTS (Vol. IV); PORTUGAL AND AFRICA (Vols. III, IV, V).

Seychelles Small nation made up of 115 islands located about 1,000 miles (1,609 km) off the coast of KENYA. Originally a French possession, the Seychelles were under British COLONIAL RULE from 1814 to 1976. Once known by Portuguese sailors as the Seven Sisters, the Seychelles were taken by France as a possession in 1756. Britain claimed the islands from France under the 1814 Treaty of Paris. In the 1830s the British abolition of

SLAVERY caused upheaval on the archipelago, as many of the inhabitants were slaveholders and the economy, based on CASH CROPS such as COTTON, was largely sustained by slave LABOR. The economy therefore switched to less-involved crops such as coconut and vanilla, as well as guano (bird droppings), which was exported for use as fertilizer. Initially administered from MAURITIUS, another former French colony, by 1903 the islands were an official crown colony in their own right.

After World War II (1939–45) the Seychelles, which had never overly interested Britain, began to gain greater political autonomy. In 1948 Britain granted limited suffrage to the landed Seychellois, known as the *grands blancs* (great whites), who were allowed to elect a four-member legislative council to advise the British governor. The "great whites" dominated the Seychelles political scene until the 1960s, when the development of an urban, professional middle class posed a challenge to the old guard. The Seychelles Democratic Party, led by Sir James Mancham (1939–), and the Seychelles People's United Party, led by France Albert René (1935–), emerged as the main political entities on the archipelago. The leaders of these parties shaped independent Seychelles in the postcolonial era.

See also: ENGLAND AND AFRICA (Vols. III, IV, V); FRANCE AND AFRICA (Vols. III, IV, V); SEYCHELLES (Vols. I, II, III, V).

Shembe, Isaiah (c. 1870–1935) *South African religious leader*

Isaiah Shembe was born in NATAL, SOUTH AFRICA. His early life was a prosperous one, and at one point he was married to four wives, which was not unusual for a prominent ZULU man. While still a young man, Shembe experienced what he believed were four messages from God, two of which were in the form of a lightning bolt. During this time Christianity was slowly spreading through South Africa, and may have influenced Shembe's visions. According to legend, the second bolt scorched his body and finally convinced him to give up wickedness as well as his four wives.

After this revelation Shembe wandered the land as a prophetic healer, eventually becoming baptized and joining the African Baptist Church, which was independent of any European missionary control or oversight. In 1911 Shembe left this church, in which he was an ordained minister, and founded the Church of Nazaretha; the members of which are known as amaNazaretha (translated as Nazarites). He preached a theology that combined the teachings of the Old Testament with the customs and beliefs of indigenous Zulu RELIGION.

In addition to his devoutness, Shembe was known for his reverence of the environment. He taught that all living creatures should be treated with the same respect as humans, and he imposed fines on his followers for misdeeds directed toward animals. Shembe established communal farms for his congregation throughout Natal, the largest at Ekuphakameni, and expected the converts to become self-sufficient farmers who did not over-cultivate or breed more livestock than necessary.

The rise of Isaiah Shembe as a religious leader was one of many prophetic movements in Africa during the late 19th and early 20th centuries. Despite Shembe's Baptist background, many of his devotees believed him to be the Messiah, a feature shared with other movements. Their beliefs most likely resulted from Shembe's reputation as a healer and, after his death, his purported resurrection.

Although Shembe was uneducated, his son, Johannes Galilee Shembe (1904–1975), who succeeded him as the Nazarites' leader, was a graduate of FORT HARE COLLEGE.

In 1960 the Church had approximately 100,000 members, but it was to expand rapidly over the next couple of decades and reach 1,000,000 members by the early 1980s.

See also: CHRISTIANITY, INFLUENCE OF (Vol. II, II, IV, V); MISSIONARIES (Vols. III, IV, V); PROPHETS AND PROPHETIC MOVEMENTS (Vol. V).

Further reading: Irving Hexham and G. C. Oosthuizen, eds., *The Story of Isaiah Shembe,* 3 vols. (Lewiston, Me.: E. Mellen Press, 1996).

Sheppard, William Henry (Reverend) (1865–1927)
African-American Protestant missionary in the Congo

William Sheppard was born in Virginia in 1865, one month after the end of the U.S. Civil War (1861–65). He was fortunate to be one of the few African-American southerners of his generation to obtain a college degree, having been educated at Stillman College and then the Presbyterian Theological Seminary for Colored Men in Tuscaloosa, Alabama. The southern Presbyterian Church selected Sheppard, an ordained minister, to be the first African-American missionary it would send to Africa. In keeping with the segregated practices of the time, however, Sheppard served under the supervision of a white missionary. In 1890, accompanied by Reverend Samuel N. Lapsley (c. 1866–1892), Sheppard arrived in the CONGO FREE STATE (present-day Democratic Republic of the CONGO). During his 20 years as a missionary he witnessed the horrific effects of the COLONIAL RULE of King LEOPOLD II (1835–1909) of Belgium.

Sheppard and Lapsley eventually set up a mission station in Congo's Kasai Province, where they learned the Kuba LANGUAGE and managed to establish good relations with the people of the Kuba ETHNIC GROUP. Up to that point the Kuba people had walled themselves off from such outsiders. Following Lapsley's untimely death from a tropical fever, Sheppard traveled back to the United States to recruit more MISSIONARIES. While in America, he married Lucy Gantt (1867–1955), who returned to the Congo with him and five other Americans.

Back in the Congo region, Sheppard found that Kuba people were being forced to seek refuge in the face of aggression from King Leopold's Force Publique, an army of African conscripts directed by European officers. Sheppard investigated the accusations of atrocities and protested to the administration, only to be brushed off. He continued to speak out, however, and in 1908 he wrote a letter to a newspaper in the Congo Free State detailing the brutal practices of European-owned CONCESSIONAIRE COMPANIES in the Congo, such as the Kasai Company. Sued for libel, Sheppard went to court, where he won his case.

Sheppard is remembered as one who informed the world of the atrocities that were being inflicted on the Congolese people during the colonial era. In 1910 he left the Congo, and in 1912 he became the minister for a Louisville, Kentucky congregation, serving in that capacity until his death in 1927.

See also: KUBA (Vol. III); BELGIUM AND AFRICA (Vol. IV); CHRISTIANITY, INFLUENCE OF (Vols. II, III, IV, V).

Further reading: Pagan Kennedy, *Black Livingstone: A True Tale of Adventure in the Nineteenth-century Congo* (New York: Viking, 2002).

Shoa (Showa, Shewa)
Province located in the mountainous central region of present-day ETHIOPIA; ADDIS ABABA, the current Ethiopian capital, is located at the center of Shoa Province. Throughout Ethiopia's long and storied history, Shoa, along with AMHARA and TIGRAY, was one of the most powerful kingdoms in what is now Ethiopia. In 1856 the newly crowned Emperor TÉWODROS II (1820–1868) attempted to consolidate his power. He had earlier established control over Amhara and other core areas and then annexed the independent kingdom of Shoa to complete the reunification of the historic Ethiopian state. For the following decade, Shoa was considered part of Téwodros's realm. To reinforce his control, he seized Sahle Mariam (1844–1913), the son of the recently deceased king of Shoa, Haile Malakot (1847–1855), and tutored him in the arts of statecraft. Eventually Téwodros even gave his daughter to him in marriage.

Sahle Mariam escaped from Téwodros's control in 1865, and three years later, after Téwodros chose suicide over the ignominy of defeat to British invaders, Sahle Mariam reasserted Shoa's autonomy with himself as king. Sahle Mariam took the name Menelik and began expanding the boundaries of his kingdom southward and establishing its Amharic-speaking cultural dominance over non-Amharic people such as the OROMO and Muslims in the state of Harar. Ethiopian Emperor YOHANNES IV (1831–1889) managed to force Menelik to acknowledge his sovereignty in 1878, but Shoa remained relatively autonomous of the central state. When Yohannes died in battle against MAHDIYYA forces invading from the Sudan in 1889, Menelik assumed the throne under the name MENELIK II.

A capable leader and statesman, Menelik II is often credited with creating modern Ethiopia. Shoa's central importance in the empire was solidified when he moved the capital from Gonder, in Amhara, to Addis Ababa, in Shoa. Geographically Shoa was the southern frontier of the old Amharic-speaking core, but it was in the center of the rapidly expanding empire that Menelik II was creating. Shoa continued to be at the center of the empire during much of the 20th century. This included the brief period of Italian COLONIAL RULE (1935–41), when Addis Ababa served as the capital of Italy's East African empire. The end of the Italian occupation of Ethiopia led to new prominence under Emperor HAILE SELASSIE (1892–1975), as Ethiopia became a leader in the continent's movement toward independence. It was only when Haile Selassie's reign began to falter after 1960 that Shoa's central role in Ethiopia began to slip somewhat.

See also: SHOA (Vol. III).

Shona Dominant ethnic group of present-day ZIMBABWE and also in part of MOZAMBIQUE. The Shona speak a number of closely related dialects of a Bantu LANGUAGE. They made up the core population of the Great Zimbabwe state, which was at its height in the 14th and 15th centuries, as well as its successor states of Mutapa and Rozwi. They referred to themselves by their various subgroupings, such as Karanga, Kalanga, and Zezeru. In the 1830s, offshoot groups from the ZULU Mfecane in SOUTH AFRICA severely disrupted the Rozwi state, which by this time was mainly a collection of smaller chiefdoms.

The appearance of the NDEBELE about 1840 established a new major state in Zimbabwe. They called the people they encountered living there by the name of "Shona," which then became the common name.

The Ndebele conquered some of the Shona chiefdoms, incorporating their populations as a lower caste in the Ndebele kingdom. They raided other Shona chiefdoms for cattle and people, but many were left undisturbed by such

depredations. The Gaza state, another Mfecane offshoot, intruded on the Shona chiefdoms in Mozambique. The European PARTITION of the continent brought new and different pressures in the 1890s. The Shona did not resist the initial incursion of the BRITISH SOUTH AFRICA COMPANY (BSAC), but in 1896 they joined the Ndebele in their rebellion against BSAC rule that has come to be called the CHIMURENGA. Among the Shona it was the spirit mediums of the Mwari cult rather than the chiefs that led the rebellion. After prolonged fighting the BSAC defeated the Chimurenga in 1897, and firmly established its COLONIAL RULE over the colony of SOUTHERN RHODESIA.

Southern Rhodesia developed a large European SETTLER population, leading to the extensive appropriation of African lands, particularly among the Shona. This especially was the case for areas near the railroads and highways. Many Shona found themselves working on white-owned commercial farms, while others lived in crowded and marginal "native reserves." Others, still, left their families in the rural areas and went to work in the urban areas or in the mines of Zimbabwe and South Africa.

The European presence also led to significant missionary activity, which led to the spread of Christianity and Western-style EDUCATION. This enabled some, such as Stanlake SAMKANGE (1922–1988) and Ndabaningi SITHOLE (1920–2000), to gain a substantial level of education that they then utilized for political leadership. By the late 1950s discontent over their economic and political status was producing a growing nationalism among the Shona.

See also: BANTU LANGUAGES (Vol. I); COLONIALISM, INFLUENCE OF (Vol. IV); GREAT ZIMBABWE (Vol. II); KARANGA (Vol. II); MFECANE (Vol. III); NATIONALISM AND INDEPENDENCE MOVEMENTS (Vol. IV); RESISTANCE AND REBELLION (Vol. IV); ROZWI (Vol. III); SHONA (Vol. II); SHONA KINGDOMS (Vol. III).

Sierra Leone Present-day country, approximately 27,700 square miles (71,700 sq km) in size, on West Africa's Atlantic coast. Bordered by GUINEA and LIBERIA, Sierra Leone began as a British colony initially settled by formerly enslaved Africans.

The Temne were the indigenous inhabitants of the region where the British Sierra Leone Company set up FREETOWN and the original colony, called the Province of Freedom. Beginning in 1787 the colony became home for numerous freed slaves from Britain, Nova Scotia, and Jamaica.

In 1808 the Sierra Leone Company began to founder, and Britain declared the settlement a crown colony and took up the responsibility of running it. The British then constructed a naval base at Freetown, which had the best natural harbor on the West African coast, to aid them in combating the SLAVE TRADE, which the British had outlawed in 1807. Human captives who had been intercepted and liberated by British vessels were taken to Freetown, and by 1864 more than 50,000 of these RECAPTIVES had joined the colony.

Between the ex-slave settlers and the recaptives, a wide variety of West African ethnic groups populated Freetown, leading the British to attempt a program of cultural unification and Christianization. Carried out primarily by Protestant MISSIONARIES of the CHURCH MISSIONARY SOCIETY, the effort was largely successful, leading to the eventual formation of a KRIO, or Creole, culture.

Krios made up a population that was distinct from the indigenous peoples of the interior. Throughout the 19th century, the colonial administration and the Church Missionary Society endeavored to make the freed slaves and recaptives a unified non-ethnic group that was Christian, Western, and, according to their patronizing notions, "civilized." Missionaries within Sierra Leone established schools such as the Annie Walsh Memorial School for girls (founded in 1816), FOURAH BAY COLLEGE (1827), and the Sierra Leone Grammar School (1845). Krios were regarded as "subjects" of the United Kingdom, a more privileged status than that accorded to the "PROTECTORATE natives" after 1896. As supposedly civilized individuals, Krios were allowed to participate in the government of Freetown, electing a mayor and members of the Municipal Council. With access to education and the governmental apparatus, the Krios of Freetown produced figures such as the noted medical doctor James Africanus Beale HORTON (1835–1883), the attorney and Freetown mayor Samuel LEWIS (1843–1903), and the first African Anglican bishop, Samuel Ajayi CROWTHER (1808–1891).

In 1896 the British declared the hinterland a protectorate, and the crown colony and the hinterland together became the present-day area of Sierra Leone. Britain proclaimed the protectorate in an effort to frustrate French encroachment into the region during the period of European PARTITION of Africa. The British protectorate, which was inhabited by about 16 other indigenous groups, was linked with the Freetown colony, forming the Colony and Protectorate of Sierra Leone, with Freetown as the colonial capital. British officials and Krios were appointed to various positions in the protectorate, and the local indigenous ethnic groups were directly ruled by traditional elites who took instructions from the British colonial administration in Freetown. Christian missionaries established missions in the interior and carried out large-scale conversions.

A railroad linking the interior to the coast was completed in 1908, encouraging the export of PALM OIL and GROUNDNUTS (peanuts), but the protectorate was otherwise not afforded the attention that the colony received. In Freetown, however, the establishment of the protectorate spelled the end for many Krio officials involved in the colonial administration. They were phased out in favor of British administrators.

In 1898 an African revolt, led by the Temne chief Bai Bureh (d. 1908), was initiated in response to the hut tax Britain had imposed to finance the protectorate. The revolt was promptly quashed, effectively ending African resistance to British COLONIAL RULE in Sierra Leone.

Following World War I (1914–18), iron and DIAMOND MINING became major industries in Sierra Leone, employing as many as 16,000 Africans by 1926, often for minimal wages and under oppressive conditions. During World War II (1939–45) Freetown served as an important navy and air base for Allied forces operating in the South Atlantic, and 7,000 Sierra Leoneans fought in the war.

After the war, in spite of Krio calls for a greater role in the government, the British passed a colonial constitution, the Stevenson Constitution, which was opposed and could not be implemented until 1950. In 1951 the Stevenson Constitution awarded more power to the indigenous Africans of the protectorate, who greatly outnumbered the Krio minority of Freetown and the rest of the original colony. Also in 1951 elections were held, with the Sierra Leone Peoples Party (SLPP), based largely in the protectorate, dominating the new government. In 1961 Sierra Leone achieved full independence within the British Commonwealth, with SLPP leader Dr. Milton MARGAI (1895–1964) as prime minister. Freetown, no longer predominantly Krio, was made the national capital.

See also: COLONIALISM, INFLUENCE OF (Vol. IV); ENGLAND AND AFRICA (Vols. III, IV, V); SIERRA LEONE (Vols. I, II, III, V).

Further reading: C. Magbaily Fyle, *The History of Sierra Leone: A Concise Introduction* (London: Evans, 1981); Aintola Wyse, *The Krio of Sierra Leone: An Interpretive History* (London: Hurst, 1989).

Sisulu, Walter (Walter Max Ulyate Sisulu)
(1912–2003) *Leading political figure in South Africa*

Walter Sisulu was born in Engcobo, Transkei, in the Eastern Cape Province, SOUTH AFRICA. Coincidentally, he was born in 1912, the same year that saw the establishment of the activist group that later became the AFRICAN NATIONAL CONGRESS (ANC), the organization to which he dedicated much of his adult life. He went to JOHANNESBURG in 1929, working several jobs, including a stint as a GOLD miner. He joined the ANC in 1940 and was responsible for recruiting Nelson MANDELA (1918–) into its ranks. Sisulu, along with Mandela and Oliver TAMBO (1917–1993), were among a small handful of young ANC members who formed the ANC Youth League in 1943.

This new arm increased the militancy of the ANC, and as a result the parent organization became more responsive to grassroots issues of concern to the masses. In 1944 Sisulu married Albertina Thetiwa (1918–   ), who became an important anti-APARTHEID activist in her own right.

Under the influence of Sisulu, the ANC Youth Leaguers undertook strikes, boycotts, and public protests in an attempt to pressure the government to grant more rights to black South Africans. Initially Sisulu favored an Africanist, or separatist, approach that excluded non-Africans from involvement in the ANC. In the 1950s, however, he gradually modified his views to the point that he was key in cementing working relations with the South African Indian Congress and other racial groups that sought to bring an end to apartheid. Throughout the rest of his career with the ANC, Sisulu was considered one of its most skillful tacticians, particularly renowned for his moderation and pragmatism.

From 1949 to 1954 he served as the secretary general of the ANC and was responsible for formulating and coordinating the Defiance Campaign of 1952, which increased ANC membership to more than 100,000. During the 1950s Sisulu wrote numerous articles for political South African NEWSPAPERS, including NEW AGE and the *Guardian*. In 1954, sponsored by the government of India, he published a book on African nationalism.

In the mid-1950s, as state repression grew more intense, Sisulu was frequently arrested. Most notably he was one of 156 individuals tried during the Treason Trial, begun in 1956 as a government effort to neutralize anti-apartheid forces. On trial again in 1964, he was sentenced to life imprisonment on Robben Island for his political activities. While in prison Sisulu read extensively, earning a secondary degree in ART history and anthropology. In 1984 he was transferred to Pollsmoor Prison, in CAPE TOWN, from which he was released in 1989.

See also: SISULU, ALBERTINA (Vol. V); SISULU, WALTER (Vol. V).

Sithole, Ndabaningi (1920–2000) *Clergyman and political leader in Southern Rhodesia (present-day Zimbabwe)*

Born to parents who adhered to indigenous SHONA religious practices and beliefs, Sithole did not become a Christian until attending a British mission school in Shabani, in 1932. Later he became a student at the Dadaya Mission school, run by the future prime minister of SOUTHERN RHODESIA, the Reverend Garfield Todd (1908–2002). A determined student, Sithole excelled in his studies and became a teacher at the Dadaya Mission school while also earning a bachelor's degree through correspondence from the University of South Africa. From 1953 to 1956 Sithole was a student at Newton Theological Seminary in Massachusetts and also toured the United States, lecturing and preaching. In 1956, having been ordained as a

Congregationalist minister, he returned to Southern Rhodesia, where he was a school principal and minister.

In 1959 Sithole published *African Nationalism,* a book that made the case against the racist white government of Southern Rhodesia. His election in 1959 to the presidency of the African Teachers' Association gave him a springboard into politics, and in 1960 he became a member of the National Democratic Party (NDP), headed by Joshua NKOMO (1917–1999).

African Nationalism argued on Christian grounds for interracial justice within the highly segregated Southern Rhodesian society, which was dominated by whites. In this sense, Sithole was reflecting the views of Garfield Todd, who believed that Christian principles required white Rhodesians to provide a fuller economic, political, and social scope for African participation in Southern Rhodesia.

As the treasurer of the NDP, Sithole became so involved in his political activities that he ultimately gave up his teaching position. His involvement in the NDP provided him a course to leadership within the turbulent world of Rhodesian politics and allowed him, in the upcoming years, to take a major part in the colony's independence from British COLONIAL RULE and white-settler political domination.

See also: CHRISTIANITY, INFLUENCE OF (Vols. IV, V); EDUCATION (Vols. IV, V); ENGLAND AND AFRICA (Vols. III, IV, V); INDEPENDENCE MOVEMENTS (Vol. V); NATIONALISM AND INDEPENDENCE MOVEMENTS (Vol. IV); SETTLERS, EUROPEAN (Vol. IV); SITHOLE, NDABANINGI (Vol. V).

Siti binti Saad (c. 1885–1950) *Legendary singer from Zanzibar*

Siti binti Saad was born into SLAVERY on rural ZANZIBAR island and given the name Mtumwa (literally, "slave"). In the late 19th century major political changes took place in Zanzibar that were to affect her and the other slaves, who made up about three-fourths of the island's population. In 1890 Britain took over Zanzibar as a PROTECTORATE, and in 1897 the European occupier compelled the governing BUSAIDI dynasty to abolish the practice of slavery. This unleashed a gradual social revolution, as the former slave population began to build and assert an identity as free people. For many, part of this process involved a move from the rural areas to ZANZIBAR CITY. The future singer joined this migration in 1911.

Siti binti Saad sold the pots that she made for a living on the streets of Zanzibar. To attract buyers she developed a performance style that included singing and reciting verses. She first attracted attention with her engaging voice, and she then began to learn the Quran and recite its verses. She was such a dynamic performer that she attracted the attention of members of the island's Omani Arab elite, who bestowed the name of *Siti* (Lady) upon her as a sign of their respect and appreciation for her performance. Thus through her MUSIC the former slave girl, Mtumwa, rose to the position of a lady.

After World War I (1914–18) Siti binti Saad formed a band that began to perform *taarab* music, but in a new, revolutionary way. *Taarab* had originated as court music sung in Arabic during the reign of Zanzibari Sultan ibn Said BARGHASH (c. 1833–1888). Siti binti Saad and her band took it out of the court and into the public sphere, performing in KISWAHILI, the LANGUAGE of the urban neighborhoods populated by former slaves. In doing so, she made *taarab* into a form of music that was quintessentially Zanzibari. While the band performed for the elite on some occasions, their songs reflected the concerns of the Zanzibari working class of both genders. The lyrics dealt with topical politics, the structure of society, and everyday concerns of marriage, family, love, and sex.

In March 1928 Siti binti Saad and her band traveled to Bombay, India, to record their music for the international recording company, HMV (His Master's Voice). Their songs, sung in Kiswahili, had gained immense popularity on their home island of Zanzibar and along the East African SWAHILI COAST and in the interior. In three sessions they recorded about 100 songs, which HMV put on records that were bought by an estimated 72,000 fans by 1931. This was the first time that East African performers had recorded their music for commercial release. Siti binti Saad thus stands as the premier East African musician of her time, and her influence is still felt today.

See also: OMANI SULTANATE (Vol. III); SLAVE TRADE ON THE SWAHILI COAST (Vol. III).

slavery The institution of slavery in Africa is as old as it is in other parts of the Eastern Hemisphere, but it has received much more attention because of the impact of the transatlantic SLAVE TRADE on the Western world. The abolition of the transatlantic trade in the 19th century did not bring about the abolition of slavery in Africa.

Many scholars who study the slave trade prefer the term "servitude" when referring to the institution of slavery in Africa. Among the Ashanti of present-day GHANA, the term *akoa* denoted different levels of servility, some of which could be loosely translated to mean servant or subject. Among the Fulbe-speaking FULANI of the Futa Jalon region of GUINEA, the words that translate as "slave" vary from *machudo* to *huwowoh*, but both mean more precisely, "agricultural worker." Among the Anyungwe of central MOZAMBIQUE, *kapolo* meant a person of inferior status,

often forced to work without pay. The persistence of words in modern African languages that denote various forms of servitude point to the complex history of slavery on the continent.

Slavery in Africa was not devoid of exploitation. Indeed, at times in some African societies, slaves were absolute property or chattel of their owners and could be denied personal freedoms, such as sexual rights. The recruiting of slaves on the continent was done generally through warfare between kingdoms, states, towns, chiefdoms, and villages. Wars and state-building efforts that spanned the 19th century often generated large numbers of slaves. For individuals such as SAMORI TOURÉ (c. 1830–1900), slaves were a by-product of his larger objectives. For others such as RABIH BIN FADLALLAH (c. 1835–1900), capturing slaves constituted a principal objective. Some-times powerful states forced weaker societies to enter into a tributary arrangement, essentially making servants of the tributary state. Sometimes crimes, harassment, debt, threats, famine, or hunger often led people to leave their homes and volunteer for servitude. Other people—criminals, for example—lost their freedom and had to become slaves.

Slaves were in demand in Africa before any recorded European involvement. Large numbers of Africans were enslaved and forced to mine GOLD in the AKAN mines in West Africa prior to European contact. By the 16th century the African owners were paying Portuguese traders in gold in exchange for the slaves they provided. Likewise, other Europeans, including the English, the Dutch, and the Danes, entered the trade and provided slaves in exchange for gold. When Britain defeated the ASHANTI EMPIRE in the ANGLO-ASHANTI WARS, thousands of slaves took advantage of the defeat of the Ashanti to escape from slavery. The DOUALA of West Africa also became involved in the trade when they needed workers in their gold mines. Gold-rich Douala kings fed, clothed, and sometimes married their slave women.

Slavery sometimes was useful in the affairs of the state. In military states, slave soldiers played a significant role in the selection of kings. In other areas, slaves became trusted advisers and administrators to royal courts. Often, African slaves were domestic servants who became members of the family and KINSHIP group of their masters, and slaves in this situation could rise above their stations. For example, JAJA (1821–1891), the powerful merchant and later ruler of Opobo in the NIGER DELTA, was born a slave.

Domestic servants were entrusted with household chores, but some of the young females might also become wives to their masters or to some other free members of society. New extended family settings were by-products of the relationship between domestic servants and their masters' families. Over time large numbers of descendants of domestic servants even became family leaders of their former masters' households. Female domestic servants were also employed to tend babies. While their children could be integrated into the households of free husbands, servant women were less likely than men to be able to escape from servitude because they were tethered in place by their children.

Colonial governments gradually instituted laws stipulating that individuals could not be born into slavery after a given date, but such decrees varied widely in terms of dates and extent. Thus, slaves in the GOLD COAST COLONY were free as of 1874, but in the interior regions of SIERRA LEONE, slavery was not abolished until 1928.

Slavery and the slave trade in Africa continued throughout the colonial period and right up to the present in various forms. The institution of slavery has been much more visible in areas where highly centralized political structures existed, such as SENEGAL, the SOKOTO CALIPHATE, EGYPT, MALI, MAURITANIA and the Nilotic Sudan. Indeed, for a number of years the British colonial government tolerated slavery in Northern NIGERIA because of its economic importance to the indigenous Muslim Fulani elite, through whom the British governed using indirect rule. Colonial governments resorted to the use of forced LABOR, very similar to slavery in some instances, to build infrastructure, including streets, railroads, and harbors.

In recent years the governments of the Republic of the SUDAN and MAURITANIA have been accused of practicing slavery. They deny the accusations while admitting to practicing some form of servitude, contending that such practices existed in the past without degenerating into anything similar to the Atlantic slave trade.

See also: SERVITUDE (Vol. I); SLAVERY (Vols. II, III).

Further reading: Trevor R. Getz, *Slavery and Reform in West Africa: Toward Emancipation in Nineteenth-Century Senegal and the Gold Coast* (Athens: Ohio University Press, 2003).

slave trade Trade in human beings was an increasingly significant and even dominant aspect of social, economic, and political developments in much of Africa between 1500 and the early 1800s. Though it declined, the slave trade continued to be significant through the remainder of the 19th century and into the early 20th century.

The Slave Trade Continues By the early part of the 19th century, a general European and American condemnation of SLAVERY and the slave trade slowly was bringing the Atlantic slave trade to a halt. Ironically, Great Britain, which had benefited greatly from the slave trade, took the

lead. In 1807 Britain enacted legislation that outlawed the involvement of British subjects in the slave trade. The following year the United States abolished its slave trade.

Although most other European nations soon followed the British and American examples, the trade continued, spurred on by conflicts in the Nilotic Sudan and southern NIGERIA, and by the continued expansion of commercial networks in the Congo and northern ANGOLA. European slavers and African middlemen continued to ship enslaved Africans to the Americas, and to Brazil and Cuba in particular. Some of the last shipments of enslaved Africans to the Americas went to Cuba, then a Spanish colony, where prices for slaves were high and the trade was legal. On Africa's eastern coast some enslaved Africans from the Sudan and eastern Africa were taken to the Middle East and others went to India and South Asia.

According to a Dutch navy officer, as many as 30,000 enslaved Africans a year continued to be exported from the coast at the mouth of the Congo River as late as 1860. Cuba imported at least 122,000 slaves in the 1850s, most of whom came from western Central Africa.

A clandestine slave trade thrived, as well. European slavers and their African collaborators would meet secretly and negotiate prices before loading ships with Africans captured in the interior and transported by road or canoe to the coast. The ships would then sail with their captives to the Americas. This sort of clandestine trade continued until the 1880s.

Abolition and Resettlement Britain championed the abolition of the transatlantic slave trade by stationing a navy squadron along the coast of SIERRA LEONE in the early part of the 19th century. Hundreds of slave ships and crews were captured on the high seas and thousands of Africans were freed and resettled in FREETOWN, Sierra Leone. A racially mixed court in Freetown often tried the crews. The liberated Africans ultimately formed part of the KRIO community. The United States joined Britain in "repatriating" both American freed slaves and RECAPTIVES in what became the Republic of LIBERIA in 1847. The French also established a similar settlement in Libreville, GABON, thus creating a third center for the liberation of freed slaves and recaptives.

The Slave Trade and Colonial Labor Needs The need for LABOR rose with the intense European demand for African NATURAL RESOURCES and CASH CROPS. West African groundnut (peanut) planters used slave labor to cultivate the crops in places such as Northern NIGERIA, SENEGAL, and The GAMBIA. Similar cash crops, such as COCOA in the GOLD COAST COLONY (now GHANA), COFFEE in UGANDA and IVORY COAST, tea in KENYA, RUBBER in the CONGO FREE STATE, and PALM OIL in Calabar (Nigeria) needed labor performed by enslaved Africans to produce the required quantity for European markets. In Portuguese-controlled territories especially, the clandestine slave trade was used to provide labor in order to produce coffee, tobacco, and sugar. However, free labor also was a feature of the cash crop industry, usually provided by small-scale African farmers.

While European individuals, companies, and governments outwardly prohibited participation in the slave trade, often they tacitly condoned, benefited from, and even participated in the use of slave labor on the continent throughout the colonial era.

The Fernando Po scandal was a typical example of European and African collaboration in the clandestine slave trade. A Spanish syndicate in search of slave labor reached an agreement in 1928 with some officials in the Liberian government to supply labor for the Spanish cocoa plantations on the island of Fernando Po. In light of the irregularity of the transaction, a League of Nations committee investigated the so-called Liberian contract labor system and condemned it as slavery.

See also: SLAVE TRADE, THE TRANSATLANTIC (Vol. III); SLAVE TRADE ON THE SWAHILI COAST (Vol. III).

Further reading: Patrick Manning, *Slavery and African Life: Occidental, Oriental, and African Slave Trade* (Cambridge, U.K.: Cambridge University Press, 1990); David Northrup, *The Atlantic Slave Trade* (Lexington, Mass.: D. C. Heath and Co., 1994).

Smuts, Jan Christian (1870–1950) *Military and political leader, and one of the founders of the Union of South Africa*

A major political figure in SOUTH AFRICA for more than half a century, Smuts was, along with Louis BOTHA (1862–1919), one of the founders of the UNION OF SOUTH AFRICA. Serving in a variety of positions, he frequently represented South Africa on the world stage and played a role in both the signing of the Treaty of Versailles, which ended World War I (1914–18), and the founding of the United Nations. Throughout his life Smuts remained a South African nationalist, albeit one who was more willing to take a moderate stance on race relations and ties with Britain than many of his fellow South Africans.

Born in the CAPE COLONY, Smuts came from a family with deep roots in the Boer community. He was, however, a British subject, and he received his education at Cambridge University. After completing his studies in law he returned to the Cape Colony, where he became a practicing attorney.

In the 1890s Smuts found himself increasingly at odds with Britain over its attempt to wrest control of southern Africa from the BOERS. The final catalyst for Smuts's break with Britain was the infamous JAMESON RAID of 1898. Led by Leander Starr Jameson and instigated by Cecil RHODES (1853–1902), this attempt to overthrow the Afrikaner government of the TRANSVAAL was purportedly taken in defense of the "oppressed" UITLANDERS, as the non-Boer immigrants to South Africa were commonly known. To Smuts, this was a clear sign of Britain's intention to carry out its territorial ambitions. Renouncing his British citizenship, he moved to the South African Republic, where he steadily became more involved in public affairs.

During the ANGLO-BOER WAR (1899–1902) Smuts commanded Boer forces in their ultimately doomed battle against the British Empire. Ever pragmatic, though, after the war Smuts came to the conclusion that hard-line Boer opposition to Britain would only lead to further disaster. Instead he advocated cooperation between Britain and the Boers, a route he followed in conjunction with Botha. Ultimately this led to the founding of the Union of South Africa, made up of the two former Boer republics of the ORANGE FREE STATE and the TRANSVAAL as well as the Cape Colony and NATAL.

With Botha as South Africa's first prime minister, Smuts assumed a variety of roles in the new nation's government, at one time serving simultaneously as defense minister, minister of the interior and mines, and minister of finance. During World War I he also assumed direct command of the South African forces fighting against German troops in GERMAN EAST AFRICA. By 1917 he had taken on an even larger role, becoming part of Britain's Imperial War Cabinet in London, as well as one of the signatories of the Treaty of Versailles.

Although Smuts succeeded Botha as prime minister after Botha's death in 1919, political dissension intensified within South Africa. Smuts's pragmatic stance, combined with his anti-LABOR policies, brought about his fall from power in 1924. However, in 1933 he returned to power in a coalition cabinet, eventually becoming South Africa's wartime prime minister at the outbreak of World War II (1939–45).

Despite being named a field marshal, he did not take command of troops in battle. Instead he spent most of the war in London, where he eventually became active in organizing the United Nations. Politically, he once again fell victim to more extreme elements, and the South African Nationalist Party defeated him and his party in the election of 1948.

See also: AFRIKANERS (Vol. V); KRUGER, PAUL (Vol. IV); VEREENIGING, TREATY OF (Vol. IV); UNITED NATIONS AND AFRICA (Vol. IV).

Further reading: J. C. Smuts, *Jan Christian Smuts: A Biography* (Westport, Conn.: Greenwood, 1973).

Sobukwe, Robert (1924–1978) *Leader of the Pan-Africanist Congress in South Africa*

Born in Graff-Reinet, Cape Province, SOUTH AFRICA, Robert Mangaliso Sobukwe was educated at the country's premier educational institutions for Africans, Healdtown secondary school and FORT HARE COLLEGE. While at Fort Hare, he joined the Youth League of the AFRICAN NATIONAL CONGRESS (ANC). At the time, this was a particularly risky thing to do, since the ANC Youth League endorsed militant popular protest to force the South African state to alter its overtly racist policies.

After graduation in 1949 Sobukwe assumed a teaching position in Standerton, TRANSVAAL, but was dismissed because of his political activism. He was able to find other employment as an instructor of ZULU at the University of Witwatersrand.

During the 1950s, as the ANC was moving toward cooperation with other racial groups in order to combat APARTHEID, Sobukwe became increasingly opposed to the organization's policy of multiracialism. Instead he advocated an Africanist, or separatist, policy, whereby Africans would rely only on themselves in their attempt to overcome the government's unjust laws.

In 1955 he became the editor of *The Africanist,* which was the official voice of the Africanist bloc within the black opposition. In 1958 he led the breakaway Africanist faction out of the ANC and helped found the PAN-AFRICANIST CONGRESS (PAC) the following year. He was elected its first president and became its leading theoretician. In March 1960 the PAC led demonstrations against the pass laws that required all Africans to carry state-issued identity documents. The protests ended in the Sharpeville massacre, in which South African police killed 69 Africans. The government banned the PAC and arrested Sobukwe, imprisoning him for the next nine years.

See also: PAN-AFRICANISM (Vol. IV); SHARPEVILLE (Vol. V); SOBUKWE, ROBERT (Vol. V).

Further reading: Gail M. Gerhart, *Black Power in South Africa: The Evolution of an Ideology* (Berkeley, Calif.: University of California Press, 1978).

Soga, John Henderson (Reverend) (1860–1941) *Author, minister, and historian of the African peoples of South Africa*

Soga was the eldest son of a XHOSA father, Tiyo SOGA (1829–1871), the first black South African to be ordained as a Christian minister. His mother, Janet Burnside, was Scottish. John Henderson Soga was born in England and grew up in the eastern Cape Province town of Mgwali. Often sick as a child, he returned to England with his mother on several occasions for medical care. In 1870 his parents sent him to Glasgow, Scotland, for his elementary education, after which he attended the University of Edinburgh. He graduated from Edinburgh in 1890 and then attended the United Presbyterian Divinity Hall. Soga became an ordained minister in 1893 and returned to South Africa as a missionary in the Mount Frere district of present-day Transkei. Later he moved to a mission in Elliottsdale. His career as a minister, and that of his father, are examples of the important role that African Christians played as MISSIONARIES to their own people.

Following in the footsteps of his father, John translated religious texts from English into Xhosa and vice versa. In 1929 he completed a Xhosa translation, begun by his father, of John Bunyan's popular Christian allegory, *Pilgrim's Progress.* In 1930 he published a Xhosa history, entitled *The South-Eastern Bantu* (1930), that has been a standard in the field ever since. His later works included *The AmaXhosa: Life and Customs* (1931) and *Bantu Literature and Life* (1935).

John Henderson Soga's younger brother Allan Kirkland Soga (d. 1938) was a journalist who was active in politics and was a founding member, in 1912, of the AFRICAN NATIONAL CONGRESS.

After a long and distinguished career as a writer, translator, and missionary in South Africa, Soga retired with his Scottish wife to England in 1936. They and their son were killed in a German air raid on Southampton in 1941.

See also: CHRISTIANITY, INFLUENCE OF (Vols. II, III, IV, V); HISTORICAL SCHOLARSHIP ON AFRICA (Vols. IV, V).

Soga, Tiyo (1829–1871) *Missionary, journalist, writer of hymns, and collector of Xhosa folklore*

A scholar and journalist as well as an evangelical preacher, Tiyo Soga was a prime force in the establishment of Presbyterian missions in SOUTH AFRICA. He was also a talented linguist who helped supervise a XHOSA translation of the Gospels. Born in Tyume, CAPE COLONY, in 1829, Tiyo was the son of one of the main advisors to the powerful Xhosa chieftain, Ngqika (c. 1775–1829). While Tiyo was a child, his mother converted to Christianity. Released from her polygamous marriage, she and her son moved to the Chumie Mission, where the boy began his schooling. In 1844 he began study at Lovedale, but the 1846–47 war between the Xhosa and the Cape Colony caused the school to close. Soon thereafter Lovedale's former principal took Tiyo to Scotland, where he attended Normal School in Glasgow and was "adopted" by the congregation of the John Street United Presbyterian Church. He was baptized in 1848.

Soga returned to the eastern Cape and, beginning in 1849, served as an evangelist, first in Chumie, and then at a new mission he opened at Uniondale. His work proved especially difficult because the people at Uniondale associated Christianity with the COLONIAL RULE they were fighting against. When another war broke out in 1850, Soga's mission was burned to the ground on Christmas Day. He then returned to Scotland to embark on further studies and enrolled at the Theological Hall, in Glasgow. He was ordained as a minister by the United Presbyterian Church in 1856, and soon married a Scotswoman, Janet Burnside.

Soga's return to the eastern Cape in 1857 coincided with the great period of turmoil known as the CATTLE KILLING. It was in the midst of the subsequent political upheaval and mass starvation that Soga started his missionary work, first at Peelton and then at Mgwali. Over the years that followed, Soga developed successful missions throughout the region. Poor health, however, hampered his ministry. During this period he also wrote hymns and translated the first part of Bunyan's *Pilgrim's Progress,* putting the words of the famous allegory into Xhosa.

Writing, in one form or another, was an important part of Soga's life and work. He was a prominent contributor to the newspaper, *Indaba,* which was published in both Xhosa and English. Many of his articles appeared under the pseudonym Nonjiba Waseluhlangeni (Dove of the Nation). He also collected dozens of Xhosa tales, legends, and sayings, putting down some of the most noteworthy of them in a volume called *The Inheritance of My Children,* which he hoped would help his children understand and appreciate their African heritage.

Some of Soga's most lasting literary accomplishments came as the result of his service on the board that oversaw revisions to the Xhosa translation of the Gospels. Here his experience as a composer of hymns as well as a journalist helped him make major contributions to a revised translation of the Gospel that influenced generations of African converts to Christianity.

In ill health for much of his life, Soga died in 1871, succumbing to tuberculosis. The legacy he left behind included his extensive missionary work and his spreading of the belief, which he passed down to his followers and children alike, that Xhosa traditions and culture were every bit as important as those of Europe. Tiyo Soga's children included Alan Kirkland Soga (d. 1938), a newspaper editor and founder of a group that became a political ancestor of the AFRICAN NATIONAL CONGRESS, and John Henderson SOGA (1860–1941), who carried on his fa-

ther's missionary and literary work. The daub-and-wattle church that Soga built in Mgwali still stands today.

See also: CHRISTIANITY, INFLUENCE OF (Vol. IV); EDUCATION (Vols. IV, V); NEWSPAPERS (Vol. IV).

Sokoto Caliphate Muslim theocratic state established in Northern NIGERIA in the early 1800s; it fell to the British in 1903 and became part of colonial Nigeria. The Sokoto Caliphate was a FULANI-led, Muslim empire established over the HAUSA States in the early 19th century, in the aftermath of the JIHAD led by Usman dan Fodio (1754–1817). Upon Usman's death, the caliphate passed to his son, Muhammad Bello (c. 1781–1837), who transformed the caliphate into a vital power. By the mid-1850s Sokoto had become the largest empire in Africa since the collapse of Songhai. Its influence spread far outside its borders, as it inspired jihads and the rise of other theocratic Muslim states in SENEGAL, MALI, IVORY COAST, CHAD, and the present-day Republic of the SUDAN.

The vigorous economy of the caliphate was based on well-established Hausa commercial activity with ties to trans-Saharan trade. Major items included salt, cloth, and leather. But it was the commerce in human beings that was its primary source of income, with the captives taken in the caliphate's regular wars being shipped to various parts of Hausaland, where they worked in everything from AGRICULTURE and herding to crafts.

Politically the caliphate was a loose confederation of semi-autonomous emirates, or Muslim states, with supreme authority over the confederation resting in the caliph, or sultan. Relatively early in its history, conflict between Muhammad Bello and his uncle, Abdullah (d. 1829), led the caliphate to become divided into eastern and western regions. Although each region had its own capital—Sokoto being the capital in the east and Gwanda the capital in the west—both recognized the supreme authority of the caliph in Sokoto.

At its peak in the 1850s, the Sokoto Caliphate was made up of 30 semi-independent emirates, as well the capital region of Sokoto. It stretched over 900 miles (1,448 km) from Dori, in present-day Mali, to Adamawa, in CAMEROON.

The state had faced internal rebellions and wars with African neighbors throughout much of its history, but French-British rivalry for territorial empire in the aftermath of the BERLIN CONFERENCE (1884–85) meant that the caliphate eventually faced forces it could not defeat. By the late 1890s the French had advanced into northern and western regions, but the greatest threat was from the British in the south, where the ROYAL NIGER COMPANY had gained sovereignty over much of the territory. When the company lost its charter in 1900, those lands were placed under direct British control, and Captain Frederick LUGARD (1858–1945) then launched major efforts to establish British COLONIAL RULE over Sokoto. In 1903 he defeated the caliph, Muhammad Attahiru (d. 1903), who died soon after. Lugard then dismantled the caliphate.

Following a policy of indirect rule that he advocated for colonial administration, Lugard allowed local emirates to remain in place as long as they acknowledged British sovereignty, abolished SLAVERY, and followed various other administrative practices.

See also: BELLO, MUHAMMAD (Vol. III); COLONIAL CONQUEST (Vol. IV); USMAN DAN FODIO (Vol. III); ENGLAND AND AFRICA (Vols. III, IV); FRANCE AND AFRICA (Vol. IV); HAUSA STATES (Vol. II, III); ISLAM, INFLUENCE OF (Vols. III, IV); PARTITION (Vol. IV); SOKOTO CALIPHATE (Vol. III).

Somalia East African country, 246,000 square miles (637,100 sq km) in size, located on the Horn of Africa; during the colonial era, the region, known as Somaliland, was hotly contested among both European and African imperial powers. Somalia is bordered by DJIBOUTI to the north, KENYA to the south, and ETHIOPIA to the west.

The late 19th century saw no fewer than five countries lay claim to portions of what is now the nation of Somalia. Britain wanted to acquire Somali territory for use in animal husbandry, specifically to supply meat to its naval port in Aden, on the Arabian Peninsula. France had established its claim to the port of Obock (in present-day Djibouti) and was seeking more territory. In 1870, EGYPT, then under the control of the Ottoman Empire, occupied portions of the Somali Coast in response to European encroachment. However in 1885, when Egypt was forced to withdraw from the region in order to combat the MAHDIYYA uprising in the Sudan, Britain stepped into the void, establishing coastal claims.

Soon both Italy and Ethiopia began to stake their own claims to Somali territory. By 1889 Italy had acquired protectorates within southern Somaliland. Between 1887 and 1897 Ethiopia, under Emperor MENELIK II (1844–1913), annexed the Muslim emirate of Harer and the region of western Somaliland known as the OGADEN, over which Ethiopia claimed sovereignty. By 1900 the entire region had been divided, resulting in BRITISH SOMALILAND to the north, FRENCH SOMALILAND (the future Djibouti) to the northwest, and ITALIAN SOMALILAND to the south. Ethi-opia claimed the Ogaden as Ethiopian Somaliland, and another portion was claimed by Britain as the Northern Frontier District of the colony of Kenya.

The Somali, among the most ethnically homogenous peoples of Africa, remained divided under COLONIAL RULE until 1935, the year Italy invaded Ethiopia. A year into World War II (1939–45), the Italians conquered British Somaliland and the Ogaden, reuniting all of the Somali territories except for French Somaliland. The reunification under Italy was brief, however, as Britain recaptured British Somaliland in 1941 and went on to liberate Ethiopia. Britain then set up a military administration over the Somali territories, and in 1948 a colonial government was once again established. That same year the Ogaden was returned to Ethiopia, derailing the desires of Somali nationalists who desired a "Greater Somalia." In 1950 Italian Somaliland was returned to Italy as a United Nations TRUST TERRITORY, under the condition that the colony become independent in 10 years.

Ethiopian and British forces were met with violent resistance in the form of the so-called dervish movement headed by the devout and militant anti-foreign Islamic leader, Muhammad Abdullah HASSAN (1864–1920). The war he led lasted until his death in 1920, and resulted in the death of approximately one-third of the northern Somali population.

While Italian Somaliland benefited from development under colonial rule, British Somaliland was largely neglected. Upon the merging of the two colonies, discrepancies in terms of economic strength and political experience caused a skew in power that favored southern Somalia.

Italy adhered to the deadline and withdrew from Italian Somaliland in 1960. Submitting to Somali nationalist fervor, Britain granted British Somaliland independence that same year, and the two former colonies merged to become the United Republic of Somalia. A coalition government was then formed in MOGADISHU, formerly the capital of Italian Somaliland, with the Somali National League and the United Somali Party representing the North, and the dominant Somali Youth League (SYL) representing the South. Aadan Abdullah Usmaan (b. 1908) of the SYL became the country's first president.

See also: COLONIALISM, INFLUENCE OF (Vol. IV); ENGLAND AND AFRICA (Vols. III, IV, V); FRANCE AND AFRICA (Vols. III, IV, V); HALLIE SELLASIE ITALY AND AFRICA (Vol. IV); NATIONALISM AND INDEPENDENCE MOVEMENTS (Vol. IV); RESISTANCE AND REBELLION (Vol. IV); SOMALI (Vol. II); SOMALIA (Vols. I, II, III, V).

Sotho One of southern Africa's largest groups speaking a Bantu-based LANGUAGE; the Sotho (pronounced *sutu*) can be divided into three separate peoples, each of which speaks its own Sotho-based language: the Basotho, the PEDI, and the TSWANA.

The Basotho Historically, the Sotho-speaking people (often called the *Basotho*) lived primarily in a region that includes present-day LESOTHO (a small independent country located completely within the borders of SOUTH AFRICA), the adjacent Free State, and, to a lesser extent, the Eastern Cape Province of South Africa. The Sotho trace their origins as a modern people to the early 1800s, when large numbers of Sotho were displaced by the ZULU Mfecane, a period of expansion for the Zulu nation. Sotho refugees were united by their leader, Mshweshwe (c. 1786–1870), who formed the Sotho kingdom by the early 1830s. The kingdom then became a British PROTECTORATE in 1868 and remained under British rule until independence, in 1966. Many Sotho people migrated to work on the diamond mines and then the GOLD mines of South Africa in the later 19th century, so that today they also live in the JOHANNESBURG urban area. Today people who speak Sesotho, as the Sotho language is called, form nearly 8 percent of the South African population. Sesotho was among the first African languages to develop a written form.

The Pedi The Pedi kingdom originated among the northern Sotho people, in the 17th century, in the region between the Vaal and Limpopo rivers in present-day South Africa. United under King Thulare (d. 1824), the Pedi dominated the TRANSVAAL and exploited the Phalaborwa mines, which yielded iron and COPPER for trade. In the 1800s NDEBELE attacks and the Zulu Mfecane forced the Pedi to resettle east of the present-day city of PRETORIA. There they battled both the BOERS and British settlers before being defeated in 1879. Subsequently many Pedi were forced to LABOR on the mines and white-owned farms. Later they suffered greatly under South Africa's APARTHEID policies. The Pedi Sotho language is spoken by almost 10 percent of today's South Africans.

The Tswana As with the Basotho and Pedi, the Tswana were also greatly affected by the Zulu Mfecane, which forced them to unite and restructure their society. The Tswana also became embroiled in the Boer and British conflicts of the late 1800s. They were ultimately dominated by the British, who established the protectorate of BECHUANALAND in 1885. Bechuanaland became independent BOTSWANA in 1966. Setswana, or Tswana, common throughout Botswana, is spoken by 8 percent of South Africans. Presently, the three languages of these groups—Sotho, Pedi and Tswana, are among the 11 national languages of South Africa.

See also: ANGLO-BOER WAR (Vol. IV); BANTU LANGUAGES (Vol. I); COLONIALISM, INFLUENCE OF (Vol. IV); COLONIAL CONQUEST (Vol. IV); ENGLAND AND AFRICA (Vols. III, IV, V); MFECANE (Vol. III); MSHWESHWE (Vol. III); PHALABORWA MINES (Vol. III); SOTHO (Vol. III).

South Africa Present-day country at the southern tip of Africa with an area of 470,700 square miles (1,219,100 sq km). South Africa completely surrounds the country of LESOTHO and is bordered by NAMIBIA to the northwest, by BOTSWANA and ZIMBABWE to the north, and by MOZAMBIQUE and SWAZILAND to the east.

During the first half of the 19th century, the ZULU period of expansion known as the Mfecane resulted in the temporary depopulation of large areas of fertile land in what later became the TRANSVAAL, the ORANGE FREE STATE (OFS), and NATAL. This allowed the BOERS, who had migrated from the CAPE COLONY to these areas during the Great Boer Trek (1835–early 1840s), to lay claim to large tracts of seemingly unoccupied land. In the mid-1840s Britain annexed Natal, which led to an exodus of Boer families to the OFS and the Transvaal. British settlers arriving in Natal in turn brought indentured Indian workers to supply LABOR on sugar plantations. In the meantime the Cape Colony continued on its path of steady if unspectacular economic growth. It also continued to expand its borders, especially eastward into the lands of the XHOSA.

African Resistance to European Expansion As the Boers migrated, the indigenous inhabitants of the region attempted to contain them. For example, the NDEBELE, led by their king, Mzilikazi (1790–1868), fought the Boers for three years near PRETORIA before retreating to an area north of the Limpopo River.

Meanwhile the Zulu impeded the movement of AFRIKANERS (another name for the Boers) into Natal. Under the leadership of CETSHWAYO (c. 1826–1884) and DINUZULU (1868–1913), Zulus also resisted British colonial actions in Natal. They inflicted heavy losses upon the British at the Battle of ISANDLWANA, but the Zulus eventually lost the ANGLO-ZULU WAR (1878–79). After the war Britain severely weakened Zululand by dividing the kingdom among 13 chiefdoms. Nearly a decade later, in 1887, Britain annexed Zululand to Natal.

Some African groups fared better against European intrusion. For example, the SOTHO battled the Boers off and on for years, ultimately retaining a homeland, BASUTOLAND (later Lesotho), with the help of the British. At the end of the century, some of the TSWANA, under the leadership of KHAMA III (1835–1923), were able to prevent the incorporation of much of BECHUANALAND (later Botswana) into the neighboring white-ruled colonies.

Unification of South Africa The importance Britain ascribed to South Africa increased dramatically with the discovery of DIAMONDS at KIMBERLEY in 1866, and the GOLD rush on the WITWATERSRAND during the 1880s. Wanting to ensure their access to the resource-rich land that sparked the MINERAL REVOLUTION, Britain favored the political unification of Cape Colony, Natal, the Transvaal, and the OFS. The AFRIKANER REPUBLICS of the Transvaal and the OFS, however, opposed unification, and the conflict of interests came to a head with the ANGLO-BOER WAR (1899–1902), thanks in large part to the heavy-handed tactics of administrator Lord Alfred MILNER (1854–1925). Though the Boers met with early success, the British, with the resources of an entire empire, eventually emerged victorious.

With peace restored to the region, Britain established the UNION OF SOUTH AFRICA in 1910. However, with no black political representation in the new parliament and an ineffective English-speaking electorate, control of the Union government fell to the Afrikaners. Generally Afrikaners practiced an austere form of Calvinism and held an unyielding belief in white supremacy. They shared a common sense of nationalism that the British colonists in South Africa lacked, and this strengthened their political resolve.

One goal of Afrikaner nationalism was to expand the legislation that gave whites a privileged position in South African society. Hence, the Native Labor Regulation Act of 1911 outlawed blacks from breaking a LABOR contract. Later that year the government passed the Mines and Works Act, which codified the long-standing practice of reserving skilled MINING jobs for whites. Then in 1913 the government passed the Native Lands Act, which created separate living areas for blacks and whites and prohibited blacks from acquiring land outside of "native reserves."

The Native Lands Act designated less than 7 percent of the land in the Union for blacks, though they made up more than two-thirds of the population. Meanwhile, the remaining land—more than 90 percent of it—was reserved for whites, who made up only one-fifth of the population.

Africans did not accept these new laws silently. In 1912 black activists founded the South African Native National Congress (SANNC), which in 1923 became the AFRICAN NATIONAL CONGRESS (ANC). The ANC vigorously protested the actions of the Union's government but, with little support among South Africa's British politicians, the Afrikaner-controlled government continued to institute its racist policies unabated.

In the elections of 1924 the union's relatively moderate prime minister, Jan Christiaan SMUTS (1870–1950), was defeated by J. B. M. HERTZOG (1866–1942), an avowed ardent Afrikaner nationalist. Hertzog quickly introduced more legislation that benefited whites, including the Wage Act of 1925, which promoted the preferential hiring of white workers.

In the 1930s Hertzog attempted to shore up his support by allying himself with his former opponent, Smuts, and formed the new United Party (UP). This did not sit well with the many Afrikaners who believed that Smuts was not a strong supporter of Afrikaner nationalism. As a result, disenchanted UP members split from the party to form the Purified National Party (PNP) under the leadership of D. F. MALAN (1874–1959), a fervent Afrikaner nationalist and white-supremacist.

World War II and its Aftermath World War II (1939–45) proved to be a divisive period for Afrikaners. Smuts believed that South Africa was bound by loyalty to the British Commonwealth and should enter the war on the side of Britain. Hertzog meanwhile, favored neutrality. Still others pushed for an alliance with Germany and a reorganization of South Africa into a Nazi state. Smuts prevailed, however, causing Hertzog to resign. Smuts again became prime minister, while Hertzog joined with Malan to form the Reunited National Party (Herenigde National Party, HNP). Following the war, in the pivotal 1948 election, the UP government was ousted in favor of the HNP.

The war had stimulated South Africa's manufacturing sector, resulting in a job explosion that drew more blacks into the urban work force. This URBANIZATION, especially marked in cities like JOHANNESBURG and DURBAN, contributed to an increase in black political activity, which became more vocal in its insistence on racial equality.

Political activity among South Africa's blacks unnerved Afrikaner nationalists, who began pushing for laws to further limit the movement of blacks into white-controlled areas. Malan, for his part, supported a ban on interracial marriage and more stringent enforcement of labor laws. Malan and the HNP grouped the tenets of their platform under a single, descriptive name, APARTHEID, which is AFRIKAANS for "aparthood," or "separateness."

The HNP soon joined with the Afrikaner Party in the reformed National Party (NP), which quickly began passing legislation that made apartheid a binding system of social, economic, and political organization. During this time, one of the system's leading proponents was Hendrik VERWOERD (1901–1966). South Africa's minister of native affairs from 1950 to 1958, Verwoerd served as the country's prime minister from 1958 until his death in 1966. With Verwoerd's support, the South African government passed laws to divide cities into racially segregated areas and to create supposedly self-governing African "Bantustans" (black homelands). Further legislation established a separate system of EDUCATION for blacks.

In response to the government's more insistent separation of the races, black political organizations also adopted stronger positions. The ANC Youth League was a younger and more militant arm of the ANC. Founded by Anton Lembede (1914–1947), it was later led by Nelson MANDELA

(1918–   ), who oversaw an increase in ANC membership from 10,000 to more than 100,000 by 1952. In concert with other political groups such as the South African Indian Congress, the ANC organized antigovernment rallies. They especially targeted the laws that made it mandatory for blacks to carry a passbook at all times.

Despite its efforts the ANC was unable to gain much ground in its fight against apartheid. Increasing frustration among some members led to the foundation of the militant PAN-AFRICANIST CONGRESS (PAC) in 1959. The following year the PAC organized a national campaign against passbooks, calling on blacks to leave their passbooks at home and rally peacefully outside police stations to invite arrest. It was hoped that the arrests would overwhelm the South African judicial system and call attention to the inequities of the system.

However, one such rally in the city of Sharpeville ended in disaster, with police opening fire, killing 69 demonstrators and wounding 200 more. The incident led to massive work stoppages and continued demonstrations. As a result the South African government declared a state of emergency, arresting thousands and outlawing both the ANC and the PAC.

After the incident at Sharpeville, the government became even harsher in dealing with opposition groups and their leaders. Annoyed by international criticism of apartheid, especially by newly independent members of the British Commonwealth, the Union of South Africa became defiant in its preservation of the system. A referendum limited to whites voted in favor of forming a republic free of all ties to Britain, and on May 30, 1961, Prime Minister Verwoerd declared the independent Republic of South Africa.

See also: ENGLAND AND AFRICA (Vols. III, IV, V); MFECANE (Vol. III); SOUTH AFRICA (Vols. I, II, III, V).

Further reading: Roger B. Beck, *The History of South Africa* (Westport, Conn.: Greenwood Press, 2000); Clifton Crais, *The Politics of Evil: Magic, State Power, and the Politi-*

Civil unrest and police repression were a large part of life in South Africa in 1957. © *AP Newsfeatures*

cal Imagination in South Africa (New York: Cambridge University Press, 2002); Robert Ross, *A Concise History of South Africa* (New York: Cambridge University Press, 1999); Leonard Thompson, *A History of South Africa,* 3rd ed. (New Haven, Conn.: Yale University Press, 2001).

Southern Rhodesia Colonial territory that became present-day ZIMBABWE. Beginning in the 1850s, the region that became Southern Rhodesia rapidly changed with the arrival of British explorers, colonists, and MISSIONARIES. In 1888 the NDEBELE king, LOBENGULA (1836–1894), signed a treaty with the BRITISH SOUTH AFRICA COMPANY (BSAC), led by Cecil RHODES (1853–1902), which permitted the company to mine GOLD in the kingdom. Within a few years, the BSAC established an administrative center at SALISBURY (now Harare) and had taken control of the whole country, renaming it Southern Rhodesia in Rhodes's honor.

Southern Rhodesia officially became a British colony in 1923, a year after a whites-only referendum chose self-government over joining the UNION OF SOUTH AFRICA to the south. Three decades later, in 1953, the whites of Southern Rhodesia supported the creation of the CENTRAL AFRICAN FEDERATION, which brought Southern Rhodesia together with the two British protectorates of NYASALAND (now MALAWI) and NORTHERN RHODESIA (now ZAMBIA). The federation was disbanded in 1963, and two years later the whites of Southern Rhodesia announced a unilateral declaration of independence, although Britain refused to recognize the new nation, now named simply Rhodesia.

The other nations of the former Central African Federation achieved independence in 1964, but the minority white rulers in Rhodesia clung to power until 1980. At that time, the majority black population won independence and renamed the nation Zimbabwe after the famous stone city of Great Zimbabwe, located on the Zimbabwe Plateau.

See also: COLONIAL RULE (Vol. IV); GREAT ZIMBABWE (Vol. II); SETTLERS, EUROPEAN (Vol. IV); UNILATERAL DECLARATION OF INDEPENDENCE (Vol. V).

South West Africa German PROTECTORATE and colony from 1884 to 1915. South West Africa was governed by SOUTH AFRICA from 1915 until 1990, the year that it became independent NAMIBIA. During the colonial era the protectorate was bordered by ANGOLA, NORTHERN RHODESIA, BECHUANALAND, and the UNION OF SOUTH AFRICA.

After South West Africa was declared a German colony in 1885, German MINING companies and their financiers began prospecting in the interior regions of the country. These territories, however, were occupied by the NAMA and HERERO peoples, who attempted to repel the outsiders. In short order German forces were dispatched to the region and, using genocide as a tactic of regional PACIFICATION, they decimated the indigenous populations of the region.

The German colony of South West Africa excluded the coastal town of WALVIS BAY, which was claimed by British settlers from CAPE COLONY, in South Africa.

After World War I (1914–18) Germany's African colonies were divided among the victorious Allies. The League of Nations authorized South Africa, which in 1915 had invaded and occupied the territory on behalf of the Allied Powers, to administer South West Africa as a MANDATE. The South African administration instituted its segregation policies that favored the white, largely AFRIKAANS- and German-speaking population of South West Africa at the expense of the country's African and mixed-race populations. The indigenous Africans were confined to nonproductive "native reserves," where they were unable to maintain a livelihood based on the traditional practices of AGRICULTURE and PASTORALISM. In particular, OVAMBO men were thus forced to engage in migrant LABOR and work for white enterprises. In contrast, the most fertile and mineral-rich lands were allocated to the minority whites and South African firms.

The white-minority South African government ruled South West Africa and after 1948 implemented the same racist APARTHEID policies that it used to maintain political and social superiority at home. For this reason, independence was very slow in coming to South West Africa's oppressed majority. Finally, in 1989, the decades-long efforts of nationalist leaders, coupled with international pressure, paid off and the country held its first national elections. Samuel Nujoma (1929–), the leader of the South West Africa People's Organization, became the country's first president, and in 1990 Nujoma declared the independent Republic of Namibia.

See also: GERMANY AND AFRICA (Vol. IV); NUJOMA, SAMUEL (Vol. V); TRUST TERRITORY (Vol. IV); UNITED NATIONS AND AFRICA (Vols. IV, V).

Soviet Union and Africa The government of what was the former United Soviet Socialist Republics, or Soviet Union, became involved in Africa in the early 20th century, not long after the Bolshevik Revolution (1917) established the communist Soviet state in Russia. From that time onward Soviet interaction with Africa took many forms.

Once the communist revolution in Russia succeeded, the newly renamed Soviet Union focused much of its energy on fomenting revolution against capitalist states around the world. The Soviet leadership made concerted efforts to send communists to Africa to reinforce the ideas of national liberation already present in the minds of African colonial subjects. The success of the Soviet revolution clearly demonstrated to the African colonies that liberation was within their reach.

By 1921 white socialists in SOUTH AFRICA organized Africa's first Communist party, which found support among South Africa's blacks and Coloured population. Before the decade was over, the Communist International, a Soviet body organized to coordinate the world's communist parties, had passed a specific resolution to support the liberation of all oppressed people in the European colonies.

For the most part, after World War II (1939–45), the European colonizers were only marginally concerned with advancing African independence movements. Because of this the Soviet Union was able to make great strides in presenting itself across the African continent as a possible post-independence benefactor.

Furthermore, the Cold War period exacerbated international tensions between the United States and the Soviet Union. Both sides of this ideological conflict were actively involved in African politics. Soviet aid came in the form of weapons, training, and financial assistance that was intended to fuel the emerging nationalist conflicts and further assist in the development of African nationalism. Soviet overtures were not entirely for the sake of national liberation, however. Africa's strategic position near the oil sources of the Middle East and its own incredible wealth of NATURAL RESOURCES, including uranium, were compelling reasons for the Soviets to have allies in Africa. Although Soviet influence in African affairs was limited during the period immediately following the Second World War, its role would increase dramatically from 1960 onward.

See also: COLD WAR AND AFRICA (Vol. V); COMMUNISM AND SOCIALISM (Vol. V); INDEPENDENCE MOVEMENTS (Vol. V); NATIONALISM AND INDEPENDENCE MOVEMENTS (Vol. IV); SOVIET UNION AND AFRICA (Vol. V).

Further reading: E. A. Tarabrin, *USSR and Countries of Africa* (Moscow: Progress Publishers, 1980).

Soyinka, Wole (Akinwande Oluwole Soyinka)
(1934–) *Nigerian playwright, novelist, and winner of the 1986 Nobel Prize in Literature*

Born in 1934, in a village in the YORUBA-speaking region of Western NIGERIA, Soyinka came from a family that was representative of the spiritual and intellectual divisions facing Africans of his generation. His mother was a Christian convert known for her religious devotion, and his father, although an agnostic, was the head of a Christian primary school. His grandfather, however, insisted that Soyinka be instructed in the traditional ways of his Yoruba culture, and saw to it that the boy went

through the appropriate Yoruba initiation rituals before being sent off to a colonial government school. As a result Soyinka grew up recognizing the validity of both the African and European traditions, not just in ART and culture, but in terms of RELIGION as well.

Eventually attending University College in IBADAN, Soyinka studied Yoruba and Greek mythology as well as dramatic literature. After publishing several poems and short stories while still an undergraduate, he went to England to study drama at Leeds University. After graduating he spent two years with London's Royal Court Theater. In 1957 Soyinka's first play, *The Invention*, was produced. A satire of colonial Africa, *The Invention* examines the confusion of the colonial authorities when people of Africa suddenly lose their black skin color. He also wrote the widely popular *Trials of Brother Jero* (1960) during this period, which came to be widely performed in both Britain and Nigeria. Soyinka returned to Nigeria in 1960, already an established playwright of some note. But his literary career was only beginning, for he was soon to become one of Africa's best-known and most widely respected contemporary writers. He also developed into a highly vocal critic of the political scene within Nigeria and of the failures of postcolonial African states to achieve for their citizens the promises of independence from COLONIAL RULE.

See also: COLONIALISM, INFLUENCE OF (Vol. IV); ENGLAND AND AFRICA (Vols. III, IV, V); IBADAN, UNIVERSITY OF (Vol. V); LITERATURE IN COLONIAL AFRICA (Vol. IV); LITERATURE IN MODERN AFRICA (Vol. V); SOYINKA, WOLE (Vol. V).

Further reading: James Gibbs, ed., *Critical Perspectives on Wole Soyinka* (Colorado Springs, Colo.: Three Continents, 1980); David E. Herdeck, *Three Dynamite Authors: Derek Walcott, Naguib Mafouz, Wole Soyinka* (Colorado Springs, Colo.: Three Continents, 1995); Margaret Laurence, *Long Drums and Cannons: Nigerian Dramatists and Novelists* (Portsmouth, N.H.: Praeger, 1968).

Spain and Africa
In general, Spain's colonial interest in Africa was limited to settlements along the Mediterranean Moroccan coast (known as SPANISH MOROCCO) and outposts on the continent's northwest Atlantic coast (known as SPANISH SAHARA). Spain's only sub-Saharan colony was SPANISH GUINEA—a small territory on the southern West African coast and offshore islands, the most important of which was Fernando Po—which later became EQUATORIAL GUINEA.

For centuries Spain had posted naval forces in the Moroccan coastal towns of Ceuta and Melilla to patrol the Mediterranean. In 1859–60, however, MOROCCO disputed the boundaries of the Spanish settlements, and the two countries came to war. Following a Spanish victory, Morocco was forced to recognize Spanish authority in the two towns and also had to cede territory along its southern coast. The international right of Spain to rule these territories (and Spanish Guinea) was officially recognized by the other European colonial powers following negotiations at the BERLIN CONFERENCE (1884–85).

The Spanish settlements in northern Morocco often faced armed resistance from indigenous BERBERS who fiercely defended their territory, known as the RIF, against colonial occupation by both Spanish and French forces.

In 1912 Morocco became a French PROTECTORATE, but Spain was allowed to continue its rule in the areas it already controlled. These included the southern coastal settlements of Villa Cisneros (now Tarfaya), and Río de Oro (now Dakhla). By 1934 Spain had suppressed indigenous Saharawi resistance and added Ifni and Laayoune, the new colonial administrative center, to its holdings. Spain also exercised control over the Canary Islands, located in the Atlantic Ocean off the coast of Spanish Sahara. Like Ceuta and Melilla, the Canaries had long been used to protect Spanish maritime interests.

During the Spanish Civil War (1936–39), control of Spain's Moroccan territories became crucial because of their proximity to the Spanish mainland. In 1936 the Spanish Republican government sent military leader Francisco Franco (1892–1975) to the Canary Islands for fear that he might lead his troops in a rebellion. The move failed, however, when Franco seized the islands within a few months. This made it possible for him to move some of his Nationalist troops to the Moroccan mainland, from which he launched air attacks against Republican forces in southern Spain. Franco's Nationalists eventually won the war.

In 1956, following the French lead, Franco returned most of Spain's former territories to Morocco. However, the discovery of huge deposits of valuable minerals in the Moroccan interior caused Spain to put off a total withdrawal from its former Saharan colonies. Further complicating the issue, local Saharawi herders and farmers claimed territorial rights in the western Sahara and renewed their armed resistance to the last vestiges of Spanish colonialism. The Saharan territorial disputes involving Spain would last until the 1976, when, under the watchful eye of the United Nations, the last Spanish forces and administrators officially withdrew from Laayoune.

See also: FERNANDO PO (Vol. III); SPAIN AND AFRICA (Vols. III, V).

Spanish Guinea
Coastal West African colony that became EQUATORIAL GUINEA in 1963. The colony was made up of a small continental region as well as five islands, including Fernando Po (present-day Bioko). In 1858 Spain took control of Fernando Po from the British. Through the Treaty of Paris (1900) Spain formalized its claims to Fernando Po and the neighboring continental territory. The colony of Spanish Guinea was Spain's only colonial possession in Africa outside MOROCCO and SPANISH SAHARA.

Spain established Spanish Guinea as an overseas territory in 1959, granting all of its inhabitants the rights and privileges of Spanish citizens. African nationalist movements led to autonomy as Equatorial Guinea in 1963, and full independence in 1968.

See also: FANG (Vols. I, II); FERNANDO PO (Vol. III); MALABO (Vol. V); SPAIN AND AFRICA (Vol. IV).

Spanish Morocco
PROTECTORATE established by Spain over portions of MOROCCO from 1912 to 1956. In 1859 Spain and Morocco fought over the disputed boundary of the Spanish city of Ceuta, on Morocco's northern Mediterranean coast, near the Strait of Gibraltar. Ultimately, Spanish troops invaded Morocco, securing Ceuta and the mountainous coastal region that included the cities of Tétouan and Melilla, home to a number of fiercely independent Berber groups. The following year Morocco, impoverished, militarily weak, and lacking decisive leadership, also ceded Tarfaya, a region along the southwestern Atlantic coast that included Río de Oro and Ifni.

In the 19th century the activity of the Barbary corsairs, or pirates, led Spain to secure the sea routes along Africa's northern Mediterranean coast. Since access to the Atlantic Ocean was so important, control over the Strait of Gibraltar, the Mediterranean gateway to the Atlantic, became a primary concern of the European powers.

In 1904 a secret treaty between Spain and France divided Morocco into a northern Spanish zone and a southern French zone. The Spanish zone, administered by Spanish-appointed Moroccan governors, covered an area from south of Tangier, in the west, to the Algerian border, in the east, and included the RIF mountains. After the treaty was signed, the BERBERS in northern Morocco grew increasingly militant in their opposition to Spanish control, and in 1909 Spain had to send 90,000 troops to Melilla to quell their resistance.

In 1912 the Moroccan sultan Moulay Hafid (r. 1908–1912) signed the Treaty of Fez, making Morocco a French protectorate governed by a resident-general. By the same treaty Spain was allowed to continue as the chief power in the mostly coastal regions it already controlled.

By 1921 the well armed and highly organized Berber resistance in the Rif was meeting with unprecedented success. The Berber military leader and respected scholar Mohamed ben ABD EL-KRIM (c. 1880–1963), who resisted both French and Spanish colonial efforts, established his independent Islamic Republic of the Rif after destroying a Spanish force sent to root him out. In 1926, however, Abd el-Krim surrendered to the French forces that were sent to aid Spain in putting an end to his rebellion.

In 1936 rebel Spanish general Francisco Franco (1892–1975) began attacking the Spanish Republic from Morocco, signaling the start of the Spanish Civil War (1936–39). Following his victory in 1939, Franco got support from Germany's Nazi government. When France fell to Germany in 1940, Spanish troops moved in to occupy Tangier. They withdrew, however, with the Allied victory in 1945.

After the war, Spain—in spite of its Fascist leadership—administered its holdings in Morocco rather liberally. The Spanish let members of the Moroccan royal family retain a nominal amount of governing power and allowed the territory's inhabitants practice their religions freely. In 1953 the French deposed King MUHAMMAD V (1910–1961), but Spain continued to recognize his rule. Following Muhammad's lead, Moroccan nationalist sentiments grew to the point that France granted Morocco its independence in 1956. Later that year, in light of France's actions, Spain also agreed to withdraw from Morocco, although the Mediterranean port cities of Ceuta and Melilla remained, and still are today, Spanish enclaves.

See also: COLONIAL RULE (Vol. IV); PARTITION (Vol. V); SPAIN AND AFRICA (Vols. III, IV); RESISTANCE AND REBELLION (Vol. IV).

Further reading: José E. Alvarez, *The Betrothed of Death: the Spanish Foreign Legion During the Rif Rebellion, 1920–1927* (Westport, Conn.: Greenwood Press, 2001); Sebastian Balfour, *Deadly Embrace: Morocco and the Road to the Spanish Civil War* (New York: Oxford University Press, 2002); Peter Gold, *Europe of Africa: A Contemporary Study of the Spanish North African Enclaves* (Liverpool, U.K.: Liverpool Univ. Press, 2001).

Spanish Sahara (1884–1976) Colonial territory in western North Africa that became WESTERN SAHARA in

1976. At the BERLIN CONFERENCE of 1884–85, Spain claimed a PROTECTORATE over territory along the Atlantic coast of what was then southern MOROCCO. Initial attempts by Spain to settle in the interior region were successfully repelled by the indigenous Saharawi BERBERS, so Spain's efforts at COLONIAL CONQUEST were confined to the coast. By 1935 Spanish Sahara included settlements at Laayoune, the administrative capital, Villa Cisneros (now Tarfaya), Río de Oro (now Dakhla), and Ifni.

In 1956 both Spain and France withdrew their colonial governments from northern Morocco and granted the nation autonomy. In the southern regions, however, Spanish business and financial interests had begun large-scale MINING of the region's valuable phosphate deposits. As a result Spain continued its COLONIAL RULE in the area, denying independence and suppressing Saharawi nationalism. Regional anti-Spain violence raged from 1956 to 1958. The situation was so dire that the Spanish forces enlisted the help of French troops, and together they finally put down the Saharawi insurgency.

Despite the successful independence efforts that swept across the African continent throughout the late 1950s and early 1960s, territorial disputes among Morocco, MAURITANIA, and Spain kept the western Sahara region under Spanish colonial control. Finally, in 1976 Spain withdrew and the territory was renamed Western Sahara, with Morocco administering the northern two-thirds of the country and Mauritania governing the southern one-third.

See also: SPAIN AND AFRICA (Vols. III, IV, V).

Speke, John Hanning (1827–1864) *British army officer and explorer*

Born in England, Speke attended military schools before joining the British army in India in 1844. Ten years later, upon completion of his tour of duty in India, Speke traveled to Africa, stopping first in the British colonial outpost of Aden, in Arabia. There he met the famed African explorer Richard burton (1821–1890), who was preparing for an expedition to Somaliland, in the Horn of Africa. Speke joined the expedition as one of Burton's forward scouts in 1855. Taken prisoner and badly beaten by Somali marauders, he escaped his captors but had to return to England to recover from his injuries. When he was again able, Speke traveled back to Africa to join Burton in further exploration. In 1857 the two men set off from zanzibar for the interior hoping to find the source of the Nile River.

Both Speke and Burton soon came down with malaria, but they continued on, eventually reaching the commercial port town of Ujiji, on the eastern shores of Lake Tanganyika. The expedition then became increasingly difficult, and Speke, nearly blind from an eye infection, decided to part ways with Burton. Speke headed north, and in August 1858 he and his party encountered a vast lake that he named Victoria in honor of the English queen. Speke was satisfied that he had found the source of the Nile and set off for Britain.

Speke's report on his findings impressed the British Royal Geographical Society, which immediately offered to fund another expedition to confirm the discoveries. Leaving less than a year after his return, Speke retraced his steps to Lake Victoria. After exploring the region the expedition found that the lake released its water northward, toward the Nile. Following the river's course the expedition passed through several kingdoms, including BUGANDA.

In his journal Speke wrote extensively of his four-month stay in Buganda at the court of Kabaka, or King, MUTESA I (c. late 1830s–1884). The two men became friendly, with Speke showing Mutesa how to hunt with firearms, and Mutesa telling Speke, through a KISWAHILI interpreter, the oral history of his people. Much of the history was reproduced in Speke's *Journal of the Discovery of the Source of the Nile,* published posthumously in 1868.

When the caravan arrived in BUNYORO, however, the king did not allow it to pass through, so Speke chose instead to travel overland, thereby losing sight of the river. Later, despite the growing body of evidence in his favor, this detour kept Speke from being able to say definitively that he discovered the source of the Nile. Nevertheless, when Speke returned to England, he was widely regarded as a hero. In 1864 he accidentally shot himself in a hunting accident and died.

See also: EXPLORATION (Vol. III); VICTORIA, LAKE (Vols. I, V).

Stanley, Henry Morton (Sir) (1841–1904) *Writer and explorer instrumental in the establishment of the Congo Free State*

Famous for locating the well-known explorer Dr. Robert LIVINGSTONE (1818–1873), who had been assumed to be "missing" while on an expedition, Stanley went on to become, in his own right, one of the late 19th century's most noted European adventurers and explorers of Africa.

Born John Rowland in Wales in 1841, the future explorer was an illegitimate child whose parents could not afford to raise him. As a result he was sent to a work-house at an early age, where he endured a bleak life of abuse and mistreatment. Determined to make something of his life, he wandered the British Isles for a while, even-

tually getting hired as a cabin boy on a merchant ship bound for the United States. Arriving in New Orleans at the age of 18, he worked for an American merchant who eventually took him in and whose name Stanley adopted. Adventurous by nature, Stanley saw military service on both the Confederate and Union sides of the U. S. Civil War (1861–65), worked on merchant ships, and finally took on assignments as a journalist in the western United States.

Stanley's experience as a journalist led to overseas assignments in Africa, where in 1868 he reported on the war in Abyssinia (present-day ETHIOPIA). His articles for the *New York Herald* gained him considerable notoriety. More important, they earned him the assignment of locating Livingstone, who had not been heard from since he went in search of the source of the Nile. Stanley set out from ZANZIBAR in March 1871, finally encountering the legendary missionary and explorer in November 1872. It was then, at Ujiji near Lake Tanganyika, that he uttered the words that have been forever linked with his name, "Dr. Livingstone, I presume."

The "discovery" of Livingstone launched Stanley on a series of expeditions of his own. Following the death of Livingstone in 1873, Stanley was hired by the *New York Herald* and London's *Daily Telegraph* to continue the late explorer's work. On an epic journey that lasted from 1874 to 1877, Stanley followed the Congo River from its source, in present-day Democratic Republic of the CONGO, to its mouth in the Atlantic Ocean. Seeking backing for further efforts in the area, Stanley was dismayed to learn that Britain was, at the time, not interested in developing a presence in the region. He therefore accepted an invitation from King LEOPOLD II (1835–1909) of Belgium to undertake another expedition that lasted from 1879 to 1884. During the course of that trip, Stanley helped lay the foundations of the CONGO FREE STATE. Later he was instrumental in gaining American support for Leopold when the Belgian monarch was given personal control of the vast Congo region following the BERLIN CONFERENCE (1884–85). Stanley's final African expedition came in 1887–89, when he went to rescue Emin Pasha, the governor of Egypt's Equatoria Province (in present-day southern Republic of the SUDAN), who had been "lost" during the Mahdist revolt.

His adventures in Africa completed, Stanley went on to a career as an author and politician. Books such as *Through the Dark Continent* (1878), *In Darkest Africa* (1890), and *The Founding of the Congo Free State* (1885) helped seal his fame. He served as a member of Parliament, from 1895 to 1900, and was knighted, in 1899. Ultimately, however, he must be remembered for his role in founding what turned out to be the most horrific example of COLONIAL RULE in Africa—the Congo Free State.

See also: BELGIUM AND AFRICA (Vol. IV); EXPLORATION (Vol. IV); STANLEYVILLE (Vol. IV).

Further readings: John Bierman, *The Life Behind the Legend of Henry Morton Stanley* (Austin: University of Texas Press, 1999); Martin Dugard, *The Epic Adventures of Stanley and Livingstone* (New York: Doubleday, 2003).

Stanleyville Port city on the Congo River named after explorer Sir Henry Morton STANLEY (1841–1904). In 1882–83 Stanley was exploring the African interior in the service of Belgian King LEOPOLD II (1835–1909) when he established an outpost, known as Falls Station, on an island in the Congo River. The station was located just downriver from Boyoma Falls (formerly Stanley Falls), which marked the upper limits of river navigation. Later moved to the north shore of the river, by 1898 the station had grown into a city called Stanleyville. At the time, the area surrounding Stanleyville was sparsely populated, dense forest. Before long, however, Stanleyville was a major center for trade to and from Kinshasa, located downriver about 770 miles (1,239 km) to the southwest.

Stanleyville continued to grow, becoming by the middle of the 20th century the third principal city of the BELGIAN CONGO, along with Kinshasa and Lubumbashi. In the 1950s it was very much a Belgian colonial city when Patrice LUMUMBA (1925–1961), a charismatic former postal clerk, gained political clout by organizing the African people of Stanleyville to demand Congolese independence from Belgium. Unmoved, Belgian colonial officials in Stanleyville had Lumumba arrested, causing a wave of civil unrest in the city. After his release Lumumba continued his political activism with the Congolese National Movement, getting elected as Congo's prime minister in 1959, and eventually leading the country to independence in 1960.

Within months, however, internal dissension among the Congo's leaders turned violent. Lumumba and his supporters retreated to Stanleyville, where they proclaimed themselves the leaders of the "free republic of the Congo." Charged with inciting a Stanleyville riot that caused 30 deaths, Lumumba was arrested again and taken away from the city. In January 1961 he was executed by unknown assailants outside the southern Congo city of Elizabethville, leaving Stanleyville, and the country, in chaos. Stanleyville was renamed Kisangani in 1966.

See also: BELGIUM AND AFRICA (Vol. IV); COLONIAL RULE (Vol. IV); URBANIZATION (Vols. IV, V).

Sudan, Republic of the Present-day country directly south of EGYPT, in northeast Africa, with an area of 966,800 square miles (2,504,000 sq km). Known during the colonial era as the Sudan, it is also bordered by the present-day countries of LIBYA, CHAD, the CENTRAL AFRICAN REPUBLIC, the Democratic Republic of the CONGO, UGANDA, KENYA, ETHIOPIA, and ERITREA.

For most of the 19th century, the Sudan was under the political authority of Egypt, which itself was a province of the Ottoman Empire until the middle of the century. In 1801 the British occupied Egypt after expelling Napoleon Bonaparte (1769–1873) and his French forces from the region. During the 1820s Egypt, under the order of the pasha Muhammad Ali (c. 1769–1849), invaded the Sudan to expel the Mamluks from the region. Ali was also interested in the prosperous SLAVE TRADE of the Sudan, and commandeered 30,000 Sudanese captives for use in the Egyptian army.

During this era of Egyptian rule, known as the Turkiyah, Egypt imposed oppressive taxes on the Sudanese people. In 1822 Ali's son, Ismail (1795–1822), who had led the Egyptian invasion, was assassinated. His death stirred the Sudanese into a mass rebellion that was brutally crushed using scorched-earth tactics. In the aftermath the Sudan was left ravaged and many of its people were either exhausted or had fled to the Ethiopian border.

After 1825 Egypt eased the despotic nature of its rule and attempted to cultivate wealth from the Sudan. The Egyptians introduced agricultural techniques such as improved irrigation in an effort to increase farmer output and, in turn, tax income. These efforts largely failed, however, as did an ill-conceived attempt at iron MINING and the fervent search for GOLD. In the end, early Egyptian rule of the Sudan was marked by increasing apathy, and except for the slave trade it was economically fruitless. Egypt, however, was successful in establishing a parasitic, multitiered bureaucracy that was headed by a governor-general stationed at KHARTOUM.

During the 1830s most of the Egyptian activity in the Sudan was in the northern region of the territory. Historically, there was a significant difference between the people in the northern and southern parts of the Sudan. Arabic-speaking Muslims were predominant in the north, and though typically of mixed descent, they viewed themselves as Arabs. In the south, most of the population was black African and followed traditional African religions. Furthermore, the people south of the Sudd, a vast, long-impenetrable swampland, had been in complete isolation before an Egyptian gold expedition finally ventured into the area in 1839.

Though it lacked the desired gold deposits, the area south of the Sudd possessed large amounts of ivory. The discovery soon drew European and Arab traders to the previously disregarded land. The population of the area, initially cordial, began to resist the intrusion of the traders. As the IVORY TRADE expanded, the supply of ivory gradually decreased, and trading posts developed as staging grounds for elephant hunts in the interior. Indigenous resistance increased and the trading posts evolved into fortified trading camps called ZARIBAS that became centers of power in the region. Traders made more frequent raids and began to take prisoners from the resisting population, eventually selling them to slavers from the north. The slaving activities of the traders resulted in the seizure of thousands of Africans and devastated the southern Sudan's social and economic structure.

During the 1860s Khedive ISMAIL (1830–1895), who succeeded Muhammad Ali, began to extend Egyptian rule into southern Sudan. In 1869 Ismail appointed Sir Samuel BAKER (1821–1893) as governor of the newly forged Equatoria Province of the upper Nile, charging him with carrying out the expansionist initiative. Under pressure from Britain, Egypt extended its rule in large part to end the southern slave trade. Baker's harsh and inconsistent tactics, however, garnered animosity from both the slave traders of the region and the Sudanese he was sent to protect. In 1874 Baker, who had become governor-general of the Sudan, was replaced by Charles George GORDON (1833–1885). Gordon's administration was just as oppressive as Baker's was, but he succeeded in ending the slave trade and crushing the resistance of defiant slavers.

The opening of the SUEZ CANAL in 1869 increased British interest in Egyptian affairs, and in 1879 the British forced Ismail to abdicate in favor of his more easily controlled son, Muhammad Tawfiq (1852–1892). In 1880 Gordon resigned his post. The feebleness of his successors and the political disarray of Egypt led to a deterioration of conditions in the Sudan.

Within this environment of instability arose the Islamic holy man Muhammad Ahmad al-MAHDI (1844–1885). Ahmad preached a strict form of Islam and advocated the expulsion of foreign forces from the Sudan. He quickly gained a strong following and eventually declared a JIHAD against the Egyptian occupation. Initially dismissed as a religious fanatic, al-Mahdi led a rebellion that by 1885 had captured Khartoum and effectively gained control of the whole Sudan. He died six months after the fall of Khartoum, but his victory was secured and initiated the era of the MAHDIYYA rule of the Sudan.

Al-Mahdi's death led to years of factional bickering among the Mahdist leadership. In 1891, however, ABDAL-LAHI IBN MUHAMMAD (1846–1899) rose to become the leader of Mahdiyya and was given the title of Khalifa (successor). Under the Khalifa, the Mahdiyya continued the jihad in an attempt to spread their version of Islam. The new jihad was largely a failure, however, and severely weakened the Mahdiyya's once overpowering army.

By the 1890s other colonial powers began to question Britain's claim over the Sudan and the headwaters of the Nile. As a result the British sought to reestablish Egyptian control over the Sudan. So, in 1896, a joint British-Egyptian invasion began under the leadership of Horatio Herbert KITCHENER (1850–1916). The Mahdists resisted but eventually were overwhelmed by British firepower. The decisive blow occurred in 1898 at the Battle of OMDURMAN, where the Mahdists lost 11,000 warriors while inflicting only 48 casualties upon the British. The Khalifa was able to escape, but he died one year later, ending coordinated Mahdist resistance.

The Sudan during the Colonial Period: Anglo-Egyptian Condominium Concerned about further revolts by the Mahdists, Britain was unwilling to allow the Sudan to revert solely to Egyptian rule. Accordingly, on July 10, 1899, Britain established an agreement of joint authority called the ANGLO-EGYPTIAN CONDOMINIUM. By the terms of this agreement, the Sudan became a political entity separate from Egypt.

Dominated from the start by the British, the condominium was not a relationship of equal partners. Though formally appointed by the khedive, the governor-general of the Sudan was named by the British. Although he officially reported to the British Foreign Office through the British diplomatic agent in CAIRO, the governor-general administered the Sudan as if it were a British colony. Most of the administrative personnel were British officers attached to the Egyptian army. Beginning in 1901 these administrators were replaced by civilians from Britain. Egyptians filled the middle-level posts, and Sudanese held the lower-level positions. In 1910 an appointive legislative council was formed that retained power until 1948, when it was superceded by a partly elected legislative assembly.

The British treated the northern and southern regions of Sudan differently. While they modernized the north—introducing technology and new styles of administration—they left the south largely unattended. Britain barred northerners from entering the south to help the region develop along indigenous lines. The British also advocated the expression of African culture in the south, while discouraging the practice of Arab customs and the religion of Islam. This separation from the north left the south isolated from commercial and educational activities and stifled modern development in the region.

During the early part of the Condominium, Britain began to shape the Sudan to its liking. The colonial power built a railway that linked northern Sudan with Egypt and was later expanded to connect the inland city of Sennar to ports along the Red Sea. This new railroad neatly complemented the changes introduced to Sudanese AGRICULTURE, the most notable of which being those related to the GEZIRA SCHEME. Begun in 1911 as a joint venture between the Sudanese government and the Sudan Plantations Syndicate, the Gezira Scheme was used to supply COTTON to British textile factories. Helped by the construction of a large dam near Sennar in 1925, cotton production in the region increased dramatically. In addition, newly constructed railroads made exporting the cash crop a relatively easy endeavor.

In 1922 Britain unilaterally declared Egypt independent. Independence was hardly complete, however, as the British maintained a strong military and retained political influence in the country. The Egyptian constitution was presented a year later, but it made no reference to Egypt's sovereignty over the Sudan. With the status of the Sudan still unanswered, Britain and Egypt entered negotiations to determine the parameters of their new relationship. The two countries were slow to reach an understanding, however, largely due to disagreement over the status of the Sudan. Unhappy with the deliberate pace of the proceedings, Egyptian nationalists rioted.

In 1924 the governor-general of the Sudan, Sir Lee Stack, was assassinated in Cairo. Britain blamed Egyptian nationalists for the murder, and the British responded by ordering all Egyptian personnel to leave the Sudan. A year later the Sudan Defense Force was formed to replace the Egyptian troops that had been stationed there.

During this time Britain increasingly used indirect rule to govern the Sudan, delegating judicial and administrative duties to local chiefs. This concerned the Sudan's educated elite, who believed that the arrangement further alienated southern Sudan and would hinder the transfer of power from colonial authorities. This dissatisfaction with British policy gradually led to an increase of Sudanese nationalism, which began in earnest during the 1930s.

In 1936 a new Anglo-Egyptian treaty allowed the return of some Egyptians to Sudanese governmental posts. The agreement angered educated Sudanese, who resented the fact that they were not consulted on issues affecting the Sudan. From their dissatisfaction arose, in 1938, the Graduates' General Congress, which was initially founded by alumni of Gordon's Memorial College but grew to accept all educated Sudanese.

The congress demanded self-determination for the Sudan once World War II (1939–45) was over, but its demands were ignored. Unable to agree on a plan of action, the congress divided into two factions that later became political parties. Ismail al-Azhari (1902–1969) founded the Ashigga, later the National Unionist Party (NUP), which favored union of the Sudan and Egypt. Ashigga gained support from Sayed Sir Ali al-Mirghani, head of a powerful religious sect that had supported a strong relationship with Egypt. Meanwhile the Umma Party also obtained the support of a religious leader, Abdur-Rahman al-Mahdi, son of Muhammad Ahmad al-Mahdi, who agreed with party's call for a fully independent Sudan.

The NUP boycotted the 1948 elections, allowing the Umma to gain decisive control of the Legislative Assembly. In 1952 they negotiated with Britain the Self-Determination Agreement, which angered Egypt and led to the dissolution of the condominium.

Independence Later that year, the Egyptian government of King FARUK (1920–1965) was overthrown by a military coup led by Muhammad Naguib (1900–1984) and Gamal Abdel NASSER (1918–1970). The new Egyptian government was accepting of Sudanese self-rule and in 1953 signed an Anglo-Egyptian treaty that created a three-year period of self-rule for the Sudan at the end of which the Sudanese would decide their fate.

A 1952 electoral victory by the NUP seemed to mark the Sudan's intention to eventually vote for unification with Egypt. Sudanese nationalism, however, eventually prevailed, as al-Azhari, who became prime minister in 1954, shifted his position on the issue to follow the changing public opinion. In 1956 the Sudanese parliament unanimously voted for a declaration of independence, with al-Azhari forming a coalition government soon after.

Al-Azhari's government was short-lived, however, as a new coalition government, led by Abd Allah Khalil (1888–1970), took control in July 1956. Two years later Ibrahim Abboud (1900–1983) led a successful military coup. Abboud created the Supreme Council, which was composed of military officers, to govern Sudan. Despite strong opposition to his rule, Abboud maintained control over the Sudan until 1964.

See also: ENGLAND AND AFRICA (Vol. IV); SUDAN, REPUBLIC OF THE (Vols. I, II, III, V); SUDAN, THE (Vol. II); SUDD (Vol. I).

Further reading: P. M. Holt and M. W. Daly, *The History of the Sudan, from the Coming of Islam to the Present Day* (New York: Longman, 1988); Deng D. Akol Ruay, *The Politics of Two Sudans: the South and the North, 1821–1969* (Uppsala, Sweden: Nordiska Afrikainstitutet, 1994).

Suez Canal Artificial waterway linking the Mediterranean Sea with the Red Sea. Although artificial waterways linking the Red Sea and the Nile River had existed in ancient times, the modern idea for the canal was born during France's invasion of EGYPT (1798–1801), led by Napoleon Bonaparte (1769–1821). However, nothing came of Napoleon's vision of a canal for more than 50 years. Then, in 1854, the French diplomat and canal builder Ferdinand de Lesseps (1805–1894) obtained permission from the viceroy of Egypt to design and construct a waterway between the Red Sea and the Mediterranean.

Planned by an international group of technicians and engineers and built with money raised by the sale of stock in the private company that was to run it, the Suez Canal took almost 10 years and the work of more than a million laborers to build. The workers endured virtually slave-like conditions and nearly 125,000 died during construction, mainly of cholera. When completed in November 1869, the canal stretched 121 miles (195 km) and linked the Mediterranean Sea with the Gulf of Suez (which opens to the Red Sea and, in turn, the Indian Ocean). The canal's opening was a gala event planned by the new viceroy, Khedive ISMAIL (1830–1895), to showcase the efforts he was making in order to transform CAIRO into a modern world capital.

In addition to new roads, grand hotels, and entire suburbs, among Ismail's plans for the grand opening of the canal was an opera house in which there would be the premiere of a work by the noted Italian composer Giusseppe Verdi (1813–1901). Unfortunately Verdi was unable to complete the opera on time, and *Aïda,* his opera about ancient Egypt, was not performed for another year, when it was staged at the Cairo Opera.

For almost a hundred years the canal was run by the Suez Canal Company, a corporation dominated, at first, by the French and Ottomans. Great Britain, which initially had opposed the construction of the canal, had no part in either its construction or its early operation. In 1875, however, in response to the financial crisis brought on by Khedive Ismail's disastrous economic policies, Britain bought the Khedive's shares in the company and assumed a dominant role.

In spite of the roles Britain and France played in the canal's operations, during its early years issues involving the Suez Canal were kept removed from politics. Indeed, according to an 1888 treaty, the Convention of Constantinople, it was to be open to the vessels of all nations, in war and peace. The canal's history during much of the 20th century, however, has been a political and, occasionally, a martial tangle.

During World War I (1914–18), for example, Britain stationed troops at the canal in order to protect it from possible falling under control of the Central Powers. Similarly, invoking clauses of its 1936 treaty with Egypt, Britain guarded the Suez Canal with troops during World War II (1939–45) and closed the canal to German, Italian, and Japanese shipping.

The situation, however, changed dramatically during the 1940s and 1950s. Although the Anglo-Egyptian treaty of 1936 assured Egypt of independence, the agreement guaranteed Britain the right to maintain troops and protect the Suez Canal. In the years following World War II, these clauses became flash points among Egyptian nationalists anxious to take control of their country's leadership. In 1951, with anti-British and antiforeign riots paralyzing Cairo, Egypt repudiated the treaty, forcing Britain to agree to withdraw its troops from the canal zone by 1956.

The issue of control of the canal was a key element in the 1952 coup d'état that overthrew King FARUK (1920–1965) and the eventual rise to power of president Gamal Abdel NASSER (1918–1970).

Hostilities peaked in 1956 when, angered over the withdrawal of British and United States aid for his ASWAN DAM project, Egyptian president Gamal Abdel Nasser nationalized the canal just days after Britain withdrew its troops from the canal zone. Replacing the long-standing canal company administration with an Egyptian Canal Authority, the government took immediate control of the waterway. Reaction to Nasser's takeover of the canal was immediate, not only from Britain, but also from France and Israel. Israel, which had been prevented from using the canal since the ARAB-ISRAELI WAR of 1947–48, attacked in October of 1956, supported by British and French air power. Days later British and French troops arrived to retake the canal.

In one of the many tests of its ability to maintain the peace during the Cold War era, the United Nations quickly sent in peacekeepers and eventually helped negotiate a settlement. With United Nations assistance, sunken ships, mines, and other obstacles were cleared

At Port Said, seen here in about 1900, Egyptian beef was loaded aboard ocean liners to pass through the Suez Canal. © *Underwood & Underwood/Library of Congress*

away and the canal was reopened in April 1957, with Egypt paying the shareholders of the old canal company for the nationalized shares. This paved the way for the relatively peaceful operation of the canal for the next decade.

See also: ARAB-ISRAELI WARS (Vol. V); COLD WAR AND AFRICA (Vol. IV, V); ENGLAND AND AFRICA (Vols. III, IV, V); FRANCE AND AFRICA (Vols. III, IV,V); MEDITERRANEAN SEA (Vol. I); NILE RIVER (Vol. I); OTTOMAN EMPIRE (Vols. III, IV); RED SEA (Vol. I); SUEZ CANAL (Vol. V); UNITED NATIONS AND AFRICA (Vols. IV, V).

Further reading: D. A. Farnie, *East and West of Suez: The Suez Canal in History, 1854–1956* (Oxford, U.K.: Oxford University Press, 1969); Muhammad H. Heikal, *Cutting the Lion's Tail: Suez through Egyptian Eyes* (New York: Arbor House, 1987); Zachary Karabell, *Parting the Desert: The Creation of the Suez Canal* (New York: Knopf, 2003).

Sufism Mystical form of Islam. African Sufism has roots that date back to the 12th century, and it still is a dominant element in the forms of Islam practiced on the African continent. During the 18th and 19th centuries, as the Turkish Ottoman Empire began to falter, African Sufi *turuq* (sing., *tariqa*), or brotherhoods, gained large followings across northern Africa. Although they weren't necessarily militant, these brotherhoods generally opposed European colonialism.

The origin of the word *Sufi* is uncertain. Since Sufis preached a purification of the heart, *Sufi* may be related to the Arabic word *safa*, meaning "to clean." It is also possible that *Sufi* came from the Arabic word *suf*, meaning "wool," since early Sufis rejected earthly pleasures and wore coarse wool shirts instead of more comfortable fabrics.

Like all Muslims, Sufis follow a path based on the life of the prophet Muhammad and on *sharia*, the laws defined by the interpretation of the Quran and Sunna. For Sufis, however, the personal, spiritual relationship with God, or Allah, is of utmost importance. In this way Sufism transcends political movements and intellectual systems.

Although all Sufis focus on spiritual development and purification of the heart, even within Sufism there is debate as to what constitutes a true practice. In Africa, where Islam was often adapted to fit better with deeper-rooted traditional beliefs, the mystical elements of Sufism have inspired numerous innovations. For example, some Sufis use MUSIC, DANCE, and mystical rituals to celebrate Allah, while others denigrate these activities as *schrick* (false practices or unnecessary additions in the teachings of Islam, which is a very serious offense among Muslims).

As in other parts of the Islamic world, Sufi leaders in Africa were usually charismatic teachers who cultivated their reputations as spiritually superior individuals. Their small group of students could then recruit others, eventually forming a *tariqa,* or brotherhood, which could then act en masse to achieve social, political, or even military objectives. Among the more influential Sufi brotherhoods in Africa during the 19th and 20th centuries were the Qadiriyya, Tijaniyya, Sanusiyya, and MAHDIYYA.

The Qadiriyya, one of the oldest Sufi brotherhoods, was especially active in West Africa in the early 19th century. Usman dan Fodio (1754–1817) was a member of the Qadiriyya, and his loyal following helped him organize his jihads to establish the SOKOTO CALIPHATE in present-day NIGERIA.

Toward the middle of the 19th century, UMAR TAL (1794–1864), a Muslim cleric of the Tijaniyya order, founded the TUKULOR EMPIRE in present-day eastern SENEGAL and southern MALI. The impact of the teachings of Qadiriyya and Tijaniyya on Usman dan Fodio and Umar Tal, respectively, instigated these two leaders to carry out successful jihads in West Africa.

About the same time, an influential North African Sufi leader, Muhammad Ali bin al-SANUSI (1787–1859), called upon his Sufi brethren to take up arms to repel French colonial encroachment in ALGERIA and Cyrenaica (now LIBYA). With a social model based on a strict reading of the Quran, the Sanusiyya found many willing recruits throughout the rural areas in the region. Their struggle was fueled by the reputation of Europeans as heathen invaders who threatened the Muslim way of life.

In the late 19th century, Cheik Amadou Bamba (c. 1850–1927), from Senegal, founded a *tariqa* that became known as Muridiyya, which emphasized obedience and hard work. The Muridiyya mixed Qadiriyya, Tijaniyya, and African practices.

In northeast Africa, the Mahdiyya Sufi brotherhood, founded by Muhammad Ahmad al-MAHDI (1844–1885), drove the non-Muslim Egyptian rulers from the region and eventually controlled most of the northern part of present-day Republic of the Sudan. Despite the Mahdi's 1898 defeat at the Battle of OMDURMAN by British and Egyptian forces, the Mahdiyya brotherhood remained an influential religious order and still wields power in contemporary Sudan.

In SOMALIA, too, Sufi brotherhoods, especially the Qadiriyya, were instrumental in social organization. Later they also led the resistance to Italian colonization. One of the prominent Qadiriyya leaders, Uways bin Muhammad al-Barawi (1847–1909), translated Arabic works into KISWAHILI, the lingua franca of East Africa, in order to spread his message.

By the beginning of the 20th century, African Sufi brotherhoods had lost much of their social and political power to the European colonial administrations that replaced them. In religious and spiritual matters, however, the brotherhoods remained strong, keeping their special Islamic practices alive for future generations.

See also: COLONIAL CONQUEST (Vol. IV); ISLAM, INFLUENCE OF (Vols. II, III, IV, V); QURAN (Vol. II); QADIRIYYA (Vol. III); SHARIA (Vol. V); SUFISM (Vols. II, III); USMAN DAN FODIO (Vol. III).

Further reading: Nehemia Levtzion and Randall L. Pouwels, eds., *The History of Islam in Africa* (Athens, Ohio: Ohio University Press, 2000).

Swahili Coast

Area varying from 12 miles (20 km) to 200 miles (320 km) wide and stretching some 1,800 miles (2,897 km) along the East African coast from southern SOMALIA to northern MOZAMBIQUE; also includes offshore islands and those in the Indian Ocean such as ZANZIBAR and the COMOROS.

The name *Swahili,* derived from the Arabic *sahel,* for "coast," means "people of the coast." It is an apt description, as the Swahili are a varied and scattered people who live in the coastal regions of East Africa. They are united by a common LANGUAGE, KISWAHILI, and by a common RELIGION, since most Swahili practice Islam. Historically, the Swahili were merchants and traders, though their influence in these areas declined as the colonial powers usurped control of commerce. Many Swahili have at one time or another asserted an Arab ancestry. This was probably done to gain the benefits of preferential treatment toward Arabs that was common during COLONIAL RULE or to distinguish themselves from their slaves. Despite these claims, historical and archaeological evidence shows that the Swahili are African in origin.

Long involved with the TRADE AND COMMERCE of the Indian Ocean, by the 1850s the Swahili coast was controlled by the Omani Sultanate. In fact, by 1840 the Omani Sultan Sayyid Said (1791–1856), realizing the vast economic potential of the lands, had completed the move of his capital to the island of Zanzibar. From there he solidified control over key coastal port towns such as MOGADISHU, MOMBASA, and BAGAMOYO, which enabled him to expand into the interior. The booming trading activity along the Swahili Coast made Zanzibar extremely wealthy. But a large portion of this trade was in captives, evidenced by the success of the infamous TIPPU TIP (c. 1830–1905).

The continuing SLAVE TRADE was increasingly untenable to the British, who in 1873 pressured the sultanate to abolish the slave trade. Weakened by declining income, a subsequent loss of control over the mainland merchant and planter communities, and growing European pressure, the sultanate of Zanzibar gradually ceded most of its territory and influence to the colonial powers as the 19th century came to an end. The Anglo-German agreement of 1886 divided the sultanate's mainland territory between GERMAN EAST AFRICA (later TANGANYIKA) and what would later become BRITISH EAST AFRICA (now KENYA). In 1889 Mogadishu and neighboring areas became a part of ITALIAN SOMALILAND. In 1890 Zanzibar itself became a British PROTECTORATE. Germany later ceded its territory along the Swahili coast after defeat in World War I (1914–18), with Britain given a League of Nations MANDATE to govern the area of Tanganyika (now part of TANZANIA).

The division of the Swahili Coast among the various colonial powers led to a final demise of the city-states that had characterized the region. Moreover, the subsequent linking of the coast to the individual colonies on the interior disrupted the Indian Ocean commercial orientation of the coastal civilization. During the colonial period the Swahili Coast's central role in trade with the interior began to decline, as advances in shipping diminished the need for the Swahili-controlled ocean trade routes. Cash crop AGRICULTURE became increasingly important throughout the region as a means for the colonial powers to tax the African population, who at the time were mainly employed as farmers. At the time of independence in the 1960s, political and economic control was transferred from the colonial authorities to elites drawn from people of the interior and not the coast. While Kiswahili had become a national language in Kenya and Tanzania, it was because it was a politically neutral language. This in turn reflected the demographic and political marginality of the coast and its peoples in the new nations.

See also: BUSAIDI (Vols. III, IV); COLONIALISM, INFLUENCE OF (Vol. IV); LEAGUE OF NATIONS AND AFRICA (Vol. IV); SAYYID SAID (Vol. III); SLAVE TRADE ON THE SWAHILI COAST (Vol. III); SWAHILI COAST (Vols. II, III).

Further reading: Jonathon Glassman, *Feasts and Riot: Revelry, Rebellion, and Popular Consciousness on the Swahili Coast, 1856–1888* (Portsmouth, N.H.: Heinemann, 1995); Mark Horton and John Middleton, *The Swahili: The Social Landscape of a Mercantile Society* (Malden, Mass.: Blackwell Publishers, 2000); Chapurukha Makohkha Kusimba, *The Rise and Fall of Swahili States* (Walnut Creek, Calif.: AltaMira Press, 1999).

Swaziland

Mountainous country that covers approximately 6,700 square miles (17,400 sq km) in southeastern Africa and is bordered by SOUTH AFRICA and MOZAMBIQUE.

The origins of present-day Swaziland date to the ZULU Mfecane of the early 1800s, which forced the Ngwane, under king Sobhuza I (c. 1795–1836), to move northward into what became Swaziland. Under Sobhuza's son, Mswati II (1820–1868), the Swazi, as they came to be called, established a stable kingdom.

Swaziland derives its name from Mswati II (also spelled Mswazi), who was called the Swazi's greatest fighting king.

By 1860 the Swazi borders reached well beyond those of the present-day nation. Mswati, in contrast to other African leaders of his time, avoided war with whites, but he sought British assistance against Zulu raids. A steady stream of European SETTLERS also entered Swaziland seeking concessions for rights to land and minerals. By 1890 the entirety of Swaziland was tied up in concessions, and the Swazi had effectively lost their independence.

The Swazi also became embroiled in the bitter struggle between the BOERS and British settlers. The Boers were seeking access to the sea, which could be achieved through Swaziland, while the British wanted to deny them such access. In 1893 Britain and the Boer South African Republic (SAR) agreed over vigorous Swazi protests that the SAR should administer all of Swaziland. However, following the ANGLO-BOER WAR (1899–1902), a much smaller Swaziland fell under British control, and beginning in 1906 the British High Commissioner to South Africa administered Swaziland, as well as BASUTOLAND and BECHUANALAND.

When the UNION OF SOUTH AFRICA was formed, in 1910, it appeared that Swaziland, along with Basutoland and Bechuanaland, would be incorporated into the new union. However, despite South Africa's requests, the British refused to transfer the colony to the union, a position that later solidified as South Africa instituted APARTHEID following its 1948 elections. Furthermore, the Swazi political system remained basically intact because it had never been defeated militarily. Under King Sobhuza II (1899–1982), who ascended the throne in 1921, the monarchy continued to exercise considerable authority. Sobhuza also sought to regain land lost through the earlier concessions, but much of the economy remained in white hands. When Swaziland became fully independent in 1968, it did so as an absolute monarchy in modern guise.

See also: AFRIKANER REPUBLICS (Vol. IV); COLONIALISM, INFLUENCE OF (Vol. IV); COLONIAL RULE (Vol. IV); ENGLAND AND AFRICA (Vols. III, IV, V); MFECANE (Vol. III); SWAZILAND (Vols. I, II, III, V).

Further reading: Richard P. Stevens, *Lesotho, Botswana, and Swaziland: The Former High Commission Territories in Southern Africa* (New York: Praeger, 1967).

Syad, William J. F. (1930–1988) *Somali statesman and poet*

Born in FRENCH SOMALILAND (today's DJIBOUTI), Syad studied at the Université de Paris, Sorbonne, France. His subsequent writings made him a leading proponent of a united SOMALIA free of both French and Italian rule. Because of these activities he ultimately was forced into exile. From 1955 to 1960 he worked for the official RADIO station of Djibouti. With the founding of a united and independent Somalia in 1960, Syad became the nation's first head of the Department of Tourism and Culture at the Ministry of Information. In the years that followed, Syad continued in government service, both at home and abroad. Meanwhile, his literary voice grew, and he produced plays and wrote four volumes of poetry. In all of these works he sought to blend Islamic and Western thought, ultimately leaving an indelible humanist mark on African literature.

See also: LITERATURE IN COLONIAL AFRICA (Vol. IV).

T

al-Tahtawi, Rifaah Rafi (Rifaa Rafé al-Tahtawi)
(1801–1873) *Egyptian scholar and educational pioneer*

Born to an aristocratic family in Tahta, upper EGYPT, Tahtawi proved himself a budding intellectual at an early age, memorizing the Quran and attending the renowned al-Azhar University at the age of 16. There he studied under Sheik Hassan Mohammed al-Attar, who believed Muslim countries could improve themselves through the study and utilization of Western SCIENCE, MEDICINE, and pedagogical methods. Tahtawi graduated in 1823 and then served as a teacher at al-Azhar until 1825. He was then appointed as the imam, or religious head, of an educational mission to Paris, where he learned French and studied translation. By 1830 he had translated 12 French works from various disciplines and produced a book entitled *A Paris Profile.*

In 1831 Tahtawi returned to Egypt and began work as a translator at the Egyptian Medicine School and later, in 1833, at the Artillery School, where he translated engineering and military texts. In 1835 he founded the Al-Alsun Translation School, which ultimately became a university. Realizing that the preservation of the past was essential to establishing a national identity, Tahtawi formulated a plan in 1835 to preserve Egypt's many ancient artifacts. Individuals who found artifacts would turn them over to Tahtawi to be added to the collection at Al-Alsun. Its courtyard gradually became the precursor to Egypt's first antiquities museum.

Continuing his efforts in translation, in 1841 Tahtawi founded the Translation Department, which focused on translations in the areas of medicine, math, social science, physics, and Turkish texts. Tahtawi was at his most productive during the reign of Khedive ISMAIL (1830–1895), working diligently as a member of Ismail's Schools Department and later as head of the National Bureau Council, where he oversaw the teaching of Arabic in Egypt.

It was during this time as well that Tahtawi made his most significant advances in pioneering women's EDUCATION. As early as 1836 Tahtawi had been gathering support for women's education, before then nonexistent in institutional form, among the Egyptian upper class. During the 1860s Khedive Ismail enlisted Tahtawi to prepare the public to accept the institutional education of women. This led, in 1872, to the publication of his *Honest Guide,* which outlined the benefits of women's education. Arguing that the oppression of Egyptian women arose from moral faults within the Muslim community, he encouraged a return to what he saw as the true meaning of Islam. In 1873, with the help of Ismail's wife Tchesme Afit Hanim, the Sufiyya School opened as the first state school for girls in Egypt. That same year Tahtawi died, leaving a legacy of both preserving Egypt's past and building its future.

Tahtawi is also known as the "father of Egyptian journalism." He founded Egypt's first newspaper, *Al-Waqal al-Misrea.*

See also: ISLAMIC CENTERS OF LEARNING (Vol. II); ISLAM, INFLUENCE OF (Vols. III, IV, V); NEWSPAPERS (Vol. IV); WOMEN IN COLONIAL AFRICA (Vol. IV).

Tambo, Oliver (1917–1993) *South African anti-apartheid activist and African National Congress leader*

Oliver Reginald Tambo was born in Bizana, in East Mpondoland of the Eastern Cape Province, SOUTH AFRICA. He attended FORT HARE COLLEGE, where, in the late 1930s, he first became acquainted with his life-long friend, Nelson MANDELA (1918–   ). Graduating with a bachelor's degree in 1941, he continued on at Fort Hare to pursue an honors degree in education, simultaneously becoming active in the politics of the national liberation movement. In 1942 Tambo was expelled—along with Mandela—for organizing a student boycott in reaction to the school's refusal to allow a democratically chosen student council. Afterward, Tambo began teaching in JOHANNESBURG, a career he stuck with until the late 1940s. He began studying law in 1948 and, with Mandela as his partner, established the first black law practice in South Africa, in 1952.

After joining the AFRICAN NATIONAL CONGRESS (ANC) in the early 1940s, Tambo, along with other young ANC members including Mandela, Walter SISULU (1912–2003), and Anton Lembede (1913–1947), founded the ANC Youth League. This organization radicalized the ANC and made it more responsive to the concerns of ordinary Africans. In 1949 Tambo was elected to the ANC national executive committee, proving instrumental in the adoption of the Program of Action, an agenda for ANC-led, mass-based resistance to APARTHEID. This new populist direction in ANC policy led to the Defiance Campaign of 1952, during which protesters courted arrest by defying what they viewed as unjust and oppressive laws.

Tambo was banned and arrested for high treason in 1956, although he was released the following year. He progressed up the organizational ladder of the ANC, occupying the position of ANC secretary-general between 1954 and 1958, before becoming deputy president in 1958. In the latter half of the 1950s, when a faction within the ANC moved toward an Africanist approach that would exclude all non-African participation in the organization, Tambo insisted on keeping the organization multiracial. As a result, in 1959, activist Robert SOBUKWE (1924–1978) established a breakaway faction and named it the PAN-AFRICANIST CONGRESS (PAC). The subsequent Sharpeville crisis of 1960, sparked by PAC anti-pass-law demonstrations, led the government to declare a state of emergency. That same year, fearing the arrest and detention of its leadership, the ANC selected Tambo to go into exile to provide leadership from abroad.

See also: TAMBO, OLIVER (Vol. V).

Tanganyika

During the colonial era, the name of the mainland portion of present-day TANZANIA. In the latter half of the 1800s, BUSAIDI rulers of ZANZIBAR claimed sovereignty over much of the coastal regions of East Africa. By 1886, however, German adventurers had established treaties with local rulers in Tanganyika, making the territory part of the colony of GERMAN EAST AFRICA. During World War I (1914–18) British forces occupied Tanganyika and, following Germany's defeat, the area was given to Britain. In 1919 British authority over the colony was confirmed under the MANDATE system of the League of Nations. The British colonial administration thus answered to the League of Nations and its successor, the United Nations (UN), which, in 1946, made Tanganyika a UN TRUST TERRITORY, also under British administration.

Following World War II (1939–45) the nationalist Tanganyikan African National Union (TANU) worked to terminate British colonial authority over the country. The leader of TANU, Julius NYERERE (1922–1999), asserted the primacy of African interests at the international level when, in 1955 and again in 1956, he pleaded Tanganyika's case before the United Nations, in New York. The United Nations finally pressured Britain to allow elections and establish a representative government. TANU won national elections in 1958 and 1959, and in 1961 Tanganyika became independent, with Nyerere as the first president.

In 1964, a year after a revolution in Zanzibar overthrew the Busaidi sultan, Tanganyika and Zanzibar merged to form the United Republic of Tanganyika and Zanzibar. Six months later the name was changed to Tanzania.

See also: COLONIAL RULE (Vol. IV); ENGLAND AND AFRICA (Vol. IV); GERMANY AND AFRICA (Vol. IV); LEAGUE OF NATIONS AND AFRICA (Vol. IV); UNITED NATIONS AND AFRICA (Vols. IV, V).

Further reading: Peter A. Dumbuya, *Tanganyika Under International Mandate, 1919–1946* (Lanham, Md.: University Press of America, 1995).

Tani, Maame Harris "Grace" (c. 1880–1958) *Cofounder of the Twelve Apostles Church, in Ghana*

Born in a coastal fishing village in the southwestern part of present-day GHANA, Tani gained a reputation as a healer in an area where hospitals were not common. In 1914 the charismatic prophet William Wade HARRIS (c. 1850–1929) baptized her when he was passing through her region (which, by that time, was the British GOLD COAST COLONY). Tani joined Harris's mission and, for a brief time, was married to him. However, when he returned to IVORY COAST, she remained in her home region to carry on his work.

Along with another of Harris's baptized converts, Papa Kwesi "John" Nackabah (c. 1870–1947), Tani founded the Twelve Apostles Church, which became the largest independent church in southern Ghana. As the two "elders" of the church, Tani and Nackabah faced opposition from colonial officials, MISSIONARIES, and even some African leaders. They were able to overcome this opposition, however, by recognizing the importance of existing indigenous religious beliefs during the challenging times of the colonial era.

See also: CHRISTIANITY, INFLUENCE OF (Vols. IV, V); COLONIAL RULE (Vol. IV); COLONIALISM, INFLUENCE OF (Vol. IV); PROPHETS AND PROPHETIC MOVEMENTS (Vols. IV, V); RELIGION (Vols. III, IV, V).

Tanzania Modern East African country made up of the former colonial territory of TANGANYIKA and the island of ZANZIBAR. Tanzania, which also includes Pemba and Mafia islands, covers approximately 342,100 square miles (886,000 sq km). It is bordered by UGANDA and KENYA to the north, MOZAMBIQUE, MALAWI (formerly NYASALAND), and ZAMBIA (formerly NORTHERN RHODESIA) to the south, and RWANDA and BURUNDI to the west. Also to the west is Lake Tanganyika, which lies between Tanzania and the Democratic Republic of the CONGO.

By the 19th century East African ports such as Tanga and BAGAMOYO were busy trading centers for East Africa's Arab merchants, who dealt in human captives and luxury items, including ivory. In the 1860s the coastal city of DAR ES SALAAM, the present-day capital of Tanzania, began to grow in importance as well.

Ngoni groups, meanwhile, conquered inland areas in southern Tanzania. About the same time, NYAMWEZI groups, many managing to avoid Ngoni conquest, expanded their influence throughout central Tanzania south of Lake Victoria. The Nyamwezi kingdom, led by MIRAMBO (c. 1840–1884), grew especially powerful by controlling the bustling trade routes that led from the interior to the trade ports along East Africa's SWAHILI COAST.

At the outset of the era of European COLONIAL CONQUEST in the 19th century, Britain began developing ties with the Arab BUSAIDI sultans, who, after 1840, used Zanzibar as the administrative center of a vast, coastal trading empire that stretched as far north as present-day SOMALIA. On the mainland, however, the German East Africa Company struck treaties with local rulers allowing them to claim Tanganyika, the territory between British Kenya and Portuguese Mozambique.

Tanzania during the Colonial Era: Tanganyika and Zanzibar In 1890, as a result of the agreements forged at the BERLIN CONFERENCE (1884–85), Germany claimed Tanganyika as a PROTECTORATE and Britain claimed Zanzibar. The German colonial administration used force to recruit African LABOR to produce tobacco, sisal, COFFEE, and COTTON for export. Britain, meanwhile, went about spreading its influence in other areas and allowed the Busaidi sultans to continue their nominal rule on Zanzibar.

Germany's colonial claims also included RUANDA-URUNDI, regions that would become the independent nations of Rwanda and Burundi in 1962.

Widespread resistance to German COLONIAL RULE in Tanganyika culminated in the MAJI-MAJI REBELLION of 1905–06. During the uprising as many as 200,000 Africans, many of them Ngoni, died in fighting and subsequent hardship. After crushing the insurgency, Germany governed its East African colony with increasing harshness. Before long, however, Germany was forced to cede its African colonies, a consequence of its defeat in World War I (1914–18). According to a League of Nations MANDATE Tanganyika was entrusted, in 1919, to Britain, which also ruled Kenya to the north. The British colonial administration answered to the League of Nations and its successor, the United Nations (UN), which, in 1946, made Tanganyika a UN TRUST TERRITORY also under British administration.

After World War II (1939–45) African NATIONALIST AND INDEPENDENCE MOVEMENTS called for the end of colonial rule throughout the continent. In 1954 former schoolteacher Julius NYERERE (1922–1999) helped organize the Tanganyikan African National Union (TANU), the first African political organization in Tanganyika. Using international diplomacy, Nyerere and TANU called upon the United Nations to pressure Britain to establish a representative government. In 1958 Tanganyika finally held national elections, in which TANU won the majority of the seats. In 1960 Britain granted Tanganyika limited autonomy, and the following year, when the country was given its independence, Nyerere became prime minister. He became Tanganyika's first president when the country became a republic, in 1962.

The road to independence was vastly different on the island of Zanzibar, where Britain's colonial policy of indirect rule left the Arab sultanate intact. In 1963 Britain granted Zanzibar its independence, reinstating the sultanate in the form of a constitutional monarchy. The African-majority population on the island resented the continuation of Arab rule, however, and within a year, a bloody revolt overturned the sultanate. By the end of 1964 Zanzibar joined with Tanganyika to form the United Republic of Tanganyika and Zanzibar, with Nyerere its president and Abeid Awani Karume (1905–1972) of Zanzibar the vice president. Six months later the name of the union was changed to Tanzania.

In northern Tanganyika (now Tanzania), Lumbwa men pose with a truck that accompanied them on a lion hunt in 1927. © *New York Times*

See also: AFRO-SHIRAZI PARTY (Vol. V); ENGLAND AND AFRICA (Vol. IV); GERMANY AND AFRICA (Vol. IV); TANZANIA (Vols. I, II, III, V); UNITED NATIONS AND AFRICA (Vol. IV).

Further reading: Helge Kjekshus, *Ecology Control & Economic Development in East African History: The Case of Tanganyika 1850–1950* (Athens, Ohio: Ohio University Press, 1996).

taxation, colonial Colonial governments levied taxes for the purposes of both meeting the costs of administration and for generating needed sources of LABOR. Africans had long been accustomed to paying different types of taxes, depending on what type of state they lived in and what the state needed in terms of revenue. Usually, though, the taxes were paid in kind or through services, since MONEY AND CURRENCY were more associated with TRADE AND COMMERCE than with the necessities of everyday life. Colonial governments introduced new forms of taxation along with the other innovations and changes they brought to African life. These systems of taxation often led to the monetization of the ECONOMY and the introduction of government-issued coins and bank notes with set values that were determined by the colonial governments.

Colonial taxation basically had two purposes. The first was to defray the high cost of administering the African colonies. Taxpayers in Europe generally opposed paying taxes to fund the colonies, and it was the taxpayers who elected the colonial governments. Those in government, therefore, had little choice but to shift the tax burden to their colonial subjects, who under the circumstances of COLONIAL RULE did not have a voice in their governments.

The imposition of taxation often sparked revolts against the colonial authorities, especially early on in the colonial era. In GERMAN EAST AFRICA, for example, the administration found itself short of both administrative personnel and funds. In 1897 it imposed a hut tax, which was enforced, sometimes using harsh violence, through local officials. This conduct led to resentment and ultimately fuelled the MAJI-MAJI REBELLION (1905–06). Similarly, the British imposition of a five-shilling hut tax in SIERRA LEONE, in 1898, provoked the Temne chief Bai Bureh (d. 1908) to lead a revolt that became known as the Hut Tax War. Even as the colonial period entered its more mature stage and methods of collecting taxes had been regularized, the imposition of a tax could provoke unrest, as happened in NIGERIA with the ABA WOMEN'S REVOLT (1929–30). Also, the NATIONAL CONGRESS OF BRITISH WEST AFRICA made taxation without representation one of their main grievances in their effort to reform colonial rule.

Another major reason that colonial officials imposed taxes was to generate LABOR for the colonial economy. Colonial officials recognized that many colonial enterprises were economically marginal to the point that they could not afford to pay living wages. As a result, rather than requiring employers to pay wages that would attract labor, administrations resorted to various taxing schemes. Levying taxes for labor purposes was particularly prevalent in southern Africa, where white commercial farmers needed workers for their large farms and the MINING industry needed large numbers of miners. By 1899, for example, the GOLD mines on South Africa's WITWATERSRAND employed 100,000 Africans. One of the reasons the colonial governments of the region imposed poll taxes, which every male over the age of 18 had to pay, was to force them into the wage-labor force.

Throughout their West African colonies, France imposed new taxes that needed to be paid in French currency. This required Africans to earn hard currency either by producing CASH CROPS for sale or by engaging in wage labor on plantations or in the urban areas. The French also imposed a policy of forced labor in order to generate workers for projects such as the building of roads, railroads, and ports.

The manner and purpose of colonial taxation reveals just how authoritarian colonial governments truly were. They did not have to respond to the people living in their colonies because they were subjects and not citizens. The arbitrary nature of colonial taxation was one of the factors that helped fuel the rise of African NATIONALISM AND INDEPENDENCE MOVEMENTS that ultimately brought an end to colonial rule.

See also: COLONIALISM, INFLUENCE OF (Vol. IV); RESISTANCE AND REBELLION (Vol. IV).

Téwodros II (Theodore II, Kassa, Lij Kassa)
(1820–1868) *Ethiopian emperor*

Born in 1820 and given the name Kassa, or Lij Kassa, the future emperor came from a family that had traditionally ruled the Qwara district of northwestern ETHIOPIA, near the Sudanese border. He was raised by his half-brother, Kinfu (d. 1839), who was one of the many feudal warlords who held sway in Ethiopia at the time. Following Kinfu's death, Kassa became a *shifta,* a warrior who refused to acknowledge the sovereignty of any particular feudal lord.

A fierce leader and brilliant strategist, Kassa soon attracted a following, which he led to a number of military successes in the late 1840s. By 1852 he had embarked on a campaign of conquest that, within three years, left him in control of all of Ethiopia. On February 11, 1855, he had himself crowned and anointed *negus nagast* (king of kings), taking the name Téwodros II after a legendary figure Ethiopians believed would someday bring peace and prosperity to the land.

As insightful as he was ruthless, Téwodros believed that only by modernizing would Ethiopia be able to restore the greatness it had realized in its past. He knew, however, that modernization was not possible without first putting an end to the feudal system that had divided the country for so long. To centralize authority and break the power of the warlords, he set up a system of governors and judges, all under his direct authority. He also established a national army that he hoped would replace the independent armies of the feudal lords. He even attempted to reform the Ethiopian Church, whose vast, tax-exempt holdings and incessant doctrinal rivalries, he believed, were a primary obstacle to modernization.

At the same time that he attempted to carry out this process of unification and centralization, Téwodros brought in European technicians, engineers, and teachers to modernize the nation. Soon, his foreign advisors were at work constructing bridges and roads and helping Ethiopians develop their own manufacturing capabilities.

Many in Ethiopia opposed Téwodros's actions. His attempts to transform the Ethiopian Church—especially to find a way to tax its holdings—angered not only religious officials but also conservative-minded farmers and peasants. Similarly, his new administrative and judicial systems, as well as his attempt to do away with private armies, cost him the support of the warlords. As a result he spent much of his time—and treasure—putting down rebellions on the part of warlords who refused to give up their traditional power. As his army grew to a force 50,000 full-time soldiers, it was not long before Ethiopia's peasants were starving in order to feed and clothe the emperor's troops.

By the 1860s Téwodros's reforms had reduced Ethiopia to poverty and chaos, and the warlords were more in control than ever. Fearing not only his own people but also invasions by the Egyptians and the Ottoman Turks, Téwodros appealed to Britain's Queen Victoria (1819–1901) for help. When his appeal went unanswered, the prickly emperor seized diplomats and other foreign nationals, taking them, along with the last remnant of his army, to his mountain fortress at Magdala. Eventually Britain sent a substantial force to Ethiopia to free the captives, launching an attack on Magdala on August 10, 1868. The specific accounts vary, especially as to whether or not Téwodros eventually released the captives or not. The final result, however, was that Téwodros's forces were easily defeated, and the emperor killed himself rather than surrender to the foreign invaders. The British then withdrew.

In the aftermath of Téwodros's defeat, a period of civil war engulfed Ethiopia until Kassa Mercha was able to defeat the other warlords and become the Emperor YOHANNES IV (1831–1889).

See also: CHRISTIANITY, INFLUENCE OF (Vols. II, III, IV, V); ENGLAND AND AFRICA (Vol. IV); ETHIOPIAN ORTHODOX CHURCH (Vol. IV); OTTOMAN EMPIRE AND AFRICA (Vol. IV).

Further reading: Richard K. P. Pankhurst, *A Social History of Ethiopia: The Northern and Central Highlands from Early Medieval Times to the Rise of Emperor Tewodros II* (Trenton, N.J.: Red Sea Press, 1993).

Things Fall Apart (1958) First novel written by the Nigerian writer Chinua ACHEBE (1930–). *Things Fall Apart* became one of the most widely read English LANGUAGE novels of the 20th century. The book's title comes from a line in the poem "Second Coming" by the Anglo-Irish poet William Butler Yeats (1865–1939) in which the poet apprehensively describes the end of European civilization after World War I (1914–18). In the novel, Achebe portrays the end of the traditional IGBO world in NIGERIA at the start of the 20th century. He describes the subtle ways through which British colonialism and Christianity undermined traditional African cultural and social values. The novel's hero, Okonkwo, grew up in a society that possessed a strong sense of communal purpose and deep religious beliefs. It also had a system of social hierarchy in which every stratum of society knew its place and purpose. In the course of the novel, Achebe shows how the religious and cultural values that the British impose on the Igbo disrupted the social hierarchy and subverted their traditional beliefs. Okonkwo's refusal to adjust to the ways of the outsiders pits him against his fellow Igbo and ultimately leads to his suicide.

Critics have noted that Achebe's novel is both an attempt to present the values of traditional Igbo culture to the outside world and a reminder to his own people that their traditional culture is a sustaining source.

See also: LITERATURE IN COLONIAL AFRICA (Vols. IV); LITERATURE IN MODERN AFRICA (Vol. V).

Further reading: Simon Gikandi, *Reading Chinua Achebe: Language & Ideology in Fiction* (London: James Currey, 1991).

Thuku, Harry (1895–1970) *Kikuyu political leader*

Born in Kiambu, KENYA, to a powerful KIKUYU family, Thuku received his education in missionary schools and went on to become a clerk for the colonial treasury in NAIROBI. Thuku's position allowed him to move to the forefront of the developing nationalist movements among Africans in Nairobi. Nairobi's growth from a shantytown to the capital of BRITISH EAST AFRICA, in 1906, had brought European SETTLERS into conflict with the indigenous Kikuyu, who suffered from the loss of their lands as well as from discriminatory taxation and LABOR policies. In response, in 1921, Thuku and fellow Kikuyu Jesse Kariuki founded the East African Association, a movement among Nairobi youths of various ethnic backgrounds. In that same year Thuku also founded the Young Kikuyu Association. Through these organizations, Thuku gave voice to a wide range of African grievances against the colonial government, challenging the overall white rule, the low-paying labor policy, the head tax, and the theft of land by white settlers. Of particular issue was the imposition of the *kipande,* a required identification card distributed by the colonial government to all Africans.

Within a year Thuku's movements were gaining significant support both within Nairobi and in surrounding areas. In 1922 colonial authorities arrested Thuku, an act that led to a massive protest and the death of over 20 Africans, who were killed when fired upon by colonial police. Thuku was forced into exile in Kismayu, SOMALIA, and the East African Association fell apart. While in exile Thuku took up farming. He later became a successful COFFEE farmer back in Kenya.

In 1928, during Thuku's absence, the Young Kikuyu Association reformed as the Kikuyu Central Association (KCA), for which Thuku remained an inspirational leader. Upon his return, in 1931, Thuku's views had become too moderate for the KCA's leadership. Because of this Thuku split from the group, in 1935, to form the Kikuyu Provincial Association. In 1944 he joined the Kenya African Union (KAU), and in 1960 he became a member of the Kenya African National Union (KANU), led by former KCA general secretary and future president of Kenya Jomo KENYATTA (c. 1891–1978). These organizations evolved from one another and stemmed from Thuku's Young Kikuyu Association. In 1963 the nationalist movement Thuku helped initiate culminated with Kenya's independence.

See also: COLONIAL RULE (Vol. IV); COLONIALISM, INFLUENCE OF (Vol. IV); ENGLAND AND AFRICA (Vols. III, IV, V); NATIONALISM AND INDEPENDENCE MOVEMENTS (Vol. IV).

Further reading: Kenneth King, ed., *Harry Thuku: An Autobiography* (Nairobi: Oxford Univeristy Press, 1970).

Tigray (Tigrai) Province in the northeastern region of ETHIOPIA and the neighboring region of southern ERITREA inhabited by Tigrinya-speaking people, who are also called the Tigray. The site of the ancient kingdom of Aksum and the 1896 Battle of ADOWA, Tigray had been largely autonomous from the greater Ethiopian state until Emperor TÉWODROS II (1820–1868) defeated its governor and incorporated it as a province in his newly reconstituted Ethiopian state. In the aftermath of Téwodros's death, in

1868, Tigray again reasserted its autonomy from the central state. Its king, Kassa Mercha, led Tigray to defeat rival Ethiopian states, and in 1872 he crowned himself *negus nagast* (king of kings, or emperor) of Ethiopia. He took the name YOHANNES IV (1831–1889). Yohannes IV made his capital the Tigrayan city of Mekele, in the Ethiopian highlands. The key to his power was his army, which he had managed to equip with modern weapons, including machine guns and mortars purchased from European allies, primarily Britain. Yohannes IV led his forces to victory over Egyptian forces in 1875 and again in 1876. His bold leadership raised his profile and kept northern Ethiopia peaceful until the late 1880s, when the MAHDIYYA invaded from the Sudan, to the west. In March 1889 Yohannes IV led the Tigrayan army to victory over the Mahdiyya, at Metema, but he died from wounds suffered in battle.

The name of this province in northern Ethiopia is sometimes spelled Tigre or Tigré, which can cause confusion. The people of Tigray speak Tigrinya, a LANGUAGE based on ancient Ge'ez. In Eritrea, the people of Tigray are also known as the Tigrinya. The Tigray are descended from the Aksumites who once ruled much of Ethiopia. Confusion arises, however, because areas in Eritrea and the Republic of the SUDAN to the north of Tigray province are inhabited by a related—but culturally distinct—ethnic group called the *Tigre.* These people speak a language called *Tigré,* also based on Ge'ez. Although related, the languages spoken by the mostly Christian Tigray and the predominantly Muslim Tigre are mutually unintelligible. The group that rebelled against Ethiopian rule in the 1960s was made up of Tigrinya-speaking people from the Tigray ethnic group.

The death of Yohannes IV was followed by a war of succession among different Tigrayan contenders. The ensuing confusion allowed MENELIK II (1845–1912), the powerful king of SHOA, a major Amharic-speaking province to the south, to seize the throne and become Ethiopia's emperor. Tigray was thrown into chaos again late in 1895, when Italian imperialist forces invaded the region from the Red Sea. Until that time, Ras Mengesha (d. 1906), the Tigray governor, had refused to recognize Menelik as emperor. However, overwhelmed by the invasion, Mengesha bowed to Menelik's authority and asked for military support from Ethiopia's central government. The following year Menelik's Ethiopian army, which included thousands of Tigrayan soldiers, routed the Italian

forces at the Battle of Adowa. The victory preserved Ethiopia's independence from European COLONIAL RULE for another four decades as well as doing much to restore Tigray's pride. Over the next few years, Ras Mengesha resumed his insubordination until Menelik finally had him arrested. In 1906 Mengesha died while under house arrest, leaving no Tigrayan claimant to the Ethiopian throne when Menelik died, in 1912.

The Ethiopian throne remained thereafter in the hands of AMHARA, with the last emperor being HAILE SELASSIE (1892–1975). Known as Ras Tafari prior to his coronation as emperor, Haile Selassie was the regent from 1916 to 1930, prior to reigning in his own name from 1930 to 1974. In 1936, in the aftermath of yet another Italian invasion of Ethiopia, Haile Selassie fled to Britain. The five-year period of Italian occupation that followed was characterized by famine, war, humiliation, and discontent among Tigray's population.

During the Italian occupation of Ethiopia, many of Tigray's famed stelae, or ceremonial stone grave markers, were transported to Italy. One of the most impressive markers, dating back to the kingdom of Aksum (500 BCE–1000 CE), decorated Mussolini's Ministry for Africa, in Rome.

Most of Ethiopia rejoiced when, in 1941, British forces invaded Ethiopia to oust the Italians and help Haile Selassie reclaim his throne. The people of Tigray, however, were not entirely pleased. First, they still felt that the rightful successor to the throne after Yohannes IV should have been from Tigray. Second, they expected their emperor to be a fierce warrior in the mold of Yohannes IV and, despite Haile Selassie's earlier valor on the battlefield, they resented his flight in the face of the Italian invasion. In response to the emperor's return, they organized an uprising known as the Weyane. When the emperor asked Britain to help him suppress the Tigrayan rebels, the British obliged, launching air strikes on Tigrayan positions. The city of Makele, the center of Tigray resistance, fell to the combined Ethiopian-British forces in October 1943, and imperial order was restored to the province.

After the overthrow of Haile Selassie, in 1974, a Tigrayan independence movement, the Tigray People's Liberation Front (TPLF), emerged. It first gained control of Tigray, reasserting its autonomy from the government in ADDIS ABABA. Then, in alliance with the Eritrea People's Liberation Front, the TPLF succeeded, in 1991, in overthrowing Mengistu Haile Mariam (c. 1937–) and installing one of its founders, Meles Zenawi (1955–) as the head of the government.

The vicious suppression of the Weyane by the Ethiopian emperor was not easily forgotten, but Haile Selassie wisely arranged a marriage between his granddaughter, Aida Desta (1927–   ), and Tigray's governor, Ras Mengesha Seyoum, the grandson of Yohannes IV. With Tigrayans thus pacified, Haile Selassie reascended the throne in a traditional ceremony in Aksum that consecrated the legitimacy of new Ethiopian emperors. However, the discontent in Tigray with Amhara dominance, emanating from Menelik's national capital of Addis Ababa, never fully disappeared.

See also: ETHNICITY AND IDENTITY (Vol. V); ITALY AND AFRICA (Vol. IV); MELES ZENAWI (Vol. V); TIGRAY (Vols. I, V); TIGRE (Vol. I); TIGRINYA (Vol. I).

Timbuktu (Timbuctoo) City in present-day northern Republic of MALI, located near the Niger River on the southern border of the Sahara desert, known for its legendary wealth as a trade center. Founded in 12th century, Timbuktu had a long history as an important center at the intersection of trans-Saharan and Sudanic West African trade routes. Timbuktu also possessed a long-standing reputation as a center for Islamic learning that began with the construction of the Great Mosque (Djinguereger), in the 14th century. Between the 15th and 19th centuries, political control of the city changed hands many times. Although Timbuktu's significance as a great trading center had declined somewhat, the city remained strategically important. In 1844 the city revolted against the Islamic state of Masina after the death of Macina's founder, AHMADU SÉKU (d. 1844). The Muslim conqueror UMAR TAL (1794–1864), however, was able to bring Timbuktu somewhat within the orbit of his TUKULOR EMPIRE after midcentury.

France gained control of Timbuktu, in 1894, as part of its COLONIAL CONQUEST of what became FRENCH WEST AFRICA. At the time the Islamic scholarly community consisted of approximately 25 famous scholars who were still residing in the city. The French attempted to restore Timbuktu under their COLONIAL RULE, but they did not make the necessary investments in road and rail connections with other cities and regions of Mali and neighboring countries. It thus remained difficult to reach, with the Niger River providing the best means of TRANSPORTATION. Camel caravans were still setting out from the city across the Sahara late into the 20th century. With approximately 6,600 inhabitants, the city became part of the Republic of Mali when the country gained independence, in 1960.

See also: FRANCE AND AFRICA (Vols. III, IV, V); ISLAM, CENTERS OF LEARNING (Vol. II); ISLAM, INFLUENCE OF (Vols. II, III, IV, V); MALI EMPIRE (Vol. II); NIGER RIVER (Vols. I, II); SAHARA (Vols. I, II); TIMBUKTU (Vols. II, III); TRANS-SAHARAN TRADE ROUTES (Vol. II); URBAN LIFE AND CULTURE (Vols. IV, V); URBANIZATION (Vols. IV, V).

Further reading: Elias N. Saad, *Social History of Timbuktu: The Role of Muslim Scholars and Notables, 1400–1900* (New York: Cambridge University Press, 1983).

Tinubu, Madame (1805–1887) *Influential trader and politician in southwestern Nigeria*

Madame Tinubu exemplifies the powerful role that women have played outside the home in many areas of West Africa. Born in the inland town ABEOKUTA, she rose to prominence as a merchant in the YORUBA-speaking region of southwestern NIGERIA, trading mainly between Abeokuta and the coastal port cities of Badagri and LAGOS. She lived in an era when African-European commercial relations were changing from the SLAVE TRADE to so-called legitimate commerce. The commodities of this trade were mostly CASH CROPS, such as COTTON and PALM OIL, which were exported as raw materials to rapidly industrializing Europe. For example, in 1856 alone, the Egba region centered on Abeokuta exported 15,000 tons of palm oil through Lagos.

In 1832 Tinubu married Adele (d. 1834) who had been, and in 1833 again became, the *olugun* (ruler) of Lagos. The Lagos throne was entering a very turbulent period, especially when British agents began inserting themselves in the succession process. When Adele died, his son Oluwole (d. 1841) assumed the throne. As a leading merchant and as the widow of Adele, Tinubu wielded considerable political power. Her influence was such that her biographer considered her a king-maker. Political power in Lagos, however, was slipping from local to British hands. Lagos soon had its own British consul, Benjamin Campbell, who in 1856 forced Olugun Docemo to expel Tinubu from Lagos. She then returned to Abeokuta, where she was prominent in commercial and political affairs.

In recognition of her role in the civic life of Abeokuta, Madame Tinubu was bestowed with the honorific title of *iyalode*, which is given only to the most powerful woman in a Yoruba community.

See also: COLONIAL CONQUEST (Vol. IV); ENGLAND AND AFRICA (Vols. III, IV, V); TRADE AND COMMERCE (Vol. IV); WOMEN IN COLONIAL AFRICA (Vol. IV).

Tippu Tip (Tipu Tib, Hamed bin Muhammed) (c. 1830–1905) *Builder of a major commercial empire in the East African interior*

Born Hamed bin Muhammed on the island of ZANZIBAR, Tippu Tip was the son of an African mother and a highly successful Afro-Arab merchant and plantation owner. By age 12 he was accompanying his father on trading ventures onto the mainland at a time of the rapid expansion of the SLAVE TRADE and IVORY TRADE. By 1850 Hamed, now known as Tippu Tip, was striking out to build his own fortune and independent base of power. He proved adept at combining the necessary commercial acumen, military skills, and leadership to become one of East Africa's leading Zanzibari traders. In the 1860s he pushed into present-day northeastern ZAMBIA and the eastern portion of the present-day Democratic Republic of the CONGO. By the early 1880s, utilizing both warfare and diplomacy, he was able to begin sending large caravans of human captives and ivory to the coast.

In 1882 Tippu Tip returned to Zanzibar, his first visit to the island in 12 years. As part of an effort to cement his claims over vast stretches of the interior, the ruler of Zanzibar, Sultan ibn Said BARGHASH (c. 1833–1888), appointed Tippu Tip governor for the eastern Congo region. The sultan's territorial ambitions, however, conflicted with increased European empire-building activities. In 1885 Germany began asserting its control over the cities of the SWAHILI COAST, its first step toward founding the colony of GERMAN EAST AFRICA. In the Congo, Belgium's King LEOPOLD II (1835–1909) was busy laying the foundations of the CONGO FREE STATE, which was not a colony but the personal possession of the king.

At first the Congo Free State's military forces were too weak to force a confrontation with Tippu Tip and his fellow Arabs. As a result he acted as an agent for King Leopold II for a few years. However, as the Congo Free State grew in strength, it no longer had need of its Arab allies. Consequently, when Tippu Tip left for Zanzibar in 1890, the Free State forced a military confrontation that led to war. By 1894 the Free State was in full control of the region.

In the later years of his life Tippu Tip wrote his autobiography, which was translated into English by W. H. Whitely in 1966. The book has since become a KISWAHILI literary classic.

See also: COLONIAL CONQUEST (Vol. IV); TRADE AND COMMERCE (Vol. IV).

Tirailleurs Sénégalais
Black, African-born troops serving in the French Army. In 1857 the governor general of FRENCH WEST AFRICA, Louis FAIDHERBE (1818–1889), faced a military manpower shortage due to the death of large numbers of his French-born soldiers from tropical diseases. Recognizing that Africans were seemingly more immune to these illnesses, Faidherbe decided to recruit Africans into a special French army unit to be used in the African service. Eventually known as the Tirailleurs Sénégalais, these troops went on to serve not only in Africa but throughout the French colonial empire and in Europe itself.

The French word *tirailleurs* can be translated as "riflemen." Although, as time went on, members of the Tirailleurs Sénégalais came from many different ethnic groups and places, the initial name Sénégalais remained the one most commonly used.

Though some of the early members of the Tirailleurs Sénégalais were recruits attracted by promises of good pay, uniforms, and booty, many were slaves purchased from African masters and trained to be soldiers. By the 1880s, however, the practice of purchasing slaves declined markedly, and the majority of the Tirailleurs were former prisoners of war, defeated soldiers who decided that serving with the victorious French forces was a better fate than the alternatives. Beginning with World War I (1914–18) and until the end of World War II (1939–45), the soldiers in the ranks were mostly conscripts. During the last 15 years of French COLONIAL RULE, however, they were volunteer, professional soldiers. In addition, although the higher-ranking positions in the units were invariably reserved for white Frenchmen, Africans eventually became accepted as both non-commissioned and lower-ranking commissioned officers. This ultimately led to enlistments by members of Africa's own ruling classes, who saw service in the army as respectable employment and even as a means of social advancement in lands now dominated by the French colonialists.

Although the soldiers of the Tirailleurs Sénégalaise came from many different ethnic groups, the majority were Bambara, with high numbers of Tukolor and MANDE speakers as well. There were so many Bambara, in fact, that the two languages used for commands in the units were pidgin French and Bombara, the Bambara tongue.

By the beginning of the 20th century, the Tirailleurs Sénégalaise had established a reputation as fierce and effective combat troops. After 1905 they began to be used outside of Africa. Because of this the established recruitment techniques were no longer supplying enough troops, and the French government had to find new ways to add to the force. As a result, by World War I conscription was used to fill the need for troops. The Tirailleurs Sénégalese ultimately played an important role in World War I, in which more than 30,000 African-born soldiers died on the battlefields of Europe in the service of France.

At the outset of World War II, some 75,000 African troops were stationed in France, with 15,000 or more becoming prisoners of war. Furthermore, the vast majority of troops in the Free French army of General Charles DE GAULLE (1890–1970) were African-born. In an ironic twist, more than half of the troops who landed in southern France to liberate that country in 1944 were African-born soldiers. In all, more than 200,000 served in the French army during the war. As military veterans, they often became active in NATIONALIST AND INDEPENDENCE MOVEMENTS because they were upset over the paltry veteran benefits they received for their wartime service.

This Tirailleur was awarded the Cross of Liberation by General Charles de Gaulle during ceremonies held in 1942 in Brazzaville, French Equatorial Africa. © *Free French Press/Office of War Information/Library of Congress*

After World War II the French reduced the size of the Tirailleurs Sénégalais to roughly 34,000 men. Africans were now serving in the middle ranks of commissioned officers. A majority of these soldiers were stationed outside French West Africa. They saw action in both ALGERIA and Indochina, and a number of them were among the French army that surrendered to the Viet Minh at Dien Bien Phu 1954. The Tirailleurs Sénégalais contingents from the various French West African colonies were to constitute the basis for the new national armies upon the breakup of French West Africa, in 1960.

See also: ARMIES, COLONIAL (Vol. IV); BAMBARA (Vols. I, II, III); COLONIALISM, INFLUENCE OF (Vol. IV); DIAGNE, BLAISE (Vol. IV); FRANCE AND AFRICA (Vol. IV); INDEPENDENCE MOVEMENTS (Vol. V).

Further reading: Myron Echenberg, *Colonial Conscripts: The Tirailleurs Sénégalais in French West Africa, 1857–1960* (Portsmouth, N.H.: Heinemann, 1991).

Tiv Largest ethnic group of the Benue State in NIGERIA. The Tiv constitute one of Nigeria's largest ethnic minorities, composing 2.5 percent of the country's population. A small number of Tiv speakers can also be found in CAMEROON. Tiv myths of origin say that they came "from the southeast" before settling in their present-day homeland, in Nigeria's Middle Belt.

For defensive purposes the Tiv lived in stockaded villages, and it was not until the period of British COLONIAL RULE that they dispersed into smaller settlements. The initial British penetration into Tivland occurred in 1906, but permanent colonial control was not firmly established until the end of World War I (1914–18). They gradually became involved in cash-crop production in addition to their earlier system of AGRICULTURE, which was centered on the production of FOOD CROPS.

Like their neighbors the IGBO, the Tiv organized a stateless society. At the local level there was no chief, and decisions concerning laws and law enforcement were made by consensus of the family elders. During the colonial period the British delegated powers of governance over the Middle Belt region to their Muslim, HAUSA-FULANI allies. The non-Muslim Tiv, resentful of Islamic, outsider control, erupted in violence in the early 1960s.

More recently the Tiv have been involved in repeated ethnic clashes with neighboring peoples, including the Jukun, who are the ethnic majority of Taraba to the east of Benue State. These clashes have resulted in thousands of deaths, as well as thousands of refugees fleeing the violence.

See also: BANTU LANGUAGES (Vol. I); LANGUAGES (Vol. I); LANGUAGE USAGE IN MODERN AFRICA (Vol. V); NIGER-CONGO LANGUAGES (Vol. I).

Togo Present-day West African country 22,000 square miles (57,000 sq km) in size, located on the Gulf of Guinea; Togo shares borders with GHANA to the west, Republic of BENIN to the east, and BURKINA FASO to the north. The area that is present-day Togo was hotly contested in the early 1800s, with the Akwamu state, the ASHANTI EMPIRE, and the kingdom of DAHOMEY competing for regional dominance.

Known by Europeans as TOGOLAND, the region was frequently raided by the Ashanti for human captives to support the SLAVE TRADE. Denmark was the controlling European presence in the coastal area until the middle of the 1800s, when German MISSIONARIES and traders began to establish settlements in Togoland's port city of Anécho. Led by the efforts of the diplomat Gustav Nachtigal (1834–1885), Germany secured treaties with coastal chiefs, and at the BERLIN CONFERENCE (1884–85) the German PROTECTORATE of Togoland was recognized.

Togo during the Colonial Era: Togoland Through the 1890s, the Germans expanded their protectorate northward, encountering little resistance. By 1904 Germany signed treaties with both France, which had colonized neighboring Dahomey (present-day Republic of Benin), and Britain, which had established the GOLD COAST COLONY to the west, thereby setting the boundaries of German Togoland.

Germany enacted an ambitious public works program in the colony, building modern roads and railways and encouraging the production of the colony's main agricultural EXPORTS, namely COTTON, RUBBER, COCOA, and palm products. The port city of Lomé, named the colonial capital in 1897, was developed extensively. Despite Germany's success in creating and administering a strong infrastructure for the colony, the brutal treatment of Africans and the policies of direct taxation and forced LABOR tarnished the image of Germany's *Musterkolonie* (model colony).

Germany maintained its colonial rule in Togoland until 1914, when, in the first victory for Allied forces in World War I (1914–18), British and French troops easily seized the colony. After the war Togoland was divided into two League of Nations mandates, with western Togoland coming under British administration and eastern Togoland going to the French. British Togoland was governed as part of the Gold Coast. French Togoland remained a separate entity until 1934, when it was linked to Dahomey and later to french west africa. In 1946 the mandates became United Nations trust territories and remained under British and French rule.

In 1947 the Ewe people, who were the majority population in southern British Togoland, began to call for a unified, independent Togo. Their people split by the colonial divisions Germany, Britain, and France had imposed on their homeland, the Ewe sought to reunite their fractured population. The plan fell apart, however, when the rest of British Togoland voted to be fully incorporated into the Gold Coast, which the British were moving quickly toward independence. In 1957 the Gold Coast and British Togoland became independent Ghana.

A sliver of land 320 miles long with a 32 mile coastline, French Togoland retained its borders and, in 1956, became an internally autonomous country within the FRENCH UNION. In 1958 the country's population voted for full independence. Sylvanus OLYMPIO (1902–1963), the head of the Committee of Togolese Unity, became president when the independent Republic of Togo was established in 1960.

See also: COLONIAL CONQUEST (Vol. IV); COLONIALISM, INFLUENCE OF (Vol. IV); DENMARK AND AFRICA (Vol. III); ENGLAND AND AFRICA (Vols. III, IV, V); EWE (Vols. II, III) FRANCE AND AFRICA (Vols. III, IV, V); GERMANY AND AFRICA (Vol. IV); LEAGUE OF NATIONS AND AFRICA (Vol. IV); SLAVE COAST (Vol. III); TOGO (Vols. I, II, III, V); TRUST TERRITROY (Vol. IV); UNITED NATIONS AND AFRICA (Vol. IV).

Togoland Colonial name of the territory that became the independent Republic of TOGO, in 1960. Beginning in the mid-1800s, German explorers, MISSIONARIES, and traders began settling along the coast of Togoland. One such explorer, Gustav Nachtigal (1834–1885), forged agreements with local leaders that gave Germany trading rights within these leaders' kingdoms. With these agreements in place, Germany's occupation of Togoland was recognized by the other European powers at the BERLIN CONFERENCE (1884–85), allowing Germany to claim the territory as a PROTECTORATE. The German colonial administration then proceeded to build railroads and develop the port facilities at Lomé, the administrative capital, in order to transport the region's agricultural products, which included COTTON, RUBBER, COCOA, and palm products.

During the course of World War I (1914–18), combined British and French forces seized Togoland, and at the end of the war the territory was divided between Britain and France to be administered as League of Nations mandates. In 1957 the western territory administered by Britain joined with the GOLD COAST COLONY to become the newly independent nation of GHANA. The eastern, French mandated territory joined the FRENCH UNION in 1956, and achieved independence from France in 1960. The new Republic of Togo was led by President Sylvanus OLYMPIO (1902–1963).

See also: GERMANY AND AFRICA (Vol. IV).

Touré, Ahmed Sékou (1922–1984) *Trade unionist and president of independent Guinea's First Republic.*

Born to a poor, Muslim family in Faranah, GUINEA, near the headwaters of the Niger River, Sékou Touré attended Quranic school before getting a Western-style education at French-speaking elementary and technical schools. In 1941 he took a postal job and four years later cofounded Guinea's first trade union for postal workers. He was exposed to Marxism by trade unionists from the French Communist party, but he disavowed Marxist-Leninist communism, claiming instead to be a socialist. In 1952 Sékou Touré founded the general Union of the Workers of Black Africa, which, while under his direction, never lost a strike. Throughout the latter half of the 1950s he continued working in prominent, union roles.

Sékou Touré's leadership of LABOR UNIONS provided him with a basis for engaging in the politics associated with African NATIONALISM AND INDEPENDENCE MOVEMENTS. In 1946, at the Bamako Conference in neighboring FRENCH SOUDAN (now MALI), he helped found the popular AFRICAN DEMOCRATIC ASSEMBLY (Rassemblement Démocratique Africain, RDA) and became the party's vice president. As the RDA emerged as the dominant African political organization in FRENCH WEST AFRICA, Sékou Touré took control of the Democratic Party of Guinea (Parti Démocratique de Guinée, PDG), the Guinea branch of the RDA.

In his campaign to become the leader of government of an independent Guinea, Sékou Touré evoked the name of the renowned hero of Guinean resistance, SAMORI TOURÉ (c. 1830–1900). Sékou Touré even falsely claimed to be his grandson.

Drawing on the prominence of Islam in Guinea, Sékou Touré unified the region's diverse ethnic groups with an unspoken promise of making Guinea an Islamic state (which, ultimately, he did not do). By advocating a greater role for African women in public office and a redistribution of land, Sékou Touré appealed to peasants, women, and youth—the audience targeted by the PDG. He opposed the rule of chiefs, claiming that they supported French COLONIAL RULE and were obstacles to reform.

In 1957 his party won 56 of the 60 seats in the Territorial Assembly, and Sékou Touré became mayor of Conakry, Guinea's capital, and representative to the French National Assembly. The following year he led the drive for a "no" vote on the referendum, called by French president Charles DE GAULLE (1890–1970), for continuing affiliation with France through membership in the FRENCH UNION. Guinea was the only French West African state to vote "no," and de Gaulle granted the country immediate independence. However, as part of his attempt to discourage other former colonies from following Guinea's lead, de Gaulle cancelled all French aid and withdrew all French personnel, equipment, and supplies from Guinea. Sékou Touré's radical decision for independence encouraged the DECOLONIZATION of the rest of France's sub-Saharan possessions and also led to the collapse of the RDA.

See also: COMMUNISM AND SOCIALISM (Vol. V); FRANCE AND AFRICA (Vols. III, IV, V); ISLAM, INFLUENCE OF (Vols II, IV, V); SÉKOU TOURÉ, AHMED (Vol. V).

Further reading: W. A. E. Skurnik, *African Political Thought: Lumumba, Nkrumah, Touré* (Denver: University of Denver, 1968).

towns and cities The colonial era saw the widespread growth of towns and cities in various parts of Africa, with many precolonial small towns growing into large ones and larger cities becoming even more densely settled. Especially in the 20th century, increasing urban populations altered the face of Africa, resulting in sweeping changes to FAMILY relations, the environment, and the African ECONOMY. These changes, very few of them entirely positive, challenged existing values, beliefs, and social norms.

See also: ABIDJAN (Vol. IV), ACCRA (Vol. IV), ADDIS ABABA (Vol. IV); ALGIERS (Vol. IV); BAMAKO (Vol. IV); BANGUI (Vol. IV); BANJUL (Vol. IV); BRAZZAVILLE (Vol. IV); CAIRO (Vol. IV); CAPE TOWN (Vol. IV); COLONIALISM, INFLUENCE OF (Vol. IV); DAKAR (Vol. IV); DAR ES SALAAM (Vol. IV); DURBAN (Vol. IV); ELIZABETHVILLE (Vol. IV); FREETOWN (Vol. IV); JOHANNESBURG (Vol. IV); KAMPALA (Vol. IV); KANKAN (Vol. IV); KANO (Vol. IV); KHARTOUM (Vol. IV); KIMBERLEY (Vol. IV); LAGOS (Vol. IV); LEOPOLDVILLE (Vol. IV); LIBREVILLE (Vol. IV); MOGADISHU (Vol. IV); MOMBASA (Vol. IV); NAIROBI (Vol. IV); STANLEYVILLE (Vol. IV); TIMBUKTU (Vol. IV); TOWNS AND CITIES (Vols. I, II, III, V); URBANIZATION (Vol. IV); URBAN LIFE AND CULTURE (Vol. IV); ZANZIBAR CITY (Vol. IV).

trade and commerce Although trade—and trade routes—had been well established in Africa for thousands of years, long-standing patterns of African trade and commerce were undergoing fundamental changes by the middle of the 19th century. This process accelerated during the colonial period.

For centuries Africans had conducted trade in everything from metals to crafts. With the arrival of Europeans, however, both international and domestic commerce became dominated by the SLAVE TRADE. In the years before 1800 this trade in human captives spread from West and Central Africa to the Atlantic, from the savanna regions south of the Sahara across the desert to North Africa, and from the Horn of Africa into the Arabian Peninsula. By 1800 this trade had expanded still further because of increases in the East African slave trade. In spite of the widespread abolition of the slave trade, which was begun by Britain in 1807, the trade continued, finally reaching a peak of 130,000 captives per year. Eventually, however, abolition of the trade took hold, and the Atlantic trade was in sharp decline by 1850. As a result, other forms of commerce, called *legitimate trade* in retrospect, took the place of the trade in human captives.

This shift away from the slave trade actually had begun in the early 1800s. At that time much of the trade involved the production of CASH CROPS for export. Industrializing Europe needed oil crops, such as GROUNDNUTS (peanuts) and oil palms, to lubricate machinery as well as for consumption. The scale of this commerce increased steadily over the course of the century, and, through the 1860s at least, the terms of trade (i.e., what one country or region could obtain as imports with a set quantity of exports) favored Africa. Ironically, and unfortunately, it was the need for LABOR in the production of cash crops that kept the internal African slave trade going throughout much of the 19th century.

As was true in the era of the international slave trade, African merchants dominated the early decades of the exporting of commodities. Initially the most prominent merchants were politically powerful individuals such as the merchant princes of the NIGER DELTA or the politically connected Madame TINUBU (1805–1887). Over time, however, a new merchant class emerged, typified by people such as Richard Beale BLAIZE (1845–1904).

The process of European colonial expansion and the establishment of formal COLONIAL RULE, however, spelled the end of the powerful African merchants. European commercial firms such as the ROYAL NIGER COMPANY and its successor, the UNITED AFRICA COMPANY, linked as they were to the colonial administrations, squeezed the African merchants out of business. Thus, in the colonial period, African commercial life centered on traders such as Madam Alimotu PELEWURA (c. 1865–1951) rather than the heads of large commercial firms.

In colonies such as the CONGO FREE STATE (later the BELGIAN CONGO) and those of FRENCH EQUATORIAL AFRICA, where the colonial governments handed out large tracts of land to CONCESSIONAIRE COMPANIES, large-scale African traders also lost out to European merchants. The European-owned companies monopolized the export-import business, leaving the collection of cash crops from small-scale African farmers and the sale of imported commodities at the local level to African traders. These traders also faced increased competition at the local, retail level, for small-scale businesspeople from Greece, Lebanon, and India began to enter the local, retail trade.

Developments in East Africa were similar to those in West Africa, but with some notable differences. One major difference was that of chronology. Both West and East Africans were involved in complex trading systems, both local and long-distance. However, while the West African slave trade was gradually slowing down, the trade in slaves was increasing at ports along the SWAHILI COAST in East Africa. In response to the demand for human captives, interior peoples such as the NYAMWEZI and the YAO opened new trade routes between the interior and the coast. Ivory, too, continued to be a major trade item along these same trade routes. In addition, Arab planters on Indian Ocean islands and along the African coast were also raising cash crops such as cloves and copra for export to Europe.

The coastal merchants were both Arabs and Swahili and operated under the political sovereignty of the BUSAIDI sultanate of ZANZIBAR. Beginning about mid-century, Zanzibari traders became more active in the interior, and by the 1870s the sultanate was attempting to expand its territorial control inland from the coast, especially in what is today TANZANIA. Under the leadership of individuals such as TIPPU TIP (c. 1830–1905), Zanzibari traders pushed into the eastern Congo by the early 1880s. The European colonial conquest of this region proved even more disruptive of African commercial life than it did in West Africa. Commercial activities changed from African and Arab hands to that of large firms such as the German East Africa Company. Throughout the colonial period, major commercial activities remained in the hands of European-owned firms. Individuals in ASIAN COMMUNITIES, however, controlled much of the business at the retail level in both the rural areas and cities.

Trade and commercial patterns were different in both southern and North Africa. The European SETTLERS of SOUTH AFRICA had a strong merchant class from the early years of British rule of the CAPE COLONY. The spread of commercial farming, with the introduction of wool-producing Merino sheep in the 1840s, and then the establishment of sugar plantations in NATAL, led to an upsurge of commercial activity. This paled, however, in comparison with the level of economic activity that the MINERAL REVOLUTION produced.

Throughout the 19th century commerce at all levels remained fully in white hands, although by late century some Indians in Natal were entering trade at the lower levels. In the 20th century trade and commerce were increasingly focused on the cities, as the pace of urbanization and industrialization quickened over the first half of the century. By 1960 approximately half of South Africa's population was urbanized, including the vast majority of whites, who had enormous purchasing power.

The situation in North Africa was much more varied. The French conquest of ALGERIA, dating from about

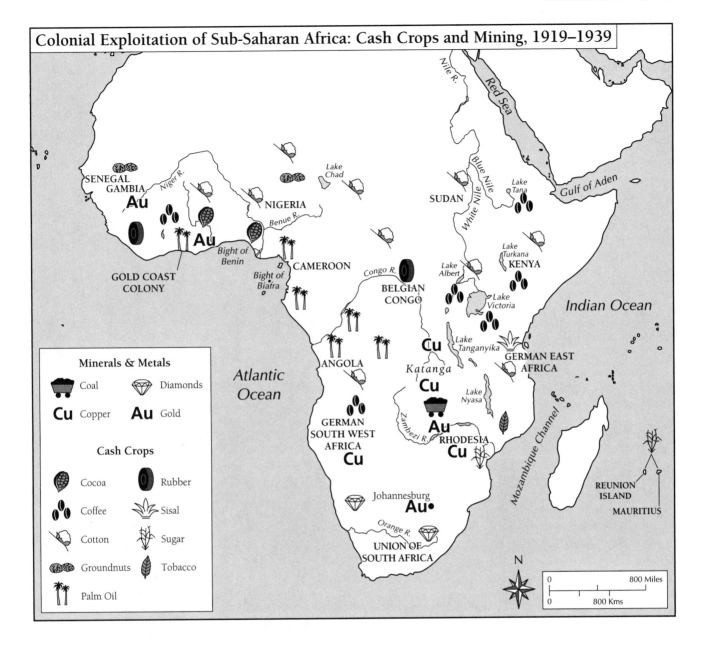

Colonial Exploitation of Sub-Saharan Africa: Cash Crops and Mining, 1919–1939

1830, led to the large-scale immigration of white settlers, know as colons. They appropriated large amounts of land and came to dominate much of the commercial agriculture. Wine made up over half of the colony's exports in the interwar period, with a small number of European producers responsible for the bulk of the production. The majority of colons settled in the coastal cities, especially ALGIERS, where they dominated commercial life just as they dominated other aspects of society. EGYPT, on the other hand, did not experience significant European settlement, and European commerce was unable to make much headway against the well-entrenched Egyptian merchant class. The establishment of the wholly Egyptian-owned Bank Misr in 1920 was a further boost to indigenous commercial life. Significant foreign capital was invested in Egypt, but much of it in Egyptian-owned firms.

The year 1960 witnessed a transformation of trade and commerce in Africa from what it had been in 1850. For the most part large-scale European firms controlled the flow of both exports and imports at the wholesale level. At the retail level the situation was more varied. In West Africa, for example, African traders still dominated local markets, but in South Africa, retail commerce was almost wholly the domain of Europeans, with some limited Indian participation. As with so many other patterns of African life, the newly independent countries inherited a very colonial system of trade and commerce.

See also: COLON (Vol. IV); ECONOMY (Vol. IV); TRADE AND COMMERCE (Vols. I, II, III, V).

transportation From 1850 onward, significant changes began to take place in the modes of transportation in Africa. These changes took the form of the mechanization of transportation that the Industrial Revolution made available in Europe earlier in the century. The navigable rivers of Africa were few in number, with only the Congo, Niger, and Nile being of major significance, although other rivers such as the Gambia and the Senegal and stretches of the Zambezi also were passable. They had long been used for transportation purposes. It was on these rivers that the first major transportation changes occurred with the introduction of steam navigation. The Nile saw the beginning of steam navigation early in the century. In 1857 the British government promoted steam navigation on the Niger River by contracting with a British trader and providing him with a subsidy to maintain a steamboat on the river. Steam navigation on the Congo quickly emerged as that river became the main transport artery for the CONGO FREE STATE. In fact the locations of both LEOPOLDVILLE and STANLEYVILLE were determined because of their locations at either end of a key navigable stretch of the river.

The first steamboat to maintain regular steamer service on the Niger was the *Dayspring*, which was put in service in 1857. The enterprise ended in failure when the *Dayspring* went aground on a large rock at Jebba, which was located hundreds of miles upstream from the mouth. Other steamers, however, were soon in service on the Niger as well as its major tributary, the Benue River.

While steam navigation was a significant transportation innovation, it had limited applicability because of the small number of navigable rivers. The major transportation changes came with the introduction of railroads. Except for EGYPT, where the government of Khedive ISMAIL (1830–1895) was able to raise the necessary capital to launch railroad construction in the Nile Delta region in the 1850s, the building of railroads in Africa was almost wholly a colonial enterprise. Railroad construction began in ALGERIA in the 1870s, largely to serve the needs of the expanding COLON population. The 1870s also witnessed the beginnings in SOUTH AFRICA of what was to become the most extensive railway system on the continent. Spurring this construction was the MINERAL REVOLUTION that was tied to the discovery of DIAMONDS and GOLD deep in the interior. Between 1897 and 1905 the BRITISH SOUTH AFRICA COMPANY oversaw the extension of lines from South Africa northward into its new colony of SOUTHERN RHODESIA.

Railway construction patterns for most of Africa were very different from those in colonies with large populations of European SETTLERS. Sometimes the purposes could be strategic. For example, part of the British military advance into the present-day Republic of the SUDAN in pursuit of the MAHDIYYA included building a railroad. Begun in 1896, that railway stretched from Wadi Halfa, at the head of navigation on the lower Nile, across the desert to the great bend above the fourth cataract. Within two years rail workers had extended the rail further south to Atbara. This enabled the British army to have a dependable supply route in preparing for the decisive Battle of OMDURMAN, in 1898. Silmilarly, beginning in 1899, the British pushed a railroad inland from MOMBASA to Lake Victoria in order to secure their hold on the region.

Once COLONIAL RULE was firmly in place, colonial governments built railroads primarily for the purpose of developing the colonial export-oriented economies. Thus, in 1898 the Congo Free State built a rail line between Leopoldville and the Atlantic Ocean port of Matadi. This enabled travelers and traders to bypass the long stretch of rapids on the lower Congo. By 1918 the government of the BELGIAN CONGO had connected ELIZABETHVILLE by rail to the navigable reaches of the upper Congo in order to export COPPER through the port at Matadi. As early as 1906 the French had established a rail link between BAMAKO on the Upper Niger and Kayes at the head of navigation on the Senegal River. This connection facilitated French administrative control of their sprawling West African colonial empire and allowed for its economic development. Colonial economic development in MALI centered on COTTON, while that in SENEGAL depended on GROUNDNUTS (peanuts). Completion of the railroad from Kayes to the port at DAKAR further facilitated the transport of these and other CASH CROPS.

Outside of the MAGHRIB and South Africa, with their large settler populations that could demand well-developed rail networks, the railroad map of colonial Africa was mainly a series of lines stretching inland from port cities to the interior. Few branch lines existed, and, except within southern and North Africa, seldom did the rail lines of one colony link with those of a neighboring colony. This was even the case when adjacent colonies were part of the same empire, as in FRENCH WEST AFRICA. Thus, at independence, African countries inherited railroads and associated port facilities that were not designed for internal communications and development but rather export-oriented economies.

Road construction began to take hold in the 1920s, as motor vehicles started to become an important means of transportation. At first the colonial governments built roads as feeder links to their railways. Soon, however, road networks began to develop more fully. They had the advantage of being cheaper and more flexible than railroads, and they also were more likely to serve the needs of local Africans.

Unlike railroads, which required large amounts of capital and extensive administration, road transport was open to small entrepreneurial enterprises. Africans, especially in the well-developed market economy of West Africa, quickly took advantage as both owner-operators and users of the new opportunities that road transport provided.

Air travel, which did not become significant on a global scale until after World War II (1939–45), was not very well developed in colonial Africa. Other than air routes between Europe and North Africa, which emerged in the aftermath of World War I (1914–18), regular air service did not come to most of the continent until the 1930s. Even then it was not very extensive. For example, in 1936 it took four days for a passenger to fly from Belgium to Leopoldville. By comparison, at that same time, the weekly mail ships reached CAPE TOWN from Southampton, England in 14 days. Even as late as 1960, most airline services linked African countries with Europe, and there were few internal flights.

Motor vehicles remained a rarity for most Africans as late as the 1950s. Only in South Africa were there more than 60 vehicles per thousand people. In the vast area of French West Africa, on the other hand, there were fewer than four vehicles per thousand people.

Colonial Railways in Sub-Saharan Africa, c. 1919–1939

See also: COLONIALISM, INFLUENCE OF (Vol. IV); CONGO RIVER (Vol. I); GAMBIA RIVER (Vol. I); NIGER RIVER (Vol. I); NILE RIVER (Vol. I); SENEGAL RIVER (Vol. I); TRADE AND COMMERCE (Vols. IV, V); TRANSPORTATION (Vol. V); ZAMBEZI RIVER (Vol. I).

Transvaal, the (1852–1902) Province of the UNION OF SOUTH AFRICA (1910–1961), located in the highveld of present-day SOUTH AFRICA, between the Vaal and Limpopo rivers. The restraints of British rule upon the BOERS of the CAPE COLONY inspired the Great Boer Trek (1835–early 1840s), a large Boer migration into the hinterland of southern Africa. Once across the Vaal River, the Boers met resistance from the area's indigenous people, especially the NDEBELE, the PEDI, and the ZULU. Tenacious and ruggedly individualistic, the Boers eventually prevailed, spreading out across the region in loosely organized settlements.

At the Sand River Convention (1852) Britain recognized the Transvaal as a sovereign state and PRETORIA was named the new republic's capital. From it inception the Transvaal encountered economic difficulties, and in 1877 the British peacefully annexed the bankrupt country as part of its confederation plans for South Africa. Three years later, frustrated by unfulfilled British promises, the Boers revolted and regained the Transvaal's independence.

In 1886 the discovery of GOLD in the WITWATERSRAND of the Transvaal precipitated a large influx of foreigners into the region. The city of JOHANNESBURG quickly sprang into existence as the center of the MINING industry. The Boers, attempting to maintain political control of the Transvaal, denied the franchise to the new immigrants, especially English-speakers, who began to outnumber the Boers. The English migrants, pejoratively called UIT-LANDERS (outsiders) by the Boers, became increasingly dissatisfied with their lack of political power. Their un-happiness culminated in the ill-advised JAMESON RAID (1895), which Cecil RHODES (1853– 1902), a principal mining capitalist and prime minister of the Cape Colony, instigated in an attempt to overthrow the Boer government.

After the failure of the Jameson Raid, relations between the Transavaal and Britain deteriorated. Hostilities culminated in the ANGLO-BOER WAR (1899–1902), which pitted the Transvaal and its fellow Boer republic, the OR-GANGE FREE STATE (OFS), against the British Empire. The Boer armies earned early victories, but superior British numbers eventually overwhelmed them. The Treaty of VEREENIGING ended the war in 1902, making the Transvaal a colony of Britain.

Led by Louis BOTHA (1862–1919), in 1907 the Transvaal received the right to a limited self-government under British authority. AFRIKANERS immediately dominated the government, protecting the advantages afforded the white population. In 1910 the Transvaal united with the OFS, NATAL, and the Cape Colony to form the Union of South Africa. The Transvaal became the economic powerhouse of the union and eventually the political powerhouse as well.

See also: AFRIKANER REPUBLICS (Vol. IV); GREAT BOER TREK (Vol. III); KRUGER, PAUL (Vol. IV).

Further reading: Herman Giliomee, *The Afrikaners: Biography of a People* (Charlottesville, Va.: Univ. of Virginia Press, 2003); Jeremy Krikler, *Revolution from Above, Rebellion from Below: The Agrarian Transvaal at the Turn of the Century* (New York: Oxford University Press, 1993); Johannes Stephanus Marais, *The Fall of Kruger's Republic* (Oxford, U.K.: Clarendon Press, 1961).

Tripoli (Tarabulus al-Gharb, in Arabic) Capital of LIBYA, located on the Mediterranean coast in the north-western part of the country. The Ottoman Empire reestablished direct rule over the province of TRIPOLITA-NIA in 1835. From 1850 to 1911 Tripoli—the only urban center in the region—was the capital of Tripolitania (the Ottoman province of Tarabulus al-Gharb). Tripoli's citizens included Turkish administrators, 4,000 Europeans from the Mediterranean island of Malta, and 25,000 Tunisians, who emigrated in 1883 to escape the newly declared French PROTECTORATE of TUNISIA to the west. The Ottoman Empire controlled the area until the Italians seized Tripoli, in 1911, during the Turko-Italian War (1911–12).

Under Italian control, many more European SETTLERS came to the city and the urban ARCHITECTURE began to reflect the colonial influence. Built using European techniques of urban construction, the new city structures eventually extended beyond the original city wall. Despite its growth Tripoli remained a relatively small colonial town until the late 1950s, when the effects of Libya's new petroleum industry began to appear.

See also: ITALY AND AFRICA (Vol. IV); OTTOMAN EM-PIRE AND AFRICA (Vols. III, IV); TRIPOLI (Vol. V).

Tripolitania Region in present-day western LIBYA located on the coast of the Mediterranean. In the late 19th and early 20th centuries, Tripolitania was governed by the Ottoman Empire and, later, by Italy. Ruled as a vassal state by the Ottomans since the 17th century, in 1835 Tripolitania became an Ottoman province directly ruled by a governor-general, who was appointed by the sultan. While the Ottoman administrators actively tended to the coastal regions, they were less interested in pacifying the Fezzan region in the interior.

After the Berlin Congress of 1878 the Italians considered Tripolitania part of their Mediterranean-sphere of influence; however, the Ottoman rulers did not relinquish control of the region. In 1879 the provinces of Tripolitania and Cyrenaica (present-day eastern Libya) were separated. Later, in the early 20th century, the Young Turk movement within the Ottoman government allowed both provinces to send representatives to the Ottoman Parliament.

In 1911 Italy engineered a crisis to undermine the Ottoman government. Claiming that the Turks had armed the indigenous peoples of Tripolitania against the Italian settlers, Italy declared war and invaded the region. Under the leadership of Mustafa Kemal Ataturk (1881–1938), the future leader of Turkey, Ottoman troops withdrew to the interior and organized indigenous resistance to the Italian invasion. However, because a separate war was threatening their empire on the Balkan Peninsula, the Ottomans sued for peace with Italy. As part of the peace agreement the Ottoman Empire granted independence to both Tripolitania and Cyrenaica in 1912, at which time the Italians formally annexed the two territories. In spite of the annexation, the Italian colonial administration maintained the Islamic Ottoman sultan as the religious leader, vesting him with the power to appoint the *qadi* (judge) in Tripoli to oversee the administration of the *sharia* courts.

In Islamic theocracies, *sharia* courts dispense justice based on civil laws that are determined by the clerical interpretation of the Quran, Islam's holy book.

In 1934 Tripolitania and Cyrenaica together became the Italian colony of Libya, and in 1939 Libya was formally made part of Italy.

See also: COLONIAL CONQUEST (Vol. IV); COLONIAL RULE (Vol. IV); ITALY AND AFRICA (Vol. IV); OTTOMAN EMPIRE AND AFRICA (Vols. III, IV).

Further reading: Mattingly, D. J., *Tripolitania*, (Ann Arbor, Mich.: University of Michigan Press, 1994).

trust territory Region or state held in trust (that is, governed on behalf of the indigenous inhabitants) by a colonial power under the auspices of the United Nations (UN) Trusteeship Council. The UN Charter established the Trusteeship Council to supervise the administration of trust territories as one of the six basic functions of the United Nations. For the most part, African trust territories were the former mandates of the defunct League of Nations. The central aims of the UN trust-territory system were to protect and support Africans as they moved toward independence.

All of the League of Nations mandates became trust territories except SOUTH WEST AFRICA (today's NAMIBIA). In that country, SOUTH AFRICA, its neighbor to the south,

continued to govern without the oversight authority of the Trusteeship Council. In addition, Italy was allowed to resume its administration of ITALIAN SOMALILAND, which it had lost to Britain early in World War II (1939–45).

Africa's UN trust territories became independent nations beginning in 1957, when the British-administered area of TOGOLAND was incorporated with the British GOLD COAST COLONY to create independent GHANA. By 1962 the former trust territories of Somaliland, French Togoland, British Cameroons, French Cameroons, TANGANYIKA, and RUANDA-URUNDI were all independent or part of independent countries.

See also: COLONIAL RULE (Vol. IV); INDEPENDENCE MOVEMENTS (Vol. V); LEAGUE OF NATIONS AND AFRICA (Vol. IV); MANDATE (Vol. IV); NATIONALISM AND INDEPENDENCE MOVEMENTS (Vol. IV); PROTECTORATE (Vol. IV); UNITED NATIONS AND AFRICA (Vols. IV, V); WORLD WAR II AND AFRICA (Vol. IV).

Tswana People of southern Africa who live primarily in BOTSWANA and SOUTH AFRICA. Today, Setswana, the LANGUAGE of the Tswana people, is spoken by approximately 4 million people in South Africa and Botswana alone. It is a Bantu language so closely related to that of the SOTHO that it sometimes is called "Western Sotho." The first of the Sotho-Tswana group of languages to be written down, Tswana was studied extensively by MISSIONARIES during the early 19th century. This resulted in a Tswana translation of the biblical gospel of Luke as early as 1830. Other biblical translations followed in the 1840s and 1850s. Beginning in 1914 the noted scholar, journalist, and political activist Sol T. PLAATJE (1876–1932) brought Tswana some notoriety with his translations of Tswana proverbs in an endeavor to promulgate pride in Tswana traditions.

During the 19th century a combination of factors led to the diminishing of Tswana power and culture. The ZULU Mfecane (The Crushing) drove a number of other peoples—primarily Nguni, Hlubi, and Ngwani—into Tswana territory, forcing the Tswana to compete for land and food. Later, military incursions by the Zulu themselves as well as by the founder of the NDEBELE nation, Mzilikazi (1790–1868), led to the devastation of much of the Tswana lands. To make matters still worse, internal disagreements led Tswana minor chieftains to split off and form their own sub-groups, further diluting Tswana power.

All of this left the Tswana vulnerable to Europeans, both BOERS and the British, who attempted to appropriate Tswana lands as they searched for pasture and farmlands and other imperial objectives. By 1886 European incursions were so extensive that the northern Tswana region had become the British PROTECTORATE of BECHUANALAND, and the southern chiefdoms had been incorporated into the CAPE COLONY. Subsequently the British colonial administration largely neglected the territory, and many Batswana were reduced to working as migrant laborers in the South African mines or as farm workers on land that was once their own in order to pay the heavy colonial taxes.

Inhabiting the western limits of the rain-fed agricultural area of the southern African interior, the Tswana have for centuries been a primarily agrarian and pastoral people. Their cattle herds have played particularly important economic and social roles, for they reflected an individual's wealth and social standing. They also developed extensive trading relationships with nearby Khoisan-speaking hunter-gatherers. The extremely well-organized Tswana society was noteworthy for its complex judicial system and its royal power, which was based on the ownership of cattle.

See also: MFECANE (Vol. III); MZILIKAZI (Vol. III); TSWANA (Vols. I, III).

Further reading: J. Mutero Chirenje, *A History of Northern Botswana, 1850–1910* (Rutherford, N.J.: Fairleigh Dickinson Univ. Press, 1977); Kevin Shillington, *The Colonisation of the Southern Tswana, 1870–1900* (Braamfontein, South Africa: Ravan Press, 1985).

Tuaregs Mostly nomadic Berber peoples who have long occupied harsh regions of the Sahara desert, engaged in camel PASTORALISM. Throughout history, Tuareg strongholds have included Gao and TIMBUKTU in present-day MALI, the Aïr Massif in NIGER, and the Ahaggar (Hoggar) Massif in southern ALGERIA.

Until the late 19th century Tuareg people were masters of the Saharan interior. Trans-Saharan trading caravans had little option but to hire local Tuaregs as guides and for protection against raiding parties (often other Tuaregs). The Tuaregs themselves also participated in the Trans-Saharan trade, exchanging GOLD, silver, and ivory jewelry—small luxury items that made their trans-Saharan crossing worthwhile—for the goods that they needed to survive.

As the 20th century progressed, however, Tuareg culture changed radically. The French colonial administration built roads through Tuareg-inhabited regions, and before long, trucks came to replace camel caravans as the preferred form of TRANSPORTATION. Later, air travel further reduced the need for desert guides.

With their shrouded faces and mysterious bearing, the Tuaregs captured the imagination of the French in the late 1800s and early 1900s. (See photo on following page.) *L'Atlantide* (Atlantis), a novel by Pierre Benoit (1886–1962), became a bestseller. In the book, a Frenchman is captivated by a Tuareg enchantress, whose castle is hidden in the Ahaggar Mountains.

Prior to French colonization, in the late 1800s, Tuaregs managed their affairs through clan confederations. But, in light of Tuareg strength, the French redrew national boundaries in the Sahara with the purpose of breaking the Tuareg confederations into smaller, less powerful bands. The Tuaregs' condition continued to deteriorate in the 20th century, as their former way of life became untenable and they became increasingly marginalized, with Tuareg grazing lands taken by the French authorities and young Tuareg men forcibly recruited for LABOR and military duty. Still, those Tuaregs living in Aïr retained their independence up until World War I (1914–18).

In 1916, however, French troops crushed a Tuareg uprising in Aïr, later capturing and executing Kawsen ag Muhammad (d. 1919), the chief who led the insurgents. Despite decreased levels of political organization, Tuaregs in Niger continued to engage French colonial forces in a fierce war. Ultimately the uprising was suppressed and many Tuaregs migrated south to NIGERIA.

In the early 1960s the Tuaregs in Mali and Niger were still dispossessed and began small-scale, armed insurrections, which were violently suppressed by the governments of those newly independent nations.

See also: COLONIAL RULE (Vol. IV); FRANCE AND AFRICA (Vols. III, IV, V); TRANS-SAHARAN TRADE ROUTES (Vol. II); TUAREGS (Vols. I, II, III, V).

Further reading: H. T. Norris, *The Tuaregs: Their Islamic Legacy and Its Diffusion in the Sahel* (Warminster, U.K.: Aris & Phillips, 1975).

Tubman, William (William Vacanarat Shadrach Tubman) (1895–1971) *Seven-term president of Liberia*

Born into a family with a long tradition of religious and government service, Tubman was educated in missionary and public schools before entering the army, in 1910, and rising to officer status. While still in the army, he worked for various civil-service agencies and studied law, eventually being appointed the Harper County attorney. Tubman was heavily involved in local politics and Liberia's major party, the True Whig Party, when he was elected to the national legislature in 1923. He served as a lawmaker until being appointed an associate justice of the Liberian Supreme Court in 1937.

William Tubman's father, Reverend Alexander Tubman, was not only a Methodist minister but also a senator, the speaker of the House of Representatives, and a general in the Liberian army.

In 1943 Tubman became the leader of the True Whig Party and was elected Liberia's president for what would be the first of seven consecutive terms. Once in office he implemented the Unification Policy—an effort to unite indigenous Liberians and descendants of settlers—and also proposed the Open Door Policy, by which LIBERIA welcomed development from foreign sources to help enrich the country. He even toured the United States, in 1954, in an attempt to build economic and political partnerships.

Tubman died in 1971 from complications related to prostate surgery. Today he is remembered for his strong international leadership and for providing the once-isolated hinterlands of Liberia with congressional representation as well as economic development.

Further reading: Tuan Weh, *Love of Liberty: The Rule of President William V. S. Tubman in Liberia 1944–1971* (New York: Universe, 1976).

Tukulor empire Muslim caliphate established by UMAR TAL (1794–1864) in the region between the upper Senegal and Niger rivers, covering parts of present-day SENEGAL, GUINEA, and the Republic of MALI. In 1826 the

The traditional indigo-dyed scarves worn by these three warriors gave the Tuaregs the name "People of the Blue Veil." This photo was taken in 1934. © *Wide World*

Tukulor Muslim cleric and reputed miracle-worker Umar Tal undertook the pilgrimage to Mecca, where the head of the Sufi Tijaniyya brotherhood named him its caliph for western Africa. On his way home, Umar Tal studied under Muhammad Bello (1781–1857), ruler of the SOKOTO CALIPHATE, and married Bello's daughter before returning to his Tukulor homeland in the Fouta Toro (in present-day Guinea). There, in 1845, he established a Muslim community and set about building an Islamic theocratic state that was to become the Tukulor empire.

The title *al-Hajj* is given to Muslims who have made the pilgrimage to the Muslim holy city of Mecca. The title of *caliph* is reserved for the supreme ruler and religious head of a Muslim group or state.

Unsuccessful in his attempts to convert the surrounding populations to Islam, Umar Tal launched a JIHAD to impose Islamic rule. By 1854 he had conquered the Bambara kingdom of Kaarta, located in the upper Senegal River basin. However, his expansion westward along the Senegal River was halted by French colonial forces under the command of governor Louis FAIDHERBE (1818–1889), who forced Umar Tal to sign a treaty establishing the Bakoye River, a tributary of the Senegal River, as the western boundary of the Tukulor empire. Between 1859 and 1861 the empire spread eastward, with Umar Tal's armies overrunning the Bambara kingdom of Segu and the FULANI Islamic state of Macina. By 1863 the empire stretched as far east as TIMBUKTU (in present-day Mali) and was nearly as large as the Sokoto Caliphate.

The empire was far from stable, however. Revolts repeatedly broke out among the conquered Bambara and Fulani peoples. Almost as soon as Umar Tal had conquered Timbuktu, it was taken by the TUAREGS. Umar Tal's attempts to maintain his empire led to the enslavement of thousands and the death of thousands more. In 1864, while battling Fulani rebels, Umar Tal was killed, and his son, AHMADU SÉKU (d. 1898), became the Tukulor ruler. Séku's control over the empire gradually crumbled,

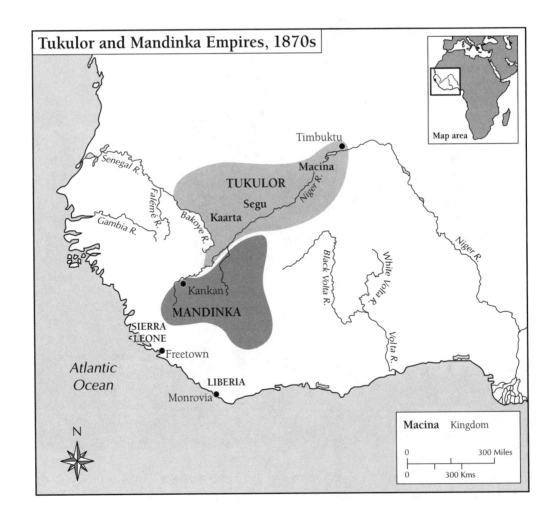

and the French, eager to expand their colonial holdings eastward, moved in. By 1893 Séku had surrendered, and the Tukulor empire was assimilated into what would become FRENCH WEST AFRICA.

See also: BELLO, MUHAMMAD (Vol. III); COLONIAL CONQUEST (Vol. IV); FRANCE AND AFRICA (Vols. III, IV, V); FULANI JIHADS (Vol. III); ISLAM (Vol. II); ISLAM, INFLUENCE OF (Vols. II, III, IV, V); JIHAD (Vols. II, V); TUAREGS (Vols. I, II, III); TUKULOR (Vols. II, III); SUFISM (Vols. III, IV).

Further reading: B. O. Oloruntimehin, *The Segu Tukulor Empire* (London: Longman, 1972); David Robinson, *The Holy War of Umar Tal: The Western Sudan in the Mid-nineteenth Century* (New York: Oxford University Press, 1985).

Tunis Capital of the North African country of TUNISIA. The city is located on an inlet of the Gulf of Tunis, on the Mediterranean Sea. Founded in the ninth century, Tunis is the country's oldest city. By the late 16th century, it was part of the Ottoman Empire, with a bey, or Ottoman governor, in charge. A majority of Arab Muslims and a small minority of Jewish residents inhabited the old Arab sector of the city, known as the Medina. The city's winding streets generally bustled with business during the day and remained relatively quiet at night. For the most part women remained inside—off the streets and out of the public eye.

Tunis became increasingly diverse as the 19th century progressed, however, with more European immigrants moving there from all over the Mediterranean region. The arrival of the foreigners caused major changes in the social, political, and economic conditions of the city. For example, a different sort of nightlife developed in the Medina, with the opening of bars and wine shops and increased public drinking. In addition, non-Muslim females frequented the streets and transformed this previously males-only domain into a space where men and women interacted regularly. At the same time, the crime rate rose, and the government responded by attempting to implement stricter control on the populace.

By 1881 the bey's control over the city had weakened sufficiently that an invasion of Tunis by French forces encountered little resistance. That same year the bey signed the Treaty of Bardo with France, acknowledging French supremacy in the region and making the city a French PROTECTORATE. Within 30 years, the city was home to significant minority groups from France, Italy, Britain, Malta, and Spain.

Although there was some resistance to French occupation, a group of young intellectuals emerged in support of ties with France. Known as the "Young Tunisians," they were in favor of modernizing the city. However, dissent grew among the general population, especially after a Muslim child was killed in a rail accident. France responded to the civil unrest by declaring martial law, which lasted from 1912 until 1921.

In the 1930s a more nationalistic group of younger, French-educated Tunis residents formed the Neo-Destour Party. Under its leadership, support for independence mounted, and in 1956 Tunis, with 410,000 inhabitants, became the capital of a newly independent Tunisia.

See also: FRANCE AND AFRICA (Vols. III, IV, V); NATIONALISM AND INDEPENDENCE MOVEMENTS (Vol. IV); OTTOMAN EMPIRE AND AFRICA (Vols. III, IV); TUNIS (Vol. II, V); URBAN LIFE AND CULTURE (Vols. IV, V); URBANIZATION (Vols. IV, V).

Tunisia Country on the Mediterranean Sea measuring approximately 60,000 square miles (155,400 sq km) and bordered by ALGERIA to the west and LIBYA to the east.

Tunisia in the 19th Century Prior to the mid-1800s a Tunisian regency ruled the country under the supervision of the Ottoman Empire. Tunisian prosperity can be measured from the rule of Bey Hammuda (1759–1814), who created an industrious nation by balancing the economic, religious, and military sectors of society. After Hammuda, between 1837 and 1855, Bey Ahmed I (1806–1855) modernized the Tunisian army and created a navy. However, Bey Ahmed I and MUSTAFA KHAZNADAR (1817–1878), the minister of the treasury, bankrupted the state by supporting the Ottoman Empire in its military campaigns during the Crimean War (1853–1856). Rejecting the modernization of his predecessors, Bey Mohammed II (1810–1859), who ruled from 1855 until his death, pushed for a return to traditional practices and declared a constitution guaranteeing equality in taxation, freedom of RELIGION, and mixed European-Tunisian courts. Despite Mohammed's efforts, however, Europeans infused themselves into Tunisia by pressuring the government to allow them—for the first time—to own land.

Bey Mohammed as Sadiq (1814–1882), who ruled from 1859 until 1882, inaugurated a new constitution that provided for a limited monarchy with cabinet ministers. Although supported by many foreigners and Tunisian reformers, the new constitution was rejected by both the religious establishment and France, which viewed it as a disguise for autocratic corruption. In 1863 Khaznadar, by that time the prime minister, and his loyal clique of financial friends negotiated a loan with the Parisian d'Erlanger Bank for the Tunisian treasury. After Khaznadar and the others received their commissions on the deal, the treasury received only one-fourth of the total loan. Consequently, in order to meet the interest payments on the loan, the Bey doubled taxes and revoked the tax-free status of churches and some businesses. During the resulting "Tax Rebellion," in 1864, Britain, France, and Italy sent troops to protect their citizens and financial investments, and in 1869 the Bey surrendered control of his country's finances to an international commission run by France, Britain, and Italy. The Bey tried unsuccessfully to retain Tunisian autonomy by petitioning the Ottoman Empire to make Tunisia a province. Khaznadar, for his part, was dismissed in 1873 and fled to France after being charged with embezzling 50 million francs from Tunisia's coffers.

KHAYR AL-DIN al-Tunisi (d. 1889), one of the great Muslim reformers of the period, became the country's new prime minister and immediately turned his focus on administrative and financial reform. He confiscated the estates of former prime minister Khaznadar and turned them into the Sadiqi College of Tunis, dedicated to the EDUCATION of future civil servants. In addition, al-Din created a government printing press to produce textbooks for the college and to reproduce Islamic legal documents. He also tried to curb government spending and eliminate abuses by tax collectors.

All of these efforts at reform went to little avail, however, for in 1878 France, the United Kingdom, and other European nations met at the Berlin Congress, where they divided Africa into "spheres of influence." As a result Tunisia and much of the rest of North Africa were designated part of France's sphere. In 1881 France invaded Tunisia, claiming that it was harboring Algerian rebels, and forced the bey to sign treaties creating a French PROTECTORATE under Governor Jules Cambon (1845–1935). Italy objected, citing that its settlers in Tunisia outnumbered those from France three to one, but it could do little to change the course of events.

Tunisia during the Colonial Era: French West Africa Burdened with the responsibility of reducing the Tunisian debt, the French retained the existing administrative structure (although the real power lay in the hands of the French resident-general, who imposed direct rule). The expectation among Tunisians was that the French protectorate was a temporary measure until the debt was paid in full.

Firmly in control of the region, France set about the PACIFICATION and development of the interior. It built new roads to open the region to commerce, attempted to control the nomadic groups by forcing them to settle, and exploited the land's phosphate mineral deposits. In light of the benefits of French modernization, and keeping in mind the temporary nature of French control, Tunisian reformers supported the protectorate. The Arab-language newspaper that was founded at the time, *al-Hadira,* supported the protectorate and promoted modernization and education for all, including females. Editorials in the newspaper encouraged the French to use qualified, young Tunisians— most of whom had graduated from the Sadiqi College—in their colonial administration. A group of these graduates, styling themselves after the reform-minded Turkish army officers known as the Young Turks, took on the name Young Tunisians. By 1911 they were politically aware enough to begin challenging French COLONIAL RULE.

Tunisia during Wartime During First World War the nationalist movement continued in Tunisia, culminating in the founding of the DESTOUR PARTY in 1920. In 1934 the radical wing of the Destour party created its own party, the Neo-Destour party, under the leadership of Habib BOURGUIBA (1903–2000). The new party organized a strong underground movement, firmly establishing itself as the political party for independence. During World War II (1939–45) Tunisia remained under Vichy control and witnessed many major battles of the North African campaign. Bourguiba and the Neo-Destour party supported Charles DE GAULLE (1890–1970) and the Free French government. Despite their wartime loyalty, however, Tunisians were not invited to share in the spoils of victory, a decision by the French that bred ill will throughout the country.

Toward Independence France tried to maintain Tunisian support and loyalty by appointing a Tunisian prime minister, who would appoint a cabinet with equal numbers of French and Tunisian ministers. However, as in the past, the power rested in the hands of the French resident-general. The Tunisians resisted, and after a violent demonstration in TUNIS, the capital, the resident-general arrested Bourguiba and other members of the Neo-Destour party. These acts of suppression were met with spontaneous protests and the massing of 3,000 Tunisian *fellagha* (freedom fighters) in the mountains. In response to this show of anti-French sentiment—and considering the difficult situations in both Indo-China and Algeria— France granted Tunisia self-government in 1955.

Full independence arrived the following year, and Bourguiba set about creating a constituent assembly to draft a new constitution. Under Bourguiba's leadership, Tunisia became a modern, secular state with a universal adult franchise and universal education with equal rights for women. Although the population was predominantly Islamic, secular laws were instituted and the influence of Muslim brotherhoods was suppressed. When Bourguiba became president of the Tunisian republic in, 1957, he outlawed opposition parties. By 1959 Bourguiba presided over a one-party state in which he had enormous executive powers. Although Bourguiba followed a pro-Western foreign policy, Tunisia's relations with France remained strained until 1962, when neighboring Algeria finally received its independence.

See also: COLONIAL CONQUEST (Vol. IV); COLONIALISM, INFLUENCE OF (Vol. IV); FRANCE AND AFRICA (Vol. IV); MAGHRIB (Vols. I, II, III, V); OTTOMAN EMPIRE AND AFRICA (Vols. III, IV), TUNISIA (Vols. I, II, III, V).

Further reading: L. Carl Brown, *The Tunisia of Ahmad Bey, 1837–1855* (Princeton, N.J.: Princeton University Press, 1974); Muhammad al-Hashimi Hamidi, Kenneth J. Perkins, *Historical Dictionary of Tunisia* (Lanham, Md.: Scarecrow Press, 1997); Norma Salem, *Habib Bourguiba, Islam, and the Creation of Tunisia* (London: Croom Helm, 1984); Lucette

Valensi, *Tunisian Peasants in the Eighteenth and Nineteenth Centuries* (Cambridge: Cambridge University Press, 1985).

Turner, Henry M. (1834–1915) *African-American religious leader*

Born in South Carolina, Turner learned to read and write through the aid of young clerks in the law office where he worked as a janitor. After a period as an itinerant preacher he joined the all-black African Methodist Episcopal Church (AME), eventually settling in Washington, D.C., where he became well known for his oratorical skills as a preacher and his outspoken statements on racial issues. During the Reconstruction Era he became increasingly disillusioned with the progress of civil rights for African-Americans, and he looked to relocation in Africa as a solution to the economic, political, and social problems confronting African-Americans.

By 1868 Turner was speaking out not only in opposition to white racism but also in favor of the establishment of an African nation inhabited by young blacks from North America. Racism, he proclaimed, was so deeply rooted in the United States that people of color could achieve respect only by leaving American soil and settling in lands containing black majorities. From the late 1860s through the 1890s he insistently preached for the creation of a new state for African-Americans on African soil. Active in the establishment of schools and churches in various places in Africa—including SOUTH AFRICA, LIBERIA, and SIERRA LEONE—Turner also founded NEWSPAPERS and other periodicals to support his cause.

By the turn of the 20th century, however, Turner's idea of massive emigration no longer seemed to appeal to most African-Americans. In 1893 his plan was rejected by a national convention of African-Americans, and news of a failed emigration effort by a large group of African-Americans in the mid 1890s further disillusioned people with the notion of relocation. The tide seemed to turn totally against Turner when, in 1895, Booker T. WASHINGTON (1856–1915) spoke at the Atlanta Exposition in favor of African-American patience and forbearance in hopes of eventual equality in American society. As Washington and his ideas gained acceptance among a majority of African-Americans, Turner's program of relocation was increasingly marginalized. In the end, Turner's idea appealed only to poor African-Americans who were, ironically, unable to afford the passage to Africa and would have lacked the money or skills needed to establish new lives for themselves once on the continent.

In his later years, although no longer in the vanguard of African-American political activities, Turner continued to remain a respected figure, drawing crowds for his frequent speaking engagements and maintaining a power base in the AME church with its 250,000 members. He died in Ontario, Canada in 1915, still convinced that African-Americans could never lead lives of true equality without removing to a place in which blacks, rather than whites, were the majority population.

See also: DUBOIS, W. E. B. (Vol. IV); BACK-TO-AFRICA MOVEMENT (Vol. IV); GARVEY, MARCUS (Vol. IV).

Further reading: Stephen W. Angell, *Bishop Henry McNeal Turner and African-American Religion in the South* (Chattanooga, Tenn.: Univ. of Tennessee Press, 1992).

Tutsi (Batutsi) Ethnic group inhabiting present-day RWANDA and BURUNDI.

There are two primary ethnic groups in Rwanda and Burundi, the Tutsi and the HUTU. Tutsi make up about 14 percent of the population in each country. Tutsi pastoralists have historically maintained monarchies that were served by the Hutu agriculturalists. Despite their superior numbers, the Hutu were considered socially inferior by the Tutsi.

During the colonial period both German and Belgian administrators observed the social superiority of the markedly leaner and lighter-skinned Tutsi and favored them within the colonial apparatus. Tutsi and Hutu share the same languages: Kinyarwanda in Rwanda and, the closely related Kirundi in Burundi.

See also: BELGIUM AND AFRICA (Vol. IV); TUTSI (Vols. II, III, V).

Tutuola, Amos (1920–1997) *Yoruba writer and folklorist from Nigeria*

Amos Tutuola was born to YORUBA parents in ABEOKUTA in southwestern NIGERIA. As a child Tutuola enjoyed listening to and telling Yoruba folktales, which would later figure largely in his writing. Due to financial difficulties and the death of his father, Tutuola only received six years of formal education. He worked as a farmer, blacksmith for the British Royal Air Force, breadseller, and messenger for the Nigerian Department of Labor. With a limited formal education and working-class background, Tutuola differed markedly from other famous and slightly later Nigerian writers such as Chinua ACHEBE (1930–) and Wole SOYINKA (1934–), both of whom were university educated. As a result he did not write in the precise English of Nigeria's educated elite.

Instead Tutuola told his stories in the English that ordinary Yoruba-speakers used when speaking English, a language that captured the cadence and syntax of Yoruba. He also drew much of his material from Yoruba folktales and traditions, which he wove into his narratives in many ways. His first published work, *The Palm-Wine Drinkard* (1952), reflected these dimensions of his writing. It is the tale of a man so enamored by palm wine that he is willing to travel to the Land of the Dead to bring back to earth a recently deceased wine maker.

The Palm-Wine Drinkard **is populated with fantastically imaginative characters derived from Yoruba folktales. They include a monstrous red fish with multiple horns and eyes, and a mysterious, handsome man who rents his body to lure women into the forest. As the women follow the man into the trees, he begins to fall apart, until all that remains is a skull. Nigerian novelist Chinua Achebe interprets** *The Palm-Wine Drinkard* **as a moral indictment of the laziness produced by Western consumerism.**

The linking of the worlds of reality and magic characterizes most of Tutuola's works, including his second book, *My Life in the Bush of Ghosts* (1954). This novel deals with a young boy's experiences in a parallel universe of magic, spirits, and ghosts. Although *The Palm-Wine Drunkard* was well received by critics in Britain and North America, making its author one of the most famous writers of Africa's postcolonial period, many Western-educated Nigerians reacted to it with hostility. Tutuola's use of the language of the streets angered some who felt it reflected badly on the people of Nigeria. Others felt that his material drew too closely upon traditional themes and images, making it almost an unacknowledged "borrowing" of that material for Tutuola's own uses. As a result none of Tutuola's subsequent works received the same accolades as initial efforts.

The criticism did not seem to bother Tutuola, however, as he continued writing his books in his own manner for the remainder of his life. Holding a minor job with the Nigerian Radio Company for most of his life, he continued to publish through the 1950s and on into the 1980s. During the 1970s and 1980s he was given various fellowships and grants that allowed him to leave his job and work on university campuses. Schools that hosted Tutuola included the University of Ife, in Nigeria, and the University of Iowa, in the United States.

See also: LANGUAGE USAGE IN MODERN AFRICA (Vol. V); LITERATURE IN COLONIAL AFRICA (Vol. IV); LITERATURE IN MODERN AFRICA (Vol. V).

Further reading: Bernth Lindfors, *Folklore in Nigerian Literature* (New York: Africana, 1973); Gerald Moore, *Seven African Writers* (London: Oxford University Press, 1962).

Twe, Didwo (c. 1879–1960) *Liberian leader*

A member of the Kru peoples from the Liberian interior, Didwo Twe was educated first at Cuttington College in LIBERIA before going to the United States to attend St. Johnsbury Academy, in Vermont, and Rhode Island State College. A brilliant student and orator, he also was a rebel against Liberia's political system that perpetuated the authority of an entrenched Americo-Liberian elite over the Kru and other indigenous peoples. Although well educated in terms of Liberia, Twe chose to associate himself with the less-privileged social realm into which he originally was born. Returning from the United States in 1910, he began working for the Liberian government and then became a member of the Liberian House of Representatives. Yet as a lawmaker he found himself powerless to get legislation introduced that would prohibit the use of forced LABOR. This issue became such a scandal that a League of Nations Commission of Inquiry went to Liberia and exposed the abuses, forcing the country's president and vice president to resign. However, instead of moving ahead with reform, the government of President Edwin Barclay, which lasted from 1930 to 1944, cracked down on Twe and other protesters. Twe had to flee to SIERRA LEONE, though he later returned, in 1936, and made his peace with the ruling establishment.

During the 1950s Twe returned to the political fray with an attempt to launch an opposition Reformation Party. He sought to challenge President William TUBMAN (1895–1971) who, as the leader of the dominant True Whig Party, had been in office since 1944 (he served until his death). Twe believed that with the support of the 1.5 million indigenous peoples of the interior he would be able to overcome Tubman and the Americo-Liberian elite. However, Twe did not take into account the fierceness of Tubman's support. Members of the Reformation Party were harassed, and the government confiscated funds and jailed officials for what the government termed seditious or unlawful behavior. Although Tubman ultimately decided to preserve the sham of democracy and allow Twe's party to participate in the election, at the last moment the Reformation Party was tossed off the ballot on a technicality.

Rather than submit, Twe protested, taking his case to the United Nations. Tubman saw to it, in 1953, that Twe was banished and forced to go into hiding. Tubman allowed Twe to return to Liberia, in 1960, and even arranged a state funeral when he died. The issues that Twe raised, however, did not die with him, as the overthrow and execution of Tubman's successor, William Tolbert (1913–1980), was to illustrate.

See also: LEAGUE OF NATIONS AND AFRICA (Vol. IV); UNITED STATES AND AFRICA (Vols. IV, V).

U

Uganda Landlocked country in East Africa, some 91,100 square miles (236,000 sq km) in size, located to the north and west of Lake Victoria. Today Uganda is bordered by the Republic of the SUDAN to the north, KENYA to the east, RWANDA and TANZANIA to the south, and the Democratic Republic of the CONGO to the west.

The people of precolonial Uganda lived in largely self-contained societies, having limited contact with outside influences. The area was made up of a few large, centralized kingdoms spread among many smaller, loosely organized clans. The two most prominent kingdoms were BUGANDA and BUNYORO, which competed for supremacy over the area.

Between the 16th and 18th centuries Bunyoro was the most powerful kingdom of the region. The area held large iron and salt deposits, which allowed the kingdom to prosper from regional trade. By the 19th century, however, the egalitarian structure of the Bunyoro ruling clan began to weaken the kingdom, as the occurrence of civil wars and secessions increased.

The kingdom of Buganda arose in the 15th century, when Bito clan aristocrats left Bunyoro and took control of a number of small chiefdoms. Buganda was initially much smaller than Bunyoro but began to grow during the 17th and 18th centuries. The expansion of the Ganda (the people of Buganda) was guided by the secure rule of the *kabaka* (king), whose authority could not be questioned. As Buganda broadened its borders, new land and people were incorporated into the kingdom under the leadership of provincial chiefs appointed by the *kabaka*.

By 1850 traders from the SWAHILI COAST were in the region in search of ivory and slaves. European visitors soon followed, beginning in 1862 with the arrival of explorer John Hanning SPEKE (1827–1864). In 1875 Kabaka MUTESA I (late 1830s–1884) gave audience to the newly arrived Henry Morton STANLEY (1841–1904), who urged Mutesa to invite MISSIONARIES to Buganda. Searching for new allies to help him defend against potential Egyptian and Sudanese invasions, as well as incursions from neighboring Bunyoro, Mutesa agreed to Stanley's proposal.

> Buganda held dominion over Lake Victoria thanks to its royal navy. Consisting of hundreds of canoes, the force could transport Ganda warriors anywhere along the lake's shores.

In 1877 a group from the Protestant CHURCH MISSIONARY SOCIETY arrived, followed two years later by representatives of the French-Catholic White Fathers missionary society. By the 1880s the Protestants and Catholics, as well as ZANZIBAR-based Muslims, successfully converted substantial numbers of Ganda. In 1888 the converts revolted against the *kabaka*, whose overthrow sparked a civil war among the Catholics, Protestants, and Muslims. Eventually, in 1892, the Protestants and Catholics joined forces to defeat the Muslims. The victorious Christians divided Buganda and controlled the kingdom as a shadow-government that ruled through a figurehead *kabaka*.

Uganda during the Colonial Period Soon after the end of the civil war, competing colonial interests, represented by the German Karl PETERS (1856–1918) and the

British Captain Frederick LUGARD (1858–1945), entered Buganda and fractured the Christian alliance. In 1892 Protestant and Catholic Ganda converts began fighting over control of the kingdom. The Catholics gained a quick advantage, but Lugard intervened and turned the tide in favor of the Protestants—and the British.

After securing Buganda the British turned their attention to the Bunyoro kingdom, which was firmly united under Kabaka KABAREGA (c. 1853–1923). Although they initially met with resistance from Kabarega's well-armed military, the British, with the help of Ganda Protestants and Sudanese mercenaries, finally came to occupy Bunyoro. British also gained control, through force and by treaty, of the outer regions of the territory, and in 1896 Britain made Uganda a PROTECTORATE.

> In 1897 the Sudanese mercenaries who had helped the British against Bunyoro mutinied. The rebellion lasted two years and was put down with the help of the Ganda Protestants. The British recognized the vital Ganda support through a treaty that allowed for limited self-government within the Uganda protectorate. The British also gave the Ganda half of the territory of the conquered Bunyoro kingdom. This arbitrary division of land was contended for decades and came back to disrupt Uganda in the 1960s.

Once the British solidified their authority in the region, they began the process of governance. To administer their protectorate the British used the Ganda as tax collectors and local organizers. The use of the Ganda as extensions of the British government created resentment in other kingdoms of the region, especially Bunyoro, which rose in rebellion in 1907. As a result of the uprising, which was called *nyangire* (refusing), the British removed the Ganda from their roles as government agents.

In the early 1900s the British focused on developing Uganda's infrastructure and encouraging AGRICULTURE production, especially COTTON. The income from cotton farming created a relatively robust economy, and, unlike cotton in most other African colonies, the crop generated a reasonable income for Uganda's farmers. Taxation on the crop had made the Ugandan colonial administration self-sufficient by the beginning of World War I (1914–18).

The war had little effect upon Uganda beyond a few British-German encounters in the outskirts of the protectorate. After the war a political movement led by young bureaucrats, the Young Ganda Association (YBA), called for a transformation of the African leadership in the protectorate. At first they aligned themselves with Kabaka

Daudi Chwa II (1897–1942), but he died before garnering significant political power. After Chwa's death, the YBA gained favor with British colonial administrators, and the older generation of African leaders was gradually replaced by younger men. This transformation culminated, in 1926, with the resignation of Buganda's chief minister, Sir Apolo KAGWA (1869–1927).

> In 1921, Britain established the Uganda Legislative Council. It disproportionately represented European special interests, however, and Africans showed little interest in sitting on the council, holding their own traditional councils in higher regard.

Despite the worldwide economic depression of the 1930s, Uganda's economy remained active and its population increased. As the protectorate evolved, Africans began to challenge colonial rules that they felt were unfair. Especially disconcerting to the African populace were the price controls on CASH CROPS, the exclusion of Africans from cotton ginning, and the lack of African representation on the Legislative Council. These objections continued through World War II (1939–45) and led to riots in 1949. Three years later the reformist colonial governor, Sir Andrew Cohen (1909–1968), answered the African grievances by eliminating price discrimination, establishing African cotton ginning, and reorganizing the Legislative Council to include popularly elected members to represent African interests.

During the 1950s Uganda moved toward independence, and new political activity began to take hold. At the time there was discussion that Uganda would join an East African federation with Kenya and TANGANYIKA (now Tanzania). The possibility alarmed many Africans, who worried that such a federation might become dominated by the racist, white settlers of Kenya.

African concerns about the federation were championed by the Buganda *kabaka* at the time, F. W. Mutesa II (1924–1969), otherwise known as "King Freddie." Before his opposition to federation, Mutesa was considered a panderer to colonial interests. His nationalist stance on the nature of Buganda independence, however, resulted in Cohen exiling him to Britain in 1953. The British expulsion of Kabaka Mutesa made him a national hero, and the lack of a suitable replacement forced Governor Cohen to restore him to the throne two years later.

Upon his return Mutesa negotiated the transfer of a considerable amount of power from the British colonial administration. A group of loyal Ganda rallied around him, calling themselves the "King's Friends." They envisioned an independent Uganda dominated by the kingdom of Buganda and headed by the *kabaka,* and they labeled those who opposed this idea as the "King's Enemies." This power grab by Buganda nationalists sparked widespread resistance to Ganda dominance. Milton OBOTE (1925–), a northerner, from the Lango ethnic group, took advantage of the prevalent anti-Buganda sentiment and, in 1960, formed the Uganda People's Congress (UPC). The UPC gained widespread popular support, and upon Uganda's independence, in 1962, Obote became the country's first prime minister, while Mutesa became the non-executive president.

See also: COLONIAL RULE (Vol. IV); COLONIALISM, INFLUENCE OF (Vol. IV); ENGLAND AND AFRICA (Vols. III, IV, V); GANDA (Vols. II, III); GREAT LAKES REGION (Vol. III); UGANDA (Vols. I, II, III, V).

Further reading: Jan Jelmert Jorgensen, *Uganda: A Modern History* (New York: St. Martin's Press, 1981); Samwiri Rubaraza Karugire, *A Political History of Uganda* (Nairobi, Kenya: Heinemann Educational Books, 1980); Donald A. Low, *Buganda in Modern History* (Berkeley, Calif.: University of California Press, 1971); Edward I. Steinhart, *Conflict and Collaboration: The Kingdoms of Western Uganda, 1890–1907* (Princeton, N.J.: Princeton University Press, 1977).

uhuru Word used to describe the NATIONALISM AND INDEPENDENCE MOVEMENTS in TANZANIA and especially KENYA. *Uhuru* comes from the KISWAHILI language and means "freedom" or "independence."

Kenyans born after independence—December 12, 1963—are now coming of age as politicians and civic activists. Their movement, often called the "Uhuru Generation," calls for a changing of the old-guard leaders who were born into a Kenya that was part of the British Empire.

Uitlanders Pejorative term used to describe foreigners who flooded into the TRANSVAAL in present-day SOUTH AFRICA in the mid-1880s, after GOLD was discovered on the WITWATERSRAND. Thousands of Uitlanders came to southern Africa from all over the world to make their fortunes as miners and entrepreneurs in what was, at the time, the world's largest gold discovery. This intrusion of outsiders into the relatively homogeneous and mainly rural Afrikaner population of the Transvaal Republic created a large cultural gulf between the two groups. AFRIKANERS resented the Uitlanders, regarding them as interlopers. They sought to exclude the Uitlanders from political power, most notably by denying them political rights until they had been residents of the Transvaal for 14 years.

The treatment of Uitlanders grew still worse in the wake of the abortive JAMESON RAID, conducted in 1895, which unsuccessfully attempted to replace Afrikaner rule of the Transvaal with British imperial rule. The already uneasy relations between the British government and the Transvaal Republic under President Paul KRUGER (1825–1904) grew worse, culminating in the outbreak of the ANGLO-BOER WAR, in 1899. Despite the Britain's victory in this war and an continued influx of British settlers, Afrikaners mobilized effectively in the postwar years and succeeded in maintaining political power in the Transvaal.

See also: COLONIAL CONQUEST (Vol. IV); MINING (Vol. IV).

Umar Tal (Al-Hajj Umar ibn Said Tall) (1794–1864) *Islamic scholar and Tukulor state builder in West Africa*

Umar Tal was born in the northern region of modern-day SENEGAL, near the Senegal River. He received a Quranic education in Arabic from his religious father. After continuing his studies with other religious scholars he embarked on a pilgrimage, at the age of 23, to the Islamic holy city of Mecca in the distant Arabian Peninsula. Preceded by his reputation as a devout religious scholar, Umar Tal was well received along his journey. His travels enabled him to see first-hand a large area of Africa as well as the core of the Islamic world. This included the contrasting situation of EGYPT under its ruler Muhammad Ali (1769–1849) and the militant Wahhabi movement, with its stress on Islamic fundamentalism. During his visit to Mecca he joined the Tijaniyya brotherhood, a strict, Sufi Islamic sect, and was eventually named its caliph (leader) for West Africa. Under his leadership the Tijaniyya brotherhood challenged the older Qadiriyya order in West Africa and formed the base for Umar Tal's later state-building efforts.

Returning to Africa in 1833, Umar Tal spent several years in the SOKOTO CALIPHATE. He endeared himself to the emir, Sultan Muhammad Bello (c. 1787–1831), and married his daughter. Bello also instructed him in the ways of political leadership. Upon Bello's death, Umar Tal, who had amassed a sizable following, moved to present-day GUINEA.

In Guinea Umar Tal organized his thoughts about converting people to Islam, wrote on religious devotion and the beliefs of the Tijaniyya brotherhood, and again increased the size of his following. In 1845, hoping to expand his influence, he returned to his homeland to preach. His efforts were largely unsuccessful, however, and in 1848 he moved, along with his followers, to Dinguiraye, a city in Guinea near the border with Senegal.

In 1854, after preaching and conversion failed to rid his homeland of adherents to traditional religious beliefs, Umar Tal ordered a JIHAD for the purpose of expanding Islam. He backed up his directive by unleashing the military might of his following. Living off the land, Umar Tal and his army terrorized the non-Muslims of the region and gradually increased his territorial holdings, initiating the birth of the TUKULOR EMPIRE.

Umar's hold over his empire was unstable, however, as the people he conquered constantly revolted. Complicating matters, his status as religious warrior became tainted when he defeated Macina, a state founded by equally devout Muslims. Even so, by 1863 Umar Tal expanded his empire as far as TIMBUKTU. A year later he died during a revolt in the city of Hamdalahi, in Macina. He was succeeded by his son, AHMADU SÉKU (d. 1898), who ruled the empire until his defeat at the hands of French colonial forces, in 1896.

See also: FULANI (Vol. II, III); FULANI JIHADS (Vol, III); ISLAM, INFLUENCE OF (Vols. II, III, IV, V); MACINA (Vol. III); QADIRIYYA (Vol. III); SUFISM (Vols. II, III, IV): TUKULOR (Vols. II, III).

Further reading: David Robinson, *The Holy War of Umar Tal: The Western Sudan in the Mid-Nineteenth Century* (Oxford, U.K.: Oxford Univ. Press, 1992).

Union Minière (Union Minière du Haut-Katanga)

World's largest COPPER-mining company in the 1930s. The Union Minière operations were run from ELIZABETHVILLE (present-day Lubumbashi) in the Katanga Province of the southeastern region of what was then the BELGIAN CONGO (today's Democratic Republic of the CONGO).

Large corporations, of which Union Minière was one of the most important, dominated the agricultural and MINING sectors of the Belgian Congo economy. Formed in 1906, the company moved quickly to exploit the rich deposits of Central Africa's COPPERBELT.

Africa's so-called Copperbelt measures some 280 miles (450 km) long and up to 160 miles (265 km) wide, running on a northwest-to-southeasterly axis from Katanga to Luanshya, in present-day ZAMBIA.

By 1910 the town of Elizabethville was established to house both the headquarters and some of the mining operations of Union Minière. Indeed, the city's history is inseparable from that of the company. In the heyday of the copper industry, Elizabethville was the Belgian Congo's boom town. It is estimated that in its first 30 years of op-eration, the company employed a total of between 180,000 and 250,000 men. In the present day, the company has been taken over by the government and run as a state-owned corporation called the Générale des Carrières et des Mines (GECAMINES), but the copper smelter's tall chimney stack and the growing mountain of slag continue to define the city. Copper in the early 21st century is not the profitable enterprise it once was, so the state-owned GECAMINES does not generate the huge profits that Union Minière did for its European colonial owners. Zinc has since replaced copper as the principal metal mined by the company.

See also: BELGIUM AND AFRICA (Vol. IV); COLONIAL RULE (Vol. IV); COLONIALISM, INFLUENCE OF (Vol. IV); CONGO CRISIS (Vol. V); COPPER MINES (Vol. II); KATANGA (Vol. V); LUBUMBASHI (Vol. V); METALS AND MINERALS (Vols. IV, V).

Union of South Africa

Political union of CAPE COLONY, NATAL, the TRANSVAAL, and the ORANGE FREE STATE (OFS) established in 1910. In 1902 the Transvaal and the OFS became colonies of Britain under the terms of the Treaty of VEREENIGING, which was signed at the end of the ANGLO-BOER WAR (1899–1902). In 1905, craving political unification of the region, Britain allowed the two former AFRIKANER REPUBLICS a limited form of self-rule as a gesture of reconciliation. The BOERS, realizing union with the other British colonies was inevitable, quickly elected an Afrikaner government to ensure that their doctrine of white supremacy would have a voice during the unification process.

Representation of black-African interests was essentially nonexistent at the national convention. While the four colonies met, however, the South African Native Convention convened in Bloemfontein, marking the initiation of the first all-inclusive, African political association in the region. After Britain failed to keep promises of equal treatment, Africans began to establish political organizations in an effort to unite the black population across ethnic and geographical divisions. In 1912 the South African Native Congress, which would later become the AFRICAN NATIONAL CONGRESS (ANC), was founded with the American-educated John L. DUBE (1871–1946) as its first president and Sol T. PLAATJE (1876–1932) as its first general secretary.

From 1908 to 1909 the representatives from the four colonies held a national convention in DURBAN, where

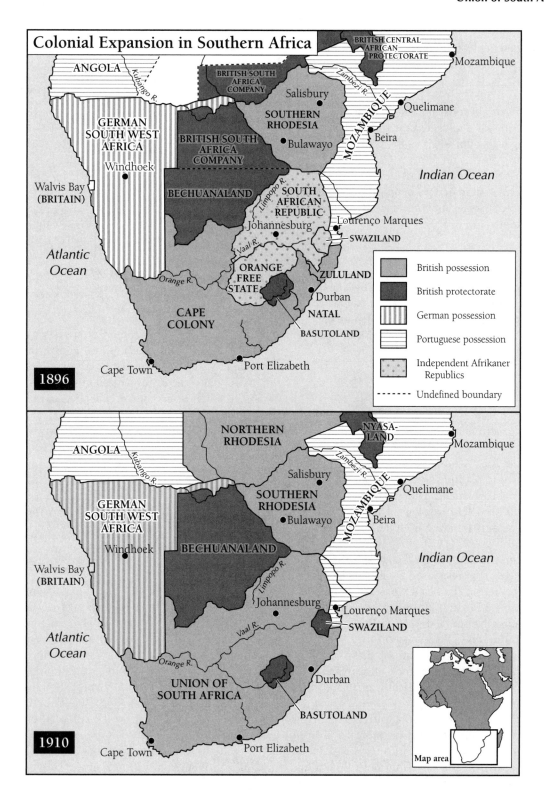

Colonial Expansion in Southern Africa

1896

	British possession
	British protectorate
	German possession
	Portuguese possession
	Independent Afrikaner Republics
- - - - -	Undefined boundary

1910

Map area

they drafted a constitution for the forthcoming union. The Afrikaner colonies staunchly opposed an extension of suffrage beyond the white-male population. As a result a compromise was struck between the colonies, and each was allowed to maintain its existing franchise rules.

In the Cape this meant that Africans and Couloureds could still vote, though they were thoroughly outnumbered by whites.

The AFRIKANERS were also successful in gaining a disproportionate amount of parliamentary representation for the rural communities, which were populated predominantly by Afrikaners at the time of unification, in 1910. This gerrymandering ensured that Afrikaners would dominate politics in SOUTH AFRICA for much of the 20th century.

Despite African efforts at political action, the Union of South Africa quickly subjugated the union's black population by using legislation such as the Native Lands Act (1913) and the Mines and Works ("Color Bar") Act (1911) and subsequent amendments to give unfair benefits to whites. This system of legal subjugation would last for decades, as racist segregation became ingrained in the culture of the union.

The goals of Afrikaner nationalism went beyond its racist segregationist policies. Afrikaners constantly fought for the supremacy of Afrikaner culture and succeeded in making AFRIKAANS an official LANGUAGE of the union in 1925.

White women were granted suffrage in 1930, but the South African government continued to infringe upon the voting rights of blacks. The 1936 Natives Representation Act removed Cape Africans from the common voters' roll and attempted to placate blacks by giving them white representatives in Parliament. The electorate was made exclusively white in 1956, when even mixed-race CAPE COLOURED PEOPLE were removed from the voting rolls.

After World War II (1939–45) Afrikaner policies were further cemented with the establishment of the APARTHEID system. In response to apartheid, South Africa's blacks embraced the Black Consciousness Movement and increased organized resistance. During the 1950s ANC leaders Nelson MANDELA (1918–), Walter SISULU (1912–2003), and Oliver TAMBO (1917–1993) coordinated workers' strikes and planned massive rallies. The white-controlled government took measures to quell the resistance, arresting black political leaders and ruthlessly suppressing demonstrations.

As apartheid became even more entrenched in the second half of the century, Britain was more vocal in its disapproval of the racist South African system. In response to anti-apartheid pressure from both Britain and the rest of the international community, in 1961 South Africa voted in favor of becoming a republic, while wishing to remain in the British Commonwealth. Its application was subsequently turned down, however, and the Union of South Africa became a republic fully independent of any ties with Britain.

See also: MINERAL REVOLUTION (Vol. IV); SWAZILAND (Vol. IV); WITWATERSRAND (Vol. IV); ZULU (Vol. IV).

United Africa Company Large commercial firm in British West Africa that was part of the multinational Unilever Corporation. The United Africa Company (UAC) was the largest of several foreign-owned firms that dominated commerce in West Africa during the colonial period. The predecessors to the UAC were the ROYAL NIGER COMPANY, founded in 1886, and the African Association, founded in 1889. (In 1919 the latter company became part of the African and Eastern Trade Corporation.)

In 1920 William Lever (1851–1925), an English soap manufacturer, acquired the Royal Niger Company because of its involvement in the British West African trade in PALM OIL, which was used for the manufacture of soap. By 1929 Lever's company had joined with the African and Eastern Trade Corporation to form the UAC, which went on to become the dominant commercial force throughout Britain's West African colonies.

Many foreign trading companies went bankrupt during the great economic depression of the 1930s. The UAC, however, survived and even grew by consolidating its operations and entering into agreements that limited competition. As a primary buyer of African-grown CASH CROPS, the company organized groups of commodity buyers to force prices down. The UAC also diversified its holdings to include breweries, ranches, and various factories for producing consumer goods, industrial goods, and pharmaceuticals.

By 1979 the United Africa Company was operating in 23 African countries.

In addition, the UAC began to Africanize its management so that, as the colonies gained independence, local UAC operations were increasingly in the hands of nationals. Because of its longevity on the continent and its African management, the UAC is sometimes perceived as an African-held company. Its profits, however, continue to flow to Europe and are not reinvested on the continent.

See also: COLONIAL RULE (Vol. IV); COLONIALISM, INFLUENCE OF (Vol. IV); CONCESSIONAIRE COMPANIES (Vol. IV); TRADE AND COMMERCE (Vols. IV, V).

Further reading: Frederick Pedler, *The Lion and the Unicorn in Africa: A History of the Origins of the United Africa Company 1787–1931* (London: Heinemann Educational, 1974).

United Gold Coast Convention (UGCC) Political party in the GOLD COAST COLONY (now GHANA) that sought independence from Britain. In 1947 the Gold Coast's first political party, the UGCC was founded by Dr. J. B. DAN-

QUAH (1895–1965), an English-educated African lawyer, and other leading figures who believed that they were the best suited to lead their country to independence. The party thus represented the African elites who were positioned to take over the governmental positions held by the British when COLONIAL RULE ended. The party participated in the political process as permitted by the British, while at the same time pressing them for independence at the earliest possible time.

The UGCC leadership believed that independence could be gained through negotiation and political maneuvering. Their belief in the gradual transfer of political power—as dictated by the British colonial administration—was marked by their slogan, "Self-government in the Shortest Time Possible."

Later in 1947, in an effort to free leadership from organizational tasks and to allow them to pursue their own professions, the UGCC appointed Kwame NKRUMAH (1909–1972) as the party's general secretary. The move backfired, as Nkrumah had a more galvanizing presence than his superiors. More appealing to working people than the party's middle-class leadership, Nkrumah quickly built a large following. In 1948 the British authorities arrested the "Big Six" of the UGCC leadership because of their role in fomenting opposition to British rule, a turn of events that Nkrumah welcomed. In 1949 Nkrumah left the party and took his supporters with him, forming the CONVENTION PEOPLE'S PARTY (CPP).

The CPP was more radical than the UGCC, evidenced by its slogan "Self-government *Now.*" In 1951 the CPP defeated the UGCC in the Legislative Assembly elections. In 1952 Nkrumah became the Gold Coast's prime minister and, in 1957, prime minister of independent Ghana.

See also: ENGLAND AND AFRICA (Vols. III, IV, V); NATIONALISM AND INDEPENDENCE MOVEMENTS (Vol. IV); POLITICAL PARTIES AND ORGANIZATIONS (Vols. IV, V).

United National Independence Party (UNIP)

Political party of NORTHERN RHODESIA (now ZAMBIA) that steered the country to independence by fighting against British colonial domination, racial segregation, and membership in the CENTRAL AFRICAN FEDERATION (CAF). The roots of UNIP date back to the earliest history of African opposition to white, minority rule in southern Africa. The British Colonial Office began ruling Northern Rhodesia as a PROTECTORATE in 1924 and, until 1963, administered the country in favor of the minority, white population. Africans often staged strikes and work stoppages to protest unfair wages and taxes and other mistreatment. In 1948 African laborers formed the first African Mineworkers Union. In the same year, Harry Mwaanga Nkumbula (1914–1983), a former school-teacher, brought together various Rhodesian welfare associations under one umbrella congress. By the early 1950s, Nkumbula had begun working with

general secretary Kenneth KAUNDA (1924–   ), also a former school teacher, to fight racial segregation and to achieve Northern Rhodesia's independence from COLONIAL RULE.

However, the Africans' situation worsened from the 1950s. A movement to consolidate the British protectorates of NYASALAND (now MALAWI) and Northern Rhodesia with the colony of SOUTHERN RHODESIA (today's ZIMBABWE) gained popularity among the white population living in these colonies.

Africans from Northern Rhodesia and Nyasaland opposed the idea, primarily because the settler colony of Southern Rhodesia had interests at odds with their own. They also believed that federation would prolong colonial-style rule. These objections, however, could not halt the movement toward federation, and in 1953 the three colonies were officially joined into the CAF.

African resistance to the federation continued, supported by existing nationalist movements in the region. In Northern Rhodesia, opposition was led by the ANC, which used boycotts to express displeasure with the CAF. Their efforts were met with harsh government retaliation.

In 1955 Nkumbula and Kaunda were jailed. By this time support for the ANC had spread, and the organization had grown into a national political party. About 1958, however, the two leaders came to a disagreement over the future direction of the organization. Kaunda, supporting a more aggressive opposition to the CAF, left the ANC and formed the Zambia African National Congress (ZANC). In 1959 ZANC boycotted the general election set for March 20, and as a result only one-quarter of eligible Africans registered to vote. The prime minister of the CAF, Sir Roy WELENSKY (1907–1991), ordered the arrest of ZANC leaders claiming they had been involved in illegal actions. Kaunda and other party leaders were arrested and ZANC was banned.

While Kaunda was in detention, ZANC was revived as the United National Independence Party (UNIP) by Mathias Mainza Chona (1930–2001), a militant nationalist, who kept the leading position for Kaunda. Upon his release in 1960, Kaunda became president of UNIP and led the party in its fight to dissolve the CAF and gain independence for Northern Rhodesia.

See also: CHONA, MATHIAS MAINZA (Vol. V); ENGLAND AND AFRICA (Vols. III, IV, V); INDEPENDENCE MOVEMENTS (Vol. V); NATIONALISM AND INDEPENDENCE MOVEMENTS (Vol. IV); POLITICAL PARTIES AND ORGANIZATIONS (Vols. IV, V); UNITED NATIONAL INDEPENDENCE PARTY (Vol. V).

Further reading: Eugenia W. Herbert, *Twilight on the Zambezi: Late Colonialism in Central Africa* (New York: Palgrave Macmillan, 2002); Robert I. Rotberg, *The Rise of Nationalism in Central Africa: The Making of Malawi and Zambia, 1873–1964* (Cambridge, Mass.: Harvard University Press, 1965).

United Nations and Africa The United Nations (UN) was founded on October 24, 1945, in the wake of World War II (1939–45). There were 51 founding members, only four of which were African states—EGYPT, ETHIOPIA, LIBERIA, and SOUTH AFRICA. As of the year 2000, UN membership has since increased to 189, with more than a quarter of the member states coming from Africa.

The United Nations has a short but important history in Africa. The present-day United Nations was a result of the League of Nations project, which was initiated after World War I (1914–18) but faltered in the years leading up to World War II. The United Nations was formed in that war's aftermath to foster the idea of collective security. The central principles of the organization include sovereign equality among nations, non-intervention, nonaggression, and respect for the independence and territory of member states.

The United Nations is a complex, international umbrella organization that includes six basic organs: the General Assembly, the Security Council, the International Court of Justice, the Economic and Social Council, the Secretariat, and the Trusteeship Council. Each organ is charged with different responsibilities.

The main purposes of the United Nations are the maintenance of international peace and security, fostering friendly relations among states, finding solutions to social and economic challenges, and developing an understanding of the respect for human rights.

When the United Nations was founded, most of what would become Africa's countries was still under COLONIAL RULE. This situation soon changed, however, and many African nations immediately joined the United Nations after achieving independence. With each newly independent country that joined the organization, Africa increasingly made its international presence felt, especially in the General Assembly, to which every member nation sent representatives.

During the 1950s the United Nations was influential in the DECOLONIZATION process. This was especially true for the Trusteeship Council, which required colonial powers to make annual reports on each UN TRUST TERRITORY they governed. At the same time colonized peoples could send delegations to the United Nations as a way to express grievances. By 1960 GHANA, LIBYA, MOROCCO, Republic of the SUDAN, and TUNISIA had gained their independence and joined the United Nations, bringing the African contingent to nine.

In 1956 the United Nations intervened in the Suez Crisis, which unfolded after Egyptian president Gamal Abdel NASSER (1918–1970) nationalized the SUEZ CANAL. When Britain, France, and Israel launched an offensive against Egypt, UN secretary-general Dag Hammarskjöld

In 1958 the secretary-general of the United Nations, Dag Hammarskjöld, meets with the president of Ghana, Kwame Nkrumah. © *New York World-Telegram & Sun Collection/ Library of Congress*

(1905–1961) helped defuse the situation by sending an international peacekeeping force made up of soldiers from member nations. The success of this UN Emergency Force set a precedent for the deployment of UN peacekeeping troops to trouble spots around the world.

Independent African countries also allied themselves with other formerly colonized countries in the BANDUNG AFRO-ASIAN CONFERENCE, which laid the foundation for the Nonaligned Movement. Founded in 1961, the Bandung Conference nations sought a position that avoided the intensifying Cold War rivalry between the United States and the Soviet Union.

Perhaps the most notable direct UN intervention in sub-Saharan Africa in its early history occurred in the former BELGIAN CONGO. Upon declaring independence as the Democratic Republic of the CONGO, in 1960, the country immediately fell into crisis, with ethnic and political rivalries making the region very unstable. Although a substantial UN military and civil presence helped keep the situation from exploding into outright civil war, the intervention also led to the death of the UN secretary general. In 1961 the plane carrying Hammarskjöld crashed en route to the Congo.

In 1958, with the establishment of the UN Economic Commission for Africa (ECA), the General Assembly took a step that, in subsequent years, had major implications for economic development. While at first the primary concern of the ECA was the economic reconstruction of countries and regions devastated by war, its later focus shifted to social, economic, and infrastructure development.

See also: COLD WAR AND AFRICA (Vol. V); CONGO CRISIS (Vol. V); DEVELOPMENT (Vol. V); INDEPENDENCE MOVEMENTS (Vol. V); LEAGUE OF NATIONS AND AFRICA (Vol. IV); MANDATE (Vol. IV); NATIONALISM AND INDEPENDENCE MOVEMENTS (Vol. IV); NONALIGNED MOVEMENT AND AFRICA (Vol. V); UNITED NATIONS AND AFRICA (Vol. V); WORLD WAR I AND AFRICA (Vol. IV); WORLD WAR II AND AFRICA (Vol. IV).

United States and Africa American involvement on the African continent was minimal during the 19th and early 20th centuries. Though American slavers were active on the western coast of Africa since the mid 1600s, United States (U.S.) involvement on the continent was relatively minimal when compared to other nations until the end of the U.S. Civil War (1861–65).

After the war, American MISSIONARIES, who initially came to Africa in the 1820s, began to arrive in greater numbers. Some, like the Reverend William H. SHEPPARD (1865–1927), who worked in the Congo region, were individual African-Americans acting under the auspices of white-run American churches—in his case the Presbyterian Church. Others were sponsored by African-American denominations such as the African Methodist Episcopal Church, which sent missionaries to southern Africa in the 1890s.

Representatives from the United States were present at the BERLIN CONFERENCE (1884–85), but they were not involved in the partition of the African continent. Still recovering from its devastating Civil War, the United States was reluctant to join in the "scramble for Africa," a phrase used to describe the colonization of Africa by European powers in the late 19th century. In general, until World War I (1914–18) the United States limited its political involvement in Africa to LIBERIA, a country founded by freed American slaves in 1822. After the war, however, the United States became more engaged in African affairs. For example, American leaders denied France and Britain the right to annex Germany's former colonies outright and pushed instead for League of Nations MANDATE status for those territories.

Between the two world wars, U.S. interest in Africa was largely economic, with investments in RUBBER operations in Liberia and mines in southern Africa. Even so, U.S. influence did go beyond the commercial realm. The BACK-TO-AFRICA MOVEMENT, for instance, encouraged the return of African-Americans to their homelands in Africa. The philosophy behind the movement was articulated as early as the second half of the 19th century by the American physician Martin Delaney (1812–1885) and gained support in the early 20th century through the efforts of Jamaican Marcus GARVEY (1887–1940).

In the first half of the 20th century, many important African nationalist leaders, including Kwame NKRUMAH (1909–1972) and Nnamdi AZIKIWE (1904–1996), received their university education in the United States

The United States landed troops in North Africa during World War II (1939–45) and helped expel German and Italian forces from the continent. After the war the United States was concerned with strengthening France and Britain, making it wary of the instability African independence could cause those nations. As a result the United States supported the short-term preservation of

European colonial possessions and a gradual move toward self-government. Later, as African nations claimed their independence, the United States became more politically involved in the continent, as it attempted to gain allies for its struggle against the Soviet Union during the Cold War.

See also: COLD WAR AND AFRICA (Vol. IV); UNITED STATES AND AFRICA (Vol. V).

Universal Negro Improvement Association (UNIA)

Black-nationalist organization founded by Marcus GARVEY (1887–1940) that became a popular African-American movement. Garvey, heavily influenced by the ideals of Booker T. WASHINGTON (1856–1915), founded UNIA in Jamaica, in 1914. Early on it had minimal success. In 1916 Garvey traveled to the United States, where he became deeply involved with the African-American struggle to achieve equal rights. Inspired, in 1917 Garvey moved the headquarters of the UNIA to Harlem, in New York City, where the UNIA then flourished.

Garvey's experiences with white racism led him to reject the possibility of integration. Instead Garvey proposed an extreme form of black nationalism that called for African-Americans and other members of the AFRICAN DIASPORA to return to Africa, reclaim it, and establish a great African nation independent and free from white control. He even sent a delegation to the League of Nations to argue that it hand over the former German colonies in Africa—lost by Germany in the wake of World War I (1914–18)—to the UNIA for the founding of his proposed independent state.

Garvey's message, with its elements of racial unity and pride in African heritage, became wildly popular, and by 1920 the UNIA had established almost a thousand local chapters throughout the United States, Canada, Central America, the Caribbean, and Africa. Africans were attracted by the focus on economic development of the continent and trading and shipping links through his Black Star and subsequent Black Cross shipping concerns. Garvey's *Negro World* newspaper, founded in 1918, further spread his ideas on the continent. At its height in the 1920s, the number of official UNIA members topped 6 million.

The size and popularity of the UNIA did not prevent it from having detractors, however. Prominent African-American leaders such as W. E. B. DU BOIS (1868–1963) and James Weldon Johnson (1871–1938) challenged Garvey's views, as did some of the more moderate African nationalists. J. Edgar Hoover (1895–1972), director of the Federal Bureau of Investigation, took a special interest in the activities of Garvey and the UNIA, and he ultimately had Garvey arrested on charges of mail fraud. Garvey was imprisoned in 1925, and then deported to Jamaica two years later. The UNIA faltered under the weight of the

scandal, and though Garvey remained involved in the organization until his death, in 1940, it never regained the influence it enjoyed in the 1920s.

See also: BACK-TO-AFRICA MOVEMENT (Vol. IV); PAN-AFRICANISM (Vol. IV); THE UNITED STATES OF AMERICA AND AFRICA (Vols. IV, V).

Upper Volta

Colonial name of the territory that gained independence from France, in 1960, as Upper Volta; it was renamed BURKINA FASO in 1984. Beginning in the 15th century, the MOSSI STATES had control over most of the region known to Europeans as Upper Volta. By the end of the 19th century, however, French colonial forces overran the most powerful Mossi kingdom, Ouagadougou, marking the beginning of French COLONIAL RULE.

> **Upper Volta was so named because it is the northern source of both the Black Volta and White Volta rivers that fill Lake Volta, to the south, in present-day GHANA.**

After World War I (1914–18) the French administration used a policy of forced LABOR with Upper Volta's peasant classes to develop a COTTON industry, even though the crop was labor-intensive and the soil was generally ill-suited for that purpose. In 1932, in order to administer the region more effectively, Upper Volta was divided and distributed among the neighboring French colonies of IVORY COAST, FRENCH SOUDAN (now MALI), and NIGER. However, after World War II (1939–45) the Mossi peoples, who wanted a separate territorial identity, pressured France to reinstate Upper Volta as part of the FRENCH UNION. The following year Upper Volta became an autonomous country within the French Community. In 1960 the fully independent Republic of Upper Volta was declared, and Maurice Yameogo (1921–1993), head of the Voltaic Democratic Union, was elected the nation's first president.

See also: FRANCE AND AFRICA (Vols. IV, V).

Urabi, Ahmad (1841–1911) *Leader of Egypt's first nationalist movement*

From a peasant background, Colonel Ahmad Urabi emerged as a nationalist leader in EGYPT under Khedive Muhammad Tawfiq Pasha (1852–1892). Egypt had been left in political turmoil when Tawfiq's predecessor, Khedive ISMAIL (1830–1895), was dismissed by the Ottoman sultan, in 1879. Ismail's overspending had placed Egypt deeply in debt to foreign creditors, and in response Britain and France had taken control of the country's treasury, railroads, and many essential services.

In 1881, seeking to establish a government more favorable to the nationalist position, Urabi led a bloodless revolution against Khedive Tawfiq. Under Urabi's leadership Egypt's unpaid junior army officers demonstrated for their pay. Urabi then mobilized his followers to make broader political demands, which included restoring the officers' choice of war minister, enlarging the army, dismissing the prime minister, and reconvening the Assembly of Delegates. Eventually forcing Khedive Tawfiq to agree to a new constitution and elections, Urabi emerged as a national hero.

In 1882 Britain and France issued a joint declaration threatening to intervene on behalf of Khedive Tawfiq. Urabi, the war minister in Tawfiq's new cabinet, resisted, inciting a popular movement for the protection of Egypt and the defense of Islam against foreigners. Although this movement did not have wide popular support, it combined social protest with RELIGION and nationalism. In July of that year nationalist sentiment increased when the presence of Anglo-French naval vessels in the Mediterranean port city of ALEXANDRIA sparked anti-European riots. When Urabi refused to remove the armaments he had positioned to fortify the harbor, the French ships withdrew. The British responded by bombarding Alexandria and landing troops. Tawfiq sought British protection and left Urabi in charge of the government. In September 1882 Urabi's army was defeated at Tel-el-Kebir, near Alexandria. Urabi surrendered and was exiled to Ceylon. The British restored Khedive Tawfiq to power. Although Egypt was still formally an independent state within the Ottoman Empire, Britain had taken over direct control of its government.

See also: COLONIAL CONQUEST (Vol. IV); OTTOMAN EMPIRE AND AFRICA (Vol. IV).

Further reading: Juan R. I. Cole, *Colonialism and Revolution in the Middle East: Social and Cultural Origins of Egypt's Urabi Movement* (Cairo: University of Cairo Press, 1999); Ronald Robinson and John Gallagher, *Africa and the Victorians: The Official Mind of Imperialism* (New York: St. Martin's Press, 1961).

urbanization Process of becoming a city. The phenomenon of urbanization is not new to the African continent. History describes great urban centers, including Great Zimbabwe in southern Africa, TIMBUKTU in West Africa, and Carthage in North Africa. These and other precolonial urban centers were places of refuge, ritual power, military force, trade, and wealth. The nature of governance in these urban areas was very different from that found in the colonial cities that developed after them. During the period of COLONIAL RULE, in the late 19th and early 20th centuries, the rate of urbanization, the motivation for urban growth, and the nature of the urban setting changed.

Colonial Administrative Centers When European colonial interests came to Africa, cities grew as administrative and industrial centers and as international and regional trading hubs. Such cities also were places for Europeans to reside. In West Africa, colonial cities grew near or around the established urban centers. Some, such as Jenne and Timbuktu, were situated along old trade routes; others, like ACCRA, developed around old ports.

In some cases the establishment of a new colonial administrative center near an ancient trading town would lead to the demise of the latter. Such was the case with BAGAMOYO, in what is now TANZANIA, when DAR ES SALAAM was made the new capital of GERMAN EAST AFRICA. The same situation came about in states not under colonial control, as well, as in the case of ETHIOPIA. There, in 1887, MENELIK II (1844–1913) moved the administrative capital of the empire from Ankober to ADDIS ABABA, and the importance of Ankober quickly faded. However, some ancient cities, including CAIRO and TUNIS, continued to thrive under colonialism.

Areas rich in NATURAL RESOURCES resulted in cities such as JOHANNESBURG and ELIZABETHVILLE (now Lubumbashi), with growing populations and TRANSPORTATION infrastructures that facilitated the extraction of their mineral resources. In eastern and southern Africa, towns emerged more as residential areas for Europeans. These urban areas included SALISBURY (present-day Harare), DURBAN, and NAIROBI. Entebbe, in UGANDA, and BAMAKO, in FRENCH SOUDAN (now MALI), are other examples of cities that developed as European administrative centers.

Urban Population Control In many of the new cities, colonial administrators implemented policies that maintained strict control over the urban activities and movement of the African population. European colonial authorities and settlers would have preferred to maintain urban centers as European spaces, but the LABOR demands brought on by increased INDUSTRIALIZATION required Europeans and Africans to reside near each other. Because of this, city officials planned segregated living areas to keep the two groups separate. This urban segregation was not a new concept in Africa, however, as ancient urban kingdoms on the continent also had maintained separate neighborhoods for different ethnic groups and economic classes.

In many East African countries colonial policies forbade Africans to reside in European-dominated urban areas. This, combined with a smaller urban base at the start of the colonial period, resulted in lower urban growth rates in that region.

Initially colonial policies were effective in separating Africans and Europeans. Over time, however, migration from rural to urban areas increased dramatically. Along with this movement of people, the rapid pace of natural population growth led to greater interaction between races and ethnic groups.

Growth rates in the urban areas usually outpaced the ability of the administration to provide services, and expansive squatter settlements often arose on the outskirts of towns. Generally these settlements were seen as illegitimate and therefore did not receive funding for public services. As a result, life in squatter settlements was tenuous. Colonial governments often rezoned these areas for industrial or commercial use, forcing the African inhabitants onto more marginal land. Further, limited resources often spurred competition that divided the residential areas by ETHNIC GROUP. Ultimately African squatter settlements were characterized by unemployment, overcrowding, poor sanitation, discrimination, and a lack of public services.

For much of the colonial period single males comprised the majority of African urban populations. This resulted from the explicit designs of colonial administrations to allow only temporary migration of laborers for industrial jobs. Colonial authorities believed that the best way to ensure that Africans did not reside in the cities permanently was to have them maintain ties to their rural homesteads by leaving their families behind. However, after 1945 more and more women began to move to the cities, and migration rates increased dramatically. For example, between 1912 and 1952 the estimated population of Casablanca, in MOROCCO grew from 20,000 to 682,000. During this period, as the lines between African and European areas began to blur, racial interaction and ethnic diversity became major features of the urban setting.

Independent Development   As squatter settlements and African urban residential areas grew, social and support networks developed, often out of necessity. By the mid-1900s African urban residents were taking it upon themselves to make up for the shortcomings they encountered in their economic and social situations. For example, unable to afford homes, they built their own housing using recycled and local materials, including mud, iron, and plastic.

Also, in an entrepreneurial sprit, they established small businesses that produced or sold much-needed, affordably priced consumer products to other poor urban Africans. This marked the beginning of an economic movement that would be known as the "informal economy" and that would come to employ great numbers of urban migrants.

Despite the rapid urban growth rates of the colonial period, during this time the majority of Africans still lived in rural areas. It is estimated that even as late as 1950 less than 15 percent of the total population of sub-Saharan Africa resided in urban centers. This would change drastically, however, with the explosive urban growth of the post-independence era.

See also: ACCRA (Vols. II, III, V); ADDIS ABABA (Vols. I, V); BAMAKO (Vols. II, III, V); CAIRO (Vols. II, III, V); CARTHAGE (Vol. I); COLONIAL CONQUEST (Vol. IV); COLONIALSIM, INFLUENCE OF (Vol. IV); DURBAN (Vol. V); ENTEBBE (Vol. V); GREAT ZIMBABWE (Vol. II); HARARE (Vol. V); INDUSTRIALIZATION (Vol. V); JENNE (Vols. II, III); JOHANNESBURG (Vol. V); LUBUMBASHI (Vol. V); NAIROBI (Vol. V); TIMBUKTU (Vols. II, III); TUNIS (Vols. II, V); SETTLERS, EUROPEAN (Vol. IV); URBAN LIFE AND CULTURE (Vols. IV, V).

Further reading: David M. Anderson and Richard Rathbone, *Africa's Urban Past* (Portsmouth, N.H.: Heinneman, 2000); Tjalling Dijkstra, *Food Trade and Urbanization in Sub-Saharan Africa: From the Early Stone Age to the Structural Adjustment Era* (Leiden, Netherlands: African Studies Centre, 1995); Jane I. Guyer, ed., *Feeding African Cities* (Bloomington, Ind.: Indiana University Press, 1987).

urban life and culture   Colonialism brought with it an increase in the growth rates of African cities and the widespread URBANIZATION of the continent that continues today. Although urban centers are not new to Africa, colonial administrators established industries and businesses for the export ECONOMY that demanded large amounts of African LABOR. African men, who migrated to the cities leaving their families in the countryside, comprised the bulk of laborers during this period. In cities like JOHANNESBURG, SOUTH AFRICA, this created a high male-to-female ratio in the urban areas and brought people from all different ethnic groups to the cities. This movement changed the feel of many urban centers from friendly, busy market centers to bustling centers of commerce composed more of strangers than neighbors.

Ethnic groups within cities tended to congregate in their own separate neighborhoods. This tendency was reinforced by migrants from the countryside who, as strangers to the city, sought out familiar surroundings in terms of language and culture. European colonizers, on the other hand, usually occupied neighborhoods with large houses and enjoyed access to more of the cities' urban infrastructure. They often employed Africans to clean their homes and serve as gardeners.

In the Arab-influenced areas of Africa, urban growth resulted in the establishment of different neighborhoods or sectors outside the walls of the traditional Arab quarters, which were known as *medinas*.

African workers often occupied organized housing for laborers, sharing small living quarters to save what little money they made to send home to their families. Merchants of different ethnic groups, who owned small shops or sold consumer goods on the streets and in open-air markets, occupied different neighborhoods as well. Initially colonizers invested only in whatever infrastructure was necessary to facilitate the export of Africa's resources. Most often this included railroads, road networks, and port facilities. Public TRANSPORTATION—other than services for moving laborers around—was not considered a priority until later in the colonial period.

After World War II (1939–45), the colonial powers began to plan for the eventual DECOLONIZATION of Africa. They then realized the need for facilities to educate the African middle class to have the skills to govern after independence. As a result, advanced educational institutions arose in the major cities across Africa. Other businesses and services developed as well, and African cities soon bustled with diverse markets, restaurants, hotels, movie houses, bookstores, and nightclubs.

From the 1940s to the 1960s, a musical movement known as HIGHLIFE became popular in West African cities, especially in ACCRA, GHANA, and LAGOS, NIGERIA. This distinctly urban and cosmopolitan musical style reflected influences from traditional African rhythms as well as from American jazz and Caribbean calypso. The lyrics of the songs, sung in both English and indigenous tongues, often told of the challenges of life in the city.

Whereas colonial cities had been the places where colonizers exhibited the most social, political, and economic control, in the late colonial period, cities came to be characterized by civil unrest. In the aftermath of World War II (1939–45), individuals and organizations from the educated, merchant classes, as well as LABOR UNIONS and student unions, agitated for the end of COLONIAL RULE. As a result political riots and strikes became an increasingly common urban phenomenon in Africa. The pattern continued into the era of independence, as the populations of African cities became even larger and more diverse.

See also: COLONIALISM, INFLUENCE OF (Vol. IV); EDUCATION (Vol. IV); INDEPENDENCE MOVEMENTS (Vol. V); URBAN LIFE AND CULTURE (Vol. V).

U Tamsi, Tchicaya (Gerald Felix Tchicaya U Tam'si) (1931–1988) *Leading Congolese nationalist and poet*

U Tamsi was born in the city of BRAZZAVILLE, when it was still the administrative capital of FRENCH EQUTORIAL AFRICA. In 1946 he moved to France, where he soon established himself as a leading, young Congolese voice. He joined the independence struggle in the 1950s, supporting the militant, nationalist politician Patrice LUMUMBA (1925–1961) and Lumumba's Congolese National Movement in its struggle to gain independence from Belgian COLONIAL RULE.

U Tamsi's sophisticated writings reflect a harsh world that is only slightly softened by hope. Stylistically he used humorous, symbolic, and surreal visions of reality as a means of commenting on the human condition. He also sought to further the exploration of NÉGRITUDE that had been begun earlier by Aimé CESAIRE (1913–   ), Leopold SENGHOR (1906–2001), and other French-speaking African and Afro-Caribbean intellectuals. By the time of his death, in 1988, U Tamsi had become one of Africa's leading poets, influencing an entirely new generation of writers.

See also: LITERATURE IN COLONIAL AFRICA (Vol. IV).

V

Vereeniging, Treaty of Peace treaty of 1902 that ended the ANGLO-BOER WAR (1899–1902), establishing TRANSVAAL and the ORANGE FREE STATE as British crown colonies and paving the way for the UNION OF SOUTH AFRICA. The Anglo-Boer War, or South African War, was the result of many years of tensions between British GOLD-mining interests on the WITWATERSRAND, and the BOERS of the Transvaal under the government of Paul KRUGER (1825–1904). Led by their high commissioner to SOUTH AFRICA, Sir Alfred MILNER (1854–1925), Britain pressured the Kruger government to yield to the British mining interests, though publicly Milner claimed to be seeking fuller civil rights for the mostly British immigrants called UITLANDERS, who had come to the Witwatersrand for economic opportunity. The British were also driven by a desire for a unified South Africa, for they were concerned about German support for the Boers. In 1899 A build-up of British troops in the CAPE COLONY was staged to provoke the Boers into declaring war. After the British defeated the Boer regular forces in the field, hostilities became marked by bloody guerrilla warfare and the atrocities of British concentration camps. On May 31, 1902, the two sides signed a peace treaty in Vereeniging, a town south of JOHANNESBURG, and the British secured victory.

The treaty resulted from tense negotiations between Milner and the Boers, who were headed by General Louis BOTHA (1862–1919). The British received full sovereignty over Transvaal and the Orange Free State, transforming the territories into crown colonies. In return, the Boers received 3 million pounds sterling toward their war debt, a protection of the Dutch LANGUAGE for official usage, and a continuance of previous property rights. The British also allowed the Boers to continue their policy of excluding non-whites in their territories from political enfranchisement. Finally, the British promised the Boers eventual self-government, which did not occur until 1910, when CAPE COLONY and NATAL merged with Transvaal and the Orange Free State to form the Union of South Africa. The union remained part of the British Empire and, later, the British Commonwealth, until 1961, but throughout this period the government was in the hands of AFRIKANERS, as the Boers came to be called.

See also: ENGLAND AND AFRICA (Vols. III, IV, V).

Verwoerd, Hendrik (Hendrik Frensch Verwoerd; H. F. Verwoerd) (1901–1966) *Prime minister of South Africa from 1958 to 1966*

Born in Amsterdam, the Netherlands, Verwoerd came to exercise great influence in the shaping of APARTHEID in SOUTH AFRICA. The son of MISSIONARIES, he emigrated with his family to South Africa in 1903. After studying in Europe, he returned to South Africa, in 1927, and became a professor of applied psychology (and later of sociology) at the University of Stellenbosch. From 1937 to 1948 he served as editor of the AFRIKAANS-language, pro-Nationalist Party newspaper, *Die Transvaaler,* which was published in JOHANNESBURG. Following the 1948 electoral victory of the Nationalist Party, with its almost exclusively white electorate, Verwoerd became a senator.

From 1950 to 1958 he held the important post of minister of native affairs. In that role, he was instrumental in formulating the policy of apartheid, which sought to maintain the supremacy of the minority, white population over the African majority. In 1958 Verwoerd was elected to the House of Assembly. Shortly thereafter, when Johannes Gerhardus Strijdom (1893–1958) died, Verwoerd took his place as prime minister of South Africa.

In an attempt to defuse the criticism aimed at apartheid, Verwoerd, in 1959, established a "homeland," or *Bantustan,* system for Africans. Under this system Africans were supposed to either already live in areas designated for their exclusive use or be resettled there. However, much of the land set aside for the homelands was among South Africa's least fertile, and resettlement into these homelands further isolated and segregated Africans from Europeans.

More than any other white South African politician of his time, Verwoerd molded the content and steered the direction of apartheid.

See also: VERWOERD, HENDRIK (Vol. V).

Further reading: Henry Kenney, *Architect of Apartheid: H. F. Verwoerd, an Appraisal* (Johannesburg: J. Ball, 1980).

Wafd Party Popular nationalist movement, initially organized by Sad Zaghlul (1857–1927), that evolved into the leading political party in EGYPT, from 1918 to 1952. The party originated in 1912, when Sad Zaghlul resigned as education minister in the PROTECTORATE government over disputes with Khedive Abbas II (1874–1944). Zaghlul and those associated with him were strongly influenced in their thinking by the Muslim philosopher and reformer Jamal al-Din al-AFGHANI (1838–1897). Once officially a part of the opposition, Zaghlul quietly worked to build support for a parliamentary government and a liberal democracy in Egypt.

The Wafd Party takes its name from the permanent delegation (*Wafd,* in Arabic) of Egyptians that Zaghlul led to London, in 1918, to argue the case for Egyptian independence. Zaghlul continued to press the nationalist cause at home and abroad until 1919, when British authorities had him exiled as a troublemaker. Political unrest, at times violent, in support of the independence movement marked the next three years. Finally, Britain decided to give up its protectorate over Egypt and unilaterally declared the country independent in 1922.

The Wafd organized itself into a political party in September 1923. Its electoral base included members of both the Muslim majority and the Coptic Christian minority. Campaigning on a platform of full independence and Egyptian control of the SUEZ CANAL and the Sudan, the Wafd Party won a landslide victory in the elections of 1924. As a result a new constitutional government emerged under King Fuad I (1868–1936), with a cabinet headed by Sad Zaghlul.

The Wafd Party remained a constant presence in Egyptian politics until 1953, when parliamentary government and liberal democracy were replaced by radical Arab nationalism. The charismatic Gamal Abdel NASSER (1918–1970) soon emerged as the leader of a new Egypt.

The Wafd Party did not completely disappear, however. In 1981 Hosni Mubarak (1938–) became president and instituted economic and political reforms. Five new political parties were established, including the reconstituted Neo-Wafd Party.

See also: NATIONALIST AND INDEPENDENCE MOVEMENTS (Vol. IV); MUBARAK, HOSNI (Vol. V).

Wallace-Johnson, I. T. A. (1895–1965) *West African labor union leader, politician, and pan-Africanist*

Born in Wilderforce, SIERRA LEONE, I. T. A. Wallace-Johnson established his country's first labor union and went on to become active in both African and international workers' causes. Educated at mission schools, he left before completing secondary school in order to support his family. After holding various jobs, in 1913 he went to work for the British colonial government. While employed as a clerk in government offices, he began his activities as a union organizer. His abilities as a public speaker, as well as his talent for organization, led to his rapid advancement in the union movement until his support of a workers' strike, in 1914, led to his dismissal from the government's customs office.

Over the next decade and a half, Wallace-Johnson served in the British Army, shipped out as a merchant sailor, and wrote for the *Daily Times,* a newspaper located in LAGOS, NIGERIA. By the 1930s, however, he had attained prominence as a spokesman for both the union movement as well as African nationalism, attending the International

Conference of Negro Workers, in Germany in 1930, as well as visiting the Soviet Union with a group of African nationalists. By the early 1930s he also had become an editor of and regular contributor to the Communist-oriented French publication, *Negro Worker.*

Later in the 1930s he became even better known when he was arrested for writing what British officials considered to be seditious material for the *African Morning Post,* in the GOLD COAST COLONY (today's GHANA). In England to appeal his conviction, he met a wide range of British intellectuals and African nationalists and took editorial positions with both *Africa and the World* and the *African Sentinel.*

In 1938, returning to FREETOWN, Sierra Leone from England, Wallace-Johnson brought with him several thousand copies of the African Sentinel, which were seized by customs officials. Using this as a rallying point, Wallace-Johnson quickly organized public appearances and demonstrations that enabled him to launch a new political party, the West African Youth League.

Back in Sierra Leone Wallace-Johnson launched a branch of the West African Youth League, aided in the effort by Constance CUMMINGS-JOHN (1918–2000). This was the nation's first effective mass political party, and it won elections for both the Freetown city council and the Sierra Leone national legislature. Wallace-Johnson seemed on his way to building a large-scale movement. Realizing the danger this represented to their authority, especially in light of the looming war clouds in Europe, British authorities moved to silence opposition. In 1939 they passed a number of new laws that severely limited civil liberties in Sierra Leone. Then, when World War II (1939–45) began, Wallace-Johnson was interned by the authorities as an "undesirable." Although Wallace-Johnson eventually was released in 1944, he never regained the power he once had. He continued to have speaking engagements, but his stands on a number of issues—including a proposed reorganization of Sierra Leone's Legislative Council—led to his marginalization as a political force. He died at the age of 70, while attending political conference in Ghana.

See also: COLONIAL RULE (Vol. IV); ENGLAND AND AFRICA (Vol. IV); LABOR UNIONS (Vols. IV, V) NATIONALISM AND INDEPENDENCE MOVEMENTS (Vol. IV); NEWSPAPERS (Vol. IV).

Further reading: John R. Cartwright, *Politics in Sierra Leone: 1947–1967* (Toronto: University of Toronto Press, 1970).

Walvis Bay City on the Atlantic coast of NAMIBIA, (formerly SOUTH WEST AFRICA) and important deepwater port. Located about 250 miles (400 km) west of the country's present capital, Windhoek, Walvis Bay is situated at the mouth of the Kuiseb River on the Atlantic Ocean. The Namib Desert surrounds Walvis Bay on three sides. Walvis Bay is one of only two ocean harbors in Namibia, the other being Lüderitz, which is located farther to the south.

Much of the settlement's history has been intricately tied to its value as a port. In 1487 Bartholomeu Dias (1450–1500), a Portuguese explorer, became the first European to enter Walvis Bay. He originally named it Conception Bay, but from the 16th century onward it became known as Whale Bay because of the high concentration of whales in the area. *Walvisbaai,* as it is known in Dutch and AFRIKAANS, also translates as "whale bay." It became a popular port for American whalers in the 18th and 19th centuries. Beginning in 1878 Walvis Bay and offshore islands in the area were claimed by Britain, though the British did not lay any claims to South West Africa overall. Then, in 1884, Walvis Bay was incorporated into the British-controlled CAPE COLONY, even though Germany had claimed the surrounding region as a colony in the same year. The area thus became a pawn in the European imperial competition that led to the colonial PARTITION of Africa.

When SOUTH AFRICA became a unified country, in 1910, Walvis Bay became part of it, specifically of the Cape Province. South Africa took over the administration of the former German colony of South West Africa after World War I (1914–18) as a MANDATE territory under the authority of the League of Nations. After 1948 South Africa continued to administer it as a TRUST TERRITORY for the United Nations.

See also: COLONIAL RULE (Vol. IV); DIAS, BARTOLOMEU (Vol. II); GERMANY AND AFRICA (Vol. IV); LEAGUE OF NATIONS AND AFRICA (Vol. IV); UNITED NATIONS AND AFRICA (Vols. IV, V).

warfare and weapons During the colonial era, war in Africa was dominated by the spread of modernized weapons. As the European powers tightened their control on their African colonies, they increasingly supported their own armed forces with indigenous African soldiers and police, whom they equipped with industrialized armaments. This gave the colonial powers the means to dominate indigenous forces. There was the occasional rare victory for a traditionally armed African army—such as the Battle of ISANDLWANA (1879), in Zululand—but it was soon clear that there was little chance of indigenous Africans winning a sustained conflict against European forces.

The ANGLO-BOER WAR (1899–1902), in SOUTH AFRICA, represented the first time in Africa that two armies fully equipped with modern weaponry conducted a prolonged war. Outside of the Anglo-Boer War modern weapons generally remained in the hands of the forces of the colonial powers. In ETHIOPIA, however, Emperor MENELIK II (1844–1913) amassed a powerful array of advanced arms, some imported and some produced in Ethiopia itself. Aided by these weapons, Menelik's forces were able to deal invading Italian forces a decisive blow at the Battle of ADOWA (1896), a victory that helped preserve Ethiopian independence until the 1930s.

As a result of this situation, except for occasional rebellions and outbreaks of violence, warfare during the colonial era was a matter of conflict between European armies. One of the few exceptions was the Italian invasion of Ethiopia during the 1930s, which saw the modern army of Mussolini's Fascist government easily defeat the ill-equipped forces of HAILE SELASSIE I (1892–1975). On the whole, however, armies on the African continent during this period were almost always led by European officers in pursuit of European aims, whether those aims be the quelling of a revolt or the more widespread conflicts of World War I and World War II.

See also: ANGLO-ASHANTI WARS (Vol. IV); ANGLO-BOER WAR (Vol. IV); ANGLO-ZULU WARS (Vol. IV); ARAB-ISRAELI WARS (Vols. IV, V); ARMIES, COLONIAL (Vol. IV); BIAFRA (Vol. V); CIVIL WARS (Vol. V); COLD WAR AND AFRICA (Vols. IV, V); COLONIAL CONQUEST (Vol. IV); ITALO-ETHIOPIAN WARS (Vol. IV); LEAGUE OF NATIONS AND AFRICA (Vol. IV); OMDURMAN, BATTLE OF (Vol. IV); PACIFICATION (Vol. IV); RESISTANCE AND REBELLION (Vol. IV); TIRAILLEURS SÉNÉGALAIS (Vol. IV); UNITED NATIONS AND AFRICA (Vol. IV); VEREENIGING, TREATY OF (Vol. IV); WARFARE AND WEAPONS (Vols. I, II, III, V); WORLD WAR I AND AFRICA (Vol. IV); WORLD WAR II AND AFRICA (Vol. IV).

Washington, Booker T. (Booker Taliaferro Washington) (1856–1915) African-American educator and activist

Washington was born into SLAVERY in Hales Ford, Virginia, in the United States. After emancipation, in 1865, he labored in salt and coal mines while also gaining an elementary education. In 1871 Washington enrolled in the Hampton Institute, a school for African-Americans in Hampton, Virginia. There he was exposed to the ideals of its principal, General Samuel C. Armstrong (1839–1893), who believed that a practical education was best for African-American students. After graduating, in 1875, Washington based his own ideology on Armstrong's theories and on the structured training he received at the Hampton Institute. Washington taught at Hampton from 1879 to 1881 before becoming the founding principal of a new school in Tuskegee, Alabama. Under his direction, the Tuskegee Normal and Industrial Institute became a major center of African-American education.

In 1895 Washington delivered what came to be known as the "Atlanta Compromise" speech in Atlanta, Georgia, in which he outlined his ideology, which had been developed and put into action over 14 years at his Tuskegee Institute. The road to equality for African-Americans, Washington declared, was through a practical, or vocational, education rather than through a higher education based on the humanities. He argued that attaining economic stability and wealth would inevitably lead to an increase in social status; it would also win the respect and acceptance of the dominant white society. In the meantime Washington felt that African-Americans should remain patient and accept the current social and political discriminations they faced.

In the year following this address, Washington went on to become the most prominent African-American in the United States. He garnered the support of wealthy, white capitalists and philanthropists, to the point where they would not contribute to other African-American causes without Washington's approval. His "Tuskegee Machine" became a central institutional force in African-American society.

Washington's high profile, and that of Tuskegee, made him influential abroad as well, especially in Africa. His autobiography, entitled *Up From Slavery* (1901), was a major inspiration to Jamaican-born activist Marcus GARVEY (1887–1940). Washington's views on industrial education as a means of self-betterment made a great impression among Africans, who related the situation of African-Americans to their own. The Ghanaian educator James E. Kwegyir AGGREY (1875–1927), who had been educated in North Carolina, became an active proponent of Washington's philosophy for Africa under COLONIAL RULE. South African schools such as the Ohlange Institute at Inanda, SOUTH AFRICA, founded by John L. DUBE (1871–1946) and the AME Wilberforce Institute, in Evanton, TRANSVAAL, were modeled on the Tuskegee Institute. In planning FORT HARE COLLEGE, South African educational officials looked to Tuskegee for ideas. Schools in KENYA and GHANA, and in non-African countries like India and Panama, also looked up to Tuskegee.

In addition to influencing the development of schools in Africa, Tuskegee also had an influence on colonial AGRICULTURE. For example, the German colonial government of TOGOLAND hired African-American agricultural demonstrators trained at Tuskegee to assist them with growing COTTON as a cash crop.

While Washington was successful in walking the narrow line between attempting to better African-Americans and not threatening whites, he earned in the process a strong opposition. African-American intellectuals such as W. E. B. DU BOIS (1868–1963) challenged Washington's moderate and outwardly accommodating beliefs, calling instead for vigorous protest of social and political conditions and supporting the virtues of a more traditional, less vocational higher education for the betterment of black society. By 1912 this opposition and the rise of the National Association for the Advancement of Colored People (NAACP) had begun to limit Washington's influence. In Africa, as well, the rise of NATIONALISM AND INDEPENDENCE MOVEMENTS meant that African political leaders and thinkers increasingly embraced the more radical views of Du Bois, while Washington's approach began to fall out of favor. In the late 20th century, however, as the continent struggled with development, some of Washington's ideas again became current.

In 1915 Washington became ill while in New York City and returned to Alabama, where he died.

See also: EDUCATION (Vol. IV); UNITED STATES AND AFRICA (Vols. IV, V).

Further reading: Kenneth J. King, *Pan-Africanism and Education: A Study of Race Philanthropy and Education in the Southern States of America and East Africa* (Oxford, U.K.: Clarendon Press, 1971).

Watch Tower Movement Anticolonialist religious movement of Central and southern Africa. The Watch Tower Movement in Africa originated with the British missionary Joseph Booth (1851–1932). In 1892 the highly unconventional Booth established a mission of the Baptist Scottish Free Church, in Blantyre, in what was then the British colony of NYASALAND (present-day MALAWI). Treating Africans as equals and paying high wages, Booth's mission was very successful.

By 1903 Booth had joined the Seventh Day Adventist Church and was upsetting colonial authorities throughout Central and southern Africa with his anticolonial messages. Fearing possible rebellions in Booth's wake, the colonial governments of MOZAMBIQUE and then Nyasaland deported him, and he landed in SOUTH AFRICA. In 1906 the Seventh Day Adventists, seeking to distance themselves from his controversial activities, excommunicated Booth.

Disenchanted, Booth turned to the ideas of Charles Taze Russell (1852–1916), an American who had founded the Watch Tower Bible and Tract Society, in 1884. Russell preached that a period of great trouble, beginning in 1874, would lead to the Biblical apocalypse, in 1914, and result in a new period of peace, in 1915.

Booth brought Russellism back to CAPE TOWN, South Africa, and set about spreading Russell's beliefs through the mail and African MISSIONARIES. One such missionary was Elliot Kamwana (1872–1956), who had been previously baptized an Adventist by Booth and joined Booth's new movement. Kamwana took the religion into Nyasaland in 1909. He applied Russell's ideas to the African situation under COLONIAL RULE, claiming that 1914 was the year that all Europeans would leave Africa. Kamwana was successful in winning converts, baptizing an estimated 10,000 people

into the religion. He then took the Watch Tower Movement into Mozambique, where he preached until 1914, when the Portuguese colonial authorities deported him back to Nyasaland. Once World War I (1914–18) began, the British accused Kamwana of interfering with the recruitment of African troops and imprisoned him in the SEYCHELLES.

By 1910 Joseph Booth had dropped Russellism in favor of becoming a Seventh Day Baptist.

The growth of the Watch Tower Movement was not dependent only on Kamwana, however. Russellism fit neatly into the events of the period, with colonialism as the time of trouble and World War I as the beginning of the final, cleansing apocalypse.

During the 1920s, in spite of the fact that the war had ended with the Europeans still firmly entrenched in Africa, the Watch Tower Movement spread into the Katanga province of the BELGIAN CONGO. Known there as the Kitwala Movement, it proceeded to find many converts among the African miners of the COPPERBELT of the Congo and NORTHERN RHODESIA (present-day ZAMBIA). Espousing racial, economic, and political equality, the movement took on highly Afro-centric political tones, equating colonialism with evil. The radicalization of the movement in Africa led the international Watch Tower Movement (whose followers became known as the Jehovah's Witnesses) to renounce its African offshoot, while colonial authorities tried without success to ban the RELIGION entirely.

The anticolonialist, antiauthoritarian attitudes of the Watch Tower Movement also influenced John CHILEMBWE (c. 1872–1915), who in 1915 launched a rebellion against colonial authorities in Nyasaland. The rebels killed three white plantation owners before British soldiers put down the revolt. Chilembwe was shot while trying to escape into Mozambique.

Kamwana returned to Nyasaland in 1937 and participated in furthering the movement into the 1950s, though by that point its influence had diminished. Even after the end of the colonial era in Africa, however, the Watch Tower Movement and its antiauthoritarian stance continued, this time opposing the authority of the African governments by refusing to pay taxes and resisting mandatory public-works projects. The Jehovah's Witnesses have since reconnected with many Watch Tower groups in Africa, though many still remain independent.

See also: CHRISTIANITY, INFLUENCE OF (Vols. II, III, IV, V); COLONIALISM, INFLUENCE OF (Vol. IV); KIMBANGU, SIMON (Vol. IV); RESISTANCE AND REBELLION (Vol. IV).

Welensky, Roy (Sir) (1907–1991) *Labor union leader and politician in Rhodesia*

A powerfully built man who, from 1926 to 1928, was Rhodesia's heavyweight boxing champion, Roy Welensky rose through the ranks of the labor-union movement to become a key figure in Central African political developments during the 1950s and early 1960s. Born in SALISBURY (renamed Harare, in 1980), in SOUTHERN RHODESIA (now ZIMBABWE), he dropped out of school at the age of 14 and eventually worked for Rhodesia Railways, first as a fireman and later as an engineer.

An active LABOR unionist, Welensky rose steadily in the power structure of the railway workers' union before entering politics, serving on both Northern Rhodesia's Legislative Council and Executive Council. During World War II (1939–45), he was instrumental in the founding of Rhodesia's Labor Party, seeking to use it to keep jobs in the hands of white workers at the expense of Africans.

During this same period Welensky began urging the establishment of a unified Rhodesia, which he believed would be able to maintain white domination of the region. When British authorities joined the Rhodesias with NYASALAND in an independent federation known as the CENTRAL AFRICAN FEDERATION, Welensky became both deputy prime minister and minister of transport, posts he held from 1953 to 1956. He became prime minister in 1956, continuing to lead the United Federal Party and the federation until its demise, in 1963.

In 1964 Welensky published *Welensky, 4000 Days.* a defense of the Central African Federation and of his government. In it, he expressed great bitterness over British policy that he thought caused the collapse of the federation.

Following the dissolution of the federation Welensky left politics, entering a long period of retirement. He became an outspoken opponent of the African-dominated states that emerged from both Nyasaland (now MALAWI) and NORTHERN RHODESIA (now ZAMBIA). A staunch believer in maintaining ties with Britain, he also opposed the radical white government of Southern Rhodesia, which broke away from the United Kingdom in 1965.

See also: ENGLAND AND AFRICA (Vol. IV); NATIONALISM AND INDEPENDENCE MOVEMENTS (Vol. IV); SETTLERS, EUROPEAN (Vol. IV).

West African Pilot
Highly influential anticolonial newspaper published in LAGOS, NIGERIA, founded by leading nationalist politician Nnamdi AZIKIWE (1904–1996). Newspaper publishing had a long tradition in West Africa. As early as 1857 an African newspaper, the *Accra Herald*, was published in GHANA. While such NEWSPAPERS dealt with political issues, they usually did so rather gingerly, since their readership was primarily the educated African elite.

Nnamdi Azikiwe broke with this tradition when, in 1937, he founded the *West African Pilot*. This occurred upon his return to Lagos from ACCRA, where he had honed his journalistic skills for two years as editor of the *African Morning Post*. The *Post* had reached out beyond the older elite to the growing number of educated young people who were increasingly anxious to end colonialism. When Azikiwe publicly voiced this discontent, Britain charged him with sedition. His trial and ultimate vindication boosted his popularity and earned him a hero's welcome when he returned to Lagos.

With the founding of the *Pilot*, Azikiwe launched a revolutionary brand of journalism. In the words of one observer, it was "a fire-eating and aggressive nationalist paper of the highest order." Within a short time it had attracted a readership of 9,000, a high number for the time. During the next decade Azikiwe established a chain of six newspapers in major Nigerian cities. While they were consistently and aggressively critical of British COLONIAL RULE, they also were run along business lines. For not only was Azikiwe a staunch political nationalist, but he was also an economic nationalist, as indicated by his role in founding the African Continental Bank, in 1944.

Newspapers such as Azikiwe's *West African Pilot* were an important factor in the rise of African NATIONALISM AND INDEPENDENCE MOVEMENTS.

See also: COLONIALISM, INFLUENCE OF (Vol. IV).

Western Sahara
Present-day country of some 103,000 square miles (266,800 sq km) bordering on the Atlantic Ocean, with MOROCCO to the north and MAURITANIA to the east and south. During the colonial era the territory was known as SPANISH SAHARA. Prior to colonization the area that became Western Sahara was dominated by Sanhaja Berber traders, the group that established the Almoravid empire in the 11th and 12th centuries. The Saharawi, a pastoralist ethnic group originally from the Arabian Peninsula, arrived later and settled in pockets throughout northwest Africa.

In 1860 a weak and financially distressed Morocco ceded some of its arid southern coastal territory to Spain. Spain, for its part, desired to protect its trading and fishing interests in the Canary Islands, located in the Atlantic Ocean off the Moroccan coast. Then in the early 1880s Spain signed treaties with local groups that allowed it to establish a coastal PROTECTORATE that stretched from Cape Bojador to Cap Blanc (at the present-day border of Western Sahara and Mauritania). In 1884–85 the other European colonial powers confirmed these holdings at the BERLIN CONFERENCE.

During the first decade of the 20th century, Spanish settlers began moving into the hinterlands from their coastal settlements, causing the Saharawi to take up arms in an effort to repel the invaders. (The fierce Saharawi resistance to the colonial efforts of both Spain and France would continue until 1958.)

In light of the political instability that was threatening the country, in 1912 the Moroccan sultan Moulay Hafid (r. 1908–1912) signed the Treaty of Fez, officially making Morocco a French protectorate. By the same treaty, however, Spain was allowed to continue as the chief power in its coastal settlements in the Western Sahara. At the time these settlements included Villa Cisneros (now Tarfaya) and Río de Oro (now Dakhla). By 1930 the Spanish had established the town of Laayoune (El Aioún), which became the colonial administrative center. Four years later Spain annexed Ifni, a relatively small region (580 square miles; 1,502 sq km) to the north of Cape Bojador.

Spain basically ignored the inland regions of Spanish Sahara until the 1950s, when Spanish MINING companies began discovering phosphate deposits. (These organic compounds are used as fertilizer and have become a highly valuable commodity.) At the same time, however, African independence movements were gaining momentum, and the European colonial powers were beginning to withdraw from the continent.

In 1956, first France and then Spain—led by Generalisimo Francisco Franco (1892–1975)—returned most of their northern Moroccan settlements to local rule. However, since influential Spanish mining companies owned the rights to the region's phosphates, the Spanish government decided to hold on to its territories in the south. In the wave of anticolonial violence that followed (1956–58), Moroccan national forces appeared to join Saharawi troops in their attempts to expel the Spanish settlers and gain independence. In the end, though, Morocco joined with Spain and France to subdue Saharawi resistance. During what became known as the Ecouvillon Operation, Moroccan forces knowingly left the Saharawi troops vulnerable to Spanish-French attacks, resulting in devastating losses. In 1958, as a reward for the cooperation, Franco awarded Morocco governing power in Villa Cisneros, a region with potential for mineral exploitation.

During the fighting for Saharawi independence, the Moroccan press accused Spanish forces of using mustard gas to kill 600 Saharawi troops.

During the 1960s, with their armed resistance effectively defeated, the Saharawi turned instead to political and diplomatic means to achieve an independent Western Sahara. Despite their efforts, however, protracted territorial disputes among the governments of Morocco, Mauritania, and Spain allowed Spain to retain its western Saharan holdings until 1976.

See also: ALMORAVIDS (Vol. II); POLISARIO (Vol. V); SAHARAWI (Vol. V); SPAIN AND AFRICA (Vol. III, IV, V); SPANISH MOROCCO (Vol. IV); WESTERN SAHARA (Vols. I, II, III, V).

white man's burden Doctrine that espoused a cultural superiority and the supposed "imperative" nature of European and American colonial expansion. In 1899 the British poet and novelist Rudyard Kipling (1865–1936) published the poem "The White Man's Burden" in *McClure's,* a popular American magazine. Intended to tilt public opinion in favor of U.S. intervention in the Philippines, the poem cast American imperialism as a noble "civilizing mission."

The racist undertones of the poem implied that the indigenous peoples inhabiting the territories being colonized were incapable of self-rule. Though the poem sparked widespread criticism and was frequently parodied, it accurately reflected a common rationalization for the European intrusion into Africa.

See also: COLONIAL CONQUEST (Vol. IV); RACE AND RACISM (Vol. IV).

Witbooi, Hendrik (1830–1905) *Last independent leader of the Oorlam people living in South West Africa (present-day Namibia)*

Hendrik Witbooi was the grandson of Kido Witbooi (c. 1780–1875), who in mid-century led his branch of the Oorlam people (who today are considered part of the CAPE COLOURED PEOPLE) to settle in southern NAMIBIA. They had moved out of the CAPE COLONY earlier in the century to avoid the increasing discrimination they were facing. In Namibia, Kido Witbooi expanded his authority through conquest to include the NAMA, another Khoikhoi people. He also converted to Christianity later in his life. Upon his death he was succeeded by his son, Hendrik's father, Moses Witbooi (1810–1888), who effectively had been the ruler for a number of years. In 1888 Moses was killed by his own son-in-law. Hendrik then killed the usurper and assumed control.

Hendrik, who was baptized by German MISSIONARIES in 1868, had already developed a substantial following by the time he became the Oorlam-Nama leader. Other Khoikhoi groups soon turned to him as they contested the HERERO for control of southern Namibia. Rivalry for dominance among African groups soon gave way to resistance against German COLONIAL CONQUEST. Between 1890 and 1894 Witbooi fought to stave off German incursions into his territory, but he was finally defeated and made to accept German COLONIAL RULE. He then worked cooperatively with Governor Theodor Leutwin (1849–1921), assisting the Germans in subordinating other African peoples. He even participated in a military campaign to subdue the BONDELSWARTS Nama.

The Herero revolt against German colonial rule that began in 1904 led to the replacement of Governor Leutwin. Witbooi, concerned by the loss of his people's land to German settlers and the harsh policies of the government and no longer tied by personal obligations to Leutwin, joined the rebellion, in 1904. He was killed in the fighting a year later, and his followers soon surrendered. After another two years of fighting German colonial rule was firmly established in its new colony of SOUTH WEST AFRICA.

See also: GERMANY AND AFRICA (Vol. IV); KHOIKHOI (Vols. II, III); MAHERERO, SAMUEL (Vol. IV); RESISTANCE AND REBELLION (Vol. IV); SETTLERS, EUROPEAN (Vol. IV).

witchcraft In many parts of Africa the use of sorcery or magic is believed to have the power to bring about desired events. It can have positive or negative connotations depending on whether it is intended to express ill will on the part of the practitioner or if it is meant to offer protection from the ill will of others. Colonial authorities, who publicly condemned both the practice of and the belief in witchcraft, had a hand in assigning negative connotations to it. The anti-witchcraft sentiment of colonial and missionary church authorities resulted in reports of witch-hunting and persecution. Some countries passed witchcraft prohibition laws. Anti-witchcraft movements, however, were as likely to be initiated and led by local Africans as by individuals acting on behalf of the colonial authorities or churches.

Among many people in Africa witchcraft is widely used to account for those things that do not have scientific explanations. In this limited sense, belief in witchcraft is not too far removed from some of the doctrines of the world's major religions.

Witchcraft practitioners use curses, the evil eye, or bad omens to supposedly cause harm, including afflictions and illness. If an individual comes down with an ill-

ness, determining whether it is the result of witchcraft involves establishing a reason why the use of witchcraft would be justified against the victim in the first place. A condition might be associated with witchcraft if it is particularly difficult to treat, reoccurring, strange, or if it results in sudden death. By the same token, if it is determined that an illness has a supernatural or human cause, among believers in witchcraft, that does not necessarily eliminate the possibility of a scientific explanation. For example, one can understand that malaria is contracted through the bite of a mosquito while at the same time crediting witchcraft as the reason why one person gets malaria while another does not. In other words, those who practice witchcraft are thought—even by those with a degree of "scientific" knowledge—to have the power to control the natural forces in the world.

The healing and religious movement launched by Simon KIMBANGU (c. 1887–1951) in the BELGIAN CONGO (today's Democratic Republic of the CONGO), in 1921, exemplified the wide popular appeal of anti-witchcraft movements. He claimed to be an "apostle" of Christ and attracted large crowds who believed in his healing powers. To be healed, people had to abandon their so-called fetishes and beliefs in sorcery. Although the Belgian authorities imprisoned Kimbangu out of fear that he was preaching an anticolonial message, the movement he launched continued. It increasingly attracted followers in the 1930s, in large part because of its opposition to witchcraft and its efforts to purify society of its ills.

For believers in witchcraft, once an illness has been attributed to it, one must seek out a person—a *diviner*, for example—who can offer a counter-treatment using the same supernatural forces. Diviners use different tools to determine the cause of the affliction and the action that is necessary to fix it. For example, some diviners shake bones or seeds into a pile and "read" their formation or placement. Cures for witchcraft can call for using herbal remedies, completing ritualized ceremonies, or even avoiding specific foods or activities.

See also: HEALTH AND HEALING IN COLONIAL AFRICA (Vol. IV); DISEASE IN COLONIAL AFRICA (Vol. IV); COLONIALISM, INFLUENCE OF (Vol. IV); MALARIA (Vol. V); PROPHETS AND PROHPETIC MOVEMENTS (Vol. IV, V); SCIENCE (Vol. IV).

Further reading: B. Hallen, *Knowledge, Belief & Witchcraft: Analytic Experiments in African Philosophy* (London: Ethnographica, 1986); Henrietta L. Moore and

Todd Sanders, eds., *Magical Interpretations, Material Realities: Modernity, Witchcraft and the Occult in Postcolonial Africa* (London: Routledge, 2001).

Witwatersrand GOLD-rich region of the TRANSVAAL, in central SOUTH AFRICA. The Witwatersrand gained international prominence for its huge, underground deposits of gold. Though Africans had mined the precious metal in the region for centuries, the first commercially viable discovery occurred in 1886. This discovery, along with the MINING of DIAMONDS at KIMBERLEY, to the west, sparked the South African MINERAL REVOLUTION. An influx of prospectors soon flooded the Witwatersrand, forming a large mining camp that would evolve into the city of JOHANNESBURG.

Witwatersrand is a Dutch word meaning "white water ridge." Ironically there is no white water near the heart of Witwatersrand, and the region is actually named for the water-like appearance of the quartzite found in the area.

See also: ANGLO-BOER WAR (Vol. IV); CAPE COLONY (Vol. IV); PRETORIA (Vols. IV, V); UNION OF SOUTH AFRICA (Vol. IV).

Wolof Large, influential ethnic group of the SENEGAL and The GAMBIA region (Senegambia) in West Africa, where they had settled by the 1300s; also the LANGUAGE they speak. In 1854 the Wolof states of the SENEGAMBIA REGION faced French colonial expansion when Major Louis FAIDHERBE (1818–1889) was appointed the new governor of French Senegal. By 1858 Faidherbe had annexed the Wolof states.

Historically, Wolof speakers have been the largest ethnic group in the Senegalese capital city of DAKAR, where a Wolof trading community predated the city's founding by the French, in 1857.

Local Wolof leaders resisted Faidherbe's attempts at further colonization by turning to Islam. By the mid-1860s, Maba Diakhou (1809–1867), a Tukulor Muslim leader, had converted many of the Wolof leaders. Among them were Lat Dior (r. 1842–1886) of Cayor, and Alboury

N'Diaye (r. 1842–?) of Djolof. They in turn led the armed resistance against the French COLONIAL CONQUEST and occupation of the Senegambia. France's final defeat of the Wolof armies and the death of Lat Dior, in 1886, enabled the French to exercise direct control over most of the Senegal region. French colonization had wide-ranging influence in the Wolof states, disrupting the former Wolof political structure and minimizing the power and prestige of the Wolof nobility. As general social upheaval took over the region, many Wolof turned to the Mouride Sufi brotherhood led by Amadou Bamba (1850–1927).

By the end of the 19th century the Wolof were both largely acculturated to Islam and subjugated by the French. The Mouride brotherhood, with membership numbering about 70,000 by the early 1900s, maintained its authority by controlling a large peasant LABOR force and the production of GROUNDNUTS (peanuts) for Senegal's colonial cash-crop economy.

During both World War I (1914–18) and World War II (1939–45), many Muslim Wolof speakers were recruited by their religious leaders to fight for France.

See also: FRANCE AND AFRICA (Vols. III, IV, V); ISLAM, INFLUENCE OF (Vols. II, III, IV, V); NIGER-CONGO LANGUAGES (Vol. I); SUFISM (Vols. II, III, IV); WOLOF (Vol. II); WOLOF EMPIRE (Vol. III); WOLOF STATES (Vol. II).

Further reading: Eunice A. Charles, *Precolonial Senegal: The Jolof Kingdom, 1800–1890,* (Brookline, Mass.: Boston University African Studies Center, 1977); Cruise O'Brien, *The Mourides of Senegal: The Political and Economic Organization of an Islamic Brotherhood,* (Oxford, U.K.: Clarendon Press, 1971); James F. Searing, *Islam and Emancipation in Senegal: The Wolof Kingdoms of Kajour and Bawol, 1859–1914* (Portsmouth, N.H.: Heinemann, 2002).

women in colonial Africa Prior to the colonial period many women in Africa enjoyed a substantial amount of public influence as leaders of social groups and traditional religions. In addition, women were often integrated into local market economies as traders, earning an income separate from their husbands'. Beyond their public activities, women were responsible for child rearing, subsistence farming, and household chores such as collecting firewood and water. However, when European colonial authorities and settlers arrived in Africa, they brought with them their own strict ideas of a female's role.

For instance, most Europeans expected African women to be totally dependent on their husbands. Therefore colonial administrators ignored or undermined female leadership positions and did not address the traditional importance of women regarding agricultural production. However, women continued to provide the food for their families, since their husbands often migrated, willingly or unwillingly, to the mines, plantations, or towns to provide cheap wage LABOR for the colonial export ECONOMY. Unless they were born in one of the older African towns such as ACCRA, in GOLD COAST COLONY (now GHANA), or MOMBASA (in KENYA), women were far less likely than men to be a part of the URBANIZATION process during the colonial era.

In the colonial era an African woman living in an agricultural community had many responsibilities. During the busy agricultural season her typical day might start before sun-up with washing and eating. After that she would walk to the field with her hand hoe and spend 8–10 hours preparing the soil, weeding, or planting. She might cook food in the field for lunch or skip eating until supper. After working in the field she would probably collect firewood and carry it back home on her head, which might take an hour, depending on the availability of wood in the area. To prepare for the evening meal she would pound or grind the grain for another hour or more and fetch water at a well that could be as far away as a few miles.

The woman would then have to light a fire and cook dinner, serving the family before feeding herself. After dinner she would wash the children, the dishes, and herself and then go to bed. Her workday might be from 11 to 14 hours long, and if she had young children, she might be doing much of the work with a baby strapped to her back.

During World War II (1939–45), with many men absent, women suddenly became the primary decision makers in their own households while continuing with their busy roles as caretakers and providers. However, with the limitations imposed by colonial policies, women had diminished access to resources such as credit, EDUCATION, and land. In addition, MISSIONARIES further increased a woman's workload by discouraging the practice of polygamy, which had served to distribute household activities among co-wives. In part, because of the colonialists ignored the public power of women, many women used the anticolonial independence movements as a way to voice their opinions and move back into the public sphere.

See also: COLONIALISM, INFLUENCE OF (Vol. IV); GENDER IN COLONIAL AFRICA (Vol. IV); POLITICAL PARTIES AND ORGANIZATIONS (Vol. IV); RELIGION (Vol. IV); WOMEN IN ANCIENT AFRICA (Vol. I); WOMEN IN MEDIEVAL AFRICA (Vol. II); WOMEN IN INDEPENDENT AFRICA (Vol. V); WOMEN IN PRECOLONIAL AFRICA (Vol. III).

Further reading: Jean Allman, Susan Geiger, and Nakanyike Musisi, *Women in African Colonial Histories* (Bloomington, Ind.: Indiana University Press, 2002).

World War I and Africa (1914–1918) Despite the fact that World War I began and ended on European soil, it profoundly affected millions of people on the African continent. This was the case because African countries were brought into the conflict by their European colonial subjugators, who relied heavily on African NATURAL RESOURCES and manpower.

Colonial Recruitment During the war Africans were engaged as porters as well as soldiers. For example, by using compulsory service for all African males, France enlisted more than 500,000 colonial subjects for the war effort. France was aided in its recruitment effort by Blaise DIAGNE (1872–1934), a Senegalese politician who enlisted more than 180,000 West African men and hoped that supporting the French cause would lead to greater rights for the Senegalese people. Britain also used forced conscription, enlisting roughly 30,000 soldiers while using more than 1 million Africans as porters. The colonial powers also utilized forced LABOR during the war, with Belgium, for example, forcing hundreds of thousands of Africans into PORTERAGE.

Not all Africans quietly accepted conscription into European armies, and resistance was manifested in various forms. Thousands of Africans went into hiding in some areas, while others took up arms against the Europeans. Beyond dragging African men into essentially foreign disputes, the war in Europe also diverted attention away form nascent anticolonial efforts in Africa.

Warfare in Africa and Abroad Troops from FRENCH WEST AFRICA, known as the TIRAILLEURS SÉNÉGALAIS, and other French African possessions greatly contributed to war, engaging the Central Powers along the Western Front in Europe. However, unlike France, Britain did not use any African soldiers in Europe.

Most African soldiers fought in Africa. France and Britain used their COLONIAL ARMIES to attack all of the German African possessions. TOGOLAND (today's TOGO) quickly fell to Anglo-French forces in 1914. That same year the UNION OF SOUTH AFRICA joined the British cause despite fervent opposition from AFRIKANERS in the TRANSVAAL and the ORANGE FREE STATE. The South African forces were sent to conquer German SOUTH WEST AFRICA (now NAMIBIA), in 1915, and quickly took control of the territory. German Kamerun (now CAMEROON) held out a little longer, falling in 1916.

The struggle for GERMAN EAST AFRICA, however, was quite different. Under the leadership of German lieutenant-colonel Paul Emil von Lettow-Vorbeck (1870–1964), the German East African forces held out against the numerically superior Allies for the duration of the war. At the beginning of the war, Lettow-Vorbeck launched forays into KENYA against the British railway. Three months later the allies responded with a massive Anglo-Indian invasion, but Lettow-Vorbeck repelled the operation through superior tactical maneuvers and strategic use of his limited number of troops.

German East Africa's army included thousands of *askari*, or African soldiers, who outnumbered German soldiers by nearly three to one.

Bolstered by South African forces led by General Jan Christiaan SMUTS (1870–1950), the allies eventually penetrated German East Africa, in 1916, and captured the major cities of the territory. In response Lettow-Vorbeck initiated a campaign of guerrilla warfare, using his *askaris'* knowledge of the terrain to live off the land. German East Africa forces continued to pester and bog down Allied troops in the region until 1918, when Lettow-Vorbeck finally surrendered, two weeks *after* the signing of the Armistice had officially ended the war.

For the most part, however, the battlefields of Africa were ruled by Allied forces. For instance, when the sultan of DARFUR, Ali Dinar (c. 1898–1916), proclaimed his kingdom's allegiance to the Ottoman Empire, a small British force quickly defeated his forces, with the sultan dying during the fighting.

Aftermath At the end of World War I the status of many African territories changed. While the Allies were eager to annex the former territories of Germany and the Ottoman Empire, U.S. president Woodrow Wilson (1856–1924) had a different agenda He introduced the Treaty of Versailles, which called for the formation of the League of Nations to maintain the hard-won peace. Under the treaty each of the former German colonies became a League of Nations MANDATE to be overseen by one of the Allies. SOUTH AFRICA took responsibility for South West Africa, while Britain oversaw parts of Cameroon and Togo as well as all of TANGANYIKA (later part of present-day TANZANIA). France received the other portions of Cameroon and Togo.

The changes brought about by the end of First World War went beyond exchanges of territory, however. Africans were emboldened by Wilson's Fourteen Points, which accompanied his League of Nations proposal and promoted the right to self-determination. Though the call for a right to independence for all people was eventually muted, the idea sparked the imagination of many Africans and was a seed to the independence movements that grew in the following decades.

See also: RESISTANCE AND REBELLION (Vol. IV); UNITED STATES AND AFRICA (Vol. IV); WARFARE AND WEAPONS (Vol. IV); WORLD WAR II AND AFRICA (Vol. IV).

Further reading: Hew Strachan, *The Oxford Illustrated History of the First World War* (Oxford, U.K.: Oxford University Press, 1998). Byron Farwell, *The Great War in Africa, 1914–1918* (New York: W. W. Norton & Company, 1989).

World War II and Africa Compared to the events of World War I (1914–18), the action affecting the African continent as well as its inhabitants during World War II (1939–45) was far greater in magnitude. African participation in World War II came in many forms. For example, the battle against the Axis of Germany and Italy came earlier to Africa than to Europe, with the invasion of ETHIOPIA by Italian forces in 1934.

The actual fighting done on African soil was more intense during World War II than in the previous world war. In the Horn of Africa the Italian conquest of Ethiopia led, with the outbreak of full hostilities in 1939, to an invasion by forces from Britain, East and West Africa, and SOUTH AFRICA. These forces, which included substantial numbers of Africans, quickly routed the Italian armies, giving the Allies their first important victory of the war.

Even more intense was the fighting in North Africa, where Germany's Afrika Korps was sent to support the Italian forces in LIBYA. With access to both oil and the SUEZ CANAL—key elements of both the Axis and Allied strategies—the fighting in North Africa was particularly fierce. Although the German Afrika Korps proved especially effective in the early stages of the war, their defeat

This photo from 1942 shows Free French artillery gunners, two of the many colonial troops who saw active service during World War II. © *Library of Congress*

by Allied forces, at the Battle of El Alamein, in 1942, eventually proved to be a turning point in the war.

Furthermore, although many African soldiers served in the armies of the European powers during the First World War, these numbers increased dramatically during World War II. For example, more than 80,000 of the well-known TIRAILLEURS SÉNÉGALAIS from FRENCH WEST AFRICA were called into immediate service in France during the early stages of the war. Between 1943 and 1945, more than 100,000 African soldiers were added to the French forces, primarily through conscription. France, of course, was not alone in its reliance on African troops. Britain recruited nearly 325,000 soldiers from East Africa alone, with one division playing an important role in the campaign in Southeast Asia. In addition, more than 200,000 white and 100,000 black South Africans served in Britain's forces, primarily in North Africa.

Beyond this, the war's impact on colonial life in Africa was astounding and affected the colonies in numerous ways. Economically, due to increased production of FOOD, Africa became more reliant on international markets. Politically, however, the changes in African society were more salient and had long-term effects on the continent.

As the war ended African soldiers returned to their homelands with new ideas about their place in the world. First, since some Africans served as equals with Europeans during the war, they began to demand equal treatment in all spheres. More importantly, however, was the impact of the ATLANTIC CHARTER of 1941, which suggested that peoples of the world have the right to national self-determination. This right to self-determination included Africans and was further guaranteed by the United Nations, which was established in 1945.

With these new ideas came radical change. African INDEPENDENCE AND NATIONALISM MOVEMENTS began to surface and Africans demanded to be free of COLONIAL RULE. Greater African participation in politics was evident as well as the increased formation of African political parties.

Over time the European nations began to relinquish control over their colonies; however, this was not always a smooth process. Examples of civil unrest and outright violent confrontation were evident in ALGERIA, the Congo region, and numerous African states. The end of World War II also brought the international political rivalry between the United States and the Soviet Union, both victors in the war. The tensions between the two countries signaled the beginning of what became known as the Cold War, which, in the 1960s and 1970s, would include proxy battles fought in Africa.

See also: ARMIES, COLONIAL (Vol. IV); COLD WAR AND AFRICA (Vol. V); COLONIAL RULE (Vol. IV); COLONIALISM, INFLUENCE OF (Vol. IV); INDEPENDENCE MOVEMENTS (Vol. V); MANDATE (Vol. IV); RESISTANCE AND REBELLION (Vol. IV); SOVIET UNION AND AFRICA (Vol. IV); UNITED STATES AND AFRICA (Vol. IV); WARFARE AND WEAPONS (Vol. V); WORLD WAR I AND AFRICA (Vol. V).

Further reading: Basil Davidson, *Modern Africa: A Social and Political History* (London: Longman Group UK Limited, 1994).

X

Xhosa People of SOUTH AFRICA descended from an Nguni group of Bantu speakers who migrated from Central Africa, probably in the third or fourth century CE. Beginning in the latter part of the 18th century and continuing into the last quarter of the 19th century, the Xhosa were engaged in a series of nine Cape Frontier Wars (1779–1878). They first fought with Boer settlers and subsequently with the British colonial government of the CAPE COLONY. These conflicts resulted from competing interests over land use and cattle. (Cattle significantly determined a man's stature in Xhosa society.) The Xhosa met with varying degrees of success in defending their homeland; in the early fighting against the BOERS, they met with relative success. The superior resources of the British, however, proved too great. While they were able to win individual battles, they ultimately lost the wars. Moreover, with each military defeat came a further loss of land to white settlers.

In 1853, after an especially bitter and bloody war, a large tract of Xhosa territory was annexed into Cape Colony. Three years later the Xhosa began the CATTLE KILLING, an ill-fated attempt to magically rid their lands of whites. The Cattle Killing caused massive starvation among the Xhosa and severely weakened their ability to resist European intrusion. As a result, over the later part of the 19th century, the remaining Xhosa territory was incorporated into Cape Colony.

The British annexation of Xhosa land and the disintegration of herding culture that resulted forced many Xhosa to migrate to work for Europeans on farms and in mines. At the same time MISSIONARIES converted many Xhosa to Christianity and spread Western ideas through new EDUCATION initiatives. Under the leadership of individuals such as John Tengo JABAVU (1859–1921), editor of the Xhosa-LANGUAGE newspaper *IMVO ZABANTSUNDU,* many among the Xhosa turned from the military struggle to the political struggle in order to secure their rights and livelihoods. However, the political arena became much more complex and challenging after the Cape Colony became part of the UNION OF SOUTH AFRICA, in 1910. As South Africa fell further into a system of racial segregation, many of the African opposition leaders who emerged came from Xhosa heritage, including Nelson MANDELA (1918–) and Steve Biko (1947–1977).

See also: BIKO, STEVE (Vol. V); CAPE FRONTIER WARS (Vol. III); CHRISTIANITY, INFLUENCE OF (Vol. IV); XHOSA (Vols. II, III, V).

Further reading: Noël Mostert, *Frontiers: The Epic of South Africa's Creation and the Tragedy of the Xhosa People* (New York: Knopf, 1992).

Yao Ethnic group primarily inhabiting the highlands of what are now southern MALAWI and northern MOZAMBIQUE; since World War II (1939–45) Yao groups also have migrated to neighboring TANZANIA, to the north. During the early 1800s Yao traders began to serve as intermediaries between the people of the south-central interior and the Arab and Swahili merchants of coastal Kilwa. Initially politically decentralized, the Yao responded to the growing warfare, slave trade, and political disruption of the 19th century by arming themselves and then establishing political control over their area. They prospered by supplying ivory and slaves to the SWAHILI COAST in exchange for firearms and other manufactured goods imported from Europe and the United States.

Following a famine in the late 1800s, however, large numbers of Yao migrated to the interior highlands of Malawi. At this time, British MISSIONARIES in the region were working to end the SLAVE TRADE, and they attempted to convert the Yao in the process. For their part the Yao largely rejected Christianity and tended to prefer conversion to Islam, the religion of the Arabic slave traders on the coast.

Malawi came under British colonial control in the 1890s, and by 1907 the region had become the PROTECTORATE of NYASALAND. Under British rule, the SLAVE TRADE was outlawed, and many Yao men were arrested and imprisoned for attempting to continue this practice. Further impinging on the Yao way of life, in 1912 the British instituted a hut tax to pay for the administration of the protectorate. In order to raise the necessary money Yao men had few options beyond working on British-owned tea and tobacco plantations; some even traveled as far as SOUTH AFRICA to work in that country's GOLD mines.

A noted Yao Christian convert was the missionary John CHILEMBWE (c. 1872–1915). In 1915 Chilembwe led a small group of Nyasaland's Africans in a failed revolt against the rule of the British colonial administration.

During World War I (1914–18) British officials caused widespread resentment among Nyasaland's indigenous peoples by forcing them to enlist in the colonial army. Despite their objections, however, Yao soldiers helped the British in their campaigns in the East African theater of operations. Yao discontent with British rule continued through World War II, ending only in 1964 with the declaration of an independent Malawi.

See also: SLAVE TRADE ON THE SWAHILI COAST (Vol. III); TRADE AND COMMERCE (Vol. IV); YAO (Vol. III).

Yohannes IV (Johannes IV, John IV, Kassa Mercha) (1831–1889) *Emperor of Ethiopia from 1872 to 1889*

After the death of the emperor TÉWODROS II (1820–1868), a four-year struggle for succession ensued. The main contenders for the throne were Tekla Giorgis of Gondar, the future Emperor MENELIK II (1844–1913), known at the time as Sahle Mariam and *negus* (king) of the SHOA kingdom, and Kassa Mercha, the governor of TIGRAY. After negotiations with Kassa Mercha and Sahle Mariam, Tekla Giorgis appeared set to succeed Téwodros

432

II as Ethiopia's emperor. However, Tekla Giorgis unwisely attempted to conquer Tigray and was defeated by a smaller but better equipped Tigrayan force. As a result Kassa Mercha ascended the throne, in 1872, and was crowned *negus nagast* (king of kings, or emperor) under the name Yohannes IV.

In order to consolidate his power Yohannes IV had to contend with the Ethiopian nobility, who exerted considerable regional control. While Yohannes had some difficulty establishing his authority in the north of the country, the main challenge to his power was Sahle Mariam in southern ETHIOPIA, who staunchly refused to recognize the new emperor.

Hailing from the Tigray region, Yohannes IV was the only non-Amharic-speaking emperor between 1270 and the end of the Ethiopian monarchy under HAILE SELASSIE (1892–1975).

Sahle Mariam persistently reinforced his control in Shoa, extending his kingdom to include the lands of the OROMO peoples to the south and west and equipping his army with European firearms. It was not until 1878 that Yohannes IV was able to win Sahle Mariam's submission. However, this was only in exchange for Yohannes's recognition of Sahle Mariam's kingship south of Shoa. Despite this truce Sahle Mariam continued to strengthen his kingdom, and in 1882 another agreement was reached, whereby Yohannes's son wedded Sahle Mariam's daughter and Sahle Mariam was established as Yohannes's successor.

Yohannes's power struggle with Sahle Mariam was minor compared to the external threats that Ethiopia faced during his reign. The first came from EGYPT, which had imperial designs on Ethiopia as part of its plan to create a "Greater Egypt." Egyptian forces attempted to invade Ethiopia in 1875, but Yohannes rallied what amounted to a Christian crusade against the Muslim Egyptian invaders, and by 1876 he had driven the Egyptians out.

Italy, with its own goals of empire, proved a more difficult foe. Having assumed control of the ports of Aseb and Massawa (on the Red Sea, in present-day ERITREA), the Italians used this foothold to launch a campaign of COLONIAL CONQUEST into Tigray. The Italian advance was checked, in 1887, after a convincing Ethiopian victory at Dogali. In spite of this, Yohannes IV did not succeed at completely driving the Italians from the region. As a result Italy was allowed to establish the colony of Eritrea, and Ethiopia was denied its only access to the coast. It also set the stage for subsequent Italo-Ethiopian hostilities that continued until World War II (1939–45).

In another attempt to impose his authority, Yohannes implemented a policy of forced conversion to the Christian ETHIOPIAN ORTHODOX CHURCH. Ethiopia's Muslims put up significant resistance to the policy, which forced them to be baptized, build churches, and pay church taxes.

Also in 1887, Sudanese Mahdists, followers of the messianic Islamic leader Muhammad Ahmad al-MAHDI (1844–1885), launched assaults on Ethiopia, destroying the city of Gondar. In response Yohannes IV led an Ethiopian invasion of Sudan, where he was killed in the Battle of Metema (1889). Just before his death Yohannes named his son as his successor, but the Shoan *negus* Sahle Mariam quickly stepped in and assumed the throne, taking the name Emperor Menelik II.

See also: ITALY AND AFRICA (Vol. IV).

Yoruba General term used to describe the LANGUAGE, peoples, and kingdoms of southwestern NIGERIA and part of neighboring Republic of BENIN. By the beginning of the 19th century the Yoruba-speaking states had reached the height of their power as an empire. With their capital at Oyo, the Yoruba dominated regions within present-day western Nigeria and Benin and controlled long-distance trade with Europeans. However, events of the early 19th century and a subsequent rise of European colonialism led to Yoruba decline.

First, Britain banned the lucrative SLAVE TRADE, in 1807, taking away what had been a source of wealth. Then, by 1817 Muslim armies from northern Nigeria had conquered the northern Yoruba state of ILORIN, installing HAUSA-speaking FULANI chiefs.

In the latter half of the 19th century, as the connections between the Yoruba states disintegrated, previously conquered kingdoms, such as DAHOMEY (present-day Benin), began refusing to pay tribute. This political crisis came to a head in 1877 with the outbreak of a civil war that lasted until 1893.

As Britain tried to persuade the region to abolish the slave trade and encourage other commerce, British commercial interests took over the Yoruba port town of LAGOS in 1851. The king of Lagos signed a treaty, in 1861, ceding the city to Britain. British efforts to ensure free trade in the region included sending troops to stop the fighting among the Yoruba states. In 1886 British authorities in Lagos held a cease-fire conference to which all the opposing forces—except Ilorin—sent representatives. The agreement reached that year ended the Yoruba infighting. Under the provision of the agreement the Yoruba kingdom of IBADAN, which was at the height of its power, became independent. However, by 1888 French traders were inserting themselves into the Yoruba trade network, so Britain forced the *alafin* of Oyo, the recognized Yoruba leader, to sign a treaty placing the Yoruba states under a British PROTECTORATE. In 1897 Ilorin and Nupe were conquered by armed forces representing the British ROYAL NIGER COMPANY. Despite resistance, by 1914 all the Yoruba states were under British rule.

In the early 20th century the British colonial government constructed a railroad through the Western Province of Nigeria to connect KANO, a Hausa state in the north, with the port at Lagos. The railroad proved a boon to AGRICULTURE, and many Yoruba farmers successfully integrated themselves into the colonial ECONOMY by growing COCOA for export.

In 1960 Nigeria became independent as a federal republic made up of three states, each dominated by a major ETHNIC GROUP. The Yoruba dominated Western Nigeria and for the most part supported the Action Group headed by Obafemi AWOLOWO (1909–1987). In spite of independence, within a few years the country's ethnic-based politics plunged it into civil war.

Some Yoruba who had been sold into the transatlantic slave trade returned as emissaries of European organizations. One such figure was Samuel Ajayi CROWTHER (1808–1891), a Yoruba recaptive who, in 1854, helped the CHURCH MISSIONARY SOCIETY establish the Niger Mission at Onitsha. Crowther later became the first African bishop of the Anglican church.

See also: ALAFIN (Vol. II); COLONIAL RULE (Vol. IV); ENGLAND AND AFRICA (Vols. III, IV, V); YORUBA (Vols. I, II, V); YORUBA STATES (Vols. II, III).

Further reading: Toyin Falola and G. O. Oguntomisin, *Yoruba Warlords of the Nineteenth Century* (Trenton, N.J.: Africa World Press, 2001); Ruth Watson, *Civil Disorder is the Disease of Ibadan: Chieftaincy & Civic Culture in a Yoruba City* (Athens, Ohio: Ohio University Press, 2003).

Z

Zambia Landlocked country located in southern Central Africa. It occupies an area of 290,600 square miles (752,700 sq km) and is mostly a plateau, rising to 8,000 ft (2,434 m) in the east. As early as the 15th century, major new waves of Bantu-speaking immigrants began arriving in Zambia, with the greatest influx occurring between the late 17th and early 19th centuries. These people came primarily from the Luba and Lunda kingdoms of what is now southern Democratic Republic of the CONGO and northern ANGOLA. They were joined in the 19th century by Ngoni peoples, from the south. Also, by the late 18th century, traders (including Arabs, Swahili, and other Africans) had penetrated the region from both the Atlantic and Indian Ocean coasts. By the middle of the 19th century the various groups were settled in Zambia in their present locations. Mainly organized into chieftaincies and monarchies, they developed a complex trading network in COPPER, ivory, iron, rhinoceros horn, and beads. The major kingdoms were those of the Bemba, Lunda, CHEWA, Ngoni, Luvale, Tonga, and LOZI.

Zambia during the Colonial Era: Northern Rhodesia The arrival of MISSIONARIES and explorers such as David LIVINGSTONE (1813–1873) changed the political climate of Zambia. In 1890 the British took control of the Zambia region through the British empire builder, Cecil RHODES (1853–1902) and his BRITISH SOUTH AFRICA COMPANY (BSAC). The Lozi king, Lubosi LEWANIKA (1845–1916), asked the British for protection against the NDEBELE to the south, while also signing a treaty giving the BSAC MINING rights. The treaty led to BSAC control of the whole territory, which it administered as NORTHERN RHODESIA, from 1911 until 1923, when Britain assumed direct COLONIAL RULE.

During the BSAC administration, vast copper ore deposits were discovered in the north-central part of Northern Rhodesia (the area now called the COPPERBELT). The discovery of these deposits made the region one of the world's most renowned areas of concentrated mining. The BSAC, which owned the mineral rights, earned royalty payments amounting to £83 million ($166 million) by 1963.

The mining of copper required a large LABOR force, which meant that Zambians from all over the country were drawn to the Copperbelt. While Africans held low-level and unskilled positions, the management of the mines and all skilled jobs were in the hands of whites, many of whom were from SOUTH AFRICA, where racism was the norm. Zambians often staged strikes and work stoppages in protest against unfair wages and taxes, and in 1948 they formed the first African Mineworkers Union.

In 1953 Britain formed the CENTRAL AFRICAN FEDERATION to bring together its colonies of Northern Rhodesia, SOUTHERN RHODESIA (now ZIMBABWE), and the PROTECTORATE of NYASALAND (now MALAWI), arguing that the federation would benefit the three countries economically. The politically dominant white settlers of Southern Rhodesia hoped that the alliance would counteract the economic hegemony of South Africa. African leaders, however, criticized the federation and mounted protests. While Britain hoped the federation would evolve into a better partnership with Africans, the Europeans, led by the federation's prime minister, Sir Roy WELENSKY (1907–1991), opposed any form of power sharing and worked against plans to establish African majority rule. When pressure from Britain and Africans increased, Welensky threatened to declare the federation independent from Britain.

Among Zambia's prominent ethnic groups are the Bemba, Luba, Lunda, and Luvale. Traditional among all of these people was a masquerade dance known as *likishi*, which involved the kind of intricate costumes and masks shown in this photo taken in 1935. © *National Archives*

Mounting African political dissatisfaction had led to the formation of the Northern Rhodesia Congress in 1948, with Harry Nkumbula (1916–1983), a former teacher, becoming its leader in 1951. His general secretary was another former schoolteacher, Kenneth KAUNDA (1924–   ). The party split in 1958, with Kaunda forming a separate party. In 1959 colonial authorities banned Kaunda's new party and sent Kaunda to prison for nine months for holding an illegal meeting. Released in 1960, Kaunda became president of yet another new party, the UNITED NATIONAL INDEPENDENCE PARTY (UNIP), which quickly grew. UNIP fought against the colonial government by launching a "master plan" of civil disobedience throughout the country, a tactic that UNIP hoped would force the British to dissolve the Central African Federation. The plan worked, and in 1963 Britain disbanded the federation and granted Northern Rhodesia and Nyasaland their independence. On October 24, 1964, Kaunda became the first president of independent Zambia.

See also: BEMBA (Vol. III); ENGLAND AND AFRICA (Vols. III, IV, V); KAUNDA, KENNETH (Vol. V); LUBA (Vol. II); LUBA EMPIRE (Vol. III); LUNDA EMPIRE (Vol. III); LUNDA KINGDOM (Vol. II); NATIONALISM AND INDEPENDENCE MOVEMENTS (Vol. IV); NGONI (Vol. III); ZAMBIA (Vols. I, II, III, V).

Further reading: Brian M. Fagan, *A Short History of Zambia: From the Earliest Times Until A.D. 1900* (Lusaka, Zambia: Oxford University Press. 1966); Kenneth Kaunda, *Zambia Shall Be Free* (London: Heinemann, 1962).

Zanzibar   Island capital of the sultanate of Zanzibar, part of present-day TANZANIA. The island is 640 square miles (1,660 sq km) in size and is located 22 miles (35 km) off the coast of East Africa. During the 18th and early 19th centuries Zanzibar, along with other East African lands, was part of the Omani Sultanate under the rule of the BUSAIDI dynasty. The Omani Sultanate was essentially a maritime trading empire that stretched from the Arabian peninsula to the SWAHILI COAST. In the 1830s Sultan Seyyid Said (1791–1856) took a great interest in the economic potential of the African possessions, and in 1841 he moved his capital to Zanzibar.

Seyyid Said's efforts to expand Zanzibar's influence were centered on trade in ivory, human captives, and spices, especially cloves, which were produced with slave LABOR on Arab-owned plantations in the coastal regions. Said's emphasis on trade strengthened the caravan routes into inland portions of eastern Africa and resulted in Zanzibar becoming the most affluent domain in the region. As a result, the island became a staging ground for explorers, including the Scottish David LIVINGSTONE (1813–1873), and his earnest pursuer, Henry Morton STANLEY (1841–1904).

Upon Seyyid Said's death, in 1856, the Omani Sultanate was partitioned. Geography guided division, with the Arabian and African territories grouped into two separate empires. Seyyid Said's son, Majid bin Said (c. 1835–1870), took over the African territories, which were named the sultanate of Zanzibar. At the time of Majid's ascension to the throne, the sultanate of Zanzibar controlled the Swahili Coast and to a lesser degree exercised influence over large areas of eastern Africa, including portions of what later became GERMAN EAST AFRICA, ITALIAN SOMALILAND (now SOMALIA), and BRITISH EAST AFRICA (now KENYA).

In 1896, after the British appointed his cousin sultan, Khaled bin Thuwain climbed through a broken window of the palace, claimed the throne for himself, and then amassed a few thousand supporters to defend his position. The British, unmoved, ordered him to surrender by 9:00 a.m. the next day. The new sultan, determined to maintain his hold on power, refused. At 9:02 a.m., August 27, British warships opened fire on the palace, eventually reducing parts of it to rubble. Sultan Khaled surrendered 38 minutes later, making the conflict, according to the *Guiness Book of World Records*, the shortest war in history.

When ibn Said BARGHASH (c. 1833–1888) succeeded his brother as sultan, Zanzibar's domain was still expanding. The upsurge of European imperial interests in East Africa in the aftermath of the BERLIN CONFERENCE (1884–85) ended in a loss of control over Zanzibar's mainland areas, and in 1890 Zanzibar became a British PROTECTORATE. Britain, however, was more interested in expanding its sphere of influence than conquering Zanzibar. The British administration kept intact the office of sultan, though the position became mostly symbolic, and they divided the sultanate's lands with Germany and Italy.

By leaving the sultanate intact, the British allowed the island's Arab nobility to continue to dominate positions of power. Although they were the minority in Zanzibar, Arab nobles had long subjugated the African inhabitants of the island, many of whom had been brought there in bondage (although the British had abolished the SLAVE TRADE). The disparity between Arabs and Africans framed the events that preceded Zanzibar's independence and the eventual end of the sultanate.

During the 1950s political activity in Zanzibar grew as the country moved towards independence. Two parties, the Zanzibar National Party (ZNP) and the Afro-Shirazi Party (ASP) came to the forefront of the political landscape. In 1957 the ZNP, ostensibly the party of the Arab population, won the first popular elections for the Zanzibar Legislative Council. A second round of elections, in 1961, resulted in neither party gaining a majority. The ZNP, however, was able to form a coalition government through an alliance with the smaller Zanzibar and Pemba Peoples Party. In 1963 Zanzibar gained its independence, and Britain, reinstating the sultanate as a constitutional monarchy, handed over control of Zanzibar to the ZNP-led government.

In 1964, however, the island's African majority, led by Abeid Awani KARUME (1905–1972) of the ASP, overthrew the sultanate and joined Zanzibar with TANGANYIKA in a new political union. Called the United Republic of Tanganyika and Zanzibar, the country was led by President Julius NYERERE (1922–1999), from Tanganyika, and Vice President Karume. Six months after unification, the republic changed its name to Tanzania.

See also: AFRO-SHIRAZI PARTY (Vol. V); OMANI SULTANATE (Vol. III); SLAVE TRADE (Vol. IV); ZANZIBAR (Vols. I, II, III, V); ZANZIBAR CITY (Vols. IV, V).

Further reading: Laur Fair, *Pastimes and Politics: Culture, Community, and Identity in Post-Abolition Urban Zanzibar* (Athens, Ohio: Ohio University Press, 2002).

Zanzibar City Capital of present-day Zanzibar West region of TANZANIA, located on the western side of the island of ZANZIBAR. The site of Zanzibar City was first used as a fishing village between the eighth and 10th centuries. Possessing a deepwater harbor, it eventually became a well-known trading town for goods transported on the Indian Ocean trade routes. The Swahili inhabitants, who were mostly Muslim, developed strong trade ties, particularly with Oman, in Saudi Arabia, and in the mid-17th century the Omani army assisted in expelling the Portuguese from the SWAHILI COAST. By 1840 the sultan of Oman, Seyyid Said (1791–1856), had transferred his capital to Zanzibar City, which soon experienced rapid growth and commercialization. It became an international center for the SLAVE TRADE, and its population grew from 50,000 in the 1850s, to 80,000 in the 1870s. Zanzibar City began to diversify as South Asians, Omanis, Swahilis from the mainland, and captured African slaves from the interior of eastern Africa migrated to the city. During this time the production of cloves, for which Zanzibar City is famous, began to flourish.

In 1890 Zanzibar became a British PROTECTORATE, and in 1897 the island's slave trade was abolished. Throughout the next several decades, former slaves abandoned the rural plantations and moved to the city in search of employment. This again dramatically increased the population of Zanzibar City. Without the lucrative slave trade, the exportation of cloves became the most important economic activity. Zanzibar gained independence in 1963, but both the city and the island were soon gripped by a violent revolution that overthrew the sultan and his government.

In 1964 the island of Zanzibar joined with TANGANYIKA to form the nation of Tanzania. Zanzibar City's importance as a port decreased when DAR ES SALAAM became the new country's capital and principal economic and commercial center.

See also: ENGLAND AND AFRICA (Vols. III, IV, V); ISLAM (Vol. II); ISLAM, INFLUENCE OF (Vols. II, III, IV, V); PORTUGAL AND AFRICA (Vols. III, IV, V); SLAVE TRADE ON THE SWAHILI COAST (Vol. III); URBAN LIFE AND CULTURE (Vols. IV, V); URBANIZATION (Vols. IV, V); ZANZIBAR, CITY OF (Vol. V).

Further readings: Abdul Sheriff, ed., *The History and Conservation of Zanzibar Stone Town* (Athens, Ohio: Ohio University Press, 1995).

zaribas Fortified camps of Sudanese slave traders in the present-day southern Republic of the SUDAN. *Zaribas* are named for the thorny hedges that surrounded the trading camps. In the 1820s Egypt invaded Sudan, seeking slave conscripts for its military. Because of this, the SLAVE TRADE, along with trade in ivory and other goods, became one of the economic mainstays of Egyptian-controlled Sudan.

Sudanese merchants from the KHARTOUM area, as well as Egyptian traders from the east, pushed southward along the White Nile into the Bahr-al-Ghazal region, setting up *zaribas* as they moved along. A highly predatory commerce developed under such merchant-commanders as Rahma Mansur al-ZUBAYR (1830–1913).

The commerce in human captives, conducted by Arabic-speaking traders from the north, helped lay the foundations for the deep division that exists in present-day Sudan, between the Arabic-speaking, Muslim north and the non-Arabic speaking, Christian and animist south. The *zariba*-based trading system continued until

the rise of the MAHDIYYA, the Islamic brotherhood that ousted Egypt from the Sudan, in 1885. After that time the *zaribas* also made convenient military outposts for both the Mahdiyya and the combined British and Egyptian forces who took control of Sudan, in 1899.

Zimbabwe Present-day country in southeastern Africa 150,900 square miles (390,800 sq km) in size and marked by a large, central plateau. Zimbabwe is bordered to the east by MOZAMBIQUE, to the south by SOUTH AFRICA, to the west by BOTSWANA (formerly BECHUANALAND), and to the north by ZAMBIA (formerly NORTHERN RHODESIA).

In the early 19th century the period of ZULU warfare known as Mfecane (The Crushing) led to a large-scale migration among the peoples of southern Africa. One of these goups, the NDEBELE, were led by King Mzilikazi (1790–1868), a former Zulu general. Finally pushed out of the TRANSVAAL region by defeat at the hands of the BOERS, the Ndebele eventually reached southern Zimbabwe, where they quickly defeated Changamire, a SHONA kingdom.

The collapse of the Changamire kingdom did not destroy the cultural identity of the Shona people, who were descendents of the Bantu speakers who migrated to the Zimbabwean plateau more than a thousand years earlier, and who later erected the walled city of Great Zimbabwe. The Shona were skilled at iron working and pottery and noted for their expert musicianship. After the Ndebele invaded, much of the Shona population moved north and resettled in what became known as Mashonaland.

By about 1840 Mzilikazi settled his people in their newly conquered territory, which came to be called Matabeleland. He was a strong ruler and cemented his power by subjugating the remaining Shona clans into a feudal, caste-based social order. The relative isolation of the people of Zimbabwe from Europeans came to an end in the late 19th century, after European prospectors discovered GOLD deposits in Matabeleland, in 1867. Although these early discoveries did not lead to a permanent white presence, they foreshadowed the developments that would follow.

Interest in the potential of Zimbabwean gold deposits increased with the 1886 discovery of the massive gold-ore deposits of the WITWATERSRAND, in the Transvaal. This development fueled European hopes for similar deposits further north, bringing more European miners and prospectors into southen Africa.

By 1888, CAPE COLONY financier and mine owner Cecil RHODES (1853–1902) had negotiated MINING rights to Matabeleland with the Ndebele king, LOBENGULA (1836–1894), who had succeeded Mzilikazi, in 1870. Rhodes used the mineral concessions to gain a charter from the British government that allowed him to form the BRITISH SOUTH AFRICAN COMPANY (BSAC). By 1890, however, Lobengula was wary of Rhodes and no longer wished to tolerate the presence of white settlers in the Ndebele kingdom. To avoid an immediate confrontation with the Ndebele, the initial group of BSAC settlers and miners, known as the Pioneer Column, avoided the Ndebele state and settled in Mashonaland in the area around SALISBURY (now Harare), a city they founded.

Despite the fact that the Europeans had settled outside of Matabeleland, the Ndebele understood the threat the BSAC presented to their kingdom. Lobengula subsequently sent agents to ask Britain's Queen Victoria to intervene on his behalf. His request fell on deaf ears, however, and in 1893 the BSAC invaded Matabeleland. The Ndebele resisted for months but eventually lost the war to superior British firepower. The Ndebele defeat, culminating in the death of Lobengula later that year, marked the demise of African sovereignty in the region. Two years later the territories of Matabeleland and Mashonaland were joined to form SOUTHERN RHODESIA, named in honor of Rhodes.

In reaction to new taxes and the BSAC expropriation of land, the Ndebele and Shona peoples rose up in a rebellion known as the CHIMURENGA. However, by 1897, the uprising had been quashed. The following year, the British created "tribal reserves." Africans were forcibly displaced to these areas, and their former lands were allotted to white settlers.

Initially the BSAC believed that the amount of gold in Southern Rhodesia would equal the massive amounts found in the Transvaal. By the early 1900s, however, it was evident that Southern Rhodesia held far less gold than the neighboring territories to the south. As a result the BSAC appropriated even more African land and focused its energies on agricultural production.

The amount of land allotted to Africans was a fraction of the amount retained for the BSAC and white settlers. Moreover, the scattered Native Reserves were assigned the least productive terrain. By World War I (1914–18) the BSAC and white settlers, who comprised 3 percent of the population, occupied 21 million acres of Southern Rhodesia's land and reserved the right to claim much of the remaining 70 million acres still in African hands.

In 1914, on the eve of World War I, the BSAC charter for Southern Rhodesia expired. Because of the exclusion of Africans from the electorate, white settlers effectively controlled the destiny of the PROTECTORATE. Opposed to joining the UNION OF SOUTH AFRICA, the settlers asked Britain to prolong their charter, which was extended for 10 years.

Zimbabwe during the Colonial Era: Southern Rhodesia In 1922, with the BSAC charter expiration just a few years away, Southern Rhodesia held a referendum to decide between joining the Union of South Africa or initiating self-government. The white settlers, who were the only ones allowed to vote on the matter, chose the latter, and in 1923 Southern Rhodesia officially became a British colony.

Southern Rhodesia prospered in the period between the two world wars, as the colony increased its revenue from mining and AGRICULTURE and expanded its infrastructure. For the Africans, however, the period marked an escalation of discriminatory practices by the white-minority-controlled government. In 1930 The Land Apportionment Act formalized the division of land based on race, with Africans having rights to 33 percent of the land, whites getting 50 percent, and the rest remaining for future allocation. Four years later a LABOR law was passed that excluded Africans from entering skilled trades, forcing them to work for marginal wages on white farms and in white-owned mines and factories. The labor situation only worsened during World War II (1939–45), as white commercial interests convinced the Southern Rhodesian government to pass the Compulsory Labor Act, which legalized African forced labor.

LABOR UNIONS in Southern Rhodesia were strictly controlled and banned in many sectors of employment. As a result Africans faced many challenges in manifesting discontent on a national scale. Even so, the Rhodesian African National Congress (RANC), founded in the 1930s, succeeded in voicing the concerns of African regarding unfair labor practices.

After the World War II, a movement among white settlers began to take root calling for the federation of Southern Rhodesia with Northern Rhodesia (now Zambia) and NYASALAND (now MALAWI). Africans were against the idea, but had no political position to voice their concerns. In 1953 the three territories joined to form the CENTRAL AFRICAN FEDERATION (CAF).

With the founding of the CAF, political opposition by black Africans in Southern Rhodesia began to increase in size and intensity. Joshua NKOMO (1917–1999), a leader within the Rhodesian African National Congress, was strongly opposed to the CAF. After the RANC was banned, Nkomo formed the National Democratic Party, which later was banned also. Along with Ndabaningi SIT-HOLE (1920–2000), Nkomo then formed the Zimbabwe African People's Union, though that, too, was banned, in 1962.

As a result of African pressure, the CAF disbanded, in 1963. Two years later the whites of Southern Rhodesia, led by Prime Minister Ian Smith (1919–), announced a Unilateral Declaration of Independence for Southern Rhodesia, now simply called Rhodesia. Britain refused to recognize the new nation, and international pressure was applied to the Smith government to make it allow greater black representation. Despite the general movement toward African independence that swept across the continent throughout the 1960s, Rhodesia remained a white-minority-ruled nation until 1980.

See also: COLONIAL RULE (Vol. IV); ENGLAND AND AFRICA (Vols. III, IV, V); GREAT ZIMBABWE (Vol. II); MFE-CANE (Vol. III); MZILIKAZI (Vol. III); SETTLERS, EUROPEAN (Vol. IV); ZIMBABWE (Vols. I, II, III, V).

Further reading: John S. Galbraith, *Crown and Charter: The Early Years of the British South Africa Company* (Berkeley, Calif.: Univ. of California Press, 1974); Paul Mosley, *The Settler Economies: Studies in the Economic History of Kenya and Southern Rhodesia, 1900–1963* (New York: Cambridge University Press, 1983); Ian Phimister, *An Economic and Social History of Zimbabwe, 1890–1948: Capital Accumulation and Class Struggle* (New York: Longman, 1988); Innocent Pikirayi and Joseph O. Vogel, *The Zimbabwe Culture: Origins and Decline of Southern Zambezian States* (Lanham, Md.: University Press of America, 2001).

al-Zubayr, Rahma Mansur (Pasha) (1830–1913)
Sudanese administrator in the Egyptian-controlled Sudan

Rahma Mansur al-Zubayr was born in the region north of KHARTOUM, the present-day capital of the Republic of the SUDAN. In 1856 he became one of a number of northern Sudanese traders who engaged in raiding and trading for ivory and captives in the Bahr-al-Ghazal region in the southern Sudan. These traders operated out of fortified posts known as ZARIBAS. To expand his own trading operations, al-Zubayr collaborated with the Baggara nomads of southern DARFUR to secure his trading route back north to Khartoum. He also began to establish political control over the region through military conquest.

As a consequence the Egyptian colonial government based in Khartoum designated him the governor over what became the Bahr-al-Ghazal Province. However, when he visited Egypt in 1875 the Egyptian ruler, Khedive IS-MAIL (1830–1895), refused to let al-Zubayr return to southern Sudan. Then, in the early 1880s, al-Zubayr was suspected of conspiring with the MAHDIYYA Islamic brotherhood and was subsequently exiled to the British fortress at Gibraltar, on the southern Mediterranean coast of Spain. In 1899, when the British reconquered Sudan, they set up the ANGLO-EGYPTIAN CONDOMINIUM to govern the country. With the region secure, they allowed al-Zubayr to return to northern Sudan, where he lived until his death.

See also: ENGLAND AND AFRICA (Vols. III, IV, V); SLAVE TRADE (Vol. III).

Zulu
Bantu-speaking people of Nguni descent in southern Africa whose kingdom reached the apex of power in the early 19th century. After the assassination of the Zulu king Shaka (1787–1828), in 1828, his half-brother Dingane (1795–1840), who had orchestrated the murder, took the throne. In December 1838, Dingane was defeated by a Boer force out to avenge the killing of more than a hundred Boer settlers earlier in the year. After his defeat Dingane fled, but he was captured and killed by the BOERS, who were abetted by Dingane's half-brother, Mpande (1798–1872). The death of Dingane and the Boer alliance with Mpande splintered the Zulu and left Mpande with the task of reuniting his people.

In 1842 Mpande withdrew his allegiance from the Boers and signed a treaty with Britain, which recognized Mpande "King of the Zulu Nation." Similar to his predecessors, Mpande frequently purged the ranks of his rivals, forcing many Zulu men to leave Zululand to escape his wrath. The emigrants took large numbers of cattle with them, and Mpande began raiding the herds of neighboring lands. In 1852 this process culminated with the invasion of SWAZILAND.

As Mpande began to age, two of his sons contested the right to succession. A prolonged struggle called the "Battle of the Princes" ended with CETSHWAYO (c. 1826–1884) emerging victorious. Though the British initially supported Cetshwayo, his growing regional influence eventually caused them, in 1878, to give him an ultimatum: pay British taxes, return stolen cattle, and put and end to raids on British settler farms, or face an invasion. Cetshwayo refused the British demands and Britain invaded Zululand.

The Zulu offered staunch resistance to the British, handing them a staggering defeat at the Battle of ISANDL-WANA (1879). However, the Zulu could not maintain their advantage, and within six months they were completely defeated at the Battle of Ulundi. Cetshwayo was captured a month later and exiled to CAPE TOWN. In an effort to dilute the power of the Zulu and prevent the rise of another Zulu king, the British divided Zululand into 13 chiefdoms.

The chiefdoms quickly were at odds, and the territory moved toward civil war. Seeking to quell the re-

This Zulu dance provides an interesting moment for U.S. sailors on a visit near Durban, South Africa, in 1948. © *New York Times*

gional tensions and protect their interests in NATAL, the British returned Cetshwayo to Zululand and installed him as the nominal ruler, in 1883. The following year Cetshwayo died and his son, Dinizulu (1868–1913), was named his successor.

Dinizulu formed an alliance with the Boers, who promised to protect him from British incursion in return for territory in Zululand. Boers began moving into the territory, raising concerns among the British settlers of nearby Natal, who clamored for British intervention. In response, in 1887 Britain annexed all of Zululand and declared it a colony. Dinizulu resisted, which sparked a war with Britain. The Zulu leader was eventually arrested and sent to St. Helena Island, off the West African coast. In 1897 Dinizulu was invited back to Zululand, though only as a British-paid "traditional leader."

In 1906, the last uprising before the Zulu fully succumbed to British rule was led by Bambatha (1856–1906), chief of the Zondi Zulu. Known as BAMBATHA'S REBELLION, the uprising was brutally crushed by Britain, with more

than 4,000 Zulu losing their lives. After the Bambatha uprising, Zulu leaders held the title of "paramount chief." Their power was nominal, however, as they were effectively salaried employees of the South African government.

For ordinary Zulu, the loss of much of their land and cattle meant that they had to enter the wage-LABOR force, taking jobs such as working the docks in the port of DURBAN or GOLD mining on the WITWATERSRAND. Some who had managed to receive an EDUCATION from MISSIONARIES were able to find employment as clerks or teachers. From the ranks of these Zulu emerged top members of political movements, including the educator John L. DUBE (1871–1946), who was the first president of the AFRICAN NATIONAL CONGRESS, as well as influential labor leaders, such as A. W. G. CHAMPION (1893–1975).

See also: BANTU LANGUAGES (Vol. I); NGONI (Vol. III); SHAKA (Vol. III); ZULU (Vols. III, V).

Further reading: John Laband, *The Rise and Fall of the Zulu Nation* (London: Arms and Armour Press, 1997).

GLOSSARY

agriculturalists Sociological term for "farmers."

agro-pastoralists People who practice both farming and animal husbandry.

alafin Yoruba word for "ruler" or "king."

Allah Arabic for "God" or "Supreme Being."

Americo-Liberian Liberians of African-American ancestry.

ancestor worship Misnomer for the traditional practice of honoring and recognizing the memory and spirits of deceased family members.

al-Andalus Arabic term for Muslim Spain.

animism Belief that inanimate objects have a soul or life force.

anglophone English speaking.

apartheid Afrikaans word that means "separateness"; a formal system and policy of racial segregation and political and economic discrimination against South Africa's nonwhite majority.

aphrodesiac Food or other agent thought to arouse or increase sexual desire.

askia Arabic word meaning "general" that was applied to the Songhai kings. Capitalized, the word refers to a dynasty of Songhai rulers.

assimilados Portuguese word for Africans who had assimilated into the colonial culture.

Australopithicus africanus Hominid species that branched off into *Homo habilis* and *A. robustus*.

Australopithicus anamensis Second-oldest species of the hominid *Australopithicus*.

Australopithicus ramadus Oldest of the apelike, hominid species of *Australopithicus*.

Australopithicus robustus A sturdy species of *Australopithicus* that came after *A. africanus* and appears to have been an evolutionary dead end. *Australopithecus robustus* roamed the Earth at the same time as *Homo habilis*.

balkanization The breaking apart of regions or units into smaller groups.

barter Trading system in which goods are exchanged for items of equal value.

bey Governor in the Ottoman Empire.

Bilad al-Sudan Arabic for "Land of the Blacks."

bride price The payment made by a groom and his family to compensate the bride's father for the loss of her services because of marriage.

British Commonwealth Organization of sovereign states that were former colonies under the British Empire.

caliph Title for Muslim rulers who claim to be the secular and religious successors of the Prophet Muhammad.

caliphate Muslim state ruled by a caliph.

caravel A small, maneuverable ship used by the Portuguese during the Age of Discovery.

caste A division of society based on wealth, privilege, rank, or occupation.

circumcision The cutting of the clitoris (also called clitorectomy or clitoridectomy) or the prepuce of the penis; a rite of passage in many African societies.

cire perdu French for "lost wax," a technique used to cast metals.

clan A group that traces its descent from a common ancestor.

conflict diamonds Gems that are sold or traded extra-legally in order to fund wars.

conquistadores Spanish for "conquerors"; term used to describe the Spanish leaders of the conquest of the Americas during the 1500s.

constitutional monarchy State with a constitution that is ruled by a king or queen.

customary law Established traditions, customs, or practices that govern daily life and interaction.

degredados Portuguese criminals who were sent to Africa by the Portuguese king to perform hazardous duties related to exploration and colonization.

dhow Arabic word for a wooden sailing vessel with a triangular sail that was commonly used to transport trade goods.

diaspora Word used to describe a large, readily distinguishable group of people settled far from their ancestral homelands.

divination The interpretation of supernatural signs, usually done by a medicine man or priest.

djembe African drum, often called "the healing drum" because of its use in healing ceremonies.

emir A Muslim ruler or commander.

emirate A state ruled by an emir.

endogamy Marriage within one's ethnic group, as required by custom or law.

enset Another name for the "false banana" plant common in Africa.

ethnic group Term used to signify people who share a common culture.

ethno-linguistic Word used to describe a group whose individuals share racial characteristics and a common language.

eunuch A man who has been castrated (had his testicles removed), generally so that he might be trusted to watch over a ruler's wife or wives.

francophone French speaking.

government transparency Feature of an open society in which the decisions and the policy-making process of leaders are open to public scrutiny.

griot Storyteller, common in West African cultures, who preserves and relates the oral history of his people, often with musical accompaniment.

gross domestic product (GDP) Total value of goods and services produced by a nation's economy, within that nation. GDP is measured within a certain time frame, usually a year.

gross national product (GNP) Total value of goods and services produced by the residents of a nation, both within the nation as well as beyond its borders. Like GDP, GNP is measured within a certain time frame, usually a year.

hajj In Islam, a pilgrimage to Mecca.

hajjiyy "Pilgrim" in Arabic.

hegira Arabic for "flight" or "exodus"; generally used to describe the move of the Muslim prophet Muhammad from Mecca to Medina.

hominid Biological term used to describe the various branches of the Hominidae, the family from which modern humans descend according to evolutionary theory.

ideology A coherent or systematic way of looking at human life and culture.

imam A spiritual and political leader of a Muslim state.

imamate The region or state ruled by an imam.

indigénat Separate legal code used by France in its judicial dealings with the indigenous African population of its colonies.

infidel Term used as an epithet to describe one who is unfaithful or an unbeliever with respect to a particular religion .

infrastructure Basic physical, economic, and social facilities and institutions of a community or country .

Janissary From the Turkish for "new soldier," a member of an elite Ottoman military corps.

jebel "Mountain" in Arabic.

kabaka The word for "king" in Babito and Buganda cultures.

kemet Egyptian for "black earth."

kora Small percussion instrument played by some griots.

kraal Enclosure for cattle or a group of houses surrounding such an enclosure.

lineage A group whose individuals trace their descent from a common ancestor; usually a subgroup of a larger clan.

lingua franca Common language used by speakers of different languages.

Luso-African Word that describes the combined Portuguese and African cultures, especially the offspring of Portuguese settlers and indigenous African women. (The Latin name for the area of the Iberian Peninsula occupied by modern Portugal was Lusitania.)

madrasa Theological school for the interpretation of Islamic law.

Mahdi Arabic word for "enlightened one," or "righteous leader"; specifically, the Muslim savior who, in Islamic belief, is to arrive shortly before the end of time.

mamluk Arabic for "one who is owned"; capitalized, it is a member of an elite military unit made up of captives enslaved and used by Islamic rulers to serve in Middle Eastern and North African armies.

mansa Mande term for "king" or "emperor."

marabout A mystical Muslim spiritual leader.

massif A mountainous geological feature.

mastaba Arabic for an inscribed stone tomb.

matrilineal Relating to descent on the maternal, or mother's, side.

medina Arabic word for the old section of a city.

megaliths Archaeological term meaning "large rocks"; used to describe stelae and such features as cairns and tumuli that mark important places or events for many ancient cultures.

mestizo Adjective meaning "of mixed blood."

mfecane Zulu word meaning "the crushing." When capitalized, the word refers to the nineteenth-century Zulu conquests that caused the mass migration of peoples in southern Africa.

microliths Archaeological term meaning "small rocks"; used to describe sharpened stone blade tools of Stone Age cultures.

Monophysite Related to the Christian tradition that holds that Jesus Christ had only one (divine) nature.

Moor An Arab or Berber conqueror of al-Andalus (Muslim Spain).

mulatto The offspring of a Negroid (black) person and a Caucasoid (white) person.

mwami Head of the Tutsi political structure, believed to be of divine lineage.

negusa negast "King of kings" in Ethiopic; traditional title given to the ruler of Ethiopia.

neocolonialism Political or economic policies by which former colonial powers maintain their control of former colonies.

Nilotic Relating to peoples of the Nile, or Nile River basin, used especially to describe the languages spoken by these peoples.

Nsibidi Secret script of the Ekoi people of Nigeria.

oba Yoruba king or chieftain.

pasha A high-ranking official in the Ottoman Empire.

pashalik Territory or province of the Ottoman Empire governed by a pasha.

pass book A feature of apartheid-era South Africa, pass books were identification documents that black Africans, but not whites, were required by law to carry at all times.

pastoralists People whose livelihood and society center on raising livestock.

patriarch Male head of a family, organization, or society.

patrilineal Relating to descent through the paternal, or father's, side.

poll tax A tax of a fixed amount per person levied on adults.

polygyny The practice of having more than one wife or female mate at one time.

prazeros Portuguese settlers in Africa who held prazos.

prazos Similar to feudal estates, parcels of land in Africa that were leased to Portuguese settlers by the Portuguese king.

primogeniture A hereditary system common in Africa by which the eldest child, or more commonly, the eldest son, receives all of a family's inheritance.

proverb A short popular expression or adage. Proverbs are tools for passing on traditional wisdom orally.

pygmy Greek for "fist," a unit of measurement; used to describe the short-statured Mbuti people.

qadi Arabic for "judge."

Quran (also spelled Koran) Arabic for "recitation," and the name of the book of Muslim sacred writings.

ras A title meaning "regional ruler" in Ethiopia.

rondavel Small, round homes common in southern Africa.

salaam Arabic for "peace."

sarki Hausa word for "king."

scarification Symbolic markings made by pricking, scraping, or cutting the skin.

secret society Formal organizations united by an oath of secrecy and constituted for political or religious purposes.

shantytowns A town or part of a town consisting mostly of crudely built dwellings.

sharia Muslim law, which governs the civil and religious behavior of believers.

sharif In Islamic culture, one of noble ancestry.

sheikh (shaykh, sheik) Arabic word for patrilineal clan leaders.

sirocco Name given to a certain type of strong wind in the Sahara Desert.

souk Arabic word for "market."

stelae Large stone objects, usually phallus-shaped, whose markings generally contain information important to those who produced them.

stratified Arranged into sharply defined classes.

stratigraphy The study of sequences of sediments, soils, and rocks; used by archaeologists to determine the approximate age of a region.

sultan The king or sovereign of a Muslim state.

sultanate The lands or territory ruled by a sultan.

syncretism The combining of religious beliefs to form a new religion.

taboo (adj.) forbidden by custom, usually because of the fear of retribution by supernatural forces; (n.) a prohibition based on morality or social custom.

tafsir Arabic for "interpretation," especially as regards the Quran.

taqwa In Islam, the internal ability to determine right from wrong.

taro Another name for the cocoyam, an edible tuber common throughout Africa.

tauf Puddled mud that, when dried, serves as the foundation for some homes in sub-Saharan Africa.

teff A grass native to Africa that can be threshed to produce flour.

theocracy Government of a state by officials who are thought to be guided by God.

ulamaa Islamic learned men, the inheritors of the tradition of the prophet Muhammad.

vizier A high-ranking official in a Muslim state, esp. within the Ottoman Empire.

SUGGESTED READINGS FOR COLONIAL AFRICA

Abun-Nasr, Jamil M. *A History of the Maghrib in the Islamic Period.* New York: Cambridge University Press, 1987.

Akyeampong, Emmanuel Kwaku. *Drink, Power, and Cultural Change: A Social History of Alcohol in Ghana, c. 1800 to Recent Times.* Portsmouth, N.H.: Heinemann, 1996.

Ajayi, J. F. Ade. *Christian Missions in Nigeria, 1841–1891: The Making of a New Elite.* London: Longmans, 1965.

_____, ed. *UNESCO General History of Africa.* Vol. VI, *Africa in the Nineteenth Century until the 1880s.* Berkeley: University of California Press, 1989.

_____ and Crowder, Michael, eds. *History of West Africa.* 2 vols. Vol 2. 2nd ed. Burnt Mill, Harlow, Essex, England: Longman, 1987.

Alpers, Edward A. *Ivory & Slaves in East Central Africa: Changing Patterns of International Trade to the Later Nineteenth Century.* London: Heinemann, 1975.

Atkins, Keletso E. *The Moon is Dead! Give Us Our Money!: The Cultural Origins of an African Work Ethic,* Natal, South Africa, 1843-1900. Portsmouth, N.H.: Heinemann, 1993.

Austen, Ralph A., and Derrick, Jonathan. *Middlemen of the Cameroons Rivers: the Duala and their Hinterland, c.1600-c.1960.* New York: Cambridge University Press, 1999.

Barnes, Teresa A. *"We Women Worked So Hard": Gender, Urbanization, and Social Reproduction in Colonial Harare, Zimbabwe, 1930–1956.* Portsmouth, N.H.: Heinemann, 1999.

Bassett, Thomas J. *The Peasant Cotton Revolution in West Africa: Cote d'Ivoire, 1880–1995.* New York: Cambridge University Press, 2001.

Bay, Edna G. *Wives of the Leopard: Gender, Politics, and Culture in the Kingdom of Dahomey.* Charlottesville, Va.: University of Virginia Press, 1998.

Beck, Roger B. *The History of South Africa.* Westport, Conn.: Greenwood Press, 2000.

Bernault, Florence, ed. *A History of Prison and Confinement in Africa.* Portsmouth, N.H.: Heinemann, 2003.

Birmingham, David. *The Decolonization of Africa.* Athens, Ohio: Ohio University Press, 1995.

_____. *Portugal and Africa.* Athens, Ohio: Ohio University Press, 2004.

_____ and Martin, Phyllis M., eds. *History of Central Africa.* 2 vols. New York: Longman, 1983.

Boahen, A. Adu, ed. *UNESCO General History of Africa.* Vol. VII, *Africa Under Colonial Domination, 1880–1935.* Berkeley: University of California Press, 1990.

Bonner, P. L. Kings, *Commoners, and Concessionaires: The Evolution and Dissolution of the Nineteenth-Century Swazi State.* Johannesburg: Ravan Press, 1983.

Brett, Michael, and Fentress, Elizabeth. *The Berbers.* Malden, Mass.: Blackwell Publishing, 1997.

Bunker, Stephen G. *Peasants Against the State: The Politics of Market Control in Bugisu, Uganda, 1900–1983.* Chicago: University of Chicago Press, 1987.

Burns, J. M. Flickering Shadows: *Cinema and Identity in Colonial Zimbabwe.* Athens, Ohio.: Ohio University Press, 2002.

Byfield, Judith A. *The Bluest Hands: A Social and Economic History of Women Dyers in Abeokuta (Nigeria), 1890–1940.* Portsmouth, N.H.: Heinemann, 2002.

Chafer, Tony. *The End of Empire in French West Africa: France's Successful Decolonization?* New York: Berg Publishers, 2002.

Chamberlain, Muriel. *The Scramble for Africa.* New York: Longman, 1999.

Chanock, Martin. *Law, Custom, and Social Order: The Colonial Experience in Malawi and Zambia.* New York: Cambridge University Press, 1985.

Cooper, Barbara M. *Marriage in Maradi: Gender and Culture in a Hausa Society in Niger, 1900–1989.* Portsmouth, N.H.: Heinemann, 1997.

Crais, Clifton C. *White Supremacy and Black Resistance in Pre-industrial South Africa: The Making of the Colonial Order in the Eastern Cape, 1770–1865.* New York: Cambridge University Press, 1992.

Crummey, Donald. *Land and Society in the Christian Kingdom of Ethiopia: From the Thirteenth to the Twentieth Century.* Urbana, Il.: University of Illinois Press, 2000.

Crush, Jonathan and Charles Ambler, eds. *Liquor and Labor in Southern Africa.* Athens, Ohio: Ohio University Press, 1992.

Daly, M. W. *Empire on the Nile: The Anglo-Egyptian Sudan, 1898–1934.* New York: Cambridge University Press, 1986.

DeCorse, Christopher R. *An Archaeology of Elmina: Africans and Europeans on the Gold Coast, 1400–1900.* Washington, D.C.: Smithsonian Institution Press, 2001.

Delius, Peter. *A Lion Amongst the Cattle: Reconstruction and Resistance in the Northern Transvaal.* Portsmouth, N.H.: Heinemann, 1996.

Echenberg, Myron. *Black Death, White Medicine: Bubonic Plague and the Politics of Public Health in Colonial Senegal, 1914–1945.* Portsmouth, N.H.: Heinemann, 2002.

_____. *Colonial Conscripts: The Tirailleurs Senegalais in French West Africa, 1857–1960.* Portsmouth, N.H.: Heinemann, 1991.

Eldredge, Elizabeth A. *A South African Kingdom: The Pursuit of Security in Nineteenth-century Lesotho.* New York: Cambridge University Press, 1993.

Elleh, Nnamdi. *African Architecture: Evolution and Transformation.* New York: McGraw-Hill, 1996.

Erlich, Hoggai and Gershoni, Israel, eds. *The Nile: Histories, Cultures, Myths.* Boulder, Colo.: Lynne Rienner, 2000.

Etherington, Norman. *The Great Treks: The Transformation of Southern Africa, 1815–1854.* New York: Longman, 2001.

Fairhead, James, and Melissa Leach. *Misreading the African Landscape: Society and Ecology in the Forest Ecology in the Forest-Savanna Mosaic.* New York: Cambridge University Press, 1996.

Falola, Toyin, ed. *Warfare and Diplomacy in Precolonial Nigeria.* Madison, Wis.: African Studies Program, University of Wisconsin, 1992.

Feierman, Steven. *The Shambaa Kingdom: A History.* Madison, Wis.: University of Wisconsin Press, 1974

Fisher, Robert B. *West African Religious Traditions.* Maryknoll, New York: Orbis Books, 1998.

Floyd, Samuel A., Jr. *The Power of Black Music.* New York: Oxford University Press, 1995.

Garretson, Peter P. *A History of Addis Ababa from its Foundation in 1886 to 1910.* Wiesbaden, Germany: Harrassowitz, 2000.

Gebru Tareke, *Ethiopia, Power and Protest: Peasant Revolts in the Twentieth Century.* New York: Cambridge University Press, 1991.

Getz, Trevor R. *Slavery and Reform in West Africa: Toward Emancipation in Nineteenth-Century Senegal and the Gold Coast.* Athens, Ohio: Ohio University Press, 2004.

Gilbert, Erik. *Dhows and the Colonial Economy in Zanzibar, 1860–1970.* Athens, Ohio: Ohio University Press, 2004.

Glassman, Jonathon. *Feasts and Riot: Revelry, Rebellion, and Popular Consciousness on the Swahili Coast, 1856–1888.* Portsmouth, N.H.: Heinemann, 1995.

Gondola, Didier. *The History of Congo.* Westport, Conn.: Greenwood Press, 2002.

Good, Charles M. *The Steamer Parish: The Rise and Fall of Missionary Medicine on an African Frontier.* Chicago: University of Chicago Press, 2004.

Gordon, Jacob U. *African Leadership in the Twentieth Century.* Lanham, Md.: University Press of America, 2002.

Gray, Christopher J. *Colonial Rule and Crisis in Equatorial Africa: Southern Gabon, ca. 1850–1940.* Rochester, NY: University of Rochester, 2002.

Harrison, Christopher. *France and Islam in West Africa, 1860–1960.* New York: Cambridge University Press, 1988.

Heywood, Linda Marinda. *Contested Power in Angola, 1840s to the Present.* Rochester, N.Y.: University of Rochester Press, 2000.

Hiskett, Mervyn. *The Development of Islam in West Africa.* New York: Longman, 1984.

_____. *The Course of Islam in Africa.* Edinburgh: Edinburgh University Press, 1994.

Hochschild, Adam. *King Leopold's Ghost.* Boston: Houghton Mifflin Co., 1998.

Hoisington, William A. Jr., *Lyautey and the French Conquest of Morocco.* New York: St. Martin's Press, 1995.

Holt, Peter Malcolm, and Daly, M. W. *The History of the Sudan, from the Coming of Islam to the Present Day.* 4th ed. New York: Longman, 1988.

Hopwood, Derek. *Habib Bourguiba of Tunisia: The Tragedy of Longevity.* New York: St. Martin's Press, 1992.

Iliffe, John. *The African Poor: A History.* New York: Cambridge University Press, 1987.

Isaacman, Allen F. *Mozambique: The Africanization of a European Institution; the Zambesi Prazos, 1750–1902.* Madison, Wis.: University of Wisconsin Press, 1972.

_____ and Richard Roberts, eds. *Cotton, Colonialism, and Social History in Sub-Saharan Africa.* Portsmouth, N.H.: Heinemann, 1995.

Isichei, Elizabeth Allo. *A History of the Igbo People.* New York: St. Martin's Press, 1976.

Iyob, Ruth. *The Eritrean Struggle for Independence: Domination, Resistance, Nationalism, 1941–1993.* New York: Cambridge University Press, 1995.

Jeeves, Alan H. and Jonathan Crush, eds. *White Farms, Black Labor: The State and Agrarian Change in Southern Africa, 1910–50.* Portsmouth, N.H.: Heinemann, 1997.

Johnson, Douglas H. *Nuer Prophets.* New York: Oxford University Press, 1994.

Kanogo, Tabitha. *Squatters and the Roots of Mau Mau, 1905–1963.* Athens, Ohio: Ohio University Press, 1987.

Karugire, Samwiri Rubaraza. *A History of the Kingdom of Nkore in Western Uganda to 1896.* Oxford, Clarendon Press, 1971.

Kimambo, I. N., and Temu, A. J. *A History of Tanzania.* Nairobi: East African Publishing House, 1969.

Kimambo, Isaria N. *A Political History of the Pare of Tanzania, c1500–1900.* Nairobi: East African Pub., 1969.

Klein, Martin A. *Slavery and Colonial Rule in French West Africa.* New York: Cambridge University Press, 1998.

Kriger, Colleen E. *Pride of Men: Ironworking in 19th Century West Central Africa.* Portsmouth, N.H.: Heinemann, 1999.

Law, Robin, ed. *From Slave Trade to "Legitimate" Commerce: The Commercial Transition in Nineteenth-Century West Africa.* New York: Cambridge University Press, 1995.

Lewis, I. M. *A Modern History of Somalia.* 4th ed. Athens, Ohio: Ohio University Press, 2003.

Lynn, Martin. *Commerce and Economic Change in West Africa: The Palm Oil Trade in the Nineteenth Century.* New York: Cambridge University Press, 1997.

Mann, Kristin and Richard Roberts, eds. *Law in Colonial Africa.* Portsmouth, N.H.: Heinemann, 1991.

Manning, P. *Francophone Sub-Saharan Africa, 1880–1995.* 2nd ed. New York: Cambridge Univ. Press, 1998.

Marcus, Harold G. *A History of Ethiopia.* Berkeley: University of California Press, 1994.

Martin, Bradford G. *Muslim Brotherhoods in Nineteenth Century Africa.* New York: Cambridge Univ. Press, 1976.

Martin, Phyllis. *The External Trade of the Loango Coast, 1576–1870.* Oxford: Clarendon Press, 1972.

Mazrui, Ali A., ed. *UNESCO General History of Africa.* Vol. VIII, *Africa Since 1935.* Berkeley: University of California Press, 1993.

Mazrui, Ali A. and Alamin M. Mazrui. *The Power of Babel: Language and Governance in the African Experience.* University of Chicago Press, 1998.

McCarthy, Justin. *The Ottoman Turks: An Introductory History to 1923.* New York: Longman, 1997.

McCaskie, T. C. *State and Society in Pre-colonial Asante.* New York: Cambridge University Press, 1995.

Miller, James, and Jerome Bookin-Weiner. *Morocco: The Arab West* (Boulder, Colo.: Westview Press, 1998).

Mudimbe, V.Y., ed. *The Surreptitious Speech: Présence Africaine and the Politics of Otherness, 1947–1987.* Chicago: University of Chicago Press, 1992.

Nasson, Bill. *The South African War, 1899–1902.* New York: Oxford University Press, 1999.

Nzongola-Ntalaja. *The Congo: From Leopold to Kabila: A People's History.* New York: Palgrave, 2002.

Pankhurst, Richard. *The Ethiopian Borderlands.* Lawrenceville, N. J.: The Red Sea Press, 1997.

Parker, John. *Making the Town: Ga State and Society in Early Colonial Accra.* Portsmouth, N.H.: Heinemann, 2000.

Parsons, Neil. King Khama, *Emperor Joe, and the Great White Queen: Victorian Britain through African Eyes.* Chicago: University of Chicago Press, 1998.

Peel, J. D. Y. *Ijeshas and Nigerians: The Incorporation of a Yoruba Kingdom, 1890s–1970s.* New York: Cambridge University Press, 1983.

_____. *Religious Encounter and the Making of the Yoruba.* Bloomington, Ind.: Indiana University Press, 2002.

Pennell, C. R., *Morocco Since 1830: A History.* New York: New York University Press, 2000.

Powell, Eve M. Troutt. *A Different Shade of Colonialism: Egypt, Great Britain, and the Mastery of the Sudan.* Berkeley: University of California Press, 2003.

Prins, Gwyn. *The Hidden Hippopotamus: Reappraisal in African History: The Early Colonial Experience in Western Zambia.* New York: Cambridge University Press, 1980.

Quataert, Donald. *The Ottoman Empire, 1700–1922.* Cambridge, Eng.: Cambridge University Press, 2000.

Reefe, Thomas Q. *The Rainbow and the Kings: A History of the Luba Empire to 1891.* Berkeley: University of California Press, 1981.

Reimer, Michael J. *Colonial Bridgehead: Government and Society in Alexandria, 1807–1882.* Boulder, Colo.: Westview Press, 1997.

Robinson, David. *Paths of Accommodation: Muslim Societies and French Colonial Authorities in Senegal and Mauritania, 1880–1920.* Athens, Ohio: Ohio University Press, 2000.

Ruedy, John Douglas. *Modern Algeria: The Origins and Development of a Nation.* Bloomington: Indiana University Press, 1992.

Ryder, Alan Frederick Charles. *Benin and the Europeans, 1485–1897.* New York: Humanities Press, 1969.

Saul, Mahir, and Patrick Royer. *West African Challenges to Empire: Culture and History in the Volta-Bani Anti-colonial War.* Athens, Ohio: Ohio University Press, 2001.

Schmidt, Elizabeth. *Peasants, Traders, and Wives: Shona Women in the History of Zimbabwe, 1870–1939.* Portsmouth, N.H.: Heinemann, 1992.

Sheriff, Abdul. *Slaves, Spices, & Ivory in Zanzibar: Integration of an East African Commercial Empire into the World Economy, 1770–1873.* Athens, Ohio: Ohio University Press, 1987.

Shick, Tom W. *Behold the Promised Land: A History of Afro-American Settler Society in Nineteenth-Century Liberia.* Baltimore: Johns Hopkins University Press, 1980.

Sikainga, Ahmad Alawad. *City of Steel and Fire: A Social History of Atbara, Sudan's Railway Town, 1906–1984.* Porstmouth, N.H.: Heineman, 2002.

Summers, Carol. *Colonial Lessons: Africans' Education in Southern Rhodesia, 1918–1940.* Portsmouth, N.H.: Heinemann, 2002.

Sunseri, Thaddeus Vilimani: *Labor Migration and Rural Change in Early Colonial Tanzania.* Portsmouth, N.H.: Heinemann, 2002.

Thompson, Leonard Monteath. *A History of South Africa.* 3rd ed. New Haven, Conn.: Yale University Press, 2001.

_____. *Survival in Two Worlds: Moshoeshoe of Lesotho, 1786–1870.* Oxford: Clarendon Press, 1975.

Tignor, Robert L. *Capitalism and Nationalism at the End of Empire: State and Business in Decolonizing Egypt, Nigeria, and Kenya, 1945–1963.* Princeton, N.J.: Princeton University Press, 1998.

Vandervort, Bruce. *Wars of Imperial Conquest in Africa, 1830–1914.* Bloomington: Indiana University Press, 1998.

Vaughan, Olufemi. *Nigerian Chiefs: Traditional Power in Modern Politics, 1890s–1990s.* Rochester, NY: University of Rochester Press, 2000.

Warwick, Peter. *Black Pople and the South African War, 1899–1902*. New York: Cambridge University Press, 1983.

Watson, Ruth. *"Civil Disorder is the Disease of Ibadan": Chieftaincy and Civic Culture in a Yoruba City*. Athens, Ohio: Ohio University Press, 2004.

Wesseling, H. L. *Divide and Rule: The Partition of Africa, 1880–1914*. Westport, Conn.: Praeger, 1996.

West, Michael. *The Rise of an African Middle Class: Colonial Zimbabwe, 1898–1965*. Bloomington, Ind.: Indiana University Press, 2002.

White, Luise. *The Comforts of Home: Prostitution in Colonial Nairobi*. Chicago: University of Chicago Press, 1990.

Wilks, Ivor. *Asante in the Nineteenth Century: The Structure and Evolution of a Political Order*. 1st ed., with new introductory material. New York: Cambridge University Press, 1989.

Wilmsen, Edwin N. *Land Filled with Flies: A Political Economy of the Kalahari*. Chicago: University of Chicago Press, 1989.

Wright, Donald R. *The World and a Very Small Place in Africa*. Armonk, N.Y.: M.E. Sharpe, 1997.

Wright, John. *Libya, a Modern History*. Baltimore, MD.: Johns Hopkins University Press, 1982.

Wrigley, Christopher. *Kingship and State: The Buganda Dynasty*. New York: Cambridge University Press, 1996.

INDEX FOR
THIS VOLUME

Bold page numbers indicate main entries. Page numbers followed by the letter *c* refer to a timeline; the letter *f* refers to illustrations; the letter *m* indicates a map; and the letter *t* indicates a table.

A

AB (Afrikaner Broederbond) 61

ABAKO (Alliance des Bakongo) 217

Aba Women's Revolt xxxviic, **1–2**, 182, 334, 384

Abbas, Ferhat **2**, 17, 294

Abbas Hilmi, Pasha. *See* Abbas II

Abbas II 128, 129

Abboud, Ibrahim 375

Abdallahi ibn Muhammad **2–3**, 22, 110, 167, 216, 251–252, 309

Abdelaziz, Mawlai 174

Abd el-Krim, Mohamed ben **3**, 278, 337, 371

Abdullahi ibn Muhammad. *See* Abdallahi ibn Muhammad

Abdurahman, Abdullah 72

Abel Karim, Muhammad ben. *See* Abd el-Krim, Mohamed ben

Abeokuta **4**, 197, 387

Abidjan **4**

abolition and resettlement 40, 83, 360, 392. *See also* British Anti-Slavery Squadron

Aborigines' Rights Protection Society (ARPS) xxxvic, **4–5**, 163, 347

Abrahams, Peter 237

Academy for Language, Literature, and Arts 10

Accra **5**, 29

Achebe, Albert C. *See* Achebe, Chinua

Achebe, Chinua xxxviiic, **5–6**, 83, 236, 385

Achimota College **6**, 13, 127

Acolatse, Alex A. 320

Action Group 37, 301

Adama 69

Addis Ababa **6–7**, 119, 135*m*, 136

Addis Ababa, Treaty of 7, 36, 136, 188

Adowa, Battle of xxxvic, 6, 7, 36, 93, 136, 188, 268, 317

AEF (Afrique Équatoriale Française). *See* French Equatorial Africa

Afar people 119

Afghani, Jamal al-Din al- **7–8**, 128

Africa in 2005 ix*m*

African Agricultural Union 179

African Anglican Church 86

"African Claims" 264

African culture, European view on 93–94

African Democratic Assembly (RDA) xxxviic, **8**, 42, 148, 180, 191, 390

African diaspora **8**, 285, 296

Africanism 316

Africanist, The 362

Africanists 10

African labor organizations 222

African Methodist Episcopal Church (AME) 403

African Mineworkers Union 411

African National Congress (ANC) xxxvic, **9–10**
   apartheid 26
   A. W. G. Champion 80
   John L. Dube 121
   Freedom Charter 149
   Albert J. Lutuli 245
   Nelson Mandela 259
   Govan Mbeki 264
   nationalism and independence movements 293
   Pan-Africanist Congress 316
   Sol T. Plaatje 321
   Walter Sisulu 357–358
   South Africa 366–367
   Oliver Tambo 381
   Union of South Africa 408

African National Congress Youth League (ANCYL) 9, 259, 358, 362, 367, 381

African Nationalism 358

African Nationalism (Sithole) 358

African Party for the Independence of Guinea and Cape Verde (PAIGC) 67, 73, 171, 324

African People's Organization (APO) 72

African Times and Orient Review, The (journal) 19

African traditional religions 331

Afrikaans **10–11**, 72

Afrikaans language 237

Afrikaner Broederbond (AB) 61

Afrikaner government of South Africa 149

Afrikaner nationalism 11–12, 21, 55, 61, 177–178

Afrikaner National Party 9–12, 26, 61, 178, 237, 254, 366. *See also* South African National Party

Afrikaner Republics **11**, 55, 195, 408. *See also* Orange Free State; Transvaal

Afrikaners **11–12**
   apartheid 25–27
   Freedom Charter 149
   Johannesburg 196–197
   Namibia 289
   South Africa 366
   the Transvaal 396
   Union of South Africa 410

Afrique Équatoriale Française. *See* French Equatorial Africa

Afro-Shirazi party (ASP) 437

age-grade systems of education 126

Age of Princes 135

Aggrey, James E. Kwegyir 6, **12–13**, 37, 422

agriculture **13–14**, 13*f*
   kingdom of Benin 50
   Republic of Benin 51–52
   Comoros 97
   economy 125
   food crops 145
   Gezira Scheme 161
   Ibadan 181
   Ilorin 182
   industrialization 183
   Italian Somaliland 187
   D. D. T. Jabavu 193
   Kikuyu 209–210

Republic of the Sudan 373

Swahili Coast 378

Booker T. Washington 422

agriculture, subsistence 144

agro-pastoralists 57, 122

Ague Festival 301

Agyiman, Ekra (J. E. Casely-Hayford) **73–74**

Ahmad I bin Mustafa Bey 209

Ahmadu ibn Umar Tal. *See* Ahmadu Séku

Ahmadu Sefu. *See* Ahmadu Séku

Ahmadu Séku xxxvc, xxxvic, **14–15**, 185, 408

Aïda (opera) 186, 376

air service in colonial Africa 395

Aja kingdoms 51

Ajayi. *See* Crowther, Samuel Ajayi

Akan **15**

Akan Doctrine of God, The (Danquah) 109

Aksum, Ethiopia 19, 28

Al-Alsun Translation School 380

Albert I, Belgium 230

Alexander High School, Monrovia 54–55

Alexandria **15**, 415

Alexandria, Battle of 130

Algeria vii*m*, viii*m*, xxxviiic, **15–17**, 292*m*
   agriculture 14
   Ahmed Ben Bella 49, 50
   colon 91
   cotton 103
   European settlers in xxxvc
   FLN 294–295
   Louis H. G. Lyautey 245
   nationalism and independence movements 293–294
   European settlers 352, 354

Algerian Muslims 16–18

Algerian Popular Union 2

Algerian Republic, Provisional Government of 294–295

Algerian Statute 17